Toucan Comparative Guide Series

The Comparative Guide to AMERICAN Elementary & Secondary SCHOOLS

Toucan Comparative Guide Series

The Comparative Guide to AMERICAN Elementary & Secondary SCHOOLS

Covers all public school districts serving 2,500 or more students

TOUCAN VALLEY PUBLICATIONS, INC.

ISBN 1-884925-63-4

Toucan Valley Publications, Inc.
142 N. Milpitas Blvd, Suit 260 ◆ Milpitas CA 95035
Phone: (800) 236-7946 ◆ Fax: (510) 498-1010
e-mail: query@toucanvalley.com

Manufactured in the United States of America
First Edition

INTRODUCTION

The Comparative Guide to American Elementary & Secondary Schools brings together pertinent evaluative and demographic statistics for each regular public school district in the United States with more than 2,500 students, and presents these statistics in one easy-to-use volume. These districts encompass approximately 80% of all the public schools in the U.S.

ARRANGEMENT

The Comparative Guide to American Elementary & Secondary Schools is arranged by state. Within each state, the arrangement is alphabetical by county. Within each county, the arrangement is alphabetical by the city in which the school district headquarters is located. If the school district name does not begin with the name of the city, then that city name is supplied in brackets before the school district name. If more than one district is located in the same city, the districts are listed alphabetically by district name.

CITY INDEX

The alphabetical CITY INDEX lists each district operating one or more schools in that city, followed by the number of schools operated by that district and the page number where full information about that school district may be found. The INDEX is especially useful for identifying the name of a school district that serves a particular city or town, or for locating in which county a particular city or town is located.

School district boundaries do not necessarily follow city limit lines or postal address lines. Some cities have several school districts. Some districts have schools in more than one city.

INFORMATION FOR EACH SCHOOL DISTRICT

Address

Location of the school district headquarters.

Telephone number

Main number for the school district headquarters. Efforts have been made to include the most recent area codes. However, changes in area codes are occurring rapidly, and may affect the area codes listed.

Web address

Web addresses are supplied for nearly 40% of the school districts. In most cases, these web sites are maintained by the school district. It should be noted that web sites are subject to frequent change.

Grade Span

All grade levels served by the school district. (PK = pre-kindergarten)

Schools

Number of schools classified by the National Center for Education Statistics as "Regular," "Special Education," and "Alternative or Vocational."

Students

Number of students enrolled in the district.

Total Teachers

Number of full-time-equivalent teachers, including classroom teachers and teachers who are not assigned to a classroom.

Student/Classroom Teacher Ratio

Total number of students in each regular school, divided by the total number of classroom teachers in that school (does *not* include teachers not assigned to a classroom), averaged for the district.

Expenditures per Student

All school district expenditures (excepting capital outlay expenditures and debt interest) divided by the number of students.

Librarians

Number of full-time-equivalent professional elementary and secondary school librarians serving in the district. The ratio of students to librarians is also given. If there are no professional school librarians in the district, the students/librarian ratio is given as ***.

Guidance Counselors

Number of full-time-equivalent elementary and secondary guidance counselors serving in the district. The ratio of students to counselors is also given. If there are no guidance counselors in the district, the students/counselor ratio is given as ***.

Ethnicity

Ethnicity of student population. "Amer Indian" includes Alaskan native students; "Asian" includes Pacific Islander students.

National Socio-Economic Status Indicator

This indicator was derived from the count of students eligible to participate in the Free Lunch Program under the National School Lunch Act. The lower the number of students eligible to participate, the higher the socio-economic status indicator. A percentile was calculated from this data. For example, a 1st percentile ranking would indicate that the school district has more students eligible for the Free Lunch Program than any other districts; a 100th percentile ranking would indicate that the district has fewer students eligible for the Free Lunch Program than other districts. This indicator is not available for the states of Alabama, Arizona, Illinois, Kentucky, Massachusetts, New Mexico, Pennsylvania, South Dakota, Tennessee, and Washington.

In any data field, "na" indicates that the statistic is not available for that district.

SOURCE OF DATA

The source of the data, except for the web address and the expenditures per student, is the National Center for Education Statistics, in the *Common Core of Data Public School Universe* and the *Common Core of Data Agency Universe* files. Both files, the most current available as of summer 1998, are from the 1995-96 school year. Raw data from these two files was programmed and re-formatted in order to present it in a manner that is easy for use in evaluating each school district.

The expenditures per student figures were derived from the U.S. Bureau of the Census, Public Elementary-Secondary Finance Data. Data, the most current as of summer 1998, is from fiscal 1995.

Web addresses were researched independently.

Autauga County

[PRATTVILLE] **AUTAUGA COUNTY S.D.**

PO BOX 130 ● PRATTVILLE AL 36067 ● (334) 365-5706

Grade Span: KG-12 **Schools**: *Regular* 10 ● *Spec Ed* 0 ● *Alt* 0 **Students**: 7,834 **Total Teachers**: 400 **Student/Classroom Teacher Ratio**: 19.6	**Expenditures/Student**: $3,294 **Librarians**: 10.0 783 students/librarian **Guidance Counselors**: 13.0 603 students/counselor	**% Amer Indian**: 0.1 **% Asian**: 0.2 **% Black**: 24.5 **% Hispanic**: 0.4 **% White**: 74.9	National ***Socio-Economic Status*** indicator percentiles are not available for the state of Alabama

Baldwin County

[BAY MINETTE] **BALDWIN COUNTY S.D.**

175 COURTHOUSE SQUARE ● BAY MINETTE AL 36507 ● (334) 937-0308 ● http://www.gulftel.net/bcbe/mainmenu.html

Grade Span: KG-12 **Schools**: *Regular* 34 ● *Spec Ed* 0 ● *Alt* 1 **Students**: 20,699 **Total Teachers**: 1,258 **Student/Classroom Teacher Ratio**: 16.5	**Expenditures/Student**: $3,940 **Librarians**: 31.0 668 students/librarian **Guidance Counselors**: 47.5 436 students/counselor	**% Amer Indian**: 0.2 **% Asian**: 0.3 **% Black**: 17.8 **% Hispanic**: 0.5 **% White**: 81.2	National ***Socio-Economic Status*** indicator percentiles are not available for the state of Alabama

Barbour County

EUFAULA CITY S.D.

420 SANFORD AVENUE ● EUFAULA AL 36027 ● (334) 687-1100 ● http://users.the-link.net/ehs

Grade Span: KG-12 **Schools**: *Regular* 5 ● *Spec Ed* 0 ● *Alt* 0 **Students**: 3,066 **Total Teachers**: 192 **Student/Classroom Teacher Ratio**: 16.1	**Expenditures/Student**: $4,336 **Librarians**: 5.0 613 students/librarian **Guidance Counselors**: 7.0 438 students/counselor	**% Amer Indian**: 0.0 **% Asian**: 0.4 **% Black**: 48.2 **% Hispanic**: 0.2 **% White**: 51.2	National ***Socio-Economic Status*** indicator percentiles are not available for the state of Alabama

Bibb County

[CENTREVILLE] **BIBB COUNTY S.D.**

103 SW DAVIDSON DRIVE ● CENTREVILLE AL 35042 ● (205) 926-9881

Grade Span: KG-12 **Schools**: *Regular* 7 ● *Spec Ed* 1 ● *Alt* 0 **Students**: 3,656 **Total Teachers**: 211 **Student/Classroom Teacher Ratio**: 18.2	**Expenditures/Student**: $3,882 **Librarians**: 7.0 522 students/librarian **Guidance Counselors**: 8.0 457 students/counselor	**% Amer Indian**: 0.0 **% Asian**: 0.1 **% Black**: 28.6 **% Hispanic**: 0.1 **% White**: 71.3	National ***Socio-Economic Status*** indicator percentiles are not available for the state of Alabama

Blount County

[ONEONTA] **BLOUNT COUNTY S.D.**

PO BOX 578 ● ONEONTA AL 35121 ● (205) 625-4102

Grade Span: KG-12 **Schools**: *Regular* 10 ● *Spec Ed* 0 ● *Alt* 0 **Students**: 6,457 **Total Teachers**: 340 **Student/Classroom Teacher Ratio**: 20.0	**Expenditures/Student**: $3,695 **Librarians**: 9.0 717 students/librarian **Guidance Counselors**: 11.0 587 students/counselor	**% Amer Indian**: 0.2 **% Asian**: 0.1 **% Black**: 0.4 **% Hispanic**: 2.8 **% White**: 96.5	National ***Socio-Economic Status*** indicator percentiles are not available for the state of Alabama

Butler County

[GREENVILLE] **BUTLER COUNTY S.D.**

215 SIMPSON STREET ● GREENVILLE AL 36037-1833 ● (334) 382-2665

Grade Span: KG-12 **Schools**: *Regular* 6 ● *Spec Ed* 0 ● *Alt* 0 **Students**: 4,173 **Total Teachers**: 245 **Student/Classroom Teacher Ratio**: 17.4	**Expenditures/Student**: $3,934 **Librarians**: 6.0 696 students/librarian **Guidance Counselors**: 9.8 426 students/counselor	**% Amer Indian**: 0.0 **% Asian**: 0.1 **% Black**: 60.1 **% Hispanic**: 0.0 **% White**: 39.8	National ***Socio-Economic Status*** indicator percentiles are not available for the state of Alabama

Calhoun County

ANNISTON CITY S.D.

PO BOX 1500 ● ANNISTON AL 36202 ● (256) 231-5000

Grade Span: KG-12 **Schools**: *Regular* 9 ● *Spec Ed* 0 ● *Alt* 0 **Students**: 3,586 **Total Teachers**: 232 **Student/Classroom Teacher Ratio**: 16.0	**Expenditures/Student**: $5,138 **Librarians**: 10.0 359 students/librarian **Guidance Counselors**: 10.0 359 students/counselor	**% Amer Indian**: 0.1 **% Asian**: 0.2 **% Black**: 81.2 **% Hispanic**: 2.6 **% White**: 15.9	National ***Socio-Economic Status*** indicator percentiles are not available for the state of Alabama

Calhoun County

[ANNISTON] **CALHOUN COUNTY S.D.**

PO BOX 2084 ● ANNISTON AL 36202 ● (256) 236-7641

Grade Span: KG-12 **Schools**: *Regular* 15 ● *Spec Ed* 0 ● *Alt* 1 **Students**: 10,426 **Total Teachers**: 533 **Student/Classroom Teacher Ratio**: 20.5	**Expenditures/Student**: $3,607 **Librarians**: 17.6 592 students/librarian **Guidance Counselors**: 18.0 579 students/counselor	**% Amer Indian**: 0.1 **% Asian**: 0.8 **% Black**: 10.1 **% Hispanic**: 0.8 **% White**: 88.1	National ***Socio-Economic Status*** indicator percentiles are not available for the state of Alabama

Calhoun County

OXFORD CITY S.D.

310 SECOND STREET E ● OXFORD AL 36203 ● (256) 831-0243

Grade Span: KG-12 **Schools**: *Regular* 3 ● *Spec Ed* 0 ● *Alt* 0 **Students**: 2,803 **Total Teachers**: 153 **Student/Classroom Teacher Ratio**: 17.9	**Expenditures/Student**: $3,706 **Librarians**: 3.9 719 students/librarian **Guidance Counselors**: 6.0 467 students/counselor	**% Amer Indian**: 0.0 **% Asian**: 0.4 **% Black**: 20.7 **% Hispanic**: 0.7 **% White**: 78.1	National ***Socio-Economic Status*** indicator percentiles are not available for the state of Alabama

Chambers County

[LAFAYETTE] **CHAMBERS COUNTY S.D.**

BOX 408D ● LAFAYETTE AL 36862 ● (334) 864-9343

Grade Span: KG-12 **Schools**: *Regular* 10 ● *Spec Ed* 0 ● *Alt* 0 **Students**: 4,149 **Total Teachers**: 248 **Student/Classroom Teacher Ratio**: 17.2	**Expenditures/Student**: $4,570 **Librarians**: 8.9 466 students/librarian **Guidance Counselors**: 7.9 525 students/counselor	**% Amer Indian**: 0.0 **% Asian**: 0.0 **% Black**: 55.9 **% Hispanic**: 0.0 **% White**: 44.0	National ***Socio-Economic Status*** indicator percentiles are not available for the state of Alabama

Cherokee County

[CENTRE] **CHEROKEE COUNTY S.D.**

130 EAST MAIN STREET ● CENTRE AL 35960 ● (256) 927-3362 ● http://www.pacers.org/schools/gaylesville

Grade Span: KG-12 **Schools**: *Regular* 7 ● *Spec Ed* 0 ● *Alt* 0 **Students**: 3,794 **Total Teachers**: 229 **Student/Classroom Teacher Ratio**: 17.9	**Expenditures/Student**: $4,100 **Librarians**: 7.0 542 students/librarian **Guidance Counselors**: 8.7 436 students/counselor	**% Amer Indian**: 0.0 **% Asian**: 0.2 **% Black**: 8.3 **% Hispanic**: 0.2 **% White**: 91.3	National ***Socio-Economic Status*** indicator percentiles are not available for the state of Alabama

Chilton County

[CLANTON] **CHILTON COUNTY S.D.**

1705 LAY DAM ROAD ● CLANTON AL 35045 ● (205) 755-3190

Grade Span: KG-12 **Schools**: *Regular* 9 ● *Spec Ed* 0 ● *Alt* 0 **Students**: 6,257 **Total Teachers**: 372 **Student/Classroom Teacher Ratio**: 17.7	**Expenditures/Student**: $3,923 **Librarians**: 8.8 711 students/librarian **Guidance Counselors**: 15.1 414 students/counselor	**% Amer Indian**: 0.0 **% Asian**: 0.1 **% Black**: 16.3 **% Hispanic**: 0.6 **% White**: 82.9	National ***Socio-Economic Status*** indicator percentiles are not available for the state of Alabama

Choctaw County

[BUTLER] **CHOCTAW COUNTY S.D.**

PO DRAWER 839 ● BUTLER AL 36904 ● (205) 459-3031

Grade Span: KG-12 **Schools**: *Regular* 7 ● *Spec Ed* 0 ● *Alt* 0 **Students**: 2,719 **Total Teachers**: 176 **Student/Classroom Teacher Ratio**: 15.6	**Expenditures/Student**: $4,477 **Librarians**: 6.0 453 students/librarian **Guidance Counselors**: 7.5 363 students/counselor	**% Amer Indian**: 0.0 **% Asian**: 0.0 **% Black**: 67.2 **% Hispanic**: 0.0 **% White**: 32.8	National ***Socio-Economic Status*** indicator percentiles are not available for the state of Alabama

Clarke County

[GROVE HILL] **CLARKE COUNTY S.D.**

BOX 936 ● GROVE HILL AL 36451 ● (334) 275-3255

Grade Span: KG-12 **Schools**: *Regular* 8 ● *Spec Ed* 0 ● *Alt* 0 **Students**: 3,971 **Total Teachers**: 240 **Student/Classroom Teacher Ratio**: 16.7	**Expenditures/Student**: $4,014 **Librarians**: 6.5 611 students/librarian **Guidance Counselors**: 6.9 576 students/counselor	**% Amer Indian**: 0.1 **% Asian**: 0.0 **% Black**: 66.2 **% Hispanic**: 0.0 **% White**: 33.7	National ***Socio-Economic Status*** indicator percentiles are not available for the state of Alabama

Clay County

[ASHLAND] **CLAY COUNTY S.D.**

PO BOX 278 ● ASHLAND AL 36251 ● (205) 354-5414

Grade Span: KG-12 **Schools**: *Regular* 7 ● *Spec Ed* 0 ● *Alt* 0 **Students**: 2,635 **Total Teachers**: 164 **Student/Classroom Teacher Ratio**: 16.6	**Expenditures/Student**: $3,939 **Librarians**: 3.0 878 students/librarian **Guidance Counselors**: 5.5 479 students/counselor	**% Amer Indian**: 0.0 **% Asian**: 0.2 **% Black**: 23.9 **% Hispanic**: 0.2 **% White**: 75.7	National ***Socio-Economic Status*** indicator percentiles are not available for the state of Alabama

Coffee County

ENTERPRISE CITY S.D.

502 EAST WATTS STREET ● ENTERPRISE AL 36330 ● (334) 347-9531

Grade Span: KG-12 **Schools**: *Regular* 10 ● *Spec Ed* 0 ● *Alt* 0 **Students**: 5,307 **Total Teachers**: 305 **Student/Classroom Teacher Ratio**: 17.7	**Expenditures/Student**: $3,815 **Librarians**: 11.0 482 students/librarian **Guidance Counselors**: 12.0 442 students/counselor	**% Amer Indian**: 0.3 **% Asian**: 1.7 **% Black**: 25.9 **% Hispanic**: 2.6 **% White**: 69.4	National ***Socio-Economic Status*** indicator percentiles are not available for the state of Alabama

Colbert County

[TUSCUMBIA] **COLBERT COUNTY S.D.**

116 WEST FIFTH STREET ● TUSCUMBIA AL 35674 ● (256) 386-8565

Grade Span: KG-12 **Schools**: *Regular* 9 ● *Spec Ed* 0 ● *Alt* 0 **Students**: 3,390 **Total Teachers**: 221 **Student/Classroom Teacher Ratio**: 15.4	**Expenditures/Student**: $4,844 **Librarians**: 8.6 394 students/librarian **Guidance Counselors**: 8.4 404 students/counselor	**% Amer Indian**: 0.1 **% Asian**: 0.1 **% Black**: 21.9 **% Hispanic**: 0.4 **% White**: 77.4	National ***Socio-Economic Status*** indicator percentiles are not available for the state of Alabama

Covington County

[ANDALUSIA] **COVINGTON COUNTY S.D.**

BOX 460 ● ANDALUSIA AL 36420 ● (334) 222-7571

Grade Span: KG-12 **Schools**: *Regular* 8 ● *Spec Ed* 0 ● *Alt* 0 **Students**: 3,245 **Total Teachers**: 189 **Student/Classroom Teacher Ratio**: 17.0	**Expenditures/Student**: $3,954 **Librarians**: 5.3 612 students/librarian **Guidance Counselors**: 8.0 406 students/counselor	**% Amer Indian**: 0.2 **% Asian**: 0.1 **% Black**: 10.6 **% Hispanic**: 0.1 **% White**: 89.0	National ***Socio-Economic Status*** indicator percentiles are not available for the state of Alabama

Cullman County
CULLMAN CITY S.D.
PO BOX 887 ● CULLMAN AL 35055 ● (256) 734-2233 ● http://www.cneti.com/~chs

Grade Span: KG-12 **Schools**: *Regular* 5 ● *Spec Ed* 0 ● *Alt* 0 **Students**: 2,739 **Total Teachers**: 155 **Student/Classroom Teacher Ratio**: 17.7	**Expenditures/Student**: $4,136 **Librarians**: 5.0 548 students/librarian **Guidance Counselors**: 5.0 548 students/counselor	**% Amer Indian**: 0.2 **% Asian**: 0.5 **% Black**: 0.0 **% Hispanic**: 0.8 **% White**: 98.4	National ***Socio-Economic Status*** indicator percentiles are not available for the state of Alabama

Cullman County
[CULLMAN] **CULLMAN COUNTY S.D.**
PO BOX 518 ● CULLMAN AL 35056-0518 ● (256) 734-2933

Grade Span: KG-12 **Schools**: *Regular* 14 ● *Spec Ed* 0 ● *Alt* 0 **Students**: 9,321 **Total Teachers**: 513 **Student/Classroom Teacher Ratio**: 16.5	**Expenditures/Student**: $3,780 **Librarians**: 12.0 777 students/librarian **Guidance Counselors**: 14.0 666 students/counselor	**% Amer Indian**: 0.1 **% Asian**: 0.1 **% Black**: 1.3 **% Hispanic**: 0.5 **% White**: 98.0	National ***Socio-Economic Status*** indicator percentiles are not available for the state of Alabama

Dale County
[OZARK] **DALE COUNTY S.D.**
PO BOX 948 ● OZARK AL 36361 ● (334) 774-2355

Grade Span: KG-12 **Schools**: *Regular* 7 ● *Spec Ed* 0 ● *Alt* 0 **Students**: 2,704 **Total Teachers**: 166 **Student/Classroom Teacher Ratio**: 16.3	**Expenditures/Student**: $4,634 **Librarians**: 6.0 451 students/librarian **Guidance Counselors**: 6.8 398 students/counselor	**% Amer Indian**: 0.1 **% Asian**: 0.3 **% Black**: 17.7 **% Hispanic**: 0.2 **% White**: 81.6	National ***Socio-Economic Status*** indicator percentiles are not available for the state of Alabama

Dale County
OZARK CITY S.D.
PO BOX 788 ● OZARK AL 36361 ● (334) 774-5197

Grade Span: KG-12 **Schools**: *Regular* 6 ● *Spec Ed* 0 ● *Alt* 0 **Students**: 3,362 **Total Teachers**: 206 **Student/Classroom Teacher Ratio**: 16.5	**Expenditures/Student**: $4,215 **Librarians**: 6.9 487 students/librarian **Guidance Counselors**: 7.8 431 students/counselor	**% Amer Indian**: 0.2 **% Asian**: 0.6 **% Black**: 38.0 **% Hispanic**: 1.3 **% White**: 59.9	National ***Socio-Economic Status*** indicator percentiles are not available for the state of Alabama

Dallas County
[SELMA] **DALLAS COUNTY S.D.**
PO BOX 1056 ● SELMA AL 36702-1056 ● (334) 875-3440

Grade Span: KG-12 **Schools**: *Regular* 12 ● *Spec Ed* 0 ● *Alt* 0 **Students**: 5,026 **Total Teachers**: 293 **Student/Classroom Teacher Ratio**: 17.6	**Expenditures/Student**: $3,697 **Librarians**: 10.5 479 students/librarian **Guidance Counselors**: 13.0 387 students/counselor	**% Amer Indian**: 0.0 **% Asian**: 0.0 **% Black**: 74.0 **% Hispanic**: 0.0 **% White**: 26.0	National ***Socio-Economic Status*** indicator percentiles are not available for the state of Alabama

Dallas County
SELMA CITY S.D.
PO BOX F ● SELMA AL 36702 ● (334) 874-1600

Grade Span: KG-12 **Schools**: *Regular* 11 ● *Spec Ed* 0 ● *Alt* 0 **Students**: 4,862 **Total Teachers**: 295 **Student/Classroom Teacher Ratio**: 16.5	**Expenditures/Student**: $4,045 **Librarians**: 12.5 389 students/librarian **Guidance Counselors**: 12.5 389 students/counselor	**% Amer Indian**: 0.0 **% Asian**: 0.3 **% Black**: 87.4 **% Hispanic**: 0.1 **% White**: 12.1	National ***Socio-Economic Status*** indicator percentiles are not available for the state of Alabama

DeKalb County

[FORT PAYNE] **DEKALB COUNTY S.D.**

BOX 777 ● FORT PAYNE AL 35967 ● (256) 845-8575

Grade Span: KG-12 **Schools**: *Regular* 12 ● *Spec Ed* 0 ● *Alt* 0 **Students**: 7,285 **Total Teachers**: 430 **Student/Classroom Teacher Ratio**: 16.8	**Expenditures/Student**: $3,903 **Librarians**: 10.5 694 students/librarian **Guidance Counselors**: 15.2 479 students/counselor	**% Amer Indian**: 15.4 **% Asian**: 0.1 **% Black**: 0.8 **% Hispanic**: 1.6 **% White**: 82.0	National ***Socio-Economic Status*** indicator percentiles are not available for the state of Alabama

DeKalb County

FORT PAYNE CITY S.D.

PO BOX 1029 ● FORT PAYNE AL 35967 ● (256) 845-0915

Grade Span: KG-12 **Schools**: *Regular* 4 ● *Spec Ed* 0 ● *Alt* 0 **Students**: 2,598 **Total Teachers**: 149 **Student/Classroom Teacher Ratio**: 17.2	**Expenditures/Student**: $3,654 **Librarians**: 4.0 650 students/librarian **Guidance Counselors**: 4.0 650 students/counselor	**% Amer Indian**: 3.4 **% Asian**: 0.6 **% Black**: 7.0 **% Hispanic**: 1.7 **% White**: 87.3	National ***Socio-Economic Status*** indicator percentiles are not available for the state of Alabama

Elmore County

[WETUMPKA] **ELMORE COUNTY S.D.**

PO BOX 617 ● WETUMPKA AL 36092 ● (334) 567-1200

Grade Span: KG-12 **Schools**: *Regular* 11 ● *Spec Ed* 0 ● *Alt* 0 **Students**: 9,026 **Total Teachers**: 493 **Student/Classroom Teacher Ratio**: 19.3	**Expenditures/Student**: $3,515 **Librarians**: 11.0 821 students/librarian **Guidance Counselors**: 18.5 488 students/counselor	**% Amer Indian**: 0.0 **% Asian**: 0.3 **% Black**: 27.4 **% Hispanic**: 0.3 **% White**: 72.0	National ***Socio-Economic Status*** indicator percentiles are not available for the state of Alabama

Escambia County

[BREWTON] **ESCAMBIA COUNTY S.D.**

PO BOX 307 ● BREWTON AL 36427 ● (334) 867-6251

Grade Span: KG-12 **Schools**: *Regular* 11 ● *Spec Ed* 0 ● *Alt* 0 **Students**: 4,982 **Total Teachers**: 286 **Student/Classroom Teacher Ratio**: 18.7	**Expenditures/Student**: $4,246 **Librarians**: 9.0 554 students/librarian **Guidance Counselors**: 12.0 415 students/counselor	**% Amer Indian**: 4.5 **% Asian**: 0.2 **% Black**: 36.5 **% Hispanic**: 0.3 **% White**: 58.5	National ***Socio-Economic Status*** indicator percentiles are not available for the state of Alabama

Etowah County

[GADSDEN] **ETOWAH COUNTY S.D.**

3200 W MEIGHAN BOULEVARD ● GADSDEN AL 35904 ● (256) 549-7577

Grade Span: KG-12 **Schools**: *Regular* 19 ● *Spec Ed* 0 ● *Alt* 0 **Students**: 8,664 **Total Teachers**: 503 **Student/Classroom Teacher Ratio**: 18.3	**Expenditures/Student**: $3,731 **Librarians**: 17.9 484 students/librarian **Guidance Counselors**: 21.0 413 students/counselor	**% Amer Indian**: 0.0 **% Asian**: 0.2 **% Black**: 1.7 **% Hispanic**: 0.3 **% White**: 97.7	National ***Socio-Economic Status*** indicator percentiles are not available for the state of Alabama

Etowah County

GADSDEN CITY S.D.

PO BOX 184 ● GADSDEN AL 35999 ● (256) 549-2904 ● http://www.gcs.k12.al.us

Grade Span: KG-12 **Schools**: *Regular* 15 ● *Spec Ed* 0 ● *Alt* 0 **Students**: 5,852 **Total Teachers**: 392 **Student/Classroom Teacher Ratio**: 15.5	**Expenditures/Student**: $4,588 **Librarians**: 14.9 393 students/librarian **Guidance Counselors**: 15.3 382 students/counselor	**% Amer Indian**: 0.1 **% Asian**: 0.4 **% Black**: 50.3 **% Hispanic**: 1.3 **% White**: 47.9	National ***Socio-Economic Status*** indicator percentiles are not available for the state of Alabama

Fayette County

[FAYETTE] **FAYETTE COUNTY S.D.**

PO BOX 599 ● FAYETTE AL 35555 ● (205) 932-4611

Grade Span: KG-12 **Schools**: *Regular* 6 ● *Spec Ed* 0 ● *Alt* 0 **Students**: 2,936 **Total Teachers**: 179 **Student/Classroom Teacher Ratio**: 18.4	**Expenditures/Student**: $4,041 **Librarians**: 6.0 489 students/librarian **Guidance Counselors**: 6.0 489 students/counselor	**% Amer Indian**: 0.0 **% Asian**: 0.1 **% Black**: 17.3 **% Hispanic**: 0.0 **% White**: 82.6	National ***Socio-Economic Status*** indicator percentiles are not available for the state of Alabama

Franklin County

[RUSSELLVILLE] **FRANKLIN COUNTY S.D.**

PO BOX 610 ● RUSSELLVILLE AL 35653 ● (256) 332-1360

Grade Span: KG-12 **Schools**: *Regular* 6 ● *Spec Ed* 0 ● *Alt* 0 **Students**: 3,225 **Total Teachers**: 203 **Student/Classroom Teacher Ratio**: 16.0	**Expenditures/Student**: $4,197 **Librarians**: 6.0 538 students/librarian **Guidance Counselors**: 5.6 576 students/counselor	**% Amer Indian**: 0.1 **% Asian**: 0.1 **% Black**: 0.4 **% Hispanic**: 1.6 **% White**: 97.8	National ***Socio-Economic Status*** indicator percentiles are not available for the state of Alabama

Geneva County

[GENEVA] **GENEVA COUNTY S.D.**

PO BOX 250 ● GENEVA AL 36340 ● (334) 684-3686

Grade Span: KG-12 **Schools**: *Regular* 10 ● *Spec Ed* 0 ● *Alt* 0 **Students**: 2,770 **Total Teachers**: 168 **Student/Classroom Teacher Ratio**: 16.2	**Expenditures/Student**: $3,907 **Librarians**: 3.6 769 students/librarian **Guidance Counselors**: 5.1 543 students/counselor	**% Amer Indian**: 0.0 **% Asian**: 0.1 **% Black**: 19.3 **% Hispanic**: 1.5 **% White**: 79.1	National ***Socio-Economic Status*** indicator percentiles are not available for the state of Alabama

Hale County

[GREENSBORO] **HALE COUNTY S.D.**

PO BOX 360 ● GREENSBORO AL 36744 ● (334) 624-8836

Grade Span: KG-12 **Schools**: *Regular* 7 ● *Spec Ed* 0 ● *Alt* 0 **Students**: 3,470 **Total Teachers**: 209 **Student/Classroom Teacher Ratio**: 17.6	**Expenditures/Student**: $4,038 **Librarians**: 8.3 418 students/librarian **Guidance Counselors**: 7.4 469 students/counselor	**% Amer Indian**: 0.0 **% Asian**: 0.0 **% Black**: 75.1 **% Hispanic**: 0.2 **% White**: 24.7	National ***Socio-Economic Status*** indicator percentiles are not available for the state of Alabama

Henry County

[ABBEVILLE] **HENRY COUNTY S.D.**

PO BOX 635 ● ABBEVILLE AL 36310 ● (334) 585-2206

Grade Span: KG-12 **Schools**: *Regular* 6 ● *Spec Ed* 0 ● *Alt* 0 **Students**: 2,842 **Total Teachers**: 166 **Student/Classroom Teacher Ratio**: 17.4	**Expenditures/Student**: $4,342 **Librarians**: 6.0 474 students/librarian **Guidance Counselors**: 5.9 482 students/counselor	**% Amer Indian**: 0.0 **% Asian**: 0.0 **% Black**: 51.0 **% Hispanic**: 0.6 **% White**: 48.4	National ***Socio-Economic Status*** indicator percentiles are not available for the state of Alabama

Houston County

DOTHAN CITY S.D.

500 DUSY STREET ● DOTHAN AL 36301 ● (334) 793-1397 ● http://www.dothan.k12.al.us

Grade Span: KG-12 **Schools**: *Regular* 17 ● *Spec Ed* 0 ● *Alt* 0 **Students**: 9,575 **Total Teachers**: 549 **Student/Classroom Teacher Ratio**: 18.1	**Expenditures/Student**: $4,822 **Librarians**: 19.0 504 students/librarian **Guidance Counselors**: 25.5 375 students/counselor	**% Amer Indian**: 0.0 **% Asian**: 1.3 **% Black**: 43.5 **% Hispanic**: 0.4 **% White**: 54.8	National ***Socio-Economic Status*** indicator percentiles are not available for the state of Alabama

Houston County

[DOTHAN] **HOUSTON COUNTY S.D.**

PO DRAWER 1688 ● DOTHAN AL 36302 ● (334) 792-8331

Grade Span: KG-12 **Schools**: *Regular* 8 ● *Spec Ed* 0 ● *Alt* 0 **Students**: 5,946 **Total Teachers**: 358 **Student/Classroom Teacher Ratio**: 17.4	**Expenditures/Student**: $4,328 **Librarians**: 7.5 793 students/librarian **Guidance Counselors**: 9.1 653 students/counselor	**% Amer Indian**: 0.2 **% Asian**: 0.2 **% Black**: 19.5 **% Hispanic**: 0.5 **% White**: 79.5	National ***Socio-Economic Status*** indicator percentiles are not available for the state of Alabama

Jackson County

[SCOTTSBORO] **JACKSON COUNTY S.D.**

COURTHOUSE-SUITE 20 ● SCOTTSBORO AL 35768 ● (256) 574-9200

Grade Span: KG-12 **Schools**: *Regular* 17 ● *Spec Ed* 0 ● *Alt* 0 **Students**: 6,392 **Total Teachers**: 378 **Student/Classroom Teacher Ratio**: 17.9	**Expenditures/Student**: $4,199 **Librarians**: 12.9 496 students/librarian **Guidance Counselors**: 12.8 499 students/counselor	**% Amer Indian**: 15.6 **% Asian**: 0.1 **% Black**: 3.7 **% Hispanic**: 0.3 **% White**: 80.4	National ***Socio-Economic Status*** indicator percentiles are not available for the state of Alabama

Jackson County

SCOTTSBORO CITY S.D.

906 SOUTH SCOTT STREET ● SCOTTSBORO AL 35768 ● (256) 259-4165

Grade Span: KG-12 **Schools**: *Regular* 6 ● *Spec Ed* 0 ● *Alt* 0 **Students**: 2,944 **Total Teachers**: 181 **Student/Classroom Teacher Ratio**: 16.5	**Expenditures/Student**: $4,556 **Librarians**: 6.0 491 students/librarian **Guidance Counselors**: 6.8 433 students/counselor	**% Amer Indian**: 0.0 **% Asian**: 0.4 **% Black**: 7.7 **% Hispanic**: 0.6 **% White**: 91.2	National ***Socio-Economic Status*** indicator percentiles are not available for the state of Alabama

Jefferson County

BESSEMER CITY S.D.

PO BOX 1230 ● BESSEMER AL 35021 ● (205) 481-9800

Grade Span: KG-12 **Schools**: *Regular* 7 ● *Spec Ed* 0 ● *Alt* 0 **Students**: 4,850 **Total Teachers**: 303 **Student/Classroom Teacher Ratio**: 16.5	**Expenditures/Student**: $4,547 **Librarians**: 7.0 693 students/librarian **Guidance Counselors**: 11.6 418 students/counselor	**% Amer Indian**: 0.0 **% Asian**: 0.0 **% Black**: 91.4 **% Hispanic**: 0.2 **% White**: 8.4	National ***Socio-Economic Status*** indicator percentiles are not available for the state of Alabama

Jefferson County

BIRMINGHAM CITY S.D.

PO BOX 10007 ● BIRMINGHAM AL 35202 ● (205) 583-4700 ● http://www.bhm.k12.al.us

Grade Span: KG-12 **Schools**: *Regular* 81 ● *Spec Ed* 7 ● *Alt* 3 **Students**: 41,824 **Total Teachers**: 2,588 **Student/Classroom Teacher Ratio**: 16.1	**Expenditures/Student**: $4,691 **Librarians**: 87.0 481 students/librarian **Guidance Counselors**: 96.0 436 students/counselor	**% Amer Indian**: 0.0 **% Asian**: 0.3 **% Black**: 92.6 **% Hispanic**: 0.1 **% White**: 6.9	National ***Socio-Economic Status*** indicator percentiles are not available for the state of Alabama

Jefferson County

[BIRMINGHAM] **JEFFERSON COUNTY S.D.**

2100 18TH STREET S ● BIRMINGHAM AL 35209-0056 ● (205) 930-3800

Grade Span: KG-12 **Schools**: *Regular* 55 ● *Spec Ed* 1 ● *Alt* 2 **Students**: 41,054 **Total Teachers**: 2,475 **Student/Classroom Teacher Ratio**: 16.9	**Expenditures/Student**: $4,399 **Librarians**: 58.0 708 students/librarian **Guidance Counselors**: 96.0 428 students/counselor	**% Amer Indian**: 0.0 **% Asian**: 0.4 **% Black**: 15.8 **% Hispanic**: 0.3 **% White**: 83.5	National ***Socio-Economic Status*** indicator percentiles are not available for the state of Alabama

Jefferson County

[BIRMINGHAM] **VESTAVIA HILLS CITY S.D.**

PO BOX 20826 ● BIRMINGHAM AL 35216 ● (205) 823-0295 ● http://www.digitrends.com/vhedu

Grade Span: KG-12	**Expenditures/Student**: $4,380	**% Amer Indian**: 0.3	National ***Socio-Economic Status*** indicator percentiles are not available for the state of Alabama
Schools: *Regular* 5 ● *Spec Ed* 0 ● *Alt* 0	**Librarians**: 6.0	**% Asian**: 3.1	
Students: 4,243	707 students/librarian	**% Black**: 4.4	
Total Teachers: 254	**Guidance Counselors**: 10.9	**% Hispanic**: 0.2	
Student/Classroom Teacher Ratio: 16.5	389 students/counselor	**% White**: 92.0	

Jefferson County

HOMEWOOD CITY S.D.

PO BOX 59366 ● HOMEWOOD AL 35259 ● (205) 870-4203

Grade Span: KG-12	**Expenditures/Student**: $4,844	**% Amer Indian**: 0.2	National ***Socio-Economic Status*** indicator percentiles are not available for the state of Alabama
Schools: *Regular* 5 ● *Spec Ed* 0 ● *Alt* 0	**Librarians**: 5.0	**% Asian**: 2.4	
Students: 3,259	652 students/librarian	**% Black**: 17.5	
Total Teachers: 226	**Guidance Counselors**: 10.0	**% Hispanic**: 1.4	
Student/Classroom Teacher Ratio: 14.4	326 students/counselor	**% White**: 78.5	

Jefferson County

HOOVER CITY S.D.

100 MUNICIPAL DRIVE SUITE 200 ● HOOVER AL 35216 ● (205) 985-2425

Grade Span: KG-12	**Expenditures/Student**: $5,576	**% Amer Indian**: 0.1	National ***Socio-Economic Status*** indicator percentiles are not available for the state of Alabama
Schools: *Regular* 11 ● *Spec Ed* 0 ● *Alt* 0	**Librarians**: 12.0	**% Asian**: 1.8	
Students: 8,235	686 students/librarian	**% Black**: 6.5	
Total Teachers: 577	**Guidance Counselors**: 23.9	**% Hispanic**: 0.8	
Student/Classroom Teacher Ratio: 14.4	345 students/counselor	**% White**: 90.8	

Jefferson County

MOUNTAIN BROOK CITY S.D.

PO BOX 130040 ● MOUNTAIN BROOK AL 35213 ● (205) 871-4608 ● http://www.mtnbrook.k12.al.us

Grade Span: KG-12	**Expenditures/Student**: $5,848	**% Amer Indian**: 0.0	National ***Socio-Economic Status*** indicator percentiles are not available for the state of Alabama
Schools: *Regular* 6 ● *Spec Ed* 0 ● *Alt* 0	**Librarians**: 7.0	**% Asian**: 0.5	
Students: 3,677	525 students/librarian	**% Black**: 0.1	
Total Teachers: 282	**Guidance Counselors**: 12.2	**% Hispanic**: 0.2	
Student/Classroom Teacher Ratio: 13.3	301 students/counselor	**% White**: 99.2	

Lamar County

[VERNON] **LAMAR COUNTY S.D.**

PO BOX 1379 ● VERNON AL 35592 ● (205) 695-7615

Grade Span: KG-12	**Expenditures/Student**: $3,794	**% Amer Indian**: 0.0	National ***Socio-Economic Status*** indicator percentiles are not available for the state of Alabama
Schools: *Regular* 3 ● *Spec Ed* 0 ● *Alt* 0	**Librarians**: 6.0	**% Asian**: 0.0	
Students: 2,957	493 students/librarian	**% Black**: 16.6	
Total Teachers: 171	**Guidance Counselors**: 6.7	**% Hispanic**: 0.2	
Student/Classroom Teacher Ratio: 18.8	441 students/counselor	**% White**: 83.2	

Lauderdale County

FLORENCE CITY S.D.

541 RIVERVIEW DRIVE ● FLORENCE AL 35630 ● (256) 766-3234

Grade Span: KG-12	**Expenditures/Student**: $5,310	**% Amer Indian**: 0.0	National ***Socio-Economic Status*** indicator percentiles are not available for the state of Alabama
Schools: *Regular* 8 ● *Spec Ed* 1 ● *Alt* 0	**Librarians**: 11.0	**% Asian**: 0.4	
Students: 4,951	450 students/librarian	**% Black**: 34.2	
Total Teachers: 339	**Guidance Counselors**: 14.0	**% Hispanic**: 0.2	
Student/Classroom Teacher Ratio: 15.2	354 students/counselor	**% White**: 65.1	

Lauderdale County

[FLORENCE] **LAUDERDALE COUNTY S.D.**

PO BOX 278 ● FLORENCE AL 35631-0278 ● (256) 760-1300

Grade Span: KG-12 **Schools**: *Regular* 12 ● *Spec Ed* 0 ● *Alt* 1 **Students**: 8,643 **Total Teachers**: 505 **Student/Classroom Teacher Ratio**: 17.8	**Expenditures/Student**: $3,804 **Librarians**: 11.5 752 students/librarian **Guidance Counselors**: 18.5 467 students/counselor	**% Amer Indian**: 0.1 **% Asian**: 0.1 **% Black**: 3.6 **% Hispanic**: 0.2 **% White**: 96.0	National ***Socio-Economic Status*** indicator percentiles are not available for the state of Alabama

Lawrence County

[MOULTON] **LAWRENCE COUNTY S.D.**

14131 MARKET STREET ● MOULTON AL 35650 ● (256) 974-1121

Grade Span: KG-12 **Schools**: *Regular* 13 ● *Spec Ed* 0 ● *Alt* 0 **Students**: 6,307 **Total Teachers**: 378 **Student/Classroom Teacher Ratio**: 17.7	**Expenditures/Student**: $4,166 **Librarians**: 13.0 485 students/librarian **Guidance Counselors**: 18.0 350 students/counselor	**% Amer Indian**: 18.9 **% Asian**: 0.0 **% Black**: 19.7 **% Hispanic**: 0.3 **% White**: 61.0	National ***Socio-Economic Status*** indicator percentiles are not available for the state of Alabama

Lee County

AUBURN CITY S.D.

PO BOX 3270 ● AUBURN AL 36831 ● (334) 887-2100

Grade Span: KG-12 **Schools**: *Regular* 7 ● *Spec Ed* 0 ● *Alt* 0 **Students**: 4,067 **Total Teachers**: 269 **Student/Classroom Teacher Ratio**: 15.2	**Expenditures/Student**: $4,981 **Librarians**: 8.0 508 students/librarian **Guidance Counselors**: 8.0 508 students/counselor	**% Amer Indian**: 0.0 **% Asian**: 5.1 **% Black**: 34.5 **% Hispanic**: 0.5 **% White**: 59.9	National ***Socio-Economic Status*** indicator percentiles are not available for the state of Alabama

Lee County

[OPELIKA] **LEE COUNTY S.D.**

BOX 120 ● OPELIKA AL 36803-0120 ● (334) 745-9770 ● http://www.lee.k12.al.us

Grade Span: KG-12 **Schools**: *Regular* 11 ● *Spec Ed* 0 ● *Alt* 0 **Students**: 7,154 **Total Teachers**: 401 **Student/Classroom Teacher Ratio**: 17.2	**Expenditures/Student**: $3,832 **Librarians**: 10.0 715 students/librarian **Guidance Counselors**: 14.0 511 students/counselor	**% Amer Indian**: 0.2 **% Asian**: 0.4 **% Black**: 23.6 **% Hispanic**: 0.7 **% White**: 75.2	National ***Socio-Economic Status*** indicator percentiles are not available for the state of Alabama

Lee County

OPELIKA CITY S.D.

PO BOX 2469 ● OPELIKA AL 36803 ● (334) 745-9700

Grade Span: KG-12 **Schools**: *Regular* 8 ● *Spec Ed* 0 ● *Alt* 0 **Students**: 4,559 **Total Teachers**: 284 **Student/Classroom Teacher Ratio**: 16.2	**Expenditures/Student**: $4,436 **Librarians**: 10.0 456 students/librarian **Guidance Counselors**: 8.6 530 students/counselor	**% Amer Indian**: 0.1 **% Asian**: 1.3 **% Black**: 56.2 **% Hispanic**: 0.3 **% White**: 42.1	National ***Socio-Economic Status*** indicator percentiles are not available for the state of Alabama

Limestone County

ATHENS CITY S.D.

313 EAST WASHINGTON STREET ● ATHENS AL 35611 ● (256) 233-6600

Grade Span: KG-12 **Schools**: *Regular* 6 ● *Spec Ed* 0 ● *Alt* 0 **Students**: 2,981 **Total Teachers**: 187 **Student/Classroom Teacher Ratio**: 15.8	**Expenditures/Student**: $5,055 **Librarians**: 6.0 497 students/librarian **Guidance Counselors**: 6.4 466 students/counselor	**% Amer Indian**: 0.1 **% Asian**: 0.7 **% Black**: 25.6 **% Hispanic**: 1.6 **% White**: 72.0	National ***Socio-Economic Status*** indicator percentiles are not available for the state of Alabama

Limestone County

[ATHENS] **LIMESTONE COUNTY S.D.**

300 SOUTH JEFFERSON STREET ● ATHENS AL 35611 ● (256) 232-5353 ● http://east2.elhs.limestone.k12.al.us/html/board.htm

Grade Span: KG-12	**Expenditures/Student**: $3,979	**% Amer Indian**: 0.0	National ***Socio-Economic***
Schools: *Regular* 10 ● *Spec Ed* 0 ● *Alt* 0	**Librarians**: 10.0	**% Asian**: 0.1	***Status*** indicator percentiles
Students: 7,474	747 students/librarian	**% Black**: 11.4	are not available for the
Total Teachers: 439	**Guidance Counselors**: 16.9	**% Hispanic**: 0.5	state of Alabama
Student/Classroom Teacher Ratio: 17.4	442 students/counselor	**% White**: 87.9	

Lowndes County

[HAYNEVILLE] **LOWNDES COUNTY S.D.**

PO BOX 755 ● HAYNEVILLE AL 36040 ● (334) 548-2131

Grade Span: KG-12	**Expenditures/Student**: $4,764	**% Amer Indian**: 0.0	National ***Socio-Economic***
Schools: *Regular* 8 ● *Spec Ed* 0 ● *Alt* 0	**Librarians**: 5.0	**% Asian**: 0.0	***Status*** indicator percentiles
Students: 2,969	594 students/librarian	**% Black**: 99.4	are not available for the
Total Teachers: 170	**Guidance Counselors**: 8.0	**% Hispanic**: 0.0	state of Alabama
Student/Classroom Teacher Ratio: 17.9	371 students/counselor	**% White**: 0.6	

Macon County

[TUSKEGEE] **MACON COUNTY S.D.**

PO BOX 90 ● TUSKEGEE AL 36083 ● (334) 727-1600 ● http://members.aol.com/bookertwhs/eagles/btw.htm

Grade Span: KG-12	**Expenditures/Student**: $4,822	**% Amer Indian**: 0.0	National ***Socio-Economic***
Schools: *Regular* 8 ● *Spec Ed* 0 ● *Alt* 0	**Librarians**: 8.0	**% Asian**: 0.0	***Status*** indicator percentiles
Students: 4,280	535 students/librarian	**% Black**: 94.2	are not available for the
Total Teachers: 252	**Guidance Counselors**: 13.0	**% Hispanic**: 0.1	state of Alabama
Student/Classroom Teacher Ratio: 16.7	329 students/counselor	**% White**: 5.7	

Madison County

HUNTSVILLE CITY S.D.

PO BOX 1256 ● HUNTSVILLE AL 35807 ● (256) 532-4640 ● http://www.hsv.tis.net/~lpearce

Grade Span: KG-12	**Expenditures/Student**: $5,158	**% Amer Indian**: 0.5	National ***Socio-Economic***
Schools: *Regular* 42 ● *Spec Ed* 0 ● *Alt* 1	**Librarians**: 46.0	**% Asian**: 3.1	***Status*** indicator percentiles
Students: 24,163	525 students/librarian	**% Black**: 38.2	are not available for the
Total Teachers: 1,690	**Guidance Counselors**: 68.0	**% Hispanic**: 1.2	state of Alabama
Student/Classroom Teacher Ratio: 14.1	355 students/counselor	**% White**: 57.0	

Madison County

[HUNTSVILLE] **MADISON COUNTY S.D.**

PO BOX 226 ● HUNTSVILLE AL 35804 ● (256) 532-3522 ● http://www.bjhs.madison.k12.al.us

Grade Span: KG-12	**Expenditures/Student**: $3,825	**% Amer Indian**: 4.1	National ***Socio-Economic***
Schools: *Regular* 21 ● *Spec Ed* 0 ● *Alt* 0	**Librarians**: 22.0	**% Asian**: 1.4	***Status*** indicator percentiles
Students: 18,182	826 students/librarian	**% Black**: 13.2	are not available for the
Total Teachers: 990	**Guidance Counselors**: 34.0	**% Hispanic**: 1.0	state of Alabama
Student/Classroom Teacher Ratio: 18.7	535 students/counselor	**% White**: 80.3	

Marion County

[HAMILTON] **MARION COUNTY S.D.**

PO BOX 189 ● HAMILTON AL 35570 ● (205) 921-3192

Grade Span: KG-12	**Expenditures/Student**: $3,705	**% Amer Indian**: 0.1	National ***Socio-Economic***
Schools: *Regular* 11 ● *Spec Ed* 0 ● *Alt* 0	**Librarians**: 8.5	**% Asian**: 0.2	***Status*** indicator percentiles
Students: 4,094	482 students/librarian	**% Black**: 3.6	are not available for the
Total Teachers: 244	**Guidance Counselors**: 7.5	**% Hispanic**: 0.4	state of Alabama
Student/Classroom Teacher Ratio: 16.8	546 students/counselor	**% White**: 95.6	

Marshall County

ALBERTVILLE CITY S.D.

PO BOX 1487 ● ALBERTVILLE AL 35950 ● (256) 891-1183

Grade Span: KG-12 **Schools**: *Regular* 6 ● *Spec Ed* 0 ● *Alt* 0 **Students**: 3,213 **Total Teachers**: 182 **Student/Classroom Teacher Ratio**: 17.8	**Expenditures/Student**: $4,051 **Librarians**: 7.0 459 students/librarian **Guidance Counselors**: 5.0 643 students/counselor	**% Amer Indian**: 0.1 **% Asian**: 0.2 **% Black**: 1.3 **% Hispanic**: 7.3 **% White**: 91.0	National ***Socio-Economic Status*** indicator percentiles are not available for the state of Alabama

Marshall County

ARAB CITY S.D.

PO DRAWER O ● ARAB AL 35016 ● (256) 586-6011 ● http://www.mindspring.com/~arabhigh

Grade Span: KG-12 **Schools**: *Regular* 4 ● *Spec Ed* 0 ● *Alt* 0 **Students**: 2,518 **Total Teachers**: 142 **Student/Classroom Teacher Ratio**: 17.9	**Expenditures/Student**: $3,588 **Librarians**: 4.0 630 students/librarian **Guidance Counselors**: 5.0 504 students/counselor	**% Amer Indian**: 0.1 **% Asian**: 0.4 **% Black**: 0.0 **% Hispanic**: 0.2 **% White**: 99.3	National ***Socio-Economic Status*** indicator percentiles are not available for the state of Alabama

Marshall County

[GUNTERSVILLE] **MARSHALL COUNTY S.D.**

12380 US HIGHWAY 431 SOUTH ● GUNTERSVILLE AL 35976 ● (256) 582-3171

Grade Span: KG-12 **Schools**: *Regular* 14 ● *Spec Ed* 0 ● *Alt* 0 **Students**: 6,793 **Total Teachers**: 408 **Student/Classroom Teacher Ratio**: 17.8	**Expenditures/Student**: $4,317 **Librarians**: 13.7 496 students/librarian **Guidance Counselors**: 14.8 459 students/counselor	**% Amer Indian**: 0.0 **% Asian**: 0.2 **% Black**: 0.3 **% Hispanic**: 1.0 **% White**: 98.5	National ***Socio-Economic Status*** indicator percentiles are not available for the state of Alabama

Mobile County

[MOBILE] **MOBILE COUNTY S.D.**

PO BOX 1327 ● MOBILE AL 36633 ● (334) 690-8227 ● http://www.mcpss.com

Grade Span: KG-12 **Schools**: *Regular* 87 ● *Spec Ed* 1 ● *Alt* 0 **Students**: 65,602 **Total Teachers**: 3,603 **Student/Classroom Teacher Ratio**: 17.9	**Expenditures/Student**: $3,832 **Librarians**: 96.9 677 students/librarian **Guidance Counselors**: 145.4 451 students/counselor	**% Amer Indian**: 0.3 **% Asian**: 1.4 **% Black**: 48.9 **% Hispanic**: 0.3 **% White**: 49.2	National ***Socio-Economic Status*** indicator percentiles are not available for the state of Alabama

Monroe County

[MONROEVILLE] **MONROE COUNTY S.D.**

BOX 967 ● MONROEVILLE AL 36461 ● (334) 575-2168

Grade Span: KG-12 **Schools**: *Regular* 11 ● *Spec Ed* 0 ● *Alt* 0 **Students**: 5,180 **Total Teachers**: 303 **Student/Classroom Teacher Ratio**: 17.2	**Expenditures/Student**: $3,731 **Librarians**: 10.0 518 students/librarian **Guidance Counselors**: 9.9 523 students/counselor	**% Amer Indian**: 0.8 **% Asian**: 0.3 **% Black**: 52.1 **% Hispanic**: 0.1 **% White**: 46.6	National ***Socio-Economic Status*** indicator percentiles are not available for the state of Alabama

Montgomery County

[MONTGOMERY] **MONTGOMERY COUNTY S.D.**

PO BOX 1991 ● MONTGOMERY AL 36102 ● (334) 269-3028

Grade Span: KG-12 **Schools**: *Regular* 49 ● *Spec Ed* 2 ● *Alt* 4 **Students**: 35,065 **Total Teachers**: 2,134 **Student/Classroom Teacher Ratio**: 16.4	**Expenditures/Student**: $3,905 **Librarians**: 58.5 599 students/librarian **Guidance Counselors**: 92.0 381 students/counselor	**% Amer Indian**: 0.1 **% Asian**: 1.0 **% Black**: 66.9 **% Hispanic**: 0.6 **% White**: 31.4	National ***Socio-Economic Status*** indicator percentiles are not available for the state of Alabama

Morgan County
DECATUR CITY S.D.
302 4TH AVENUE NE ● DECATUR AL 35601 ● (256) 552-3000 ● http://www.ptc.dcs.edu

Grade Span: KG-12 **Schools**: *Regular* 17 ● *Spec Ed* 0 ● *Alt* 0 **Students**: 8,690 **Total Teachers**: 574 **Student/Classroom Teacher Ratio**: 15.2	**Expenditures/Student**: $5,137 **Librarians**: 19.0 457 students/librarian **Guidance Counselors**: 23.0 378 students/counselor	**% Amer Indian**: 0.3 **% Asian**: 1.1 **% Black**: 27.1 **% Hispanic**: 1.9 **% White**: 69.6	National ***Socio-Economic Status*** indicator percentiles are not available for the state of Alabama

Morgan County
[DECATUR] **MORGAN COUNTY S.D.**
1325 POINT MALLARD PKWY SE ● DECATUR AL 35601 ● (256) 353-6442

Grade Span: KG-12 **Schools**: *Regular* 14 ● *Spec Ed* 0 ● *Alt* 0 **Students**: 7,537 **Total Teachers**: 496 **Student/Classroom Teacher Ratio**: 15.2	**Expenditures/Student**: $4,718 **Librarians**: 13.4 562 students/librarian **Guidance Counselors**: 18.0 419 students/counselor	**% Amer Indian**: 0.1 **% Asian**: 0.2 **% Black**: 3.3 **% Hispanic**: 0.4 **% White**: 96.0	National ***Socio-Economic Status*** indicator percentiles are not available for the state of Alabama

Morgan County
HARTSELLE CITY S.D.
109 COLLEGE STREET NW ● HARTSELLE AL 35640 ● (256) 773-5419

Grade Span: KG-12 **Schools**: *Regular* 5 ● *Spec Ed* 0 ● *Alt* 0 **Students**: 2,955 **Total Teachers**: 196 **Student/Classroom Teacher Ratio**: 15.4	**Expenditures/Student**: $4,606 **Librarians**: 5.0 591 students/librarian **Guidance Counselors**: 8.0 369 students/counselor	**% Amer Indian**: 0.2 **% Asian**: 0.2 **% Black**: 5.2 **% Hispanic**: 0.4 **% White**: 94.0	National ***Socio-Economic Status*** indicator percentiles are not available for the state of Alabama

Pickens County
[CARROLLTON] **PICKENS COUNTY S.D.**
PO BOX 32 ● CARROLLTON AL 35447 ● (205) 367-2080

Grade Span: KG-12 **Schools**: *Regular* 9 ● *Spec Ed* 0 ● *Alt* 0 **Students**: 3,954 **Total Teachers**: 228 **Student/Classroom Teacher Ratio**: 17.5	**Expenditures/Student**: $4,041 **Librarians**: 8.0 494 students/librarian **Guidance Counselors**: 11.0 359 students/counselor	**% Amer Indian**: 0.0 **% Asian**: 0.2 **% Black**: 65.2 **% Hispanic**: 0.0 **% White**: 34.6	National ***Socio-Economic Status*** indicator percentiles are not available for the state of Alabama

Pike County
[TROY] **PIKE COUNTY S.D.**
109 EAST CHURCH STREET ● TROY AL 36081 ● (334) 566-1850

Grade Span: KG-12 **Schools**: *Regular* 5 ● *Spec Ed* 0 ● *Alt* 0 **Students**: 2,527 **Total Teachers**: 162 **Student/Classroom Teacher Ratio**: 16.1	**Expenditures/Student**: $4,746 **Librarians**: 5.0 505 students/librarian **Guidance Counselors**: 4.9 516 students/counselor	**% Amer Indian**: 0.1 **% Asian**: 0.2 **% Black**: 53.0 **% Hispanic**: 0.0 **% White**: 46.7	National ***Socio-Economic Status*** indicator percentiles are not available for the state of Alabama

Russell County
PHENIX CITY CITY S.D.
PO BOX 460 ● PHENIX CITY AL 36867 ● (334) 298-0534

Grade Span: KG-12 **Schools**: *Regular* 9 ● *Spec Ed* 0 ● *Alt* 0 **Students**: 5,023 **Total Teachers**: 285 **Student/Classroom Teacher Ratio**: 17.9	**Expenditures/Student**: $4,607 **Librarians**: 10.0 502 students/librarian **Guidance Counselors**: 14.9 337 students/counselor	**% Amer Indian**: 0.0 **% Asian**: 0.2 **% Black**: 54.4 **% Hispanic**: 0.4 **% White**: 44.9	National ***Socio-Economic Status*** indicator percentiles are not available for the state of Alabama

Russell County

[PHENIX CITY] **RUSSELL COUNTY S.D.**

PO BOX 400 ● PHENIX CITY AL 36868 ● (334) 298-8791 ● http://www.mindspring.com/~endfingerb

Grade Span: KG-12 **Schools**: *Regular* 8 ● *Spec Ed* 0 ● *Alt* 0 **Students**: 3,749 **Total Teachers**: 211 **Student/Classroom Teacher Ratio**: 17.3	**Expenditures/Student**: $3,994 **Librarians**: 6.5 577 students/librarian **Guidance Counselors**: 7.0 536 students/counselor	**% Amer Indian**: 0.0 **% Asian**: 0.2 **% Black**: 43.2 **% Hispanic**: 0.6 **% White**: 55.9	National ***Socio-Economic Status*** indicator percentiles are not available for the state of Alabama

St. Clair County

[ASHVILLE] **ST. CLAIR COUNTY S.D.**

PO BOX 248 ● ASHVILLE AL 35953 ● (205) 594-5693

Grade Span: KG-12 **Schools**: *Regular* 12 ● *Spec Ed* 0 ● *Alt* 1 **Students**: 6,506 **Total Teachers**: 350 **Student/Classroom Teacher Ratio**: 19.6	**Expenditures/Student**: $3,440 **Librarians**: 11.0 591 students/librarian **Guidance Counselors**: 13.8 471 students/counselor	**% Amer Indian**: 0.1 **% Asian**: 0.2 **% Black**: 8.5 **% Hispanic**: 0.7 **% White**: 90.6	National ***Socio-Economic Status*** indicator percentiles are not available for the state of Alabama

St. Clair County

PELL CITY CITY S.D.

25-12TH STREET S ● PELL CITY AL 35125 ● (205) 884-4440

Grade Span: KG-12 **Schools**: *Regular* 5 ● *Spec Ed* 0 ● *Alt* 0 **Students**: 3,618 **Total Teachers**: 193 **Student/Classroom Teacher Ratio**: 18.9	**Expenditures/Student**: $3,809 **Librarians**: 5.0 724 students/librarian **Guidance Counselors**: 7.0 517 students/counselor	**% Amer Indian**: 0.1 **% Asian**: 0.2 **% Black**: 14.8 **% Hispanic**: 0.2 **% White**: 84.8	National ***Socio-Economic Status*** indicator percentiles are not available for the state of Alabama

Shelby County

[COLUMBIANA] **SHELBY COUNTY S.D.**

P O BOX 429 ● COLUMBIANA AL 35051 ● (205) 669-5600

Grade Span: KG-12 **Schools**: *Regular* 27 ● *Spec Ed* 1 ● *Alt* 0 **Students**: 18,132 **Total Teachers**: 1,056 **Student/Classroom Teacher Ratio**: 17.8	**Expenditures/Student**: $4,193 **Librarians**: 29.0 625 students/librarian **Guidance Counselors**: 41.0 442 students/counselor	**% Amer Indian**: 0.2 **% Asian**: 0.7 **% Black**: 12.3 **% Hispanic**: 0.4 **% White**: 86.5	National ***Socio-Economic Status*** indicator percentiles are not available for the state of Alabama

Sumter County

[LIVINGSTON] **SUMTER COUNTY S.D.**

PO BOX 10 ● LIVINGSTON AL 35470 ● (205) 652-9605

Grade Span: KG-12 **Schools**: *Regular* 6 ● *Spec Ed* 0 ● *Alt* 0 **Students**: 2,878 **Total Teachers**: 170 **Student/Classroom Teacher Ratio**: 17.2	**Expenditures/Student**: $4,808 **Librarians**: 5.9 488 students/librarian **Guidance Counselors**: 9.0 320 students/counselor	**% Amer Indian**: 0.0 **% Asian**: 0.0 **% Black**: 99.5 **% Hispanic**: 0.1 **% White**: 0.4	National ***Socio-Economic Status*** indicator percentiles are not available for the state of Alabama

Talladega County

SYLACAUGA CITY S.D.

PO DRAWER 1127 ● SYLACAUGA AL 35150 ● (256) 245-5256

Grade Span: KG-12 **Schools**: *Regular* 5 ● *Spec Ed* 0 ● *Alt* 0 **Students**: 2,607 **Total Teachers**: 154 **Student/Classroom Teacher Ratio**: 17.2	**Expenditures/Student**: $4,299 **Librarians**: 5.0 521 students/librarian **Guidance Counselors**: 6.0 435 students/counselor	**% Amer Indian**: 0.1 **% Asian**: 0.2 **% Black**: 38.1 **% Hispanic**: 0.1 **% White**: 61.5	National ***Socio-Economic Status*** indicator percentiles are not available for the state of Alabama

Talladega County
TALLADEGA CITY S.D.
PO BOX 946 ● TALLADEGA AL 35160 ● (256) 362-2203

Grade Span: KG-12	**Expenditures/Student**: $4,101	**% Amer Indian**: 0.1	National ***Socio-Economic Status*** indicator percentiles are not available for the state of Alabama
Schools: *Regular* 8 ● *Spec Ed* 0 ● *Alt* 0	**Librarians**: 9.0	**% Asian**: 0.2	
Students: 3,623	403 students/librarian	**% Black**: 49.9	
Total Teachers: 210	**Guidance Counselors**: 7.0	**% Hispanic**: 0.4	
Student/Classroom Teacher Ratio: 17.5	518 students/counselor	**% White**: 49.4	

Talladega County
[TALLADEGA] **TALLADEGA COUNTY S.D.**
PO BOX 887 ● TALLADEGA AL 35160 ● (256) 362-1401

Grade Span: KG-12	**Expenditures/Student**: $4,046	**% Amer Indian**: 0.0	National ***Socio-Economic Status*** indicator percentiles are not available for the state of Alabama
Schools: *Regular* 15 ● *Spec Ed* 0 ● *Alt* 0	**Librarians**: 16.0	**% Asian**: 0.1	
Students: 7,733	483 students/librarian	**% Black**: 40.9	
Total Teachers: 436	**Guidance Counselors**: 16.9	**% Hispanic**: 0.1	
Student/Classroom Teacher Ratio: 18.0	458 students/counselor	**% White**: 58.8	

Tallapoosa County
ALEXANDER CITY CITY S.D.
PO BOX 1205 ● ALEXANDER CITY AL 35010 ● (256) 234-5074

Grade Span: KG-12	**Expenditures/Student**: $3,911	**% Amer Indian**: 0.0	National ***Socio-Economic Status*** indicator percentiles are not available for the state of Alabama
Schools: *Regular* 5 ● *Spec Ed* 0 ● *Alt* 0	**Librarians**: 5.0	**% Asian**: 0.4	
Students: 3,812	762 students/librarian	**% Black**: 36.0	
Total Teachers: 226	**Guidance Counselors**: 10.0	**% Hispanic**: 0.2	
Student/Classroom Teacher Ratio: 18.0	381 students/counselor	**% White**: 63.4	

Tallapoosa County
[DADEVILLE] **TALLAPOOSA COUNTY S.D.**
COURTHOUSE ● DADEVILLE AL 36853 ● (256) 825-1020

Grade Span: KG-12	**Expenditures/Student**: $3,915	**% Amer Indian**: 0.2	National ***Socio-Economic Status*** indicator percentiles are not available for the state of Alabama
Schools: *Regular* 5 ● *Spec Ed* 0 ● *Alt* 0	**Librarians**: 5.0	**% Asian**: 0.1	
Students: 3,419	684 students/librarian	**% Black**: 38.3	
Total Teachers: 203	**Guidance Counselors**: 6.1	**% Hispanic**: 0.1	
Student/Classroom Teacher Ratio: 16.5	560 students/counselor	**% White**: 61.2	

Tuscaloosa County
TUSCALOOSA CITY S.D.
1100 21ST STREET E ● TUSCALOOSA AL 35404 ● (205) 759-3510

Grade Span: KG-12	**Expenditures/Student**: $4,941	**% Amer Indian**: 0.0	National ***Socio-Economic Status*** indicator percentiles are not available for the state of Alabama
Schools: *Regular* 18 ● *Spec Ed* 0 ● *Alt* 1	**Librarians**: 20.0	**% Asian**: 1.1	
Students: 10,302	515 students/librarian	**% Black**: 66.2	
Total Teachers: 713	**Guidance Counselors**: 28.7	**% Hispanic**: 0.3	
Student/Classroom Teacher Ratio: 14.1	359 students/counselor	**% White**: 32.5	

Tuscaloosa County
[TUSCALOOSA] **TUSCALOOSA COUNTY S.D.**
PO DRAWER 2568 ● TUSCALOOSA AL 35403 ● (205) 758-0411

Grade Span: KG-12	**Expenditures/Student**: $4,093	**% Amer Indian**: 0.0	National ***Socio-Economic Status*** indicator percentiles are not available for the state of Alabama
Schools: *Regular* 23 ● *Spec Ed* 2 ● *Alt* 2	**Librarians**: 23.5	**% Asian**: 0.3	
Students: 15,168	645 students/librarian	**% Black**: 21.7	
Total Teachers: 931	**Guidance Counselors**: 33.0	**% Hispanic**: 0.2	
Student/Classroom Teacher Ratio: 16.7	460 students/counselor	**% White**: 77.8	

Walker County

JASPER CITY S.D.

PO BOX 500 ● JASPER AL 35501 ● (205) 384-6021

Grade Span: KG-12 **Schools**: *Regular* 5 ● *Spec Ed* 1 ● *Alt* 0 **Students**: 2,571 **Total Teachers**: 170 **Student/Classroom Teacher Ratio**: 15.6	**Expenditures/Student**: $4,887 **Librarians**: 6.0 429 students/librarian **Guidance Counselors**: 9.0 286 students/counselor	**% Amer Indian**: 0.0 **% Asian**: 0.6 **% Black**: 21.0 **% Hispanic**: 0.4 **% White**: 78.0	National ***Socio-Economic Status*** indicator percentiles are not available for the state of Alabama

Walker County

[JASPER] **WALKER COUNTY S.D.**

PO BOX 311 ● JASPER AL 35502 ● (205) 387-0555

Grade Span: KG-12 **Schools**: *Regular* 22 ● *Spec Ed* 0 ● *Alt* 0 **Students**: 9,193 **Total Teachers**: 565 **Student/Classroom Teacher Ratio**: 16.9	**Expenditures/Student**: $4,203 **Librarians**: 8.8 1,045 students/librarian **Guidance Counselors**: 19.0 484 students/counselor	**% Amer Indian**: 0.0 **% Asian**: 0.0 **% Black**: 7.1 **% Hispanic**: 0.2 **% White**: 92.6	National ***Socio-Economic Status*** indicator percentiles are not available for the state of Alabama

Washington County

[CHATOM] **WASHINGTON COUNTY S.D.**

PO BOX 1359 ● CHATOM AL 36518 ● (334) 847-2401

Grade Span: KG-12 **Schools**: *Regular* 10 ● *Spec Ed* 0 ● *Alt* 0 **Students**: 3,803 **Total Teachers**: 237 **Student/Classroom Teacher Ratio**: 16.6	**Expenditures/Student**: $4,275 **Librarians**: 8.7 437 students/librarian **Guidance Counselors**: 9.5 400 students/counselor	**% Amer Indian**: 7.3 **% Asian**: 0.2 **% Black**: 35.4 **% Hispanic**: 0.1 **% White**: 57.0	National ***Socio-Economic Status*** indicator percentiles are not available for the state of Alabama

Wilcox County

[CAMDEN] **WILCOX COUNTY S.D.**

PO BOX 160 ● CAMDEN AL 36726 ● (334) 682-4716

Grade Span: KG-12 **Schools**: *Regular* 7 ● *Spec Ed* 0 ● *Alt* 0 **Students**: 2,799 **Total Teachers**: 169 **Student/Classroom Teacher Ratio**: 16.0	**Expenditures/Student**: $4,559 **Librarians**: 3.8 737 students/librarian **Guidance Counselors**: 6.0 467 students/counselor	**% Amer Indian**: 0.0 **% Asian**: 0.0 **% Black**: 99.1 **% Hispanic**: 0.0 **% White**: 0.9	National ***Socio-Economic Status*** indicator percentiles are not available for the state of Alabama

Winston County

[DOUBLE SPRINGS] **WINSTON COUNTY S.D.**

PO BOX 9 ● DOUBLE SPRINGS AL 35553 ● (205) 489-5018

Grade Span: KG-12 **Schools**: *Regular* 5 ● *Spec Ed* 0 ● *Alt* 0 **Students**: 2,772 **Total Teachers**: 168 **Student/Classroom Teacher Ratio**: 17.5	**Expenditures/Student**: $4,327 **Librarians**: 5.0 554 students/librarian **Guidance Counselors**: 6.0 462 students/counselor	**% Amer Indian**: 0.0 **% Asian**: 0.0 **% Black**: 0.0 **% Hispanic**: 0.0 **% White**: 100.0	National ***Socio-Economic Status*** indicator percentiles are not available for the state of Alabama

Anchorage Borough

ANCHORAGE S.D.

PO BOX 196614 ● ANCHORAGE AK 99519-6614 ● (907) 333-9561 ● http://www.asd.k12.ak.us

Grade Span: PK-12 **Schools**: *Regular* 71 ● *Spec Ed* 2 ● *Alt* 11 **Students**: 47,318 **Total Teachers**: 2,461 **Student/Classroom Teacher Ratio**: 19.8	**Expenditures/Student**: $6,227 **Librarians**: 58.0 816 students/librarian **Guidance Counselors**: 69.6 680 students/counselor	**% Amer Indian**: 10.8 **% Asian**: 7.2 **% Black**: 8.6 **% Hispanic**: 4.5 **% White**: 68.9	National ***Socio-Economic Status*** indicator percentile (100=high): 69th

Bethel Census Area

[BETHEL] **LOWER KUSKOKWIM S.D.**

PO BOX 305 ● BETHEL AK 99559-0305 ● (907) 543-4800 ● http://www.lksd.org

Grade Span: PK-12 **Schools**: *Regular* 25 ● *Spec Ed* 0 ● *Alt* 1 **Students**: 3,466 **Total Teachers**: 252 **Student/Classroom Teacher Ratio**: 13.1	**Expenditures/Student**: $13,160 **Librarians**: 2.0 1,733 students/librarian **Guidance Counselors**: 3.0 1,155 students/counselor	**% Amer Indian**: 91.7 **% Asian**: 0.6 **% Black**: 0.3 **% Hispanic**: 0.2 **% White**: 7.2	National ***Socio-Economic Status*** indicator percentile (100=high): 9th

Fairbanks North Star Borough

FAIRBANKS NORTH STAR BOROUGH S.D.

520 FIFTH AVENUE ● FAIRBANKS AK 99701 ● (907) 452-2000 ● http://www.northstar.k12.ak.us

Grade Span: PK-12 **Schools**: *Regular* 27 ● *Spec Ed* 0 ● *Alt* 3 **Students**: 15,968 **Total Teachers**: 862 **Student/Classroom Teacher Ratio**: 18.6	**Expenditures/Student**: $6,972 **Librarians**: 7.5 2,129 students/librarian **Guidance Counselors**: 38.8 412 students/counselor	**% Amer Indian**: 10.6 **% Asian**: 3.0 **% Black**: 8.5 **% Hispanic**: 3.3 **% White**: 74.7	National ***Socio-Economic Status*** indicator percentile (100=high): 63rd

Juneau Borough

JUNEAU BOROUGH S.D.

10014 CRAZY HORSE DRIVE ● JUNEAU AK 99801 ● (907) 463-1700 ● http://www.jsd.k12.ak.us

Grade Span: PK-12 **Schools**: *Regular* 8 ● *Spec Ed* 0 ● *Alt* 1 **Students**: 5,531 **Total Teachers**: 286 **Student/Classroom Teacher Ratio**: 20.6	**Expenditures/Student**: $7,726 **Librarians**: 4.5 1,229 students/librarian **Guidance Counselors**: 7.5 737 students/counselor	**% Amer Indian**: 20.4 **% Asian**: 6.0 **% Black**: 1.6 **% Hispanic**: 2.5 **% White**: 69.5	National ***Socio-Economic Status*** indicator percentile (100=high): 85th

Kenai Peninsula Borough

[SOLDOTNA] **KENAI PENINSULA BOROUGH S.D.**

148 NORTH BINKLEY STREET ● SOLDOTNA AK 99669 ● (907) 262-5846 ● http://www.kpbsd.k12.ak.us

Grade Span: PK-12 **Schools**: *Regular* 36 ● *Spec Ed* 0 ● *Alt* 2 **Students**: 10,314 **Total Teachers**: 608 **Student/Classroom Teacher Ratio**: 16.4	**Expenditures/Student**: $8,086 **Librarians**: 19.8 521 students/librarian **Guidance Counselors**: 16.5 625 students/counselor	**% Amer Indian**: 9.8 **% Asian**: 1.9 **% Black**: 0.6 **% Hispanic**: 1.4 **% White**: 86.2	National ***Socio-Economic Status*** indicator percentile (100=high): 60th

Ketchikan Gateway Borough

KETCHIKAN GATEWAY BOROUGH S.D.

POUCH Z ● KETCHIKAN AK 99901 ● (907) 225-2118

Grade Span: PK-12 **Schools**: *Regular* 7 ● *Spec Ed* 0 ● *Alt* 1 **Students**: 2,890 **Total Teachers**: 156 **Student/Classroom Teacher Ratio**: 20.4	**Expenditures/Student**: $6,522 **Librarians**: 2.0 1,445 students/librarian **Guidance Counselors**: 6.5 445 students/counselor	**% Amer Indian**: 21.3 **% Asian**: 4.9 **% Black**: 0.6 **% Hispanic**: 1.3 **% White**: 71.9	National ***Socio-Economic Status*** indicator percentile (100=high): 76th

Kodiak Island Borough

KODIAK ISLAND BOROUGH S.D.

722 MILL BAY ROAD ● KODIAK AK 99615 ● (907) 486-9220 ● http://www.kodiak.k12.ak.us

Grade Span: PK-12	**Expenditures/Student**: $7,843	**% Amer Indian**: 19.9	
Schools: *Regular* 15 ● *Spec Ed* 0 ● *Alt* 1	**Librarians**: 1.0	**% Asian**: 17.3	National ***Socio-Economic***
Students: 2,910	2,910 students/librarian	**% Black**: 1.0	***Status*** indicator percentile
Total Teachers: 166	**Guidance Counselors**: 5.5	**% Hispanic**: 3.7	(100=high): 66th
Student/Classroom Teacher Ratio: 15.2	529 students/counselor	**% White**: 58.1	

Matanuska-Susitna Borough

[PALMER] MATANUSKA-SUSITNA BOROUGH S.D.

125 WEST EVERGREEN ● PALMER AK 99645 ● (907) 746-9255 ● http://MSB.mat-su.k12.ak.us

Grade Span: PK-12	**Expenditures/Student**: $7,175	**% Amer Indian**: 8.0	
Schools: *Regular* 27 ● *Spec Ed* 0 ● *Alt* 1	**Librarians**: 19.5	**% Asian**: 0.8	National ***Socio-Economic***
Students: 12,338	633 students/librarian	**% Black**: 0.9	***Status*** indicator percentile
Total Teachers: 700	**Guidance Counselors**: 18.5	**% Hispanic**: 1.5	(100=high): 58th
Student/Classroom Teacher Ratio: 18.6	667 students/counselor	**% White**: 88.8	

ARIZONA (Apache County -- Coconino County)

Apache County
CHINLE UNIFIED S.D.
P O BOX 587 ● CHINLE AZ 86503-0587 ● (520) 674-9400 ● http://chinleusd.k12.az.us

Grade Span: PK-12 **Schools**: *Regular* 7 ● *Spec Ed* 0 ● *Alt* 0 **Students**: 5,124 **Total Teachers**: 265 **Student/Classroom Teacher Ratio**: 17.8	**Expenditures/Student**: $6,083 **Librarians**: 5.0 1,025 students/librarian **Guidance Counselors**: 11.0 466 students/counselor	**% Amer Indian**: 97.4 **% Asian**: 0.1 **% Black**: 0.1 **% Hispanic**: 0.4 **% White**: 1.9	National ***Socio-Economic Status*** indicator percentiles are not available for the state of Arizona

Apache County
[FORT DEFIANCE] **WINDOW ROCK UNIFIED S.D.**
P O BOX 559 ● FORT DEFIANCE AZ 86504-0559 ● (520) 729-5705

Grade Span: PK-12 **Schools**: *Regular* 5 ● *Spec Ed* 0 ● *Alt* 0 **Students**: 3,134 **Total Teachers**: 211 **Student/Classroom Teacher Ratio**: 15.1	**Expenditures/Student**: $5,969 **Librarians**: 2.0 1,567 students/librarian **Guidance Counselors**: 10.0 313 students/counselor	**% Amer Indian**: 98.6 **% Asian**: 0.2 **% Black**: 0.0 **% Hispanic**: 0.0 **% White**: 1.1	National ***Socio-Economic Status*** indicator percentiles are not available for the state of Arizona

Apache County
[SPRINGERVILLE] **ROUND VALLEY UNIFIED S.D.**
P O BOX 610 ● SPRINGERVILLE AZ 85938-0610 ● (520) 333-2632

Grade Span: PK-12 **Schools**: *Regular* 3 ● *Spec Ed* 0 ● *Alt* 1 **Students**: 2,637 **Total Teachers**: 100 **Student/Classroom Teacher Ratio**: 28.1	**Expenditures/Student**: $4,370 **Librarians**: 4.0 659 students/librarian **Guidance Counselors**: 4.0 659 students/counselor	**% Amer Indian**: 34.4 **% Asian**: 0.4 **% Black**: 0.1 **% Hispanic**: 10.8 **% White**: 54.3	National ***Socio-Economic Status*** indicator percentiles are not available for the state of Arizona

Cochise County
DOUGLAS UNIFIED S.D.
P O BOX 1237 ● DOUGLAS AZ 85607 ● (520) 364-2447

Grade Span: PK-12 **Schools**: *Regular* 12 ● *Spec Ed* 0 ● *Alt* 0 **Students**: 4,437 **Total Teachers**: 241 **Student/Classroom Teacher Ratio**: 19.2	**Expenditures/Student**: $3,958 **Librarians**: 3.0 1,479 students/librarian **Guidance Counselors**: 8.9 499 students/counselor	**% Amer Indian**: 0.0 **% Asian**: 0.5 **% Black**: 0.3 **% Hispanic**: 92.9 **% White**: 6.4	National ***Socio-Economic Status*** indicator percentiles are not available for the state of Arizona

Cochise County
SIERRA VISTA UNIFIED S.D.
3555 FRY BLVD ● SIERRA VISTA AZ 85635-2972 ● (520) 515-2700 ● http://www.c2i2.com/~svps/welcome/svps.html

Grade Span: PK-12 **Schools**: *Regular* 9 ● *Spec Ed* 0 ● *Alt* 0 **Students**: 7,182 **Total Teachers**: 392 **Student/Classroom Teacher Ratio**: 17.9	**Expenditures/Student**: $3,861 **Librarians**: 10.0 718 students/librarian **Guidance Counselors**: 16.2 443 students/counselor	**% Amer Indian**: 0.7 **% Asian**: 4.9 **% Black**: 11.6 **% Hispanic**: 18.6 **% White**: 64.3	National ***Socio-Economic Status*** indicator percentiles are not available for the state of Arizona

Coconino County
FLAGSTAFF UNIFIED S.D.
3285 E SPARROW AVE ● FLAGSTAFF AZ 86004 ● (520) 527-6000 ● http://www.flagstaff.k12.az.us

Grade Span: PK-12 **Schools**: *Regular* 17 ● *Spec Ed* 0 ● *Alt* 0 **Students**: 12,150 **Total Teachers**: 661 **Student/Classroom Teacher Ratio**: 18.6	**Expenditures/Student**: $4,107 **Librarians**: 19.0 639 students/librarian **Guidance Counselors**: 37.9 321 students/counselor	**% Amer Indian**: 20.0 **% Asian**: 1.2 **% Black**: 2.4 **% Hispanic**: 14.4 **% White**: 62.0	National ***Socio-Economic Status*** indicator percentiles are not available for the state of Arizona

Coconino County

PAGE UNIFIED S.D.

P O BOX 1927 ● PAGE AZ 86040-1927 ● (520) 608-4100 ● http://www.isdnet.com/pageud/info/pusdhrd.htm

Grade Span: PK-12 **Schools**: *Regular* 4 ● *Spec Ed* 0 ● *Alt* 0 **Students**: 3,532 **Total Teachers**: 196 **Student/Classroom Teacher Ratio**: 18.5	**Expenditures/Student**: $4,654 **Librarians**: 0.0 *** students/librarian **Guidance Counselors**: 3.0 1,177 students/counselor	**% Amer Indian**: 61.3 **% Asian**: 0.4 **% Black**: 0.2 **% Hispanic**: 2.3 **% White**: 35.7	National ***Socio-Economic Status*** indicator percentiles are not available for the state of Arizona

Coconino County

TUBA CITY UNIFIED S.D.

P O BOX 67 ● TUBA CITY AZ 86045-0067 ● (520) 283-4211

Grade Span: KG-12 **Schools**: *Regular* 6 ● *Spec Ed* 0 ● *Alt* 0 **Students**: 2,781 **Total Teachers**: 186 **Student/Classroom Teacher Ratio**: 14.9	**Expenditures/Student**: $6,358 **Librarians**: 5.0 556 students/librarian **Guidance Counselors**: 4.9 568 students/counselor	**% Amer Indian**: 96.3 **% Asian**: 0.3 **% Black**: 0.0 **% Hispanic**: 0.9 **% White**: 2.4	National ***Socio-Economic Status*** indicator percentiles are not available for the state of Arizona

Gila County

PAYSON UNIFIED S.D.

P O BOX 919 ● PAYSON AZ 85547-0919 ● (520) 474-2463

Grade Span: PK-12 **Schools**: *Regular* 4 ● *Spec Ed* 0 ● *Alt* 0 **Students**: 2,546 **Total Teachers**: 128 **Student/Classroom Teacher Ratio**: 20.1	**Expenditures/Student**: $3,998 **Librarians**: 4.0 637 students/librarian **Guidance Counselors**: 4.0 637 students/counselor	**% Amer Indian**: 2.6 **% Asian**: 0.8 **% Black**: 0.2 **% Hispanic**: 5.1 **% White**: 91.3	National ***Socio-Economic Status*** indicator percentiles are not available for the state of Arizona

Graham County

SAFFORD UNIFIED S.D.

734 11TH ST ● SAFFORD AZ 85546-2967 ● (520) 428-2950

Grade Span: PK-12 **Schools**: *Regular* 4 ● *Spec Ed* 0 ● *Alt* 0 **Students**: 3,697 **Total Teachers**: 145 **Student/Classroom Teacher Ratio**: 20.7	**Expenditures/Student**: $3,476 **Librarians**: 3.0 1,232 students/librarian **Guidance Counselors**: 3.0 1,232 students/counselor	**% Amer Indian**: 0.6 **% Asian**: 0.9 **% Black**: 1.3 **% Hispanic**: 42.0 **% White**: 55.2	National ***Socio-Economic Status*** indicator percentiles are not available for the state of Arizona

Maricopa County

AVONDALE ELEMENTARY S.D.

235 W WESTERN AVE ● AVONDALE AZ 85323-1848 ● (602) 932-0840

Grade Span: KG-08 **Schools**: *Regular* 5 ● *Spec Ed* 0 ● *Alt* 0 **Students**: 2,753 **Total Teachers**: 140 **Student/Classroom Teacher Ratio**: 23.3	**Expenditures/Student**: $4,057 **Librarians**: 1.5 1,835 students/librarian **Guidance Counselors**: 1.0 2,753 students/counselor	**% Amer Indian**: 0.9 **% Asian**: 0.4 **% Black**: 6.4 **% Hispanic**: 63.9 **% White**: 28.5	National ***Socio-Economic Status*** indicator percentiles are not available for the state of Arizona

Maricopa County

CHANDLER UNIFIED S.D.

1525 W FRYE RD ● CHANDLER AZ 85224-6178 ● (602) 786-7000 ● http://www.chandler.k12.az.us

Grade Span: PK-12 **Schools**: *Regular* 16 ● *Spec Ed* 0 ● *Alt* 1 **Students**: 15,390 **Total Teachers**: 749 **Student/Classroom Teacher Ratio**: 20.9	**Expenditures/Student**: $3,896 **Librarians**: 17.0 905 students/librarian **Guidance Counselors**: 25.0 616 students/counselor	**% Amer Indian**: 1.9 **% Asian**: 1.9 **% Black**: 3.7 **% Hispanic**: 31.8 **% White**: 60.7	National ***Socio-Economic Status*** indicator percentiles are not available for the state of Arizona

Maricopa County
[EL MIRAGE] **DYSART UNIFIED S.D.**
11405 N DYSART RD ● EL MIRAGE AZ 85335 ● (602) 876-7000

Grade Span: PK-12 **Schools**: *Regular* 6 ● *Spec Ed* 0 ● *Alt* 0 **Students**: 4,339 **Total Teachers**: 227 **Student/Classroom Teacher Ratio**: 19.3	**Expenditures/Student**: $4,645 **Librarians**: 6.0 723 students/librarian **Guidance Counselors**: 5.9 735 students/counselor	**% Amer Indian**: 0.5 **% Asian**: 1.4 **% Black**: 5.4 **% Hispanic**: 66.7 **% White**: 26.0	National ***Socio-Economic Status*** indicator percentiles are not available for the state of Arizona

Maricopa County
GILBERT UNIFIED S.D.
140 S GILBERT RD ● GILBERT AZ 85296-6724 ● (602) 497-3300

Grade Span: PK-12 **Schools**: *Regular* 15 ● *Spec Ed* 0 ● *Alt* 0 **Students**: 15,440 **Total Teachers**: 895 **Student/Classroom Teacher Ratio**: na	**Expenditures/Student**: $3,657 **Librarians**: 20.0 0 students/librarian **Guidance Counselors**: 17.0 0 students/counselor	**% Amer Indian**: na **% Asian**: na **% Black**: na **% Hispanic**: na **% White**: na	National ***Socio-Economic Status*** indicator percentiles are not available for the state of Arizona

Maricopa County
GLENDALE ELEMENTARY S.D.
7301 N 58TH AVE ● GLENDALE AZ 85301-1893 ● (602) 842-8100 ● http://www.gesd.k12.az.us

Grade Span: PK-08 **Schools**: *Regular* 12 ● *Spec Ed* 0 ● *Alt* 1 **Students**: 10,512 **Total Teachers**: 545 **Student/Classroom Teacher Ratio**: 19.6	**Expenditures/Student**: $3,990 **Librarians**: 13.0 809 students/librarian **Guidance Counselors**: 2.0 5,256 students/counselor	**% Amer Indian**: 1.8 **% Asian**: 1.4 **% Black**: 7.8 **% Hispanic**: 44.0 **% White**: 45.0	National ***Socio-Economic Status*** indicator percentiles are not available for the state of Arizona

Maricopa County
GLENDALE UNION HIGH S.D.
7650 N 43RD AVE ● GLENDALE AZ 85301-1697 ● (602) 435-6000

Grade Span: 09-12 **Schools**: *Regular* 10 ● *Spec Ed* 0 ● *Alt* 0 **Students**: 11,728 **Total Teachers**: 626 **Student/Classroom Teacher Ratio**: 21.0	**Expenditures/Student**: $4,899 **Librarians**: 8.0 1,466 students/librarian **Guidance Counselors**: 33.4 351 students/counselor	**% Amer Indian**: 1.6 **% Asian**: 3.2 **% Black**: 4.1 **% Hispanic**: 18.8 **% White**: 72.3	National ***Socio-Economic Status*** indicator percentiles are not available for the state of Arizona

Maricopa County
MESA UNIFIED S.D.
549 N STAPLEY DR ● MESA AZ 85203-7297 ● (602) 898-7700 ● http://www.mesa.k12.az.us

Grade Span: PK-12 **Schools**: *Regular* 65 ● *Spec Ed* 2 ● *Alt* 4 **Students**: 70,035 **Total Teachers**: 3,327 **Student/Classroom Teacher Ratio**: 21.1	**Expenditures/Student**: $3,921 **Librarians**: 63.7 1,099 students/librarian **Guidance Counselors**: 83.4 840 students/counselor	**% Amer Indian**: 3.1 **% Asian**: 1.7 **% Black**: 2.8 **% Hispanic**: 16.3 **% White**: 76.2	National ***Socio-Economic Status*** indicator percentiles are not available for the state of Arizona

Maricopa County
PEORIA UNIFIED S.D.
P O BOX 39 ● PEORIA AZ 85380 ● (602) 486-6000 ● http://www.peoriaud.k12.az.us

Grade Span: PK-12 **Schools**: *Regular* 24 ● *Spec Ed* 0 ● *Alt* 1 **Students**: 27,052 **Total Teachers**: 1,288 **Student/Classroom Teacher Ratio**: 20.6	**Expenditures/Student**: $3,689 **Librarians**: 27.0 1,002 students/librarian **Guidance Counselors**: 35.1 771 students/counselor	**% Amer Indian**: 0.6 **% Asian**: 2.3 **% Black**: 3.2 **% Hispanic**: 16.4 **% White**: 77.5	National ***Socio-Economic Status*** indicator percentiles are not available for the state of Arizona

Maricopa County
[PHOENIX] ALHAMBRA ELEMENTARY S.D.
4510 N 37TH AVE ● PHOENIX AZ 85019 ● (602) 336-2920 ● http://www.alhambraesd.com

Grade Span: PK-08 **Schools**: *Regular* 11 ● *Spec Ed* 0 ● *Alt* 0 **Students**: 10,503 **Total Teachers**: 496 **Student/Classroom Teacher Ratio**: 21.3	**Expenditures/Student**: $3,902 **Librarians**: 11.1 946 students/librarian **Guidance Counselors**: 7.5 1,400 students/counselor	**% Amer Indian**: 6.1 **% Asian**: 3.1 **% Black**: 10.1 **% Hispanic**: 40.8 **% White**: 39.9	National ***Socio-Economic Status*** indicator percentiles are not available for the state of Arizona

Maricopa County
[PHOENIX] BALSZ ELEMENTARY S.D.
515 N 48TH ST SUITE 1 ● PHOENIX AZ 85008-5499 ● (602) 275-4457

Grade Span: PK-08 **Schools**: *Regular* 4 ● *Spec Ed* 1 ● *Alt* 0 **Students**: 2,768 **Total Teachers**: 135 **Student/Classroom Teacher Ratio**: 20.5	**Expenditures/Student**: $9,275 **Librarians**: 4.0 692 students/librarian **Guidance Counselors**: 0.0 *** students/counselor	**% Amer Indian**: 7.6 **% Asian**: 1.2 **% Black**: 10.7 **% Hispanic**: 54.9 **% White**: 25.7	National ***Socio-Economic Status*** indicator percentiles are not available for the state of Arizona

Maricopa County
[PHOENIX] CARTWRIGHT ELEMENTARY S.D.
3401 N 67TH AVE ● PHOENIX AZ 85033-4599 ● (602) 846-2800

Grade Span: PK-08 **Schools**: *Regular* 17 ● *Spec Ed* 1 ● *Alt* 0 **Students**: 16,328 **Total Teachers**: 789 **Student/Classroom Teacher Ratio**: 20.4	**Expenditures/Student**: $3,678 **Librarians**: 4.0 4,082 students/librarian **Guidance Counselors**: 6.0 2,721 students/counselor	**% Amer Indian**: 1.6 **% Asian**: 1.2 **% Black**: 11.6 **% Hispanic**: 49.1 **% White**: 36.6	National ***Socio-Economic Status*** indicator percentiles are not available for the state of Arizona

Maricopa County
[PHOENIX] CREIGHTON ELEMENTARY S.D.
2702 E FLOWER ST ● PHOENIX AZ 85016-7498 ● (602) 381-6000 ● http://www.creighton.k12.az.us

Grade Span: PK-08 **Schools**: *Regular* 7 ● *Spec Ed* 0 ● *Alt* 0 **Students**: 7,584 **Total Teachers**: 331 **Student/Classroom Teacher Ratio**: 23.1	**Expenditures/Student**: $4,350 **Librarians**: 6.0 1,264 students/librarian **Guidance Counselors**: 0.0 *** students/counselor	**% Amer Indian**: 5.0 **% Asian**: 1.3 **% Black**: 6.8 **% Hispanic**: 61.3 **% White**: 25.6	National ***Socio-Economic Status*** indicator percentiles are not available for the state of Arizona

Maricopa County
[PHOENIX] DEER VALLEY UNIFIED S.D.
20402 N 15TH AVE ● PHOENIX AZ 85027-3699 ● (602) 581-7700 ● http://www.dvusd.k12.az.us

Grade Span: PK-12 **Schools**: *Regular* 19 ● *Spec Ed* 0 ● *Alt* 1 **Students**: 20,420 **Total Teachers**: 1,068 **Student/Classroom Teacher Ratio**: 18.9	**Expenditures/Student**: $4,019 **Librarians**: 21.0 972 students/librarian **Guidance Counselors**: 22.5 908 students/counselor	**% Amer Indian**: 0.6 **% Asian**: 1.9 **% Black**: 1.8 **% Hispanic**: 7.7 **% White**: 88.0	National ***Socio-Economic Status*** indicator percentiles are not available for the state of Arizona

Maricopa County
[PHOENIX] ISAAC ELEMENTARY S.D.
3348 W MC DOWELL ● PHOENIX AZ 85009-2390 ● (602) 484-4700 ● http://www.IsaacELD.k12.az.us

Grade Span: PK-08 **Schools**: *Regular* 8 ● *Spec Ed* 0 ● *Alt* 0 **Students**: 7,616 **Total Teachers**: 350 **Student/Classroom Teacher Ratio**: 20.5	**Expenditures/Student**: $4,247 **Librarians**: 6.0 1,269 students/librarian **Guidance Counselors**: 1.0 7,616 students/counselor	**% Amer Indian**: 2.1 **% Asian**: 1.0 **% Black**: 6.7 **% Hispanic**: 80.0 **% White**: 10.2	National ***Socio-Economic Status*** indicator percentiles are not available for the state of Arizona

Maricopa County
[PHOENIX] **MADISON ELEMENTARY S.D.**
5601 N 16TH ST ● PHOENIX AZ 85016-2999 ● (602) 264-5951 ● http://www.msd38.k12.az.us

Grade Span: KG-08 **Schools**: *Regular* 6 ● *Spec Ed* 0 ● *Alt* 0 **Students**: 4,446 **Total Teachers**: 211 **Student/Classroom Teacher Ratio**: 21.0	**Expenditures/Student**: $4,412 **Librarians**: 6.0 741 students/librarian **Guidance Counselors**: 0.0 *** students/counselor	**% Amer Indian**: 5.2 **% Asian**: 2.6 **% Black**: 4.7 **% Hispanic**: 16.5 **% White**: 71.0	National ***Socio-Economic Status*** indicator percentiles are not available for the state of Arizona

Maricopa County
[PHOENIX] **MURPHY ELEMENTARY S.D.**
2615 W BUCKEYE RD ● PHOENIX AZ 85009-5783 ● (602) 484-4000 ● http://msd.k12.az.us

Grade Span: PK-08 **Schools**: *Regular* 4 ● *Spec Ed* 0 ● *Alt* 0 **Students**: 2,533 **Total Teachers**: 133 **Student/Classroom Teacher Ratio**: 18.9	**Expenditures/Student**: $4,844 **Librarians**: 3.0 844 students/librarian **Guidance Counselors**: 1.0 2,533 students/counselor	**% Amer Indian**: 1.7 **% Asian**: 0.2 **% Black**: 4.2 **% Hispanic**: 87.8 **% White**: 6.0	National ***Socio-Economic Status*** indicator percentiles are not available for the state of Arizona

Maricopa County
[PHOENIX] **OSBORN ELEMENTARY S.D.**
1226 W OSBORN RD ● PHOENIX AZ 85013-3618 ● (602) 234-3366

Grade Span: PK-08 **Schools**: *Regular* 5 ● *Spec Ed* 0 ● *Alt* 0 **Students**: 4,085 **Total Teachers**: 210 **Student/Classroom Teacher Ratio**: 19.4	**Expenditures/Student**: $4,430 **Librarians**: 5.0 817 students/librarian **Guidance Counselors**: 1.0 4,085 students/counselor	**% Amer Indian**: 12.8 **% Asian**: 2.9 **% Black**: 8.0 **% Hispanic**: 40.7 **% White**: 35.6	National ***Socio-Economic Status*** indicator percentiles are not available for the state of Arizona

Maricopa County
[PHOENIX] **PARADISE VALLEY UNIFIED S.D.**
15002 N 32ND ST ● PHOENIX AZ 85032-4441 ● (602) 867-5100

Grade Span: PK-12 **Schools**: *Regular* 32 ● *Spec Ed* 0 ● *Alt* 1 **Students**: 32,099 **Total Teachers**: 1,615 **Student/Classroom Teacher Ratio**: 20.1	**Expenditures/Student**: $4,078 **Librarians**: 32.0 1,003 students/librarian **Guidance Counselors**: 21.0 1,529 students/counselor	**% Amer Indian**: 0.6 **% Asian**: 2.2 **% Black**: 1.7 **% Hispanic**: 8.1 **% White**: 87.5	National ***Socio-Economic Status*** indicator percentiles are not available for the state of Arizona

Maricopa County
[PHOENIX] **PENDERGAST ELEMENTARY S.D.**
3802 N 91ST AVE ● PHOENIX AZ 85037 ● (602) 872-8484

Grade Span: PK-08 **Schools**: *Regular* 6 ● *Spec Ed* 0 ● *Alt* 0 **Students**: 5,621 **Total Teachers**: 279 **Student/Classroom Teacher Ratio**: 20.1	**Expenditures/Student**: $3,572 **Librarians**: 5.0 1,124 students/librarian **Guidance Counselors**: 6.0 937 students/counselor	**% Amer Indian**: 1.6 **% Asian**: 2.0 **% Black**: 7.8 **% Hispanic**: 27.4 **% White**: 61.1	National ***Socio-Economic Status*** indicator percentiles are not available for the state of Arizona

Maricopa County
PHOENIX ELEMENTARY S.D.
1817 N 7TH ST ● PHOENIX AZ 85006 ● (602) 257-3755

Grade Span: KG-08 **Schools**: *Regular* 15 ● *Spec Ed* 0 ● *Alt* 1 **Students**: 9,144 **Total Teachers**: 463 **Student/Classroom Teacher Ratio**: 21.0	**Expenditures/Student**: $4,840 **Librarians**: 4.0 2,286 students/librarian **Guidance Counselors**: 6.0 1,524 students/counselor	**% Amer Indian**: 3.7 **% Asian**: 0.7 **% Black**: 8.2 **% Hispanic**: 80.5 **% White**: 7.0	National ***Socio-Economic Status*** indicator percentiles are not available for the state of Arizona

Maricopa County
PHOENIX UNION HIGH S.D.
4502 N CENTRAL AVE ● PHOENIX AZ 85012 ● (602) 271-3100

Grade Span: 09-12	**Expenditures/Student**: $6,563	**% Amer Indian**: 3.5	National ***Socio-Economic Status*** indicator percentiles are not available for the state of Arizona
Schools: *Regular* 9 ● *Spec Ed* 1 ● *Alt* 4	**Librarians**: 18.0	**% Asian**: 2.2	
Students: 21,083	1,171 students/librarian	**% Black**: 11.9	
Total Teachers: 1,171	**Guidance Counselors**: 90.0	**% Hispanic**: 55.1	
Student/Classroom Teacher Ratio: 21.4	234 students/counselor	**% White**: 27.3	

Maricopa County
[PHOENIX] ROOSEVELT ELEMENTARY S.D.
6000 S 7TH ST ● PHOENIX AZ 85040-4294 ● (602) 243-4800

Grade Span: PK-08	**Expenditures/Student**: $4,411	**% Amer Indian**: 0.9	National ***Socio-Economic Status*** indicator percentiles are not available for the state of Arizona
Schools: *Regular* 17 ● *Spec Ed* 2 ● *Alt* 0	**Librarians**: 17.0	**% Asian**: 0.2	
Students: 11,598	682 students/librarian	**% Black**: 22.1	
Total Teachers: 612	**Guidance Counselors**: 1.0	**% Hispanic**: 70.0	
Student/Classroom Teacher Ratio: 19.1	11,598 students/counselor	**% White**: 6.7	

Maricopa County
[PHOENIX] SCOTTSDALE UNIFIED S.D.
3811 N 44TH ST ● PHOENIX AZ 85018-5489 ● (602) 952-6100 ● http://www.scottsdale.org

Grade Span: PK-12	**Expenditures/Student**: $4,381	**% Amer Indian**: 0.9	National ***Socio-Economic Status*** indicator percentiles are not available for the state of Arizona
Schools: *Regular* 26 ● *Spec Ed* 0 ● *Alt* 0	**Librarians**: 24.5	**% Asian**: 2.5	
Students: 24,467	999 students/librarian	**% Black**: 1.4	
Total Teachers: 1,249	**Guidance Counselors**: 29.5	**% Hispanic**: 7.9	
Student/Classroom Teacher Ratio: 19.5	829 students/counselor	**% White**: 87.2	

Maricopa County
[PHOENIX] WASHINGTON ELEMENTARY S.D.
8610 N 19TH AVE ● PHOENIX AZ 85021-4295 ● (602) 864-2600 ● http://www.wesd.k12.az.us/1/district

Grade Span: PK-08	**Expenditures/Student**: $4,060	**% Amer Indian**: 1.9	National ***Socio-Economic Status*** indicator percentiles are not available for the state of Arizona
Schools: *Regular* 32 ● *Spec Ed* 0 ● *Alt* 0	**Librarians**: 30.5	**% Asian**: 2.3	
Students: 24,587	806 students/librarian	**% Black**: 3.9	
Total Teachers: 1,358	**Guidance Counselors**: 0.0	**% Hispanic**: 16.6	
Student/Classroom Teacher Ratio: 17.9	*** students/counselor	**% White**: 75.3	

Maricopa County
[TEMPE] KYRENE ELEMENTARY S.D.
8700 S KYRENE RD ● TEMPE AZ 85284-2197 ● (602) 496-4600 ● http://www.kyrene.k12.az.us

Grade Span: PK-08	**Expenditures/Student**: $3,826	**% Amer Indian**: 0.9	National ***Socio-Economic Status*** indicator percentiles are not available for the state of Arizona
Schools: *Regular* 17 ● *Spec Ed* 0 ● *Alt* 1	**Librarians**: 14.0	**% Asian**: 4.4	
Students: 17,493	1,250 students/librarian	**% Black**: 3.3	
Total Teachers: 879	**Guidance Counselors**: 8.0	**% Hispanic**: 10.5	
Student/Classroom Teacher Ratio: 19.9	2,187 students/counselor	**% White**: 80.9	

Maricopa County
TEMPE ELEMENTARY S.D.
P O BOX 27708 ● TEMPE AZ 85285 ● (602) 730-7100

Grade Span: PK-08	**Expenditures/Student**: $4,582	**% Amer Indian**: 8.1	National ***Socio-Economic Status*** indicator percentiles are not available for the state of Arizona
Schools: *Regular* 23 ● *Spec Ed* 0 ● *Alt* 0	**Librarians**: 18.6	**% Asian**: 3.2	
Students: 13,324	716 students/librarian	**% Black**: 9.8	
Total Teachers: 833	**Guidance Counselors**: 21.5	**% Hispanic**: 29.5	
Student/Classroom Teacher Ratio: 15.7	620 students/counselor	**% White**: 49.3	

Maricopa County

TEMPE UNION HIGH S.D.

500 W GUADALUPE RD ● TEMPE AZ 85283-3599 ● (602) 839-0292 ● http://www.tuhsd.k12.az.us

Grade Span: 09-12 **Schools**: *Regular* 5 ● *Spec Ed* 0 ● *Alt* 1 **Students**: 10,824 **Total Teachers**: 517 **Student/Classroom Teacher Ratio**: 21.3	**Expenditures/Student**: $4,542 **Librarians**: 16.0 677 students/librarian **Guidance Counselors**: 29.9 362 students/counselor	**% Amer Indian**: 2.5 **% Asian**: 4.2 **% Black**: 6.3 **% Hispanic**: 17.5 **% White**: 69.4	National ***Socio-Economic Status*** indicator percentiles are not available for the state of Arizona

Maricopa County

TOLLESON UNION HIGH S.D.

9419 W VAN BUREN ST ● TOLLESON AZ 85353-2898 ● (602) 247-4222

Grade Span: 09-12 **Schools**: *Regular* 2 ● *Spec Ed* 0 ● *Alt* 0 **Students**: 3,250 **Total Teachers**: 166 **Student/Classroom Teacher Ratio**: 19.9	**Expenditures/Student**: $4,665 **Librarians**: 2.0 1,625 students/librarian **Guidance Counselors**: 9.0 361 students/counselor	**% Amer Indian**: 2.3 **% Asian**: 2.0 **% Black**: 6.1 **% Hispanic**: 40.2 **% White**: 49.4	National ***Socio-Economic Status*** indicator percentiles are not available for the state of Arizona

Mohave County

BULLHEAD CITY ELEMENTARY S.D.

1004 E HANCOCK RD ● BULLHEAD CITY AZ 86442-5901 ● (520) 758-3961

Grade Span: KG-08 **Schools**: *Regular* 4 ● *Spec Ed* 0 ● *Alt* 0 **Students**: 3,256 **Total Teachers**: 155 **Student/Classroom Teacher Ratio**: 20.1	**Expenditures/Student**: $2,954 **Librarians**: 5.0 651 students/librarian **Guidance Counselors**: 3.0 1,085 students/counselor	**% Amer Indian**: 1.5 **% Asian**: 0.7 **% Black**: 1.7 **% Hispanic**: 20.9 **% White**: 75.2	National ***Socio-Economic Status*** indicator percentiles are not available for the state of Arizona

Mohave County

KINGMAN ELEMENTARY S.D.

3033 MCDONALD ● KINGMAN AZ 86401-4298 ● (520) 753-5678

Grade Span: PK-08 **Schools**: *Regular* 8 ● *Spec Ed* 0 ● *Alt* 0 **Students**: 5,096 **Total Teachers**: 274 **Student/Classroom Teacher Ratio**: 19.0	**Expenditures/Student**: $3,439 **Librarians**: 6.1 835 students/librarian **Guidance Counselors**: 2.6 1,960 students/counselor	**% Amer Indian**: 2.1 **% Asian**: 1.2 **% Black**: 0.6 **% Hispanic**: 7.8 **% White**: 88.3	National ***Socio-Economic Status*** indicator percentiles are not available for the state of Arizona

Mohave County

[LAKE HAVASU CITY] **LAKE HAVASU UNIFIED S.D.**

2200 HAVASUPAI BLVD ● LAKE HAVASU CITY AZ 86403-3798 ● (520) 855-7861 ● http://www.Havasu.K12.AZ.US

Grade Span: PK-12 **Schools**: *Regular* 7 ● *Spec Ed* 0 ● *Alt* 0 **Students**: 5,350 **Total Teachers**: 258 **Student/Classroom Teacher Ratio**: 20.5	**Expenditures/Student**: $3,410 **Librarians**: 2.0 2,675 students/librarian **Guidance Counselors**: 5.0 1,070 students/counselor	**% Amer Indian**: 1.2 **% Asian**: 1.1 **% Black**: 0.4 **% Hispanic**: 9.4 **% White**: 87.9	National ***Socio-Economic Status*** indicator percentiles are not available for the state of Arizona

Navajo County

KAYENTA UNIFIED S.D.

P O BOX 337 ● KAYENTA AZ 86033-0337 ● (520) 697-3251 ● http://www.kayenta.k12.az.us

Grade Span: PK-12 **Schools**: *Regular* 4 ● *Spec Ed* 0 ● *Alt* 0 **Students**: 2,713 **Total Teachers**: 168 **Student/Classroom Teacher Ratio**: 16.7	**Expenditures/Student**: $6,199 **Librarians**: 4.0 678 students/librarian **Guidance Counselors**: 7.0 388 students/counselor	**% Amer Indian**: 97.6 **% Asian**: 0.1 **% Black**: 0.0 **% Hispanic**: 0.1 **% White**: 2.1	National ***Socio-Economic Status*** indicator percentiles are not available for the state of Arizona

Navajo County

SNOWFLAKE UNIFIED S.D.

P O BOX 1100 ● SNOWFLAKE AZ 85937-1100 ● (520) 536-4156

Grade Span: PK-12	**Expenditures/Student**: $3,862	**% Amer Indian**: 7.9	National ***Socio-Economic***
Schools: *Regular* 7 ● *Spec Ed* 0 ● *Alt* 0	**Librarians**: 1.0	**% Asian**: 0.3	***Status*** indicator percentiles
Students: 2,583	2,583 students/librarian	**% Black**: 0.4	are not available for the
Total Teachers: 141	**Guidance Counselors**: 2.0	**% Hispanic**: 6.9	state of Arizona
Student/Classroom Teacher Ratio: 17.5	1,292 students/counselor	**% White**: 84.4	

Navajo County

WHITERIVER UNIFIED S.D.

P O BOX 190 ● WHITERIVER AZ 85941-0190 ● (520) 338-4842 ● http://wusd.k12.az.us

Grade Span: PK-12	**Expenditures/Student**: $5,147	**% Amer Indian**: 98.7	National ***Socio-Economic***
Schools: *Regular* 4 ● *Spec Ed* 0 ● *Alt* 0	**Librarians**: 3.0	**% Asian**: 0.0	***Status*** indicator percentiles
Students: 2,625	875 students/librarian	**% Black**: 0.1	are not available for the
Total Teachers: 152	**Guidance Counselors**: 6.0	**% Hispanic**: 0.1	state of Arizona
Student/Classroom Teacher Ratio: 18.3	438 students/counselor	**% White**: 1.1	

Navajo County

WINSLOW UNIFIED S.D.

P O BOX 580 ● WINSLOW AZ 86047-0580 ● (520) 289-3375

Grade Span: PK-12	**Expenditures/Student**: $3,677	**% Amer Indian**: 40.4	National ***Socio-Economic***
Schools: *Regular* 5 ● *Spec Ed* 0 ● *Alt* 0	**Librarians**: 3.0	**% Asian**: 0.8	***Status*** indicator percentiles
Students: 2,741	914 students/librarian	**% Black**: 2.9	are not available for the
Total Teachers: 140	**Guidance Counselors**: 2.9	**% Hispanic**: 21.3	state of Arizona
Student/Classroom Teacher Ratio: 20.4	945 students/counselor	**% White**: 34.6	

Pima County

MARANA UNIFIED S.D.

11279 W GRIER RD ● MARANA AZ 85653-9776 ● (520) 682-3243

Grade Span: PK-12	**Expenditures/Student**: $3,750	**% Amer Indian**: 1.3	National ***Socio-Economic***
Schools: *Regular* 12 ● *Spec Ed* 0 ● *Alt* 0	**Librarians**: 12.0	**% Asian**: 1.4	***Status*** indicator percentiles
Students: 10,599	883 students/librarian	**% Black**: 2.1	are not available for the
Total Teachers: 525	**Guidance Counselors**: 14.0	**% Hispanic**: 17.2	state of Arizona
Student/Classroom Teacher Ratio: 20.3	757 students/counselor	**% White**: 78.1	

Pima County

[TUCSON] **AMPHITHEATER UNIFIED S.D.**

701 W WETMORE ● TUCSON AZ 85705-1547 ● (520) 292-4200 ● http://sun1.wetmore.amphi.com

Grade Span: PK-12	**Expenditures/Student**: $4,093	**% Amer Indian**: 1.7	National ***Socio-Economic***
Schools: *Regular* 17 ● *Spec Ed* 1 ● *Alt* 0	**Librarians**: 9.0	**% Asian**: 2.7	***Status*** indicator percentiles
Students: 15,451	1,717 students/librarian	**% Black**: 3.2	are not available for the
Total Teachers: 788	**Guidance Counselors**: 16.2	**% Hispanic**: 23.3	state of Arizona
Student/Classroom Teacher Ratio: 19.7	954 students/counselor	**% White**: 69.0	

Pima County

[TUCSON] **CATALINA FOOTHILLS UNIFIED S.D.**

2101 E RIVER RD ● TUCSON AZ 85718-6597 ● (520) 299-6446 ● http://www.cfsd.k12.az.us

Grade Span: PK-12	**Expenditures/Student**: $4,867	**% Amer Indian**: 0.1	National ***Socio-Economic***
Schools: *Regular* 7 ● *Spec Ed* 0 ● *Alt* 0	**Librarians**: 7.0	**% Asian**: 5.3	***Status*** indicator percentiles
Students: 4,581	654 students/librarian	**% Black**: 0.7	are not available for the
Total Teachers: 262	**Guidance Counselors**: 8.1	**% Hispanic**: 7.1	state of Arizona
Student/Classroom Teacher Ratio: 16.1	566 students/counselor	**% White**: 86.8	

ARIZONA (Pima County -- Pinal County)

Pima County

[TUCSON] FLOWING WELLS UNIFIED S.D.

1556 W PRINCE RD ● TUCSON AZ 85705-3024 ● (520) 690-2200 ● http://www.azstarnet.com/~fwhs/admin/index.htm

Grade Span: PK-12 **Schools**: *Regular* 7 ● *Spec Ed* 0 ● *Alt* 1 **Students**: 6,028 **Total Teachers**: 286 **Student/Classroom Teacher Ratio**: 20.9	**Expenditures/Student**: $3,783 **Librarians**: 2.0 3,014 students/librarian **Guidance Counselors**: 14.0 431 students/counselor	**% Amer Indian**: 1.9 **% Asian**: 1.2 **% Black**: 2.3 **% Hispanic**: 24.0 **% White**: 70.6	National ***Socio-Economic Status*** indicator percentiles are not available for the state of Arizona

Pima County

[TUCSON] SUNNYSIDE UNIFIED S.D.

2238 E GINTER RD ● TUCSON AZ 85706-5806 ● (520) 741-2500 ● http://wacky.ccit.arizona.edu/~susd/dvstats.html

Grade Span: PK-12 **Schools**: *Regular* 18 ● *Spec Ed* 0 ● *Alt* 0 **Students**: 14,476 **Total Teachers**: 727 **Student/Classroom Teacher Ratio**: 20.0	**Expenditures/Student**: $4,434 **Librarians**: 17.0 852 students/librarian **Guidance Counselors**: 36.9 392 students/counselor	**% Amer Indian**: 4.4 **% Asian**: 0.6 **% Black**: 2.6 **% Hispanic**: 77.1 **% White**: 15.3	National ***Socio-Economic Status*** indicator percentiles are not available for the state of Arizona

Pima County

TUCSON UNIFIED S.D.

1010 E TENTH ST ● TUCSON AZ 85717-0400 ● (520) 617-7233 ● http://www.tusd.k12.az.us

Grade Span: PK-12 **Schools**: *Regular* 102 ● *Spec Ed* 1 ● *Alt* 7 **Students**: 62,317 **Total Teachers**: 3,179 **Student/Classroom Teacher Ratio**: 22.3	**Expenditures/Student**: $4,304 **Librarians**: 101.2 616 students/librarian **Guidance Counselors**: 156.5 398 students/counselor	**% Amer Indian**: 3.7 **% Asian**: 2.3 **% Black**: 6.5 **% Hispanic**: 40.8 **% White**: 46.7	National ***Socio-Economic Status*** indicator percentiles are not available for the state of Arizona

Pinal County

APACHE JUNCTION UNIFIED S.D.

P O BOX 879 ● APACHE JUNCTION AZ 85217-0879 ● (602) 982-1110

Grade Span: PK-12 **Schools**: *Regular* 6 ● *Spec Ed* 0 ● *Alt* 0 **Students**: 4,540 **Total Teachers**: 237 **Student/Classroom Teacher Ratio**: 19.9	**Expenditures/Student**: $4,059 **Librarians**: 6.0 757 students/librarian **Guidance Counselors**: 7.0 649 students/counselor	**% Amer Indian**: 0.9 **% Asian**: 0.7 **% Black**: 0.7 **% Hispanic**: 8.7 **% White**: 89.0	National ***Socio-Economic Status*** indicator percentiles are not available for the state of Arizona

Pinal County

CASA GRANDE ELEMENTARY S.D.

1460 N PINAL AVE ● CASA GRANDE AZ 85222-3397 ● (520) 836-2111

Grade Span: PK-08 **Schools**: *Regular* 8 ● *Spec Ed* 0 ● *Alt* 0 **Students**: 5,077 **Total Teachers**: 274 **Student/Classroom Teacher Ratio**: 18.4	**Expenditures/Student**: $3,805 **Librarians**: 8.0 635 students/librarian **Guidance Counselors**: 4.8 1,058 students/counselor	**% Amer Indian**: 7.9 **% Asian**: 0.5 **% Black**: 4.8 **% Hispanic**: 42.6 **% White**: 44.2	National ***Socio-Economic Status*** indicator percentiles are not available for the state of Arizona

Pinal County

COOLIDGE UNIFIED S.D.

450 N ARIZONA BLVD ● COOLIDGE AZ 85228 ● (520) 723-9349

Grade Span: KG-12 **Schools**: *Regular* 5 ● *Spec Ed* 0 ● *Alt* 0 **Students**: 3,530 **Total Teachers**: 164 **Student/Classroom Teacher Ratio**: 17.7	**Expenditures/Student**: $4,416 **Librarians**: 3.0 1,177 students/librarian **Guidance Counselors**: 3.0 1,177 students/counselor	**% Amer Indian**: 20.6 **% Asian**: 0.5 **% Black**: 9.7 **% Hispanic**: 34.8 **% White**: 34.4	National ***Socio-Economic Status*** indicator percentiles are not available for the state of Arizona

Santa Cruz County

NOGALES UNIFIED S.D.

310 W PLUM ST ● NOGALES AZ 85621-2611 ● (520) 287-0800 ● http://www.nusd.k12.az.us

Grade Span: PK-12	**Expenditures/Student**: $3,746	**% Amer Indian**: 0.0	National ***Socio-Economic***
Schools: *Regular* 8 ● *Spec Ed* 1 ● *Alt* 1	**Librarians**: 4.0	**% Asian**: 0.1	***Status*** indicator percentiles
Students: 6,381	1,595 students/librarian	**% Black**: 0.1	are not available for the
Total Teachers: 317	**Guidance Counselors**: 8.3	**% Hispanic**: 96.8	state of Arizona
Student/Classroom Teacher Ratio: 21.4	769 students/counselor	**% White**: 3.0	

Yavapai County

[DEWEY] **HUMBOLDT UNIFIED S.D.**

12150 TURQUOISE CIR ● DEWEY AZ 86327 ● (520) 772-9200

Grade Span: PK-12	**Expenditures/Student**: $3,430	**% Amer Indian**: 0.8	National ***Socio-Economic***
Schools: *Regular* 6 ● *Spec Ed* 0 ● *Alt* 0	**Librarians**: 4.0	**% Asian**: 0.7	***Status*** indicator percentiles
Students: 4,245	1,061 students/librarian	**% Black**: 0.5	are not available for the
Total Teachers: 222	**Guidance Counselors**: 6.0	**% Hispanic**: 11.0	state of Arizona
Student/Classroom Teacher Ratio: 20.1	708 students/counselor	**% White**: 87.0	

Yavapai County

PRESCOTT UNIFIED S.D.

146 S GRANITE ST ● PRESCOTT AZ 86303-4786 ● (520) 445-5400 ● http://www.primenet.com/~lincoln/pusd1.html

Grade Span: PK-12	**Expenditures/Student**: $4,268	**% Amer Indian**: 2.1	National ***Socio-Economic***
Schools: *Regular* 9 ● *Spec Ed* 2 ● *Alt* 0	**Librarians**: 3.0	**% Asian**: 0.8	***Status*** indicator percentiles
Students: 5,448	1,816 students/librarian	**% Black**: 0.5	are not available for the
Total Teachers: 287	**Guidance Counselors**: 8.5	**% Hispanic**: 7.5	state of Arizona
Student/Classroom Teacher Ratio: 19.5	641 students/counselor	**% White**: 89.0	

Yuma County

[YUMA] **CRANE ELEMENTARY S.D.**

4250 W 16TH ST ● YUMA AZ 85364-4099 ● (520) 782-5183

Grade Span: PK-08	**Expenditures/Student**: $3,779	**% Amer Indian**: 0.8	National ***Socio-Economic***
Schools: *Regular* 6 ● *Spec Ed* 0 ● *Alt* 0	**Librarians**: 1.0	**% Asian**: 0.9	***Status*** indicator percentiles
Students: 5,087	5,087 students/librarian	**% Black**: 2.4	are not available for the
Total Teachers: 265	**Guidance Counselors**: 7.4	**% Hispanic**: 60.1	state of Arizona
Student/Classroom Teacher Ratio: 29.5	687 students/counselor	**% White**: 35.8	

Yuma County

YUMA ELEMENTARY S.D.

450 SIXTH ST ● YUMA AZ 85364-2973 ● (520) 782-6581 ● http://www.yuma.org

Grade Span: PK-08	**Expenditures/Student**: $3,959	**% Amer Indian**: 0.9	National ***Socio-Economic***
Schools: *Regular* 15 ● *Spec Ed* 0 ● *Alt* 0	**Librarians**: 10.0	**% Asian**: 1.2	***Status*** indicator percentiles
Students: 9,322	932 students/librarian	**% Black**: 3.8	are not available for the
Total Teachers: 458	**Guidance Counselors**: 4.0	**% Hispanic**: 56.2	state of Arizona
Student/Classroom Teacher Ratio: 20.2	2,331 students/counselor	**% White**: 37.8	

Yuma County

YUMA UNION HIGH S.D.

3150 AVE A ● YUMA AZ 85364-7928 ● (520) 726-1733

Grade Span: 09-12	**Expenditures/Student**: $4,551	**% Amer Indian**: 1.4	National ***Socio-Economic***
Schools: *Regular* 3 ● *Spec Ed* 0 ● *Alt* 1	**Librarians**: 6.0	**% Asian**: 1.0	***Status*** indicator percentiles
Students: 7,271	1,212 students/librarian	**% Black**: 2.1	are not available for the
Total Teachers: 346	**Guidance Counselors**: 19.4	**% Hispanic**: 64.5	state of Arizona
Student/Classroom Teacher Ratio: 21.1	375 students/counselor	**% White**: 31.0	

Ashley County
CROSSETT S.D.
301 W. 9TH AVENUE ● CROSSETT AR 71635 ● (870) 364-3112

Grade Span: PK-12 **Schools**: *Regular* 6 ● *Spec Ed* 0 ● *Alt* 0 **Students**: 2,563 **Total Teachers**: 153 **Student/Classroom Teacher Ratio**: 17.9	**Expenditures/Student**: $3,675 **Librarians**: 6.0 427 students/librarian **Guidance Counselors**: 7.0 366 students/counselor	**% Amer Indian**: 0.2 **% Asian**: 0.4 **% Black**: 33.0 **% Hispanic**: 0.5 **% White**: 65.9	National ***Socio-Economic Status*** indicator percentile (100=high): 43rd

Baxter County
MOUNTAIN HOME S.D.
1230 S. MAPLE STREET ● MOUNTAIN HOME AR 72653 ● (870) 425-1201 ● http://www.mtncom.com/mthoschl/index.ssi

Grade Span: KG-12 **Schools**: *Regular* 7 ● *Spec Ed* 0 ● *Alt* 0 **Students**: 3,901 **Total Teachers**: 193 **Student/Classroom Teacher Ratio**: 19.8	**Expenditures/Student**: $3,944 **Librarians**: 6.5 600 students/librarian **Guidance Counselors**: 8.7 448 students/counselor	**% Amer Indian**: 0.1 **% Asian**: 0.2 **% Black**: 0.0 **% Hispanic**: 0.2 **% White**: 99.5	National ***Socio-Economic Status*** indicator percentile (100=high): 48th

Benton County
BENTONVILLE S.D.
400 N.W. SECOND STREET ● BENTONVILLE AR 72712 ● (501) 271-1100

Grade Span: PK-12 **Schools**: *Regular* 9 ● *Spec Ed* 0 ● *Alt* 0 **Students**: 6,020 **Total Teachers**: 278 **Student/Classroom Teacher Ratio**: 19.4	**Expenditures/Student**: $4,014 **Librarians**: 8.5 708 students/librarian **Guidance Counselors**: 11.3 533 students/counselor	**% Amer Indian**: 0.5 **% Asian**: 1.3 **% Black**: 0.6 **% Hispanic**: 2.6 **% White**: 95.0	National ***Socio-Economic Status*** indicator percentile (100=high): 64th

Benton County
ROGERS S.D.
220 S. FIFTH STREET ● ROGERS AR 72756 ● (501) 636-3910 ● http://icu.nwsc.k12.ar.us

Grade Span: KG-12 **Schools**: *Regular* 14 ● *Spec Ed* 0 ● *Alt* 0 **Students**: 9,380 **Total Teachers**: 453 **Student/Classroom Teacher Ratio**: 20.4	**Expenditures/Student**: $3,664 **Librarians**: 14.0 670 students/librarian **Guidance Counselors**: 22.1 424 students/counselor	**% Amer Indian**: 0.6 **% Asian**: 1.5 **% Black**: 0.1 **% Hispanic**: 9.3 **% White**: 88.5	National ***Socio-Economic Status*** indicator percentile (100=high): 53rd

Benton County
SILOAM SPRINGS S.D.
P.O. BOX 798 ● SILOAM SPRINGS AR 72761 ● (501) 524-3191 ● http://pride.nwsc.k12.ar.us

Grade Span: KG-12 **Schools**: *Regular* 5 ● *Spec Ed* 0 ● *Alt* 0 **Students**: 2,609 **Total Teachers**: 131 **Student/Classroom Teacher Ratio**: 20.6	**Expenditures/Student**: $3,778 **Librarians**: 4.0 652 students/librarian **Guidance Counselors**: 6.3 414 students/counselor	**% Amer Indian**: 4.0 **% Asian**: 0.4 **% Black**: 0.0 **% Hispanic**: 7.3 **% White**: 88.2	National ***Socio-Economic Status*** indicator percentile (100=high): 51st

Boone County
HARRISON S.D.
400 S. SYCAMORE STREET ● HARRISON AR 72601 ● (870) 741-7600

Grade Span: KG-12 **Schools**: *Regular* 7 ● *Spec Ed* 0 ● *Alt* 0 **Students**: 2,798 **Total Teachers**: 162 **Student/Classroom Teacher Ratio**: 17.0	**Expenditures/Student**: $3,868 **Librarians**: 6.6 424 students/librarian **Guidance Counselors**: 7.6 368 students/counselor	**% Amer Indian**: 0.1 **% Asian**: 0.4 **% Black**: 0.0 **% Hispanic**: 0.4 **% White**: 99.1	National ***Socio-Economic Status*** indicator percentile (100=high): 61st

Columbia County

MAGNOLIA S.D.

P.O. BOX 649 ● MAGNOLIA AR 71753 ● (870) 234-4933

Grade Span: KG-12 **Schools**: *Regular* 4 ● *Spec Ed* 0 ● *Alt* 0 **Students**: 3,150 **Total Teachers**: 164 **Student/Classroom Teacher Ratio**: 19.1	**Expenditures/Student**: $3,513 **Librarians**: 4.0 788 students/librarian **Guidance Counselors**: 8.1 389 students/counselor	**% Amer Indian**: 0.0 **% Asian**: 0.3 **% Black**: 38.2 **% Hispanic**: 0.1 **% White**: 61.4	National ***Socio-Economic Status*** indicator percentile (100=high): 34th

Conway County

[MORRILTON] SOUTH CONWAY COUNTY S.D.

704 E. CHURCH STREET ● MORRILTON AR 72110 ● (501) 354-9400

Grade Span: KG-12 **Schools**: *Regular* 6 ● *Spec Ed* 0 ● *Alt* 0 **Students**: 2,703 **Total Teachers**: 150 **Student/Classroom Teacher Ratio**: 18.2	**Expenditures/Student**: $4,102 **Librarians**: 5.5 491 students/librarian **Guidance Counselors**: 7.0 386 students/counselor	**% Amer Indian**: 0.1 **% Asian**: 0.6 **% Black**: 26.2 **% Hispanic**: 1.1 **% White**: 72.1	National ***Socio-Economic Status*** indicator percentile (100=high): 40th

Craighead County

JONESBORO S.D.

1307 S. FLINT STREET ● JONESBORO AR 72401 ● (870) 933-5800

Grade Span: KG-12 **Schools**: *Regular* 9 ● *Spec Ed* 0 ● *Alt* 0 **Students**: 4,774 **Total Teachers**: 282 **Student/Classroom Teacher Ratio**: 17.6	**Expenditures/Student**: $4,301 **Librarians**: 9.0 530 students/librarian **Guidance Counselors**: 15.2 314 students/counselor	**% Amer Indian**: 0.3 **% Asian**: 1.0 **% Black**: 21.9 **% Hispanic**: 0.8 **% White**: 75.9	National ***Socio-Economic Status*** indicator percentile (100=high): 30th

Crawford County

ALMA S.D.

P.O. BOX 2359 ● ALMA AR 72921 ● (501) 632-4791

Grade Span: KG-12 **Schools**: *Regular* 4 ● *Spec Ed* 0 ● *Alt* 0 **Students**: 2,624 **Total Teachers**: 150 **Student/Classroom Teacher Ratio**: 17.6	**Expenditures/Student**: $3,943 **Librarians**: 4.0 656 students/librarian **Guidance Counselors**: 6.1 430 students/counselor	**% Amer Indian**: 0.2 **% Asian**: 0.2 **% Black**: 1.3 **% Hispanic**: 0.6 **% White**: 97.8	National ***Socio-Economic Status*** indicator percentile (100=high): 39th

Crawford County

VAN BUREN S.D.

2221 POINTER TRAIL EAST ● VAN BUREN AR 72956 ● (501) 474-7942

Grade Span: KG-12 **Schools**: *Regular* 10 ● *Spec Ed* 0 ● *Alt* 0 **Students**: 5,090 **Total Teachers**: 291 **Student/Classroom Teacher Ratio**: 17.4	**Expenditures/Student**: $3,882 **Librarians**: 10.0 509 students/librarian **Guidance Counselors**: 15.1 337 students/counselor	**% Amer Indian**: 1.1 **% Asian**: 3.2 **% Black**: 1.5 **% Hispanic**: 2.7 **% White**: 91.4	National ***Socio-Economic Status*** indicator percentile (100=high): 46th

Crittenden County

MARION S.D.

76 ELM STREET ● MARION AR 72364 ● (870) 739-5100

Grade Span: KG-12 **Schools**: *Regular* 7 ● *Spec Ed* 0 ● *Alt* 0 **Students**: 2,874 **Total Teachers**: 151 **Student/Classroom Teacher Ratio**: 18.9	**Expenditures/Student**: $3,810 **Librarians**: 6.0 479 students/librarian **Guidance Counselors**: 7.1 405 students/counselor	**% Amer Indian**: 0.0 **% Asian**: 0.2 **% Black**: 21.9 **% Hispanic**: 1.2 **% White**: 76.8	National ***Socio-Economic Status*** indicator percentile (100=high): 47th

Crittenden County

WEST MEMPHIS S.D.

P.O. BOX 826 ● WEST MEMPHIS AR 72303 ● (870) 735-1915

Grade Span: KG-12 **Schools**: *Regular* 12 ● *Spec Ed* 0 ● *Alt* 0 **Students**: 6,016 **Total Teachers**: 361 **Student/Classroom Teacher Ratio**: 16.6	**Expenditures/Student**: $3,927 **Librarians**: 12.0 501 students/librarian **Guidance Counselors**: 15.6 386 students/counselor	**% Amer Indian**: 0.0 **% Asian**: 0.1 **% Black**: 72.2 **% Hispanic**: 0.3 **% White**: 27.3	National ***Socio-Economic Status*** indicator percentile (100=high): 10th

Cross County

WYNNE S.D.

P.O. BOX 69 ● WYNNE AR 72396 ● (870) 238-5000

Grade Span: KG-12 **Schools**: *Regular* 4 ● *Spec Ed* 0 ● *Alt* 0 **Students**: 2,847 **Total Teachers**: 164 **Student/Classroom Teacher Ratio**: 17.3	**Expenditures/Student**: $3,661 **Librarians**: 4.0 712 students/librarian **Guidance Counselors**: 8.6 331 students/counselor	**% Amer Indian**: 0.0 **% Asian**: 0.1 **% Black**: 32.5 **% Hispanic**: 0.1 **% White**: 67.3	National ***Socio-Economic Status*** indicator percentile (100=high): 27th

Faulkner County

CONWAY S.D.

2220 PRINCE STREET ● CONWAY AR 72032 ● (501) 450-4800

Grade Span: KG-12 **Schools**: *Regular* 11 ● *Spec Ed* 0 ● *Alt* 0 **Students**: 7,288 **Total Teachers**: 405 **Student/Classroom Teacher Ratio**: 17.0	**Expenditures/Student**: $3,866 **Librarians**: 11.0 663 students/librarian **Guidance Counselors**: 17.5 416 students/counselor	**% Amer Indian**: 0.2 **% Asian**: 0.9 **% Black**: 15.3 **% Hispanic**: 0.6 **% White**: 83.1	National ***Socio-Economic Status*** indicator percentile (100=high): 60th

Garland County

HOT SPRINGS S.D.

140 N. BORDER TERRACE ● HOT SPRINGS AR 71901 ● (501) 624-3372

Grade Span: KG-12 **Schools**: *Regular* 6 ● *Spec Ed* 0 ● *Alt* 0 **Students**: 3,342 **Total Teachers**: 203 **Student/Classroom Teacher Ratio**: 16.5	**Expenditures/Student**: $4,517 **Librarians**: 7.0 477 students/librarian **Guidance Counselors**: 8.4 398 students/counselor	**% Amer Indian**: 0.2 **% Asian**: 0.4 **% Black**: 39.7 **% Hispanic**: 1.6 **% White**: 58.0	National ***Socio-Economic Status*** indicator percentile (100=high): 11th

Garland County

[PEARCY] LAKE HAMILTON S.D.

300 WOLF STREET ● PEARCY AR 71964 ● (501) 767-2306 ● http://orion.dsc.k12.ar.us

Grade Span: KG-12 **Schools**: *Regular* 5 ● *Spec Ed* 0 ● *Alt* 0 **Students**: 3,640 **Total Teachers**: 170 **Student/Classroom Teacher Ratio**: 21.2	**Expenditures/Student**: $3,961 **Librarians**: 5.0 728 students/librarian **Guidance Counselors**: 9.0 404 students/counselor	**% Amer Indian**: 0.2 **% Asian**: 0.1 **% Black**: 1.7 **% Hispanic**: 1.5 **% White**: 96.6	National ***Socio-Economic Status*** indicator percentile (100=high): 57th

Grant County

SHERIDAN S.D.

400 N. ROCK STREET ● SHERIDAN AR 72150 ● (870) 942-3135 ● http://jackets.arsc.k12.ar.us

Grade Span: KG-12 **Schools**: *Regular* 5 ● *Spec Ed* 0 ● *Alt* 0 **Students**: 3,821 **Total Teachers**: 202 **Student/Classroom Teacher Ratio**: 18.8	**Expenditures/Student**: $3,767 **Librarians**: 5.0 764 students/librarian **Guidance Counselors**: 9.0 425 students/counselor	**% Amer Indian**: 0.1 **% Asian**: 0.7 **% Black**: 2.5 **% Hispanic**: 0.4 **% White**: 96.2	National ***Socio-Economic Status*** indicator percentile (100=high): 57th

Greene County

[PARAGOULD] **NORTHEAST ARKANSAS S.D.**

631 W. COURT STREET ● PARAGOULD AR 72450 ● (870) 239-2105

Grade Span: KG-12 **Schools**: *Regular* 7 ● *Spec Ed* 0 ● *Alt* 0 **Students**: 2,777 **Total Teachers**: 162 **Student/Classroom Teacher Ratio**: 15.8	**Expenditures/Student**: $4,497 **Librarians**: 6.0 463 students/librarian **Guidance Counselors**: 7.2 386 students/counselor	**% Amer Indian**: 0.0 **% Asian**: 0.0 **% Black**: 0.1 **% Hispanic**: 0.6 **% White**: 99.3	National ***Socio-Economic Status*** indicator percentile (100=high): 37th

Hempstead County

HOPE S.D.

117 E. SECOND STREET ● HOPE AR 71801 ● (870) 777-2251

Grade Span: PK-12 **Schools**: *Regular* 4 ● *Spec Ed* 0 ● *Alt* 0 **Students**: 3,177 **Total Teachers**: 176 **Student/Classroom Teacher Ratio**: 18.3	**Expenditures/Student**: $3,961 **Librarians**: 4.0 794 students/librarian **Guidance Counselors**: 8.0 397 students/counselor	**% Amer Indian**: 0.1 **% Asian**: 0.2 **% Black**: 46.0 **% Hispanic**: 4.4 **% White**: 49.3	National ***Socio-Economic Status*** indicator percentile (100=high): 22nd

Hot Spring County

MALVERN S.D.

1517 S. MAIN STREET ● MALVERN AR 72104 ● (501) 332-7500

Grade Span: KG-12 **Schools**: *Regular* 6 ● *Spec Ed* 0 ● *Alt* 0 **Students**: 2,655 **Total Teachers**: 160 **Student/Classroom Teacher Ratio**: 16.5	**Expenditures/Student**: $4,049 **Librarians**: 6.0 443 students/librarian **Guidance Counselors**: 7.5 354 students/counselor	**% Amer Indian**: 0.3 **% Asian**: 0.3 **% Black**: 29.2 **% Hispanic**: 0.5 **% White**: 69.8	National ***Socio-Economic Status*** indicator percentile (100=high): 29th

Jefferson County

PINE BLUFF S.D.

P. O. BOX 7678 ● PINE BLUFF AR 71611 ● (870) 543-4200

Grade Span: KG-12 **Schools**: *Regular* 16 ● *Spec Ed* 0 ● *Alt* 0 **Students**: 7,292 **Total Teachers**: 421 **Student/Classroom Teacher Ratio**: 16.5	**Expenditures/Student**: $4,760 **Librarians**: 15.0 486 students/librarian **Guidance Counselors**: 19.1 382 students/counselor	**% Amer Indian**: 0.0 **% Asian**: 0.6 **% Black**: 80.4 **% Hispanic**: 0.2 **% White**: 18.8	National ***Socio-Economic Status*** indicator percentile (100=high): 14th

Jefferson County

[PINE BLUFF] **WATSON CHAPEL S.D.**

4100 CAMDEN ROAD ● PINE BLUFF AR 71603 ● (870) 879-0220

Grade Span: KG-12 **Schools**: *Regular* 5 ● *Spec Ed* 0 ● *Alt* 0 **Students**: 3,452 **Total Teachers**: 195 **Student/Classroom Teacher Ratio**: 17.6	**Expenditures/Student**: $4,242 **Librarians**: 5.0 690 students/librarian **Guidance Counselors**: 9.0 384 students/counselor	**% Amer Indian**: 0.1 **% Asian**: 0.2 **% Black**: 51.2 **% Hispanic**: 0.1 **% White**: 48.3	National ***Socio-Economic Status*** indicator percentile (100=high): 25th

Jefferson County

WHITE HALL S.D.

1020 W. HOLLAND AVENUE ● WHITE HALL AR 71602 ● (501) 247-2002 ● http://whte.arsc.k12.ar.us

Grade Span: KG-12 **Schools**: *Regular* 7 ● *Spec Ed* 0 ● *Alt* 0 **Students**: 2,937 **Total Teachers**: 170 **Student/Classroom Teacher Ratio**: 17.8	**Expenditures/Student**: $4,319 **Librarians**: 7.0 420 students/librarian **Guidance Counselors**: 7.3 402 students/counselor	**% Amer Indian**: 0.0 **% Asian**: 0.4 **% Black**: 7.0 **% Hispanic**: 0.8 **% White**: 91.7	National ***Socio-Economic Status*** indicator percentile (100=high): 67th

Lonoke County

CABOT S.D.

404 N. SECOND STREET ● CABOT AR 72023 ● (501) 843-3363

Grade Span: KG-12 **Schools**: *Regular* 10 ● *Spec Ed* 0 ● *Alt* 0 **Students**: 6,212 **Total Teachers**: 322 **Student/Classroom Teacher Ratio**: 18.2	**Expenditures/Student**: $3,615 **Librarians**: 10.0 621 students/librarian **Guidance Counselors**: 15.7 396 students/counselor	**% Amer Indian**: 0.5 **% Asian**: 1.1 **% Black**: 0.3 **% Hispanic**: 0.9 **% White**: 97.2	National ***Socio-Economic Status*** indicator percentile (100=high): 71st

Miller County

TEXARKANA S.D.

P. O. BOX 9050 ● TEXARKANA AR 75505-9050 ● (870) 772-3371 ● http://darkstar.swsc.k12.ar.us

Grade Span: KG-12 **Schools**: *Regular* 10 ● *Spec Ed* 0 ● *Alt* 0 **Students**: 5,332 **Total Teachers**: 369 **Student/Classroom Teacher Ratio**: 14.5	**Expenditures/Student**: $4,257 **Librarians**: 10.5 508 students/librarian **Guidance Counselors**: 16.5 323 students/counselor	**% Amer Indian**: 0.2 **% Asian**: 0.3 **% Black**: 43.0 **% Hispanic**: 0.8 **% White**: 55.7	National ***Socio-Economic Status*** indicator percentile (100=high): 23rd

Mississippi County

BLYTHEVILLE S.D.

200 S. LAKE STREET ● BLYTHEVILLE AR 72315 ● (870) 762-2053

Grade Span: KG-12 **Schools**: *Regular* 8 ● *Spec Ed* 0 ● *Alt* 0 **Students**: 4,051 **Total Teachers**: 236 **Student/Classroom Teacher Ratio**: 16.9	**Expenditures/Student**: $4,157 **Librarians**: 7.5 540 students/librarian **Guidance Counselors**: 11.5 352 students/counselor	**% Amer Indian**: 0.0 **% Asian**: 0.5 **% Black**: 69.0 **% Hispanic**: 0.4 **% White**: 30.1	National ***Socio-Economic Status*** indicator percentile (100=high): 9th

Ouachita County

CAMDEN FAIRVIEW S.D.

625 CLIFTON STREET ● CAMDEN AR 71701 ● (870) 836-4193

Grade Span: KG-12 **Schools**: *Regular* 7 ● *Spec Ed* 0 ● *Alt* 0 **Students**: 3,914 **Total Teachers**: 230 **Student/Classroom Teacher Ratio**: 16.5	**Expenditures/Student**: $4,616 **Librarians**: 6.5 602 students/librarian **Guidance Counselors**: 11.1 353 students/counselor	**% Amer Indian**: 0.0 **% Asian**: 0.2 **% Black**: 55.4 **% Hispanic**: 0.2 **% White**: 44.1	National ***Socio-Economic Status*** indicator percentile (100=high): 25th

Phillips County

HELENA-WEST HELENA S.D.

P.O. BOX 369 ● HELENA AR 72342 ● (870) 338-8172

Grade Span: KG-12 **Schools**: *Regular* 6 ● *Spec Ed* 0 ● *Alt* 0 **Students**: 4,039 **Total Teachers**: 242 **Student/Classroom Teacher Ratio**: 17.5	**Expenditures/Student**: $4,405 **Librarians**: 8.0 505 students/librarian **Guidance Counselors**: 11.0 367 students/counselor	**% Amer Indian**: 0.1 **% Asian**: 0.3 **% Black**: 83.5 **% Hispanic**: 0.5 **% White**: 15.5	National ***Socio-Economic Status*** indicator percentile (100=high): 5th

Pope County

RUSSELLVILLE S.D.

P.O. BOX 928 ● RUSSELLVILLE AR 72811 ● (501) 968-1306 ● http://rsd.afsc.k12.ar.us

Grade Span: KG-12 **Schools**: *Regular* 10 ● *Spec Ed* 0 ● *Alt* 0 **Students**: 5,369 **Total Teachers**: 300 **Student/Classroom Teacher Ratio**: 17.7	**Expenditures/Student**: $4,107 **Librarians**: 10.0 537 students/librarian **Guidance Counselors**: 15.0 358 students/counselor	**% Amer Indian**: 0.2 **% Asian**: 1.3 **% Black**: 5.9 **% Hispanic**: 1.4 **% White**: 91.1	National ***Socio-Economic Status*** indicator percentile (100=high): 53rd

Pulaski County

LITTLE ROCK S.D.

810 W. MARKHAM STREET ● LITTLE ROCK AR 72201 ● (501) 324-2000 ● http://www.lrsd.k12.ar.us

Grade Span: PK-12 **Schools**: *Regular* 48 ● *Spec Ed* 0 ● *Alt* 0 **Students**: 24,901 **Total Teachers**: 1,628 **Student/Classroom Teacher Ratio**: 15.8	**Expenditures/Student**: $6,051 **Librarians**: 50.0 498 students/librarian **Guidance Counselors**: 77.1 323 students/counselor	**% Amer Indian**: 0.1 **% Asian**: 1.0 **% Black**: 66.5 **% Hispanic**: 1.1 **% White**: 31.3	National ***Socio-Economic Status*** indicator percentile (100=high): 24th

Pulaski County

[LITTLE ROCK] **PULASKI COUNTY SPECIAL S.D.**

P.O. BOX 8601 ● LITTLE ROCK AR 72216 ● (501) 490-2000

Grade Span: PK-12 **Schools**: *Regular* 37 ● *Spec Ed* 0 ● *Alt* 0 **Students**: 20,534 **Total Teachers**: 1,169 **Student/Classroom Teacher Ratio**: 17.5	**Expenditures/Student**: $5,303 **Librarians**: 38.0 540 students/librarian **Guidance Counselors**: 62.9 326 students/counselor	**% Amer Indian**: 0.1 **% Asian**: 0.5 **% Black**: 32.3 **% Hispanic**: 0.5 **% White**: 66.6	National ***Socio-Economic Status*** indicator percentile (100=high): 39th

Pulaski County

NORTH LITTLE ROCK S.D.

P.O. BOX 687 ● NORTH LITTLE ROCK AR 72115 ● (501) 771-8000

Grade Span: KG-12 **Schools**: *Regular* 21 ● *Spec Ed* 0 ● *Alt* 0 **Students**: 8,802 **Total Teachers**: 543 **Student/Classroom Teacher Ratio**: 16.3	**Expenditures/Student**: $5,216 **Librarians**: 16.5 533 students/librarian **Guidance Counselors**: 24.9 353 students/counselor	**% Amer Indian**: 0.1 **% Asian**: 0.4 **% Black**: 54.1 **% Hispanic**: 1.0 **% White**: 44.4	National ***Socio-Economic Status*** indicator percentile (100=high): 18th

St. Francis County

FORREST CITY S.D.

334 GRAHAM STREET ● FORREST CITY AR 72335 ● (870) 633-1485

Grade Span: PK-12 **Schools**: *Regular* 8 ● *Spec Ed* 0 ● *Alt* 0 **Students**: 4,767 **Total Teachers**: 263 **Student/Classroom Teacher Ratio**: 18.5	**Expenditures/Student**: $4,355 **Librarians**: 8.0 596 students/librarian **Guidance Counselors**: 13.1 364 students/counselor	**% Amer Indian**: 0.0 **% Asian**: 0.2 **% Black**: 68.8 **% Hispanic**: 0.4 **% White**: 30.5	National ***Socio-Economic Status*** indicator percentile (100=high): 8th

Saline County

BENTON S.D.

P.O. BOX 939 ● BENTON AR 72018 ● (501) 778-4861 ● http://www.bentonark.com/sindex.html

Grade Span: KG-12 **Schools**: *Regular* 7 ● *Spec Ed* 0 ● *Alt* 0 **Students**: 4,375 **Total Teachers**: 229 **Student/Classroom Teacher Ratio**: 18.9	**Expenditures/Student**: $3,636 **Librarians**: 7.0 625 students/librarian **Guidance Counselors**: 12.1 362 students/counselor	**% Amer Indian**: 0.2 **% Asian**: 0.3 **% Black**: 5.3 **% Hispanic**: 0.7 **% White**: 93.5	National ***Socio-Economic Status*** indicator percentile (100=high): 70th

Saline County

BRYANT S.D.

200 N.W. 4TH STREET ● BRYANT AR 72022 ● (501) 847-5600

Grade Span: KG-12 **Schools**: *Regular* 8 ● *Spec Ed* 0 ● *Alt* 0 **Students**: 5,634 **Total Teachers**: 278 **Student/Classroom Teacher Ratio**: 19.8	**Expenditures/Student**: $3,571 **Librarians**: 8.0 704 students/librarian **Guidance Counselors**: 13.0 433 students/counselor	**% Amer Indian**: 0.3 **% Asian**: 0.5 **% Black**: 0.9 **% Hispanic**: 0.9 **% White**: 97.5	National ***Socio-Economic Status*** indicator percentile (100=high): 74th

Sebastian County

FORT SMITH S.D.

P.O. BOX 1948 ● FORT SMITH AR 72902 ● (501) 785-2501 ● http://clx.fssc.k12.ar.us

Grade Span: KG-12 **Schools**: *Regular* 27 ● *Spec Ed* 0 ● *Alt* 0 **Students**: 12,570 **Total Teachers**: 705 **Student/Classroom Teacher Ratio**: 18.2	**Expenditures/Student**: $4,451 **Librarians**: 23.0 547 students/librarian **Guidance Counselors**: 34.2 368 students/counselor	**% Amer Indian**: 3.5 **% Asian**: 7.8 **% Black**: 13.7 **% Hispanic**: 4.0 **% White**: 71.0	National ***Socio-Economic Status*** indicator percentile (100=high): 36th

Sebastian County

GREENWOOD S.D.

444 E. GARY STREET ● GREENWOOD AR 72936 ● (501) 996-4142 ● http://www.gwol.com/schools.html

Grade Span: KG-12 **Schools**: *Regular* 4 ● *Spec Ed* 0 ● *Alt* 0 **Students**: 2,923 **Total Teachers**: 145 **Student/Classroom Teacher Ratio**: 19.9	**Expenditures/Student**: $3,909 **Librarians**: 4.0 731 students/librarian **Guidance Counselors**: 7.0 418 students/counselor	**% Amer Indian**: 0.4 **% Asian**: 0.2 **% Black**: 0.1 **% Hispanic**: 0.4 **% White**: 98.8	National ***Socio-Economic Status*** indicator percentile (100=high): 73rd

Union County

EL DORADO S.D.

200 W. OAK STREET ● EL DORADO AR 71730 ● (870) 864-5001

Grade Span: KG-12 **Schools**: *Regular* 9 ● *Spec Ed* 0 ● *Alt* 0 **Students**: 4,814 **Total Teachers**: 292 **Student/Classroom Teacher Ratio**: 16.4	**Expenditures/Student**: $4,159 **Librarians**: 9.0 535 students/librarian **Guidance Counselors**: 13.1 367 students/counselor	**% Amer Indian**: 0.0 **% Asian**: 0.3 **% Black**: 54.0 **% Hispanic**: 0.5 **% White**: 45.2	National ***Socio-Economic Status*** indicator percentile (100=high): 18th

Washington County

FAYETTEVILLE S.D.

P.O. BOX 849 ● FAYETTEVILLE AR 72702-0849 ● (501) 444-3000 ● http://fps.nwsc.k12.ar.us

Grade Span: KG-12 **Schools**: *Regular* 14 ● *Spec Ed* 0 ● *Alt* 0 **Students**: 7,681 **Total Teachers**: 416 **Student/Classroom Teacher Ratio**: 18.3	**Expenditures/Student**: $4,094 **Librarians**: 15.0 512 students/librarian **Guidance Counselors**: 17.8 432 students/counselor	**% Amer Indian**: 1.0 **% Asian**: 1.8 **% Black**: 5.8 **% Hispanic**: 2.6 **% White**: 88.8	National ***Socio-Economic Status*** indicator percentile (100=high): 57th

Washington County

SPRINGDALE S.D.

202 W. EMMA AVENUE ● SPRINGDALE AR 72764 ● (501) 750-8800

Grade Span: KG-12 **Schools**: *Regular* 14 ● *Spec Ed* 0 ● *Alt* 0 **Students**: 9,342 **Total Teachers**: 462 **Student/Classroom Teacher Ratio**: 20.0	**Expenditures/Student**: $3,974 **Librarians**: 15.0 623 students/librarian **Guidance Counselors**: 21.6 432 students/counselor	**% Amer Indian**: 1.0 **% Asian**: 2.7 **% Black**: 0.4 **% Hispanic**: 5.4 **% White**: 90.6	National ***Socio-Economic Status*** indicator percentile (100=high): 58th

White County

SEARCY S.D.

801 N. ELM STREET ● SEARCY AR 72143 ● (501) 268-3517 ● http://ssweb.wmsc.k12.ar.us

Grade Span: KG-12 **Schools**: *Regular* 6 ● *Spec Ed* 0 ● *Alt* 0 **Students**: 3,628 **Total Teachers**: 195 **Student/Classroom Teacher Ratio**: 18.7	**Expenditures/Student**: $3,672 **Librarians**: 6.0 605 students/librarian **Guidance Counselors**: 8.1 448 students/counselor	**% Amer Indian**: 0.1 **% Asian**: 0.6 **% Black**: 5.0 **% Hispanic**: 0.8 **% White**: 93.4	National ***Socio-Economic Status*** indicator percentile (100=high): 57th

Alameda County
ALAMEDA CITY UNIFIED S.D.
2200 CENTRAL AVE. ● ALAMEDA CA 94501-4450 ● (510) 337-7060 ● http://www.alameda.k12.ca.us

Grade Span: KG-12	**Expenditures/Student**: $4,907	**% Amer Indian**: 1.0	
Schools: *Regular* 17 ● *Spec Ed* 0 ● *Alt* 1	**Librarians**: 11.0	**% Asian**: 33.6	National ***Socio-Economic***
Students: 10,370	943 students/librarian	**% Black**: 15.9	***Status*** indicator percentile
Total Teachers: 435	**Guidance Counselors**: 8.0	**% Hispanic**: 10.3	(100=high): 33rd
Student/Classroom Teacher Ratio: 25.4	1,296 students/counselor	**% White**: 39.3	

Alameda County
ALBANY CITY UNIFIED S.D.
904 TALBOT AVE. ● ALBANY CA 94706-2020 ● (510) 559-6500

Grade Span: KG-12	**Expenditures/Student**: $5,505	**% Amer Indian**: 0.5	
Schools: *Regular* 5 ● *Spec Ed* 0 ● *Alt* 1	**Librarians**: 1.8	**% Asian**: 27.7	National ***Socio-Economic***
Students: 2,983	1,657 students/librarian	**% Black**: 10.9	***Status*** indicator percentile
Total Teachers: 137	**Guidance Counselors**: 5.1	**% Hispanic**: 9.0	(100=high): 64th
Student/Classroom Teacher Ratio: 21.9	585 students/counselor	**% White**: 51.9	

Alameda County
BERKELEY UNIFIED S.D.
2134 MARTIN LUTHER KING, JR. WAY ● BERKELEY CA 94704-1109 ● (510) 644-6147 ● http://www.berkeley.k12.ca.us

Grade Span: KG-12	**Expenditures/Student**: $7,693	**% Amer Indian**: 0.5	
Schools: *Regular* 14 ● *Spec Ed* 0 ● *Alt* 1	**Librarians**: 2.8	**% Asian**: 11.2	National ***Socio-Economic***
Students: 8,308	2,967 students/librarian	**% Black**: 40.9	***Status*** indicator percentile
Total Teachers: 414	**Guidance Counselors**: 6.8	**% Hispanic**: 12.7	(100=high): 36th
Student/Classroom Teacher Ratio: 22.0	1,222 students/counselor	**% White**: 34.7	

Alameda County
CASTRO VALLEY UNIFIED S.D.
P.O. BOX 2146 ● CASTRO VALLEY CA 94546-0146 ● (510) 537-3000

Grade Span: KG-12	**Expenditures/Student**: $4,660	**% Amer Indian**: 1.4	
Schools: *Regular* 11 ● *Spec Ed* 1 ● *Alt* 1	**Librarians**: 2.0	**% Asian**: 16.1	National ***Socio-Economic***
Students: 6,986	3,493 students/librarian	**% Black**: 3.7	***Status*** indicator percentile
Total Teachers: 293	**Guidance Counselors**: 10.3	**% Hispanic**: 10.2	(100=high): 76th
Student/Classroom Teacher Ratio: 26.1	678 students/counselor	**% White**: 68.5	

Alameda County
DUBLIN UNIFIED S.D.
7471 LARKDALE AVE. ● DUBLIN CA 94568-1500 ● (925) 426-5500

Grade Span: KG-12	**Expenditures/Student**: $5,894	**% Amer Indian**: 1.9	
Schools: *Regular* 5 ● *Spec Ed* 0 ● *Alt* 1	**Librarians**: 1.0	**% Asian**: 10.7	National ***Socio-Economic***
Students: 3,651	3,651 students/librarian	**% Black**: 5.0	***Status*** indicator percentile
Total Teachers: 167	**Guidance Counselors**: 3.0	**% Hispanic**: 12.6	(100=high): 74th
Student/Classroom Teacher Ratio: 22.1	1,217 students/counselor	**% White**: 69.9	

Alameda County
FREMONT UNIFIED S.D.
P.O. BOX 5008 ● FREMONT CA 94537-5008 ● (510) 657-2350

Grade Span: KG-12	**Expenditures/Student**: $4,539	**% Amer Indian**: 0.5	
Schools: *Regular* 38 ● *Spec Ed* 0 ● *Alt* 2	**Librarians**: 0.0	**% Asian**: 29.4	National ***Socio-Economic***
Students: 29,587	*** students/librarian	**% Black**: 5.1	***Status*** indicator percentile
Total Teachers: 1,192	**Guidance Counselors**: 0.4	**% Hispanic**: 13.3	(100=high): 57th
Student/Classroom Teacher Ratio: 26.0	73,968 students/counselor	**% White**: 51.6	

Alameda County
HAYWARD UNIFIED S.D.
P.O. BOX 5000 ● HAYWARD CA 94540-0001 ● (510) 784-2600 ● http://www.tdl.com/~husd

Grade Span: KG-12 **Schools**: *Regular* 31 ● *Spec Ed* 0 ● *Alt* 1 **Students**: 20,511 **Total Teachers**: 857 **Student/Classroom Teacher Ratio**: 23.8	**Expenditures/Student**: $4,798 **Librarians**: 0.5 41,022 students/librarian **Guidance Counselors**: 10.0 2,051 students/counselor	**% Amer Indian**: 0.7 **% Asian**: 18.2 **% Black**: 20.0 **% Hispanic**: 35.0 **% White**: 26.1	National ***Socio-Economic Status*** indicator percentile (100=high): 13th

Alameda County
LIVERMORE VALLEY JOINT UNIFIED S.D.
685 E. JACK LONDON BLVD. ● LIVERMORE CA 94550-1800 ● (925) 606-3200 ● http://www.lvjusd.k12.ca.us

Grade Span: KG-12 **Schools**: *Regular* 16 ● *Spec Ed* 0 ● *Alt* 3 **Students**: 11,705 **Total Teachers**: 454 **Student/Classroom Teacher Ratio**: 27.0	**Expenditures/Student**: $5,035 **Librarians**: 1.0 11,705 students/librarian **Guidance Counselors**: 0.0 *** students/counselor	**% Amer Indian**: 0.5 **% Asian**: 6.0 **% Black**: 2.7 **% Hispanic**: 12.4 **% White**: 78.3	National ***Socio-Economic Status*** indicator percentile (100=high): 68th

Alameda County
NEWARK UNIFIED S.D.
P.O. BOX 385 ● NEWARK CA 94560-0385 ● (510) 794-2141 ● http://www.nusd.k12.ca.us

Grade Span: KG-12 **Schools**: *Regular* 10 ● *Spec Ed* 0 ● *Alt* 2 **Students**: 7,432 **Total Teachers**: 336 **Student/Classroom Teacher Ratio**: 22.6	**Expenditures/Student**: $4,938 **Librarians**: 1.0 7,432 students/librarian **Guidance Counselors**: 2.0 3,716 students/counselor	**% Amer Indian**: 0.7 **% Asian**: 18.9 **% Black**: 6.8 **% Hispanic**: 29.9 **% White**: 43.7	National ***Socio-Economic Status*** indicator percentile (100=high): 41st

Alameda County
OAKLAND UNIFIED S.D.
1025 SECOND AVE. ● OAKLAND CA 94606-2212 ● (510) 836-8100 ● http://www.ousd.k12.ca.us

Grade Span: KG-12 **Schools**: *Regular* 80 ● *Spec Ed* 3 ● *Alt* 6 **Students**: 52,452 **Total Teachers**: 2,262 **Student/Classroom Teacher Ratio**: 24.2	**Expenditures/Student**: $5,666 **Librarians**: 15.3 3,428 students/librarian **Guidance Counselors**: 67.1 782 students/counselor	**% Amer Indian**: 0.5 **% Asian**: 20.5 **% Black**: 51.6 **% Hispanic**: 20.7 **% White**: 6.7	National ***Socio-Economic Status*** indicator percentile (100=high): 9th

Alameda County
PIEDMONT CITY UNIFIED S.D.
760 MAGNOLIA AVE. ● PIEDMONT CA 94611-4047 ● (510) 420-3600

Grade Span: KG-12 **Schools**: *Regular* 5 ● *Spec Ed* 0 ● *Alt* 1 **Students**: 2,603 **Total Teachers**: 134 **Student/Classroom Teacher Ratio**: 19.8	**Expenditures/Student**: $5,050 **Librarians**: 3.0 868 students/librarian **Guidance Counselors**: 4.3 605 students/counselor	**% Amer Indian**: 0.4 **% Asian**: 20.0 **% Black**: 1.9 **% Hispanic**: 2.5 **% White**: 75.2	National ***Socio-Economic Status*** indicator percentile (100=high): na

Alameda County
PLEASANTON UNIFIED S.D.
4665 BERNAL AVE. ● PLEASANTON CA 94566-7449 ● (925) 426-5500 ● http://www.pleasanton.k12.ca.us

Grade Span: KG-12 **Schools**: *Regular* 11 ● *Spec Ed* 0 ● *Alt* 1 **Students**: 10,615 **Total Teachers**: 433 **Student/Classroom Teacher Ratio**: 24.9	**Expenditures/Student**: $5,512 **Librarians**: 3.0 3,538 students/librarian **Guidance Counselors**: 12.7 836 students/counselor	**% Amer Indian**: 0.9 **% Asian**: 8.5 **% Black**: 2.0 **% Hispanic**: 6.9 **% White**: 81.7	National ***Socio-Economic Status*** indicator percentile (100=high): 92nd

Alameda County

SAN LEANDRO UNIFIED S.D.

14735 JUNIPER ST. ● SAN LEANDRO CA 94579-1222 ● (510) 667-3500

Grade Span: KG-12 **Schools**: *Regular* 10 ● *Spec Ed* 0 ● *Alt* 1 **Students**: 7,233 **Total Teachers**: 304 **Student/Classroom Teacher Ratio**: 23.9	**Expenditures/Student**: $4,499 **Librarians**: 1.8 4,018 students/librarian **Guidance Counselors**: 9.2 786 students/counselor	**% Amer Indian**: 0.9 **% Asian**: 21.0 **% Black**: 18.0 **% Hispanic**: 23.2 **% White**: 37.0	National ***Socio-Economic Status*** indicator percentile (100=high): 43rd

Alameda County

SAN LORENZO UNIFIED S.D.

P.O. BOX 37 ● SAN LORENZO CA 94580 ● (510) 481-4600 ● http://www.sanlorenzousd.k12.ca.us

Grade Span: KG-12 **Schools**: *Regular* 11 ● *Spec Ed* 0 ● *Alt* 1 **Students**: 9,862 **Total Teachers**: 429 **Student/Classroom Teacher Ratio**: 24.7	**Expenditures/Student**: $4,515 **Librarians**: 2.0 4,931 students/librarian **Guidance Counselors**: 9.0 1,096 students/counselor	**% Amer Indian**: 1.1 **% Asian**: 15.7 **% Black**: 14.2 **% Hispanic**: 28.5 **% White**: 40.5	National ***Socio-Economic Status*** indicator percentile (100=high): 29th

Alameda County

[UNION CITY] **NEW HAVEN UNIFIED S.D.**

34200 ALVARADO-NILES ROAD ● UNION CITY CA 94587-4402 ● (510) 471-1100 ● http://www.nhusd.k12.ca.us

Grade Span: KG-12 **Schools**: *Regular* 10 ● *Spec Ed* 0 ● *Alt* 1 **Students**: 13,469 **Total Teachers**: 609 **Student/Classroom Teacher Ratio**: 22.5	**Expenditures/Student**: $4,882 **Librarians**: 1.0 13,469 students/librarian **Guidance Counselors**: 15.0 898 students/counselor	**% Amer Indian**: 0.3 **% Asian**: 34.4 **% Black**: 12.7 **% Hispanic**: 28.1 **% White**: 24.4	National ***Socio-Economic Status*** indicator percentile (100=high): 35th

Amador County

[JACKSON] **AMADOR COUNTY UNIFIED S.D.**

217 REX AVE., NO. 7 ● JACKSON CA 95642-2020 ● (209) 223-1750

Grade Span: KG-12 **Schools**: *Regular* 10 ● *Spec Ed* 0 ● *Alt* 1 **Students**: 4,773 **Total Teachers**: 185 **Student/Classroom Teacher Ratio**: 26.0	**Expenditures/Student**: $4,316 **Librarians**: 1.0 4,773 students/librarian **Guidance Counselors**: 6.9 692 students/counselor	**% Amer Indian**: 2.9 **% Asian**: 0.7 **% Black**: 0.7 **% Hispanic**: 6.4 **% White**: 89.2	National ***Socio-Economic Status*** indicator percentile (100=high): 57th

Butte County

CHICO UNIFIED S.D.

1163 E. SEVENTH ST. ● CHICO CA 95928-5903 ● (530) 891-3000 ● http://www.cusd.chico.k12.ca.us

Grade Span: KG-12 **Schools**: *Regular* 20 ● *Spec Ed* 0 ● *Alt* 2 **Students**: 13,882 **Total Teachers**: 572 **Student/Classroom Teacher Ratio**: 24.4	**Expenditures/Student**: $4,160 **Librarians**: 5.0 2,776 students/librarian **Guidance Counselors**: 14.8 938 students/counselor	**% Amer Indian**: 1.4 **% Asian**: 7.6 **% Black**: 2.6 **% Hispanic**: 11.9 **% White**: 76.6	National ***Socio-Economic Status*** indicator percentile (100=high): 35th

Butte County

OROVILLE CITY ELEMENTARY S.D.

2795 YARD ST. ● OROVILLE CA 95966-5113 ● (530) 533-0495

Grade Span: KG-08 **Schools**: *Regular* 7 ● *Spec Ed* 0 ● *Alt* 0 **Students**: 3,893 **Total Teachers**: 161 **Student/Classroom Teacher Ratio**: 26.0	**Expenditures/Student**: $4,162 **Librarians**: 0.0 *** students/librarian **Guidance Counselors**: 1.0 3,893 students/counselor	**% Amer Indian**: 3.4 **% Asian**: 16.9 **% Black**: 5.1 **% Hispanic**: 5.9 **% White**: 68.7	National ***Socio-Economic Status*** indicator percentile (100=high): 4th

Butte County
PARADISE UNIFIED S.D.
5665 RECREATION DR. ● PARADISE CA 95969-5103 ● (530) 872-6400 ● http://paradisedirect.com/pusd

Grade Span: KG-12 **Schools**: *Regular* 7 ● *Spec Ed* 0 ● *Alt* 2 **Students**: 5,489 **Total Teachers**: 237 **Student/Classroom Teacher Ratio**: 24.5	**Expenditures/Student**: $4,225 **Librarians**: 0.0 *** students/librarian **Guidance Counselors**: 5.8 946 students/counselor	**% Amer Indian**: 1.9 **% Asian**: 1.8 **% Black**: 0.4 **% Hispanic**: 4.5 **% White**: 91.5	National ***Socio-Economic Status*** indicator percentile (100=high): 32nd

Calaveras County
[SAN ANDREAS] **CALAVERAS UNIFIED S.D.**
P.O. BOX 788 ● SAN ANDREAS CA 95249-0788 ● (209) 754-3504

Grade Span: KG-12 **Schools**: *Regular* 8 ● *Spec Ed* 0 ● *Alt* 3 **Students**: 3,806 **Total Teachers**: 144 **Student/Classroom Teacher Ratio**: 26.6	**Expenditures/Student**: $4,096 **Librarians**: 0.0 *** students/librarian **Guidance Counselors**: 1.0 3,806 students/counselor	**% Amer Indian**: 1.1 **% Asian**: 0.9 **% Black**: 0.9 **% Hispanic**: 6.6 **% White**: 90.6	National ***Socio-Economic Status*** indicator percentile (100=high): 28th

Contra Costa County
ANTIOCH UNIFIED S.D.
P.O. BOX 768 ● ANTIOCH CA 94509-0904 ● (925) 706-4100 ● http://www.antioch.k12.ca.us

Grade Span: KG-12 **Schools**: *Regular* 14 ● *Spec Ed* 0 ● *Alt* 2 **Students**: 15,491 **Total Teachers**: 643 **Student/Classroom Teacher Ratio**: 24.7	**Expenditures/Student**: $4,386 **Librarians**: 1.8 8,606 students/librarian **Guidance Counselors**: 1.0 15,491 students/counselor	**% Amer Indian**: 1.6 **% Asian**: 7.7 **% Black**: 7.8 **% Hispanic**: 19.4 **% White**: 63.5	National ***Socio-Economic Status*** indicator percentile (100=high): 38th

Contra Costa County
BRENTWOOD UNION ELEMENTARY S.D.
255 GUTHRIE LANE ● BRENTWOOD CA 94513-1610 ● (925) 634-1168

Grade Span: KG-08 **Schools**: *Regular* 5 ● *Spec Ed* 0 ● *Alt* 0 **Students**: 2,673 **Total Teachers**: 111 **Student/Classroom Teacher Ratio**: 24.5	**Expenditures/Student**: $4,612 **Librarians**: 0.0 *** students/librarian **Guidance Counselors**: 2.8 955 students/counselor	**% Amer Indian**: 0.8 **% Asian**: 2.0 **% Black**: 0.8 **% Hispanic**: 34.7 **% White**: 61.7	National ***Socio-Economic Status*** indicator percentile (100=high): 42nd

Contra Costa County
[BRENTWOOD] **LIBERTY UNION HIGH S.D.**
20 OAK ST. ● BRENTWOOD CA 94513-1379 ● (925) 634-2166

Grade Span: 09-12 **Schools**: *Regular* 1 ● *Spec Ed* 0 ● *Alt* 1 **Students**: 2,678 **Total Teachers**: 106 **Student/Classroom Teacher Ratio**: 26.2	**Expenditures/Student**: $5,320 **Librarians**: 1.0 2,678 students/librarian **Guidance Counselors**: 4.9 547 students/counselor	**% Amer Indian**: 0.9 **% Asian**: 3.3 **% Black**: 2.3 **% Hispanic**: 23.3 **% White**: 70.2	National ***Socio-Economic Status*** indicator percentile (100=high): 83rd

Contra Costa County
[CONCORD] **MT. DIABLO UNIFIED S.D.**
1936 CARLOTTA DR. ● CONCORD CA 94519-1358 ● (925) 682-8000 ● http://www.cccoe.k12.ca.us/mddist/welcome.html

Grade Span: KG-12 **Schools**: *Regular* 43 ● *Spec Ed* 2 ● *Alt* 9 **Students**: 35,258 **Total Teachers**: 1,576 **Student/Classroom Teacher Ratio**: 24.6	**Expenditures/Student**: $4,668 **Librarians**: 29.1 1,212 students/librarian **Guidance Counselors**: 10.0 3,526 students/counselor	**% Amer Indian**: 0.4 **% Asian**: 11.5 **% Black**: 4.6 **% Hispanic**: 14.7 **% White**: 68.8	National ***Socio-Economic Status*** indicator percentile (100=high): 53rd

Contra Costa County
[DANVILLE] **SAN RAMON VALLEY UNIFIED S.D.**
699 OLD ORCHARD DR. ● DANVILLE CA 94526-4331 ● (925) 837-1511 ● http://www.srvusd.k12.ca.us

Grade Span: KG-12	**Expenditures/Student**: $4,355	**% Amer Indian**: 0.5	
Schools: *Regular* 22 ● *Spec Ed* 0 ● *Alt* 2	**Librarians**: 7.3	**% Asian**: 11.9	National ***Socio-Economic***
Students: 18,361	2,515 students/librarian	**% Black**: 1.5	***Status*** indicator percentile
Total Teachers: 737	**Guidance Counselors**: 11.5	**% Hispanic**: 4.2	(100=high): 98th
Student/Classroom Teacher Ratio: 25.9	1,597 students/counselor	**% White**: 81.9	

Contra Costa County
[LAFAYETTE] **ACALANES UNION HIGH S.D.**
1212 PLEASANT HILL ROAD ● LAFAYETTE CA 94549-2623 ● (925) 935-2800 ● http://www.acalanes.k12.ca.us

Grade Span: 09-12	**Expenditures/Student**: $5,848	**% Amer Indian**: 0.4	
Schools: *Regular* 4 ● *Spec Ed* 0 ● *Alt* 1	**Librarians**: 3.4	**% Asian**: 14.2	National ***Socio-Economic***
Students: 4,465	1,313 students/librarian	**% Black**: 1.3	***Status*** indicator percentile
Total Teachers: 202	**Guidance Counselors**: 11.0	**% Hispanic**: 5.3	(100=high): 98th
Student/Classroom Teacher Ratio: 22.6	406 students/counselor	**% White**: 78.8	

Contra Costa County
LAFAYETTE ELEMENTARY S.D.
P.O. BOX 1029 ● LAFAYETTE CA 94549-1029 ● (925) 284-7011 ● http://www.lafsd.k12.ca.us

Grade Span: KG-08	**Expenditures/Student**: $4,100	**% Amer Indian**: 0.4	
Schools: *Regular* 5 ● *Spec Ed* 0 ● *Alt* 0	**Librarians**: 1.0	**% Asian**: 8.8	National ***Socio-Economic***
Students: 3,310	3,310 students/librarian	**% Black**: 1.1	***Status*** indicator percentile
Total Teachers: 146	**Guidance Counselors**: 1.0	**% Hispanic**: 2.8	(100=high): 100th
Student/Classroom Teacher Ratio: 22.7	3,310 students/counselor	**% White**: 87.0	

Contra Costa County
MARTINEZ UNIFIED S.D.
921 SUSANA ST. ● MARTINEZ CA 94553-1848 ● (925) 313-0480

Grade Span: KG-12	**Expenditures/Student**: $5,599	**% Amer Indian**: 2.4	
Schools: *Regular* 6 ● *Spec Ed* 0 ● *Alt* 1	**Librarians**: 1.0	**% Asian**: 4.1	National ***Socio-Economic***
Students: 3,985	3,985 students/librarian	**% Black**: 3.9	***Status*** indicator percentile
Total Teachers: 181	**Guidance Counselors**: 4.6	**% Hispanic**: 13.6	(100=high): 54th
Student/Classroom Teacher Ratio: 22.5	866 students/counselor	**% White**: 75.9	

Contra Costa County
OAKLEY UNION ELEMENTARY S.D.
P.O. BOX 7 ● OAKLEY CA 94561-0007 ● (925) 625-0700

Grade Span: KG-08	**Expenditures/Student**: $3,928	**% Amer Indian**: 1.0	
Schools: *Regular* 5 ● *Spec Ed* 0 ● *Alt* 0	**Librarians**: 0.0	**% Asian**: 3.6	National ***Socio-Economic***
Students: 3,903	*** students/librarian	**% Black**: 2.9	***Status*** indicator percentile
Total Teachers: 157	**Guidance Counselors**: 4.5	**% Hispanic**: 21.3	(100=high): 42nd
Student/Classroom Teacher Ratio: 25.4	867 students/counselor	**% White**: 71.2	

Contra Costa County
PITTSBURG UNIFIED S.D.
2000 RAILROAD AVE. ● PITTSBURG CA 94565-3830 ● (925) 473-4231 ● http://www.pittsburg.k12.ca.us

Grade Span: KG-12	**Expenditures/Student**: $4,681	**% Amer Indian**: 0.3	
Schools: *Regular* 10 ● *Spec Ed* 0 ● *Alt* 1	**Librarians**: 2.0	**% Asian**: 14.5	National ***Socio-Economic***
Students: 9,132	4,566 students/librarian	**% Black**: 26.6	***Status*** indicator percentile
Total Teachers: 383	**Guidance Counselors**: 10.0	**% Hispanic**: 33.4	(100=high): 13th
Student/Classroom Teacher Ratio: 24.4	913 students/counselor	**% White**: 25.2	

Contra Costa County

[RICHMOND] **WEST CONTRA COSTA UNIFIED S.D.**

1108 BISSELL AVE. ● RICHMOND CA 94801-3135 ● (510) 234-3825 ● http://www.wccusd.k12.ca.us

Grade Span: KG-12	**Expenditures/Student**: $4,819	**% Amer Indian**: 0.3	
Schools: *Regular* 49 ● *Spec Ed* 1 ● *Alt* 7	**Librarians**: 4.3	**% Asian**: 19.0	National ***Socio-Economic***
Students: 31,894	7,417 students/librarian	**% Black**: 35.1	***Status*** indicator percentile
Total Teachers: 1,326	**Guidance Counselors**: 27.6	**% Hispanic**: 21.9	(100=high): 13th
Student/Classroom Teacher Ratio: 25.9	1,156 students/counselor	**% White**: 23.7	

Contra Costa County

WALNUT CREEK ELEMENTARY S.D.

960 YGNACIO VALLEY ROAD ● WALNUT CREEK CA 94596-3892 ● (925) 944-6850

Grade Span: KG-08	**Expenditures/Student**: $3,880	**% Amer Indian**: 0.7	
Schools: *Regular* 6 ● *Spec Ed* 0 ● *Alt* 0	**Librarians**: 0.0	**% Asian**: 6.9	National ***Socio-Economic***
Students: 3,097	*** students/librarian	**% Black**: 1.6	***Status*** indicator percentile
Total Teachers: 128	**Guidance Counselors**: 3.0	**% Hispanic**: 7.3	(100=high): 79th
Student/Classroom Teacher Ratio: 24.3	1,032 students/counselor	**% White**: 83.5	

Del Norte County

[CRESCENT CITY] **DEL NORTE COUNTY UNIFIED S.D.**

301 W. WASHINGTON BLVD. ● CRESCENT CITY CA 95531-8340 ● (707) 464-6141 ● http://www.delnorte.k12.ca.us

Grade Span: KG-12	**Expenditures/Student**: $4,564	**% Amer Indian**: 11.7	
Schools: *Regular* 10 ● *Spec Ed* 0 ● *Alt* 1	**Librarians**: 0.0	**% Asian**: 4.7	National ***Socio-Economic***
Students: 5,248	*** students/librarian	**% Black**: 0.7	***Status*** indicator percentile
Total Teachers: 228	**Guidance Counselors**: 4.0	**% Hispanic**: 10.1	(100=high): 23rd
Student/Classroom Teacher Ratio: 23.5	1,312 students/counselor	**% White**: 72.8	

El Dorado County

[DIAMOND SPRINGS] **EL DORADO UNION HIGH S.D.**

P.O. BOX 1450 ● DIAMOND SPRINGS CA 95619-1450 ● (916) 622-5081

Grade Span: 09-12	**Expenditures/Student**: $4,946	**% Amer Indian**: 2.6	
Schools: *Regular* 3 ● *Spec Ed* 0 ● *Alt* 3	**Librarians**: 3.0	**% Asian**: 1.8	National ***Socio-Economic***
Students: 5,760	1,920 students/librarian	**% Black**: 0.6	***Status*** indicator percentile
Total Teachers: 249	**Guidance Counselors**: 16.4	**% Hispanic**: 4.8	(100=high): 88th
Student/Classroom Teacher Ratio: 23.4	351 students/counselor	**% White**: 90.2	

El Dorado County

RESCUE UNION ELEMENTARY S.D.

2390 BASS LAKE ROAD ● RESCUE CA 95672-9608 ● (530) 933-0129

Grade Span: KG-08	**Expenditures/Student**: $3,986	**% Amer Indian**: 1.1	
Schools: *Regular* 5 ● *Spec Ed* 0 ● *Alt* 0	**Librarians**: 1.0	**% Asian**: 2.9	National ***Socio-Economic***
Students: 2,838	2,838 students/librarian	**% Black**: 1.1	***Status*** indicator percentile
Total Teachers: 119	**Guidance Counselors**: 1.2	**% Hispanic**: 4.9	(100=high): 78th
Student/Classroom Teacher Ratio: 23.9	2,365 students/counselor	**% White**: 90.1	

El Dorado County

[SHINGLE SPRINGS] **BUCKEYE UNION ELEMENTARY S.D.**

P.O. BOX 547 ● SHINGLE SPRINGS CA 95682-0547 ● (530) 677-2261

Grade Span: KG-08	**Expenditures/Student**: $3,744	**% Amer Indian**: 1.1	
Schools: *Regular* 6 ● *Spec Ed* 0 ● *Alt* 0	**Librarians**: 1.0	**% Asian**: 1.6	National ***Socio-Economic***
Students: 3,451	3,451 students/librarian	**% Black**: 0.5	***Status*** indicator percentile
Total Teachers: 141	**Guidance Counselors**: 3.1	**% Hispanic**: 1.7	(100=high): 81st
Student/Classroom Teacher Ratio: 24.4	1,113 students/counselor	**% White**: 95.1	

El Dorado County

[SOUTH LAKE TAHOE] **LAKE TAHOE UNIFIED S.D.**

P.O. BOX 14426 ● SOUTH LAKE TAHOE CA 96151-4426 ● (530) 541-2850

Grade Span: KG-12 **Schools**: *Regular* 7 ● *Spec Ed* 0 ● *Alt* 2 **Students**: 5,845 **Total Teachers**: 243 **Student/Classroom Teacher Ratio**: 25.2	**Expenditures/Student**: $4,357 **Librarians**: 0.0 *** students/librarian **Guidance Counselors**: 6.0 974 students/counselor	**% Amer Indian**: 0.9 **% Asian**: 5.6 **% Black**: 0.9 **% Hispanic**: 24.4 **% White**: 68.1	National ***Socio-Economic Status*** indicator percentile (100=high): 18th

Fresno County

CLOVIS UNIFIED S.D.

1450 HERNDON AVE. ● CLOVIS CA 93611-0567 ● (209) 297-4000 ● http://www.clovisusd.k12.ca.us

Grade Span: KG-12 **Schools**: *Regular* 28 ● *Spec Ed* 0 ● *Alt* 2 **Students**: 29,522 **Total Teachers**: 1,181 **Student/Classroom Teacher Ratio**: 25.6	**Expenditures/Student**: $4,737 **Librarians**: 0.0 *** students/librarian **Guidance Counselors**: 27.0 1,093 students/counselor	**% Amer Indian**: 1.4 **% Asian**: 12.5 **% Black**: 2.9 **% Hispanic**: 18.2 **% White**: 65.0	National ***Socio-Economic Status*** indicator percentile (100=high): 51st

Fresno County

COALINGA-HURON JOINT UNIFIED S.D.

657 SUNSET ST. ● COALINGA CA 93210-2927 ● (209) 935-7500

Grade Span: KG-12 **Schools**: *Regular* 7 ● *Spec Ed* 0 ● *Alt* 2 **Students**: 3,995 **Total Teachers**: 166 **Student/Classroom Teacher Ratio**: 24.9	**Expenditures/Student**: $4,444 **Librarians**: 0.0 *** students/librarian **Guidance Counselors**: 2.0 1,998 students/counselor	**% Amer Indian**: 0.1 **% Asian**: 1.3 **% Black**: 0.8 **% Hispanic**: 67.1 **% White**: 30.6	National ***Socio-Economic Status*** indicator percentile (100=high): 9th

Fresno County

[FRESNO] **CENTRAL UNIFIED S.D.**

4605 N. POLK AVE. ● FRESNO CA 93722-5334 ● (209) 276-5200 ● http://www.csd.k12.ca.us

Grade Span: KG-12 **Schools**: *Regular* 11 ● *Spec Ed* 0 ● *Alt* 2 **Students**: 7,742 **Total Teachers**: 329 **Student/Classroom Teacher Ratio**: 23.1	**Expenditures/Student**: $4,225 **Librarians**: 0.0 *** students/librarian **Guidance Counselors**: 7.0 1,106 students/counselor	**% Amer Indian**: 0.5 **% Asian**: 9.6 **% Black**: 6.5 **% Hispanic**: 42.3 **% White**: 41.1	National ***Socio-Economic Status*** indicator percentile (100=high): 14th

Fresno County

FRESNO UNIFIED S.D.

ED. CNTR., TULARE & M STS ● FRESNO CA 93721 ● (209) 441-3000 ● http://www.fresno.k12.ca.us

Grade Span: KG-12 **Schools**: *Regular* 82 ● *Spec Ed* 2 ● *Alt* 5 **Students**: 77,880 **Total Teachers**: 3,295 **Student/Classroom Teacher Ratio**: 24.1	**Expenditures/Student**: $5,088 **Librarians**: 21.0 3,709 students/librarian **Guidance Counselors**: 62.9 1,238 students/counselor	**% Amer Indian**: 0.8 **% Asian**: 23.1 **% Black**: 10.8 **% Hispanic**: 41.5 **% White**: 23.9	National ***Socio-Economic Status*** indicator percentile (100=high): 7th

Fresno County

KERMAN UNIFIED S.D.

151 S. FIRST ST. ● KERMAN CA 93630-1029 ● (209) 846-5383

Grade Span: KG-12 **Schools**: *Regular* 4 ● *Spec Ed* 0 ● *Alt* 1 **Students**: 3,367 **Total Teachers**: 140 **Student/Classroom Teacher Ratio**: 25.1	**Expenditures/Student**: $4,721 **Librarians**: 1.0 3,367 students/librarian **Guidance Counselors**: 0.0 *** students/counselor	**% Amer Indian**: 0.0 **% Asian**: 5.8 **% Black**: 0.2 **% Hispanic**: 67.0 **% White**: 27.0	National ***Socio-Economic Status*** indicator percentile (100=high): 4th

Fresno County

PARLIER UNIFIED S.D.

900 NEWMARK AVE. ● PARLIER CA 93648-2034 ● (209) 646-2731

Grade Span: KG-12 **Schools**: *Regular* 4 ● *Spec Ed* 0 ● *Alt* 1 **Students**: 2,561 **Total Teachers**: 125 **Student/Classroom Teacher Ratio**: 20.5	**Expenditures/Student**: $5,503 **Librarians**: 0.0 *** students/librarian **Guidance Counselors**: 2.0 1,281 students/counselor	**% Amer Indian**: 0.0 **% Asian**: 0.1 **% Black**: 0.0 **% Hispanic**: 99.4 **% White**: 0.5	National ***Socio-Economic Status*** indicator percentile (100=high): 0th

Fresno County

[REEDLEY] **KINGS CANYON JOINT UNIFIED S.D.**

675 W. MANNING AVE. ● REEDLEY CA 93654-2427 ● (209) 637-1200

Grade Span: KG-12 **Schools**: *Regular* 14 ● *Spec Ed* 0 ● *Alt* 2 **Students**: 8,230 **Total Teachers**: 357 **Student/Classroom Teacher Ratio**: 23.7	**Expenditures/Student**: $4,568 **Librarians**: 1.0 8,230 students/librarian **Guidance Counselors**: 5.8 1,419 students/counselor	**% Amer Indian**: 0.8 **% Asian**: 2.8 **% Black**: 0.6 **% Hispanic**: 68.2 **% White**: 27.6	National ***Socio-Economic Status*** indicator percentile (100=high): 5th

Fresno County

SANGER UNIFIED S.D.

1905 SEVENTH ST. ● SANGER CA 93657-2806 ● (209) 875-6521

Grade Span: KG-12 **Schools**: *Regular* 12 ● *Spec Ed* 0 ● *Alt* 2 **Students**: 7,633 **Total Teachers**: 324 **Student/Classroom Teacher Ratio**: 24.5	**Expenditures/Student**: $4,570 **Librarians**: 0.0 *** students/librarian **Guidance Counselors**: 8.2 931 students/counselor	**% Amer Indian**: 0.3 **% Asian**: 4.3 **% Black**: 0.4 **% Hispanic**: 70.3 **% White**: 24.6	National ***Socio-Economic Status*** indicator percentile (100=high): 10th

Fresno County

SELMA UNIFIED S.D.

3036 THOMPSON AVE. ● SELMA CA 93662-2497 ● (209) 896-6500

Grade Span: KG-12 **Schools**: *Regular* 10 ● *Spec Ed* 0 ● *Alt* 1 **Students**: 5,327 **Total Teachers**: 235 **Student/Classroom Teacher Ratio**: 23.7	**Expenditures/Student**: $4,464 **Librarians**: 0.0 *** students/librarian **Guidance Counselors**: 1.4 3,805 students/counselor	**% Amer Indian**: 1.1 **% Asian**: 4.1 **% Black**: 1.2 **% Hispanic**: 74.4 **% White**: 19.2	National ***Socio-Economic Status*** indicator percentile (100=high): 3rd

Humboldt County

EUREKA CITY ELEMENTARY S.D.

3200 WALFORD AVE. ● EUREKA CA 95503-4828 ● (707) 441-2400

Grade Span: KG-06 **Schools**: *Regular* 8 ● *Spec Ed* 0 ● *Alt* 0 **Students**: 2,839 **Total Teachers**: 136 **Student/Classroom Teacher Ratio**: 21.4	**Expenditures/Student**: $na **Librarians**: 0.0 *** students/librarian **Guidance Counselors**: 2.1 1,352 students/counselor	**% Amer Indian**: 13.4 **% Asian**: 12.2 **% Black**: 1.6 **% Hispanic**: 6.4 **% White**: 66.4	National ***Socio-Economic Status*** indicator percentile (100=high): 7th

Humboldt County

EUREKA CITY HIGH S.D.

3200 WALFORD AVE. ● EUREKA CA 95503-4828 ● (707) 441-2400

Grade Span: 07-12 **Schools**: *Regular* 3 ● *Spec Ed* 1 ● *Alt* 2 **Students**: 3,256 **Total Teachers**: 157 **Student/Classroom Teacher Ratio**: 20.9	**Expenditures/Student**: $9,428 **Librarians**: 2.0 1,628 students/librarian **Guidance Counselors**: 5.0 651 students/counselor	**% Amer Indian**: 8.8 **% Asian**: 6.5 **% Black**: 1.7 **% Hispanic**: 5.0 **% White**: 78.1	National ***Socio-Economic Status*** indicator percentile (100=high): 49th

Imperial County
BRAWLEY ELEMENTARY S.D.
261 D ST. ● BRAWLEY CA 92227-1912 ● (760) 344-2330

Grade Span: KG-08 **Schools**: *Regular* 3 ● *Spec Ed* 0 ● *Alt* 0 **Students**: 3,713 **Total Teachers**: 156 **Student/Classroom Teacher Ratio**: 23.6	**Expenditures/Student**: $4,548 **Librarians**: 0.0 *** students/librarian **Guidance Counselors**: 3.0 1,238 students/counselor	**% Amer Indian**: 0.1 **% Asian**: 0.8 **% Black**: 3.4 **% Hispanic**: 80.4 **% White**: 15.2	National ***Socio-Economic Status*** indicator percentile (100=high): 4th

Imperial County
CALEXICO UNIFIED S.D.
P.O. BOX 792 ● CALEXICO CA 92232-0792 ● (760) 357-7351

Grade Span: KG-12 **Schools**: *Regular* 9 ● *Spec Ed* 0 ● *Alt* 1 **Students**: 7,171 **Total Teachers**: 289 **Student/Classroom Teacher Ratio**: 25.4	**Expenditures/Student**: $4,818 **Librarians**: 0.0 *** students/librarian **Guidance Counselors**: 14.0 512 students/counselor	**% Amer Indian**: 0.0 **% Asian**: 1.4 **% Black**: 0.1 **% Hispanic**: 97.6 **% White**: 0.8	National ***Socio-Economic Status*** indicator percentile (100=high): 21st

Imperial County
[EL CENTRO] **CENTRAL UNION HIGH S.D.**
1001 BRIGHTON AVE. ● EL CENTRO CA 92243-3110 ● (760) 352-2471

Grade Span: 09-12 **Schools**: *Regular* 2 ● *Spec Ed* 0 ● *Alt* 1 **Students**: 3,295 **Total Teachers**: 139 **Student/Classroom Teacher Ratio**: 23.2	**Expenditures/Student**: $5,396 **Librarians**: 1.0 3,295 students/librarian **Guidance Counselors**: 10.5 314 students/counselor	**% Amer Indian**: 0.1 **% Asian**: 1.1 **% Black**: 2.9 **% Hispanic**: 79.3 **% White**: 16.6	National ***Socio-Economic Status*** indicator percentile (100=high): 18th

Imperial County
EL CENTRO ELEMENTARY S.D.
1256 BROADWAY ● EL CENTRO CA 92243-2317 ● (760) 352-5712

Grade Span: KG-08 **Schools**: *Regular* 10 ● *Spec Ed* 0 ● *Alt* 0 **Students**: 6,457 **Total Teachers**: 261 **Student/Classroom Teacher Ratio**: 24.9	**Expenditures/Student**: $4,324 **Librarians**: 0.0 *** students/librarian **Guidance Counselors**: 2.0 3,229 students/counselor	**% Amer Indian**: 0.1 **% Asian**: 1.9 **% Black**: 3.4 **% Hispanic**: 82.4 **% White**: 12.2	National ***Socio-Economic Status*** indicator percentile (100=high): 4th

Kern County
ARVIN UNION ELEMENTARY S.D.
737 BEAR MOUNTAIN BLVD. ● ARVIN CA 93203-1413 ● (805) 854-6500

Grade Span: KG-08 **Schools**: *Regular* 3 ● *Spec Ed* 0 ● *Alt* 0 **Students**: 2,512 **Total Teachers**: 102 **Student/Classroom Teacher Ratio**: 24.7	**Expenditures/Student**: $4,280 **Librarians**: 0.0 *** students/librarian **Guidance Counselors**: 0.0 *** students/counselor	**% Amer Indian**: 0.0 **% Asian**: 1.3 **% Black**: 0.4 **% Hispanic**: 89.3 **% White**: 9.0	National ***Socio-Economic Status*** indicator percentile (100=high): 0th

Kern County
BAKERSFIELD CITY ELEMENTARY S.D.
1300 BAKER ST. ● BAKERSFIELD CA 93305-4326 ● (805) 631-4600 ● http://www.bcsd.k12.ca.us

Grade Span: KG-08 **Schools**: *Regular* 36 ● *Spec Ed* 1 ● *Alt* 0 **Students**: 26,232 **Total Teachers**: 1,129 **Student/Classroom Teacher Ratio**: 24.1	**Expenditures/Student**: $4,536 **Librarians**: 2.0 13,116 students/librarian **Guidance Counselors**: 30.0 874 students/counselor	**% Amer Indian**: 1.3 **% Asian**: 2.4 **% Black**: 13.7 **% Hispanic**: 57.4 **% White**: 25.2	National ***Socio-Economic Status*** indicator percentile (100=high): 1st

Kern County

[BAKERSFIELD] **GREENFIELD UNION ELEMENTARY S.D.**

1624 FAIRVIEW ROAD ● BAKERSFIELD CA 93307-5512 ● (805) 832-2450

Grade Span: KG-08 **Schools**: *Regular* 9 ● *Spec Ed* 0 ● *Alt* 0 **Students**: 5,551 **Total Teachers**: 227 **Student/Classroom Teacher Ratio**: 24.5	**Expenditures/Student**: $3,957 **Librarians**: 0.0 *** students/librarian **Guidance Counselors**: 4.0 1,388 students/counselor	**% Amer Indian**: 1.5 **% Asian**: 4.6 **% Black**: 12.4 **% Hispanic**: 40.5 **% White**: 41.0	National ***Socio-Economic Status*** indicator percentile (100=high): 9th

Kern County

[BAKERSFIELD] **KERN UNION HIGH S.D.**

2000 24TH ST. ● BAKERSFIELD CA 93301-3815 ● (805) 631-3100 ● http://www.khsd.k12.ca.us

Grade Span: 09-12 **Schools**: *Regular* 13 ● *Spec Ed* 2 ● *Alt* 7 **Students**: 24,714 **Total Teachers**: 918 **Student/Classroom Teacher Ratio**: 27.3	**Expenditures/Student**: $5,543 **Librarians**: 1.0 24,714 students/librarian **Guidance Counselors**: 48.9 505 students/counselor	**% Amer Indian**: 1.1 **% Asian**: 3.0 **% Black**: 7.4 **% Hispanic**: 38.9 **% White**: 49.7	National ***Socio-Economic Status*** indicator percentile (100=high): 39th

Kern County

[BAKERSFIELD] **PANAMA BUENA VISTA UNION ELEMENTARY S.D.**

4200 ASHE ROAD ● BAKERSFIELD CA 93313-2029 ● (805) 831-8331 ● http://www.pbvusd.k12.ca.us

Grade Span: KG-08 **Schools**: *Regular* 17 ● *Spec Ed* 0 ● *Alt* 0 **Students**: 11,769 **Total Teachers**: 504 **Student/Classroom Teacher Ratio**: 23.5	**Expenditures/Student**: $4,390 **Librarians**: 1.0 11,769 students/librarian **Guidance Counselors**: 4.0 2,942 students/counselor	**% Amer Indian**: 0.8 **% Asian**: 5.5 **% Black**: 10.5 **% Hispanic**: 19.2 **% White**: 64.1	National ***Socio-Economic Status*** indicator percentile (100=high): 44th

Kern County

[BAKERSFIELD] **ROSEDALE UNION ELEMENTARY S.D.**

2553 OLD FARM RD. ● BAKERSFIELD CA 93312-3531 ● (805) 588-6000

Grade Span: KG-08 **Schools**: *Regular* 5 ● *Spec Ed* 0 ● *Alt* 0 **Students**: 3,168 **Total Teachers**: 127 **Student/Classroom Teacher Ratio**: 25.0	**Expenditures/Student**: $3,408 **Librarians**: 1.0 3,168 students/librarian **Guidance Counselors**: 1.0 3,168 students/counselor	**% Amer Indian**: 0.3 **% Asian**: 2.7 **% Black**: 1.6 **% Hispanic**: 11.2 **% White**: 84.2	National ***Socio-Economic Status*** indicator percentile (100=high): 82nd

Kern County

[BAKERSFIELD] **STANDARD ELEMENTARY S.D.**

1200 N. CHESTER AVE. ● BAKERSFIELD CA 93308-3521 ● (805) 392-2110

Grade Span: KG-08 **Schools**: *Regular* 4 ● *Spec Ed* 0 ● *Alt* 0 **Students**: 2,527 **Total Teachers**: 112 **Student/Classroom Teacher Ratio**: 22.8	**Expenditures/Student**: $4,888 **Librarians**: 0.0 *** students/librarian **Guidance Counselors**: 1.7 1,486 students/counselor	**% Amer Indian**: 0.6 **% Asian**: 0.6 **% Black**: 0.0 **% Hispanic**: 8.5 **% White**: 90.2	National ***Socio-Economic Status*** indicator percentile (100=high): 15th

Kern County

DELANO JOINT UNION HIGH S.D.

1747 PRINCETON ST. ● DELANO CA 93215-1501 ● (805) 725-4000

Grade Span: 09-12 **Schools**: *Regular* 1 ● *Spec Ed* 0 ● *Alt* 2 **Students**: 2,694 **Total Teachers**: 91 **Student/Classroom Teacher Ratio**: 27.3	**Expenditures/Student**: $5,775 **Librarians**: 0.0 *** students/librarian **Guidance Counselors**: 4.8 561 students/counselor	**% Amer Indian**: 0.7 **% Asian**: 19.9 **% Black**: 2.3 **% Hispanic**: 72.4 **% White**: 4.7	National ***Socio-Economic Status*** indicator percentile (100=high): 34th

Kern County
DELANO UNION ELEMENTARY S.D.
1405 12TH AVE. ● DELANO CA 93215-2416 ● (805) 721-5000

Grade Span: KG-08 **Schools**: *Regular* 7 ● *Spec Ed* 0 ● *Alt* 0 **Students**: 5,282 **Total Teachers**: 210 **Student/Classroom Teacher Ratio**: 25.1	**Expenditures/Student**: $4,180 **Librarians**: 0.0 *** students/librarian **Guidance Counselors**: 0.0 *** students/counselor	**% Amer Indian**: 0.1 **% Asian**: 15.3 **% Black**: 1.9 **% Hispanic**: 78.4 **% White**: 4.3	National ***Socio-Economic Status*** indicator percentile (100=high): 1st

Kern County
LAMONT ELEMENTARY S.D.
8201 PALM AVE. ● LAMONT CA 93241-2118 ● (805) 845-0751

Grade Span: KG-08 **Schools**: *Regular* 4 ● *Spec Ed* 0 ● *Alt* 0 **Students**: 2,670 **Total Teachers**: 104 **Student/Classroom Teacher Ratio**: 26.1	**Expenditures/Student**: $4,205 **Librarians**: 0.0 *** students/librarian **Guidance Counselors**: 0.0 *** students/counselor	**% Amer Indian**: 0.0 **% Asian**: 1.2 **% Black**: 0.1 **% Hispanic**: 91.5 **% White**: 7.2	National ***Socio-Economic Status*** indicator percentile (100=high): 0th

Kern County
MOJAVE UNIFIED S.D.
3500 DOUGLAS AVE. ● MOJAVE CA 93501-1143 ● (805) 824-4001

Grade Span: KG-12 **Schools**: *Regular* 6 ● *Spec Ed* 0 ● *Alt* 2 **Students**: 3,005 **Total Teachers**: 118 **Student/Classroom Teacher Ratio**: 25.6	**Expenditures/Student**: $4,406 **Librarians**: 0.0 *** students/librarian **Guidance Counselors**: 3.0 1,002 students/counselor	**% Amer Indian**: 0.7 **% Asian**: 3.0 **% Black**: 14.0 **% Hispanic**: 22.3 **% White**: 60.1	National ***Socio-Economic Status*** indicator percentile (100=high): 23rd

Kern County
[NORTH EDWARDS] **MUROC JOINT UNIFIED S.D.**
P.O. BOX 833 ● NORTH EDWARDS CA 93523-0833 ● (760) 769-4821

Grade Span: KG-12 **Schools**: *Regular* 6 ● *Spec Ed* 0 ● *Alt* 1 **Students**: 2,580 **Total Teachers**: 118 **Student/Classroom Teacher Ratio**: 22.8	**Expenditures/Student**: $5,454 **Librarians**: 0.0 *** students/librarian **Guidance Counselors**: 2.0 1,290 students/counselor	**% Amer Indian**: 1.3 **% Asian**: 6.1 **% Black**: 11.9 **% Hispanic**: 7.1 **% White**: 73.6	National ***Socio-Economic Status*** indicator percentile (100=high): 36th

Kern County
[RIDGECREST] **SIERRA SANDS UNIFIED S.D.**
113 FELSPAR ● RIDGECREST CA 93555-3520 ● (760) 375-3363

Grade Span: KG-12 **Schools**: *Regular* 11 ● *Spec Ed* 0 ● *Alt* 1 **Students**: 6,761 **Total Teachers**: 302 **Student/Classroom Teacher Ratio**: 23.5	**Expenditures/Student**: $4,552 **Librarians**: 0.0 *** students/librarian **Guidance Counselors**: 6.6 1,024 students/counselor	**% Amer Indian**: 1.6 **% Asian**: 5.2 **% Black**: 4.6 **% Hispanic**: 10.0 **% White**: 78.5	National ***Socio-Economic Status*** indicator percentile (100=high): 36th

Kern County
[ROSAMOND] **SOUTHERN KERN UNIFIED S.D.**
P.O. DRAWER CC ● ROSAMOND CA 93560-0640 ● (805) 256-5000

Grade Span: KG-12 **Schools**: *Regular* 4 ● *Spec Ed* 0 ● *Alt* 2 **Students**: 3,390 **Total Teachers**: 134 **Student/Classroom Teacher Ratio**: 24.2	**Expenditures/Student**: $4,515 **Librarians**: 0.0 *** students/librarian **Guidance Counselors**: 0.2 16,950 students/counselor	**% Amer Indian**: 0.5 **% Asian**: 3.1 **% Black**: 6.3 **% Hispanic**: 32.1 **% White**: 58.1	National ***Socio-Economic Status*** indicator percentile (100=high): 13th

Kern County

TEHACHAPI UNIFIED S.D.

400 S. SNYDER ● TEHACHAPI CA 93561-1519 ● (805) 822-2100 ● http://www.tminet.com/~jwalsh/home.html

Grade Span: KG-12	**Expenditures/Student**: $4,447	**% Amer Indian**: 1.0	
Schools: *Regular* 6 ● *Spec Ed* 0 ● *Alt* 1	**Librarians**: 1.0	**% Asian**: 1.1	National ***Socio-Economic***
Students: 5,045	5,045 students/librarian	**% Black**: 2.2	***Status*** indicator percentile
Total Teachers: 213	**Guidance Counselors**: 5.0	**% Hispanic**: 17.5	(100=high): 48th
Student/Classroom Teacher Ratio: 23.8	1,009 students/counselor	**% White**: 78.2	

Kern County

WASCO UNION ELEMENTARY S.D.

639 BROADWAY ● WASCO CA 93280-1899 ● (805) 758-7100

Grade Span: KG-08	**Expenditures/Student**: $4,205	**% Amer Indian**: 0.1	
Schools: *Regular* 4 ● *Spec Ed* 0 ● *Alt* 0	**Librarians**: 0.0	**% Asian**: 0.9	National ***Socio-Economic***
Students: 2,549	*** students/librarian	**% Black**: 5.0	***Status*** indicator percentile
Total Teachers: 107	**Guidance Counselors**: 0.0	**% Hispanic**: 79.0	(100=high): 4th
Student/Classroom Teacher Ratio: 24.5	*** students/counselor	**% White**: 15.1	

Kings County

CORCORAN JOINT UNIFIED S.D.

1520 PATTERSON AVE. ● CORCORAN CA 93212-1722 ● (209) 992-3104

Grade Span: KG-12	**Expenditures/Student**: $4,401	**% Amer Indian**: 0.1	
Schools: *Regular* 5 ● *Spec Ed* 0 ● *Alt* 1	**Librarians**: 0.0	**% Asian**: 0.7	National ***Socio-Economic***
Students: 3,281	*** students/librarian	**% Black**: 4.2	***Status*** indicator percentile
Total Teachers: 148	**Guidance Counselors**: 3.0	**% Hispanic**: 76.3	(100=high): 6th
Student/Classroom Teacher Ratio: 22.5	1,094 students/counselor	**% White**: 18.7	

Kings County

HANFORD ELEMENTARY S.D.

P.O. BOX G-1067 ● HANFORD CA 93232 ● (209) 585-2265

Grade Span: KG-08	**Expenditures/Student**: $4,292	**% Amer Indian**: 0.3	
Schools: *Regular* 8 ● *Spec Ed* 0 ● *Alt* 0	**Librarians**: 0.0	**% Asian**: 2.6	National ***Socio-Economic***
Students: 4,884	*** students/librarian	**% Black**: 8.5	***Status*** indicator percentile
Total Teachers: 184	**Guidance Counselors**: 0.0	**% Hispanic**: 47.9	(100=high): 7th
Student/Classroom Teacher Ratio: 26.6	*** students/counselor	**% White**: 40.7	

Kings County

HANFORD JOINT UNION HIGH S.D.

120 E. GRANGEVILLE ROAD ● HANFORD CA 93230-3067 ● (209) 582-4401 ● http://www.kings.k12.ca.us/huhsd

Grade Span: 09-12	**Expenditures/Student**: $5,024	**% Amer Indian**: 0.3	
Schools: *Regular* 1 ● *Spec Ed* 0 ● *Alt* 2	**Librarians**: 0.0	**% Asian**: 5.2	National ***Socio-Economic***
Students: 2,813	*** students/librarian	**% Black**: 5.3	***Status*** indicator percentile
Total Teachers: 115	**Guidance Counselors**: 6.0	**% Hispanic**: 35.9	(100=high): 70th
Student/Classroom Teacher Ratio: 23.6	469 students/counselor	**% White**: 53.3	

Kings County

LEMOORE UNION ELEMENTARY S.D.

100 VINE ST. ● LEMOORE CA 93245-3418 ● (209) 924-6800 ● http://www.luhsd.k12.ca.us

Grade Span: KG-08	**Expenditures/Student**: $3,893	**% Amer Indian**: 0.6	
Schools: *Regular* 4 ● *Spec Ed* 0 ● *Alt* 0	**Librarians**: 0.0	**% Asian**: 9.0	National ***Socio-Economic***
Students: 2,799	*** students/librarian	**% Black**: 10.0	***Status*** indicator percentile
Total Teachers: 101	**Guidance Counselors**: 1.0	**% Hispanic**: 33.2	(100=high): 14th
Student/Classroom Teacher Ratio: 27.8	2,799 students/counselor	**% White**: 47.2	

Lake County

[CLEARLAKE] **KONOCTI UNIFIED S.D.**

P.O. BOX 6630 ● CLEARLAKE CA 95422-6630 ● (707) 994-6475

Grade Span: KG-12 **Schools**: *Regular* 6 ● *Spec Ed* 0 ● *Alt* 2 **Students**: 3,289 **Total Teachers**: 149 **Student/Classroom Teacher Ratio**: 22.2	**Expenditures/Student**: $4,700 **Librarians**: 0.0 *** students/librarian **Guidance Counselors**: 4.0 822 students/counselor	**% Amer Indian**: 7.1 **% Asian**: 2.2 **% Black**: 5.9 **% Hispanic**: 8.7 **% White**: 76.1	National ***Socio-Economic Status*** indicator percentile (100=high): 3rd

Los Angeles County

ALHAMBRA CITY ELEMENTARY S.D.

P.O. BOX 110 ● ALHAMBRA CA 91802-2110 ● (818) 308-2200

Grade Span: KG-08 **Schools**: *Regular* 13 ● *Spec Ed* 0 ● *Alt* 0 **Students**: 11,403 **Total Teachers**: 453 **Student/Classroom Teacher Ratio**: 26.5	**Expenditures/Student**: $5,239 **Librarians**: 0.0 *** students/librarian **Guidance Counselors**: 1.5 7,602 students/counselor	**% Amer Indian**: 0.1 **% Asian**: 45.8 **% Black**: 0.9 **% Hispanic**: 42.1 **% White**: 11.0	National ***Socio-Economic Status*** indicator percentile (100=high): 8th

Los Angeles County

ALHAMBRA CITY HIGH S.D.

P.O. BOX 110 ● ALHAMBRA CA 91802-2110 ● (818) 308-2200

Grade Span: 09-12 **Schools**: *Regular* 3 ● *Spec Ed* 0 ● *Alt* 2 **Students**: 8,427 **Total Teachers**: 352 **Student/Classroom Teacher Ratio**: 24.6	**Expenditures/Student**: $na **Librarians**: 3.0 2,809 students/librarian **Guidance Counselors**: 19.3 437 students/counselor	**% Amer Indian**: 0.3 **% Asian**: 56.1 **% Black**: 0.8 **% Hispanic**: 36.0 **% White**: 6.8	National ***Socio-Economic Status*** indicator percentile (100=high): 9th

Los Angeles County

ARCADIA UNIFIED S.D.

234 CAMPUS DR. ● ARCADIA CA 91007-6902 ● (626) 447-9223 ● http://www.ausd.k12.ca.us

Grade Span: KG-12 **Schools**: *Regular* 10 ● *Spec Ed* 0 ● *Alt* 1 **Students**: 8,945 **Total Teachers**: 344 **Student/Classroom Teacher Ratio**: 26.8	**Expenditures/Student**: $4,320 **Librarians**: 1.0 8,945 students/librarian **Guidance Counselors**: 8.5 1,052 students/counselor	**% Amer Indian**: 0.0 **% Asian**: 50.2 **% Black**: 1.2 **% Hispanic**: 10.6 **% White**: 38.0	National ***Socio-Economic Status*** indicator percentile (100=high): 84th

Los Angeles County

AZUSA UNIFIED S.D.

P.O. BOX 500 ● AZUSA CA 91702-0500 ● (626) 967-6211

Grade Span: KG-12 **Schools**: *Regular* 17 ● *Spec Ed* 0 ● *Alt* 1 **Students**: 11,527 **Total Teachers**: 470 **Student/Classroom Teacher Ratio**: 26.7	**Expenditures/Student**: $4,676 **Librarians**: 0.0 *** students/librarian **Guidance Counselors**: 11.0 1,048 students/counselor	**% Amer Indian**: 0.1 **% Asian**: 3.2 **% Black**: 3.7 **% Hispanic**: 75.3 **% White**: 17.7	National ***Socio-Economic Status*** indicator percentile (100=high): 4th

Los Angeles County

BALDWIN PARK UNIFIED S.D.

3699 N. HOLLY AVE. ● BALDWIN PARK CA 91706-5397 ● (626) 926-3311

Grade Span: KG-12 **Schools**: *Regular* 19 ● *Spec Ed* 0 ● *Alt* 1 **Students**: 16,311 **Total Teachers**: 586 **Student/Classroom Teacher Ratio**: 28.6	**Expenditures/Student**: $4,785 **Librarians**: 2.5 6,524 students/librarian **Guidance Counselors**: 11.5 1,418 students/counselor	**% Amer Indian**: 0.3 **% Asian**: 8.6 **% Black**: 1.9 **% Hispanic**: 83.7 **% White**: 5.4	National ***Socio-Economic Status*** indicator percentile (100=high): 7th

Los Angeles County

BELLFLOWER UNIFIED S.D.

16703 S. CLARK AVE. ● BELLFLOWER CA 90706-5203 ● (310) 866-9011

Grade Span: KG-12 **Schools**: *Regular* 11 ● *Spec Ed* 0 ● *Alt* 1 **Students**: 12,623 **Total Teachers**: 467 **Student/Classroom Teacher Ratio**: 27.4	**Expenditures/Student**: $4,494 **Librarians**: 1.0 12,623 students/librarian **Guidance Counselors**: 9.3 1,357 students/counselor	**% Amer Indian**: 0.4 **% Asian**: 10.1 **% Black**: 16.3 **% Hispanic**: 33.5 **% White**: 39.7	National ***Socio-Economic Status*** indicator percentile (100=high): 16th

Los Angeles County

BEVERLY HILLS UNIFIED S.D.

255 S. LASKY DR. ● BEVERLY HILLS CA 90212-3644 ● (562) 277-5900 ● http://www.beverlyhills.k12.ca.us

Grade Span: KG-12 **Schools**: *Regular* 5 ● *Spec Ed* 0 ● *Alt* 1 **Students**: 5,178 **Total Teachers**: 274 **Student/Classroom Teacher Ratio**: 18.6	**Expenditures/Student**: $7,103 **Librarians**: 1.0 5,178 students/librarian **Guidance Counselors**: 5.8 893 students/counselor	**% Amer Indian**: 0.1 **% Asian**: 10.6 **% Black**: 4.3 **% Hispanic**: 3.8 **% White**: 81.2	National ***Socio-Economic Status*** indicator percentile (100=high): 80th

Los Angeles County

BURBANK UNIFIED S.D.

330 N. BUENA VISTA ST. ● BURBANK CA 91505-3607 ● (818) 558-4600

Grade Span: KG-12 **Schools**: *Regular* 16 ● *Spec Ed* 0 ● *Alt* 1 **Students**: 13,835 **Total Teachers**: 578 **Student/Classroom Teacher Ratio**: 24.6	**Expenditures/Student**: $4,773 **Librarians**: 0.0 *** students/librarian **Guidance Counselors**: 10.6 1,305 students/counselor	**% Amer Indian**: 0.1 **% Asian**: 7.9 **% Black**: 3.1 **% Hispanic**: 37.2 **% White**: 51.8	National ***Socio-Economic Status*** indicator percentile (100=high): 28th

Los Angeles County

[CALABASAS] **LAS VIRGENES UNIFIED S.D.**

4111 N. LAS VIRGENES RD. ● CALABASAS CA 91302-1929 ● (818) 880-4000 ● http://www.lvusd.k12.ca.us

Grade Span: KG-12 **Schools**: *Regular* 12 ● *Spec Ed* 0 ● *Alt* 1 **Students**: 10,970 **Total Teachers**: 434 **Student/Classroom Teacher Ratio**: 26.9	**Expenditures/Student**: $4,473 **Librarians**: 4.0 2,743 students/librarian **Guidance Counselors**: 11.2 979 students/counselor	**% Amer Indian**: 0.2 **% Asian**: 8.6 **% Black**: 1.3 **% Hispanic**: 4.7 **% White**: 85.1	National ***Socio-Economic Status*** indicator percentile (100=high): 97th

Los Angeles County

[CANYON COUNTRY] **SULPHUR SPRINGS UNION ELEMENTARY S.D.**

17866 SIERRA HWY. ● CANYON COUNTRY CA 91351-1671 ● (805) 252-5131 ● http://www.sssd.k12.ca.us

Grade Span: KG-06 **Schools**: *Regular* 7 ● *Spec Ed* 0 ● *Alt* 0 **Students**: 4,435 **Total Teachers**: 168 **Student/Classroom Teacher Ratio**: 26.0	**Expenditures/Student**: $4,176 **Librarians**: 0.0 *** students/librarian **Guidance Counselors**: 0.0 *** students/counselor	**% Amer Indian**: 0.2 **% Asian**: 3.6 **% Black**: 4.5 **% Hispanic**: 17.9 **% White**: 73.8	National ***Socio-Economic Status*** indicator percentile (100=high): 41st

Los Angeles County

[CERRITOS] **ABC UNIFIED S.D.**

16700 NORWALK BLVD. ● CERRITOS CA 90703-1838 ● (562) 926-5566 ● http://www.abcusd.k12.ca.us

Grade Span: KG-12 **Schools**: *Regular* 28 ● *Spec Ed* 0 ● *Alt* 2 **Students**: 21,819 **Total Teachers**: 900 **Student/Classroom Teacher Ratio**: 25.7	**Expenditures/Student**: $4,784 **Librarians**: 0.0 *** students/librarian **Guidance Counselors**: 14.7 1,484 students/counselor	**% Amer Indian**: 0.3 **% Asian**: 39.4 **% Black**: 9.8 **% Hispanic**: 30.7 **% White**: 19.8	National ***Socio-Economic Status*** indicator percentile (100=high): 38th

Los Angeles County

[CITY OF INDUSTRY] **HACIENDA LA PUENTE UNIFIED S.D.**

P.O. BOX 60002 ● CITY OF INDUSTRY CA 91716-0002 ● (626) 333-2201 ● http://www.hlpusd.k12.ca.us

Grade Span: KG-12 **Schools**: *Regular* 32 ● *Spec Ed* 1 ● *Alt* 2 **Students**: 21,943 **Total Teachers**: 831 **Student/Classroom Teacher Ratio**: 27.3	**Expenditures/Student**: $5,691 **Librarians**: 1.6 13,714 students/librarian **Guidance Counselors**: 21.9 1,002 students/counselor	**% Amer Indian**: 0.5 **% Asian**: 19.1 **% Black**: 2.8 **% Hispanic**: 65.7 **% White**: 11.9	National ***Socio-Economic Status*** indicator percentile (100=high): 24th

Los Angeles County

CLAREMONT UNIFIED S.D.

2080 N. MOUNTAIN AVE. ● CLAREMONT CA 91711-2643 ● (909) 398-0609

Grade Span: KG-12 **Schools**: *Regular* 9 ● *Spec Ed* 1 ● *Alt* 1 **Students**: 6,493 **Total Teachers**: 270 **Student/Classroom Teacher Ratio**: 25.0	**Expenditures/Student**: $5,262 **Librarians**: 0.0 *** students/librarian **Guidance Counselors**: 7.0 928 students/counselor	**% Amer Indian**: 0.3 **% Asian**: 11.8 **% Black**: 11.2 **% Hispanic**: 17.2 **% White**: 59.6	National ***Socio-Economic Status*** indicator percentile (100=high): 57th

Los Angeles County

COMPTON UNIFIED S.D.

604 S. TAMARIND AVE. ● COMPTON CA 90220-3826 ● (310) 639-4321 ● http://www.compton.k12.ca.us

Grade Span: KG-12 **Schools**: *Regular* 33 ● *Spec Ed* 0 ● *Alt* 2 **Students**: 28,133 **Total Teachers**: 945 **Student/Classroom Teacher Ratio**: 29.9	**Expenditures/Student**: $4,739 **Librarians**: 4.0 7,033 students/librarian **Guidance Counselors**: 28.0 1,005 students/counselor	**% Amer Indian**: 0.0 **% Asian**: 1.4 **% Black**: 37.8 **% Hispanic**: 60.6 **% White**: 0.2	National ***Socio-Economic Status*** indicator percentile (100=high): 2nd

Los Angeles County

[COVINA] **CHARTER OAK UNIFIED S.D.**

P.O. BOX 9 ● COVINA CA 91723-0009 ● (626) 966-8331 ● http://www.cousd.k12.ca.us/index.html

Grade Span: KG-12 **Schools**: *Regular* 7 ● *Spec Ed* 0 ● *Alt* 1 **Students**: 6,272 **Total Teachers**: 228 **Student/Classroom Teacher Ratio**: 28.3	**Expenditures/Student**: $4,677 **Librarians**: 1.0 6,272 students/librarian **Guidance Counselors**: 7.0 896 students/counselor	**% Amer Indian**: 0.2 **% Asian**: 7.8 **% Black**: 4.7 **% Hispanic**: 33.8 **% White**: 53.5	National ***Socio-Economic Status*** indicator percentile (100=high): 49th

Los Angeles County

COVINA-VALLEY UNIFIED S.D.

P.O. BOX 269 ● COVINA CA 91723-0269 ● (626) 331-3371 ● http://www.cvusd.k12.ca.us

Grade Span: KG-12 **Schools**: *Regular* 18 ● *Spec Ed* 0 ● *Alt* 2 **Students**: 12,849 **Total Teachers**: 494 **Student/Classroom Teacher Ratio**: 26.2	**Expenditures/Student**: $4,733 **Librarians**: 1.0 12,849 students/librarian **Guidance Counselors**: 13.2 973 students/counselor	**% Amer Indian**: 0.3 **% Asian**: 11.3 **% Black**: 6.2 **% Hispanic**: 46.5 **% White**: 35.7	National ***Socio-Economic Status*** indicator percentile (100=high): 28th

Los Angeles County

CULVER CITY UNIFIED S.D.

4034 IRVING PL. ● CULVER CITY CA 90232-2810 ● (562) 842-4221 ● http://www.ccusd.k12.ca.us

Grade Span: KG-12 **Schools**: *Regular* 7 ● *Spec Ed* 0 ● *Alt* 2 **Students**: 5,607 **Total Teachers**: 227 **Student/Classroom Teacher Ratio**: 25.7	**Expenditures/Student**: $5,315 **Librarians**: 0.0 *** students/librarian **Guidance Counselors**: 6.0 935 students/counselor	**% Amer Indian**: 0.4 **% Asian**: 12.8 **% Black**: 17.4 **% Hispanic**: 35.2 **% White**: 34.3	National ***Socio-Economic Status*** indicator percentile (100=high): 34th

Los Angeles County

DOWNEY UNIFIED S.D.

P.O. BOX 7017 ● DOWNEY CA 90241-7017 ● (562) 904-3500

Grade Span: KG-12	**Expenditures/Student**: $4,429	**% Amer Indian**: 0.8	
Schools: *Regular* 19 ● *Spec Ed* 1 ● *Alt* 1	**Librarians**: 5.0	**% Asian**: 9.0	National ***Socio-Economic***
Students: 18,522	3,704 students/librarian	**% Black**: 5.2	***Status*** indicator percentile
Total Teachers: 735	**Guidance Counselors**: 17.7	**% Hispanic**: 57.0	(100=high): 22nd
Student/Classroom Teacher Ratio: 25.2	1,046 students/counselor	**% White**: 28.0	

Los Angeles County

DUARTE UNIFIED S.D.

1620 HUNTINGTON DRIVE ● DUARTE CA 91010-2534 ● (626) 358-1191

Grade Span: KG-12	**Expenditures/Student**: $4,814	**% Amer Indian**: 0.2	
Schools: *Regular* 7 ● *Spec Ed* 0 ● *Alt* 1	**Librarians**: 0.0	**% Asian**: 6.7	National ***Socio-Economic***
Students: 4,614	*** students/librarian	**% Black**: 12.2	***Status*** indicator percentile
Total Teachers: 176	**Guidance Counselors**: 2.0	**% Hispanic**: 60.9	(100=high): 7th
Student/Classroom Teacher Ratio: 26.8	2,307 students/counselor	**% White**: 19.9	

Los Angeles County

EL MONTE CITY ELEMENTARY S.D.

3540 N. LEXINGTON AVE. ● EL MONTE CA 91731-2684 ● (626) 453-3799

Grade Span: KG-08	**Expenditures/Student**: $4,566	**% Amer Indian**: 0.2	
Schools: *Regular* 17 ● *Spec Ed* 1 ● *Alt* 0	**Librarians**: 0.0	**% Asian**: 13.7	National ***Socio-Economic***
Students: 11,378	*** students/librarian	**% Black**: 1.1	***Status*** indicator percentile
Total Teachers: 457	**Guidance Counselors**: 0.0	**% Hispanic**: 76.4	(100=high): 1st
Student/Classroom Teacher Ratio: 25.6	*** students/counselor	**% White**: 8.5	

Los Angeles County

EL MONTE UNION HIGH S.D.

3537 JOHNSON AVE. ● EL MONTE CA 91731-3290 ● (626) 444-9005

Grade Span: 09-12	**Expenditures/Student**: $5,977	**% Amer Indian**: 0.3	
Schools: *Regular* 5 ● *Spec Ed* 0 ● *Alt* 1	**Librarians**: 0.5	**% Asian**: 17.5	National ***Socio-Economic***
Students: 9,148	18,296 students/librarian	**% Black**: 0.6	***Status*** indicator percentile
Total Teachers: 341	**Guidance Counselors**: 24.0	**% Hispanic**: 74.7	(100=high): 9th
Student/Classroom Teacher Ratio: 26.2	381 students/counselor	**% White**: 7.0	

Los Angeles County

[EL MONTE] MOUNTAIN VIEW ELEMENTARY S.D.

3320 GILMAN RD. ● EL MONTE CA 91732-3226 ● (626) 575-2151

Grade Span: KG-08	**Expenditures/Student**: $4,393	**% Amer Indian**: 0.1	
Schools: *Regular* 12 ● *Spec Ed* 0 ● *Alt* 0	**Librarians**: 1.0	**% Asian**: 7.7	National ***Socio-Economic***
Students: 9,290	9,290 students/librarian	**% Black**: 0.5	***Status*** indicator percentile
Total Teachers: 355	**Guidance Counselors**: 3.0	**% Hispanic**: 89.3	(100=high): 0th
Student/Classroom Teacher Ratio: 27.5	3,097 students/counselor	**% White**: 2.5	

Los Angeles County

GLENDALE UNIFIED S.D.

223 N. JACKSON ST. ● GLENDALE CA 91206-4334 ● (626) 241-3111

Grade Span: KG-12	**Expenditures/Student**: $4,424	**% Amer Indian**: 0.2	
Schools: *Regular* 26 ● *Spec Ed* 1 ● *Alt* 2	**Librarians**: 1.0	**% Asian**: 16.4	National ***Socio-Economic***
Students: 29,747	29,747 students/librarian	**% Black**: 1.1	***Status*** indicator percentile
Total Teachers: 1,142	**Guidance Counselors**: 11.5	**% Hispanic**: 23.0	(100=high): 14th
Student/Classroom Teacher Ratio: 27.5	2,587 students/counselor	**% White**: 59.3	

Los Angeles County
GLENDORA UNIFIED S.D.
500 N. LORAINE AVE. ● GLENDORA CA 91741-2964 ● (626) 963-1611

Grade Span: KG-12 **Schools**: *Regular* 9 ● *Spec Ed* 0 ● *Alt* 1 **Students**: 7,453 **Total Teachers**: 277 **Student/Classroom Teacher Ratio**: 26.4	**Expenditures/Student**: $4,171 **Librarians**: 1.0 7,453 students/librarian **Guidance Counselors**: 4.0 1,863 students/counselor	**% Amer Indian**: 0.1 **% Asian**: 5.6 **% Black**: 1.4 **% Hispanic**: 15.5 **% White**: 77.3	National ***Socio-Economic Status*** indicator percentile (100=high): 70th

Los Angeles County
HAWTHORNE ELEMENTARY S.D.
4301 W. 129TH ST. ● HAWTHORNE CA 90250-5210 ● (310) 676-2276

Grade Span: KG-08 **Schools**: *Regular* 9 ● *Spec Ed* 0 ● *Alt* 0 **Students**: 7,864 **Total Teachers**: 316 **Student/Classroom Teacher Ratio**: 25.2	**Expenditures/Student**: $3,874 **Librarians**: 0.1 78,640 students/librarian **Guidance Counselors**: 4.0 1,966 students/counselor	**% Amer Indian**: 0.1 **% Asian**: 8.0 **% Black**: 36.1 **% Hispanic**: 47.8 **% White**: 8.0	National ***Socio-Economic Status*** indicator percentile (100=high): 1st

Los Angeles County
INGLEWOOD UNIFIED S.D.
401 S. INGLEWOOD AVE. ● INGLEWOOD CA 90301-2501 ● (562) 419-2500

Grade Span: KG-12 **Schools**: *Regular* 17 ● *Spec Ed* 0 ● *Alt* 1 **Students**: 16,285 **Total Teachers**: 593 **Student/Classroom Teacher Ratio**: 27.6	**Expenditures/Student**: $4,602 **Librarians**: 1.7 9,579 students/librarian **Guidance Counselors**: 12.0 1,357 students/counselor	**% Amer Indian**: 0.1 **% Asian**: 1.3 **% Black**: 43.6 **% Hispanic**: 54.5 **% White**: 0.5	National ***Socio-Economic Status*** indicator percentile (100=high): 4th

Los Angeles County
LA CANADA UNIFIED S.D.
5039 PALM DR. ● LA CANADA CA 91011-1518 ● (818) 952-8300 ● http://www.lcusd.k12.ca.us

Grade Span: KG-12 **Schools**: *Regular* 4 ● *Spec Ed* 0 ● *Alt* 1 **Students**: 4,009 **Total Teachers**: 157 **Student/Classroom Teacher Ratio**: 26.0	**Expenditures/Student**: $4,549 **Librarians**: 1.0 4,009 students/librarian **Guidance Counselors**: 3.8 1,055 students/counselor	**% Amer Indian**: 0.0 **% Asian**: 25.9 **% Black**: 0.8 **% Hispanic**: 3.0 **% White**: 70.2	National ***Socio-Economic Status*** indicator percentile (100=high): 99th

Los Angeles County
[LA PUENTE] **BASSETT UNIFIED S.D.**
904 N. WILLOW AVE. ● LA PUENTE CA 91746-1615 ● (626) 918-3131 ● http://sunkistschool.hypermart.net/BUSD

Grade Span: KG-12 **Schools**: *Regular* 7 ● *Spec Ed* 0 ● *Alt* 1 **Students**: 5,875 **Total Teachers**: 226 **Student/Classroom Teacher Ratio**: 26.9	**Expenditures/Student**: $5,586 **Librarians**: 0.0 *** students/librarian **Guidance Counselors**: 4.0 1,469 students/counselor	**% Amer Indian**: 0.5 **% Asian**: 5.6 **% Black**: 2.5 **% Hispanic**: 87.1 **% White**: 4.3	National ***Socio-Economic Status*** indicator percentile (100=high): 1st

Los Angeles County
[LANCASTER] **ANTELOPE VALLEY UNION HIGH S.D.**
44811 NORTH SIERRA HWY. ● LANCASTER CA 93534-3226 ● (805) 948-7655 ● http://avdistrict.org

Grade Span: 09-12 **Schools**: *Regular* 6 ● *Spec Ed* 0 ● *Alt* 1 **Students**: 14,638 **Total Teachers**: 482 **Student/Classroom Teacher Ratio**: 30.1	**Expenditures/Student**: $4,089 **Librarians**: 0.0 *** students/librarian **Guidance Counselors**: 32.5 450 students/counselor	**% Amer Indian**: 0.5 **% Asian**: 4.3 **% Black**: 13.6 **% Hispanic**: 25.7 **% White**: 55.9	National ***Socio-Economic Status*** indicator percentile (100=high): 53rd

Los Angeles County
LANCASTER ELEMENTARY S.D.
44711 N. CEDAR AVE. ● LANCASTER CA 93534-3210 ● (805) 948-4661 ● http://www.lancaster.k12.ca.us

Grade Span: KG-08 **Schools**: *Regular* 14 ● *Spec Ed* 0 ● *Alt* 0 **Students**: 13,238 **Total Teachers**: 483 **Student/Classroom Teacher Ratio**: 27.6	**Expenditures/Student**: $4,117 **Librarians**: 0.0 *** students/librarian **Guidance Counselors**: 0.0 *** students/counselor	**% Amer Indian**: 0.8 **% Asian**: 3.8 **% Black**: 18.8 **% Hispanic**: 23.9 **% White**: 52.7	National ***Socio-Economic Status*** indicator percentile (100=high): 17th

Los Angeles County
[LANCASTER] WESTSIDE UNION ELEMENTARY S.D.
46809 N. 70TH ST. WEST ● LANCASTER CA 93535-7836 ● (805) 948-2669

Grade Span: KG-08 **Schools**: *Regular* 10 ● *Spec Ed* 0 ● *Alt* 0 **Students**: 5,879 **Total Teachers**: 230 **Student/Classroom Teacher Ratio**: 25.4	**Expenditures/Student**: $3,904 **Librarians**: 1.0 5,879 students/librarian **Guidance Counselors**: 1.0 5,879 students/counselor	**% Amer Indian**: 1.3 **% Asian**: 4.5 **% Black**: 9.9 **% Hispanic**: 13.5 **% White**: 70.8	National ***Socio-Economic Status*** indicator percentile (100=high): 52nd

Los Angeles County
[LAWNDALE] CENTINELA VALLEY UNION HIGH S.D.
14901 S. INGLEWOOD AVE. ● LAWNDALE CA 90260-1251 ● (310) 970-7700

Grade Span: 09-12 **Schools**: *Regular* 2 ● *Spec Ed* 0 ● *Alt* 1 **Students**: 5,994 **Total Teachers**: 223 **Student/Classroom Teacher Ratio**: 26.8	**Expenditures/Student**: $5,278 **Librarians**: 0.0 *** students/librarian **Guidance Counselors**: 11.9 504 students/counselor	**% Amer Indian**: 0.3 **% Asian**: 9.6 **% Black**: 19.7 **% Hispanic**: 63.7 **% White**: 6.6	National ***Socio-Economic Status*** indicator percentile (100=high): 73rd

Los Angeles County
LAWNDALE ELEMENTARY S.D.
4161 W. 147TH ST. ● LAWNDALE CA 90260-1709 ● (310) 973-1300 ● http://www.lawndale.k12.ca.us

Grade Span: KG-08 **Schools**: *Regular* 7 ● *Spec Ed* 0 ● *Alt* 0 **Students**: 5,092 **Total Teachers**: 213 **Student/Classroom Teacher Ratio**: 24.0	**Expenditures/Student**: $4,452 **Librarians**: 1.0 5,092 students/librarian **Guidance Counselors**: 1.0 5,092 students/counselor	**% Amer Indian**: 0.6 **% Asian**: 13.7 **% Black**: 20.3 **% Hispanic**: 49.1 **% White**: 16.2	National ***Socio-Economic Status*** indicator percentile (100=high): 1st

Los Angeles County
LENNOX ELEMENTARY S.D.
10319 S. FIRMONA AVE. ● LENNOX CA 90304-1419 ● (310) 330-4950

Grade Span: KG-08 **Schools**: *Regular* 6 ● *Spec Ed* 0 ● *Alt* 0 **Students**: 6,171 **Total Teachers**: 241 **Student/Classroom Teacher Ratio**: 26.0	**Expenditures/Student**: $4,302 **Librarians**: 0.0 *** students/librarian **Guidance Counselors**: 8.0 771 students/counselor	**% Amer Indian**: 0.0 **% Asian**: 2.3 **% Black**: 3.3 **% Hispanic**: 93.7 **% White**: 0.7	National ***Socio-Economic Status*** indicator percentile (100=high): 0th

Los Angeles County
LONG BEACH UNIFIED S.D.
701 LOCUST AVE. ● LONG BEACH CA 90813-4316 ● (562) 436-9931 ● http://www.lbusd.k12.ca.us

Grade Span: KG-12 **Schools**: *Regular* 79 ● *Spec Ed* 0 ● *Alt* 3 **Students**: 80,520 **Total Teachers**: 3,249 **Student/Classroom Teacher Ratio**: 25.0	**Expenditures/Student**: $4,949 **Librarians**: 4.5 17,893 students/librarian **Guidance Counselors**: 125.6 641 students/counselor	**% Amer Indian**: 0.4 **% Asian**: 20.6 **% Black**: 20.9 **% Hispanic**: 37.3 **% White**: 20.7	National ***Socio-Economic Status*** indicator percentile (100=high): 6th

Los Angeles County
LOS ANGELES UNIFIED S.D.
450 N. GRAND AVE. ● LOS ANGELES CA 90012-2100 ● (213) 625-6251 ● http://www.lausd.k12.ca.us/welcome.html

Grade Span: KG-12 **Schools**: *Regular* 562 ● *Spec Ed* 18 ● *Alt* 62 **Students**: 647,612 **Total Teachers**: 26,438 **Student/Classroom Teacher Ratio**: 25.2	**Expenditures/Student**: $5,539 **Librarians**: 66.0 9,812 students/librarian **Guidance Counselors**: 758.5 854 students/counselor	**% Amer Indian**: 0.3 **% Asian**: 6.9 **% Black**: 13.9 **% Hispanic**: 67.9 **% White**: 11.0	National ***Socio-Economic Status*** indicator percentile (100=high): 3rd

Los Angeles County
LYNWOOD UNIFIED S.D.
11321 BULLIS RD. ● LYNWOOD CA 90262-3600 ● (562) 886-1600 ● http://www.lynwood.k12.ca.us

Grade Span: KG-12 **Schools**: *Regular* 11 ● *Spec Ed* 0 ● *Alt* 1 **Students**: 15,333 **Total Teachers**: 538 **Student/Classroom Teacher Ratio**: 29.2	**Expenditures/Student**: $4,105 **Librarians**: 1.0 15,333 students/librarian **Guidance Counselors**: 12.0 1,278 students/counselor	**% Amer Indian**: 0.3 **% Asian**: 0.7 **% Black**: 13.7 **% Hispanic**: 84.7 **% White**: 0.5	National ***Socio-Economic Status*** indicator percentile (100=high): 9th

Los Angeles County
MANHATTAN BEACH UNIFIED S.D.
1501 REDONDO AVE. ● MANHATTAN BEACH CA 90266-4214 ● (310) 546-3488

Grade Span: KG-12 **Schools**: *Regular* 6 ● *Spec Ed* 0 ● *Alt* 0 **Students**: 4,988 **Total Teachers**: 218 **Student/Classroom Teacher Ratio**: 24.9	**Expenditures/Student**: $5,443 **Librarians**: 1.0 4,988 students/librarian **Guidance Counselors**: 8.9 560 students/counselor	**% Amer Indian**: 0.2 **% Asian**: 7.5 **% Black**: 1.6 **% Hispanic**: 9.3 **% White**: 81.5	National ***Socio-Economic Status*** indicator percentile (100=high): 86th

Los Angeles County
MONROVIA UNIFIED S.D.
325 E. HUNTINGTON DR. ● MONROVIA CA 91016-3585 ● (626) 359-9181

Grade Span: KG-12 **Schools**: *Regular* 8 ● *Spec Ed* 0 ● *Alt* 1 **Students**: 5,965 **Total Teachers**: 224 **Student/Classroom Teacher Ratio**: 27.5	**Expenditures/Student**: $4,734 **Librarians**: 1.0 5,965 students/librarian **Guidance Counselors**: 5.0 1,193 students/counselor	**% Amer Indian**: 0.4 **% Asian**: 3.4 **% Black**: 15.3 **% Hispanic**: 44.5 **% White**: 36.5	National ***Socio-Economic Status*** indicator percentile (100=high): 10th

Los Angeles County
MONTEBELLO UNIFIED S.D.
123 S. MONTEBELLO BLVD. ● MONTEBELLO CA 90640-4729 ● (213) 726-1225 ● http://www.montebello.k12.ca.us

Grade Span: KG-12 **Schools**: *Regular* 26 ● *Spec Ed* 0 ● *Alt* 3 **Students**: 32,801 **Total Teachers**: 1,091 **Student/Classroom Teacher Ratio**: 29.9	**Expenditures/Student**: $4,720 **Librarians**: 2.0 16,401 students/librarian **Guidance Counselors**: 38.6 850 students/counselor	**% Amer Indian**: 0.1 **% Asian**: 5.8 **% Black**: 0.5 **% Hispanic**: 89.4 **% White**: 4.1	National ***Socio-Economic Status*** indicator percentile (100=high): 2nd

Los Angeles County
NORWALK-LA MIRADA UNIFIED S.D.
12820 PIONEER BLVD. ● NORWALK CA 90650-2894 ● (562) 868-0431

Grade Span: KG-12 **Schools**: *Regular* 25 ● *Spec Ed* 0 ● *Alt* 1 **Students**: 20,885 **Total Teachers**: 802 **Student/Classroom Teacher Ratio**: 26.8	**Expenditures/Student**: $4,832 **Librarians**: 0.0 *** students/librarian **Guidance Counselors**: 24.8 842 students/counselor	**% Amer Indian**: 0.2 **% Asian**: 8.4 **% Black**: 5.0 **% Hispanic**: 60.6 **% White**: 25.8	National ***Socio-Economic Status*** indicator percentile (100=high): 21st

Los Angeles County
PALMDALE ELEMENTARY S.D.
39139 10TH ST. EAST. ● PALMDALE CA 93550-3419 ● (805) 947-7191

Grade Span: KG-08	**Expenditures/Student**: $4,146	**% Amer Indian**: 1.0	
Schools: *Regular* 18 ● *Spec Ed* 0 ● *Alt* 0	**Librarians**: 0.0	**% Asian**: 4.0	National ***Socio-Economic***
Students: 18,004	*** students/librarian	**% Black**: 14.1	***Status*** indicator percentile
Total Teachers: 630	**Guidance Counselors**: 1.0	**% Hispanic**: 36.1	(100=high): 22nd
Student/Classroom Teacher Ratio: 29.2	18,004 students/counselor	**% White**: 44.7	

Los Angeles County
[PALOS VERDES ESTATES] **PALOS VERDES PENINSULA UNIFIED S.D.**
3801 VIA LA SELVA ● PALOS VERDES ESTATES CA 90274-1119 ● (310) 378-9966 ● http://www.pvpusd.k12.ca.us

Grade Span: KG-12	**Expenditures/Student**: $4,373	**% Amer Indian**: 0.1	
Schools: *Regular* 13 ● *Spec Ed* 0 ● *Alt* 1	**Librarians**: 1.0	**% Asian**: 32.6	National ***Socio-Economic***
Students: 8,901	8,901 students/librarian	**% Black**: 1.6	***Status*** indicator percentile
Total Teachers: 354	**Guidance Counselors**: 9.0	**% Hispanic**: 3.8	(100=high): 98th
Student/Classroom Teacher Ratio: 26.2	989 students/counselor	**% White**: 61.9	

Los Angeles County
PARAMOUNT UNIFIED S.D.
15110 CALIFORNIA AVE. ● PARAMOUNT CA 90723-4320 ● (562) 602-6000

Grade Span: KG-12	**Expenditures/Student**: $4,387	**% Amer Indian**: 0.3	
Schools: *Regular* 13 ● *Spec Ed* 0 ● *Alt* 1	**Librarians**: 1.0	**% Asian**: 4.2	National ***Socio-Economic***
Students: 15,082	15,082 students/librarian	**% Black**: 14.6	***Status*** indicator percentile
Total Teachers: 535	**Guidance Counselors**: 17.0	**% Hispanic**: 74.8	(100=high): 10th
Student/Classroom Teacher Ratio: 29.0	887 students/counselor	**% White**: 6.1	

Los Angeles County
PASADENA UNIFIED S.D.
351 S. HUDSON AVE. ● PASADENA CA 91101-3507 ● (626) 795-6981 ● http://www.pasadena.k12.ca.us

Grade Span: KG-12	**Expenditures/Student**: $5,198	**% Amer Indian**: 0.1	
Schools: *Regular* 28 ● *Spec Ed* 0 ● *Alt* 3	**Librarians**: 7.2	**% Asian**: 3.9	National ***Socio-Economic***
Students: 22,136	3,074 students/librarian	**% Black**: 33.6	***Status*** indicator percentile
Total Teachers: 862	**Guidance Counselors**: 23.5	**% Hispanic**: 45.5	(100=high): 7th
Student/Classroom Teacher Ratio: 26.5	942 students/counselor	**% White**: 16.9	

Los Angeles County
[PEARBLOSSOM] **KEPPEL UNION ELEMENTARY S.D.**
P.O. BOX 186 ● PEARBLOSSOM CA 93553-0186 ● (805) 944-2155

Grade Span: KG-08	**Expenditures/Student**: $3,989	**% Amer Indian**: 1.5	
Schools: *Regular* 6 ● *Spec Ed* 0 ● *Alt* 0	**Librarians**: 0.0	**% Asian**: 1.6	National ***Socio-Economic***
Students: 3,037	*** students/librarian	**% Black**: 9.3	***Status*** indicator percentile
Total Teachers: 109	**Guidance Counselors**: 0.0	**% Hispanic**: 41.9	(100=high): 6th
Student/Classroom Teacher Ratio: 28.3	*** students/counselor	**% White**: 45.8	

Los Angeles County
[PICO RIVERA] **EL RANCHO UNIFIED S.D.**
9333 LOCH LOMOND DR. ● PICO RIVERA CA 90660-2913 ● (562) 942-1500 ● http://www.erusd.k12.ca.us

Grade Span: KG-12	**Expenditures/Student**: $4,784	**% Amer Indian**: 0.1	
Schools: *Regular* 13 ● *Spec Ed* 0 ● *Alt* 1	**Librarians**: 0.0	**% Asian**: 1.7	National ***Socio-Economic***
Students: 11,139	*** students/librarian	**% Black**: 0.6	***Status*** indicator percentile
Total Teachers: 438	**Guidance Counselors**: 8.0	**% Hispanic**: 93.7	(100=high): 5th
Student/Classroom Teacher Ratio: 26.5	1,392 students/counselor	**% White**: 3.8	

Los Angeles County
POMONA UNIFIED S.D.
P.O. BOX 2900 ● POMONA CA 91769-2900 ● (909) 397-4700 ● http://www.pomona.k12.ca.us

Grade Span: KG-12	**Expenditures/Student**: $4,990	**% Amer Indian**: 0.1	National ***Socio-Economic Status*** indicator percentile (100=high): 3rd
Schools: *Regular* 34 ● *Spec Ed* 0 ● *Alt* 2	**Librarians**: 4.0	**% Asian**: 8.4	
Students: 30,625	7,656 students/librarian	**% Black**: 11.8	
Total Teachers: 1,158	**Guidance Counselors**: 16.0	**% Hispanic**: 69.1	
Student/Classroom Teacher Ratio: 26.9	1,914 students/counselor	**% White**: 10.5	

Los Angeles County
REDONDO BEACH UNIFIED S.D.
1401 INGLEWOOD AVE. ● REDONDO BEACH CA 90278-3912 ● (310) 379-5449 ● http://www.bnet.org/rbsd

Grade Span: KG-12	**Expenditures/Student**: $5,931	**% Amer Indian**: 0.3	National ***Socio-Economic Status*** indicator percentile (100=high): 47th
Schools: *Regular* 11 ● *Spec Ed* 0 ● *Alt* 1	**Librarians**: 1.0	**% Asian**: 8.6	
Students: 7,032	7,032 students/librarian	**% Black**: 5.0	
Total Teachers: 309	**Guidance Counselors**: 12.0	**% Hispanic**: 21.9	
Student/Classroom Teacher Ratio: 23.9	586 students/counselor	**% White**: 64.2	

Los Angeles County
[ROSEMEAD] **GARVEY ELEMENTARY S.D.**
2730 N. DEL MAR ● ROSEMEAD CA 91770-3026 ● (626) 307-3400

Grade Span: KG-08	**Expenditures/Student**: $5,086	**% Amer Indian**: 0.2	National ***Socio-Economic Status*** indicator percentile (100=high): 3rd
Schools: *Regular* 13 ● *Spec Ed* 1 ● *Alt* 0	**Librarians**: 0.6	**% Asian**: 46.2	
Students: 7,259	12,098 students/librarian	**% Black**: 0.5	
Total Teachers: 283	**Guidance Counselors**: 1.7	**% Hispanic**: 49.8	
Student/Classroom Teacher Ratio: 25.9	4,270 students/counselor	**% White**: 3.3	

Los Angeles County
ROSEMEAD ELEMENTARY S.D.
3640 N. RIO HONDO AVE. ● ROSEMEAD CA 91770-2041 ● (626) 443-0173

Grade Span: KG-08	**Expenditures/Student**: $4,206	**% Amer Indian**: 0.0	National ***Socio-Economic Status*** indicator percentile (100=high): 3rd
Schools: *Regular* 5 ● *Spec Ed* 0 ● *Alt* 0	**Librarians**: 0.0	**% Asian**: 36.2	
Students: 3,092	*** students/librarian	**% Black**: 1.2	
Total Teachers: 120	**Guidance Counselors**: 0.0	**% Hispanic**: 53.2	
Student/Classroom Teacher Ratio: 25.8	*** students/counselor	**% White**: 9.4	

Los Angeles County
[ROWLAND HEIGHTS] **ROWLAND UNIFIED S.D.**
P.O. BOX 8490 ● ROWLAND HEIGHTS CA 91748-0490 ● (818) 965-2541 ● http://www.rowland-unified.org

Grade Span: KG-12	**Expenditures/Student**: $4,534	**% Amer Indian**: 0.2	National ***Socio-Economic Status*** indicator percentile (100=high): 33rd
Schools: *Regular* 20 ● *Spec Ed* 0 ● *Alt* 1	**Librarians**: 2.5	**% Asian**: 26.1	
Students: 18,558	7,423 students/librarian	**% Black**: 7.4	
Total Teachers: 700	**Guidance Counselors**: 11.0	**% Hispanic**: 53.2	
Student/Classroom Teacher Ratio: 27.9	1,687 students/counselor	**% White**: 13.1	

Los Angeles County
[SAN DIMAS] **BONITA UNIFIED S.D.**
115 W. ALLEN AVE. ● SAN DIMAS CA 91773-1437 ● (909) 599-6787 ● http://www.bonita.k12.ca.us

Grade Span: KG-12	**Expenditures/Student**: $4,683	**% Amer Indian**: 0.5	National ***Socio-Economic Status*** indicator percentile (100=high): 48th
Schools: *Regular* 12 ● *Spec Ed* 0 ● *Alt* 1	**Librarians**: 2.0	**% Asian**: 8.5	
Students: 9,894	4,947 students/librarian	**% Black**: 4.8	
Total Teachers: 371	**Guidance Counselors**: 6.8	**% Hispanic**: 25.2	
Student/Classroom Teacher Ratio: 30.0	1,455 students/counselor	**% White**: 61.1	

Los Angeles County
SAN GABRIEL UNIFIED S.D.
102 E. BROADWAY ● SAN GABRIEL CA 91776-4500 ● (626) 285-3111

Grade Span: KG-10 **Schools**: *Regular* 7 ● *Spec Ed* 0 ● *Alt* 0 **Students**: 4,413 **Total Teachers**: 189 **Student/Classroom Teacher Ratio**: 23.9	**Expenditures/Student**: $5,381 **Librarians**: 0.0 *** students/librarian **Guidance Counselors**: 3.9 1,132 students/counselor	**% Amer Indian**: 0.3 **% Asian**: 37.1 **% Black**: 1.8 **% Hispanic**: 44.0 **% White**: 16.8	National ***Socio-Economic Status*** indicator percentile (100=high): 13th

Los Angeles County
SAN MARINO UNIFIED S.D.
1665 WEST DR. ● SAN MARINO CA 91108-2594 ● (626) 281-3691 ● http://www.san-marino.k12.ca.us

Grade Span: KG-12 **Schools**: *Regular* 4 ● *Spec Ed* 0 ● *Alt* 0 **Students**: 3,015 **Total Teachers**: 130 **Student/Classroom Teacher Ratio**: 23.1	**Expenditures/Student**: $4,505 **Librarians**: 0.0 *** students/librarian **Guidance Counselors**: 4.0 754 students/counselor	**% Amer Indian**: 0.0 **% Asian**: 60.9 **% Black**: 0.4 **% Hispanic**: 3.4 **% White**: 35.4	National ***Socio-Economic Status*** indicator percentile (100=high): 100th

Los Angeles County
[SANTA CLARITA] **SAUGUS UNION ELEMENTARY S.D.**
24930 AVENUE STANFORD . ● SANTA CLARITA CA 91355-1272 ● (805) 294-7500 ● http://www.saugus.k12.ca.us

Grade Span: KG-06 **Schools**: *Regular* 11 ● *Spec Ed* 0 ● *Alt* 0 **Students**: 7,045 **Total Teachers**: 257 **Student/Classroom Teacher Ratio**: 27.6	**Expenditures/Student**: $4,102 **Librarians**: 0.0 *** students/librarian **Guidance Counselors**: 0.0 *** students/counselor	**% Amer Indian**: 0.1 **% Asian**: 6.1 **% Black**: 2.0 **% Hispanic**: 13.8 **% White**: 78.0	National ***Socio-Economic Status*** indicator percentile (100=high): 83rd

Los Angeles County
[SANTA CLARITA] **WILLIAM S. HART UNION HIGH S.D.**
21515 REDVIEW DR. ● SANTA CLARITA CA 91350-2948 ● (805) 259-0033

Grade Span: 07-12 **Schools**: *Regular* 8 ● *Spec Ed* 0 ● *Alt* 2 **Students**: 12,331 **Total Teachers**: 496 **Student/Classroom Teacher Ratio**: 24.8	**Expenditures/Student**: $4,886 **Librarians**: 6.0 2,055 students/librarian **Guidance Counselors**: 29.1 424 students/counselor	**% Amer Indian**: 0.2 **% Asian**: 5.1 **% Black**: 2.6 **% Hispanic**: 17.5 **% White**: 74.7	National ***Socio-Economic Status*** indicator percentile (100=high): 81st

Los Angeles County
[SANTA FE SPRINGS] **LITTLE LAKE CITY ELEMENTARY S.D.**
10515 S. PIONEER BLVD. ● SANTA FE SPRINGS CA 90670-3703 ● (562) 868-8241

Grade Span: KG-08 **Schools**: *Regular* 9 ● *Spec Ed* 0 ● *Alt* 0 **Students**: 4,696 **Total Teachers**: 184 **Student/Classroom Teacher Ratio**: 26.3	**Expenditures/Student**: $5,043 **Librarians**: 0.0 *** students/librarian **Guidance Counselors**: 3.4 1,381 students/counselor	**% Amer Indian**: 0.4 **% Asian**: 6.2 **% Black**: 2.5 **% Hispanic**: 71.9 **% White**: 18.9	National ***Socio-Economic Status*** indicator percentile (100=high): 18th

Los Angeles County
SANTA MONICA-MALIBU UNIFIED S.D.
1651 16TH ST. ● SANTA MONICA CA 90404-3891 ● (310) 450-8338 ● http://www.smmusd.org

Grade Span: KG-12 **Schools**: *Regular* 13 ● *Spec Ed* 0 ● *Alt* 2 **Students**: 10,590 **Total Teachers**: 450 **Student/Classroom Teacher Ratio**: 24.0	**Expenditures/Student**: $5,957 **Librarians**: 1.0 10,590 students/librarian **Guidance Counselors**: 11.2 946 students/counselor	**% Amer Indian**: 0.2 **% Asian**: 6.8 **% Black**: 8.6 **% Hispanic**: 27.7 **% White**: 56.7	National ***Socio-Economic Status*** indicator percentile (100=high): 46th

Los Angeles County
SOUTH PASADENA UNIFIED S.D.
1020 EL CENTRO ST. • SOUTH PASADENA CA 91030-3118 • (626) 441-5703

Grade Span: KG-12 **Schools**: *Regular* 5 • *Spec Ed* 0 • *Alt* 0 **Students**: 3,699 **Total Teachers**: 150 **Student/Classroom Teacher Ratio**: 25.2	**Expenditures/Student**: $4,254 **Librarians**: 2.0 1,850 students/librarian **Guidance Counselors**: 7.0 528 students/counselor	**% Amer Indian**: 0.4 **% Asian**: 33.9 **% Black**: 4.5 **% Hispanic**: 17.8 **% White**: 43.3	National ***Socio-Economic Status*** indicator percentile (100=high): 76th

Los Angeles County
TEMPLE CITY UNIFIED S.D.
9516 E. LONGDEN AVE. • TEMPLE CITY CA 91780-1610 • (626) 285-2111

Grade Span: KG-12 **Schools**: *Regular* 6 • *Spec Ed* 0 • *Alt* 1 **Students**: 5,168 **Total Teachers**: 198 **Student/Classroom Teacher Ratio**: 26.6	**Expenditures/Student**: $4,208 **Librarians**: 0.8 6,460 students/librarian **Guidance Counselors**: 5.0 1,034 students/counselor	**% Amer Indian**: 0.2 **% Asian**: 35.7 **% Black**: 1.9 **% Hispanic**: 19.7 **% White**: 42.5	National ***Socio-Economic Status*** indicator percentile (100=high): 44th

Los Angeles County
TORRANCE UNIFIED S.D.
2335 PLAZA DEL AMO • TORRANCE CA 90501-3420 • (310) 533-4200

Grade Span: KG-12 **Schools**: *Regular* 29 • *Spec Ed* 0 • *Alt* 1 **Students**: 22,619 **Total Teachers**: 930 **Student/Classroom Teacher Ratio**: 25.0	**Expenditures/Student**: $4,542 **Librarians**: 5.6 4,039 students/librarian **Guidance Counselors**: 31.5 718 students/counselor	**% Amer Indian**: 0.4 **% Asian**: 30.8 **% Black**: 4.1 **% Hispanic**: 14.3 **% White**: 50.3	National ***Socio-Economic Status*** indicator percentile (100=high): 63rd

Los Angeles County
[VALENCIA] NEWHALL ELEMENTARY S.D.
25375 ORCHARD VILLAGE,STE. 200 • VALENCIA CA 91355-3055 • (805) 286-2200

Grade Span: KG-06 **Schools**: *Regular* 7 • *Spec Ed* 0 • *Alt* 0 **Students**: 5,267 **Total Teachers**: 197 **Student/Classroom Teacher Ratio**: 27.9	**Expenditures/Student**: $3,912 **Librarians**: 0.0 *** students/librarian **Guidance Counselors**: 0.0 *** students/counselor	**% Amer Indian**: 0.0 **% Asian**: 5.0 **% Black**: 1.3 **% Hispanic**: 22.7 **% White**: 71.0	National ***Socio-Economic Status*** indicator percentile (100=high): 45th

Los Angeles County
WALNUT VALLEY UNIFIED S.D.
880 S. LEMON AVE. • WALNUT CA 91789-2931 • (909) 595-1261

Grade Span: KG-12 **Schools**: *Regular* 14 • *Spec Ed* 0 • *Alt* 1 **Students**: 13,830 **Total Teachers**: 520 **Student/Classroom Teacher Ratio**: 27.7	**Expenditures/Student**: $4,358 **Librarians**: 0.0 *** students/librarian **Guidance Counselors**: 14.1 981 students/counselor	**% Amer Indian**: 0.0 **% Asian**: 45.6 **% Black**: 5.5 **% Hispanic**: 17.9 **% White**: 31.0	National ***Socio-Economic Status*** indicator percentile (100=high): 89th

Los Angeles County
WEST COVINA UNIFIED S.D.
1717 W. MERCED AVE. • WEST COVINA CA 91790-3406 • (626) 338-8411

Grade Span: KG-12 **Schools**: *Regular* 11 • *Spec Ed* 0 • *Alt* 1 **Students**: 8,764 **Total Teachers**: 335 **Student/Classroom Teacher Ratio**: 26.6	**Expenditures/Student**: $4,037 **Librarians**: 0.0 *** students/librarian **Guidance Counselors**: 10.0 876 students/counselor	**% Amer Indian**: 0.4 **% Asian**: 13.7 **% Black**: 10.5 **% Hispanic**: 53.4 **% White**: 21.9	National ***Socio-Economic Status*** indicator percentile (100=high): 17th

Los Angeles County

[WHITTIER] **EAST WHITTIER CITY ELEMENTARY S.D.**

14535 E. WHITTIER BLVD. ● WHITTIER CA 90605-2130 ● (562) 698-0351

Grade Span: KG-08 **Schools**: *Regular* 13 ● *Spec Ed* 0 ● *Alt* 0 **Students**: 8,231 **Total Teachers**: 320 **Student/Classroom Teacher Ratio**: 25.5	**Expenditures/Student**: $4,065 **Librarians**: 0.0 *** students/librarian **Guidance Counselors**: 1.0 8,231 students/counselor	**% Amer Indian**: 0.5 **% Asian**: 3.4 **% Black**: 1.4 **% Hispanic**: 54.7 **% White**: 40.1	National ***Socio-Economic Status*** indicator percentile (100=high): 28th

Los Angeles County

[WHITTIER] **LOWELL JOINT ELEMENTARY S.D.**

11019 VALLEY HOME AVE. ● WHITTIER CA 90603-3042 ● (562) 943-0211

Grade Span: KG-08 **Schools**: *Regular* 5 ● *Spec Ed* 0 ● *Alt* 0 **Students**: 3,009 **Total Teachers**: 124 **Student/Classroom Teacher Ratio**: 24.7	**Expenditures/Student**: $4,120 **Librarians**: 0.0 *** students/librarian **Guidance Counselors**: 0.0 *** students/counselor	**% Amer Indian**: 0.2 **% Asian**: 3.5 **% Black**: 1.3 **% Hispanic**: 27.6 **% White**: 67.4	National ***Socio-Economic Status*** indicator percentile (100=high): 69th

Los Angeles County

[WHITTIER] **SOUTH WHITTIER ELEMENTARY S.D.**

P.O. BOX 3037 ● WHITTIER CA 90605-0037 ● (562) 944-6231

Grade Span: KG-08 **Schools**: *Regular* 7 ● *Spec Ed* 0 ● *Alt* 0 **Students**: 3,932 **Total Teachers**: 156 **Student/Classroom Teacher Ratio**: 25.8	**Expenditures/Student**: $4,297 **Librarians**: 0.0 *** students/librarian **Guidance Counselors**: 1.0 3,932 students/counselor	**% Amer Indian**: 0.6 **% Asian**: 2.4 **% Black**: 1.6 **% Hispanic**: 85.1 **% White**: 10.3	National ***Socio-Economic Status*** indicator percentile (100=high): 3rd

Los Angeles County

WHITTIER CITY ELEMENTARY S.D.

7211 S. WHITTIER AVE. ● WHITTIER CA 90602-1123 ● (562) 698-9531

Grade Span: KG-08 **Schools**: *Regular* 13 ● *Spec Ed* 0 ● *Alt* 0 **Students**: 6,606 **Total Teachers**: 256 **Student/Classroom Teacher Ratio**: 26.8	**Expenditures/Student**: $4,291 **Librarians**: 0.0 *** students/librarian **Guidance Counselors**: 4.5 1,468 students/counselor	**% Amer Indian**: 0.3 **% Asian**: 2.6 **% Black**: 1.3 **% Hispanic**: 80.4 **% White**: 15.4	National ***Socio-Economic Status*** indicator percentile (100=high): 4th

Los Angeles County

WHITTIER UNION HIGH S.D.

9401 S. PAINTER AVE. ● WHITTIER CA 90605-2798 ● (562) 698-8121

Grade Span: 09-12 **Schools**: *Regular* 5 ● *Spec Ed* 0 ● *Alt* 2 **Students**: 9,912 **Total Teachers**: 370 **Student/Classroom Teacher Ratio**: 26.2	**Expenditures/Student**: $7,666 **Librarians**: 1.0 9,912 students/librarian **Guidance Counselors**: 23.0 431 students/counselor	**% Amer Indian**: 0.6 **% Asian**: 4.1 **% Black**: 1.3 **% Hispanic**: 67.2 **% White**: 26.8	National ***Socio-Economic Status*** indicator percentile (100=high): 37th

Madera County

MADERA UNIFIED S.D.

1902 HOWARD ROAD ● MADERA CA 93637-5123 ● (209) 675-4500

Grade Span: KG-12 **Schools**: *Regular* 17 ● *Spec Ed* 0 ● *Alt* 1 **Students**: 15,459 **Total Teachers**: 599 **Student/Classroom Teacher Ratio**: 25.7	**Expenditures/Student**: $4,508 **Librarians**: 2.0 7,730 students/librarian **Guidance Counselors**: 16.5 937 students/counselor	**% Amer Indian**: 0.2 **% Asian**: 1.4 **% Black**: 3.9 **% Hispanic**: 65.1 **% White**: 29.4	National ***Socio-Economic Status*** indicator percentile (100=high): 7th

Marin County

[LARKSPUR] **TAMALPAIS UNION HIGH S.D.**

P.O. BOX 605 ● LARKSPUR CA 94977-0605 ● (415) 924-1800 ● http://redwood.org/rhs/district/district.htm

Grade Span: 08-12 **Schools**: *Regular* 3 ● *Spec Ed* 0 ● *Alt* 2 **Students**: 3,074 **Total Teachers**: 156 **Student/Classroom Teacher Ratio**: 19.9	**Expenditures/Student**: $8,329 **Librarians**: 2.0 1,537 students/librarian **Guidance Counselors**: 9.1 338 students/counselor	**% Amer Indian**: 0.9 **% Asian**: 6.3 **% Black**: 3.9 **% Hispanic**: 5.3 **% White**: 83.5	National ***Socio-Economic Status*** indicator percentile (100=high): 95th

Marin County

NOVATO UNIFIED S.D.

1015 SEVENTH ST. ● NOVATO CA 94945-2205 ● (415) 897-4201 ● http://nusd.marin.k12.ca.us/nusd/index.html

Grade Span: KG-12 **Schools**: *Regular* 13 ● *Spec Ed* 0 ● *Alt* 2 **Students**: 7,727 **Total Teachers**: 329 **Student/Classroom Teacher Ratio**: 24.8	**Expenditures/Student**: $4,692 **Librarians**: 4.6 1,680 students/librarian **Guidance Counselors**: 3.0 2,576 students/counselor	**% Amer Indian**: 0.3 **% Asian**: 5.9 **% Black**: 3.8 **% Hispanic**: 9.6 **% White**: 80.4	National ***Socio-Economic Status*** indicator percentile (100=high): 69th

Marin County

SAN RAFAEL CITY ELEMENTARY S.D.

225 WOODLAND AVE. ● SAN RAFAEL CA 94901-6017 ● (415) 485-2300 ● http://srcs.marin.k12.ca.us

Grade Span: KG-08 **Schools**: *Regular* 7 ● *Spec Ed* 0 ● *Alt* 0 **Students**: 3,150 **Total Teachers**: 143 **Student/Classroom Teacher Ratio**: 22.2	**Expenditures/Student**: $4,531 **Librarians**: 0.0 *** students/librarian **Guidance Counselors**: 2.2 1,432 students/counselor	**% Amer Indian**: 0.3 **% Asian**: 9.7 **% Black**: 5.5 **% Hispanic**: 36.8 **% White**: 47.6	National ***Socio-Economic Status*** indicator percentile (100=high): 20th

Mariposa County

[MARIPOSA] **MARIPOSA COUNTY UNIFIED S.D.**

P.O. BOX 8 ● MARIPOSA CA 95338-0008 ● (209) 742-0250

Grade Span: KG-12 **Schools**: *Regular* 11 ● *Spec Ed* 0 ● *Alt* 1 **Students**: 2,707 **Total Teachers**: 119 **Student/Classroom Teacher Ratio**: 20.6	**Expenditures/Student**: $4,887 **Librarians**: 0.0 *** students/librarian **Guidance Counselors**: 2.5 1,083 students/counselor	**% Amer Indian**: 4.1 **% Asian**: 1.0 **% Black**: 0.4 **% Hispanic**: 5.8 **% White**: 88.6	National ***Socio-Economic Status*** indicator percentile (100=high): 45th

Mendocino County

UKIAH UNIFIED S.D.

925 N. STATE ST. ● UKIAH CA 95482-3411 ● (707) 463-5211

Grade Span: KG-12 **Schools**: *Regular* 9 ● *Spec Ed* 0 ● *Alt* 1 **Students**: 6,721 **Total Teachers**: 305 **Student/Classroom Teacher Ratio**: 21.7	**Expenditures/Student**: $5,312 **Librarians**: 0.0 *** students/librarian **Guidance Counselors**: 5.0 1,344 students/counselor	**% Amer Indian**: 6.3 **% Asian**: 1.2 **% Black**: 1.1 **% Hispanic**: 20.7 **% White**: 70.6	National ***Socio-Economic Status*** indicator percentile (100=high): 17th

Mendocino County

WILLITS UNIFIED S.D.

48 W. COMMERCIAL ST. ● WILLITS CA 95490-3007 ● (707) 459-5314

Grade Span: KG-12 **Schools**: *Regular* 7 ● *Spec Ed* 0 ● *Alt* 2 **Students**: 2,600 **Total Teachers**: 122 **Student/Classroom Teacher Ratio**: 17.9	**Expenditures/Student**: $4,565 **Librarians**: 1.0 2,600 students/librarian **Guidance Counselors**: 1.7 1,529 students/counselor	**% Amer Indian**: 6.0 **% Asian**: 1.1 **% Black**: 0.9 **% Hispanic**: 10.5 **% White**: 81.5	National ***Socio-Economic Status*** indicator percentile (100=high): 17th

Merced County

ATWATER ELEMENTARY S.D.

1601 GROVE AVE. ● ATWATER CA 95301-3535 ● (209) 357-6100

Grade Span: KG-08 **Schools**: *Regular* 8 ● *Spec Ed* 0 ● *Alt* 0 **Students**: 4,279 **Total Teachers**: 177 **Student/Classroom Teacher Ratio**: 25.3	**Expenditures/Student**: $4,396 **Librarians**: 1.0 4,279 students/librarian **Guidance Counselors**: 3.0 1,426 students/counselor	**% Amer Indian**: 0.6 **% Asian**: 13.8 **% Black**: 6.4 **% Hispanic**: 36.2 **% White**: 43.0	National ***Socio-Economic Status*** indicator percentile (100=high): 6th

Merced County

DOS PALOS ORO LOMA JOINT UNIFIED S.D.

2041 ALMOND ST. ● DOS PALOS CA 93620-2303 ● (209) 392-6101 ● http://www.dpol.k12.ca.us

Grade Span: KG-12 **Schools**: *Regular* 5 ● *Spec Ed* 0 ● *Alt* 1 **Students**: 2,592 **Total Teachers**: 122 **Student/Classroom Teacher Ratio**: 21.9	**Expenditures/Student**: $5,345 **Librarians**: 0.0 *** students/librarian **Guidance Counselors**: 2.5 1,037 students/counselor	**% Amer Indian**: 0.1 **% Asian**: 0.7 **% Black**: 7.0 **% Hispanic**: 61.5 **% White**: 30.7	National ***Socio-Economic Status*** indicator percentile (100=high): 8th

Merced County

LOS BANOS UNIFIED S.D.

1717 S. 11TH ST. ● LOS BANOS CA 93635-4800 ● (209) 826-3801 ● http://userzweb.lightspeed.net/~rdavis

Grade Span: KG-12 **Schools**: *Regular* 7 ● *Spec Ed* 0 ● *Alt* 1 **Students**: 5,602 **Total Teachers**: 237 **Student/Classroom Teacher Ratio**: 23.8	**Expenditures/Student**: $4,203 **Librarians**: 0.0 *** students/librarian **Guidance Counselors**: 1.0 5,602 students/counselor	**% Amer Indian**: 0.1 **% Asian**: 2.4 **% Black**: 4.6 **% Hispanic**: 51.0 **% White**: 41.8	National ***Socio-Economic Status*** indicator percentile (100=high): 13th

Merced County

MERCED CITY ELEMENTARY S.D.

444 W. 23RD ST. ● MERCED CA 95340-3723 ● (209) 385-6600 ● http://mercedcity.k12.ca.us

Grade Span: KG-08 **Schools**: *Regular* 15 ● *Spec Ed* 0 ● *Alt* 0 **Students**: 11,424 **Total Teachers**: 405 **Student/Classroom Teacher Ratio**: 28.6	**Expenditures/Student**: $4,515 **Librarians**: 15.0 762 students/librarian **Guidance Counselors**: 6.7 1,705 students/counselor	**% Amer Indian**: 0.2 **% Asian**: 29.6 **% Black**: 6.7 **% Hispanic**: 37.1 **% White**: 26.5	National ***Socio-Economic Status*** indicator percentile (100=high): 2nd

Merced County

MERCED UNION HIGH S.D.

P.O. BOX 2147 ● MERCED CA 95344-0147 ● (209) 385-6412 ● http://www.muhsd.k12.ca.us

Grade Span: 09-12 **Schools**: *Regular* 4 ● *Spec Ed* 0 ● *Alt* 2 **Students**: 8,668 **Total Teachers**: 365 **Student/Classroom Teacher Ratio**: 24.2	**Expenditures/Student**: $4,989 **Librarians**: 4.0 2,167 students/librarian **Guidance Counselors**: 15.5 559 students/counselor	**% Amer Indian**: 0.8 **% Asian**: 17.6 **% Black**: 5.5 **% Hispanic**: 39.7 **% White**: 36.5	National ***Socio-Economic Status*** indicator percentile (100=high): 16th

Monterey County

MONTEREY PENINSULA UNIFIED S.D.

700 PACIFIC ST. ● MONTEREY CA 93942-1031 ● (831) 649-1562

Grade Span: KG-12 **Schools**: *Regular* 18 ● *Spec Ed* 0 ● *Alt* 2 **Students**: 11,596 **Total Teachers**: 538 **Student/Classroom Teacher Ratio**: 21.6	**Expenditures/Student**: $6,265 **Librarians**: 10.5 1,104 students/librarian **Guidance Counselors**: 17.6 659 students/counselor	**% Amer Indian**: 0.7 **% Asian**: 18.6 **% Black**: 16.1 **% Hispanic**: 22.5 **% White**: 42.2	National ***Socio-Economic Status*** indicator percentile (100=high): 26th

Monterey County
[MOSS LANDING] **NORTH MONTEREY COUNTY UNIFIED S.D.**
P.O. BOX 49 ● MOSS LANDING CA 95039-0049 ● (831) 633-4286

Grade Span: KG-12 **Schools**: *Regular* 7 ● *Spec Ed* 0 ● *Alt* 3 **Students**: 5,700 **Total Teachers**: 238 **Student/Classroom Teacher Ratio**: 24.1	**Expenditures/Student**: $4,673 **Librarians**: 1.0 5,700 students/librarian **Guidance Counselors**: 7.0 814 students/counselor	**% Amer Indian**: 0.5 **% Asian**: 4.2 **% Black**: 1.5 **% Hispanic**: 47.5 **% White**: 46.4	National ***Socio-Economic Status*** indicator percentile (100=high): 20th

Monterey County
[SALINAS] **ALISAL UNION ELEMENTARY S.D.**
1205 E. MARKET ST. ● SALINAS CA 93905-2831 ● (831) 753-5700

Grade Span: KG-06 **Schools**: *Regular* 7 ● *Spec Ed* 0 ● *Alt* 0 **Students**: 6,144 **Total Teachers**: 230 **Student/Classroom Teacher Ratio**: 26.7	**Expenditures/Student**: $4,379 **Librarians**: 0.0 *** students/librarian **Guidance Counselors**: 1.0 6,144 students/counselor	**% Amer Indian**: 0.2 **% Asian**: 2.9 **% Black**: 0.8 **% Hispanic**: 91.5 **% White**: 4.6	National ***Socio-Economic Status*** indicator percentile (100=high): 0th

Monterey County
SALINAS CITY ELEMENTARY S.D.
431 W. ALISAL ST. ● SALINAS CA 93901-1624 ● (831) 753-5600

Grade Span: KG-06 **Schools**: *Regular* 13 ● *Spec Ed* 0 ● *Alt* 0 **Students**: 8,745 **Total Teachers**: 346 **Student/Classroom Teacher Ratio**: 25.2	**Expenditures/Student**: $4,261 **Librarians**: 0.0 *** students/librarian **Guidance Counselors**: 0.0 *** students/counselor	**% Amer Indian**: 0.1 **% Asian**: 6.9 **% Black**: 3.0 **% Hispanic**: 65.9 **% White**: 24.2	National ***Socio-Economic Status*** indicator percentile (100=high): 7th

Monterey County
SALINAS UNION HIGH S.D.
431 W. ALISAL ST. ● SALINAS CA 93901-1624 ● (831) 753-4100

Grade Span: 07-12 **Schools**: *Regular* 7 ● *Spec Ed* 0 ● *Alt* 1 **Students**: 10,364 **Total Teachers**: 416 **Student/Classroom Teacher Ratio**: 25.0	**Expenditures/Student**: $5,709 **Librarians**: 2.4 4,318 students/librarian **Guidance Counselors**: 19.0 545 students/counselor	**% Amer Indian**: 0.5 **% Asian**: 7.1 **% Black**: 2.4 **% Hispanic**: 69.6 **% White**: 20.4	National ***Socio-Economic Status*** indicator percentile (100=high): 23rd

Napa County
NAPA VALLEY UNIFIED S.D.
2425 JEFFERSON ST. ● NAPA CA 94558-4931 ● (707) 253-3511

Grade Span: KG-12 **Schools**: *Regular* 26 ● *Spec Ed* 0 ● *Alt* 3 **Students**: 15,378 **Total Teachers**: 672 **Student/Classroom Teacher Ratio**: 24.3	**Expenditures/Student**: $4,418 **Librarians**: 3.0 5,126 students/librarian **Guidance Counselors**: 8.9 1,728 students/counselor	**% Amer Indian**: 0.9 **% Asian**: 3.8 **% Black**: 1.6 **% Hispanic**: 24.5 **% White**: 69.3	National ***Socio-Economic Status*** indicator percentile (100=high): 35th

Nevada County
[GRASS VALLEY] **NEVADA JOINT UNION HIGH S.D.**
11645 RIDGE ROAD ● GRASS VALLEY CA 95945-5024 ● (530) 273-3351

Grade Span: 08-12 **Schools**: *Regular* 2 ● *Spec Ed* 0 ● *Alt* 7 **Students**: 4,357 **Total Teachers**: 192 **Student/Classroom Teacher Ratio**: 23.6	**Expenditures/Student**: $5,392 **Librarians**: 2.0 2,179 students/librarian **Guidance Counselors**: 11.2 389 students/counselor	**% Amer Indian**: 1.2 **% Asian**: 1.3 **% Black**: 0.4 **% Hispanic**: 2.9 **% White**: 94.3	National ***Socio-Economic Status*** indicator percentile (100=high): 79th

Orange County
ANAHEIM ELEMENTARY S.D.
1001 S. EAST ST. ● ANAHEIM CA 92805-5749 ● (714) 535-6001

Grade Span: KG-06 **Schools**: *Regular* 21 ● *Spec Ed* 0 ● *Alt* 0 **Students**: 18,356 **Total Teachers**: 716 **Student/Classroom Teacher Ratio**: 25.6	**Expenditures/Student**: $3,897 **Librarians**: 1.0 18,356 students/librarian **Guidance Counselors**: 1.0 18,356 students/counselor	**% Amer Indian**: 0.3 **% Asian**: 7.1 **% Black**: 2.5 **% Hispanic**: 71.5 **% White**: 18.6	National ***Socio-Economic Status*** indicator percentile (100=high): 2nd

Orange County
ANAHEIM UNION HIGH S.D.
P.O. BOX 3520 ● ANAHEIM CA 92803-3520 ● (714) 999-3511

Grade Span: 07-12 **Schools**: *Regular* 16 ● *Spec Ed* 1 ● *Alt* 3 **Students**: 24,412 **Total Teachers**: 895 **Student/Classroom Teacher Ratio**: 28.3	**Expenditures/Student**: $5,328 **Librarians**: 5.0 4,882 students/librarian **Guidance Counselors**: 37.0 660 students/counselor	**% Amer Indian**: 0.6 **% Asian**: 16.8 **% Black**: 3.8 **% Hispanic**: 43.7 **% White**: 35.1	National ***Socio-Economic Status*** indicator percentile (100=high): 22nd

Orange County
[ANAHEIM] MAGNOLIA ELEMENTARY S.D.
2705 W. ORANGE AVE. ● ANAHEIM CA 92804-3203 ● (714) 761-5533

Grade Span: KG-06 **Schools**: *Regular* 8 ● *Spec Ed* 0 ● *Alt* 0 **Students**: 5,749 **Total Teachers**: 240 **Student/Classroom Teacher Ratio**: 24.1	**Expenditures/Student**: $4,279 **Librarians**: 0.0 *** students/librarian **Guidance Counselors**: 1.0 5,749 students/counselor	**% Amer Indian**: 0.8 **% Asian**: 15.0 **% Black**: 4.4 **% Hispanic**: 48.0 **% White**: 31.9	National ***Socio-Economic Status*** indicator percentile (100=high): 4th

Orange County
BREA-OLINDA UNIFIED S.D.
P.O. BOX 300 ● BREA CA 92622-0300 ● (714) 990-7800

Grade Span: KG-12 **Schools**: *Regular* 8 ● *Spec Ed* 0 ● *Alt* 1 **Students**: 5,830 **Total Teachers**: 220 **Student/Classroom Teacher Ratio**: 27.1	**Expenditures/Student**: $4,183 **Librarians**: 0.0 *** students/librarian **Guidance Counselors**: 4.5 1,296 students/counselor	**% Amer Indian**: 0.4 **% Asian**: 9.3 **% Black**: 2.0 **% Hispanic**: 20.1 **% White**: 68.2	National ***Socio-Economic Status*** indicator percentile (100=high): 66th

Orange County
BUENA PARK ELEMENTARY S.D.
6885 ORANGETHORPE AVE. ● BUENA PARK CA 90620-1348 ● (714) 522-8412

Grade Span: KG-08 **Schools**: *Regular* 7 ● *Spec Ed* 0 ● *Alt* 0 **Students**: 5,096 **Total Teachers**: 196 **Student/Classroom Teacher Ratio**: 26.4	**Expenditures/Student**: $4,122 **Librarians**: 0.0 *** students/librarian **Guidance Counselors**: 0.0 *** students/counselor	**% Amer Indian**: 0.1 **% Asian**: 13.9 **% Black**: 7.5 **% Hispanic**: 44.9 **% White**: 33.6	National ***Socio-Economic Status*** indicator percentile (100=high): 14th

Orange County
[BUENA PARK] CENTRALIA ELEMENTARY S.D.
6625 LA PALMA AVE. ● BUENA PARK CA 90620-2859 ● (714) 228-3100

Grade Span: KG-06 **Schools**: *Regular* 9 ● *Spec Ed* 0 ● *Alt* 0 **Students**: 4,859 **Total Teachers**: 188 **Student/Classroom Teacher Ratio**: 26.7	**Expenditures/Student**: $4,535 **Librarians**: 0.0 *** students/librarian **Guidance Counselors**: 1.0 4,859 students/counselor	**% Amer Indian**: 0.6 **% Asian**: 18.3 **% Black**: 4.4 **% Hispanic**: 29.1 **% White**: 47.6	National ***Socio-Economic Status*** indicator percentile (100=high): 26th

Orange County
CYPRESS ELEMENTARY S.D.
9470 MOODY ST. ● CYPRESS CA 90630-2919 ● (714) 220-6900 ● http://www.cypsd.k12.ca.us

Grade Span: KG-06 **Schools**: *Regular* 10 ● *Spec Ed* 0 ● *Alt* 0 **Students**: 4,499 **Total Teachers**: 191 **Student/Classroom Teacher Ratio**: 23.9	**Expenditures/Student**: $4,310 **Librarians**: 0.0 *** students/librarian **Guidance Counselors**: 0.0 *** students/counselor	**% Amer Indian**: 1.0 **% Asian**: 17.8 **% Black**: 5.0 **% Hispanic**: 17.6 **% White**: 58.7	National ***Socio-Economic Status*** indicator percentile (100=high): 53rd

Orange County
FOUNTAIN VALLEY ELEMENTARY S.D.
17210 OAK ST. ● FOUNTAIN VALLEY CA 92708-3405 ● (714) 843-3200 ● http://www.fvsd.k12.ca.us

Grade Span: KG-08 **Schools**: *Regular* 11 ● *Spec Ed* 0 ● *Alt* 0 **Students**: 6,027 **Total Teachers**: 234 **Student/Classroom Teacher Ratio**: 25.7	**Expenditures/Student**: $4,568 **Librarians**: 1.0 6,027 students/librarian **Guidance Counselors**: 2.0 3,014 students/counselor	**% Amer Indian**: 0.6 **% Asian**: 19.1 **% Black**: 1.7 **% Hispanic**: 9.8 **% White**: 68.8	National ***Socio-Economic Status*** indicator percentile (100=high): 65th

Orange County
FULLERTON ELEMENTARY S.D.
1401 W. VALENCIA DR. ● FULLERTON CA 92633-3938 ● (714) 447-7400 ● http://www.fsd.k12.ca.us

Grade Span: KG-08 **Schools**: *Regular* 17 ● *Spec Ed* 0 ● *Alt* 0 **Students**: 11,498 **Total Teachers**: 474 **Student/Classroom Teacher Ratio**: 24.6	**Expenditures/Student**: $4,304 **Librarians**: 0.0 *** students/librarian **Guidance Counselors**: 3.4 3,382 students/counselor	**% Amer Indian**: 0.4 **% Asian**: 17.7 **% Black**: 2.5 **% Hispanic**: 35.8 **% White**: 43.6	National ***Socio-Economic Status*** indicator percentile (100=high): 34th

Orange County
FULLERTON JOINT UNION HIGH S.D.
780 BEECHWOOD AVE. ● FULLERTON CA 92635-2777 ● (714) 671-4331

Grade Span: 09-12 **Schools**: *Regular* 6 ● *Spec Ed* 0 ● *Alt* 2 **Students**: 12,934 **Total Teachers**: 453 **Student/Classroom Teacher Ratio**: 24.3	**Expenditures/Student**: $5,010 **Librarians**: 6.0 2,156 students/librarian **Guidance Counselors**: 13.1 987 students/counselor	**% Amer Indian**: 0.4 **% Asian**: 19.8 **% Black**: 2.9 **% Hispanic**: 33.6 **% White**: 43.3	National ***Socio-Economic Status*** indicator percentile (100=high): 91st

Orange County
GARDEN GROVE UNIFIED S.D.
10331 STANFORD AVE. ● GARDEN GROVE CA 92640-6351 ● (714) 633-6000 ● http://www.ggusd.k12.ca.us/schooldistrict

Grade Span: KG-12 **Schools**: *Regular* 59 ● *Spec Ed* 2 ● *Alt* 2 **Students**: 43,413 **Total Teachers**: 1,659 **Student/Classroom Teacher Ratio**: 26.4	**Expenditures/Student**: $4,591 **Librarians**: 15.2 2,856 students/librarian **Guidance Counselors**: 33.7 1,288 students/counselor	**% Amer Indian**: 0.3 **% Asian**: 31.7 **% Black**: 1.4 **% Hispanic**: 41.2 **% White**: 25.4	National ***Socio-Economic Status*** indicator percentile (100=high): 16th

Orange County
HUNTINGTON BEACH CITY ELEMENTARY S.D.
P.O. BOX 71 ● HUNTINGTON BEACH CA 92648-0071 ● (714) 964-8888

Grade Span: KG-08 **Schools**: *Regular* 8 ● *Spec Ed* 0 ● *Alt* 0 **Students**: 6,037 **Total Teachers**: 229 **Student/Classroom Teacher Ratio**: 26.3	**Expenditures/Student**: $4,096 **Librarians**: 0.0 *** students/librarian **Guidance Counselors**: 0.0 *** students/counselor	**% Amer Indian**: 0.1 **% Asian**: 8.0 **% Black**: 0.7 **% Hispanic**: 11.6 **% White**: 79.6	National ***Socio-Economic Status*** indicator percentile (100=high): 66th

Orange County
HUNTINGTON BEACH UNION HIGH S.D.
10251 YORKTOWN AVE. ● HUNTINGTON BEACH CA 92646-2999 ● (714) 964-3339 ● http://www.hbuhsd.k12.ca.us

Grade Span: 09-12 **Schools**: *Regular* 6 ● *Spec Ed* 0 ● *Alt* 2 **Students**: 13,251 **Total Teachers**: 504 **Student/Classroom Teacher Ratio**: 26.5	**Expenditures/Student**: $6,322 **Librarians**: 3.0 4,417 students/librarian **Guidance Counselors**: 6.5 2,039 students/counselor	**% Amer Indian**: 7.4 **% Asian**: 23.2 **% Black**: 1.2 **% Hispanic**: 16.3 **% White**: 51.9	National ***Socio-Economic Status*** indicator percentile (100=high): 70th

Orange County
[HUNTINGTON BEACH] **OCEAN VIEW ELEMENTARY S.D.**
17200 PINEHURST LANE ● HUNTINGTON BEACH CA 92647-5569 ● (714) 847-2551 ● http://users.deltanet.com/users/ovsd/index.htm

Grade Span: KG-08 **Schools**: *Regular* 15 ● *Spec Ed* 0 ● *Alt* 0 **Students**: 9,241 **Total Teachers**: 378 **Student/Classroom Teacher Ratio**: 24.8	**Expenditures/Student**: $4,210 **Librarians**: 0.0 *** students/librarian **Guidance Counselors**: 0.0 *** students/counselor	**% Amer Indian**: 0.8 **% Asian**: 13.8 **% Black**: 1.5 **% Hispanic**: 23.0 **% White**: 60.9	National ***Socio-Economic Status*** indicator percentile (100=high): 39th

Orange County
IRVINE UNIFIED S.D.
5050 BARRANCA PARKWAY ● IRVINE CA 92714-4652 ● (714) 651-0444 ● http://www.iusd.k12.ca.us

Grade Span: KG-12 **Schools**: *Regular* 29 ● *Spec Ed* 0 ● *Alt* 2 **Students**: 21,975 **Total Teachers**: 875 **Student/Classroom Teacher Ratio**: 27.1	**Expenditures/Student**: $4,883 **Librarians**: 9.5 2,313 students/librarian **Guidance Counselors**: 16.0 1,373 students/counselor	**% Amer Indian**: 0.4 **% Asian**: 24.5 **% Black**: 3.4 **% Hispanic**: 6.8 **% White**: 64.9	National ***Socio-Economic Status*** indicator percentile (100=high): 79th

Orange County
LA HABRA CITY ELEMENTARY S.D.
P.O. BOX 307 ● LA HABRA CA 90633-0307 ● (562) 690-2300

Grade Span: KG-08 **Schools**: *Regular* 8 ● *Spec Ed* 0 ● *Alt* 0 **Students**: 5,583 **Total Teachers**: 236 **Student/Classroom Teacher Ratio**: 24.3	**Expenditures/Student**: $4,257 **Librarians**: 0.0 *** students/librarian **Guidance Counselors**: 0.0 *** students/counselor	**% Amer Indian**: 0.0 **% Asian**: 2.5 **% Black**: 1.6 **% Hispanic**: 62.3 **% White**: 33.6	National ***Socio-Economic Status*** indicator percentile (100=high): 8th

Orange County
LAGUNA BEACH UNIFIED S.D.
550 BLUMONT ST. ● LAGUNA BEACH CA 92651-2356 ● (714) 497-7770

Grade Span: KG-12 **Schools**: *Regular* 4 ● *Spec Ed* 0 ● *Alt* 0 **Students**: 2,501 **Total Teachers**: 117 **Student/Classroom Teacher Ratio**: 21.4	**Expenditures/Student**: $5,945 **Librarians**: 0.0 *** students/librarian **Guidance Counselors**: 4.0 625 students/counselor	**% Amer Indian**: 0.5 **% Asian**: 3.2 **% Black**: 0.9 **% Hispanic**: 8.8 **% White**: 86.6	National ***Socio-Economic Status*** indicator percentile (100=high): 82nd

Orange County
LOS ALAMITOS UNIFIED S.D.
10293 BLOOMFIELD ST. ● LOS ALAMITOS CA 90720-2264 ● (562) 430-1021

Grade Span: KG-12 **Schools**: *Regular* 8 ● *Spec Ed* 0 ● *Alt* 1 **Students**: 8,155 **Total Teachers**: 325 **Student/Classroom Teacher Ratio**: 25.6	**Expenditures/Student**: $4,698 **Librarians**: 2.0 4,078 students/librarian **Guidance Counselors**: 6.0 1,359 students/counselor	**% Amer Indian**: 0.2 **% Asian**: 11.1 **% Black**: 3.5 **% Hispanic**: 11.0 **% White**: 74.1	National ***Socio-Economic Status*** indicator percentile (100=high): 76th

Orange County
[MISSION VIEJO] **SADDLEBACK VALLEY UNIFIED S.D.**
25631 DISENO DR. ● MISSION VIEJO CA 92691-3199 ● (949) 586-1234 ● http://www.svusd.k12.ca.us

Grade Span: KG-12 **Schools**: *Regular* 33 ● *Spec Ed* 1 ● *Alt* 1 **Students**: 30,116 **Total Teachers**: 1,236 **Student/Classroom Teacher Ratio**: 24.8	**Expenditures/Student**: $4,260 **Librarians**: 0.0 *** students/librarian **Guidance Counselors**: 10.8 2,789 students/counselor	**% Amer Indian**: 0.3 **% Asian**: 10.4 **% Black**: 2.1 **% Hispanic**: 13.4 **% White**: 73.9	National ***Socio-Economic Status*** indicator percentile (100=high): 79th

Orange County
[NEWPORT BEACH] **NEWPORT-MESA UNIFIED S.D.**
P.O. BOX 1368 ● NEWPORT BEACH CA 92659-0368 ● (949) 760-3200 ● http://www.nmusd.k12.ca.us

Grade Span: KG-12 **Schools**: *Regular* 24 ● *Spec Ed* 1 ● *Alt* 2 **Students**: 18,552 **Total Teachers**: 771 **Student/Classroom Teacher Ratio**: 24.8	**Expenditures/Student**: $4,866 **Librarians**: 6.0 3,092 students/librarian **Guidance Counselors**: 15.3 1,213 students/counselor	**% Amer Indian**: 0.1 **% Asian**: 6.8 **% Black**: 1.1 **% Hispanic**: 31.9 **% White**: 60.1	National ***Socio-Economic Status*** indicator percentile (100=high): 26th

Orange County
ORANGE UNIFIED S.D.
P.O. BOX 11022 ● ORANGE CA 92668-8122 ● (714) 997-6100 ● http://www.orangeusd.k12.ca.us

Grade Span: KG-12 **Schools**: *Regular* 35 ● *Spec Ed* 1 ● *Alt* 1 **Students**: 27,432 **Total Teachers**: 1,061 **Student/Classroom Teacher Ratio**: 26.0	**Expenditures/Student**: $4,263 **Librarians**: 9.0 3,048 students/librarian **Guidance Counselors**: 24.0 1,143 students/counselor	**% Amer Indian**: 0.3 **% Asian**: 13.0 **% Black**: 2.1 **% Hispanic**: 34.4 **% White**: 50.2	National ***Socio-Economic Status*** indicator percentile (100=high): 30th

Orange County
PLACENTIA-YORBA LINDA UNIFIED S.D.
1301 E. ORANGETHORPE AVE. ● PLACENTIA CA 92670-5302 ● (714) 996-2550

Grade Span: KG-12 **Schools**: *Regular* 26 ● *Spec Ed* 1 ● *Alt* 1 **Students**: 23,632 **Total Teachers**: 919 **Student/Classroom Teacher Ratio**: 26.0	**Expenditures/Student**: $4,496 **Librarians**: 3.0 7,877 students/librarian **Guidance Counselors**: 9.0 2,626 students/counselor	**% Amer Indian**: 0.3 **% Asian**: 9.2 **% Black**: 1.9 **% Hispanic**: 24.2 **% White**: 64.4	National ***Socio-Economic Status*** indicator percentile (100=high): 57th

Orange County
[SAN JUAN CAPISTRANO] **CAPISTRANO UNIFIED S.D.**
32972 CALLE PERFECTO ● SAN JUAN CAPISTRANO CA 92675-4706 ● (949) 489-7000 ● http://intergate.capousd.k12.ca.us/Welcome.shtml

Grade Span: KG-12 **Schools**: *Regular* 34 ● *Spec Ed* 0 ● *Alt* 1 **Students**: 34,929 **Total Teachers**: 1,399 **Student/Classroom Teacher Ratio**: 26.0	**Expenditures/Student**: $4,278 **Librarians**: 1.3 26,868 students/librarian **Guidance Counselors**: 6.0 5,822 students/counselor	**% Amer Indian**: 0.4 **% Asian**: 5.7 **% Black**: 1.5 **% Hispanic**: 15.8 **% White**: 76.6	National ***Socio-Economic Status*** indicator percentile (100=high): 64th

Orange County
SANTA ANA UNIFIED S.D.
1601 E. CHESTNUT AVE. ● SANTA ANA CA 92701-6322 ● (949) 558-5501 ● http://www.sausd.k12.ca.us

Grade Span: KG-12 **Schools**: *Regular* 41 ● *Spec Ed* 1 ● *Alt* 2 **Students**: 50,268 **Total Teachers**: 1,844 **Student/Classroom Teacher Ratio**: 28.0	**Expenditures/Student**: $4,271 **Librarians**: 4.4 11,425 students/librarian **Guidance Counselors**: 29.5 1,704 students/counselor	**% Amer Indian**: 0.0 **% Asian**: 5.9 **% Black**: 1.3 **% Hispanic**: 88.9 **% White**: 3.9	National ***Socio-Economic Status*** indicator percentile (100=high): 3rd

Orange County

TUSTIN UNIFIED S.D.

300 SOUTH C ST. ● TUSTIN CA 92680-3633 ● (714) 730-7301 ● http://www.tustin.k12.ca.us

Grade Span: KG-12 **Schools**: *Regular* 17 ● *Spec Ed* 0 ● *Alt* 1 **Students**: 13,432 **Total Teachers**: 505 **Student/Classroom Teacher Ratio**: 27.1	**Expenditures/Student**: $4,094 **Librarians**: 2.0 6,716 students/librarian **Guidance Counselors**: 12.0 1,119 students/counselor	**% Amer Indian**: 0.5 **% Asian**: 11.7 **% Black**: 4.8 **% Hispanic**: 37.8 **% White**: 45.2	National ***Socio-Economic Status*** indicator percentile (100=high): 40th

Orange County

WESTMINSTER ELEMENTARY S.D.

14121 CEDARWOOD AVE. ● WESTMINSTER CA 92683-4482 ● (714) 894-7311

Grade Span: KG-08 **Schools**: *Regular* 16 ● *Spec Ed* 0 ● *Alt* 0 **Students**: 8,999 **Total Teachers**: 367 **Student/Classroom Teacher Ratio**: 25.7	**Expenditures/Student**: $4,520 **Librarians**: 1.0 8,999 students/librarian **Guidance Counselors**: 4.0 2,250 students/counselor	**% Amer Indian**: 1.3 **% Asian**: 35.5 **% Black**: 1.6 **% Hispanic**: 30.8 **% White**: 30.9	National ***Socio-Economic Status*** indicator percentile (100=high): 9th

Placer County

AUBURN UNION ELEMENTARY S.D.

55 COLLEGE WAY ● AUBURN CA 95603 ● (530) 885-7242

Grade Span: KG-08 **Schools**: *Regular* 5 ● *Spec Ed* 0 ● *Alt* 0 **Students**: 2,970 **Total Teachers**: 115 **Student/Classroom Teacher Ratio**: 25.8	**Expenditures/Student**: $4,705 **Librarians**: 0.0 *** students/librarian **Guidance Counselors**: 2.0 1,485 students/counselor	**% Amer Indian**: 2.5 **% Asian**: 2.0 **% Black**: 0.9 **% Hispanic**: 4.3 **% White**: 90.4	National ***Socio-Economic Status*** indicator percentile (100=high): 38th

Placer County

[AUBURN] **PLACER UNION HIGH S.D.**

P.O. BOX 5048 ● AUBURN CA 95604-5048 ● (530) 885-7986 ● http://www.puhsd.k12.ca.us

Grade Span: 09-12 **Schools**: *Regular* 3 ● *Spec Ed* 1 ● *Alt* 2 **Students**: 4,595 **Total Teachers**: 196 **Student/Classroom Teacher Ratio**: 23.3	**Expenditures/Student**: $5,036 **Librarians**: 1.0 4,595 students/librarian **Guidance Counselors**: 8.5 541 students/counselor	**% Amer Indian**: 1.8 **% Asian**: 1.9 **% Black**: 0.3 **% Hispanic**: 4.8 **% White**: 91.2	National ***Socio-Economic Status*** indicator percentile (100=high): 72nd

Placer County

[GRANITE BAY] **EUREKA UNION ELEMENTARY S.D.**

5477 EUREKA ROAD ● GRANITE BAY CA 95746-8808 ● (916) 791-4939

Grade Span: KG-08 **Schools**: *Regular* 5 ● *Spec Ed* 0 ● *Alt* 0 **Students**: 2,866 **Total Teachers**: 118 **Student/Classroom Teacher Ratio**: 24.3	**Expenditures/Student**: $3,541 **Librarians**: 0.0 *** students/librarian **Guidance Counselors**: 0.0 *** students/counselor	**% Amer Indian**: 0.5 **% Asian**: 4.8 **% Black**: 1.6 **% Hispanic**: 3.2 **% White**: 89.8	National ***Socio-Economic Status*** indicator percentile (100=high): 96th

Placer County

[LINCOLN] **WESTERN PLACER UNIFIED S.D.**

630 SIXTH ST. ● LINCOLN CA 95648-1825 ● (916) 645-6350

Grade Span: KG-12 **Schools**: *Regular* 5 ● *Spec Ed* 0 ● *Alt* 3 **Students**: 3,510 **Total Teachers**: 156 **Student/Classroom Teacher Ratio**: 22.8	**Expenditures/Student**: $3,760 **Librarians**: 0.0 *** students/librarian **Guidance Counselors**: 3.0 1,170 students/counselor	**% Amer Indian**: 0.7 **% Asian**: 0.8 **% Black**: 0.3 **% Hispanic**: 22.3 **% White**: 75.8	National ***Socio-Economic Status*** indicator percentile (100=high): 30th

Placer County

ROCKLIN UNIFIED S.D.

5035 MEYERS ST. ● ROCKLIN CA 95677-2811 ● (916) 624-2428 ● http://www.rocklin.k12.ca.us

Grade Span: KG-11 **Schools**: *Regular* 7 ● *Spec Ed* 0 ● *Alt* 0 **Students**: 5,182 **Total Teachers**: 214 **Student/Classroom Teacher Ratio**: 24.7	**Expenditures/Student**: $4,256 **Librarians**: 2.0 2,591 students/librarian **Guidance Counselors**: 4.0 1,296 students/counselor	**% Amer Indian**: 0.4 **% Asian**: 4.6 **% Black**: 1.4 **% Hispanic**: 7.6 **% White**: 86.0	National ***Socio-Economic Status*** indicator percentile (100=high): 65th

Placer County

[ROSEVILLE] **DRY CREEK JOINT ELEMENTARY S.D.**

9707 COOK RIOLO RD. ● ROSEVILLE CA 95747-9793 ● (916) 771-0646

Grade Span: KG-08 **Schools**: *Regular* 5 ● *Spec Ed* 0 ● *Alt* 0 **Students**: 3,670 **Total Teachers**: 137 **Student/Classroom Teacher Ratio**: 26.2	**Expenditures/Student**: $3,804 **Librarians**: 0.0 *** students/librarian **Guidance Counselors**: 1.0 3,670 students/counselor	**% Amer Indian**: 0.6 **% Asian**: 9.2 **% Black**: 6.3 **% Hispanic**: 7.6 **% White**: 76.2	National ***Socio-Economic Status*** indicator percentile (100=high): 71st

Placer County

ROSEVILLE CITY ELEMENTARY S.D.

1000 DARLING WAY ● ROSEVILLE CA 95678-4341 ● (916) 786-5090

Grade Span: KG-08 **Schools**: *Regular* 10 ● *Spec Ed* 0 ● *Alt* 0 **Students**: 5,262 **Total Teachers**: 212 **Student/Classroom Teacher Ratio**: 24.4	**Expenditures/Student**: $4,016 **Librarians**: 0.0 *** students/librarian **Guidance Counselors**: 1.0 5,262 students/counselor	**% Amer Indian**: 0.2 **% Asian**: 3.1 **% Black**: 1.1 **% Hispanic**: 14.2 **% White**: 81.5	National ***Socio-Economic Status*** indicator percentile (100=high): 38th

Placer County

ROSEVILLE JOINT UNION HIGH S.D.

1750 CIRBY WAY ● ROSEVILLE CA 95661-5520 ● (916) 786-2681

Grade Span: 09-12 **Schools**: *Regular* 3 ● *Spec Ed* 0 ● *Alt* 3 **Students**: 4,998 **Total Teachers**: 210 **Student/Classroom Teacher Ratio**: 24.9	**Expenditures/Student**: $4,505 **Librarians**: 1.0 4,998 students/librarian **Guidance Counselors**: 11.9 420 students/counselor	**% Amer Indian**: 1.5 **% Asian**: 5.3 **% Black**: 2.9 **% Hispanic**: 9.4 **% White**: 80.9	National ***Socio-Economic Status*** indicator percentile (100=high): 90th

Placer County

[TRUCKEE] **TAHOE-TRUCKEE UNIFIED S.D.**

11839 DONNER PASS ROAD ● TRUCKEE CA 96161-4951 ● (530) 587-3561

Grade Span: KG-12 **Schools**: *Regular* 10 ● *Spec Ed* 0 ● *Alt* 1 **Students**: 4,761 **Total Teachers**: 235 **Student/Classroom Teacher Ratio**: 19.9	**Expenditures/Student**: $4,907 **Librarians**: 1.0 4,761 students/librarian **Guidance Counselors**: 7.3 652 students/counselor	**% Amer Indian**: 0.4 **% Asian**: 0.6 **% Black**: 0.3 **% Hispanic**: 16.9 **% White**: 81.9	National ***Socio-Economic Status*** indicator percentile (100=high): 52nd

Plumas County

[QUINCY] **PLUMAS UNIFIED S.D.**

P.O. BOX 10330 ● QUINCY CA 95971-6009 ● (530) 283-6500

Grade Span: KG-12 **Schools**: *Regular* 14 ● *Spec Ed* 0 ● *Alt* 4 **Students**: 3,655 **Total Teachers**: 152 **Student/Classroom Teacher Ratio**: 24.9	**Expenditures/Student**: $4,713 **Librarians**: 0.0 *** students/librarian **Guidance Counselors**: 0.9 4,061 students/counselor	**% Amer Indian**: 4.6 **% Asian**: 1.4 **% Black**: 1.4 **% Hispanic**: 6.0 **% White**: 86.6	National ***Socio-Economic Status*** indicator percentile (100=high): 29th

Riverside County
BANNING UNIFIED S.D.
161 W. WILLIAMS ST. ● BANNING CA 92220-4746 ● (909) 922-0201

Grade Span: KG-12 **Schools**: *Regular* 7 ● *Spec Ed* 0 ● *Alt* 1 **Students**: 4,671 **Total Teachers**: 195 **Student/Classroom Teacher Ratio**: 24.0	**Expenditures/Student**: $4,773 **Librarians**: 0.0 *** students/librarian **Guidance Counselors**: 5.0 934 students/counselor	**% Amer Indian**: 5.4 **% Asian**: 14.6 **% Black**: 13.4 **% Hispanic**: 34.3 **% White**: 32.3	National ***Socio-Economic Status*** indicator percentile (100=high): 2nd

Riverside County
BEAUMONT UNIFIED S.D.
P.O. BOX 187 ● BEAUMONT CA 92223-0187 ● (909) 845-1631

Grade Span: KG-12 **Schools**: *Regular* 6 ● *Spec Ed* 0 ● *Alt* 1 **Students**: 3,510 **Total Teachers**: 136 **Student/Classroom Teacher Ratio**: 26.3	**Expenditures/Student**: $4,263 **Librarians**: 0.0 *** students/librarian **Guidance Counselors**: 2.5 1,404 students/counselor	**% Amer Indian**: 0.6 **% Asian**: 1.6 **% Black**: 3.7 **% Hispanic**: 32.4 **% White**: 61.8	National ***Socio-Economic Status*** indicator percentile (100=high): 10th

Riverside County
[BLYTHE] **PALO VERDE UNIFIED S.D.**
187 N. SEVENTH ST. ● BLYTHE CA 92225-1824 ● (760) 922-4164

Grade Span: KG-12 **Schools**: *Regular* 5 ● *Spec Ed* 0 ● *Alt* 1 **Students**: 3,949 **Total Teachers**: 159 **Student/Classroom Teacher Ratio**: 25.4	**Expenditures/Student**: $4,649 **Librarians**: 0.0 *** students/librarian **Guidance Counselors**: 3.0 1,316 students/counselor	**% Amer Indian**: 0.5 **% Asian**: 0.5 **% Black**: 10.4 **% Hispanic**: 51.4 **% White**: 37.2	National ***Socio-Economic Status*** indicator percentile (100=high): 11th

Riverside County
HEMET UNIFIED S.D.
2350 W. LATHAM AVE. ● HEMET CA 92545-3632 ● (909) 765-5100

Grade Span: KG-12 **Schools**: *Regular* 15 ● *Spec Ed* 0 ● *Alt* 2 **Students**: 14,910 **Total Teachers**: 589 **Student/Classroom Teacher Ratio**: 25.1	**Expenditures/Student**: $4,208 **Librarians**: 1.6 9,319 students/librarian **Guidance Counselors**: 13.8 1,080 students/counselor	**% Amer Indian**: 0.6 **% Asian**: 2.2 **% Black**: 2.4 **% Hispanic**: 27.1 **% White**: 67.7	National ***Socio-Economic Status*** indicator percentile (100=high): 7th

Riverside County
[INDIO] **DESERT SANDS UNIFIED S.D.**
82-879 HWY. 111 ● INDIO CA 92201-5639 ● (760) 775-3500 ● http://www.dsusd.k12.ca.us

Grade Span: KG-12 **Schools**: *Regular* 20 ● *Spec Ed* 0 ● *Alt* 1 **Students**: 19,662 **Total Teachers**: 747 **Student/Classroom Teacher Ratio**: 26.3	**Expenditures/Student**: $4,982 **Librarians**: 3.0 6,554 students/librarian **Guidance Counselors**: 26.9 731 students/counselor	**% Amer Indian**: 0.5 **% Asian**: 1.9 **% Black**: 2.2 **% Hispanic**: 57.9 **% White**: 37.4	National ***Socio-Economic Status*** indicator percentile (100=high): 11th

Riverside County
LAKE ELSINORE UNIFIED S.D.
545 CHANEY ST. ● LAKE ELSINORE CA 92530-2723 ● (909) 674-7731 ● http://www.leusd.k12.ca.us

Grade Span: KG-12 **Schools**: *Regular* 15 ● *Spec Ed* 0 ● *Alt* 1 **Students**: 14,133 **Total Teachers**: 527 **Student/Classroom Teacher Ratio**: 27.1	**Expenditures/Student**: $4,502 **Librarians**: 0.0 *** students/librarian **Guidance Counselors**: 12.0 1,178 students/counselor	**% Amer Indian**: 0.9 **% Asian**: 2.9 **% Black**: 3.4 **% Hispanic**: 26.9 **% White**: 65.9	National ***Socio-Economic Status*** indicator percentile (100=high): 27th

Riverside County
MENIFEE UNION ELEMENTARY S.D.
30205 MENIFEE RD. ● MENIFEE CA 92584-8109 ● (909) 672-1851

Grade Span: KG-08	**Expenditures/Student**: $4,020	**% Amer Indian**: 0.9	
Schools: *Regular* 4 ● *Spec Ed* 0 ● *Alt* 0	**Librarians**: 0.0	**% Asian**: 2.8	National ***Socio-Economic***
Students: 4,025	*** students/librarian	**% Black**: 2.0	***Status*** indicator percentile
Total Teachers: 156	**Guidance Counselors**: 1.0	**% Hispanic**: 21.7	(100=high): 39th
Student/Classroom Teacher Ratio: 26.1	4,025 students/counselor	**% White**: 72.6	

Riverside County
MORENO VALLEY UNIFIED S.D.
13911 PERRIS BLVD. ● MORENO VALLEY CA 92553-4306 ● (909) 485-5600 ● http://www.mvusd.k12.ca.us

Grade Span: KG-12	**Expenditures/Student**: $4,425	**% Amer Indian**: 0.4	
Schools: *Regular* 32 ● *Spec Ed* 0 ● *Alt* 2	**Librarians**: 0.0	**% Asian**: 6.7	National ***Socio-Economic***
Students: 31,503	*** students/librarian	**% Black**: 21.6	***Status*** indicator percentile
Total Teachers: 1,268	**Guidance Counselors**: 47.0	**% Hispanic**: 30.8	(100=high): 22nd
Student/Classroom Teacher Ratio: 24.7	670 students/counselor	**% White**: 40.5	

Riverside County
MURRIETA VALLEY UNIFIED S.D.
26396 BECKMAN CT. ● MURRIETA CA 92562-7021 ● (909) 696-1600

Grade Span: KG-12	**Expenditures/Student**: $3,971	**% Amer Indian**: 0.3	
Schools: *Regular* 8 ● *Spec Ed* 0 ● *Alt* 1	**Librarians**: 2.0	**% Asian**: 4.7	National ***Socio-Economic***
Students: 8,399	4,200 students/librarian	**% Black**: 2.9	***Status*** indicator percentile
Total Teachers: 324	**Guidance Counselors**: 6.6	**% Hispanic**: 17.6	(100=high): 63rd
Student/Classroom Teacher Ratio: 26.7	1,273 students/counselor	**% White**: 74.5	

Riverside County
[NORCO] CORONA-NORCO UNIFIED S.D.
2820 CLARK AVE. ● NORCO CA 91760-1903 ● (909) 736-5000 ● http://www.cnusd.k12.ca.us

Grade Span: KG-12	**Expenditures/Student**: $4,238	**% Amer Indian**: 0.6	
Schools: *Regular* 27 ● *Spec Ed* 1 ● *Alt* 6	**Librarians**: 4.0	**% Asian**: 5.4	National ***Socio-Economic***
Students: 28,014	7,004 students/librarian	**% Black**: 3.5	***Status*** indicator percentile
Total Teachers: 1,081	**Guidance Counselors**: 26.2	**% Hispanic**: 40.2	(100=high): 24th
Student/Classroom Teacher Ratio: 26.7	1,069 students/counselor	**% White**: 50.4	

Riverside County
PALM SPRINGS UNIFIED S.D.
333 S. FARRELL DR. ● PALM SPRINGS CA 92262-7905 ● (760) 327-1581 ● http://www.palmspringsusd.org

Grade Span: KG-12	**Expenditures/Student**: $4,606	**% Amer Indian**: 1.0	
Schools: *Regular* 19 ● *Spec Ed* 0 ● *Alt* 2	**Librarians**: 5.2	**% Asian**: 3.6	National ***Socio-Economic***
Students: 17,589	3,383 students/librarian	**% Black**: 6.1	***Status*** indicator percentile
Total Teachers: 683	**Guidance Counselors**: 14.4	**% Hispanic**: 50.0	(100=high): 7th
Student/Classroom Teacher Ratio: 27.3	1,221 students/counselor	**% White**: 39.2	

Riverside County
PERRIS ELEMENTARY S.D.
143 E. FIRST ST. ● PERRIS CA 92570-2113 ● (909) 657-3118

Grade Span: KG-06	**Expenditures/Student**: $4,327	**% Amer Indian**: 0.5	
Schools: *Regular* 5 ● *Spec Ed* 0 ● *Alt* 0	**Librarians**: 0.0	**% Asian**: 2.6	National ***Socio-Economic***
Students: 4,011	*** students/librarian	**% Black**: 18.9	***Status*** indicator percentile
Total Teachers: 149	**Guidance Counselors**: 2.0	**% Hispanic**: 56.4	(100=high): 1st
Student/Classroom Teacher Ratio: 27.1	2,006 students/counselor	**% White**: 21.5	

Riverside County
PERRIS UNION HIGH S.D.
1151 NORTH A ST. ● PERRIS CA 92570-1909 ● (909) 943-6369

Grade Span: 07-12 **Schools**: *Regular* 3 ● *Spec Ed* 0 ● *Alt* 2 **Students**: 4,794 **Total Teachers**: 156 **Student/Classroom Teacher Ratio**: 32.3	**Expenditures/Student**: $4,969 **Librarians**: 2.0 2,397 students/librarian **Guidance Counselors**: 4.0 1,199 students/counselor	**% Amer Indian**: 1.1 **% Asian**: 2.5 **% Black**: 11.5 **% Hispanic**: 45.9 **% White**: 39.0	National ***Socio-Economic Status*** indicator percentile (100=high): 38th

Riverside County
[PERRIS] VAL VERDE UNIFIED S.D.
975 E. MORGAN ROAD ● PERRIS CA 92571-3103 ● (909) 940-6100 ● http://www.valverde.edu

Grade Span: KG-12 **Schools**: *Regular* 9 ● *Spec Ed* 0 ● *Alt* 1 **Students**: 8,134 **Total Teachers**: 301 **Student/Classroom Teacher Ratio**: 27.3	**Expenditures/Student**: $4,730 **Librarians**: 0.0 *** students/librarian **Guidance Counselors**: 7.0 1,162 students/counselor	**% Amer Indian**: 0.7 **% Asian**: 5.6 **% Black**: 22.7 **% Hispanic**: 41.0 **% White**: 30.0	National ***Socio-Economic Status*** indicator percentile (100=high): 11th

Riverside County
[RIVERSIDE] ALVORD UNIFIED S.D.
10365 KELLER AVE ● RIVERSIDE CA 92505-1349 ● (909) 351-9367

Grade Span: KG-12 **Schools**: *Regular* 16 ● *Spec Ed* 0 ● *Alt* 1 **Students**: 16,356 **Total Teachers**: 621 **Student/Classroom Teacher Ratio**: 27.5	**Expenditures/Student**: $3,991 **Librarians**: 3.5 4,673 students/librarian **Guidance Counselors**: 13.0 1,258 students/counselor	**% Amer Indian**: 0.4 **% Asian**: 7.0 **% Black**: 6.8 **% Hispanic**: 43.3 **% White**: 42.5	National ***Socio-Economic Status*** indicator percentile (100=high): 23rd

Riverside County
[RIVERSIDE] JURUPA UNIFIED S.D.
3924 RIVERVIEW DR. ● RIVERSIDE CA 92509-6611 ● (909) 222-7768

Grade Span: KG-12 **Schools**: *Regular* 20 ● *Spec Ed* 0 ● *Alt* 2 **Students**: 17,305 **Total Teachers**: 669 **Student/Classroom Teacher Ratio**: 26.7	**Expenditures/Student**: $4,220 **Librarians**: 2.0 8,653 students/librarian **Guidance Counselors**: 13.5 1,282 students/counselor	**% Amer Indian**: 0.2 **% Asian**: 2.0 **% Black**: 5.7 **% Hispanic**: 49.0 **% White**: 43.1	National ***Socio-Economic Status*** indicator percentile (100=high): 15th

Riverside County
RIVERSIDE UNIFIED S.D.
P.O. BOX 2800 ● RIVERSIDE CA 92516-2800 ● (909) 788-7134 ● http://www.rusd.k12.ca.us

Grade Span: KG-12 **Schools**: *Regular* 37 ● *Spec Ed* 1 ● *Alt* 4 **Students**: 35,055 **Total Teachers**: 1,403 **Student/Classroom Teacher Ratio**: 25.4	**Expenditures/Student**: $4,530 **Librarians**: 7.4 4,737 students/librarian **Guidance Counselors**: 29.4 1,192 students/counselor	**% Amer Indian**: 0.6 **% Asian**: 4.9 **% Black**: 10.3 **% Hispanic**: 38.2 **% White**: 46.0	National ***Socio-Economic Status*** indicator percentile (100=high): 16th

Riverside County
SAN JACINTO UNIFIED S.D.
600 E. MAIN ● SAN JACINTO CA 92583-4322 ● (909) 654-2785

Grade Span: KG-12 **Schools**: *Regular* 6 ● *Spec Ed* 0 ● *Alt* 1 **Students**: 4,623 **Total Teachers**: 177 **Student/Classroom Teacher Ratio**: 27.1	**Expenditures/Student**: $4,047 **Librarians**: 0.0 *** students/librarian **Guidance Counselors**: 4.4 1,051 students/counselor	**% Amer Indian**: 4.1 **% Asian**: 1.3 **% Black**: 2.9 **% Hispanic**: 48.2 **% White**: 43.5	National ***Socio-Economic Status*** indicator percentile (100=high): 7th

Riverside County

TEMECULA VALLEY UNIFIED S.D.

31350 RANCHO VISTA ROAD ● TEMECULA CA 92592-6202 ● (909) 676-2661

Grade Span: KG-12 **Schools**: *Regular* 11 ● *Spec Ed* 0 ● *Alt* 2 **Students**: 12,295 **Total Teachers**: 488 **Student/Classroom Teacher Ratio**: 25.7	**Expenditures/Student**: $4,376 **Librarians**: 1.0 12,295 students/librarian **Guidance Counselors**: 9.5 1,294 students/counselor	**% Amer Indian**: 2.2 **% Asian**: 5.0 **% Black**: 3.0 **% Hispanic**: 17.5 **% White**: 72.3	National ***Socio-Economic Status*** indicator percentile (100=high): 62nd

Riverside County

[THERMAL] **COACHELLA VALLEY UNIFIED S.D.**

P.O. BOX 847 ● THERMAL CA 92274-0847 ● (760) 399-5137

Grade Span: KG-12 **Schools**: *Regular* 13 ● *Spec Ed* 0 ● *Alt* 1 **Students**: 10,659 **Total Teachers**: 403 **Student/Classroom Teacher Ratio**: 25.9	**Expenditures/Student**: $4,589 **Librarians**: 0.0 *** students/librarian **Guidance Counselors**: 6.0 1,777 students/counselor	**% Amer Indian**: 0.6 **% Asian**: 0.4 **% Black**: 0.3 **% Hispanic**: 95.6 **% White**: 3.1	National ***Socio-Economic Status*** indicator percentile (100=high): 1st

Sacramento County

[ANTELOPE] **CENTER JOINT UNIFIED S.D.**

8408 WATT AVE. ● ANTELOPE CA 95843-9116 ● (916) 338-6400 ● http://www.ns.net/~fortune

Grade Span: KG-12 **Schools**: *Regular* 6 ● *Spec Ed* 0 ● *Alt* 1 **Students**: 5,231 **Total Teachers**: 225 **Student/Classroom Teacher Ratio**: 23.6	**Expenditures/Student**: $4,210 **Librarians**: 1.0 5,231 students/librarian **Guidance Counselors**: 3.0 1,744 students/counselor	**% Amer Indian**: 1.3 **% Asian**: 12.7 **% Black**: 14.9 **% Hispanic**: 9.3 **% White**: 61.8	National ***Socio-Economic Status*** indicator percentile (100=high): 40th

Sacramento County

[CARMICHAEL] **SAN JUAN UNIFIED S.D.**

P.O. BOX 477 ● CARMICHAEL CA 95609-0477 ● (916) 971-7700 ● http://www.sanjuan.edu

Grade Span: KG-12 **Schools**: *Regular* 72 ● *Spec Ed* 4 ● *Alt* 11 **Students**: 47,581 **Total Teachers**: 2,049 **Student/Classroom Teacher Ratio**: 26.2	**Expenditures/Student**: $4,768 **Librarians**: 6.6 7,209 students/librarian **Guidance Counselors**: 47.0 1,012 students/counselor	**% Amer Indian**: 1.9 **% Asian**: 6.0 **% Black**: 5.5 **% Hispanic**: 8.3 **% White**: 78.4	National ***Socio-Economic Status*** indicator percentile (100=high): 42nd

Sacramento County

ELK GROVE UNIFIED S.D.

9510 ELK GROVE-FLORIN RD. ● ELK GROVE CA 95624-1801 ● (916) 686-7700 ● http://www.egusd.k12.ca.us

Grade Span: KG-12 **Schools**: *Regular* 33 ● *Spec Ed* 1 ● *Alt* 6 **Students**: 35,936 **Total Teachers**: 1,497 **Student/Classroom Teacher Ratio**: 24.7	**Expenditures/Student**: $4,853 **Librarians**: 6.0 5,989 students/librarian **Guidance Counselors**: 40.4 890 students/counselor	**% Amer Indian**: 1.3 **% Asian**: 21.6 **% Black**: 18.2 **% Hispanic**: 14.8 **% White**: 44.1	National ***Socio-Economic Status*** indicator percentile (100=high): 30th

Sacramento County

FOLSOM-CORDOVA UNIFIED S.D.

125 EAST BIDWELL ST. ● FOLSOM CA 95630-3241 ● (916) 355-1100

Grade Span: KG-12 **Schools**: *Regular* 20 ● *Spec Ed* 1 ● *Alt* 3 **Students**: 13,349 **Total Teachers**: 542 **Student/Classroom Teacher Ratio**: 24.8	**Expenditures/Student**: $4,583 **Librarians**: 3.4 3,926 students/librarian **Guidance Counselors**: 15.3 872 students/counselor	**% Amer Indian**: 0.4 **% Asian**: 7.3 **% Black**: 9.8 **% Hispanic**: 8.3 **% White**: 74.1	National ***Socio-Economic Status*** indicator percentile (100=high): 46th

Sacramento County
GALT JOINT UNION ELEMENTARY S.D.
21 C ST. ● GALT CA 95632-2090 ● (209) 745-2911

Grade Span: KG-08 **Schools**: *Regular* 4 ● *Spec Ed* 0 ● *Alt* 0 **Students**: 3,177 **Total Teachers**: 145 **Student/Classroom Teacher Ratio**: 22.3	**Expenditures/Student**: $3,779 **Librarians**: 0.0 *** students/librarian **Guidance Counselors**: 1.0 3,177 students/counselor	**% Amer Indian**: 0.7 **% Asian**: 2.1 **% Black**: 0.6 **% Hispanic**: 26.7 **% White**: 69.9	National ***Socio-Economic Status*** indicator percentile (100=high): 25th

Sacramento County
RIO LINDA UNION ELEMENTARY S.D.
627 L ST. ● RIO LINDA CA 95673-3430 ● (916) 991-1704

Grade Span: KG-07 **Schools**: *Regular* 21 ● *Spec Ed* 0 ● *Alt* 0 **Students**: 10,177 **Total Teachers**: 432 **Student/Classroom Teacher Ratio**: 25.6	**Expenditures/Student**: $4,329 **Librarians**: 1.0 10,177 students/librarian **Guidance Counselors**: 4.6 2,212 students/counselor	**% Amer Indian**: 1.1 **% Asian**: 6.4 **% Black**: 14.2 **% Hispanic**: 11.6 **% White**: 66.7	National ***Socio-Economic Status*** indicator percentile (100=high): 12th

Sacramento County
[SACRAMENTO] **GRANT JOINT UNION HIGH S.D.**
1333 GRAND AVE. ● SACRAMENTO CA 95838-3697 ● (916) 263-6206

Grade Span: 07-12 **Schools**: *Regular* 9 ● *Spec Ed* 1 ● *Alt* 2 **Students**: 11,005 **Total Teachers**: 470 **Student/Classroom Teacher Ratio**: 23.3	**Expenditures/Student**: $5,289 **Librarians**: 4.0 2,751 students/librarian **Guidance Counselors**: 26.6 414 students/counselor	**% Amer Indian**: 1.5 **% Asian**: 16.6 **% Black**: 18.2 **% Hispanic**: 15.6 **% White**: 48.1	National ***Socio-Economic Status*** indicator percentile (100=high): 28th

Sacramento County
[SACRAMENTO] **NATOMAS UNIFIED S.D.**
1515 SPORTS DR., SUITE 1 ● SACRAMENTO CA 95834-1905 ● (916) 641-3300

Grade Span: KG-10 **Schools**: *Regular* 6 ● *Spec Ed* 0 ● *Alt* 0 **Students**: 3,541 **Total Teachers**: 155 **Student/Classroom Teacher Ratio**: 22.8	**Expenditures/Student**: $4,772 **Librarians**: 0.0 *** students/librarian **Guidance Counselors**: 2.6 1,362 students/counselor	**% Amer Indian**: 0.9 **% Asian**: 11.0 **% Black**: 30.0 **% Hispanic**: 24.4 **% White**: 33.7	National ***Socio-Economic Status*** indicator percentile (100=high): 28th

Sacramento County
[SACRAMENTO] **NORTH SACRAMENTO ELEMENTARY S.D.**
670 DIXIEANNE AVE. ● SACRAMENTO CA 95815-3023 ● (916) 924-3502

Grade Span: KG-06 **Schools**: *Regular* 10 ● *Spec Ed* 0 ● *Alt* 0 **Students**: 5,013 **Total Teachers**: 228 **Student/Classroom Teacher Ratio**: 23.0	**Expenditures/Student**: $4,758 **Librarians**: 0.0 *** students/librarian **Guidance Counselors**: 3.0 1,671 students/counselor	**% Amer Indian**: 1.1 **% Asian**: 18.2 **% Black**: 17.5 **% Hispanic**: 29.3 **% White**: 33.9	National ***Socio-Economic Status*** indicator percentile (100=high): 1st

Sacramento County
SACRAMENTO CITY UNIFIED S.D.
P.O. BOX 2271 ● SACRAMENTO CA 95812-2271 ● (916) 264-4305 ● http://www.scusd.edu

Grade Span: KG-12 **Schools**: *Regular* 73 ● *Spec Ed* 0 ● *Alt* 2 **Students**: 50,104 **Total Teachers**: 1,944 **Student/Classroom Teacher Ratio**: 26.3	**Expenditures/Student**: $4,987 **Librarians**: 10.4 4,818 students/librarian **Guidance Counselors**: 23.0 2,178 students/counselor	**% Amer Indian**: 1.4 **% Asian**: 26.8 **% Black**: 21.0 **% Hispanic**: 22.1 **% White**: 28.6	National ***Socio-Economic Status*** indicator percentile (100=high): 9th

San Benito County
HOLLISTER ELEMENTARY S.D.
761 SOUTH ST. ● HOLLISTER CA 95023-4570 ● (831) 636-4400

Grade Span: KG-08 **Schools**: *Regular* 7 ● *Spec Ed* 0 ● *Alt* 0 **Students**: 4,821 **Total Teachers**: 198 **Student/Classroom Teacher Ratio**: 25.5	**Expenditures/Student**: $3,962 **Librarians**: 0.0 *** students/librarian **Guidance Counselors**: 2.0 2,411 students/counselor	**% Amer Indian**: 0.3 **% Asian**: 1.6 **% Black**: 0.6 **% Hispanic**: 60.3 **% White**: 37.2	National ***Socio-Economic Status*** indicator percentile (100=high): 17th

San Bernardino County
ADELANTO ELEMENTARY S.D.
P.O. BOX 70 ● ADELANTO CA 92301-0070 ● (619) 246-8691

Grade Span: KG-06 **Schools**: *Regular* 5 ● *Spec Ed* 0 ● *Alt* 0 **Students**: 3,303 **Total Teachers**: 134 **Student/Classroom Teacher Ratio**: 24.5	**Expenditures/Student**: $4,700 **Librarians**: 0.0 *** students/librarian **Guidance Counselors**: 0.0 *** students/counselor	**% Amer Indian**: 1.0 **% Asian**: 3.6 **% Black**: 12.7 **% Hispanic**: 41.4 **% White**: 41.3	National ***Socio-Economic Status*** indicator percentile (100=high): 9th

San Bernardino County
ALTA LOMA ELEMENTARY S.D.
P.O. BOX 370 ● ALTA LOMA CA 91701-0370 ● (909) 987-0766

Grade Span: KG-08 **Schools**: *Regular* 9 ● *Spec Ed* 0 ● *Alt* 0 **Students**: 7,874 **Total Teachers**: 286 **Student/Classroom Teacher Ratio**: 27.8	**Expenditures/Student**: $4,078 **Librarians**: 0.0 *** students/librarian **Guidance Counselors**: 2.5 3,150 students/counselor	**% Amer Indian**: 0.2 **% Asian**: 4.5 **% Black**: 7.5 **% Hispanic**: 18.0 **% White**: 69.7	National ***Socio-Economic Status*** indicator percentile (100=high): 68th

San Bernardino County
APPLE VALLEY UNIFIED S.D.
22974 BEAR VALLEY ROAD ● APPLE VALLEY CA 92308-7423 ● (760) 247-8001 ● http://www.avstc.org/stchtml/schools/avusd_m.htm

Grade Span: KG-12 **Schools**: *Regular* 12 ● *Spec Ed* 0 ● *Alt* 1 **Students**: 12,236 **Total Teachers**: 481 **Student/Classroom Teacher Ratio**: 26.1	**Expenditures/Student**: $4,427 **Librarians**: 0.0 *** students/librarian **Guidance Counselors**: 11.0 1,112 students/counselor	**% Amer Indian**: 0.5 **% Asian**: 2.6 **% Black**: 8.4 **% Hispanic**: 19.2 **% White**: 69.3	National ***Socio-Economic Status*** indicator percentile (100=high): 22nd

San Bernardino County
BARSTOW UNIFIED S.D.
551 S. AVENUE H ● BARSTOW CA 92311-2500 ● (760) 256-0611

Grade Span: KG-12 **Schools**: *Regular* 11 ● *Spec Ed* 0 ● *Alt* 1 **Students**: 7,050 **Total Teachers**: 288 **Student/Classroom Teacher Ratio**: 25.2	**Expenditures/Student**: $4,603 **Librarians**: 2.0 3,525 students/librarian **Guidance Counselors**: 9.2 766 students/counselor	**% Amer Indian**: 2.0 **% Asian**: 2.9 **% Black**: 11.7 **% Hispanic**: 36.1 **% White**: 47.4	National ***Socio-Economic Status*** indicator percentile (100=high): 14th

San Bernardino County
[BIG BEAR LAKE] BEAR VALLEY UNIFIED S.D.
BOX 1529 ● BIG BEAR LAKE CA 92315-1529 ● (909) 866-4631

Grade Span: KG-12 **Schools**: *Regular* 7 ● *Spec Ed* 0 ● *Alt* 1 **Students**: 3,469 **Total Teachers**: 132 **Student/Classroom Teacher Ratio**: 25.9	**Expenditures/Student**: $4,182 **Librarians**: 0.0 *** students/librarian **Guidance Counselors**: 3.0 1,156 students/counselor	**% Amer Indian**: 1.2 **% Asian**: 0.9 **% Black**: 0.7 **% Hispanic**: 9.9 **% White**: 87.3	National ***Socio-Economic Status*** indicator percentile (100=high): 26th

San Bernardino County
CHINO UNIFIED S.D.
5130 RIVERSIDE DR. ● CHINO CA 91710-4130 ● (909) 628-1201

Grade Span: KG-12 **Schools**: *Regular* 28 ● *Spec Ed* 0 ● *Alt* 2 **Students**: 28,514 **Total Teachers**: 1,117 **Student/Classroom Teacher Ratio**: 26.0	**Expenditures/Student**: $4,410 **Librarians**: 3.0 9,505 students/librarian **Guidance Counselors**: 16.6 1,718 students/counselor	**% Amer Indian**: 0.1 **% Asian**: 8.7 **% Black**: 5.0 **% Hispanic**: 35.5 **% White**: 50.8	National ***Socio-Economic Status*** indicator percentile (100=high): 48th

San Bernardino County
COLTON JOINT UNIFIED S.D.
1212 VALENCIA DR. ● COLTON CA 92324-1798 ● (909) 876-4227

Grade Span: KG-12 **Schools**: *Regular* 22 ● *Spec Ed* 0 ● *Alt* 2 **Students**: 18,818 **Total Teachers**: 750 **Student/Classroom Teacher Ratio**: 25.6	**Expenditures/Student**: $4,310 **Librarians**: 3.0 6,273 students/librarian **Guidance Counselors**: 23.4 804 students/counselor	**% Amer Indian**: 0.6 **% Asian**: 3.8 **% Black**: 8.4 **% Hispanic**: 60.2 **% White**: 27.0	National ***Socio-Economic Status*** indicator percentile (100=high): 19th

San Bernardino County
ETIWANDA ELEMENTARY S.D.
P.O. BOX 248 ● ETIWANDA CA 91739-0248 ● (909) 899-2451

Grade Span: KG-08 **Schools**: *Regular* 8 ● *Spec Ed* 0 ● *Alt* 0 **Students**: 4,943 **Total Teachers**: 192 **Student/Classroom Teacher Ratio**: 26.2	**Expenditures/Student**: $3,545 **Librarians**: 0.0 *** students/librarian **Guidance Counselors**: 0.0 *** students/counselor	**% Amer Indian**: 0.4 **% Asian**: 11.7 **% Black**: 12.1 **% Hispanic**: 28.1 **% White**: 47.6	National ***Socio-Economic Status*** indicator percentile (100=high): 68th

San Bernardino County
FONTANA UNIFIED S.D.
9680 CITRUS AVE. ● FONTANA CA 92335-5571 ● (909) 357-5000 ● http://www.fontana.k12.ca.us

Grade Span: KG-12 **Schools**: *Regular* 28 ● *Spec Ed* 0 ● *Alt* 2 **Students**: 30,979 **Total Teachers**: 1,224 **Student/Classroom Teacher Ratio**: 26.5	**Expenditures/Student**: $4,414 **Librarians**: 0.0 *** students/librarian **Guidance Counselors**: 41.8 741 students/counselor	**% Amer Indian**: 0.4 **% Asian**: 2.6 **% Black**: 12.0 **% Hispanic**: 60.0 **% White**: 24.9	National ***Socio-Economic Status*** indicator percentile (100=high): 25th

San Bernardino County
HESPERIA UNIFIED S.D.
9144 THIRD ST. ● HESPERIA CA 92345-3643 ● (760) 244-9323

Grade Span: KG-12 **Schools**: *Regular* 15 ● *Spec Ed* 0 ● *Alt* 1 **Students**: 14,837 **Total Teachers**: 561 **Student/Classroom Teacher Ratio**: 27.6	**Expenditures/Student**: $4,241 **Librarians**: 1.0 14,837 students/librarian **Guidance Counselors**: 11.0 1,349 students/counselor	**% Amer Indian**: 0.5 **% Asian**: 1.5 **% Black**: 5.1 **% Hispanic**: 30.2 **% White**: 62.8	National ***Socio-Economic Status*** indicator percentile (100=high): 17th

San Bernardino County
[LAKE ARROWHEAD] **RIM OF THE WORLD UNIFIED S.D.**
P.O. BOX 430 ● LAKE ARROWHEAD CA 92352-0430 ● (909) 336-2031

Grade Span: KG-12 **Schools**: *Regular* 7 ● *Spec Ed* 0 ● *Alt* 1 **Students**: 5,931 **Total Teachers**: 232 **Student/Classroom Teacher Ratio**: 26.0	**Expenditures/Student**: $5,372 **Librarians**: 1.6 3,707 students/librarian **Guidance Counselors**: 5.0 1,186 students/counselor	**% Amer Indian**: 0.5 **% Asian**: 1.5 **% Black**: 0.9 **% Hispanic**: 11.9 **% White**: 85.2	National ***Socio-Economic Status*** indicator percentile (100=high): 49th

San Bernardino County
[ONTARIO] **CHAFFEY UNION HIGH S.D.**
211 W. FIFTH ST. ● ONTARIO CA 91762-1698 ● (909) 988-8511

Grade Span: 09-12 **Schools**: *Regular* 6 ● *Spec Ed* 0 ● *Alt* 1 **Students**: 16,162 **Total Teachers**: 618 **Student/Classroom Teacher Ratio**: 26.2	**Expenditures/Student**: $4,756 **Librarians**: 6.0 2,694 students/librarian **Guidance Counselors**: 36.0 449 students/counselor	**% Amer Indian**: 0.9 **% Asian**: 7.4 **% Black**: 9.9 **% Hispanic**: 41.6 **% White**: 40.3	National ***Socio-Economic Status*** indicator percentile (100=high): 59th

San Bernardino County
[ONTARIO] **MOUNTAIN VIEW ELEMENTARY S.D.**
2947-A S. TURNER AVE. ● ONTARIO CA 91761-8146 ● (909) 947-2992

Grade Span: KG-08 **Schools**: *Regular* 4 ● *Spec Ed* 0 ● *Alt* 0 **Students**: 2,839 **Total Teachers**: 114 **Student/Classroom Teacher Ratio**: 25.3	**Expenditures/Student**: $3,787 **Librarians**: 0.0 *** students/librarian **Guidance Counselors**: 0.0 *** students/counselor	**% Amer Indian**: 0.5 **% Asian**: 7.3 **% Black**: 16.2 **% Hispanic**: 39.0 **% White**: 37.0	National ***Socio-Economic Status*** indicator percentile (100=high): 47th

San Bernardino County
ONTARIO-MONTCLAIR ELEMENTARY S.D.
950 WEST D ST. ● ONTARIO CA 91762-3026 ● (909) 983-9501 ● http://www.omsd.k12.ca.us

Grade Span: KG-08 **Schools**: *Regular* 30 ● *Spec Ed* 1 ● *Alt* 0 **Students**: 23,682 **Total Teachers**: 935 **Student/Classroom Teacher Ratio**: 27.0	**Expenditures/Student**: $4,173 **Librarians**: 0.0 *** students/librarian **Guidance Counselors**: 9.0 2,631 students/counselor	**% Amer Indian**: 0.6 **% Asian**: 4.3 **% Black**: 8.0 **% Hispanic**: 68.1 **% White**: 19.0	National ***Socio-Economic Status*** indicator percentile (100=high): 2nd

San Bernardino County
[PHELAN] **SNOWLINE JOINT UNIFIED S.D.**
P.O. BOX 296000 ● PHELAN CA 92329-6000 ● (760) 868-5817

Grade Span: KG-12 **Schools**: *Regular* 8 ● *Spec Ed* 0 ● *Alt* 4 **Students**: 6,300 **Total Teachers**: 263 **Student/Classroom Teacher Ratio**: 24.4	**Expenditures/Student**: $3,110 **Librarians**: 0.0 *** students/librarian **Guidance Counselors**: 5.4 1,167 students/counselor	**% Amer Indian**: 1.0 **% Asian**: 1.0 **% Black**: 1.8 **% Hispanic**: 16.6 **% White**: 79.5	National ***Socio-Economic Status*** indicator percentile (100=high): 53rd

San Bernardino County
[RANCHO CUCAMONGA] **CENTRAL ELEMENTARY S.D.**
10601 CHURCH ST., SUITE 112 ● RANCHO CUCAMONGA CA 91730-6863 ● (909) 989-8541

Grade Span: KG-08 **Schools**: *Regular* 7 ● *Spec Ed* 0 ● *Alt* 0 **Students**: 4,964 **Total Teachers**: 191 **Student/Classroom Teacher Ratio**: 26.1	**Expenditures/Student**: $3,847 **Librarians**: 0.0 *** students/librarian **Guidance Counselors**: 7.0 709 students/counselor	**% Amer Indian**: 0.2 **% Asian**: 4.9 **% Black**: 11.8 **% Hispanic**: 28.3 **% White**: 54.8	National ***Socio-Economic Status*** indicator percentile (100=high): 43rd

San Bernardino County
REDLANDS UNIFIED S.D.
P.O. BOX 3008 ● REDLANDS CA 92373-1508 ● (909) 307-5300 ● http://www.redlands.k12.ca.us/district/dist.html

Grade Span: KG-12 **Schools**: *Regular* 16 ● *Spec Ed* 0 ● *Alt* 1 **Students**: 17,628 **Total Teachers**: 706 **Student/Classroom Teacher Ratio**: 26.2	**Expenditures/Student**: $4,302 **Librarians**: 3.0 5,876 students/librarian **Guidance Counselors**: 18.9 933 students/counselor	**% Amer Indian**: 0.8 **% Asian**: 10.6 **% Black**: 7.8 **% Hispanic**: 29.3 **% White**: 51.5	National ***Socio-Economic Status*** indicator percentile (100=high): 33rd

San Bernardino County
RIALTO UNIFIED S.D.
182 E. WALNUT AVE. ● RIALTO CA 92376-3530 ● (909) 820-7700 ● http://www.rialto.k12.ca.us

Grade Span: KG-12 **Schools**: *Regular* 22 ● *Spec Ed* 0 ● *Alt* 2 **Students**: 23,830 **Total Teachers**: 924 **Student/Classroom Teacher Ratio**: 26.5	**Expenditures/Student**: $4,341 **Librarians**: 4.0 5,958 students/librarian **Guidance Counselors**: 23.0 1,036 students/counselor	**% Amer Indian**: 0.2 **% Asian**: 4.1 **% Black**: 27.2 **% Hispanic**: 48.3 **% White**: 20.2	National ***Socio-Economic Status*** indicator percentile (100=high): 10th

San Bernardino County
SAN BERNARDINO CITY UNIFIED S.D.
777 NORTH F ST. ● SAN BERNARDINO CA 92410-3017 ● (909) 381-1100

Grade Span: KG-12 **Schools**: *Regular* 52 ● *Spec Ed* 3 ● *Alt* 3 **Students**: 45,091 **Total Teachers**: 1,855 **Student/Classroom Teacher Ratio**: 25.0	**Expenditures/Student**: $4,826 **Librarians**: 11.3 3,990 students/librarian **Guidance Counselors**: 66.5 678 students/counselor	**% Amer Indian**: 1.5 **% Asian**: 4.8 **% Black**: 18.6 **% Hispanic**: 48.5 **% White**: 26.6	National ***Socio-Economic Status*** indicator percentile (100=high): 4th

San Bernardino County
[TWENTYNINE PALMS] **MORONGO UNIFIED S.D.**
P.O. BOX 1209 ● TWENTYNINE PALMS CA 92277-0980 ● (760) 367-9191

Grade Span: KG-12 **Schools**: *Regular* 15 ● *Spec Ed* 0 ● *Alt* 2 **Students**: 9,961 **Total Teachers**: 436 **Student/Classroom Teacher Ratio**: 23.2	**Expenditures/Student**: $4,716 **Librarians**: 1.0 9,961 students/librarian **Guidance Counselors**: 8.0 1,245 students/counselor	**% Amer Indian**: 0.8 **% Asian**: 4.3 **% Black**: 8.0 **% Hispanic**: 13.1 **% White**: 73.8	National ***Socio-Economic Status*** indicator percentile (100=high): 18th

San Bernardino County
UPLAND UNIFIED S.D.
P.O. BOX 1239 ● UPLAND CA 91785-1239 ● (909) 985-1864 ● http://www.upland.k12.ca.us

Grade Span: KG-12 **Schools**: *Regular* 13 ● *Spec Ed* 0 ● *Alt* 1 **Students**: 11,528 **Total Teachers**: 459 **Student/Classroom Teacher Ratio**: 26.0	**Expenditures/Student**: $4,298 **Librarians**: 1.0 11,528 students/librarian **Guidance Counselors**: 12.3 937 students/counselor	**% Amer Indian**: 0.4 **% Asian**: 8.8 **% Black**: 10.7 **% Hispanic**: 25.9 **% White**: 54.2	National ***Socio-Economic Status*** indicator percentile (100=high): 38th

San Bernardino County
[VICTORVILLE] **VICTOR ELEMENTARY S.D.**
15579 EIGHTH ST. ● VICTORVILLE CA 92392-3348 ● (760) 245-1691

Grade Span: KG-06 **Schools**: *Regular* 9 ● *Spec Ed* 0 ● *Alt* 0 **Students**: 7,997 **Total Teachers**: 295 **Student/Classroom Teacher Ratio**: 27.8	**Expenditures/Student**: $3,913 **Librarians**: 0.0 *** students/librarian **Guidance Counselors**: 3.0 2,666 students/counselor	**% Amer Indian**: 0.5 **% Asian**: 3.3 **% Black**: 14.7 **% Hispanic**: 33.9 **% White**: 47.6	National ***Socio-Economic Status*** indicator percentile (100=high): 16th

San Bernardino County
[VICTORVILLE] **VICTOR VALLEY UNION HIGH S.D.**
16350 MOJAVE DR. ● VICTORVILLE CA 92392-3655 ● (760) 955-3200 ● http://vvuhsd.k12.ca.us

Grade Span: 07-12 **Schools**: *Regular* 4 ● *Spec Ed* 0 ● *Alt* 3 **Students**: 7,308 **Total Teachers**: 274 **Student/Classroom Teacher Ratio**: 25.5	**Expenditures/Student**: $5,334 **Librarians**: 0.0 *** students/librarian **Guidance Counselors**: 13.9 526 students/counselor	**% Amer Indian**: 1.3 **% Asian**: 4.5 **% Black**: 13.2 **% Hispanic**: 38.0 **% White**: 43.1	National ***Socio-Economic Status*** indicator percentile (100=high): 22nd

San Bernardino County
[YERMO] SILVER VALLEY UNIFIED S.D.
P.O. BOX 847 ● YERMO CA 92398-0847 ● (760) 254-2916

Grade Span: KG-12	**Expenditures/Student**: $5,135	**% Amer Indian**: 1.5	
Schools: *Regular* 6 ● *Spec Ed* 0 ● *Alt* 1	**Librarians**: 0.0	**% Asian**: 4.7	National ***Socio-Economic***
Students: 2,734	*** students/librarian	**% Black**: 17.8	***Status*** indicator percentile
Total Teachers: 134	**Guidance Counselors**: 4.0	**% Hispanic**: 15.3	(100=high): 18th
Student/Classroom Teacher Ratio: 20.5	684 students/counselor	**% White**: 60.7	

San Bernardino County
YUCAIPA-CALIMESA JOINT UNIFIED S.D.
12797 THIRD ST. ● YUCAIPA CA 92399-4544 ● (909) 797-0174 ● http://www.eee.org/gov/yuc-cal/school/yucamis1.htm

Grade Span: KG-12	**Expenditures/Student**: $4,460	**% Amer Indian**: 0.7	
Schools: *Regular* 8 ● *Spec Ed* 0 ● *Alt* 1	**Librarians**: 1.0	**% Asian**: 1.3	National ***Socio-Economic***
Students: 7,954	7,954 students/librarian	**% Black**: 0.5	***Status*** indicator percentile
Total Teachers: 311	**Guidance Counselors**: 6.0	**% Hispanic**: 17.8	(100=high): 43rd
Student/Classroom Teacher Ratio: 26.0	1,326 students/counselor	**% White**: 79.7	

San Diego County
CARLSBAD UNIFIED S.D.
801 PINE AVE. ● CARLSBAD CA 92008-2430 ● (760) 729-9291 ● http://www.stan-co.k12.ca.us/ceres/cusd.htm

Grade Span: KG-12	**Expenditures/Student**: $4,824	**% Amer Indian**: 0.3	
Schools: *Regular* 9 ● *Spec Ed* 0 ● *Alt* 1	**Librarians**: 0.0	**% Asian**: 3.5	National ***Socio-Economic***
Students: 7,384	*** students/librarian	**% Black**: 1.9	***Status*** indicator percentile
Total Teachers: 300	**Guidance Counselors**: 4.5	**% Hispanic**: 26.9	(100=high): 45th
Student/Classroom Teacher Ratio: 25.4	1,641 students/counselor	**% White**: 67.3	

San Diego County
CHULA VISTA ELEMENTARY S.D.
84 EAST J ST. ● CHULA VISTA CA 91910-6115 ● (619) 425-9600 ● http://www.cvesd.k12.ca.us

Grade Span: KG-06	**Expenditures/Student**: $4,333	**% Amer Indian**: 0.7	
Schools: *Regular* 33 ● *Spec Ed* 0 ● *Alt* 0	**Librarians**: 10.5	**% Asian**: 11.0	National ***Socio-Economic***
Students: 19,347	1,843 students/librarian	**% Black**: 5.9	***Status*** indicator percentile
Total Teachers: 783	**Guidance Counselors**: 0.5	**% Hispanic**: 55.1	(100=high): 19th
Student/Classroom Teacher Ratio: 24.8	38,694 students/counselor	**% White**: 27.3	

San Diego County
[CHULA VISTA] SWEETWATER UNION HIGH S.D.
1130 FIFTH AVE. ● CHULA VISTA CA 91911-2812 ● (619) 691-5500 ● http://www.suhsd.k12.ca.us

Grade Span: 07-12	**Expenditures/Student**: $5,351	**% Amer Indian**: 0.6	
Schools: *Regular* 18 ● *Spec Ed* 0 ● *Alt* 1	**Librarians**: 16.4	**% Asian**: 13.2	National ***Socio-Economic***
Students: 29,567	1,803 students/librarian	**% Black**: 4.7	***Status*** indicator percentile
Total Teachers: 1,251	**Guidance Counselors**: 80.5	**% Hispanic**: 62.5	(100=high): 22nd
Student/Classroom Teacher Ratio: 24.1	367 students/counselor	**% White**: 19.0	

San Diego County
CORONADO UNIFIED S.D.
555 D AVE. ● CORONADO CA 92118-1714 ● (619) 522-8900

Grade Span: KG-12	**Expenditures/Student**: $4,838	**% Amer Indian**: 0.4	
Schools: *Regular* 4 ● *Spec Ed* 0 ● *Alt* 0	**Librarians**: 0.8	**% Asian**: 6.3	National ***Socio-Economic***
Students: 2,622	3,278 students/librarian	**% Black**: 2.0	***Status*** indicator percentile
Total Teachers: 119	**Guidance Counselors**: 3.5	**% Hispanic**: 11.3	(100=high): 73rd
Student/Classroom Teacher Ratio: 22.9	749 students/counselor	**% White**: 80.1	

San Diego County
[EL CAJON] CAJON VALLEY UNION ELEMENTARY S.D.
P.O. BOX 1007 ● EL CAJON CA 92022-1007 ● (619) 588-3000

Grade Span: KG-08 **Schools**: *Regular* 26 ● *Spec Ed* 0 ● *Alt* 0 **Students**: 18,780 **Total Teachers**: 749 **Student/Classroom Teacher Ratio**: 25.9	**Expenditures/Student**: $4,343 **Librarians**: 0.5 37,560 students/librarian **Guidance Counselors**: 11.6 1,619 students/counselor	**% Amer Indian**: 1.4 **% Asian**: 3.3 **% Black**: 5.7 **% Hispanic**: 19.3 **% White**: 70.2	National ***Socio-Economic Status*** indicator percentile (100=high): 13th

San Diego County
ENCINITAS UNION ELEMENTARY S.D.
101 SOUTH RANCHO SANTA FE RD. ● ENCINITAS CA 92024-4308 ● (760) 944-4300 ● http://intergate.eusd.k12.ca.us

Grade Span: KG-06 **Schools**: *Regular* 9 ● *Spec Ed* 0 ● *Alt* 0 **Students**: 4,982 **Total Teachers**: 193 **Student/Classroom Teacher Ratio**: 25.9	**Expenditures/Student**: $3,363 **Librarians**: 0.0 *** students/librarian **Guidance Counselors**: 0.0 *** students/counselor	**% Amer Indian**: 5.8 **% Asian**: 3.1 **% Black**: 0.8 **% Hispanic**: 17.5 **% White**: 72.9	National ***Socio-Economic Status*** indicator percentile (100=high): 62nd

San Diego County
[ENCINITAS] SAN DIEGUITO UNION HIGH S.D.
710 ENCINITAS BLVD. ● ENCINITAS CA 92024-3357 ● (760) 753-6491 ● http://www.sduhsd.k12.ca.us

Grade Span: 07-12 **Schools**: *Regular* 5 ● *Spec Ed* 0 ● *Alt* 2 **Students**: 8,063 **Total Teachers**: 334 **Student/Classroom Teacher Ratio**: 24.6	**Expenditures/Student**: $5,136 **Librarians**: 5.0 1,613 students/librarian **Guidance Counselors**: 15.5 520 students/counselor	**% Amer Indian**: 0.1 **% Asian**: 6.5 **% Black**: 0.7 **% Hispanic**: 13.0 **% White**: 79.7	National ***Socio-Economic Status*** indicator percentile (100=high): 81st

San Diego County
ESCONDIDO UNION ELEMENTARY S.D.
1330 E. GRAND AVE. ● ESCONDIDO CA 92027-3099 ● (760) 432-2432 ● http://www.escusd.k12.ca.us

Grade Span: KG-08 **Schools**: *Regular* 18 ● *Spec Ed* 1 ● *Alt* 0 **Students**: 17,051 **Total Teachers**: 696 **Student/Classroom Teacher Ratio**: 25.1	**Expenditures/Student**: $3,942 **Librarians**: 0.5 34,102 students/librarian **Guidance Counselors**: 8.4 2,030 students/counselor	**% Amer Indian**: 0.5 **% Asian**: 4.5 **% Black**: 2.7 **% Hispanic**: 43.4 **% White**: 48.9	National ***Socio-Economic Status*** indicator percentile (100=high): 14th

San Diego County
ESCONDIDO UNION HIGH S.D.
302 N. MIDWAY DR. ● ESCONDIDO CA 92027-2741 ● (760) 480-3000

Grade Span: 09-12 **Schools**: *Regular* 3 ● *Spec Ed* 0 ● *Alt* 2 **Students**: 7,279 **Total Teachers**: 280 **Student/Classroom Teacher Ratio**: 25.6	**Expenditures/Student**: $5,144 **Librarians**: 0.0 *** students/librarian **Guidance Counselors**: 15.6 467 students/counselor	**% Amer Indian**: 2.0 **% Asian**: 5.7 **% Black**: 1.5 **% Hispanic**: 32.8 **% White**: 58.0	National ***Socio-Economic Status*** indicator percentile (100=high): 52nd

San Diego County
FALLBROOK UNION ELEMENTARY S.D.
P.O. BOX 698 ● FALLBROOK CA 92088-0698 ● (760) 723-7000

Grade Span: KG-08 **Schools**: *Regular* 7 ● *Spec Ed* 0 ● *Alt* 0 **Students**: 5,806 **Total Teachers**: 227 **Student/Classroom Teacher Ratio**: 26.0	**Expenditures/Student**: $4,565 **Librarians**: 0.0 *** students/librarian **Guidance Counselors**: 4.4 1,320 students/counselor	**% Amer Indian**: 0.5 **% Asian**: 3.3 **% Black**: 6.2 **% Hispanic**: 33.9 **% White**: 56.1	National ***Socio-Economic Status*** indicator percentile (100=high): 10th

San Diego County

[IMPERIAL BEACH] **SOUTH BAY UNION ELEMENTARY S.D.**

601 ELM AVE. ● IMPERIAL BEACH CA 91932-2029 ● (619) 575-5900 ● http://intergate.sbusd.k12.ca.us

Grade Span: KG-06 **Schools**: *Regular* 12 ● *Spec Ed* 0 ● *Alt* 0 **Students**: 9,937 **Total Teachers**: 403 **Student/Classroom Teacher Ratio**: 24.8	**Expenditures/Student**: $4,690 **Librarians**: 0.0 *** students/librarian **Guidance Counselors**: 1.0 9,937 students/counselor	**% Amer Indian**: 0.6 **% Asian**: 11.1 **% Black**: 7.9 **% Hispanic**: 62.4 **% White**: 18.0	National ***Socio-Economic Status*** indicator percentile (100=high): 4th

San Diego County

[LA MESA] **GROSSMONT UNION HIGH S.D.**

P.O. BOX 1043 ● LA MESA CA 91944-1043 ● (619) 465-3131 ● http://www.grossmont.k12.ca.us

Grade Span: 09-12 **Schools**: *Regular* 10 ● *Spec Ed* 1 ● *Alt* 2 **Students**: 21,431 **Total Teachers**: 860 **Student/Classroom Teacher Ratio**: 26.6	**Expenditures/Student**: $5,118 **Librarians**: 11.6 1,848 students/librarian **Guidance Counselors**: 28.0 765 students/counselor	**% Amer Indian**: 1.5 **% Asian**: 5.4 **% Black**: 5.6 **% Hispanic**: 16.9 **% White**: 70.6	National ***Socio-Economic Status*** indicator percentile (100=high): 56th

San Diego County

LA MESA-SPRING VALLEY S.D.

4750 DATE AVE. ● LA MESA CA 91941-5214 ● (619) 463-5700

Grade Span: KG-08 **Schools**: *Regular* 22 ● *Spec Ed* 0 ● *Alt* 0 **Students**: 14,486 **Total Teachers**: 598 **Student/Classroom Teacher Ratio**: 24.8	**Expenditures/Student**: $4,536 **Librarians**: 2.1 6,898 students/librarian **Guidance Counselors**: 24.0 604 students/counselor	**% Amer Indian**: 0.6 **% Asian**: 7.3 **% Black**: 12.2 **% Hispanic**: 22.5 **% White**: 57.4	National ***Socio-Economic Status*** indicator percentile (100=high): 20th

San Diego County

LAKESIDE UNION ELEMENTARY S.D.

P.O. BOX 578 ● LAKESIDE CA 92040-0578 ● (619) 390-2600

Grade Span: KG-08 **Schools**: *Regular* 9 ● *Spec Ed* 0 ● *Alt* 0 **Students**: 4,856 **Total Teachers**: 201 **Student/Classroom Teacher Ratio**: 24.5	**Expenditures/Student**: $4,385 **Librarians**: 0.1 48,560 students/librarian **Guidance Counselors**: 3.4 1,428 students/counselor	**% Amer Indian**: 2.1 **% Asian**: 1.2 **% Black**: 1.1 **% Hispanic**: 9.3 **% White**: 86.2	National ***Socio-Economic Status*** indicator percentile (100=high): 70th

San Diego County

LEMON GROVE ELEMENTARY S.D.

8025 LINCOLN ST. ● LEMON GROVE CA 91945-2515 ● (619) 589-5600 ● http://www.lgsd.k12.ca.us

Grade Span: KG-08 **Schools**: *Regular* 8 ● *Spec Ed* 0 ● *Alt* 0 **Students**: 4,325 **Total Teachers**: 179 **Student/Classroom Teacher Ratio**: 24.2	**Expenditures/Student**: $4,298 **Librarians**: 1.0 4,325 students/librarian **Guidance Counselors**: 0.0 *** students/counselor	**% Amer Indian**: 0.6 **% Asian**: 6.9 **% Black**: 18.3 **% Hispanic**: 27.3 **% White**: 46.8	National ***Socio-Economic Status*** indicator percentile (100=high): 14th

San Diego County

[NATIONAL CITY] **NATIONAL ELEMENTARY S.D.**

1500 N AVE. ● NATIONAL CITY CA 91950-4827 ● (619) 474-6791 ● http://www.sdcoe.k12.ca.us/districts/national/index.html

Grade Span: KG-06 **Schools**: *Regular* 10 ● *Spec Ed* 0 ● *Alt* 0 **Students**: 6,329 **Total Teachers**: 250 **Student/Classroom Teacher Ratio**: 25.7	**Expenditures/Student**: $4,740 **Librarians**: 0.0 *** students/librarian **Guidance Counselors**: 0.8 7,911 students/counselor	**% Amer Indian**: 0.5 **% Asian**: 14.6 **% Black**: 5.4 **% Hispanic**: 73.5 **% White**: 6.0	National ***Socio-Economic Status*** indicator percentile (100=high): 0th

San Diego County
OCEANSIDE CITY UNIFIED S.D.
2111 MISSION AVE. ● OCEANSIDE CA 92054-2326 ● (760) 757-2560

Grade Span: KG-12 **Schools**: *Regular* 21 ● *Spec Ed* 0 ● *Alt* 1 **Students**: 19,468 **Total Teachers**: 780 **Student/Classroom Teacher Ratio**: 25.7	**Expenditures/Student**: $4,453 **Librarians**: 0.4 48,670 students/librarian **Guidance Counselors**: 14.0 1,391 students/counselor	**% Amer Indian**: 0.8 **% Asian**: 8.9 **% Black**: 15.1 **% Hispanic**: 39.4 **% White**: 35.8	National ***Socio-Economic Status*** indicator percentile (100=high): 11th

San Diego County
POWAY UNIFIED S.D.
13626 TWIN PEAKS ROAD ● POWAY CA 92064-3034 ● (619) 748-0010 ● http://powayusd.sdcoe.k12.ca.us

Grade Span: KG-12 **Schools**: *Regular* 27 ● *Spec Ed* 0 ● *Alt* 1 **Students**: 30,043 **Total Teachers**: 1,234 **Student/Classroom Teacher Ratio**: 25.1	**Expenditures/Student**: $4,505 **Librarians**: 8.0 3,755 students/librarian **Guidance Counselors**: 34.0 884 students/counselor	**% Amer Indian**: 0.5 **% Asian**: 16.5 **% Black**: 2.8 **% Hispanic**: 7.4 **% White**: 72.9	National ***Socio-Economic Status*** indicator percentile (100=high): 79th

San Diego County
RAMONA CITY UNIFIED S.D.
720 NINTH ST. ● RAMONA CA 92065-2348 ● (760) 788-5000

Grade Span: KG-12 **Schools**: *Regular* 7 ● *Spec Ed* 0 ● *Alt* 2 **Students**: 6,764 **Total Teachers**: 281 **Student/Classroom Teacher Ratio**: 24.3	**Expenditures/Student**: $4,686 **Librarians**: 2.0 3,382 students/librarian **Guidance Counselors**: 5.0 1,353 students/counselor	**% Amer Indian**: 1.0 **% Asian**: 2.3 **% Black**: 0.8 **% Hispanic**: 19.2 **% White**: 76.7	National ***Socio-Economic Status*** indicator percentile (100=high): 31st

San Diego County
SAN DIEGO CITY UNIFIED S.D.
4100 NORMAL ST. ● SAN DIEGO CA 92103-2653 ● (619) 293-8686 ● http://www.sdcs.k12.ca.us

Grade Span: KG-12 **Schools**: *Regular* 155 ● *Spec Ed* 3 ● *Alt* 6 **Students**: 130,360 **Total Teachers**: 5,786 **Student/Classroom Teacher Ratio**: 23.5	**Expenditures/Student**: $5,297 **Librarians**: 42.0 3,104 students/librarian **Guidance Counselors**: 243.9 534 students/counselor	**% Amer Indian**: 0.7 **% Asian**: 19.4 **% Black**: 16.7 **% Hispanic**: 33.3 **% White**: 29.9	National ***Socio-Economic Status*** indicator percentile (100=high): 7th

San Diego County
SAN MARCOS UNIFIED S.D.
1 CIVIC CENTER DR., SUITE 300 ● SAN MARCOS CA 92069-4076 ● (760) 744-4776

Grade Span: KG-12 **Schools**: *Regular* 9 ● *Spec Ed* 0 ● *Alt* 2 **Students**: 10,953 **Total Teachers**: 421 **Student/Classroom Teacher Ratio**: 26.0	**Expenditures/Student**: $4,377 **Librarians**: 1.0 10,953 students/librarian **Guidance Counselors**: 8.2 1,336 students/counselor	**% Amer Indian**: 0.8 **% Asian**: 4.8 **% Black**: 2.6 **% Hispanic**: 41.1 **% White**: 50.7	National ***Socio-Economic Status*** indicator percentile (100=high): 15th

San Diego County
SAN YSIDRO ELEMENTARY S.D.
4350 OTAY MESA ROAD ● SAN YSIDRO CA 92173-1617 ● (619) 428-4476 ● http://www.sysd.k12.ca.us

Grade Span: KG-08 **Schools**: *Regular* 6 ● *Spec Ed* 0 ● *Alt* 0 **Students**: 3,828 **Total Teachers**: 153 **Student/Classroom Teacher Ratio**: 25.4	**Expenditures/Student**: $4,941 **Librarians**: 0.2 19,140 students/librarian **Guidance Counselors**: 0.0 *** students/counselor	**% Amer Indian**: 0.1 **% Asian**: 0.8 **% Black**: 2.2 **% Hispanic**: 94.9 **% White**: 2.0	National ***Socio-Economic Status*** indicator percentile (100=high): 0th

San Diego County
SANTEE ELEMENTARY S.D.
9625 CUYAMACA ST. ● SANTEE CA 92071-2674 ● (619) 258-2300

Grade Span: KG-08	**Expenditures/Student**: $4,594	**% Amer Indian**: 0.4	
Schools: *Regular* 10 ● *Spec Ed* 0 ● *Alt* 1	**Librarians**: 1.0	**% Asian**: 2.9	National ***Socio-Economic***
Students: 8,242	8,242 students/librarian	**% Black**: 1.1	***Status*** indicator percentile
Total Teachers: 329	**Guidance Counselors**: 1.0	**% Hispanic**: 8.5	(100=high): 48th
Student/Classroom Teacher Ratio: 25.2	8,242 students/counselor	**% White**: 87.1	

San Diego County
VALLEY CENTER UNION ELEMENTARY S.D.
28751 COLE GRADE ROAD ● VALLEY CENTER CA 92082-6575 ● (760) 749-0464

Grade Span: KG-08	**Expenditures/Student**: $4,502	**% Amer Indian**: 9.4	
Schools: *Regular* 4 ● *Spec Ed* 0 ● *Alt* 0	**Librarians**: 0.0	**% Asian**: 0.9	National ***Socio-Economic***
Students: 2,657	*** students/librarian	**% Black**: 0.1	***Status*** indicator percentile
Total Teachers: 121	**Guidance Counselors**: 1.0	**% Hispanic**: 27.4	(100=high): 23rd
Student/Classroom Teacher Ratio: 22.1	2,657 students/counselor	**% White**: 62.1	

San Diego County
VISTA UNIFIED S.D.
1234 ARCADIA AVE. ● VISTA CA 92084-3404 ● (760) 726-2170 ● http://www.vusd.k12.ca.us

Grade Span: KG-12	**Expenditures/Student**: $4,373	**% Amer Indian**: 0.7	
Schools: *Regular* 20 ● *Spec Ed* 2 ● *Alt* 3	**Librarians**: 2.7	**% Asian**: 5.6	National ***Socio-Economic***
Students: 24,094	8,924 students/librarian	**% Black**: 6.2	***Status*** indicator percentile
Total Teachers: 958	**Guidance Counselors**: 28.3	**% Hispanic**: 35.1	(100=high): 25th
Student/Classroom Teacher Ratio: 26.4	851 students/counselor	**% White**: 52.4	

San Francisco County
SAN FRANCISCO UNIFIED S.D.
135 VAN NESS AVE. ● SAN FRANCISCO CA 94102-5207 ● (415) 241-6000 ● http://www.sfusd.k12.ca.us

Grade Span: KG-12	**Expenditures/Student**: $5,541	**% Amer Indian**: 0.7	
Schools: *Regular* 107 ● *Spec Ed* 0 ● *Alt* 4	**Librarians**: 0.0	**% Asian**: 48.6	National ***Socio-Economic***
Students: 61,889	*** students/librarian	**% Black**: 17.1	***Status*** indicator percentile
Total Teachers: 2,972	**Guidance Counselors**: 59.0	**% Hispanic**: 20.4	(100=high): 6th
Student/Classroom Teacher Ratio: 22.2	1,049 students/counselor	**% White**: 13.2	

San Joaquin County
ESCALON UNIFIED S.D.
1520 YOSEMITE AVE. ● ESCALON CA 95320-1753 ● (209) 838-3591

Grade Span: KG-12	**Expenditures/Student**: $4,078	**% Amer Indian**: 0.7	
Schools: *Regular* 6 ● *Spec Ed* 0 ● *Alt* 1	**Librarians**: 0.0	**% Asian**: 1.4	National ***Socio-Economic***
Students: 2,955	*** students/librarian	**% Black**: 0.7	***Status*** indicator percentile
Total Teachers: 120	**Guidance Counselors**: 3.5	**% Hispanic**: 27.4	(100=high): 30th
Student/Classroom Teacher Ratio: 26.6	844 students/counselor	**% White**: 69.8	

San Joaquin County
LODI UNIFIED S.D.
1305 E. VINE ST. ● LODI CA 95240-3148 ● (209) 331-7000 ● http://www.lodiusd.k12.ca.us

Grade Span: KG-12	**Expenditures/Student**: $4,453	**% Amer Indian**: 0.6	
Schools: *Regular* 32 ● *Spec Ed* 1 ● *Alt* 2	**Librarians**: 2.0	**% Asian**: 24.7	National ***Socio-Economic***
Students: 25,500	12,750 students/librarian	**% Black**: 5.6	***Status*** indicator percentile
Total Teachers: 1,150	**Guidance Counselors**: 35.0	**% Hispanic**: 22.7	(100=high): 15th
Student/Classroom Teacher Ratio: 24.4	729 students/counselor	**% White**: 46.4	

San Joaquin County
MANTECA UNIFIED S.D.
P.O. BOX 32 ● MANTECA CA 95336-0032 ● (209) 825-3200 ● http://www.sjcoe.k12.ca.us:80/MUSD/MUSDHomepage.html

Grade Span: KG-12 **Schools**: *Regular* 17 ● *Spec Ed* 0 ● *Alt* 1 **Students**: 15,094 **Total Teachers**: 592 **Student/Classroom Teacher Ratio**: 26.0	**Expenditures/Student**: $4,303 **Librarians**: 3.0 5,031 students/librarian **Guidance Counselors**: 16.0 943 students/counselor	**% Amer Indian**: 1.5 **% Asian**: 6.5 **% Black**: 3.9 **% Hispanic**: 27.4 **% White**: 60.7	National ***Socio-Economic Status*** indicator percentile (100=high): 32nd

San Joaquin County
[STOCKTON] **LINCOLN UNIFIED S.D.**
2010 W. SWAIN RD. ● STOCKTON CA 95207-4055 ● (209) 953-8700 ● http://www.lincolnusd.k12.ca.us

Grade Span: KG-12 **Schools**: *Regular* 11 ● *Spec Ed* 0 ● *Alt* 1 **Students**: 8,688 **Total Teachers**: 370 **Student/Classroom Teacher Ratio**: 23.3	**Expenditures/Student**: $4,382 **Librarians**: 2.0 4,344 students/librarian **Guidance Counselors**: 12.6 690 students/counselor	**% Amer Indian**: 0.3 **% Asian**: 23.2 **% Black**: 10.9 **% Hispanic**: 16.0 **% White**: 49.7	National ***Socio-Economic Status*** indicator percentile (100=high): 20th

San Joaquin County
STOCKTON CITY UNIFIED S.D.
701 N. MADISON ST. ● STOCKTON CA 95202-1634 ● (209) 953-4050 ● http://www.stockton.k12.ca.us

Grade Span: KG-12 **Schools**: *Regular* 38 ● *Spec Ed* 2 ● *Alt* 1 **Students**: 34,637 **Total Teachers**: 1,460 **Student/Classroom Teacher Ratio**: 24.1	**Expenditures/Student**: $5,001 **Librarians**: 3.5 9,896 students/librarian **Guidance Counselors**: 59.8 579 students/counselor	**% Amer Indian**: 1.7 **% Asian**: 28.4 **% Black**: 12.9 **% Hispanic**: 39.9 **% White**: 17.1	National ***Socio-Economic Status*** indicator percentile (100=high): 4th

San Joaquin County
TRACY ELEMENTARY S.D.
315 E. 11TH ST. ● TRACY CA 95376-4017 ● (209) 831-5000 ● http://www.tracy.k12.ca.us

Grade Span: KG-08 **Schools**: *Regular* 12 ● *Spec Ed* 0 ● *Alt* 0 **Students**: 7,314 **Total Teachers**: 298 **Student/Classroom Teacher Ratio**: 25.0	**Expenditures/Student**: $3,713 **Librarians**: 1.0 7,314 students/librarian **Guidance Counselors**: 3.0 2,438 students/counselor	**% Amer Indian**: 1.7 **% Asian**: 8.1 **% Black**: 5.9 **% Hispanic**: 26.3 **% White**: 57.9	National ***Socio-Economic Status*** indicator percentile (100=high): 41st

San Joaquin County
TRACY JOINT UNION HIGH S.D.
315 E. 11TH ST. ● TRACY CA 95376-4017 ● (209) 831-5000 ● http://www.tracy.k12.ca.us

Grade Span: 09-12 **Schools**: *Regular* 2 ● *Spec Ed* 0 ● *Alt* 3 **Students**: 3,066 **Total Teachers**: 124 **Student/Classroom Teacher Ratio**: 25.5	**Expenditures/Student**: $5,102 **Librarians**: 1.0 3,066 students/librarian **Guidance Counselors**: 6.0 511 students/counselor	**% Amer Indian**: 1.2 **% Asian**: 6.3 **% Black**: 5.0 **% Hispanic**: 26.9 **% White**: 60.5	National ***Socio-Economic Status*** indicator percentile (100=high): 58th

San Luis Obispo County
[ARROYO GRANDE] **LUCIA MAR UNIFIED S.D.**
602 ORCHARD ST. ● ARROYO GRANDE CA 93420-4000 ● (805) 473-4300

Grade Span: KG-12 **Schools**: *Regular* 14 ● *Spec Ed* 0 ● *Alt* 1 **Students**: 10,419 **Total Teachers**: 460 **Student/Classroom Teacher Ratio**: 23.0	**Expenditures/Student**: $4,481 **Librarians**: 0.0 *** students/librarian **Guidance Counselors**: 8.8 1,184 students/counselor	**% Amer Indian**: 0.7 **% Asian**: 2.8 **% Black**: 1.3 **% Hispanic**: 29.1 **% White**: 65.9	National ***Socio-Economic Status*** indicator percentile (100=high): 28th

San Luis Obispo County
ATASCADERO UNIFIED S.D.
5601 WEST MALL ● ATASCADERO CA 93422-4234 ● (805) 466-0393

Grade Span: KG-12 **Schools**: *Regular* 9 ● *Spec Ed* 0 ● *Alt* 2 **Students**: 6,136 **Total Teachers**: 252 **Student/Classroom Teacher Ratio**: 24.0	**Expenditures/Student**: $4,184 **Librarians**: 0.5 12,272 students/librarian **Guidance Counselors**: 6.5 944 students/counselor	**% Amer Indian**: 0.6 **% Asian**: 1.7 **% Black**: 1.2 **% Hispanic**: 8.5 **% White**: 88.1	National ***Socio-Economic Status*** indicator percentile (100=high): 62nd

San Luis Obispo County
PASO ROBLES UNION ELEMENTARY S.D.
P.O. BOX 7010 ● PASO ROBLES CA 93447-7010 ● (805) 238-2222

Grade Span: KG-08 **Schools**: *Regular* 7 ● *Spec Ed* 0 ● *Alt* 0 **Students**: 3,980 **Total Teachers**: 165 **Student/Classroom Teacher Ratio**: 24.1	**Expenditures/Student**: $5,568 **Librarians**: 2.0 1,990 students/librarian **Guidance Counselors**: 2.0 1,990 students/counselor	**% Amer Indian**: 0.8 **% Asian**: 1.9 **% Black**: 4.8 **% Hispanic**: 27.8 **% White**: 64.7	National ***Socio-Economic Status*** indicator percentile (100=high): 23rd

San Luis Obispo County
[SAN LUIS OBISPO] **SAN LUIS COASTAL UNIFIED S.D.**
1499 SAN LUIS DR. ● SAN LUIS OBISPO CA 93401-3060 ● (805) 543-2010 ● http://www.slocs.k12.ca.us

Grade Span: KG-12 **Schools**: *Regular* 17 ● *Spec Ed* 1 ● *Alt* 1 **Students**: 8,257 **Total Teachers**: 372 **Student/Classroom Teacher Ratio**: 22.5	**Expenditures/Student**: $6,319 **Librarians**: 3.7 2,232 students/librarian **Guidance Counselors**: 9.3 888 students/counselor	**% Amer Indian**: 0.4 **% Asian**: 4.0 **% Black**: 2.0 **% Hispanic**: 11.4 **% White**: 82.2	National ***Socio-Economic Status*** indicator percentile (100=high): 53rd

San Mateo County
[DALY CITY] **JEFFERSON ELEMENTARY S.D.**
101 LINCOLN AVE. ● DALY CITY CA 94015-3934 ● (415) 991-1270

Grade Span: KG-08 **Schools**: *Regular* 15 ● *Spec Ed* 0 ● *Alt* 0 **Students**: 8,129 **Total Teachers**: 323 **Student/Classroom Teacher Ratio**: 25.3	**Expenditures/Student**: $4,141 **Librarians**: 0.9 9,032 students/librarian **Guidance Counselors**: 2.0 4,065 students/counselor	**% Amer Indian**: 0.7 **% Asian**: 46.2 **% Black**: 9.1 **% Hispanic**: 33.4 **% White**: 10.6	National ***Socio-Economic Status*** indicator percentile (100=high): 11th

San Mateo County
[DALY CITY] **JEFFERSON UNION HIGH S.D.**
699 SERRAMONTE BLVD.,SUITE 100 ● DALY CITY CA 94015-4132 ● (415) 756-0300 ● http://www.juhsd.k12.ca.us

Grade Span: 09-12 **Schools**: *Regular* 4 ● *Spec Ed* 0 ● *Alt* 1 **Students**: 5,272 **Total Teachers**: 211 **Student/Classroom Teacher Ratio**: 24.9	**Expenditures/Student**: $5,107 **Librarians**: 4.0 1,318 students/librarian **Guidance Counselors**: 9.0 586 students/counselor	**% Amer Indian**: 0.3 **% Asian**: 42.1 **% Black**: 8.6 **% Hispanic**: 25.2 **% White**: 23.8	National ***Socio-Economic Status*** indicator percentile (100=high): 60th

San Mateo County
[EAST PALO ALTO] **RAVENSWOOD CITY ELEMENTARY S.D.**
2160 EUCLID AVE. ● EAST PALO ALTO CA 94303-1703 ● (650) 329-2800

Grade Span: KG-08 **Schools**: *Regular* 9 ● *Spec Ed* 0 ● *Alt* 0 **Students**: 4,693 **Total Teachers**: 185 **Student/Classroom Teacher Ratio**: 25.3	**Expenditures/Student**: $5,108 **Librarians**: 0.0 *** students/librarian **Guidance Counselors**: 0.0 *** students/counselor	**% Amer Indian**: 0.3 **% Asian**: 10.9 **% Black**: 28.0 **% Hispanic**: 59.9 **% White**: 0.9	National ***Socio-Economic Status*** indicator percentile (100=high): 2nd

San Mateo County

[HALF MOON BAY] **CABRILLO UNIFIED S.D.**

498 KELLY AVE. ● HALF MOON BAY CA 94019-1636 ● (650) 712-7100 ● http://www.coastside.net/cusd

Grade Span: KG-12 **Schools**: *Regular* 6 ● *Spec Ed* 0 ● *Alt* 1 **Students**: 3,668 **Total Teachers**: 159 **Student/Classroom Teacher Ratio**: 24.0	**Expenditures/Student**: $4,454 **Librarians**: 0.0 *** students/librarian **Guidance Counselors**: 4.0 917 students/counselor	**% Amer Indian**: 0.4 **% Asian**: 4.1 **% Black**: 0.6 **% Hispanic**: 23.7 **% White**: 71.3	National ***Socio-Economic Status*** indicator percentile (100=high): 60th

San Mateo County

[PACIFICA] **LAGUNA SALADA UNION ELEMENTARY S.D.**

375 REINA DEL MAR ● PACIFICA CA 94044-3052 ● (650) 359-1641

Grade Span: KG-08 **Schools**: *Regular* 10 ● *Spec Ed* 0 ● *Alt* 0 **Students**: 3,984 **Total Teachers**: 157 **Student/Classroom Teacher Ratio**: 27.0	**Expenditures/Student**: $4,054 **Librarians**: 0.0 *** students/librarian **Guidance Counselors**: 2.0 1,992 students/counselor	**% Amer Indian**: 0.5 **% Asian**: 16.3 **% Black**: 7.1 **% Hispanic**: 15.8 **% White**: 60.3	National ***Socio-Economic Status*** indicator percentile (100=high): 55th

San Mateo County

REDWOOD CITY ELEMENTARY S.D.

815 ALLERTON ST. ● REDWOOD CITY CA 94063-1360 ● (650) 365-1550 ● http://www.rcsd.k12.ca.us

Grade Span: KG-08 **Schools**: *Regular* 14 ● *Spec Ed* 0 ● *Alt* 0 **Students**: 8,672 **Total Teachers**: 416 **Student/Classroom Teacher Ratio**: 21.7	**Expenditures/Student**: $4,749 **Librarians**: 0.0 *** students/librarian **Guidance Counselors**: 2.0 4,336 students/counselor	**% Amer Indian**: 0.4 **% Asian**: 6.3 **% Black**: 3.0 **% Hispanic**: 56.8 **% White**: 33.6	National ***Socio-Economic Status*** indicator percentile (100=high): 17th

San Mateo County

[REDWOOD CITY] **SEQUOIA UNION HIGH S.D.**

480 JAMES AVE. ● REDWOOD CITY CA 94062-1041 ● (650) 369-1411

Grade Span: 09-12 **Schools**: *Regular* 4 ● *Spec Ed* 0 ● *Alt* 1 **Students**: 6,783 **Total Teachers**: 319 **Student/Classroom Teacher Ratio**: 21.5	**Expenditures/Student**: $6,302 **Librarians**: 4.0 1,696 students/librarian **Guidance Counselors**: 15.0 452 students/counselor	**% Amer Indian**: 0.4 **% Asian**: 10.8 **% Black**: 11.4 **% Hispanic**: 37.7 **% White**: 39.7	National ***Socio-Economic Status*** indicator percentile (100=high): 75th

San Mateo County

SAN BRUNO PARK ELEMENTARY S.D.

500 ACACIA AVE. ● SAN BRUNO CA 94066-4298 ● (650) 244-0133

Grade Span: KG-08 **Schools**: *Regular* 7 ● *Spec Ed* 0 ● *Alt* 0 **Students**: 2,809 **Total Teachers**: 115 **Student/Classroom Teacher Ratio**: 24.9	**Expenditures/Student**: $4,192 **Librarians**: 0.0 *** students/librarian **Guidance Counselors**: 2.3 1,221 students/counselor	**% Amer Indian**: 0.2 **% Asian**: 22.9 **% Black**: 2.2 **% Hispanic**: 24.5 **% White**: 50.2	National ***Socio-Economic Status*** indicator percentile (100=high): 43rd

San Mateo County

SAN MATEO UNION HIGH S.D.

650 N. DELAWARE ST. ● SAN MATEO CA 94401-1795 ● (650) 348-8834

Grade Span: 09-12 **Schools**: *Regular* 6 ● *Spec Ed* 0 ● *Alt* 1 **Students**: 8,116 **Total Teachers**: 359 **Student/Classroom Teacher Ratio**: 23.2	**Expenditures/Student**: $6,845 **Librarians**: 6.0 1,353 students/librarian **Guidance Counselors**: 15.6 520 students/counselor	**% Amer Indian**: 0.3 **% Asian**: 26.9 **% Black**: 3.5 **% Hispanic**: 19.0 **% White**: 50.2	National ***Socio-Economic Status*** indicator percentile (100=high): 88th

San Mateo County
SAN MATEO-FOSTER CITY ELEMENTARY S.D.
P.O. BOX K ● SAN MATEO CA 94402-0058 ● (650) 312-7700 ● http://www.smfc.k12.ca.us

Grade Span: KG-08 **Schools**: *Regular* 19 ● *Spec Ed* 0 ● *Alt* 0 **Students**: 10,498 **Total Teachers**: 471 **Student/Classroom Teacher Ratio**: 22.9	**Expenditures/Student**: $4,781 **Librarians**: 3.1 3,386 students/librarian **Guidance Counselors**: 10.5 1,000 students/counselor	**% Amer Indian**: 0.3 **% Asian**: 21.7 **% Black**: 4.6 **% Hispanic**: 24.1 **% White**: 49.4	National ***Socio-Economic Status*** indicator percentile (100=high): 44th

San Mateo County
SOUTH SAN FRANCISCO UNIFIED S.D.
398 B ST. ● SOUTH SAN FRANCISCO CA 94080-4423 ● (650) 877-8770

Grade Span: KG-12 **Schools**: *Regular* 15 ● *Spec Ed* 0 ● *Alt* 1 **Students**: 10,011 **Total Teachers**: 407 **Student/Classroom Teacher Ratio**: 24.9	**Expenditures/Student**: $4,392 **Librarians**: 2.0 5,006 students/librarian **Guidance Counselors**: 8.8 1,138 students/counselor	**% Amer Indian**: 0.4 **% Asian**: 34.7 **% Black**: 5.2 **% Hispanic**: 33.5 **% White**: 26.1	National ***Socio-Economic Status*** indicator percentile (100=high): 37th

Santa Barbara County
CARPINTERIA UNIFIED S.D.
1400 LINDON AVE. ● CARPINTERIA CA 93013-1414 ● (805) 684-4511

Grade Span: KG-12 **Schools**: *Regular* 6 ● *Spec Ed* 0 ● *Alt* 1 **Students**: 2,961 **Total Teachers**: 122 **Student/Classroom Teacher Ratio**: 24.9	**Expenditures/Student**: $4,148 **Librarians**: 0.0 *** students/librarian **Guidance Counselors**: 2.6 1,139 students/counselor	**% Amer Indian**: 0.2 **% Asian**: 1.9 **% Black**: 1.2 **% Hispanic**: 51.3 **% White**: 45.5	National ***Socio-Economic Status*** indicator percentile (100=high): 26th

Santa Barbara County
GOLETA UNION ELEMENTARY S.D.
401 N. FAIRVIEW AVE. ● GOLETA CA 93117-1732 ● (805) 681-1210

Grade Span: KG-06 **Schools**: *Regular* 8 ● *Spec Ed* 0 ● *Alt* 0 **Students**: 4,299 **Total Teachers**: 176 **Student/Classroom Teacher Ratio**: 24.6	**Expenditures/Student**: $4,724 **Librarians**: 0.0 *** students/librarian **Guidance Counselors**: 0.0 *** students/counselor	**% Amer Indian**: 0.7 **% Asian**: 7.7 **% Black**: 2.2 **% Hispanic**: 35.5 **% White**: 53.9	National ***Socio-Economic Status*** indicator percentile (100=high): 34th

Santa Barbara County
LOMPOC UNIFIED S.D.
P.O. BOX 8000 ● LOMPOC CA 93438-8000 ● (805) 736-2371 ● http://server1.sbceo.k12.ca.us/%7Elusdprch

Grade Span: KG-12 **Schools**: *Regular* 14 ● *Spec Ed* 0 ● *Alt* 1 **Students**: 10,774 **Total Teachers**: 498 **Student/Classroom Teacher Ratio**: 22.5	**Expenditures/Student**: $4,358 **Librarians**: 2.0 5,387 students/librarian **Guidance Counselors**: 11.9 905 students/counselor	**% Amer Indian**: 1.3 **% Asian**: 7.3 **% Black**: 8.9 **% Hispanic**: 30.0 **% White**: 52.4	National ***Socio-Economic Status*** indicator percentile (100=high): 31st

Santa Barbara County
ORCUTT UNION ELEMENTARY S.D.
P.O. BOX 2310 ● ORCUTT CA 93457-2310 ● (805) 937-6345

Grade Span: KG-08 **Schools**: *Regular* 8 ● *Spec Ed* 0 ● *Alt* 0 **Students**: 4,545 **Total Teachers**: 181 **Student/Classroom Teacher Ratio**: 25.4	**Expenditures/Student**: $3,944 **Librarians**: 1.0 4,545 students/librarian **Guidance Counselors**: 1.0 4,545 students/counselor	**% Amer Indian**: 0.5 **% Asian**: 4.4 **% Black**: 2.1 **% Hispanic**: 18.1 **% White**: 75.0	National ***Socio-Economic Status*** indicator percentile (100=high): 52nd

Santa Barbara County
SANTA BARBARA ELEMENTARY S.D.
723 E. COTA ST. ● SANTA BARBARA CA 93103-3173 ● (805) 963-4331

Grade Span: KG-08 **Schools**: *Regular* 11 ● *Spec Ed* 0 ● *Alt* 0 **Students**: 5,765 **Total Teachers**: 243 **Student/Classroom Teacher Ratio**: 24.9	**Expenditures/Student**: $5,213 **Librarians**: 8.2 703 students/librarian **Guidance Counselors**: 0.0 *** students/counselor	**% Amer Indian**: 1.1 **% Asian**: 1.8 **% Black**: 2.8 **% Hispanic**: 65.7 **% White**: 28.6	National ***Socio-Economic Status*** indicator percentile (100=high): 14th

Santa Barbara County
SANTA BARBARA HIGH S.D.
723 E. COTA ST. ● SANTA BARBARA CA 93103-3173 ● (805) 963-4331

Grade Span: 06-12 **Schools**: *Regular* 7 ● *Spec Ed* 0 ● *Alt* 4 **Students**: 8,974 **Total Teachers**: 383 **Student/Classroom Teacher Ratio**: 23.4	**Expenditures/Student**: $4,505 **Librarians**: 7.0 1,282 students/librarian **Guidance Counselors**: 17.9 501 students/counselor	**% Amer Indian**: 0.6 **% Asian**: 4.9 **% Black**: 2.5 **% Hispanic**: 43.4 **% White**: 48.6	National ***Socio-Economic Status*** indicator percentile (100=high): 51st

Santa Barbara County
SANTA MARIA JOINT UNION HIGH S.D.
829 S. LINCOLN ● SANTA MARIA CA 93454-6112 ● (805) 922-4573

Grade Span: 09-12 **Schools**: *Regular* 2 ● *Spec Ed* 0 ● *Alt* 1 **Students**: 5,108 **Total Teachers**: 196 **Student/Classroom Teacher Ratio**: 27.0	**Expenditures/Student**: $4,600 **Librarians**: 0.0 *** students/librarian **Guidance Counselors**: 0.0 *** students/counselor	**% Amer Indian**: 1.1 **% Asian**: 6.5 **% Black**: 1.8 **% Hispanic**: 53.8 **% White**: 36.6	National ***Socio-Economic Status*** indicator percentile (100=high): 51st

Santa Barbara County
SANTA MARIA-BONITA ELEMENTARY S.D.
708 S. MILLER ST. ● SANTA MARIA CA 93454-6230 ● (805) 928-1783

Grade Span: KG-08 **Schools**: *Regular* 14 ● *Spec Ed* 0 ● *Alt* 0 **Students**: 9,859 **Total Teachers**: 401 **Student/Classroom Teacher Ratio**: 25.3	**Expenditures/Student**: $4,739 **Librarians**: 1.0 9,859 students/librarian **Guidance Counselors**: 4.0 2,465 students/counselor	**% Amer Indian**: 0.8 **% Asian**: 4.2 **% Black**: 2.4 **% Hispanic**: 74.4 **% White**: 18.2	National ***Socio-Economic Status*** indicator percentile (100=high): 2nd

Santa Clara County
CAMPBELL UNION ELEMENTARY S.D.
155 N. THIRD ST. ● CAMPBELL CA 95008-2044 ● (408) 364-4200 ● http://www.campbellusd.k12.ca.us

Grade Span: KG-08 **Schools**: *Regular* 11 ● *Spec Ed* 0 ● *Alt* 0 **Students**: 7,620 **Total Teachers**: 311 **Student/Classroom Teacher Ratio**: 25.1	**Expenditures/Student**: $4,353 **Librarians**: 0.0 *** students/librarian **Guidance Counselors**: 1.0 7,620 students/counselor	**% Amer Indian**: 0.3 **% Asian**: 11.5 **% Black**: 7.0 **% Hispanic**: 26.0 **% White**: 55.2	National ***Socio-Economic Status*** indicator percentile (100=high): 17th

Santa Clara County
CUPERTINO UNION ELEMENTARY S.D.
10301 VISTA DR. ● CUPERTINO CA 95014-2040 ● (408) 252-3000 ● http://www.cupertino.k12.ca.us

Grade Span: KG-08 **Schools**: *Regular* 23 ● *Spec Ed* 0 ● *Alt* 0 **Students**: 14,472 **Total Teachers**: 568 **Student/Classroom Teacher Ratio**: 26.2	**Expenditures/Student**: $4,345 **Librarians**: 0.0 *** students/librarian **Guidance Counselors**: 4.0 3,618 students/counselor	**% Amer Indian**: 0.1 **% Asian**: 37.5 **% Black**: 1.7 **% Hispanic**: 4.0 **% White**: 56.8	National ***Socio-Economic Status*** indicator percentile (100=high): 86th

Santa Clara County
GILROY UNIFIED S.D.
7810 ARROYO CIRCLE ● GILROY CA 95020-7313 ● (408) 847-2700

Grade Span: KG-12 **Schools**: *Regular* 12 ● *Spec Ed* 0 ● *Alt* 1 **Students**: 8,767 **Total Teachers**: 358 **Student/Classroom Teacher Ratio**: 24.3	**Expenditures/Student**: $4,451 **Librarians**: 1.3 6,744 students/librarian **Guidance Counselors**: 14.1 622 students/counselor	**% Amer Indian**: 0.5 **% Asian**: 3.4 **% Black**: 1.3 **% Hispanic**: 60.5 **% White**: 34.3	National ***Socio-Economic Status*** indicator percentile (100=high): 20th

Santa Clara County
LOS ALTOS ELEMENTARY S.D.
201 COVINGTON ROAD ● LOS ALTOS CA 94024-4030 ● (650) 941-4010

Grade Span: KG-08 **Schools**: *Regular* 8 ● *Spec Ed* 0 ● *Alt* 0 **Students**: 3,491 **Total Teachers**: 160 **Student/Classroom Teacher Ratio**: 22.3	**Expenditures/Student**: $4,716 **Librarians**: 0.0 *** students/librarian **Guidance Counselors**: 0.0 *** students/counselor	**% Amer Indian**: 0.0 **% Asian**: 18.6 **% Black**: 1.8 **% Hispanic**: 3.4 **% White**: 76.1	National ***Socio-Economic Status*** indicator percentile (100=high): 98th

Santa Clara County
LOS GATOS UNION ELEMENTARY S.D.
15766 POPPY LANE ● LOS GATOS CA 95030-3228 ● (408) 395-5570

Grade Span: KG-08 **Schools**: *Regular* 5 ● *Spec Ed* 0 ● *Alt* 0 **Students**: 2,547 **Total Teachers**: 115 **Student/Classroom Teacher Ratio**: 22.6	**Expenditures/Student**: $4,671 **Librarians**: 0.6 4,245 students/librarian **Guidance Counselors**: 1.2 2,123 students/counselor	**% Amer Indian**: 0.8 **% Asian**: 7.7 **% Black**: 0.6 **% Hispanic**: 4.9 **% White**: 86.0	National ***Socio-Economic Status*** indicator percentile (100=high): 90th

Santa Clara County
MILPITAS UNIFIED S.D.
1331 E. CALAVERAS BLVD. ● MILPITAS CA 95035-5707 ● (408) 945-2300

Grade Span: KG-12 **Schools**: *Regular* 12 ● *Spec Ed* 0 ● *Alt* 1 **Students**: 9,490 **Total Teachers**: 400 **Student/Classroom Teacher Ratio**: 24.7	**Expenditures/Student**: $4,882 **Librarians**: 2.0 4,745 students/librarian **Guidance Counselors**: 5.0 1,898 students/counselor	**% Amer Indian**: 0.8 **% Asian**: 45.4 **% Black**: 6.3 **% Hispanic**: 18.5 **% White**: 29.0	National ***Socio-Economic Status*** indicator percentile (100=high): 42nd

Santa Clara County
MORGAN HILL UNIFIED S.D.
15600 CONCORD CIRCLE ● MORGAN HILL CA 95037-7110 ● (408) 779-5272 ● http://www.mhu.k12.ca.us

Grade Span: KG-12 **Schools**: *Regular* 12 ● *Spec Ed* 0 ● *Alt* 1 **Students**: 8,994 **Total Teachers**: 368 **Student/Classroom Teacher Ratio**: 24.6	**Expenditures/Student**: $4,908 **Librarians**: 1.0 8,994 students/librarian **Guidance Counselors**: 8.2 1,097 students/counselor	**% Amer Indian**: 0.3 **% Asian**: 6.4 **% Black**: 2.7 **% Hispanic**: 32.2 **% White**: 58.4	National ***Socio-Economic Status*** indicator percentile (100=high): 51st

Santa Clara County
MOUNTAIN VIEW ELEMENTARY S.D.
220 VIEW ST. ● MOUNTAIN VIEW CA 94041-1344 ● (650) 968-6565

Grade Span: KG-08 **Schools**: *Regular* 5 ● *Spec Ed* 0 ● *Alt* 0 **Students**: 3,269 **Total Teachers**: 139 **Student/Classroom Teacher Ratio**: 23.6	**Expenditures/Student**: $4,914 **Librarians**: 0.0 *** students/librarian **Guidance Counselors**: 0.0 *** students/counselor	**% Amer Indian**: 0.3 **% Asian**: 14.2 **% Black**: 6.8 **% Hispanic**: 39.5 **% White**: 39.2	National ***Socio-Economic Status*** indicator percentile (100=high): 18th

Santa Clara County
MOUNTAIN VIEW-LOS ALTOS UNION S.D.
1299 BRYANT AVE. ● MOUNTAIN VIEW CA 94040-4527 ● (650) 940-4650

Grade Span: 09-12 **Schools**: *Regular* 2 ● *Spec Ed* 0 ● *Alt* 2 **Students**: 2,901 **Total Teachers**: 146 **Student/Classroom Teacher Ratio**: 20.1	**Expenditures/Student**: $8,011 **Librarians**: 1.0 2,901 students/librarian **Guidance Counselors**: 9.4 309 students/counselor	**% Amer Indian**: 0.2 **% Asian**: 19.8 **% Black**: 5.0 **% Hispanic**: 20.5 **% White**: 54.5	National ***Socio-Economic Status*** indicator percentile (100=high): 69th

Santa Clara County
PALO ALTO UNIFIED S.D.
25 CHURCHILL AVE. ● PALO ALTO CA 94306-1005 ● (650) 329-3700

Grade Span: KG-12 **Schools**: *Regular* 15 ● *Spec Ed* 0 ● *Alt* 1 **Students**: 8,715 **Total Teachers**: 469 **Student/Classroom Teacher Ratio**: 21.0	**Expenditures/Student**: $7,322 **Librarians**: 10.2 854 students/librarian **Guidance Counselors**: 9.4 927 students/counselor	**% Amer Indian**: 0.3 **% Asian**: 17.5 **% Black**: 5.2 **% Hispanic**: 6.4 **% White**: 70.6	National ***Socio-Economic Status*** indicator percentile (100=high): 85th

Santa Clara County
[SAN JOSE] **ALUM ROCK UNION ELEMENTARY S.D.**
2930 GAY AVE. ● SAN JOSE CA 95127-2322 ● (408) 258-4923 ● http://www.alumrock.k12.ca.us

Grade Span: KG-08 **Schools**: *Regular* 25 ● *Spec Ed* 0 ● *Alt* 0 **Students**: 15,834 **Total Teachers**: 572 **Student/Classroom Teacher Ratio**: 28.9	**Expenditures/Student**: $4,565 **Librarians**: 1.0 15,834 students/librarian **Guidance Counselors**: 3.0 5,278 students/counselor	**% Amer Indian**: 0.9 **% Asian**: 22.1 **% Black**: 3.5 **% Hispanic**: 65.5 **% White**: 8.0	National ***Socio-Economic Status*** indicator percentile (100=high): 3rd

Santa Clara County
[SAN JOSE] **BERRYESSA UNION ELEMENTARY S.D.**
1376 PIEDMONT ROAD ● SAN JOSE CA 95132-2427 ● (408) 923-1800 ● http://www.berryessa.k12.ca.us

Grade Span: KG-08 **Schools**: *Regular* 13 ● *Spec Ed* 0 ● *Alt* 0 **Students**: 9,011 **Total Teachers**: 355 **Student/Classroom Teacher Ratio**: 25.9	**Expenditures/Student**: $4,428 **Librarians**: 0.0 *** students/librarian **Guidance Counselors**: 6.0 1,502 students/counselor	**% Amer Indian**: 0.5 **% Asian**: 53.7 **% Black**: 4.8 **% Hispanic**: 18.8 **% White**: 22.2	National ***Socio-Economic Status*** indicator percentile (100=high): 49th

Santa Clara County
[SAN JOSE] **CAMBRIAN ELEMENTARY S.D.**
4115 JACKSOL DR. ● SAN JOSE CA 95124-3312 ● (408) 377-2103

Grade Span: KG-08 **Schools**: *Regular* 5 ● *Spec Ed* 0 ● *Alt* 0 **Students**: 2,773 **Total Teachers**: 112 **Student/Classroom Teacher Ratio**: 25.1	**Expenditures/Student**: $3,887 **Librarians**: 0.0 *** students/librarian **Guidance Counselors**: 1.0 2,773 students/counselor	**% Amer Indian**: 1.0 **% Asian**: 9.7 **% Black**: 5.8 **% Hispanic**: 13.7 **% White**: 69.8	National ***Socio-Economic Status*** indicator percentile (100=high): 52nd

Santa Clara County
[SAN JOSE] **CAMPBELL UNION HIGH S.D.**
3235 UNION AVE ● SAN JOSE CA 95124-2009 ● (408) 371-0960

Grade Span: 09-12 **Schools**: *Regular* 4 ● *Spec Ed* 0 ● *Alt* 1 **Students**: 6,477 **Total Teachers**: 273 **Student/Classroom Teacher Ratio**: 24.0	**Expenditures/Student**: $5,733 **Librarians**: 2.0 3,239 students/librarian **Guidance Counselors**: 5.2 1,246 students/counselor	**% Amer Indian**: 0.8 **% Asian**: 14.8 **% Black**: 5.0 **% Hispanic**: 17.1 **% White**: 62.4	National ***Socio-Economic Status*** indicator percentile (100=high): 74th

Santa Clara County
[SAN JOSE] **EAST SIDE UNION HIGH S.D.**
830 N. CAPITOL AVE. ● SAN JOSE CA 95133-1316 ● (408) 272-6400 ● http://sun.sjen.org

Grade Span: 09-12 **Schools**: *Regular* 10 ● *Spec Ed* 0 ● *Alt* 4 **Students**: 22,082 **Total Teachers**: 963 **Student/Classroom Teacher Ratio**: 23.3	**Expenditures/Student**: $5,633 **Librarians**: 6.4 3,450 students/librarian **Guidance Counselors**: 33.4 661 students/counselor	**% Amer Indian**: 1.1 **% Asian**: 34.8 **% Black**: 6.1 **% Hispanic**: 37.5 **% White**: 20.5	National ***Socio-Economic Status*** indicator percentile (100=high): 75th

Santa Clara County
[SAN JOSE] **EVERGREEN ELEMENTARY S.D.**
3188 QUIMBY ROAD ● SAN JOSE CA 95148-3022 ● (408) 270-6800 ● http://www.do.esd.k12.ca.us

Grade Span: KG-08 **Schools**: *Regular* 15 ● *Spec Ed* 0 ● *Alt* 0 **Students**: 11,052 **Total Teachers**: 423 **Student/Classroom Teacher Ratio**: 26.5	**Expenditures/Student**: $4,143 **Librarians**: 4.3 2,570 students/librarian **Guidance Counselors**: 0.0 *** students/counselor	**% Amer Indian**: 0.5 **% Asian**: 44.6 **% Black**: 6.9 **% Hispanic**: 31.0 **% White**: 17.0	National ***Socio-Economic Status*** indicator percentile (100=high): 33rd

Santa Clara County
[SAN JOSE] **FRANKLIN-MCKINLEY ELEMENTARY S.D.**
645 WOOL CREEK DR. ● SAN JOSE CA 95112-2617 ● (408) 283-6000 ● http://www.fmsd.k12.ca.us

Grade Span: KG-08 **Schools**: *Regular* 13 ● *Spec Ed* 0 ● *Alt* 0 **Students**: 10,643 **Total Teachers**: 391 **Student/Classroom Teacher Ratio**: 28.4	**Expenditures/Student**: $4,630 **Librarians**: 0.0 *** students/librarian **Guidance Counselors**: 3.0 3,548 students/counselor	**% Amer Indian**: 0.4 **% Asian**: 36.2 **% Black**: 4.3 **% Hispanic**: 52.1 **% White**: 7.0	National ***Socio-Economic Status*** indicator percentile (100=high): 3rd

Santa Clara County
[SAN JOSE] **MORELAND ELEMENTARY S.D.**
4710 CAMPBELL AVE. ● SAN JOSE CA 95130-1709 ● (408) 379-1370 ● http://www.moreland.k12.ca.us

Grade Span: KG-08 **Schools**: *Regular* 9 ● *Spec Ed* 0 ● *Alt* 0 **Students**: 4,446 **Total Teachers**: 184 **Student/Classroom Teacher Ratio**: 24.5	**Expenditures/Student**: $4,211 **Librarians**: 0.0 *** students/librarian **Guidance Counselors**: 0.0 *** students/counselor	**% Amer Indian**: 0.4 **% Asian**: 20.9 **% Black**: 4.4 **% Hispanic**: 15.9 **% White**: 58.4	National ***Socio-Economic Status*** indicator percentile (100=high): 46th

Santa Clara County
[SAN JOSE] **MT. PLEASANT ELEMENTARY S.D.**
3434 MARTEN AVE. ● SAN JOSE CA 95148 ● (408) 928-1200

Grade Span: KG-08 **Schools**: *Regular* 5 ● *Spec Ed* 0 ● *Alt* 0 **Students**: 2,737 **Total Teachers**: 110 **Student/Classroom Teacher Ratio**: 25.0	**Expenditures/Student**: $4,192 **Librarians**: 0.0 *** students/librarian **Guidance Counselors**: 0.0 *** students/counselor	**% Amer Indian**: 0.3 **% Asian**: 21.2 **% Black**: 7.1 **% Hispanic**: 56.6 **% White**: 14.7	National ***Socio-Economic Status*** indicator percentile (100=high): 10th

Santa Clara County
[SAN JOSE] **OAK GROVE ELEMENTARY S.D.**
6578 SANTA TERESA BLVD. ● SAN JOSE CA 95119-1204 ● (408) 227-8300

Grade Span: KG-08 **Schools**: *Regular* 20 ● *Spec Ed* 0 ● *Alt* 0 **Students**: 12,231 **Total Teachers**: 487 **Student/Classroom Teacher Ratio**: 25.6	**Expenditures/Student**: $4,617 **Librarians**: 0.5 24,462 students/librarian **Guidance Counselors**: 7.3 1,675 students/counselor	**% Amer Indian**: 0.6 **% Asian**: 18.8 **% Black**: 6.5 **% Hispanic**: 28.8 **% White**: 45.2	National ***Socio-Economic Status*** indicator percentile (100=high): 36th

Santa Clara County
SAN JOSE UNIFIED S.D.
855 LENZEN AVE. ● SAN JOSE CA 95126-2736 ● (408) 998-6000 ● http://www.sjusd.k12.ca.us

Grade Span: KG-12 **Schools**: *Regular* 41 ● *Spec Ed* 0 ● *Alt* 8 **Students**: 32,160 **Total Teachers**: 1,404 **Student/Classroom Teacher Ratio**: 23.5	**Expenditures/Student**: $5,668 **Librarians**: 9.0 3,573 students/librarian **Guidance Counselors**: 26.7 1,204 students/counselor	**% Amer Indian**: 1.8 **% Asian**: 14.7 **% Black**: 3.5 **% Hispanic**: 47.2 **% White**: 32.9	National ***Socio-Economic Status*** indicator percentile (100=high): 22nd

Santa Clara County
[SAN JOSE] **UNION ELEMENTARY S.D.**
5175 UNION AVE. ● SAN JOSE CA 95124-5434 ● (408) 377-8010

Grade Span: KG-08 **Schools**: *Regular* 10 ● *Spec Ed* 0 ● *Alt* 0 **Students**: 4,839 **Total Teachers**: 212 **Student/Classroom Teacher Ratio**: 23.2	**Expenditures/Student**: $4,543 **Librarians**: 0.1 48,390 students/librarian **Guidance Counselors**: 2.0 2,420 students/counselor	**% Amer Indian**: 0.8 **% Asian**: 8.9 **% Black**: 2.9 **% Hispanic**: 10.4 **% White**: 77.0	National ***Socio-Economic Status*** indicator percentile (100=high): 63rd

Santa Clara County
SANTA CLARA UNIFIED S.D.
P.O. BOX 397 ● SANTA CLARA CA 95052-0397 ● (408) 983-2000 ● http://www.scu.k12.ca.us

Grade Span: KG-12 **Schools**: *Regular* 20 ● *Spec Ed* 0 ● *Alt* 2 **Students**: 14,018 **Total Teachers**: 567 **Student/Classroom Teacher Ratio**: 24.9	**Expenditures/Student**: $5,199 **Librarians**: 5.0 2,804 students/librarian **Guidance Counselors**: 11.6 1,208 students/counselor	**% Amer Indian**: 1.1 **% Asian**: 26.5 **% Black**: 4.5 **% Hispanic**: 24.6 **% White**: 43.4	National ***Socio-Economic Status*** indicator percentile (100=high): 24th

Santa Clara County
[SUNNYVALE] **FREMONT UNION HIGH S.D.**
P.O. BOX F ● SUNNYVALE CA 94087 ● (408) 522-2200 ● http://www.fuhsd.org

Grade Span: 09-12 **Schools**: *Regular* 5 ● *Spec Ed* 0 ● *Alt* 0 **Students**: 8,199 **Total Teachers**: 362 **Student/Classroom Teacher Ratio**: 22.6	**Expenditures/Student**: $6,177 **Librarians**: 0.0 *** students/librarian **Guidance Counselors**: 2.0 4,100 students/counselor	**% Amer Indian**: 1.0 **% Asian**: 37.1 **% Black**: 3.3 **% Hispanic**: 12.9 **% White**: 45.7	National ***Socio-Economic Status*** indicator percentile (100=high): 88th

Santa Clara County
SUNNYVALE ELEMENTARY S.D.
P.O. BOX 3217 ● SUNNYVALE CA 94088-3217 ● (408) 522-8200

Grade Span: KG-08 **Schools**: *Regular* 9 ● *Spec Ed* 0 ● *Alt* 0 **Students**: 5,896 **Total Teachers**: 243 **Student/Classroom Teacher Ratio**: 24.7	**Expenditures/Student**: $5,387 **Librarians**: 0.0 *** students/librarian **Guidance Counselors**: 0.0 *** students/counselor	**% Amer Indian**: 0.8 **% Asian**: 27.2 **% Black**: 7.3 **% Hispanic**: 32.7 **% White**: 32.1	National ***Socio-Economic Status*** indicator percentile (100=high): 28th

Santa Cruz County
[FELTON] **SAN LORENZO VALLEY UNIFIED S.D.**
6134 HIGHWAY 9 ● FELTON CA 95018-9704 ● (831) 335-4701 ● http://www.slv.k12.ca.us

Grade Span: KG-12 **Schools**: *Regular* 6 ● *Spec Ed* 0 ● *Alt* 1 **Students**: 4,143 **Total Teachers**: 173 **Student/Classroom Teacher Ratio**: 23.8	**Expenditures/Student**: $4,189 **Librarians**: 0.0 *** students/librarian **Guidance Counselors**: 3.6 1,151 students/counselor	**% Amer Indian**: 1.6 **% Asian**: 2.8 **% Black**: 1.1 **% Hispanic**: 5.2 **% White**: 89.3	National ***Socio-Economic Status*** indicator percentile (100=high): 69th

Santa Cruz County
SANTA CRUZ CITY ELEMENTARY S.D.
133 MISSION ST. ● SANTA CRUZ CA 95060-3747 ● (831) 429-3800 ● http://www.sccs.santacruz.k12.ca.us

Grade Span: KG-06 **Schools**: *Regular* 6 ● *Spec Ed* 0 ● *Alt* 1 **Students**: 3,395 **Total Teachers**: 141 **Student/Classroom Teacher Ratio**: 24.5	**Expenditures/Student**: $4,491 **Librarians**: 5.0 679 students/librarian **Guidance Counselors**: 0.0 *** students/counselor	**% Amer Indian**: 0.5 **% Asian**: 4.6 **% Black**: 3.3 **% Hispanic**: 28.2 **% White**: 63.4	National ***Socio-Economic Status*** indicator percentile (100=high): 29th

Santa Cruz County
SANTA CRUZ CITY HIGH S.D.
133 MISSION ST. ● SANTA CRUZ CA 95060-3788 ● (831) 429-3800 ● http://www.sccs.santacruz.k12.ca.us

Grade Span: 07-12 **Schools**: *Regular* 5 ● *Spec Ed* 0 ● *Alt* 2 **Students**: 5,490 **Total Teachers**: 224 **Student/Classroom Teacher Ratio**: 24.6	**Expenditures/Student**: $na **Librarians**: 4.0 1,373 students/librarian **Guidance Counselors**: 10.0 549 students/counselor	**% Amer Indian**: 0.8 **% Asian**: 4.7 **% Black**: 3.1 **% Hispanic**: 17.2 **% White**: 74.2	National ***Socio-Economic Status*** indicator percentile (100=high): 75th

Santa Cruz County
[WATSONVILLE] **PAJARO VALLEY JOINT UNIFIED S.D.**
P.O. BOX 50010 ● WATSONVILLE CA 95077-5010 ● (831) 728-6230

Grade Span: KG-12 **Schools**: *Regular* 22 ● *Spec Ed* 0 ● *Alt* 1 **Students**: 17,736 **Total Teachers**: 722 **Student/Classroom Teacher Ratio**: 25.4	**Expenditures/Student**: $4,761 **Librarians**: 0.0 *** students/librarian **Guidance Counselors**: 2.8 6,334 students/counselor	**% Amer Indian**: 0.2 **% Asian**: 2.8 **% Black**: 0.7 **% Hispanic**: 70.1 **% White**: 26.2	National ***Socio-Economic Status*** indicator percentile (100=high): 11th

Shasta County
[REDDING] **ENTERPRISE ELEMENTARY S.D.**
1155 MISTLETOE LANE ● REDDING CA 96002-0749 ● (530) 224-4100

Grade Span: KG-08 **Schools**: *Regular* 7 ● *Spec Ed* 0 ● *Alt* 0 **Students**: 3,932 **Total Teachers**: 165 **Student/Classroom Teacher Ratio**: 25.0	**Expenditures/Student**: $4,297 **Librarians**: 1.0 3,932 students/librarian **Guidance Counselors**: 1.0 3,932 students/counselor	**% Amer Indian**: 3.0 **% Asian**: 9.0 **% Black**: 2.0 **% Hispanic**: 4.7 **% White**: 81.4	National ***Socio-Economic Status*** indicator percentile (100=high): 11th

Shasta County
[REDDING] **GATEWAY UNIFIED S.D.**
4411 MOUNTAIN LAKES BLVD. ● REDDING CA 96003-1446 ● (530) 275-7900 ● http://www.gsd.k12.ca.us

Grade Span: KG-12 **Schools**: *Regular* 9 ● *Spec Ed* 0 ● *Alt* 2 **Students**: 4,415 **Total Teachers**: 190 **Student/Classroom Teacher Ratio**: 23.6	**Expenditures/Student**: $4,722 **Librarians**: 1.0 4,415 students/librarian **Guidance Counselors**: 4.5 981 students/counselor	**% Amer Indian**: 9.0 **% Asian**: 1.8 **% Black**: 1.3 **% Hispanic**: 4.3 **% White**: 83.6	National ***Socio-Economic Status*** indicator percentile (100=high): 15th

Shasta County
REDDING ELEMENTARY S.D.
P.O. BOX 992418 ● REDDING CA 96099-2418 ● (530) 225-0011

Grade Span: KG-08 **Schools**: *Regular* 7 ● *Spec Ed* 0 ● *Alt* 0 **Students**: 3,271 **Total Teachers**: 129 **Student/Classroom Teacher Ratio**: 25.6	**Expenditures/Student**: $4,326 **Librarians**: 0.0 *** students/librarian **Guidance Counselors**: 2.5 1,308 students/counselor	**% Amer Indian**: 2.6 **% Asian**: 9.9 **% Black**: 2.0 **% Hispanic**: 4.7 **% White**: 80.7	National ***Socio-Economic Status*** indicator percentile (100=high): 13th

Shasta County

[REDDING] **SHASTA UNION HIGH S.D.**

1313 YUBA ST. ● REDDING CA 96001-1012 ● (530) 241-3261

Grade Span: 09-12 **Schools**: *Regular* 3 ● *Spec Ed* 0 ● *Alt* 2 **Students**: 4,565 **Total Teachers**: 173 **Student/Classroom Teacher Ratio**: 28.1	**Expenditures/Student**: $4,970 **Librarians**: 1.0 4,565 students/librarian **Guidance Counselors**: 12.0 380 students/counselor	**% Amer Indian**: 4.3 **% Asian**: 5.4 **% Black**: 1.3 **% Hispanic**: 3.7 **% White**: 85.3	National ***Socio-Economic Status*** indicator percentile (100=high): 65th

Solano County

BENICIA UNIFIED S.D.

350 EAST K ST. ● BENICIA CA 94510-3437 ● (707) 747-8300

Grade Span: KG-12 **Schools**: *Regular* 7 ● *Spec Ed* 0 ● *Alt* 1 **Students**: 5,112 **Total Teachers**: 232 **Student/Classroom Teacher Ratio**: 23.1	**Expenditures/Student**: $4,280 **Librarians**: 0.5 10,224 students/librarian **Guidance Counselors**: 5.0 1,022 students/counselor	**% Amer Indian**: 0.2 **% Asian**: 10.9 **% Black**: 7.8 **% Hispanic**: 9.5 **% White**: 71.7	National ***Socio-Economic Status*** indicator percentile (100=high): 77th

Solano County

DIXON UNIFIED S.D.

305 N. ALMOND ST. ● DIXON CA 95620-2702 ● (916) 678-5582

Grade Span: KG-12 **Schools**: *Regular* 5 ● *Spec Ed* 0 ● *Alt* 1 **Students**: 3,295 **Total Teachers**: 155 **Student/Classroom Teacher Ratio**: 21.6	**Expenditures/Student**: $4,398 **Librarians**: 0.6 5,492 students/librarian **Guidance Counselors**: 4.1 804 students/counselor	**% Amer Indian**: 0.2 **% Asian**: 2.6 **% Black**: 1.5 **% Hispanic**: 40.4 **% White**: 55.4	National ***Socio-Economic Status*** indicator percentile (100=high): 25th

Solano County

FAIRFIELD-SUISUN UNIFIED S.D.

1125 MISSOURI ST. ● FAIRFIELD CA 94533-6000 ● (707) 421-4000

Grade Span: KG-12 **Schools**: *Regular* 24 ● *Spec Ed* 0 ● *Alt* 2 **Students**: 20,999 **Total Teachers**: 901 **Student/Classroom Teacher Ratio**: 23.7	**Expenditures/Student**: $4,009 **Librarians**: 8.0 2,625 students/librarian **Guidance Counselors**: 6.5 3,231 students/counselor	**% Amer Indian**: 0.7 **% Asian**: 15.6 **% Black**: 19.2 **% Hispanic**: 16.1 **% White**: 48.4	National ***Socio-Economic Status*** indicator percentile (100=high): 42nd

Solano County

[TRAVIS AFB] **TRAVIS UNIFIED S.D.**

2751 DE RONDE DR. ● TRAVIS AFB CA 94533-9710 ● (707) 437-4604

Grade Span: KG-12 **Schools**: *Regular* 7 ● *Spec Ed* 0 ● *Alt* 1 **Students**: 4,601 **Total Teachers**: 218 **Student/Classroom Teacher Ratio**: 21.9	**Expenditures/Student**: $4,778 **Librarians**: 3.5 1,315 students/librarian **Guidance Counselors**: 4.8 959 students/counselor	**% Amer Indian**: 0.9 **% Asian**: 11.1 **% Black**: 17.3 **% Hispanic**: 9.5 **% White**: 61.2	National ***Socio-Economic Status*** indicator percentile (100=high): 53rd

Solano County

VACAVILLE UNIFIED S.D.

751 SCHOOL ST. ● VACAVILLE CA 95688-3945 ● (707) 453-6100

Grade Span: KG-12 **Schools**: *Regular* 17 ● *Spec Ed* 0 ● *Alt* 2 **Students**: 14,136 **Total Teachers**: 621 **Student/Classroom Teacher Ratio**: 22.0	**Expenditures/Student**: $4,156 **Librarians**: 3.0 4,712 students/librarian **Guidance Counselors**: 17.7 799 students/counselor	**% Amer Indian**: 1.3 **% Asian**: 5.1 **% Black**: 7.5 **% Hispanic**: 14.9 **% White**: 71.3	National ***Socio-Economic Status*** indicator percentile (100=high): 51st

Solano County

VALLEJO CITY UNIFIED S.D.

211 VALLE VISTA ● VALLEJO CA 94590-3256 ● (707) 644-8921

Grade Span: KG-12	**Expenditures/Student**: $4,889	**% Amer Indian**: 0.9	National ***Socio-Economic Status*** indicator percentile (100=high): 31st
Schools: *Regular* 23 ● *Spec Ed* 1 ● *Alt* 1	**Librarians**: 6.0	**% Asian**: 28.2	
Students: 19,083	3,181 students/librarian	**% Black**: 33.2	
Total Teachers: 766	**Guidance Counselors**: 4.0	**% Hispanic**: 13.9	
Student/Classroom Teacher Ratio: 26.3	4,771 students/counselor	**% White**: 23.8	

Sonoma County

COTATI-ROHNERT PARK UNIFIED S.D.

1601 E. COTATI AVE. ● COTATI CA 94928 ● (707) 792-4720

Grade Span: KG-12	**Expenditures/Student**: $4,097	**% Amer Indian**: 1.3	National ***Socio-Economic Status*** indicator percentile (100=high): 59th
Schools: *Regular* 12 ● *Spec Ed* 0 ● *Alt* 2	**Librarians**: 2.0	**% Asian**: 6.4	
Students: 7,959	3,980 students/librarian	**% Black**: 3.6	
Total Teachers: 314	**Guidance Counselors**: 7.5	**% Hispanic**: 11.6	
Student/Classroom Teacher Ratio: 26.0	1,061 students/counselor	**% White**: 77.1	

Sonoma County

HEALDSBURG UNIFIED S.D.

925 UNIVERSITY ST. ● HEALDSBURG CA 95448-3528 ● (707) 431-3488

Grade Span: KG-12	**Expenditures/Student**: $na	**% Amer Indian**: 1.0	National ***Socio-Economic Status*** indicator percentile (100=high): 55th
Schools: *Regular* 5 ● *Spec Ed* 0 ● *Alt* 1	**Librarians**: 0.0	**% Asian**: 1.3	
Students: 3,238	*** students/librarian	**% Black**: 0.4	
Total Teachers: 141	**Guidance Counselors**: 5.8	**% Hispanic**: 29.4	
Student/Classroom Teacher Ratio: 22.8	558 students/counselor	**% White**: 67.9	

Sonoma County

PETALUMA JOINT UNION HIGH S.D.

11 FIFTH ST. ● PETALUMA CA 94952-3007 ● (707) 778-4604 ● http://www.rpnet.net/~psd

Grade Span: 07-12	**Expenditures/Student**: $na	**% Amer Indian**: 0.6	National ***Socio-Economic Status*** indicator percentile (100=high): 81st
Schools: *Regular* 4 ● *Spec Ed* 0 ● *Alt* 4	**Librarians**: 1.9	**% Asian**: 4.1	
Students: 4,739	2,494 students/librarian	**% Black**: 1.3	
Total Teachers: 197	**Guidance Counselors**: 12.4	**% Hispanic**: 10.9	
Student/Classroom Teacher Ratio: 24.2	382 students/counselor	**% White**: 83.2	

Sonoma County

[SANTA ROSA] **RINCON VALLEY UNION ELEMENTARY S.D.**

1000 YULUPA AVE. ● SANTA ROSA CA 95405-7020 ● (707) 542-7375

Grade Span: KG-06	**Expenditures/Student**: $4,159	**% Amer Indian**: 0.5	National ***Socio-Economic Status*** indicator percentile (100=high): 48th
Schools: *Regular* 7 ● *Spec Ed* 0 ● *Alt* 0	**Librarians**: 0.0	**% Asian**: 4.0	
Students: 2,631	*** students/librarian	**% Black**: 3.2	
Total Teachers: 104	**Guidance Counselors**: 0.0	**% Hispanic**: 7.1	
Student/Classroom Teacher Ratio: 26.1	*** students/counselor	**% White**: 85.2	

Sonoma County

SANTA ROSA ELEMENTARY S.D.

P.O. BOX 940 ● SANTA ROSA CA 95402-0940 ● (707) 528-5181

Grade Span: KG-06	**Expenditures/Student**: $5,631	**% Amer Indian**: 3.3	National ***Socio-Economic Status*** indicator percentile (100=high): 13th
Schools: *Regular* 12 ● *Spec Ed* 1 ● *Alt* 0	**Librarians**: 0.5	**% Asian**: 7.6	
Students: 5,122	10,244 students/librarian	**% Black**: 4.4	
Total Teachers: 240	**Guidance Counselors**: 2.4	**% Hispanic**: 27.8	
Student/Classroom Teacher Ratio: 23.7	2,134 students/counselor	**% White**: 57.0	

Sonoma County
SANTA ROSA HIGH S.D.
P.O. BOX 940 ● SANTA ROSA CA 95402-0940 ● (707) 528-5181

Grade Span: 07-12 **Schools**: *Regular* 9 ● *Spec Ed* 0 ● *Alt* 5 **Students**: 11,278 **Total Teachers**: 496 **Student/Classroom Teacher Ratio**: 23.5	**Expenditures/Student**: $na **Librarians**: 4.5 2,506 students/librarian **Guidance Counselors**: 31.1 363 students/counselor	**% Amer Indian**: 2.0 **% Asian**: 6.3 **% Black**: 3.2 **% Hispanic**: 16.9 **% White**: 71.5	National ***Socio-Economic Status*** indicator percentile (100=high): 50th

Sonoma County
SONOMA VALLEY UNIFIED S.D.
721 W. NAPA ST. ● SONOMA CA 95476-6412 ● (707) 935-6000 ● http://www.sonomavly.k12.ca.us

Grade Span: KG-12 **Schools**: *Regular* 8 ● *Spec Ed* 0 ● *Alt* 1 **Students**: 5,182 **Total Teachers**: 235 **Student/Classroom Teacher Ratio**: 22.6	**Expenditures/Student**: $4,415 **Librarians**: 1.0 5,182 students/librarian **Guidance Counselors**: 7.8 664 students/counselor	**% Amer Indian**: 0.3 **% Asian**: 2.2 **% Black**: 0.8 **% Hispanic**: 19.0 **% White**: 77.7	National ***Socio-Economic Status*** indicator percentile (100=high): 38th

Sonoma County
WINDSOR UNIFIED S.D.
7650 BELL ROAD ● WINDSOR CA 95492-8998 ● (707) 837-7701

Grade Span: KG-09 **Schools**: *Regular* 5 ● *Spec Ed* 0 ● *Alt* 0 **Students**: 2,670 **Total Teachers**: 114 **Student/Classroom Teacher Ratio**: 23.6	**Expenditures/Student**: $4,284 **Librarians**: 0.0 *** students/librarian **Guidance Counselors**: 1.8 1,483 students/counselor	**% Amer Indian**: 2.5 **% Asian**: 1.9 **% Black**: 1.1 **% Hispanic**: 26.3 **% White**: 68.3	National ***Socio-Economic Status*** indicator percentile (100=high): 34th

Stanislaus County
CERES UNIFIED S.D.
P.O. BOX 307 ● CERES CA 95307-0307 ● (209) 538-0141 ● http://www.carlsbadusd.k12.ca.us

Grade Span: KG-12 **Schools**: *Regular* 10 ● *Spec Ed* 0 ● *Alt* 2 **Students**: 9,044 **Total Teachers**: 372 **Student/Classroom Teacher Ratio**: 25.1	**Expenditures/Student**: $4,305 **Librarians**: 1.0 9,044 students/librarian **Guidance Counselors**: 8.2 1,103 students/counselor	**% Amer Indian**: 1.5 **% Asian**: 5.3 **% Black**: 3.2 **% Hispanic**: 37.4 **% White**: 52.6	National ***Socio-Economic Status*** indicator percentile (100=high): 13th

Stanislaus County
[MODESTO] **EMPIRE UNION ELEMENTARY S.D.**
116 N. MCCLURE RD. ● MODESTO CA 95357-1329 ● (209) 521-2800

Grade Span: KG-08 **Schools**: *Regular* 6 ● *Spec Ed* 0 ● *Alt* 0 **Students**: 3,999 **Total Teachers**: 170 **Student/Classroom Teacher Ratio**: 24.0	**Expenditures/Student**: $4,799 **Librarians**: 1.0 3,999 students/librarian **Guidance Counselors**: 6.0 667 students/counselor	**% Amer Indian**: 0.4 **% Asian**: 10.8 **% Black**: 6.1 **% Hispanic**: 27.7 **% White**: 55.1	National ***Socio-Economic Status*** indicator percentile (100=high): na

Stanislaus County
MODESTO CITY ELEMENTARY S.D.
426 LOCUST ST. ● MODESTO CA 95351-2631 ● (209) 576-4011

Grade Span: KG-08 **Schools**: *Regular* 27 ● *Spec Ed* 0 ● *Alt* 0 **Students**: 18,152 **Total Teachers**: 769 **Student/Classroom Teacher Ratio**: 23.7	**Expenditures/Student**: $4,431 **Librarians**: 9.6 1,891 students/librarian **Guidance Counselors**: 1.0 18,152 students/counselor	**% Amer Indian**: 0.7 **% Asian**: 13.0 **% Black**: 4.4 **% Hispanic**: 39.5 **% White**: 42.4	National ***Socio-Economic Status*** indicator percentile (100=high): 4th

Stanislaus County

MODESTO CITY HIGH S.D.

426 LOCUST ST. ● MODESTO CA 95351-2631 ● (209) 576-4011

Grade Span: 08-12 **Schools**: *Regular* 5 ● *Spec Ed* 0 ● *Alt* 1 **Students**: 12,571 **Total Teachers**: 496 **Student/Classroom Teacher Ratio**: 26.1	**Expenditures/Student**: $na **Librarians**: 5.4 2,328 students/librarian **Guidance Counselors**: 20.3 619 students/counselor	**% Amer Indian**: 0.7 **% Asian**: 12.0 **% Black**: 3.9 **% Hispanic**: 26.7 **% White**: 56.7	National ***Socio-Economic Status*** indicator percentile (100=high): 42nd

Stanislaus County

[MODESTO] **STANISLAUS UNION ELEMENTARY S.D.**

3601 CARVER ROAD ● MODESTO CA 95356-0926 ● (209) 529-9546

Grade Span: KG-08 **Schools**: *Regular* 6 ● *Spec Ed* 0 ● *Alt* 0 **Students**: 3,237 **Total Teachers**: 139 **Student/Classroom Teacher Ratio**: 23.5	**Expenditures/Student**: $4,038 **Librarians**: 0.0 *** students/librarian **Guidance Counselors**: 0.0 *** students/counselor	**% Amer Indian**: 0.4 **% Asian**: 16.5 **% Black**: 7.5 **% Hispanic**: 20.2 **% White**: 55.4	National ***Socio-Economic Status*** indicator percentile (100=high): 19th

Stanislaus County

[MODESTO] **SYLVAN UNION ELEMENTARY S.D.**

605 SYLVAN AVE. ● MODESTO CA 95350-1517 ● (209) 524-9407

Grade Span: KG-08 **Schools**: *Regular* 9 ● *Spec Ed* 0 ● *Alt* 0 **Students**: 6,385 **Total Teachers**: 288 **Student/Classroom Teacher Ratio**: 22.5	**Expenditures/Student**: $4,132 **Librarians**: 2.0 3,193 students/librarian **Guidance Counselors**: 3.1 2,060 students/counselor	**% Amer Indian**: 0.4 **% Asian**: 6.2 **% Black**: 3.8 **% Hispanic**: 14.6 **% White**: 75.0	National ***Socio-Economic Status*** indicator percentile (100=high): 41st

Stanislaus County

OAKDALE UNION ELEMENTARY S.D.

168 S. THIRD AVE. ● OAKDALE CA 95361-3223 ● (209) 847-4226

Grade Span: KG-08 **Schools**: *Regular* 4 ● *Spec Ed* 0 ● *Alt* 0 **Students**: 2,953 **Total Teachers**: 116 **Student/Classroom Teacher Ratio**: 26.1	**Expenditures/Student**: $3,964 **Librarians**: 0.0 *** students/librarian **Guidance Counselors**: 1.0 2,953 students/counselor	**% Amer Indian**: 0.3 **% Asian**: 1.8 **% Black**: 0.7 **% Hispanic**: 18.5 **% White**: 78.7	National ***Socio-Economic Status*** indicator percentile (100=high): 26th

Stanislaus County

PATTERSON JOINT UNIFIED S.D.

P.O. BOX 547 ● PATTERSON CA 95363-0547 ● (209) 892-3700

Grade Span: KG-12 **Schools**: *Regular* 7 ● *Spec Ed* 0 ● *Alt* 1 **Students**: 3,445 **Total Teachers**: 138 **Student/Classroom Teacher Ratio**: 23.7	**Expenditures/Student**: $4,019 **Librarians**: 0.0 *** students/librarian **Guidance Counselors**: 4.0 861 students/counselor	**% Amer Indian**: 0.2 **% Asian**: 1.4 **% Black**: 1.2 **% Hispanic**: 62.0 **% White**: 35.2	National ***Socio-Economic Status*** indicator percentile (100=high): 11th

Stanislaus County

TURLOCK JOINT ELEMENTARY S.D.

P.O. BOX 1105 ● TURLOCK CA 95381-1105 ● (209) 667-0632 ● http://www.turlock.k12.ca.us

Grade Span: KG-08 **Schools**: *Regular* 9 ● *Spec Ed* 0 ● *Alt* 0 **Students**: 7,616 **Total Teachers**: 318 **Student/Classroom Teacher Ratio**: 25.0	**Expenditures/Student**: $3,960 **Librarians**: 0.0 *** students/librarian **Guidance Counselors**: 5.3 1,437 students/counselor	**% Amer Indian**: 1.1 **% Asian**: 5.7 **% Black**: 2.0 **% Hispanic**: 35.9 **% White**: 55.3	National ***Socio-Economic Status*** indicator percentile (100=high): 12th

Stanislaus County

TURLOCK JOINT UNION HIGH S.D.

PO BOX 1105 ● TURLOCK CA 95381-1105 ● (209) 667-0632 ● http://www.turlock.k12.ca.us

Grade Span: 09-12 **Schools**: *Regular* 1 ● *Spec Ed* 0 ● *Alt* 1 **Students**: 3,581 **Total Teachers**: 140 **Student/Classroom Teacher Ratio**: 26.1	**Expenditures/Student**: $4,839 **Librarians**: 0.0 *** students/librarian **Guidance Counselors**: 8.0 448 students/counselor	**% Amer Indian**: 1.6 **% Asian**: 6.1 **% Black**: 1.2 **% Hispanic**: 27.9 **% White**: 63.1	National ***Socio-Economic Status*** indicator percentile (100=high): 65th

Sutter County

YUBA CITY UNIFIED S.D.

750 PALORA AVE. ● YUBA CITY CA 95991-3627 ● (530) 741-5200

Grade Span: KG-12 **Schools**: *Regular* 14 ● *Spec Ed* 0 ● *Alt* 2 **Students**: 10,557 **Total Teachers**: 443 **Student/Classroom Teacher Ratio**: 23.1	**Expenditures/Student**: $4,483 **Librarians**: 1.0 10,557 students/librarian **Guidance Counselors**: 12.0 880 students/counselor	**% Amer Indian**: 1.3 **% Asian**: 14.3 **% Black**: 3.2 **% Hispanic**: 24.6 **% White**: 56.6	National ***Socio-Economic Status*** indicator percentile (100=high): 15th

Tulare County

DINUBA ELEMENTARY S.D.

1327 E. EL MONTE BLVD. ● DINUBA CA 93618-1825 ● (209) 591-3334

Grade Span: KG-08 **Schools**: *Regular* 6 ● *Spec Ed* 0 ● *Alt* 0 **Students**: 3,190 **Total Teachers**: 134 **Student/Classroom Teacher Ratio**: 25.0	**Expenditures/Student**: $4,195 **Librarians**: 0.0 *** students/librarian **Guidance Counselors**: 2.5 1,276 students/counselor	**% Amer Indian**: 0.1 **% Asian**: 1.6 **% Black**: 0.3 **% Hispanic**: 78.8 **% White**: 19.1	National ***Socio-Economic Status*** indicator percentile (100=high): 2nd

Tulare County

LINDSAY UNIFIED S.D.

519 E. HONOLULU ● LINDSAY CA 93247-2143 ● (209) 562-5111

Grade Span: KG-12 **Schools**: *Regular* 5 ● *Spec Ed* 0 ● *Alt* 2 **Students**: 3,322 **Total Teachers**: 149 **Student/Classroom Teacher Ratio**: 22.3	**Expenditures/Student**: $4,818 **Librarians**: 0.0 *** students/librarian **Guidance Counselors**: 6.0 554 students/counselor	**% Amer Indian**: 0.0 **% Asian**: 2.5 **% Black**: 0.0 **% Hispanic**: 80.5 **% White**: 17.0	National ***Socio-Economic Status*** indicator percentile (100=high): 2nd

Tulare County

[OROSI] CUTLER-OROSI JOINT UNIFIED S.D.

41855 ROAD 128 ● OROSI CA 93647-2008 ● (209) 528-6763

Grade Span: KG-12 **Schools**: *Regular* 6 ● *Spec Ed* 0 ● *Alt* 3 **Students**: 3,635 **Total Teachers**: 159 **Student/Classroom Teacher Ratio**: 22.1	**Expenditures/Student**: $5,566 **Librarians**: 0.0 *** students/librarian **Guidance Counselors**: 2.0 1,818 students/counselor	**% Amer Indian**: 0.0 **% Asian**: 5.9 **% Black**: 0.1 **% Hispanic**: 88.8 **% White**: 5.1	National ***Socio-Economic Status*** indicator percentile (100=high): 1st

Tulare County

PORTERVILLE ELEMENTARY S.D.

589 W. VINE ● PORTERVILLE CA 93257-4500 ● (209) 782-7000 ● http://porterville.k12.ca.us/dist/Home.html

Grade Span: KG-08 **Schools**: *Regular* 10 ● *Spec Ed* 0 ● *Alt* 0 **Students**: 6,879 **Total Teachers**: 294 **Student/Classroom Teacher Ratio**: 24.2	**Expenditures/Student**: $4,682 **Librarians**: 0.0 *** students/librarian **Guidance Counselors**: 2.0 3,440 students/counselor	**% Amer Indian**: 2.7 **% Asian**: 6.8 **% Black**: 0.7 **% Hispanic**: 59.0 **% White**: 30.9	National ***Socio-Economic Status*** indicator percentile (100=high): 1st

Tulare County

PORTERVILLE UNION HIGH S.D.

589 W. VINE ST. ● PORTERVILLE CA 93257-4500 ● (209) 782-7000 ● http://porterville.k12.ca.us/dist/Home.html

Grade Span: 09-12 **Schools**: *Regular* 2 ● *Spec Ed* 0 ● *Alt* 1 **Students**: 4,769 **Total Teachers**: 202 **Student/Classroom Teacher Ratio**: 24.2	**Expenditures/Student**: $5,408 **Librarians**: 1.0 4,769 students/librarian **Guidance Counselors**: 6.0 795 students/counselor	**% Amer Indian**: 2.4 **% Asian**: 6.9 **% Black**: 0.8 **% Hispanic**: 48.2 **% White**: 41.8	National ***Socio-Economic Status*** indicator percentile (100=high): 9th

Tulare County

TULARE CITY ELEMENTARY S.D.

600 N. CHERRY AVE. ● TULARE CA 93274-2920 ● (209) 685-7200 ● http://www.tcsd.k12.ca.us

Grade Span: KG-08 **Schools**: *Regular* 11 ● *Spec Ed* 0 ● *Alt* 0 **Students**: 7,105 **Total Teachers**: 315 **Student/Classroom Teacher Ratio**: 22.6	**Expenditures/Student**: $4,539 **Librarians**: 0.0 *** students/librarian **Guidance Counselors**: 3.0 2,368 students/counselor	**% Amer Indian**: 0.7 **% Asian**: 4.2 **% Black**: 7.8 **% Hispanic**: 49.9 **% White**: 37.3	National ***Socio-Economic Status*** indicator percentile (100=high): 5th

Tulare County

TULARE JOINT UNION HIGH S.D.

426 N. BLACKSTONE ● TULARE CA 93274-4449 ● (209) 688-2021

Grade Span: 09-12 **Schools**: *Regular* 2 ● *Spec Ed* 0 ● *Alt* 3 **Students**: 3,839 **Total Teachers**: 155 **Student/Classroom Teacher Ratio**: 24.4	**Expenditures/Student**: $5,787 **Librarians**: 2.0 1,920 students/librarian **Guidance Counselors**: 13.4 286 students/counselor	**% Amer Indian**: 0.4 **% Asian**: 3.1 **% Black**: 5.4 **% Hispanic**: 44.1 **% White**: 47.0	National ***Socio-Economic Status*** indicator percentile (100=high): 63rd

Tulare County

VISALIA UNIFIED S.D.

315 E. ACEQUIA ST. ● VISALIA CA 93291-6341 ● (209) 730-7551 ● http://vusd-1.visalia.k12.ca.us

Grade Span: KG-12 **Schools**: *Regular* 28 ● *Spec Ed* 1 ● *Alt* 2 **Students**: 24,232 **Total Teachers**: 997 **Student/Classroom Teacher Ratio**: 25.9	**Expenditures/Student**: $4,614 **Librarians**: 4.0 6,058 students/librarian **Guidance Counselors**: 19.5 1,243 students/counselor	**% Amer Indian**: 0.8 **% Asian**: 8.7 **% Black**: 1.7 **% Hispanic**: 40.7 **% White**: 48.1	National ***Socio-Economic Status*** indicator percentile (100=high): 20th

Ventura County

[CAMARILLO] PLEASANT VALLEY ELEMENTARY S.D.

600 TEMPLE AVE. ● CAMARILLO CA 93010-4835 ● (805) 482-2763 ● http://www.pvsd.ca.us/~pvsd/default.html

Grade Span: KG-08 **Schools**: *Regular* 14 ● *Spec Ed* 0 ● *Alt* 0 **Students**: 6,930 **Total Teachers**: 304 **Student/Classroom Teacher Ratio**: 23.2	**Expenditures/Student**: $4,115 **Librarians**: 1.0 6,930 students/librarian **Guidance Counselors**: 2.3 3,013 students/counselor	**% Amer Indian**: 0.5 **% Asian**: 7.2 **% Black**: 2.3 **% Hispanic**: 18.2 **% White**: 71.7	National ***Socio-Economic Status*** indicator percentile (100=high): 72nd

Ventura County

FILLMORE UNIFIED S.D.

P.O. BOX 697 ● FILLMORE CA 93016-0697 ● (805) 524-0280 ● http://www.fillmore.k12.ca.us

Grade Span: KG-12 **Schools**: *Regular* 5 ● *Spec Ed* 0 ● *Alt* 1 **Students**: 3,515 **Total Teachers**: 146 **Student/Classroom Teacher Ratio**: 24.4	**Expenditures/Student**: $4,291 **Librarians**: 1.0 3,515 students/librarian **Guidance Counselors**: 2.2 1,598 students/counselor	**% Amer Indian**: 1.1 **% Asian**: 1.0 **% Black**: 0.2 **% Hispanic**: 75.4 **% White**: 22.3	National ***Socio-Economic Status*** indicator percentile (100=high): 14th

Ventura County
MOORPARK UNIFIED S.D.
30 FLORY AVE. ● MOORPARK CA 93021-1862 ● (805) 378-6300

Grade Span: KG-12 **Schools**: *Regular* 8 ● *Spec Ed* 0 ● *Alt* 1 **Students**: 6,587 **Total Teachers**: 266 **Student/Classroom Teacher Ratio**: 25.4	**Expenditures/Student**: $4,273 **Librarians**: 0.0 *** students/librarian **Guidance Counselors**: 5.5 1,198 students/counselor	**% Amer Indian**: 0.3 **% Asian**: 5.3 **% Black**: 1.9 **% Hispanic**: 28.5 **% White**: 64.0	National ***Socio-Economic Status*** indicator percentile (100=high): 53rd

Ventura County
OAK PARK UNIFIED S.D.
5801 E. CONIFER ST. ● OAK PARK CA 91301-1002 ● (818) 707-7900 ● http://www.opusd.k12.ca.us

Grade Span: KG-12 **Schools**: *Regular* 5 ● *Spec Ed* 0 ● *Alt* 1 **Students**: 2,967 **Total Teachers**: 128 **Student/Classroom Teacher Ratio**: 23.9	**Expenditures/Student**: $4,333 **Librarians**: 0.0 *** students/librarian **Guidance Counselors**: 3.8 781 students/counselor	**% Amer Indian**: 0.2 **% Asian**: 6.4 **% Black**: 1.4 **% Hispanic**: 2.1 **% White**: 90.0	National ***Socio-Economic Status*** indicator percentile (100=high): 99th

Ventura County
OJAI UNIFIED S.D.
P.O. BOX 878 ● OJAI CA 93024-0878 ● (805) 640-4300

Grade Span: KG-12 **Schools**: *Regular* 7 ● *Spec Ed* 0 ● *Alt* 1 **Students**: 4,132 **Total Teachers**: 162 **Student/Classroom Teacher Ratio**: 27.2	**Expenditures/Student**: $4,140 **Librarians**: 0.0 *** students/librarian **Guidance Counselors**: 4.6 898 students/counselor	**% Amer Indian**: 0.5 **% Asian**: 1.5 **% Black**: 0.8 **% Hispanic**: 17.5 **% White**: 79.6	National ***Socio-Economic Status*** indicator percentile (100=high): 51st

Ventura County
OXNARD ELEMENTARY S.D.
1051 SOUTH A ST. ● OXNARD CA 93030-7442 ● (805) 487-3918 ● http://www.oxnardsd.org

Grade Span: KG-08 **Schools**: *Regular* 15 ● *Spec Ed* 1 ● *Alt* 0 **Students**: 13,683 **Total Teachers**: 507 **Student/Classroom Teacher Ratio**: 26.5	**Expenditures/Student**: $4,590 **Librarians**: 0.0 *** students/librarian **Guidance Counselors**: 0.0 *** students/counselor	**% Amer Indian**: 0.2 **% Asian**: 3.9 **% Black**: 4.2 **% Hispanic**: 76.9 **% White**: 14.9	National ***Socio-Economic Status*** indicator percentile (100=high): 3rd

Ventura County
OXNARD UNION HIGH S.D.
309 SOUTH K ST. ● OXNARD CA 93030-5212 ● (805) 385-2500 ● http://www.ouhsd.k12.ca.us

Grade Span: 09-12 **Schools**: *Regular* 5 ● *Spec Ed* 0 ● *Alt* 1 **Students**: 12,983 **Total Teachers**: 486 **Student/Classroom Teacher Ratio**: 26.7	**Expenditures/Student**: $4,937 **Librarians**: 5.0 2,597 students/librarian **Guidance Counselors**: 23.8 546 students/counselor	**% Amer Indian**: 0.9 **% Asian**: 9.0 **% Black**: 4.7 **% Hispanic**: 54.2 **% White**: 31.2	National ***Socio-Economic Status*** indicator percentile (100=high): 34th

Ventura County
[OXNARD] RIO ELEMENTARY S.D.
3300 CORTEZ ST. ● OXNARD CA 93030-1309 ● (805) 485-3111

Grade Span: KG-08 **Schools**: *Regular* 5 ● *Spec Ed* 0 ● *Alt* 0 **Students**: 2,796 **Total Teachers**: 107 **Student/Classroom Teacher Ratio**: 26.2	**Expenditures/Student**: $4,256 **Librarians**: 0.0 *** students/librarian **Guidance Counselors**: 0.0 *** students/counselor	**% Amer Indian**: 0.3 **% Asian**: 2.3 **% Black**: 2.5 **% Hispanic**: 78.6 **% White**: 16.3	National ***Socio-Economic Status*** indicator percentile (100=high): 6th

Ventura County

[PORT HUENEME] **HUENEME ELEMENTARY S.D.**

205 NORTH VENTURA RD. ● PORT HUENEME CA 93041-3065 ● (805) 488-3588 ● http://www.huensd.k12.ca.us

Grade Span: KG-08 **Schools**: *Regular* 11 ● *Spec Ed* 0 ● *Alt* 0 **Students**: 8,020 **Total Teachers**: 310 **Student/Classroom Teacher Ratio**: 26.2	**Expenditures/Student**: $4,059 **Librarians**: 0.0 *** students/librarian **Guidance Counselors**: 1.4 5,729 students/counselor	**% Amer Indian**: 0.6 **% Asian**: 11.0 **% Black**: 5.6 **% Hispanic**: 62.3 **% White**: 20.4	National ***Socio-Economic Status*** indicator percentile (100=high): 5th

Ventura County

SANTA PAULA ELEMENTARY S.D.

P.O. BOX 710 ● SANTA PAULA CA 93061-0710 ● (805) 933-5342 ● http://www.spesd.k12.ca.us

Grade Span: KG-08 **Schools**: *Regular* 7 ● *Spec Ed* 0 ● *Alt* 0 **Students**: 3,448 **Total Teachers**: 134 **Student/Classroom Teacher Ratio**: 26.5	**Expenditures/Student**: $4,714 **Librarians**: 0.0 *** students/librarian **Guidance Counselors**: 2.5 1,379 students/counselor	**% Amer Indian**: 0.1 **% Asian**: 0.3 **% Black**: 0.4 **% Hispanic**: 82.1 **% White**: 17.1	National ***Socio-Economic Status*** indicator percentile (100=high): 2nd

Ventura County

SIMI VALLEY UNIFIED S.D.

875 E. COCHRAN ● SIMI VALLEY CA 93065-0999 ● (805) 520-6500 ● http://www.qtime.com/~svusd

Grade Span: KG-12 **Schools**: *Regular* 25 ● *Spec Ed* 0 ● *Alt* 2 **Students**: 18,627 **Total Teachers**: 719 **Student/Classroom Teacher Ratio**: 26.8	**Expenditures/Student**: $4,618 **Librarians**: 2.0 9,314 students/librarian **Guidance Counselors**: 15.0 1,242 students/counselor	**% Amer Indian**: 1.1 **% Asian**: 7.0 **% Black**: 1.9 **% Hispanic**: 16.5 **% White**: 73.6	National ***Socio-Economic Status*** indicator percentile (100=high): 67th

Ventura County

[THOUSAND OAKS] **CONEJO VALLEY UNIFIED S.D.**

1400 E JANSS RD ● THOUSAND OAKS CA 91362-2133 ● (805) 497-9511

Grade Span: KG-12 **Schools**: *Regular* 25 ● *Spec Ed* 0 ● *Alt* 2 **Students**: 17,993 **Total Teachers**: 675 **Student/Classroom Teacher Ratio**: 28.4	**Expenditures/Student**: $4,472 **Librarians**: 3.0 5,998 students/librarian **Guidance Counselors**: 9.0 1,999 students/counselor	**% Amer Indian**: 0.6 **% Asian**: 6.7 **% Black**: 1.4 **% Hispanic**: 13.3 **% White**: 77.9	National ***Socio-Economic Status*** indicator percentile (100=high): 75th

Ventura County

VENTURA UNIFIED S.D.

120 E. SANTA CLARA ST. ● VENTURA CA 93001-2716 ● (805) 641-5000

Grade Span: KG-12 **Schools**: *Regular* 23 ● *Spec Ed* 0 ● *Alt* 4 **Students**: 16,560 **Total Teachers**: 622 **Student/Classroom Teacher Ratio**: 26.2	**Expenditures/Student**: $4,607 **Librarians**: 6.1 2,715 students/librarian **Guidance Counselors**: 18.3 905 students/counselor	**% Amer Indian**: 1.1 **% Asian**: 3.3 **% Black**: 2.3 **% Hispanic**: 31.3 **% White**: 62.0	National ***Socio-Economic Status*** indicator percentile (100=high): 27th

Yolo County

DAVIS JOINT UNIFIED S.D.

526 B ST. ● DAVIS CA 95616-3811 ● (530) 757-5300

Grade Span: KG-12 **Schools**: *Regular* 11 ● *Spec Ed* 0 ● *Alt* 2 **Students**: 7,453 **Total Teachers**: 333 **Student/Classroom Teacher Ratio**: 23.8	**Expenditures/Student**: $4,493 **Librarians**: 5.4 1,380 students/librarian **Guidance Counselors**: 9.7 768 students/counselor	**% Amer Indian**: 0.8 **% Asian**: 10.1 **% Black**: 3.5 **% Hispanic**: 13.0 **% White**: 72.5	National ***Socio-Economic Status*** indicator percentile (100=high): 62nd

Yolo County

[WEST SACRAMENTO] **WASHINGTON UNIFIED S.D.**

930 WEST ACRES RD. ● WEST SACRAMENTO CA 95691-3224 ● (916) 371-9300

Grade Span: KG-12 **Schools**: *Regular* 8 ● *Spec Ed* 0 ● *Alt* 2 **Students**: 5,474 **Total Teachers**: 251 **Student/Classroom Teacher Ratio**: 22.1	**Expenditures/Student**: $4,821 **Librarians**: 1.0 5,474 students/librarian **Guidance Counselors**: 7.0 782 students/counselor	**% Amer Indian**: 2.6 **% Asian**: 16.2 **% Black**: 2.9 **% Hispanic**: 31.6 **% White**: 46.7	National ***Socio-Economic Status*** indicator percentile (100=high): 7th

Yolo County

WOODLAND JOINT UNIFIED S.D.

526 MARSHALL AVE. ● WOODLAND CA 95695-4853 ● (530) 662-0201

Grade Span: KG-12 **Schools**: *Regular* 14 ● *Spec Ed* 0 ● *Alt* 1 **Students**: 8,974 **Total Teachers**: 377 **Student/Classroom Teacher Ratio**: 23.7	**Expenditures/Student**: $4,152 **Librarians**: 0.0 *** students/librarian **Guidance Counselors**: 14.8 606 students/counselor	**% Amer Indian**: 0.7 **% Asian**: 3.8 **% Black**: 1.6 **% Hispanic**: 43.7 **% White**: 50.2	National ***Socio-Economic Status*** indicator percentile (100=high): 22nd

Yuba County

MARYSVILLE JOINT UNIFIED S.D.

1919 B ST. ● MARYSVILLE CA 95901-3731 ● (530) 741-6030

Grade Span: KG-12 **Schools**: *Regular* 19 ● *Spec Ed* 0 ● *Alt* 3 **Students**: 10,579 **Total Teachers**: 423 **Student/Classroom Teacher Ratio**: 25.0	**Expenditures/Student**: $4,689 **Librarians**: 0.0 *** students/librarian **Guidance Counselors**: 7.0 1,511 students/counselor	**% Amer Indian**: 6.8 **% Asian**: 21.5 **% Black**: 2.7 **% Hispanic**: 15.1 **% White**: 53.9	National ***Socio-Economic Status*** indicator percentile (100=high): 3rd

Adams County
BRIGHTON S.D. 27J
630 SOUTH EIGHTH STREET ● BRIGHTON CO 80601-3295 ● (303) 659-4820

Grade Span: PK-12 **Schools**: *Regular* 8 ● *Spec Ed* 0 ● *Alt* 2 **Students**: 4,468 **Total Teachers**: 220 **Student/Classroom Teacher Ratio**: 21.3	**Expenditures/Student**: $4,764 **Librarians**: 3.0 1,489 students/librarian **Guidance Counselors**: 5.6 798 students/counselor	**% Amer Indian**: 0.5 **% Asian**: 1.0 **% Black**: 0.5 **% Hispanic**: 36.0 **% White**: 62.0	National ***Socio-Economic Status*** indicator percentile (100=high): 54th

Adams County
[COMMERCE CITY] **ADAMS COUNTY S.D. 14**
4720 EAST 69TH AVENUE ● COMMERCE CITY CO 80022 ● (303) 289-3950 ● http://www.acsd14.k12.co.us

Grade Span: PK-12 **Schools**: *Regular* 12 ● *Spec Ed* 0 ● *Alt* 2 **Students**: 6,157 **Total Teachers**: 323 **Student/Classroom Teacher Ratio**: 23.9	**Expenditures/Student**: $5,125 **Librarians**: 3.0 2,052 students/librarian **Guidance Counselors**: 7.0 880 students/counselor	**% Amer Indian**: 1.9 **% Asian**: 0.6 **% Black**: 2.8 **% Hispanic**: 50.0 **% White**: 44.7	National ***Socio-Economic Status*** indicator percentile (100=high): 21st

Adams County
[DENVER] **MAPLETON S.D. 1**
591 EAST 80TH AVENUE ● DENVER CO 80229-5806 ● (303) 288-6681

Grade Span: PK-12 **Schools**: *Regular* 10 ● *Spec Ed* 0 ● *Alt* 1 **Students**: 4,991 **Total Teachers**: 244 **Student/Classroom Teacher Ratio**: 20.8	**Expenditures/Student**: $4,521 **Librarians**: 3.0 1,664 students/librarian **Guidance Counselors**: 7.0 713 students/counselor	**% Amer Indian**: 2.4 **% Asian**: 2.2 **% Black**: 1.6 **% Hispanic**: 31.5 **% White**: 62.2	National ***Socio-Economic Status*** indicator percentile (100=high): 49th

Adams County
NORTHGLENN-THORNTON S.D. 12
11285 HIGHLINE DRIVE ● NORTHGLENN CO 80233 ● (303) 451-1561 ● http://www.ad12.k12.co.us

Grade Span: PK-12 **Schools**: *Regular* 36 ● *Spec Ed* 0 ● *Alt* 4 **Students**: 24,603 **Total Teachers**: 1,238 **Student/Classroom Teacher Ratio**: 19.8	**Expenditures/Student**: $4,737 **Librarians**: 35.0 703 students/librarian **Guidance Counselors**: 26.3 935 students/counselor	**% Amer Indian**: 1.2 **% Asian**: 3.0 **% Black**: 1.8 **% Hispanic**: 17.8 **% White**: 76.2	National ***Socio-Economic Status*** indicator percentile (100=high): 66th

Adams County
WESTMINSTER S.D. 50
4476 WEST 68TH AVENUE ● WESTMINSTER CO 80030 ● (303) 428-3511

Grade Span: PK-12 **Schools**: *Regular* 23 ● *Spec Ed* 0 ● *Alt* 3 **Students**: 11,406 **Total Teachers**: 640 **Student/Classroom Teacher Ratio**: 18.8	**Expenditures/Student**: $4,447 **Librarians**: 9.0 1,267 students/librarian **Guidance Counselors**: 16.0 713 students/counselor	**% Amer Indian**: 1.2 **% Asian**: 8.7 **% Black**: 1.7 **% Hispanic**: 30.4 **% White**: 58.0	National ***Socio-Economic Status*** indicator percentile (100=high): 44th

Alamosa County
ALAMOSA S.D. RE-11J
209 VICTORIA AVENUE ● ALAMOSA CO 81101 ● (719) 589-6634

Grade Span: PK-12 **Schools**: *Regular* 5 ● *Spec Ed* 0 ● *Alt* 1 **Students**: 2,500 **Total Teachers**: 146 **Student/Classroom Teacher Ratio**: 17.2	**Expenditures/Student**: $4,516 **Librarians**: 2.0 1,250 students/librarian **Guidance Counselors**: 8.0 313 students/counselor	**% Amer Indian**: 0.5 **% Asian**: 0.9 **% Black**: 0.7 **% Hispanic**: 50.1 **% White**: 47.8	National ***Socio-Economic Status*** indicator percentile (100=high): 24th

Arapahoe County

[AURORA] **ADAMS-ARAPAHOE S.D. 28J**

1085 PEORIA STREET ● AURORA CO 80011-6297 ● (303) 344-8060

Grade Span: PK-12 **Schools**: *Regular* 42 ● *Spec Ed* 0 ● *Alt* 2 **Students**: 27,825 **Total Teachers**: 1,480 **Student/Classroom Teacher Ratio**: 21.5	**Expenditures/Student**: $5,123 **Librarians**: 36.3 767 students/librarian **Guidance Counselors**: 60.3 461 students/counselor	**% Amer Indian**: 1.1 **% Asian**: 5.2 **% Black**: 23.3 **% Hispanic**: 12.8 **% White**: 57.7	National ***Socio-Economic Status*** indicator percentile (100=high): 50th

Arapahoe County

[ENGLEWOOD] **CHERRY CREEK S.D. 5**

4700 SOUTH YOSEMITE STREET ● ENGLEWOOD CO 80111-1394 ● (303) 773-1184 ● http://www.ccsd.k12.co.us

Grade Span: PK-12 **Schools**: *Regular* 42 ● *Spec Ed* 0 ● *Alt* 3 **Students**: 35,761 **Total Teachers**: 1,921 **Student/Classroom Teacher Ratio**: 18.8	**Expenditures/Student**: $5,562 **Librarians**: 42.2 847 students/librarian **Guidance Counselors**: 49.4 724 students/counselor	**% Amer Indian**: 0.3 **% Asian**: 4.9 **% Black**: 6.5 **% Hispanic**: 4.5 **% White**: 83.9	National ***Socio-Economic Status*** indicator percentile (100=high): 91st

Arapahoe County

ENGLEWOOD S.D. 1

4101 SOUTH BANNOCK STREET ● ENGLEWOOD CO 80110-4600 ● (303) 761-7050

Grade Span: PK-12 **Schools**: *Regular* 9 ● *Spec Ed* 0 ● *Alt* 2 **Students**: 4,704 **Total Teachers**: 222 **Student/Classroom Teacher Ratio**: 19.7	**Expenditures/Student**: $4,649 **Librarians**: 1.0 4,704 students/librarian **Guidance Counselors**: 9.0 523 students/counselor	**% Amer Indian**: 1.9 **% Asian**: 1.7 **% Black**: 2.3 **% Hispanic**: 13.0 **% White**: 81.1	National ***Socio-Economic Status*** indicator percentile (100=high): 55th

Arapahoe County

LITTLETON S.D. 6

5776 SOUTH CROCKER STREET ● LITTLETON CO 80120 ● (303) 347-3300 ● http://www.lps.k12.co.us

Grade Span: PK-12 **Schools**: *Regular* 23 ● *Spec Ed* 0 ● *Alt* 0 **Students**: 15,863 **Total Teachers**: 833 **Student/Classroom Teacher Ratio**: 19.3	**Expenditures/Student**: $4,895 **Librarians**: 18.0 881 students/librarian **Guidance Counselors**: 23.5 675 students/counselor	**% Amer Indian**: 0.4 **% Asian**: 2.7 **% Black**: 1.2 **% Hispanic**: 4.6 **% White**: 91.0	National ***Socio-Economic Status*** indicator percentile (100=high): 89th

Boulder County

BOULDER VALLEY S.D. RE-2

P O BOX 9011 ● BOULDER CO 80301 ● (303) 447-1010 ● http://bvsd.k12.co.us

Grade Span: PK-12 **Schools**: *Regular* 48 ● *Spec Ed* 1 ● *Alt* 1 **Students**: 25,230 **Total Teachers**: 1,352 **Student/Classroom Teacher Ratio**: 19.5	**Expenditures/Student**: $5,276 **Librarians**: 35.9 703 students/librarian **Guidance Counselors**: 36.3 695 students/counselor	**% Amer Indian**: 0.9 **% Asian**: 4.4 **% Black**: 1.7 **% Hispanic**: 9.6 **% White**: 83.4	National ***Socio-Economic Status*** indicator percentile (100=high): 80th

Boulder County

[LONGMONT] **ST. VRAIN VALLEY S.D. RE-1J**

395 SOUTH PRATT PARKWAY ● LONGMONT CO 80501 ● (303) 776-6200

Grade Span: KG-12 **Schools**: *Regular* 29 ● *Spec Ed* 0 ● *Alt* 4 **Students**: 16,790 **Total Teachers**: 884 **Student/Classroom Teacher Ratio**: 19.3	**Expenditures/Student**: $4,749 **Librarians**: 12.0 1,399 students/librarian **Guidance Counselors**: 33.3 504 students/counselor	**% Amer Indian**: 1.0 **% Asian**: 1.7 **% Black**: 0.4 **% Hispanic**: 16.7 **% White**: 80.3	National ***Socio-Economic Status*** indicator percentile (100=high): 69th

Delta County

[DELTA] **DELTA COUNTY S.D. 50J**

765 2075 ROAD ● DELTA CO 81416 ● (970) 874-4438

Grade Span: PK-12	**Expenditures/Student**: $5,102	**% Amer Indian**: 0.6	
Schools: *Regular* 15 ● *Spec Ed* 0 ● *Alt* 1	**Librarians**: 1.0	**% Asian**: 0.6	National ***Socio-Economic***
Students: 4,758	4,758 students/librarian	**% Black**: 0.3	***Status*** indicator percentile
Total Teachers: 264	**Guidance Counselors**: 6.0	**% Hispanic**: 14.2	(100=high): 39th
Student/Classroom Teacher Ratio: 18.5	793 students/counselor	**% White**: 84.3	

Denver County

[DENVER] **DENVER COUNTY S.D. 1**

900 GRANT STREET ● DENVER CO 80203-2996 ● (303) 764-3200 ● http://www.denver.k12.co.us

Grade Span: PK-12	**Expenditures/Student**: $5,691	**% Amer Indian**: 1.3	
Schools: *Regular* 108 ● *Spec Ed* 0 ● *Alt* 4	**Librarians**: 65.5	**% Asian**: 3.9	National ***Socio-Economic***
Students: 64,322	982 students/librarian	**% Black**: 21.3	***Status*** indicator percentile
Total Teachers: 3,271	**Guidance Counselors**: 51.5	**% Hispanic**: 46.3	(100=high): 14th
Student/Classroom Teacher Ratio: 20.4	1,249 students/counselor	**% White**: 27.2	

Douglas County

[CASTLE ROCK] **DOUGLAS COUNTY S.D. RE-1**

620 WILCOX STREET ● CASTLE ROCK CO 80104-1739 ● (303) 688-3195 ● http://www.dcsd.k12.co.us

Grade Span: PK-12	**Expenditures/Student**: $4,829	**% Amer Indian**: 0.5	
Schools: *Regular* 32 ● *Spec Ed* 1 ● *Alt* 2	**Librarians**: 5.0	**% Asian**: 1.9	National ***Socio-Economic***
Students: 22,032	4,406 students/librarian	**% Black**: 0.9	***Status*** indicator percentile
Total Teachers: 1,213	**Guidance Counselors**: 26.3	**% Hispanic**: 3.1	(100=high): 98th
Student/Classroom Teacher Ratio: 18.0	838 students/counselor	**% White**: 93.6	

Eagle County

[EAGLE] **EAGLE COUNTY S.D. RE-50**

P O BOX 740 ● EAGLE CO 81631 ● (970) 328-6321

Grade Span: PK-12	**Expenditures/Student**: $5,790	**% Amer Indian**: 0.3	
Schools: *Regular* 10 ● *Spec Ed* 0 ● *Alt* 0	**Librarians**: 8.6	**% Asian**: 0.5	National ***Socio-Economic***
Students: 3,865	449 students/librarian	**% Black**: 0.5	***Status*** indicator percentile
Total Teachers: 237	**Guidance Counselors**: 10.0	**% Hispanic**: 26.6	(100=high): 68th
Student/Classroom Teacher Ratio: 17.7	387 students/counselor	**% White**: 72.2	

El Paso County

[COLORADO SPRINGS] **ACADEMY S.D. 20**

7610 NORTH UNION BOULEVARD ● COLORADO SPRINGS CO 80920-3899 ● (719) 598-2566 ● http://www.d20.co.edu

Grade Span: KG-12	**Expenditures/Student**: $4,625	**% Amer Indian**: 1.1	
Schools: *Regular* 19 ● *Spec Ed* 0 ● *Alt* 2	**Librarians**: 7.0	**% Asian**: 2.6	National ***Socio-Economic***
Students: 14,049	2,007 students/librarian	**% Black**: 3.1	***Status*** indicator percentile
Total Teachers: 768	**Guidance Counselors**: 36.7	**% Hispanic**: 3.9	(100=high): 96th
Student/Classroom Teacher Ratio: 18.6	383 students/counselor	**% White**: 89.4	

El Paso County

[COLORADO SPRINGS] **CHEYENNE MOUNTAIN S.D. 12**

1118 WEST CHEYENNE ROAD ● COLORADO SPRINGS CO 80906-2497 ● (719) 475-6100 ● http://www.cmsd.k12.co.us

Grade Span: PK-12	**Expenditures/Student**: $4,411	**% Amer Indian**: 0.5	
Schools: *Regular* 7 ● *Spec Ed* 0 ● *Alt* 0	**Librarians**: 5.0	**% Asian**: 3.0	National ***Socio-Economic***
Students: 3,301	660 students/librarian	**% Black**: 2.1	***Status*** indicator percentile
Total Teachers: 163	**Guidance Counselors**: 9.0	**% Hispanic**: 5.3	(100=high): 96th
Student/Classroom Teacher Ratio: 21.3	367 students/counselor	**% White**: 89.2	

COLORADO (El Paso County)

El Paso County

COLORADO SPRINGS S.D. 11

1115 NORTH EL PASO STREET ● COLORADO SPRINGS CO 80903-2599 ● (719) 520-2000 ● http://www.cssd11.k12.co.us

Grade Span: PK-12 **Schools**: *Regular* 54 ● *Spec Ed* 0 ● *Alt* 5 **Students**: 32,960 **Total Teachers**: 1,691 **Student/Classroom Teacher Ratio**: 18.9	**Expenditures/Student**: $4,520 **Librarians**: 14.0 2,354 students/librarian **Guidance Counselors**: 38.3 861 students/counselor	**% Amer Indian**: 1.0 **% Asian**: 2.3 **% Black**: 9.8 **% Hispanic**: 13.1 **% White**: 73.8	National ***Socio-Economic Status*** indicator percentile (100=high): 52nd

El Paso County

[COLORADO SPRINGS] **HARRISON S.D. 2**

1060 HARRISON ROAD ● COLORADO SPRINGS CO 80906-3586 ● (719) 576-8360 ● http://www.harrison.k12.co.us

Grade Span: PK-12 **Schools**: *Regular* 17 ● *Spec Ed* 0 ● *Alt* 2 **Students**: 10,686 **Total Teachers**: 643 **Student/Classroom Teacher Ratio**: 16.2	**Expenditures/Student**: $4,846 **Librarians**: 5.0 2,137 students/librarian **Guidance Counselors**: 23.0 465 students/counselor	**% Amer Indian**: 1.2 **% Asian**: 5.1 **% Black**: 24.4 **% Hispanic**: 18.4 **% White**: 50.9	National ***Socio-Economic Status*** indicator percentile (100=high): 29th

El Paso County

[COLORADO SPRINGS] **WIDEFIELD S.D. 3**

1820 MAIN STREET ● COLORADO SPRINGS CO 80911-1152 ● (719) 392-3481 ● http://wsd3.k12.co.us

Grade Span: PK-12 **Schools**: *Regular* 14 ● *Spec Ed* 0 ● *Alt* 1 **Students**: 8,353 **Total Teachers**: 441 **Student/Classroom Teacher Ratio**: 19.5	**Expenditures/Student**: $4,183 **Librarians**: 5.0 1,671 students/librarian **Guidance Counselors**: 22.0 380 students/counselor	**% Amer Indian**: 1.2 **% Asian**: 5.1 **% Black**: 15.5 **% Hispanic**: 11.9 **% White**: 66.3	National ***Socio-Economic Status*** indicator percentile (100=high): 68th

El Paso County

FALCON S.D. 49

10850 WOODMAN ROAD ● FALCON CO 80831-8127 ● (719) 495-3601

Grade Span: PK-12 **Schools**: *Regular* 7 ● *Spec Ed* 0 ● *Alt* 0 **Students**: 3,621 **Total Teachers**: 203 **Student/Classroom Teacher Ratio**: 21.6	**Expenditures/Student**: $4,005 **Librarians**: 6.0 604 students/librarian **Guidance Counselors**: 8.0 453 students/counselor	**% Amer Indian**: 1.0 **% Asian**: 4.8 **% Black**: 7.4 **% Hispanic**: 6.2 **% White**: 80.6	National ***Socio-Economic Status*** indicator percentile (100=high): 78th

El Paso County

FOUNTAIN S.D. 8

425 WEST ALABAMA AVENUE ● FOUNTAIN CO 80817-1703 ● (719) 382-5631

Grade Span: PK-12 **Schools**: *Regular* 9 ● *Spec Ed* 0 ● *Alt* 1 **Students**: 4,449 **Total Teachers**: 264 **Student/Classroom Teacher Ratio**: 17.3	**Expenditures/Student**: $4,648 **Librarians**: 2.0 2,225 students/librarian **Guidance Counselors**: 9.0 494 students/counselor	**% Amer Indian**: 1.3 **% Asian**: 2.8 **% Black**: 20.2 **% Hispanic**: 14.0 **% White**: 61.7	National ***Socio-Economic Status*** indicator percentile (100=high): 39th

El Paso County

[MONUMENT] **LEWIS-PALMER S.D. 38**

P O BOX B 146 JEFFERSON ST ● MONUMENT CO 80132-0040 ● (719) 488-4700 ● http://www.lpsd.k12.co.us

Grade Span: PK-12 **Schools**: *Regular* 6 ● *Spec Ed* 0 ● *Alt* 0 **Students**: 3,515 **Total Teachers**: 170 **Student/Classroom Teacher Ratio**: 20.6	**Expenditures/Student**: $3,897 **Librarians**: 3.0 1,172 students/librarian **Guidance Counselors**: 10.0 352 students/counselor	**% Amer Indian**: 0.5 **% Asian**: 1.6 **% Black**: 0.9 **% Hispanic**: 2.9 **% White**: 94.2	National ***Socio-Economic Status*** indicator percentile (100=high): 95th

Fremont County

CANON CITY S.D. RE-1

101 NORTH 14TH STREET ● CANON CITY CO 81212 ● (719) 269-6400

Grade Span: KG-12 **Schools**: *Regular* 8 ● *Spec Ed* 0 ● *Alt* 2 **Students**: 4,011 **Total Teachers**: 227 **Student/Classroom Teacher Ratio**: 18.5	**Expenditures/Student**: $4,246 **Librarians**: 2.0 2,006 students/librarian **Guidance Counselors**: 6.0 669 students/counselor	**% Amer Indian**: 4.1 **% Asian**: 0.7 **% Black**: 0.5 **% Hispanic**: 6.2 **% White**: 88.4	National ***Socio-Economic Status*** indicator percentile (100=high): 53rd

Garfield County

[GLENWOOD SPRINGS] ROARING FORK S.D. RE-1

1405 GRAND AVENUE ● GLENWOOD SPRINGS CO 81601-0820 ● (970) 945-6558

Grade Span: PK-12 **Schools**: *Regular* 10 ● *Spec Ed* 0 ● *Alt* 1 **Students**: 4,688 **Total Teachers**: 280 **Student/Classroom Teacher Ratio**: 16.7	**Expenditures/Student**: $5,019 **Librarians**: 8.0 586 students/librarian **Guidance Counselors**: 11.0 426 students/counselor	**% Amer Indian**: 0.3 **% Asian**: 0.9 **% Black**: 0.3 **% Hispanic**: 14.3 **% White**: 84.2	National ***Socio-Economic Status*** indicator percentile (100=high): 83rd

Garfield County

[RIFLE] GARFIELD S.D. RE-2

839 WHITERIVER ● RIFLE CO 81650 ● (970) 625-1595 ● http://www.garfieldre2.k12.co.us

Grade Span: PK-12 **Schools**: *Regular* 7 ● *Spec Ed* 0 ● *Alt* 0 **Students**: 3,139 **Total Teachers**: 160 **Student/Classroom Teacher Ratio**: 19.7	**Expenditures/Student**: $3,882 **Librarians**: 2.0 1,570 students/librarian **Guidance Counselors**: 6.0 523 students/counselor	**% Amer Indian**: 0.6 **% Asian**: 0.6 **% Black**: 0.3 **% Hispanic**: 10.6 **% White**: 87.8	National ***Socio-Economic Status*** indicator percentile (100=high): 64th

Jefferson County

[GOLDEN] JEFFERSON COUNTY S.D. R-1

P O BOX 4001 ● GOLDEN CO 80401-0001 ● (303) 982-6500 ● http://jeffco.k12.co.us

Grade Span: PK-12 **Schools**: *Regular* 135 ● *Spec Ed* 2 ● *Alt* 5 **Students**: 85,495 **Total Teachers**: 4,005 **Student/Classroom Teacher Ratio**: 21.9	**Expenditures/Student**: $4,963 **Librarians**: 122.0 701 students/librarian **Guidance Counselors**: 108.0 792 students/counselor	**% Amer Indian**: 0.7 **% Asian**: 2.8 **% Black**: 1.1 **% Hispanic**: 8.8 **% White**: 86.6	National ***Socio-Economic Status*** indicator percentile (100=high): 80th

La Plata County

DURANGO S.D. 9R

P O BOX 2467 ● DURANGO CO 81302 ● (970) 247-5411 ● http://www.durango.k12.co.us

Grade Span: PK-12 **Schools**: *Regular* 12 ● *Spec Ed* 0 ● *Alt* 1 **Students**: 4,735 **Total Teachers**: 294 **Student/Classroom Teacher Ratio**: 15.4	**Expenditures/Student**: $5,181 **Librarians**: 9.0 526 students/librarian **Guidance Counselors**: 12.5 379 students/counselor	**% Amer Indian**: 2.9 **% Asian**: 0.5 **% Black**: 0.4 **% Hispanic**: 10.0 **% White**: 86.2	National ***Socio-Economic Status*** indicator percentile (100=high): 70th

Larimer County

[FORT COLLINS] POUDRE S.D. R-1

2407 LA PORTE AVENUE ● FORT COLLINS CO 80521-2297 ● (970) 482-7420 ● http://www.psd.k12.co.us

Grade Span: KG-12 **Schools**: *Regular* 41 ● *Spec Ed* 1 ● *Alt* 2 **Students**: 21,283 **Total Teachers**: 1,004 **Student/Classroom Teacher Ratio**: 21.3	**Expenditures/Student**: $4,438 **Librarians**: 20.6 1,033 students/librarian **Guidance Counselors**: 50.1 425 students/counselor	**% Amer Indian**: 0.9 **% Asian**: 2.5 **% Black**: 1.1 **% Hispanic**: 9.8 **% White**: 85.6	National ***Socio-Economic Status*** indicator percentile (100=high): 71st

Larimer County

[LOVELAND] **THOMPSON S.D. RE-2J**

535 NORTH DOUGLAS AVENUE ● LOVELAND CO 80537-5396 ● (970) 669-3940 ● http://www.thompson.k12.co.us

Grade Span: KG-12 **Schools**: *Regular* 25 ● *Spec Ed* 0 ● *Alt* 2 **Students**: 13,405 **Total Teachers**: 691 **Student/Classroom Teacher Ratio**: 19.6	**Expenditures/Student**: $4,354 **Librarians**: 7.0 1,915 students/librarian **Guidance Counselors**: 20.5 654 students/counselor	**% Amer Indian**: 0.9 **% Asian**: 1.0 **% Black**: 0.5 **% Hispanic**: 17.7 **% White**: 79.9	National ***Socio-Economic Status*** indicator percentile (100=high): 72nd

Logan County

[STERLING] **VALLEY S.D. RE-1**

119 NORTH THIRD AVENUE ● STERLING CO 80751-0910 ● (970) 522-0792

Grade Span: PK-12 **Schools**: *Regular* 8 ● *Spec Ed* 0 ● *Alt* 2 **Students**: 2,855 **Total Teachers**: 176 **Student/Classroom Teacher Ratio**: 16.2	**Expenditures/Student**: $4,721 **Librarians**: 1.0 2,855 students/librarian **Guidance Counselors**: 3.0 952 students/counselor	**% Amer Indian**: 0.6 **% Asian**: 0.4 **% Black**: 0.2 **% Hispanic**: 16.5 **% White**: 82.2	National ***Socio-Economic Status*** indicator percentile (100=high): 44th

Mesa County

[GRAND JUNCTION] **MESA COUNTY VALLEY S.D. 51**

2115 GRAND AVENUE ● GRAND JUNCTION CO 81501-8063 ● (970) 245-2422

Grade Span: PK-12 **Schools**: *Regular* 32 ● *Spec Ed* 1 ● *Alt* 4 **Students**: 18,643 **Total Teachers**: 1,033 **Student/Classroom Teacher Ratio**: 17.9	**Expenditures/Student**: $4,379 **Librarians**: 12.0 1,554 students/librarian **Guidance Counselors**: 32.9 567 students/counselor	**% Amer Indian**: 0.9 **% Asian**: 0.8 **% Black**: 0.6 **% Hispanic**: 11.2 **% White**: 86.5	National ***Socio-Economic Status*** indicator percentile (100=high): 33rd

Moffat County

[CRAIG] **MOFFAT COUNTY S.D. RE-1**

775 YAMPA AVENUE ● CRAIG CO 81625-2532 ● (970) 824-3268 ● http://www.colosys.net/mcsd

Grade Span: PK-12 **Schools**: *Regular* 8 ● *Spec Ed* 0 ● *Alt* 0 **Students**: 2,815 **Total Teachers**: 150 **Student/Classroom Teacher Ratio**: 15.5	**Expenditures/Student**: $4,961 **Librarians**: 2.0 1,408 students/librarian **Guidance Counselors**: 4.0 704 students/counselor	**% Amer Indian**: 0.5 **% Asian**: 0.6 **% Black**: 0.1 **% Hispanic**: 8.0 **% White**: 90.8	National ***Socio-Economic Status*** indicator percentile (100=high): 72nd

Montezuma County

[CORTEZ] **MONTEZUMA-CORTEZ S.D. RE-1**

DRAWER R ● CORTEZ CO 81321 ● (970) 565-7282

Grade Span: PK-12 **Schools**: *Regular* 12 ● *Spec Ed* 0 ● *Alt* 1 **Students**: 3,492 **Total Teachers**: 199 **Student/Classroom Teacher Ratio**: 18.9	**Expenditures/Student**: $4,559 **Librarians**: 2.0 1,746 students/librarian **Guidance Counselors**: 10.0 349 students/counselor	**% Amer Indian**: 19.7 **% Asian**: 0.6 **% Black**: 0.2 **% Hispanic**: 10.7 **% White**: 68.8	National ***Socio-Economic Status*** indicator percentile (100=high): 35th

Montrose County

[MONTROSE] **MONTROSE COUNTY S.D. RE-1J**

P O BOX 219 ● MONTROSE CO 81402-0219 ● (970) 249-7726

Grade Span: PK-12 **Schools**: *Regular* 12 ● *Spec Ed* 0 ● *Alt* 2 **Students**: 5,165 **Total Teachers**: 286 **Student/Classroom Teacher Ratio**: 18.4	**Expenditures/Student**: $4,284 **Librarians**: 2.0 2,583 students/librarian **Guidance Counselors**: 10.6 487 students/counselor	**% Amer Indian**: 0.3 **% Asian**: 0.7 **% Black**: 0.5 **% Hispanic**: 17.8 **% White**: 80.7	National ***Socio-Economic Status*** indicator percentile (100=high): 48th

Morgan County
FORT MORGAN S.D. RE-3
230 WALNUT STREET ● FORT MORGAN CO 80701-2640 ● (970) 867-5633

Grade Span: PK-12 **Schools**: *Regular* 6 ● *Spec Ed* 0 ● *Alt* 0 **Students**: 2,938 **Total Teachers**: 185 **Student/Classroom Teacher Ratio**: 16.5	**Expenditures/Student**: $4,947 **Librarians**: 1.7 1,728 students/librarian **Guidance Counselors**: 5.0 588 students/counselor	**% Amer Indian**: 0.7 **% Asian**: 0.4 **% Black**: 0.2 **% Hispanic**: 35.3 **% White**: 63.5	National ***Socio-Economic Status*** indicator percentile (100=high): 29th

Pueblo County
PUEBLO CITY S.D. 60
315 WEST 11TH STREET ● PUEBLO CO 81003 ● (719) 549-7100

Grade Span: PK-12 **Schools**: *Regular* 32 ● *Spec Ed* 0 ● *Alt* 3 **Students**: 17,817 **Total Teachers**: 948 **Student/Classroom Teacher Ratio**: 18.8	**Expenditures/Student**: $4,830 **Librarians**: 31.0 575 students/librarian **Guidance Counselors**: 41.0 435 students/counselor	**% Amer Indian**: 1.4 **% Asian**: 0.7 **% Black**: 2.0 **% Hispanic**: 50.1 **% White**: 45.8	National ***Socio-Economic Status*** indicator percentile (100=high): 24th

Pueblo County
[PUEBLO] **PUEBLO COUNTY RURAL S.D. 70**
24951 EAST HIGHWAY 50 ● PUEBLO CO 81006 ● (719) 542-0220

Grade Span: PK-12 **Schools**: *Regular* 16 ● *Spec Ed* 0 ● *Alt* 1 **Students**: 5,160 **Total Teachers**: 261 **Student/Classroom Teacher Ratio**: 19.5	**Expenditures/Student**: $4,676 **Librarians**: 7.0 737 students/librarian **Guidance Counselors**: 12.0 430 students/counselor	**% Amer Indian**: 0.4 **% Asian**: 0.5 **% Black**: 0.6 **% Hispanic**: 23.7 **% White**: 74.7	National ***Socio-Economic Status*** indicator percentile (100=high): 59th

Teller County
WOODLAND PARK S.D. RE-2
P O BOX 99 ● WOODLAND PARK CO 80866 ● (719) 687-6048

Grade Span: PK-12 **Schools**: *Regular* 5 ● *Spec Ed* 0 ● *Alt* 0 **Students**: 3,064 **Total Teachers**: 155 **Student/Classroom Teacher Ratio**: 19.6	**Expenditures/Student**: $4,628 **Librarians**: 5.1 601 students/librarian **Guidance Counselors**: 8.0 383 students/counselor	**% Amer Indian**: 0.7 **% Asian**: 0.8 **% Black**: 0.8 **% Hispanic**: 3.9 **% White**: 93.9	National ***Socio-Economic Status*** indicator percentile (100=high): 84th

Weld County
FORT LUPTON S.D. RE-8
301 REYNOLDS STREET ● FORT LUPTON CO 80621 ● (303) 857-6291

Grade Span: PK-12 **Schools**: *Regular* 4 ● *Spec Ed* 0 ● *Alt* 1 **Students**: 2,576 **Total Teachers**: 142 **Student/Classroom Teacher Ratio**: 18.3	**Expenditures/Student**: $4,203 **Librarians**: 4.0 644 students/librarian **Guidance Counselors**: 5.0 515 students/counselor	**% Amer Indian**: 0.2 **% Asian**: 0.4 **% Black**: 0.4 **% Hispanic**: 47.1 **% White**: 51.8	National ***Socio-Economic Status*** indicator percentile (100=high): 19th

Weld County
GREELEY S.D. 6
811 15TH STREET ● GREELEY CO 80631-4686 ● (970) 352-1543

Grade Span: PK-12 **Schools**: *Regular* 22 ● *Spec Ed* 1 ● *Alt* 3 **Students**: 13,223 **Total Teachers**: 626 **Student/Classroom Teacher Ratio**: 28.1	**Expenditures/Student**: $4,349 **Librarians**: 16.0 826 students/librarian **Guidance Counselors**: 17.7 747 students/counselor	**% Amer Indian**: 0.5 **% Asian**: 0.9 **% Black**: 0.7 **% Hispanic**: 35.9 **% White**: 62.0	National ***Socio-Economic Status*** indicator percentile (100=high): 31st

Fairfield County
BETHEL S.D.
9 NASHVILLE ROAD, BOX 253 ● BETHEL CT 06801-0253 ● (203) 794-8601 ● http://www.bethel.k12.ct.us

Grade Span: PK-12 **Schools**: *Regular* 5 ● *Spec Ed* 0 ● *Alt* 0 **Students**: 3,185 **Total Teachers**: 210 **Student/Classroom Teacher Ratio**: 15.9	**Expenditures/Student**: $7,064 **Librarians**: 6.0 531 students/librarian **Guidance Counselors**: 8.5 375 students/counselor	**% Amer Indian**: 0.6 **% Asian**: 4.9 **% Black**: 1.5 **% Hispanic**: 3.3 **% White**: 89.7	National ***Socio-Economic Status*** indicator percentile (100=high): 90th

Fairfield County
BRIDGEPORT S.D.
45 LYON TERRACE, RM 303 ● BRIDGEPORT CT 06604-4060 ● (203) 576-7301

Grade Span: PK-12 **Schools**: *Regular* 35 ● *Spec Ed* 1 ● *Alt* 4 **Students**: 21,519 **Total Teachers**: 1,402 **Student/Classroom Teacher Ratio**: 18.0	**Expenditures/Student**: $7,981 **Librarians**: 18.6 1,157 students/librarian **Guidance Counselors**: 37.6 572 students/counselor	**% Amer Indian**: 0.1 **% Asian**: 3.5 **% Black**: 41.9 **% Hispanic**: 42.9 **% White**: 11.6	National ***Socio-Economic Status*** indicator percentile (100=high): 3rd

Fairfield County
BROOKFIELD S.D.
MUNICIPAL CENTER ● BROOKFIELD CT 06804-3331 ● (203) 775-2300

Grade Span: PK-12 **Schools**: *Regular* 4 ● *Spec Ed* 0 ● *Alt* 0 **Students**: 2,597 **Total Teachers**: 171 **Student/Classroom Teacher Ratio**: 16.0	**Expenditures/Student**: $7,403 **Librarians**: 3.0 866 students/librarian **Guidance Counselors**: 7.6 342 students/counselor	**% Amer Indian**: 0.0 **% Asian**: 3.4 **% Black**: 1.2 **% Hispanic**: 1.3 **% White**: 94.1	National ***Socio-Economic Status*** indicator percentile (100=high): 93rd

Fairfield County
DANBURY S.D.
63 BEAVER BROOK ROAD ● DANBURY CT 06810-6211 ● (203) 797-4701 ● http://www.danbury.org/org/dhs

Grade Span: PK-12 **Schools**: *Regular* 16 ● *Spec Ed* 0 ● *Alt* 1 **Students**: 8,659 **Total Teachers**: 590 **Student/Classroom Teacher Ratio**: 15.9	**Expenditures/Student**: $7,742 **Librarians**: 20.0 433 students/librarian **Guidance Counselors**: 16.0 541 students/counselor	**% Amer Indian**: 0.2 **% Asian**: 9.1 **% Black**: 12.5 **% Hispanic**: 17.7 **% White**: 60.4	National ***Socio-Economic Status*** indicator percentile (100=high): 37th

Fairfield County
DARIEN S.D.
2 RENSHAW ROAD, BOX 1167 ● DARIEN CT 06820-1167 ● (203) 656-7400

Grade Span: PK-12 **Schools**: *Regular* 7 ● *Spec Ed* 0 ● *Alt* 0 **Students**: 3,125 **Total Teachers**: 234 **Student/Classroom Teacher Ratio**: 15.6	**Expenditures/Student**: $9,940 **Librarians**: 6.3 496 students/librarian **Guidance Counselors**: 7.3 428 students/counselor	**% Amer Indian**: 0.0 **% Asian**: 3.7 **% Black**: 0.2 **% Hispanic**: 1.9 **% White**: 94.2	National ***Socio-Economic Status*** indicator percentile (100=high): 99th

Fairfield County
FAIRFIELD S.D.
BOX 220, 760 STILLSON ROAD ● FAIRFIELD CT 06430-0220 ● (203) 255-8371

Grade Span: PK-12 **Schools**: *Regular* 12 ● *Spec Ed* 0 ● *Alt* 0 **Students**: 7,186 **Total Teachers**: 518 **Student/Classroom Teacher Ratio**: 14.8	**Expenditures/Student**: $8,490 **Librarians**: 10.9 659 students/librarian **Guidance Counselors**: 13.4 536 students/counselor	**% Amer Indian**: 0.3 **% Asian**: 3.1 **% Black**: 1.4 **% Hispanic**: 2.7 **% White**: 92.6	National ***Socio-Economic Status*** indicator percentile (100=high): 88th

Fairfield County
GREENWICH S.D.
HAVEMEYER BUILDING ● GREENWICH CT 06830-6521 ● (203) 625-7425 ● http://gps.lhric.org

Grade Span: PK-12	**Expenditures/Student**: $11,103	**% Amer Indian**: 0.0	
Schools: *Regular* 14 ● *Spec Ed* 0 ● *Alt* 1	**Librarians**: 23.4	**% Asian**: 8.4	National ***Socio-Economic***
Students: 7,459	319 students/librarian	**% Black**: 3.2	***Status*** indicator percentile
Total Teachers: 578	**Guidance Counselors**: 22.5	**% Hispanic**: 8.3	(100=high): 85th
Student/Classroom Teacher Ratio: 14.8	332 students/counselor	**% White**: 80.1	

Fairfield County
MONROE S.D.
375 MONROE TURNPIKE ● MONROE CT 06468-2362 ● (203) 268-3914

Grade Span: PK-12	**Expenditures/Student**: $7,435	**% Amer Indian**: 0.1	
Schools: *Regular* 5 ● *Spec Ed* 0 ● *Alt* 0	**Librarians**: 2.0	**% Asian**: 1.7	National ***Socio-Economic***
Students: 3,541	1,771 students/librarian	**% Black**: 1.3	***Status*** indicator percentile
Total Teachers: 219	**Guidance Counselors**: 6.9	**% Hispanic**: 2.0	(100=high): 96th
Student/Classroom Teacher Ratio: 16.8	513 students/counselor	**% White**: 94.9	

Fairfield County
NEW CANAAN S.D.
39 LOCUST AVENUE ● NEW CANAAN CT 06840-4723 ● (203) 972-4400 ● http://www.i84.net/~mawdsley

Grade Span: PK-12	**Expenditures/Student**: $9,870	**% Amer Indian**: 0.0	
Schools: *Regular* 5 ● *Spec Ed* 0 ● *Alt* 0	**Librarians**: 6.5	**% Asian**: 1.8	National ***Socio-Economic***
Students: 3,018	464 students/librarian	**% Black**: 0.9	***Status*** indicator percentile
Total Teachers: 228	**Guidance Counselors**: 7.6	**% Hispanic**: 1.2	(100=high): 100th
Student/Classroom Teacher Ratio: 13.8	397 students/counselor	**% White**: 96.1	

Fairfield County
NEW FAIRFIELD S.D.
3 BRUSH HILL ROAD ● NEW FAIRFIELD CT 06812-2597 ● (203) 796-1842

Grade Span: PK-12	**Expenditures/Student**: $6,703	**% Amer Indian**: 0.2	
Schools: *Regular* 4 ● *Spec Ed* 0 ● *Alt* 0	**Librarians**: 3.0	**% Asian**: 2.3	National ***Socio-Economic***
Students: 2,656	885 students/librarian	**% Black**: 0.6	***Status*** indicator percentile
Total Teachers: 173	**Guidance Counselors**: 4.0	**% Hispanic**: 0.6	(100=high): 95th
Student/Classroom Teacher Ratio: 17.2	664 students/counselor	**% White**: 96.3	

Fairfield County
NEWTOWN S.D.
11 QUEEN STREET ● NEWTOWN CT 06470-2151 ● (203) 426-7621

Grade Span: PK-12	**Expenditures/Student**: $7,308	**% Amer Indian**: 0.0	
Schools: *Regular* 6 ● *Spec Ed* 0 ● *Alt* 0	**Librarians**: 5.0	**% Asian**: 1.3	National ***Socio-Economic***
Students: 3,984	797 students/librarian	**% Black**: 0.8	***Status*** indicator percentile
Total Teachers: 265	**Guidance Counselors**: 7.6	**% Hispanic**: 1.0	(100=high): 95th
Student/Classroom Teacher Ratio: 16.9	524 students/counselor	**% White**: 96.8	

Fairfield County
NORWALK S.D.
125 EAST AVENUE, BOX 6001 ● NORWALK CT 06852-6001 ● (203) 854-4001

Grade Span: PK-12	**Expenditures/Student**: $9,196	**% Amer Indian**: 0.1	
Schools: *Regular* 19 ● *Spec Ed* 0 ● *Alt* 2	**Librarians**: 4.0	**% Asian**: 3.3	National ***Socio-Economic***
Students: 10,455	2,614 students/librarian	**% Black**: 27.8	***Status*** indicator percentile
Total Teachers: 739	**Guidance Counselors**: 27.1	**% Hispanic**: 15.6	(100=high): 50th
Student/Classroom Teacher Ratio: 15.0	386 students/counselor	**% White**: 53.2	

Fairfield County
RIDGEFIELD S.D.
BOX 629, 40 FLORIDA ROAD ● RIDGEFIELD CT 06877-0629 ● (203) 544-9881

Grade Span: KG-12 **Schools**: *Regular* 6 ● *Spec Ed* 0 ● *Alt* 0 **Students**: 4,084 **Total Teachers**: 279 **Student/Classroom Teacher Ratio**: 15.4	**Expenditures/Student**: $8,949 **Librarians**: 9.0 454 students/librarian **Guidance Counselors**: 13.8 296 students/counselor	**% Amer Indian**: 0.1 **% Asian**: 2.1 **% Black**: 0.8 **% Hispanic**: 1.8 **% White**: 95.2	National ***Socio-Economic Status*** indicator percentile (100=high): 99th

Fairfield County
SHELTON S.D.
PO BOX 846, 124 MEADOW STREET ● SHELTON CT 06484-0846 ● (203) 924-1023

Grade Span: PK-12 **Schools**: *Regular* 8 ● *Spec Ed* 1 ● *Alt* 0 **Students**: 5,282 **Total Teachers**: 331 **Student/Classroom Teacher Ratio**: 17.7	**Expenditures/Student**: $7,044 **Librarians**: 2.0 2,641 students/librarian **Guidance Counselors**: 9.0 587 students/counselor	**% Amer Indian**: 0.1 **% Asian**: 2.6 **% Black**: 1.8 **% Hispanic**: 3.4 **% White**: 92.1	National ***Socio-Economic Status*** indicator percentile (100=high): 82nd

Fairfield County
STAMFORD S.D.
888 WASHINGTON BLVD, BOX 9310 ● STAMFORD CT 06901-9310 ● (203) 977-4105

Grade Span: PK-12 **Schools**: *Regular* 20 ● *Spec Ed* 0 ● *Alt* 1 **Students**: 13,932 **Total Teachers**: 1,017 **Student/Classroom Teacher Ratio**: 15.1	**Expenditures/Student**: $9,240 **Librarians**: 17.3 805 students/librarian **Guidance Counselors**: 27.0 516 students/counselor	**% Amer Indian**: 0.0 **% Asian**: 3.1 **% Black**: 34.4 **% Hispanic**: 17.0 **% White**: 45.5	National ***Socio-Economic Status*** indicator percentile (100=high): 43rd

Fairfield County
STRATFORD S.D.
1000 EAST BROADWAY ● STRATFORD CT 06497-5998 ● (203) 385-4210

Grade Span: PK-12 **Schools**: *Regular* 13 ● *Spec Ed* 0 ● *Alt* 0 **Students**: 6,743 **Total Teachers**: 431 **Student/Classroom Teacher Ratio**: 17.1	**Expenditures/Student**: $8,284 **Librarians**: 11.2 602 students/librarian **Guidance Counselors**: 12.5 539 students/counselor	**% Amer Indian**: 0.2 **% Asian**: 2.1 **% Black**: 15.8 **% Hispanic**: 6.3 **% White**: 75.6	National ***Socio-Economic Status*** indicator percentile (100=high): 52nd

Fairfield County
TRUMBULL S.D.
6254 MAIN STREET ● TRUMBULL CT 06611-2052 ● (203) 261-3801

Grade Span: PK-12 **Schools**: *Regular* 8 ● *Spec Ed* 0 ● *Alt* 2 **Students**: 5,275 **Total Teachers**: 333 **Student/Classroom Teacher Ratio**: 18.0	**Expenditures/Student**: $8,053 **Librarians**: 10.0 528 students/librarian **Guidance Counselors**: 14.6 361 students/counselor	**% Amer Indian**: 0.2 **% Asian**: 2.5 **% Black**: 2.5 **% Hispanic**: 2.5 **% White**: 92.2	National ***Socio-Economic Status*** indicator percentile (100=high): 96th

Fairfield County
WESTPORT S.D.
110 MYRTLE AVENUE ● WESTPORT CT 06880-3513 ● (203) 227-8451

Grade Span: PK-12 **Schools**: *Regular* 5 ● *Spec Ed* 1 ● *Alt* 0 **Students**: 3,797 **Total Teachers**: 303 **Student/Classroom Teacher Ratio**: 13.9	**Expenditures/Student**: $11,341 **Librarians**: 6.0 633 students/librarian **Guidance Counselors**: 5.6 678 students/counselor	**% Amer Indian**: 0.1 **% Asian**: 2.8 **% Black**: 1.1 **% Hispanic**: 1.9 **% White**: 94.1	National ***Socio-Economic Status*** indicator percentile (100=high): 97th

Fairfield County

WILTON S.D.

395 DANBURY ROAD, BOX 277 ● WILTON CT 06897-0277 ● (203) 762-3381

Grade Span: KG-12 **Schools**: *Regular* 5 ● *Spec Ed* 0 ● *Alt* 0 **Students**: 3,150 **Total Teachers**: 210 **Student/Classroom Teacher Ratio**: 16.0	**Expenditures/Student**: $9,012 **Librarians**: 6.0 525 students/librarian **Guidance Counselors**: 6.8 463 students/counselor	**% Amer Indian**: 0.0 **% Asian**: 3.1 **% Black**: 0.5 **% Hispanic**: 1.4 **% White**: 95.0	National ***Socio-Economic Status*** indicator percentile (100=high): na

Hartford County

BERLIN S.D.

240 KENSINGTON ROAD ● BERLIN CT 06037-2648 ● (860) 828-6581 ● http://www.berlinwall.org:3280

Grade Span: PK-12 **Schools**: *Regular* 5 ● *Spec Ed* 0 ● *Alt* 0 **Students**: 3,019 **Total Teachers**: 204 **Student/Classroom Teacher Ratio**: 15.6	**Expenditures/Student**: $7,332 **Librarians**: 4.8 629 students/librarian **Guidance Counselors**: 6.4 472 students/counselor	**% Amer Indian**: 0.0 **% Asian**: 2.6 **% Black**: 0.8 **% Hispanic**: 1.2 **% White**: 95.5	National ***Socio-Economic Status*** indicator percentile (100=high): 92nd

Hartford County

BRISTOL S.D.

129 CHURCH STREET, BOX 450 ● BRISTOL CT 06011-0450 ● (860) 584-7700 ● http://www.bristol.k12.ct.us

Grade Span: PK-12 **Schools**: *Regular* 15 ● *Spec Ed* 0 ● *Alt* 1 **Students**: 8,296 **Total Teachers**: 566 **Student/Classroom Teacher Ratio**: 15.4	**Expenditures/Student**: $7,368 **Librarians**: 5.8 1,430 students/librarian **Guidance Counselors**: 17.2 482 students/counselor	**% Amer Indian**: 0.1 **% Asian**: 1.8 **% Black**: 4.5 **% Hispanic**: 6.5 **% White**: 87.0	National ***Socio-Economic Status*** indicator percentile (100=high): 55th

Hartford County

EAST HARTFORD S.D.

31 SCHOOL STREET ● EAST HARTFORD CT 06108-2681 ● (860) 282-3107

Grade Span: KG-12 **Schools**: *Regular* 12 ● *Spec Ed* 0 ● *Alt* 2 **Students**: 6,798 **Total Teachers**: 455 **Student/Classroom Teacher Ratio**: 16.8	**Expenditures/Student**: $8,013 **Librarians**: 3.6 1,888 students/librarian **Guidance Counselors**: 10.0 680 students/counselor	**% Amer Indian**: 0.1 **% Asian**: 4.8 **% Black**: 26.2 **% Hispanic**: 18.5 **% White**: 50.4	National ***Socio-Economic Status*** indicator percentile (100=high): 28th

Hartford County

ENFIELD S.D.

27 SHAKER ROAD ● ENFIELD CT 06082-3199 ● (860) 741-3551

Grade Span: PK-12 **Schools**: *Regular* 13 ● *Spec Ed* 0 ● *Alt* 0 **Students**: 6,684 **Total Teachers**: 442 **Student/Classroom Teacher Ratio**: 15.5	**Expenditures/Student**: $7,817 **Librarians**: 5.0 1,337 students/librarian **Guidance Counselors**: 17.8 376 students/counselor	**% Amer Indian**: 0.3 **% Asian**: 2.0 **% Black**: 2.8 **% Hispanic**: 1.9 **% White**: 93.0	National ***Socio-Economic Status*** indicator percentile (100=high): 69th

Hartford County

FARMINGTON S.D.

1 MONTEITH DRIVE ● FARMINGTON CT 06032-1041 ● (860) 673-8268

Grade Span: PK-12 **Schools**: *Regular* 6 ● *Spec Ed* 0 ● *Alt* 0 **Students**: 3,575 **Total Teachers**: 235 **Student/Classroom Teacher Ratio**: 15.6	**Expenditures/Student**: $7,350 **Librarians**: 6.0 596 students/librarian **Guidance Counselors**: 8.6 416 students/counselor	**% Amer Indian**: 0.2 **% Asian**: 3.7 **% Black**: 5.4 **% Hispanic**: 1.8 **% White**: 88.8	National ***Socio-Economic Status*** indicator percentile (100=high): 90th

Hartford County
GLASTONBURY S.D.
232 WILLIAMS STREET ● GLASTONBURY CT 06033-2354 ● (860) 652-7961

Grade Span: PK-12 **Schools**: *Regular* 8 ● *Spec Ed* 0 ● *Alt* 0 **Students**: 5,268 **Total Teachers**: 347 **Student/Classroom Teacher Ratio**: 16.0	**Expenditures/Student**: $7,647 **Librarians**: 9.0 585 students/librarian **Guidance Counselors**: 12.3 428 students/counselor	**% Amer Indian**: 0.2 **% Asian**: 4.1 **% Black**: 3.4 **% Hispanic**: 3.9 **% White**: 88.4	National ***Socio-Economic Status*** indicator percentile (100=high): 91st

Hartford County
HARTFORD S.D.
249 HIGH STREET ● HARTFORD CT 06103-1095 ● (860) 722-8500 ● http://www.ntplx.net/~hphs

Grade Span: PK-12 **Schools**: *Regular* 33 ● *Spec Ed* 1 ● *Alt* 1 **Students**: 23,791 **Total Teachers**: 1,676 **Student/Classroom Teacher Ratio**: 14.9	**Expenditures/Student**: $10,082 **Librarians**: 22.6 1,053 students/librarian **Guidance Counselors**: 36.2 657 students/counselor	**% Amer Indian**: 0.1 **% Asian**: 1.1 **% Black**: 42.9 **% Hispanic**: 51.1 **% White**: 4.8	National ***Socio-Economic Status*** indicator percentile (100=high): 6th

Hartford County
MANCHESTER S.D.
45 NORTH SCHOOL STREET ● MANCHESTER CT 06040-2022 ● (860) 647-3441

Grade Span: PK-12 **Schools**: *Regular* 13 ● *Spec Ed* 2 ● *Alt* 0 **Students**: 7,754 **Total Teachers**: 507 **Student/Classroom Teacher Ratio**: 17.1	**Expenditures/Student**: $7,813 **Librarians**: 7.6 1,020 students/librarian **Guidance Counselors**: 16.8 462 students/counselor	**% Amer Indian**: 0.2 **% Asian**: 2.6 **% Black**: 14.6 **% Hispanic**: 8.0 **% White**: 74.6	National ***Socio-Economic Status*** indicator percentile (100=high): 51st

Hartford County
NEW BRITAIN S.D.
1 LIBERTY SQUARE ● NEW BRITAIN CT 06051-2641 ● (860) 827-2204

Grade Span: PK-12 **Schools**: *Regular* 14 ● *Spec Ed* 0 ● *Alt* 0 **Students**: 9,241 **Total Teachers**: 589 **Student/Classroom Teacher Ratio**: 17.8	**Expenditures/Student**: $8,391 **Librarians**: 10.8 856 students/librarian **Guidance Counselors**: 16.0 578 students/counselor	**% Amer Indian**: 0.1 **% Asian**: 2.8 **% Black**: 15.5 **% Hispanic**: 46.1 **% White**: 35.6	National ***Socio-Economic Status*** indicator percentile (100=high): 11th

Hartford County
NEWINGTON S.D.
131 CEDAR STREET ● NEWINGTON CT 06111-2698 ● (860) 667-2000

Grade Span: PK-12 **Schools**: *Regular* 7 ● *Spec Ed* 0 ● *Alt* 0 **Students**: 4,052 **Total Teachers**: 266 **Student/Classroom Teacher Ratio**: 15.3	**Expenditures/Student**: $8,073 **Librarians**: 8.0 507 students/librarian **Guidance Counselors**: 11.6 349 students/counselor	**% Amer Indian**: 0.1 **% Asian**: 3.8 **% Black**: 3.6 **% Hispanic**: 3.5 **% White**: 89.0	National ***Socio-Economic Status*** indicator percentile (100=high): 85th

Hartford County
PLAINVILLE S.D.
47 ROBERT HOLCOMB WAY ● PLAINVILLE CT 06062-2398 ● (860) 793-3202

Grade Span: PK-12 **Schools**: *Regular* 5 ● *Spec Ed* 0 ● *Alt* 0 **Students**: 2,543 **Total Teachers**: 172 **Student/Classroom Teacher Ratio**: 15.6	**Expenditures/Student**: $8,076 **Librarians**: 3.0 848 students/librarian **Guidance Counselors**: 6.0 424 students/counselor	**% Amer Indian**: 0.4 **% Asian**: 1.5 **% Black**: 5.5 **% Hispanic**: 3.4 **% White**: 89.3	National ***Socio-Economic Status*** indicator percentile (100=high): 69th

Hartford County

SIMSBURY S.D.

933 HOPMEADOW STREET ● SIMSBURY CT 06070-1897 ● (860) 651-3361 ● http://www.simsbury.org

Grade Span: PK-12 **Schools**: *Regular* 7 ● *Spec Ed* 0 ● *Alt* 0 **Students**: 4,286 **Total Teachers**: 286 **Student/Classroom Teacher Ratio**: 16.1	**Expenditures/Student**: $7,375 **Librarians**: 6.0 714 students/librarian **Guidance Counselors**: 10.1 424 students/counselor	**% Amer Indian**: 0.0 **% Asian**: 2.6 **% Black**: 2.2 **% Hispanic**: 0.9 **% White**: 94.3	National ***Socio-Economic Status*** indicator percentile (100=high): 89th

Hartford County

SOUTH WINDSOR S.D.

1737 MAIN STREET ● SOUTH WINDSOR CT 06074-1093 ● (860) 291-1205

Grade Span: PK-12 **Schools**: *Regular* 7 ● *Spec Ed* 0 ● *Alt* 0 **Students**: 4,351 **Total Teachers**: 282 **Student/Classroom Teacher Ratio**: 16.8	**Expenditures/Student**: $7,624 **Librarians**: 3.0 1,450 students/librarian **Guidance Counselors**: 10.0 435 students/counselor	**% Amer Indian**: 0.6 **% Asian**: 3.3 **% Black**: 3.2 **% Hispanic**: 1.7 **% White**: 91.2	National ***Socio-Economic Status*** indicator percentile (100=high): 89th

Hartford County

SOUTHINGTON S.D.

49 BEECHER STREET ● SOUTHINGTON CT 06489-3097 ● (860) 628-3202 ● http://www.sboe.k12.southington.ct.us

Grade Span: PK-12 **Schools**: *Regular* 12 ● *Spec Ed* 0 ● *Alt* 0 **Students**: 6,441 **Total Teachers**: 450 **Student/Classroom Teacher Ratio**: 15.7	**Expenditures/Student**: $7,118 **Librarians**: 10.0 644 students/librarian **Guidance Counselors**: 17.7 364 students/counselor	**% Amer Indian**: 0.1 **% Asian**: 1.4 **% Black**: 1.4 **% Hispanic**: 2.1 **% White**: 95.0	National ***Socio-Economic Status*** indicator percentile (100=high): 86th

Hartford County

WEST HARTFORD S.D.

28 SOUTH MAIN STREET ● WEST HARTFORD CT 06107-2447 ● (860) 523-3500 ● http://www.connix.com/~cbacon

Grade Span: KG-12 **Schools**: *Regular* 15 ● *Spec Ed* 0 ● *Alt* 0 **Students**: 8,477 **Total Teachers**: 578 **Student/Classroom Teacher Ratio**: 15.1	**Expenditures/Student**: $8,209 **Librarians**: 17.0 499 students/librarian **Guidance Counselors**: 18.0 471 students/counselor	**% Amer Indian**: 0.2 **% Asian**: 5.6 **% Black**: 6.5 **% Hispanic**: 8.9 **% White**: 78.7	National ***Socio-Economic Status*** indicator percentile (100=high): 72nd

Hartford County

WETHERSFIELD S.D.

51 WILLOW STREET ● WETHERSFIELD CT 06109-2798 ● (860) 563-8181

Grade Span: PK-12 **Schools**: *Regular* 7 ● *Spec Ed* 0 ● *Alt* 0 **Students**: 3,090 **Total Teachers**: 218 **Student/Classroom Teacher Ratio**: 16.9	**Expenditures/Student**: $9,221 **Librarians**: 2.0 1,545 students/librarian **Guidance Counselors**: 7.0 441 students/counselor	**% Amer Indian**: 0.2 **% Asian**: 2.3 **% Black**: 2.7 **% Hispanic**: 4.9 **% White**: 90.0	National ***Socio-Economic Status*** indicator percentile (100=high): 87th

Hartford County

WINDSOR S.D.

601 MATIANUK AVENUE, BOX 10 ● WINDSOR CT 06095-0010 ● (860) 688-3631 ● http://www.hs.windsor.k12.ct.us

Grade Span: PK-12 **Schools**: *Regular* 6 ● *Spec Ed* 0 ● *Alt* 0 **Students**: 4,467 **Total Teachers**: 291 **Student/Classroom Teacher Ratio**: 16.8	**Expenditures/Student**: $6,784 **Librarians**: 6.4 698 students/librarian **Guidance Counselors**: 10.0 447 students/counselor	**% Amer Indian**: 0.2 **% Asian**: 3.2 **% Black**: 33.3 **% Hispanic**: 5.6 **% White**: 57.6	National ***Socio-Economic Status*** indicator percentile (100=high): 72nd

Litchfield County

NEW MILFORD S.D.

50 EAST STREET ● NEW MILFORD CT 06776-3099 ● (860) 355-8406 ● http://k12.wcsu.ctstateu.edu/~nm_page/index.html

Grade Span: PK-12 **Schools**: *Regular* 5 ● *Spec Ed* 0 ● *Alt* 0 **Students**: 4,660 **Total Teachers**: 298 **Student/Classroom Teacher Ratio**: 16.5	**Expenditures/Student**: $7,174 **Librarians**: 3.2 1,456 students/librarian **Guidance Counselors**: 12.5 373 students/counselor	**% Amer Indian**: 0.6 **% Asian**: 2.3 **% Black**: 1.9 **% Hispanic**: 1.6 **% White**: 93.5	National ***Socio-Economic Status*** indicator percentile (100=high): 84th

Litchfield County

TORRINGTON S.D.

355 MIGEON AVENUE ● TORRINGTON CT 06790-4822 ● (860) 489-2327 ● http://www.torrington.org

Grade Span: PK-12 **Schools**: *Regular* 8 ● *Spec Ed* 0 ● *Alt* 0 **Students**: 4,867 **Total Teachers**: 299 **Student/Classroom Teacher Ratio**: 17.5	**Expenditures/Student**: $7,012 **Librarians**: 4.0 1,217 students/librarian **Guidance Counselors**: 10.0 487 students/counselor	**% Amer Indian**: 0.5 **% Asian**: 2.3 **% Black**: 3.3 **% Hispanic**: 2.4 **% White**: 91.4	National ***Socio-Economic Status*** indicator percentile (100=high): 58th

Litchfield County

WATERTOWN S.D.

10 DEFOREST STREET ● WATERTOWN CT 06795-2190 ● (860) 945-4801

Grade Span: PK-12 **Schools**: *Regular* 7 ● *Spec Ed* 0 ● *Alt* 0 **Students**: 3,486 **Total Teachers**: 223 **Student/Classroom Teacher Ratio**: 16.5	**Expenditures/Student**: $6,673 **Librarians**: 2.0 1,743 students/librarian **Guidance Counselors**: 5.5 634 students/counselor	**% Amer Indian**: 0.2 **% Asian**: 1.2 **% Black**: 0.7 **% Hispanic**: 1.4 **% White**: 96.6	National ***Socio-Economic Status*** indicator percentile (100=high): 78th

Middlesex County

MIDDLETOWN S.D.

311 HUNTING HILL AVENUE ● MIDDLETOWN CT 06457-4356 ● (860) 638-1401

Grade Span: PK-12 **Schools**: *Regular* 12 ● *Spec Ed* 0 ● *Alt* 0 **Students**: 4,710 **Total Teachers**: 325 **Student/Classroom Teacher Ratio**: 15.1	**Expenditures/Student**: $8,192 **Librarians**: 5.0 942 students/librarian **Guidance Counselors**: 8.0 589 students/counselor	**% Amer Indian**: 0.1 **% Asian**: 3.1 **% Black**: 25.6 **% Hispanic**: 8.1 **% White**: 63.1	National ***Socio-Economic Status*** indicator percentile (100=high): 32nd

New Haven County

BRANFORD S.D.

1111 MAIN STREET ● BRANFORD CT 06405-3698 ● (203) 488-7276

Grade Span: KG-12 **Schools**: *Regular* 6 ● *Spec Ed* 0 ● *Alt* 0 **Students**: 3,613 **Total Teachers**: 248 **Student/Classroom Teacher Ratio**: 16.3	**Expenditures/Student**: $7,651 **Librarians**: 7.0 516 students/librarian **Guidance Counselors**: 8.0 452 students/counselor	**% Amer Indian**: 0.3 **% Asian**: 3.4 **% Black**: 2.1 **% Hispanic**: 1.8 **% White**: 92.4	National ***Socio-Economic Status*** indicator percentile (100=high): 74th

New Haven County

CHESHIRE S.D.

29 MAIN STREET ● CHESHIRE CT 06410-2495 ● (203) 250-2430 ● http://www.pcnet.com/~cheshigh

Grade Span: PK-12 **Schools**: *Regular* 7 ● *Spec Ed* 1 ● *Alt* 0 **Students**: 4,513 **Total Teachers**: 307 **Student/Classroom Teacher Ratio**: 15.8	**Expenditures/Student**: $7,971 **Librarians**: 6.0 752 students/librarian **Guidance Counselors**: 13.3 339 students/counselor	**% Amer Indian**: 0.1 **% Asian**: 3.1 **% Black**: 1.1 **% Hispanic**: 0.7 **% White**: 95.0	National ***Socio-Economic Status*** indicator percentile (100=high): 96th

New Haven County

EAST HAVEN S.D.

HUDSON STREET ● EAST HAVEN CT 06512-1597 ● (203) 468-3261 ● http://www.connix.com/easthavenhighschool

Grade Span: PK-12 **Schools**: *Regular* 10 ● *Spec Ed* 0 ● *Alt* 0 **Students**: 3,905 **Total Teachers**: 235 **Student/Classroom Teacher Ratio**: 18.4	**Expenditures/Student**: $7,502 **Librarians**: 6.6 592 students/librarian **Guidance Counselors**: 7.0 558 students/counselor	**% Amer Indian**: 0.3 **% Asian**: 1.7 **% Black**: 0.9 **% Hispanic**: 3.4 **% White**: 93.7	National ***Socio-Economic Status*** indicator percentile (100=high): 56th

New Haven County

GUILFORD S.D.

BOX 367, NEW ENGLAND ROAD ● GUILFORD CT 06437-0367 ● (203) 453-8200 ● http://www.guilford.k12.ct.us

Grade Span: PK-12 **Schools**: *Regular* 7 ● *Spec Ed* 0 ● *Alt* 0 **Students**: 3,492 **Total Teachers**: 238 **Student/Classroom Teacher Ratio**: 16.5	**Expenditures/Student**: $7,839 **Librarians**: 7.0 499 students/librarian **Guidance Counselors**: 8.6 406 students/counselor	**% Amer Indian**: 0.1 **% Asian**: 1.5 **% Black**: 1.1 **% Hispanic**: 1.5 **% White**: 95.7	National ***Socio-Economic Status*** indicator percentile (100=high): 95th

New Haven County

HAMDEN S.D.

60 PUTNAM AVENUE ● HAMDEN CT 06517-2825 ● (203) 288-8473

Grade Span: PK-12 **Schools**: *Regular* 11 ● *Spec Ed* 0 ● *Alt* 0 **Students**: 6,267 **Total Teachers**: 423 **Student/Classroom Teacher Ratio**: 16.1	**Expenditures/Student**: $8,819 **Librarians**: 11.0 570 students/librarian **Guidance Counselors**: 9.0 696 students/counselor	**% Amer Indian**: 0.1 **% Asian**: 3.2 **% Black**: 20.3 **% Hispanic**: 3.7 **% White**: 72.7	National ***Socio-Economic Status*** indicator percentile (100=high): 57th

New Haven County

MADISON S.D.

10 CAMPUS DRIVE, DRAWER 71 ● MADISON CT 06443-2562 ● (203) 245-6300

Grade Span: PK-12 **Schools**: *Regular* 6 ● *Spec Ed* 0 ● *Alt* 0 **Students**: 2,950 **Total Teachers**: 195 **Student/Classroom Teacher Ratio**: 16.6	**Expenditures/Student**: $8,211 **Librarians**: 4.0 738 students/librarian **Guidance Counselors**: 6.6 447 students/counselor	**% Amer Indian**: 0.1 **% Asian**: 1.4 **% Black**: 0.6 **% Hispanic**: 0.9 **% White**: 97.1	National ***Socio-Economic Status*** indicator percentile (100=high): 98th

New Haven County

MERIDEN S.D.

22 LIBERTY STREET, BOX 848 ● MERIDEN CT 06450-0848 ● (203) 630-4171

Grade Span: PK-12 **Schools**: *Regular* 12 ● *Spec Ed* 0 ● *Alt* 1 **Students**: 8,342 **Total Teachers**: 542 **Student/Classroom Teacher Ratio**: 16.8	**Expenditures/Student**: $7,759 **Librarians**: 10.0 834 students/librarian **Guidance Counselors**: 23.0 363 students/counselor	**% Amer Indian**: 0.1 **% Asian**: 1.7 **% Black**: 9.5 **% Hispanic**: 30.2 **% White**: 58.5	National ***Socio-Economic Status*** indicator percentile (100=high): 31st

New Haven County

[MIDDLEBURY] **REGIONAL S.D. 15**

286 WHITTEMORE ROAD, BOX 395 ● MIDDLEBURY CT 06762-0395 ● (203) 758-8258

Grade Span: PK-12 **Schools**: *Regular* 6 ● *Spec Ed* 0 ● *Alt* 0 **Students**: 3,553 **Total Teachers**: 231 **Student/Classroom Teacher Ratio**: 16.1	**Expenditures/Student**: $7,709 **Librarians**: 6.0 592 students/librarian **Guidance Counselors**: 11.2 317 students/counselor	**% Amer Indian**: 0.2 **% Asian**: 1.9 **% Black**: 0.3 **% Hispanic**: 1.3 **% White**: 96.3	National ***Socio-Economic Status*** indicator percentile (100=high): 96th

New Haven County

MILFORD S.D.

70 WEST RIVER STREET ● MILFORD CT 06460-3364 ● (203) 783-3401

Grade Span: PK-12 **Schools**: *Regular* 14 ● *Spec Ed* 0 ● *Alt* 0 **Students**: 7,089 **Total Teachers**: 474 **Student/Classroom Teacher Ratio**: 15.7	**Expenditures/Student**: $8,358 **Librarians**: 11.6 611 students/librarian **Guidance Counselors**: 12.0 591 students/counselor	**% Amer Indian**: 0.2 **% Asian**: 2.0 **% Black**: 2.3 **% Hispanic**: 2.7 **% White**: 92.8	National ***Socio-Economic Status*** indicator percentile (100=high): 68th

New Haven County

NAUGATUCK S.D.

380 CHURCH STREET ● NAUGATUCK CT 06770-2887 ● (203) 720-5265

Grade Span: PK-12 **Schools**: *Regular* 12 ● *Spec Ed* 0 ● *Alt* 0 **Students**: 5,673 **Total Teachers**: 317 **Student/Classroom Teacher Ratio**: 18.2	**Expenditures/Student**: $6,869 **Librarians**: 3.8 1,493 students/librarian **Guidance Counselors**: 10.0 567 students/counselor	**% Amer Indian**: 0.4 **% Asian**: 1.2 **% Black**: 3.5 **% Hispanic**: 3.6 **% White**: 91.4	National ***Socio-Economic Status*** indicator percentile (100=high): 58th

New Haven County

NEW HAVEN S.D.

54 MEADOW STREET ● NEW HAVEN CT 06519-1743 ● (203) 787-8888 ● http://www.nhps.com

Grade Span: PK-12 **Schools**: *Regular* 38 ● *Spec Ed* 1 ● *Alt* 7 **Students**: 18,777 **Total Teachers**: 1,230 **Student/Classroom Teacher Ratio**: 17.7	**Expenditures/Student**: $9,136 **Librarians**: 21.0 894 students/librarian **Guidance Counselors**: 34.0 552 students/counselor	**% Amer Indian**: 0.0 **% Asian**: 1.9 **% Black**: 58.6 **% Hispanic**: 26.6 **% White**: 12.9	National ***Socio-Economic Status*** indicator percentile (100=high): 3rd

New Haven County

NORTH HAVEN S.D.

5 LINSLEY STREET ● NORTH HAVEN CT 06473-2586 ● (203) 239-2581 ● http://www.connix.com/~nhhlmc

Grade Span: PK-12 **Schools**: *Regular* 6 ● *Spec Ed* 0 ● *Alt* 0 **Students**: 3,337 **Total Teachers**: 233 **Student/Classroom Teacher Ratio**: 14.9	**Expenditures/Student**: $8,286 **Librarians**: 7.8 428 students/librarian **Guidance Counselors**: 7.6 439 students/counselor	**% Amer Indian**: 0.2 **% Asian**: 3.7 **% Black**: 3.0 **% Hispanic**: 1.6 **% White**: 91.5	National ***Socio-Economic Status*** indicator percentile (100=high): 87th

New Haven County

SEYMOUR S.D.

98 BANK STREET, ANNEX BUILDING ● SEYMOUR CT 06483-2892 ● (203) 888-4565

Grade Span: PK-12 **Schools**: *Regular* 5 ● *Spec Ed* 0 ● *Alt* 0 **Students**: 2,554 **Total Teachers**: 152 **Student/Classroom Teacher Ratio**: 17.5	**Expenditures/Student**: $6,604 **Librarians**: 1.0 2,554 students/librarian **Guidance Counselors**: 6.0 426 students/counselor	**% Amer Indian**: 0.2 **% Asian**: 1.6 **% Black**: 1.4 **% Hispanic**: 2.3 **% White**: 94.5	National ***Socio-Economic Status*** indicator percentile (100=high): 72nd

New Haven County

WALLINGFORD S.D.

142 HOPE HILL ROAD ● WALLINGFORD CT 06492-2254 ● (203) 949-6500

Grade Span: PK-12 **Schools**: *Regular* 11 ● *Spec Ed* 0 ● *Alt* 0 **Students**: 6,786 **Total Teachers**: 448 **Student/Classroom Teacher Ratio**: 16.4	**Expenditures/Student**: $7,434 **Librarians**: 10.5 646 students/librarian **Guidance Counselors**: 13.5 503 students/counselor	**% Amer Indian**: 0.2 **% Asian**: 1.9 **% Black**: 1.4 **% Hispanic**: 4.3 **% White**: 92.2	National ***Socio-Economic Status*** indicator percentile (100=high): 77th

New Haven County

WATERBURY S.D.

236 GRAND STREET ● WATERBURY CT 06702-1972 ● (203) 574-8004

Grade Span: PK-12 **Schools**: *Regular* 25 ● *Spec Ed* 1 ● *Alt* 0 **Students**: 14,315 **Total Teachers**: 1,001 **Student/Classroom Teacher Ratio**: 15.6	**Expenditures/Student**: $8,631 **Librarians**: 16.6 862 students/librarian **Guidance Counselors**: 16.0 895 students/counselor	**% Amer Indian**: 0.3 **% Asian**: 1.4 **% Black**: 24.9 **% Hispanic**: 33.0 **% White**: 40.4	National ***Socio-Economic Status*** indicator percentile (100=high): 9th

New Haven County

WEST HAVEN S.D.

25 OGDEN STREET ● WEST HAVEN CT 06516-1800 ● (203) 934-6631

Grade Span: PK-12 **Schools**: *Regular* 12 ● *Spec Ed* 0 ● *Alt* 0 **Students**: 7,308 **Total Teachers**: 441 **Student/Classroom Teacher Ratio**: 17.6	**Expenditures/Student**: $7,592 **Librarians**: 9.0 812 students/librarian **Guidance Counselors**: 10.4 703 students/counselor	**% Amer Indian**: 0.4 **% Asian**: 2.2 **% Black**: 23.7 **% Hispanic**: 8.9 **% White**: 64.8	National ***Socio-Economic Status*** indicator percentile (100=high): 27th

New Haven County

WOLCOTT S.D.

154 CENTER STREET ● WOLCOTT CT 06716-2035 ● (203) 879-8180

Grade Span: PK-12 **Schools**: *Regular* 5 ● *Spec Ed* 0 ● *Alt* 0 **Students**: 2,814 **Total Teachers**: 180 **Student/Classroom Teacher Ratio**: 17.0	**Expenditures/Student**: $6,863 **Librarians**: 2.0 1,407 students/librarian **Guidance Counselors**: 7.3 385 students/counselor	**% Amer Indian**: 0.2 **% Asian**: 0.9 **% Black**: 1.8 **% Hispanic**: 1.0 **% White**: 96.2	National ***Socio-Economic Status*** indicator percentile (100=high): 80th

New London County

EAST LYME S.D.

BOX 176, BOSTON POST ROAD ● EAST LYME CT 06333-0176 ● (860) 739-3966

Grade Span: PK-12 **Schools**: *Regular* 5 ● *Spec Ed* 0 ● *Alt* 0 **Students**: 2,844 **Total Teachers**: 193 **Student/Classroom Teacher Ratio**: 16.3	**Expenditures/Student**: $7,302 **Librarians**: 5.6 508 students/librarian **Guidance Counselors**: 7.0 406 students/counselor	**% Amer Indian**: 0.9 **% Asian**: 2.4 **% Black**: 1.1 **% Hispanic**: 1.4 **% White**: 94.3	National ***Socio-Economic Status*** indicator percentile (100=high): 90th

New London County

GROTON S.D.

PO BOX K ● GROTON CT 06340-1411 ● (860) 572-5840 ● http://www.groton.k12.ct.us

Grade Span: PK-12 **Schools**: *Regular* 14 ● *Spec Ed* 0 ● *Alt* 0 **Students**: 6,143 **Total Teachers**: 446 **Student/Classroom Teacher Ratio**: 14.7	**Expenditures/Student**: $7,956 **Librarians**: 15.0 410 students/librarian **Guidance Counselors**: 10.0 614 students/counselor	**% Amer Indian**: 0.5 **% Asian**: 3.0 **% Black**: 11.6 **% Hispanic**: 4.8 **% White**: 80.1	National ***Socio-Economic Status*** indicator percentile (100=high): 49th

New London County

LEDYARD S.D.

4 BLONDER BOULEVARD ● LEDYARD CT 06339-1504 ● (860) 464-9255 ● http://www.ledyardschools.org

Grade Span: PK-12 **Schools**: *Regular* 6 ● *Spec Ed* 0 ● *Alt* 0 **Students**: 3,140 **Total Teachers**: 209 **Student/Classroom Teacher Ratio**: 16.0	**Expenditures/Student**: $7,141 **Librarians**: 4.0 785 students/librarian **Guidance Counselors**: 9.0 349 students/counselor	**% Amer Indian**: 2.6 **% Asian**: 2.4 **% Black**: 3.5 **% Hispanic**: 2.2 **% White**: 89.4	National ***Socio-Economic Status*** indicator percentile (100=high): 98th

New London County

NEW LONDON S.D.

134 WILLIAMS STREET ● NEW LONDON CT 06320-5296 ● (860) 447-1435

Grade Span: KG-12 **Schools**: *Regular* 8 ● *Spec Ed* 1 ● *Alt* 0 **Students**: 2,944 **Total Teachers**: 229 **Student/Classroom Teacher Ratio**: 13.7	**Expenditures/Student**: $9,845 **Librarians**: 2.0 1,472 students/librarian **Guidance Counselors**: 7.0 421 students/counselor	**% Amer Indian**: 0.7 **% Asian**: 1.3 **% Black**: 37.0 **% Hispanic**: 30.5 **% White**: 30.4	National ***Socio-Economic Status*** indicator percentile (100=high): 7th

New London County

NORWICH S.D.

MAHAN DRIVE ● NORWICH CT 06360-2498 ● (860) 823-4245

Grade Span: PK-08 **Schools**: *Regular* 12 ● *Spec Ed* 0 ● *Alt* 1 **Students**: 4,330 **Total Teachers**: 292 **Student/Classroom Teacher Ratio**: 16.1	**Expenditures/Student**: $7,953 **Librarians**: 7.0 619 students/librarian **Guidance Counselors**: 7.0 619 students/counselor	**% Amer Indian**: 1.5 **% Asian**: 1.4 **% Black**: 13.0 **% Hispanic**: 8.2 **% White**: 75.8	National ***Socio-Economic Status*** indicator percentile (100=high): 23rd

New London County

[OAKDALE] **MONTVILLE S.D.**

OLD COLCHESTER ROAD ● OAKDALE CT 06370-0078 ● (860) 848-1228

Grade Span: PK-12 **Schools**: *Regular* 5 ● *Spec Ed* 0 ● *Alt* 2 **Students**: 2,802 **Total Teachers**: 194 **Student/Classroom Teacher Ratio**: 15.5	**Expenditures/Student**: $7,950 **Librarians**: 5.0 560 students/librarian **Guidance Counselors**: 6.3 445 students/counselor	**% Amer Indian**: 1.5 **% Asian**: 1.4 **% Black**: 3.4 **% Hispanic**: 2.6 **% White**: 91.1	National ***Socio-Economic Status*** indicator percentile (100=high): 75th

New London County

WATERFORD S.D.

15 ROPE FERRY ROAD ● WATERFORD CT 06385-2886 ● (860) 444-5801

Grade Span: KG-12 **Schools**: *Regular* 8 ● *Spec Ed* 0 ● *Alt* 0 **Students**: 2,657 **Total Teachers**: 210 **Student/Classroom Teacher Ratio**: 12.6	**Expenditures/Student**: $10,521 **Librarians**: 3.0 886 students/librarian **Guidance Counselors**: 7.0 380 students/counselor	**% Amer Indian**: 0.5 **% Asian**: 2.7 **% Black**: 3.4 **% Hispanic**: 1.2 **% White**: 92.1	National ***Socio-Economic Status*** indicator percentile (100=high): 67th

Tolland County

VERNON S.D.

30 PARK STREET, BOX 600 ● VERNON CT 06066-3244 ● (860) 872-7361

Grade Span: PK-12 **Schools**: *Regular* 7 ● *Spec Ed* 1 ● *Alt* 0 **Students**: 4,188 **Total Teachers**: 310 **Student/Classroom Teacher Ratio**: 14.8	**Expenditures/Student**: $8,024 **Librarians**: 0.9 4,653 students/librarian **Guidance Counselors**: 9.6 436 students/counselor	**% Amer Indian**: 0.6 **% Asian**: 3.7 **% Black**: 5.7 **% Hispanic**: 3.9 **% White**: 86.0	National ***Socio-Economic Status*** indicator percentile (100=high): 55th

Windham County

[CENTRAL VILLAGE] **PLAINFIELD S.D.**

99 PUTNAM ROAD, BOX 705 ● CENTRAL VILLAGE CT 06332-0705 ● (860) 564-6403

Grade Span: PK-12 **Schools**: *Regular* 5 ● *Spec Ed* 0 ● *Alt* 0 **Students**: 2,903 **Total Teachers**: 195 **Student/Classroom Teacher Ratio**: 15.3	**Expenditures/Student**: $6,950 **Librarians**: 2.0 1,452 students/librarian **Guidance Counselors**: 8.0 363 students/counselor	**% Amer Indian**: 0.4 **% Asian**: 0.6 **% Black**: 1.9 **% Hispanic**: 2.0 **% White**: 95.1	National ***Socio-Economic Status*** indicator percentile (100=high): 56th

Windham County

[DANIELSON] **KILLINGLY S.D.**

PO BOX 210, 369 MAIN STREET ● DANIELSON CT 06239-0210 ● (860) 774-9034

Grade Span: KG-12 **Schools**: *Regular* 5 ● *Spec Ed* 0 ● *Alt* 0 **Students**: 3,059 **Total Teachers**: 210 **Student/Classroom Teacher Ratio**: 14.3	**Expenditures/Student**: $7,638 **Librarians**: 3.8 805 students/librarian **Guidance Counselors**: 7.4 413 students/counselor	**% Amer Indian**: 0.7 **% Asian**: 2.3 **% Black**: 1.9 **% Hispanic**: 1.5 **% White**: 93.6	National ***Socio-Economic Status*** indicator percentile (100=high): 47th

Windham County

[WILLIMANTIC] **WINDHAM S.D.**

322 PROSPECT STREET ● WILLIMANTIC CT 06226-2202 ● (860) 465-2300 ● http://www.windham.k12.ct.us

Grade Span: KG-12 **Schools**: *Regular* 7 ● *Spec Ed* 0 ● *Alt* 0 **Students**: 3,446 **Total Teachers**: 279 **Student/Classroom Teacher Ratio**: 12.7	**Expenditures/Student**: $9,138 **Librarians**: 2.0 1,723 students/librarian **Guidance Counselors**: 9.0 383 students/counselor	**% Amer Indian**: 0.1 **% Asian**: 0.9 **% Black**: 4.7 **% Hispanic**: 39.3 **% White**: 55.1	National ***Socio-Economic Status*** indicator percentile (100=high): 14th

Kent County

[CAMDEN-WYOMING] **CAESAR RODNEY S.D.**

OLD NORTH ROAD BOX 188 ● CAMDEN-WYOMING DE 19934-0188 ● (302) 697-2173

Grade Span: PK-12 **Schools**: *Regular* 11 ● *Spec Ed* 1 ● *Alt* 0 **Students**: 6,580 **Total Teachers**: 392 **Student/Classroom Teacher Ratio**: 17.5	**Expenditures/Student**: $6,123 **Librarians**: 10.0 658 students/librarian **Guidance Counselors**: 14.5 454 students/counselor	**% Amer Indian**: 0.3 **% Asian**: 2.1 **% Black**: 23.3 **% Hispanic**: 2.9 **% White**: 71.4	National ***Socio-Economic Status*** indicator percentile (100=high): 56th

Kent County

[DOVER] **CAPITAL S.D.**

945 FOREST STREET ● DOVER DE 19901-3498 ● (302) 672-1556

Grade Span: PK-12 **Schools**: *Regular* 9 ● *Spec Ed* 2 ● *Alt* 0 **Students**: 6,313 **Total Teachers**: 372 **Student/Classroom Teacher Ratio**: 17.1	**Expenditures/Student**: $6,090 **Librarians**: 3.0 2,104 students/librarian **Guidance Counselors**: 8.0 789 students/counselor	**% Amer Indian**: 0.8 **% Asian**: 1.6 **% Black**: 39.5 **% Hispanic**: 2.9 **% White**: 55.2	National ***Socio-Economic Status*** indicator percentile (100=high): 37th

Kent County

[FELTON] **LAKE FOREST S.D.**

R.D. 12 ● FELTON DE 19943-9801 ● (302) 284-3020

Grade Span: PK-12 **Schools**: *Regular* 5 ● *Spec Ed* 1 ● *Alt* 0 **Students**: 3,525 **Total Teachers**: 229 **Student/Classroom Teacher Ratio**: 17.1	**Expenditures/Student**: $6,370 **Librarians**: 3.0 1,175 students/librarian **Guidance Counselors**: 9.0 392 students/counselor	**% Amer Indian**: 0.1 **% Asian**: 1.2 **% Black**: 20.3 **% Hispanic**: 1.2 **% White**: 77.3	National ***Socio-Economic Status*** indicator percentile (100=high): 37th

Kent County

MILFORD S.D.

906 LAKEVIEW AVENUE ● MILFORD DE 19963-1799 ● (302) 422-1600 ● http://www.k12.de.us/k12/milford/milfhs/www/default.htm

Grade Span: PK-12 **Schools**: *Regular* 5 ● *Spec Ed* 1 ● *Alt* 0 **Students**: 3,825 **Total Teachers**: 225 **Student/Classroom Teacher Ratio**: 17.3	**Expenditures/Student**: $5,566 **Librarians**: 4.0 956 students/librarian **Guidance Counselors**: 7.0 546 students/counselor	**% Amer Indian**: 0.1 **% Asian**: 0.5 **% Black**: 26.4 **% Hispanic**: 4.2 **% White**: 68.8	National ***Socio-Economic Status*** indicator percentile (100=high): 38th

Kent County

SMYRNA S.D.

22 SOUTH MAIN STREET ● SMYRNA DE 19977-1493 ● (302) 653-8585

Grade Span: PK-12 **Schools**: *Regular* 5 ● *Spec Ed* 0 ● *Alt* 0 **Students**: 3,202 **Total Teachers**: 183 **Student/Classroom Teacher Ratio**: 19.5	**Expenditures/Student**: $5,629 **Librarians**: 3.0 1,067 students/librarian **Guidance Counselors**: 9.0 356 students/counselor	**% Amer Indian**: 0.0 **% Asian**: 0.5 **% Black**: 11.8 **% Hispanic**: 1.8 **% White**: 85.8	National ***Socio-Economic Status*** indicator percentile (100=high): 62nd

New Castle County

[CLAYMONT] **BRANDYWINE S.D.**

1000 PENNSYLVANIA AVENUE ● CLAYMONT DE 19703-1237 ● (302) 792-3800

Grade Span: PK-12 **Schools**: *Regular* 17 ● *Spec Ed* 3 ● *Alt* 0 **Students**: 11,354 **Total Teachers**: 655 **Student/Classroom Teacher Ratio**: 17.6	**Expenditures/Student**: $6,940 **Librarians**: 14.0 811 students/librarian **Guidance Counselors**: 29.0 392 students/counselor	**% Amer Indian**: 0.1 **% Asian**: 2.7 **% Black**: 33.7 **% Hispanic**: 2.0 **% White**: 61.6	National ***Socio-Economic Status*** indicator percentile (100=high): 48th

New Castle County
[MIDDLETOWN] **APPOQUINIMINK S.D.**
230 EAST LAKE STREET ● MIDDLETOWN DE 19709-1135 ● (302) 378-5010

Grade Span: PK-12 **Schools**: *Regular* 5 ● *Spec Ed* 1 ● *Alt* 0 **Students**: 3,590 **Total Teachers**: 199 **Student/Classroom Teacher Ratio**: 18.0	**Expenditures/Student**: $5,085 **Librarians**: 1.0 3,590 students/librarian **Guidance Counselors**: 6.0 598 students/counselor	**% Amer Indian**: 0.0 **% Asian**: 0.5 **% Black**: 8.5 **% Hispanic**: 0.5 **% White**: 90.5	National ***Socio-Economic Status*** indicator percentile (100=high): 79th

New Castle County
[NEW CASTLE] **COLONIAL S.D.**
318 EAST BASIN ROAD ● NEW CASTLE DE 19720-4200 ● (302) 323-2700

Grade Span: PK-12 **Schools**: *Regular* 14 ● *Spec Ed* 2 ● *Alt* 0 **Students**: 10,230 **Total Teachers**: 576 **Student/Classroom Teacher Ratio**: 18.5	**Expenditures/Student**: $6,618 **Librarians**: 15.0 682 students/librarian **Guidance Counselors**: 24.0 426 students/counselor	**% Amer Indian**: 0.1 **% Asian**: 1.3 **% Black**: 36.4 **% Hispanic**: 3.5 **% White**: 58.8	National ***Socio-Economic Status*** indicator percentile (100=high): 32nd

New Castle County
[NEWARK] **CHRISTINA S.D.**
83 EAST MAIN STREET ● NEWARK DE 19711-4671 ● (302) 454-2000

Grade Span: PK-12 **Schools**: *Regular* 24 ● *Spec Ed* 4 ● *Alt* 2 **Students**: 19,868 **Total Teachers**: 1,156 **Student/Classroom Teacher Ratio**: 17.7	**Expenditures/Student**: $6,949 **Librarians**: 26.5 750 students/librarian **Guidance Counselors**: 15.0 1,325 students/counselor	**% Amer Indian**: 0.1 **% Asian**: 2.8 **% Black**: 30.3 **% Hispanic**: 3.9 **% White**: 63.0	National ***Socio-Economic Status*** indicator percentile (100=high): 44th

New Castle County
[WILMINGTON] **RED CLAY CONSOLIDATED S.D.**
1400 WASHINGTON STREET ● WILMINGTON DE 19801-1037 ● (302) 651-2600

Grade Span: PK-12 **Schools**: *Regular* 23 ● *Spec Ed* 3 ● *Alt* 0 **Students**: 15,112 **Total Teachers**: 860 **Student/Classroom Teacher Ratio**: 19.6	**Expenditures/Student**: $6,985 **Librarians**: 17.0 889 students/librarian **Guidance Counselors**: 27.0 560 students/counselor	**% Amer Indian**: 0.1 **% Asian**: 2.7 **% Black**: 30.3 **% Hispanic**: 10.6 **% White**: 56.2	National ***Socio-Economic Status*** indicator percentile (100=high): 32nd

Sussex County
[FRANKFORD] **INDIAN RIVER S.D.**
RD 2, BOX 236 ● FRANKFORD DE 19945-9667 ● (302) 436-1000

Grade Span: PK-12 **Schools**: *Regular* 9 ● *Spec Ed* 2 ● *Alt* 0 **Students**: 7,073 **Total Teachers**: 455 **Student/Classroom Teacher Ratio**: 16.1	**Expenditures/Student**: $6,173 **Librarians**: 8.0 884 students/librarian **Guidance Counselors**: 13.0 544 students/counselor	**% Amer Indian**: 0.5 **% Asian**: 1.2 **% Black**: 24.8 **% Hispanic**: 3.7 **% White**: 69.8	National ***Socio-Economic Status*** indicator percentile (100=high): 39th

Sussex County
[LEWES] **CAPE HENLOPEN S.D.**
1270 KINGS HIGHWAY ● LEWES DE 19958-1798 ● (302) 645-6686

Grade Span: PK-12 **Schools**: *Regular* 6 ● *Spec Ed* 2 ● *Alt* 0 **Students**: 4,092 **Total Teachers**: 246 **Student/Classroom Teacher Ratio**: 17.8	**Expenditures/Student**: $6,790 **Librarians**: 3.0 1,364 students/librarian **Guidance Counselors**: 7.0 585 students/counselor	**% Amer Indian**: 0.2 **% Asian**: 0.8 **% Black**: 22.2 **% Hispanic**: 2.4 **% White**: 74.4	National ***Socio-Economic Status*** indicator percentile (100=high): 36th

Sussex County

SEAFORD S.D.

DELAWARE PLACE ● SEAFORD DE 19973-1433 ● (302) 629-4587 ● http://www.seaford.k12.de.us

Grade Span: PK-12 **Schools**: *Regular* 5 ● *Spec Ed* 2 ● *Alt* 0 **Students**: 3,730 **Total Teachers**: 219 **Student/Classroom Teacher Ratio**: 17.4	**Expenditures/Student**: $5,974 **Librarians**: 4.0 933 students/librarian **Guidance Counselors**: 10.0 373 students/counselor	**% Amer Indian**: 0.1 **% Asian**: 0.8 **% Black**: 34.3 **% Hispanic**: 1.8 **% White**: 62.9	National ***Socio-Economic Status*** indicator percentile (100=high): 28th

District of Columbia

[WASHINGTON] **DISTRICT OF COLUMBIA PUBLIC S.D.**

415 12TH STREET, NW ● WASHINGTON DC 20004 ● (202) 724-4222 ● http://www.k12.dc.us

Grade Span: PK-12 **Schools**: *Regular* 167 ● *Spec Ed* 11 ● *Alt* 8 **Students**: 79,802 **Total Teachers**: 5,305 **Student/Classroom Teacher Ratio**: 20.2	**Expenditures/Student**: $8,404 **Librarians**: 143.0 558 students/librarian **Guidance Counselors**: 217.0 368 students/counselor	**% Amer Indian**: 0.0 **% Asian**: 1.4 **% Black**: 87.4 **% Hispanic**: 7.2 **% White**: 4.0	National ***Socio-Economic Status*** indicator percentile (100=high): 5th

Alachua County

[GAINESVILLE] **ALACHUA COUNTY S.D.**

620 EAST UNIVERSITY AVENUE ● GAINESVILLE FL 32601-5498 ● (352) 336-3527 ● http://www.sbac.edu

Grade Span: PK-12 **Schools**: *Regular* 36 ● *Spec Ed* 2 ● *Alt* 4 **Students**: 29,166 **Total Teachers**: 1,622 **Student/Classroom Teacher Ratio**: 18.0	**Expenditures/Student**: $4,962 **Librarians**: 48.0 608 students/librarian **Guidance Counselors**: 68.0 429 students/counselor	**% Amer Indian**: 0.2 **% Asian**: 2.3 **% Black**: 35.8 **% Hispanic**: 3.1 **% White**: 58.7	National ***Socio-Economic Status*** indicator percentile (100=high): 27th

Baker County

[MACCLENNY] **BAKER COUNTY S.D.**

392 SOUTH BOULEVARD EAST ● MACCLENNY FL 32063-2540 ● (904) 259-6251

Grade Span: PK-12 **Schools**: *Regular* 5 ● *Spec Ed* 1 ● *Alt* 0 **Students**: 4,635 **Total Teachers**: 231 **Student/Classroom Teacher Ratio**: 20.7	**Expenditures/Student**: $4,680 **Librarians**: 6.0 773 students/librarian **Guidance Counselors**: 9.0 515 students/counselor	**% Amer Indian**: 0.1 **% Asian**: 0.2 **% Black**: 17.3 **% Hispanic**: 0.1 **% White**: 82.3	National ***Socio-Economic Status*** indicator percentile (100=high): 30th

Bay County

[PANAMA CITY] **BAY COUNTY S.D.**

PO DRAWER 820 ● PANAMA CITY FL 32402-0820 ● (850) 872-4100 ● http://www.bay.k12.fl.us

Grade Span: PK-12 **Schools**: *Regular* 29 ● *Spec Ed* 3 ● *Alt* 3 **Students**: 25,228 **Total Teachers**: 1,443 **Student/Classroom Teacher Ratio**: 18.2	**Expenditures/Student**: $5,002 **Librarians**: 39.0 647 students/librarian **Guidance Counselors**: 68.0 371 students/counselor	**% Amer Indian**: 0.3 **% Asian**: 2.3 **% Black**: 15.1 **% Hispanic**: 1.3 **% White**: 81.1	National ***Socio-Economic Status*** indicator percentile (100=high): 33rd

Bradford County

[STARKE] **BRADFORD COUNTY S.D.**

582 NORTH TEMPLE AVENUE ● STARKE FL 32091-2610 ● (904) 964-6800 ● http://www.daccess.net/starknet/school.html

Grade Span: PK-12 **Schools**: *Regular* 7 ● *Spec Ed* 0 ● *Alt* 2 **Students**: 4,119 **Total Teachers**: 238 **Student/Classroom Teacher Ratio**: 18.1	**Expenditures/Student**: $4,797 **Librarians**: 9.0 458 students/librarian **Guidance Counselors**: 9.0 458 students/counselor	**% Amer Indian**: 0.1 **% Asian**: 0.7 **% Black**: 21.7 **% Hispanic**: 0.6 **% White**: 76.9	National ***Socio-Economic Status*** indicator percentile (100=high): 25th

Brevard County

[MELBOURNE] **BREVARD COUNTY S.D.**

2700 SAINT JOHNS STREET ● MELBOURNE FL 32940-6699 ● (407) 631-1911 ● http://www.brevard.k12.fl.us

Grade Span: PK-12 **Schools**: *Regular* 72 ● *Spec Ed* 6 ● *Alt* 5 **Students**: 65,621 **Total Teachers**: 3,568 **Student/Classroom Teacher Ratio**: 17.6	**Expenditures/Student**: $4,670 **Librarians**: 90.0 729 students/librarian **Guidance Counselors**: 133.0 493 students/counselor	**% Amer Indian**: 0.2 **% Asian**: 1.8 **% Black**: 14.5 **% Hispanic**: 3.5 **% White**: 79.9	National ***Socio-Economic Status*** indicator percentile (100=high): 50th

Broward County

[FORT LAUDERDALE] **BROWARD COUNTY S.D.**

600 SE THIRD AVENUE ● FORT LAUDERDALE FL 33301-3125 ● (954) 765-6271 ● http://browardschools.com

Grade Span: PK-12 **Schools**: *Regular* 173 ● *Spec Ed* 10 ● *Alt* 9 **Students**: 208,359 **Total Teachers**: 9,897 **Student/Classroom Teacher Ratio**: 21.7	**Expenditures/Student**: $5,393 **Librarians**: 193.0 1,080 students/librarian **Guidance Counselors**: 403.0 517 students/counselor	**% Amer Indian**: 0.3 **% Asian**: 2.6 **% Black**: 34.8 **% Hispanic**: 13.3 **% White**: 49.1	National ***Socio-Economic Status*** indicator percentile (100=high): 37th

Charlotte County

[PORT CHARLOTTE] **CHARLOTTE COUNTY S.D.**

1445 PIATTI DRIVE ● PORT CHARLOTTE FL 33948-1053 ● (941) 255-0808 ● http://www.ccps.k12.fl.us

Grade Span: PK-12 **Schools**: *Regular* 18 ● *Spec Ed* 1 ● *Alt* 2 **Students**: 15,593 **Total Teachers**: 829 **Student/Classroom Teacher Ratio**: 19.9	**Expenditures/Student**: $5,275 **Librarians**: 18.0 866 students/librarian **Guidance Counselors**: 33.0 473 students/counselor	**% Amer Indian**: 0.2 **% Asian**: 1.2 **% Black**: 8.5 **% Hispanic**: 2.9 **% White**: 87.1	National ***Socio-Economic Status*** indicator percentile (100=high): 39th

Citrus County

[INVERNESS] **CITRUS COUNTY S.D.**

1007 WEST MAIN STREET ● INVERNESS FL 34450-4698 ● (352) 726-1931

Grade Span: PK-12 **Schools**: *Regular* 16 ● *Spec Ed* 1 ● *Alt* 1 **Students**: 13,934 **Total Teachers**: 790 **Student/Classroom Teacher Ratio**: 17.4	**Expenditures/Student**: $4,956 **Librarians**: 20.0 697 students/librarian **Guidance Counselors**: 31.0 449 students/counselor	**% Amer Indian**: 0.2 **% Asian**: 1.1 **% Black**: 4.6 **% Hispanic**: 2.4 **% White**: 91.7	National ***Socio-Economic Status*** indicator percentile (100=high): 30th

Clay County

[GREEN COVE SPRINGS] **CLAY COUNTY S.D.**

900 WALNUT STREET ● GREEN COVE SPRINGS FL 32043-3129 ● (904) 284-6510 ● http://www.clay.k12.fl.us

Grade Span: PK-12 **Schools**: *Regular* 26 ● *Spec Ed* 0 ● *Alt* 1 **Students**: 24,875 **Total Teachers**: 1,237 **Student/Classroom Teacher Ratio**: 19.0	**Expenditures/Student**: $4,195 **Librarians**: 26.0 957 students/librarian **Guidance Counselors**: 43.0 578 students/counselor	**% Amer Indian**: 0.2 **% Asian**: 1.9 **% Black**: 9.0 **% Hispanic**: 2.3 **% White**: 86.6	National ***Socio-Economic Status*** indicator percentile (100=high): 65th

Collier County

[NAPLES] **COLLIER COUNTY S.D.**

3710 ESTEY AVENUE ● NAPLES FL 33942-4457 ● (941) 643-2700 ● http://www.naples.net/educate/zedmain.htm

Grade Span: PK-12 **Schools**: *Regular* 33 ● *Spec Ed* 0 ● *Alt* 6 **Students**: 26,376 **Total Teachers**: 1,375 **Student/Classroom Teacher Ratio**: 17.5	**Expenditures/Student**: $6,106 **Librarians**: 33.0 799 students/librarian **Guidance Counselors**: 71.0 371 students/counselor	**% Amer Indian**: 0.4 **% Asian**: 0.4 **% Black**: 10.8 **% Hispanic**: 23.7 **% White**: 64.7	National ***Socio-Economic Status*** indicator percentile (100=high): 34th

Columbia County

[LAKE CITY] **COLUMBIA COUNTY S.D.**

PO BOX 1148 ● LAKE CITY FL 32056-1148 ● (904) 755-8000

Grade Span: PK-12 **Schools**: *Regular* 11 ● *Spec Ed* 0 ● *Alt* 1 **Students**: 9,137 **Total Teachers**: 481 **Student/Classroom Teacher Ratio**: 18.6	**Expenditures/Student**: $4,701 **Librarians**: 12.0 761 students/librarian **Guidance Counselors**: 16.0 571 students/counselor	**% Amer Indian**: 0.2 **% Asian**: 0.7 **% Black**: 24.6 **% Hispanic**: 1.8 **% White**: 72.7	National ***Socio-Economic Status*** indicator percentile (100=high): 20th

Dade County

[MIAMI] **DADE COUNTY S.D.**

1450 NE 2ND AVENUE SUITE 403 ● MIAMI FL 33132-1308 ● (305) 995-1429 ● http://dcps.dade.k12.fl.us

Grade Span: PK-12 **Schools**: *Regular* 285 ● *Spec Ed* 4 ● *Alt* 33 **Students**: 333,817 **Total Teachers**: 16,648 **Student/Classroom Teacher Ratio**: 19.3	**Expenditures/Student**: $6,053 **Librarians**: 323.0 1,033 students/librarian **Guidance Counselors**: 874.0 382 students/counselor	**% Amer Indian**: 0.1 **% Asian**: 1.3 **% Black**: 33.8 **% Hispanic**: 50.5 **% White**: 14.4	National ***Socio-Economic Status*** indicator percentile (100=high): 13th

DeSoto County

[ARCADIA] **DE SOTO COUNTY S.D.**

530 LA SOLONA AVENUE ● ARCADIA FL 33821-4911 ● (941) 494-4222 ● http://www.desoto.net/schools/schools.htm

Grade Span: PK-12 **Schools**: *Regular* 7 ● *Spec Ed* 1 ● *Alt* 3 **Students**: 4,508 **Total Teachers**: 259 **Student/Classroom Teacher Ratio**: 19.5	**Expenditures/Student**: $5,514 **Librarians**: 5.0 902 students/librarian **Guidance Counselors**: 8.0 564 students/counselor	**% Amer Indian**: 0.2 **% Asian**: 0.5 **% Black**: 21.8 **% Hispanic**: 15.4 **% White**: 62.1	National ***Socio-Economic Status*** indicator percentile (100=high): 13th

Duval County

[JACKSONVILLE] **DUVAL COUNTY S.D.**

1701 PRUDENTIAL DRIVE ● JACKSONVILLE FL 32207-8154 ● (904) 390-2115 ● http://www2.duval.k12.fl.us

Grade Span: PK-12 **Schools**: *Regular* 144 ● *Spec Ed* 5 ● *Alt* 6 **Students**: 123,910 **Total Teachers**: 6,090 **Student/Classroom Teacher Ratio**: 20.1	**Expenditures/Student**: $4,681 **Librarians**: 141.0 879 students/librarian **Guidance Counselors**: 201.0 616 students/counselor	**% Amer Indian**: 0.1 **% Asian**: 2.7 **% Black**: 39.7 **% Hispanic**: 2.6 **% White**: 55.0	National ***Socio-Economic Status*** indicator percentile (100=high): 28th

Escambia County

[PENSACOLA] **ESCAMBIA COUNTY S.D.**

PO BOX 1470 ● PENSACOLA FL 32597-1470 ● (850) 469-6130 ● http://www.escambia.k12.fl.us

Grade Span: PK-12 **Schools**: *Regular* 63 ● *Spec Ed* 3 ● *Alt* 6 **Students**: 45,215 **Total Teachers**: 2,547 **Student/Classroom Teacher Ratio**: 18.0	**Expenditures/Student**: $5,023 **Librarians**: 62.0 729 students/librarian **Guidance Counselors**: 99.0 457 students/counselor	**% Amer Indian**: 0.5 **% Asian**: 2.9 **% Black**: 34.0 **% Hispanic**: 1.1 **% White**: 61.4	National ***Socio-Economic Status*** indicator percentile (100=high): 19th

Flagler County

[BUNNELL] **FLAGLER COUNTY S.D.**

PO BOX 755 ● BUNNELL FL 32110-0755 ● (904) 437-3351

Grade Span: PK-12 **Schools**: *Regular* 5 ● *Spec Ed* 0 ● *Alt* 1 **Students**: 5,361 **Total Teachers**: 313 **Student/Classroom Teacher Ratio**: 17.1	**Expenditures/Student**: $6,111 **Librarians**: 5.0 1,072 students/librarian **Guidance Counselors**: 12.0 447 students/counselor	**% Amer Indian**: 0.2 **% Asian**: 1.6 **% Black**: 15.0 **% Hispanic**: 4.8 **% White**: 78.4	National ***Socio-Economic Status*** indicator percentile (100=high): 36th

Gadsden County

[QUINCY] **GADSDEN COUNTY S.D.**

PO BOX 1499 ● QUINCY FL 32353-1499 ● (850) 627-9651

Grade Span: PK-12 **Schools**: *Regular* 15 ● *Spec Ed* 0 ● *Alt* 5 **Students**: 8,674 **Total Teachers**: 472 **Student/Classroom Teacher Ratio**: 18.5	**Expenditures/Student**: $5,118 **Librarians**: 12.0 723 students/librarian **Guidance Counselors**: 20.0 434 students/counselor	**% Amer Indian**: 0.0 **% Asian**: 0.1 **% Black**: 85.0 **% Hispanic**: 6.1 **% White**: 8.8	National ***Socio-Economic Status*** indicator percentile (100=high): 5th

Gilchrist County

[TRENTON] **GILCHRIST COUNTY S.D.**

PO BOX 67 ● TRENTON FL 32693-0067 ● (352) 463-3200

Grade Span: PK-12 **Schools**: *Regular* 4 ● *Spec Ed* 0 ● *Alt* 0 **Students**: 2,529 **Total Teachers**: 138 **Student/Classroom Teacher Ratio**: 18.6	**Expenditures/Student**: $5,078 **Librarians**: 4.0 632 students/librarian **Guidance Counselors**: 4.0 632 students/counselor	**% Amer Indian**: 0.1 **% Asian**: 0.0 **% Black**: 5.5 **% Hispanic**: 0.8 **% White**: 93.6	National ***Socio-Economic Status*** indicator percentile (100=high): 24th

Hardee County

[WAUCHULA] **HARDEE COUNTY S.D.**

PO DRAWER 1678 ● WAUCHULA FL 33873-1678 ● (941) 773-9058 ● http://www.firn.edu/schools/hardee/hardee_csb

Grade Span: PK-12 **Schools**: *Regular* 7 ● *Spec Ed* 0 ● *Alt* 3 **Students**: 5,325 **Total Teachers**: 292 **Student/Classroom Teacher Ratio**: 21.4	**Expenditures/Student**: $5,813 **Librarians**: 6.0 888 students/librarian **Guidance Counselors**: 11.0 484 students/counselor	**% Amer Indian**: 0.2 **% Asian**: 0.1 **% Black**: 8.8 **% Hispanic**: 43.6 **% White**: 47.3	National ***Socio-Economic Status*** indicator percentile (100=high): 30th

Hendry County

[LA BELLE] **HENDRY COUNTY S.D.**

PO BOX 1980 ● LA BELLE FL 33935-1980 ● (941) 675-5266

Grade Span: PK-12 **Schools**: *Regular* 9 ● *Spec Ed* 1 ● *Alt* 1 **Students**: 7,064 **Total Teachers**: 346 **Student/Classroom Teacher Ratio**: 19.5	**Expenditures/Student**: $5,219 **Librarians**: 9.0 785 students/librarian **Guidance Counselors**: 15.0 471 students/counselor	**% Amer Indian**: 0.5 **% Asian**: 0.6 **% Black**: 19.8 **% Hispanic**: 33.1 **% White**: 45.9	National ***Socio-Economic Status*** indicator percentile (100=high): 16th

Hernando County

[BROOKSVILLE] **HERNANDO COUNTY S.D.**

919 NORTH BROAD STREET ● BROOKSVILLE FL 34601-2397 ● (352) 796-6761 ● http://hernando.com/moton/brooksville/schools/HernandoSchools.html

Grade Span: PK-12 **Schools**: *Regular* 18 ● *Spec Ed* 0 ● *Alt* 0 **Students**: 15,393 **Total Teachers**: 757 **Student/Classroom Teacher Ratio**: 19.0	**Expenditures/Student**: $4,657 **Librarians**: 17.0 905 students/librarian **Guidance Counselors**: 40.0 385 students/counselor	**% Amer Indian**: 0.1 **% Asian**: 0.8 **% Black**: 7.9 **% Hispanic**: 4.6 **% White**: 86.6	National ***Socio-Economic Status*** indicator percentile (100=high): 31st

Highlands County

[SEBRING] **HIGHLANDS COUNTY S.D.**

426 SCHOOL STREET ● SEBRING FL 33870-4048 ● (941) 382-1121

Grade Span: PK-12 **Schools**: *Regular* 14 ● *Spec Ed* 0 ● *Alt* 1 **Students**: 10,758 **Total Teachers**: 530 **Student/Classroom Teacher Ratio**: 18.8	**Expenditures/Student**: $5,328 **Librarians**: 15.0 717 students/librarian **Guidance Counselors**: 25.0 430 students/counselor	**% Amer Indian**: 0.5 **% Asian**: 0.7 **% Black**: 21.2 **% Hispanic**: 11.9 **% White**: 65.8	National ***Socio-Economic Status*** indicator percentile (100=high): 19th

Hillsborough County

[TAMPA] **HILLSBOROUGH COUNTY S.D.**

PO BOX 3408 ● TAMPA FL 33601-3408 ● (813) 272-4050 ● http://www.ideas-classroom.org

Grade Span: PK-12 **Schools**: *Regular* 151 ● *Spec Ed* 10 ● *Alt* 11 **Students**: 143,192 **Total Teachers**: 8,492 **Student/Classroom Teacher Ratio**: 17.4	**Expenditures/Student**: $5,646 **Librarians**: 185.0 774 students/librarian **Guidance Counselors**: 356.0 402 students/counselor	**% Amer Indian**: 0.3 **% Asian**: 1.9 **% Black**: 23.6 **% Hispanic**: 16.8 **% White**: 57.3	National ***Socio-Economic Status*** indicator percentile (100=high): 24th

Holmes County

[BONIFAY] **HOLMES COUNTY S.D.**

211 WEST IOWA AVENUE ● BONIFAY FL 32425-2103 ● (850) 547-9341

Grade Span: PK-12 **Schools**: *Regular* 7 ● *Spec Ed* 0 ● *Alt* 1 **Students**: 3,759 **Total Teachers**: 213 **Student/Classroom Teacher Ratio**: 16.8	**Expenditures/Student**: $4,772 **Librarians**: 8.0 470 students/librarian **Guidance Counselors**: 7.0 537 students/counselor	**% Amer Indian**: 0.1 **% Asian**: 0.2 **% Black**: 2.7 **% Hispanic**: 0.5 **% White**: 96.4	National ***Socio-Economic Status*** indicator percentile (100=high): 17th

Indian River County

[VERO BEACH] **INDIAN RIVER COUNTY S.D.**

1990 25TH STREET ● VERO BEACH FL 32960-3367 ● (561) 567-7165

Grade Span: PK-12 **Schools**: *Regular* 19 ● *Spec Ed* 2 ● *Alt* 0 **Students**: 13,665 **Total Teachers**: 752 **Student/Classroom Teacher Ratio**: 17.8	**Expenditures/Student**: $5,157 **Librarians**: 21.0 651 students/librarian **Guidance Counselors**: 22.0 621 students/counselor	**% Amer Indian**: 0.2 **% Asian**: 0.7 **% Black**: 17.6 **% Hispanic**: 6.1 **% White**: 75.5	National ***Socio-Economic Status*** indicator percentile (100=high): 31st

Jackson County

[MARIANNA] **JACKSON COUNTY S.D.**

PO BOX 5958 ● MARIANNA FL 32446-5958 ● (850) 482-1200

Grade Span: PK-12 **Schools**: *Regular* 13 ● *Spec Ed* 4 ● *Alt* 1 **Students**: 7,991 **Total Teachers**: 512 **Student/Classroom Teacher Ratio**: 16.8	**Expenditures/Student**: $4,967 **Librarians**: 12.0 666 students/librarian **Guidance Counselors**: 22.0 363 students/counselor	**% Amer Indian**: 0.2 **% Asian**: 0.2 **% Black**: 33.1 **% Hispanic**: 1.1 **% White**: 65.3	National ***Socio-Economic Status*** indicator percentile (100=high): 24th

Lake County

[TAVARES] **LAKE COUNTY S.D.**

201 WEST BURLEIGH BOULEVARD ● TAVARES FL 32778-2496 ● (352) 343-3531

Grade Span: PK-12 **Schools**: *Regular* 32 ● *Spec Ed* 3 ● *Alt* 6 **Students**: 24,827 **Total Teachers**: 1,261 **Student/Classroom Teacher Ratio**: 19.3	**Expenditures/Student**: $4,579 **Librarians**: 34.0 730 students/librarian **Guidance Counselors**: 62.0 400 students/counselor	**% Amer Indian**: 0.2 **% Asian**: 0.8 **% Black**: 17.5 **% Hispanic**: 5.2 **% White**: 76.4	National ***Socio-Economic Status*** indicator percentile (100=high): 32nd

Lee County

[FORT MYERS] **LEE COUNTY S.D.**

2055 CENTRAL AVENUE ● FORT MYERS FL 33901-3916 ● (941) 337-8301 ● http://www.lee.k12.fl.us

Grade Span: PK-12 **Schools**: *Regular* 59 ● *Spec Ed* 4 ● *Alt* 8 **Students**: 50,945 **Total Teachers**: 2,571 **Student/Classroom Teacher Ratio**: 19.1	**Expenditures/Student**: $5,506 **Librarians**: 73.0 698 students/librarian **Guidance Counselors**: 121.0 421 students/counselor	**% Amer Indian**: 0.2 **% Asian**: 1.0 **% Black**: 15.2 **% Hispanic**: 10.9 **% White**: 72.7	National ***Socio-Economic Status*** indicator percentile (100=high): 32nd

Leon County

[TALLAHASSEE] **LEON COUNTY S.D.**

2757 WEST PENSACOLA STREET ● TALLAHASSEE FL 32304-2907 ● (850) 487-7250 ● http://www.leon.k12.fl.us

Grade Span: PK-12 **Schools**: *Regular* 36 ● *Spec Ed* 4 ● *Alt* 7 **Students**: 31,335 **Total Teachers**: 1,718 **Student/Classroom Teacher Ratio**: 18.5	**Expenditures/Student**: $5,290 **Librarians**: 44.0 712 students/librarian **Guidance Counselors**: 78.0 402 students/counselor	**% Amer Indian**: 0.1 **% Asian**: 1.6 **% Black**: 37.5 **% Hispanic**: 1.6 **% White**: 59.2	National ***Socio-Economic Status*** indicator percentile (100=high): 54th

Levy County

[BRONSON] **LEVY COUNTY S.D.**

PO DRAWER 129 ● BRONSON FL 32621-0129 ● (352) 486-2151

Grade Span: PK-12 **Schools**: *Regular* 12 ● *Spec Ed* 0 ● *Alt* 2 **Students**: 5,734 **Total Teachers**: 316 **Student/Classroom Teacher Ratio**: 18.5	**Expenditures/Student**: $4,978 **Librarians**: 10.0 573 students/librarian **Guidance Counselors**: 12.0 478 students/counselor	**% Amer Indian**: 0.1 **% Asian**: 0.3 **% Black**: 18.6 **% Hispanic**: 2.0 **% White**: 78.9	National ***Socio-Economic Status*** indicator percentile (100=high): 16th

Madison County

[MADISON] **MADISON COUNTY S.D.**

PO BOX 449 ● MADISON FL 32340-0449 ● (850) 973-4081 ● http://sy2000.madison.k12.fl.us

Grade Span: PK-12 **Schools**: *Regular* 7 ● *Spec Ed* 0 ● *Alt* 2 **Students**: 3,434 **Total Teachers**: 191 **Student/Classroom Teacher Ratio**: 17.4	**Expenditures/Student**: $5,035 **Librarians**: 4.0 859 students/librarian **Guidance Counselors**: 7.0 491 students/counselor	**% Amer Indian**: 0.0 **% Asian**: 0.1 **% Black**: 57.8 **% Hispanic**: 0.8 **% White**: 41.4	National ***Socio-Economic Status*** indicator percentile (100=high): 8th

Manatee County

[BRADENTON] **MANATEE COUNTY S.D.**

PO BOX 9069 ● BRADENTON FL 34206-9069 ● (941) 741-7235 ● http://www.manatee.k12.fl.us

Grade Span: PK-12 **Schools**: *Regular* 38 ● *Spec Ed* 9 ● *Alt* 14 **Students**: 31,805 **Total Teachers**: 1,660 **Student/Classroom Teacher Ratio**: 19.2	**Expenditures/Student**: $4,984 **Librarians**: 39.0 816 students/librarian **Guidance Counselors**: 64.0 497 students/counselor	**% Amer Indian**: 0.1 **% Asian**: 0.8 **% Black**: 17.2 **% Hispanic**: 10.6 **% White**: 71.3	National ***Socio-Economic Status*** indicator percentile (100=high): 30th

Marion County

[OCALA] **MARION COUNTY S.D.**

PO BOX 670 ● OCALA FL 32678-0670 ● (352) 620-7702 ● http://www.marionschoolsk12.org

Grade Span: PK-12 **Schools**: *Regular* 41 ● *Spec Ed* 2 ● *Alt* 4 **Students**: 35,526 **Total Teachers**: 1,888 **Student/Classroom Teacher Ratio**: 18.1	**Expenditures/Student**: $4,806 **Librarians**: 42.0 846 students/librarian **Guidance Counselors**: 66.0 538 students/counselor	**% Amer Indian**: 0.2 **% Asian**: 0.6 **% Black**: 21.8 **% Hispanic**: 5.2 **% White**: 72.1	National ***Socio-Economic Status*** indicator percentile (100=high): 23rd

Martin County

[STUART] **MARTIN COUNTY S.D.**

PO BOX 1049 ● STUART FL 34995-1049 ● (561) 287-0101 ● http://www.martin.k12.fl.us

Grade Span: PK-12 **Schools**: *Regular* 17 ● *Spec Ed* 2 ● *Alt* 5 **Students**: 14,369 **Total Teachers**: 832 **Student/Classroom Teacher Ratio**: 18.8	**Expenditures/Student**: $5,917 **Librarians**: 18.0 798 students/librarian **Guidance Counselors**: 28.0 513 students/counselor	**% Amer Indian**: 0.1 **% Asian**: 0.8 **% Black**: 12.6 **% Hispanic**: 8.8 **% White**: 77.7	National ***Socio-Economic Status*** indicator percentile (100=high): 48th

Monroe County

[KEY WEST] **MONROE COUNTY S.D.**

PO BOX 1788 ● KEY WEST FL 33041-1788 ● (305) 293-1440 ● http://www.monroe.k12.fl.us

Grade Span: PK-12 **Schools**: *Regular* 12 ● *Spec Ed* 1 ● *Alt* 0 **Students**: 9,508 **Total Teachers**: 541 **Student/Classroom Teacher Ratio**: 17.9	**Expenditures/Student**: $5,911 **Librarians**: 6.0 1,585 students/librarian **Guidance Counselors**: 18.0 528 students/counselor	**% Amer Indian**: 0.2 **% Asian**: 1.1 **% Black**: 9.4 **% Hispanic**: 15.9 **% White**: 73.4	National ***Socio-Economic Status*** indicator percentile (100=high): 43rd

Nassau County

[FERNANDINA BEACH] **NASSAU COUNTY S.D.**

1201 ATLANTIC AVENUE ● FERNANDINA BEACH FL 32034-3499 ● (904) 261-5761

Grade Span: PK-12 **Schools**: *Regular* 15 ● *Spec Ed* 0 ● *Alt* 3 **Students**: 9,579 **Total Teachers**: 464 **Student/Classroom Teacher Ratio**: 20.2	**Expenditures/Student**: $4,363 **Librarians**: 15.0 639 students/librarian **Guidance Counselors**: 22.0 435 students/counselor	**% Amer Indian**: 0.1 **% Asian**: 0.4 **% Black**: 12.1 **% Hispanic**: 0.7 **% White**: 86.7	National ***Socio-Economic Status*** indicator percentile (100=high): 49th

Okaloosa County

[FORT WALTON BEACH] **OKALOOSA COUNTY S.D.**

120 LOWERY PLACE SE ● FORT WALTON BEACH FL 32548-5547 ● (850) 833-3109 ● http://www.okaloosa.k12.fl.us

Grade Span: PK-12 **Schools**: *Regular* 33 ● *Spec Ed* 1 ● *Alt* 2 **Students**: 29,454 **Total Teachers**: 1,604 **Student/Classroom Teacher Ratio**: 19.0	**Expenditures/Student**: $4,405 **Librarians**: 40.0 736 students/librarian **Guidance Counselors**: 61.0 483 students/counselor	**% Amer Indian**: 0.4 **% Asian**: 3.4 **% Black**: 12.6 **% Hispanic**: 3.0 **% White**: 80.6	National ***Socio-Economic Status*** indicator percentile (100=high): 55th

Okeechobee County

[OKEECHOBEE] **OKEECHOBEE COUNTY S.D.**

100 SW 5TH AVENUE ● OKEECHOBEE FL 33474-4299 ● (941) 763-3157

Grade Span: PK-12 **Schools**: *Regular* 9 ● *Spec Ed* 0 ● *Alt* 2 **Students**: 6,456 **Total Teachers**: 334 **Student/Classroom Teacher Ratio**: 17.7	**Expenditures/Student**: $5,015 **Librarians**: 7.0 922 students/librarian **Guidance Counselors**: 14.0 461 students/counselor	**% Amer Indian**: 1.9 **% Asian**: 0.5 **% Black**: 8.6 **% Hispanic**: 18.2 **% White**: 70.8	National ***Socio-Economic Status*** indicator percentile (100=high): 18th

Orange County

[ORLANDO] **ORANGE COUNTY S.D.**

PO BOX 271 ● ORLANDO FL 32802-0271 ● (407) 849-3209 ● http://www.ocps.k12.fl.us

Grade Span: PK-12 **Schools**: *Regular* 125 ● *Spec Ed* 6 ● *Alt* 26 **Students**: 123,165 **Total Teachers**: 6,394 **Student/Classroom Teacher Ratio**: 19.0	**Expenditures/Student**: $5,193 **Librarians**: 133.0 926 students/librarian **Guidance Counselors**: 266.0 463 students/counselor	**% Amer Indian**: 0.3 **% Asian**: 3.4 **% Black**: 27.4 **% Hispanic**: 16.2 **% White**: 52.7	National ***Socio-Economic Status*** indicator percentile (100=high): 36th

Osceola County

[KISSIMMEE] **OSCEOLA COUNTY S.D.**

817 BILL BECK BOULEVARD ● KISSIMMEE FL 32744-4495 ● (407) 870-4008 ● http://www.osceola.k12.fl.us

Grade Span: PK-12 **Schools**: *Regular* 24 ● *Spec Ed* 0 ● *Alt* 7 **Students**: 25,670 **Total Teachers**: 1,194 **Student/Classroom Teacher Ratio**: 20.6	**Expenditures/Student**: $4,582 **Librarians**: 26.0 987 students/librarian **Guidance Counselors**: 60.0 428 students/counselor	**% Amer Indian**: 0.2 **% Asian**: 2.6 **% Black**: 9.7 **% Hispanic**: 26.7 **% White**: 60.8	National ***Socio-Economic Status*** indicator percentile (100=high): 35th

Palm Beach County

[WEST PALM BEACH] **PALM BEACH COUNTY S.D.**

3340 FOREST HILL BOULEVARD ● WEST PALM BEACH FL 33406-5869 ● (561) 434-8200 ● http://www.palmbeach.k12.fl.us

Grade Span: PK-12 **Schools**: *Regular* 122 ● *Spec Ed* 1 ● *Alt* 10 **Students**: 132,215 **Total Teachers**: 7,090 **Student/Classroom Teacher Ratio**: 18.2	**Expenditures/Student**: $5,750 **Librarians**: 122.0 1,084 students/librarian **Guidance Counselors**: 246.0 537 students/counselor	**% Amer Indian**: 0.3 **% Asian**: 2.0 **% Black**: 28.8 **% Hispanic**: 13.6 **% White**: 55.3	National ***Socio-Economic Status*** indicator percentile (100=high): 39th

Pasco County

[LAND O'LAKES] **PASCO COUNTY S.D.**

7227 LAND O LAKES BOULEVARD ● LAND O'LAKES FL 34639-2805 ● (813) 996-3600 ● http://www.pasco.k12.fl.us

Grade Span: PK-12 **Schools**: *Regular* 42 ● *Spec Ed* 0 ● *Alt* 3 **Students**: 41,791 **Total Teachers**: 2,202 **Student/Classroom Teacher Ratio**: 18.1	**Expenditures/Student**: $4,953 **Librarians**: 54.0 774 students/librarian **Guidance Counselors**: 105.0 398 students/counselor	**% Amer Indian**: 0.2 **% Asian**: 1.1 **% Black**: 4.0 **% Hispanic**: 5.7 **% White**: 89.1	National ***Socio-Economic Status*** indicator percentile (100=high): 31st

Pinellas County

[LARGO] PINELLAS COUNTY S.D.

301 FOURTH STREET SW ● LARGO FL 34640-3536 ● (813) 588-6011 ● http://www.pinellas.k12.fl.us

Grade Span: PK-12	**Expenditures/Student**: $5,380	**% Amer Indian**: 0.2	
Schools: *Regular* 116 ● *Spec Ed* 4 ● *Alt* 27	**Librarians**: 135.0	**% Asian**: 2.6	National ***Socio-Economic***
Students: 104,335	773 students/librarian	**% Black**: 18.5	***Status*** indicator percentile
Total Teachers: 6,030	**Guidance Counselors**: 226.0	**% Hispanic**: 2.7	(100=high): 39th
Student/Classroom Teacher Ratio: 18.9	462 students/counselor	**% White**: 76.0	

Polk County

[BARTOW] POLK COUNTY S.D.

PO BOX 391 ● BARTOW FL 33830-0391 ● (941) 534-0521 ● http://www.pcsb.k12.fl.us

Grade Span: PK-12	**Expenditures/Student**: $4,791	**% Amer Indian**: 0.2	
Schools: *Regular* 94 ● *Spec Ed* 3 ● *Alt* 22	**Librarians**: 106.0	**% Asian**: 0.9	National ***Socio-Economic***
Students: 72,807	687 students/librarian	**% Black**: 22.8	***Status*** indicator percentile
Total Teachers: 4,029	**Guidance Counselors**: 170.0	**% Hispanic**: 7.7	(100=high): 21st
Student/Classroom Teacher Ratio: 18.6	428 students/counselor	**% White**: 68.5	

Putnam County

[PALATKA] PUTNAM COUNTY S.D.

200 SOUTH 7TH STREET ● PALATKA FL 32077 ● (904) 329-0510

Grade Span: PK-12	**Expenditures/Student**: $4,631	**% Amer Indian**: 0.2	
Schools: *Regular* 16 ● *Spec Ed* 1 ● *Alt* 2	**Librarians**: 18.0	**% Asian**: 0.6	National ***Socio-Economic***
Students: 12,935	719 students/librarian	**% Black**: 28.1	***Status*** indicator percentile
Total Teachers: 714	**Guidance Counselors**: 34.0	**% Hispanic**: 6.6	(100=high): 12th
Student/Classroom Teacher Ratio: 19.5	380 students/counselor	**% White**: 64.6	

St. Johns County

[ST. AUGUSTINE] ST. JOHNS COUNTY S.D.

40 ORANGE STREET ● ST. AUGUSTINE FL 32084-3633 ● (904) 824-7201 ● http://macserver.stjohns.k12.fl.us/NetCloak.acgi

Grade Span: PK-12	**Expenditures/Student**: $5,373	**% Amer Indian**: 0.1	
Schools: *Regular* 21 ● *Spec Ed* 0 ● *Alt* 3	**Librarians**: 21.0	**% Asian**: 0.8	National ***Socio-Economic***
Students: 15,396	733 students/librarian	**% Black**: 11.8	***Status*** indicator percentile
Total Teachers: 850	**Guidance Counselors**: 45.0	**% Hispanic**: 1.7	(100=high): 59th
Student/Classroom Teacher Ratio: 17.3	342 students/counselor	**% White**: 85.5	

St. Lucie County

[FORT PIERCE] ST. LUCIE COUNTY S.D.

2909 DELAWARE AVENUE ● FORT PIERCE FL 34947-7299 ● (561) 468-5000 ● http://plato.stlucie.k12.fl.us

Grade Span: PK-12	**Expenditures/Student**: $5,083	**% Amer Indian**: 0.2	
Schools: *Regular* 28 ● *Spec Ed* 1 ● *Alt* 6	**Librarians**: 33.0	**% Asian**: 0.9	National ***Socio-Economic***
Students: 27,044	820 students/librarian	**% Black**: 30.9	***Status*** indicator percentile
Total Teachers: 1,781	**Guidance Counselors**: 51.0	**% Hispanic**: 6.9	(100=high): 23rd
Student/Classroom Teacher Ratio: 19.9	530 students/counselor	**% White**: 61.0	

Santa Rosa County

[MILTON] SANTA ROSA COUNTY S.D.

603 CANAL STREET ● MILTON FL 32570-6706 ● (850) 623-3663 ● http://www.santarosa.k12.fl.us

Grade Span: PK-12	**Expenditures/Student**: $4,539	**% Amer Indian**: 0.4	
Schools: *Regular* 25 ● *Spec Ed* 0 ● *Alt* 4	**Librarians**: 27.0	**% Asian**: 1.3	National ***Socio-Economic***
Students: 19,762	732 students/librarian	**% Black**: 5.3	***Status*** indicator percentile
Total Teachers: 1,058	**Guidance Counselors**: 43.0	**% Hispanic**: 1.2	(100=high): 49th
Student/Classroom Teacher Ratio: 18.2	460 students/counselor	**% White**: 91.8	

Sarasota County

[SARASOTA] **SARASOTA COUNTY S.D.**

2418 HATTON STREET ● SARASOTA FL 34237-8126 ● (941) 953-5000 ● http://www.sarasota.k12.fl.us

Grade Span: PK-12 **Schools**: *Regular* 30 ● *Spec Ed* 3 ● *Alt* 5 **Students**: 31,035 **Total Teachers**: 1,612 **Student/Classroom Teacher Ratio**: 18.8	**Expenditures/Student**: $6,121 **Librarians**: 17.0 1,826 students/librarian **Guidance Counselors**: 48.0 647 students/counselor	**% Amer Indian**: 0.1 **% Asian**: 1.2 **% Black**: 10.8 **% Hispanic**: 4.2 **% White**: 83.7	National ***Socio-Economic Status*** indicator percentile (100=high): 47th

Seminole County

[SANFORD] **SEMINOLE COUNTY S.D.**

1211 MELLONVILLE AVENUE SOUTH ● SANFORD FL 32771-2240 ● (407) 322-1252 ● http://www.scps.k12.fl.us

Grade Span: PK-12 **Schools**: *Regular* 46 ● *Spec Ed* 2 ● *Alt* 7 **Students**: 54,603 **Total Teachers**: 2,664 **Student/Classroom Teacher Ratio**: 19.7	**Expenditures/Student**: $4,283 **Librarians**: 53.0 1,030 students/librarian **Guidance Counselors**: 114.0 479 students/counselor	**% Amer Indian**: 0.2 **% Asian**: 2.8 **% Black**: 14.0 **% Hispanic**: 10.1 **% White**: 72.9	National ***Socio-Economic Status*** indicator percentile (100=high): 59th

Sumter County

[BUSHNELL] **SUMTER COUNTY S.D.**

202 NORTH FLORIDA STREET ● BUSHNELL FL 33513-9401 ● (352) 793-2315

Grade Span: PK-12 **Schools**: *Regular* 9 ● *Spec Ed* 1 ● *Alt* 0 **Students**: 5,767 **Total Teachers**: 295 **Student/Classroom Teacher Ratio**: 18.7	**Expenditures/Student**: $4,749 **Librarians**: 9.0 641 students/librarian **Guidance Counselors**: 10.0 577 students/counselor	**% Amer Indian**: 0.3 **% Asian**: 0.4 **% Black**: 27.2 **% Hispanic**: 3.6 **% White**: 68.5	National ***Socio-Economic Status*** indicator percentile (100=high): 12th

Suwannee County

[LIVE OAK] **SUWANNEE COUNTY S.D.**

224 PARSHLEY STREET SW ● LIVE OAK FL 32060-2396 ● (904) 364-2601 ● http://www.firn.edu/schools/suwannee/suwann_csb

Grade Span: PK-12 **Schools**: *Regular* 5 ● *Spec Ed* 0 ● *Alt* 3 **Students**: 5,690 **Total Teachers**: 291 **Student/Classroom Teacher Ratio**: 21.1	**Expenditures/Student**: $5,020 **Librarians**: 6.0 948 students/librarian **Guidance Counselors**: 13.0 438 students/counselor	**% Amer Indian**: 0.1 **% Asian**: 0.2 **% Black**: 18.8 **% Hispanic**: 2.1 **% White**: 78.8	National ***Socio-Economic Status*** indicator percentile (100=high): 29th

Taylor County

[PERRY] **TAYLOR COUNTY S.D.**

PO BOX 509 ● PERRY FL 32347-0509 ● (850) 584-2009 ● http://www.taylor.k12.fl.us

Grade Span: PK-12 **Schools**: *Regular* 5 ● *Spec Ed* 0 ● *Alt* 3 **Students**: 3,889 **Total Teachers**: 200 **Student/Classroom Teacher Ratio**: 22.9	**Expenditures/Student**: $5,154 **Librarians**: 4.0 972 students/librarian **Guidance Counselors**: 6.0 648 students/counselor	**% Amer Indian**: 0.4 **% Asian**: 0.3 **% Black**: 27.8 **% Hispanic**: 0.6 **% White**: 70.9	National ***Socio-Economic Status*** indicator percentile (100=high): 21st

Volusia County

[DELAND] **VOLUSIA COUNTY S.D.**

PO BOX 2118 ● DELAND FL 32721-2118 ● (904) 734-7190 ● http://www.volusia.k12.fl.us

Grade Span: PK-12 **Schools**: *Regular* 60 ● *Spec Ed* 1 ● *Alt* 10 **Students**: 56,788 **Total Teachers**: 3,236 **Student/Classroom Teacher Ratio**: 16.6	**Expenditures/Student**: $4,873 **Librarians**: 95.0 598 students/librarian **Guidance Counselors**: 137.0 415 students/counselor	**% Amer Indian**: 0.2 **% Asian**: 1.0 **% Black**: 16.0 **% Hispanic**: 6.7 **% White**: 76.1	National ***Socio-Economic Status*** indicator percentile (100=high): 35th

Wakulla County

[CRAWFORDVILLE] **WAKULLA COUNTY S.D.**

PO BOX 100 ● CRAWFORDVILLE FL 32327-0100 ● (850) 926-7131

Grade Span: PK-12	**Expenditures/Student**: $4,554	**% Amer Indian**: 0.2	
Schools: *Regular* 5 ● *Spec Ed* 0 ● *Alt* 1	**Librarians**: 6.0	**% Asian**: 0.3	National ***Socio-Economic***
Students: 4,270	712 students/librarian	**% Black**: 13.3	***Status*** indicator percentile
Total Teachers: 213	**Guidance Counselors**: 7.0	**% Hispanic**: 0.2	(100=high): 43rd
Student/Classroom Teacher Ratio: 18.8	610 students/counselor	**% White**: 86.0	

Walton County

[DEFUNIAK SPRINGS] **WALTON COUNTY S.D.**

9 EAST SLOSS AVENUE ● DEFUNIAK SPRINGS FL 32433-1995 ● (850) 892-3141 ● http://www.walton.k12.fl.us

Grade Span: PK-12	**Expenditures/Student**: $4,889	**% Amer Indian**: 0.5	
Schools: *Regular* 8 ● *Spec Ed* 0 ● *Alt* 1	**Librarians**: 8.0	**% Asian**: 1.0	National ***Socio-Economic***
Students: 5,233	654 students/librarian	**% Black**: 10.7	***Status*** indicator percentile
Total Teachers: 294	**Guidance Counselors**: 7.0	**% Hispanic**: 1.3	(100=high): 20th
Student/Classroom Teacher Ratio: 17.9	748 students/counselor	**% White**: 86.5	

Washington County

[CHIPLEY] **WASHINGTON COUNTY S.D.**

206 NORTH 3RD STREET ● CHIPLEY FL 32428 ● (850) 638-6222

Grade Span: PK-12	**Expenditures/Student**: $7,006	**% Amer Indian**: 0.5	
Schools: *Regular* 6 ● *Spec Ed* 0 ● *Alt* 2	**Librarians**: 5.0	**% Asian**: 0.8	National ***Socio-Economic***
Students: 3,174	635 students/librarian	**% Black**: 19.1	***Status*** indicator percentile
Total Teachers: 199	**Guidance Counselors**: 10.0	**% Hispanic**: 0.7	(100=high): 22nd
Student/Classroom Teacher Ratio: 20.7	317 students/counselor	**% White**: 78.8	

Appling County

[BAXLEY] APPLING COUNTY S.D.

ROUTE 7 BOX 36 HIGHWAY 15 ● BAXLEY GA 31513 ● (912) 367-8600

Grade Span: PK-12 **Schools**: *Regular* 6 ● *Spec Ed* 0 ● *Alt* 0 **Students**: 3,516 **Total Teachers**: 236 **Student/Classroom Teacher Ratio**: 15.0	**Expenditures/Student**: $5,055 **Librarians**: 6.0 586 students/librarian **Guidance Counselors**: 6.0 586 students/counselor	**% Amer Indian**: 0.0 **% Asian**: 0.3 **% Black**: 30.1 **% Hispanic**: 1.9 **% White**: 67.7	National ***Socio-Economic Status*** indicator percentile (100=high): 21st

Baldwin County

[MILLEDGEVILLE] BALDWIN COUNTY S.D.

PO BOX 1188 ● MILLEDGEVILLE GA 31061 ● (912) 453-4176 ● http://www.baldwin-county-schools.com

Grade Span: PK-12 **Schools**: *Regular* 9 ● *Spec Ed* 0 ● *Alt* 0 **Students**: 6,361 **Total Teachers**: 388 **Student/Classroom Teacher Ratio**: 16.4	**Expenditures/Student**: $4,701 **Librarians**: 9.0 707 students/librarian **Guidance Counselors**: 9.0 707 students/counselor	**% Amer Indian**: 0.0 **% Asian**: 0.9 **% Black**: 59.6 **% Hispanic**: 0.3 **% White**: 39.2	National ***Socio-Economic Status*** indicator percentile (100=high): 18th

Barrow County

[WINDER] BARROW COUNTY S.D.

PO BOX 767 ● WINDER GA 30680 ● (770) 867-4527 ● http://www.mindspring.com/~jmoates/bcsindex.html

Grade Span: PK-12 **Schools**: *Regular* 10 ● *Spec Ed* 0 ● *Alt* 0 **Students**: 6,871 **Total Teachers**: 436 **Student/Classroom Teacher Ratio**: 16.4	**Expenditures/Student**: $4,583 **Librarians**: 11.0 625 students/librarian **Guidance Counselors**: 8.0 859 students/counselor	**% Amer Indian**: 0.0 **% Asian**: 1.5 **% Black**: 12.3 **% Hispanic**: 1.1 **% White**: 85.1	National ***Socio-Economic Status*** indicator percentile (100=high): 50th

Bartow County

[CARTERSVILLE] BARTOW COUNTY S.D.

PO BOX 200007 ● CARTERSVILLE GA 30120 ● (770) 382-3813 ● http://www.bartow.k12.ga.us

Grade Span: PK-12 **Schools**: *Regular* 14 ● *Spec Ed* 0 ● *Alt* 0 **Students**: 9,820 **Total Teachers**: 650 **Student/Classroom Teacher Ratio**: 14.9	**Expenditures/Student**: $4,749 **Librarians**: 16.0 614 students/librarian **Guidance Counselors**: 20.4 481 students/counselor	**% Amer Indian**: 0.1 **% Asian**: 0.4 **% Black**: 7.2 **% Hispanic**: 0.6 **% White**: 91.6	National ***Socio-Economic Status*** indicator percentile (100=high): 47th

Bartow County

CARTERSVILLE CITY S.D.

310 OLD MILL ROAD ● CARTERSVILLE GA 30120 ● (770) 382-5880 ● http://www.cartersville.k12.ga.us/cityschl.html

Grade Span: PK-12 **Schools**: *Regular* 4 ● *Spec Ed* 0 ● *Alt* 0 **Students**: 3,175 **Total Teachers**: 190 **Student/Classroom Teacher Ratio**: 16.5	**Expenditures/Student**: $4,764 **Librarians**: 4.0 794 students/librarian **Guidance Counselors**: 6.0 529 students/counselor	**% Amer Indian**: 0.2 **% Asian**: 0.4 **% Black**: 23.5 **% Hispanic**: 2.1 **% White**: 73.8	National ***Socio-Economic Status*** indicator percentile (100=high): 48th

Ben Hill County

[FITZGERALD] BEN HILL COUNTY S.D.

PO DRAWER 5189 ● FITZGERALD GA 31750 ● (912) 423-3320

Grade Span: PK-12 **Schools**: *Regular* 4 ● *Spec Ed* 0 ● *Alt* 0 **Students**: 3,704 **Total Teachers**: 246 **Student/Classroom Teacher Ratio**: 15.6	**Expenditures/Student**: $4,359 **Librarians**: 4.7 788 students/librarian **Guidance Counselors**: 2.0 1,852 students/counselor	**% Amer Indian**: 0.1 **% Asian**: 0.2 **% Black**: 43.1 **% Hispanic**: 0.4 **% White**: 56.2	National ***Socio-Economic Status*** indicator percentile (100=high): 17th

Berrien County

[NASHVILLE] **BERRIEN COUNTY S.D.**

BOX 625 ● NASHVILLE GA 31639 ● (912) 686-2081

Grade Span: PK-12 **Schools**: *Regular* 4 ● *Spec Ed* 0 ● *Alt* 0 **Students**: 2,944 **Total Teachers**: 194 **Student/Classroom Teacher Ratio**: 15.3	**Expenditures/Student**: $4,736 **Librarians**: 5.0 589 students/librarian **Guidance Counselors**: 5.0 589 students/counselor	**% Amer Indian**: 0.2 **% Asian**: 0.2 **% Black**: 17.4 **% Hispanic**: 0.8 **% White**: 81.4	National ***Socio-Economic Status*** indicator percentile (100=high): 23rd

Bibb County

[MACON] **BIBB COUNTY S.D.**

BOX 6157 ● MACON GA 31213 ● (912) 741-8502 ● http://www.bibbcountyschools.com

Grade Span: PK-12 **Schools**: *Regular* 39 ● *Spec Ed* 1 ● *Alt* 0 **Students**: 25,066 **Total Teachers**: 1,521 **Student/Classroom Teacher Ratio**: 17.0	**Expenditures/Student**: $4,874 **Librarians**: 44.0 570 students/librarian **Guidance Counselors**: 58.0 432 students/counselor	**% Amer Indian**: 0.1 **% Asian**: 0.4 **% Black**: 66.1 **% Hispanic**: 0.4 **% White**: 32.9	National ***Socio-Economic Status*** indicator percentile (100=high): 11th

Brantley County

[NAHUNTA] **BRANTLEY COUNTY S.D.**

PO BOX 613 ● NAHUNTA GA 31553 ● (912) 462-6176

Grade Span: PK-12 **Schools**: *Regular* 5 ● *Spec Ed* 0 ● *Alt* 0 **Students**: 2,826 **Total Teachers**: 175 **Student/Classroom Teacher Ratio**: 15.6	**Expenditures/Student**: $4,033 **Librarians**: 5.0 565 students/librarian **Guidance Counselors**: 3.0 942 students/counselor	**% Amer Indian**: 0.1 **% Asian**: 0.1 **% Black**: 5.1 **% Hispanic**: 0.4 **% White**: 94.3	National ***Socio-Economic Status*** indicator percentile (100=high): 23rd

Brooks County

[QUITMAN] **BROOKS COUNTY S.D.**

PO BOX 511 ● QUITMAN GA 31643 ● (912) 263-7531 ● http://www.datasys.net/brooks_schools/brooks1.html

Grade Span: PK-12 **Schools**: *Regular* 4 ● *Spec Ed* 0 ● *Alt* 0 **Students**: 2,722 **Total Teachers**: 167 **Student/Classroom Teacher Ratio**: 16.4	**Expenditures/Student**: $4,608 **Librarians**: 4.0 681 students/librarian **Guidance Counselors**: 3.0 907 students/counselor	**% Amer Indian**: 0.0 **% Asian**: 0.1 **% Black**: 66.5 **% Hispanic**: 1.3 **% White**: 32.1	National ***Socio-Economic Status*** indicator percentile (100=high): 3rd

Bryan County

[PEMBROKE] **BRYAN COUNTY S.D.**

PO BOX 768 ● PEMBROKE GA 31321 ● (912) 653-4381

Grade Span: PK-12 **Schools**: *Regular* 6 ● *Spec Ed* 0 ● *Alt* 0 **Students**: 5,092 **Total Teachers**: 289 **Student/Classroom Teacher Ratio**: 18.2	**Expenditures/Student**: $3,963 **Librarians**: 8.0 637 students/librarian **Guidance Counselors**: 8.0 637 students/counselor	**% Amer Indian**: 0.0 **% Asian**: 0.7 **% Black**: 16.5 **% Hispanic**: 0.7 **% White**: 82.1	National ***Socio-Economic Status*** indicator percentile (100=high): 42nd

Bulloch County

[STATESBORO] **BULLOCH COUNTY S.D.**

500 NORTHSIDE DRIVE ● STATESBORO GA 30458 ● (912) 764-6201

Grade Span: PK-12 **Schools**: *Regular* 13 ● *Spec Ed* 0 ● *Alt* 0 **Students**: 8,325 **Total Teachers**: 532 **Student/Classroom Teacher Ratio**: 15.7	**Expenditures/Student**: $4,504 **Librarians**: 15.0 555 students/librarian **Guidance Counselors**: 17.0 490 students/counselor	**% Amer Indian**: 0.1 **% Asian**: 0.7 **% Black**: 39.0 **% Hispanic**: 0.5 **% White**: 59.7	National ***Socio-Economic Status*** indicator percentile (100=high): 20th

Burke County

[WAYNESBORO] **BURKE COUNTY S.D.**

PO BOX 908 ● WAYNESBORO GA 30830 ● (706) 554-5101

Grade Span: PK-12	**Expenditures/Student**: $4,773	**% Amer Indian**: 0.0	
Schools: *Regular* 5 ● *Spec Ed* 0 ● *Alt* 0	**Librarians**: 6.0	**% Asian**: 0.1	National ***Socio-Economic***
Students: 4,898	816 students/librarian	**% Black**: 68.5	***Status*** indicator percentile
Total Teachers: 283	**Guidance Counselors**: 9.0	**% Hispanic**: 0.6	(100=high): 5th
Student/Classroom Teacher Ratio: 17.4	544 students/counselor	**% White**: 30.7	

Butts County

[JACKSON] **BUTTS COUNTY S.D.**

181 NORTH MULBERRY STREET ● JACKSON GA 30233 ● (770) 775-7532

Grade Span: PK-12	**Expenditures/Student**: $4,396	**% Amer Indian**: 0.0	
Schools: *Regular* 4 ● *Spec Ed* 0 ● *Alt* 0	**Librarians**: 4.0	**% Asian**: 0.4	National ***Socio-Economic***
Students: 3,124	781 students/librarian	**% Black**: 41.6	***Status*** indicator percentile
Total Teachers: 174	**Guidance Counselors**: 5.0	**% Hispanic**: 0.4	(100=high): 28th
Student/Classroom Teacher Ratio: 18.2	625 students/counselor	**% White**: 57.6	

Camden County

[KINGSLAND] **CAMDEN COUNTY S.D.**

PO BOX 1329 ● KINGSLAND GA 31548 ● (912) 729-5687

Grade Span: PK-12	**Expenditures/Student**: $4,210	**% Amer Indian**: 0.5	
Schools: *Regular* 10 ● *Spec Ed* 0 ● *Alt* 0	**Librarians**: 10.0	**% Asian**: 1.1	National ***Socio-Economic***
Students: 8,608	861 students/librarian	**% Black**: 23.5	***Status*** indicator percentile
Total Teachers: 477	**Guidance Counselors**: 15.0	**% Hispanic**: 2.1	(100=high): 45th
Student/Classroom Teacher Ratio: 17.8	574 students/counselor	**% White**: 72.9	

Carroll County

[CARROLLTON] **CARROLL COUNTY S.D.**

164 INDEPENDENCE DRIVE ● CARROLLTON GA 30117 ● (770) 832-3568

Grade Span: PK-12	**Expenditures/Student**: $4,783	**% Amer Indian**: 0.3	
Schools: *Regular* 17 ● *Spec Ed* 0 ● *Alt* 0	**Librarians**: 19.0	**% Asian**: 0.2	National ***Socio-Economic***
Students: 11,053	582 students/librarian	**% Black**: 17.2	***Status*** indicator percentile
Total Teachers: 660	**Guidance Counselors**: 22.0	**% Hispanic**: 0.4	(100=high): 34th
Student/Classroom Teacher Ratio: 27.2	502 students/counselor	**% White**: 82.0	

Carroll County

CARROLLTON CITY S.D.

PO BOX 740 ● CARROLLTON GA 30117 ● (770) 832-9633 ● http://www.co.Carrollton.K12.GA.US

Grade Span: KG-12	**Expenditures/Student**: $4,887	**% Amer Indian**: 0.1	
Schools: *Regular* 3 ● *Spec Ed* 0 ● *Alt* 0	**Librarians**: 5.0	**% Asian**: 1.3	National ***Socio-Economic***
Students: 3,586	717 students/librarian	**% Black**: 35.9	***Status*** indicator percentile
Total Teachers: 202	**Guidance Counselors**: 7.4	**% Hispanic**: 1.8	(100=high): 33rd
Student/Classroom Teacher Ratio: 18.2	485 students/counselor	**% White**: 60.9	

Catoosa County

[RINGGOLD] **CATOOSA COUNTY S.D.**

BOX 130 ● RINGGOLD GA 30736 ● (706) 965-2297 ● http://hub.catoosa.k12.ga.us

Grade Span: PK-12	**Expenditures/Student**: $4,228	**% Amer Indian**: 0.0	
Schools: *Regular* 12 ● *Spec Ed* 0 ● *Alt* 0	**Librarians**: 16.0	**% Asian**: 0.4	National ***Socio-Economic***
Students: 8,526	533 students/librarian	**% Black**: 1.0	***Status*** indicator percentile
Total Teachers: 482	**Guidance Counselors**: 11.0	**% Hispanic**: 0.3	(100=high): 52nd
Student/Classroom Teacher Ratio: 17.2	775 students/counselor	**% White**: 98.3	

Chatham County

[SAVANNAH] CHATHAM COUNTY S.D.

208 BULL STREET ● SAVANNAH GA 30401 ● (912) 651-7000 ● http://www.savannah.chatham.k12.ga.us

Grade Span: PK-12 **Schools**: *Regular* 44 ● *Spec Ed* 0 ● *Alt* 0 **Students**: 35,860 **Total Teachers**: 2,141 **Student/Classroom Teacher Ratio**: 16.7	**Expenditures/Student**: $5,480 **Librarians**: 55.0 652 students/librarian **Guidance Counselors**: 67.0 535 students/counselor	**% Amer Indian**: 0.2 **% Asian**: 1.3 **% Black**: 61.8 **% Hispanic**: 1.2 **% White**: 35.4	National ***Socio-Economic Status*** indicator percentile (100=high): 14th

Chattooga County

[SUMMERVILLE] CHATTOOGA COUNTY S.D.

PO BOX 30 ● SUMMERVILLE GA 30747 ● (404) 857-3447

Grade Span: PK-12 **Schools**: *Regular* 7 ● *Spec Ed* 0 ● *Alt* 0 **Students**: 3,020 **Total Teachers**: 214 **Student/Classroom Teacher Ratio**: 14.2	**Expenditures/Student**: $4,885 **Librarians**: 7.0 431 students/librarian **Guidance Counselors**: 5.0 604 students/counselor	**% Amer Indian**: 0.1 **% Asian**: 0.1 **% Black**: 15.1 **% Hispanic**: 0.3 **% White**: 84.4	National ***Socio-Economic Status*** indicator percentile (100=high): 26th

Cherokee County

[CANTON] CHEROKEE COUNTY S.D.

PO BOX 769 ● CANTON GA 30114 ● (770) 479-1871

Grade Span: PK-12 **Schools**: *Regular* 26 ● *Spec Ed* 1 ● *Alt* 0 **Students**: 20,893 **Total Teachers**: 1,209 **Student/Classroom Teacher Ratio**: 18.7	**Expenditures/Student**: $4,469 **Librarians**: 28.0 746 students/librarian **Guidance Counselors**: 39.5 529 students/counselor	**% Amer Indian**: 0.6 **% Asian**: 0.1 **% Black**: 2.2 **% Hispanic**: 1.6 **% White**: 95.5	National ***Socio-Economic Status*** indicator percentile (100=high): 76th

Clarke County

[ATHENS] CLARKE COUNTY S.D.

PO BOX 1708 ● ATHENS GA 30603 ● (706) 546-7721

Grade Span: PK-12 **Schools**: *Regular* 19 ● *Spec Ed* 0 ● *Alt* 1 **Students**: 11,316 **Total Teachers**: 767 **Student/Classroom Teacher Ratio**: 14.3	**Expenditures/Student**: $5,673 **Librarians**: 22.0 514 students/librarian **Guidance Counselors**: 15.0 754 students/counselor	**% Amer Indian**: 0.1 **% Asian**: 2.9 **% Black**: 55.0 **% Hispanic**: 3.4 **% White**: 38.7	National ***Socio-Economic Status*** indicator percentile (100=high): 14th

Clayton County

[JONESBORO] CLAYTON COUNTY S.D.

120 SMITH STREET ● JONESBORO GA 30236 ● (770) 473-2700 ● http://www.ccps.ga.net

Grade Span: PK-12 **Schools**: *Regular* 44 ● *Spec Ed* 0 ● *Alt* 0 **Students**: 40,562 **Total Teachers**: 2,383 **Student/Classroom Teacher Ratio**: 17.3	**Expenditures/Student**: $4,770 **Librarians**: 51.0 795 students/librarian **Guidance Counselors**: 81.0 501 students/counselor	**% Amer Indian**: 0.2 **% Asian**: 4.5 **% Black**: 47.3 **% Hispanic**: 2.8 **% White**: 45.2	National ***Socio-Economic Status*** indicator percentile (100=high): 29th

Cobb County

[MARIETTA] COBB COUNTY S.D.

PO BOX 1088 ● MARIETTA GA 30060 ● (404) 422-9171 ● http://www.cobb.k12.ga.us

Grade Span: PK-12 **Schools**: *Regular* 85 ● *Spec Ed* 0 ● *Alt* 1 **Students**: 82,870 **Total Teachers**: 4,889 **Student/Classroom Teacher Ratio**: 16.5	**Expenditures/Student**: $4,740 **Librarians**: 111.0 747 students/librarian **Guidance Counselors**: 172.5 480 students/counselor	**% Amer Indian**: 0.2 **% Asian**: 2.8 **% Black**: 16.8 **% Hispanic**: 2.6 **% White**: 77.7	National ***Socio-Economic Status*** indicator percentile (100=high): 72nd

Cobb County

MARIETTA CITY S.D.

PO BOX 1265 ● MARIETTA GA 30061 ● (404) 422-3500

Grade Span: PK-12 **Schools**: *Regular* 8 ● *Spec Ed* 0 ● *Alt* 1 **Students**: 6,217 **Total Teachers**: 403 **Student/Classroom Teacher Ratio**: 16.1	**Expenditures/Student**: $5,655 **Librarians**: 9.0 691 students/librarian **Guidance Counselors**: 16.0 389 students/counselor	**% Amer Indian**: 0.2 **% Asian**: 2.3 **% Black**: 46.2 **% Hispanic**: 8.6 **% White**: 42.7	National ***Socio-Economic Status*** indicator percentile (100=high): 24th

Coffee County

[DOUGLAS] COFFEE COUNTY S.D.

PO BOX 959 ● DOUGLAS GA 31533 ● (912) 384-2086

Grade Span: PK-12 **Schools**: *Regular* 10 ● *Spec Ed* 0 ● *Alt* 0 **Students**: 7,260 **Total Teachers**: 452 **Student/Classroom Teacher Ratio**: 15.9	**Expenditures/Student**: $4,699 **Librarians**: 10.0 726 students/librarian **Guidance Counselors**: 10.0 726 students/counselor	**% Amer Indian**: 0.0 **% Asian**: 0.4 **% Black**: 35.0 **% Hispanic**: 2.5 **% White**: 62.0	National ***Socio-Economic Status*** indicator percentile (100=high): 14th

Colquitt County

[MOULTRIE] COLQUITT COUNTY S.D.

PO BOX 1806 ● MOULTRIE GA 31768 ● (912) 890-6206 ● http://colquitt.k12.ga.us

Grade Span: PK-12 **Schools**: *Regular* 13 ● *Spec Ed* 0 ● *Alt* 0 **Students**: 8,238 **Total Teachers**: 515 **Student/Classroom Teacher Ratio**: 15.7	**Expenditures/Student**: $4,460 **Librarians**: 15.0 549 students/librarian **Guidance Counselors**: 12.0 687 students/counselor	**% Amer Indian**: 0.0 **% Asian**: 0.1 **% Black**: 33.8 **% Hispanic**: 5.1 **% White**: 61.0	National ***Socio-Economic Status*** indicator percentile (100=high): 16th

Columbia County

[APPLING] COLUMBIA COUNTY S.D.

PO BOX 10 ● APPLING GA 30802 ● (706) 541-0650 ● http://www.ccboe.net

Grade Span: PK-12 **Schools**: *Regular* 20 ● *Spec Ed* 0 ● *Alt* 0 **Students**: 17,523 **Total Teachers**: 963 **Student/Classroom Teacher Ratio**: 18.2	**Expenditures/Student**: $4,017 **Librarians**: 23.0 762 students/librarian **Guidance Counselors**: 34.0 515 students/counselor	**% Amer Indian**: 0.2 **% Asian**: 3.6 **% Black**: 12.5 **% Hispanic**: 1.6 **% White**: 82.1	National ***Socio-Economic Status*** indicator percentile (100=high): 70th

Cook County

[ADEL] COOK COUNTY S.D.

PO BOX 152 ● ADEL GA 31620 ● (912) 896-2294

Grade Span: PK-12 **Schools**: *Regular* 3 ● *Spec Ed* 0 ● *Alt* 0 **Students**: 2,929 **Total Teachers**: 183 **Student/Classroom Teacher Ratio**: 16.4	**Expenditures/Student**: $4,466 **Librarians**: 3.0 976 students/librarian **Guidance Counselors**: 4.0 732 students/counselor	**% Amer Indian**: 0.0 **% Asian**: 0.1 **% Black**: 41.0 **% Hispanic**: 1.0 **% White**: 57.9	National ***Socio-Economic Status*** indicator percentile (100=high): 14th

Coweta County

[NEWNAN] COWETA COUNTY S.D.

PO BOX 280 ● NEWNAN GA 30263 ● (770) 254-2800 ● http://www.coweta.k12.ga.us

Grade Span: PK-12 **Schools**: *Regular* 19 ● *Spec Ed* 0 ● *Alt* 0 **Students**: 13,484 **Total Teachers**: 785 **Student/Classroom Teacher Ratio**: 17.2	**Expenditures/Student**: $4,545 **Librarians**: 22.0 613 students/librarian **Guidance Counselors**: 28.0 482 students/counselor	**% Amer Indian**: 0.1 **% Asian**: 0.3 **% Black**: 27.1 **% Hispanic**: 0.5 **% White**: 72.1	National ***Socio-Economic Status*** indicator percentile (100=high): 46th

Crisp County

[CORDELE] CRISP COUNTY S.D.

PO BOX 729 ● CORDELE GA 31015 ● (912) 273-1611

Grade Span: PK-12 **Schools**: *Regular* 5 ● *Spec Ed* 0 ● *Alt* 0 **Students**: 4,605 **Total Teachers**: 298 **Student/Classroom Teacher Ratio**: 16.3	**Expenditures/Student**: $4,671 **Librarians**: 6.0 768 students/librarian **Guidance Counselors**: 6.0 768 students/counselor	**% Amer Indian**: 0.1 **% Asian**: 0.4 **% Black**: 58.6 **% Hispanic**: 0.2 **% White**: 40.7	National ***Socio-Economic Status*** indicator percentile (100=high): 8th

DeKalb County

[DECATUR] DE KALB COUNTY S.D.

3770 NORTH DECATUR ROAD ● DECATUR GA 30032 ● (404) 297-2300 ● http://rehoboth.co.dekalb.k12.ga.us

Grade Span: PK-12 **Schools**: *Regular* 101 ● *Spec Ed* 4 ● *Alt* 1 **Students**: 87,291 **Total Teachers**: 5,279 **Student/Classroom Teacher Ratio**: 17.1	**Expenditures/Student**: $5,796 **Librarians**: 135.0 647 students/librarian **Guidance Counselors**: 198.9 439 students/counselor	**% Amer Indian**: 0.1 **% Asian**: 4.2 **% Black**: 74.4 **% Hispanic**: 3.8 **% White**: 17.4	National ***Socio-Economic Status*** indicator percentile (100=high): 23rd

DeKalb County

DECATUR CITY S.D.

320 NORTH MCDONOUGH ST ● DECATUR GA 30030 ● (404) 373-5344 ● http://www.tvq.com/dsw

Grade Span: PK-12 **Schools**: *Regular* 9 ● *Spec Ed* 0 ● *Alt* 0 **Students**: 2,832 **Total Teachers**: 182 **Student/Classroom Teacher Ratio**: 16.7	**Expenditures/Student**: $6,699 **Librarians**: 7.0 405 students/librarian **Guidance Counselors**: 5.5 515 students/counselor	**% Amer Indian**: 0.0 **% Asian**: 0.9 **% Black**: 62.6 **% Hispanic**: 0.2 **% White**: 36.3	National ***Socio-Economic Status*** indicator percentile (100=high): 18th

Decatur County

[BAINBRIDGE] DECATUR COUNTY S.D.

PO DRAWER 1406 ● BAINBRIDGE GA 31717 ● (912) 246-5898

Grade Span: PK-12 **Schools**: *Regular* 9 ● *Spec Ed* 0 ● *Alt* 0 **Students**: 5,929 **Total Teachers**: 367 **Student/Classroom Teacher Ratio**: 15.8	**Expenditures/Student**: $4,101 **Librarians**: 10.0 593 students/librarian **Guidance Counselors**: 8.0 741 students/counselor	**% Amer Indian**: 0.1 **% Asian**: 0.1 **% Black**: 50.2 **% Hispanic**: 2.4 **% White**: 47.2	National ***Socio-Economic Status*** indicator percentile (100=high): 12th

Dodge County

[EASTMAN] DODGE COUNTY S.D.

PO BOX 1029 ● EASTMAN GA 31023 ● (912) 374-3783

Grade Span: PK-12 **Schools**: *Regular* 4 ● *Spec Ed* 0 ● *Alt* 0 **Students**: 3,474 **Total Teachers**: 219 **Student/Classroom Teacher Ratio**: 16.5	**Expenditures/Student**: $4,628 **Librarians**: 4.0 869 students/librarian **Guidance Counselors**: 4.0 869 students/counselor	**% Amer Indian**: 0.0 **% Asian**: 0.1 **% Black**: 34.1 **% Hispanic**: 0.6 **% White**: 65.1	National ***Socio-Economic Status*** indicator percentile (100=high): 18th

Dougherty County

[ALBANY] DOUGHERTY S.D.

BOX 1470 ● ALBANY GA 31703 ● (912) 431-1286

Grade Span: PK-12 **Schools**: *Regular* 26 ● *Spec Ed* 0 ● *Alt* 0 **Students**: 18,027 **Total Teachers**: 1,053 **Student/Classroom Teacher Ratio**: 18.6	**Expenditures/Student**: $5,118 **Librarians**: 27.0 668 students/librarian **Guidance Counselors**: 29.0 622 students/counselor	**% Amer Indian**: 0.1 **% Asian**: 0.2 **% Black**: 75.6 **% Hispanic**: 0.2 **% White**: 23.8	National ***Socio-Economic Status*** indicator percentile (100=high): 12th

Douglas County

[DOUGLASVILLE] **DOUGLAS COUNTY S.D.**

PO BOX 1077 ● DOUGLASVILLE GA 30133 ● (404) 942-5411

Grade Span: PK-12 **Schools**: *Regular* 21 ● *Spec Ed* 0 ● *Alt* 0 **Students**: 15,536 **Total Teachers**: 935 **Student/Classroom Teacher Ratio**: 16.5	**Expenditures/Student**: $4,544 **Librarians**: 24.0 647 students/librarian **Guidance Counselors**: 29.0 536 students/counselor	**% Amer Indian**: 0.6 **% Asian**: 0.3 **% Black**: 14.3 **% Hispanic**: 0.8 **% White**: 83.9	National ***Socio-Economic Status*** indicator percentile (100=high): 58th

Early County

[BLAKELY] **EARLY COUNTY S.D.**

503 COLUMBIA ROAD ● BLAKELY GA 31723 ● (912) 723-4337

Grade Span: PK-12 **Schools**: *Regular* 3 ● *Spec Ed* 0 ● *Alt* 0 **Students**: 2,751 **Total Teachers**: 172 **Student/Classroom Teacher Ratio**: 16.3	**Expenditures/Student**: $4,646 **Librarians**: 3.0 917 students/librarian **Guidance Counselors**: 4.0 688 students/counselor	**% Amer Indian**: 0.0 **% Asian**: 0.2 **% Black**: 61.9 **% Hispanic**: 0.2 **% White**: 37.7	National ***Socio-Economic Status*** indicator percentile (100=high): 6th

Effingham County

[SPRINGFIELD] **EFFINGHAM COUNTY S.D.**

PO BOX 346 ● SPRINGFIELD GA 31329 ● (912) 754-6491

Grade Span: PK-12 **Schools**: *Regular* 9 ● *Spec Ed* 0 ● *Alt* 0 **Students**: 7,179 **Total Teachers**: 403 **Student/Classroom Teacher Ratio**: 17.1	**Expenditures/Student**: $4,100 **Librarians**: 12.0 598 students/librarian **Guidance Counselors**: 12.0 598 students/counselor	**% Amer Indian**: 0.1 **% Asian**: 0.3 **% Black**: 16.4 **% Hispanic**: 0.3 **% White**: 83.0	National ***Socio-Economic Status*** indicator percentile (100=high): 52nd

Elbert County

[ELBERTON] **ELBERT COUNTY S.D.**

50 LAUREL DRIVE ● ELBERTON GA 30635 ● (706) 283-1904 ● http://www.elbert.k12.ga.us

Grade Span: PK-12 **Schools**: *Regular* 6 ● *Spec Ed* 0 ● *Alt* 0 **Students**: 3,962 **Total Teachers**: 251 **Student/Classroom Teacher Ratio**: 16.6	**Expenditures/Student**: $4,580 **Librarians**: 7.0 566 students/librarian **Guidance Counselors**: 5.0 792 students/counselor	**% Amer Indian**: 0.0 **% Asian**: 0.4 **% Black**: 41.3 **% Hispanic**: 0.5 **% White**: 57.8	National ***Socio-Economic Status*** indicator percentile (100=high): 18th

Emanuel County

[SWAINSBORO] **EMANUEL COUNTY S.D.**

PO BOX 130 ● SWAINSBORO GA 30401 ● (912) 237-6674

Grade Span: PK-12 **Schools**: *Regular* 8 ● *Spec Ed* 0 ● *Alt* 0 **Students**: 5,017 **Total Teachers**: 311 **Student/Classroom Teacher Ratio**: 16.6	**Expenditures/Student**: $4,483 **Librarians**: 8.5 590 students/librarian **Guidance Counselors**: 7.0 717 students/counselor	**% Amer Indian**: 0.1 **% Asian**: 0.4 **% Black**: 45.8 **% Hispanic**: 0.3 **% White**: 53.4	National ***Socio-Economic Status*** indicator percentile (100=high): 10th

Fannin County

[BLUE RIDGE] **FANNIN COUNTY S.D.**

PO BOX 606 ● BLUE RIDGE GA 30513 ● (706) 632-3771

Grade Span: PK-12 **Schools**: *Regular* 5 ● *Spec Ed* 0 ● *Alt* 0 **Students**: 3,065 **Total Teachers**: 183 **Student/Classroom Teacher Ratio**: 16.8	**Expenditures/Student**: $4,487 **Librarians**: 5.0 613 students/librarian **Guidance Counselors**: 6.0 511 students/counselor	**% Amer Indian**: 0.1 **% Asian**: 0.3 **% Black**: 0.0 **% Hispanic**: 0.5 **% White**: 99.1	National ***Socio-Economic Status*** indicator percentile (100=high): 32nd

Fayette County

[FAYETTEVILLE] **FAYETTE COUNTY S.D.**

210 STONEWALL AVENUE ● FAYETTEVILLE GA 30214 ● (404) 461-8171 ● http://www.fcboe.org

Grade Span: PK-12 **Schools**: *Regular* 21 ● *Spec Ed* 0 ● *Alt* 0 **Students**: 16,725 **Total Teachers**: 1,073 **Student/Classroom Teacher Ratio**: 16.7	**Expenditures/Student**: $4,520 **Librarians**: 24.0 697 students/librarian **Guidance Counselors**: 36.0 465 students/counselor	**% Amer Indian**: 0.2 **% Asian**: 2.1 **% Black**: 9.7 **% Hispanic**: 1.3 **% White**: 86.7	National ***Socio-Economic Status*** indicator percentile (100=high): 91st

Floyd County

[ROME] **FLOYD COUNTY S.D.**

600 RIVERSIDE PARKWAY NE ● ROME GA 30161 ● (706) 234-1031 ● http://www.fcboe.ga.net

Grade Span: PK-12 **Schools**: *Regular* 16 ● *Spec Ed* 0 ● *Alt* 1 **Students**: 9,553 **Total Teachers**: 620 **Student/Classroom Teacher Ratio**: 15.6	**Expenditures/Student**: $4,822 **Librarians**: 17.0 562 students/librarian **Guidance Counselors**: 24.5 390 students/counselor	**% Amer Indian**: 0.6 **% Asian**: 0.2 **% Black**: 4.4 **% Hispanic**: 1.5 **% White**: 93.4	National ***Socio-Economic Status*** indicator percentile (100=high): 52nd

Floyd County

ROME CITY S.D.

508 EAST SECOND STREET ● ROME GA 30161 ● (706) 236-5050

Grade Span: PK-12 **Schools**: *Regular* 10 ● *Spec Ed* 0 ● *Alt* 0 **Students**: 4,792 **Total Teachers**: 327 **Student/Classroom Teacher Ratio**: 14.1	**Expenditures/Student**: $5,264 **Librarians**: 12.0 399 students/librarian **Guidance Counselors**: 11.0 436 students/counselor	**% Amer Indian**: 0.1 **% Asian**: 2.0 **% Black**: 51.0 **% Hispanic**: 3.8 **% White**: 43.1	National ***Socio-Economic Status*** indicator percentile (100=high): 14th

Forsyth County

[CUMMING] **FORSYTH COUNTY S.D.**

101 SCHOOL STREET ● CUMMING GA 30130 ● (770) 887-2461 ● http://www.forsyth.k12.ga.us

Grade Span: PK-12 **Schools**: *Regular* 14 ● *Spec Ed* 0 ● *Alt* 1 **Students**: 10,342 **Total Teachers**: 596 **Student/Classroom Teacher Ratio**: 17.2	**Expenditures/Student**: $4,776 **Librarians**: 14.0 739 students/librarian **Guidance Counselors**: 20.0 517 students/counselor	**% Amer Indian**: 0.0 **% Asian**: 0.1 **% Black**: 0.1 **% Hispanic**: 1.8 **% White**: 97.9	National ***Socio-Economic Status*** indicator percentile (100=high): 72nd

Franklin County

[CARNESVILLE] **FRANKLIN COUNTY S.D.**

PO BOX 99 ● CARNESVILLE GA 30521 ● (706) 384-4554

Grade Span: PK-12 **Schools**: *Regular* 5 ● *Spec Ed* 0 ● *Alt* 0 **Students**: 3,385 **Total Teachers**: 216 **Student/Classroom Teacher Ratio**: 15.7	**Expenditures/Student**: $4,458 **Librarians**: 5.0 677 students/librarian **Guidance Counselors**: 5.0 677 students/counselor	**% Amer Indian**: 0.1 **% Asian**: 0.2 **% Black**: 14.3 **% Hispanic**: 0.4 **% White**: 85.0	National ***Socio-Economic Status*** indicator percentile (100=high): 34th

Fulton County

ATLANTA CITY S.D.

210 PRYOR STREET SW ● ATLANTA GA 30335 ● (404) 827-8000 ● http://www.atlanta.k12.ga.us

Grade Span: PK-12 **Schools**: *Regular* 99 ● *Spec Ed* 0 ● *Alt* 3 **Students**: 60,209 **Total Teachers**: 3,637 **Student/Classroom Teacher Ratio**: 16.4	**Expenditures/Student**: $6,995 **Librarians**: 117.0 515 students/librarian **Guidance Counselors**: 109.0 552 students/counselor	**% Amer Indian**: 0.1 **% Asian**: 1.2 **% Black**: 90.4 **% Hispanic**: 1.8 **% White**: 6.6	National ***Socio-Economic Status*** indicator percentile (100=high): 3rd

Fulton County

[ATLANTA] **FULTON COUNTY S.D.**

786 CLEVELAND AVENUE SW ● ATLANTA GA 30315 ● (404) 768-3600 ● http://www.fulton.k12.ga.us

Grade Span: PK-12 **Schools**: *Regular* 53 ● *Spec Ed* 0 ● *Alt* 2 **Students**: 56,338 **Total Teachers**: 3,509 **Student/Classroom Teacher Ratio**: 15.8	**Expenditures/Student**: $5,942 **Librarians**: 78.0 722 students/librarian **Guidance Counselors**: 123.0 458 students/counselor	**% Amer Indian**: 0.1 **% Asian**: 3.4 **% Black**: 42.5 **% Hispanic**: 3.0 **% White**: 51.0	National ***Socio-Economic Status*** indicator percentile (100=high): 43rd

Gilmer County

[ELLIJAY] **GILMER COUNTY S.D.**

275 BOBCAT TRAIL ● ELLIJAY GA 30540 ● (706) 276-5000

Grade Span: PK-12 **Schools**: *Regular* 5 ● *Spec Ed* 0 ● *Alt* 0 **Students**: 3,082 **Total Teachers**: 178 **Student/Classroom Teacher Ratio**: 17.4	**Expenditures/Student**: $4,424 **Librarians**: 5.0 616 students/librarian **Guidance Counselors**: 4.0 771 students/counselor	**% Amer Indian**: 0.0 **% Asian**: 0.3 **% Black**: 0.0 **% Hispanic**: 2.1 **% White**: 97.6	National ***Socio-Economic Status*** indicator percentile (100=high): 32nd

Glynn County

[BRUNSWICK] **GLYNN COUNTY S.D.**

PO BOX 1677 ● BRUNSWICK GA 31520 ● (912) 267-4100 ● http://www.glynn.k12.ga.us

Grade Span: KG-12 **Schools**: *Regular* 14 ● *Spec Ed* 0 ● *Alt* 1 **Students**: 11,356 **Total Teachers**: 734 **Student/Classroom Teacher Ratio**: 15.9	**Expenditures/Student**: $5,348 **Librarians**: 17.0 668 students/librarian **Guidance Counselors**: 23.0 494 students/counselor	**% Amer Indian**: 0.4 **% Asian**: 0.0 **% Black**: 38.1 **% Hispanic**: 0.7 **% White**: 60.8	National ***Socio-Economic Status*** indicator percentile (100=high): 32nd

Gordon County

[CALHOUN] **GORDON COUNTY S.D.**

PO BOX 127 ● CALHOUN GA 30701 ● (706) 629-7366

Grade Span: PK-12 **Schools**: *Regular* 8 ● *Spec Ed* 0 ● *Alt* 0 **Students**: 5,439 **Total Teachers**: 325 **Student/Classroom Teacher Ratio**: 16.6	**Expenditures/Student**: $4,740 **Librarians**: 10.0 544 students/librarian **Guidance Counselors**: 10.0 544 students/counselor	**% Amer Indian**: 0.1 **% Asian**: 0.1 **% Black**: 1.7 **% Hispanic**: 0.9 **% White**: 97.2	National ***Socio-Economic Status*** indicator percentile (100=high): 45th

Grady County

[CAIRO] **GRADY COUNTY S.D.**

PO BOX 300 ● CAIRO GA 31728 ● (912) 377-3701

Grade Span: PK-12 **Schools**: *Regular* 7 ● *Spec Ed* 0 ● *Alt* 0 **Students**: 4,599 **Total Teachers**: 302 **Student/Classroom Teacher Ratio**: 15.2	**Expenditures/Student**: $4,312 **Librarians**: 8.0 575 students/librarian **Guidance Counselors**: 8.0 575 students/counselor	**% Amer Indian**: 0.2 **% Asian**: 0.0 **% Black**: 40.0 **% Hispanic**: 2.0 **% White**: 57.8	National ***Socio-Economic Status*** indicator percentile (100=high): 15th

Greene County

[GREENSBORO] **GREENE COUNTY S.D.**

201 NORTH MAIN STREET ● GREENSBORO GA 30642 ● (706) 453-7688

Grade Span: PK-12 **Schools**: *Regular* 4 ● *Spec Ed* 0 ● *Alt* 0 **Students**: 2,538 **Total Teachers**: 162 **Student/Classroom Teacher Ratio**: 17.1	**Expenditures/Student**: $5,291 **Librarians**: 4.0 635 students/librarian **Guidance Counselors**: 3.0 846 students/counselor	**% Amer Indian**: 0.0 **% Asian**: 0.0 **% Black**: 78.0 **% Hispanic**: 1.0 **% White**: 21.0	National ***Socio-Economic Status*** indicator percentile (100=high): 3rd

Gwinnett County

[LAWRENCEVILLE] **GWINNETT COUNTY S.D.**

52 GWINNETT DRIVE ● LAWRENCEVILLE GA 30245 ● (404) 963-8651 ● http://www.gwinnett.k12.ga.us

Grade Span: PK-12 **Schools**: *Regular* 68 ● *Spec Ed* 2 ● *Alt* 1 **Students**: 84,555 **Total Teachers**: 4,820 **Student/Classroom Teacher Ratio**: 17.4	**Expenditures/Student**: $4,663 **Librarians**: 82.0 1,031 students/librarian **Guidance Counselors**: 179.2 472 students/counselor	**% Amer Indian**: 0.1 **% Asian**: 6.1 **% Black**: 9.4 **% Hispanic**: 3.9 **% White**: 80.5	National ***Socio-Economic Status*** indicator percentile (100=high): 79th

Habersham County

[CLARKESVILLE] **HABERSHAM COUNTY S.D.**

PO BOX 467 ● CLARKESVILLE GA 30523 ● (706) 754-2118 ● http://www.habersham.k12.ga.us

Grade Span: KG-12 **Schools**: *Regular* 10 ● *Spec Ed* 0 ● *Alt* 0 **Students**: 5,381 **Total Teachers**: 322 **Student/Classroom Teacher Ratio**: 16.0	**Expenditures/Student**: $4,612 **Librarians**: 10.5 512 students/librarian **Guidance Counselors**: 10.0 538 students/counselor	**% Amer Indian**: 0.1 **% Asian**: 2.8 **% Black**: 2.2 **% Hispanic**: 3.8 **% White**: 91.2	National ***Socio-Economic Status*** indicator percentile (100=high): 52nd

Hall County

GAINESVILLE CITY S.D.

850 CENTURY PLACE ● GAINESVILLE GA 30505 ● (770) 536-5275 ● http://www.gcss.org

Grade Span: KG-12 **Schools**: *Regular* 5 ● *Spec Ed* 0 ● *Alt* 0 **Students**: 3,119 **Total Teachers**: 227 **Student/Classroom Teacher Ratio**: 13.9	**Expenditures/Student**: $5,777 **Librarians**: 4.0 780 students/librarian **Guidance Counselors**: 6.0 520 students/counselor	**% Amer Indian**: 0.1 **% Asian**: 2.7 **% Black**: 37.6 **% Hispanic**: 20.7 **% White**: 39.0	National ***Socio-Economic Status*** indicator percentile (100=high): 16th

Hall County

[GAINESVILLE] **HALL COUNTY S.D.**

711 GREEN STREET SUITE 100 ● GAINESVILLE GA 30501 ● (770) 534-1080

Grade Span: PK-12 **Schools**: *Regular* 25 ● *Spec Ed* 0 ● *Alt* 0 **Students**: 16,863 **Total Teachers**: 1,009 **Student/Classroom Teacher Ratio**: 16.7	**Expenditures/Student**: $4,346 **Librarians**: 26.0 649 students/librarian **Guidance Counselors**: 26.0 649 students/counselor	**% Amer Indian**: 0.2 **% Asian**: 0.9 **% Black**: 5.9 **% Hispanic**: 9.1 **% White**: 83.9	National ***Socio-Economic Status*** indicator percentile (100=high): 50th

Haralson County

[BUCHANAN] **HARALSON COUNTY S.D.**

PO BOX 508 ● BUCHANAN GA 30113 ● (770) 646-3882

Grade Span: PK-12 **Schools**: *Regular* 6 ● *Spec Ed* 0 ● *Alt* 0 **Students**: 3,334 **Total Teachers**: 195 **Student/Classroom Teacher Ratio**: 16.9	**Expenditures/Student**: $4,300 **Librarians**: 6.0 556 students/librarian **Guidance Counselors**: 5.0 667 students/counselor	**% Amer Indian**: 0.0 **% Asian**: 0.4 **% Black**: 5.0 **% Hispanic**: 0.1 **% White**: 94.5	National ***Socio-Economic Status*** indicator percentile (100=high): 27th

Harris County

[HAMILTON] **HARRIS COUNTY S.D.**

PO BOX 388 ● HAMILTON GA 31811 ● (706) 628-4206

Grade Span: PK-12 **Schools**: *Regular* 5 ● *Spec Ed* 0 ● *Alt* 0 **Students**: 3,532 **Total Teachers**: 212 **Student/Classroom Teacher Ratio**: 17.1	**Expenditures/Student**: $4,463 **Librarians**: 5.0 706 students/librarian **Guidance Counselors**: 8.0 442 students/counselor	**% Amer Indian**: 0.0 **% Asian**: 0.2 **% Black**: 27.7 **% Hispanic**: 0.4 **% White**: 71.7	National ***Socio-Economic Status*** indicator percentile (100=high): 31st

Hart County

[HARTWELL] **HART COUNTY S.D.**

PO BOX 696 ● HARTWELL GA 30643 ● (706) 376-5141

Grade Span: PK-12 **Schools**: *Regular* 7 ● *Spec Ed* 0 ● *Alt* 1 **Students**: 3,374 **Total Teachers**: 218 **Student/Classroom Teacher Ratio**: 15.8	**Expenditures/Student**: $4,699 **Librarians**: 7.0 482 students/librarian **Guidance Counselors**: 5.0 675 students/counselor	**% Amer Indian**: 0.0 **% Asian**: 0.3 **% Black**: 28.8 **% Hispanic**: 0.3 **% White**: 70.6	National ***Socio-Economic Status*** indicator percentile (100=high): 31st

Henry County

[MCDONOUGH] **HENRY COUNTY S.D.**

396 TOMLINSON STREET ● MCDONOUGH GA 30253 ● (770) 957-6601 ● http://www.henry.k12.ga.us

Grade Span: KG-12 **Schools**: *Regular* 19 ● *Spec Ed* 0 ● *Alt* 1 **Students**: 15,754 **Total Teachers**: 891 **Student/Classroom Teacher Ratio**: 17.5	**Expenditures/Student**: $4,375 **Librarians**: 23.0 685 students/librarian **Guidance Counselors**: 33.0 477 students/counselor	**% Amer Indian**: 0.1 **% Asian**: 0.8 **% Black**: 12.7 **% Hispanic**: 1.1 **% White**: 85.3	National ***Socio-Economic Status*** indicator percentile (100=high): 67th

Houston County

[PERRY] **HOUSTON COUNTY S.D.**

1211 WASHINGTON STREET ● PERRY GA 31069 ● (912) 987-1929

Grade Span: PK-12 **Schools**: *Regular* 26 ● *Spec Ed* 0 ● *Alt* 1 **Students**: 19,331 **Total Teachers**: 1,209 **Student/Classroom Teacher Ratio**: 15.3	**Expenditures/Student**: $4,727 **Librarians**: 29.0 667 students/librarian **Guidance Counselors**: 41.0 471 students/counselor	**% Amer Indian**: 0.1 **% Asian**: 1.3 **% Black**: 31.0 **% Hispanic**: 1.0 **% White**: 66.6	National ***Socio-Economic Status*** indicator percentile (100=high): 42nd

Jackson County

[JEFFERSON] **JACKSON COUNTY S.D.**

PO BOX 279 ● JEFFERSON GA 30549 ● (706) 367-5151

Grade Span: PK-12 **Schools**: *Regular* 7 ● *Spec Ed* 0 ● *Alt* 1 **Students**: 4,437 **Total Teachers**: 273 **Student/Classroom Teacher Ratio**: 15.5	**Expenditures/Student**: $4,671 **Librarians**: 8.0 555 students/librarian **Guidance Counselors**: 9.0 493 students/counselor	**% Amer Indian**: 0.2 **% Asian**: 0.3 **% Black**: 5.4 **% Hispanic**: 0.8 **% White**: 93.2	National ***Socio-Economic Status*** indicator percentile (100=high): 25th

Jeff Davis County

[HAZLEHURST] **JEFF DAVIS COUNTY S.D.**

PO BOX 571 ● HAZLEHURST GA 31539 ● (912) 375-4286

Grade Span: PK-12 **Schools**: *Regular* 4 ● *Spec Ed* 0 ● *Alt* 0 **Students**: 2,668 **Total Teachers**: 168 **Student/Classroom Teacher Ratio**: 16.0	**Expenditures/Student**: $4,322 **Librarians**: 4.0 667 students/librarian **Guidance Counselors**: 5.0 534 students/counselor	**% Amer Indian**: 0.1 **% Asian**: 0.1 **% Black**: 18.6 **% Hispanic**: 2.7 **% White**: 78.4	National ***Socio-Economic Status*** indicator percentile (100=high): 25th

Jefferson County

[LOUISVILLE] **JEFFERSON COUNTY S.D.**

PO BOX 449 ● LOUISVILLE GA 30434 ● (912) 625-7626

Grade Span: PK-12 **Schools**: *Regular* 6 ● *Spec Ed* 0 ● *Alt* 0 **Students**: 3,876 **Total Teachers**: 237 **Student/Classroom Teacher Ratio**: 15.8	**Expenditures/Student**: $4,193 **Librarians**: 6.0 646 students/librarian **Guidance Counselors**: 6.0 646 students/counselor	**% Amer Indian**: 0.0 **% Asian**: 0.1 **% Black**: 75.1 **% Hispanic**: 0.1 **% White**: 24.8	National ***Socio-Economic Status*** indicator percentile (100=high): 6th

Jones County

[GRAY] **JONES COUNTY S.D.**

PO BOX 519 ● GRAY GA 31032 ● (912) 986-6580

Grade Span: PK-12 **Schools**: *Regular* 4 ● *Spec Ed* 0 ● *Alt* 0 **Students**: 4,416 **Total Teachers**: 231 **Student/Classroom Teacher Ratio**: 19.5	**Expenditures/Student**: $3,585 **Librarians**: 4.0 1,104 students/librarian **Guidance Counselors**: 5.0 883 students/counselor	**% Amer Indian**: 0.0 **% Asian**: 0.2 **% Black**: 27.3 **% Hispanic**: 1.2 **% White**: 71.3	National ***Socio-Economic Status*** indicator percentile (100=high): 43rd

Laurens County

DUBLIN CITY S.D.

207 SHAMROCK DRIVE ● DUBLIN GA 31021 ● (912) 272-3440

Grade Span: PK-12 **Schools**: *Regular* 7 ● *Spec Ed* 0 ● *Alt* 0 **Students**: 3,956 **Total Teachers**: 242 **Student/Classroom Teacher Ratio**: 16.2	**Expenditures/Student**: $4,675 **Librarians**: 8.0 495 students/librarian **Guidance Counselors**: 8.5 465 students/counselor	**% Amer Indian**: 0.1 **% Asian**: 0.8 **% Black**: 61.3 **% Hispanic**: 0.4 **% White**: 37.4	National ***Socio-Economic Status*** indicator percentile (100=high): 14th

Laurens County

[DUBLIN] **LAURENS COUNTY S.D.**

PO BOX 2128 ● DUBLIN GA 31040 ● (912) 272-4767

Grade Span: PK-12 **Schools**: *Regular* 7 ● *Spec Ed* 0 ● *Alt* 0 **Students**: 5,131 **Total Teachers**: 320 **Student/Classroom Teacher Ratio**: 15.9	**Expenditures/Student**: $4,867 **Librarians**: 7.4 693 students/librarian **Guidance Counselors**: 9.0 570 students/counselor	**% Amer Indian**: 0.0 **% Asian**: 0.1 **% Black**: 34.1 **% Hispanic**: 0.5 **% White**: 65.3	National ***Socio-Economic Status*** indicator percentile (100=high): 15th

Lee County

[LEESBURG] **LEE COUNTY S.D.**

PO BOX 236 ● LEESBURG GA 31763 ● (912) 759-6414

Grade Span: PK-12 **Schools**: *Regular* 5 ● *Spec Ed* 0 ● *Alt* 0 **Students**: 4,890 **Total Teachers**: 247 **Student/Classroom Teacher Ratio**: 20.4	**Expenditures/Student**: $3,892 **Librarians**: 6.0 815 students/librarian **Guidance Counselors**: 9.0 543 students/counselor	**% Amer Indian**: 0.1 **% Asian**: 0.4 **% Black**: 17.2 **% Hispanic**: 0.3 **% White**: 82.0	National ***Socio-Economic Status*** indicator percentile (100=high): 56th

Liberty County

[HINESVILLE] **LIBERTY COUNTY S.D.**

110 SOUTH GAUSE STREET ● HINESVILLE GA 31313 ● (912) 876-2161

Grade Span: PK-12 **Schools**: *Regular* 11 ● *Spec Ed* 0 ● *Alt* 0 **Students**: 10,874 **Total Teachers**: 645 **Student/Classroom Teacher Ratio**: 17.1	**Expenditures/Student**: $4,351 **Librarians**: 15.0 725 students/librarian **Guidance Counselors**: 18.0 604 students/counselor	**% Amer Indian**: 0.2 **% Asian**: 2.1 **% Black**: 54.3 **% Hispanic**: 5.4 **% White**: 38.0	National ***Socio-Economic Status*** indicator percentile (100=high): 33rd

Lowndes County

[VALDOSTA] **LOWNDES COUNTY S.D.**

BOX 1227 ● VALDOSTA GA 31601 ● (912) 242-8760

Grade Span: PK-12 **Schools**: *Regular* 9 ● *Spec Ed* 0 ● *Alt* 0 **Students**: 8,323 **Total Teachers**: 519 **Student/Classroom Teacher Ratio**: 16.7	**Expenditures/Student**: $4,486 **Librarians**: 12.0 694 students/librarian **Guidance Counselors**: 14.0 595 students/counselor	**% Amer Indian**: 0.4 **% Asian**: 0.3 **% Black**: 21.9 **% Hispanic**: 1.9 **% White**: 75.5	National ***Socio-Economic Status*** indicator percentile (100=high): 38th

Lowndes County

VALDOSTA CITY S.D.

PO BOX 5407 ● VALDOSTA GA 31603 ● (912) 333-8500

Grade Span: PK-12	**Expenditures/Student**: $3,976	**% Amer Indian**: 0.1	National ***Socio-Economic Status*** indicator percentile (100=high): 16th
Schools: *Regular* 9 ● *Spec Ed* 0 ● *Alt* 0	**Librarians**: 12.0	**% Asian**: 1.0	
Students: 7,561	630 students/librarian	**% Black**: 67.1	
Total Teachers: 460	**Guidance Counselors**: 14.0	**% Hispanic**: 0.8	
Student/Classroom Teacher Ratio: 16.7	540 students/counselor	**% White**: 31.1	

Lumpkin County

[DAHLONEGA] **LUMPKIN COUNTY S.D.**

101 MOUNTAIN VIEW DRIVE ● DAHLONEGA GA 30533 ● (706) 864-3611

Grade Span: PK-12	**Expenditures/Student**: $4,368	**% Amer Indian**: 0.2	National ***Socio-Economic Status*** indicator percentile (100=high): 43rd
Schools: *Regular* 4 ● *Spec Ed* 0 ● *Alt* 0	**Librarians**: 4.0	**% Asian**: 0.3	
Students: 2,893	723 students/librarian	**% Black**: 1.5	
Total Teachers: 182	**Guidance Counselors**: 5.5	**% Hispanic**: 1.8	
Student/Classroom Teacher Ratio: 16.3	526 students/counselor	**% White**: 96.1	

McDuffie County

[THOMSON] **MCDUFFIE COUNTY S.D.**

PO BOX 957 ● THOMSON GA 30824 ● (706) 595-1918

Grade Span: PK-12	**Expenditures/Student**: $4,223	**% Amer Indian**: 0.0	National ***Socio-Economic Status*** indicator percentile (100=high): 17th
Schools: *Regular* 6 ● *Spec Ed* 0 ● *Alt* 0	**Librarians**: 8.0	**% Asian**: 0.3	
Students: 4,459	557 students/librarian	**% Black**: 47.4	
Total Teachers: 271	**Guidance Counselors**: 9.0	**% Hispanic**: 0.2	
Student/Classroom Teacher Ratio: 16.6	495 students/counselor	**% White**: 52.2	

Macon County

[OGLETHORPE] **MACON COUNTY S.D.**

PO BOX 488 ● OGLETHORPE GA 31068 ● (912) 472-8188

Grade Span: PK-12	**Expenditures/Student**: $4,541	**% Amer Indian**: 0.0	National ***Socio-Economic Status*** indicator percentile (100=high): 3rd
Schools: *Regular* 7 ● *Spec Ed* 0 ● *Alt* 0	**Librarians**: 6.0	**% Asian**: 0.4	
Students: 2,523	421 students/librarian	**% Black**: 80.6	
Total Teachers: 156	**Guidance Counselors**: 4.0	**% Hispanic**: 1.1	
Student/Classroom Teacher Ratio: 15.1	631 students/counselor	**% White**: 17.9	

Madison County

[DANIELSVILLE] **MADISON COUNTY S.D.**

PO BOX 37 ● DANIELSVILLE GA 30633 ● (706) 795-2191

Grade Span: PK-12	**Expenditures/Student**: $4,214	**% Amer Indian**: 0.0	National ***Socio-Economic Status*** indicator percentile (100=high): 38th
Schools: *Regular* 6 ● *Spec Ed* 0 ● *Alt* 0	**Librarians**: 8.0	**% Asian**: 0.2	
Students: 4,330	541 students/librarian	**% Black**: 9.3	
Total Teachers: 252	**Guidance Counselors**: 4.0	**% Hispanic**: 0.7	
Student/Classroom Teacher Ratio: 17.6	1,083 students/counselor	**% White**: 89.8	

Meriwether County

[GREENVILLE] **MERIWETHER COUNTY S.D.**

PO BOX 70 ● GREENVILLE GA 30222 ● (706) 672-4297

Grade Span: PK-12	**Expenditures/Student**: $4,735	**% Amer Indian**: 0.0	National ***Socio-Economic Status*** indicator percentile (100=high): 10th
Schools: *Regular* 9 ● *Spec Ed* 0 ● *Alt* 0	**Librarians**: 9.0	**% Asian**: 0.1	
Students: 4,209	468 students/librarian	**% Black**: 64.6	
Total Teachers: 281	**Guidance Counselors**: 5.0	**% Hispanic**: 0.1	
Student/Classroom Teacher Ratio: 15.3	842 students/counselor	**% White**: 35.1	

Mitchell County

[CAMILLA] **MITCHELL COUNTY S.D.**

PO BOX 588 ● CAMILLA GA 31730 ● (912) 336-5641

Grade Span: PK-12 **Schools**: *Regular* 3 ● *Spec Ed* 0 ● *Alt* 0 **Students**: 3,001 **Total Teachers**: 192 **Student/Classroom Teacher Ratio**: 15.8	**Expenditures/Student**: $4,452 **Librarians**: 4.0 750 students/librarian **Guidance Counselors**: 4.0 750 students/counselor	**% Amer Indian**: 0.0 **% Asian**: 0.1 **% Black**: 72.9 **% Hispanic**: 0.7 **% White**: 26.3	National ***Socio-Economic Status*** indicator percentile (100=high): 5th

Monroe County

[FORSYTH] **MONROE COUNTY S.D.**

PO BOX 1308 ● FORSYTH GA 31029 ● (912) 994-2031

Grade Span: PK-12 **Schools**: *Regular* 4 ● *Spec Ed* 0 ● *Alt* 0 **Students**: 3,660 **Total Teachers**: 217 **Student/Classroom Teacher Ratio**: 16.7	**Expenditures/Student**: $4,577 **Librarians**: 4.0 915 students/librarian **Guidance Counselors**: 6.0 610 students/counselor	**% Amer Indian**: 0.0 **% Asian**: 0.3 **% Black**: 36.4 **% Hispanic**: 0.1 **% White**: 63.2	National ***Socio-Economic Status*** indicator percentile (100=high): 32nd

Morgan County

[MADISON] **MORGAN COUNTY S.D.**

1065 EAST AVENUE ● MADISON GA 30650 ● (706) 342-0752

Grade Span: PK-12 **Schools**: *Regular* 4 ● *Spec Ed* 0 ● *Alt* 0 **Students**: 2,640 **Total Teachers**: 177 **Student/Classroom Teacher Ratio**: 15.0	**Expenditures/Student**: $5,247 **Librarians**: 4.0 660 students/librarian **Guidance Counselors**: 4.0 660 students/counselor	**% Amer Indian**: 0.0 **% Asian**: 0.1 **% Black**: 38.8 **% Hispanic**: 0.5 **% White**: 60.6	National ***Socio-Economic Status*** indicator percentile (100=high): 26th

Murray County

[CHATSWORTH] **MURRAY COUNTY S.D.**

PO BOX 40 ● CHATSWORTH GA 30705 ● (706) 695-4531

Grade Span: PK-12 **Schools**: *Regular* 8 ● *Spec Ed* 0 ● *Alt* 0 **Students**: 6,001 **Total Teachers**: 357 **Student/Classroom Teacher Ratio**: 16.3	**Expenditures/Student**: $4,162 **Librarians**: 8.0 750 students/librarian **Guidance Counselors**: 6.0 1,000 students/counselor	**% Amer Indian**: 0.0 **% Asian**: 0.2 **% Black**: 0.3 **% Hispanic**: 1.4 **% White**: 98.0	National ***Socio-Economic Status*** indicator percentile (100=high): 40th

Muscogee County

[COLUMBUS] **MUSCOGEE COUNTY S.D.**

PO BOX 2427 ● COLUMBUS GA 31994 ● (706) 649-0500 ● http://www.columbusga.com/mcsd

Grade Span: PK-12 **Schools**: *Regular* 49 ● *Spec Ed* 0 ● *Alt* 1 **Students**: 33,117 **Total Teachers**: 1,969 **Student/Classroom Teacher Ratio**: 17.6	**Expenditures/Student**: $5,141 **Librarians**: 60.0 552 students/librarian **Guidance Counselors**: 74.5 445 students/counselor	**% Amer Indian**: 0.2 **% Asian**: 1.1 **% Black**: 57.6 **% Hispanic**: 2.8 **% White**: 38.3	National ***Socio-Economic Status*** indicator percentile (100=high): 17th

Newton County

[COVINGTON] **NEWTON COUNTY S.D.**

PO BOX 1469 ● COVINGTON GA 30209 ● (770) 787-1330

Grade Span: PK-12 **Schools**: *Regular* 12 ● *Spec Ed* 0 ● *Alt* 1 **Students**: 9,223 **Total Teachers**: 566 **Student/Classroom Teacher Ratio**: 16.7	**Expenditures/Student**: $4,676 **Librarians**: 12.0 769 students/librarian **Guidance Counselors**: 14.0 659 students/counselor	**% Amer Indian**: 0.2 **% Asian**: 0.2 **% Black**: 29.4 **% Hispanic**: 0.8 **% White**: 69.4	National ***Socio-Economic Status*** indicator percentile (100=high): 29th

Oconee County

[WATKINSVILLE] **OCONEE COUNTY S.D.**

PO BOX 146 ● WATKINSVILLE GA 30677 ● (706) 769-5130

Grade Span: PK-12 **Schools**: *Regular* 5 ● *Spec Ed* 0 ● *Alt* 0 **Students**: 4,571 **Total Teachers**: 253 **Student/Classroom Teacher Ratio**: 17.9	**Expenditures/Student**: $4,003 **Librarians**: 5.0 914 students/librarian **Guidance Counselors**: 8.0 571 students/counselor	**% Amer Indian**: 0.0 **% Asian**: 0.8 **% Black**: 7.2 **% Hispanic**: 2.1 **% White**: 89.9	National ***Socio-Economic Status*** indicator percentile (100=high): 68th

Paulding County

[DALLAS] **PAULDING COUNTY S.D.**

522 HARDEE STREET ● DALLAS GA 30132 ● (770) 445-2051 ● http://www.paulding.k12.ga.us

Grade Span: PK-12 **Schools**: *Regular* 14 ● *Spec Ed* 0 ● *Alt* 0 **Students**: 11,256 **Total Teachers**: 647 **Student/Classroom Teacher Ratio**: 17.1	**Expenditures/Student**: $4,201 **Librarians**: 15.0 750 students/librarian **Guidance Counselors**: 22.5 500 students/counselor	**% Amer Indian**: 0.3 **% Asian**: 0.1 **% Black**: 4.8 **% Hispanic**: 0.7 **% White**: 94.1	National ***Socio-Economic Status*** indicator percentile (100=high): 62nd

Peach County

[FORT VALLEY] **PEACH COUNTY S.D.**

PO BOX 1018 ● FORT VALLEY GA 31030 ● (912) 825-5933

Grade Span: PK-12 **Schools**: *Regular* 5 ● *Spec Ed* 0 ● *Alt* 0 **Students**: 4,478 **Total Teachers**: 285 **Student/Classroom Teacher Ratio**: 15.5	**Expenditures/Student**: $4,174 **Librarians**: 7.0 640 students/librarian **Guidance Counselors**: 9.0 498 students/counselor	**% Amer Indian**: 0.2 **% Asian**: 0.3 **% Black**: 53.2 **% Hispanic**: 2.1 **% White**: 44.2	National ***Socio-Economic Status*** indicator percentile (100=high): 15th

Pickens County

[JASPER] **PICKENS COUNTY S.D.**

488 STEGALL DRIVE ● JASPER GA 30143 ● (706) 692-2532

Grade Span: KG-12 **Schools**: *Regular* 4 ● *Spec Ed* 0 ● *Alt* 0 **Students**: 3,220 **Total Teachers**: 200 **Student/Classroom Teacher Ratio**: 15.9	**Expenditures/Student**: $4,787 **Librarians**: 4.0 805 students/librarian **Guidance Counselors**: 6.0 537 students/counselor	**% Amer Indian**: 0.0 **% Asian**: 0.2 **% Black**: 2.0 **% Hispanic**: 0.2 **% White**: 97.5	National ***Socio-Economic Status*** indicator percentile (100=high): 40th

Pierce County

[BLACKSHEAR] **PIERCE COUNTY S.D.**

PO BOX 349 ● BLACKSHEAR GA 31516 ● (912) 449-5564 ● http://www.almatel.net/~levance

Grade Span: PK-12 **Schools**: *Regular* 4 ● *Spec Ed* 0 ● *Alt* 0 **Students**: 3,048 **Total Teachers**: 173 **Student/Classroom Teacher Ratio**: 17.2	**Expenditures/Student**: $4,174 **Librarians**: 5.0 610 students/librarian **Guidance Counselors**: 4.0 762 students/counselor	**% Amer Indian**: 0.0 **% Asian**: 0.0 **% Black**: 14.4 **% Hispanic**: 1.1 **% White**: 84.5	National ***Socio-Economic Status*** indicator percentile (100=high): 21st

Polk County

[CEDARTOWN] **POLK COUNTY S.D.**

PO BOX 128 ● CEDARTOWN GA 30125 ● (770) 748-3821

Grade Span: PK-12 **Schools**: *Regular* 11 ● *Spec Ed* 0 ● *Alt* 0 **Students**: 6,826 **Total Teachers**: 389 **Student/Classroom Teacher Ratio**: 17.1	**Expenditures/Student**: $4,131 **Librarians**: 12.0 569 students/librarian **Guidance Counselors**: 11.0 621 students/counselor	**% Amer Indian**: 0.1 **% Asian**: 0.1 **% Black**: 18.6 **% Hispanic**: 3.8 **% White**: 77.4	National ***Socio-Economic Status*** indicator percentile (100=high): 28th

Richmond County

[AUGUSTA] RICHMOND COUNTY S.D.

2083 HECKLE STREET ● AUGUSTA GA 30910 ● (706) 737-7200 ● http://www.richmond.k12.ga.us

Grade Span: PK-12 **Schools**: *Regular* 56 ● *Spec Ed* 0 ● *Alt* 0 **Students**: 36,359 **Total Teachers**: 2,125 **Student/Classroom Teacher Ratio**: 17.4	**Expenditures/Student**: $4,508 **Librarians**: 56.9 639 students/librarian **Guidance Counselors**: 52.0 699 students/counselor	**% Amer Indian**: 0.1 **% Asian**: 0.9 **% Black**: 64.1 **% Hispanic**: 1.9 **% White**: 33.0	National ***Socio-Economic Status*** indicator percentile (100=high): 12th

Rockdale County

[CONYERS] ROCKDALE COUNTY S.D.

PO DRAWER 1199 ● CONYERS GA 30207 ● (404) 483-4713 ● http://www.rockdale.k12.ga.us/index.htm

Grade Span: PK-12 **Schools**: *Regular* 15 ● *Spec Ed* 0 ● *Alt* 0 **Students**: 12,530 **Total Teachers**: 753 **Student/Classroom Teacher Ratio**: 16.4	**Expenditures/Student**: $4,985 **Librarians**: 22.0 570 students/librarian **Guidance Counselors**: 27.0 464 students/counselor	**% Amer Indian**: 0.4 **% Asian**: 1.2 **% Black**: 13.1 **% Hispanic**: 1.6 **% White**: 83.8	National ***Socio-Economic Status*** indicator percentile (100=high): 65th

Screven County

[SYLVANIA] SCREVEN COUNTY S.D.

PO BOX 1668 ● SYLVANIA GA 30467 ● (912) 564-7114

Grade Span: PK-12 **Schools**: *Regular* 3 ● *Spec Ed* 0 ● *Alt* 0 **Students**: 3,291 **Total Teachers**: 209 **Student/Classroom Teacher Ratio**: 15.5	**Expenditures/Student**: $4,584 **Librarians**: 4.0 823 students/librarian **Guidance Counselors**: 6.0 549 students/counselor	**% Amer Indian**: 0.0 **% Asian**: 0.1 **% Black**: 56.2 **% Hispanic**: 0.2 **% White**: 43.5	National ***Socio-Economic Status*** indicator percentile (100=high): 11th

Spalding County

[GRIFFIN] SPALDING COUNTY S.D.

PO DRAWER N ● GRIFFIN GA 30224 ● (770) 227-9478

Grade Span: PK-12 **Schools**: *Regular* 16 ● *Spec Ed* 0 ● *Alt* 0 **Students**: 10,391 **Total Teachers**: 633 **Student/Classroom Teacher Ratio**: 16.5	**Expenditures/Student**: $5,317 **Librarians**: 17.4 597 students/librarian **Guidance Counselors**: 23.4 444 students/counselor	**% Amer Indian**: 0.1 **% Asian**: 0.5 **% Black**: 57.3 **% Hispanic**: 0.6 **% White**: 41.5	National ***Socio-Economic Status*** indicator percentile (100=high): 21st

Stephens County

[TOCCOA] STEPHENS COUNTY S.D.

ROUTE 1 BOX 75 ● TOCCOA GA 30577 ● (706) 886-3783

Grade Span: PK-12 **Schools**: *Regular* 6 ● *Spec Ed* 0 ● *Alt* 0 **Students**: 4,221 **Total Teachers**: 277 **Student/Classroom Teacher Ratio**: 15.4	**Expenditures/Student**: $4,719 **Librarians**: 7.0 603 students/librarian **Guidance Counselors**: 10.0 422 students/counselor	**% Amer Indian**: 0.0 **% Asian**: 0.6 **% Black**: 16.4 **% Hispanic**: 0.6 **% White**: 82.4	National ***Socio-Economic Status*** indicator percentile (100=high): 36th

Sumter County

[AMERICUS] SUMTER COUNTY S.D.

210 INDUSTRIAL WAY ● AMERICUS GA 31709 ● (912) 924-6949

Grade Span: KG-12 **Schools**: *Regular* 7 ● *Spec Ed* 0 ● *Alt* 0 **Students**: 5,700 **Total Teachers**: 351 **Student/Classroom Teacher Ratio**: 17.2	**Expenditures/Student**: $3,137 **Librarians**: 7.0 814 students/librarian **Guidance Counselors**: 11.0 518 students/counselor	**% Amer Indian**: 0.2 **% Asian**: 0.3 **% Black**: 70.3 **% Hispanic**: 1.6 **% White**: 27.5	National ***Socio-Economic Status*** indicator percentile (100=high): 6th

Tattnall County

[REIDSVILLE] **TATTNALL COUNTY S.D.**

PO BOX 157 • REIDSVILLE GA 30453 • (912) 557-4726

Grade Span: PK-12 **Schools**: *Regular* 4 • *Spec Ed* 0 • *Alt* 0 **Students**: 3,386 **Total Teachers**: 211 **Student/Classroom Teacher Ratio**: 16.0	**Expenditures/Student**: $4,297 **Librarians**: 4.0 847 students/librarian **Guidance Counselors**: 6.0 564 students/counselor	**% Amer Indian**: 0.1 **% Asian**: 0.3 **% Black**: 36.5 **% Hispanic**: 6.2 **% White**: 57.0	National ***Socio-Economic Status*** indicator percentile (100=high): 10th

Thomas County

[THOMASVILLE] **THOMAS COUNTY S.D.**

PO BOX 2300 • THOMASVILLE GA 31792 • (912) 225-4380 • http://home.rose.net/~tcs/county/index.html

Grade Span: PK-12 **Schools**: *Regular* 4 • *Spec Ed* 0 • *Alt* 0 **Students**: 5,089 **Total Teachers**: 312 **Student/Classroom Teacher Ratio**: 18.5	**Expenditures/Student**: $4,792 **Librarians**: 5.0 1,018 students/librarian **Guidance Counselors**: 7.0 727 students/counselor	**% Amer Indian**: 0.1 **% Asian**: 0.3 **% Black**: 33.4 **% Hispanic**: 1.7 **% White**: 64.5	National ***Socio-Economic Status*** indicator percentile (100=high): 19th

Thomas County

THOMASVILLE CITY S.D.

915 EAST JACKSON STREET • THOMASVILLE GA 31799 • (912) 226-1601

Grade Span: PK-12 **Schools**: *Regular* 6 • *Spec Ed* 0 • *Alt* 0 **Students**: 3,801 **Total Teachers**: 236 **Student/Classroom Teacher Ratio**: 17.3	**Expenditures/Student**: $4,664 **Librarians**: 6.0 634 students/librarian **Guidance Counselors**: 6.0 634 students/counselor	**% Amer Indian**: 0.0 **% Asian**: 0.1 **% Black**: 72.1 **% Hispanic**: 0.2 **% White**: 27.5	National ***Socio-Economic Status*** indicator percentile (100=high): 12th

Tift County

[TIFTON] **TIFT COUNTY S.D.**

PO BOX 389 • TIFTON GA 31794 • (912) 382-4000

Grade Span: PK-12 **Schools**: *Regular* 10 • *Spec Ed* 0 • *Alt* 0 **Students**: 7,566 **Total Teachers**: 442 **Student/Classroom Teacher Ratio**: 16.9	**Expenditures/Student**: $4,033 **Librarians**: 12.0 631 students/librarian **Guidance Counselors**: 11.0 688 students/counselor	**% Amer Indian**: 0.1 **% Asian**: 0.4 **% Black**: 39.1 **% Hispanic**: 3.9 **% White**: 56.5	National ***Socio-Economic Status*** indicator percentile (100=high): 22nd

Toombs County

[LYONS] **TOOMBS COUNTY S.D.**

PO BOX 440 • LYONS GA 30436 • (912) 526-3141

Grade Span: PK-12 **Schools**: *Regular* 4 • *Spec Ed* 0 • *Alt* 0 **Students**: 2,619 **Total Teachers**: 171 **Student/Classroom Teacher Ratio**: 16.4	**Expenditures/Student**: $4,328 **Librarians**: 4.0 655 students/librarian **Guidance Counselors**: 5.0 524 students/counselor	**% Amer Indian**: 0.0 **% Asian**: 0.0 **% Black**: 23.7 **% Hispanic**: 8.7 **% White**: 67.5	National ***Socio-Economic Status*** indicator percentile (100=high): 12th

Toombs County

VIDALIA CITY S.D.

208 COLLEGE STREET • VIDALIA GA 30474 • (912) 537-3088

Grade Span: KG-12 **Schools**: *Regular* 4 • *Spec Ed* 0 • *Alt* 0 **Students**: 2,580 **Total Teachers**: 156 **Student/Classroom Teacher Ratio**: 16.3	**Expenditures/Student**: $4,033 **Librarians**: 4.0 645 students/librarian **Guidance Counselors**: 4.0 645 students/counselor	**% Amer Indian**: 0.7 **% Asian**: 0.3 **% Black**: 45.9 **% Hispanic**: 1.0 **% White**: 52.2	National ***Socio-Economic Status*** indicator percentile (100=high): 21st

Troup County

[LA GRANGE] **TROUP COUNTY S.D.**

PO BOX 1228 ● LA GRANGE GA 30240 ● (706) 812-7900

Grade Span: PK-12 **Schools**: *Regular* 17 ● *Spec Ed* 0 ● *Alt* 0 **Students**: 11,279 **Total Teachers**: 733 **Student/Classroom Teacher Ratio**: 15.0	**Expenditures/Student**: $4,857 **Librarians**: 20.0 564 students/librarian **Guidance Counselors**: 22.0 513 students/counselor	**% Amer Indian**: 0.1 **% Asian**: 0.2 **% Black**: 40.5 **% Hispanic**: 0.2 **% White**: 59.0	National ***Socio-Economic Status*** indicator percentile (100=high): 23rd

Upson County

[THOMASTON] **UPSON COUNTY S.D.**

205 CIVIC CENTER DRIVE ● THOMASTON GA 30286 ● (706) 647-9621 ● http://www.upson.k12.ga.us

Grade Span: PK-12 **Schools**: *Regular* 4 ● *Spec Ed* 0 ● *Alt* 0 **Students**: 5,032 **Total Teachers**: 288 **Student/Classroom Teacher Ratio**: 17.5	**Expenditures/Student**: $4,058 **Librarians**: 7.0 719 students/librarian **Guidance Counselors**: 9.0 559 students/counselor	**% Amer Indian**: 0.0 **% Asian**: 0.4 **% Black**: 34.4 **% Hispanic**: 0.1 **% White**: 65.0	National ***Socio-Economic Status*** indicator percentile (100=high): 26th

Walker County

[LA FAYETTE] **WALKER COUNTY S.D.**

PO BOX 29 ● LA FAYETTE GA 30728 ● (706) 638-1240 ● http://www.walkerschools.org/index.html

Grade Span: PK-12 **Schools**: *Regular* 16 ● *Spec Ed* 0 ● *Alt* 0 **Students**: 8,746 **Total Teachers**: 550 **Student/Classroom Teacher Ratio**: 15.8	**Expenditures/Student**: $4,518 **Librarians**: 17.5 500 students/librarian **Guidance Counselors**: 18.0 486 students/counselor	**% Amer Indian**: 0.0 **% Asian**: 0.4 **% Black**: 5.1 **% Hispanic**: 0.5 **% White**: 94.1	National ***Socio-Economic Status*** indicator percentile (100=high): 35th

Walton County

[MONROE] **WALTON COUNTY S.D.**

115 OAK STREET ● MONROE GA 30655 ● (770) 267-6544

Grade Span: PK-12 **Schools**: *Regular* 10 ● *Spec Ed* 0 ● *Alt* 0 **Students**: 8,226 **Total Teachers**: 483 **Student/Classroom Teacher Ratio**: 17.1	**Expenditures/Student**: $3,914 **Librarians**: 10.0 823 students/librarian **Guidance Counselors**: 14.0 588 students/counselor	**% Amer Indian**: 0.1 **% Asian**: 0.3 **% Black**: 21.2 **% Hispanic**: 0.4 **% White**: 77.9	National ***Socio-Economic Status*** indicator percentile (100=high): 43rd

Ware County

[WAYCROSS] **WARE COUNTY S.D.**

PO BOX 1789 ● WAYCROSS GA 31501 ● (912) 283-8656

Grade Span: PK-12 **Schools**: *Regular* 10 ● *Spec Ed* 0 ● *Alt* 0 **Students**: 6,711 **Total Teachers**: 443 **Student/Classroom Teacher Ratio**: 15.3	**Expenditures/Student**: $5,140 **Librarians**: 12.0 559 students/librarian **Guidance Counselors**: 11.0 610 students/counselor	**% Amer Indian**: 0.1 **% Asian**: 0.5 **% Black**: 36.8 **% Hispanic**: 0.7 **% White**: 61.9	National ***Socio-Economic Status*** indicator percentile (100=high): 18th

Washington County

[SANDERSVILLE] **WASHINGTON COUNTY S.D.**

PO BOX 716 ● SANDERSVILLE GA 31082 ● (912) 552-3981

Grade Span: PK-12 **Schools**: *Regular* 6 ● *Spec Ed* 0 ● *Alt* 0 **Students**: 3,832 **Total Teachers**: 225 **Student/Classroom Teacher Ratio**: 16.6	**Expenditures/Student**: $4,768 **Librarians**: 6.0 639 students/librarian **Guidance Counselors**: 7.0 547 students/counselor	**% Amer Indian**: 0.0 **% Asian**: 0.1 **% Black**: 69.8 **% Hispanic**: 0.1 **% White**: 30.1	National ***Socio-Economic Status*** indicator percentile (100=high): 9th

Wayne County

[JESUP] **WAYNE COUNTY S.D.**

555 SOUTH SUNSET BLVD ● JESUP GA 31545 ● (912) 427-4244

Grade Span: PK-12 **Schools**: *Regular* 8 ● *Spec Ed* 0 ● *Alt* 0 **Students**: 5,117 **Total Teachers**: 298 **Student/Classroom Teacher Ratio**: 18.2	**Expenditures/Student**: $4,235 **Librarians**: 8.0 640 students/librarian **Guidance Counselors**: 9.0 569 students/counselor	**% Amer Indian**: 0.0 **% Asian**: 0.3 **% Black**: 26.9 **% Hispanic**: 1.4 **% White**: 71.4	National ***Socio-Economic Status*** indicator percentile (100=high): 22nd

White County

[CLEVELAND] **WHITE COUNTY S.D.**

113 NORTH BROOK STREET ● CLEVELAND GA 30528 ● (404) 865-2315

Grade Span: PK-12 **Schools**: *Regular* 4 ● *Spec Ed* 0 ● *Alt* 0 **Students**: 2,792 **Total Teachers**: 160 **Student/Classroom Teacher Ratio**: 17.3	**Expenditures/Student**: $4,603 **Librarians**: 4.0 698 students/librarian **Guidance Counselors**: 5.0 558 students/counselor	**% Amer Indian**: 0.2 **% Asian**: 0.3 **% Black**: 3.3 **% Hispanic**: 0.4 **% White**: 95.8	National ***Socio-Economic Status*** indicator percentile (100=high): 44th

Whitfield County

DALTON CITY S.D.

PO BOX 1408 ● DALTON GA 30720 ● (706) 278-8766

Grade Span: PK-12 **Schools**: *Regular* 8 ● *Spec Ed* 0 ● *Alt* 1 **Students**: 4,448 **Total Teachers**: 295 **Student/Classroom Teacher Ratio**: 15.4	**Expenditures/Student**: $6,785 **Librarians**: 9.0 494 students/librarian **Guidance Counselors**: 10.0 445 students/counselor	**% Amer Indian**: 0.2 **% Asian**: 1.7 **% Black**: 11.9 **% Hispanic**: 27.2 **% White**: 59.0	National ***Socio-Economic Status*** indicator percentile (100=high): 29th

Whitfield County

[DALTON] **WHITFIELD COUNTY S.D.**

PO BOX 2167 ● DALTON GA 30720 ● (706) 278-8070 ● http://www.whitfield.k12.ga.us

Grade Span: PK-12 **Schools**: *Regular* 17 ● *Spec Ed* 0 ● *Alt* 0 **Students**: 10,512 **Total Teachers**: 613 **Student/Classroom Teacher Ratio**: 19.5	**Expenditures/Student**: $4,545 **Librarians**: 18.0 584 students/librarian **Guidance Counselors**: 24.0 438 students/counselor	**% Amer Indian**: 0.2 **% Asian**: 0.3 **% Black**: 1.2 **% Hispanic**: 5.4 **% White**: 92.9	National ***Socio-Economic Status*** indicator percentile (100=high): 48th

Worth County

[SYLVESTER] **WORTH COUNTY S.D.**

204-A EAST FRANKLIN STREET ● SYLVESTER GA 31791 ● (912) 776-8600

Grade Span: KG-12 **Schools**: *Regular* 5 ● *Spec Ed* 0 ● *Alt* 0 **Students**: 4,635 **Total Teachers**: 259 **Student/Classroom Teacher Ratio**: 17.9	**Expenditures/Student**: $4,104 **Librarians**: 6.0 773 students/librarian **Guidance Counselors**: 8.0 579 students/counselor	**% Amer Indian**: 0.1 **% Asian**: 0.2 **% Black**: 40.5 **% Hispanic**: 0.7 **% White**: 58.4	National ***Socio-Economic Status*** indicator percentile (100=high): 15th

Honolulu County

[HONOLULU] HAWAII DEPARTMENT OF EDUCATION

PO BOX 2360 ● HONOLULU HI 96804 ● (808) 832-5880 ● http://www.k12.hi.us

Grade Span: PK-12 **Schools**: *Regular* 241 ● *Spec Ed* 4 ● *Alt* 1 **Students**: 187,104 **Total Teachers**: 10,500 **Student/Classroom Teacher Ratio**: 18.1	**Expenditures/Student**: $5,778 **Librarians**: 287.0 652 students/librarian **Guidance Counselors**: 540.0 346 students/counselor	**% Amer Indian**: 0.4 **% Asian**: 69.3 **% Black**: 2.6 **% Hispanic**: 4.9 **% White**: 22.9	National ***Socio-Economic Status*** indicator percentile (100=high): 68th

Ada County

BOISE CITY INDEPENDENT S.D. 1

1207 WEST FORT STREET ● BOISE ID 83702 ● (208) 338-3400 ● http://www.sd01.k12.id.us

Grade Span: PK-12 **Schools**: *Regular* 42 ● *Spec Ed* 1 ● *Alt* 3 **Students**: 26,714 **Total Teachers**: 1,396 **Student/Classroom Teacher Ratio**: 19.0	**Expenditures/Student**: $4,401 **Librarians**: 10.0 2,671 students/librarian **Guidance Counselors**: 54.9 487 students/counselor	**% Amer Indian**: na **% Asian**: na **% Black**: na **% Hispanic**: na **% White**: na	National ***Socio-Economic Status*** indicator percentile (100=high): 66th

Ada County

MERIDIAN JOINT S.D. 2

911 NORTH MERIDIAN ROAD ● MERIDIAN ID 83642 ● (208) 888-6701 ● http://www.sd02.k12.id.us

Grade Span: PK-12 **Schools**: *Regular* 23 ● *Spec Ed* 0 ● *Alt* 1 **Students**: 18,641 **Total Teachers**: 918 **Student/Classroom Teacher Ratio**: 20.0	**Expenditures/Student**: $3,368 **Librarians**: 6.8 2,741 students/librarian **Guidance Counselors**: 46.5 401 students/counselor	**% Amer Indian**: na **% Asian**: na **% Black**: na **% Hispanic**: na **% White**: na	National ***Socio-Economic Status*** indicator percentile (100=high): 85th

Bannock County

POCATELLO S.D. 25

3115 POLE LINE ROAD ● POCATELLO ID 83204 ● (208) 232-3563 ● http://www.d25.k12.id.us

Grade Span: PK-12 **Schools**: *Regular* 22 ● *Spec Ed* 2 ● *Alt* 5 **Students**: 13,820 **Total Teachers**: 669 **Student/Classroom Teacher Ratio**: 21.0	**Expenditures/Student**: $3,940 **Librarians**: 13.0 1,063 students/librarian **Guidance Counselors**: 33.5 413 students/counselor	**% Amer Indian**: na **% Asian**: na **% Black**: na **% Hispanic**: na **% White**: na	National ***Socio-Economic Status*** indicator percentile (100=high): 59th

Bingham County

BLACKFOOT S.D. 55

270 EAST BRIDGE STREET ● BLACKFOOT ID 83221 ● (208) 785-8800

Grade Span: PK-12 **Schools**: *Regular* 10 ● *Spec Ed* 1 ● *Alt* 1 **Students**: 4,594 **Total Teachers**: 234 **Student/Classroom Teacher Ratio**: 20.0	**Expenditures/Student**: $3,991 **Librarians**: 2.0 2,297 students/librarian **Guidance Counselors**: 9.5 484 students/counselor	**% Amer Indian**: na **% Asian**: na **% Black**: na **% Hispanic**: na **% White**: na	National ***Socio-Economic Status*** indicator percentile (100=high): 34th

Blaine County

[HAILEY] **BLAINE COUNTY S.D. 61**

PO BOX 1008 ● HAILEY ID 83333 ● (208) 788-2296 ● http://webtrack.bcsd.k12.id.us

Grade Span: PK-12 **Schools**: *Regular* 6 ● *Spec Ed* 2 ● *Alt* 1 **Students**: 2,852 **Total Teachers**: 182 **Student/Classroom Teacher Ratio**: 15.7	**Expenditures/Student**: $5,166 **Librarians**: 2.3 1,240 students/librarian **Guidance Counselors**: 3.4 839 students/counselor	**% Amer Indian**: na **% Asian**: na **% Black**: na **% Hispanic**: na **% White**: na	National ***Socio-Economic Status*** indicator percentile (100=high): 75th

Bonner County

[SANDPOINT] **BONNER COUNTY S.D. 82**

1123 LAKE STREET, SUITE 2 ● SANDPOINT ID 83864 ● (208) 263-2184

Grade Span: PK-12 **Schools**: *Regular* 14 ● *Spec Ed* 0 ● *Alt* 1 **Students**: 6,167 **Total Teachers**: 315 **Student/Classroom Teacher Ratio**: 19.3	**Expenditures/Student**: $3,749 **Librarians**: 6.6 934 students/librarian **Guidance Counselors**: 13.3 464 students/counselor	**% Amer Indian**: na **% Asian**: na **% Black**: na **% Hispanic**: na **% White**: na	National ***Socio-Economic Status*** indicator percentile (100=high): 47th

Bonneville County
[IDAHO FALLS] **BONNEVILLE JOINT S.D. 93**
3497 NORTH AMMON ROAD ● IDAHO FALLS ID 83401 ● (208) 525-4400 ● http://d93.k12.id.us

Grade Span: PK-12 **Schools**: *Regular* 13 ● *Spec Ed* 1 ● *Alt* 1 **Students**: 7,736 **Total Teachers**: 395 **Student/Classroom Teacher Ratio**: 20.1	**Expenditures/Student**: $3,492 **Librarians**: 3.7 2,091 students/librarian **Guidance Counselors**: 16.0 484 students/counselor	**% Amer Indian**: na **% Asian**: na **% Black**: na **% Hispanic**: na **% White**: na	National ***Socio-Economic Status*** indicator percentile (100=high): 60th

Bonneville County
IDAHO FALLS S.D. 91
690 JOHN ADAMS PKWY ● IDAHO FALLS ID 83401 ● (208) 525-7500 ● http://www.d91.k12.id.us

Grade Span: PK-12 **Schools**: *Regular* 19 ● *Spec Ed* 0 ● *Alt* 2 **Students**: 11,211 **Total Teachers**: 552 **Student/Classroom Teacher Ratio**: 20.2	**Expenditures/Student**: $3,889 **Librarians**: 5.0 2,242 students/librarian **Guidance Counselors**: 14.0 801 students/counselor	**% Amer Indian**: na **% Asian**: na **% Black**: na **% Hispanic**: na **% White**: na	National ***Socio-Economic Status*** indicator percentile (100=high): 64th

Canyon County
CALDWELL S.D. 132
1101 CLEVELAND BOULEVARD ● CALDWELL ID 83605 ● (208) 455-3300

Grade Span: PK-12 **Schools**: *Regular* 7 ● *Spec Ed* 0 ● *Alt* 2 **Students**: 4,988 **Total Teachers**: 253 **Student/Classroom Teacher Ratio**: 20.4	**Expenditures/Student**: $3,824 **Librarians**: 2.5 1,995 students/librarian **Guidance Counselors**: 12.8 390 students/counselor	**% Amer Indian**: na **% Asian**: na **% Black**: na **% Hispanic**: na **% White**: na	National ***Socio-Economic Status*** indicator percentile (100=high): 25th

Canyon County
[CALDWELL] **VALLIVUE S.D. 139**
2423 SOUTH GEORGIA ● CALDWELL ID 83605 ● (208) 454-0445

Grade Span: PK-12 **Schools**: *Regular* 5 ● *Spec Ed* 0 ● *Alt* 0 **Students**: 2,970 **Total Teachers**: 156 **Student/Classroom Teacher Ratio**: 19.3	**Expenditures/Student**: $3,865 **Librarians**: 1.9 1,563 students/librarian **Guidance Counselors**: 7.9 376 students/counselor	**% Amer Indian**: na **% Asian**: na **% Black**: na **% Hispanic**: na **% White**: na	National ***Socio-Economic Status*** indicator percentile (100=high): 29th

Canyon County
NAMPA S.D. 131
619 SOUTH CANYON ● NAMPA ID 83686 ● (208) 465-2700

Grade Span: PK-12 **Schools**: *Regular* 14 ● *Spec Ed* 0 ● *Alt* 2 **Students**: 8,771 **Total Teachers**: 428 **Student/Classroom Teacher Ratio**: 20.9	**Expenditures/Student**: $3,400 **Librarians**: 2.9 3,024 students/librarian **Guidance Counselors**: 14.0 627 students/counselor	**% Amer Indian**: na **% Asian**: na **% Black**: na **% Hispanic**: na **% White**: na	National ***Socio-Economic Status*** indicator percentile (100=high): 40th

Cassia County
[BURLEY] **CASSIA COUNTY JOINT S.D. 151**
237 EAST 19TH STREET ● BURLEY ID 83318 ● (208) 678-6600

Grade Span: PK-12 **Schools**: *Regular* 14 ● *Spec Ed* 0 ● *Alt* 0 **Students**: 5,397 **Total Teachers**: 279 **Student/Classroom Teacher Ratio**: 19.4	**Expenditures/Student**: $3,710 **Librarians**: 5.3 1,018 students/librarian **Guidance Counselors**: 11.5 469 students/counselor	**% Amer Indian**: na **% Asian**: na **% Black**: na **% Hispanic**: na **% White**: na	National ***Socio-Economic Status*** indicator percentile (100=high): 44th

Elmore County

MOUNTAIN HOME S.D. 193

140 NORTH 3RD EAST ● MOUNTAIN HOME ID 83647 ● (208) 587-2580

Grade Span: PK-12 **Schools**: *Regular* 10 ● *Spec Ed* 0 ● *Alt* 1 **Students**: 4,255 **Total Teachers**: 241 **Student/Classroom Teacher Ratio**: 15.5	**Expenditures/Student**: $3,996 **Librarians**: 2.7 1,576 students/librarian **Guidance Counselors**: 10.0 426 students/counselor	**% Amer Indian**: na **% Asian**: na **% Black**: na **% Hispanic**: na **% White**: na	National ***Socio-Economic Status*** indicator percentile (100=high): 58th

Fremont County

[ST. ANTHONY] FREMONT COUNTY JOINT S.D. 215

147 NORTH 2ND WEST STREET ● ST. ANTHONY ID 83445 ● (208) 624-7542

Grade Span: PK-12 **Schools**: *Regular* 7 ● *Spec Ed* 0 ● *Alt* 1 **Students**: 2,634 **Total Teachers**: 138 **Student/Classroom Teacher Ratio**: 18.9	**Expenditures/Student**: $4,019 **Librarians**: 2.4 1,098 students/librarian **Guidance Counselors**: 5.6 470 students/counselor	**% Amer Indian**: na **% Asian**: na **% Black**: na **% Hispanic**: na **% White**: na	National ***Socio-Economic Status*** indicator percentile (100=high): 38th

Gem County

EMMETT S.D. 221

601 EAST 3RD STREET ● EMMETT ID 83617 ● (208) 365-6301 ● http://www.sd221.k12.id.us

Grade Span: PK-12 **Schools**: *Regular* 8 ● *Spec Ed* 0 ● *Alt* 1 **Students**: 2,827 **Total Teachers**: 144 **Student/Classroom Teacher Ratio**: 19.0	**Expenditures/Student**: $3,742 **Librarians**: 1.9 1,488 students/librarian **Guidance Counselors**: 5.0 565 students/counselor	**% Amer Indian**: na **% Asian**: na **% Black**: na **% Hispanic**: na **% White**: na	National ***Socio-Economic Status*** indicator percentile (100=high): 42nd

Jefferson County

[RIGBY] JEFFERSON COUNTY JOINT S.D. 251

201 IDAHO AVENUE ● RIGBY ID 83442 ● (208) 745-6693

Grade Span: PK-12 **Schools**: *Regular* 8 ● *Spec Ed* 0 ● *Alt* 0 **Students**: 4,171 **Total Teachers**: 193 **Student/Classroom Teacher Ratio**: 21.8	**Expenditures/Student**: $3,175 **Librarians**: 1.8 2,317 students/librarian **Guidance Counselors**: 9.8 426 students/counselor	**% Amer Indian**: na **% Asian**: na **% Black**: na **% Hispanic**: na **% White**: na	National ***Socio-Economic Status*** indicator percentile (100=high): 49th

Jerome County

JEROME JOINT S.D. 261

107 WEST 3RD STREET ● JEROME ID 83338 ● (208) 324-2392 ● http://www.d261.k12.id.us

Grade Span: PK-12 **Schools**: *Regular* 6 ● *Spec Ed* 0 ● *Alt* 1 **Students**: 3,154 **Total Teachers**: 155 **Student/Classroom Teacher Ratio**: 18.6	**Expenditures/Student**: $3,458 **Librarians**: 3.0 1,051 students/librarian **Guidance Counselors**: 5.0 631 students/counselor	**% Amer Indian**: na **% Asian**: na **% Black**: na **% Hispanic**: na **% White**: na	National ***Socio-Economic Status*** indicator percentile (100=high): 36th

Kootenai County

COEUR D'ALENE S.D. 271

311 NORTH 10TH STREET ● COEUR D'ALENE ID 83814 ● (208) 664-8241 ● http://www.sd271.k12.id.us/cda1.html

Grade Span: PK-12 **Schools**: *Regular* 13 ● *Spec Ed* 0 ● *Alt* 2 **Students**: 8,496 **Total Teachers**: 423 **Student/Classroom Teacher Ratio**: 20.3	**Expenditures/Student**: $4,009 **Librarians**: 3.6 2,360 students/librarian **Guidance Counselors**: 19.9 427 students/counselor	**% Amer Indian**: na **% Asian**: na **% Black**: na **% Hispanic**: na **% White**: na	National ***Socio-Economic Status*** indicator percentile (100=high): 65th

Kootenai County
POST FALLS S.D. 273
206 WEST MULLAN AVENUE ● POST FALLS ID 83854 ● (208) 773-1658

Grade Span: KG-12 **Schools**: *Regular* 6 ● *Spec Ed* 0 ● *Alt* 1 **Students**: 3,931 **Total Teachers**: 190 **Student/Classroom Teacher Ratio**: 22.8	**Expenditures/Student**: $3,508 **Librarians**: 3.0 1,310 students/librarian **Guidance Counselors**: 8.4 468 students/counselor	**% Amer Indian**: na **% Asian**: na **% Black**: na **% Hispanic**: na **% White**: na	National ***Socio-Economic Status*** indicator percentile (100=high): 61st

Kootenai County
[RATHDRUM] **LAKELAND S.D. 272**
1564 WASHINGTON STREET ● RATHDRUM ID 83858 ● (208) 687-0431

Grade Span: PK-12 **Schools**: *Regular* 7 ● *Spec Ed* 0 ● *Alt* 1 **Students**: 3,529 **Total Teachers**: 173 **Student/Classroom Teacher Ratio**: 20.6	**Expenditures/Student**: $3,241 **Librarians**: 3.0 1,176 students/librarian **Guidance Counselors**: 8.2 430 students/counselor	**% Amer Indian**: na **% Asian**: na **% Black**: na **% Hispanic**: na **% White**: na	National ***Socio-Economic Status*** indicator percentile (100=high): na

Latah County
MOSCOW S.D. 281
410 EAST THIRD STREET ● MOSCOW ID 83843 ● (208) 882-1120

Grade Span: KG-12 **Schools**: *Regular* 7 ● *Spec Ed* 0 ● *Alt* 1 **Students**: 2,709 **Total Teachers**: 161 **Student/Classroom Teacher Ratio**: 16.1	**Expenditures/Student**: $4,839 **Librarians**: 3.0 903 students/librarian **Guidance Counselors**: 6.5 417 students/counselor	**% Amer Indian**: na **% Asian**: na **% Black**: na **% Hispanic**: na **% White**: na	National ***Socio-Economic Status*** indicator percentile (100=high): 74th

Madison County
[REXBURG] **MADISON S.D. 321**
290 NORTH 1ST EAST ● REXBURG ID 83440 ● (208) 359-3300 ● http://d321.k12.id.us

Grade Span: KG-12 **Schools**: *Regular* 10 ● *Spec Ed* 0 ● *Alt* 1 **Students**: 4,337 **Total Teachers**: 213 **Student/Classroom Teacher Ratio**: 19.6	**Expenditures/Student**: $3,390 **Librarians**: 3.0 1,446 students/librarian **Guidance Counselors**: 8.2 529 students/counselor	**% Amer Indian**: na **% Asian**: na **% Black**: na **% Hispanic**: na **% White**: na	National ***Socio-Economic Status*** indicator percentile (100=high): 51st

Minidoka County
[RUPERT] **MINIDOKA COUNTY JOINT S.D. 331**
633 FREMONT AVENUE ● RUPERT ID 83350 ● (208) 436-4727 ● http://www.sd331.k12.id.us/default.tmpl

Grade Span: PK-12 **Schools**: *Regular* 10 ● *Spec Ed* 0 ● *Alt* 2 **Students**: 5,295 **Total Teachers**: 278 **Student/Classroom Teacher Ratio**: 18.2	**Expenditures/Student**: $3,410 **Librarians**: 2.4 2,206 students/librarian **Guidance Counselors**: 6.8 779 students/counselor	**% Amer Indian**: na **% Asian**: na **% Black**: na **% Hispanic**: na **% White**: na	National ***Socio-Economic Status*** indicator percentile (100=high): 29th

Nez Perce County
LEWISTON INDEPENDENT S.D. 340
3317 12TH STREET ● LEWISTON ID 83501 ● (208) 746-2337 ● http://www.lewiston.k12.id.us

Grade Span: PK-12 **Schools**: *Regular* 10 ● *Spec Ed* 0 ● *Alt* 2 **Students**: 5,103 **Total Teachers**: 289 **Student/Classroom Teacher Ratio**: 18.2	**Expenditures/Student**: $4,860 **Librarians**: 4.0 1,276 students/librarian **Guidance Counselors**: 10.5 486 students/counselor	**% Amer Indian**: na **% Asian**: na **% Black**: na **% Hispanic**: na **% White**: na	National ***Socio-Economic Status*** indicator percentile (100=high): 69th

Twin Falls County

TWIN FALLS S.D. 411

201 MAIN AVENUE WEST ● TWIN FALLS ID 83301 ● (208) 733-6900

Grade Span: PK-12 **Schools**: *Regular* 10 ● *Spec Ed* 1 ● *Alt* 2 **Students**: 7,057 **Total Teachers**: 354 **Student/Classroom Teacher Ratio**: 20.1	**Expenditures/Student**: $3,553 **Librarians**: 3.7 1,907 students/librarian **Guidance Counselors**: 15.4 458 students/counselor	**% Amer Indian**: na **% Asian**: na **% Black**: na **% Hispanic**: na **% White**: na	National ***Socio-Economic Status*** indicator percentile (100=high): 51st

Adams County

QUINCY S.D. 172

1444 MAINE ST ● QUINCY IL 62301-4261 ● (217) 223-8700

Grade Span: PK-12 **Schools**: *Regular* 11 ● *Spec Ed* 4 ● *Alt* 1 **Students**: 7,751 **Total Teachers**: 412 **Student/Classroom Teacher Ratio**: 17.6	**Expenditures/Student**: $4,902 **Librarians**: 2.0 3,876 students/librarian **Guidance Counselors**: 13.0 596 students/counselor	**% Amer Indian**: 0.1 **% Asian**: 0.9 **% Black**: 8.5 **% Hispanic**: 0.5 **% White**: 90.0	National ***Socio-Economic Status*** indicator percentiles are not available for the state of Illinois

Boone County

BELVIDERE COMMUNITY UNIT S.D. 100

1201 5TH AVE ● BELVIDERE IL 61008-5125 ● (815) 544-0301 ● http://www.belvidere100.k12.il.us

Grade Span: PK-12 **Schools**: *Regular* 9 ● *Spec Ed* 0 ● *Alt* 0 **Students**: 5,476 **Total Teachers**: 266 **Student/Classroom Teacher Ratio**: 20.1	**Expenditures/Student**: $3,801 **Librarians**: 5.0 1,095 students/librarian **Guidance Counselors**: 3.0 1,825 students/counselor	**% Amer Indian**: 0.1 **% Asian**: 0.5 **% Black**: 0.9 **% Hispanic**: 13.0 **% White**: 85.5	National ***Socio-Economic Status*** indicator percentiles are not available for the state of Illinois

Champaign County

CHAMPAIGN COMMUNITY UNIT S.D. 4

703 S NEW ST ● CHAMPAIGN IL 61820-5899 ● (217) 351-3838 ● http://www.cmi.k12.il.us/Champaign/Champaign.htm

Grade Span: PK-12 **Schools**: *Regular* 15 ● *Spec Ed* 2 ● *Alt* 0 **Students**: 9,057 **Total Teachers**: 566 **Student/Classroom Teacher Ratio**: 16.3	**Expenditures/Student**: $4,287 **Librarians**: 10.0 906 students/librarian **Guidance Counselors**: 14.0 647 students/counselor	**% Amer Indian**: 0.1 **% Asian**: 4.5 **% Black**: 31.6 **% Hispanic**: 0.8 **% White**: 63.0	National ***Socio-Economic Status*** indicator percentiles are not available for the state of Illinois

Champaign County

MAHOMET-SEYMOUR COMMUNITY UNIT S.D. 3

BX229 101 N DIVISION ● MAHOMET IL 61853 ● (217) 586-4995

Grade Span: PK-12 **Schools**: *Regular* 5 ● *Spec Ed* 0 ● *Alt* 0 **Students**: 2,636 **Total Teachers**: 149 **Student/Classroom Teacher Ratio**: 19.9	**Expenditures/Student**: $3,754 **Librarians**: 4.0 659 students/librarian **Guidance Counselors**: 4.0 659 students/counselor	**% Amer Indian**: 0.1 **% Asian**: 0.7 **% Black**: 0.2 **% Hispanic**: 0.4 **% White**: 98.5	National ***Socio-Economic Status*** indicator percentiles are not available for the state of Illinois

Champaign County

URBANA S.D. 116

BX 3039 205 N RACE ● URBANA IL 61801-2669 ● (217) 384-3636 ● http://squire.cmi.k12.il.us/Urbana/Urbana.htm

Grade Span: PK-12 **Schools**: *Regular* 8 ● *Spec Ed* 1 ● *Alt* 0 **Students**: 4,997 **Total Teachers**: 337 **Student/Classroom Teacher Ratio**: 15.9	**Expenditures/Student**: $5,974 **Librarians**: 8.0 625 students/librarian **Guidance Counselors**: 7.0 714 students/counselor	**% Amer Indian**: 0.1 **% Asian**: 8.3 **% Black**: 24.0 **% Hispanic**: 2.7 **% White**: 64.8	National ***Socio-Economic Status*** indicator percentiles are not available for the state of Illinois

Christian County

TAYLORVILLE COMMUNITY UNIT S.D. 3

101 E ADAMS ST ● TAYLORVILLE IL 62568-2288 ● (217) 824-4951

Grade Span: PK-12 **Schools**: *Regular* 8 ● *Spec Ed* 0 ● *Alt* 0 **Students**: 3,139 **Total Teachers**: 171 **Student/Classroom Teacher Ratio**: 19.9	**Expenditures/Student**: $4,292 **Librarians**: 3.0 1,046 students/librarian **Guidance Counselors**: 3.0 1,046 students/counselor	**% Amer Indian**: 0.1 **% Asian**: 0.2 **% Black**: 1.0 **% Hispanic**: 0.3 **% White**: 98.5	National ***Socio-Economic Status*** indicator percentiles are not available for the state of Illinois

Coles County

CHARLESTON COMMUNITY UNIT S.D. 1

410 W POLK AVE ● CHARLESTON IL 61920-2557 ● (217) 345-2106

Grade Span: PK-12 **Schools**: *Regular* 8 ● *Spec Ed* 0 ● *Alt* 0 **Students**: 3,400 **Total Teachers**: 171 **Student/Classroom Teacher Ratio**: 21.3	**Expenditures/Student**: $4,734 **Librarians**: 3.0 1,133 students/librarian **Guidance Counselors**: 3.0 1,133 students/counselor	**% Amer Indian**: 0.2 **% Asian**: 1.2 **% Black**: 2.6 **% Hispanic**: 0.5 **% White**: 95.4	National ***Socio-Economic Status*** indicator percentiles are not available for the state of Illinois

Coles County

MATTOON COMMUNITY UNIT S.D. 2

100 N 22ND ST ● MATTOON IL 61938-2760 ● (217) 235-5446

Grade Span: PK-12 **Schools**: *Regular* 9 ● *Spec Ed* 1 ● *Alt* 0 **Students**: 3,732 **Total Teachers**: 229 **Student/Classroom Teacher Ratio**: 16.3	**Expenditures/Student**: $4,610 **Librarians**: 3.0 1,244 students/librarian **Guidance Counselors**: 5.0 746 students/counselor	**% Amer Indian**: 0.2 **% Asian**: 0.7 **% Black**: 2.8 **% Hispanic**: 1.5 **% White**: 94.8	National ***Socio-Economic Status*** indicator percentiles are not available for the state of Illinois

Cook County

ARLINGTON HEIGHTS S.D. 25

301 W SOUTH ST ● ARLINGTON HEIGHTS IL 60005-1893 ● (847) 398-4200 ● http://nsn.nslsilus.org/ahkhome/ahsd25

Grade Span: PK-08 **Schools**: *Regular* 9 ● *Spec Ed* 0 ● *Alt* 0 **Students**: 4,450 **Total Teachers**: 282 **Student/Classroom Teacher Ratio**: 16.0	**Expenditures/Student**: $6,579 **Librarians**: 0.0 *** students/librarian **Guidance Counselors**: 0.0 *** students/counselor	**% Amer Indian**: 0.0 **% Asian**: 4.4 **% Black**: 0.8 **% Hispanic**: 2.7 **% White**: 92.1	National ***Socio-Economic Status*** indicator percentiles are not available for the state of Illinois

Cook County

[ARLINGTON HEIGHTS] COMMUNITY CONSOLIDATED S.D. 59

2123 S ARLINGTON HTS ● ARLINGTON HEIGHTS IL 60005-4596 ● (708) 593-4300

Grade Span: PK-08 **Schools**: *Regular* 13 ● *Spec Ed* 0 ● *Alt* 0 **Students**: 6,354 **Total Teachers**: 385 **Student/Classroom Teacher Ratio**: 16.6	**Expenditures/Student**: $6,998 **Librarians**: 1.0 6,354 students/librarian **Guidance Counselors**: 0.0 *** students/counselor	**% Amer Indian**: 0.3 **% Asian**: 12.6 **% Black**: 3.7 **% Hispanic**: 17.0 **% White**: 66.5	National ***Socio-Economic Status*** indicator percentiles are not available for the state of Illinois

Cook County

[ARLINGTON HEIGHTS] TOWNSHIP HIGH S.D. 214

2121 S GOEBBERT RD ● ARLINGTON HEIGHTS IL 60005-4297 ● (708) 437-4600 ● http://www.dist214.k12.il.us

Grade Span: 09-12 **Schools**: *Regular* 6 ● *Spec Ed* 4 ● *Alt* 0 **Students**: 10,665 **Total Teachers**: 692 **Student/Classroom Teacher Ratio**: 15.8	**Expenditures/Student**: $11,720 **Librarians**: 16.5 646 students/librarian **Guidance Counselors**: 52.3 204 students/counselor	**% Amer Indian**: 0.2 **% Asian**: 8.8 **% Black**: 2.2 **% Hispanic**: 10.3 **% White**: 78.4	National ***Socio-Economic Status*** indicator percentiles are not available for the state of Illinois

Cook County

BELLWOOD S.D. 88

640 EASTERN AVE ● BELLWOOD IL 60104-1031 ● (708) 344-9344

Grade Span: PK-08 **Schools**: *Regular* 7 ● *Spec Ed* 2 ● *Alt* 0 **Students**: 3,093 **Total Teachers**: 158 **Student/Classroom Teacher Ratio**: 22.4	**Expenditures/Student**: $4,609 **Librarians**: 1.0 3,093 students/librarian **Guidance Counselors**: 0.0 *** students/counselor	**% Amer Indian**: 0.1 **% Asian**: 1.3 **% Black**: 69.1 **% Hispanic**: 26.3 **% White**: 3.1	National ***Socio-Economic Status*** indicator percentiles are not available for the state of Illinois

Cook County
[BLUE ISLAND] **COOK COUNTY S.D. 130**
12300 GREENWOOD AVE ● BLUE ISLAND IL 60406-1567 ● (708) 385-6800

Grade Span: PK-08 **Schools**: *Regular* 9 ● *Spec Ed* 1 ● *Alt* 0 **Students**: 3,365 **Total Teachers**: 175 **Student/Classroom Teacher Ratio**: 22.8	**Expenditures/Student**: $4,585 **Librarians**: 4.0 841 students/librarian **Guidance Counselors**: 0.0 *** students/counselor	**% Amer Indian**: 0.0 **% Asian**: 0.1 **% Black**: 22.6 **% Hispanic**: 33.2 **% White**: 44.1	National ***Socio-Economic Status*** indicator percentiles are not available for the state of Illinois

Cook County
BURBANK S.D. 111
7600 S CENTRAL AVE ● BURBANK IL 60459-1397 ● (708) 496-0500

Grade Span: PK-08 **Schools**: *Regular* 7 ● *Spec Ed* 0 ● *Alt* 0 **Students**: 3,104 **Total Teachers**: 170 **Student/Classroom Teacher Ratio**: 18.5	**Expenditures/Student**: $4,788 **Librarians**: 3.0 1,035 students/librarian **Guidance Counselors**: 0.0 *** students/counselor	**% Amer Indian**: 0.1 **% Asian**: 1.7 **% Black**: 0.1 **% Hispanic**: 8.2 **% White**: 90.0	National ***Socio-Economic Status*** indicator percentiles are not available for the state of Illinois

Cook County
[CALUMET CITY] **DOLTON S.D. 149**
292 TORRENCE AVENUE ● CALUMET CITY IL 60409-1941 ● (708) 868-7861

Grade Span: PK-08 **Schools**: *Regular* 5 ● *Spec Ed* 0 ● *Alt* 0 **Students**: 3,175 **Total Teachers**: 147 **Student/Classroom Teacher Ratio**: 22.3	**Expenditures/Student**: $5,017 **Librarians**: 1.0 3,175 students/librarian **Guidance Counselors**: 0.0 *** students/counselor	**% Amer Indian**: 0.0 **% Asian**: 0.3 **% Black**: 92.9 **% Hispanic**: 3.2 **% White**: 3.7	National ***Socio-Economic Status*** indicator percentiles are not available for the state of Illinois

Cook County
[CALUMET CITY] **THORNTON FRACTIONAL TOWNSHIP HIGH S.D. 215**
1601 WENTWORTH AVE ● CALUMET CITY IL 60409-6399 ● (708) 418-1906

Grade Span: 09-12 **Schools**: *Regular* 2 ● *Spec Ed* 1 ● *Alt* 0 **Students**: 2,684 **Total Teachers**: 150 **Student/Classroom Teacher Ratio**: 18.5	**Expenditures/Student**: $7,559 **Librarians**: 2.0 1,342 students/librarian **Guidance Counselors**: 7.0 383 students/counselor	**% Amer Indian**: 0.7 **% Asian**: 1.0 **% Black**: 20.3 **% Hispanic**: 10.7 **% White**: 67.3	National ***Socio-Economic Status*** indicator percentiles are not available for the state of Illinois

Cook County
[CHICAGO] **CITY OF CHICAGO S.D. 299**
1819 W PERSHING RD ● CHICAGO IL 60609-2317 ● (312) 535-8000 ● http://www.cps.k12.il.us

Grade Span: PK-12 **Schools**: *Regular* 531 ● *Spec Ed* 24 ● *Alt* 0 **Students**: 412,921 **Total Teachers**: 22,941 **Student/Classroom Teacher Ratio**: 18.3	**Expenditures/Student**: $6,181 **Librarians**: 498.0 829 students/librarian **Guidance Counselors**: 899.4 459 students/counselor	**% Amer Indian**: 0.2 **% Asian**: 3.2 **% Black**: 54.3 **% Hispanic**: 31.4 **% White**: 10.8	National ***Socio-Economic Status*** indicator percentiles are not available for the state of Illinois

Cook County
[CHICAGO HEIGHTS] **BLOOM TOWNSHIP HIGH S.D. 206**
100 W 10TH ● CHICAGO HEIGHTS IL 60411 ● (708) 755-7010

Grade Span: 09-12 **Schools**: *Regular* 2 ● *Spec Ed* 1 ● *Alt* 0 **Students**: 3,128 **Total Teachers**: 137 **Student/Classroom Teacher Ratio**: 24.6	**Expenditures/Student**: $8,274 **Librarians**: 2.0 1,564 students/librarian **Guidance Counselors**: 6.0 521 students/counselor	**% Amer Indian**: 0.8 **% Asian**: 0.4 **% Black**: 41.3 **% Hispanic**: 16.7 **% White**: 40.9	National ***Socio-Economic Status*** indicator percentiles are not available for the state of Illinois

Cook County

CHICAGO HEIGHTS S.D. 170

30 W 16TH ST ● CHICAGO HEIGHTS IL 60411-3412 ● (708) 756-4165

Grade Span: PK-08	**Expenditures/Student**: $5,629	**% Amer Indian**: 0.1	National ***Socio-Economic Status*** indicator percentiles are not available for the state of Illinois
Schools: *Regular* 11 ● *Spec Ed* 1 ● *Alt* 0	**Librarians**: 1.0	**% Asian**: 0.2	
Students: 3,080	3,080 students/librarian	**% Black**: 54.6	
Total Teachers: 201	**Guidance Counselors**: 2.0	**% Hispanic**: 31.7	
Student/Classroom Teacher Ratio: 16.0	1,540 students/counselor	**% White**: 13.4	

Cook County

CICERO S.D. 99

5110 W 24TH ST ● CICERO IL 60650-2931 ● (708) 863-4856

Grade Span: PK-08	**Expenditures/Student**: $3,775	**% Amer Indian**: 0.1	National ***Socio-Economic Status*** indicator percentiles are not available for the state of Illinois
Schools: *Regular* 13 ● *Spec Ed* 0 ● *Alt* 0	**Librarians**: 9.0	**% Asian**: 1.3	
Students: 10,227	1,136 students/librarian	**% Black**: 0.3	
Total Teachers: 454	**Guidance Counselors**: 0.0	**% Hispanic**: 82.0	
Student/Classroom Teacher Ratio: 23.6	*** students/counselor	**% White**: 16.4	

Cook County

[CICERO] **J S MORTON HIGH S.D. 201**

2423 S AUSTIN BLVD ● CICERO IL 60650-2627 ● (708) 656-2300 ● http://kato.theramp.net/dist201

Grade Span: 09-12	**Expenditures/Student**: $6,482	**% Amer Indian**: 0.6	National ***Socio-Economic Status*** indicator percentiles are not available for the state of Illinois
Schools: *Regular* 2 ● *Spec Ed* 0 ● *Alt* 0	**Librarians**: 4.0	**% Asian**: 1.4	
Students: 5,634	1,409 students/librarian	**% Black**: 0.1	
Total Teachers: 294	**Guidance Counselors**: 16.0	**% Hispanic**: 56.6	
Student/Classroom Teacher Ratio: 20.1	352 students/counselor	**% White**: 41.3	

Cook County

DES PLAINES COMMUNITY CONSOLIDATED S.D. 62

777 E ALGONQUIN RD ● DES PLAINES IL 60016-6296 ● (847) 824-1136

Grade Span: PK-08	**Expenditures/Student**: $7,708	**% Amer Indian**: 0.0	National ***Socio-Economic Status*** indicator percentiles are not available for the state of Illinois
Schools: *Regular* 11 ● *Spec Ed* 0 ● *Alt* 0	**Librarians**: 11.0	**% Asian**: 7.3	
Students: 4,490	408 students/librarian	**% Black**: 2.8	
Total Teachers: 286	**Guidance Counselors**: 3.0	**% Hispanic**: 19.0	
Student/Classroom Teacher Ratio: 15.7	1,497 students/counselor	**% White**: 70.8	

Cook County

[DES PLAINES] **EAST MAINE S.D. 63**

10150 DEE RD ● DES PLAINES IL 60016-1597 ● (847) 299-1900

Grade Span: PK-08	**Expenditures/Student**: $5,675	**% Amer Indian**: 0.2	National ***Socio-Economic Status*** indicator percentiles are not available for the state of Illinois
Schools: *Regular* 5 ● *Spec Ed* 1 ● *Alt* 0	**Librarians**: 3.2	**% Asian**: 31.2	
Students: 3,456	1,080 students/librarian	**% Black**: 4.5	
Total Teachers: 191	**Guidance Counselors**: 2.0	**% Hispanic**: 8.7	
Student/Classroom Teacher Ratio: 18.2	1,728 students/counselor	**% White**: 55.4	

Cook County

DOLTON S.D. 148

PO BOX 160 ● DOLTON IL 60419-1096 ● (708) 841-2290

Grade Span: PK-08	**Expenditures/Student**: $4,194	**% Amer Indian**: 0.1	National ***Socio-Economic Status*** indicator percentiles are not available for the state of Illinois
Schools: *Regular* 8 ● *Spec Ed* 1 ● *Alt* 0	**Librarians**: 0.0	**% Asian**: 0.3	
Students: 2,700	*** students/librarian	**% Black**: 87.9	
Total Teachers: 147	**Guidance Counselors**: 0.0	**% Hispanic**: 3.6	
Student/Classroom Teacher Ratio: 19.1	*** students/counselor	**% White**: 8.1	

Cook County
ELMWOOD PARK COMMUNITY UNIT S.D. 401
8201 W FULLERTON AVE ● ELMWOOD PARK IL 60635-2499 ● (708) 452-7272 ● http://www.epcusd.w-cook.k12.il.us

Grade Span: PK-12	**Expenditures/Student**: $6,252	**% Amer Indian**: 0.2	National ***Socio-Economic Status*** indicator percentiles are not available for the state of Illinois
Schools: *Regular* 4 ● *Spec Ed* 0 ● *Alt* 0	**Librarians**: 1.0	**% Asian**: 1.3	
Students: 2,643	2,643 students/librarian	**% Black**: 0.2	
Total Teachers: 139	**Guidance Counselors**: 2.0	**% Hispanic**: 10.3	
Student/Classroom Teacher Ratio: 19.9	1,322 students/counselor	**% White**: 88.1	

Cook County
EVANSTON COMMUNITY CONSOLIDATED S.D. 65
1314 RIDGE AVE ● EVANSTON IL 60201-4198 ● (847) 492-5870 ● http://www.d65.k12.il.us

Grade Span: PK-08	**Expenditures/Student**: $8,240	**% Amer Indian**: 0.2	National ***Socio-Economic Status*** indicator percentiles are not available for the state of Illinois
Schools: *Regular* 15 ● *Spec Ed* 3 ● *Alt* 0	**Librarians**: 14.0	**% Asian**: 3.3	
Students: 7,148	511 students/librarian	**% Black**: 42.8	
Total Teachers: 514	**Guidance Counselors**: 0.0	**% Hispanic**: 7.0	
Student/Classroom Teacher Ratio: 14.4	*** students/counselor	**% White**: 46.7	

Cook County
EVANSTON TOWNSHIP HIGH S.D. 202
1600 DODGE AVE ● EVANSTON IL 60204 ● (847) 492-3856

Grade Span: 09-12	**Expenditures/Student**: $13,244	**% Amer Indian**: 0.0	National ***Socio-Economic Status*** indicator percentiles are not available for the state of Illinois
Schools: *Regular* 1 ● *Spec Ed* 0 ● *Alt* 0	**Librarians**: 4.0	**% Asian**: 3.1	
Students: 2,624	656 students/librarian	**% Black**: 43.4	
Total Teachers: 211	**Guidance Counselors**: 14.0	**% Hispanic**: 6.5	
Student/Classroom Teacher Ratio: 12.5	187 students/counselor	**% White**: 47.0	

Cook County
[FRANKLIN PARK] LEYDEN COMMUNITY HIGH S.D. 212
3400 ROSE ST ● FRANKLIN PARK IL 60131-2155 ● (847) 451-3000

Grade Span: 09-12	**Expenditures/Student**: $9,943	**% Amer Indian**: 0.3	National ***Socio-Economic Status*** indicator percentiles are not available for the state of Illinois
Schools: *Regular* 2 ● *Spec Ed* 0 ● *Alt* 0	**Librarians**: 5.0	**% Asian**: 3.8	
Students: 2,994	599 students/librarian	**% Black**: 1.3	
Total Teachers: 175	**Guidance Counselors**: 10.0	**% Hispanic**: 28.6	
Student/Classroom Teacher Ratio: 17.0	299 students/counselor	**% White**: 66.0	

Cook County
[FRANKLIN PARK] MANNHEIM S.D. 83
10401 GRAND AVE ● FRANKLIN PARK IL 60131-2294 ● (847) 455-4413

Grade Span: KG-08	**Expenditures/Student**: $6,604	**% Amer Indian**: 0.3	National ***Socio-Economic Status*** indicator percentiles are not available for the state of Illinois
Schools: *Regular* 4 ● *Spec Ed* 1 ● *Alt* 0	**Librarians**: 3.0	**% Asian**: 3.3	
Students: 2,652	884 students/librarian	**% Black**: 2.1	
Total Teachers: 178	**Guidance Counselors**: 0.0	**% Hispanic**: 43.7	
Student/Classroom Teacher Ratio: 15.5	*** students/counselor	**% White**: 50.7	

Cook County
GLENVIEW COMMUNITY CONSOLIDATED S.D. 34
1401 GREENWOOD RD ● GLENVIEW IL 60025-1599 ● (847) 998-5000 ● http://www.ncook.k12.il.us

Grade Span: PK-08	**Expenditures/Student**: $6,581	**% Amer Indian**: 0.3	National ***Socio-Economic Status*** indicator percentiles are not available for the state of Illinois
Schools: *Regular* 7 ● *Spec Ed* 0 ● *Alt* 0	**Librarians**: 2.0	**% Asian**: 11.6	
Students: 3,571	1,786 students/librarian	**% Black**: 2.5	
Total Teachers: 220	**Guidance Counselors**: 0.0	**% Hispanic**: 6.9	
Student/Classroom Teacher Ratio: 16.4	*** students/counselor	**% White**: 78.7	

Cook County

[GLENVIEW] **NORTHFIELD TOWNSHIP HIGH S.D. 225**

1835 LANDWEHR RD ● GLENVIEW IL 60025-1289 ● (847) 486-4700

Grade Span: 09-12	**Expenditures/Student**: $11,607	**% Amer Indian**: 0.1	National ***Socio-Economic***
Schools: *Regular* 2 ● *Spec Ed* 2 ● *Alt* 0	**Librarians**: 8.5	**% Asian**: 18.2	***Status*** indicator percentiles
Students: 4,055	477 students/librarian	**% Black**: 1.1	are not available for the
Total Teachers: 283	**Guidance Counselors**: 15.2	**% Hispanic**: 3.6	state of Illinois
Student/Classroom Teacher Ratio: 14.2	267 students/counselor	**% White**: 77.0	

Cook County

HARVEY S.D. 152

15147 S MYRTLE AVE ● HARVEY IL 60426 ● (708) 333-0300

Grade Span: PK-08	**Expenditures/Student**: $4,396	**% Amer Indian**: 0.0	National ***Socio-Economic***
Schools: *Regular* 8 ● *Spec Ed* 0 ● *Alt* 0	**Librarians**: 1.0	**% Asian**: 0.2	***Status*** indicator percentiles
Students: 3,210	3,210 students/librarian	**% Black**: 90.7	are not available for the
Total Teachers: 158	**Guidance Counselors**: 2.0	**% Hispanic**: 7.7	state of Illinois
Student/Classroom Teacher Ratio: 20.9	1,605 students/counselor	**% White**: 1.4	

Cook County

[HARVEY] **THORNTON TOWNSHIP HIGH S.D. 205**

151ST & BROADWAY ● HARVEY IL 60426 ● (708) 596-1000

Grade Span: 09-12	**Expenditures/Student**: $8,961	**% Amer Indian**: 0.0	National ***Socio-Economic***
Schools: *Regular* 3 ● *Spec Ed* 0 ● *Alt* 0	**Librarians**: 7.0	**% Asian**: 0.5	***Status*** indicator percentiles
Students: 7,069	1,010 students/librarian	**% Black**: 82.6	are not available for the
Total Teachers: 450	**Guidance Counselors**: 15.0	**% Hispanic**: 3.5	state of Illinois
Student/Classroom Teacher Ratio: 15.9	471 students/counselor	**% White**: 13.3	

Cook County

[HAZEL CREST] **PRAIRIE-HILLS ELEMENTARY S.D. 144**

P O BOX 233 ● HAZEL CREST IL 60429-0233 ● (708) 210-2888

Grade Span: PK-08	**Expenditures/Student**: $4,954	**% Amer Indian**: 0.0	National ***Socio-Economic***
Schools: *Regular* 7 ● *Spec Ed* 0 ● *Alt* 0	**Librarians**: 0.0	**% Asian**: 0.8	***Status*** indicator percentiles
Students: 2,906	*** students/librarian	**% Black**: 86.1	are not available for the
Total Teachers: 160	**Guidance Counselors**: 1.0	**% Hispanic**: 1.4	state of Illinois
Student/Classroom Teacher Ratio: 18.2	2,906 students/counselor	**% White**: 11.7	

Cook County

[JUSTICE] **INDIAN SPRINGS S.D. 109**

80TH ST & 82ND AVE ● JUSTICE IL 60458-1599 ● (708) 496-8700

Grade Span: PK-08	**Expenditures/Student**: $4,600	**% Amer Indian**: 0.3	National ***Socio-Economic***
Schools: *Regular* 5 ● *Spec Ed* 1 ● *Alt* 0	**Librarians**: 0.0	**% Asian**: 1.2	***Status*** indicator percentiles
Students: 2,636	*** students/librarian	**% Black**: 12.1	are not available for the
Total Teachers: 140	**Guidance Counselors**: 0.0	**% Hispanic**: 6.8	state of Illinois
Student/Classroom Teacher Ratio: 19.1	*** students/counselor	**% White**: 79.7	

Cook County

[LA GRANGE] **LYONS TOWNSHIP HIGH S.D. 204**

100 S BRAINARD AVE ● LA GRANGE IL 60525-2113 ● (708) 579-6300

Grade Span: 09-12	**Expenditures/Student**: $11,041	**% Amer Indian**: 0.1	National ***Socio-Economic***
Schools: *Regular* 1 ● *Spec Ed* 0 ● *Alt* 0	**Librarians**: 6.0	**% Asian**: 1.3	***Status*** indicator percentiles
Students: 2,903	484 students/librarian	**% Black**: 3.3	are not available for the
Total Teachers: 205	**Guidance Counselors**: 15.0	**% Hispanic**: 4.4	state of Illinois
Student/Classroom Teacher Ratio: 14.2	194 students/counselor	**% White**: 90.9	

Cook County

[LA GRANGE PARK] **LA GRANGE S.D. 102**

333 N PARK RD ● LA GRANGE PARK IL 60526-1898 ● (708) 482-2400

Grade Span: PK-08	**Expenditures/Student**: $5,349	**% Amer Indian**: 0.0	National ***Socio-Economic***
Schools: *Regular* 5 ● *Spec Ed* 0 ● *Alt* 0	**Librarians**: 4.0	**% Asian**: 1.9	***Status*** indicator percentiles
Students: 2,610	653 students/librarian	**% Black**: 8.1	are not available for the
Total Teachers: 171	**Guidance Counselors**: 0.0	**% Hispanic**: 4.6	state of Illinois
Student/Classroom Teacher Ratio: 15.6	*** students/counselor	**% White**: 85.4	

Cook County

MAYWOOD-MELROSE PARK-BROADVIEW S.D.

1133 S 8TH AVE ● MAYWOOD IL 60153-1997 ● (708) 450-2000

Grade Span: PK-08	**Expenditures/Student**: $4,205	**% Amer Indian**: 0.0	National ***Socio-Economic***
Schools: *Regular* 10 ● *Spec Ed* 0 ● *Alt* 0	**Librarians**: 2.0	**% Asian**: 0.6	***Status*** indicator percentiles
Students: 5,091	2,546 students/librarian	**% Black**: 65.3	are not available for the
Total Teachers: 232	**Guidance Counselors**: 0.0	**% Hispanic**: 26.0	state of Illinois
Student/Classroom Teacher Ratio: 22.0	*** students/counselor	**% White**: 8.1	

Cook County

[MAYWOOD] **PROVISO TOWNSHIP HIGH S.D. 209**

807 S 1ST AVE ● MAYWOOD IL 60153-2307 ● (708) 344-7000

Grade Span: 09-12	**Expenditures/Student**: $7,888	**% Amer Indian**: 0.6	National ***Socio-Economic***
Schools: *Regular* 2 ● *Spec Ed* 0 ● *Alt* 0	**Librarians**: 4.0	**% Asian**: 1.8	***Status*** indicator percentiles
Students: 4,416	1,104 students/librarian	**% Black**: 70.5	are not available for the
Total Teachers: 269	**Guidance Counselors**: 8.0	**% Hispanic**: 17.6	state of Illinois
Student/Classroom Teacher Ratio: 16.4	552 students/counselor	**% White**: 9.5	

Cook County

[MIDLOTHIAN] **BREMEN COMMUNITY HIGH S.D. 228**

15233 PULASKI RD ● MIDLOTHIAN IL 60445-3799 ● (708) 389-1175

Grade Span: 09-12	**Expenditures/Student**: $6,913	**% Amer Indian**: 0.3	National ***Socio-Economic***
Schools: *Regular* 4 ● *Spec Ed* 0 ● *Alt* 0	**Librarians**: 4.0	**% Asian**: 1.7	***Status*** indicator percentiles
Students: 4,916	1,229 students/librarian	**% Black**: 34.3	are not available for the
Total Teachers: 226	**Guidance Counselors**: 13.0	**% Hispanic**: 4.1	state of Illinois
Student/Classroom Teacher Ratio: 21.9	378 students/counselor	**% White**: 59.7	

Cook County

[OAK LAWN] **COMMUNITY HIGH S.D. 218**

10701 KILPATRICK AVE ● OAK LAWN IL 60453-5464 ● (708) 424-2000

Grade Span: 09-12	**Expenditures/Student**: $9,034	**% Amer Indian**: 0.2	National ***Socio-Economic***
Schools: *Regular* 3 ● *Spec Ed* 1 ● *Alt* 0	**Librarians**: 2.0	**% Asian**: 1.6	***Status*** indicator percentiles
Students: 4,849	2,425 students/librarian	**% Black**: 27.2	are not available for the
Total Teachers: 303	**Guidance Counselors**: 17.0	**% Hispanic**: 12.5	state of Illinois
Student/Classroom Teacher Ratio: 16.7	285 students/counselor	**% White**: 58.5	

Cook County

OAK LAWN-HOMETOWN S.D. 123

4201 93RD ST ● OAK LAWN IL 60453-1907 ● (708) 423-0150

Grade Span: PK-08	**Expenditures/Student**: $5,364	**% Amer Indian**: 0.1	National ***Socio-Economic***
Schools: *Regular* 6 ● *Spec Ed* 0 ● *Alt* 0	**Librarians**: 6.0	**% Asian**: 1.0	***Status*** indicator percentiles
Students: 2,602	434 students/librarian	**% Black**: 0.2	are not available for the
Total Teachers: 172	**Guidance Counselors**: 0.0	**% Hispanic**: 3.5	state of Illinois
Student/Classroom Teacher Ratio: 16.0	*** students/counselor	**% White**: 95.2	

Cook County

OAK PARK ELEMENTARY S.D. 97

970 MADISON ST ● OAK PARK IL 60302-4480 ● (708) 524-3000

Grade Span: PK-08 **Schools**: *Regular* 10 ● *Spec Ed* 0 ● *Alt* 0 **Students**: 5,243 **Total Teachers**: 318 **Student/Classroom Teacher Ratio**: 17.0	**Expenditures/Student**: $6,640 **Librarians**: 8.0 655 students/librarian **Guidance Counselors**: 0.0 *** students/counselor	**% Amer Indian**: 0.2 **% Asian**: 2.7 **% Black**: 33.5 **% Hispanic**: 3.2 **% White**: 60.5	National ***Socio-Economic Status*** indicator percentiles are not available for the state of Illinois

Cook County

OAK PARK-RIVER FOREST S.D. 200

201 N SCOVILLE AVE ● OAK PARK IL 60302-2296 ● (708) 383-0700

Grade Span: 09-12 **Schools**: *Regular* 1 ● *Spec Ed* 0 ● *Alt* 0 **Students**: 2,747 **Total Teachers**: 149 **Student/Classroom Teacher Ratio**: 18.4	**Expenditures/Student**: $10,576 **Librarians**: 3.0 916 students/librarian **Guidance Counselors**: 12.5 220 students/counselor	**% Amer Indian**: 0.3 **% Asian**: 4.1 **% Black**: 28.4 **% Hispanic**: 3.9 **% White**: 63.3	National ***Socio-Economic Status*** indicator percentiles are not available for the state of Illinois

Cook County

[OLYMPIA FIELDS] RICH TOWNSHIP HIGH S.D. 227

20290 GOVERNORS HIWY ● OLYMPIA FIELDS IL 60461 ● (708) 747-2600

Grade Span: 09-12 **Schools**: *Regular* 3 ● *Spec Ed* 0 ● *Alt* 0 **Students**: 3,472 **Total Teachers**: 181 **Student/Classroom Teacher Ratio**: 19.3	**Expenditures/Student**: $8,476 **Librarians**: 3.0 1,157 students/librarian **Guidance Counselors**: 12.0 289 students/counselor	**% Amer Indian**: 0.1 **% Asian**: 1.4 **% Black**: 60.6 **% Hispanic**: 2.4 **% White**: 35.6	National ***Socio-Economic Status*** indicator percentiles are not available for the state of Illinois

Cook County

[ORLAND PARK] CONSOLIDATED HIGH S.D. 230

15100 S 94TH AVE ● ORLAND PARK IL 60462-3820 ● (708) 349-5750 ● http://www.d230.s-cook.k12.il.us

Grade Span: 09-12 **Schools**: *Regular* 4 ● *Spec Ed* 0 ● *Alt* 0 **Students**: 7,345 **Total Teachers**: 437 **Student/Classroom Teacher Ratio**: 16.2	**Expenditures/Student**: $8,010 **Librarians**: 5.0 1,469 students/librarian **Guidance Counselors**: 23.5 313 students/counselor	**% Amer Indian**: 0.1 **% Asian**: 2.6 **% Black**: 1.0 **% Hispanic**: 2.4 **% White**: 94.0	National ***Socio-Economic Status*** indicator percentiles are not available for the state of Illinois

Cook County

[ORLAND PARK] ORLAND S.D. 135

15100 S 94TH AVE ● ORLAND PARK IL 60462 ● (708) 349-5700

Grade Span: PK-08 **Schools**: *Regular* 9 ● *Spec Ed* 0 ● *Alt* 0 **Students**: 5,373 **Total Teachers**: 284 **Student/Classroom Teacher Ratio**: 20.8	**Expenditures/Student**: $5,492 **Librarians**: 6.0 896 students/librarian **Guidance Counselors**: 4.0 1,343 students/counselor	**% Amer Indian**: 0.3 **% Asian**: 4.1 **% Black**: 1.8 **% Hispanic**: 1.8 **% White**: 92.1	National ***Socio-Economic Status*** indicator percentiles are not available for the state of Illinois

Cook County

PALATINE COMMUNITY CONSOLIDATED S.D. 15

580 N FIRST BANK DR ● PALATINE IL 60067-8108 ● (847) 934-2770 ● http://www.ccsd15.k12.il.us

Grade Span: PK-08 **Schools**: *Regular* 20 ● *Spec Ed* 1 ● *Alt* 0 **Students**: 11,958 **Total Teachers**: 641 **Student/Classroom Teacher Ratio**: 19.3	**Expenditures/Student**: $5,926 **Librarians**: 10.0 1,196 students/librarian **Guidance Counselors**: 2.0 5,979 students/counselor	**% Amer Indian**: 0.1 **% Asian**: 7.3 **% Black**: 4.0 **% Hispanic**: 13.5 **% White**: 75.1	National ***Socio-Economic Status*** indicator percentiles are not available for the state of Illinois

Cook County
[PALATINE] **TOWNSHIP HIGH S.D. 211**
1750 S ROSELLE RD ● PALATINE IL 60067-7336 ● (847) 359-3300

Grade Span: 09-12 **Schools**: *Regular* 5 ● *Spec Ed* 1 ● *Alt* 0 **Students**: 11,762 **Total Teachers**: 666 **Student/Classroom Teacher Ratio**: 17.7	**Expenditures/Student**: $9,227 **Librarians**: 15.0 784 students/librarian **Guidance Counselors**: 41.6 283 students/counselor	**% Amer Indian**: 0.2 **% Asian**: 10.7 **% Black**: 4.6 **% Hispanic**: 7.0 **% White**: 77.4	National ***Socio-Economic Status*** indicator percentiles are not available for the state of Illinois

Cook County
[PARK RIDGE] **MAINE TOWNSHIP HIGH S.D. 207**
1131 S DEE RD ● PARK RIDGE IL 60068-4398 ● (847) 696-3600 ● http://www.park-ridge.il.us/mwest

Grade Span: 09-12 **Schools**: *Regular* 3 ● *Spec Ed* 3 ● *Alt* 0 **Students**: 5,888 **Total Teachers**: 394 **Student/Classroom Teacher Ratio**: 15.8	**Expenditures/Student**: $12,576 **Librarians**: 9.0 654 students/librarian **Guidance Counselors**: 22.0 268 students/counselor	**% Amer Indian**: 0.2 **% Asian**: 14.3 **% Black**: 2.0 **% Hispanic**: 8.5 **% White**: 74.9	National ***Socio-Economic Status*** indicator percentiles are not available for the state of Illinois

Cook County
PARK RIDGE COMMUNITY CONSOLIDATED S.D. 64
164 S PROSPECT AVE ● PARK RIDGE IL 60068-4079 ● (847) 318-4300

Grade Span: PK-08 **Schools**: *Regular* 6 ● *Spec Ed* 0 ● *Alt* 0 **Students**: 3,475 **Total Teachers**: 225 **Student/Classroom Teacher Ratio**: 15.8	**Expenditures/Student**: $6,720 **Librarians**: 6.5 535 students/librarian **Guidance Counselors**: 2.0 1,738 students/counselor	**% Amer Indian**: 0.0 **% Asian**: 3.4 **% Black**: 0.3 **% Hispanic**: 1.8 **% White**: 94.6	National ***Socio-Economic Status*** indicator percentiles are not available for the state of Illinois

Cook County
SCHAUMBURG COMMUNITY CONSOLIDATED S.D. 54
524 E SCHAUMBURG RD ● SCHAUMBURG IL 60194-3510 ● (847) 885-6700

Grade Span: PK-08 **Schools**: *Regular* 26 ● *Spec Ed* 2 ● *Alt* 0 **Students**: 16,101 **Total Teachers**: 942 **Student/Classroom Teacher Ratio**: 17.6	**Expenditures/Student**: $6,664 **Librarians**: 0.0 *** students/librarian **Guidance Counselors**: 7.5 2,147 students/counselor	**% Amer Indian**: 0.1 **% Asian**: 12.2 **% Black**: 6.2 **% Hispanic**: 5.9 **% White**: 75.5	National ***Socio-Economic Status*** indicator percentiles are not available for the state of Illinois

Cook County
[SKOKIE] **NILES TOWNSHIP COMMUNITY HIGH S.D. 219**
7700 GROSS POINT RD ● SKOKIE IL 60077 ● (847) 965-9131

Grade Span: 09-12 **Schools**: *Regular* 2 ● *Spec Ed* 0 ● *Alt* 0 **Students**: 4,111 **Total Teachers**: 258 **Student/Classroom Teacher Ratio**: 16.5	**Expenditures/Student**: $11,424 **Librarians**: 8.0 514 students/librarian **Guidance Counselors**: 17.0 242 students/counselor	**% Amer Indian**: 0.2 **% Asian**: 31.7 **% Black**: 1.7 **% Hispanic**: 5.4 **% White**: 61.0	National ***Socio-Economic Status*** indicator percentiles are not available for the state of Illinois

Cook County
[TINLEY PARK] **KIRBY S.D. 140**
16931 S GRISSOM DR ● TINLEY PARK IL 60477-0098 ● (708) 532-6462

Grade Span: PK-08 **Schools**: *Regular* 7 ● *Spec Ed* 0 ● *Alt* 0 **Students**: 4,586 **Total Teachers**: 224 **Student/Classroom Teacher Ratio**: 20.6	**Expenditures/Student**: $3,734 **Librarians**: 5.0 917 students/librarian **Guidance Counselors**: 2.0 2,293 students/counselor	**% Amer Indian**: 0.1 **% Asian**: 1.9 **% Black**: 0.5 **% Hispanic**: 2.6 **% White**: 94.9	National ***Socio-Economic Status*** indicator percentiles are not available for the state of Illinois

Cook County

TINLEY PARK COMMUNITY S.D. 146

17316 OAK PARK AVE ● TINLEY PARK IL 60477-3404 ● (708) 614-4500

Grade Span: PK-08	**Expenditures/Student**: $5,365	**% Amer Indian**: 0.0	National ***Socio-Economic***
Schools: *Regular* 6 ● *Spec Ed* 0 ● *Alt* 0	**Librarians**: 4.0	**% Asian**: 2.3	***Status*** indicator percentiles
Students: 2,508	627 students/librarian	**% Black**: 1.5	are not available for the
Total Teachers: 165	**Guidance Counselors**: 0.0	**% Hispanic**: 2.7	state of Illinois
Student/Classroom Teacher Ratio: 15.7	*** students/counselor	**% White**: 93.5	

Cook County

WHEELING COMMUNITY CONSOLIDATED S.D. 21

999 W DUNDEE RD ● WHEELING IL 60090-3997 ● (847) 537-8270

Grade Span: PK-08	**Expenditures/Student**: $6,156	**% Amer Indian**: 0.0	National ***Socio-Economic***
Schools: *Regular* 12 ● *Spec Ed* 0 ● *Alt* 0	**Librarians**: 9.0	**% Asian**: 6.5	***Status*** indicator percentiles
Students: 6,847	761 students/librarian	**% Black**: 3.1	are not available for the
Total Teachers: 436	**Guidance Counselors**: 1.0	**% Hispanic**: 19.1	state of Illinois
Student/Classroom Teacher Ratio: 16.4	6,847 students/counselor	**% White**: 71.4	

Cook County

WILMETTE S.D. 39

615 LOCUST RD ● WILMETTE IL 60091-2299 ● (847) 256-2450 ● http://wilmette.newtrier.k12.il.us

Grade Span: KG-08	**Expenditures/Student**: $6,464	**% Amer Indian**: 0.1	National ***Socio-Economic***
Schools: *Regular* 6 ● *Spec Ed* 0 ● *Alt* 0	**Librarians**: 3.0	**% Asian**: 7.7	***Status*** indicator percentiles
Students: 3,226	1,075 students/librarian	**% Black**: 0.6	are not available for the
Total Teachers: 198	**Guidance Counselors**: 1.0	**% Hispanic**: 1.6	state of Illinois
Student/Classroom Teacher Ratio: 16.7	3,226 students/counselor	**% White**: 90.1	

Cook County

[WINNETKA] NEW TRIER TOWNSHIP HIGH S.D. 203

385 WINNETKA AVE ● WINNETKA IL 60093-4295 ● (847) 446-7000

Grade Span: 09-12	**Expenditures/Student**: $13,181	**% Amer Indian**: 0.1	National ***Socio-Economic***
Schools: *Regular* 1 ● *Spec Ed* 1 ● *Alt* 0	**Librarians**: 6.0	**% Asian**: 11.8	***Status*** indicator percentiles
Students: 2,993	499 students/librarian	**% Black**: 1.0	are not available for the
Total Teachers: 249	**Guidance Counselors**: 5.0	**% Hispanic**: 2.1	state of Illinois
Student/Classroom Teacher Ratio: 12.2	599 students/counselor	**% White**: 85.1	

DeKalb County

[DE KALB] DEKALB COMMUNITY UNIT S.D. 428

901 S FOURTH ST ● DE KALB IL 60115 ● (815) 754-2350 ● http://dist428.dekalb.k12.il.us

Grade Span: PK-12	**Expenditures/Student**: $5,154	**% Amer Indian**: 0.1	National ***Socio-Economic***
Schools: *Regular* 9 ● *Spec Ed* 0 ● *Alt* 0	**Librarians**: 1.0	**% Asian**: 3.7	***Status*** indicator percentiles
Students: 4,211	4,211 students/librarian	**% Black**: 7.5	are not available for the
Total Teachers: 234	**Guidance Counselors**: 7.0	**% Hispanic**: 8.3	state of Illinois
Student/Classroom Teacher Ratio: 18.9	602 students/counselor	**% White**: 80.4	

DeKalb County

SYCAMORE COMMUNITY UNIT S.D. 427

245 W EXCHANGE ST ● SYCAMORE IL 60178-1406 ● (815) 899-8103

Grade Span: KG-12	**Expenditures/Student**: $4,660	**% Amer Indian**: 0.2	National ***Socio-Economic***
Schools: *Regular* 5 ● *Spec Ed* 0 ● *Alt* 0	**Librarians**: 2.0	**% Asian**: 1.0	***Status*** indicator percentiles
Students: 2,898	1,449 students/librarian	**% Black**: 3.4	are not available for the
Total Teachers: 170	**Guidance Counselors**: 4.0	**% Hispanic**: 2.4	state of Illinois
Student/Classroom Teacher Ratio: 17.9	725 students/counselor	**% White**: 93.0	

DuPage County
ADDISON S.D. 4
222 N KENNEDY DR ● ADDISON IL 60101-2497 ● (630) 628-2500

Grade Span: PK-08 **Schools**: *Regular* 8 ● *Spec Ed* 1 ● *Alt* 0 **Students**: 3,743 **Total Teachers**: 215 **Student/Classroom Teacher Ratio**: 19.5	**Expenditures/Student**: $5,231 **Librarians**: 0.0 *** students/librarian **Guidance Counselors**: 1.0 3,743 students/counselor	**% Amer Indian**: 0.0 **% Asian**: 5.2 **% Black**: 1.6 **% Hispanic**: 28.1 **% White**: 65.1	National ***Socio-Economic Status*** indicator percentiles are not available for the state of Illinois

DuPage County
[CAROL STREAM] **COMMUNITY CONSOLIDATED S.D. 93**
P O BOX 88093 ● CAROL STREAM IL 60188-0093 ● (630) 462-8900

Grade Span: PK-08 **Schools**: *Regular* 7 ● *Spec Ed* 0 ● *Alt* 0 **Students**: 5,047 **Total Teachers**: 239 **Student/Classroom Teacher Ratio**: 21.5	**Expenditures/Student**: $3,849 **Librarians**: 6.0 841 students/librarian **Guidance Counselors**: 2.5 2,019 students/counselor	**% Amer Indian**: 0.1 **% Asian**: 11.5 **% Black**: 3.4 **% Hispanic**: 5.3 **% White**: 79.8	National ***Socio-Economic Status*** indicator percentiles are not available for the state of Illinois

DuPage County
[DOWNERS GROVE] **COMMUNITY HIGH S.D. 99**
6301 SPRINGSIDE ● DOWNERS GROVE IL 60516-2489 ● (630) 271-6699 ● http://d99-netra.csd99.k12.il.us

Grade Span: 09-12 **Schools**: *Regular* 2 ● *Spec Ed* 0 ● *Alt* 0 **Students**: 5,015 **Total Teachers**: 274 **Student/Classroom Teacher Ratio**: 18.5	**Expenditures/Student**: $7,904 **Librarians**: 6.0 836 students/librarian **Guidance Counselors**: 16.0 313 students/counselor	**% Amer Indian**: 0.0 **% Asian**: 11.1 **% Black**: 5.9 **% Hispanic**: 3.8 **% White**: 79.2	National ***Socio-Economic Status*** indicator percentiles are not available for the state of Illinois

DuPage County
DOWNERS GROVE GRADED S.D. 58
1860 63RD ST ● DOWNERS GROVE IL 60516-2403 ● (630) 719-5800

Grade Span: PK-08 **Schools**: *Regular* 12 ● *Spec Ed* 0 ● *Alt* 0 **Students**: 5,221 **Total Teachers**: 272 **Student/Classroom Teacher Ratio**: 19.5	**Expenditures/Student**: $5,055 **Librarians**: 2.0 2,611 students/librarian **Guidance Counselors**: 3.0 1,740 students/counselor	**% Amer Indian**: 0.2 **% Asian**: 6.8 **% Black**: 2.6 **% Hispanic**: 2.9 **% White**: 87.5	National ***Socio-Economic Status*** indicator percentiles are not available for the state of Illinois

DuPage County
ELMHURST S.D. 205
130 WEST MADISON ST ● ELMHURST IL 60126-3320 ● (630) 834-4530

Grade Span: PK-12 **Schools**: *Regular* 12 ● *Spec Ed* 0 ● *Alt* 0 **Students**: 6,343 **Total Teachers**: 415 **Student/Classroom Teacher Ratio**: 15.7	**Expenditures/Student**: $6,958 **Librarians**: 13.0 488 students/librarian **Guidance Counselors**: 15.0 423 students/counselor	**% Amer Indian**: 0.0 **% Asian**: 5.6 **% Black**: 1.0 **% Hispanic**: 3.9 **% White**: 89.5	National ***Socio-Economic Status*** indicator percentiles are not available for the state of Illinois

DuPage County
GLEN ELLYN COMMUNITY CONSOLIDATED S.D. 89
789 SHEEHAN AVE ● GLEN ELLYN IL 60137-6332 ● (630) 469-8900

Grade Span: PK-08 **Schools**: *Regular* 5 ● *Spec Ed* 0 ● *Alt* 0 **Students**: 2,617 **Total Teachers**: 150 **Student/Classroom Teacher Ratio**: 17.5	**Expenditures/Student**: $5,268 **Librarians**: 3.0 872 students/librarian **Guidance Counselors**: 2.0 1,309 students/counselor	**% Amer Indian**: 0.0 **% Asian**: 10.0 **% Black**: 4.1 **% Hispanic**: 1.8 **% White**: 84.1	National ***Socio-Economic Status*** indicator percentiles are not available for the state of Illinois

DuPage County

GLEN ELLYN S.D. 41

793 N MAIN ST ● GLEN ELLYN IL 60137-3999 ● (630) 790-6406

Grade Span: PK-08 **Schools**: *Regular* 5 ● *Spec Ed* 0 ● *Alt* 0 **Students**: 3,032 **Total Teachers**: 160 **Student/Classroom Teacher Ratio**: 20.5	**Expenditures/Student**: $4,904 **Librarians**: 4.0 758 students/librarian **Guidance Counselors**: 2.0 1,516 students/counselor	**% Amer Indian**: 0.0 **% Asian**: 3.4 **% Black**: 3.6 **% Hispanic**: 3.0 **% White**: 90.0	National ***Socio-Economic Status*** indicator percentiles are not available for the state of Illinois

DuPage County

[GLEN ELLYN] GLENBARD TOWNSHIP HIGH S.D. 87

800 ROOSEVELT BLDG-E ● GLEN ELLYN IL 60137-5854 ● (630) 469-9100

Grade Span: 09-12 **Schools**: *Regular* 4 ● *Spec Ed* 0 ● *Alt* 0 **Students**: 7,730 **Total Teachers**: 456 **Student/Classroom Teacher Ratio**: 16.8	**Expenditures/Student**: $8,388 **Librarians**: 11.0 703 students/librarian **Guidance Counselors**: 31.2 248 students/counselor	**% Amer Indian**: 0.4 **% Asian**: 12.1 **% Black**: 4.8 **% Hispanic**: 5.9 **% White**: 76.8	National ***Socio-Economic Status*** indicator percentiles are not available for the state of Illinois

DuPage County

[GLENDALE HEIGHTS] MARQUARDT S.D. 15

1890 GLEN ELLYN RD ● GLENDALE HEIGHTS IL 60139-2261 ● (630) 858-1166

Grade Span: PK-08 **Schools**: *Regular* 5 ● *Spec Ed* 0 ● *Alt* 0 **Students**: 2,724 **Total Teachers**: 137 **Student/Classroom Teacher Ratio**: 20.1	**Expenditures/Student**: $4,662 **Librarians**: 2.5 1,090 students/librarian **Guidance Counselors**: 1.0 2,724 students/counselor	**% Amer Indian**: 0.0 **% Asian**: 17.1 **% Black**: 8.3 **% Hispanic**: 13.4 **% White**: 61.2	National ***Socio-Economic Status*** indicator percentiles are not available for the state of Illinois

DuPage County

HINSDALE COMMUNITY CONSOLIDATED S.D. 181

5905 S COUNTY LN RD ● HINSDALE IL 60521-4870 ● (630) 887-1070

Grade Span: PK-08 **Schools**: *Regular* 8 ● *Spec Ed* 0 ● *Alt* 0 **Students**: 3,094 **Total Teachers**: 187 **Student/Classroom Teacher Ratio**: 17.3	**Expenditures/Student**: $6,901 **Librarians**: 8.0 387 students/librarian **Guidance Counselors**: 0.0 *** students/counselor	**% Amer Indian**: 0.0 **% Asian**: 4.1 **% Black**: 0.4 **% Hispanic**: 1.1 **% White**: 94.4	National ***Socio-Economic Status*** indicator percentiles are not available for the state of Illinois

DuPage County

HINSDALE TOWNSHIP HIGH S.D. 86

55TH & GRANT ST ● HINSDALE IL 60521-4577 ● (630) 655-6100 ● http://www.district86.k12.il.us/district86_home_page.html

Grade Span: 09-12 **Schools**: *Regular* 2 ● *Spec Ed* 0 ● *Alt* 0 **Students**: 3,518 **Total Teachers**: 232 **Student/Classroom Teacher Ratio**: 15.2	**Expenditures/Student**: $10,517 **Librarians**: 6.0 586 students/librarian **Guidance Counselors**: 16.0 220 students/counselor	**% Amer Indian**: 0.0 **% Asian**: 15.1 **% Black**: 3.7 **% Hispanic**: 2.6 **% White**: 78.5	National ***Socio-Economic Status*** indicator percentiles are not available for the state of Illinois

DuPage County

LOMBARD S.D. 44

150 W MADISON ST ● LOMBARD IL 60148-3379 ● (630) 620-3700

Grade Span: PK-08 **Schools**: *Regular* 7 ● *Spec Ed* 0 ● *Alt* 0 **Students**: 3,119 **Total Teachers**: 178 **Student/Classroom Teacher Ratio**: 17.6	**Expenditures/Student**: $5,841 **Librarians**: 2.0 1,560 students/librarian **Guidance Counselors**: 3.0 1,040 students/counselor	**% Amer Indian**: 0.1 **% Asian**: 7.1 **% Black**: 3.2 **% Hispanic**: 4.8 **% White**: 84.8	National ***Socio-Economic Status*** indicator percentiles are not available for the state of Illinois

DuPage County
[NAPERVILLE] **INDIAN PRAIRIE COMMUNITY UNIT S.D. 204**
P O BOX 3990 ● NAPERVILLE IL 60567-3990 ● (630) 851-6161 ● http://www.ipsd.org

Grade Span: PK-12	**Expenditures/Student**: $4,545	**% Amer Indian**: 0.1	National ***Socio-Economic***
Schools: *Regular* 17 ● *Spec Ed* 0 ● *Alt* 0	**Librarians**: 5.0	**% Asian**: 5.6	***Status*** indicator percentiles
Students: 13,744	2,749 students/librarian	**% Black**: 5.8	are not available for the
Total Teachers: 764	**Guidance Counselors**: 17.0	**% Hispanic**: 2.5	state of Illinois
Student/Classroom Teacher Ratio: 18.4	808 students/counselor	**% White**: 86.1	

DuPage County
NAPERVILLE COMMUNITY UNIT S.D. 203
203 W HILLSIDE ● NAPERVILLE IL 60540-6589 ● (630) 420-6300

Grade Span: PK-12	**Expenditures/Student**: $5,202	**% Amer Indian**: 0.1	National ***Socio-Economic***
Schools: *Regular* 21 ● *Spec Ed* 0 ● *Alt* 0	**Librarians**: 9.0	**% Asian**: 8.9	***Status*** indicator percentiles
Students: 17,921	1,991 students/librarian	**% Black**: 2.4	are not available for the
Total Teachers: 940	**Guidance Counselors**: 30.9	**% Hispanic**: 1.3	state of Illinois
Student/Classroom Teacher Ratio: 19.6	580 students/counselor	**% White**: 87.3	

DuPage County
[ROSELLE] **LAKE PARK COMMUNITY HIGH S.D. 108**
450 SPRING COURT ● ROSELLE IL 60172-1978 ● (630) 529-4500

Grade Span: 09-12	**Expenditures/Student**: $8,137	**% Amer Indian**: 0.4	National ***Socio-Economic***
Schools: *Regular* 1 ● *Spec Ed* 0 ● *Alt* 0	**Librarians**: 3.0	**% Asian**: 7.6	***Status*** indicator percentiles
Students: 2,741	914 students/librarian	**% Black**: 3.1	are not available for the
Total Teachers: 139	**Guidance Counselors**: 8.0	**% Hispanic**: 3.9	state of Illinois
Student/Classroom Teacher Ratio: 19.8	343 students/counselor	**% White**: 85.1	

DuPage County
[VILLA PARK] **DU PAGE HIGH S.D. 88**
101 W HIGH RIDGE RD ● VILLA PARK IL 60181-3205 ● (630) 530-3981

Grade Span: 09-12	**Expenditures/Student**: $8,531	**% Amer Indian**: 0.2	National ***Socio-Economic***
Schools: *Regular* 2 ● *Spec Ed* 0 ● *Alt* 0	**Librarians**: 3.0	**% Asian**: 6.3	***Status*** indicator percentiles
Students: 3,592	1,197 students/librarian	**% Black**: 1.8	are not available for the
Total Teachers: 209	**Guidance Counselors**: 14.0	**% Hispanic**: 11.2	state of Illinois
Student/Classroom Teacher Ratio: 17.3	257 students/counselor	**% White**: 80.5	

DuPage County
VILLA PARK S.D. 45
255 W VERMONT ST ● VILLA PARK IL 60181-1943 ● (630) 530-6200

Grade Span: PK-08	**Expenditures/Student**: $5,278	**% Amer Indian**: 0.1	National ***Socio-Economic***
Schools: *Regular* 8 ● *Spec Ed* 0 ● *Alt* 0	**Librarians**: 0.0	**% Asian**: 5.2	***Status*** indicator percentiles
Students: 3,724	*** students/librarian	**% Black**: 5.0	are not available for the
Total Teachers: 211	**Guidance Counselors**: 2.0	**% Hispanic**: 10.4	state of Illinois
Student/Classroom Teacher Ratio: 18.7	1,862 students/counselor	**% White**: 79.4	

DuPage County
WEST CHICAGO S.D. 33
312 E FOREST AVE ● WEST CHICAGO IL 60185-3599 ● (630) 293-6000

Grade Span: PK-08	**Expenditures/Student**: $5,229	**% Amer Indian**: 0.0	National ***Socio-Economic***
Schools: *Regular* 7 ● *Spec Ed* 0 ● *Alt* 0	**Librarians**: 7.0	**% Asian**: 1.9	***Status*** indicator percentiles
Students: 3,619	517 students/librarian	**% Black**: 2.3	are not available for the
Total Teachers: 199	**Guidance Counselors**: 1.0	**% Hispanic**: 39.8	state of Illinois
Student/Classroom Teacher Ratio: 18.6	3,619 students/counselor	**% White**: 56.0	

DuPage County

[WHEATON] **COMMUNITY UNIT S.D. 200**

130 W PARK AVE ● WHEATON IL 60187-6460 ● (630) 682-2002

Grade Span: PK-12 **Schools**: *Regular* 19 ● *Spec Ed* 0 ● *Alt* 0 **Students**: 13,358 **Total Teachers**: 704 **Student/Classroom Teacher Ratio**: 20.1	**Expenditures/Student**: $5,087 **Librarians**: 21.0 636 students/librarian **Guidance Counselors**: 19.0 703 students/counselor	**% Amer Indian**: 0.1 **% Asian**: 5.1 **% Black**: 4.1 **% Hispanic**: 4.0 **% White**: 86.7	National ***Socio-Economic Status*** indicator percentiles are not available for the state of Illinois

DuPage County

WOODRIDGE S.D. 68

7925 JANES AVE ● WOODRIDGE IL 60517-1699 ● (630) 985-7925

Grade Span: PK-08 **Schools**: *Regular* 7 ● *Spec Ed* 0 ● *Alt* 0 **Students**: 3,650 **Total Teachers**: 190 **Student/Classroom Teacher Ratio**: 19.6	**Expenditures/Student**: $4,545 **Librarians**: 6.0 608 students/librarian **Guidance Counselors**: 2.0 1,825 students/counselor	**% Amer Indian**: 0.0 **% Asian**: 7.6 **% Black**: 12.5 **% Hispanic**: 6.4 **% White**: 73.5	National ***Socio-Economic Status*** indicator percentiles are not available for the state of Illinois

Effingham County

EFFINGHAM COMMUNITY UNIT S.D. 40

PO BOX 130 ● EFFINGHAM IL 62401-0130 ● (217) 342-2163 ● http://www.effingham.k12.il.us

Grade Span: PK-12 **Schools**: *Regular* 7 ● *Spec Ed* 1 ● *Alt* 0 **Students**: 3,119 **Total Teachers**: 163 **Student/Classroom Teacher Ratio**: 19.5	**Expenditures/Student**: $3,994 **Librarians**: 2.0 1,560 students/librarian **Guidance Counselors**: 4.0 780 students/counselor	**% Amer Indian**: 0.0 **% Asian**: 0.8 **% Black**: 0.3 **% Hispanic**: 0.5 **% White**: 98.3	National ***Socio-Economic Status*** indicator percentiles are not available for the state of Illinois

Fulton County

CANTON UNION S.D. 66

20 W WALNUT ST ● CANTON IL 61520-2591 ● (309) 647-9411

Grade Span: PK-12 **Schools**: *Regular* 5 ● *Spec Ed* 1 ● *Alt* 0 **Students**: 2,848 **Total Teachers**: 174 **Student/Classroom Teacher Ratio**: 16.4	**Expenditures/Student**: $4,278 **Librarians**: 1.0 2,848 students/librarian **Guidance Counselors**: 4.0 712 students/counselor	**% Amer Indian**: 0.0 **% Asian**: 0.8 **% Black**: 1.0 **% Hispanic**: 0.5 **% White**: 97.6	National ***Socio-Economic Status*** indicator percentiles are not available for the state of Illinois

Henry County

GENESEO COMMUNITY UNIT S.D. 228

209 S COLLEGE AVE ● GENESEO IL 61254-1405 ● (309) 944-2159

Grade Span: PK-12 **Schools**: *Regular* 6 ● *Spec Ed* 0 ● *Alt* 0 **Students**: 3,100 **Total Teachers**: 159 **Student/Classroom Teacher Ratio**: 19.9	**Expenditures/Student**: $4,009 **Librarians**: 3.0 1,033 students/librarian **Guidance Counselors**: 4.0 775 students/counselor	**% Amer Indian**: 0.0 **% Asian**: 0.3 **% Black**: 0.4 **% Hispanic**: 1.5 **% White**: 97.8	National ***Socio-Economic Status*** indicator percentiles are not available for the state of Illinois

Jackson County

MURPHYSBORO COMMUNITY UNIT S.D. 186

9TH & WALNUT STS ● MURPHYSBORO IL 62966-2005 ● (618) 684-3781 ● http://www.lth6.k12.il.us/schools/murphysboro/default.htm

Grade Span: PK-12 **Schools**: *Regular* 6 ● *Spec Ed* 0 ● *Alt* 0 **Students**: 2,657 **Total Teachers**: 141 **Student/Classroom Teacher Ratio**: 19.2	**Expenditures/Student**: $5,072 **Librarians**: 2.0 1,329 students/librarian **Guidance Counselors**: 4.0 664 students/counselor	**% Amer Indian**: 0.0 **% Asian**: 0.0 **% Black**: 14.0 **% Hispanic**: 0.6 **% White**: 85.3	National ***Socio-Economic Status*** indicator percentiles are not available for the state of Illinois

Jersey County

[JERSEYVILLE] **JERSEY COMMUNITY UNIT S.D. 100**

100 LINCOLN STREET ● JERSEYVILLE IL 62052-1425 ● (618) 498-5561

Grade Span: PK-12	**Expenditures/Student**: $4,062	**% Amer Indian**: 0.0	National ***Socio-Economic Status*** indicator percentiles are not available for the state of Illinois
Schools: *Regular* 8 ● *Spec Ed* 0 ● *Alt* 0	**Librarians**: 4.0	**% Asian**: 0.1	
Students: 3,273	818 students/librarian	**% Black**: 0.4	
Total Teachers: 175	**Guidance Counselors**: 4.0	**% Hispanic**: 0.0	
Student/Classroom Teacher Ratio: 18.7	818 students/counselor	**% White**: 99.5	

Kane County

AURORA EAST UNIT S.D. 131

417 FIFTH ST ● AURORA IL 60505-4744 ● (630) 844-5550

Grade Span: PK-12	**Expenditures/Student**: $4,300	**% Amer Indian**: 0.3	National ***Socio-Economic Status*** indicator percentiles are not available for the state of Illinois
Schools: *Regular* 16 ● *Spec Ed* 0 ● *Alt* 0	**Librarians**: 3.0	**% Asian**: 1.0	
Students: 9,207	3,069 students/librarian	**% Black**: 18.9	
Total Teachers: 488	**Guidance Counselors**: 9.0	**% Hispanic**: 58.4	
Student/Classroom Teacher Ratio: 19.5	1,023 students/counselor	**% White**: 21.5	

Kane County

AURORA WEST UNIT S.D. 129

80 SO RIVER ST ● AURORA IL 60506-4108 ● (630) 844-4431

Grade Span: PK-12	**Expenditures/Student**: $4,533	**% Amer Indian**: 0.0	National ***Socio-Economic Status*** indicator percentiles are not available for the state of Illinois
Schools: *Regular* 14 ● *Spec Ed* 1 ● *Alt* 0	**Librarians**: 6.0	**% Asian**: 2.0	
Students: 8,973	1,496 students/librarian	**% Black**: 20.0	
Total Teachers: 497	**Guidance Counselors**: 10.0	**% Hispanic**: 22.5	
Student/Classroom Teacher Ratio: 18.1	897 students/counselor	**% White**: 55.5	

Kane County

BATAVIA UNIT S.D. 101

12 WEST WILSON ● BATAVIA IL 60510-1998 ● (630) 879-4645

Grade Span: PK-12	**Expenditures/Student**: $4,538	**% Amer Indian**: 0.1	National ***Socio-Economic Status*** indicator percentiles are not available for the state of Illinois
Schools: *Regular* 7 ● *Spec Ed* 0 ● *Alt* 0	**Librarians**: 7.0	**% Asian**: 1.3	
Students: 4,627	661 students/librarian	**% Black**: 2.8	
Total Teachers: 242	**Guidance Counselors**: 5.0	**% Hispanic**: 4.1	
Student/Classroom Teacher Ratio: 19.2	925 students/counselor	**% White**: 91.7	

Kane County

[CARPENTERSVILLE] **COMMUNITY UNIT S.D. 300**

300 CLEVELAND AVE ● CARPENTERSVILLE IL 60110-1943 ● (847) 426-1300 ● http://www.d300.kane.k12.il.us

Grade Span: PK-12	**Expenditures/Student**: $4,542	**% Amer Indian**: 0.4	National ***Socio-Economic Status*** indicator percentiles are not available for the state of Illinois
Schools: *Regular* 18 ● *Spec Ed* 1 ● *Alt* 0	**Librarians**: 7.0	**% Asian**: 1.2	
Students: 13,857	1,980 students/librarian	**% Black**: 3.8	
Total Teachers: 709	**Guidance Counselors**: 14.0	**% Hispanic**: 12.9	
Student/Classroom Teacher Ratio: 20.5	990 students/counselor	**% White**: 81.7	

Kane County

[ELGIN] **S.D. 46**

355 E CHICAGO ST ● ELGIN IL 60120-6543 ● (847) 888-5000

Grade Span: PK-12	**Expenditures/Student**: $4,664	**% Amer Indian**: 0.1	National ***Socio-Economic Status*** indicator percentiles are not available for the state of Illinois
Schools: *Regular* 44 ● *Spec Ed* 6 ● *Alt* 0	**Librarians**: 9.0	**% Asian**: 5.9	
Students: 31,168	3,463 students/librarian	**% Black**: 8.0	
Total Teachers: 1,500	**Guidance Counselors**: 22.0	**% Hispanic**: 23.7	
Student/Classroom Teacher Ratio: 24.9	1,417 students/counselor	**% White**: 62.2	

Kane County
GENEVA COMMUNITY UNIT S.D. 304
400 MCKINLEY AVE ● GENEVA IL 60134-1213 ● (630) 232-0678 ● http://www.chicago.avenew.com/comnity/educate/kane.d304/home.htm

Grade Span: PK-12	**Expenditures/Student**: $4,779	**% Amer Indian**: 0.0	National ***Socio-Economic Status*** indicator percentiles are not available for the state of Illinois
Schools: *Regular* 5 ● *Spec Ed* 1 ● *Alt* 0	**Librarians**: 4.8	**% Asian**: 0.9	
Students: 3,800	792 students/librarian	**% Black**: 0.1	
Total Teachers: 189	**Guidance Counselors**: 4.0	**% Hispanic**: 0.9	
Student/Classroom Teacher Ratio: 20.2	950 students/counselor	**% White**: 98.1	

Kane County
ST. CHARLES COMMUNITY UNIT S.D. 303
201 S 7TH STREET ● ST. CHARLES IL 60174-1489 ● (630) 513-3030 ● http://www.chicago.avenew.com/comnity/educate/kane.d303/home.htm

Grade Span: PK-12	**Expenditures/Student**: $5,107	**% Amer Indian**: 0.1	National ***Socio-Economic Status*** indicator percentiles are not available for the state of Illinois
Schools: *Regular* 14 ● *Spec Ed* 0 ● *Alt* 0	**Librarians**: 13.0	**% Asian**: 1.8	
Students: 9,503	731 students/librarian	**% Black**: 0.6	
Total Teachers: 505	**Guidance Counselors**: 14.0	**% Hispanic**: 2.4	
Student/Classroom Teacher Ratio: 20.1	679 students/counselor	**% White**: 95.1	

Kankakee County
KANKAKEE S.D. 111
240 WARREN AVE ● KANKAKEE IL 60901-4319 ● (815) 933-0700

Grade Span: PK-12	**Expenditures/Student**: $5,283	**% Amer Indian**: 0.1	National ***Socio-Economic Status*** indicator percentiles are not available for the state of Illinois
Schools: *Regular* 11 ● *Spec Ed* 3 ● *Alt* 0	**Librarians**: 2.0	**% Asian**: 0.5	
Students: 5,967	2,984 students/librarian	**% Black**: 59.2	
Total Teachers: 312	**Guidance Counselors**: 5.0	**% Hispanic**: 6.1	
Student/Classroom Teacher Ratio: 18.6	1,193 students/counselor	**% White**: 34.2	

Kendall County
OSWEGO COMMUNITY UNIT S.D. 308
4209 RT 71 B0X 729 ● OSWEGO IL 60543-0729 ● (630) 554-3447

Grade Span: PK-12	**Expenditures/Student**: $4,536	**% Amer Indian**: 0.8	National ***Socio-Economic Status*** indicator percentiles are not available for the state of Illinois
Schools: *Regular* 6 ● *Spec Ed* 0 ● *Alt* 0	**Librarians**: 6.0	**% Asian**: 1.1	
Students: 4,994	832 students/librarian	**% Black**: 1.6	
Total Teachers: 245	**Guidance Counselors**: 6.0	**% Hispanic**: 6.0	
Student/Classroom Teacher Ratio: 20.4	832 students/counselor	**% White**: 90.5	

Knox County
GALESBURG COMMUNITY UNIT S.D. 205
P O B0X 1206 ● GALESBURG IL 61402-1206 ● (309) 343-1151

Grade Span: PK-12	**Expenditures/Student**: $4,341	**% Amer Indian**: 0.1	National ***Socio-Economic Status*** indicator percentiles are not available for the state of Illinois
Schools: *Regular* 9 ● *Spec Ed* 3 ● *Alt* 0	**Librarians**: 0.0	**% Asian**: 0.8	
Students: 5,282	*** students/librarian	**% Black**: 10.9	
Total Teachers: 302	**Guidance Counselors**: 4.0	**% Hispanic**: 4.0	
Student/Classroom Teacher Ratio: 17.2	1,321 students/counselor	**% White**: 84.2	

Lake County
BARRINGTON COMMUNITY UNIT S.D. 220
310 JAMES ST ● BARRINGTON IL 60010-1799 ● (847) 381-6300 ● http://www.cusd220.lake.k12.il.us

Grade Span: PK-12	**Expenditures/Student**: $6,981	**% Amer Indian**: 0.0	National ***Socio-Economic Status*** indicator percentiles are not available for the state of Illinois
Schools: *Regular* 11 ● *Spec Ed* 0 ● *Alt* 0	**Librarians**: 9.0	**% Asian**: 5.2	
Students: 7,514	835 students/librarian	**% Black**: 1.3	
Total Teachers: 435	**Guidance Counselors**: 13.0	**% Hispanic**: 5.4	
Student/Classroom Teacher Ratio: 17.6	578 students/counselor	**% White**: 88.0	

Lake County

[BUFFALO GROVE] **KILDEER COUNTRYSIDE COMMUNITY CONSOLIDATED S.D. 96**

1050 IVY HALL LANE ● BUFFALO GROVE IL 60089-1700 ● (847) 459-4260 ● http://www.district96.k12.il.us

Grade Span: PK-08	**Expenditures/Student**: $4,739	**% Amer Indian**: 0.1	National ***Socio-Economic***
Schools: *Regular* 5 ● *Spec Ed* 0 ● *Alt* 0	**Librarians**: 1.0	**% Asian**: 6.1	***Status*** indicator percentiles
Students: 3,410	3,410 students/librarian	**% Black**: 1.3	are not available for the
Total Teachers: 187	**Guidance Counselors**: 1.0	**% Hispanic**: 1.3	state of Illinois
Student/Classroom Teacher Ratio: 18.4	3,410 students/counselor	**% White**: 91.2	

Lake County

DEERFIELD S.D. 109

517 DEERFIELD RD ● DEERFIELD IL 60015-4419 ● (847) 945-1844

Grade Span: PK-08	**Expenditures/Student**: $7,162	**% Amer Indian**: 0.0	National ***Socio-Economic***
Schools: *Regular* 6 ● *Spec Ed* 0 ● *Alt* 0	**Librarians**: 6.0	**% Asian**: 2.4	***Status*** indicator percentiles
Students: 2,582	430 students/librarian	**% Black**: 0.3	are not available for the
Total Teachers: 168	**Guidance Counselors**: 1.8	**% Hispanic**: 1.0	state of Illinois
Student/Classroom Teacher Ratio: 15.8	1,434 students/counselor	**% White**: 96.3	

Lake County

[GAGES LAKE] **WOODLAND COMMUNITY CONSOLIDATED S.D. 50**

17370 W GAGES LK RD ● GAGES LAKE IL 60030-1898 ● (847) 816-2532 ● http://www.d50.lake.k12.il.us

Grade Span: PK-08	**Expenditures/Student**: $4,157	**% Amer Indian**: 0.4	National ***Socio-Economic***
Schools: *Regular* 4 ● *Spec Ed* 0 ● *Alt* 0	**Librarians**: 0.0	**% Asian**: 6.6	***Status*** indicator percentiles
Students: 4,498	*** students/librarian	**% Black**: 4.0	are not available for the
Total Teachers: 233	**Guidance Counselors**: 0.0	**% Hispanic**: 7.9	state of Illinois
Student/Classroom Teacher Ratio: 19.9	*** students/counselor	**% White**: 81.2	

Lake County

[HIGHLAND PARK] **NORTH SHORE S.D. 112**

530 RED OAK LANE ● HIGHLAND PARK IL 60035 ● (847) 831-4370

Grade Span: PK-08	**Expenditures/Student**: $8,250	**% Amer Indian**: 0.1	National ***Socio-Economic***
Schools: *Regular* 11 ● *Spec Ed* 0 ● *Alt* 0	**Librarians**: 12.0	**% Asian**: 2.6	***Status*** indicator percentiles
Students: 4,216	351 students/librarian	**% Black**: 3.2	are not available for the
Total Teachers: 306	**Guidance Counselors**: 4.0	**% Hispanic**: 12.6	state of Illinois
Student/Classroom Teacher Ratio: 14.6	1,054 students/counselor	**% White**: 81.5	

Lake County

[HIGHLAND PARK] **TOWNSHIP HIGH S.D. 113**

1040 PARK AVE WEST ● HIGHLAND PARK IL 60035-2283 ● (847) 432-6510

Grade Span: 09-12	**Expenditures/Student**: $14,255	**% Amer Indian**: 0.1	National ***Socio-Economic***
Schools: *Regular* 2 ● *Spec Ed* 0 ● *Alt* 0	**Librarians**: 6.0	**% Asian**: 3.4	***Status*** indicator percentiles
Students: 2,772	462 students/librarian	**% Black**: 1.7	are not available for the
Total Teachers: 199	**Guidance Counselors**: 13.8	**% Hispanic**: 7.3	state of Illinois
Student/Classroom Teacher Ratio: 13.9	201 students/counselor	**% White**: 87.6	

Lake County

LAKE ZURICH COMMUNITY UNIT S.D. 95

66 CHURCH ST ● LAKE ZURICH IL 60047-1572 ● (847) 438-2831 ● http://www.lz95.lake.k12.il.us

Grade Span: PK-12	**Expenditures/Student**: $4,969	**% Amer Indian**: 0.2	National ***Socio-Economic***
Schools: *Regular* 8 ● *Spec Ed* 0 ● *Alt* 0	**Librarians**: 8.0	**% Asian**: 2.5	***Status*** indicator percentiles
Students: 5,269	659 students/librarian	**% Black**: 1.2	are not available for the
Total Teachers: 284	**Guidance Counselors**: 8.0	**% Hispanic**: 3.1	state of Illinois
Student/Classroom Teacher Ratio: 18.9	659 students/counselor	**% White**: 93.0	

Lake County
[LINCOLNSHIRE] **ADLAI E STEVENSON S.D. 125**
TWO STEVENSON DR ● LINCOLNSHIRE IL 60069 ● (847) 634-4000

Grade Span: 09-12	**Expenditures/Student**: $8,973	**% Amer Indian**: 0.1	National ***Socio-Economic Status*** indicator percentiles are not available for the state of Illinois
Schools: *Regular* 1 ● *Spec Ed* 0 ● *Alt* 0	**Librarians**: 3.0	**% Asian**: 10.0	
Students: 2,958	986 students/librarian	**% Black**: 1.6	
Total Teachers: 175	**Guidance Counselors**: 14.0	**% Hispanic**: 2.5	
Student/Classroom Teacher Ratio: 17.0	211 students/counselor	**% White**: 85.8	

Lake County
NORTH CHICAGO S.D. 187
2000 LEWIS AVE ● NORTH CHICAGO IL 60064-2543 ● (847) 689-8150

Grade Span: PK-12	**Expenditures/Student**: $5,640	**% Amer Indian**: 0.1	National ***Socio-Economic Status*** indicator percentiles are not available for the state of Illinois
Schools: *Regular* 9 ● *Spec Ed* 0 ● *Alt* 0	**Librarians**: 1.0	**% Asian**: 3.7	
Students: 3,977	3,977 students/librarian	**% Black**: 61.8	
Total Teachers: 219	**Guidance Counselors**: 6.0	**% Hispanic**: 14.4	
Student/Classroom Teacher Ratio: 17.8	663 students/counselor	**% White**: 19.9	

Lake County
ROUND LAKE AREA S.D. 116
316 S ROSEDALE CT ● ROUND LAKE IL 60073-2999 ● (847) 546-5522

Grade Span: PK-12	**Expenditures/Student**: $4,531	**% Amer Indian**: 0.5	National ***Socio-Economic Status*** indicator percentiles are not available for the state of Illinois
Schools: *Regular* 8 ● *Spec Ed* 1 ● *Alt* 0	**Librarians**: 0.0	**% Asian**: 0.9	
Students: 5,275	*** students/librarian	**% Black**: 2.4	
Total Teachers: 280	**Guidance Counselors**: 3.0	**% Hispanic**: 27.2	
Student/Classroom Teacher Ratio: 21.9	1,758 students/counselor	**% White**: 69.0	

Lake County
[VERNON HILLS] **HAWTHORN COMMUNITY CONSOLIDATED S.D. 73**
201 HAWTHORN PARKWAY ● VERNON HILLS IL 60061-1497 ● (847) 367-3226

Grade Span: PK-08	**Expenditures/Student**: $5,850	**% Amer Indian**: 0.1	National ***Socio-Economic Status*** indicator percentiles are not available for the state of Illinois
Schools: *Regular* 5 ● *Spec Ed* 0 ● *Alt* 0	**Librarians**: 4.6	**% Asian**: 9.0	
Students: 3,266	710 students/librarian	**% Black**: 3.2	
Total Teachers: 191	**Guidance Counselors**: 0.0	**% Hispanic**: 16.1	
Student/Classroom Teacher Ratio: 19.6	*** students/counselor	**% White**: 71.6	

Lake County
WAUCONDA COMMUNITY UNIT S.D. 118
555 N MAIN ST ● WAUCONDA IL 60084-1299 ● (847) 526-7690

Grade Span: PK-12	**Expenditures/Student**: $4,877	**% Amer Indian**: 0.3	National ***Socio-Economic Status*** indicator percentiles are not available for the state of Illinois
Schools: *Regular* 5 ● *Spec Ed* 0 ● *Alt* 0	**Librarians**: 2.0	**% Asian**: 1.5	
Students: 3,124	1,562 students/librarian	**% Black**: 0.7	
Total Teachers: 171	**Guidance Counselors**: 5.0	**% Hispanic**: 5.8	
Student/Classroom Teacher Ratio: 19.1	625 students/counselor	**% White**: 91.8	

Lake County
WAUKEGAN COMMUNITY UNIT S.D. 60
1201 N SHERIDAN RD ● WAUKEGAN IL 60085-2099 ● (847) 336-3100 ● http://www.nslsilus.org/Washington/district60.html

Grade Span: PK-12	**Expenditures/Student**: $4,655	**% Amer Indian**: 0.3	National ***Socio-Economic Status*** indicator percentiles are not available for the state of Illinois
Schools: *Regular* 20 ● *Spec Ed* 2 ● *Alt* 0	**Librarians**: 9.5	**% Asian**: 2.7	
Students: 13,175	1,387 students/librarian	**% Black**: 28.1	
Total Teachers: 704	**Guidance Counselors**: 16.0	**% Hispanic**: 47.3	
Student/Classroom Teacher Ratio: 21.8	823 students/counselor	**% White**: 21.7	

Lake County

ZION ELEMENTARY S.D.

2200 BETHESDA BLVD ● ZION IL 60099-2589 ● (847) 872-5455

Grade Span: PK-08	**Expenditures/Student**: $5,199	**% Amer Indian**: 0.2	National ***Socio-Economic Status*** indicator percentiles are not available for the state of Illinois
Schools: *Regular* 6 ● *Spec Ed* 1 ● *Alt* 0	**Librarians**: 1.0	**% Asian**: 1.5	
Students: 2,701	2,701 students/librarian	**% Black**: 40.5	
Total Teachers: 157	**Guidance Counselors**: 0.0	**% Hispanic**: 10.5	
Student/Classroom Teacher Ratio: 17.3	*** students/counselor	**% White**: 47.2	

Lee County

DIXON UNIT S.D. 170

1335 FRANKLIN GR RD ● DIXON IL 61021-9149 ● (815) 284-7722

Grade Span: PK-12	**Expenditures/Student**: $4,405	**% Amer Indian**: 0.1	National ***Socio-Economic Status*** indicator percentiles are not available for the state of Illinois
Schools: *Regular* 6 ● *Spec Ed* 1 ● *Alt* 0	**Librarians**: 1.0	**% Asian**: 1.6	
Students: 3,332	3,332 students/librarian	**% Black**: 3.2	
Total Teachers: 178	**Guidance Counselors**: 4.0	**% Hispanic**: 2.3	
Student/Classroom Teacher Ratio: 19.6	833 students/counselor	**% White**: 92.9	

McHenry County

CARY COMMUNITY CONSOLIDATED S.D. 26

15 S 2ND ST ● CARY IL 60013-2810 ● (847) 639-7788 ● http://www.nsn.org/cpqhome/schools/index.html

Grade Span: PK-08	**Expenditures/Student**: $4,088	**% Amer Indian**: 0.1	National ***Socio-Economic Status*** indicator percentiles are not available for the state of Illinois
Schools: *Regular* 5 ● *Spec Ed* 0 ● *Alt* 0	**Librarians**: 4.0	**% Asian**: 1.3	
Students: 3,046	762 students/librarian	**% Black**: 0.1	
Total Teachers: 162	**Guidance Counselors**: 1.0	**% Hispanic**: 3.5	
Student/Classroom Teacher Ratio: 18.8	3,046 students/counselor	**% White**: 94.9	

McHenry County

[CRYSTAL LAKE] COMMUNITY HIGH S.D. 155

1 S VIRGINIA ROAD ● CRYSTAL LAKE IL 60014-6195 ● (815) 455-8500

Grade Span: 09-12	**Expenditures/Student**: $6,965	**% Amer Indian**: 0.1	National ***Socio-Economic Status*** indicator percentiles are not available for the state of Illinois
Schools: *Regular* 3 ● *Spec Ed* 0 ● *Alt* 0	**Librarians**: 6.0	**% Asian**: 1.5	
Students: 4,513	752 students/librarian	**% Black**: 0.4	
Total Teachers: 249	**Guidance Counselors**: 15.0	**% Hispanic**: 2.5	
Student/Classroom Teacher Ratio: 18.3	301 students/counselor	**% White**: 95.5	

McHenry County

CRYSTAL LAKE COMMUNITY CONSOLIDATED S.D. 47

221 LIBERTY RD ● CRYSTAL LAKE IL 60014-8032 ● (815) 459-6070

Grade Span: PK-08	**Expenditures/Student**: $3,975	**% Amer Indian**: 0.0	National ***Socio-Economic Status*** indicator percentiles are not available for the state of Illinois
Schools: *Regular* 9 ● *Spec Ed* 0 ● *Alt* 0	**Librarians**: 5.0	**% Asian**: 1.8	
Students: 7,418	1,484 students/librarian	**% Black**: 0.6	
Total Teachers: 354	**Guidance Counselors**: 0.0	**% Hispanic**: 3.7	
Student/Classroom Teacher Ratio: 21.5	*** students/counselor	**% White**: 93.8	

McHenry County

MCHENRY COMMUNITY CONSOLIDATED S.D. 15

1011 N GREEN ST ● MCHENRY IL 60050-5243 ● (815) 385-7210

Grade Span: PK-08	**Expenditures/Student**: $3,544	**% Amer Indian**: 0.1	National ***Socio-Economic Status*** indicator percentiles are not available for the state of Illinois
Schools: *Regular* 7 ● *Spec Ed* 0 ● *Alt* 0	**Librarians**: 3.0	**% Asian**: 0.9	
Students: 4,406	1,469 students/librarian	**% Black**: 0.4	
Total Teachers: 218	**Guidance Counselors**: 0.0	**% Hispanic**: 2.9	
Student/Classroom Teacher Ratio: 20.2	*** students/counselor	**% White**: 95.7	

McHenry County
WOODSTOCK COMMUNITY UNIT S.D. 200
501 W SOUTH ST ● WOODSTOCK IL 60098-3799 ● (815) 337-5406 ● http://www.d200.mchenry.k12.il.us

Grade Span: PK-12	**Expenditures/Student**: $4,702	**% Amer Indian**: 0.0	National ***Socio-Economic Status*** indicator percentiles are not available for the state of Illinois
Schools: *Regular* 8 ● *Spec Ed* 0 ● *Alt* 0	**Librarians**: 2.0	**% Asian**: 1.1	
Students: 4,997	2,499 students/librarian	**% Black**: 0.4	
Total Teachers: 235	**Guidance Counselors**: 8.0	**% Hispanic**: 11.8	
Student/Classroom Teacher Ratio: 22.6	625 students/counselor	**% White**: 86.7	

McLean County
BLOOMINGTON S.D. 87
BOX 249 300 E MONROE ● BLOOMINGTON IL 61702-0249 ● (309) 827-6031 ● http://www.dave-world.net/community/dist87

Grade Span: PK-12	**Expenditures/Student**: $4,938	**% Amer Indian**: 0.1	National ***Socio-Economic Status*** indicator percentiles are not available for the state of Illinois
Schools: *Regular* 8 ● *Spec Ed* 1 ● *Alt* 0	**Librarians**: 6.0	**% Asian**: 1.1	
Students: 5,903	984 students/librarian	**% Black**: 20.4	
Total Teachers: 330	**Guidance Counselors**: 12.0	**% Hispanic**: 2.6	
Student/Classroom Teacher Ratio: 18.5	492 students/counselor	**% White**: 75.9	

McLean County
[NORMAL] **MCLEAN COUNTY UNIT S.D. 5**
1809 W HOVEY AVENUE ● NORMAL IL 61761-4339 ● (309) 452-4476 ● http://unit5.mclean.k12.il.us

Grade Span: PK-12	**Expenditures/Student**: $4,340	**% Amer Indian**: 0.2	National ***Socio-Economic Status*** indicator percentiles are not available for the state of Illinois
Schools: *Regular* 17 ● *Spec Ed* 0 ● *Alt* 0	**Librarians**: 6.8	**% Asian**: 2.0	
Students: 8,753	1,287 students/librarian	**% Black**: 6.5	
Total Teachers: 504	**Guidance Counselors**: 11.0	**% Hispanic**: 1.9	
Student/Classroom Teacher Ratio: 18.2	796 students/counselor	**% White**: 89.4	

Macon County
DECATUR S.D. 61
101 W CERRO GORDO ST ● DECATUR IL 62523-1001 ● (217) 424-3000 ● http://www.dps61.org

Grade Span: PK-12	**Expenditures/Student**: $4,610	**% Amer Indian**: 0.1	National ***Socio-Economic Status*** indicator percentiles are not available for the state of Illinois
Schools: *Regular* 25 ● *Spec Ed* 2 ● *Alt* 0	**Librarians**: 22.0	**% Asian**: 0.6	
Students: 12,108	550 students/librarian	**% Black**: 36.3	
Total Teachers: 565	**Guidance Counselors**: 13.4	**% Hispanic**: 0.3	
Student/Classroom Teacher Ratio: 21.8	904 students/counselor	**% White**: 62.7	

Madison County
ALTON COMMUNITY UNIT S.D. 11
PO BOX 9028 ● ALTON IL 62002-9028 ● (618) 474-2600

Grade Span: PK-12	**Expenditures/Student**: $4,649	**% Amer Indian**: 0.1	National ***Socio-Economic Status*** indicator percentiles are not available for the state of Illinois
Schools: *Regular* 16 ● *Spec Ed* 2 ● *Alt* 0	**Librarians**: 6.0	**% Asian**: 0.5	
Students: 7,570	1,262 students/librarian	**% Black**: 30.5	
Total Teachers: 414	**Guidance Counselors**: 6.0	**% Hispanic**: 0.5	
Student/Classroom Teacher Ratio: 18.3	1,262 students/counselor	**% White**: 68.4	

Madison County
BETHALTO COMMUNITY UNIT S.D. 8
322 E CENTRAL ST ● BETHALTO IL 62010-1399 ● (618) 377-7200 ● http://bethalto.madison.k12.il.us

Grade Span: PK-12	**Expenditures/Student**: $3,905	**% Amer Indian**: 0.2	National ***Socio-Economic Status*** indicator percentiles are not available for the state of Illinois
Schools: *Regular* 7 ● *Spec Ed* 1 ● *Alt* 0	**Librarians**: 2.0	**% Asian**: 0.2	
Students: 2,986	1,493 students/librarian	**% Black**: 2.0	
Total Teachers: 152	**Guidance Counselors**: 3.0	**% Hispanic**: 0.3	
Student/Classroom Teacher Ratio: 20.2	995 students/counselor	**% White**: 97.3	

Madison County

COLLINSVILLE COMMUNITY UNIT S.D. 10

201 W CLAY ST ● COLLINSVILLE IL 62234-3219 ● (618) 346-6350

Grade Span: PK-12	**Expenditures/Student**: $4,219	**% Amer Indian**: 0.1	National ***Socio-Economic***
Schools: *Regular* 12 ● *Spec Ed* 0 ● *Alt* 0	**Librarians**: 2.0	**% Asian**: 0.4	***Status*** indicator percentiles
Students: 5,938	2,969 students/librarian	**% Black**: 5.8	are not available for the
Total Teachers: 303	**Guidance Counselors**: 8.0	**% Hispanic**: 2.8	state of Illinois
Student/Classroom Teacher Ratio: 19.8	742 students/counselor	**% White**: 90.9	

Madison County

EDWARDSVILLE COMMUNITY UNIT S.D. 7

708 ST LOUIS ST ● EDWARDSVILLE IL 62025-1427 ● (618) 656-1182

Grade Span: PK-12	**Expenditures/Student**: $3,918	**% Amer Indian**: 0.2	National ***Socio-Economic***
Schools: *Regular* 9 ● *Spec Ed* 1 ● *Alt* 0	**Librarians**: 5.0	**% Asian**: 1.4	***Status*** indicator percentiles
Students: 5,953	1,191 students/librarian	**% Black**: 9.3	are not available for the
Total Teachers: 301	**Guidance Counselors**: 8.0	**% Hispanic**: 0.6	state of Illinois
Student/Classroom Teacher Ratio: 20.1	744 students/counselor	**% White**: 88.6	

Madison County

GRANITE CITY COMMUNITY UNIT S.D. 9

1947 ADAMS STREET ● GRANITE CITY IL 62040-3397 ● (618) 451-5800

Grade Span: PK-12	**Expenditures/Student**: $4,272	**% Amer Indian**: 0.1	National ***Socio-Economic***
Schools: *Regular* 12 ● *Spec Ed* 0 ● *Alt* 0	**Librarians**: 3.0	**% Asian**: 0.8	***Status*** indicator percentiles
Students: 8,376	2,792 students/librarian	**% Black**: 2.5	are not available for the
Total Teachers: 400	**Guidance Counselors**: 8.0	**% Hispanic**: 1.7	state of Illinois
Student/Classroom Teacher Ratio: 21.0	1,047 students/counselor	**% White**: 94.9	

Madison County

HIGHLAND COMMUNITY UNIT S.D. 5

1800 LINDENTHAL ● HIGHLAND IL 62249-0149 ● (618) 654-2106 ● http://www.highland.madison.k12.il.us

Grade Span: PK-12	**Expenditures/Student**: $4,088	**% Amer Indian**: 0.0	National ***Socio-Economic***
Schools: *Regular* 7 ● *Spec Ed* 0 ● *Alt* 0	**Librarians**: 3.0	**% Asian**: 0.7	***Status*** indicator percentiles
Students: 2,878	959 students/librarian	**% Black**: 0.1	are not available for the
Total Teachers: 162	**Guidance Counselors**: 3.0	**% Hispanic**: 0.0	state of Illinois
Student/Classroom Teacher Ratio: 16.7	959 students/counselor	**% White**: 99.2	

Madison County

[ST. JACOB] **TRIAD COMMUNITY UNIT S.D. 2**

9539 US HWY 40 ● ST. JACOB IL 62281-9773 ● (618) 644-3771

Grade Span: PK-12	**Expenditures/Student**: $3,533	**% Amer Indian**: 0.2	National ***Socio-Economic***
Schools: *Regular* 7 ● *Spec Ed* 0 ● *Alt* 0	**Librarians**: 1.0	**% Asian**: 1.0	***Status*** indicator percentiles
Students: 3,252	3,252 students/librarian	**% Black**: 0.6	are not available for the
Total Teachers: 168	**Guidance Counselors**: 3.0	**% Hispanic**: 0.5	state of Illinois
Student/Classroom Teacher Ratio: 20.1	1,084 students/counselor	**% White**: 97.7	

Morgan County

JACKSONVILLE S.D. 117

516 JORDAN ST ● JACKSONVILLE IL 62650-1941 ● (217) 243-9411

Grade Span: PK-12	**Expenditures/Student**: $4,104	**% Amer Indian**: 0.0	National ***Socio-Economic***
Schools: *Regular* 10 ● *Spec Ed* 1 ● *Alt* 0	**Librarians**: 3.0	**% Asian**: 0.6	***Status*** indicator percentiles
Students: 4,215	1,405 students/librarian	**% Black**: 8.5	are not available for the
Total Teachers: 244	**Guidance Counselors**: 7.0	**% Hispanic**: 1.0	state of Illinois
Student/Classroom Teacher Ratio: 17.7	602 students/counselor	**% White**: 89.9	

Peoria County
PEORIA S.D. 150
3202 N WISCONSIN AVE ● PEORIA IL 61603-1260 ● (309) 672-6767

Grade Span: PK-12 **Schools**: *Regular* 32 ● *Spec Ed* 12 ● *Alt* 0 **Students**: 16,517 **Total Teachers**: 1,002 **Student/Classroom Teacher Ratio**: 17.3	**Expenditures/Student**: $5,380 **Librarians**: 5.5 3,003 students/librarian **Guidance Counselors**: 13.0 1,271 students/counselor	**% Amer Indian**: 0.1 **% Asian**: 1.8 **% Black**: 49.4 **% Hispanic**: 1.8 **% White**: 46.9	National ***Socio-Economic Status*** indicator percentiles are not available for the state of Illinois

Rock Island County
EAST MOLINE S.D. 37
836 17TH AVE ● EAST MOLINE IL 61244-2199 ● (309) 755-4533

Grade Span: PK-08 **Schools**: *Regular* 5 ● *Spec Ed* 0 ● *Alt* 0 **Students**: 2,639 **Total Teachers**: 164 **Student/Classroom Teacher Ratio**: 16.5	**Expenditures/Student**: $4,599 **Librarians**: 2.0 1,320 students/librarian **Guidance Counselors**: 3.0 880 students/counselor	**% Amer Indian**: 0.4 **% Asian**: 1.9 **% Black**: 13.2 **% Hispanic**: 15.6 **% White**: 68.9	National ***Socio-Economic Status*** indicator percentiles are not available for the state of Illinois

Rock Island County
MOLINE UNIT S.D. 40
1619 11TH AVE ● MOLINE IL 61265-3198 ● (309) 757-3500 ● http://www.moline.lth2.k12.il.us

Grade Span: PK-12 **Schools**: *Regular* 16 ● *Spec Ed* 2 ● *Alt* 0 **Students**: 8,428 **Total Teachers**: 458 **Student/Classroom Teacher Ratio**: 18.9	**Expenditures/Student**: $4,311 **Librarians**: 12.0 702 students/librarian **Guidance Counselors**: 11.0 766 students/counselor	**% Amer Indian**: 0.3 **% Asian**: 1.0 **% Black**: 4.2 **% Hispanic**: 10.7 **% White**: 83.8	National ***Socio-Economic Status*** indicator percentiles are not available for the state of Illinois

Rock Island County
ROCK ISLAND S.D. 41
2101 6TH AVENUE ● ROCK ISLAND IL 61201-8116 ● (309) 793-5900

Grade Span: PK-12 **Schools**: *Regular* 15 ● *Spec Ed* 4 ● *Alt* 0 **Students**: 7,197 **Total Teachers**: 416 **Student/Classroom Teacher Ratio**: 17.7	**Expenditures/Student**: $5,388 **Librarians**: 1.0 7,197 students/librarian **Guidance Counselors**: 10.0 720 students/counselor	**% Amer Indian**: 0.3 **% Asian**: 0.7 **% Black**: 30.8 **% Hispanic**: 5.6 **% White**: 62.7	National ***Socio-Economic Status*** indicator percentiles are not available for the state of Illinois

St. Clair County
BELLEVILLE S.D. 118
105 W A ST ● BELLEVILLE IL 62220-1326 ● (618) 233-2830

Grade Span: PK-08 **Schools**: *Regular* 11 ● *Spec Ed* 0 ● *Alt* 0 **Students**: 3,803 **Total Teachers**: 201 **Student/Classroom Teacher Ratio**: 20.5	**Expenditures/Student**: $4,711 **Librarians**: 0.0 *** students/librarian **Guidance Counselors**: 0.0 *** students/counselor	**% Amer Indian**: 0.4 **% Asian**: 1.1 **% Black**: 20.8 **% Hispanic**: 0.7 **% White**: 77.0	National ***Socio-Economic Status*** indicator percentiles are not available for the state of Illinois

St. Clair County
BELLEVILLE TOWNSHIP HIGH S.D. 201
2600 W MAIN ST ● BELLEVILLE IL 62223-6687 ● (618) 233-5070

Grade Span: 09-12 **Schools**: *Regular* 2 ● *Spec Ed* 1 ● *Alt* 0 **Students**: 4,603 **Total Teachers**: 216 **Student/Classroom Teacher Ratio**: 20.3	**Expenditures/Student**: $5,044 **Librarians**: 3.0 1,534 students/librarian **Guidance Counselors**: 10.0 460 students/counselor	**% Amer Indian**: 0.3 **% Asian**: 1.7 **% Black**: 14.2 **% Hispanic**: 1.3 **% White**: 82.5	National ***Socio-Economic Status*** indicator percentiles are not available for the state of Illinois

St. Clair County
CAHOKIA COMMUNITY UNIT S.D. 187
1700 JEROME LN ● CAHOKIA IL 62206-2329 ● (618) 332-3700

Grade Span: PK-12 **Schools**: *Regular* 9 ● *Spec Ed* 1 ● *Alt* 0 **Students**: 5,061 **Total Teachers**: 260 **Student/Classroom Teacher Ratio**: 19.5	**Expenditures/Student**: $4,829 **Librarians**: 2.0 2,531 students/librarian **Guidance Counselors**: 6.0 844 students/counselor	**% Amer Indian**: 0.0 **% Asian**: 0.3 **% Black**: 56.7 **% Hispanic**: 0.8 **% White**: 42.1	National ***Socio-Economic Status*** indicator percentiles are not available for the state of Illinois

St. Clair County
EAST ST. LOUIS S.D. 189
1005 STATE ST ● EAST ST. LOUIS IL 62201-1907 ● (618) 583-8200

Grade Span: PK-12 **Schools**: *Regular* 26 ● *Spec Ed* 3 ● *Alt* 0 **Students**: 12,964 **Total Teachers**: 706 **Student/Classroom Teacher Ratio**: 20.0	**Expenditures/Student**: $5,269 **Librarians**: 5.0 2,593 students/librarian **Guidance Counselors**: 12.0 1,080 students/counselor	**% Amer Indian**: 0.0 **% Asian**: 0.0 **% Black**: 99.4 **% Hispanic**: 0.4 **% White**: 0.1	National ***Socio-Economic Status*** indicator percentiles are not available for the state of Illinois

St. Clair County
MASCOUTAH COMMUNITY UNIT S.D. 19
720 W HARNETT ST ● MASCOUTAH IL 62258-1121 ● (618) 566-7414 ● http://mascoutah19.k12.il.us

Grade Span: PK-12 **Schools**: *Regular* 5 ● *Spec Ed* 0 ● *Alt* 0 **Students**: 3,031 **Total Teachers**: 175 **Student/Classroom Teacher Ratio**: 17.2	**Expenditures/Student**: $5,018 **Librarians**: 2.0 1,516 students/librarian **Guidance Counselors**: 4.0 758 students/counselor	**% Amer Indian**: 0.2 **% Asian**: 1.1 **% Black**: 12.5 **% Hispanic**: 4.7 **% White**: 81.5	National ***Socio-Economic Status*** indicator percentiles are not available for the state of Illinois

Sangamon County
[CHATHAM] BALL CHATHAM COMMUNITY UNIT S.D. 5
201 W MULBERRY ● CHATHAM IL 62629-1615 ● (217) 483-2416

Grade Span: PK-12 **Schools**: *Regular* 4 ● *Spec Ed* 0 ● *Alt* 0 **Students**: 3,621 **Total Teachers**: 182 **Student/Classroom Teacher Ratio**: 20.1	**Expenditures/Student**: $3,949 **Librarians**: 4.0 905 students/librarian **Guidance Counselors**: 5.5 658 students/counselor	**% Amer Indian**: 0.0 **% Asian**: 1.2 **% Black**: 1.1 **% Hispanic**: 0.4 **% White**: 97.2	National ***Socio-Economic Status*** indicator percentiles are not available for the state of Illinois

Sangamon County
SPRINGFIELD S.D. 186
1900 W MONROE ST ● SPRINGFIELD IL 62704-1599 ● (217) 525-3002 ● http://www.springfield.k12.il.us

Grade Span: PK-12 **Schools**: *Regular* 31 ● *Spec Ed* 5 ● *Alt* 0 **Students**: 15,550 **Total Teachers**: 933 **Student/Classroom Teacher Ratio**: 16.5	**Expenditures/Student**: $5,914 **Librarians**: 16.0 972 students/librarian **Guidance Counselors**: 0.0 *** students/counselor	**% Amer Indian**: 0.1 **% Asian**: 1.5 **% Black**: 29.2 **% Hispanic**: 0.8 **% White**: 68.5	National ***Socio-Economic Status*** indicator percentiles are not available for the state of Illinois

Stephenson County
FREEPORT S.D. 145
BX387 501 E SOUTH ST ● FREEPORT IL 61032-0387 ● (815) 232-0308

Grade Span: PK-12 **Schools**: *Regular* 9 ● *Spec Ed* 1 ● *Alt* 0 **Students**: 5,096 **Total Teachers**: 281 **Student/Classroom Teacher Ratio**: 20.6	**Expenditures/Student**: $5,275 **Librarians**: 3.0 1,699 students/librarian **Guidance Counselors**: 7.0 728 students/counselor	**% Amer Indian**: 0.1 **% Asian**: 1.4 **% Black**: 20.2 **% Hispanic**: 1.0 **% White**: 77.3	National ***Socio-Economic Status*** indicator percentiles are not available for the state of Illinois

Tazewell County
MORTON COMMUNITY UNIT S.D. 709
235 E JACKSON ST ● MORTON IL 61550-1625 ● (309) 263-2581

Grade Span: PK-12 **Schools**: *Regular* 6 ● *Spec Ed* 0 ● *Alt* 0 **Students**: 2,924 **Total Teachers**: 169 **Student/Classroom Teacher Ratio**: 17.7	**Expenditures/Student**: $4,905 **Librarians**: 3.0 975 students/librarian **Guidance Counselors**: 4.0 731 students/counselor	**% Amer Indian**: 0.2 **% Asian**: 1.5 **% Black**: 0.1 **% Hispanic**: 0.5 **% White**: 97.7	National ***Socio-Economic Status*** indicator percentiles are not available for the state of Illinois

Tazewell County
PEKIN PUBLIC S.D. 108
501 WASHINGTON ST ● PEKIN IL 61554-4239 ● (309) 346-3151 ● http://www.pekin.net/pekin108

Grade Span: PK-08 **Schools**: *Regular* 10 ● *Spec Ed* 0 ● *Alt* 0 **Students**: 4,150 **Total Teachers**: 246 **Student/Classroom Teacher Ratio**: 16.8	**Expenditures/Student**: $4,409 **Librarians**: 10.0 415 students/librarian **Guidance Counselors**: 5.0 830 students/counselor	**% Amer Indian**: 0.1 **% Asian**: 0.6 **% Black**: 0.3 **% Hispanic**: 0.4 **% White**: 98.6	National ***Socio-Economic Status*** indicator percentiles are not available for the state of Illinois

Vermilion County
DANVILLE COMMUNITY CONSOLIDATED S.D. 118
516 N JACKSON ST ● DANVILLE IL 61832-4684 ● (217) 431-5406

Grade Span: PK-12 **Schools**: *Regular* 11 ● *Spec Ed* 0 ● *Alt* 0 **Students**: 6,308 **Total Teachers**: 407 **Student/Classroom Teacher Ratio**: 15.5	**Expenditures/Student**: $5,102 **Librarians**: 1.0 6,308 students/librarian **Guidance Counselors**: 8.0 789 students/counselor	**% Amer Indian**: 0.2 **% Asian**: 1.8 **% Black**: 30.9 **% Hispanic**: 3.9 **% White**: 63.2	National ***Socio-Economic Status*** indicator percentiles are not available for the state of Illinois

Whiteside County
STERLING COMMUNITY UNIT S.D. 5
1800 6TH AVE ● STERLING IL 61081-1399 ● (815) 625-3620

Grade Span: PK-12 **Schools**: *Regular* 6 ● *Spec Ed* 1 ● *Alt* 0 **Students**: 3,860 **Total Teachers**: 215 **Student/Classroom Teacher Ratio**: 17.6	**Expenditures/Student**: $4,610 **Librarians**: 2.0 1,930 students/librarian **Guidance Counselors**: 5.0 772 students/counselor	**% Amer Indian**: 0.4 **% Asian**: 1.0 **% Black**: 2.7 **% Hispanic**: 16.4 **% White**: 79.4	National ***Socio-Economic Status*** indicator percentiles are not available for the state of Illinois

Will County
CRETE MONEE COMMUNITY UNIT S.D. 201U
1742 DIXIE HWY ● CRETE IL 60417-3997 ● (708) 672-2670 ● http://www.cm201u.will.k12.il.us

Grade Span: PK-12 **Schools**: *Regular* 7 ● *Spec Ed* 0 ● *Alt* 0 **Students**: 4,226 **Total Teachers**: 225 **Student/Classroom Teacher Ratio**: 18.8	**Expenditures/Student**: $5,428 **Librarians**: 1.0 4,226 students/librarian **Guidance Counselors**: 6.2 682 students/counselor	**% Amer Indian**: 0.2 **% Asian**: 0.7 **% Black**: 37.0 **% Hispanic**: 3.2 **% White**: 58.9	National ***Socio-Economic Status*** indicator percentiles are not available for the state of Illinois

Will County
JOLIET S.D. 86
420 N RAYNOR AVE ● JOLIET IL 60435-6097 ● (815) 740-3196

Grade Span: PK-08 **Schools**: *Regular* 20 ● *Spec Ed* 2 ● *Alt* 0 **Students**: 8,396 **Total Teachers**: 402 **Student/Classroom Teacher Ratio**: 22.1	**Expenditures/Student**: $4,721 **Librarians**: 4.0 2,099 students/librarian **Guidance Counselors**: 0.0 *** students/counselor	**% Amer Indian**: 0.0 **% Asian**: 1.4 **% Black**: 40.2 **% Hispanic**: 23.7 **% White**: 34.7	National ***Socio-Economic Status*** indicator percentiles are not available for the state of Illinois

Will County

JOLIET TOWNSHIP HIGH S.D. 204

201 E JEFFERSON ST ● JOLIET IL 60432-2848 ● (815) 727-6970

Grade Span: 09-12	**Expenditures/Student**: $7,054	**% Amer Indian**: 0.6	National ***Socio-Economic Status*** indicator percentiles are not available for the state of Illinois
Schools: *Regular* 2 ● *Spec Ed* 1 ● *Alt* 0	**Librarians**: 5.0	**% Asian**: 2.1	
Students: 4,604	921 students/librarian	**% Black**: 32.3	
Total Teachers: 247	**Guidance Counselors**: 12.0	**% Hispanic**: 18.1	
Student/Classroom Teacher Ratio: 19.5	384 students/counselor	**% White**: 47.0	

Will County

[LOCKPORT] **HOMER COMMUNITY CONSOLIDATED S.D. 33C**

15733 BELL RD ● LOCKPORT IL 60441-8414 ● (708) 301-3034 ● http://www.homer33.will.k12.il.us/Homer33/default.htm

Grade Span: PK-08	**Expenditures/Student**: $3,881	**% Amer Indian**: 0.1	National ***Socio-Economic Status*** indicator percentiles are not available for the state of Illinois
Schools: *Regular* 4 ● *Spec Ed* 0 ● *Alt* 0	**Librarians**: 1.0	**% Asian**: 2.0	
Students: 2,727	2,727 students/librarian	**% Black**: 0.3	
Total Teachers: 123	**Guidance Counselors**: 2.0	**% Hispanic**: 2.4	
Student/Classroom Teacher Ratio: 22.3	1,364 students/counselor	**% White**: 95.2	

Will County

LOCKPORT TOWNSHIP HIGH S.D. 205

1323 E 7TH ST ● LOCKPORT IL 60441-3899 ● (815) 834-4400

Grade Span: 09-12	**Expenditures/Student**: $6,753	**% Amer Indian**: 0.1	National ***Socio-Economic Status*** indicator percentiles are not available for the state of Illinois
Schools: *Regular* 1 ● *Spec Ed* 0 ● *Alt* 0	**Librarians**: 2.0	**% Asian**: 2.2	
Students: 2,604	1,302 students/librarian	**% Black**: 5.9	
Total Teachers: 129	**Guidance Counselors**: 9.0	**% Hispanic**: 3.1	
Student/Classroom Teacher Ratio: 20.2	289 students/counselor	**% White**: 88.7	

Will County

[NEW LENOX] **LINCOLN WAY COMMUNITY HIGH S.D. 210**

1801 E LINCOLN HIWAY ● NEW LENOX IL 60451-2098 ● (815) 485-7600

Grade Span: 09-12	**Expenditures/Student**: $5,769	**% Amer Indian**: 0.1	National ***Socio-Economic Status*** indicator percentiles are not available for the state of Illinois
Schools: *Regular* 2 ● *Spec Ed* 0 ● *Alt* 0	**Librarians**: 2.0	**% Asian**: 0.9	
Students: 3,861	1,931 students/librarian	**% Black**: 0.5	
Total Teachers: 201	**Guidance Counselors**: 11.6	**% Hispanic**: 2.4	
Student/Classroom Teacher Ratio: 19.3	333 students/counselor	**% White**: 96.2	

Will County

NEW LENOX S.D. 122

809 N CEDAR RD ● NEW LENOX IL 60451-1499 ● (815) 485-2169

Grade Span: PK-08	**Expenditures/Student**: $3,482	**% Amer Indian**: 0.1	National ***Socio-Economic Status*** indicator percentiles are not available for the state of Illinois
Schools: *Regular* 8 ● *Spec Ed* 0 ● *Alt* 0	**Librarians**: 5.0	**% Asian**: 0.6	
Students: 3,414	683 students/librarian	**% Black**: 0.2	
Total Teachers: 139	**Guidance Counselors**: 4.0	**% Hispanic**: 2.5	
Student/Classroom Teacher Ratio: 30.7	854 students/counselor	**% White**: 96.6	

Will County

PLAINFIELD S.D. 202

500 W FORT BEGGS DR ● PLAINFIELD IL 60544 ● (815) 439-3240 ● http://www.plainfield.will.k12.il.us

Grade Span: PK-12	**Expenditures/Student**: $4,290	**% Amer Indian**: 0.0	National ***Socio-Economic Status*** indicator percentiles are not available for the state of Illinois
Schools: *Regular* 6 ● *Spec Ed* 0 ● *Alt* 0	**Librarians**: 5.0	**% Asian**: 0.9	
Students: 5,680	1,136 students/librarian	**% Black**: 0.2	
Total Teachers: 248	**Guidance Counselors**: 6.8	**% Hispanic**: 3.4	
Student/Classroom Teacher Ratio: 23.4	835 students/counselor	**% White**: 95.4	

Will County

[ROMEOVILLE] **VALLEY VIEW COMMUNITY UNIT S.D. 365U**

755 LUTHER DR ● ROMEOVILLE IL 60441-1156 ● (815) 886-2700

Grade Span: PK-12 **Schools**: *Regular* 14 ● *Spec Ed* 0 ● *Alt* 0 **Students**: 12,041 **Total Teachers**: 563 **Student/Classroom Teacher Ratio**: 22.0	**Expenditures/Student**: $4,808 **Librarians**: 12.0 1,003 students/librarian **Guidance Counselors**: 9.0 1,338 students/counselor	**% Amer Indian**: 0.0 **% Asian**: 4.8 **% Black**: 20.5 **% Hispanic**: 8.5 **% White**: 66.1	National ***Socio-Economic Status*** indicator percentiles are not available for the state of Illinois

Williamson County

MARION COMMUNITY UNIT S.D. 2

1410 W HENDRICKSON ● MARION IL 62959-1545 ● (618) 993-2321

Grade Span: PK-12 **Schools**: *Regular* 7 ● *Spec Ed* 0 ● *Alt* 0 **Students**: 3,925 **Total Teachers**: 171 **Student/Classroom Teacher Ratio**: 22.6	**Expenditures/Student**: $3,450 **Librarians**: 3.0 1,308 students/librarian **Guidance Counselors**: 8.0 491 students/counselor	**% Amer Indian**: 0.0 **% Asian**: 0.7 **% Black**: 4.6 **% Hispanic**: 0.8 **% White**: 93.9	National ***Socio-Economic Status*** indicator percentiles are not available for the state of Illinois

Winnebago County

[ROCKFORD] **HARLEM UNIT S.D. 122**

BOX 2021 8605 N 2ND ● ROCKFORD IL 61130-2021 ● (815) 654-4500 ● http://harlem.winbgo.k12.il.us

Grade Span: PK-12 **Schools**: *Regular* 10 ● *Spec Ed* 1 ● *Alt* 0 **Students**: 6,636 **Total Teachers**: 383 **Student/Classroom Teacher Ratio**: 18.7	**Expenditures/Student**: $4,650 **Librarians**: 4.5 1,475 students/librarian **Guidance Counselors**: 8.0 830 students/counselor	**% Amer Indian**: 0.2 **% Asian**: 1.1 **% Black**: 2.3 **% Hispanic**: 3.3 **% White**: 93.1	National ***Socio-Economic Status*** indicator percentiles are not available for the state of Illinois

Winnebago County

ROCKFORD S.D. 205

201 S MADISON ST ● ROCKFORD IL 61104-2092 ● (815) 966-3101 ● http://www.rps205.com

Grade Span: PK-12 **Schools**: *Regular* 46 ● *Spec Ed* 4 ● *Alt* 0 **Students**: 27,637 **Total Teachers**: 1,674 **Student/Classroom Teacher Ratio**: 17.4	**Expenditures/Student**: $6,130 **Librarians**: 12.0 2,303 students/librarian **Guidance Counselors**: 41.0 674 students/counselor	**% Amer Indian**: 0.2 **% Asian**: 2.8 **% Black**: 26.2 **% Hispanic**: 8.2 **% White**: 62.5	National ***Socio-Economic Status*** indicator percentiles are not available for the state of Illinois

Adams County

[DECATUR] NORTH ADAMS COMMUNITY S.D.

625 STADIUM DR PO BOX 191 ● DECATUR IN 46733-0191 ● (219) 724-7146 ● http://neptune.esc.k12.in.us/adams/nacs/nacs.html

Grade Span: KG-12 **Schools**: *Regular* 5 ● *Spec Ed* 0 ● *Alt* 0 **Students**: 2,551 **Total Teachers**: 134 **Student/Classroom Teacher Ratio**: 20.2	**Expenditures/Student**: $5,882 **Librarians**: 2.3 1,109 students/librarian **Guidance Counselors**: 7.0 364 students/counselor	**% Amer Indian**: 0.1 **% Asian**: 0.2 **% Black**: 0.5 **% Hispanic**: 5.5 **% White**: 93.7	National ***Socio-Economic Status*** indicator percentile (100=high): 73rd

Allen County

FORT WAYNE COMMUNITY S.D.

1200 S CLINTON ST ● FORT WAYNE IN 46802-3594 ● (219) 425-7272

Grade Span: PK-12 **Schools**: *Regular* 50 ● *Spec Ed* 2 ● *Alt* 1 **Students**: 31,748 **Total Teachers**: 1,719 **Student/Classroom Teacher Ratio**: 19.1	**Expenditures/Student**: $5,685 **Librarians**: 1.0 31,748 students/librarian **Guidance Counselors**: 35.1 905 students/counselor	**% Amer Indian**: 0.3 **% Asian**: 1.6 **% Black**: 24.4 **% Hispanic**: 3.6 **% White**: 70.2	National ***Socio-Economic Status*** indicator percentile (100=high): 37th

Allen County

[FORT WAYNE] METROPOLITAN S.D. OF SOUTHWEST ALLEN COUNTY

4824 HOMESTEAD RD ● FORT WAYNE IN 46804-5455 ● (219) 431-2010

Grade Span: KG-12 **Schools**: *Regular* 9 ● *Spec Ed* 0 ● *Alt* 0 **Students**: 5,215 **Total Teachers**: 309 **Student/Classroom Teacher Ratio**: 16.5	**Expenditures/Student**: $6,981 **Librarians**: 4.0 1,304 students/librarian **Guidance Counselors**: 15.0 348 students/counselor	**% Amer Indian**: 0.2 **% Asian**: 2.2 **% Black**: 1.7 **% Hispanic**: 1.4 **% White**: 94.5	National ***Socio-Economic Status*** indicator percentile (100=high): 99th

Allen County

[FORT WAYNE] NORTHWEST ALLEN COUNTY S.D.

13119 COLDWATER RD ● FORT WAYNE IN 46845-9632 ● (219) 637-3155 ● http://www.nacs.k12.in.us

Grade Span: KG-12 **Schools**: *Regular* 6 ● *Spec Ed* 0 ● *Alt* 1 **Students**: 3,497 **Total Teachers**: 182 **Student/Classroom Teacher Ratio**: 19.3	**Expenditures/Student**: $4,942 **Librarians**: 2.0 1,749 students/librarian **Guidance Counselors**: 8.0 437 students/counselor	**% Amer Indian**: 0.0 **% Asian**: 0.6 **% Black**: 0.6 **% Hispanic**: 0.7 **% White**: 98.2	National ***Socio-Economic Status*** indicator percentile (100=high): 95th

Allen County

[NEW HAVEN] EAST ALLEN COUNTY S.D.

1240 US 30 E ● NEW HAVEN IN 46774-1732 ● (219) 493-3761

Grade Span: PK-12 **Schools**: *Regular* 17 ● *Spec Ed* 1 ● *Alt* 0 **Students**: 9,206 **Total Teachers**: 528 **Student/Classroom Teacher Ratio**: 17.7	**Expenditures/Student**: $5,503 **Librarians**: 7.5 1,227 students/librarian **Guidance Counselors**: 25.8 357 students/counselor	**% Amer Indian**: 0.2 **% Asian**: 0.6 **% Black**: 15.4 **% Hispanic**: 1.4 **% White**: 82.4	National ***Socio-Economic Status*** indicator percentile (100=high): 67th

Bartholomew County

[COLUMBUS] BARTHOLOMEW CONSOLIDATED S.D.

2650 HOME AVE ● COLUMBUS IN 47201-3152 ● (812) 376-4220 ● http://columbus.hsonline.net/schools/bcsc.htm

Grade Span: PK-12 **Schools**: *Regular* 15 ● *Spec Ed* 0 ● *Alt* 2 **Students**: 10,435 **Total Teachers**: 634 **Student/Classroom Teacher Ratio**: 17.1	**Expenditures/Student**: $6,359 **Librarians**: 9.0 1,159 students/librarian **Guidance Counselors**: 21.0 497 students/counselor	**% Amer Indian**: 0.1 **% Asian**: 1.9 **% Black**: 2.6 **% Hispanic**: 1.2 **% White**: 94.2	National ***Socio-Economic Status*** indicator percentile (100=high): 68th

Boone County

LEBANON COMMUNITY S.D.

404 N MERIDAN ST ● LEBANON IN 46052-2241 ● (765) 482-0380 ● http://www.bccn.boone.in.us/lcsc

Grade Span: PK-12 **Schools**: *Regular* 6 ● *Spec Ed* 0 ● *Alt* 0 **Students**: 3,169 **Total Teachers**: 173 **Student/Classroom Teacher Ratio**: 18.4	**Expenditures/Student**: $5,363 **Librarians**: 5.0 634 students/librarian **Guidance Counselors**: 3.9 813 students/counselor	**% Amer Indian**: 0.1 **% Asian**: 0.5 **% Black**: 0.1 **% Hispanic**: 1.1 **% White**: 98.2	National ***Socio-Economic Status*** indicator percentile (100=high): 75th

Boone County

[ZIONSVILLE] **EAGLE-UNION COMMUNITY S.D.**

690 BEECH ST ● ZIONSVILLE IN 46077-1278 ● (317) 873-2858 ● http://www.eucsc.k12.in.us

Grade Span: KG-12 **Schools**: *Regular* 5 ● *Spec Ed* 0 ● *Alt* 0 **Students**: 2,641 **Total Teachers**: 130 **Student/Classroom Teacher Ratio**: 19.7	**Expenditures/Student**: $4,766 **Librarians**: 3.0 880 students/librarian **Guidance Counselors**: 3.5 755 students/counselor	**% Amer Indian**: 0.1 **% Asian**: 0.5 **% Black**: 0.1 **% Hispanic**: 0.3 **% White**: 99.0	National ***Socio-Economic Status*** indicator percentile (100=high): 98th

Cass County

LOGANSPORT COMMUNITY S.D.

2829 GEORGE ST ● LOGANSPORT IN 46947-3997 ● (219) 722-2911 ● http://www.cqc.com/~lcsc

Grade Span: PK-12 **Schools**: *Regular* 7 ● *Spec Ed* 1 ● *Alt* 1 **Students**: 4,138 **Total Teachers**: 327 **Student/Classroom Teacher Ratio**: 19.5	**Expenditures/Student**: $7,199 **Librarians**: 7.0 591 students/librarian **Guidance Counselors**: 4.0 1,035 students/counselor	**% Amer Indian**: 0.2 **% Asian**: 0.7 **% Black**: 1.2 **% Hispanic**: 1.6 **% White**: 96.3	National ***Socio-Economic Status*** indicator percentile (100=high): 46th

Clark County

[JEFFERSONVILLE] **GREATER CLARK COUNTY S.D.**

2710 HWY 62 ● JEFFERSONVILLE IN 47130-6010 ● (812) 283-0701

Grade Span: PK-12 **Schools**: *Regular* 18 ● *Spec Ed* 0 ● *Alt* 0 **Students**: 9,864 **Total Teachers**: 592 **Student/Classroom Teacher Ratio**: 17.7	**Expenditures/Student**: $6,229 **Librarians**: 12.0 822 students/librarian **Guidance Counselors**: 16.0 617 students/counselor	**% Amer Indian**: 0.2 **% Asian**: 0.6 **% Black**: 13.0 **% Hispanic**: 0.7 **% White**: 85.4	National ***Socio-Economic Status*** indicator percentile (100=high): 42nd

Clark County

[SELLERSBURG] **WEST CLARK COMMUNITY S.D.**

601 RENZ AVE ● SELLERSBURG IN 47172-1398 ● (812) 246-3375 ● http://www.venus.net/~wclark

Grade Span: KG-12 **Schools**: *Regular* 8 ● *Spec Ed* 0 ● *Alt* 0 **Students**: 3,087 **Total Teachers**: 166 **Student/Classroom Teacher Ratio**: 18.2	**Expenditures/Student**: $5,236 **Librarians**: 3.5 882 students/librarian **Guidance Counselors**: 4.5 686 students/counselor	**% Amer Indian**: 0.0 **% Asian**: 0.0 **% Black**: 0.1 **% Hispanic**: 0.2 **% White**: 99.7	National ***Socio-Economic Status*** indicator percentile (100=high): 66th

Clay County

[KNIGHTSVILLE] **CLAY COMMUNITY S.D.**

PO BOX 169 ● KNIGHTSVILLE IN 47857-0169 ● (812) 443-4461

Grade Span: PK-12 **Schools**: *Regular* 10 ● *Spec Ed* 0 ● *Alt* 0 **Students**: 4,764 **Total Teachers**: 260 **Student/Classroom Teacher Ratio**: 18.8	**Expenditures/Student**: $5,521 **Librarians**: 6.0 794 students/librarian **Guidance Counselors**: 7.0 681 students/counselor	**% Amer Indian**: 0.0 **% Asian**: 0.0 **% Black**: 0.1 **% Hispanic**: 0.1 **% White**: 99.7	National ***Socio-Economic Status*** indicator percentile (100=high): 61st

Clinton County

[FRANKFORT] **COMMUNITY S.D. OF FRANKFORT**

50 S MAISH RD ● FRANKFORT IN 46041-2824 ● (765) 654-5585

Grade Span: KG-12 **Schools**: *Regular* 7 ● *Spec Ed* 0 ● *Alt* 0 **Students**: 3,144 **Total Teachers**: 174 **Student/Classroom Teacher Ratio**: 18.4	**Expenditures/Student**: $5,382 **Librarians**: 6.0 524 students/librarian **Guidance Counselors**: 8.0 393 students/counselor	**% Amer Indian**: 0.1 **% Asian**: 0.3 **% Black**: 0.3 **% Hispanic**: 6.3 **% White**: 92.9	National ***Socio-Economic Status*** indicator percentile (100=high): 48th

Daviess County

WASHINGTON COMMUNITY S.D.

301 E SOUTH ST ● WASHINGTON IN 47501-3294 ● (812) 254-5536

Grade Span: KG-12 **Schools**: *Regular* 6 ● *Spec Ed* 0 ● *Alt* 0 **Students**: 2,529 **Total Teachers**: 125 **Student/Classroom Teacher Ratio**: 20.5	**Expenditures/Student**: $5,113 **Librarians**: 2.0 1,265 students/librarian **Guidance Counselors**: 4.0 632 students/counselor	**% Amer Indian**: 0.0 **% Asian**: 0.2 **% Black**: 0.8 **% Hispanic**: 1.0 **% White**: 98.1	National ***Socio-Economic Status*** indicator percentile (100=high): 45th

De Kalb County

[WATERLOO] **DEKALB COUNTY CENTRAL UNITED S.D.**

PO BOX 420 ● WATERLOO IN 46793-0420 ● (219) 925-3914 ● http://www.dekalb.k12.in.us

Grade Span: PK-12 **Schools**: *Regular* 8 ● *Spec Ed* 0 ● *Alt* 0 **Students**: 3,965 **Total Teachers**: 210 **Student/Classroom Teacher Ratio**: 17.8	**Expenditures/Student**: $5,337 **Librarians**: 2.5 1,586 students/librarian **Guidance Counselors**: 6.0 661 students/counselor	**% Amer Indian**: 0.0 **% Asian**: 0.4 **% Black**: 0.0 **% Hispanic**: 0.5 **% White**: 99.1	National ***Socio-Economic Status*** indicator percentile (100=high): 86th

Dearborn County

[AURORA] **SOUTH DEARBORN COMMMUNITY S.D.**

408 GREEN BLVD ● AURORA IN 47001-1499 ● (812) 926-2090 ● http://www.venus.net/~sdearad1

Grade Span: KG-12 **Schools**: *Regular* 6 ● *Spec Ed* 0 ● *Alt* 0 **Students**: 3,105 **Total Teachers**: 164 **Student/Classroom Teacher Ratio**: 18.7	**Expenditures/Student**: $5,023 **Librarians**: 3.0 1,035 students/librarian **Guidance Counselors**: 2.0 1,553 students/counselor	**% Amer Indian**: 0.0 **% Asian**: 0.2 **% Black**: 0.0 **% Hispanic**: 0.1 **% White**: 99.7	National ***Socio-Economic Status*** indicator percentile (100=high): 55th

Dearborn County

SUNMAN-DEARBORN COMMUNITY S.D.

PO BOX 210 ● SUNMAN IN 47041-0210 ● (812) 623-2291

Grade Span: PK-12 **Schools**: *Regular* 5 ● *Spec Ed* 1 ● *Alt* 0 **Students**: 3,724 **Total Teachers**: 195 **Student/Classroom Teacher Ratio**: 19.4	**Expenditures/Student**: $5,740 **Librarians**: 5.0 745 students/librarian **Guidance Counselors**: 8.0 466 students/counselor	**% Amer Indian**: 0.0 **% Asian**: 0.0 **% Black**: 0.2 **% Hispanic**: 0.1 **% White**: 99.6	National ***Socio-Economic Status*** indicator percentile (100=high): 86th

Delaware County

[MUNCIE] **DELAWARE COMMUNITY S.D.**

7821 SR 3 N ● MUNCIE IN 47303-9803 ● (765) 284-5074

Grade Span: KG-12 **Schools**: *Regular* 6 ● *Spec Ed* 0 ● *Alt* 0 **Students**: 2,916 **Total Teachers**: 158 **Student/Classroom Teacher Ratio**: 18.8	**Expenditures/Student**: $5,380 **Librarians**: 2.0 1,458 students/librarian **Guidance Counselors**: 7.0 417 students/counselor	**% Amer Indian**: 0.0 **% Asian**: 0.5 **% Black**: 1.1 **% Hispanic**: 0.3 **% White**: 98.0	National ***Socio-Economic Status*** indicator percentile (100=high): 76th

Delaware County
MUNCIE COMMUNITY S.D.
2501 N OAKWOOD AVE ● MUNCIE IN 47304-2399 ● (765) 747-5205

Grade Span: PK-12 **Schools**: *Regular* 16 ● *Spec Ed* 0 ● *Alt* 1 **Students**: 8,711 **Total Teachers**: 529 **Student/Classroom Teacher Ratio**: 17.4	**Expenditures/Student**: $7,119 **Librarians**: 9.0 968 students/librarian **Guidance Counselors**: 21.0 415 students/counselor	**% Amer Indian**: 0.1 **% Asian**: 0.6 **% Black**: 18.5 **% Hispanic**: 0.8 **% White**: 80.1	National ***Socio-Economic Status*** indicator percentile (100=high): 21st

Dubois County
[JASPER] **GREATER JASPER CONSOLIDATED S.D.**
1520 ST CHARLES ST SUITE 1 ● JASPER IN 47546 ● (812) 482-1801

Grade Span: PK-12 **Schools**: *Regular* 5 ● *Spec Ed* 1 ● *Alt* 0 **Students**: 2,970 **Total Teachers**: 181 **Student/Classroom Teacher Ratio**: 20.6	**Expenditures/Student**: $7,465 **Librarians**: 3.5 849 students/librarian **Guidance Counselors**: 3.3 900 students/counselor	**% Amer Indian**: 0.0 **% Asian**: 0.2 **% Black**: 0.1 **% Hispanic**: 0.8 **% White**: 98.8	National ***Socio-Economic Status*** indicator percentile (100=high): 93rd

Elkhart County
[ELKHART] **CONCORD COMMUNITY S.D.**
59040 MINUTEMAN WAY ● ELKHART IN 46517-3499 ● (219) 875-5161

Grade Span: KG-12 **Schools**: *Regular* 6 ● *Spec Ed* 0 ● *Alt* 0 **Students**: 3,970 **Total Teachers**: 201 **Student/Classroom Teacher Ratio**: 19.6	**Expenditures/Student**: $5,816 **Librarians**: 1.0 3,970 students/librarian **Guidance Counselors**: 10.0 397 students/counselor	**% Amer Indian**: 0.4 **% Asian**: 1.5 **% Black**: 5.1 **% Hispanic**: 3.3 **% White**: 89.7	National ***Socio-Economic Status*** indicator percentile (100=high): 79th

Elkhart County
ELKHART COMMUNITY S.D.
2720 CALIFORNIA RD ● ELKHART IN 46514-1297 ● (219) 262-5500 ● http://www.elkhart.k12.in.us

Grade Span: PK-12 **Schools**: *Regular* 19 ● *Spec Ed* 0 ● *Alt* 1 **Students**: 12,084 **Total Teachers**: 674 **Student/Classroom Teacher Ratio**: 19.1	**Expenditures/Student**: $6,108 **Librarians**: 6.0 2,014 students/librarian **Guidance Counselors**: 18.0 671 students/counselor	**% Amer Indian**: 0.1 **% Asian**: 1.5 **% Black**: 17.3 **% Hispanic**: 4.1 **% White**: 77.0	National ***Socio-Economic Status*** indicator percentile (100=high): 42nd

Elkhart County
GOSHEN COMMUNITY S.D.
721 E MADISON ST ● GOSHEN IN 46526-3521 ● (219) 533-8631 ● http://www.goshenschools.org

Grade Span: KG-12 **Schools**: *Regular* 9 ● *Spec Ed* 0 ● *Alt* 0 **Students**: 5,077 **Total Teachers**: 294 **Student/Classroom Teacher Ratio**: 18.6	**Expenditures/Student**: $6,662 **Librarians**: 3.0 1,692 students/librarian **Guidance Counselors**: 11.9 427 students/counselor	**% Amer Indian**: 0.3 **% Asian**: 1.0 **% Black**: 1.1 **% Hispanic**: 10.0 **% White**: 87.6	National ***Socio-Economic Status*** indicator percentile (100=high): 57th

Elkhart County
MIDDLEBURY COMMUNITY S.D.
57853 NORTHRIDGE DR ● MIDDLEBURY IN 46540-9408 ● (219) 825-9425

Grade Span: KG-12 **Schools**: *Regular* 6 ● *Spec Ed* 0 ● *Alt* 0 **Students**: 3,209 **Total Teachers**: 171 **Student/Classroom Teacher Ratio**: 18.7	**Expenditures/Student**: $5,899 **Librarians**: 3.0 1,070 students/librarian **Guidance Counselors**: 7.0 458 students/counselor	**% Amer Indian**: 0.0 **% Asian**: 0.9 **% Black**: 0.0 **% Hispanic**: 0.8 **% White**: 98.2	National ***Socio-Economic Status*** indicator percentile (100=high): 86th

Elkhart County

[NAPPANEE] WA-NEE COMMUNITY S.D.

1300 N MAIN ST ● NAPPANEE IN 46550-1986 ● (219) 773-3131

Grade Span: KG-12	**Expenditures/Student**: $5,684	**% Amer Indian**: 0.0	National *Socio-Economic Status* indicator percentile (100=high): 88th
Schools: *Regular* 5 ● *Spec Ed* 0 ● *Alt* 0	**Librarians**: 3.0	**% Asian**: 0.5	
Students: 2,858	953 students/librarian	**% Black**: 0.2	
Total Teachers: 156	**Guidance Counselors**: 6.6	**% Hispanic**: 1.7	
Student/Classroom Teacher Ratio: 18.4	433 students/counselor	**% White**: 97.6	

Fayette County

[CONNERSVILLE] FAYETTE COUNTY S.D.

1401 SPARTAN DR ● CONNERSVILLE IN 47331-1008 ● (765) 825-2178 ● http://fayette.k12.in.us

Grade Span: PK-12	**Expenditures/Student**: $8,129	**% Amer Indian**: 0.1	National *Socio-Economic Status* indicator percentile (100=high): 40th
Schools: *Regular* 10 ● *Spec Ed* 1 ● *Alt* 1	**Librarians**: 3.0	**% Asian**: 0.3	
Students: 4,449	1,483 students/librarian	**% Black**: 1.7	
Total Teachers: 376	**Guidance Counselors**: 10.0	**% Hispanic**: 0.1	
Student/Classroom Teacher Ratio: 16.8	445 students/counselor	**% White**: 97.9	

Floyd County

[NEW ALBANY] NEW ALBANY-FLOYD COUNTY CONSOLIDATED S.D.

2813 GRANT LINE PO BOX 1087 ● NEW ALBANY IN 47150-1087 ● (812) 949-4200

Grade Span: PK-12	**Expenditures/Student**: $5,824	**% Amer Indian**: 0.0	National *Socio-Economic Status* indicator percentile (100=high): 51st
Schools: *Regular* 18 ● *Spec Ed* 0 ● *Alt* 1	**Librarians**: 5.0	**% Asian**: 0.3	
Students: 11,312	2,262 students/librarian	**% Black**: 6.6	
Total Teachers: 614	**Guidance Counselors**: 22.0	**% Hispanic**: 0.3	
Student/Classroom Teacher Ratio: 19.1	514 students/counselor	**% White**: 92.7	

Franklin County

[BROOKVILLE] FRANKLIN COUNTY COMMUNITY S.D.

PO BOX I ● BROOKVILLE IN 47012-0309 ● (765) 647-4128 ● http://www.franklin.cnz.com/education

Grade Span: PK-12	**Expenditures/Student**: $5,452	**% Amer Indian**: 0.1	National *Socio-Economic Status* indicator percentile (100=high): 55th
Schools: *Regular* 5 ● *Spec Ed* 0 ● *Alt* 0	**Librarians**: 3.0	**% Asian**: 0.1	
Students: 2,816	939 students/librarian	**% Black**: 0.0	
Total Teachers: 143	**Guidance Counselors**: 3.0	**% Hispanic**: 0.0	
Student/Classroom Teacher Ratio: 19.5	939 students/counselor	**% White**: 99.8	

Grant County

MARION COMMUNITY S.D.

1240 S ADAMS PO BOX 2020 ● MARION IN 46952-8420 ● (765) 662-2546

Grade Span: PK-12	**Expenditures/Student**: $6,289	**% Amer Indian**: 0.2	National *Socio-Economic Status* indicator percentile (100=high): 39th
Schools: *Regular* 11 ● *Spec Ed* 1 ● *Alt* 1	**Librarians**: 4.0	**% Asian**: 0.9	
Students: 6,386	1,597 students/librarian	**% Black**: 20.2	
Total Teachers: 388	**Guidance Counselors**: 9.0	**% Hispanic**: 3.8	
Student/Classroom Teacher Ratio: 17.3	710 students/counselor	**% White**: 74.9	

Hamilton County

CARMEL CLAY S.D.

5201 E 131ST ST ● CARMEL IN 46033 ● (317) 844-9961 ● http://www.ccs.k12.in.us

Grade Span: PK-12	**Expenditures/Student**: $6,533	**% Amer Indian**: 0.1	National *Socio-Economic Status* indicator percentile (100=high): 99th
Schools: *Regular* 11 ● *Spec Ed* 2 ● *Alt* 0	**Librarians**: 13.5	**% Asian**: 3.5	
Students: 10,050	744 students/librarian	**% Black**: 0.9	
Total Teachers: 632	**Guidance Counselors**: 22.5	**% Hispanic**: 0.7	
Student/Classroom Teacher Ratio: 19.5	447 students/counselor	**% White**: 94.9	

Hamilton County

[FISHERS] **HAMILTON SOUTHEASTERN S.D.**

13485 CUMBERLAND RD ● FISHERS IN 46038 ● (317) 594-4100 ● http://www.hse.k12.in.us

Grade Span: PK-12 **Schools**: *Regular* 9 ● *Spec Ed* 0 ● *Alt* 0 **Students**: 5,493 **Total Teachers**: 304 **Student/Classroom Teacher Ratio**: 17.6	**Expenditures/Student**: $6,372 **Librarians**: 8.8 624 students/librarian **Guidance Counselors**: 14.8 371 students/counselor	**% Amer Indian**: 0.1 **% Asian**: 1.9 **% Black**: 0.9 **% Hispanic**: 0.6 **% White**: 96.6	National ***Socio-Economic Status*** indicator percentile (100=high): 98th

Hamilton County

NOBLESVILLE S.D.

1775 FIELD DR ● NOBLESVILLE IN 46060-1797 ● (317) 773-3171 ● http://www.nobl.k12.in.us

Grade Span: PK-12 **Schools**: *Regular* 7 ● *Spec Ed* 0 ● *Alt* 0 **Students**: 5,712 **Total Teachers**: 297 **Student/Classroom Teacher Ratio**: 19.4	**Expenditures/Student**: $4,889 **Librarians**: 8.0 714 students/librarian **Guidance Counselors**: 10.0 571 students/counselor	**% Amer Indian**: 0.1 **% Asian**: 0.7 **% Black**: 0.7 **% Hispanic**: 0.4 **% White**: 98.1	National ***Socio-Economic Status*** indicator percentile (100=high): 85th

Hancock County

GREENFIELD-CENTRAL COMMUNITY S.D.

110 W NORTH ST ● GREENFIELD IN 46140-2391 ● (317) 462-4434

Grade Span: PK-12 **Schools**: *Regular* 7 ● *Spec Ed* 1 ● *Alt* 0 **Students**: 3,538 **Total Teachers**: 271 **Student/Classroom Teacher Ratio**: 20.2	**Expenditures/Student**: $6,351 **Librarians**: 1.0 3,538 students/librarian **Guidance Counselors**: 6.0 590 students/counselor	**% Amer Indian**: 0.0 **% Asian**: 0.2 **% Black**: 0.1 **% Hispanic**: 0.3 **% White**: 99.4	National ***Socio-Economic Status*** indicator percentile (100=high): 82nd

Harrison County

[CORYDON] **SOUTH HARRISON COMMUNITY S.D.**

315 S HARRISON DR ● CORYDON IN 47112-8417 ● (812) 738-2168

Grade Span: KG-12 **Schools**: *Regular* 8 ● *Spec Ed* 1 ● *Alt* 0 **Students**: 3,073 **Total Teachers**: 172 **Student/Classroom Teacher Ratio**: 18.4	**Expenditures/Student**: $5,501 **Librarians**: 2.0 1,537 students/librarian **Guidance Counselors**: 4.0 768 students/counselor	**% Amer Indian**: 0.1 **% Asian**: 0.4 **% Black**: 0.3 **% Hispanic**: 0.2 **% White**: 99.1	National ***Socio-Economic Status*** indicator percentile (100=high): 60th

Hendricks County

AVON COMMUNITY S.D.

7203 E US HWY 36 ● AVON IN 46168 ● (317) 272-2920

Grade Span: KG-12 **Schools**: *Regular* 6 ● *Spec Ed* 0 ● *Alt* 0 **Students**: 3,649 **Total Teachers**: 189 **Student/Classroom Teacher Ratio**: 19.1	**Expenditures/Student**: $5,404 **Librarians**: 6.0 608 students/librarian **Guidance Counselors**: 6.5 561 students/counselor	**% Amer Indian**: 0.0 **% Asian**: 0.2 **% Black**: 0.2 **% Hispanic**: 0.7 **% White**: 98.8	National ***Socio-Economic Status*** indicator percentile (100=high): 88th

Hendricks County

BROWNSBURG COMMUNITY S.D.

225 S SCHOOL ST ● BROWNSBURG IN 46112-1360 ● (317) 852-5726

Grade Span: KG-12 **Schools**: *Regular* 6 ● *Spec Ed* 0 ● *Alt* 0 **Students**: 4,102 **Total Teachers**: 216 **Student/Classroom Teacher Ratio**: 19.3	**Expenditures/Student**: $5,174 **Librarians**: 6.0 684 students/librarian **Guidance Counselors**: 7.0 586 students/counselor	**% Amer Indian**: 0.0 **% Asian**: 0.6 **% Black**: 0.1 **% Hispanic**: 0.3 **% White**: 99.0	National ***Socio-Economic Status*** indicator percentile (100=high): 94th

Hendricks County

PLAINFIELD COMMUNITY S.D.

985 S LONGFELLOW DR ● PLAINFIELD IN 46168-1443 ● (317) 839-2578 ● http://www.plainfield.k12.in.us

Grade Span: KG-12 **Schools**: *Regular* 6 ● *Spec Ed* 0 ● *Alt* 0 **Students**: 3,515 **Total Teachers**: 191 **Student/Classroom Teacher Ratio**: 21.8	**Expenditures/Student**: $5,028 **Librarians**: 4.0 879 students/librarian **Guidance Counselors**: 5.0 703 students/counselor	**% Amer Indian**: 0.0 **% Asian**: 0.5 **% Black**: 0.3 **% Hispanic**: 0.2 **% White**: 98.9	National ***Socio-Economic Status*** indicator percentile (100=high): 89th

Henry County

NEW CASTLE COMMUNITY S.D.

522 ELLIOTT AVE ● NEW CASTLE IN 47362-4878 ● (765) 521-7201 ● http://nccsc.k12.in.us

Grade Span: KG-12 **Schools**: *Regular* 10 ● *Spec Ed* 0 ● *Alt* 2 **Students**: 4,224 **Total Teachers**: 265 **Student/Classroom Teacher Ratio**: 18.7	**Expenditures/Student**: $6,464 **Librarians**: 3.0 1,408 students/librarian **Guidance Counselors**: 6.0 704 students/counselor	**% Amer Indian**: 0.0 **% Asian**: 0.3 **% Black**: 1.9 **% Hispanic**: 0.8 **% White**: 97.0	National ***Socio-Economic Status*** indicator percentile (100=high): 40th

Howard County

KOKOMO-CENTER TOWNSHIP CONSOLIDATED S.D.

100 W LINCOLN PO BOX 2188 ● KOKOMO IN 46904-2188 ● (765) 455-8000 ● http://www.kokomo.k12.in.us

Grade Span: PK-12 **Schools**: *Regular* 14 ● *Spec Ed* 0 ● *Alt* 1 **Students**: 7,453 **Total Teachers**: 476 **Student/Classroom Teacher Ratio**: 16.0	**Expenditures/Student**: $6,402 **Librarians**: 5.0 1,491 students/librarian **Guidance Counselors**: 9.0 828 students/counselor	**% Amer Indian**: 0.5 **% Asian**: 0.7 **% Black**: 13.3 **% Hispanic**: 2.1 **% White**: 83.4	National ***Socio-Economic Status*** indicator percentile (100=high): 35th

Huntington County

[HUNTINGTON] HUNTINGTON COUNTY COMMUNITY S.D.

1360 N WARREN RD ● HUNTINGTON IN 46750-2192 ● (219) 356-7812

Grade Span: KG-12 **Schools**: *Regular* 11 ● *Spec Ed* 0 ● *Alt* 0 **Students**: 6,870 **Total Teachers**: 384 **Student/Classroom Teacher Ratio**: 18.1	**Expenditures/Student**: $4,956 **Librarians**: 4.5 1,527 students/librarian **Guidance Counselors**: 16.0 429 students/counselor	**% Amer Indian**: 0.1 **% Asian**: 0.3 **% Black**: 0.1 **% Hispanic**: 0.7 **% White**: 98.8	National ***Socio-Economic Status*** indicator percentile (100=high): 77th

Jackson County

SEYMOUR COMMUNITY S.D.

1638 S WALNUT ST PO BOX 366 ● SEYMOUR IN 47274-0366 ● (812) 522-3340 ● http://www.seymour.org/schools.htm

Grade Span: PK-12 **Schools**: *Regular* 7 ● *Spec Ed* 0 ● *Alt* 0 **Students**: 3,712 **Total Teachers**: 185 **Student/Classroom Teacher Ratio**: 18.9	**Expenditures/Student**: $5,073 **Librarians**: 2.0 1,856 students/librarian **Guidance Counselors**: 6.0 619 students/counselor	**% Amer Indian**: 0.3 **% Asian**: 1.4 **% Black**: 0.5 **% Hispanic**: 0.8 **% White**: 97.0	National ***Socio-Economic Status*** indicator percentile (100=high): 65th

Jasper County

[WHEATFIELD] KANKAKEE VALLEY S.D.

PO BOX 278 ● WHEATFIELD IN 46392-0278 ● (219) 987-4711

Grade Span: KG-12 **Schools**: *Regular* 4 ● *Spec Ed* 0 ● *Alt* 0 **Students**: 3,039 **Total Teachers**: 175 **Student/Classroom Teacher Ratio**: 18.1	**Expenditures/Student**: $6,103 **Librarians**: 4.0 760 students/librarian **Guidance Counselors**: 7.0 434 students/counselor	**% Amer Indian**: 0.2 **% Asian**: 0.2 **% Black**: 0.1 **% Hispanic**: 2.2 **% White**: 97.3	National ***Socio-Economic Status*** indicator percentile (100=high): 71st

Jay County

[PORTLAND] **JAY S.D.**

404 E ARCH ● PORTLAND IN 47371-3239 ● (219) 726-9341

Grade Span: PK-12 **Schools**: *Regular* 10 ● *Spec Ed* 0 ● *Alt* 0 **Students**: 4,022 **Total Teachers**: 239 **Student/Classroom Teacher Ratio**: 16.7	**Expenditures/Student**: $5,342 **Librarians**: 5.0 804 students/librarian **Guidance Counselors**: 5.5 731 students/counselor	**% Amer Indian**: 0.1 **% Asian**: 0.3 **% Black**: 0.1 **% Hispanic**: 0.5 **% White**: 99.0	National ***Socio-Economic Status*** indicator percentile (100=high): 54th

Jefferson County

MADISON CONSOLIDATED S.D.

2421 WILSON AVE ● MADISON IN 47250 ● (812) 273-8511 ● http://www.venus.net/~madadm3/mchs.html

Grade Span: PK-12 **Schools**: *Regular* 10 ● *Spec Ed* 0 ● *Alt* 0 **Students**: 3,379 **Total Teachers**: 199 **Student/Classroom Teacher Ratio**: 16.6	**Expenditures/Student**: $5,871 **Librarians**: 4.0 845 students/librarian **Guidance Counselors**: 5.5 614 students/counselor	**% Amer Indian**: 0.0 **% Asian**: 0.7 **% Black**: 1.2 **% Hispanic**: 0.1 **% White**: 98.0	National ***Socio-Economic Status*** indicator percentile (100=high): 56th

Jennings County

[NORTH VERNON] **JENNINGS COUNTY S.D.**

34 MAIN ST ● NORTH VERNON IN 47265 ● (812) 346-4483

Grade Span: PK-12 **Schools**: *Regular* 8 ● *Spec Ed* 0 ● *Alt* 0 **Students**: 4,630 **Total Teachers**: 216 **Student/Classroom Teacher Ratio**: 23.9	**Expenditures/Student**: $4,807 **Librarians**: 3.0 1,543 students/librarian **Guidance Counselors**: 7.5 617 students/counselor	**% Amer Indian**: 0.5 **% Asian**: 0.5 **% Black**: 0.7 **% Hispanic**: 0.1 **% White**: 98.3	National ***Socio-Economic Status*** indicator percentile (100=high): 56th

Johnson County

FRANKLIN COMMUNITY S.D.

998 GRIZZLY CUB DR ● FRANKLIN IN 46131-1398 ● (317) 738-5800

Grade Span: KG-12 **Schools**: *Regular* 7 ● *Spec Ed* 0 ● *Alt* 0 **Students**: 3,627 **Total Teachers**: 166 **Student/Classroom Teacher Ratio**: 22.0	**Expenditures/Student**: $5,042 **Librarians**: 2.0 1,814 students/librarian **Guidance Counselors**: 6.2 585 students/counselor	**% Amer Indian**: 0.1 **% Asian**: 0.5 **% Black**: 1.1 **% Hispanic**: 0.4 **% White**: 98.0	National ***Socio-Economic Status*** indicator percentile (100=high): 71st

Johnson County

[GREENWOOD] **CENTER GROVE COMMUNITY S.D.**

2929 S MORGANTOWN RD ● GREENWOOD IN 46143-9100 ● (317) 881-9326

Grade Span: KG-12 **Schools**: *Regular* 7 ● *Spec Ed* 0 ● *Alt* 0 **Students**: 6,173 **Total Teachers**: 288 **Student/Classroom Teacher Ratio**: 21.8	**Expenditures/Student**: $5,252 **Librarians**: 6.0 1,029 students/librarian **Guidance Counselors**: 8.0 772 students/counselor	**% Amer Indian**: 0.1 **% Asian**: 0.7 **% Black**: 0.0 **% Hispanic**: 0.5 **% White**: 98.7	National ***Socio-Economic Status*** indicator percentile (100=high): 93rd

Johnson County

GREENWOOD COMMUNITY S.D.

PO BOX 218 ● GREENWOOD IN 46142-0218 ● (317) 889-4060 ● http://oak.gws.k12.in.us

Grade Span: KG-12 **Schools**: *Regular* 5 ● *Spec Ed* 0 ● *Alt* 0 **Students**: 3,439 **Total Teachers**: 171 **Student/Classroom Teacher Ratio**: 20.3	**Expenditures/Student**: $4,767 **Librarians**: 4.0 860 students/librarian **Guidance Counselors**: 5.0 688 students/counselor	**% Amer Indian**: 0.2 **% Asian**: 1.3 **% Black**: 0.2 **% Hispanic**: 1.0 **% White**: 97.3	National ***Socio-Economic Status*** indicator percentile (100=high): 75th

Johnson County

[WHITELAND] **CLARK-PLEASANT COMMUNITY S.D.**

50 CENTER ST • WHITELAND IN 46184-1698 • (317) 535-7579 • http://www.cpcsc.k12.in.us

Grade Span: KG-12 **Schools**: *Regular* 5 • *Spec Ed* 0 • *Alt* 0 **Students**: 2,741 **Total Teachers**: 145 **Student/Classroom Teacher Ratio**: 19.2	**Expenditures/Student**: $5,452 **Librarians**: 2.0 1,371 students/librarian **Guidance Counselors**: 5.0 548 students/counselor	**% Amer Indian**: 0.1 **% Asian**: 0.5 **% Black**: 0.1 **% Hispanic**: 0.8 **% White**: 98.5	National ***Socio-Economic Status*** indicator percentile (100=high): 85th

Knox County

VINCENNES COMMUNITY S.D.

PO BOX 1267 • VINCENNES IN 47591-1267 • (812) 882-4844

Grade Span: KG-12 **Schools**: *Regular* 7 • *Spec Ed* 0 • *Alt* 0 **Students**: 3,426 **Total Teachers**: 202 **Student/Classroom Teacher Ratio**: 16.4	**Expenditures/Student**: $5,775 **Librarians**: 2.0 1,713 students/librarian **Guidance Counselors**: 5.0 685 students/counselor	**% Amer Indian**: 0.0 **% Asian**: 0.6 **% Black**: 2.2 **% Hispanic**: 0.1 **% White**: 97.1	National ***Socio-Economic Status*** indicator percentile (100=high): 45th

Kosciusko County

[SYRACUSE] **WAWASEE COMMUNITY S.D.**

12659 N SYRACUSE WEBSTER RD • SYRACUSE IN 46567-9131 • (219) 457-3188

Grade Span: KG-12 **Schools**: *Regular* 5 • *Spec Ed* 0 • *Alt* 0 **Students**: 3,590 **Total Teachers**: 194 **Student/Classroom Teacher Ratio**: 18.5	**Expenditures/Student**: $5,833 **Librarians**: 2.0 1,795 students/librarian **Guidance Counselors**: 7.0 513 students/counselor	**% Amer Indian**: 0.0 **% Asian**: 0.3 **% Black**: 0.2 **% Hispanic**: 2.5 **% White**: 97.0	National ***Socio-Economic Status*** indicator percentile (100=high): 79th

Kosciusko County

WARSAW COMMUNITY S.D.

1 ADMINISTRATION DR POB 288 • WARSAW IN 46581-0288 • (219) 267-3238 • http://www.warsaw.k12.in.us

Grade Span: KG-12 **Schools**: *Regular* 13 • *Spec Ed* 1 • *Alt* 1 **Students**: 6,365 **Total Teachers**: 358 **Student/Classroom Teacher Ratio**: 17.6	**Expenditures/Student**: $6,141 **Librarians**: 4.0 1,591 students/librarian **Guidance Counselors**: 8.6 740 students/counselor	**% Amer Indian**: 0.1 **% Asian**: 0.8 **% Black**: 1.2 **% Hispanic**: 3.4 **% White**: 94.5	National ***Socio-Economic Status*** indicator percentile (100=high): 75th

La Porte County

[LA PORTE] **LAPORTE COMMUNITY S.D.**

1921 A ST • LA PORTE IN 46350-6697 • (219) 362-7056 • http://www.lpcsc.k12.in.us

Grade Span: PK-12 **Schools**: *Regular* 12 • *Spec Ed* 0 • *Alt* 0 **Students**: 6,550 **Total Teachers**: 355 **Student/Classroom Teacher Ratio**: 17.7	**Expenditures/Student**: $5,786 **Librarians**: 5.0 1,310 students/librarian **Guidance Counselors**: 14.0 468 students/counselor	**% Amer Indian**: 0.6 **% Asian**: 0.6 **% Black**: 1.8 **% Hispanic**: 2.7 **% White**: 94.3	National ***Socio-Economic Status*** indicator percentile (100=high): 66th

La Porte County

MICHIGAN CITY AREA S.D.

408 S CARROLL AVE • MICHIGAN CITY IN 46360-5345 • (219) 873-2000

Grade Span: PK-12 **Schools**: *Regular* 16 • *Spec Ed* 0 • *Alt* 2 **Students**: 7,447 **Total Teachers**: 481 **Student/Classroom Teacher Ratio**: 15.6	**Expenditures/Student**: $6,163 **Librarians**: 7.0 1,064 students/librarian **Guidance Counselors**: 22.0 339 students/counselor	**% Amer Indian**: 0.1 **% Asian**: 0.5 **% Black**: 27.3 **% Hispanic**: 1.3 **% White**: 70.6	National ***Socio-Economic Status*** indicator percentile (100=high): 52nd

Lake County
CROWN POINT COMMUNITY S.D.
200 E NORTH ST ● CROWN POINT IN 46307-4016 ● (219) 663-3371

Grade Span: KG-12 **Schools**: *Regular* 8 ● *Spec Ed* 0 ● *Alt* 0 **Students**: 5,508 **Total Teachers**: 256 **Student/Classroom Teacher Ratio**: 21.4	**Expenditures/Student**: $4,627 **Librarians**: 4.0 1,377 students/librarian **Guidance Counselors**: 7.0 787 students/counselor	**% Amer Indian**: 0.2 **% Asian**: 0.7 **% Black**: 0.1 **% Hispanic**: 1.9 **% White**: 97.2	National ***Socio-Economic Status*** indicator percentile (100=high): 86th

Lake County
[EAST CHICAGO] **CITY S.D. OF EAST CHICAGO**
210 E COLUMBUS DR ● EAST CHICAGO IN 46312-2799 ● (219) 391-4100

Grade Span: PK-12 **Schools**: *Regular* 10 ● *Spec Ed* 0 ● *Alt* 0 **Students**: 6,291 **Total Teachers**: 366 **Student/Classroom Teacher Ratio**: 17.6	**Expenditures/Student**: $7,639 **Librarians**: 4.0 1,573 students/librarian **Guidance Counselors**: 8.0 786 students/counselor	**% Amer Indian**: 0.1 **% Asian**: 0.2 **% Black**: 42.6 **% Hispanic**: 51.9 **% White**: 5.3	National ***Socio-Economic Status*** indicator percentile (100=high): 5th

Lake County
GARY COMMUNITY S.D.
620 E 10TH PL ● GARY IN 46402-2731 ● (219) 881-5401 ● http://www.surfnetinc.com/gary_schools

Grade Span: PK-12 **Schools**: *Regular* 39 ● *Spec Ed* 1 ● *Alt* 3 **Students**: 22,489 **Total Teachers**: 1,175 **Student/Classroom Teacher Ratio**: 20.0	**Expenditures/Student**: $6,113 **Librarians**: 42.0 535 students/librarian **Guidance Counselors**: 54.0 416 students/counselor	**% Amer Indian**: 0.0 **% Asian**: 0.1 **% Black**: 96.4 **% Hispanic**: 2.5 **% White**: 1.1	National ***Socio-Economic Status*** indicator percentile (100=high): 12th

Lake County
[GARY] **LAKE RIDGE S.D.**
6111 W RIDGE RD ● GARY IN 46408-1797 ● (219) 838-1819 ● http://www.lakeridge.k12.in.us

Grade Span: KG-12 **Schools**: *Regular* 6 ● *Spec Ed* 0 ● *Alt* 0 **Students**: 2,703 **Total Teachers**: 132 **Student/Classroom Teacher Ratio**: 20.2	**Expenditures/Student**: $6,317 **Librarians**: 2.0 1,352 students/librarian **Guidance Counselors**: 3.0 901 students/counselor	**% Amer Indian**: 0.3 **% Asian**: 0.1 **% Black**: 13.6 **% Hispanic**: 10.5 **% White**: 75.5	National ***Socio-Economic Status*** indicator percentile (100=high): 23rd

Lake County
GRIFFITH S.D.
132 N BROAD ST ● GRIFFITH IN 46319-2289 ● (219) 924-4250

Grade Span: KG-12 **Schools**: *Regular* 6 ● *Spec Ed* 0 ● *Alt* 0 **Students**: 2,894 **Total Teachers**: 143 **Student/Classroom Teacher Ratio**: 20.2	**Expenditures/Student**: $4,749 **Librarians**: 2.0 1,447 students/librarian **Guidance Counselors**: 4.0 724 students/counselor	**% Amer Indian**: 0.2 **% Asian**: 0.5 **% Black**: 4.4 **% Hispanic**: 6.1 **% White**: 88.7	National ***Socio-Economic Status*** indicator percentile (100=high): 87th

Lake County
[HAMMOND] **CITY S.D. OF HAMMOND**
41 WILLIAMS ST ● HAMMOND IN 46320-1948 ● (219) 933-2400 ● http://hammond.k12.in.us

Grade Span: PK-12 **Schools**: *Regular* 23 ● *Spec Ed* 0 ● *Alt* 1 **Students**: 13,493 **Total Teachers**: 787 **Student/Classroom Teacher Ratio**: 17.3	**Expenditures/Student**: $6,312 **Librarians**: 21.3 633 students/librarian **Guidance Counselors**: 19.0 710 students/counselor	**% Amer Indian**: 0.1 **% Asian**: 0.5 **% Black**: 18.5 **% Hispanic**: 20.6 **% White**: 60.3	National ***Socio-Economic Status*** indicator percentile (100=high): 21st

Lake County

[HIGHLAND] **TOWN S.D. OF HIGHLAND**

9145 KENNEDY AVE ● HIGHLAND IN 46322-2796 ● (219) 922-5605 ● http://stoh.highland.k12.in.us

Grade Span: KG-12 **Schools**: *Regular* 6 ● *Spec Ed* 0 ● *Alt* 0 **Students**: 3,270 **Total Teachers**: 159 **Student/Classroom Teacher Ratio**: 21.1	**Expenditures/Student**: $5,577 **Librarians**: 2.0 1,635 students/librarian **Guidance Counselors**: 7.0 467 students/counselor	**% Amer Indian**: 0.2 **% Asian**: 1.0 **% Black**: 0.5 **% Hispanic**: 5.2 **% White**: 93.2	National ***Socio-Economic Status*** indicator percentile (100=high): 89th

Lake County

[HOBART] **CITY S.D. OF HOBART**

32 E 7TH ST ● HOBART IN 46342-5197 ● (219) 942-8885

Grade Span: KG-12 **Schools**: *Regular* 6 ● *Spec Ed* 0 ● *Alt* 0 **Students**: 3,532 **Total Teachers**: 178 **Student/Classroom Teacher Ratio**: 19.1	**Expenditures/Student**: $5,715 **Librarians**: 2.0 1,766 students/librarian **Guidance Counselors**: 5.0 706 students/counselor	**% Amer Indian**: 0.1 **% Asian**: 0.5 **% Black**: 0.5 **% Hispanic**: 7.3 **% White**: 91.6	National ***Socio-Economic Status*** indicator percentile (100=high): 75th

Lake County

[LOWELL] **TRI-CREEK S.D.**

690 S BURR ST ● LOWELL IN 46356-1964 ● (219) 696-6661

Grade Span: KG-12 **Schools**: *Regular* 5 ● *Spec Ed* 0 ● *Alt* 0 **Students**: 3,183 **Total Teachers**: 143 **Student/Classroom Teacher Ratio**: 22.5	**Expenditures/Student**: $4,917 **Librarians**: 2.0 1,592 students/librarian **Guidance Counselors**: 4.0 796 students/counselor	**% Amer Indian**: 0.5 **% Asian**: 0.3 **% Black**: 0.0 **% Hispanic**: 1.4 **% White**: 97.9	National ***Socio-Economic Status*** indicator percentile (100=high): 83rd

Lake County

MERRILLVILLE COMMUNITY S.D.

6701 DELAWARE ST ● MERRILLVILLE IN 46410-3586 ● (219) 736-4830

Grade Span: KG-12 **Schools**: *Regular* 8 ● *Spec Ed* 0 ● *Alt* 0 **Students**: 5,998 **Total Teachers**: 295 **Student/Classroom Teacher Ratio**: 19.7	**Expenditures/Student**: $5,873 **Librarians**: 4.0 1,500 students/librarian **Guidance Counselors**: 7.0 857 students/counselor	**% Amer Indian**: 0.4 **% Asian**: 1.9 **% Black**: 13.3 **% Hispanic**: 9.6 **% White**: 74.8	National ***Socio-Economic Status*** indicator percentile (100=high): 83rd

Lake County

[MUNSTER] **TOWN S.D. OF MUNSTER**

8616 COLUMBIA AVE ● MUNSTER IN 46321-2597 ● (219) 836-9111 ● http://www.munster.k12.in.us

Grade Span: KG-12 **Schools**: *Regular* 5 ● *Spec Ed* 0 ● *Alt* 0 **Students**: 3,214 **Total Teachers**: 199 **Student/Classroom Teacher Ratio**: 19.1	**Expenditures/Student**: $5,652 **Librarians**: 3.0 1,071 students/librarian **Guidance Counselors**: 6.0 536 students/counselor	**% Amer Indian**: 0.1 **% Asian**: 5.8 **% Black**: 0.6 **% Hispanic**: 3.5 **% White**: 90.0	National ***Socio-Economic Status*** indicator percentile (100=high): 98th

Lake County

[ST. JOHN] **LAKE CENTRAL S.D.**

8260 WICKER AVE ● ST. JOHN IN 46373-9711 ● (219) 365-8507

Grade Span: PK-12 **Schools**: *Regular* 9 ● *Spec Ed* 1 ● *Alt* 0 **Students**: 7,697 **Total Teachers**: 388 **Student/Classroom Teacher Ratio**: 20.1	**Expenditures/Student**: $6,381 **Librarians**: 3.5 2,199 students/librarian **Guidance Counselors**: 9.0 855 students/counselor	**% Amer Indian**: 0.3 **% Asian**: 1.3 **% Black**: 0.8 **% Hispanic**: 4.7 **% White**: 92.9	National ***Socio-Economic Status*** indicator percentile (100=high): 94th

Lawrence County

[BEDFORD] **NORTH LAWRENCE COMMUNITY S.D.**

PO BOX 729 ● BEDFORD IN 47421-0729 ● (812) 279-3521

Grade Span: PK-12 **Schools**: *Regular* 14 ● *Spec Ed* 1 ● *Alt* 1 **Students**: 5,530 **Total Teachers**: 318 **Student/Classroom Teacher Ratio**: 18.6	**Expenditures/Student**: $6,100 **Librarians**: 3.0 1,843 students/librarian **Guidance Counselors**: 6.5 851 students/counselor	**% Amer Indian**: 0.1 **% Asian**: 0.3 **% Black**: 0.5 **% Hispanic**: 1.0 **% White**: 98.0	National ***Socio-Economic Status*** indicator percentile (100=high): 51st

Madison County

ANDERSON COMMUNITY S.D.

30 W 11TH ST ● ANDERSON IN 46016-1479 ● (765) 641-2000 ● http://www.acsc.net

Grade Span: PK-12 **Schools**: *Regular* 23 ● *Spec Ed* 0 ● *Alt* 1 **Students**: 11,169 **Total Teachers**: 739 **Student/Classroom Teacher Ratio**: 15.4	**Expenditures/Student**: $6,107 **Librarians**: 15.4 725 students/librarian **Guidance Counselors**: 14.0 798 students/counselor	**% Amer Indian**: 0.1 **% Asian**: 0.4 **% Black**: 18.4 **% Hispanic**: 0.7 **% White**: 80.4	National ***Socio-Economic Status*** indicator percentile (100=high): 31st

Madison County

[PENDLETON] **SOUTH MADISON COMMUNITY S.D.**

201 S EAST ST ● PENDLETON IN 46064 ● (765) 778-2152

Grade Span: KG-12 **Schools**: *Regular* 4 ● *Spec Ed* 0 ● *Alt* 0 **Students**: 3,399 **Total Teachers**: 160 **Student/Classroom Teacher Ratio**: 21.7	**Expenditures/Student**: $4,739 **Librarians**: 3.0 1,133 students/librarian **Guidance Counselors**: 3.0 1,133 students/counselor	**% Amer Indian**: 0.0 **% Asian**: 0.4 **% Black**: 0.1 **% Hispanic**: 0.3 **% White**: 99.2	National ***Socio-Economic Status*** indicator percentile (100=high): 87th

Marion County

[INDIANAPOLIS] **FRANKLIN TOWNSHIP COMMUNITY S.D.**

6141 S FRANKLIN RD ● INDIANAPOLIS IN 46259-1399 ● (317) 862-2411

Grade Span: PK-12 **Schools**: *Regular* 7 ● *Spec Ed* 0 ● *Alt* 0 **Students**: 4,896 **Total Teachers**: 237 **Student/Classroom Teacher Ratio**: 20.6	**Expenditures/Student**: $5,385 **Librarians**: 3.5 1,399 students/librarian **Guidance Counselors**: 12.0 408 students/counselor	**% Amer Indian**: 0.2 **% Asian**: 0.7 **% Black**: 7.6 **% Hispanic**: 0.3 **% White**: 91.2	National ***Socio-Economic Status*** indicator percentile (100=high): 84th

Marion County

INDIANAPOLIS PUBLIC S.D.

120 E WALNUT ST ● INDIANAPOLIS IN 46204-1389 ● (317) 226-4411 ● http://www.ips.k12.in.us

Grade Span: PK-12 **Schools**: *Regular* 84 ● *Spec Ed* 6 ● *Alt* 5 **Students**: 44,896 **Total Teachers**: 2,796 **Student/Classroom Teacher Ratio**: 18.9	**Expenditures/Student**: $6,970 **Librarians**: 38.8 1,157 students/librarian **Guidance Counselors**: 83.6 537 students/counselor	**% Amer Indian**: 0.1 **% Asian**: 0.7 **% Black**: 57.1 **% Hispanic**: 1.4 **% White**: 40.6	National ***Socio-Economic Status*** indicator percentile (100=high): 7th

Marion County

[INDIANAPOLIS] **METROPOLITAN S.D. OF DECATUR TOWNSHIP**

7523 MOORESVILLE RD ● INDIANAPOLIS IN 46221 ● (317) 856-5265

Grade Span: PK-12 **Schools**: *Regular* 6 ● *Spec Ed* 0 ● *Alt* 0 **Students**: 5,014 **Total Teachers**: 255 **Student/Classroom Teacher Ratio**: 21.1	**Expenditures/Student**: $5,734 **Librarians**: 4.0 1,254 students/librarian **Guidance Counselors**: 6.0 836 students/counselor	**% Amer Indian**: 0.2 **% Asian**: 0.4 **% Black**: 11.8 **% Hispanic**: 0.6 **% White**: 87.0	National ***Socio-Economic Status*** indicator percentile (100=high): 44th

Marion County

[INDIANAPOLIS] METROPOLITAN S.D. OF LAWRENCE TOWNSHIP

7601 E 56TH ST ● INDIANAPOLIS IN 46226-1306 ● (317) 546-4921

Grade Span: PK-12 **Schools**: *Regular* 15 ● *Spec Ed* 0 ● *Alt* 0 **Students**: 13,685 **Total Teachers**: 790 **Student/Classroom Teacher Ratio**: 19.2	**Expenditures/Student**: $6,564 **Librarians**: 15.4 889 students/librarian **Guidance Counselors**: 21.5 637 students/counselor	**% Amer Indian**: 0.1 **% Asian**: 2.1 **% Black**: 22.9 **% Hispanic**: 1.6 **% White**: 73.2	National ***Socio-Economic Status*** indicator percentile (100=high): 77th

Marion County

[INDIANAPOLIS] METROPOLITAN S.D. OF PERRY TOWNSHIP

1130 E EPLER AVE ● INDIANAPOLIS IN 46227-4290 ● (317) 780-4203 ● http://www.msdpt.k12.in.us/etspages/MSDPTHomepage/index.html

Grade Span: PK-12 **Schools**: *Regular* 13 ● *Spec Ed* 1 ● *Alt* 1 **Students**: 11,802 **Total Teachers**: 648 **Student/Classroom Teacher Ratio**: 22.3	**Expenditures/Student**: $6,463 **Librarians**: 14.5 814 students/librarian **Guidance Counselors**: 15.0 787 students/counselor	**% Amer Indian**: 0.2 **% Asian**: 1.0 **% Black**: 10.4 **% Hispanic**: 0.8 **% White**: 87.7	National ***Socio-Economic Status*** indicator percentile (100=high): 59th

Marion County

[INDIANAPOLIS] METROPOLITAN S.D. OF PIKE TOWNSHIP

6901 ZIONSVILLE RD ● INDIANAPOLIS IN 46268-2467 ● (317) 293-0393

Grade Span: PK-12 **Schools**: *Regular* 11 ● *Spec Ed* 0 ● *Alt* 0 **Students**: 6,980 **Total Teachers**: 395 **Student/Classroom Teacher Ratio**: 18.1	**Expenditures/Student**: $6,817 **Librarians**: 12.0 582 students/librarian **Guidance Counselors**: 18.0 388 students/counselor	**% Amer Indian**: 0.5 **% Asian**: 4.3 **% Black**: 37.2 **% Hispanic**: 1.1 **% White**: 56.8	National ***Socio-Economic Status*** indicator percentile (100=high): 74th

Marion County

[INDIANAPOLIS] METROPOLITAN S.D. OF WARREN TOWNSHIP

9301 E 18TH ST ● INDIANAPOLIS IN 46229-2032 ● (317) 898-5935 ● http://ideanet.doe.state.in.us/~msdwarr/district/index.html

Grade Span: PK-12 **Schools**: *Regular* 14 ● *Spec Ed* 0 ● *Alt* 3 **Students**: 9,777 **Total Teachers**: 618 **Student/Classroom Teacher Ratio**: 16.8	**Expenditures/Student**: $7,114 **Librarians**: 6.0 1,630 students/librarian **Guidance Counselors**: 21.0 466 students/counselor	**% Amer Indian**: 0.2 **% Asian**: 1.4 **% Black**: 25.2 **% Hispanic**: 0.8 **% White**: 72.6	National ***Socio-Economic Status*** indicator percentile (100=high): 56th

Marion County

[INDIANAPOLIS] METROPOLITAN S.D. OF WASHINGTON TOWNSHIP

3801 E 79TH ST ● INDIANAPOLIS IN 46240-3407 ● (317) 845-9400 ● http://www.msdwt.k12.in.us

Grade Span: KG-12 **Schools**: *Regular* 12 ● *Spec Ed* 0 ● *Alt* 2 **Students**: 10,190 **Total Teachers**: 562 **Student/Classroom Teacher Ratio**: 19.4	**Expenditures/Student**: $6,481 **Librarians**: 14.0 728 students/librarian **Guidance Counselors**: 17.7 576 students/counselor	**% Amer Indian**: 0.1 **% Asian**: 2.0 **% Black**: 32.0 **% Hispanic**: 1.1 **% White**: 64.8	National ***Socio-Economic Status*** indicator percentile (100=high): 71st

Marion County

[INDIANAPOLIS] METROPOLITAN S.D. OF WAYNE TOWNSHIP

1220 S HIGH SCH RD ● INDIANAPOLIS IN 46241-3199 ● (317) 243-8251

Grade Span: PK-12 **Schools**: *Regular* 14 ● *Spec Ed* 1 ● *Alt* 0 **Students**: 12,694 **Total Teachers**: 718 **Student/Classroom Teacher Ratio**: 18.8	**Expenditures/Student**: $5,962 **Librarians**: 14.0 907 students/librarian **Guidance Counselors**: 23.5 540 students/counselor	**% Amer Indian**: 0.3 **% Asian**: 1.1 **% Black**: 20.8 **% Hispanic**: 1.2 **% White**: 76.6	National ***Socio-Economic Status*** indicator percentile (100=high): 38th

Marshall County

PLYMOUTH COMMUNITY S.D.

701 E BERKLEY ST ● PLYMOUTH IN 46563-1897 ● (219) 936-3115

Grade Span: PK-12 **Schools**: *Regular* 6 ● *Spec Ed* 0 ● *Alt* 0 **Students**: 3,308 **Total Teachers**: 158 **Student/Classroom Teacher Ratio**: 20.6	**Expenditures/Student**: $5,669 **Librarians**: 3.0 1,103 students/librarian **Guidance Counselors**: 5.0 662 students/counselor	**% Amer Indian**: 0.0 **% Asian**: 0.8 **% Black**: 0.1 **% Hispanic**: 6.5 **% White**: 92.7	National ***Socio-Economic Status*** indicator percentile (100=high): 59th

Miami County

PERU COMMUNITY S.D.

2 N BROADWAY ● PERU IN 46970-2272 ● (765) 473-3081 ● http://www.peru.k12.in.us

Grade Span: PK-12 **Schools**: *Regular* 7 ● *Spec Ed* 0 ● *Alt* 0 **Students**: 2,818 **Total Teachers**: 154 **Student/Classroom Teacher Ratio**: 18.5	**Expenditures/Student**: $5,494 **Librarians**: 3.0 939 students/librarian **Guidance Counselors**: 3.0 939 students/counselor	**% Amer Indian**: 3.2 **% Asian**: 0.6 **% Black**: 4.1 **% Hispanic**: 1.7 **% White**: 90.5	National ***Socio-Economic Status*** indicator percentile (100=high): 42nd

Monroe County

[BLOOMINGTON] MONROE COUNTY COMMUNITY S.D.

315 NORTH DR ● BLOOMINGTON IN 47401-6595 ● (812) 330-7700 ● http://www.mccsc.edu

Grade Span: PK-12 **Schools**: *Regular* 19 ● *Spec Ed* 0 ● *Alt* 1 **Students**: 10,604 **Total Teachers**: 585 **Student/Classroom Teacher Ratio**: 18.0	**Expenditures/Student**: $5,709 **Librarians**: 14.2 747 students/librarian **Guidance Counselors**: 15.4 689 students/counselor	**% Amer Indian**: 0.4 **% Asian**: 3.1 **% Black**: 4.3 **% Hispanic**: 1.5 **% White**: 90.7	National ***Socio-Economic Status*** indicator percentile (100=high): 61st

Monroe County

[ELLETTSVILLE] RICHLAND-BEAN BLOSSOM COMMUNITY S.D.

EDGEWOOD DR ● ELLETTSVILLE IN 47429-0374 ● (812) 876-7100 ● http://www.rbbcsc.k12.in.us

Grade Span: PK-12 **Schools**: *Regular* 5 ● *Spec Ed* 1 ● *Alt* 0 **Students**: 2,836 **Total Teachers**: 157 **Student/Classroom Teacher Ratio**: 21.3	**Expenditures/Student**: $5,363 **Librarians**: 2.0 1,418 students/librarian **Guidance Counselors**: 4.0 709 students/counselor	**% Amer Indian**: 0.1 **% Asian**: 0.2 **% Black**: 1.1 **% Hispanic**: 0.5 **% White**: 98.2	National ***Socio-Economic Status*** indicator percentile (100=high): 75th

Morgan County

[MARTINSVILLE] METROPOLITAN S.D. OF MARTINSVILLE

PO BOX 1416 ● MARTINSVILLE IN 46151-1416 ● (765) 342-6641 ● http://www.scican.net/mville

Grade Span: PK-12 **Schools**: *Regular* 11 ● *Spec Ed* 0 ● *Alt* 0 **Students**: 5,398 **Total Teachers**: 271 **Student/Classroom Teacher Ratio**: 21.0	**Expenditures/Student**: $4,962 **Librarians**: 3.0 1,799 students/librarian **Guidance Counselors**: 8.0 675 students/counselor	**% Amer Indian**: 0.0 **% Asian**: 0.1 **% Black**: 0.0 **% Hispanic**: 0.3 **% White**: 99.6	National ***Socio-Economic Status*** indicator percentile (100=high): 72nd

Morgan County

MOORESVILLE CONSOLIDATED S.D.

320 N INDIANA ST ● MOORESVILLE IN 46158-1509 ● (317) 831-0950 ● http://mcsc.k12.in.us

Grade Span: PK-12 **Schools**: *Regular* 7 ● *Spec Ed* 0 ● *Alt* 0 **Students**: 3,903 **Total Teachers**: 215 **Student/Classroom Teacher Ratio**: 17.8	**Expenditures/Student**: $4,592 **Librarians**: 3.0 1,301 students/librarian **Guidance Counselors**: 8.0 488 students/counselor	**% Amer Indian**: 0.0 **% Asian**: 0.0 **% Black**: 0.1 **% Hispanic**: 14.3 **% White**: 85.6	National ***Socio-Economic Status*** indicator percentile (100=high): 74th

Noble County

[KENDALLVILLE] **EAST NOBLE S.D.**

702 E DOWLING ST ● KENDALLVILLE IN 46755-1298 ● (219) 347-2502 ● http://www.enoble.k12.in.us

Grade Span: KG-12 **Schools**: *Regular* 8 ● *Spec Ed* 0 ● *Alt* 0 **Students**: 3,983 **Total Teachers**: 205 **Student/Classroom Teacher Ratio**: 19.8	**Expenditures/Student**: $4,786 **Librarians**: 4.0 996 students/librarian **Guidance Counselors**: 9.0 443 students/counselor	**% Amer Indian**: 0.0 **% Asian**: 0.4 **% Black**: 0.4 **% Hispanic**: 0.8 **% White**: 98.4	National ***Socio-Economic Status*** indicator percentile (100=high): 76th

Owen County

SPENCER-OWEN COMMUNITY S.D.

205 E HILLSIDE ● SPENCER IN 47460-1099 ● (812) 829-2233

Grade Span: PK-12 **Schools**: *Regular* 5 ● *Spec Ed* 0 ● *Alt* 0 **Students**: 3,132 **Total Teachers**: 175 **Student/Classroom Teacher Ratio**: 18.0	**Expenditures/Student**: $5,295 **Librarians**: 3.8 824 students/librarian **Guidance Counselors**: 6.0 522 students/counselor	**% Amer Indian**: 0.0 **% Asian**: 0.1 **% Black**: 0.0 **% Hispanic**: 0.2 **% White**: 99.7	National ***Socio-Economic Status*** indicator percentile (100=high): 56th

Porter County

[CHESTERTON] **DUNELAND S.D.**

700 W PORTER AVE ● CHESTERTON IN 46304-2205 ● (219) 926-1104 ● http://www.duneland.k12.in.us

Grade Span: KG-12 **Schools**: *Regular* 8 ● *Spec Ed* 0 ● *Alt* 0 **Students**: 5,320 **Total Teachers**: 250 **Student/Classroom Teacher Ratio**: 21.1	**Expenditures/Student**: $6,102 **Librarians**: 10.0 532 students/librarian **Guidance Counselors**: 10.5 507 students/counselor	**% Amer Indian**: 0.6 **% Asian**: 0.5 **% Black**: 0.3 **% Hispanic**: 2.3 **% White**: 96.3	National ***Socio-Economic Status*** indicator percentile (100=high): 87th

Porter County

PORTAGE TOWNSHIP S.D.

6240 US HWY 6 ● PORTAGE IN 46368-5057 ● (219) 762-6511 ● http://birch.palni.edu/~duhamell/pts/pts.htm

Grade Span: PK-12 **Schools**: *Regular* 11 ● *Spec Ed* 0 ● *Alt* 0 **Students**: 8,199 **Total Teachers**: 381 **Student/Classroom Teacher Ratio**: 21.2	**Expenditures/Student**: $5,481 **Librarians**: 5.0 1,640 students/librarian **Guidance Counselors**: 9.0 911 students/counselor	**% Amer Indian**: 0.4 **% Asian**: 0.6 **% Black**: 0.4 **% Hispanic**: 7.3 **% White**: 91.3	National ***Socio-Economic Status*** indicator percentile (100=high): 67th

Porter County

VALPARAISO COMMUNITY S.D.

405 N CAMPBELL ST ● VALPARAISO IN 46383-4699 ● (219) 531-3000 ● http://www.valpo.k12.in.us

Grade Span: KG-12 **Schools**: *Regular* 11 ● *Spec Ed* 0 ● *Alt* 1 **Students**: 5,926 **Total Teachers**: 313 **Student/Classroom Teacher Ratio**: 19.7	**Expenditures/Student**: $6,693 **Librarians**: 4.0 1,482 students/librarian **Guidance Counselors**: 10.0 593 students/counselor	**% Amer Indian**: 0.1 **% Asian**: 1.8 **% Black**: 0.9 **% Hispanic**: 1.9 **% White**: 95.3	National ***Socio-Economic Status*** indicator percentile (100=high): 82nd

Posey County

[MOUNT VERNON] **METROPOLITAN S.D. OF MOUNT VERNON**

1000 W 4TH ST ● MOUNT VERNON IN 47620-1696 ● (812) 838-4471

Grade Span: PK-12 **Schools**: *Regular* 6 ● *Spec Ed* 0 ● *Alt* 0 **Students**: 2,884 **Total Teachers**: 177 **Student/Classroom Teacher Ratio**: 16.7	**Expenditures/Student**: $8,314 **Librarians**: 4.0 721 students/librarian **Guidance Counselors**: 4.5 641 students/counselor	**% Amer Indian**: 0.1 **% Asian**: 0.3 **% Black**: 2.0 **% Hispanic**: 0.2 **% White**: 97.5	National ***Socio-Economic Status*** indicator percentile (100=high): 64th

Rush County

[RUSHVILLE] **RUSH COUNTY S.D.**

330 W 8TH ST ● RUSHVILLE IN 46173 ● (765) 932-4186

Grade Span: KG-12	**Expenditures/Student**: $5,375	**% Amer Indian**: 0.0	
Schools: *Regular* 6 ● *Spec Ed* 0 ● *Alt* 0	**Librarians**: 5.0	**% Asian**: 0.4	National ***Socio-Economic***
Students: 2,881	576 students/librarian	**% Black**: 0.5	***Status*** indicator percentile
Total Teachers: 161	**Guidance Counselors**: 4.0	**% Hispanic**: 0.1	(100=high): 67th
Student/Classroom Teacher Ratio: 17.4	720 students/counselor	**% White**: 99.0	

St. Joseph County

[MISHAWAKA] **CITY S.D. OF MISHAWAKA**

1402 S MAIN ST ● MISHAWAKA IN 46544-5297 ● (219) 258-3000

Grade Span: PK-12	**Expenditures/Student**: $5,994	**% Amer Indian**: 0.4	
Schools: *Regular* 10 ● *Spec Ed* 2 ● *Alt* 0	**Librarians**: 2.0	**% Asian**: 0.5	National ***Socio-Economic***
Students: 5,390	2,695 students/librarian	**% Black**: 1.7	***Status*** indicator percentile
Total Teachers: 332	**Guidance Counselors**: 8.0	**% Hispanic**: 1.3	(100=high): 45th
Student/Classroom Teacher Ratio: 18.7	674 students/counselor	**% White**: 96.1	

St. Joseph County

[MISHAWAKA] **PENN-HARRIS-MADISON S.D.**

55900 BITTERSWEET RD ● MISHAWAKA IN 46545 ● (219) 259-7941

Grade Span: KG-12	**Expenditures/Student**: $5,529	**% Amer Indian**: 0.2	
Schools: *Regular* 12 ● *Spec Ed* 0 ● *Alt* 0	**Librarians**: 0.0	**% Asian**: 1.5	National ***Socio-Economic***
Students: 9,221	*** students/librarian	**% Black**: 1.6	***Status*** indicator percentile
Total Teachers: 459	**Guidance Counselors**: 16.0	**% Hispanic**: 0.8	(100=high): 85th
Student/Classroom Teacher Ratio: 20.1	576 students/counselor	**% White**: 95.9	

St. Joseph County

SOUTH BEND COMMUNITY S.D.

635 S MAIN ST ● SOUTH BEND IN 46601-2295 ● (219) 282-4000 ● http://www.sbcsc.k12.in.us

Grade Span: PK-12	**Expenditures/Student**: $5,856	**% Amer Indian**: 0.6	
Schools: *Regular* 34 ● *Spec Ed* 1 ● *Alt* 1	**Librarians**: 22.0	**% Asian**: 1.5	National ***Socio-Economic***
Students: 21,136	961 students/librarian	**% Black**: 32.5	***Status*** indicator percentile
Total Teachers: 1,245	**Guidance Counselors**: 36.0	**% Hispanic**: 6.1	(100=high): 24th
Student/Classroom Teacher Ratio: 17.4	587 students/counselor	**% White**: 59.4	

Scott County

[SCOTTSBURG] **SCOTT COUNTY S.D. 2**

375 E MCCLAIN AVE ● SCOTTSBURG IN 47170-1798 ● (812) 752-8921

Grade Span: KG-12	**Expenditures/Student**: $5,272	**% Amer Indian**: 0.1	
Schools: *Regular* 6 ● *Spec Ed* 0 ● *Alt* 0	**Librarians**: 3.0	**% Asian**: 0.4	National ***Socio-Economic***
Students: 2,808	936 students/librarian	**% Black**: 0.0	***Status*** indicator percentile
Total Teachers: 135	**Guidance Counselors**: 7.0	**% Hispanic**: 0.2	(100=high): 54th
Student/Classroom Teacher Ratio: 20.9	401 students/counselor	**% White**: 99.3	

Shelby County

SHELBYVILLE CENTRAL S.D.

54 W BROADWAY ● SHELBYVILLE IN 46176-1295 ● (765) 392-2505

Grade Span: KG-12	**Expenditures/Student**: $4,977	**% Amer Indian**: 0.0	
Schools: *Regular* 6 ● *Spec Ed* 0 ● *Alt* 0	**Librarians**: 1.0	**% Asian**: 0.9	National ***Socio-Economic***
Students: 3,625	3,625 students/librarian	**% Black**: 2.1	***Status*** indicator percentile
Total Teachers: 178	**Guidance Counselors**: 5.0	**% Hispanic**: 0.5	(100=high): 63rd
Student/Classroom Teacher Ratio: 20.0	725 students/counselor	**% White**: 96.4	

Steuben County

[ANGOLA] METROPOLITAN S.D. OF STEUBEN COUNTY

400 S MARTHA ST ● ANGOLA IN 46703 ● (219) 665-2854 ● http://www.msdsteuben.k12.in.us

Grade Span: KG-12 **Schools**: *Regular* 5 ● *Spec Ed* 0 ● *Alt* 0 **Students**: 2,836 **Total Teachers**: 154 **Student/Classroom Teacher Ratio**: 18.7	**Expenditures/Student**: $5,706 **Librarians**: 3.0 945 students/librarian **Guidance Counselors**: 6.0 473 students/counselor	**% Amer Indian**: 0.4 **% Asian**: 0.5 **% Black**: 0.3 **% Hispanic**: 1.0 **% White**: 98.0	National ***Socio-Economic Status*** indicator percentile (100=high): 71st

Tippecanoe County

LAFAYETTE S.D.

2300 CASON ST ● LAFAYETTE IN 47904-2692 ● (765) 449-3200 ● http://www.lsc.k12.in.us

Grade Span: PK-12 **Schools**: *Regular* 14 ● *Spec Ed* 1 ● *Alt* 0 **Students**: 7,555 **Total Teachers**: 508 **Student/Classroom Teacher Ratio**: 17.3	**Expenditures/Student**: $6,901 **Librarians**: 14.0 540 students/librarian **Guidance Counselors**: 20.5 369 students/counselor	**% Amer Indian**: 0.2 **% Asian**: 0.7 **% Black**: 3.7 **% Hispanic**: 4.2 **% White**: 91.2	National ***Socio-Economic Status*** indicator percentile (100=high): 55th

Tippecanoe County

[LAFAYETTE] TIPPECANOE S.D.

21 ELSTON RD ● LAFAYETTE IN 47905-2899 ● (765) 474-2481 ● http://wvec.k12.in.us/TSC

Grade Span: KG-12 **Schools**: *Regular* 14 ● *Spec Ed* 0 ● *Alt* 0 **Students**: 8,522 **Total Teachers**: 423 **Student/Classroom Teacher Ratio**: 20.6	**Expenditures/Student**: $5,059 **Librarians**: 14.3 596 students/librarian **Guidance Counselors**: 18.0 473 students/counselor	**% Amer Indian**: 0.7 **% Asian**: 1.6 **% Black**: 1.0 **% Hispanic**: 1.6 **% White**: 95.0	National ***Socio-Economic Status*** indicator percentile (100=high): 77th

Vanderburgh County

EVANSVILLE-VANDERBURGH S.D.

1 SE 9TH ST ● EVANSVILLE IN 47708-1821 ● (812) 435-8477 ● http://www.evsc.k12.in.us

Grade Span: PK-12 **Schools**: *Regular* 35 ● *Spec Ed* 1 ● *Alt* 4 **Students**: 23,713 **Total Teachers**: 1,418 **Student/Classroom Teacher Ratio**: 17.2	**Expenditures/Student**: $5,696 **Librarians**: 29.0 818 students/librarian **Guidance Counselors**: 44.8 529 students/counselor	**% Amer Indian**: 0.2 **% Asian**: 0.6 **% Black**: 14.0 **% Hispanic**: 0.5 **% White**: 84.8	National ***Socio-Economic Status*** indicator percentile (100=high): 39th

Vigo County

[TERRE HAUTE] VIGO COUNTY S.D.

961 LAFAYETTE AVE PO BOX 4331 ● TERRE HAUTE IN 47808-4331 ● (812) 462-4216 ● http://www.vigoco.k12.in.us

Grade Span: PK-12 **Schools**: *Regular* 29 ● *Spec Ed* 0 ● *Alt* 1 **Students**: 16,971 **Total Teachers**: 968 **Student/Classroom Teacher Ratio**: 17.2	**Expenditures/Student**: $5,004 **Librarians**: 29.0 585 students/librarian **Guidance Counselors**: 33.5 507 students/counselor	**% Amer Indian**: 0.1 **% Asian**: 1.2 **% Black**: 6.6 **% Hispanic**: 0.6 **% White**: 91.5	National ***Socio-Economic Status*** indicator percentile (100=high): 44th

Wabash County

[WABASH] METROPOLITAN S.D. OF WABASH COUNTY

204 N 300 W ● WABASH IN 46992-8689 ● (219) 563-7438 ● http://www.r8esc.k12.in.us/wabash/msdwc/msd/msdhome.html

Grade Span: KG-12 **Schools**: *Regular* 6 ● *Spec Ed* 1 ● *Alt* 1 **Students**: 2,799 **Total Teachers**: 181 **Student/Classroom Teacher Ratio**: 19.8	**Expenditures/Student**: $6,200 **Librarians**: 3.0 933 students/librarian **Guidance Counselors**: 5.3 528 students/counselor	**% Amer Indian**: 0.0 **% Asian**: 0.4 **% Black**: 0.2 **% Hispanic**: 0.7 **% White**: 98.7	National ***Socio-Economic Status*** indicator percentile (100=high): 80th

Warrick County

[BOONVILLE] WARRICK COUNTY S.D.

PO BOX 809 ● BOONVILLE IN 47601-0809 ● (812) 897-0400

Grade Span: KG-12 **Schools**: *Regular* 15 ● *Spec Ed* 0 ● *Alt* 1 **Students**: 8,971 **Total Teachers**: 462 **Student/Classroom Teacher Ratio**: 19.2	**Expenditures/Student**: $5,348 **Librarians**: 6.0 1,495 students/librarian **Guidance Counselors**: 10.5 854 students/counselor	**% Amer Indian**: 0.0 **% Asian**: 0.5 **% Black**: 0.7 **% Hispanic**: 0.1 **% White**: 98.6	National ***Socio-Economic Status*** indicator percentile (100=high): 74th

Wayne County

RICHMOND COMMUNITY S.D.

300 HUB ETCHISON PKY ● RICHMOND IN 47374-5399 ● (765) 973-3300 ● http://www.rcs.k12.in.us

Grade Span: PK-12 **Schools**: *Regular* 15 ● *Spec Ed* 2 ● *Alt* 2 **Students**: 6,756 **Total Teachers**: 340 **Student/Classroom Teacher Ratio**: 21.5	**Expenditures/Student**: $5,732 **Librarians**: 15.5 436 students/librarian **Guidance Counselors**: 12.0 563 students/counselor	**% Amer Indian**: 0.2 **% Asian**: 0.8 **% Black**: 12.4 **% Hispanic**: 0.7 **% White**: 86.0	National ***Socio-Economic Status*** indicator percentile (100=high): 30th

Wells County

[OSSIAN] NORTHERN WELLS COMMUNITY S.D.

PO BOX 386 ● OSSIAN IN 46777-0386 ● (219) 622-4125

Grade Span: PK-12 **Schools**: *Regular* 4 ● *Spec Ed* 0 ● *Alt* 0 **Students**: 2,659 **Total Teachers**: 142 **Student/Classroom Teacher Ratio**: 18.9	**Expenditures/Student**: $5,090 **Librarians**: 1.0 2,659 students/librarian **Guidance Counselors**: 6.5 409 students/counselor	**% Amer Indian**: 0.0 **% Asian**: 0.5 **% Black**: 0.0 **% Hispanic**: 0.8 **% White**: 98.8	National ***Socio-Economic Status*** indicator percentile (100=high): 85th

White County

[MONTICELLO] TWIN LAKES S.D.

565 S MAIN ST ● MONTICELLO IN 47960-2446 ● (219) 583-7211 ● http://www.twinlakes.k12.in.us

Grade Span: PK-12 **Schools**: *Regular* 6 ● *Spec Ed* 0 ● *Alt* 0 **Students**: 2,675 **Total Teachers**: 141 **Student/Classroom Teacher Ratio**: 19.2	**Expenditures/Student**: $5,753 **Librarians**: 2.0 1,338 students/librarian **Guidance Counselors**: 8.0 334 students/counselor	**% Amer Indian**: 0.0 **% Asian**: 0.2 **% Black**: 0.3 **% Hispanic**: 2.0 **% White**: 97.4	National ***Socio-Economic Status*** indicator percentile (100=high): 74th

Whitley County

[COLUMBIA CITY] WHITLEY COUNTY CONSOLIDATED S.D.

400 N WHITLEY ST ● COLUMBIA CITY IN 46725-1729 ● (219) 244-5772

Grade Span: PK-12 **Schools**: *Regular* 7 ● *Spec Ed* 0 ● *Alt* 0 **Students**: 3,678 **Total Teachers**: 193 **Student/Classroom Teacher Ratio**: 18.7	**Expenditures/Student**: $5,534 **Librarians**: 4.5 817 students/librarian **Guidance Counselors**: 7.5 490 students/counselor	**% Amer Indian**: 0.2 **% Asian**: 0.2 **% Black**: 0.3 **% Hispanic**: 0.8 **% White**: 98.5	National ***Socio-Economic Status*** indicator percentile (100=high): 85th

Black Hawk County

CEDAR FALLS COMMUNITY S.D.

1002 WEST FIRST STREET ● CEDAR FALLS IA 50613 ● (319) 277-8800 ● http://www.cedar-falls.k12.ia.us

Grade Span: PK-12 **Schools**: *Regular* 10 ● *Spec Ed* 0 ● *Alt* 0 **Students**: 4,960 **Total Teachers**: 255 **Student/Classroom Teacher Ratio**: 17.4	**Expenditures/Student**: $5,086 **Librarians**: 9.0 551 students/librarian **Guidance Counselors**: 14.5 342 students/counselor	**% Amer Indian**: 0.5 **% Asian**: 2.7 **% Black**: 2.4 **% Hispanic**: 0.8 **% White**: 93.7	National ***Socio-Economic Status*** indicator percentile (100=high): 72nd

Black Hawk County

WATERLOO COMMUNITY S.D.

1516 WASHINGTON STREET ● WATERLOO IA 50702 ● (319) 291-4800 ● http://home.forbin.com/~sailors

Grade Span: PK-12 **Schools**: *Regular* 21 ● *Spec Ed* 0 ● *Alt* 2 **Students**: 10,878 **Total Teachers**: 582 **Student/Classroom Teacher Ratio**: 17.6	**Expenditures/Student**: $5,845 **Librarians**: 23.0 473 students/librarian **Guidance Counselors**: 27.5 396 students/counselor	**% Amer Indian**: 0.3 **% Asian**: 1.2 **% Black**: 25.6 **% Hispanic**: 1.5 **% White**: 71.4	National ***Socio-Economic Status*** indicator percentile (100=high): 26th

Cerro Gordo County

MASON CITY COMMUNITY S.D.

1515 S PENNSYLVANIA AVE ● MASON CITY IA 50401 ● (515) 421-4400

Grade Span: PK-12 **Schools**: *Regular* 9 ● *Spec Ed* 0 ● *Alt* 1 **Students**: 4,784 **Total Teachers**: 282 **Student/Classroom Teacher Ratio**: 15.9	**Expenditures/Student**: $5,281 **Librarians**: 7.0 683 students/librarian **Guidance Counselors**: 11.0 435 students/counselor	**% Amer Indian**: 0.0 **% Asian**: 1.3 **% Black**: 2.2 **% Hispanic**: 4.6 **% White**: 92.0	National ***Socio-Economic Status*** indicator percentile (100=high): 56th

Clinton County

CLINTON COMMUNITY S.D.

600 SOUTH 4TH STREET ● CLINTON IA 52732 ● (319) 243-9600 ● http://ccs-dist-serv.clinton.k12.ia.us/ccs/chskq.html

Grade Span: PK-12 **Schools**: *Regular* 10 ● *Spec Ed* 1 ● *Alt* 2 **Students**: 4,987 **Total Teachers**: 302 **Student/Classroom Teacher Ratio**: 18.8	**Expenditures/Student**: $5,159 **Librarians**: 8.0 623 students/librarian **Guidance Counselors**: 13.0 384 students/counselor	**% Amer Indian**: 0.3 **% Asian**: 1.2 **% Black**: 5.3 **% Hispanic**: 1.3 **% White**: 91.9	National ***Socio-Economic Status*** indicator percentile (100=high): 52nd

Des Moines County

BURLINGTON COMMUNITY S.D.

1429 WEST AVENUE ● BURLINGTON IA 52601 ● (319) 753-6791 ● http://www.aea16.k12.ia.us/GR_Schools/burl.html

Grade Span: PK-12 **Schools**: *Regular* 14 ● *Spec Ed* 0 ● *Alt* 1 **Students**: 5,336 **Total Teachers**: 327 **Student/Classroom Teacher Ratio**: 15.0	**Expenditures/Student**: $5,233 **Librarians**: 5.0 1,067 students/librarian **Guidance Counselors**: 9.0 593 students/counselor	**% Amer Indian**: 0.5 **% Asian**: 1.3 **% Black**: 8.7 **% Hispanic**: 1.7 **% White**: 87.9	National ***Socio-Economic Status*** indicator percentile (100=high): 48th

Dubuque County

DUBUQUE COMMUNITY S.D.

2300 CHANEY ● DUBUQUE IA 52001 ● (319) 588-5100

Grade Span: PK-12 **Schools**: *Regular* 17 ● *Spec Ed* 0 ● *Alt* 1 **Students**: 9,946 **Total Teachers**: 587 **Student/Classroom Teacher Ratio**: 16.3	**Expenditures/Student**: $5,260 **Librarians**: 1.0 9,946 students/librarian **Guidance Counselors**: 28.0 355 students/counselor	**% Amer Indian**: 0.4 **% Asian**: 1.2 **% Black**: 1.9 **% Hispanic**: 0.5 **% White**: 96.0	National ***Socio-Economic Status*** indicator percentile (100=high): 60th

Dubuque County

[FARLEY] WESTERN DUBUQUE COMMUNITY S.D.

BOX 279 ● FARLEY IA 52046 ● (319) 744-3885 ● http://www.wdhs.ml.org

Grade Span: PK-12 **Schools**: *Regular* 8 ● *Spec Ed* 1 ● *Alt* 0 **Students**: 2,729 **Total Teachers**: 178 **Student/Classroom Teacher Ratio**: 17.5	**Expenditures/Student**: $5,824 **Librarians**: 3.0 910 students/librarian **Guidance Counselors**: 6.0 455 students/counselor	**% Amer Indian**: 0.0 **% Asian**: 0.1 **% Black**: 0.1 **% Hispanic**: 0.1 **% White**: 99.5	National ***Socio-Economic Status*** indicator percentile (100=high): 66th

Jasper County

NEWTON COMMUNITY S.D.

807 S 6TH AVENUE WEST ● NEWTON IA 50208 ● (515) 792-5809

Grade Span: PK-12 **Schools**: *Regular* 7 ● *Spec Ed* 0 ● *Alt* 1 **Students**: 3,620 **Total Teachers**: 218 **Student/Classroom Teacher Ratio**: 18.7	**Expenditures/Student**: $5,185 **Librarians**: 5.0 724 students/librarian **Guidance Counselors**: 12.0 302 students/counselor	**% Amer Indian**: 0.2 **% Asian**: 1.2 **% Black**: 0.5 **% Hispanic**: 0.7 **% White**: 97.4	National ***Socio-Economic Status*** indicator percentile (100=high): 70th

Johnson County

IOWA CITY COMMUNITY S.D.

509 S DUBUQUE STREET ● IOWA CITY IA 52240 ● (319) 339-6800 ● http://www.iowa-city.k12.ia.us

Grade Span: PK-12 **Schools**: *Regular* 20 ● *Spec Ed* 0 ● *Alt* 1 **Students**: 10,322 **Total Teachers**: 596 **Student/Classroom Teacher Ratio**: 19.6	**Expenditures/Student**: $5,330 **Librarians**: 15.5 666 students/librarian **Guidance Counselors**: 29.5 350 students/counselor	**% Amer Indian**: 0.5 **% Asian**: 5.2 **% Black**: 4.9 **% Hispanic**: 2.7 **% White**: 86.7	National ***Socio-Economic Status*** indicator percentile (100=high): 78th

Lee County

FORT MADISON COMMUNITY S.D.

PO BOX 1423 ● FORT MADISON IA 52627 ● (319) 372-7252 ● http://www.ft-madison.k12.ia.us

Grade Span: PK-12 **Schools**: *Regular* 6 ● *Spec Ed* 0 ● *Alt* 1 **Students**: 2,825 **Total Teachers**: 181 **Student/Classroom Teacher Ratio**: 16.0	**Expenditures/Student**: $5,229 **Librarians**: 3.0 942 students/librarian **Guidance Counselors**: 5.0 565 students/counselor	**% Amer Indian**: 0.1 **% Asian**: 0.8 **% Black**: 3.5 **% Hispanic**: 4.1 **% White**: 91.5	National ***Socio-Economic Status*** indicator percentile (100=high): 58th

Lee County

KEOKUK COMMUNITY S.D.

727 WASHINGTON ● KEOKUK IA 52632 ● (319) 524-1402 ● http://www.keokuk.k12.ia.us

Grade Span: PK-12 **Schools**: *Regular* 7 ● *Spec Ed* 0 ● *Alt* 0 **Students**: 2,521 **Total Teachers**: 150 **Student/Classroom Teacher Ratio**: 15.6	**Expenditures/Student**: $5,151 **Librarians**: 3.0 840 students/librarian **Guidance Counselors**: 6.0 420 students/counselor	**% Amer Indian**: 0.4 **% Asian**: 1.0 **% Black**: 5.9 **% Hispanic**: 0.6 **% White**: 92.1	National ***Socio-Economic Status*** indicator percentile (100=high): 36th

Linn County

CEDAR RAPIDS COMMUNITY S.D.

346 2ND AVENUE SW ● CEDAR RAPIDS IA 52404 ● (319) 398-2000 ● http://www.cedar-rapids.k12.ia.us

Grade Span: PK-12 **Schools**: *Regular* 31 ● *Spec Ed* 1 ● *Alt* 1 **Students**: 17,786 **Total Teachers**: 995 **Student/Classroom Teacher Ratio**: 17.8	**Expenditures/Student**: $5,475 **Librarians**: 31.5 565 students/librarian **Guidance Counselors**: 44.0 404 students/counselor	**% Amer Indian**: 0.5 **% Asian**: 2.3 **% Black**: 6.9 **% Hispanic**: 1.6 **% White**: 88.7	National ***Socio-Economic Status*** indicator percentile (100=high): 57th

Linn County

[CEDAR RAPIDS] **COLLEGE COMMUNITY S.D.**

401 76TH AVENUE SW ● CEDAR RAPIDS IA 52404 ● (319) 848-5201 ● http://www.ccs.k12.ia.us

Grade Span: PK-12 **Schools**: *Regular* 5 ● *Spec Ed* 1 ● *Alt* 0 **Students**: 2,985 **Total Teachers**: 161 **Student/Classroom Teacher Ratio**: 17.9	**Expenditures/Student**: $5,394 **Librarians**: 3.0 995 students/librarian **Guidance Counselors**: 6.5 459 students/counselor	**% Amer Indian**: 0.5 **% Asian**: 1.2 **% Black**: 2.5 **% Hispanic**: 1.2 **% White**: 94.7	National ***Socio-Economic Status*** indicator percentile (100=high): 69th

Linn County

[MARION] **LINN-MAR COMMUNITY S.D.**

3333 NORTH 10TH STREET ● MARION IA 52302 ● (319) 377-7373 ● http://www.linnmar.k12.ia.us

Grade Span: PK-12 **Schools**: *Regular* 7 ● *Spec Ed* 0 ● *Alt* 0 **Students**: 3,904 **Total Teachers**: 227 **Student/Classroom Teacher Ratio**: 18.7	**Expenditures/Student**: $5,079 **Librarians**: 7.0 558 students/librarian **Guidance Counselors**: 8.0 488 students/counselor	**% Amer Indian**: 0.2 **% Asian**: 2.5 **% Black**: 0.7 **% Hispanic**: 0.8 **% White**: 95.7	National ***Socio-Economic Status*** indicator percentile (100=high): 87th

Mahaska County

OSKALOOSA COMMUNITY S.D.

PO BOX 710 ● OSKALOOSA IA 52577 ● (515) 673-8345

Grade Span: KG-12 **Schools**: *Regular* 8 ● *Spec Ed* 0 ● *Alt* 0 **Students**: 2,579 **Total Teachers**: 153 **Student/Classroom Teacher Ratio**: 16.6	**Expenditures/Student**: $4,859 **Librarians**: 2.0 1,290 students/librarian **Guidance Counselors**: 6.0 430 students/counselor	**% Amer Indian**: 0.0 **% Asian**: 1.7 **% Black**: 0.5 **% Hispanic**: 0.5 **% White**: 97.3	National ***Socio-Economic Status*** indicator percentile (100=high): 51st

Marshall County

MARSHALLTOWN COMMUNITY S.D.

317 COLUMBUS DRIVE ● MARSHALLTOWN IA 50158 ● (515) 754-1000 ● http://www.marshalltown.k12.ia.us

Grade Span: PK-12 **Schools**: *Regular* 9 ● *Spec Ed* 0 ● *Alt* 0 **Students**: 4,976 **Total Teachers**: 286 **Student/Classroom Teacher Ratio**: 18.3	**Expenditures/Student**: $5,473 **Librarians**: 8.0 622 students/librarian **Guidance Counselors**: 12.0 415 students/counselor	**% Amer Indian**: 0.7 **% Asian**: 1.9 **% Black**: 1.8 **% Hispanic**: 6.9 **% White**: 88.7	National ***Socio-Economic Status*** indicator percentile (100=high): 47th

Muscatine County

MUSCATINE COMMUNITY S.D.

1403 PARK AVENUE ● MUSCATINE IA 52761 ● (319) 263-7223 ● http://www.muscatine.k12.ia.us

Grade Span: PK-12 **Schools**: *Regular* 12 ● *Spec Ed* 0 ● *Alt* 0 **Students**: 5,492 **Total Teachers**: 355 **Student/Classroom Teacher Ratio**: 18.7	**Expenditures/Student**: $5,273 **Librarians**: 7.0 785 students/librarian **Guidance Counselors**: 14.0 392 students/counselor	**% Amer Indian**: 0.2 **% Asian**: 0.7 **% Black**: 1.5 **% Hispanic**: 14.4 **% White**: 83.2	National ***Socio-Economic Status*** indicator percentile (100=high): 48th

Polk County

ANKENY COMMUNITY S.D.

PO BOX 189 ● ANKENY IA 50021 ● (515) 965-9600 ● http://www.ankeny.k12.ia.us

Grade Span: PK-12 **Schools**: *Regular* 9 ● *Spec Ed* 0 ● *Alt* 0 **Students**: 5,150 **Total Teachers**: 277 **Student/Classroom Teacher Ratio**: 22.2	**Expenditures/Student**: $4,863 **Librarians**: 7.0 736 students/librarian **Guidance Counselors**: 15.0 343 students/counselor	**% Amer Indian**: 0.1 **% Asian**: 1.0 **% Black**: 1.3 **% Hispanic**: 0.6 **% White**: 97.0	National ***Socio-Economic Status*** indicator percentile (100=high): 95th

Polk County

DES MOINES INDEPENDENT COMMUNITY S.D.

1800 GRAND AVENUE ● DES MOINES IA 50309 ● (515) 242-7911 ● http://www.des-moines.k12.ia.us

Grade Span: PK-12 **Schools**: *Regular* 60 ● *Spec Ed* 5 ● *Alt* 0 **Students**: 32,414 **Total Teachers**: 2,132 **Student/Classroom Teacher Ratio**: 15.9	**Expenditures/Student**: $6,159 **Librarians**: 16.5 1,964 students/librarian **Guidance Counselors**: 111.5 291 students/counselor	**% Amer Indian**: 0.6 **% Asian**: 5.2 **% Black**: 13.6 **% Hispanic**: 4.4 **% White**: 76.1	National ***Socio-Economic Status*** indicator percentile (100=high): 37th

Polk County

JOHNSTON COMMUNITY S.D.

PO BOX 10 ● JOHNSTON IA 50131 ● (515) 278-0470 ● http://www.johnston.k12.ia.us

Grade Span: PK-12 **Schools**: *Regular* 4 ● *Spec Ed* 0 ● *Alt* 1 **Students**: 3,207 **Total Teachers**: 176 **Student/Classroom Teacher Ratio**: 20.2	**Expenditures/Student**: $4,797 **Librarians**: 4.0 802 students/librarian **Guidance Counselors**: 8.0 401 students/counselor	**% Amer Indian**: 0.3 **% Asian**: 1.9 **% Black**: 1.3 **% Hispanic**: 0.8 **% White**: 95.7	National ***Socio-Economic Status*** indicator percentile (100=high): 95th

Polk County

[RUNNELLS] **SOUTHEAST POLK COMMUNITY S.D.**

RR 2 ● RUNNELLS IA 50237 ● (515) 967-4294 ● http://www.se-polk.k12.ia.us

Grade Span: PK-12 **Schools**: *Regular* 9 ● *Spec Ed* 0 ● *Alt* 0 **Students**: 4,010 **Total Teachers**: 231 **Student/Classroom Teacher Ratio**: 15.4	**Expenditures/Student**: $4,938 **Librarians**: 1.0 4,010 students/librarian **Guidance Counselors**: 11.0 365 students/counselor	**% Amer Indian**: 0.2 **% Asian**: 0.8 **% Black**: 0.5 **% Hispanic**: 1.7 **% White**: 96.8	National ***Socio-Economic Status*** indicator percentile (100=high): 81st

Polk County

URBANDALE COMMUNITY S.D.

MERLE HAY CTR 500 WEST ● URBANDALE IA 50322 ● (515) 253-2300 ● http://www.urbandale.k12.ia.us

Grade Span: PK-12 **Schools**: *Regular* 7 ● *Spec Ed* 0 ● *Alt* 0 **Students**: 3,504 **Total Teachers**: 205 **Student/Classroom Teacher Ratio**: 17.1	**Expenditures/Student**: $5,189 **Librarians**: 2.0 1,752 students/librarian **Guidance Counselors**: 9.0 389 students/counselor	**% Amer Indian**: 0.2 **% Asian**: 2.1 **% Black**: 1.6 **% Hispanic**: 1.1 **% White**: 95.1	National ***Socio-Economic Status*** indicator percentile (100=high): 96th

Polk County

WEST DES MOINES COMMUNITY S.D.

3550 GEORGE M MILLS ● WEST DES MOINES IA 50265 ● (515) 226-2700 ● http://www.wdm.k12.ia.us

Grade Span: PK-12 **Schools**: *Regular* 13 ● *Spec Ed* 0 ● *Alt* 1 **Students**: 8,257 **Total Teachers**: 486 **Student/Classroom Teacher Ratio**: 16.9	**Expenditures/Student**: $5,203 **Librarians**: 7.0 1,180 students/librarian **Guidance Counselors**: 19.0 435 students/counselor	**% Amer Indian**: 0.1 **% Asian**: 3.2 **% Black**: 2.1 **% Hispanic**: 1.7 **% White**: 92.9	National ***Socio-Economic Status*** indicator percentile (100=high): 91st

Pottawattamie County

COUNCIL BLUFFS COMMUNITY S.D.

12 SCOTT STREET ● COUNCIL BLUFFS IA 51503 ● (712) 328-6418 ● http://www.council-bluffs.k12.ia.us

Grade Span: PK-12 **Schools**: *Regular* 18 ● *Spec Ed* 0 ● *Alt* 2 **Students**: 10,474 **Total Teachers**: 603 **Student/Classroom Teacher Ratio**: 19.8	**Expenditures/Student**: $5,146 **Librarians**: 7.0 1,496 students/librarian **Guidance Counselors**: 26.5 395 students/counselor	**% Amer Indian**: 0.5 **% Asian**: 0.5 **% Black**: 1.3 **% Hispanic**: 2.7 **% White**: 94.9	National ***Socio-Economic Status*** indicator percentile (100=high): 38th

Pottawattamie County
[COUNCIL BLUFFS] **LEWIS CENTRAL COMMUNITY S.D.**
1600 E S OMAHA BRDG RD ● COUNCIL BLUFFS IA 51503 ● (712) 366-8202 ● http://www.lewiscentral.k12.ia.us

Grade Span: PK-12 **Schools**: *Regular* 5 ● *Spec Ed* 0 ● *Alt* 0 **Students**: 2,735 **Total Teachers**: 147 **Student/Classroom Teacher Ratio**: 16.9	**Expenditures/Student**: $5,205 **Librarians**: 3.0 912 students/librarian **Guidance Counselors**: 5.0 547 students/counselor	**% Amer Indian**: 0.1 **% Asian**: 0.7 **% Black**: 0.3 **% Hispanic**: 1.6 **% White**: 97.3	National ***Socio-Economic Status*** indicator percentile (100=high): 56th

Scott County
BETTENDORF COMMUNITY S.D.
3311 CENTRAL AVENUE ● BETTENDORF IA 52722 ● (319) 359-3681 ● http://www.bettendorf.k12.ia.us

Grade Span: PK-12 **Schools**: *Regular* 8 ● *Spec Ed* 0 ● *Alt* 0 **Students**: 4,624 **Total Teachers**: 254 **Student/Classroom Teacher Ratio**: 18.9	**Expenditures/Student**: $5,376 **Librarians**: 6.5 711 students/librarian **Guidance Counselors**: 11.5 402 students/counselor	**% Amer Indian**: 0.3 **% Asian**: 2.1 **% Black**: 2.8 **% Hispanic**: 2.4 **% White**: 92.4	National ***Socio-Economic Status*** indicator percentile (100=high): 84th

Scott County
DAVENPORT COMMUNITY S.D.
1001 HARRISON STREET ● DAVENPORT IA 52803 ● (319) 323-9951

Grade Span: PK-12 **Schools**: *Regular* 33 ● *Spec Ed* 1 ● *Alt* 2 **Students**: 17,566 **Total Teachers**: 1,123 **Student/Classroom Teacher Ratio**: 15.3	**Expenditures/Student**: $5,393 **Librarians**: 24.5 717 students/librarian **Guidance Counselors**: 38.5 456 students/counselor	**% Amer Indian**: 1.3 **% Asian**: 2.2 **% Black**: 16.5 **% Hispanic**: 5.0 **% White**: 75.1	National ***Socio-Economic Status*** indicator percentile (100=high): 35th

Scott County
[ELDRIDGE] **NORTH SCOTT COMMUNITY S.D.**
251 E IOWA STREET ● ELDRIDGE IA 52748 ● (319) 285-4819 ● http://www.north-scott.k12.ia.us

Grade Span: PK-12 **Schools**: *Regular* 7 ● *Spec Ed* 0 ● *Alt* 0 **Students**: 3,118 **Total Teachers**: 184 **Student/Classroom Teacher Ratio**: 17.6	**Expenditures/Student**: $5,943 **Librarians**: 5.0 624 students/librarian **Guidance Counselors**: 7.5 416 students/counselor	**% Amer Indian**: 0.0 **% Asian**: 0.6 **% Black**: 0.4 **% Hispanic**: 0.5 **% White**: 98.6	National ***Socio-Economic Status*** indicator percentile (100=high): 82nd

Scott County
PLEASANT VALLEY COMMUNITY S.D.
PO BOX 332 ● PLEASANT VALLEY IA 52767 ● (319) 332-5550

Grade Span: PK-12 **Schools**: *Regular* 6 ● *Spec Ed* 0 ● *Alt* 0 **Students**: 3,055 **Total Teachers**: 166 **Student/Classroom Teacher Ratio**: 17.8	**Expenditures/Student**: $5,091 **Librarians**: 4.0 764 students/librarian **Guidance Counselors**: 7.5 407 students/counselor	**% Amer Indian**: 0.4 **% Asian**: 1.5 **% Black**: 0.8 **% Hispanic**: 2.4 **% White**: 94.8	National ***Socio-Economic Status*** indicator percentile (100=high): 88th

Story County
AMES COMMUNITY S.D.
120 SOUTH KELLOGG ● AMES IA 50010 ● (515) 239-3700 ● http://www.ames.k12.ia.us

Grade Span: PK-12 **Schools**: *Regular* 10 ● *Spec Ed* 1 ● *Alt* 0 **Students**: 5,221 **Total Teachers**: 292 **Student/Classroom Teacher Ratio**: 19.5	**Expenditures/Student**: $5,369 **Librarians**: 10.5 497 students/librarian **Guidance Counselors**: 11.0 475 students/counselor	**% Amer Indian**: 0.3 **% Asian**: 7.0 **% Black**: 4.3 **% Hispanic**: 2.3 **% White**: 86.1	National ***Socio-Economic Status*** indicator percentile (100=high): 73rd

Wapello County

OTTUMWA COMMUNITY S.D.

422 MCCARROLL DRIVE ● OTTUMWA IA 52501 ● (515) 684-6596 ● http://www.kca.net/ocsd

Grade Span: PK-12 **Schools**: *Regular* 11 ● *Spec Ed* 1 ● *Alt* 1 **Students**: 4,990 **Total Teachers**: 300 **Student/Classroom Teacher Ratio**: 18.6	**Expenditures/Student**: $5,418 **Librarians**: 3.0 1,663 students/librarian **Guidance Counselors**: 10.0 499 students/counselor	**% Amer Indian**: 0.4 **% Asian**: 1.3 **% Black**: 1.7 **% Hispanic**: 0.8 **% White**: 95.8	National ***Socio-Economic Status*** indicator percentile (100=high): 43rd

Warren County

INDIANOLA COMMUNITY S.D.

1304 EAST SECOND AVENUE ● INDIANOLA IA 50125 ● (515) 961-9500 ● http://www.indianola.ia.us/k12

Grade Span: PK-12 **Schools**: *Regular* 6 ● *Spec Ed* 0 ● *Alt* 1 **Students**: 3,301 **Total Teachers**: 189 **Student/Classroom Teacher Ratio**: 16.2	**Expenditures/Student**: $4,697 **Librarians**: 3.5 943 students/librarian **Guidance Counselors**: 8.0 413 students/counselor	**% Amer Indian**: 0.1 **% Asian**: 0.6 **% Black**: 0.7 **% Hispanic**: 0.7 **% White**: 98.0	National ***Socio-Economic Status*** indicator percentile (100=high): 84th

Webster County

FORT DODGE COMMUNITY S.D.

104 SOUTH 17TH STREET ● FORT DODGE IA 50501 ● (515) 576-1161 ● http://www.fort-dodge.k12.ia.us

Grade Span: KG-12 **Schools**: *Regular* 10 ● *Spec Ed* 0 ● *Alt* 0 **Students**: 4,561 **Total Teachers**: 297 **Student/Classroom Teacher Ratio**: 17.5	**Expenditures/Student**: $5,552 **Librarians**: 3.0 1,520 students/librarian **Guidance Counselors**: 14.0 326 students/counselor	**% Amer Indian**: 0.2 **% Asian**: 1.3 **% Black**: 6.4 **% Hispanic**: 1.6 **% White**: 90.5	National ***Socio-Economic Status*** indicator percentile (100=high): 51st

Woodbury County

SIOUX CITY COMMUNITY S.D.

1221 PIERCE STREET ● SIOUX CITY IA 51105 ● (712) 279-6642 ● http://www.siouxlan.com/siouxlan/education/highschool/whs/index.html

Grade Span: PK-12 **Schools**: *Regular* 30 ● *Spec Ed* 1 ● *Alt* 0 **Students**: 14,513 **Total Teachers**: 881 **Student/Classroom Teacher Ratio**: 17.4	**Expenditures/Student**: $5,062 **Librarians**: 10.0 1,451 students/librarian **Guidance Counselors**: 29.5 492 students/counselor	**% Amer Indian**: 4.4 **% Asian**: 3.6 **% Black**: 4.6 **% Hispanic**: 8.7 **% White**: 78.7	National ***Socio-Economic Status*** indicator percentile (100=high): 46th

Barton County

GREAT BEND UNIFIED S.D.

201 PATTON ROAD ● GREAT BEND KS 67530 ● (316) 793-1500

Grade Span: PK-12 **Schools**: *Regular* 10 ● *Spec Ed* 0 ● *Alt* 0 **Students**: 3,432 **Total Teachers**: 237 **Student/Classroom Teacher Ratio**: 15.5	**Expenditures/Student**: $4,867 **Librarians**: 6.0 572 students/librarian **Guidance Counselors**: 7.0 490 students/counselor	**% Amer Indian**: 0.5 **% Asian**: 0.9 **% Black**: 2.4 **% Hispanic**: 11.4 **% White**: 84.9	National ***Socio-Economic Status*** indicator percentile (100=high): 28th

Cowley County

ARKANSAS CITY UNIFIED S.D.

119 W WASHINGTON PO BOX 1028 ● ARKANSAS CITY KS 67005 ● (316) 441-2000 ● http://www.arkcity.com

Grade Span: PK-12 **Schools**: *Regular* 9 ● *Spec Ed* 0 ● *Alt* 0 **Students**: 3,215 **Total Teachers**: 169 **Student/Classroom Teacher Ratio**: 16.9	**Expenditures/Student**: $4,463 **Librarians**: 5.0 643 students/librarian **Guidance Counselors**: 6.0 536 students/counselor	**% Amer Indian**: 7.5 **% Asian**: 2.1 **% Black**: 5.3 **% Hispanic**: 3.6 **% White**: 81.5	National ***Socio-Economic Status*** indicator percentile (100=high): 24th

Cowley County

WINFIELD UNIFIED S.D.

920 MILLINGTON ● WINFIELD KS 67156 ● (316) 221-5100

Grade Span: PK-12 **Schools**: *Regular* 8 ● *Spec Ed* 1 ● *Alt* 0 **Students**: 2,772 **Total Teachers**: 224 **Student/Classroom Teacher Ratio**: 14.9	**Expenditures/Student**: $6,584 **Librarians**: 4.0 693 students/librarian **Guidance Counselors**: 3.5 792 students/counselor	**% Amer Indian**: 0.9 **% Asian**: 4.2 **% Black**: 3.2 **% Hispanic**: 4.0 **% White**: 87.7	National ***Socio-Economic Status*** indicator percentile (100=high): 37th

Crawford County

PITTSBURG UNIFIED S.D.

DRAWER 75 ● PITTSBURG KS 66762 ● (316) 235-3100 ● http://www.usd250.k12.ks.us

Grade Span: PK-12 **Schools**: *Regular* 7 ● *Spec Ed* 0 ● *Alt* 0 **Students**: 2,875 **Total Teachers**: 253 **Student/Classroom Teacher Ratio**: na	**Expenditures/Student**: $6,668 **Librarians**: 7.6 378 students/librarian **Guidance Counselors**: 10.0 288 students/counselor	**% Amer Indian**: 0.6 **% Asian**: 1.8 **% Black**: 4.7 **% Hispanic**: 1.3 **% White**: 91.6	National ***Socio-Economic Status*** indicator percentile (100=high): 28th

Douglas County

LAWRENCE UNIFIED S.D.

3705 CLINTON PARKWAY ● LAWRENCE KS 66047 ● (785) 832-5000 ● http://www.usd497.k12.ks.us

Grade Span: PK-12 **Schools**: *Regular* 24 ● *Spec Ed* 0 ● *Alt* 0 **Students**: 9,863 **Total Teachers**: 667 **Student/Classroom Teacher Ratio**: 14.7	**Expenditures/Student**: $5,289 **Librarians**: 22.0 448 students/librarian **Guidance Counselors**: 26.1 378 students/counselor	**% Amer Indian**: 4.1 **% Asian**: 3.2 **% Black**: 9.1 **% Hispanic**: 2.5 **% White**: 81.0	National ***Socio-Economic Status*** indicator percentile (100=high): 42nd

Ellis County

HAYS UNIFIED S.D.

323 W 12TH ST ● HAYS KS 67601 ● (785) 623-2400 ● http://www.hays489.k12.ks.us

Grade Span: PK-12 **Schools**: *Regular* 11 ● *Spec Ed* 0 ● *Alt* 0 **Students**: 3,597 **Total Teachers**: 279 **Student/Classroom Teacher Ratio**: 11.9	**Expenditures/Student**: $5,849 **Librarians**: 9.0 400 students/librarian **Guidance Counselors**: 8.0 450 students/counselor	**% Amer Indian**: 0.1 **% Asian**: 1.2 **% Black**: 1.2 **% Hispanic**: 1.4 **% White**: 96.0	National ***Socio-Economic Status*** indicator percentile (100=high): 53rd

Finney County

GARDEN CITY UNIFIED S.D.

1205 FLEMING ST ● GARDEN CITY KS 67846 ● (316) 276-5100 ● http://www.gckschools.com

Grade Span: PK-12 **Schools**: *Regular* 16 ● *Spec Ed* 0 ● *Alt* 2 **Students**: 7,370 **Total Teachers**: 422 **Student/Classroom Teacher Ratio**: 17.7	**Expenditures/Student**: $4,579 **Librarians**: 14.0 526 students/librarian **Guidance Counselors**: 19.0 388 students/counselor	**% Amer Indian**: 0.4 **% Asian**: 4.5 **% Black**: 1.7 **% Hispanic**: 43.2 **% White**: 50.1	National ***Socio-Economic Status*** indicator percentile (100=high): 26th

Ford County

DODGE CITY UNIFIED S.D.

1000 SECOND AVE BOX 460 ● DODGE CITY KS 67801 ● (316) 227-1620 ● http://www.usd443.org

Grade Span: PK-12 **Schools**: *Regular* 10 ● *Spec Ed* 0 ● *Alt* 0 **Students**: 5,074 **Total Teachers**: 249 **Student/Classroom Teacher Ratio**: 18.5	**Expenditures/Student**: $3,959 **Librarians**: 6.0 846 students/librarian **Guidance Counselors**: 12.0 423 students/counselor	**% Amer Indian**: 0.2 **% Asian**: 3.4 **% Black**: 3.0 **% Hispanic**: 37.1 **% White**: 56.3	National ***Socio-Economic Status*** indicator percentile (100=high): 20th

Geary County

JUNCTION CITY UNIFIED S.D.

BOX 370 ● JUNCTION CITY KS 66441 ● (785) 238-6184

Grade Span: PK-12 **Schools**: *Regular* 17 ● *Spec Ed* 0 ● *Alt* 1 **Students**: 6,665 **Total Teachers**: 405 **Student/Classroom Teacher Ratio**: 18.2	**Expenditures/Student**: $4,601 **Librarians**: 16.0 417 students/librarian **Guidance Counselors**: 10.0 667 students/counselor	**% Amer Indian**: 0.9 **% Asian**: 4.5 **% Black**: 36.0 **% Hispanic**: 8.4 **% White**: 50.1	National ***Socio-Economic Status*** indicator percentile (100=high): 10th

Harvey County

NEWTON UNIFIED S.D.

124 W 7TH BOX 307 ● NEWTON KS 67114 ● (316) 284-6200

Grade Span: PK-12 **Schools**: *Regular* 11 ● *Spec Ed* 0 ● *Alt* 0 **Students**: 3,577 **Total Teachers**: 225 **Student/Classroom Teacher Ratio**: 18.8	**Expenditures/Student**: $5,007 **Librarians**: 8.0 447 students/librarian **Guidance Counselors**: 8.0 447 students/counselor	**% Amer Indian**: 0.8 **% Asian**: 1.3 **% Black**: 4.4 **% Hispanic**: 12.6 **% White**: 80.9	National ***Socio-Economic Status*** indicator percentile (100=high): 34th

Johnson County

OLATHE UNIFIED S.D.

PO BOX 2000 ● OLATHE KS 66063 ● (913) 780-7000 ● http://www.olathe.k12.ks.us

Grade Span: PK-12 **Schools**: *Regular* 31 ● *Spec Ed* 0 ● *Alt* 1 **Students**: 17,709 **Total Teachers**: 1,204 **Student/Classroom Teacher Ratio**: 14.7	**Expenditures/Student**: $5,289 **Librarians**: 33.0 537 students/librarian **Guidance Counselors**: 40.3 439 students/counselor	**% Amer Indian**: 0.5 **% Asian**: 2.5 **% Black**: 4.2 **% Hispanic**: 1.9 **% White**: 90.9	National ***Socio-Economic Status*** indicator percentile (100=high): 80th

Johnson County

[OVERLAND PARK] **BLUE VALLEY UNIFIED S.D.**

BOX 23901 ● OVERLAND PARK KS 66223 ● (913) 681-4000 ● http://www.bluevalleyk12.org

Grade Span: PK-12 **Schools**: *Regular* 22 ● *Spec Ed* 0 ● *Alt* 0 **Students**: 13,561 **Total Teachers**: 851 **Student/Classroom Teacher Ratio**: 16.3	**Expenditures/Student**: $5,728 **Librarians**: 24.0 565 students/librarian **Guidance Counselors**: 34.9 389 students/counselor	**% Amer Indian**: 0.4 **% Asian**: 3.2 **% Black**: 1.7 **% Hispanic**: 0.9 **% White**: 93.8	National ***Socio-Economic Status*** indicator percentile (100=high): 97th

Johnson County

[OVERLAND PARK] SHAWNEE MISSION UNIFIED S.D.

7235 ANTIOCH ● OVERLAND PARK KS 66204 ● (913) 831-1900 ● http://www.smsd.k12.ks.us

Grade Span: PK-12 **Schools**: *Regular* 57 ● *Spec Ed* 0 ● *Alt* 1 **Students**: 31,844 **Total Teachers**: 1,966 **Student/Classroom Teacher Ratio**: 15.6	**Expenditures/Student**: $5,190 **Librarians**: 58.6 543 students/librarian **Guidance Counselors**: 67.0 475 students/counselor	**% Amer Indian**: 0.3 **% Asian**: 2.6 **% Black**: 3.5 **% Hispanic**: 2.9 **% White**: 90.6	National ***Socio-Economic Status*** indicator percentile (100=high): 77th

Leavenworth County

LEAVENWORTH UNIFIED S.D.

200 N 4TH ● LEAVENWORTH KS 66048 ● (913) 684-1400

Grade Span: PK-12 **Schools**: *Regular* 12 ● *Spec Ed* 0 ● *Alt* 0 **Students**: 4,501 **Total Teachers**: 347 **Student/Classroom Teacher Ratio**: 15.7	**Expenditures/Student**: $5,539 **Librarians**: 8.0 563 students/librarian **Guidance Counselors**: 8.0 563 students/counselor	**% Amer Indian**: 0.6 **% Asian**: 2.0 **% Black**: 22.1 **% Hispanic**: 4.1 **% White**: 71.1	National ***Socio-Economic Status*** indicator percentile (100=high): 31st

Lyon County

EMPORIA UNIFIED S.D.

BOX 1008 ● EMPORIA KS 66801 ● (316) 341-2200

Grade Span: KG-12 **Schools**: *Regular* 11 ● *Spec Ed* 0 ● *Alt* 0 **Students**: 4,768 **Total Teachers**: 331 **Student/Classroom Teacher Ratio**: 16.4	**Expenditures/Student**: $5,764 **Librarians**: 5.2 917 students/librarian **Guidance Counselors**: 10.1 472 students/counselor	**% Amer Indian**: 0.4 **% Asian**: 3.9 **% Black**: 3.7 **% Hispanic**: 17.1 **% White**: 74.9	National ***Socio-Economic Status*** indicator percentile (100=high): 25th

McPherson County

MCPHERSON UNIFIED S.D.

514 N MAIN PO BOX 1147 ● MCPHERSON KS 67460 ● (316) 241-9400 ● http://www.mcpherson.com/418

Grade Span: PK-12 **Schools**: *Regular* 5 ● *Spec Ed* 0 ● *Alt* 1 **Students**: 2,809 **Total Teachers**: 198 **Student/Classroom Teacher Ratio**: 14.7	**Expenditures/Student**: $5,294 **Librarians**: 5.0 562 students/librarian **Guidance Counselors**: 7.0 401 students/counselor	**% Amer Indian**: 0.4 **% Asian**: 1.0 **% Black**: 2.0 **% Hispanic**: 2.8 **% White**: 93.9	National ***Socio-Economic Status*** indicator percentile (100=high): 63rd

Reno County

HUTCHINSON UNIFIED S.D.

1520 NORTH PLUM BOX 1908 ● HUTCHINSON KS 67501 ● (316) 665-4400

Grade Span: PK-12 **Schools**: *Regular* 13 ● *Spec Ed* 0 ● *Alt* 0 **Students**: 5,325 **Total Teachers**: 336 **Student/Classroom Teacher Ratio**: 15.3	**Expenditures/Student**: $5,099 **Librarians**: 8.0 666 students/librarian **Guidance Counselors**: 14.0 380 students/counselor	**% Amer Indian**: 0.4 **% Asian**: 0.8 **% Black**: 6.1 **% Hispanic**: 8.4 **% White**: 84.4	National ***Socio-Economic Status*** indicator percentile (100=high): 22nd

Riley County

MANHATTAN UNIFIED S.D.

2031 POYNTZ ● MANHATTAN KS 66502 ● (785) 587-2000 ● http://www.manhattan.k12.ks.us

Grade Span: PK-12 **Schools**: *Regular* 12 ● *Spec Ed* 0 ● *Alt* 0 **Students**: 6,597 **Total Teachers**: 408 **Student/Classroom Teacher Ratio**: 16.3	**Expenditures/Student**: $4,915 **Librarians**: 13.5 489 students/librarian **Guidance Counselors**: 8.0 825 students/counselor	**% Amer Indian**: 0.5 **% Asian**: 4.1 **% Black**: 10.0 **% Hispanic**: 3.1 **% White**: 82.4	National ***Socio-Economic Status*** indicator percentile (100=high): 38th

Saline County

SALINA UNIFIED S.D.

BOX 797 ● SALINA KS 67402 ● (785) 826-4700

Grade Span: PK-12 **Schools**: *Regular* 18 ● *Spec Ed* 0 ● *Alt* 0 **Students**: 7,578 **Total Teachers**: 513 **Student/Classroom Teacher Ratio**: 16.4	**Expenditures/Student**: $5,233 **Librarians**: 15.5 489 students/librarian **Guidance Counselors**: 22.0 344 students/counselor	**% Amer Indian**: 0.6 **% Asian**: 2.7 **% Black**: 5.8 **% Hispanic**: 3.9 **% White**: 86.9	National ***Socio-Economic Status*** indicator percentile (100=high): 32nd

Sedgwick County

DERBY UNIFIED S.D.

120 E WASHINGTON ● DERBY KS 67037 ● (316) 788-8400 ● http://www.derby.k12.ks.us/home.html

Grade Span: PK-12 **Schools**: *Regular* 11 ● *Spec Ed* 0 ● *Alt* 1 **Students**: 6,729 **Total Teachers**: 395 **Student/Classroom Teacher Ratio**: 16.9	**Expenditures/Student**: $4,507 **Librarians**: 11.0 612 students/librarian **Guidance Counselors**: 7.0 961 students/counselor	**% Amer Indian**: 1.4 **% Asian**: 3.5 **% Black**: 6.5 **% Hispanic**: 3.6 **% White**: 85.0	National ***Socio-Economic Status*** indicator percentile (100=high): 46th

Sedgwick County

GODDARD UNIFIED S.D.

201 SOUTH MAIN BOX 249 ● GODDARD KS 67052 ● (316) 794-2267

Grade Span: KG-12 **Schools**: *Regular* 4 ● *Spec Ed* 0 ● *Alt* 0 **Students**: 2,688 **Total Teachers**: 139 **Student/Classroom Teacher Ratio**: 18.1	**Expenditures/Student**: $4,337 **Librarians**: 4.0 672 students/librarian **Guidance Counselors**: 6.0 448 students/counselor	**% Amer Indian**: 0.8 **% Asian**: 0.9 **% Black**: 0.8 **% Hispanic**: 2.7 **% White**: 94.9	National ***Socio-Economic Status*** indicator percentile (100=high): 82nd

Sedgwick County

HAYSVILLE UNIFIED S.D.

1745 W GRAND AVE ● HAYSVILLE KS 67060 ● (316) 524-0831

Grade Span: PK-12 **Schools**: *Regular* 6 ● *Spec Ed* 0 ● *Alt* 0 **Students**: 3,984 **Total Teachers**: 226 **Student/Classroom Teacher Ratio**: 18.3	**Expenditures/Student**: $4,848 **Librarians**: 5.5 724 students/librarian **Guidance Counselors**: 7.8 511 students/counselor	**% Amer Indian**: 1.5 **% Asian**: 1.7 **% Black**: 1.2 **% Hispanic**: 2.9 **% White**: 92.7	National ***Socio-Economic Status*** indicator percentile (100=high): 49th

Sedgwick County

MAIZE UNIFIED S.D.

201 S PARK ● MAIZE KS 67101 ● (316) 722-0614 ● http://www.usd266.com

Grade Span: PK-12 **Schools**: *Regular* 5 ● *Spec Ed* 0 ● *Alt* 0 **Students**: 4,339 **Total Teachers**: 226 **Student/Classroom Teacher Ratio**: 19.5	**Expenditures/Student**: $4,388 **Librarians**: 5.0 868 students/librarian **Guidance Counselors**: 12.0 362 students/counselor	**% Amer Indian**: 1.2 **% Asian**: 1.4 **% Black**: 0.9 **% Hispanic**: 2.5 **% White**: 94.1	National ***Socio-Economic Status*** indicator percentile (100=high): 89th

Sedgwick County

WICHITA UNIFIED S.D.

201 N WATER ST ● WICHITA KS 67202 ● (316) 833-4003 ● http://www.usd259.com

Grade Span: PK-12 **Schools**: *Regular* 95 ● *Spec Ed* 0 ● *Alt* 11 **Students**: 45,626 **Total Teachers**: 2,707 **Student/Classroom Teacher Ratio**: 19.4	**Expenditures/Student**: $5,392 **Librarians**: 76.6 596 students/librarian **Guidance Counselors**: 84.2 542 students/counselor	**% Amer Indian**: 1.9 **% Asian**: 4.8 **% Black**: 22.2 **% Hispanic**: 10.4 **% White**: 60.7	National ***Socio-Economic Status*** indicator percentile (100=high): 24th

Seward County

LIBERAL UNIFIED S.D.

BOX 949 ● LIBERAL KS 67901 ● (316) 626-3800

Grade Span: PK-12 **Schools**: *Regular* 10 ● *Spec Ed* 0 ● *Alt* 0 **Students**: 4,245 **Total Teachers**: 258 **Student/Classroom Teacher Ratio**: 16.8	**Expenditures/Student**: $4,574 **Librarians**: 4.0 1,061 students/librarian **Guidance Counselors**: 7.5 566 students/counselor	**% Amer Indian**: 1.0 **% Asian**: 3.4 **% Black**: 6.6 **% Hispanic**: 38.2 **% White**: 50.8	National ***Socio-Economic Status*** indicator percentile (100=high): 18th

Shawnee County

[TECUMSEH] **SHAWNEE HEIGHTS UNIFIED S.D.**

4401 SE SHAWNEE HEIGHTS ROAD ● TECUMSEH KS 66542 ● (785) 379-0584

Grade Span: PK-12 **Schools**: *Regular* 7 ● *Spec Ed* 0 ● *Alt* 0 **Students**: 3,529 **Total Teachers**: 213 **Student/Classroom Teacher Ratio**: 16.3	**Expenditures/Student**: $4,821 **Librarians**: 7.0 504 students/librarian **Guidance Counselors**: 10.0 353 students/counselor	**% Amer Indian**: 0.6 **% Asian**: 0.5 **% Black**: 5.6 **% Hispanic**: 5.2 **% White**: 88.1	National ***Socio-Economic Status*** indicator percentile (100=high): 69th

Shawnee County

[TOPEKA] **AUBURN WASHBURN UNIFIED S.D.**

5928 SOUTHWEST 53RD ● TOPEKA KS 66610 ● (785) 862-0419

Grade Span: PK-12 **Schools**: *Regular* 8 ● *Spec Ed* 0 ● *Alt* 0 **Students**: 5,075 **Total Teachers**: 325 **Student/Classroom Teacher Ratio**: 15.3	**Expenditures/Student**: $4,650 **Librarians**: 9.0 564 students/librarian **Guidance Counselors**: 7.4 686 students/counselor	**% Amer Indian**: 1.1 **% Asian**: 1.8 **% Black**: 4.0 **% Hispanic**: 2.7 **% White**: 90.4	National ***Socio-Economic Status*** indicator percentile (100=high): 65th

Shawnee County

[TOPEKA] **SEAMAN UNIFIED S.D.**

901 NW LYMAN ● TOPEKA KS 66608 ● (785) 575-8600

Grade Span: PK-12 **Schools**: *Regular* 11 ● *Spec Ed* 0 ● *Alt* 0 **Students**: 3,558 **Total Teachers**: 227 **Student/Classroom Teacher Ratio**: 15.8	**Expenditures/Student**: $4,724 **Librarians**: 8.0 445 students/librarian **Guidance Counselors**: 9.0 395 students/counselor	**% Amer Indian**: 1.1 **% Asian**: 0.4 **% Black**: 2.1 **% Hispanic**: 3.0 **% White**: 93.4	National ***Socio-Economic Status*** indicator percentile (100=high): 64th

Shawnee County

TOPEKA UNIFIED S.D.

624 W 24TH ● TOPEKA KS 66611 ● (785) 233-0313 ● http://www.topeka.k12.ks.us

Grade Span: PK-12 **Schools**: *Regular* 35 ● *Spec Ed* 0 ● *Alt* 0 **Students**: 14,085 **Total Teachers**: 1,089 **Student/Classroom Teacher Ratio**: 15.8	**Expenditures/Student**: $5,836 **Librarians**: 33.0 427 students/librarian **Guidance Counselors**: 37.5 376 students/counselor	**% Amer Indian**: 3.5 **% Asian**: 1.2 **% Black**: 23.4 **% Hispanic**: 10.0 **% White**: 61.9	National ***Socio-Economic Status*** indicator percentile (100=high): 7th

Wyandotte County

KANSAS CITY UNIFIED S.D.

LIBRARY BUILDING 625 MINNESOTA ● KANSAS CITY KS 66101 ● (913) 551-3200 ● http://www.kckps.k12.ks.us

Grade Span: PK-12 **Schools**: *Regular* 48 ● *Spec Ed* 0 ● *Alt* 0 **Students**: 21,670 **Total Teachers**: 1,463 **Student/Classroom Teacher Ratio**: 16.8	**Expenditures/Student**: $5,972 **Librarians**: 28.0 774 students/librarian **Guidance Counselors**: 39.0 556 students/counselor	**% Amer Indian**: 0.3 **% Asian**: 2.7 **% Black**: 54.1 **% Hispanic**: 11.0 **% White**: 31.9	National ***Socio-Economic Status*** indicator percentile (100=high): 7th

Wyandotte County

[KANSAS CITY] **TURNER-KANSAS CITY UNIFIED S.D.**

800 S 55TH ● KANSAS CITY KS 66106 ● (913) 287-7500 ● http://www.sunflower.org/~turnersd

Grade Span: PK-12 **Schools**: *Regular* 10 ● *Spec Ed* 0 ● *Alt* 0 **Students**: 4,041 **Total Teachers**: 266 **Student/Classroom Teacher Ratio**: 17.4	**Expenditures/Student**: $5,015 **Librarians**: 7.0 577 students/librarian **Guidance Counselors**: 9.0 449 students/counselor	**% Amer Indian**: 1.0 **% Asian**: 1.3 **% Black**: 9.6 **% Hispanic**: 7.8 **% White**: 80.3	National ***Socio-Economic Status*** indicator percentile (100=high): 33rd

Adair County

[COLUMBIA] **ADAIR COUNTY S.D.**

GREENSBURG ST ● COLUMBIA KY 42728 ● (502) 384-2476

Grade Span: KG-12	**Expenditures/Student**: $5,348	**% Amer Indian**: 0.0	National ***Socio-Economic Status*** indicator percentiles are not available for the state of Kentucky
Schools: *Regular* 6 ● *Spec Ed* 0 ● *Alt* 0	**Librarians**: 5.0	**% Asian**: 0.1	
Students: 2,623	525 students/librarian	**% Black**: 2.8	
Total Teachers: 173	**Guidance Counselors**: 4.5	**% Hispanic**: 0.2	
Student/Classroom Teacher Ratio: 14.2	583 students/counselor	**% White**: 96.9	

Allen County

[SCOTTSVILLE] **ALLEN COUNTY S.D.**

238 BG RD ● SCOTTSVILLE KY 42164 ● (502) 237-3181

Grade Span: KG-12	**Expenditures/Student**: $4,284	**% Amer Indian**: 0.0	National ***Socio-Economic Status*** indicator percentiles are not available for the state of Kentucky
Schools: *Regular* 4 ● *Spec Ed* 0 ● *Alt* 1	**Librarians**: 5.0	**% Asian**: 0.2	
Students: 2,854	571 students/librarian	**% Black**: 1.5	
Total Teachers: 152	**Guidance Counselors**: 3.4	**% Hispanic**: 0.3	
Student/Classroom Teacher Ratio: 19.0	839 students/counselor	**% White**: 98.0	

Anderson County

[LAWRENCEBURG] **ANDERSON COUNTY S.D.**

103 N MAIN ● LAWRENCEBURG KY 40342 ● (502) 839-3406 ● http://www.anderson.k12.ky.us

Grade Span: KG-12	**Expenditures/Student**: $3,654	**% Amer Indian**: 0.0	National ***Socio-Economic Status*** indicator percentiles are not available for the state of Kentucky
Schools: *Regular* 5 ● *Spec Ed* 0 ● *Alt* 0	**Librarians**: 4.0	**% Asian**: 0.2	
Students: 3,080	770 students/librarian	**% Black**: 2.6	
Total Teachers: 173	**Guidance Counselors**: 5.0	**% Hispanic**: 0.7	
Student/Classroom Teacher Ratio: 16.9	616 students/counselor	**% White**: 96.5	

Barren County

[GLASGOW] **BARREN COUNTY S.D.**

PO BOX 879 ● GLASGOW KY 42142 ● (502) 651-3787 ● http://www.bcms.barren.k12.ky.us

Grade Span: KG-12	**Expenditures/Student**: $4,800	**% Amer Indian**: 0.0	National ***Socio-Economic Status*** indicator percentiles are not available for the state of Kentucky
Schools: *Regular* 9 ● *Spec Ed* 0 ● *Alt* 0	**Librarians**: 7.3	**% Asian**: 0.0	
Students: 3,303	452 students/librarian	**% Black**: 1.0	
Total Teachers: 212	**Guidance Counselors**: 6.0	**% Hispanic**: 0.4	
Student/Classroom Teacher Ratio: 15.4	551 students/counselor	**% White**: 98.5	

Bell County

[PINEVILLE] **BELL COUNTY S.D.**

BOX 340 ● PINEVILLE KY 40977 ● (606) 337-7051

Grade Span: KG-12	**Expenditures/Student**: $5,902	**% Amer Indian**: 0.0	National ***Socio-Economic Status*** indicator percentiles are not available for the state of Kentucky
Schools: *Regular* 13 ● *Spec Ed* 0 ● *Alt* 0	**Librarians**: 9.0	**% Asian**: 0.1	
Students: 3,465	385 students/librarian	**% Black**: 0.3	
Total Teachers: 241	**Guidance Counselors**: 6.0	**% Hispanic**: 0.0	
Student/Classroom Teacher Ratio: 13.1	578 students/counselor	**% White**: 99.6	

Boone County

[FLORENCE] **BOONE COUNTY S.D.**

8330 US 42 ● FLORENCE KY 41042 ● (606) 283-1003 ● http://www.boone.k12.ky.us

Grade Span: KG-12	**Expenditures/Student**: $4,116	**% Amer Indian**: 0.1	National ***Socio-Economic Status*** indicator percentiles are not available for the state of Kentucky
Schools: *Regular* 16 ● *Spec Ed* 0 ● *Alt* 3	**Librarians**: 16.0	**% Asian**: 0.6	
Students: 11,564	723 students/librarian	**% Black**: 0.9	
Total Teachers: 636	**Guidance Counselors**: 19.8	**% Hispanic**: 0.7	
Student/Classroom Teacher Ratio: 18.1	584 students/counselor	**% White**: 97.8	

Bourbon County

[PARIS] BOURBON COUNTY S.D.

3343 LEXINGTON RD ● PARIS KY 40361 ● (606) 987-2180 ● http://www.bourbon.k12.ky.us

Grade Span: KG-12	**Expenditures/Student**: $5,770	**% Amer Indian**: 0.0	National ***Socio-Economic Status*** indicator percentiles are not available for the state of Kentucky
Schools: *Regular* 6 ● *Spec Ed* 0 ● *Alt* 0	**Librarians**: 6.0	**% Asian**: 0.3	
Students: 2,713	452 students/librarian	**% Black**: 2.7	
Total Teachers: 174	**Guidance Counselors**: 4.0	**% Hispanic**: 1.1	
Student/Classroom Teacher Ratio: 15.3	678 students/counselor	**% White**: 95.9	

Boyd County

ASHLAND INDEPENDENT S.D.

1420 CENTRAL AV ● ASHLAND KY 41101 ● (606) 327-2720

Grade Span: KG-12	**Expenditures/Student**: $4,161	**% Amer Indian**: 0.0	National ***Socio-Economic Status*** indicator percentiles are not available for the state of Kentucky
Schools: *Regular* 8 ● *Spec Ed* 0 ● *Alt* 1	**Librarians**: 8.0	**% Asian**: 0.8	
Students: 3,599	450 students/librarian	**% Black**: 4.0	
Total Teachers: 215	**Guidance Counselors**: 10.1	**% Hispanic**: 0.2	
Student/Classroom Teacher Ratio: 16.6	356 students/counselor	**% White**: 95.1	

Boyd County

[ASHLAND] BOYD COUNTY S.D.

1104 MCCULLOUGH ● ASHLAND KY 41102 ● (606) 928-4141 ● http://www.boyd.k12.ky.us

Grade Span: KG-12	**Expenditures/Student**: $4,264	**% Amer Indian**: 0.1	National ***Socio-Economic Status*** indicator percentiles are not available for the state of Kentucky
Schools: *Regular* 7 ● *Spec Ed* 0 ● *Alt* 2	**Librarians**: 6.5	**% Asian**: 0.2	
Students: 3,829	589 students/librarian	**% Black**: 0.6	
Total Teachers: 251	**Guidance Counselors**: 6.5	**% Hispanic**: 0.1	
Student/Classroom Teacher Ratio: 15.7	589 students/counselor	**% White**: 99.1	

Boyle County

[DANVILLE] BOYLE COUNTY S.D.

BOX 520 ● DANVILLE KY 40423 ● (606) 236-6634

Grade Span: KG-12	**Expenditures/Student**: $4,778	**% Amer Indian**: 0.1	National ***Socio-Economic Status*** indicator percentiles are not available for the state of Kentucky
Schools: *Regular* 5 ● *Spec Ed* 0 ● *Alt* 0	**Librarians**: 5.0	**% Asian**: 0.6	
Students: 2,579	516 students/librarian	**% Black**: 1.4	
Total Teachers: 161	**Guidance Counselors**: 6.0	**% Hispanic**: 0.4	
Student/Classroom Teacher Ratio: 15.8	430 students/counselor	**% White**: 97.6	

Breathitt County

[JACKSON] BREATHITT COUNTY S.D.

PO BOX 750 ● JACKSON KY 41339 ● (606) 666-2491 ● http://www.breathitt.k12.ky.us

Grade Span: KG-12	**Expenditures/Student**: $5,834	**% Amer Indian**: 0.0	National ***Socio-Economic Status*** indicator percentiles are not available for the state of Kentucky
Schools: *Regular* 6 ● *Spec Ed* 0 ● *Alt* 0	**Librarians**: 5.0	**% Asian**: 0.0	
Students: 2,645	529 students/librarian	**% Black**: 0.1	
Total Teachers: 183	**Guidance Counselors**: 4.0	**% Hispanic**: 0.0	
Student/Classroom Teacher Ratio: 13.8	661 students/counselor	**% White**: 99.8	

Breckinridge County

[HARDINSBURG] BRECKINRIDGE COUNTY S.D.

PO BOX 148 ● HARDINSBURG KY 40143 ● (502) 756-2186

Grade Span: KG-12	**Expenditures/Student**: $5,688	**% Amer Indian**: 0.2	National ***Socio-Economic Status*** indicator percentiles are not available for the state of Kentucky
Schools: *Regular* 7 ● *Spec Ed* 0 ● *Alt* 0	**Librarians**: 5.0	**% Asian**: 0.0	
Students: 2,791	558 students/librarian	**% Black**: 3.9	
Total Teachers: 165	**Guidance Counselors**: 5.6	**% Hispanic**: 0.8	
Student/Classroom Teacher Ratio: 16.3	498 students/counselor	**% White**: 95.1	

Bullitt County

[SHEPHERDSVILLE] BULLITT COUNTY S.D.

1040 HWY 44E ● SHEPHERDSVILLE KY 40165 ● (502) 543-2271 ● http://www.bullitt.k12.ky.us

Grade Span: KG-12 **Schools**: *Regular* 18 ● *Spec Ed* 0 ● *Alt* 0 **Students**: 10,041 **Total Teachers**: 542 **Student/Classroom Teacher Ratio**: 18.0	**Expenditures/Student**: $4,296 **Librarians**: 16.0 628 students/librarian **Guidance Counselors**: 21.0 478 students/counselor	**% Amer Indian**: 0.1 **% Asian**: 0.3 **% Black**: 0.4 **% Hispanic**: 0.2 **% White**: 99.0	National ***Socio-Economic Status*** indicator percentiles are not available for the state of Kentucky

Calloway County

[MURRAY] CALLOWAY COUNTY S.D.

BOX 800 ● MURRAY KY 42071 ● (502) 753-3033

Grade Span: KG-12 **Schools**: *Regular* 6 ● *Spec Ed* 0 ● *Alt* 1 **Students**: 3,251 **Total Teachers**: 200 **Student/Classroom Teacher Ratio**: 17.2	**Expenditures/Student**: $5,030 **Librarians**: 5.0 650 students/librarian **Guidance Counselors**: 6.0 542 students/counselor	**% Amer Indian**: 0.0 **% Asian**: 0.2 **% Black**: 1.5 **% Hispanic**: 0.5 **% White**: 97.7	National ***Socio-Economic Status*** indicator percentiles are not available for the state of Kentucky

Campbell County

[ALEXANDRIA] CAMPBELL COUNTY S.D.

101 ORCHARD ● ALEXANDRIA KY 41001 ● (606) 635-2173 ● http://www.campbell.k12.ky.us

Grade Span: KG-12 **Schools**: *Regular* 8 ● *Spec Ed* 0 ● *Alt* 3 **Students**: 4,823 **Total Teachers**: 270 **Student/Classroom Teacher Ratio**: 18.1	**Expenditures/Student**: $4,136 **Librarians**: 6.0 804 students/librarian **Guidance Counselors**: 8.0 603 students/counselor	**% Amer Indian**: 0.0 **% Asian**: 0.3 **% Black**: 0.2 **% Hispanic**: 0.1 **% White**: 99.4	National ***Socio-Economic Status*** indicator percentiles are not available for the state of Kentucky

Campbell County

NEWPORT INDEPENDENT S.D.

301 E 8TH ST ● NEWPORT KY 41071 ● (606) 292-3004

Grade Span: KG-12 **Schools**: *Regular* 6 ● *Spec Ed* 0 ● *Alt* 1 **Students**: 3,038 **Total Teachers**: 210 **Student/Classroom Teacher Ratio**: 20.2	**Expenditures/Student**: $5,609 **Librarians**: 5.0 608 students/librarian **Guidance Counselors**: 5.5 552 students/counselor	**% Amer Indian**: 0.0 **% Asian**: 0.2 **% Black**: 8.4 **% Hispanic**: 0.1 **% White**: 91.2	National ***Socio-Economic Status*** indicator percentiles are not available for the state of Kentucky

Carter County

[GRAYSON] CARTER COUNTY S.D.

228 CAROL MALONE ● GRAYSON KY 41143 ● (606) 474-6696 ● http://www.carter.k12.ky.us

Grade Span: KG-12 **Schools**: *Regular* 11 ● *Spec Ed* 0 ● *Alt* 1 **Students**: 5,086 **Total Teachers**: 307 **Student/Classroom Teacher Ratio**: 15.2	**Expenditures/Student**: $4,468 **Librarians**: 8.0 636 students/librarian **Guidance Counselors**: 12.5 407 students/counselor	**% Amer Indian**: 0.1 **% Asian**: 0.1 **% Black**: 0.1 **% Hispanic**: 0.1 **% White**: 99.6	National ***Socio-Economic Status*** indicator percentiles are not available for the state of Kentucky

Christian County

[HOPKINSVILLE] CHRISTIAN COUNTY S.D.

BOX 609 ● HOPKINSVILLE KY 42240 ● (502) 887-1300 ● http://www.christian.k12.ky.us

Grade Span: KG-12 **Schools**: *Regular* 16 ● *Spec Ed* 0 ● *Alt* 1 **Students**: 9,017 **Total Teachers**: 534 **Student/Classroom Teacher Ratio**: 17.1	**Expenditures/Student**: $5,108 **Librarians**: 18.0 501 students/librarian **Guidance Counselors**: 19.0 475 students/counselor	**% Amer Indian**: 0.2 **% Asian**: 0.8 **% Black**: 35.1 **% Hispanic**: 1.3 **% White**: 62.6	National ***Socio-Economic Status*** indicator percentiles are not available for the state of Kentucky

Clark County

[WINCHESTER] CLARK COUNTY S.D.

1600 W LEX ● WINCHESTER KY 40391 ● (606) 744-4545

Grade Span: KG-12 **Schools**: *Regular* 12 ● *Spec Ed* 0 ● *Alt* 0 **Students**: 5,372 **Total Teachers**: 311 **Student/Classroom Teacher Ratio**: 16.5	**Expenditures/Student**: $4,515 **Librarians**: 11.0 488 students/librarian **Guidance Counselors**: 15.0 358 students/counselor	**% Amer Indian**: 0.1 **% Asian**: 0.3 **% Black**: 6.6 **% Hispanic**: 0.5 **% White**: 92.5	National ***Socio-Economic Status*** indicator percentiles are not available for the state of Kentucky

Clay County

[MANCHESTER] CLAY COUNTY S.D.

128 RICHMOND R ● MANCHESTER KY 40962 ● (606) 598-2168 ● http://www.clay.k12.ky.us

Grade Span: KG-12 **Schools**: *Regular* 11 ● *Spec Ed* 0 ● *Alt* 0 **Students**: 4,561 **Total Teachers**: 307 **Student/Classroom Teacher Ratio**: 14.1	**Expenditures/Student**: $5,646 **Librarians**: 12.0 380 students/librarian **Guidance Counselors**: 5.0 912 students/counselor	**% Amer Indian**: 0.0 **% Asian**: 0.2 **% Black**: 1.3 **% Hispanic**: 0.1 **% White**: 98.4	National ***Socio-Economic Status*** indicator percentiles are not available for the state of Kentucky

Daviess County

[OWENSBORO] DAVIESS COUNTY S.D.

BOX 1510 ● OWENSBORO KY 42302 ● (502) 685-3161 ● http://www.daviess.k12.ky.us

Grade Span: KG-12 **Schools**: *Regular* 19 ● *Spec Ed* 0 ● *Alt* 4 **Students**: 10,190 **Total Teachers**: 569 **Student/Classroom Teacher Ratio**: 18.4	**Expenditures/Student**: $5,231 **Librarians**: 15.5 657 students/librarian **Guidance Counselors**: 20.5 497 students/counselor	**% Amer Indian**: 0.1 **% Asian**: 0.5 **% Black**: 2.2 **% Hispanic**: 0.3 **% White**: 97.0	National ***Socio-Economic Status*** indicator percentiles are not available for the state of Kentucky

Daviess County

OWENSBORO INDEPENDENT S.D.

PO BOX 746 ● OWENSBORO KY 42302 ● (502) 686-1000 ● http://www.owensboro.k12.ky.us

Grade Span: KG-12 **Schools**: *Regular* 11 ● *Spec Ed* 3 ● *Alt* 2 **Students**: 4,452 **Total Teachers**: 310 **Student/Classroom Teacher Ratio**: 15.5	**Expenditures/Student**: $6,243 **Librarians**: 8.0 557 students/librarian **Guidance Counselors**: 8.4 530 students/counselor	**% Amer Indian**: 0.3 **% Asian**: 0.5 **% Black**: 18.5 **% Hispanic**: 0.3 **% White**: 80.4	National ***Socio-Economic Status*** indicator percentiles are not available for the state of Kentucky

Estill County

[IRVINE] ESTILL COUNTY S.D.

BOX 391 ● IRVINE KY 40336 ● (606) 723-2181

Grade Span: KG-12 **Schools**: *Regular* 8 ● *Spec Ed* 0 ● *Alt* 0 **Students**: 2,786 **Total Teachers**: 193 **Student/Classroom Teacher Ratio**: 13.7	**Expenditures/Student**: $5,310 **Librarians**: 5.0 557 students/librarian **Guidance Counselors**: 6.0 464 students/counselor	**% Amer Indian**: 0.0 **% Asian**: 0.0 **% Black**: 0.2 **% Hispanic**: 0.1 **% White**: 99.6	National ***Socio-Economic Status*** indicator percentiles are not available for the state of Kentucky

Fayette County

[LEXINGTON] FAYETTE COUNTY S.D.

701 E MAIN ST ● LEXINGTON KY 40502 ● (606) 281-0100 ● http://www.fayette.k12.ky.us

Grade Span: KG-12 **Schools**: *Regular* 52 ● *Spec Ed* 1 ● *Alt* 4 **Students**: 32,880 **Total Teachers**: 2,092 **Student/Classroom Teacher Ratio**: 15.0	**Expenditures/Student**: $5,380 **Librarians**: 58.6 561 students/librarian **Guidance Counselors**: 84.0 391 students/counselor	**% Amer Indian**: 0.1 **% Asian**: 2.2 **% Black**: 23.0 **% Hispanic**: 0.8 **% White**: 74.0	National ***Socio-Economic Status*** indicator percentiles are not available for the state of Kentucky

Floyd County

[PRESTONSBURG] **FLOYD COUNTY S.D.**

ARNOLD AVE ● PRESTONSBURG KY 41653 ● (606) 886-2354 ● http://www.floyd.k12.ky.us

Grade Span: KG-12 **Schools**: *Regular* 20 ● *Spec Ed* 0 ● *Alt* 0 **Students**: 8,144 **Total Teachers**: 534 **Student/Classroom Teacher Ratio**: 14.6	**Expenditures/Student**: $5,594 **Librarians**: 14.9 547 students/librarian **Guidance Counselors**: 16.4 497 students/counselor	**% Amer Indian**: 0.0 **% Asian**: 0.1 **% Black**: 0.3 **% Hispanic**: 0.1 **% White**: 99.5	National ***Socio-Economic Status*** indicator percentiles are not available for the state of Kentucky

Franklin County

[FRANKFORT] **FRANKLIN COUNTY S.D.**

916 E MAIN ST ● FRANKFORT KY 40601 ● (502) 695-6700 ● http://www.franklin.k12.ky.us

Grade Span: KG-12 **Schools**: *Regular* 10 ● *Spec Ed* 0 ● *Alt* 1 **Students**: 5,976 **Total Teachers**: 348 **Student/Classroom Teacher Ratio**: 17.0	**Expenditures/Student**: $4,143 **Librarians**: 9.0 664 students/librarian **Guidance Counselors**: 14.0 427 students/counselor	**% Amer Indian**: 0.0 **% Asian**: 0.3 **% Black**: 8.3 **% Hispanic**: 0.2 **% White**: 91.2	National ***Socio-Economic Status*** indicator percentiles are not available for the state of Kentucky

Grant County

[WILLIAMSTOWN] **GRANT COUNTY S.D.**

BOX 369 ● WILLIAMSTOWN KY 41097 ● (606) 824-3323

Grade Span: KG-12 **Schools**: *Regular* 5 ● *Spec Ed* 0 ● *Alt* 0 **Students**: 3,375 **Total Teachers**: 179 **Student/Classroom Teacher Ratio**: 18.7	**Expenditures/Student**: $4,598 **Librarians**: 5.0 675 students/librarian **Guidance Counselors**: 6.0 563 students/counselor	**% Amer Indian**: 0.0 **% Asian**: 0.1 **% Black**: 0.3 **% Hispanic**: 0.3 **% White**: 99.3	National ***Socio-Economic Status*** indicator percentiles are not available for the state of Kentucky

Graves County

[MAYFIELD] **GRAVES COUNTY S.D.**

1007 CUBA RD ● MAYFIELD KY 42066 ● (502) 247-2656

Grade Span: KG-12 **Schools**: *Regular* 8 ● *Spec Ed* 0 ● *Alt* 1 **Students**: 4,346 **Total Teachers**: 226 **Student/Classroom Teacher Ratio**: 19.8	**Expenditures/Student**: $3,992 **Librarians**: 6.0 724 students/librarian **Guidance Counselors**: 8.5 511 students/counselor	**% Amer Indian**: 0.0 **% Asian**: 0.2 **% Black**: 1.2 **% Hispanic**: 0.4 **% White**: 98.2	National ***Socio-Economic Status*** indicator percentiles are not available for the state of Kentucky

Grayson County

[LEITCHFIELD] **GRAYSON COUNTY S.D.**

P O BOX 4009 ● LEITCHFIELD KY 42754 ● (502) 259-4011

Grade Span: KG-12 **Schools**: *Regular* 7 ● *Spec Ed* 0 ● *Alt* 1 **Students**: 4,052 **Total Teachers**: 233 **Student/Classroom Teacher Ratio**: 15.3	**Expenditures/Student**: $4,495 **Librarians**: 6.0 675 students/librarian **Guidance Counselors**: 8.0 507 students/counselor	**% Amer Indian**: 0.0 **% Asian**: 0.2 **% Black**: 0.6 **% Hispanic**: 0.3 **% White**: 98.9	National ***Socio-Economic Status*** indicator percentiles are not available for the state of Kentucky

Greenup County

[GREENUP] **GREENUP COUNTY S.D.**

3449 OLD DAM CT ● GREENUP KY 41144 ● (606) 473-9819

Grade Span: KG-12 **Schools**: *Regular* 9 ● *Spec Ed* 0 ● *Alt* 0 **Students**: 3,504 **Total Teachers**: 219 **Student/Classroom Teacher Ratio**: 15.1	**Expenditures/Student**: $4,951 **Librarians**: 6.5 539 students/librarian **Guidance Counselors**: 9.0 389 students/counselor	**% Amer Indian**: 0.0 **% Asian**: 0.1 **% Black**: 0.9 **% Hispanic**: 0.3 **% White**: 98.7	National ***Socio-Economic Status*** indicator percentiles are not available for the state of Kentucky

Hardin County

[ELIZABETHTOWN] HARDIN COUNTY S.D.

110 S MAIN ● ELIZABETHTOWN KY 42701 ● (502) 769-8800 ● http://www.hardin.k12.ky.us

Grade Span: KG-12 **Schools**: *Regular* 22 ● *Spec Ed* 0 ● *Alt* 2 **Students**: 13,367 **Total Teachers**: 781 **Student/Classroom Teacher Ratio**: 15.9	**Expenditures/Student**: $4,679 **Librarians**: 25.0 535 students/librarian **Guidance Counselors**: 31.2 428 students/counselor	**% Amer Indian**: 0.4 **% Asian**: 2.6 **% Black**: 14.8 **% Hispanic**: 2.3 **% White**: 80.0	National ***Socio-Economic Status*** indicator percentiles are not available for the state of Kentucky

Harlan County

[HARLAN] HARLAN COUNTY S.D.

102 BALL PARK RD ● HARLAN KY 40831 ● (606) 573-4330

Grade Span: KG-12 **Schools**: *Regular* 16 ● *Spec Ed* 0 ● *Alt* 0 **Students**: 5,894 **Total Teachers**: 423 **Student/Classroom Teacher Ratio**: 13.5	**Expenditures/Student**: $5,672 **Librarians**: 14.4 409 students/librarian **Guidance Counselors**: 8.5 693 students/counselor	**% Amer Indian**: 0.0 **% Asian**: 0.1 **% Black**: 2.7 **% Hispanic**: 0.1 **% White**: 97.1	National ***Socio-Economic Status*** indicator percentiles are not available for the state of Kentucky

Harrison County

[CYNTHIANA] HARRISON COUNTY S.D.

RT 7 BOX 158 ● CYNTHIANA KY 41031 ● (606) 234-7110 ● http://www.harrison.k12.ky.us

Grade Span: KG-12 **Schools**: *Regular* 6 ● *Spec Ed* 0 ● *Alt* 0 **Students**: 3,137 **Total Teachers**: 193 **Student/Classroom Teacher Ratio**: 15.6	**Expenditures/Student**: $4,731 **Librarians**: 6.0 523 students/librarian **Guidance Counselors**: 5.7 550 students/counselor	**% Amer Indian**: 0.1 **% Asian**: 0.1 **% Black**: 3.7 **% Hispanic**: 0.6 **% White**: 95.5	National ***Socio-Economic Status*** indicator percentiles are not available for the state of Kentucky

Henderson County

[HENDERSON] HENDERSON COUNTY S.D.

1805 2ND ST ● HENDERSON KY 42420 ● (502) 831-5000

Grade Span: KG-12 **Schools**: *Regular* 17 ● *Spec Ed* 0 ● *Alt* 0 **Students**: 7,649 **Total Teachers**: 422 **Student/Classroom Teacher Ratio**: 17.4	**Expenditures/Student**: $4,687 **Librarians**: 15.0 510 students/librarian **Guidance Counselors**: 17.8 430 students/counselor	**% Amer Indian**: 0.0 **% Asian**: 0.3 **% Black**: 9.1 **% Hispanic**: 0.2 **% White**: 90.3	National ***Socio-Economic Status*** indicator percentiles are not available for the state of Kentucky

Hopkins County

[MADISONVILLE] HOPKINS COUNTY S.D.

PO BOX 509 ● MADISONVILLE KY 42431 ● (502) 825-6060 ● http://www.hopkins.k12.ky.us

Grade Span: KG-12 **Schools**: *Regular* 17 ● *Spec Ed* 0 ● *Alt* 0 **Students**: 7,437 **Total Teachers**: 442 **Student/Classroom Teacher Ratio**: 16.2	**Expenditures/Student**: $4,988 **Librarians**: 14.0 531 students/librarian **Guidance Counselors**: 15.0 496 students/counselor	**% Amer Indian**: 0.1 **% Asian**: 0.5 **% Black**: 9.6 **% Hispanic**: 0.2 **% White**: 89.7	National ***Socio-Economic Status*** indicator percentiles are not available for the state of Kentucky

Jefferson County

[LOUISVILLE] JEFFERSON COUNTY S.D.

PO BOX 34020 ● LOUISVILLE KY 40232 ● (502) 473-3251 ● http://www.jefferson.k12.ky.us

Grade Span: KG-12 **Schools**: *Regular* 139 ● *Spec Ed* 3 ● *Alt* 8 **Students**: 93,070 **Total Teachers**: 5,516 **Student/Classroom Teacher Ratio**: 16.9	**Expenditures/Student**: $5,474 **Librarians**: 152.5 610 students/librarian **Guidance Counselors**: 203.0 458 students/counselor	**% Amer Indian**: 0.1 **% Asian**: 1.2 **% Black**: 31.5 **% Hispanic**: 0.5 **% White**: 66.8	National ***Socio-Economic Status*** indicator percentiles are not available for the state of Kentucky

Jessamine County

[NICHOLASVILLE] **JESSAMINE COUNTY S.D.**

501 E MAPLE ● NICHOLASVILLE KY 40356 ● (606) 885-4179 ● http://www.jessamine.k12.ky.us

Grade Span: KG-12	**Expenditures/Student**: $3,983	**% Amer Indian**: 0.1	National ***Socio-Economic***
Schools: *Regular* 8 ● *Spec Ed* 0 ● *Alt* 0	**Librarians**: 8.0	**% Asian**: 0.5	***Status*** indicator percentiles
Students: 6,239	780 students/librarian	**% Black**: 4.0	are not available for the
Total Teachers: 358	**Guidance Counselors**: 14.0	**% Hispanic**: 0.4	state of Kentucky
Student/Classroom Teacher Ratio: 17.3	446 students/counselor	**% White**: 95.1	

Johnson County

[PAINTSVILLE] **JOHNSON COUNTY S.D.**

253 N MAYO ● PAINTSVILLE KY 41240 ● (606) 789-2530 ● http://www.johnson.k12.ky.us

Grade Span: KG-12	**Expenditures/Student**: $5,207	**% Amer Indian**: 0.0	National ***Socio-Economic***
Schools: *Regular* 9 ● *Spec Ed* 0 ● *Alt* 0	**Librarians**: 6.0	**% Asian**: 0.0	***Status*** indicator percentiles
Students: 3,935	656 students/librarian	**% Black**: 0.1	are not available for the
Total Teachers: 258	**Guidance Counselors**: 7.1	**% Hispanic**: 0.1	state of Kentucky
Student/Classroom Teacher Ratio: 14.0	554 students/counselor	**% White**: 99.8	

Kenton County

COVINGTON INDEPENDENT S.D.

25 E 7TH ST ● COVINGTON KY 41011 ● (606) 292-5800

Grade Span: KG-12	**Expenditures/Student**: $6,162	**% Amer Indian**: 0.0	National ***Socio-Economic***
Schools: *Regular* 11 ● *Spec Ed* 0 ● *Alt* 2	**Librarians**: 9.0	**% Asian**: 0.3	***Status*** indicator percentiles
Students: 5,334	593 students/librarian	**% Black**: 16.9	are not available for the
Total Teachers: 321	**Guidance Counselors**: 9.0	**% Hispanic**: 0.4	state of Kentucky
Student/Classroom Teacher Ratio: 16.6	593 students/counselor	**% White**: 82.4	

Kenton County

[ERLANGER] **KENTON COUNTY S.D.**

20 KENTON LANDS ● ERLANGER KY 41018 ● (606) 344-8888 ● http://www.kenton.k12.ky.us

Grade Span: KG-12	**Expenditures/Student**: $4,327	**% Amer Indian**: 0.1	National ***Socio-Economic***
Schools: *Regular* 19 ● *Spec Ed* 1 ● *Alt* 1	**Librarians**: 19.0	**% Asian**: 0.4	***Status*** indicator percentiles
Students: 12,052	634 students/librarian	**% Black**: 0.9	are not available for the
Total Teachers: 656	**Guidance Counselors**: 21.4	**% Hispanic**: 0.3	state of Kentucky
Student/Classroom Teacher Ratio: 18.1	563 students/counselor	**% White**: 98.3	

Knott County

[HINDMAN] **KNOTT COUNTY S.D.**

PO BOX 869 ● HINDMAN KY 41822 ● (606) 785-3153

Grade Span: KG-12	**Expenditures/Student**: $5,556	**% Amer Indian**: 0.0	National ***Socio-Economic***
Schools: *Regular* 11 ● *Spec Ed* 0 ● *Alt* 0	**Librarians**: 9.0	**% Asian**: 0.0	***Status*** indicator percentiles
Students: 3,422	380 students/librarian	**% Black**: 1.3	are not available for the
Total Teachers: 230	**Guidance Counselors**: 7.9	**% Hispanic**: 0.0	state of Kentucky
Student/Classroom Teacher Ratio: 13.4	433 students/counselor	**% White**: 98.6	

Knox County

[BARBOURVILLE] **KNOX COUNTY S.D.**

PO BOX 700 ● BARBOURVILLE KY 40906 ● (606) 546-3157

Grade Span: KG-12	**Expenditures/Student**: $5,825	**% Amer Indian**: 0.0	National ***Socio-Economic***
Schools: *Regular* 11 ● *Spec Ed* 0 ● *Alt* 0	**Librarians**: 11.0	**% Asian**: 0.0	***Status*** indicator percentiles
Students: 4,756	432 students/librarian	**% Black**: 0.7	are not available for the
Total Teachers: 330	**Guidance Counselors**: 8.8	**% Hispanic**: 0.0	state of Kentucky
Student/Classroom Teacher Ratio: 13.2	540 students/counselor	**% White**: 99.2	

Laurel County

[LONDON] **LAUREL COUNTY S.D.**

275 S LAUREL RD ● LONDON KY 40741 ● (606) 864-5114

Grade Span: KG-12 **Schools**: *Regular* 15 ● *Spec Ed* 0 ● *Alt* 1 **Students**: 8,512 **Total Teachers**: 494 **Student/Classroom Teacher Ratio**: 18.2	**Expenditures/Student**: $4,721 **Librarians**: 17.0 501 students/librarian **Guidance Counselors**: 18.0 473 students/counselor	**% Amer Indian**: 0.1 **% Asian**: 0.2 **% Black**: 0.7 **% Hispanic**: 0.2 **% White**: 98.8	National ***Socio-Economic Status*** indicator percentiles are not available for the state of Kentucky

Lawrence County

[LOUISA] **LAWRENCE COUNTY S.D.**

BOX 607 ● LOUISA KY 41230 ● (606) 638-9671

Grade Span: KG-12 **Schools**: *Regular* 5 ● *Spec Ed* 0 ● *Alt* 0 **Students**: 2,763 **Total Teachers**: 183 **Student/Classroom Teacher Ratio**: 14.8	**Expenditures/Student**: $4,862 **Librarians**: 5.0 553 students/librarian **Guidance Counselors**: 5.0 553 students/counselor	**% Amer Indian**: 0.0 **% Asian**: 0.1 **% Black**: 0.2 **% Hispanic**: 0.0 **% White**: 99.6	National ***Socio-Economic Status*** indicator percentiles are not available for the state of Kentucky

Leslie County

[HYDEN] **LESLIE COUNTY S.D.**

PO BOX 949 ● HYDEN KY 41749 ● (606) 672-2397 ● http://leslie.k12.ky.us

Grade Span: KG-12 **Schools**: *Regular* 8 ● *Spec Ed* 0 ● *Alt* 0 **Students**: 2,621 **Total Teachers**: 177 **Student/Classroom Teacher Ratio**: 13.9	**Expenditures/Student**: $5,511 **Librarians**: 6.5 403 students/librarian **Guidance Counselors**: 3.9 672 students/counselor	**% Amer Indian**: 0.0 **% Asian**: 0.2 **% Black**: 0.2 **% Hispanic**: 0.0 **% White**: 99.7	National ***Socio-Economic Status*** indicator percentiles are not available for the state of Kentucky

Letcher County

[WHITESBURG] **LETCHER COUNTY S.D.**

BOX 788 ● WHITESBURG KY 41858 ● (606) 633-4455 ● http://www.letcher.k12.ky.us

Grade Span: KG-12 **Schools**: *Regular* 15 ● *Spec Ed* 0 ● *Alt* 0 **Students**: 4,391 **Total Teachers**: 270 **Student/Classroom Teacher Ratio**: 15.3	**Expenditures/Student**: $5,499 **Librarians**: 9.0 488 students/librarian **Guidance Counselors**: 10.2 430 students/counselor	**% Amer Indian**: 0.0 **% Asian**: 0.1 **% Black**: 0.2 **% Hispanic**: 0.1 **% White**: 99.6	National ***Socio-Economic Status*** indicator percentiles are not available for the state of Kentucky

Lewis County

[VANCEBURG] **LEWIS COUNTY S.D.**

PO BOX 159 ● VANCEBURG KY 41179 ● (606) 796-2811

Grade Span: KG-12 **Schools**: *Regular* 6 ● *Spec Ed* 0 ● *Alt* 1 **Students**: 2,532 **Total Teachers**: 159 **Student/Classroom Teacher Ratio**: 15.3	**Expenditures/Student**: $5,055 **Librarians**: 5.0 506 students/librarian **Guidance Counselors**: 4.5 563 students/counselor	**% Amer Indian**: 0.0 **% Asian**: 0.1 **% Black**: 0.2 **% Hispanic**: 0.2 **% White**: 99.5	National ***Socio-Economic Status*** indicator percentiles are not available for the state of Kentucky

Lincoln County

[STANFORD] **LINCOLN COUNTY S.D.**

PO BOX 265 ● STANFORD KY 40484 ● (606) 365-2124 ● http://lincoln.k12.ky.us

Grade Span: KG-12 **Schools**: *Regular* 9 ● *Spec Ed* 0 ● *Alt* 0 **Students**: 3,907 **Total Teachers**: 256 **Student/Classroom Teacher Ratio**: 14.6	**Expenditures/Student**: $5,592 **Librarians**: 7.0 558 students/librarian **Guidance Counselors**: 7.0 558 students/counselor	**% Amer Indian**: 0.0 **% Asian**: 0.0 **% Black**: 3.1 **% Hispanic**: 0.2 **% White**: 96.7	National ***Socio-Economic Status*** indicator percentiles are not available for the state of Kentucky

Logan County

[RUSSELLVILLE] **LOGAN COUNTY S.D.**

P O BOX 417 ● RUSSELLVILLE KY 42276 ● (502) 726-2436

Grade Span: KG-12 **Schools**: *Regular* 11 ● *Spec Ed* 0 ● *Alt* 0 **Students**: 3,160 **Total Teachers**: 186 **Student/Classroom Teacher Ratio**: 16.5	**Expenditures/Student**: $5,232 **Librarians**: 4.5 702 students/librarian **Guidance Counselors**: 5.5 575 students/counselor	**% Amer Indian**: 0.2 **% Asian**: 0.0 **% Black**: 4.9 **% Hispanic**: 0.0 **% White**: 94.8	National ***Socio-Economic Status*** indicator percentiles are not available for the state of Kentucky

McCracken County

[PADUCAH] **MCCRACKEN COUNTY S.D.**

260 BLEICH RD ● PADUCAH KY 42003 ● (502) 554-6800 ● http://www.mccracken.k12.ky.us

Grade Span: KG-12 **Schools**: *Regular* 12 ● *Spec Ed* 0 ● *Alt* 0 **Students**: 6,921 **Total Teachers**: 370 **Student/Classroom Teacher Ratio**: 18.7	**Expenditures/Student**: $4,374 **Librarians**: 12.0 577 students/librarian **Guidance Counselors**: 13.5 513 students/counselor	**% Amer Indian**: 0.0 **% Asian**: 0.6 **% Black**: 1.9 **% Hispanic**: 0.6 **% White**: 96.9	National ***Socio-Economic Status*** indicator percentiles are not available for the state of Kentucky

McCracken County

PADUCAH INDEPENDENT S.D.

P O BOX 2550 ● PADUCAH KY 42002 ● (502) 444-5606 ● http://www.paducah.k12.ky.us

Grade Span: KG-12 **Schools**: *Regular* 7 ● *Spec Ed* 0 ● *Alt* 0 **Students**: 3,322 **Total Teachers**: 224 **Student/Classroom Teacher Ratio**: 16.1	**Expenditures/Student**: $5,856 **Librarians**: 7.0 475 students/librarian **Guidance Counselors**: 4.5 738 students/counselor	**% Amer Indian**: 0.1 **% Asian**: 0.4 **% Black**: 46.4 **% Hispanic**: 0.4 **% White**: 52.7	National ***Socio-Economic Status*** indicator percentiles are not available for the state of Kentucky

McCreary County

[STEARNS] **MCCREARY COUNTY S.D.**

HC 69 BOX 24 ● STEARNS KY 42647 ● (606) 376-2591

Grade Span: KG-12 **Schools**: *Regular* 10 ● *Spec Ed* 0 ● *Alt* 0 **Students**: 3,483 **Total Teachers**: 232 **Student/Classroom Teacher Ratio**: 13.2	**Expenditures/Student**: $5,903 **Librarians**: 6.3 553 students/librarian **Guidance Counselors**: 6.9 505 students/counselor	**% Amer Indian**: 0.0 **% Asian**: 0.0 **% Black**: 0.1 **% Hispanic**: 0.0 **% White**: 99.9	National ***Socio-Economic Status*** indicator percentiles are not available for the state of Kentucky

Madison County

[RICHMOND] **MADISON COUNTY S.D.**

PO BOX 768 ● RICHMOND KY 40475 ● (606) 624-4500 ● http://www.madison.k12.ky.us

Grade Span: KG-12 **Schools**: *Regular* 16 ● *Spec Ed* 0 ● *Alt* 1 **Students**: 8,544 **Total Teachers**: 511 **Student/Classroom Teacher Ratio**: 18.3	**Expenditures/Student**: $4,742 **Librarians**: 14.7 581 students/librarian **Guidance Counselors**: 17.8 480 students/counselor	**% Amer Indian**: 0.1 **% Asian**: 0.4 **% Black**: 5.8 **% Hispanic**: 0.4 **% White**: 93.4	National ***Socio-Economic Status*** indicator percentiles are not available for the state of Kentucky

Magoffin County

[SALYERSVILLE] **MAGOFFIN COUNTY S.D.**

PO BOX 109 ● SALYERSVILLE KY 41465 ● (606) 349-6117

Grade Span: KG-12 **Schools**: *Regular* 9 ● *Spec Ed* 0 ● *Alt* 0 **Students**: 2,841 **Total Teachers**: 201 **Student/Classroom Teacher Ratio**: 13.3	**Expenditures/Student**: $5,171 **Librarians**: 6.0 474 students/librarian **Guidance Counselors**: 4.0 710 students/counselor	**% Amer Indian**: 0.0 **% Asian**: 0.0 **% Black**: 0.0 **% Hispanic**: 0.0 **% White**: 100.0	National ***Socio-Economic Status*** indicator percentiles are not available for the state of Kentucky

Marion County

[LEBANON] MARION COUNTY S.D.

223 N SPALDING ● LEBANON KY 40033 ● (502) 692-3721

Grade Span: KG-12 **Schools**: *Regular* 7 ● *Spec Ed* 0 ● *Alt* 0 **Students**: 2,891 **Total Teachers**: 193 **Student/Classroom Teacher Ratio**: 15.1	**Expenditures/Student**: $5,330 **Librarians**: 6.3 459 students/librarian **Guidance Counselors**: 7.0 413 students/counselor	**% Amer Indian**: 0.0 **% Asian**: 0.2 **% Black**: 8.6 **% Hispanic**: 0.1 **% White**: 91.1	National ***Socio-Economic Status*** indicator percentiles are not available for the state of Kentucky

Marshall County

[BENTON] MARSHALL COUNTY S.D.

86 HIGH SCHOOL RD ● BENTON KY 42025 ● (502) 527-8628 ● http://www.marshall.k12.ky.us

Grade Span: KG-12 **Schools**: *Regular* 10 ● *Spec Ed* 0 ● *Alt* 1 **Students**: 5,155 **Total Teachers**: 282 **Student/Classroom Teacher Ratio**: 16.4	**Expenditures/Student**: $3,958 **Librarians**: 8.5 606 students/librarian **Guidance Counselors**: 11.5 448 students/counselor	**% Amer Indian**: 0.0 **% Asian**: 0.2 **% Black**: 0.0 **% Hispanic**: 0.2 **% White**: 99.6	National ***Socio-Economic Status*** indicator percentiles are not available for the state of Kentucky

Martin County

[INEZ] MARTIN COUNTY S.D.

PO BOX 366 ● INEZ KY 41224 ● (606) 298-3572 ● http://www.martin.k12.ky.us

Grade Span: KG-12 **Schools**: *Regular* 11 ● *Spec Ed* 0 ● *Alt* 0 **Students**: 2,891 **Total Teachers**: 186 **Student/Classroom Teacher Ratio**: 13.7	**Expenditures/Student**: $5,034 **Librarians**: 4.9 590 students/librarian **Guidance Counselors**: 4.6 628 students/counselor	**% Amer Indian**: 0.0 **% Asian**: 0.0 **% Black**: 0.2 **% Hispanic**: 0.0 **% White**: 99.8	National ***Socio-Economic Status*** indicator percentiles are not available for the state of Kentucky

Mason County

[MAYSVILLE] MASON COUNTY S.D.

PO BOX 99 ● MAYSVILLE KY 41056 ● (606) 564-5563 ● http://www.mason.k12.ky.us

Grade Span: KG-12 **Schools**: *Regular* 5 ● *Spec Ed* 0 ● *Alt* 0 **Students**: 2,813 **Total Teachers**: 185 **Student/Classroom Teacher Ratio**: 13.3	**Expenditures/Student**: $4,354 **Librarians**: 4.0 703 students/librarian **Guidance Counselors**: 4.0 703 students/counselor	**% Amer Indian**: 0.0 **% Asian**: 0.2 **% Black**: 12.1 **% Hispanic**: 0.2 **% White**: 87.5	National ***Socio-Economic Status*** indicator percentiles are not available for the state of Kentucky

Meade County

[BRANDENBURG] MEADE COUNTY S.D.

PO BOX 337 ● BRANDENBURG KY 40108 ● (502) 422-3366

Grade Span: KG-12 **Schools**: *Regular* 9 ● *Spec Ed* 0 ● *Alt* 0 **Students**: 4,330 **Total Teachers**: 242 **Student/Classroom Teacher Ratio**: 16.7	**Expenditures/Student**: $3,968 **Librarians**: 6.0 722 students/librarian **Guidance Counselors**: 8.0 541 students/counselor	**% Amer Indian**: 0.5 **% Asian**: 0.7 **% Black**: 3.5 **% Hispanic**: 0.8 **% White**: 94.4	National ***Socio-Economic Status*** indicator percentiles are not available for the state of Kentucky

Montgomery County

[MOUNT STERLING] MONTGOMERY COUNTY S.D.

640 WOODFORD ● MOUNT STERLING KY 40353 ● (606) 498-8760 ● http://www.montgomery.k12.ky.us

Grade Span: KG-12 **Schools**: *Regular* 6 ● *Spec Ed* 0 ● *Alt* 0 **Students**: 3,648 **Total Teachers**: 234 **Student/Classroom Teacher Ratio**: 14.4	**Expenditures/Student**: $5,225 **Librarians**: 5.3 688 students/librarian **Guidance Counselors**: 8.5 429 students/counselor	**% Amer Indian**: 0.0 **% Asian**: 0.2 **% Black**: 4.5 **% Hispanic**: 0.4 **% White**: 94.9	National ***Socio-Economic Status*** indicator percentiles are not available for the state of Kentucky

Muhlenberg County

[GREENVILLE] MUHLENBERG COUNTY S.D.

BOX 167 ● GREENVILLE KY 42345 ● (502) 338-2871

Grade Span: KG-12 **Schools**: *Regular* 13 ● *Spec Ed* 0 ● *Alt* 0 **Students**: 5,481 **Total Teachers**: 378 **Student/Classroom Teacher Ratio**: 13.1	**Expenditures/Student**: $4,497 **Librarians**: 13.5 406 students/librarian **Guidance Counselors**: 10.5 522 students/counselor	**% Amer Indian**: 0.0 **% Asian**: 0.2 **% Black**: 4.7 **% Hispanic**: 0.1 **% White**: 95.0	National ***Socio-Economic Status*** indicator percentiles are not available for the state of Kentucky

Nelson County

[BARDSTOWN] NELSON COUNTY S.D.

1200 CARDINAL ● BARDSTOWN KY 40004 ● (502) 349-7000

Grade Span: KG-12 **Schools**: *Regular* 11 ● *Spec Ed* 0 ● *Alt* 0 **Students**: 4,306 **Total Teachers**: 247 **Student/Classroom Teacher Ratio**: 16.2	**Expenditures/Student**: $4,374 **Librarians**: 8.4 513 students/librarian **Guidance Counselors**: 7.6 567 students/counselor	**% Amer Indian**: 0.0 **% Asian**: 0.2 **% Black**: 2.6 **% Hispanic**: 0.3 **% White**: 97.0	National ***Socio-Economic Status*** indicator percentiles are not available for the state of Kentucky

Ohio County

[HARTFORD] OHIO COUNTY S.D.

P O BOX 70 ● HARTFORD KY 42347 ● (502) 298-3249

Grade Span: KG-12 **Schools**: *Regular* 8 ● *Spec Ed* 0 ● *Alt* 0 **Students**: 4,101 **Total Teachers**: 245 **Student/Classroom Teacher Ratio**: 16.1	**Expenditures/Student**: $4,509 **Librarians**: 6.0 684 students/librarian **Guidance Counselors**: 4.0 1,025 students/counselor	**% Amer Indian**: 0.0 **% Asian**: 0.2 **% Black**: 1.1 **% Hispanic**: 0.2 **% White**: 98.5	National ***Socio-Economic Status*** indicator percentiles are not available for the state of Kentucky

Oldham County

[BUCKNER] OLDHAM COUNTY S.D.

PO BOX 218 ● BUCKNER KY 40010 ● (502) 222-8880 ● http://www.oldham.k12.ky.us

Grade Span: KG-12 **Schools**: *Regular* 12 ● *Spec Ed* 0 ● *Alt* 0 **Students**: 7,418 **Total Teachers**: 429 **Student/Classroom Teacher Ratio**: 16.9	**Expenditures/Student**: $4,081 **Librarians**: 13.0 571 students/librarian **Guidance Counselors**: 16.6 447 students/counselor	**% Amer Indian**: 0.2 **% Asian**: 0.3 **% Black**: 2.6 **% Hispanic**: 0.4 **% White**: 96.6	National ***Socio-Economic Status*** indicator percentiles are not available for the state of Kentucky

Pendleton County

[FALMOUTH] PENDLETON COUNTY S.D.

RT 5 ● FALMOUTH KY 41040 ● (606) 654-6911 ● http://www.pendleton.k12.ky.us

Grade Span: KG-12 **Schools**: *Regular* 4 ● *Spec Ed* 0 ● *Alt* 0 **Students**: 2,709 **Total Teachers**: 149 **Student/Classroom Teacher Ratio**: 18.2	**Expenditures/Student**: $4,829 **Librarians**: 4.0 677 students/librarian **Guidance Counselors**: 5.0 542 students/counselor	**% Amer Indian**: 0.0 **% Asian**: 0.1 **% Black**: 0.5 **% Hispanic**: 0.3 **% White**: 99.1	National ***Socio-Economic Status*** indicator percentiles are not available for the state of Kentucky

Perry County

[HAZARD] PERRY COUNTY S.D.

315 PARK AVE ● HAZARD KY 41701 ● (606) 439-5814 ● http://www.perry.k12.ky.us

Grade Span: KG-12 **Schools**: *Regular* 14 ● *Spec Ed* 0 ● *Alt* 0 **Students**: 5,252 **Total Teachers**: 347 **Student/Classroom Teacher Ratio**: 14.1	**Expenditures/Student**: $5,291 **Librarians**: 12.3 427 students/librarian **Guidance Counselors**: 11.0 477 students/counselor	**% Amer Indian**: 0.0 **% Asian**: 0.1 **% Black**: 0.6 **% Hispanic**: 0.2 **% White**: 99.2	National ***Socio-Economic Status*** indicator percentiles are not available for the state of Kentucky

Pike County

[PIKEVILLE] **PIKE COUNTY S.D.**

BOX 3097 ● PIKEVILLE KY 41501 ● (606) 432-7700 ● http://pike.k12.ky.us

Grade Span: KG-12	**Expenditures/Student**: $5,232	**% Amer Indian**: 0.0	National ***Socio-Economic***
Schools: *Regular* 32 ● *Spec Ed* 0 ● *Alt* 0	**Librarians**: 26.5	**% Asian**: 0.1	***Status*** indicator percentiles
Students: 12,029	454 students/librarian	**% Black**: 0.2	are not available for the
Total Teachers: 794	**Guidance Counselors**: 16.3	**% Hispanic**: 0.0	state of Kentucky
Student/Classroom Teacher Ratio: 14.8	738 students/counselor	**% White**: 99.7	

Powell County

[STANTON] **POWELL COUNTY S.D.**

P O BOX 430 ● STANTON KY 40380 ● (606) 663-3300 ● http://www.powell.k12.ky.us

Grade Span: KG-12	**Expenditures/Student**: $4,904	**% Amer Indian**: 0.0	National ***Socio-Economic***
Schools: *Regular* 5 ● *Spec Ed* 0 ● *Alt* 0	**Librarians**: 10.0	**% Asian**: 0.2	***Status*** indicator percentiles
Students: 2,664	266 students/librarian	**% Black**: 0.9	are not available for the
Total Teachers: 156	**Guidance Counselors**: 6.0	**% Hispanic**: 0.3	state of Kentucky
Student/Classroom Teacher Ratio: 16.8	444 students/counselor	**% White**: 98.6	

Pulaski County

[SOMERSET] **PULASKI COUNTY S.D.**

P O BOX P ● SOMERSET KY 42502 ● (606) 679-1123 ● http://www.pulaski.k12.ky.us

Grade Span: KG-12	**Expenditures/Student**: $4,017	**% Amer Indian**: 0.0	National ***Socio-Economic***
Schools: *Regular* 13 ● *Spec Ed* 0 ● *Alt* 0	**Librarians**: 11.4	**% Asian**: 0.2	***Status*** indicator percentiles
Students: 7,151	627 students/librarian	**% Black**: 0.6	are not available for the
Total Teachers: 439	**Guidance Counselors**: 14.2	**% Hispanic**: 0.1	state of Kentucky
Student/Classroom Teacher Ratio: 15.7	504 students/counselor	**% White**: 99.1	

Rockcastle County

[MOUNT VERNON] **ROCKCASTLE COUNTY S.D.**

245 RICHMOND ST ● MOUNT VERNON KY 40456 ● (606) 256-2125

Grade Span: KG-12	**Expenditures/Student**: $5,207	**% Amer Indian**: 0.0	National ***Socio-Economic***
Schools: *Regular* 5 ● *Spec Ed* 0 ● *Alt* 0	**Librarians**: 5.0	**% Asian**: 0.2	***Status*** indicator percentiles
Students: 2,987	597 students/librarian	**% Black**: 0.3	are not available for the
Total Teachers: 184	**Guidance Counselors**: 5.5	**% Hispanic**: 0.0	state of Kentucky
Student/Classroom Teacher Ratio: 16.4	543 students/counselor	**% White**: 99.5	

Rowan County

[MOREHEAD] **ROWAN COUNTY S.D.**

121 E SECOND ST ● MOREHEAD KY 40351 ● (606) 784-8928

Grade Span: KG-12	**Expenditures/Student**: $5,139	**% Amer Indian**: 0.2	National ***Socio-Economic***
Schools: *Regular* 7 ● *Spec Ed* 0 ● *Alt* 1	**Librarians**: 6.0	**% Asian**: 0.2	***Status*** indicator percentiles
Students: 3,153	526 students/librarian	**% Black**: 0.7	are not available for the
Total Teachers: 200	**Guidance Counselors**: 6.5	**% Hispanic**: 0.2	state of Kentucky
Student/Classroom Teacher Ratio: 15.7	485 students/counselor	**% White**: 98.7	

Russell County

[JAMESTOWN] **RUSSELL COUNTY S.D.**

P O BOX 260 ● JAMESTOWN KY 42629 ● (502) 343-3191 ● http://www.blue.net/~goose/board.htm

Grade Span: KG-12	**Expenditures/Student**: $5,231	**% Amer Indian**: 0.0	National ***Socio-Economic***
Schools: *Regular* 7 ● *Spec Ed* 0 ● *Alt* 0	**Librarians**: 4.0	**% Asian**: 0.1	***Status*** indicator percentiles
Students: 2,789	697 students/librarian	**% Black**: 0.5	are not available for the
Total Teachers: 188	**Guidance Counselors**: 6.0	**% Hispanic**: 0.4	state of Kentucky
Student/Classroom Teacher Ratio: 13.3	465 students/counselor	**% White**: 99.0	

Scott County

[GEORGETOWN] **SCOTT COUNTY S.D.**

BOX 561 ● GEORGETOWN KY 40324 ● (502) 863-3663 ● http://www.scott.k12.ky.us

Grade Span: KG-12 **Schools**: *Regular* 10 ● *Spec Ed* 0 ● *Alt* 0 **Students**: 5,100 **Total Teachers**: 309 **Student/Classroom Teacher Ratio**: 15.5	**Expenditures/Student**: $4,944 **Librarians**: 11.0 464 students/librarian **Guidance Counselors**: 12.0 425 students/counselor	**% Amer Indian**: 0.0 **% Asian**: 0.3 **% Black**: 6.7 **% Hispanic**: 0.3 **% White**: 92.6	National ***Socio-Economic Status*** indicator percentiles are not available for the state of Kentucky

Shelby County

[SHELBYVILLE] **SHELBY COUNTY S.D.**

BOX 159 ● SHELBYVILLE KY 40065 ● (502) 633-2375 ● http://www.shelby.k12.ky.us

Grade Span: KG-12 **Schools**: *Regular* 9 ● *Spec Ed* 0 ● *Alt* 1 **Students**: 4,617 **Total Teachers**: 268 **Student/Classroom Teacher Ratio**: 17.4	**Expenditures/Student**: $4,481 **Librarians**: 9.0 513 students/librarian **Guidance Counselors**: 11.5 401 students/counselor	**% Amer Indian**: 0.2 **% Asian**: 0.6 **% Black**: 11.1 **% Hispanic**: 0.8 **% White**: 87.4	National ***Socio-Economic Status*** indicator percentiles are not available for the state of Kentucky

Simpson County

[FRANKLIN] **SIMPSON COUNTY S.D.**

BOX 467 ● FRANKLIN KY 42135 ● (502) 586-8877

Grade Span: KG-12 **Schools**: *Regular* 5 ● *Spec Ed* 0 ● *Alt* 0 **Students**: 2,947 **Total Teachers**: 174 **Student/Classroom Teacher Ratio**: 17.3	**Expenditures/Student**: $6,077 **Librarians**: 5.5 536 students/librarian **Guidance Counselors**: 6.0 491 students/counselor	**% Amer Indian**: 0.1 **% Asian**: 0.2 **% Black**: 13.6 **% Hispanic**: 0.3 **% White**: 85.7	National ***Socio-Economic Status*** indicator percentiles are not available for the state of Kentucky

Taylor County

[CAMPBELLSVILLE] **TAYLOR COUNTY S.D.**

1209 E BRDWY ● CAMPBELLSVILLE KY 42718 ● (502) 465-5371

Grade Span: KG-12 **Schools**: *Regular* 4 ● *Spec Ed* 0 ● *Alt* 0 **Students**: 2,556 **Total Teachers**: 162 **Student/Classroom Teacher Ratio**: 15.1	**Expenditures/Student**: $4,437 **Librarians**: 3.5 730 students/librarian **Guidance Counselors**: 4.0 639 students/counselor	**% Amer Indian**: 0.0 **% Asian**: 0.2 **% Black**: 2.0 **% Hispanic**: 0.3 **% White**: 97.6	National ***Socio-Economic Status*** indicator percentiles are not available for the state of Kentucky

Union County

[MORGANFIELD] **UNION COUNTY S.D.**

510 S MART ● MORGANFIELD KY 42437 ● (502) 389-1694 ● http://www.union.k12.ky.us

Grade Span: KG-12 **Schools**: *Regular* 5 ● *Spec Ed* 0 ● *Alt* 0 **Students**: 2,807 **Total Teachers**: 187 **Student/Classroom Teacher Ratio**: 14.8	**Expenditures/Student**: $5,260 **Librarians**: 5.0 561 students/librarian **Guidance Counselors**: 9.0 312 students/counselor	**% Amer Indian**: 0.0 **% Asian**: 0.2 **% Black**: 10.2 **% Hispanic**: 0.5 **% White**: 89.1	National ***Socio-Economic Status*** indicator percentiles are not available for the state of Kentucky

Warren County

BOWLING GREEN INDEPENDENT S.D.

1211 CENTER ST ● BOWLING GREEN KY 42101 ● (502) 781-2254 ● http://www.b-g.k12.ky.us

Grade Span: KG-12 **Schools**: *Regular* 9 ● *Spec Ed* 0 ● *Alt* 0 **Students**: 3,367 **Total Teachers**: 213 **Student/Classroom Teacher Ratio**: 15.0	**Expenditures/Student**: $5,193 **Librarians**: 8.0 421 students/librarian **Guidance Counselors**: 7.5 449 students/counselor	**% Amer Indian**: 0.1 **% Asian**: 2.9 **% Black**: 22.9 **% Hispanic**: 1.8 **% White**: 72.3	National ***Socio-Economic Status*** indicator percentiles are not available for the state of Kentucky

Warren County

[BOWLING GREEN] **WARREN COUNTY S.D.**

806 KENTON ● BOWLING GREEN KY 42101 ● (502) 781-5150 ● http://www.warren.k12.ky.us

Grade Span: KG-12 **Schools**: *Regular* 17 ● *Spec Ed* 0 ● *Alt* 4 **Students**: 10,377 **Total Teachers**: 601 **Student/Classroom Teacher Ratio**: 17.5	**Expenditures/Student**: $4,195 **Librarians**: 18.5 561 students/librarian **Guidance Counselors**: 21.0 494 students/counselor	**% Amer Indian**: 0.2 **% Asian**: 1.1 **% Black**: 7.0 **% Hispanic**: 0.5 **% White**: 91.2	National ***Socio-Economic Status*** indicator percentiles are not available for the state of Kentucky

Wayne County

[MONTICELLO] **WAYNE COUNTY S.D.**

BOX 437 ● MONTICELLO KY 42633 ● (606) 348-8484

Grade Span: KG-12 **Schools**: *Regular* 6 ● *Spec Ed* 0 ● *Alt* 3 **Students**: 2,795 **Total Teachers**: 190 **Student/Classroom Teacher Ratio**: 16.0	**Expenditures/Student**: $5,601 **Librarians**: 5.0 559 students/librarian **Guidance Counselors**: 6.0 466 students/counselor	**% Amer Indian**: 0.2 **% Asian**: 0.1 **% Black**: 1.3 **% Hispanic**: 0.4 **% White**: 98.0	National ***Socio-Economic Status*** indicator percentiles are not available for the state of Kentucky

Whitley County

[WILLIAMSBURG] **WHITLEY COUNTY S.D.**

116 N 4TH ● WILLIAMSBURG KY 40769 ● (606) 549-7000 ● http://whitley.k12.ky.us

Grade Span: KG-12 **Schools**: *Regular* 11 ● *Spec Ed* 0 ● *Alt* 0 **Students**: 4,328 **Total Teachers**: 260 **Student/Classroom Teacher Ratio**: 16.0	**Expenditures/Student**: $5,331 **Librarians**: 10.0 433 students/librarian **Guidance Counselors**: 3.0 1,443 students/counselor	**% Amer Indian**: 0.0 **% Asian**: 0.1 **% Black**: 0.0 **% Hispanic**: 0.1 **% White**: 99.8	National ***Socio-Economic Status*** indicator percentiles are not available for the state of Kentucky

Woodford County

[VERSAILLES] **WOODFORD COUNTY S.D.**

131 MAPLE ST ● VERSAILLES KY 40383 ● (606) 873-4701 ● http://www.woodford.k12.ky.us

Grade Span: KG-12 **Schools**: *Regular* 6 ● *Spec Ed* 0 ● *Alt* 0 **Students**: 3,839 **Total Teachers**: 209 **Student/Classroom Teacher Ratio**: 17.9	**Expenditures/Student**: $4,281 **Librarians**: 7.0 548 students/librarian **Guidance Counselors**: 7.8 492 students/counselor	**% Amer Indian**: 0.1 **% Asian**: 0.3 **% Black**: 6.7 **% Hispanic**: 1.0 **% White**: 91.9	National ***Socio-Economic Status*** indicator percentiles are not available for the state of Kentucky

Acadia Parish

[CROWLEY] **ACADIA PARISH S.D.**

PO DRAWER 3099 ● CROWLEY LA 70527-0309 ● (318) 783-3664

Grade Span: PK-12	**Expenditures/Student**: $3,636	**% Amer Indian**: 0.1	
Schools: *Regular* 25 ● *Spec Ed* 0 ● *Alt* 0	**Librarians**: 20.0	**% Asian**: 0.1	National ***Socio-Economic***
Students: 10,955	548 students/librarian	**% Black**: 28.4	***Status*** indicator percentile
Total Teachers: 642	**Guidance Counselors**: 28.1	**% Hispanic**: 0.3	(100=high): 13th
Student/Classroom Teacher Ratio: 18.2	390 students/counselor	**% White**: 71.2	

Allen Parish

[OBERLIN] **ALLEN PARISH S.D.**

PO DRAWER C ● OBERLIN LA 70655 ● (318) 639-2904

Grade Span: PK-12	**Expenditures/Student**: $4,193	**% Amer Indian**: 0.2	
Schools: *Regular* 10 ● *Spec Ed* 0 ● *Alt* 0	**Librarians**: 10.0	**% Asian**: 0.1	National ***Socio-Economic***
Students: 4,551	455 students/librarian	**% Black**: 24.3	***Status*** indicator percentile
Total Teachers: 295	**Guidance Counselors**: 13.0	**% Hispanic**: 0.7	(100=high): 20th
Student/Classroom Teacher Ratio: 16.1	350 students/counselor	**% White**: 74.7	

Ascension Parish

[DONALDSONVILLE] **ASCENSION PARISH S.D.**

PO BOX 189 ● DONALDSONVILLE LA 70346 ● (504) 473-7981

Grade Span: PK-12	**Expenditures/Student**: $4,425	**% Amer Indian**: 0.1	
Schools: *Regular* 15 ● *Spec Ed* 0 ● *Alt* 3	**Librarians**: 19.0	**% Asian**: 0.4	National ***Socio-Economic***
Students: 14,394	758 students/librarian	**% Black**: 34.6	***Status*** indicator percentile
Total Teachers: 866	**Guidance Counselors**: 73.9	**% Hispanic**: 0.7	(100=high): 28th
Student/Classroom Teacher Ratio: 16.4	195 students/counselor	**% White**: 64.3	

Assumption Parish

[NAPOLEONVILLE] **ASSUMPTION PARISH S.D.**

PO DRAWER B ● NAPOLEONVILLE LA 70390 ● (504) 369-7252 ● http://www.assumption.k12.la.us

Grade Span: PK-12	**Expenditures/Student**: $4,354	**% Amer Indian**: 0.0	
Schools: *Regular* 11 ● *Spec Ed* 0 ● *Alt* 1	**Librarians**: 2.0	**% Asian**: 0.6	National ***Socio-Economic***
Students: 5,008	2,504 students/librarian	**% Black**: 44.0	***Status*** indicator percentile
Total Teachers: 309	**Guidance Counselors**: 9.0	**% Hispanic**: 0.2	(100=high): 10th
Student/Classroom Teacher Ratio: 16.1	556 students/counselor	**% White**: 55.1	

Avoyelles Parish

[MARKSVILLE] **AVOYELLES PARISH S.D.**

201 TUNICA DRIVE WEST ● MARKSVILLE LA 71351 ● (318) 253-5982

Grade Span: PK-12	**Expenditures/Student**: $3,786	**% Amer Indian**: 0.2	
Schools: *Regular* 12 ● *Spec Ed* 0 ● *Alt* 0	**Librarians**: 12.0	**% Asian**: 0.2	National ***Socio-Economic***
Students: 7,669	639 students/librarian	**% Black**: 39.9	***Status*** indicator percentile
Total Teachers: 422	**Guidance Counselors**: 15.0	**% Hispanic**: 0.4	(100=high): 6th
Student/Classroom Teacher Ratio: 18.7	511 students/counselor	**% White**: 59.2	

Beauregard Parish

[DERIDDER] **BEAUREGARD PARISH S.D.**

PO DRAWER 938 ● DERIDDER LA 70634 ● (318) 463-5551

Grade Span: PK-12	**Expenditures/Student**: $4,310	**% Amer Indian**: 0.2	
Schools: *Regular* 11 ● *Spec Ed* 0 ● *Alt* 0	**Librarians**: 11.0	**% Asian**: 0.4	National ***Socio-Economic***
Students: 6,546	595 students/librarian	**% Black**: 17.0	***Status*** indicator percentile
Total Teachers: 404	**Guidance Counselors**: 23.0	**% Hispanic**: 0.7	(100=high): 36th
Student/Classroom Teacher Ratio: 16.2	285 students/counselor	**% White**: 81.8	

Bienville Parish

[ARCADIA] **BIENVILLE PARISH S.D.**

PO BOX 418 ● ARCADIA LA 71001 ● (318) 263-9416

Grade Span: PK-12 **Schools**: *Regular* 8 ● *Spec Ed* 1 ● *Alt* 0 **Students**: 3,037 **Total Teachers**: 194 **Student/Classroom Teacher Ratio**: 16.3	**Expenditures/Student**: $4,531 **Librarians**: 4.0 759 students/librarian **Guidance Counselors**: 9.0 337 students/counselor	**% Amer Indian**: 0.1 **% Asian**: 0.0 **% Black**: 60.6 **% Hispanic**: 0.0 **% White**: 39.3	National ***Socio-Economic Status*** indicator percentile (100=high): 5th

Bossier Parish

[BENTON] **BOSSIER PARISH S.D.**

PO BOX 2000 ● BENTON LA 71006 ● (318) 965-2281 ● http://www.shreveport.net/edu

Grade Span: PK-12 **Schools**: *Regular* 27 ● *Spec Ed* 0 ● *Alt* 3 **Students**: 18,741 **Total Teachers**: 1,037 **Student/Classroom Teacher Ratio**: 18.4	**Expenditures/Student**: $4,449 **Librarians**: 29.0 646 students/librarian **Guidance Counselors**: 58.0 323 students/counselor	**% Amer Indian**: 0.2 **% Asian**: 1.2 **% Black**: 28.9 **% Hispanic**: 1.6 **% White**: 68.1	National ***Socio-Economic Status*** indicator percentile (100=high): 37th

Caddo Parish

[SHREVEPORT] **CADDO PARISH S.D.**

PO BOX 32000 ● SHREVEPORT LA 71130-2000 ● (318) 636-0210

Grade Span: PK-12 **Schools**: *Regular* 63 ● *Spec Ed* 2 ● *Alt* 9 **Students**: 49,578 **Total Teachers**: 2,910 **Student/Classroom Teacher Ratio**: 16.9	**Expenditures/Student**: $4,393 **Librarians**: 79.0 628 students/librarian **Guidance Counselors**: 236.5 210 students/counselor	**% Amer Indian**: 0.1 **% Asian**: 0.4 **% Black**: 63.4 **% Hispanic**: 0.5 **% White**: 35.7	National ***Socio-Economic Status*** indicator percentile (100=high): 13th

Calcasieu Parish

[LAKE CHARLES] **CALCASIEU PARISH S.D.**

PO BOX 800 ● LAKE CHARLES LA 70602 ● (318) 491-1645 ● http://hal.calc.k12.la.us

Grade Span: PK-12 **Schools**: *Regular* 57 ● *Spec Ed* 1 ● *Alt* 1 **Students**: 34,163 **Total Teachers**: 2,070 **Student/Classroom Teacher Ratio**: 16.5	**Expenditures/Student**: $4,081 **Librarians**: 63.0 542 students/librarian **Guidance Counselors**: 139.1 246 students/counselor	**% Amer Indian**: 0.1 **% Asian**: 0.4 **% Black**: 31.0 **% Hispanic**: 0.3 **% White**: 68.1	National ***Socio-Economic Status*** indicator percentile (100=high): 32nd

Claiborne Parish

[HOMER] **CLAIBORNE PARISH S.D.**

PO BOX 600 ● HOMER LA 71040 ● (318) 927-3502

Grade Span: PK-12 **Schools**: *Regular* 9 ● *Spec Ed* 0 ● *Alt* 0 **Students**: 3,029 **Total Teachers**: 205 **Student/Classroom Teacher Ratio**: 15.4	**Expenditures/Student**: $4,325 **Librarians**: 2.0 1,515 students/librarian **Guidance Counselors**: 8.4 361 students/counselor	**% Amer Indian**: 0.3 **% Asian**: 0.2 **% Black**: 63.5 **% Hispanic**: 0.1 **% White**: 35.9	National ***Socio-Economic Status*** indicator percentile (100=high): 9th

Concordia Parish

[VIDALIA] **CONCORDIA PARISH S.D.**

PO BOX 950 ● VIDALIA LA 71373 ● (318) 336-4226

Grade Span: PK-12 **Schools**: *Regular* 11 ● *Spec Ed* 0 ● *Alt* 0 **Students**: 4,442 **Total Teachers**: 277 **Student/Classroom Teacher Ratio**: 16.8	**Expenditures/Student**: $4,445 **Librarians**: 9.0 494 students/librarian **Guidance Counselors**: 10.0 444 students/counselor	**% Amer Indian**: 0.0 **% Asian**: 0.0 **% Black**: 50.7 **% Hispanic**: 0.2 **% White**: 49.1	National ***Socio-Economic Status*** indicator percentile (100=high): 8th

De Soto Parish

[MANSFIELD] **DESOTO PARISH S.D.**

PO BOX 631 ● MANSFIELD LA 71052 ● (318) 872-2836 ● http://www.desoto.k12.la.us

Grade Span: PK-12 **Schools**: *Regular* 8 ● *Spec Ed* 1 ● *Alt* 0 **Students**: 5,434 **Total Teachers**: 346 **Student/Classroom Teacher Ratio**: 16.0	**Expenditures/Student**: $4,485 **Librarians**: 11.0 494 students/librarian **Guidance Counselors**: 11.0 494 students/counselor	**% Amer Indian**: 0.0 **% Asian**: 0.1 **% Black**: 55.4 **% Hispanic**: 0.7 **% White**: 43.8	National ***Socio-Economic Status*** indicator percentile (100=high): 36th

East Baton Rouge Parish

[BATON ROUGE] **EAST BATON ROUGE PARISH S.D.**

PO BOX 2950 ● BATON ROUGE LA 70821 ● (504) 922-5400 ● http://isis.ebrps.subr.edu

Grade Span: PK-12 **Schools**: *Regular* 95 ● *Spec Ed* 3 ● *Alt* 7 **Students**: 60,761 **Total Teachers**: 3,693 **Student/Classroom Teacher Ratio**: 16.2	**Expenditures/Student**: $4,776 **Librarians**: 107.0 568 students/librarian **Guidance Counselors**: 269.0 226 students/counselor	**% Amer Indian**: 0.0 **% Asian**: 2.0 **% Black**: 61.6 **% Hispanic**: 0.4 **% White**: 35.9	National ***Socio-Economic Status*** indicator percentile (100=high): 18th

East Feliciana Parish

[CLINTON] **EAST FELICIANA PARISH S.D.**

PO BOX 397 ● CLINTON LA 70722 ● (504) 683-8277

Grade Span: PK-12 **Schools**: *Regular* 5 ● *Spec Ed* 0 ● *Alt* 0 **Students**: 3,066 **Total Teachers**: 196 **Student/Classroom Teacher Ratio**: 16.7	**Expenditures/Student**: $3,845 **Librarians**: 4.0 767 students/librarian **Guidance Counselors**: 9.0 341 students/counselor	**% Amer Indian**: 0.0 **% Asian**: 0.1 **% Black**: 75.2 **% Hispanic**: 0.1 **% White**: 24.6	National ***Socio-Economic Status*** indicator percentile (100=high): 4th

Evangeline Parish

[VILLE PLATTE] **EVANGELINE PARISH S.D.**

1101 TE MAMOU ROAD ● VILLE PLATTE LA 70586 ● (318) 363-6651

Grade Span: PK-12 **Schools**: *Regular* 14 ● *Spec Ed* 0 ● *Alt* 1 **Students**: 7,122 **Total Teachers**: 449 **Student/Classroom Teacher Ratio**: 16.3	**Expenditures/Student**: $3,967 **Librarians**: 11.0 647 students/librarian **Guidance Counselors**: 24.0 297 students/counselor	**% Amer Indian**: 0.1 **% Asian**: 0.1 **% Black**: 38.8 **% Hispanic**: 0.0 **% White**: 60.9	National ***Socio-Economic Status*** indicator percentile (100=high): 7th

Franklin Parish

[WINNSBORO] **FRANKLIN PARISH S.D.**

1809 PRAIRIE ROAD ● WINNSBORO LA 71295 ● (318) 435-9046 ● http://cust.iamerica.net/tleonard

Grade Span: PK-12 **Schools**: *Regular* 12 ● *Spec Ed* 0 ● *Alt* 0 **Students**: 4,688 **Total Teachers**: 308 **Student/Classroom Teacher Ratio**: 15.3	**Expenditures/Student**: $4,172 **Librarians**: 3.0 1,563 students/librarian **Guidance Counselors**: 2.7 1,736 students/counselor	**% Amer Indian**: 0.0 **% Asian**: 0.0 **% Black**: 44.9 **% Hispanic**: 0.2 **% White**: 54.8	National ***Socio-Economic Status*** indicator percentile (100=high): 8th

Grant Parish

[COLFAX] **GRANT PARISH S.D.**

PO BOX 208 ● COLFAX LA 71417-0208 ● (318) 627-3274

Grade Span: PK-12 **Schools**: *Regular* 9 ● *Spec Ed* 0 ● *Alt* 0 **Students**: 3,691 **Total Teachers**: 230 **Student/Classroom Teacher Ratio**: 15.8	**Expenditures/Student**: $3,847 **Librarians**: 3.0 1,230 students/librarian **Guidance Counselors**: 7.0 527 students/counselor	**% Amer Indian**: 0.2 **% Asian**: 0.0 **% Black**: 17.7 **% Hispanic**: 0.1 **% White**: 81.8	National ***Socio-Economic Status*** indicator percentile (100=high): 16th

Iberia Parish

[NEW IBERIA] IBERIA PARISH S.D.

200 SCHOOL BOARD DRIVE ● NEW IBERIA LA 70560 ● (318) 365-2341

Grade Span: PK-12 **Schools**: *Regular* 31 ● *Spec Ed* 1 ● *Alt* 1 **Students**: 15,763 **Total Teachers**: 989 **Student/Classroom Teacher Ratio**: 17.1	**Expenditures/Student**: $4,154 **Librarians**: 25.0 631 students/librarian **Guidance Counselors**: 59.3 266 students/counselor	**% Amer Indian**: 0.1 **% Asian**: 3.1 **% Black**: 39.3 **% Hispanic**: 0.4 **% White**: 57.1	National ***Socio-Economic Status*** indicator percentile (100=high): 13th

Iberville Parish

[PLAQUEMINE] IBERVILLE PARISH S.D.

PO BOX 151 ● PLAQUEMINE LA 70764-0151 ● (504) 687-4341 ● http://www.ipsb.net

Grade Span: PK-12 **Schools**: *Regular* 8 ● *Spec Ed* 0 ● *Alt* 0 **Students**: 5,453 **Total Teachers**: 341 **Student/Classroom Teacher Ratio**: 16.0	**Expenditures/Student**: $5,279 **Librarians**: 8.0 682 students/librarian **Guidance Counselors**: 15.0 364 students/counselor	**% Amer Indian**: 0.0 **% Asian**: 0.1 **% Black**: 71.1 **% Hispanic**: 0.2 **% White**: 28.6	National ***Socio-Economic Status*** indicator percentile (100=high): 5th

Jackson Parish

[JONESBORO] JACKSON PARISH S.D.

PO BOX 705 ● JONESBORO LA 71251 ● (318) 259-4456

Grade Span: PK-12 **Schools**: *Regular* 9 ● *Spec Ed* 0 ● *Alt* 0 **Students**: 2,956 **Total Teachers**: 210 **Student/Classroom Teacher Ratio**: 14.3	**Expenditures/Student**: $4,262 **Librarians**: 0.0 *** students/librarian **Guidance Counselors**: 6.0 493 students/counselor	**% Amer Indian**: 0.0 **% Asian**: 0.0 **% Black**: 35.7 **% Hispanic**: 0.1 **% White**: 64.2	National ***Socio-Economic Status*** indicator percentile (100=high): 21st

Jefferson Davis Parish

[JENNINGS] JEFFERSON DAVIS PARISH S.D.

PO BOX 640 ● JENNINGS LA 70546 ● (318) 824-1834

Grade Span: PK-12 **Schools**: *Regular* 14 ● *Spec Ed* 0 ● *Alt* 0 **Students**: 6,707 **Total Teachers**: 404 **Student/Classroom Teacher Ratio**: 17.2	**Expenditures/Student**: $4,181 **Librarians**: 13.0 516 students/librarian **Guidance Counselors**: 22.0 305 students/counselor	**% Amer Indian**: 1.2 **% Asian**: 0.1 **% Black**: 24.6 **% Hispanic**: 0.4 **% White**: 73.8	National ***Socio-Economic Status*** indicator percentile (100=high): 17th

Jefferson Parish

[HARVEY] JEFFERSON PARISH S.D.

501 MANHATTAN BOULEVARD ● HARVEY LA 70058 ● (504) 367-3120

Grade Span: PK-12 **Schools**: *Regular* 79 ● *Spec Ed* 4 ● *Alt* 0 **Students**: 56,021 **Total Teachers**: 3,423 **Student/Classroom Teacher Ratio**: 17.0	**Expenditures/Student**: $4,894 **Librarians**: 36.0 1,556 students/librarian **Guidance Counselors**: 213.0 263 students/counselor	**% Amer Indian**: 0.5 **% Asian**: 4.2 **% Black**: 41.5 **% Hispanic**: 6.4 **% White**: 47.4	National ***Socio-Economic Status*** indicator percentile (100=high): 14th

La Salle Parish

[JENA] LASALLE PARISH S.D.

PO DRAWER 90 ● JENA LA 71342 ● (318) 992-2161

Grade Span: PK-12 **Schools**: *Regular* 9 ● *Spec Ed* 0 ● *Alt* 0 **Students**: 2,947 **Total Teachers**: 177 **Student/Classroom Teacher Ratio**: 17.1	**Expenditures/Student**: $3,998 **Librarians**: 6.0 491 students/librarian **Guidance Counselors**: 4.0 737 students/counselor	**% Amer Indian**: 1.0 **% Asian**: 0.3 **% Black**: 11.9 **% Hispanic**: 0.1 **% White**: 86.7	National ***Socio-Economic Status*** indicator percentile (100=high): 33rd

Lafayette Parish

LAFAYETTE PARISH S.D.

PO DRAWER 2158 ● LAFAYETTE LA 70502 ● (318) 236-6800 ● http://www.lft.k12.la.us

Grade Span: PK-12 **Schools**: *Regular* 39 ● *Spec Ed* 0 ● *Alt* 2 **Students**: 32,011 **Total Teachers**: 1,806 **Student/Classroom Teacher Ratio**: 17.9	**Expenditures/Student**: $3,924 **Librarians**: 44.0 728 students/librarian **Guidance Counselors**: 115.0 278 students/counselor	**% Amer Indian**: 0.1 **% Asian**: 1.0 **% Black**: 33.9 **% Hispanic**: 0.7 **% White**: 64.2	National ***Socio-Economic Status*** indicator percentile (100=high): 25th

Lafourche Parish

[THIBODAUX] LAFOURCHE PARISH S.D.

PO BOX 879 ● THIBODAUX LA 70302 ● (504) 446-5631 ● http://lafourche.k12.la.us

Grade Span: PK-12 **Schools**: *Regular* 27 ● *Spec Ed* 0 ● *Alt* 1 **Students**: 16,412 **Total Teachers**: 1,022 **Student/Classroom Teacher Ratio**: 16.7	**Expenditures/Student**: $3,898 **Librarians**: 25.1 654 students/librarian **Guidance Counselors**: 43.3 379 students/counselor	**% Amer Indian**: 3.4 **% Asian**: 1.3 **% Black**: 21.1 **% Hispanic**: 0.5 **% White**: 73.7	National ***Socio-Economic Status*** indicator percentile (100=high): 21st

Lincoln Parish

[RUSTON] LINCOLN PARISH S.D.

410 SOUTH FARMERVILLE SOU ● RUSTON LA 71270-4699 ● (318) 255-1430

Grade Span: PK-12 **Schools**: *Regular* 16 ● *Spec Ed* 0 ● *Alt* 1 **Students**: 7,164 **Total Teachers**: 456 **Student/Classroom Teacher Ratio**: 16.0	**Expenditures/Student**: $4,101 **Librarians**: 11.0 651 students/librarian **Guidance Counselors**: 10.0 716 students/counselor	**% Amer Indian**: 0.1 **% Asian**: 0.9 **% Black**: 47.1 **% Hispanic**: 0.5 **% White**: 51.3	National ***Socio-Economic Status*** indicator percentile (100=high): 24th

Livingston Parish

LIVINGSTON PARISH S.D.

PO BOX 128 ● LIVINGSTON LA 70754 ● (504) 686-7044

Grade Span: PK-12 **Schools**: *Regular* 33 ● *Spec Ed* 1 ● *Alt* 0 **Students**: 18,252 **Total Teachers**: 1,008 **Student/Classroom Teacher Ratio**: 18.7	**Expenditures/Student**: $3,521 **Librarians**: 15.0 1,217 students/librarian **Guidance Counselors**: 44.0 415 students/counselor	**% Amer Indian**: 0.1 **% Asian**: 0.2 **% Black**: 6.4 **% Hispanic**: 0.2 **% White**: 93.1	National ***Socio-Economic Status*** indicator percentile (100=high): 40th

Madison Parish

[TALLULAH] MADISON PARISH S.D.

PO BOX 1620 ● TALLULAH LA 71282 ● (318) 574-3616

Grade Span: PK-12 **Schools**: *Regular* 6 ● *Spec Ed* 0 ● *Alt* 2 **Students**: 3,316 **Total Teachers**: 151 **Student/Classroom Teacher Ratio**: 19.9	**Expenditures/Student**: $3,504 **Librarians**: 6.0 553 students/librarian **Guidance Counselors**: 6.0 553 students/counselor	**% Amer Indian**: 0.0 **% Asian**: 0.0 **% Black**: 83.4 **% Hispanic**: 0.9 **% White**: 15.6	National ***Socio-Economic Status*** indicator percentile (100=high): 2nd

Morehouse Parish

[BASTROP] MOREHOUSE PARISH S.D.

PO BOX 872 ● BASTROP LA 71220 ● (318) 281-5784 ● http://cust.iamerica.net/bastroph

Grade Span: PK-12 **Schools**: *Regular* 16 ● *Spec Ed* 0 ● *Alt* 0 **Students**: 6,025 **Total Teachers**: 360 **Student/Classroom Teacher Ratio**: 17.8	**Expenditures/Student**: $3,990 **Librarians**: 4.0 1,506 students/librarian **Guidance Counselors**: 16.0 377 students/counselor	**% Amer Indian**: 0.0 **% Asian**: 0.0 **% Black**: 64.9 **% Hispanic**: 0.2 **% White**: 34.9	National ***Socio-Economic Status*** indicator percentile (100=high): 9th

Natchitoches Parish

NATCHITOCHES PARISH S.D.

PO BOX 16 ● NATCHITOCHES LA 71457 ● (318) 352-2358 ● http://www.nat.k12.la.us

Grade Span: PK-12 **Schools**: *Regular* 14 ● *Spec Ed* 1 ● *Alt* 0 **Students**: 7,572 **Total Teachers**: 502 **Student/Classroom Teacher Ratio**: 15.7	**Expenditures/Student**: $4,255 **Librarians**: 16.0 473 students/librarian **Guidance Counselors**: 8.0 947 students/counselor	**% Amer Indian**: 0.2 **% Asian**: 0.3 **% Black**: 53.9 **% Hispanic**: 0.6 **% White**: 44.9	National ***Socio-Economic Status*** indicator percentile (100=high): 12th

Orleans Parish

[NEW ORLEANS] **ORLEANS PARISH S.D.**

4100 TOURO STREET ● NEW ORLEANS LA 70122 ● (504) 286-2700

Grade Span: PK-12 **Schools**: *Regular* 109 ● *Spec Ed* 2 ● *Alt* 10 **Students**: 85,596 **Total Teachers**: 3,876 **Student/Classroom Teacher Ratio**: 22.1	**Expenditures/Student**: $4,370 **Librarians**: 94.1 910 students/librarian **Guidance Counselors**: 252.7 339 students/counselor	**% Amer Indian**: 0.0 **% Asian**: 2.5 **% Black**: 90.7 **% Hispanic**: 1.3 **% White**: 5.5	National ***Socio-Economic Status*** indicator percentile (100=high): 3rd

Ouachita Parish

[MONROE] **CITY OF MONROE PARISH S.D.**

PO BOX 4180 ● MONROE LA 71211-4180 ● (318) 325-0601 ● http://monroe.k12.la.us

Grade Span: PK-12 **Schools**: *Regular* 19 ● *Spec Ed* 0 ● *Alt* 1 **Students**: 11,229 **Total Teachers**: 657 **Student/Classroom Teacher Ratio**: 18.6	**Expenditures/Student**: $4,235 **Librarians**: 21.0 535 students/librarian **Guidance Counselors**: 33.4 336 students/counselor	**% Amer Indian**: 0.0 **% Asian**: 0.2 **% Black**: 88.4 **% Hispanic**: 0.2 **% White**: 11.2	National ***Socio-Economic Status*** indicator percentile (100=high): 3rd

Ouachita Parish

[MONROE] **OUACHITA PARISH S.D.**

PO BOX 1642 ● MONROE LA 71201 ● (318) 388-2711

Grade Span: PK-12 **Schools**: *Regular* 30 ● *Spec Ed* 0 ● *Alt* 1 **Students**: 17,958 **Total Teachers**: 1,111 **Student/Classroom Teacher Ratio**: 16.3	**Expenditures/Student**: $3,765 **Librarians**: 32.0 561 students/librarian **Guidance Counselors**: 42.5 423 students/counselor	**% Amer Indian**: 0.0 **% Asian**: 0.6 **% Black**: 23.2 **% Hispanic**: 0.4 **% White**: 75.8	National ***Socio-Economic Status*** indicator percentile (100=high): 37th

Plaquemines Parish

[BELLE CHASSE] **PLAQUEMINES PARISH S.D.**

PO BOX 69 ● BELLE CHASSE LA 70037 ● (504) 392-4970

Grade Span: PK-12 **Schools**: *Regular* 8 ● *Spec Ed* 0 ● *Alt* 0 **Students**: 5,275 **Total Teachers**: 313 **Student/Classroom Teacher Ratio**: 17.3	**Expenditures/Student**: $4,640 **Librarians**: 8.0 659 students/librarian **Guidance Counselors**: 10.0 528 students/counselor	**% Amer Indian**: 1.0 **% Asian**: 3.6 **% Black**: 33.1 **% Hispanic**: 0.5 **% White**: 61.9	National ***Socio-Economic Status*** indicator percentile (100=high): 23rd

Pointe Coupee Parish

[NEW ROADS] **POINTE COUPEE PARISH S.D.**

PO DRAWER 579 ● NEW ROADS LA 70760 ● (504) 638-8674

Grade Span: PK-12 **Schools**: *Regular* 8 ● *Spec Ed* 0 ● *Alt* 0 **Students**: 3,657 **Total Teachers**: 218 **Student/Classroom Teacher Ratio**: 16.7	**Expenditures/Student**: $4,434 **Librarians**: 7.0 522 students/librarian **Guidance Counselors**: 16.0 229 students/counselor	**% Amer Indian**: 0.1 **% Asian**: 0.0 **% Black**: 66.6 **% Hispanic**: 0.1 **% White**: 33.2	National ***Socio-Economic Status*** indicator percentile (100=high): 5th

Rapides Parish

[ALEXANDRIA] **RAPIDES PARISH S.D.**

PO BOX 1230 ● ALEXANDRIA LA 71309-1230 ● (318) 487-0888

Grade Span: PK-12 **Schools**: *Regular* 50 ● *Spec Ed* 2 ● *Alt* 2 **Students**: 24,792 **Total Teachers**: 1,601 **Student/Classroom Teacher Ratio**: 16.1	**Expenditures/Student**: $4,551 **Librarians**: 52.0 477 students/librarian **Guidance Counselors**: 56.0 443 students/counselor	**% Amer Indian**: 1.0 **% Asian**: 1.1 **% Black**: 40.6 **% Hispanic**: 0.4 **% White**: 56.9	National ***Socio-Economic Status*** indicator percentile (100=high): 16th

Richland Parish

[RAYVILLE] **RICHLAND PARISH S.D.**

PO BOX 599 ● RAYVILLE LA 71269 ● (318) 728-5964

Grade Span: PK-12 **Schools**: *Regular* 11 ● *Spec Ed* 1 ● *Alt* 0 **Students**: 4,280 **Total Teachers**: 281 **Student/Classroom Teacher Ratio**: 15.9	**Expenditures/Student**: $3,991 **Librarians**: 2.0 2,140 students/librarian **Guidance Counselors**: 8.0 535 students/counselor	**% Amer Indian**: 0.0 **% Asian**: 0.0 **% Black**: 55.4 **% Hispanic**: 0.3 **% White**: 44.2	National ***Socio-Economic Status*** indicator percentile (100=high): 8th

Sabine Parish

[MANY] **SABINE PARISH S.D.**

PO BOX 1079 ● MANY LA 71449 ● (318) 256-9228 ● http://www.sabine.k12.la.us

Grade Span: PK-12 **Schools**: *Regular* 12 ● *Spec Ed* 0 ● *Alt* 0 **Students**: 4,860 **Total Teachers**: 295 **Student/Classroom Teacher Ratio**: 16.4	**Expenditures/Student**: $4,250 **Librarians**: 11.0 442 students/librarian **Guidance Counselors**: 10.0 486 students/counselor	**% Amer Indian**: 8.7 **% Asian**: 0.1 **% Black**: 27.6 **% Hispanic**: 8.3 **% White**: 55.2	National ***Socio-Economic Status*** indicator percentile (100=high): 13th

St. Bernard Parish

[CHALMETTE] **ST. BERNARD PARISH S.D.**

#67 E. CHALMETTE CIRCLE ● CHALMETTE LA 70043 ● (504) 271-2533 ● http://home.gnofn.org/~sbpsb

Grade Span: PK-12 **Schools**: *Regular* 17 ● *Spec Ed* 0 ● *Alt* 0 **Students**: 9,567 **Total Teachers**: 562 **Student/Classroom Teacher Ratio**: 17.4	**Expenditures/Student**: $4,325 **Librarians**: 18.3 523 students/librarian **Guidance Counselors**: 32.7 293 students/counselor	**% Amer Indian**: 0.9 **% Asian**: 1.7 **% Black**: 10.7 **% Hispanic**: 3.4 **% White**: 83.2	National ***Socio-Economic Status*** indicator percentile (100=high): 24th

St. Charles Parish

[LULING] **ST. CHARLES PARISH S.D.**

PO BOX 46 ● LULING LA 70070-0046 ● (504) 785-6289 ● http://stcharles.k12.la.us

Grade Span: PK-12 **Schools**: *Regular* 19 ● *Spec Ed* 0 ● *Alt* 0 **Students**: 9,973 **Total Teachers**: 639 **Student/Classroom Teacher Ratio**: 15.8	**Expenditures/Student**: $5,855 **Librarians**: 28.0 356 students/librarian **Guidance Counselors**: 38.1 262 students/counselor	**% Amer Indian**: 0.1 **% Asian**: 0.5 **% Black**: 33.8 **% Hispanic**: 1.4 **% White**: 64.1	National ***Socio-Economic Status*** indicator percentile (100=high): 31st

St. James Parish

[LUTCHER] **ST. JAMES PARISH S.D.**

PO BOX 338 ● LUTCHER LA 70071 ● (504) 869-5375

Grade Span: PK-12 **Schools**: *Regular* 12 ● *Spec Ed* 0 ● *Alt* 0 **Students**: 4,289 **Total Teachers**: 275 **Student/Classroom Teacher Ratio**: 15.9	**Expenditures/Student**: $5,150 **Librarians**: 12.0 357 students/librarian **Guidance Counselors**: 16.0 268 students/counselor	**% Amer Indian**: 0.0 **% Asian**: 0.0 **% Black**: 69.4 **% Hispanic**: 0.1 **% White**: 30.5	National ***Socio-Economic Status*** indicator percentile (100=high): 8th

St. John the Baptist Parish

[RESERVE] **ST. JOHN PARISH S.D.**

PO DRAWER AL ● RESERVE LA 70084 ● (504) 536-1106

Grade Span: PK-12 **Schools**: *Regular* 13 ● *Spec Ed* 0 ● *Alt* 0 **Students**: 7,230 **Total Teachers**: 453 **Student/Classroom Teacher Ratio**: 16.8	**Expenditures/Student**: $4,685 **Librarians**: 6.0 1,205 students/librarian **Guidance Counselors**: 24.0 301 students/counselor	**% Amer Indian**: 0.2 **% Asian**: 0.2 **% Black**: 66.9 **% Hispanic**: 1.6 **% White**: 31.0	National ***Socio-Economic Status*** indicator percentile (100=high): 8th

St. Landry Parish

[OPELOUSAS] **ST. LANDRY PARISH S.D.**

PO BOX 310 ● OPELOUSAS LA 70571-0310 ● (318) 948-3657

Grade Span: PK-12 **Schools**: *Regular* 35 ● *Spec Ed* 0 ● *Alt* 2 **Students**: 17,640 **Total Teachers**: 1,053 **Student/Classroom Teacher Ratio**: 16.2	**Expenditures/Student**: $3,865 **Librarians**: 20.0 882 students/librarian **Guidance Counselors**: 61.0 289 students/counselor	**% Amer Indian**: 0.1 **% Asian**: 0.2 **% Black**: 53.6 **% Hispanic**: 0.2 **% White**: 46.0	National ***Socio-Economic Status*** indicator percentile (100=high): 7th

St. Martin Parish

[ST. MARTINVILLE] **ST. MARTIN PARISH S.D.**

PO BOX 859 ● ST. MARTINVILLE LA 70582 ● (318) 394-6261

Grade Span: PK-12 **Schools**: *Regular* 17 ● *Spec Ed* 0 ● *Alt* 0 **Students**: 9,252 **Total Teachers**: 543 **Student/Classroom Teacher Ratio**: 17.4	**Expenditures/Student**: $3,898 **Librarians**: 16.0 578 students/librarian **Guidance Counselors**: 21.0 441 students/counselor	**% Amer Indian**: 0.0 **% Asian**: 1.1 **% Black**: 45.5 **% Hispanic**: 0.2 **% White**: 53.2	National ***Socio-Economic Status*** indicator percentile (100=high): 10th

St. Mary Parish

[CENTERVILLE] **ST. MARY PARISH S.D.**

PO BOX 170 ● CENTERVILLE LA 70522 ● (318) 836-9661 ● http://www.stmary.k12.la.us

Grade Span: PK-12 **Schools**: *Regular* 25 ● *Spec Ed* 0 ● *Alt* 1 **Students**: 11,874 **Total Teachers**: 683 **Student/Classroom Teacher Ratio**: 17.9	**Expenditures/Student**: $4,229 **Librarians**: 26.5 448 students/librarian **Guidance Counselors**: 34.0 349 students/counselor	**% Amer Indian**: 0.9 **% Asian**: 3.0 **% Black**: 45.4 **% Hispanic**: 0.9 **% White**: 49.9	National ***Socio-Economic Status*** indicator percentile (100=high): 10th

St. Tammany Parish

[COVINGTON] **ST. TAMMANY PARISH S.D.**

PO BOX 940 ● COVINGTON LA 70434 ● (504) 892-2276

Grade Span: PK-12 **Schools**: *Regular* 45 ● *Spec Ed* 1 ● *Alt* 2 **Students**: 31,984 **Total Teachers**: 2,045 **Student/Classroom Teacher Ratio**: 15.9	**Expenditures/Student**: $4,455 **Librarians**: 53.0 603 students/librarian **Guidance Counselors**: 158.0 202 students/counselor	**% Amer Indian**: 0.1 **% Asian**: 0.5 **% Black**: 15.0 **% Hispanic**: 0.8 **% White**: 83.6	National ***Socio-Economic Status*** indicator percentile (100=high): 54th

Tangipahoa Parish

[AMITE] **TANGIPAHOA PARISH S.D.**

PO BOX 457 ● AMITE LA 70422 ● (504) 748-7153 ● http://www.i-55.com/~cheraddi/schools

Grade Span: PK-12 **Schools**: *Regular* 33 ● *Spec Ed* 0 ● *Alt* 2 **Students**: 18,209 **Total Teachers**: 1,040 **Student/Classroom Teacher Ratio**: 17.1	**Expenditures/Student**: $3,780 **Librarians**: 31.0 587 students/librarian **Guidance Counselors**: 35.0 520 students/counselor	**% Amer Indian**: 0.0 **% Asian**: 0.4 **% Black**: 44.4 **% Hispanic**: 0.5 **% White**: 54.6	National ***Socio-Economic Status*** indicator percentile (100=high): 9th

Terrebonne Parish

[HOUMA] **TERREBONNE PARISH S.D.**

PO BOX 5097 ● HOUMA LA 70361 ● (504) 876-7400

Grade Span: PK-12 **Schools**: *Regular* 36 ● *Spec Ed* 1 ● *Alt* 5 **Students**: 22,194 **Total Teachers**: 1,113 **Student/Classroom Teacher Ratio**: 19.5	**Expenditures/Student**: $3,356 **Librarians**: 27.9 795 students/librarian **Guidance Counselors**: 60.4 367 students/counselor	**% Amer Indian**: 7.9 **% Asian**: 1.1 **% Black**: 25.1 **% Hispanic**: 0.5 **% White**: 65.3	National ***Socio-Economic Status*** indicator percentile (100=high): 18th

Union Parish

[FARMERVILLE] **UNION PARISH S.D.**

PO BOX 308 ● FARMERVILLE LA 71241 ● (318) 368-9715

Grade Span: PK-12 **Schools**: *Regular* 10 ● *Spec Ed* 0 ● *Alt* 0 **Students**: 4,043 **Total Teachers**: 229 **Student/Classroom Teacher Ratio**: 18.2	**Expenditures/Student**: $3,653 **Librarians**: 0.0 *** students/librarian **Guidance Counselors**: 5.0 809 students/counselor	**% Amer Indian**: 0.1 **% Asian**: 0.1 **% Black**: 41.5 **% Hispanic**: 0.8 **% White**: 57.5	National ***Socio-Economic Status*** indicator percentile (100=high): 15th

Vermilion Parish

[ABBEVILLE] **VERMILION PARISH S.D.**

PO DRAWER 520 ● ABBEVILLE LA 70511-0520 ● (318) 893-3973 ● http://www.vrml.k12.la.us

Grade Span: PK-12 **Schools**: *Regular* 20 ● *Spec Ed* 0 ● *Alt* 0 **Students**: 9,769 **Total Teachers**: 594 **Student/Classroom Teacher Ratio**: 16.4	**Expenditures/Student**: $4,135 **Librarians**: 18.0 543 students/librarian **Guidance Counselors**: 38.0 257 students/counselor	**% Amer Indian**: 0.0 **% Asian**: 2.7 **% Black**: 20.7 **% Hispanic**: 0.3 **% White**: 76.3	National ***Socio-Economic Status*** indicator percentile (100=high): 21st

Vernon Parish

[LEESVILLE] **VERNON PARISH S.D.**

201 BELVIEW ROAD ● LEESVILLE LA 71446 ● (318) 239-3401

Grade Span: PK-12 **Schools**: *Regular* 18 ● *Spec Ed* 0 ● *Alt* 0 **Students**: 11,320 **Total Teachers**: 704 **Student/Classroom Teacher Ratio**: 16.2	**Expenditures/Student**: $4,467 **Librarians**: 18.0 629 students/librarian **Guidance Counselors**: 31.5 359 students/counselor	**% Amer Indian**: 0.4 **% Asian**: 2.1 **% Black**: 24.3 **% Hispanic**: 4.1 **% White**: 69.1	National ***Socio-Economic Status*** indicator percentile (100=high): 35th

Washington Parish

[BOGALUSA] **CITY OF BOGALUSA PARISH S.D.**

PO BOX 310 ● BOGALUSA LA 70427 ● (504) 735-1392

Grade Span: PK-12 **Schools**: *Regular* 9 ● *Spec Ed* 0 ● *Alt* 0 **Students**: 3,579 **Total Teachers**: 229 **Student/Classroom Teacher Ratio**: 16.8	**Expenditures/Student**: $4,280 **Librarians**: 0.0 *** students/librarian **Guidance Counselors**: 3.0 1,193 students/counselor	**% Amer Indian**: 0.0 **% Asian**: 0.1 **% Black**: 46.5 **% Hispanic**: 0.2 **% White**: 53.2	National ***Socio-Economic Status*** indicator percentile (100=high): 5th

Washington Parish

[FRANKLINTON] **WASHINGTON PARISH S.D.**

PO BOX 587 ● FRANKLINTON LA 70438 ● (504) 839-3436

Grade Span: PK-12 **Schools**: *Regular* 12 ● *Spec Ed* 0 ● *Alt* 0 **Students**: 5,141 **Total Teachers**: 332 **Student/Classroom Teacher Ratio**: 15.8	**Expenditures/Student**: $4,261 **Librarians**: 0.0 *** students/librarian **Guidance Counselors**: 16.0 321 students/counselor	**% Amer Indian**: 0.0 **% Asian**: 0.1 **% Black**: 40.7 **% Hispanic**: 0.3 **% White**: 59.0	National ***Socio-Economic Status*** indicator percentile (100=high): 4th

Webster Parish

[MINDEN] **WEBSTER PARISH S.D.**

PO BOX 520 ● MINDEN LA 71058 ● (318) 377-7052

Grade Span: PK-12	**Expenditures/Student**: $3,616	**% Amer Indian**: 0.0	
Schools: *Regular* 21 ● *Spec Ed* 0 ● *Alt* 1	**Librarians**: 20.0	**% Asian**: 0.1	National ***Socio-Economic***
Students: 8,409	420 students/librarian	**% Black**: 41.4	***Status*** indicator percentile
Total Teachers: 490	**Guidance Counselors**: 34.0	**% Hispanic**: 0.2	(100=high): 27th
Student/Classroom Teacher Ratio: 17.5	247 students/counselor	**% White**: 58.3	

West Baton Rouge Parish

[PORT ALLEN] **WEST BATON ROUGE PARISH S.D.**

670 ROSEDALE STREET ● PORT ALLEN LA 70767 ● (504) 343-8309

Grade Span: PK-12	**Expenditures/Student**: $4,230	**% Amer Indian**: 0.0	
Schools: *Regular* 10 ● *Spec Ed* 0 ● *Alt* 1	**Librarians**: 10.0	**% Asian**: 0.2	National ***Socio-Economic***
Students: 4,156	416 students/librarian	**% Black**: 48.0	***Status*** indicator percentile
Total Teachers: 214	**Guidance Counselors**: 12.0	**% Hispanic**: 0.4	(100=high): 15th
Student/Classroom Teacher Ratio: 19.0	346 students/counselor	**% White**: 51.4	

West Carroll Parish

[OAK GROVE] **WEST CARROLL PARISH S.D.**

PO BOX 220 ● OAK GROVE LA 71263 ● (318) 428-2378

Grade Span: PK-12	**Expenditures/Student**: $3,828	**% Amer Indian**: 0.1	
Schools: *Regular* 8 ● *Spec Ed* 0 ● *Alt* 0	**Librarians**: 4.0	**% Asian**: 0.0	National ***Socio-Economic***
Students: 2,770	693 students/librarian	**% Black**: 22.2	***Status*** indicator percentile
Total Teachers: 185	**Guidance Counselors**: 5.0	**% Hispanic**: 0.4	(100=high): 15th
Student/Classroom Teacher Ratio: 14.9	554 students/counselor	**% White**: 77.4	

Winn Parish

[WINNFIELD] **WINN PARISH S.D.**

PO DRAWER 430 ● WINNFIELD LA 71483 ● (318) 628-6936

Grade Span: PK-12	**Expenditures/Student**: $4,524	**% Amer Indian**: 0.1	
Schools: *Regular* 8 ● *Spec Ed* 0 ● *Alt* 0	**Librarians**: 7.0	**% Asian**: 0.0	National ***Socio-Economic***
Students: 3,311	473 students/librarian	**% Black**: 36.7	***Status*** indicator percentile
Total Teachers: 206	**Guidance Counselors**: 7.0	**% Hispanic**: 0.5	(100=high): 15th
Student/Classroom Teacher Ratio: 16.5	473 students/counselor	**% White**: 62.8	

Androscoggin County
AUBURN S.D.
23 HIGH ST PO BOX 800 ● AUBURN ME 04212 ● (207) 784-6431 ● http://www.auburnschl.edu

Grade Span: KG-12 **Schools**: *Regular* 13 ● *Spec Ed* 0 ● *Alt* 0 **Students**: 4,455 **Total Teachers**: 308 **Student/Classroom Teacher Ratio**: 17.1	**Expenditures/Student**: $5,347 **Librarians**: 2.0 2,228 students/librarian **Guidance Counselors**: 14.8 301 students/counselor	**% Amer Indian**: 0.3 **% Asian**: 1.1 **% Black**: 1.4 **% Hispanic**: 0.3 **% White**: 97.0	National ***Socio-Economic Status*** indicator percentile (100=high): 57th

Androscoggin County
LEWISTON S.D.
DINGLEY BLDG 36 OAK ST ● LEWISTON ME 04240 ● (207) 795-4100

Grade Span: KG-12 **Schools**: *Regular* 9 ● *Spec Ed* 0 ● *Alt* 1 **Students**: 4,675 **Total Teachers**: 338 **Student/Classroom Teacher Ratio**: 17.1	**Expenditures/Student**: $6,635 **Librarians**: 3.0 1,558 students/librarian **Guidance Counselors**: 15.9 294 students/counselor	**% Amer Indian**: 0.3 **% Asian**: 0.7 **% Black**: 2.0 **% Hispanic**: 1.0 **% White**: 96.0	National ***Socio-Economic Status*** indicator percentile (100=high): 33rd

Cumberland County
BRUNSWICK S.D.
35 UNION STREET ● BRUNSWICK ME 04011 ● (207) 729-4148

Grade Span: KG-12 **Schools**: *Regular* 6 ● *Spec Ed* 0 ● *Alt* 0 **Students**: 3,143 **Total Teachers**: 200 **Student/Classroom Teacher Ratio**: 17.3	**Expenditures/Student**: $6,113 **Librarians**: 5.4 582 students/librarian **Guidance Counselors**: 8.9 353 students/counselor	**% Amer Indian**: 0.3 **% Asian**: 1.4 **% Black**: 2.2 **% Hispanic**: 1.2 **% White**: 95.0	National ***Socio-Economic Status*** indicator percentile (100=high): 70th

Cumberland County
PORTLAND S.D.
331 VERANDA STREET ● PORTLAND ME 04103 ● (207) 874-8100

Grade Span: PK-12 **Schools**: *Regular* 19 ● *Spec Ed* 0 ● *Alt* 1 **Students**: 8,266 **Total Teachers**: 620 **Student/Classroom Teacher Ratio**: 15.2	**Expenditures/Student**: $7,904 **Librarians**: 12.1 683 students/librarian **Guidance Counselors**: 17.9 462 students/counselor	**% Amer Indian**: 0.5 **% Asian**: 6.2 **% Black**: 4.1 **% Hispanic**: 1.6 **% White**: 87.6	National ***Socio-Economic Status*** indicator percentile (100=high): 38th

Cumberland County
SOUTH PORTLAND S.D.
130 WESCOTT ROAD ● SOUTH PORTLAND ME 04106 ● (207) 871-0555

Grade Span: KG-12 **Schools**: *Regular* 10 ● *Spec Ed* 0 ● *Alt* 0 **Students**: 3,457 **Total Teachers**: 245 **Student/Classroom Teacher Ratio**: 16.2	**Expenditures/Student**: $6,686 **Librarians**: 3.0 1,152 students/librarian **Guidance Counselors**: 11.0 314 students/counselor	**% Amer Indian**: 0.2 **% Asian**: 1.5 **% Black**: 0.8 **% Hispanic**: 0.3 **% White**: 97.3	National ***Socio-Economic Status*** indicator percentile (100=high): 72nd

Cumberland County
WESTBROOK S.D.
596 MAIN STREET ● WESTBROOK ME 04092 ● (207) 854-0800

Grade Span: KG-12 **Schools**: *Regular* 6 ● *Spec Ed* 0 ● *Alt* 1 **Students**: 2,824 **Total Teachers**: 207 **Student/Classroom Teacher Ratio**: 15.9	**Expenditures/Student**: $6,655 **Librarians**: 2.0 1,412 students/librarian **Guidance Counselors**: 6.9 409 students/counselor	**% Amer Indian**: 0.0 **% Asian**: 1.1 **% Black**: 1.6 **% Hispanic**: 0.4 **% White**: 97.0	National ***Socio-Economic Status*** indicator percentile (100=high): 51st

Cumberland County

WINDHAM S.D.

228 WINDHAM CENTER ROAD ● WINDHAM ME 04062 ● (207) 892-1800 ● http://www.windham.k12.me.us

Grade Span: KG-12 **Schools**: *Regular* 5 ● *Spec Ed* 0 ● *Alt* 0 **Students**: 2,615 **Total Teachers**: 173 **Student/Classroom Teacher Ratio**: 14.7	**Expenditures/Student**: $5,488 **Librarians**: 2.0 1,308 students/librarian **Guidance Counselors**: 7.0 374 students/counselor	**% Amer Indian**: 0.4 **% Asian**: 0.3 **% Black**: 0.6 **% Hispanic**: 0.3 **% White**: 98.4	National ***Socio-Economic Status*** indicator percentile (100=high): 75th

Franklin County

[NEW SHARON] SCHOOL ADMINISTRATIVE DISTRICT 9

RR 1 BOX 1775 ● NEW SHARON ME 04955 ● (207) 778-6571 ● http://route2.com/msad9.htm

Grade Span: KG-12 **Schools**: *Regular* 8 ● *Spec Ed* 0 ● *Alt* 1 **Students**: 3,059 **Total Teachers**: 212 **Student/Classroom Teacher Ratio**: 17.6	**Expenditures/Student**: $5,277 **Librarians**: 4.0 765 students/librarian **Guidance Counselors**: 7.0 437 students/counselor	**% Amer Indian**: 0.1 **% Asian**: 0.7 **% Black**: 0.2 **% Hispanic**: 0.2 **% White**: 98.8	National ***Socio-Economic Status*** indicator percentile (100=high): 46th

Kennebec County

AUGUSTA S.D.

RFD 7 BOX 2525 ● AUGUSTA ME 04330 ● (207) 626-2468

Grade Span: KG-12 **Schools**: *Regular* 7 ● *Spec Ed* 0 ● *Alt* 1 **Students**: 3,017 **Total Teachers**: 244 **Student/Classroom Teacher Ratio**: 15.9	**Expenditures/Student**: $7,017 **Librarians**: 1.8 1,676 students/librarian **Guidance Counselors**: 12.0 251 students/counselor	**% Amer Indian**: 0.2 **% Asian**: 1.9 **% Black**: 0.7 **% Hispanic**: 0.3 **% White**: 96.9	National ***Socio-Economic Status*** indicator percentile (100=high): 42nd

Kennebec County

[GARDINER] SCHOOL ADMINISTRATIVE DISTRICT 11

150 HIGHLAND AVENUE ● GARDINER ME 04345 ● (207) 582-5346

Grade Span: KG-12 **Schools**: *Regular* 8 ● *Spec Ed* 0 ● *Alt* 0 **Students**: 2,670 **Total Teachers**: 173 **Student/Classroom Teacher Ratio**: 16.5	**Expenditures/Student**: $5,344 **Librarians**: 1.9 1,405 students/librarian **Guidance Counselors**: 8.9 300 students/counselor	**% Amer Indian**: 0.8 **% Asian**: 0.3 **% Black**: 0.4 **% Hispanic**: 0.3 **% White**: 98.2	National ***Socio-Economic Status*** indicator percentile (100=high): 56th

Kennebec County

[OAKLAND] SCHOOL ADMINISTRATIVE DISTRICT 47

20 HEATH STREET ● OAKLAND ME 04963 ● (207) 465-7384 ● http://www.mint.net/sad47

Grade Span: KG-12 **Schools**: *Regular* 5 ● *Spec Ed* 0 ● *Alt* 0 **Students**: 2,535 **Total Teachers**: 163 **Student/Classroom Teacher Ratio**: 17.6	**Expenditures/Student**: $4,778 **Librarians**: 3.6 704 students/librarian **Guidance Counselors**: 10.3 246 students/counselor	**% Amer Indian**: 0.0 **% Asian**: 0.3 **% Black**: 0.2 **% Hispanic**: 0.4 **% White**: 99.1	National ***Socio-Economic Status*** indicator percentile (100=high): 64th

Oxford County

[SOUTH PARIS] SCHOOL ADMINISTRATIVE DISTRICT 17

23 MARKET SQUARE ● SOUTH PARIS ME 04281 ● (207) 743-8972

Grade Span: KG-12 **Schools**: *Regular* 11 ● *Spec Ed* 0 ● *Alt* 0 **Students**: 3,811 **Total Teachers**: 257 **Student/Classroom Teacher Ratio**: 17.4	**Expenditures/Student**: $5,092 **Librarians**: 3.0 1,270 students/librarian **Guidance Counselors**: 12.4 307 students/counselor	**% Amer Indian**: 0.2 **% Asian**: 0.2 **% Black**: 0.2 **% Hispanic**: 0.1 **% White**: 99.2	National ***Socio-Economic Status*** indicator percentile (100=high): 49th

Penobscot County

BANGOR S.D.

73 HARLOW STREET ● BANGOR ME 04401 ● (207) 945-4400

Grade Span: KG-12 **Schools**: *Regular* 10 ● *Spec Ed* 0 ● *Alt* 0 **Students**: 4,349 **Total Teachers**: 324 **Student/Classroom Teacher Ratio**: 15.4	**Expenditures/Student**: $6,300 **Librarians**: 3.0 1,450 students/librarian **Guidance Counselors**: 11.5 378 students/counselor	**% Amer Indian**: 0.9 **% Asian**: 1.3 **% Black**: 1.4 **% Hispanic**: 0.6 **% White**: 95.9	National ***Socio-Economic Status*** indicator percentile (100=high): 43rd

Sagadahoc County

[TOPSHAM] **SCHOOL ADMINISTRATAIVE DISTRICT 75**

ONE MAIN ST PO BOX 475 ● TOPSHAM ME 04086 ● (207) 729-9961 ● http://www.col.k12.me.us/msad75

Grade Span: KG-12 **Schools**: *Regular* 8 ● *Spec Ed* 0 ● *Alt* 0 **Students**: 3,373 **Total Teachers**: 229 **Student/Classroom Teacher Ratio**: 16.6	**Expenditures/Student**: $6,142 **Librarians**: 4.9 688 students/librarian **Guidance Counselors**: 11.3 298 students/counselor	**% Amer Indian**: 0.1 **% Asian**: 1.5 **% Black**: 1.2 **% Hispanic**: 0.7 **% White**: 96.5	National ***Socio-Economic Status*** indicator percentile (100=high): 80th

Somerset County

[FAIRFIELD] **SCHOOL ADMINISTRATIVE DISTRICT 49**

SCHOOL STREET ● FAIRFIELD ME 04937 ● (207) 453-4200 ● http://www.mint.net/sad49

Grade Span: PK-12 **Schools**: *Regular* 6 ● *Spec Ed* 0 ● *Alt* 0 **Students**: 2,865 **Total Teachers**: 205 **Student/Classroom Teacher Ratio**: 18.8	**Expenditures/Student**: $5,639 **Librarians**: 2.9 988 students/librarian **Guidance Counselors**: 7.8 367 students/counselor	**% Amer Indian**: 0.1 **% Asian**: 0.5 **% Black**: 0.5 **% Hispanic**: 0.2 **% White**: 98.7	National ***Socio-Economic Status*** indicator percentile (100=high): 46th

Somerset County

[SKOWHEGAN] **SCHOOL ADMINISTRATIVE DISTRICT 54**

PO BOX 69 ● SKOWHEGAN ME 04976 ● (207) 474-9508 ● http://www.msad54.k12.me.us

Grade Span: KG-12 **Schools**: *Regular* 10 ● *Spec Ed* 0 ● *Alt* 1 **Students**: 3,282 **Total Teachers**: 219 **Student/Classroom Teacher Ratio**: 18.4	**Expenditures/Student**: $6,043 **Librarians**: 1.4 2,344 students/librarian **Guidance Counselors**: 5.9 556 students/counselor	**% Amer Indian**: 0.1 **% Asian**: 0.7 **% Black**: 0.5 **% Hispanic**: 0.3 **% White**: 98.5	National ***Socio-Economic Status*** indicator percentile (100=high): 37th

York County

[BAR MILLS] **SCHOOL ADMINISTRATIVE DISTRICT 6**

PO BOX 38 ● BAR MILLS ME 04004 ● (207) 929-9108 ● http://www.sad6.k12.me.us

Grade Span: KG-12 **Schools**: *Regular* 12 ● *Spec Ed* 0 ● *Alt* 0 **Students**: 4,604 **Total Teachers**: 283 **Student/Classroom Teacher Ratio**: 19.1	**Expenditures/Student**: $5,337 **Librarians**: 7.0 658 students/librarian **Guidance Counselors**: 12.7 363 students/counselor	**% Amer Indian**: 0.0 **% Asian**: 0.4 **% Black**: 0.5 **% Hispanic**: 0.1 **% White**: 98.9	National ***Socio-Economic Status*** indicator percentile (100=high): 61st

York County

BIDDEFORD S.D.

205 MAIN ST PO BOX 1865 ● BIDDEFORD ME 04005 ● (207) 282-8280

Grade Span: PK-12 **Schools**: *Regular* 4 ● *Spec Ed* 0 ● *Alt* 1 **Students**: 2,914 **Total Teachers**: 203 **Student/Classroom Teacher Ratio**: 17.1	**Expenditures/Student**: $5,900 **Librarians**: 2.9 1,005 students/librarian **Guidance Counselors**: 8.1 360 students/counselor	**% Amer Indian**: 0.2 **% Asian**: 1.6 **% Black**: 0.9 **% Hispanic**: 0.2 **% White**: 97.0	National ***Socio-Economic Status*** indicator percentile (100=high): 34th

York County

[ELIOT] **SCHOOL ADMINISTRATIVE DISTRICT 35**

RTE 236 ELIOT COMMONS ● ELIOT ME 03903 ● (207) 439-2438

Grade Span: PK-12 **Schools**: *Regular* 4 ● *Spec Ed* 0 ● *Alt* 0 **Students**: 2,660 **Total Teachers**: 158 **Student/Classroom Teacher Ratio**: 17.9	**Expenditures/Student**: $4,703 **Librarians**: 2.0 1,330 students/librarian **Guidance Counselors**: 6.0 443 students/counselor	**% Amer Indian**: 0.1 **% Asian**: 0.1 **% Black**: 0.9 **% Hispanic**: 0.2 **% White**: 98.8	National ***Socio-Economic Status*** indicator percentile (100=high): 87th

York County

[NORTH BERWICK] **SCHOOL ADMINISTRATAIVE DISTRICT 60**

PO BOX 819 ● NORTH BERWICK ME 03906 ● (207) 676-2234

Grade Span: KG-12 **Schools**: *Regular* 6 ● *Spec Ed* 0 ● *Alt* 0 **Students**: 3,269 **Total Teachers**: 236 **Student/Classroom Teacher Ratio**: 14.6	**Expenditures/Student**: $5,508 **Librarians**: 3.0 1,090 students/librarian **Guidance Counselors**: 10.0 327 students/counselor	**% Amer Indian**: 0.0 **% Asian**: 0.7 **% Black**: 0.3 **% Hispanic**: 0.1 **% White**: 98.9	National ***Socio-Economic Status*** indicator percentile (100=high): 66th

York County

SANFORD S.D.

263 MAIN STREET ● SANFORD ME 04073 ● (207) 324-2810

Grade Span: KG-12 **Schools**: *Regular* 9 ● *Spec Ed* 0 ● *Alt* 1 **Students**: 3,966 **Total Teachers**: 273 **Student/Classroom Teacher Ratio**: 17.0	**Expenditures/Student**: $5,182 **Librarians**: 5.0 793 students/librarian **Guidance Counselors**: 11.8 336 students/counselor	**% Amer Indian**: 0.1 **% Asian**: 3.5 **% Black**: 0.4 **% Hispanic**: 0.6 **% White**: 95.5	National ***Socio-Economic Status*** indicator percentile (100=high): 43rd

York County

[WATERBORO] **SCHOOL ADMINISTRATIVE DISTRICT 57**

PO BOX 499 ● WATERBORO ME 04087 ● (207) 247-3221

Grade Span: KG-12 **Schools**: *Regular* 8 ● *Spec Ed* 0 ● *Alt* 0 **Students**: 3,353 **Total Teachers**: 215 **Student/Classroom Teacher Ratio**: 19.3	**Expenditures/Student**: $5,030 **Librarians**: 3.0 1,118 students/librarian **Guidance Counselors**: 9.6 349 students/counselor	**% Amer Indian**: 0.1 **% Asian**: 0.1 **% Black**: 0.6 **% Hispanic**: 0.3 **% White**: 98.9	National ***Socio-Economic Status*** indicator percentile (100=high): 61st

Allegany County

[CUMBERLAND] **ALLEGANY COUNTY S.D.**

108 WASHINGTÓN STREET ● CUMBERLAND MD 21502 ● (301) 759-2000 ● http://boe.allconet.org

Grade Span: PK-12	**Expenditures/Student**: $5,925	**% Amer Indian**: 0.2	
Schools: *Regular* 23 ● *Spec Ed* 0 ● *Alt* 2	**Librarians**: 23.0	**% Asian**: 0.7	National ***Socio-Economic***
Students: 11,300	491 students/librarian	**% Black**: 2.9	***Status*** indicator percentile
Total Teachers: 692	**Guidance Counselors**: 24.0	**% Hispanic**: 0.2	(100=high): 33rd
Student/Classroom Teacher Ratio: 17.3	471 students/counselor	**% White**: 96.1	

Anne Arundel County

[ANNAPOLIS] **ANNE ARUNDEL COUNTY S.D.**

2644 RIVA ROAD ● ANNAPOLIS MD 21401 ● (410) 224-5000

Grade Span: PK-12	**Expenditures/Student**: $6,296	**% Amer Indian**: 0.1	
Schools: *Regular* 106 ● *Spec Ed* 4 ● *Alt* 1	**Librarians**: 106.1	**% Asian**: 2.2	National ***Socio-Economic***
Students: 71,383	673 students/librarian	**% Black**: 17.4	***Status*** indicator percentile
Total Teachers: 4,144	**Guidance Counselors**: 182.0	**% Hispanic**: 1.4	(100=high): 77th
Student/Classroom Teacher Ratio: 19.1	392 students/counselor	**% White**: 78.8	

Baltimore County

[TOWSON] **BALTIMORE COUNTY S.D.**

6901 NORTH CHARLES STREET ● TOWSON MD 21204 ● (410) 887-4074 ● http://www.bcps.org

Grade Span: PK-12	**Expenditures/Student**: $6,433	**% Amer Indian**: 0.2	
Schools: *Regular* 141 ● *Spec Ed* 6 ● *Alt* 11	**Librarians**: 132.1	**% Asian**: 3.4	National ***Socio-Economic***
Students: 101,564	769 students/librarian	**% Black**: 24.8	***Status*** indicator percentile
Total Teachers: 6,302	**Guidance Counselors**: 248.3	**% Hispanic**: 1.1	(100=high): 59th
Student/Classroom Teacher Ratio: 17.9	409 students/counselor	**% White**: 70.5	

Baltimore Independent City

BALTIMORE CITY S.D.

200 EAST NORTH AVENUE ● BALTIMORE MD 21202 ● (410) 396-8803 ● http://www.bcps.k12.md.us

Grade Span: PK-12	**Expenditures/Student**: $5,934	**% Amer Indian**: 0.5	
Schools: *Regular* 161 ● *Spec Ed* 11 ● *Alt* 8	**Librarians**: 89.9	**% Asian**: 0.6	National ***Socio-Economic***
Students: 109,980	1,223 students/librarian	**% Black**: 83.7	***Status*** indicator percentile
Total Teachers: 6,291	**Guidance Counselors**: 159.5	**% Hispanic**: 0.4	(100=high): 6th
Student/Classroom Teacher Ratio: 19.5	690 students/counselor	**% White**: 14.8	

Calvert County

[PRINCE FREDERICK] **CALVERT COUNTY S.D.**

DARES BEACH ROAD ● PRINCE FREDERICK MD 20678 ● (410) 535-1700 ● http://calvertnet.k12.md.us

Grade Span: PK-12	**Expenditures/Student**: $5,826	**% Amer Indian**: 0.2	
Schools: *Regular* 16 ● *Spec Ed* 1 ● *Alt* 0	**Librarians**: 15.0	**% Asian**: 0.5	National ***Socio-Economic***
Students: 13,496	900 students/librarian	**% Black**: 16.9	***Status*** indicator percentile
Total Teachers: 708	**Guidance Counselors**: 26.0	**% Hispanic**: 0.5	(100=high): 76th
Student/Classroom Teacher Ratio: 21.1	519 students/counselor	**% White**: 81.9	

Caroline County

[DENTON] **CAROLINE COUNTY S.D.**

112 MARKET STREET ● DENTON MD 21629 ● (410) 479-1460 ● http://cl.k12.md.us

Grade Span: PK-12	**Expenditures/Student**: $5,556	**% Amer Indian**: 0.0	
Schools: *Regular* 9 ● *Spec Ed* 0 ● *Alt* 0	**Librarians**: 9.0	**% Asian**: 0.5	National ***Socio-Economic***
Students: 5,521	613 students/librarian	**% Black**: 21.4	***Status*** indicator percentile
Total Teachers: 307	**Guidance Counselors**: 15.0	**% Hispanic**: 0.7	(100=high): 37th
Student/Classroom Teacher Ratio: 18.8	368 students/counselor	**% White**: 77.4	

Carroll County

[WESTMINSTER] **CARROLL COUNTY S.D.**

55 NORTH COURT STREET ● WESTMINSTER MD 21157 ● (410) 848-8280 ● http://www.carr.lib.md.us/ccps/welcome.htm

Grade Span: PK-12 **Schools**: *Regular* 31 ● *Spec Ed* 1 ● *Alt* 1 **Students**: 25,408 **Total Teachers**: 1,436 **Student/Classroom Teacher Ratio**: 19.2	**Expenditures/Student**: $5,872 **Librarians**: 33.4 761 students/librarian **Guidance Counselors**: 59.0 431 students/counselor	**% Amer Indian**: 0.2 **% Asian**: 0.8 **% Black**: 2.2 **% Hispanic**: 0.6 **% White**: 96.2	National ***Socio-Economic Status*** indicator percentile (100=high): 87th

Cecil County

[ELKTON] **CECIL COUNTY S.D.**

BOOTH STREET CENTER ● ELKTON MD 21921-5684 ● (410) 996-5400 ● http://www.ccps.org

Grade Span: PK-12 **Schools**: *Regular* 27 ● *Spec Ed* 0 ● *Alt* 0 **Students**: 14,640 **Total Teachers**: 890 **Student/Classroom Teacher Ratio**: 17.4	**Expenditures/Student**: $5,723 **Librarians**: 25.0 586 students/librarian **Guidance Counselors**: 37.0 396 students/counselor	**% Amer Indian**: 0.1 **% Asian**: 0.6 **% Black**: 5.1 **% Hispanic**: 1.1 **% White**: 93.1	National ***Socio-Economic Status*** indicator percentile (100=high): 63rd

Charles County

[LA PLATA] **CHARLES COUNTY S.D.**

PO BOX D ● LA PLATA MD 20646 ● (301) 932-6610 ● http://www.ccboe.com

Grade Span: PK-12 **Schools**: *Regular* 30 ● *Spec Ed* 0 ● *Alt* 1 **Students**: 20,966 **Total Teachers**: 1,153 **Student/Classroom Teacher Ratio**: 19.8	**Expenditures/Student**: $6,214 **Librarians**: 28.0 749 students/librarian **Guidance Counselors**: 55.0 381 students/counselor	**% Amer Indian**: 1.0 **% Asian**: 1.7 **% Black**: 25.7 **% Hispanic**: 1.3 **% White**: 70.3	National ***Socio-Economic Status*** indicator percentile (100=high): 62nd

Dorchester County

[CAMBRIDGE] **DORCHESTER COUNTY S.D.**

700 GLASGLOW STREET ● CAMBRIDGE MD 21613 ● (410) 228-4747

Grade Span: PK-12 **Schools**: *Regular* 10 ● *Spec Ed* 1 ● *Alt* 1 **Students**: 5,216 **Total Teachers**: 309 **Student/Classroom Teacher Ratio**: 17.9	**Expenditures/Student**: $6,090 **Librarians**: 10.0 522 students/librarian **Guidance Counselors**: 11.0 474 students/counselor	**% Amer Indian**: 0.2 **% Asian**: 0.4 **% Black**: 39.9 **% Hispanic**: 0.5 **% White**: 59.0	National ***Socio-Economic Status*** indicator percentile (100=high): 29th

Frederick County

[FREDERICK] **FREDERICK COUNTY S.D.**

115 EAST CHURCH STREET ● FREDERICK MD 21701 ● (301) 694-1000 ● http://www.frederick.k12.md.us

Grade Span: PK-12 **Schools**: *Regular* 47 ● *Spec Ed* 2 ● *Alt* 0 **Students**: 32,766 **Total Teachers**: 1,987 **Student/Classroom Teacher Ratio**: 17.3	**Expenditures/Student**: $5,818 **Librarians**: 44.2 741 students/librarian **Guidance Counselors**: 64.6 507 students/counselor	**% Amer Indian**: 0.1 **% Asian**: 1.5 **% Black**: 7.6 **% Hispanic**: 1.5 **% White**: 89.3	National ***Socio-Economic Status*** indicator percentile (100=high): 79th

Garrett County

[OAKLAND] **GARRETT COUNTY S.D.**

40 SOUTH FOURTH STREET, BOX 59 ● OAKLAND MD 21550-0059 ● (301) 334-8900

Grade Span: PK-12 **Schools**: *Regular* 16 ● *Spec Ed* 0 ● *Alt* 1 **Students**: 5,190 **Total Teachers**: 364 **Student/Classroom Teacher Ratio**: 15.4	**Expenditures/Student**: $6,122 **Librarians**: 2.0 2,595 students/librarian **Guidance Counselors**: 11.0 472 students/counselor	**% Amer Indian**: 0.0 **% Asian**: 0.1 **% Black**: 0.3 **% Hispanic**: 0.1 **% White**: 99.5	National ***Socio-Economic Status*** indicator percentile (100=high): 34th

Harford County

[BEL AIR] **HARFORD COUNTY S.D.**

45 EAST GORDON STREET ● BEL AIR MD 21014 ● (410) 838-7300 ● http://www.hcps.org

Grade Span: PK-12 **Schools**: *Regular* 47 ● *Spec Ed* 1 ● *Alt* 3 **Students**: 36,820 **Total Teachers**: 2,250 **Student/Classroom Teacher Ratio**: 17.3	**Expenditures/Student**: $5,658 **Librarians**: 50.6 728 students/librarian **Guidance Counselors**: 86.0 428 students/counselor	**% Amer Indian**: 0.5 **% Asian**: 1.7 **% Black**: 11.9 **% Hispanic**: 1.8 **% White**: 84.1	National ***Socio-Economic Status*** indicator percentile (100=high): 75th

Howard County

[ELLICOTT CITY] **HOWARD COUNTY S.D.**

10910 ROUTE 108 ● ELLICOTT CITY MD 21042 ● (410) 313-6600 ● http://www.howard.k12.md.us

Grade Span: PK-12 **Schools**: *Regular* 55 ● *Spec Ed* 1 ● *Alt* 0 **Students**: 37,547 **Total Teachers**: 2,372 **Student/Classroom Teacher Ratio**: 16.6	**Expenditures/Student**: $6,988 **Librarians**: 64.0 587 students/librarian **Guidance Counselors**: 87.0 432 students/counselor	**% Amer Indian**: 0.1 **% Asian**: 7.5 **% Black**: 15.9 **% Hispanic**: 1.7 **% White**: 74.9	National ***Socio-Economic Status*** indicator percentile (100=high): 86th

Kent County

[CHESTERTOWN] **KENT COUNTY S.D.**

WASHINGTON AVENUE ● CHESTERTOWN MD 21620 ● (410) 778-1595

Grade Span: PK-12 **Schools**: *Regular* 8 ● *Spec Ed* 0 ● *Alt* 0 **Students**: 2,863 **Total Teachers**: 177 **Student/Classroom Teacher Ratio**: 16.8	**Expenditures/Student**: $6,602 **Librarians**: 4.5 636 students/librarian **Guidance Counselors**: 7.0 409 students/counselor	**% Amer Indian**: 0.0 **% Asian**: 0.4 **% Black**: 26.5 **% Hispanic**: 2.2 **% White**: 70.9	National ***Socio-Economic Status*** indicator percentile (100=high): 44th

Montgomery County

[ROCKVILLE] **MONTGOMERY COUNTY S.D.**

850 HUNGERFORD DRIVE ● ROCKVILLE MD 20850 ● (301) 279-3000 ● http://mcps.k12.md.us

Grade Span: PK-12 **Schools**: *Regular* 174 ● *Spec Ed* 6 ● *Alt* 1 **Students**: 120,291 **Total Teachers**: 7,188 **Student/Classroom Teacher Ratio**: 18.3	**Expenditures/Student**: $7,840 **Librarians**: 184.6 652 students/librarian **Guidance Counselors**: 326.7 368 students/counselor	**% Amer Indian**: 0.3 **% Asian**: 12.6 **% Black**: 19.2 **% Hispanic**: 12.0 **% White**: 55.9	National ***Socio-Economic Status*** indicator percentile (100=high): 65th

Prince George's County

[UPPER MARLBORO] **PRINCE GEORGES COUNTY S.D.**

14201 SCHOOL LANE ● UPPER MARLBORO MD 20772 ● (301) 952-6000 ● http://www.pgcps.pg.k12.md.us

Grade Span: PK-12 **Schools**: *Regular* 166 ● *Spec Ed* 9 ● *Alt* 4 **Students**: 122,415 **Total Teachers**: 7,054 **Student/Classroom Teacher Ratio**: 19.3	**Expenditures/Student**: $6,599 **Librarians**: 119.6 1,024 students/librarian **Guidance Counselors**: 280.0 437 students/counselor	**% Amer Indian**: 0.4 **% Asian**: 3.9 **% Black**: 71.7 **% Hispanic**: 5.4 **% White**: 18.6	National ***Socio-Economic Status*** indicator percentile (100=high): 37th

Queen Anne's County

[CENTREVILLE] **QUEEN ANNES COUNTY S.D.**

BOX 80 AND 110 ● CENTREVILLE MD 21617 ● (410) 758-2403 ● http://boe.qacps.k12.md.us

Grade Span: PK-12 **Schools**: *Regular* 10 ● *Spec Ed* 0 ● *Alt* 1 **Students**: 6,271 **Total Teachers**: 369 **Student/Classroom Teacher Ratio**: 17.7	**Expenditures/Student**: $6,078 **Librarians**: 8.0 784 students/librarian **Guidance Counselors**: 15.0 418 students/counselor	**% Amer Indian**: 0.1 **% Asian**: 0.5 **% Black**: 13.3 **% Hispanic**: 0.5 **% White**: 85.6	National ***Socio-Economic Status*** indicator percentile (100=high): 70th

St. Mary's County

[LEONARDTOWN] **ST. MARYS COUNTY S.D.**

PO BOX 641 ● LEONARDTOWN MD 20650 ● (301) 475-4250 ● http://www.smcps.k12.md.us

Grade Span: PK-12	**Expenditures/Student**: $6,187	**% Amer Indian**: 0.4	
Schools: *Regular* 22 ● *Spec Ed* 1 ● *Alt* 1	**Librarians**: 27.8	**% Asian**: 1.4	National ***Socio-Economic***
Students: 13,950	502 students/librarian	**% Black**: 19.3	***Status*** indicator percentile
Total Teachers: 829	**Guidance Counselors**: 28.0	**% Hispanic**: 1.1	(100=high): 58th
Student/Classroom Teacher Ratio: 18.1	498 students/counselor	**% White**: 77.7	

Somerset County

[PRINCESS ANNE] **SOMERSET COUNTY S.D.**

PRINCE WILLIAM STREET ● PRINCESS ANNE MD 21853 ● (410) 651-1616

Grade Span: PK-12	**Expenditures/Student**: $6,556	**% Amer Indian**: 0.0	
Schools: *Regular* 11 ● *Spec Ed* 0 ● *Alt* 0	**Librarians**: 4.0	**% Asian**: 0.0	National ***Socio-Economic***
Students: 3,277	819 students/librarian	**% Black**: 45.4	***Status*** indicator percentile
Total Teachers: 211	**Guidance Counselors**: 7.0	**% Hispanic**: 0.5	(100=high): 18th
Student/Classroom Teacher Ratio: 17.6	468 students/counselor	**% White**: 54.0	

Talbot County

[EASTON] **TALBOT COUNTY S.D.**

PO BOX 1029 WASHINGTON STREET ● EASTON MD 21601 ● (410) 822-0330

Grade Span: PK-12	**Expenditures/Student**: $5,772	**% Amer Indian**: 0.1	
Schools: *Regular* 9 ● *Spec Ed* 0 ● *Alt* 0	**Librarians**: 5.5	**% Asian**: 0.9	National ***Socio-Economic***
Students: 4,427	805 students/librarian	**% Black**: 25.7	***Status*** indicator percentile
Total Teachers: 267	**Guidance Counselors**: 14.0	**% Hispanic**: 0.7	(100=high): 54th
Student/Classroom Teacher Ratio: 17.4	316 students/counselor	**% White**: 72.6	

Washington County

[HAGERSTOWN] **WASHINGTON COUNTY S.D.**

PO BOX 730, 820 COMMONWEALTH ● HAGERSTOWN MD 21741 ● (301) 791-4000 ● http://www.wcboe.k12.md.us

Grade Span: PK-12	**Expenditures/Student**: $5,830	**% Amer Indian**: 0.0	
Schools: *Regular* 40 ● *Spec Ed* 2 ● *Alt* 2	**Librarians**: 39.0	**% Asian**: 1.1	National ***Socio-Economic***
Students: 19,824	508 students/librarian	**% Black**: 5.9	***Status*** indicator percentile
Total Teachers: 1,223	**Guidance Counselors**: 44.5	**% Hispanic**: 1.0	(100=high): 52nd
Student/Classroom Teacher Ratio: 17.9	445 students/counselor	**% White**: 91.9	

Wicomico County

[SALISBURY] **WICOMICO COUNTY S.D.**

PO BOX 1538, 101 LONG AVENUE ● SALISBURY MD 21801 ● (410) 742-5128

Grade Span: PK-12	**Expenditures/Student**: $5,572	**% Amer Indian**: 0.0	
Schools: *Regular* 21 ● *Spec Ed* 0 ● *Alt* 0	**Librarians**: 7.0	**% Asian**: 1.6	National ***Socio-Economic***
Students: 13,796	1,971 students/librarian	**% Black**: 34.0	***Status*** indicator percentile
Total Teachers: 881	**Guidance Counselors**: 23.2	**% Hispanic**: 0.9	(100=high): 41st
Student/Classroom Teacher Ratio: 17.1	595 students/counselor	**% White**: 63.5	

Worcester County

[NEWARK] **WORCESTER COUNTY S.D.**

6270 WORCESTER HIGHWAY ● NEWARK MD 21841 ● (410) 632-2582

Grade Span: PK-12	**Expenditures/Student**: $6,414	**% Amer Indian**: 0.0	
Schools: *Regular* 11 ● *Spec Ed* 1 ● *Alt* 0	**Librarians**: 11.0	**% Asian**: 1.0	National ***Socio-Economic***
Students: 6,633	603 students/librarian	**% Black**: 30.6	***Status*** indicator percentile
Total Teachers: 419	**Guidance Counselors**: 19.1	**% Hispanic**: 0.9	(100=high): 41st
Student/Classroom Teacher Ratio: 17.3	347 students/counselor	**% White**: 67.5	

Barnstable County

[EAST FALMOUTH] **FALMOUTH S.D.**

340 TEATICKET HWY ● EAST FALMOUTH MA 02536 ● (508) 548-0151

Grade Span: PK-12	**Expenditures/Student**: $5,811	**% Amer Indian**: 1.2	National ***Socio-Economic Status*** indicator percentiles are not available for the state of Massachusetts
Schools: *Regular* 7 ● *Spec Ed* 0 ● *Alt* 0	**Librarians**: 0.0	**% Asian**: 1.0	
Students: 5,207	*** students/librarian	**% Black**: 4.1	
Total Teachers: 307	**Guidance Counselors**: 8.5	**% Hispanic**: 2.0	
Student/Classroom Teacher Ratio: na	613 students/counselor	**% White**: 91.8	

Barnstable County

[HYANNIS] **BARNSTABLE S.D.**

P O BOX 955 ● HYANNIS MA 02601 ● (508) 790-9802

Grade Span: PK-12	**Expenditures/Student**: $6,038	**% Amer Indian**: 0.3	National ***Socio-Economic Status*** indicator percentiles are not available for the state of Massachusetts
Schools: *Regular* 13 ● *Spec Ed* 0 ● *Alt* 0	**Librarians**: 4.0	**% Asian**: 0.9	
Students: 7,063	1,766 students/librarian	**% Black**: 6.8	
Total Teachers: 478	**Guidance Counselors**: 19.0	**% Hispanic**: 3.2	
Student/Classroom Teacher Ratio: na	372 students/counselor	**% White**: 88.7	

Barnstable County

SANDWICH S.D.

16 DEWEY AVENUE ● SANDWICH MA 02563 ● (508) 888-1054

Grade Span: PK-12	**Expenditures/Student**: $5,680	**% Amer Indian**: 0.3	National ***Socio-Economic Status*** indicator percentiles are not available for the state of Massachusetts
Schools: *Regular* 4 ● *Spec Ed* 0 ● *Alt* 0	**Librarians**: 4.0	**% Asian**: 0.7	
Students: 3,642	911 students/librarian	**% Black**: 0.9	
Total Teachers: 198	**Guidance Counselors**: 3.0	**% Hispanic**: 0.3	
Student/Classroom Teacher Ratio: na	1,214 students/counselor	**% White**: 97.8	

Barnstable County

[SOUTH YARMOUTH] **DENNIS-YARMOUTH S.D.**

296 STATION AVE ● SOUTH YARMOUTH MA 02664 ● (508) 398-7605 ● http://www.dy-regional.k12.ma.us

Grade Span: PK-12	**Expenditures/Student**: $6,228	**% Amer Indian**: 0.3	National ***Socio-Economic Status*** indicator percentiles are not available for the state of Massachusetts
Schools: *Regular* 8 ● *Spec Ed* 0 ● *Alt* 0	**Librarians**: 7.0	**% Asian**: 0.8	
Students: 4,631	662 students/librarian	**% Black**: 4.1	
Total Teachers: 304	**Guidance Counselors**: 4.0	**% Hispanic**: 3.4	
Student/Classroom Teacher Ratio: na	1,158 students/counselor	**% White**: 91.3	

Berkshire County

[DALTON] **CENTRAL BERKSHIRE S.D.**

BOX 299,20 CLEVELAND ● DALTON MA 01227 ● (413) 684-0320

Grade Span: PK-12	**Expenditures/Student**: $6,166	**% Amer Indian**: 0.1	National ***Socio-Economic Status*** indicator percentiles are not available for the state of Massachusetts
Schools: *Regular* 7 ● *Spec Ed* 0 ● *Alt* 0	**Librarians**: 2.0	**% Asian**: 0.8	
Students: 2,516	1,258 students/librarian	**% Black**: 0.9	
Total Teachers: 157	**Guidance Counselors**: 6.1	**% Hispanic**: 0.3	
Student/Classroom Teacher Ratio: na	412 students/counselor	**% White**: 97.9	

Berkshire County

PITTSFIELD S.D.

269 FIRST ● PITTSFIELD MA 01201 ● (413) 499-9512

Grade Span: PK-12	**Expenditures/Student**: $6,383	**% Amer Indian**: 0.1	National ***Socio-Economic Status*** indicator percentiles are not available for the state of Massachusetts
Schools: *Regular* 12 ● *Spec Ed* 0 ● *Alt* 2	**Librarians**: 6.0	**% Asian**: 1.0	
Students: 6,928	1,155 students/librarian	**% Black**: 7.5	
Total Teachers: 483	**Guidance Counselors**: 12.0	**% Hispanic**: 1.9	
Student/Classroom Teacher Ratio: na	577 students/counselor	**% White**: 89.5	

Bristol County
ATTLEBORO S.D.
RATHBUN WILLARD DR ● ATTLEBORO MA 02703 ● (508) 222-0012 ● http://home.ici.net/customers/aps12/aps12.html

Grade Span: PK-12 **Schools**: *Regular* 10 ● *Spec Ed* 0 ● *Alt* 1 **Students**: 6,431 **Total Teachers**: 390 **Student/Classroom Teacher Ratio**: na	**Expenditures/Student**: $5,419 **Librarians**: 4.0 1,608 students/librarian **Guidance Counselors**: 7.2 893 students/counselor	**% Amer Indian**: 0.2 **% Asian**: 5.8 **% Black**: 1.9 **% Hispanic**: 4.5 **% White**: 87.6	National ***Socio-Economic Status*** indicator percentiles are not available for the state of Massachusetts

Bristol County
FALL RIVER S.D.
417 ROCK ● FALL RIVER MA 02720 ● (508) 675-8442 ● http://www.fallriver.mec.edu/schools1.html

Grade Span: PK-12 **Schools**: *Regular* 34 ● *Spec Ed* 0 ● *Alt* 2 **Students**: 12,327 **Total Teachers**: 923 **Student/Classroom Teacher Ratio**: na	**Expenditures/Student**: $6,361 **Librarians**: 6.8 1,813 students/librarian **Guidance Counselors**: 22.0 560 students/counselor	**% Amer Indian**: 0.5 **% Asian**: 4.7 **% Black**: 3.2 **% Hispanic**: 3.5 **% White**: 88.0	National ***Socio-Economic Status*** indicator percentiles are not available for the state of Massachusetts

Bristol County
MANSFIELD S.D.
2 PARK ROW ● MANSFIELD MA 02048 ● (508) 261-7500

Grade Span: PK-12 **Schools**: *Regular* 5 ● *Spec Ed* 0 ● *Alt* 0 **Students**: 3,650 **Total Teachers**: 242 **Student/Classroom Teacher Ratio**: na	**Expenditures/Student**: $5,603 **Librarians**: 0.0 *** students/librarian **Guidance Counselors**: 5.0 730 students/counselor	**% Amer Indian**: 0.0 **% Asian**: 1.2 **% Black**: 3.6 **% Hispanic**: 0.6 **% White**: 94.6	National ***Socio-Economic Status*** indicator percentiles are not available for the state of Massachusetts

Bristol County
NEW BEDFORD S.D.
455 COUNTY ● NEW BEDFORD MA 02740 ● (508) 997-4511 ● http://www.newbedford.k12.ma.us

Grade Span: PK-12 **Schools**: *Regular* 28 ● *Spec Ed* 0 ● *Alt* 0 **Students**: 14,595 **Total Teachers**: 1,048 **Student/Classroom Teacher Ratio**: na	**Expenditures/Student**: $6,735 **Librarians**: 1.0 14,595 students/librarian **Guidance Counselors**: 28.9 505 students/counselor	**% Amer Indian**: 0.2 **% Asian**: 0.7 **% Black**: 13.8 **% Hispanic**: 13.3 **% White**: 72.0	National ***Socio-Economic Status*** indicator percentiles are not available for the state of Massachusetts

Bristol County
NORTH ATTLEBOROUGH S.D.
570 LANDRY AVE ● NORTH ATTLEBOROUGH MA 02760 ● (508) 643-2100

Grade Span: KG-12 **Schools**: *Regular* 9 ● *Spec Ed* 0 ● *Alt* 0 **Students**: 4,287 **Total Teachers**: 240 **Student/Classroom Teacher Ratio**: na	**Expenditures/Student**: $5,086 **Librarians**: 2.0 2,144 students/librarian **Guidance Counselors**: 5.6 766 students/counselor	**% Amer Indian**: 0.0 **% Asian**: 1.4 **% Black**: 1.0 **% Hispanic**: 0.4 **% White**: 97.2	National ***Socio-Economic Status*** indicator percentiles are not available for the state of Massachusetts

Bristol County
[NORTH DIGHTON] DIGHTON-REHOBOTH S.D.
2700 REGIONAL RD ● NORTH DIGHTON MA 02764 ● (508) 252-5000

Grade Span: PK-12 **Schools**: *Regular* 5 ● *Spec Ed* 0 ● *Alt* 0 **Students**: 2,921 **Total Teachers**: 190 **Student/Classroom Teacher Ratio**: na	**Expenditures/Student**: $5,924 **Librarians**: 5.0 584 students/librarian **Guidance Counselors**: 6.0 487 students/counselor	**% Amer Indian**: 0.0 **% Asian**: 0.3 **% Black**: 0.7 **% Hispanic**: 0.1 **% White**: 98.8	National ***Socio-Economic Status*** indicator percentiles are not available for the state of Massachusetts

Bristol County

[NORTH EASTON] **EASTON S.D.**

50 OLIVER ST/POB 359 ● NORTH EASTON MA 02356 ● (508) 230-3202

Grade Span: PK-12 **Schools**: *Regular* 7 ● *Spec Ed* 0 ● *Alt* 0 **Students**: 3,460 **Total Teachers**: 198 **Student/Classroom Teacher Ratio**: na	**Expenditures/Student**: $5,561 **Librarians**: 1.0 3,460 students/librarian **Guidance Counselors**: 6.0 577 students/counselor	**% Amer Indian**: 0.1 **% Asian**: 1.6 **% Black**: 2.7 **% Hispanic**: 0.8 **% White**: 94.8	National ***Socio-Economic Status*** indicator percentiles are not available for the state of Massachusetts

Bristol County

NORTON S.D.

64 WEST MAIN ● NORTON MA 02766 ● (508) 285-0100

Grade Span: PK-12 **Schools**: *Regular* 4 ● *Spec Ed* 0 ● *Alt* 0 **Students**: 2,572 **Total Teachers**: 147 **Student/Classroom Teacher Ratio**: na	**Expenditures/Student**: $5,504 **Librarians**: 1.0 2,572 students/librarian **Guidance Counselors**: 4.1 627 students/counselor	**% Amer Indian**: 0.0 **% Asian**: 0.8 **% Black**: 1.8 **% Hispanic**: 0.9 **% White**: 96.5	National ***Socio-Economic Status*** indicator percentiles are not available for the state of Massachusetts

Bristol County

SOMERSET S.D.

580 WHETSTONE HILL ● SOMERSET MA 02726 ● (508) 324-3100 ● http://musictown.mec.edu/SchoolFrontEnd/index.html

Grade Span: PK-12 **Schools**: *Regular* 6 ● *Spec Ed* 0 ● *Alt* 0 **Students**: 2,894 **Total Teachers**: 311 **Student/Classroom Teacher Ratio**: na	**Expenditures/Student**: $6,877 **Librarians**: 2.0 1,447 students/librarian **Guidance Counselors**: 10.0 289 students/counselor	**% Amer Indian**: 0.2 **% Asian**: 0.3 **% Black**: 0.3 **% Hispanic**: 0.6 **% White**: 98.6	National ***Socio-Economic Status*** indicator percentiles are not available for the state of Massachusetts

Bristol County

[SOUTH DARTMOUTH] **DARTMOUTH S.D.**

8 BUSH ● SOUTH DARTMOUTH MA 02748 ● (508) 997-3391

Grade Span: PK-12 **Schools**: *Regular* 6 ● *Spec Ed* 0 ● *Alt* 0 **Students**: 3,968 **Total Teachers**: 265 **Student/Classroom Teacher Ratio**: na	**Expenditures/Student**: $5,461 **Librarians**: 2.0 1,984 students/librarian **Guidance Counselors**: 10.0 397 students/counselor	**% Amer Indian**: 0.8 **% Asian**: 1.3 **% Black**: 1.8 **% Hispanic**: 0.6 **% White**: 95.5	National ***Socio-Economic Status*** indicator percentiles are not available for the state of Massachusetts

Bristol County

TAUNTON S.D.

50 WILLIAMS ● TAUNTON MA 02780 ● (508) 821-1100 ● http://members.aol.com/Taunschool/index.html

Grade Span: PK-12 **Schools**: *Regular* 14 ● *Spec Ed* 0 ● *Alt* 0 **Students**: 7,380 **Total Teachers**: 470 **Student/Classroom Teacher Ratio**: na	**Expenditures/Student**: $6,191 **Librarians**: 7.0 1,054 students/librarian **Guidance Counselors**: 23.0 321 students/counselor	**% Amer Indian**: 0.0 **% Asian**: 0.6 **% Black**: 6.0 **% Hispanic**: 4.9 **% White**: 88.5	National ***Socio-Economic Status*** indicator percentiles are not available for the state of Massachusetts

Essex County

AMESBURY S.D.

9 SCHOOL ● AMESBURY MA 01913 ● (978) 388-0507

Grade Span: PK-12 **Schools**: *Regular* 5 ● *Spec Ed* 0 ● *Alt* 0 **Students**: 2,785 **Total Teachers**: 172 **Student/Classroom Teacher Ratio**: na	**Expenditures/Student**: $5,498 **Librarians**: 1.8 1,547 students/librarian **Guidance Counselors**: 3.6 774 students/counselor	**% Amer Indian**: 0.1 **% Asian**: 0.4 **% Black**: 1.0 **% Hispanic**: 0.9 **% White**: 97.7	National ***Socio-Economic Status*** indicator percentiles are not available for the state of Massachusetts

Essex County

ANDOVER S.D.

36 BARTLET ● ANDOVER MA 01810 ● (978) 623-8501

Grade Span: PK-12 **Schools**: *Regular* 8 ● *Spec Ed* 0 ● *Alt* 0 **Students**: 5,461 **Total Teachers**: 339 **Student/Classroom Teacher Ratio**: na	**Expenditures/Student**: $6,301 **Librarians**: 5.0 1,092 students/librarian **Guidance Counselors**: 11.3 483 students/counselor	**% Amer Indian**: 0.1 **% Asian**: 6.0 **% Black**: 1.0 **% Hispanic**: 2.2 **% White**: 90.7	National ***Socio-Economic Status*** indicator percentiles are not available for the state of Massachusetts

Essex County

BEVERLY S.D.

4 COLON ● BEVERLY MA 01915 ● (508) 921-6100

Grade Span: PK-12 **Schools**: *Regular* 11 ● *Spec Ed* 0 ● *Alt* 0 **Students**: 4,811 **Total Teachers**: 318 **Student/Classroom Teacher Ratio**: na	**Expenditures/Student**: $6,330 **Librarians**: 5.0 962 students/librarian **Guidance Counselors**: 7.0 687 students/counselor	**% Amer Indian**: 0.1 **% Asian**: 0.9 **% Black**: 2.3 **% Hispanic**: 2.4 **% White**: 94.3	National ***Socio-Economic Status*** indicator percentiles are not available for the state of Massachusetts

Essex County

[BYFIELD] **TRITON S.D.**

112 ELM ● BYFIELD MA 01922 ● (978) 465-5084 ● http://www.Triton.org

Grade Span: PK-12 **Schools**: *Regular* 7 ● *Spec Ed* 0 ● *Alt* 0 **Students**: 3,162 **Total Teachers**: 213 **Student/Classroom Teacher Ratio**: na	**Expenditures/Student**: $6,362 **Librarians**: 1.0 3,162 students/librarian **Guidance Counselors**: 5.0 632 students/counselor	**% Amer Indian**: 0.2 **% Asian**: 0.7 **% Black**: 0.9 **% Hispanic**: 0.8 **% White**: 97.5	National ***Socio-Economic Status*** indicator percentiles are not available for the state of Massachusetts

Essex County

DANVERS S.D.

64 CABOT ROAD ● DANVERS MA 01923 ● (978) 777-4539

Grade Span: PK-12 **Schools**: *Regular* 7 ● *Spec Ed* 0 ● *Alt* 1 **Students**: 3,535 **Total Teachers**: 228 **Student/Classroom Teacher Ratio**: na	**Expenditures/Student**: $6,596 **Librarians**: 1.0 3,535 students/librarian **Guidance Counselors**: 5.0 707 students/counselor	**% Amer Indian**: 0.0 **% Asian**: 1.3 **% Black**: 0.7 **% Hispanic**: 0.9 **% White**: 97.1	National ***Socio-Economic Status*** indicator percentiles are not available for the state of Massachusetts

Essex County

GLOUCESTER S.D.

6 SCHOOL HOUSE RD ● GLOUCESTER MA 01930 ● (978) 281-9800

Grade Span: PK-12 **Schools**: *Regular* 7 ● *Spec Ed* 0 ● *Alt* 1 **Students**: 3,977 **Total Teachers**: 286 **Student/Classroom Teacher Ratio**: na	**Expenditures/Student**: $6,809 **Librarians**: 1.0 3,977 students/librarian **Guidance Counselors**: 5.0 795 students/counselor	**% Amer Indian**: 0.0 **% Asian**: 0.4 **% Black**: 1.4 **% Hispanic**: 0.9 **% White**: 97.3	National ***Socio-Economic Status*** indicator percentiles are not available for the state of Massachusetts

Essex County

HAVERHILL S.D.

4 SUMMER ● HAVERHILL MA 01830 ● (978) 374-3400

Grade Span: PK-12 **Schools**: *Regular* 21 ● *Spec Ed* 0 ● *Alt* 0 **Students**: 8,067 **Total Teachers**: 464 **Student/Classroom Teacher Ratio**: na	**Expenditures/Student**: $5,944 **Librarians**: 2.0 4,034 students/librarian **Guidance Counselors**: 11.0 733 students/counselor	**% Amer Indian**: 0.1 **% Asian**: 1.4 **% Black**: 3.2 **% Hispanic**: 13.2 **% White**: 82.0	National ***Socio-Economic Status*** indicator percentiles are not available for the state of Massachusetts

Essex County
LAWRENCE S.D.
255 ESSEX ● LAWRENCE MA 01840 ● (978) 975-5900

Grade Span: PK-12 **Schools**: *Regular* 17 ● *Spec Ed* 0 ● *Alt* 0 **Students**: 11,355 **Total Teachers**: 758 **Student/Classroom Teacher Ratio**: na	**Expenditures/Student**: $7,021 **Librarians**: 1.0 11,355 students/librarian **Guidance Counselors**: 25.0 454 students/counselor	**% Amer Indian**: 0.0 **% Asian**: 3.3 **% Black**: 2.7 **% Hispanic**: 77.3 **% White**: 16.6	National ***Socio-Economic Status*** indicator percentiles are not available for the state of Massachusetts

Essex County
LYNN S.D.
42 FRANKLIN ● LYNN MA 01902 ● (781) 593-1680

Grade Span: PK-12 **Schools**: *Regular* 24 ● *Spec Ed* 0 ● *Alt* 2 **Students**: 13,642 **Total Teachers**: 886 **Student/Classroom Teacher Ratio**: na	**Expenditures/Student**: $6,164 **Librarians**: 10.8 1,263 students/librarian **Guidance Counselors**: 23.9 571 students/counselor	**% Amer Indian**: 0.2 **% Asian**: 12.7 **% Black**: 14.2 **% Hispanic**: 22.9 **% White**: 50.0	National ***Socio-Economic Status*** indicator percentiles are not available for the state of Massachusetts

Essex County
MARBLEHEAD S.D.
2 HUMPHREY ● MARBLEHEAD MA 01945 ● (781) 639-3141

Grade Span: PK-12 **Schools**: *Regular* 7 ● *Spec Ed* 0 ● *Alt* 0 **Students**: 2,684 **Total Teachers**: 210 **Student/Classroom Teacher Ratio**: na	**Expenditures/Student**: $6,470 **Librarians**: 0.0 *** students/librarian **Guidance Counselors**: 8.0 336 students/counselor	**% Amer Indian**: 0.0 **% Asian**: 0.8 **% Black**: 3.1 **% Hispanic**: 0.7 **% White**: 95.4	National ***Socio-Economic Status*** indicator percentiles are not available for the state of Massachusetts

Essex County
METHUEN S.D.
160 MERRIMACK ● METHUEN MA 01844 ● (978) 681-1317

Grade Span: PK-12 **Schools**: *Regular* 9 ● *Spec Ed* 0 ● *Alt* 0 **Students**: 6,337 **Total Teachers**: 352 **Student/Classroom Teacher Ratio**: na	**Expenditures/Student**: $5,811 **Librarians**: 1.0 6,337 students/librarian **Guidance Counselors**: 6.0 1,056 students/counselor	**% Amer Indian**: 0.2 **% Asian**: 2.8 **% Black**: 1.4 **% Hispanic**: 13.2 **% White**: 82.3	National ***Socio-Economic Status*** indicator percentiles are not available for the state of Massachusetts

Essex County
NORTH ANDOVER S.D.
675 CHICKERING RD ● NORTH ANDOVER MA 01845 ● (978) 794-1503

Grade Span: PK-12 **Schools**: *Regular* 8 ● *Spec Ed* 0 ● *Alt* 0 **Students**: 3,874 **Total Teachers**: 218 **Student/Classroom Teacher Ratio**: na	**Expenditures/Student**: $5,901 **Librarians**: 4.0 969 students/librarian **Guidance Counselors**: 9.2 421 students/counselor	**% Amer Indian**: 0.1 **% Asian**: 3.4 **% Black**: 0.9 **% Hispanic**: 2.4 **% White**: 93.2	National ***Socio-Economic Status*** indicator percentiles are not available for the state of Massachusetts

Essex County
PEABODY S.D.
70 ENDICOTT ST ● PEABODY MA 01960 ● (978) 531-1600

Grade Span: PK-12 **Schools**: *Regular* 10 ● *Spec Ed* 0 ● *Alt* 1 **Students**: 6,176 **Total Teachers**: 406 **Student/Classroom Teacher Ratio**: na	**Expenditures/Student**: $6,947 **Librarians**: 2.0 3,088 students/librarian **Guidance Counselors**: 16.0 386 students/counselor	**% Amer Indian**: 0.1 **% Asian**: 1.7 **% Black**: 0.9 **% Hispanic**: 5.3 **% White**: 91.9	National ***Socio-Economic Status*** indicator percentiles are not available for the state of Massachusetts

Essex County
SALEM S.D.
29 HIGHLAND AVE ● SALEM MA 01970 ● (978) 740-1212

Grade Span: PK-12 **Schools**: *Regular* 10 ● *Spec Ed* 0 ● *Alt* 0 **Students**: 4,756 **Total Teachers**: 342 **Student/Classroom Teacher Ratio**: na	**Expenditures/Student**: $6,971 **Librarians**: 3.0 1,585 students/librarian **Guidance Counselors**: 5.8 820 students/counselor	**% Amer Indian**: 0.4 **% Asian**: 2.3 **% Black**: 3.7 **% Hispanic**: 23.2 **% White**: 70.3	National ***Socio-Economic Status*** indicator percentiles are not available for the state of Massachusetts

Essex County
SAUGUS S.D.
23 MAIN ● SAUGUS MA 01906 ● (781) 231-5000

Grade Span: PK-12 **Schools**: *Regular* 8 ● *Spec Ed* 0 ● *Alt* 0 **Students**: 3,279 **Total Teachers**: 245 **Student/Classroom Teacher Ratio**: na	**Expenditures/Student**: $6,646 **Librarians**: 1.0 3,279 students/librarian **Guidance Counselors**: 8.0 410 students/counselor	**% Amer Indian**: 0.2 **% Asian**: 1.3 **% Black**: 0.7 **% Hispanic**: 0.5 **% White**: 97.4	National ***Socio-Economic Status*** indicator percentiles are not available for the state of Massachusetts

Essex County
[WEST NEWBURY] WEST MEWBURY S.D.
22 MAIN STREET ● WEST NEWBURY MA 01985 ● (978) 363-2280

Grade Span: PK-12 **Schools**: *Regular* 6 ● *Spec Ed* 0 ● *Alt* 0 **Students**: 3,096 **Total Teachers**: 210 **Student/Classroom Teacher Ratio**: na	**Expenditures/Student**: $5,321 **Librarians**: 5.0 619 students/librarian **Guidance Counselors**: 6.1 508 students/counselor	**% Amer Indian**: 0.0 **% Asian**: 0.6 **% Black**: 0.4 **% Hispanic**: 0.5 **% White**: 98.5	National ***Socio-Economic Status*** indicator percentiles are not available for the state of Massachusetts

Franklin County
GREENFIELD S.D.
141 DAVIS ● GREENFIELD MA 01301 ● (413) 772-1300 ● http://www.greenfield.k14.mass.edu

Grade Span: PK-12 **Schools**: *Regular* 8 ● *Spec Ed* 0 ● *Alt* 0 **Students**: 2,520 **Total Teachers**: 172 **Student/Classroom Teacher Ratio**: na	**Expenditures/Student**: $6,083 **Librarians**: 1.0 2,520 students/librarian **Guidance Counselors**: 4.0 630 students/counselor	**% Amer Indian**: 0.1 **% Asian**: 0.8 **% Black**: 2.9 **% Hispanic**: 6.1 **% White**: 90.1	National ***Socio-Economic Status*** indicator percentiles are not available for the state of Massachusetts

Hampden County
CHICOPEE S.D.
180 BROADWAY ● CHICOPEE MA 01020 ● (413) 594-3410

Grade Span: PK-12 **Schools**: *Regular* 15 ● *Spec Ed* 0 ● *Alt* 1 **Students**: 7,556 **Total Teachers**: 524 **Student/Classroom Teacher Ratio**: na	**Expenditures/Student**: $6,694 **Librarians**: 4.0 1,889 students/librarian **Guidance Counselors**: 22.0 343 students/counselor	**% Amer Indian**: 0.1 **% Asian**: 0.7 **% Black**: 2.7 **% Hispanic**: 10.9 **% White**: 85.6	National ***Socio-Economic Status*** indicator percentiles are not available for the state of Massachusetts

Hampden County
EAST LONGMEADOW S.D.
180 MAPLE ● EAST LONGMEADOW MA 01028 ● (413) 525-5450

Grade Span: PK-12 **Schools**: *Regular* 5 ● *Spec Ed* 0 ● *Alt* 0 **Students**: 2,584 **Total Teachers**: 157 **Student/Classroom Teacher Ratio**: na	**Expenditures/Student**: $5,793 **Librarians**: 1.6 1,615 students/librarian **Guidance Counselors**: 6.8 380 students/counselor	**% Amer Indian**: 0.0 **% Asian**: 0.5 **% Black**: 2.5 **% Hispanic**: 0.5 **% White**: 96.5	National ***Socio-Economic Status*** indicator percentiles are not available for the state of Massachusetts

Hampden County
[FEEDING HILLS] **AGAWAM S.D.**
1305 SPRINGFIELD ● FEEDING HILLS MA 01030 ● (413) 789-1400

Grade Span: KG-12 **Schools**: *Regular* 7 ● *Spec Ed* 0 ● *Alt* 0 **Students**: 4,258 **Total Teachers**: 260 **Student/Classroom Teacher Ratio**: na	**Expenditures/Student**: $5,563 **Librarians**: 3.0 1,419 students/librarian **Guidance Counselors**: 7.0 608 students/counselor	**% Amer Indian**: 0.1 **% Asian**: 1.1 **% Black**: 0.8 **% Hispanic**: 1.6 **% White**: 96.4	National ***Socio-Economic Status*** indicator percentiles are not available for the state of Massachusetts

Hampden County
HOLYOKE S.D.
57 SUFFOLK ● HOLYOKE MA 01040 ● (413) 534-2005

Grade Span: PK-12 **Schools**: *Regular* 11 ● *Spec Ed* 0 ● *Alt* 3 **Students**: 7,716 **Total Teachers**: 732 **Student/Classroom Teacher Ratio**: na	**Expenditures/Student**: $7,415 **Librarians**: 5.0 1,543 students/librarian **Guidance Counselors**: 18.0 429 students/counselor	**% Amer Indian**: 0.1 **% Asian**: 0.7 **% Black**: 4.1 **% Hispanic**: 69.4 **% White**: 25.8	National ***Socio-Economic Status*** indicator percentiles are not available for the state of Massachusetts

Hampden County
LONGMEADOW S.D.
811 LONGMEADOW ● LONGMEADOW MA 01106 ● (413) 565-4200

Grade Span: KG-12 **Schools**: *Regular* 6 ● *Spec Ed* 0 ● *Alt* 0 **Students**: 2,919 **Total Teachers**: 221 **Student/Classroom Teacher Ratio**: na	**Expenditures/Student**: $6,925 **Librarians**: 3.0 973 students/librarian **Guidance Counselors**: 6.0 487 students/counselor	**% Amer Indian**: 0.0 **% Asian**: 3.2 **% Black**: 2.4 **% Hispanic**: 0.7 **% White**: 93.7	National ***Socio-Economic Status*** indicator percentiles are not available for the state of Massachusetts

Hampden County
LUDLOW S.D.
63 CHESTNUT ● LUDLOW MA 01056 ● (413) 583-8372

Grade Span: PK-12 **Schools**: *Regular* 5 ● *Spec Ed* 0 ● *Alt* 0 **Students**: 2,973 **Total Teachers**: 189 **Student/Classroom Teacher Ratio**: na	**Expenditures/Student**: $5,848 **Librarians**: 2.0 1,487 students/librarian **Guidance Counselors**: 6.4 465 students/counselor	**% Amer Indian**: 0.0 **% Asian**: 0.4 **% Black**: 0.5 **% Hispanic**: 1.5 **% White**: 97.6	National ***Socio-Economic Status*** indicator percentiles are not available for the state of Massachusetts

Hampden County
SPRINGFIELD S.D.
195 STATE, BOX 1410 ● SPRINGFIELD MA 01102 ● (413) 787-7087

Grade Span: PK-12 **Schools**: *Regular* 38 ● *Spec Ed* 0 ● *Alt* 5 **Students**: 23,584 **Total Teachers**: 1,953 **Student/Classroom Teacher Ratio**: na	**Expenditures/Student**: $7,665 **Librarians**: 26.0 907 students/librarian **Guidance Counselors**: 40.0 590 students/counselor	**% Amer Indian**: 0.1 **% Asian**: 2.3 **% Black**: 30.6 **% Hispanic**: 37.4 **% White**: 29.6	National ***Socio-Economic Status*** indicator percentiles are not available for the state of Massachusetts

Hampden County
WEST SPRINGFIELD S.D.
26 CENTRAL ● WEST SPRINGFIELD MA 01089 ● (413) 263-3289

Grade Span: PK-12 **Schools**: *Regular* 9 ● *Spec Ed* 0 ● *Alt* 0 **Students**: 3,904 **Total Teachers**: 227 **Student/Classroom Teacher Ratio**: na	**Expenditures/Student**: $5,544 **Librarians**: 3.0 1,301 students/librarian **Guidance Counselors**: 8.0 488 students/counselor	**% Amer Indian**: 0.1 **% Asian**: 2.9 **% Black**: 3.5 **% Hispanic**: 7.1 **% White**: 86.4	National ***Socio-Economic Status*** indicator percentiles are not available for the state of Massachusetts

Hampden County
WESTFIELD S.D.
22 ASHLEY ● WESTFIELD MA 01085 ● (413) 572-6403

Grade Span: PK-12 **Schools**: *Regular* 11 ● *Spec Ed* 0 ● *Alt* 1 **Students**: 6,496 **Total Teachers**: 421 **Student/Classroom Teacher Ratio**: na	**Expenditures/Student**: $5,578 **Librarians**: 3.0 2,165 students/librarian **Guidance Counselors**: 9.9 656 students/counselor	**% Amer Indian**: 0.0 **% Asian**: 1.2 **% Black**: 1.2 **% Hispanic**: 7.9 **% White**: 89.7	National ***Socio-Economic Status*** indicator percentiles are not available for the state of Massachusetts

Hampden County
[WILBRAHAM] **HAMPDEN-WILBRAHAM S.D.**
621 MAIN ● WILBRAHAM MA 01095 ● (413) 596-3884

Grade Span: PK-12 **Schools**: *Regular* 7 ● *Spec Ed* 0 ● *Alt* 0 **Students**: 3,423 **Total Teachers**: 218 **Student/Classroom Teacher Ratio**: na	**Expenditures/Student**: $5,930 **Librarians**: 4.4 778 students/librarian **Guidance Counselors**: 8.3 412 students/counselor	**% Amer Indian**: 0.0 **% Asian**: 2.0 **% Black**: 2.3 **% Hispanic**: 0.5 **% White**: 95.2	National ***Socio-Economic Status*** indicator percentiles are not available for the state of Massachusetts

Hampshire County
NORTHAMPTON S.D.
212 MAIN ● NORTHAMPTON MA 01060 ● (413) 586-6970

Grade Span: PK-12 **Schools**: *Regular* 6 ● *Spec Ed* 0 ● *Alt* 0 **Students**: 3,082 **Total Teachers**: 229 **Student/Classroom Teacher Ratio**: na	**Expenditures/Student**: $6,590 **Librarians**: 2.0 1,541 students/librarian **Guidance Counselors**: 11.5 268 students/counselor	**% Amer Indian**: 0.7 **% Asian**: 4.3 **% Black**: 2.7 **% Hispanic**: 12.6 **% White**: 79.7	National ***Socio-Economic Status*** indicator percentiles are not available for the state of Massachusetts

Middlesex County
ARLINGTON S.D.
P O BOX 167 ● ARLINGTON MA 02174 ● (781) 646-1000

Grade Span: KG-12 **Schools**: *Regular* 9 ● *Spec Ed* 0 ● *Alt* 0 **Students**: 4,059 **Total Teachers**: 283 **Student/Classroom Teacher Ratio**: na	**Expenditures/Student**: $8,060 **Librarians**: 3.6 1,128 students/librarian **Guidance Counselors**: 7.0 580 students/counselor	**% Amer Indian**: 0.0 **% Asian**: 5.6 **% Black**: 5.3 **% Hispanic**: 2.9 **% White**: 86.1	National ***Socio-Economic Status*** indicator percentiles are not available for the state of Massachusetts

Middlesex County
BELMONT S.D.
644 PLEASANT ● BELMONT MA 02178 ● (617) 484-4180

Grade Span: PK-12 **Schools**: *Regular* 6 ● *Spec Ed* 0 ● *Alt* 0 **Students**: 3,397 **Total Teachers**: 213 **Student/Classroom Teacher Ratio**: na	**Expenditures/Student**: $7,017 **Librarians**: 2.9 1,171 students/librarian **Guidance Counselors**: 12.6 270 students/counselor	**% Amer Indian**: 0.0 **% Asian**: 5.7 **% Black**: 4.1 **% Hispanic**: 1.1 **% White**: 89.1	National ***Socio-Economic Status*** indicator percentiles are not available for the state of Massachusetts

Middlesex County
BILLERICA S.D.
365 BOSTON RD ● BILLERICA MA 01821 ● (978) 436-9500

Grade Span: KG-12 **Schools**: *Regular* 9 ● *Spec Ed* 0 ● *Alt* 0 **Students**: 6,039 **Total Teachers**: 262 **Student/Classroom Teacher Ratio**: na	**Expenditures/Student**: $6,174 **Librarians**: 0.0 *** students/librarian **Guidance Counselors**: 15.0 403 students/counselor	**% Amer Indian**: 0.1 **% Asian**: 2.1 **% Black**: 0.7 **% Hispanic**: 1.2 **% White**: 95.9	National ***Socio-Economic Status*** indicator percentiles are not available for the state of Massachusetts

Middlesex County
BURLINGTON S.D.
123 CAMBRIDGE ● BURLINGTON MA 01803 ● (781) 270-1800

Grade Span: KG-12	**Expenditures/Student**: $7,622	**% Amer Indian**: 0.0	National ***Socio-Economic***
Schools: *Regular* 6 ● *Spec Ed* 0 ● *Alt* 0	**Librarians**: 1.0	**% Asian**: 6.6	***Status*** indicator percentiles
Students: 3,413	3,413 students/librarian	**% Black**: 1.8	are not available for the
Total Teachers: 283	**Guidance Counselors**: 6.0	**% Hispanic**: 0.6	state of Massachusetts
Student/Classroom Teacher Ratio: na	569 students/counselor	**% White**: 90.9	

Middlesex County
CAMBRIDGE S.D.
159 THORNDIKE ● CAMBRIDGE MA 02141 ● (617) 349-6400 ● http://www.cps.ci.cambridge.ma.us

Grade Span: PK-12	**Expenditures/Student**: $11,621	**% Amer Indian**: 0.2	National ***Socio-Economic***
Schools: *Regular* 14 ● *Spec Ed* 0 ● *Alt* 2	**Librarians**: 12.0	**% Asian**: 8.7	***Status*** indicator percentiles
Students: 8,004	667 students/librarian	**% Black**: 34.7	are not available for the
Total Teachers: 764	**Guidance Counselors**: 14.0	**% Hispanic**: 15.3	state of Massachusetts
Student/Classroom Teacher Ratio: na	572 students/counselor	**% White**: 41.1	

Middlesex County
DRACUT S.D.
2063 LAKEVIEW AVE ● DRACUT MA 01826 ● (978) 957-2660

Grade Span: PK-12	**Expenditures/Student**: $5,310	**% Amer Indian**: 0.2	National ***Socio-Economic***
Schools: *Regular* 6 ● *Spec Ed* 0 ● *Alt* 0	**Librarians**: 2.0	**% Asian**: 3.2	***Status*** indicator percentiles
Students: 3,960	1,980 students/librarian	**% Black**: 0.9	are not available for the
Total Teachers: 230	**Guidance Counselors**: 4.0	**% Hispanic**: 1.4	state of Massachusetts
Student/Classroom Teacher Ratio: na	990 students/counselor	**% White**: 94.3	

Middlesex County
EVERETT S.D.
121 VINE ● EVERETT MA 02149 ● (617) 389-7950

Grade Span: PK-12	**Expenditures/Student**: $6,016	**% Amer Indian**: 0.1	National ***Socio-Economic***
Schools: *Regular* 10 ● *Spec Ed* 0 ● *Alt* 0	**Librarians**: 0.0	**% Asian**: 4.5	***Status*** indicator percentiles
Students: 4,806	*** students/librarian	**% Black**: 6.2	are not available for the
Total Teachers: 318	**Guidance Counselors**: 16.0	**% Hispanic**: 8.0	state of Massachusetts
Student/Classroom Teacher Ratio: na	300 students/counselor	**% White**: 81.1	

Middlesex County
FRAMINGHAM S.D.
454 WATER ● FRAMINGHAM MA 01701 ● (508) 626-9117

Grade Span: PK-12	**Expenditures/Student**: $8,331	**% Amer Indian**: 0.1	National ***Socio-Economic***
Schools: *Regular* 12 ● *Spec Ed* 0 ● *Alt* 0	**Librarians**: 5.0	**% Asian**: 5.0	***Status*** indicator percentiles
Students: 7,504	1,501 students/librarian	**% Black**: 8.8	are not available for the
Total Teachers: 573	**Guidance Counselors**: 24.0	**% Hispanic**: 15.7	state of Massachusetts
Student/Classroom Teacher Ratio: na	313 students/counselor	**% White**: 70.4	

Middlesex County
HOLLISTON S.D.
100 LINDEN ● HOLLISTON MA 01746 ● (508) 429-0654

Grade Span: PK-12	**Expenditures/Student**: $5,438	**% Amer Indian**: 0.2	National ***Socio-Economic***
Schools: *Regular* 5 ● *Spec Ed* 0 ● *Alt* 0	**Librarians**: 3.0	**% Asian**: 1.7	***Status*** indicator percentiles
Students: 3,035	1,012 students/librarian	**% Black**: 1.2	are not available for the
Total Teachers: 194	**Guidance Counselors**: 9.0	**% Hispanic**: 1.1	state of Massachusetts
Student/Classroom Teacher Ratio: na	337 students/counselor	**% White**: 95.8	

Middlesex County
HUDSON S.D.
155 APSLEY ● HUDSON MA 01749 ● (978) 567-6100

Grade Span: PK-12	**Expenditures/Student**: $6,916	**% Amer Indian**: 0.0	National ***Socio-Economic***
Schools: *Regular* 6 ● *Spec Ed* 0 ● *Alt* 0	**Librarians**: 4.0	**% Asian**: 1.4	***Status*** indicator percentiles
Students: 2,535	634 students/librarian	**% Black**: 0.7	are not available for the
Total Teachers: 179	**Guidance Counselors**: 5.5	**% Hispanic**: 2.0	state of Massachusetts
Student/Classroom Teacher Ratio: na	461 students/counselor	**% White**: 95.8	

Middlesex County
LEXINGTON S.D.
1557 MASS AVE ● LEXINGTON MA 02173 ● (781) 861-2550 ● http://lps.lexingtonma.org

Grade Span: KG-12	**Expenditures/Student**: $8,034	**% Amer Indian**: 0.2	National ***Socio-Economic***
Schools: *Regular* 9 ● *Spec Ed* 0 ● *Alt* 0	**Librarians**: 0.0	**% Asian**: 12.4	***Status*** indicator percentiles
Students: 5,274	*** students/librarian	**% Black**: 7.0	are not available for the
Total Teachers: 420	**Guidance Counselors**: 17.9	**% Hispanic**: 1.1	state of Massachusetts
Student/Classroom Teacher Ratio: na	295 students/counselor	**% White**: 79.2	

Middlesex County
LOWELL S.D.
89 APPLETON ● LOWELL MA 01852 ● (978) 937-7647

Grade Span: PK-12	**Expenditures/Student**: $6,658	**% Amer Indian**: 0.1	National ***Socio-Economic***
Schools: *Regular* 28 ● *Spec Ed* 0 ● *Alt* 1	**Librarians**: 2.0	**% Asian**: 28.8	***Status*** indicator percentiles
Students: 15,298	7,649 students/librarian	**% Black**: 3.4	are not available for the
Total Teachers: 1,036	**Guidance Counselors**: 19.0	**% Hispanic**: 21.6	state of Massachusetts
Student/Classroom Teacher Ratio: na	805 students/counselor	**% White**: 46.1	

Middlesex County
MALDEN S.D.
77 SALEM ● MALDEN MA 02148 ● (781) 397-7204

Grade Span: PK-12	**Expenditures/Student**: $6,622	**% Amer Indian**: 0.2	National ***Socio-Economic***
Schools: *Regular* 10 ● *Spec Ed* 0 ● *Alt* 0	**Librarians**: 1.0	**% Asian**: 15.8	***Status*** indicator percentiles
Students: 5,579	5,579 students/librarian	**% Black**: 11.4	are not available for the
Total Teachers: 385	**Guidance Counselors**: 6.0	**% Hispanic**: 5.4	state of Massachusetts
Student/Classroom Teacher Ratio: na	930 students/counselor	**% White**: 67.1	

Middlesex County
MARLBOROUGH S.D.
255 MAIN ● MARLBOROUGH MA 01752 ● (508) 460-3509

Grade Span: PK-12	**Expenditures/Student**: $6,970	**% Amer Indian**: 0.4	National ***Socio-Economic***
Schools: *Regular* 7 ● *Spec Ed* 0 ● *Alt* 0	**Librarians**: 1.0	**% Asian**: 2.2	***Status*** indicator percentiles
Students: 4,169	4,169 students/librarian	**% Black**: 3.0	are not available for the
Total Teachers: 292	**Guidance Counselors**: 12.0	**% Hispanic**: 7.3	state of Massachusetts
Student/Classroom Teacher Ratio: na	347 students/counselor	**% White**: 87.1	

Middlesex County
MEDFORD S.D.
489 WINTHROP ● MEDFORD MA 02155 ● (781) 393-2200

Grade Span: PK-12	**Expenditures/Student**: $7,623	**% Amer Indian**: 0.2	National ***Socio-Economic***
Schools: *Regular* 14 ● *Spec Ed* 0 ● *Alt* 1	**Librarians**: 2.0	**% Asian**: 3.0	***Status*** indicator percentiles
Students: 5,337	2,669 students/librarian	**% Black**: 9.7	are not available for the
Total Teachers: 456	**Guidance Counselors**: 9.8	**% Hispanic**: 2.3	state of Massachusetts
Student/Classroom Teacher Ratio: na	545 students/counselor	**% White**: 84.9	

Middlesex County
MELROSE S.D.
235 WEST FOSTER ● MELROSE MA 02176 ● (781) 979-2293

Grade Span: PK-12	**Expenditures/Student**: $6,952	**% Amer Indian**: 0.1	National ***Socio-Economic***
Schools: *Regular* 9 ● *Spec Ed* 0 ● *Alt* 0	**Librarians**: 2.0	**% Asian**: 1.5	***Status*** indicator percentiles
Students: 3,594	1,797 students/librarian	**% Black**: 3.1	are not available for the
Total Teachers: 237	**Guidance Counselors**: 5.0	**% Hispanic**: 0.9	state of Massachusetts
Student/Classroom Teacher Ratio: na	719 students/counselor	**% White**: 94.4	

Middlesex County
NATICK S.D.
13 EAST CENTRAL ● NATICK MA 01760 ● (508) 651-7104 ● http://www.natick.k12.ma.us

Grade Span: PK-12	**Expenditures/Student**: $8,128	**% Amer Indian**: 0.1	National ***Socio-Economic***
Schools: *Regular* 8 ● *Spec Ed* 0 ● *Alt* 1	**Librarians**: 0.0	**% Asian**: 3.4	***Status*** indicator percentiles
Students: 3,898	*** students/librarian	**% Black**: 2.9	are not available for the
Total Teachers: 258	**Guidance Counselors**: 13.2	**% Hispanic**: 1.3	state of Massachusetts
Student/Classroom Teacher Ratio: na	295 students/counselor	**% White**: 92.3	

Middlesex County
[NEWTONVILLE] NEWTON S.D.
100 WALNUT ● NEWTONVILLE MA 02160 ● (617) 552-7591 ● http://www.newton.mec.edu

Grade Span: KG-12	**Expenditures/Student**: $7,852	**% Amer Indian**: 0.1	National ***Socio-Economic***
Schools: *Regular* 20 ● *Spec Ed* 0 ● *Alt* 0	**Librarians**: 19.3	**% Asian**: 6.0	***Status*** indicator percentiles
Students: 10,675	553 students/librarian	**% Black**: 8.5	are not available for the
Total Teachers: 750	**Guidance Counselors**: 46.2	**% Hispanic**: 2.4	state of Massachusetts
Student/Classroom Teacher Ratio: na	231 students/counselor	**% White**: 83.0	

Middlesex County
[NORTH CHELMSFORD] CHELMSFORD S.D.
190 RICHARDSON RD ● NORTH CHELMSFORD MA 01863 ● (978) 251-5100

Grade Span: KG-12	**Expenditures/Student**: $6,183	**% Amer Indian**: 0.0	National ***Socio-Economic***
Schools: *Regular* 7 ● *Spec Ed* 0 ● *Alt* 0	**Librarians**: 4.0	**% Asian**: 4.2	***Status*** indicator percentiles
Students: 5,378	1,345 students/librarian	**% Black**: 0.5	are not available for the
Total Teachers: 326	**Guidance Counselors**: 12.8	**% Hispanic**: 0.6	state of Massachusetts
Student/Classroom Teacher Ratio: na	420 students/counselor	**% White**: 94.7	

Middlesex County
READING S.D.
82 OAKLAND RD ● READING MA 01867 ● (781) 944-5800

Grade Span: PK-12	**Expenditures/Student**: $5,807	**% Amer Indian**: 0.1	National ***Socio-Economic***
Schools: *Regular* 7 ● *Spec Ed* 0 ● *Alt* 0	**Librarians**: 7.0	**% Asian**: 1.7	***Status*** indicator percentiles
Students: 3,988	570 students/librarian	**% Black**: 2.5	are not available for the
Total Teachers: 245	**Guidance Counselors**: 12.0	**% Hispanic**: 0.4	state of Massachusetts
Student/Classroom Teacher Ratio: na	332 students/counselor	**% White**: 95.4	

Middlesex County
SOMERVILLE S.D.
93 SCHOOL ● SOMERVILLE MA 02143 ● (617) 625-6600

Grade Span: PK-12	**Expenditures/Student**: $7,593	**% Amer Indian**: 0.2	National ***Socio-Economic***
Schools: *Regular* 11 ● *Spec Ed* 0 ● *Alt* 2	**Librarians**: 9.0	**% Asian**: 4.6	***Status*** indicator percentiles
Students: 6,703	745 students/librarian	**% Black**: 14.9	are not available for the
Total Teachers: 495	**Guidance Counselors**: 11.0	**% Hispanic**: 15.5	state of Massachusetts
Student/Classroom Teacher Ratio: na	609 students/counselor	**% White**: 64.7	

Middlesex County
STONEHAM S.D.
149 FRANKLIN ● STONEHAM MA 02180 ● (781) 279-3800

Grade Span: PK-12 **Schools**: *Regular* 6 ● *Spec Ed* 0 ● *Alt* 0 **Students**: 2,763 **Total Teachers**: 170 **Student/Classroom Teacher Ratio**: na	**Expenditures/Student**: $6,512 **Librarians**: 2.0 1,382 students/librarian **Guidance Counselors**: 8.5 325 students/counselor	**% Amer Indian**: 0.0 **% Asian**: 1.2 **% Black**: 1.4 **% Hispanic**: 2.0 **% White**: 95.4	National ***Socio-Economic Status*** indicator percentiles are not available for the state of Massachusetts

Middlesex County
TEWKSBURY S.D.
139 PLEASANT ● TEWKSBURY MA 01876 ● (978) 851-7347 ● http://www.mec.edu/tewksbury

Grade Span: KG-12 **Schools**: *Regular* 6 ● *Spec Ed* 0 ● *Alt* 0 **Students**: 3,954 **Total Teachers**: 233 **Student/Classroom Teacher Ratio**: na	**Expenditures/Student**: $6,229 **Librarians**: 3.0 1,318 students/librarian **Guidance Counselors**: 5.0 791 students/counselor	**% Amer Indian**: 0.0 **% Asian**: 1.4 **% Black**: 1.0 **% Hispanic**: 0.7 **% White**: 97.0	National ***Socio-Economic Status*** indicator percentiles are not available for the state of Massachusetts

Middlesex County
[TOWNSEND] NORTH MIDDLESEX S.D.
23 MAIN ● TOWNSEND MA 01469 ● (978) 597-8713

Grade Span: PK-12 **Schools**: *Regular* 7 ● *Spec Ed* 0 ● *Alt* 0 **Students**: 4,718 **Total Teachers**: 296 **Student/Classroom Teacher Ratio**: na	**Expenditures/Student**: $5,267 **Librarians**: 7.0 674 students/librarian **Guidance Counselors**: 13.0 363 students/counselor	**% Amer Indian**: 0.0 **% Asian**: 0.3 **% Black**: 0.9 **% Hispanic**: 0.3 **% White**: 98.5	National ***Socio-Economic Status*** indicator percentiles are not available for the state of Massachusetts

Middlesex County
WAKEFIELD S.D.
60 FARM ● WAKEFIELD MA 01880 ● (781) 246-6400

Grade Span: PK-12 **Schools**: *Regular* 9 ● *Spec Ed* 0 ● *Alt* 0 **Students**: 3,451 **Total Teachers**: 229 **Student/Classroom Teacher Ratio**: na	**Expenditures/Student**: $6,731 **Librarians**: 3.0 1,150 students/librarian **Guidance Counselors**: 6.0 575 students/counselor	**% Amer Indian**: 0.1 **% Asian**: 1.3 **% Black**: 1.7 **% Hispanic**: 0.6 **% White**: 96.3	National ***Socio-Economic Status*** indicator percentiles are not available for the state of Massachusetts

Middlesex County
WALTHAM S.D.
617 LEXINGTON ● WALTHAM MA 02254 ● (781) 893-8050

Grade Span: PK-12 **Schools**: *Regular* 12 ● *Spec Ed* 0 ● *Alt* 1 **Students**: 5,364 **Total Teachers**: 468 **Student/Classroom Teacher Ratio**: na	**Expenditures/Student**: $8,560 **Librarians**: 10.2 526 students/librarian **Guidance Counselors**: 10.5 511 students/counselor	**% Amer Indian**: 0.0 **% Asian**: 6.4 **% Black**: 8.7 **% Hispanic**: 15.0 **% White**: 69.9	National ***Socio-Economic Status*** indicator percentiles are not available for the state of Massachusetts

Middlesex County
WATERTOWN S.D.
30 COMMON ● WATERTOWN MA 02172 ● (617) 926-7700 ● http://www.watertown.k12.ma.us

Grade Span: PK-12 **Schools**: *Regular* 5 ● *Spec Ed* 0 ● *Alt* 0 **Students**: 2,686 **Total Teachers**: 204 **Student/Classroom Teacher Ratio**: na	**Expenditures/Student**: $8,365 **Librarians**: 3.0 895 students/librarian **Guidance Counselors**: 10.6 253 students/counselor	**% Amer Indian**: 0.2 **% Asian**: 3.8 **% Black**: 2.7 **% Hispanic**: 2.8 **% White**: 90.5	National ***Socio-Economic Status*** indicator percentiles are not available for the state of Massachusetts

Middlesex County
WESTFORD S.D.
35 TOWN FARM RD ● WESTFORD MA 01886 ● (978) 692-5560

Grade Span: PK-12 **Schools**: *Regular* 6 ● *Spec Ed* 0 ● *Alt* 0 **Students**: 3,556 **Total Teachers**: 212 **Student/Classroom Teacher Ratio**: na	**Expenditures/Student**: $5,724 **Librarians**: 0.0 *** students/librarian **Guidance Counselors**: 10.4 342 students/counselor	**% Amer Indian**: 0.1 **% Asian**: 2.6 **% Black**: 0.4 **% Hispanic**: 0.7 **% White**: 96.2	National ***Socio-Economic Status*** indicator percentiles are not available for the state of Massachusetts

Middlesex County
WILMINGTON S.D.
161 CHURCH ● WILMINGTON MA 01887 ● (978) 694-6000

Grade Span: PK-12 **Schools**: *Regular* 7 ● *Spec Ed* 0 ● *Alt* 0 **Students**: 3,197 **Total Teachers**: 191 **Student/Classroom Teacher Ratio**: na	**Expenditures/Student**: $6,217 **Librarians**: 3.0 1,066 students/librarian **Guidance Counselors**: 8.0 400 students/counselor	**% Amer Indian**: 0.0 **% Asian**: 2.0 **% Black**: 0.5 **% Hispanic**: 0.6 **% White**: 96.9	National ***Socio-Economic Status*** indicator percentiles are not available for the state of Massachusetts

Middlesex County
WINCHESTER S.D.
154 HORN POND BRK RD ● WINCHESTER MA 01890 ● (781) 721-7004

Grade Span: PK-12 **Schools**: *Regular* 7 ● *Spec Ed* 0 ● *Alt* 0 **Students**: 3,097 **Total Teachers**: 200 **Student/Classroom Teacher Ratio**: na	**Expenditures/Student**: $7,103 **Librarians**: 0.0 *** students/librarian **Guidance Counselors**: 6.0 516 students/counselor	**% Amer Indian**: 0.0 **% Asian**: 4.4 **% Black**: 1.3 **% Hispanic**: 0.8 **% White**: 93.4	National ***Socio-Economic Status*** indicator percentiles are not available for the state of Massachusetts

Middlesex County
WOBURN S.D.
55 LOCUST ST ● WOBURN MA 01801 ● (781) 937-8200

Grade Span: PK-12 **Schools**: *Regular* 12 ● *Spec Ed* 0 ● *Alt* 0 **Students**: 4,614 **Total Teachers**: 333 **Student/Classroom Teacher Ratio**: na	**Expenditures/Student**: $6,765 **Librarians**: 0.0 *** students/librarian **Guidance Counselors**: 9.0 513 students/counselor	**% Amer Indian**: 0.1 **% Asian**: 2.4 **% Black**: 1.5 **% Hispanic**: 4.6 **% White**: 91.4	National ***Socio-Economic Status*** indicator percentiles are not available for the state of Massachusetts

Norfolk County
BELLINGHAM S.D.
60 HARPIN ● BELLINGHAM MA 02019 ● (508) 883-1706

Grade Span: PK-12 **Schools**: *Regular* 5 ● *Spec Ed* 0 ● *Alt* 1 **Students**: 2,588 **Total Teachers**: 162 **Student/Classroom Teacher Ratio**: na	**Expenditures/Student**: $5,812 **Librarians**: 1.0 2,588 students/librarian **Guidance Counselors**: 4.0 647 students/counselor	**% Amer Indian**: 0.1 **% Asian**: 1.1 **% Black**: 1.6 **% Hispanic**: 1.5 **% White**: 95.8	National ***Socio-Economic Status*** indicator percentiles are not available for the state of Massachusetts

Norfolk County
BRAINTREE S.D.
482 WASHINGTON ● BRAINTREE MA 02184 ● (781) 380-0130

Grade Span: KG-12 **Schools**: *Regular* 11 ● *Spec Ed* 0 ● *Alt* 0 **Students**: 4,698 **Total Teachers**: 324 **Student/Classroom Teacher Ratio**: na	**Expenditures/Student**: $6,690 **Librarians**: 0.0 *** students/librarian **Guidance Counselors**: 18.9 249 students/counselor	**% Amer Indian**: 0.1 **% Asian**: 2.7 **% Black**: 2.4 **% Hispanic**: 1.1 **% White**: 93.8	National ***Socio-Economic Status*** indicator percentiles are not available for the state of Massachusetts

Norfolk County
BROOKLINE S.D.
333 WASHINGTON ● BROOKLINE MA 02146 ● (617) 730-2403 ● http://www.brookline.mec.edu/schools/schools.html

Grade Span: KG-12	**Expenditures/Student**: $8,848	**% Amer Indian**: 0.1	National ***Socio-Economic***
Schools: *Regular* 9 ● *Spec Ed* 0 ● *Alt* 0	**Librarians**: 11.5	**% Asian**: 14.0	***Status*** indicator percentiles
Students: 6,039	525 students/librarian	**% Black**: 10.2	are not available for the
Total Teachers: 423	**Guidance Counselors**: 20.6	**% Hispanic**: 4.3	state of Massachusetts
Student/Classroom Teacher Ratio: na	293 students/counselor	**% White**: 71.4	

Norfolk County
CANTON S.D.
960 WASHINGTON ● CANTON MA 02021 ● (781) 821-5060

Grade Span: PK-12	**Expenditures/Student**: $6,919	**% Amer Indian**: 0.0	National ***Socio-Economic***
Schools: *Regular* 5 ● *Spec Ed* 0 ● *Alt* 0	**Librarians**: 2.0	**% Asian**: 2.1	***Status*** indicator percentiles
Students: 2,733	1,367 students/librarian	**% Black**: 4.2	are not available for the
Total Teachers: 207	**Guidance Counselors**: 6.0	**% Hispanic**: 0.8	state of Massachusetts
Student/Classroom Teacher Ratio: na	456 students/counselor	**% White**: 92.8	

Norfolk County
DEDHAM S.D.
30 WHITING AVE ● DEDHAM MA 02026 ● (781) 326-5622 ● http://www.dedham.com/Studentweb/indexallpages.html

Grade Span: PK-12	**Expenditures/Student**: $7,657	**% Amer Indian**: 0.4	National ***Socio-Economic***
Schools: *Regular* 7 ● *Spec Ed* 0 ● *Alt* 0	**Librarians**: 4.0	**% Asian**: 1.8	***Status*** indicator percentiles
Students: 2,970	743 students/librarian	**% Black**: 2.1	are not available for the
Total Teachers: 212	**Guidance Counselors**: 6.0	**% Hispanic**: 2.3	state of Massachusetts
Student/Classroom Teacher Ratio: na	495 students/counselor	**% White**: 93.3	

Norfolk County
FOXBOROUGH S.D.
60 SOUTH ● FOXBOROUGH MA 02035 ● (508) 543-1660 ● http://foxborough.k12.ma.us

Grade Span: PK-12	**Expenditures/Student**: $6,265	**% Amer Indian**: 0.0	National ***Socio-Economic***
Schools: *Regular* 5 ● *Spec Ed* 0 ● *Alt* 0	**Librarians**: 0.0	**% Asian**: 1.4	***Status*** indicator percentiles
Students: 2,784	*** students/librarian	**% Black**: 2.2	are not available for the
Total Teachers: 170	**Guidance Counselors**: 7.0	**% Hispanic**: 1.2	state of Massachusetts
Student/Classroom Teacher Ratio: na	398 students/counselor	**% White**: 95.1	

Norfolk County
FRANKLIN S.D.
OAK ● FRANKLIN MA 02038 ● (508) 528-5600

Grade Span: PK-12	**Expenditures/Student**: $4,856	**% Amer Indian**: 0.0	National ***Socio-Economic***
Schools: *Regular* 7 ● *Spec Ed* 0 ● *Alt* 0	**Librarians**: 2.0	**% Asian**: 1.3	***Status*** indicator percentiles
Students: 4,398	2,199 students/librarian	**% Black**: 0.7	are not available for the
Total Teachers: 256	**Guidance Counselors**: 9.0	**% Hispanic**: 0.4	state of Massachusetts
Student/Classroom Teacher Ratio: na	489 students/counselor	**% White**: 97.6	

Norfolk County
MILTON S.D.
391 BROOK RD ● MILTON MA 02186 ● (617) 696-4809

Grade Span: PK-12	**Expenditures/Student**: $5,991	**% Amer Indian**: 0.0	National ***Socio-Economic***
Schools: *Regular* 6 ● *Spec Ed* 0 ● *Alt* 0	**Librarians**: 3.5	**% Asian**: 2.6	***Status*** indicator percentiles
Students: 3,736	1,067 students/librarian	**% Black**: 13.2	are not available for the
Total Teachers: 258	**Guidance Counselors**: 11.0	**% Hispanic**: 1.0	state of Massachusetts
Student/Classroom Teacher Ratio: na	340 students/counselor	**% White**: 83.2	

Norfolk County
NEEDHAM S.D.
1330 HIGHLAND AVE ● NEEDHAM MA 02192 ● (781) 455-0435 ● http://www.needham.mec.edu

Grade Span: PK-12 **Schools**: *Regular* 7 ● *Spec Ed* 0 ● *Alt* 0 **Students**: 4,087 **Total Teachers**: 253 **Student/Classroom Teacher Ratio**: na	**Expenditures/Student**: $7,615 **Librarians**: 0.0 *** students/librarian **Guidance Counselors**: 14.4 284 students/counselor	**% Amer Indian**: 0.0 **% Asian**: 3.6 **% Black**: 4.5 **% Hispanic**: 1.5 **% White**: 90.4	National ***Socio-Economic Status*** indicator percentiles are not available for the state of Massachusetts

Norfolk County
NORWOOD S.D.
100 WESTOVER PARKWAY ● NORWOOD MA 02062 ● (781) 762-0251

Grade Span: PK-12 **Schools**: *Regular* 7 ● *Spec Ed* 0 ● *Alt* 0 **Students**: 3,678 **Total Teachers**: 236 **Student/Classroom Teacher Ratio**: na	**Expenditures/Student**: $7,082 **Librarians**: 4.5 817 students/librarian **Guidance Counselors**: 9.0 409 students/counselor	**% Amer Indian**: 0.0 **% Asian**: 3.6 **% Black**: 4.4 **% Hispanic**: 2.8 **% White**: 89.3	National ***Socio-Economic Status*** indicator percentiles are not available for the state of Massachusetts

Norfolk County
QUINCY S.D.
70 CODDINGTON ● QUINCY MA 02169 ● (617) 984-8700

Grade Span: PK-12 **Schools**: *Regular* 17 ● *Spec Ed* 0 ● *Alt* 0 **Students**: 8,696 **Total Teachers**: 597 **Student/Classroom Teacher Ratio**: na	**Expenditures/Student**: $6,916 **Librarians**: 0.0 *** students/librarian **Guidance Counselors**: 33.0 264 students/counselor	**% Amer Indian**: 0.4 **% Asian**: 17.2 **% Black**: 3.4 **% Hispanic**: 3.0 **% White**: 76.0	National ***Socio-Economic Status*** indicator percentiles are not available for the state of Massachusetts

Norfolk County
RANDOLPH S.D.
40 HIGHLAND AVE ● RANDOLPH MA 02368 ● (781) 961-6205

Grade Span: KG-12 **Schools**: *Regular* 7 ● *Spec Ed* 0 ● *Alt* 0 **Students**: 3,985 **Total Teachers**: 250 **Student/Classroom Teacher Ratio**: na	**Expenditures/Student**: $5,920 **Librarians**: 0.0 *** students/librarian **Guidance Counselors**: 7.0 569 students/counselor	**% Amer Indian**: 0.3 **% Asian**: 11.4 **% Black**: 22.6 **% Hispanic**: 5.6 **% White**: 60.0	National ***Socio-Economic Status*** indicator percentiles are not available for the state of Massachusetts

Norfolk County
SHARON S.D.
1 SCHOOL ● SHARON MA 02067 ● (781) 784-1570

Grade Span: KG-12 **Schools**: *Regular* 5 ● *Spec Ed* 0 ● *Alt* 0 **Students**: 3,045 **Total Teachers**: 193 **Student/Classroom Teacher Ratio**: na	**Expenditures/Student**: $6,003 **Librarians**: 3.6 846 students/librarian **Guidance Counselors**: 6.6 461 students/counselor	**% Amer Indian**: 0.0 **% Asian**: 3.9 **% Black**: 5.7 **% Hispanic**: 1.2 **% White**: 89.2	National ***Socio-Economic Status*** indicator percentiles are not available for the state of Massachusetts

Norfolk County
STOUGHTON S.D.
232 PEARL ● STOUGHTON MA 02072 ● (781) 344-4000

Grade Span: PK-12 **Schools**: *Regular* 8 ● *Spec Ed* 0 ● *Alt* 0 **Students**: 4,092 **Total Teachers**: 278 **Student/Classroom Teacher Ratio**: na	**Expenditures/Student**: $6,233 **Librarians**: 1.0 4,092 students/librarian **Guidance Counselors**: 10.0 409 students/counselor	**% Amer Indian**: 0.3 **% Asian**: 1.6 **% Black**: 7.0 **% Hispanic**: 2.0 **% White**: 89.1	National ***Socio-Economic Status*** indicator percentiles are not available for the state of Massachusetts

Norfolk County

WALPOLE S.D.

SCHOOL ● WALPOLE MA 02081 ● (508) 660-7200

Grade Span: KG-12	**Expenditures/Student**: $5,699	**% Amer Indian**: 0.0	National ***Socio-Economic Status*** indicator percentiles are not available for the state of Massachusetts
Schools: *Regular* 6 ● *Spec Ed* 0 ● *Alt* 0	**Librarians**: 0.0	**% Asian**: 0.7	
Students: 3,519	*** students/librarian	**% Black**: 2.0	
Total Teachers: 215	**Guidance Counselors**: 8.0	**% Hispanic**: 0.7	
Student/Classroom Teacher Ratio: na	440 students/counselor	**% White**: 96.6	

Norfolk County

WELLESLEY S.D.

40 KINGSBURY ● WELLESLEY MA 02181 ● (781) 446-6226

Grade Span: KG-12	**Expenditures/Student**: $8,092	**% Amer Indian**: 0.1	National ***Socio-Economic Status*** indicator percentiles are not available for the state of Massachusetts
Schools: *Regular* 8 ● *Spec Ed* 0 ● *Alt* 0	**Librarians**: 8.0	**% Asian**: 4.2	
Students: 3,326	416 students/librarian	**% Black**: 4.1	
Total Teachers: 229	**Guidance Counselors**: 8.4	**% Hispanic**: 1.7	
Student/Classroom Teacher Ratio: na	396 students/counselor	**% White**: 89.8	

Norfolk County

WEYMOUTH S.D.

111 MIDDLE ● WEYMOUTH MA 02189 ● (781) 335-1460

Grade Span: PK-12	**Expenditures/Student**: $6,194	**% Amer Indian**: 0.0	National ***Socio-Economic Status*** indicator percentiles are not available for the state of Massachusetts
Schools: *Regular* 13 ● *Spec Ed* 0 ● *Alt* 0	**Librarians**: 6.0	**% Asian**: 1.6	
Students: 6,635	1,106 students/librarian	**% Black**: 2.2	
Total Teachers: 518	**Guidance Counselors**: 12.0	**% Hispanic**: 1.3	
Student/Classroom Teacher Ratio: na	553 students/counselor	**% White**: 94.9	

Plymouth County

BROCKTON S.D.

43 CRESCENT ● BROCKTON MA 02401 ● (508) 580-7511

Grade Span: PK-12	**Expenditures/Student**: $6,355	**% Amer Indian**: 0.5	National ***Socio-Economic Status*** indicator percentiles are not available for the state of Massachusetts
Schools: *Regular* 23 ● *Spec Ed* 0 ● *Alt* 1	**Librarians**: 11.0	**% Asian**: 3.0	
Students: 15,035	1,367 students/librarian	**% Black**: 32.1	
Total Teachers: 851	**Guidance Counselors**: 23.5	**% Hispanic**: 13.7	
Student/Classroom Teacher Ratio: na	640 students/counselor	**% White**: 50.8	

Plymouth County

DUXBURY S.D.

130 ST GEORGE ● DUXBURY MA 02332 ● (781) 934-7600

Grade Span: PK-12	**Expenditures/Student**: $6,545	**% Amer Indian**: 0.0	National ***Socio-Economic Status*** indicator percentiles are not available for the state of Massachusetts
Schools: *Regular* 3 ● *Spec Ed* 0 ● *Alt* 0	**Librarians**: 2.0	**% Asian**: 1.0	
Students: 2,816	1,408 students/librarian	**% Black**: 0.6	
Total Teachers: 172	**Guidance Counselors**: 7.3	**% Hispanic**: 0.5	
Student/Classroom Teacher Ratio: na	386 students/counselor	**% White**: 97.9	

Plymouth County

HINGHAM S.D.

14 MAIN ● HINGHAM MA 02043 ● (781) 741-1500

Grade Span: PK-12	**Expenditures/Student**: $6,563	**% Amer Indian**: 0.0	National ***Socio-Economic Status*** indicator percentiles are not available for the state of Massachusetts
Schools: *Regular* 5 ● *Spec Ed* 0 ● *Alt* 0	**Librarians**: 0.0	**% Asian**: 0.9	
Students: 3,296	*** students/librarian	**% Black**: 1.5	
Total Teachers: 213	**Guidance Counselors**: 9.0	**% Hispanic**: 0.5	
Student/Classroom Teacher Ratio: na	366 students/counselor	**% White**: 97.2	

Plymouth County
[KINGSTON] **SILVER LAKE S.D.**
130 PEMBROKE ST ● KINGSTON MA 02364 ● (781) 585-4313

Grade Span: 07-12	**Expenditures/Student**: $6,974	**% Amer Indian**: 0.0	National ***Socio-Economic Status*** indicator percentiles are not available for the state of Massachusetts
Schools: *Regular* 2 ● *Spec Ed* 0 ● *Alt* 0	**Librarians**: 2.0	**% Asian**: 0.9	
Students: 2,574	1,287 students/librarian	**% Black**: 1.7	
Total Teachers: 186	**Guidance Counselors**: 11.5	**% Hispanic**: 0.6	
Student/Classroom Teacher Ratio: na	224 students/counselor	**% White**: 96.8	

Plymouth County
MARSHFIELD S.D.
SOUTH RIVER ● MARSHFIELD MA 02050 ● (781) 834-5010

Grade Span: PK-12	**Expenditures/Student**: $5,372	**% Amer Indian**: 0.1	National ***Socio-Economic Status*** indicator percentiles are not available for the state of Massachusetts
Schools: *Regular* 7 ● *Spec Ed* 0 ● *Alt* 0	**Librarians**: 1.0	**% Asian**: 0.8	
Students: 4,292	4,292 students/librarian	**% Black**: 1.1	
Total Teachers: 273	**Guidance Counselors**: 7.0	**% Hispanic**: 0.7	
Student/Classroom Teacher Ratio: na	613 students/counselor	**% White**: 97.3	

Plymouth County
MIDDLEBOROUGH S.D.
10 NICKERSON AVE ● MIDDLEBOROUGH MA 02346 ● (508) 946-2000 ● http://www.middleboro.k12.ma.us

Grade Span: KG-12	**Expenditures/Student**: $5,428	**% Amer Indian**: 0.1	National ***Socio-Economic Status*** indicator percentiles are not available for the state of Massachusetts
Schools: *Regular* 7 ● *Spec Ed* 0 ● *Alt* 0	**Librarians**: 0.0	**% Asian**: 0.2	
Students: 3,515	*** students/librarian	**% Black**: 2.2	
Total Teachers: 187	**Guidance Counselors**: 6.5	**% Hispanic**: 1.0	
Student/Classroom Teacher Ratio: na	541 students/counselor	**% White**: 96.5	

Plymouth County
PLYMOUTH S.D.
253 SOUTH MEADOW RD ● PLYMOUTH MA 02360 ● (508) 830-4300

Grade Span: PK-12	**Expenditures/Student**: $6,477	**% Amer Indian**: 0.6	National ***Socio-Economic Status*** indicator percentiles are not available for the state of Massachusetts
Schools: *Regular* 12 ● *Spec Ed* 0 ● *Alt* 1	**Librarians**: 3.0	**% Asian**: 0.9	
Students: 8,740	2,913 students/librarian	**% Black**: 3.4	
Total Teachers: 578	**Guidance Counselors**: 24.9	**% Hispanic**: 1.3	
Student/Classroom Teacher Ratio: na	351 students/counselor	**% White**: 93.7	

Plymouth County
[RAYNHAM] **BRIDGEWATER-RAYNHAM S.D.**
687 PLEASANT ST. ● RAYNHAM MA 02767 ● (508) 824-2730

Grade Span: PK-12	**Expenditures/Student**: $5,478	**% Amer Indian**: 0.0	National ***Socio-Economic Status*** indicator percentiles are not available for the state of Massachusetts
Schools: *Regular* 11 ● *Spec Ed* 0 ● *Alt* 0	**Librarians**: 2.0	**% Asian**: 0.8	
Students: 5,455	2,728 students/librarian	**% Black**: 2.1	
Total Teachers: 286	**Guidance Counselors**: 7.0	**% Hispanic**: 0.5	
Student/Classroom Teacher Ratio: na	779 students/counselor	**% White**: 96.5	

Plymouth County
ROCKLAND S.D.
34 MACKINLAY WAY ● ROCKLAND MA 02370 ● (781) 878-3893

Grade Span: PK-12	**Expenditures/Student**: $6,149	**% Amer Indian**: 0.0	National ***Socio-Economic Status*** indicator percentiles are not available for the state of Massachusetts
Schools: *Regular* 5 ● *Spec Ed* 0 ● *Alt* 0	**Librarians**: 1.0	**% Asian**: 1.4	
Students: 2,721	2,721 students/librarian	**% Black**: 2.5	
Total Teachers: 148	**Guidance Counselors**: 0.9	**% Hispanic**: 1.3	
Student/Classroom Teacher Ratio: na	3,023 students/counselor	**% White**: 94.8	

Plymouth County

SCITUATE S.D.

606 C J CUSHING HWY ● SCITUATE MA 02066 ● (781) 545-8759

Grade Span: PK-12	**Expenditures/Student**: $6,324	**% Amer Indian**: 0.1	National ***Socio-Economic Status*** indicator percentiles are not available for the state of Massachusetts
Schools: *Regular* 5 ● *Spec Ed* 0 ● *Alt* 0	**Librarians**: 0.0	**% Asian**: 0.3	
Students: 2,879	*** students/librarian	**% Black**: 2.5	
Total Teachers: 187	**Guidance Counselors**: 10.0	**% Hispanic**: 1.6	
Student/Classroom Teacher Ratio: na	288 students/counselor	**% White**: 95.4	

Plymouth County

WAREHAM S.D.

54 MARION RD ● WAREHAM MA 02571 ● (508) 291-3500

Grade Span: PK-12	**Expenditures/Student**: $6,124	**% Amer Indian**: 1.1	National ***Socio-Economic Status*** indicator percentiles are not available for the state of Massachusetts
Schools: *Regular* 5 ● *Spec Ed* 0 ● *Alt* 0	**Librarians**: 0.0	**% Asian**: 0.8	
Students: 3,458	*** students/librarian	**% Black**: 10.6	
Total Teachers: 207	**Guidance Counselors**: 8.0	**% Hispanic**: 2.0	
Student/Classroom Teacher Ratio: na	432 students/counselor	**% White**: 85.6	

Plymouth County

WHITMAN-HANSON S.D.

FRANKLIN ● WHITMAN MA 02382 ● (781) 447-7000 ● http://www.whrsd.k12.ma.us

Grade Span: PK-12	**Expenditures/Student**: $5,870	**% Amer Indian**: 0.2	National ***Socio-Economic Status*** indicator percentiles are not available for the state of Massachusetts
Schools: *Regular* 8 ● *Spec Ed* 0 ● *Alt* 0	**Librarians**: 2.5	**% Asian**: 0.4	
Students: 4,238	1,695 students/librarian	**% Black**: 1.5	
Total Teachers: 266	**Guidance Counselors**: 5.0	**% Hispanic**: 0.7	
Student/Classroom Teacher Ratio: na	848 students/counselor	**% White**: 97.2	

Suffolk County

BOSTON S.D.

26 COURT ● BOSTON MA 02108 ● (617) 635-9050 ● http://www.boston.k12.ma.us

Grade Span: KG-12	**Expenditures/Student**: $8,756	**% Amer Indian**: 0.4	National ***Socio-Economic Status*** indicator percentiles are not available for the state of Massachusetts
Schools: *Regular* 116 ● *Spec Ed* 1 ● *Alt* 6	**Librarians**: 20.0	**% Asian**: 9.3	
Students: 63,293	3,165 students/librarian	**% Black**: 47.8	
Total Teachers: 4,080	**Guidance Counselors**: 70.0	**% Hispanic**: 24.7	
Student/Classroom Teacher Ratio: na	904 students/counselor	**% White**: 17.8	

Suffolk County

CHELSEA S.D.

208 CITY HALL ● CHELSEA MA 02150 ● (617) 889-8415

Grade Span: PK-12	**Expenditures/Student**: $6,426	**% Amer Indian**: 0.5	National ***Socio-Economic Status*** indicator percentiles are not available for the state of Massachusetts
Schools: *Regular* 10 ● *Spec Ed* 0 ● *Alt* 1	**Librarians**: 1.0	**% Asian**: 9.0	
Students: 4,763	4,763 students/librarian	**% Black**: 6.9	
Total Teachers: 320	**Guidance Counselors**: 10.0	**% Hispanic**: 63.4	
Student/Classroom Teacher Ratio: na	476 students/counselor	**% White**: 20.1	

Suffolk County

REVERE S.D.

101 SCHOOL ● REVERE MA 02151 ● (781) 286-8226

Grade Span: PK-12	**Expenditures/Student**: $6,277	**% Amer Indian**: 0.0	National ***Socio-Economic Status*** indicator percentiles are not available for the state of Massachusetts
Schools: *Regular* 6 ● *Spec Ed* 0 ● *Alt* 1	**Librarians**: 0.0	**% Asian**: 5.2	
Students: 5,421	*** students/librarian	**% Black**: 2.9	
Total Teachers: 326	**Guidance Counselors**: 6.0	**% Hispanic**: 9.3	
Student/Classroom Teacher Ratio: na	904 students/counselor	**% White**: 82.6	

Worcester County
[BARRE] **QUABBIN S.D.**
40 WEST ● BARRE MA 01005 ● (978) 355-4668

Grade Span: PK-12 **Schools**: *Regular* 6 ● *Spec Ed* 0 ● *Alt* 0 **Students**: 2,846 **Total Teachers**: 171 **Student/Classroom Teacher Ratio**: na	**Expenditures/Student**: $5,481 **Librarians**: 0.0 *** students/librarian **Guidance Counselors**: 7.7 370 students/counselor	**% Amer Indian**: 0.1 **% Asian**: 0.7 **% Black**: 0.8 **% Hispanic**: 0.8 **% White**: 97.5	National ***Socio-Economic Status*** indicator percentiles are not available for the state of Massachusetts

Worcester County
[BOLTON] **NASHOBA REGIONAL S.D.**
626 MAIN STREET ● BOLTON MA 01740 ● (978) 779-0539

Grade Span: PK-12 **Schools**: *Regular* 7 ● *Spec Ed* 0 ● *Alt* 0 **Students**: 2,742 **Total Teachers**: 198 **Student/Classroom Teacher Ratio**: na	**Expenditures/Student**: $7,105 **Librarians**: 2.0 1,371 students/librarian **Guidance Counselors**: 5.6 490 students/counselor	**% Amer Indian**: 0.0 **% Asian**: 1.9 **% Black**: 1.7 **% Hispanic**: 2.4 **% White**: 94.0	National ***Socio-Economic Status*** indicator percentiles are not available for the state of Massachusetts

Worcester County
DUDLEY-CHARLTON S.D.
68 DUDLEY-OXFORD RD ● DUDLEY MA 01571 ● (508) 943-6888

Grade Span: PK-12 **Schools**: *Regular* 6 ● *Spec Ed* 0 ● *Alt* 0 **Students**: 3,658 **Total Teachers**: 216 **Student/Classroom Teacher Ratio**: na	**Expenditures/Student**: $4,874 **Librarians**: 1.0 3,658 students/librarian **Guidance Counselors**: 9.0 406 students/counselor	**% Amer Indian**: 0.1 **% Asian**: 0.3 **% Black**: 0.4 **% Hispanic**: 1.1 **% White**: 98.2	National ***Socio-Economic Status*** indicator percentiles are not available for the state of Massachusetts

Worcester County
FITCHBURG S.D.
376 SOUTH ST ● FITCHBURG MA 01420 ● (978) 345-3200

Grade Span: PK-12 **Schools**: *Regular* 9 ● *Spec Ed* 0 ● *Alt* 0 **Students**: 5,244 **Total Teachers**: 357 **Student/Classroom Teacher Ratio**: na	**Expenditures/Student**: $6,501 **Librarians**: 2.5 2,098 students/librarian **Guidance Counselors**: 16.0 328 students/counselor	**% Amer Indian**: 0.1 **% Asian**: 7.7 **% Black**: 6.6 **% Hispanic**: 24.6 **% White**: 61.0	National ***Socio-Economic Status*** indicator percentiles are not available for the state of Massachusetts

Worcester County
GARDNER S.D.
130 ELM/ SAUTER SCH ● GARDNER MA 01440 ● (978) 632-1000

Grade Span: PK-12 **Schools**: *Regular* 6 ● *Spec Ed* 0 ● *Alt* 0 **Students**: 2,981 **Total Teachers**: 173 **Student/Classroom Teacher Ratio**: na	**Expenditures/Student**: $4,962 **Librarians**: 1.0 2,981 students/librarian **Guidance Counselors**: 9.0 331 students/counselor	**% Amer Indian**: 0.3 **% Asian**: 1.4 **% Black**: 2.2 **% Hispanic**: 3.1 **% White**: 93.1	National ***Socio-Economic Status*** indicator percentiles are not available for the state of Massachusetts

Worcester County
LEOMINSTER S.D.
24 CHURCH ST ● LEOMINSTER MA 01453 ● (978) 534-7700

Grade Span: PK-12 **Schools**: *Regular* 8 ● *Spec Ed* 0 ● *Alt* 1 **Students**: 5,729 **Total Teachers**: 386 **Student/Classroom Teacher Ratio**: na	**Expenditures/Student**: $5,450 **Librarians**: 6.0 955 students/librarian **Guidance Counselors**: 21.0 273 students/counselor	**% Amer Indian**: 0.2 **% Asian**: 2.7 **% Black**: 3.0 **% Hispanic**: 13.3 **% White**: 80.9	National ***Socio-Economic Status*** indicator percentiles are not available for the state of Massachusetts

Worcester County
MILFORD S.D.
31 WEST FOUNTAIN ● MILFORD MA 01757 ● (508) 478-1100

Grade Span: KG-12 **Schools**: *Regular* 6 ● *Spec Ed* 0 ● *Alt* 0 **Students**: 3,946 **Total Teachers**: 282 **Student/Classroom Teacher Ratio**: na	**Expenditures/Student**: $6,658 **Librarians**: 1.0 3,946 students/librarian **Guidance Counselors**: 7.0 564 students/counselor	**% Amer Indian**: 0.1 **% Asian**: 1.6 **% Black**: 1.3 **% Hispanic**: 6.0 **% White**: 90.9	National ***Socio-Economic Status*** indicator percentiles are not available for the state of Massachusetts

Worcester County
[PRINCETON] **WACHUSETT S.D.**
206 WORCESTER RD ● PRINCETON MA 01541 ● (978) 829-6631

Grade Span: PK-12 **Schools**: *Regular* 11 ● *Spec Ed* 0 ● *Alt* 0 **Students**: 6,159 **Total Teachers**: 399 **Student/Classroom Teacher Ratio**: na	**Expenditures/Student**: $6,455 **Librarians**: 1.5 4,106 students/librarian **Guidance Counselors**: 12.5 493 students/counselor	**% Amer Indian**: 0.1 **% Asian**: 1.0 **% Black**: 0.8 **% Hispanic**: 0.9 **% White**: 97.3	National ***Socio-Economic Status*** indicator percentiles are not available for the state of Massachusetts

Worcester County
SHREWSBURY S.D.
100 MAPLE AVE ● SHREWSBURY MA 01545 ● (508) 845-5721

Grade Span: PK-12 **Schools**: *Regular* 6 ● *Spec Ed* 0 ● *Alt* 0 **Students**: 3,888 **Total Teachers**: 320 **Student/Classroom Teacher Ratio**: na	**Expenditures/Student**: $5,875 **Librarians**: 3.0 1,296 students/librarian **Guidance Counselors**: 4.0 972 students/counselor	**% Amer Indian**: 0.1 **% Asian**: 5.5 **% Black**: 1.9 **% Hispanic**: 2.6 **% White**: 89.9	National ***Socio-Economic Status*** indicator percentiles are not available for the state of Massachusetts

Worcester County
SOUTHBRIDGE S.D.
41 ELM P O 665 ● SOUTHBRIDGE MA 01550 ● (508) 764-5414

Grade Span: KG-12 **Schools**: *Regular* 5 ● *Spec Ed* 0 ● *Alt* 0 **Students**: 2,614 **Total Teachers**: 200 **Student/Classroom Teacher Ratio**: na	**Expenditures/Student**: $6,759 **Librarians**: 2.0 1,307 students/librarian **Guidance Counselors**: 8.0 327 students/counselor	**% Amer Indian**: 0.0 **% Asian**: 1.8 **% Black**: 0.2 **% Hispanic**: 32.2 **% White**: 65.8	National ***Socio-Economic Status*** indicator percentiles are not available for the state of Massachusetts

Worcester County
WESTBOROUGH S.D.
45 W MAIN, POB 1152 ● WESTBOROUGH MA 01581 ● (508) 836-7700 ● http://www.westborough.org

Grade Span: KG-12 **Schools**: *Regular* 5 ● *Spec Ed* 0 ● *Alt* 0 **Students**: 2,766 **Total Teachers**: 179 **Student/Classroom Teacher Ratio**: na	**Expenditures/Student**: $6,909 **Librarians**: 3.0 922 students/librarian **Guidance Counselors**: 10.0 277 students/counselor	**% Amer Indian**: 0.1 **% Asian**: 5.6 **% Black**: 2.2 **% Hispanic**: 2.4 **% White**: 89.6	National ***Socio-Economic Status*** indicator percentiles are not available for the state of Massachusetts

Worcester County
WORCESTER S.D.
20 IRVING ● WORCESTER MA 01609 ● (508) 799-3116

Grade Span: PK-12 **Schools**: *Regular* 49 ● *Spec Ed* 0 ● *Alt* 0 **Students**: 23,419 **Total Teachers**: 1,782 **Student/Classroom Teacher Ratio**: na	**Expenditures/Student**: $6,812 **Librarians**: 16.0 1,464 students/librarian **Guidance Counselors**: 71.0 330 students/counselor	**% Amer Indian**: 0.5 **% Asian**: 6.9 **% Black**: 9.2 **% Hispanic**: 25.6 **% White**: 57.9	National ***Socio-Economic Status*** indicator percentiles are not available for the state of Massachusetts

Allegan County

ALLEGAN S.D.

550 FIFTH STREET ● ALLEGAN MI 49010 ● (616) 673-5431

Grade Span: PK-12	**Expenditures/Student**: $5,009	**% Amer Indian**: 0.5	
Schools: *Regular* 7 ● *Spec Ed* 0 ● *Alt* 0	**Librarians**: 1.0	**% Asian**: 0.4	National ***Socio-Economic***
Students: 2,870	2,870 students/librarian	**% Black**: 3.7	***Status*** indicator percentile
Total Teachers: 147	**Guidance Counselors**: 7.0	**% Hispanic**: 2.1	(100=high): 64th
Student/Classroom Teacher Ratio: 21.3	410 students/counselor	**% White**: 93.2	

Allegan County

PLAINWELL COMMUNITY S.D.

600 SCHOOL DRIVE ● PLAINWELL MI 49080 ● (616) 685-5823

Grade Span: PK-12	**Expenditures/Student**: $5,822	**% Amer Indian**: 0.0	
Schools: *Regular* 6 ● *Spec Ed* 0 ● *Alt* 0	**Librarians**: 3.0	**% Asian**: 0.9	National ***Socio-Economic***
Students: 2,604	868 students/librarian	**% Black**: 0.5	***Status*** indicator percentile
Total Teachers: 143	**Guidance Counselors**: 6.0	**% Hispanic**: 1.9	(100=high): 78th
Student/Classroom Teacher Ratio: 19.0	434 students/counselor	**% White**: 96.7	

Allegan County

WAYLAND UNION S.D.

835 EAST SUPERIOR STREET ● WAYLAND MI 49348 ● (616) 792-2181

Grade Span: KG-12	**Expenditures/Student**: $5,388	**% Amer Indian**: 2.0	
Schools: *Regular* 7 ● *Spec Ed* 0 ● *Alt* 0	**Librarians**: 4.0	**% Asian**: 0.3	National ***Socio-Economic***
Students: 3,004	751 students/librarian	**% Black**: 0.3	***Status*** indicator percentile
Total Teachers: 157	**Guidance Counselors**: 3.0	**% Hispanic**: 1.5	(100=high): 78th
Student/Classroom Teacher Ratio: 19.0	1,001 students/counselor	**% White**: 95.8	

Alpena County

ALPENA S.D.

2373 GORDON ROAD ● ALPENA MI 49707 ● (517) 356-4863 ● http://www.oweb.com/upnorth/aps

Grade Span: KG-12	**Expenditures/Student**: $4,985	**% Amer Indian**: 0.5	
Schools: *Regular* 12 ● *Spec Ed* 0 ● *Alt* 0	**Librarians**: 3.0	**% Asian**: 0.6	National ***Socio-Economic***
Students: 5,829	1,943 students/librarian	**% Black**: 0.6	***Status*** indicator percentile
Total Teachers: 286	**Guidance Counselors**: 7.0	**% Hispanic**: 0.4	(100=high): 49th
Student/Classroom Teacher Ratio: 19.7	833 students/counselor	**% White**: 97.9	

Barry County

HASTINGS AREA S.D.

232 WEST GRAND STREET ● HASTINGS MI 49058 ● (616) 948-4400

Grade Span: KG-12	**Expenditures/Student**: $5,208	**% Amer Indian**: 0.2	
Schools: *Regular* 6 ● *Spec Ed* 0 ● *Alt* 0	**Librarians**: 1.0	**% Asian**: 0.4	National ***Socio-Economic***
Students: 3,467	3,467 students/librarian	**% Black**: 0.7	***Status*** indicator percentile
Total Teachers: 191	**Guidance Counselors**: 7.0	**% Hispanic**: 0.7	(100=high): 67th
Student/Classroom Teacher Ratio: 19.4	495 students/counselor	**% White**: 98.0	

Barry County

[MIDDLEVILLE] **THORNAPPLE KELLOGG S.D.**

3885 BENDER ROAD ● MIDDLEVILLE MI 49333 ● (616) 795-3313

Grade Span: KG-12	**Expenditures/Student**: $5,270	**% Amer Indian**: 0.4	
Schools: *Regular* 5 ● *Spec Ed* 0 ● *Alt* 1	**Librarians**: 2.0	**% Asian**: 0.6	National ***Socio-Economic***
Students: 2,538	1,269 students/librarian	**% Black**: 0.5	***Status*** indicator percentile
Total Teachers: 127	**Guidance Counselors**: 3.0	**% Hispanic**: 0.8	(100=high): 81st
Student/Classroom Teacher Ratio: 21.1	846 students/counselor	**% White**: 97.8	

Bay County

[BAY CITY] **BANGOR TOWNSHIP S.D.**

3520 OLD KAWKAWLIN ROAD ● BAY CITY MI 48706 ● (517) 684-8121

Grade Span: KG-12 **Schools**: *Regular* 6 ● *Spec Ed* 0 ● *Alt* 0 **Students**: 2,622 **Total Teachers**: 116 **Student/Classroom Teacher Ratio**: 23.4	**Expenditures/Student**: $5,607 **Librarians**: 2.0 1,311 students/librarian **Guidance Counselors**: 6.0 437 students/counselor	**% Amer Indian**: 0.2 **% Asian**: 1.2 **% Black**: 0.6 **% Hispanic**: 2.2 **% White**: 95.9	National ***Socio-Economic Status*** indicator percentile (100=high): 55th

Bay County

BAY CITY S.D.

910 NORTH WALNUT STREET ● BAY CITY MI 48706 ● (517) 686-9700

Grade Span: KG-12 **Schools**: *Regular* 19 ● *Spec Ed* 1 ● *Alt* 1 **Students**: 10,375 **Total Teachers**: 468 **Student/Classroom Teacher Ratio**: 22.9	**Expenditures/Student**: $5,361 **Librarians**: 6.0 1,729 students/librarian **Guidance Counselors**: 20.0 519 students/counselor	**% Amer Indian**: 1.5 **% Asian**: 0.9 **% Black**: 2.9 **% Hispanic**: 5.9 **% White**: 88.7	National ***Socio-Economic Status*** indicator percentile (100=high): 39th

Berrien County

BENTON HARBOR AREA S.D.

711 EAST BRITAIN AVENUE ● BENTON HARBOR MI 49022 ● (616) 927-0600 ● http://www.remc11.k12.mi.us/bhas

Grade Span: PK-12 **Schools**: *Regular* 15 ● *Spec Ed* 0 ● *Alt* 4 **Students**: 6,245 **Total Teachers**: 352 **Student/Classroom Teacher Ratio**: 18.6	**Expenditures/Student**: $6,759 **Librarians**: 4.0 1,561 students/librarian **Guidance Counselors**: 7.0 892 students/counselor	**% Amer Indian**: 0.0 **% Asian**: 0.1 **% Black**: 87.5 **% Hispanic**: 1.5 **% White**: 11.0	National ***Socio-Economic Status*** indicator percentile (100=high): 1st

Berrien County

NILES COMMUNITY S.D.

111 SPRUCE STREET ● NILES MI 49120 ● (616) 683-0732

Grade Span: PK-12 **Schools**: *Regular* 8 ● *Spec Ed* 2 ● *Alt* 0 **Students**: 4,043 **Total Teachers**: 229 **Student/Classroom Teacher Ratio**: 18.4	**Expenditures/Student**: $5,878 **Librarians**: 3.0 1,348 students/librarian **Guidance Counselors**: 6.0 674 students/counselor	**% Amer Indian**: 0.8 **% Asian**: 0.7 **% Black**: 12.8 **% Hispanic**: 2.3 **% White**: 83.4	National ***Socio-Economic Status*** indicator percentile (100=high): 39th

Berrien County

ST. JOSEPH S.D.

2214 SOUTH STATE STREET ● ST. JOSEPH MI 49085 ● (616) 982-4621

Grade Span: KG-12 **Schools**: *Regular* 6 ● *Spec Ed* 0 ● *Alt* 0 **Students**: 2,639 **Total Teachers**: 143 **Student/Classroom Teacher Ratio**: 23.4	**Expenditures/Student**: $6,089 **Librarians**: 3.0 880 students/librarian **Guidance Counselors**: 4.0 660 students/counselor	**% Amer Indian**: 0.1 **% Asian**: 3.0 **% Black**: 1.5 **% Hispanic**: 0.8 **% White**: 94.5	National ***Socio-Economic Status*** indicator percentile (100=high): 93rd

Berrien County

[STEVENSVILLE] **LAKESHORE S.D.**

5771 CLEVELAND AVENUE ● STEVENSVILLE MI 49127 ● (616) 428-1400

Grade Span: KG-12 **Schools**: *Regular* 5 ● *Spec Ed* 0 ● *Alt* 0 **Students**: 2,986 **Total Teachers**: 140 **Student/Classroom Teacher Ratio**: 23.0	**Expenditures/Student**: $4,673 **Librarians**: 2.0 1,493 students/librarian **Guidance Counselors**: 5.0 597 students/counselor	**% Amer Indian**: 0.1 **% Asian**: 2.0 **% Black**: 0.9 **% Hispanic**: 1.1 **% White**: 95.9	National ***Socio-Economic Status*** indicator percentile (100=high): 88th

Branch County

COLDWATER COMMUNITY S.D.

175 SOUTH MICHIGAN AVENUE ● COLDWATER MI 49036 ● (517) 279-5910 ● http://www.remc12.k12.mi.us/coldwater

Grade Span: PK-12 **Schools**: *Regular* 8 ● *Spec Ed* 0 ● *Alt* 1 **Students**: 3,523 **Total Teachers**: 181 **Student/Classroom Teacher Ratio**: 22.0	**Expenditures/Student**: $5,602 **Librarians**: 2.0 1,762 students/librarian **Guidance Counselors**: 6.0 587 students/counselor	**% Amer Indian**: 0.6 **% Asian**: 0.8 **% Black**: 0.3 **% Hispanic**: 1.0 **% White**: 97.4	National ***Socio-Economic Status*** indicator percentile (100=high): 64th

Calhoun County

BATTLE CREEK S.D.

3 WEST VAN BUREN STREET ● BATTLE CREEK MI 49017 ● (616) 965-9500

Grade Span: PK-12 **Schools**: *Regular* 24 ● *Spec Ed* 0 ● *Alt* 2 **Students**: 8,868 **Total Teachers**: 582 **Student/Classroom Teacher Ratio**: 16.3	**Expenditures/Student**: $8,831 **Librarians**: 4.0 2,217 students/librarian **Guidance Counselors**: 14.0 633 students/counselor	**% Amer Indian**: 1.1 **% Asian**: 0.5 **% Black**: 33.7 **% Hispanic**: 3.0 **% White**: 61.6	National ***Socio-Economic Status*** indicator percentile (100=high): 17th

Calhoun County

[BATTLE CREEK] **HARPER CREEK COMMUNITY S.D.**

7290 B DRIVE NORTH ● BATTLE CREEK MI 49017 ● (616) 979-1136

Grade Span: KG-12 **Schools**: *Regular* 5 ● *Spec Ed* 0 ● *Alt* 0 **Students**: 2,615 **Total Teachers**: 131 **Student/Classroom Teacher Ratio**: 20.4	**Expenditures/Student**: $5,601 **Librarians**: 1.0 2,615 students/librarian **Guidance Counselors**: 4.0 654 students/counselor	**% Amer Indian**: 0.6 **% Asian**: 0.5 **% Black**: 0.9 **% Hispanic**: 0.5 **% White**: 97.5	National ***Socio-Economic Status*** indicator percentile (100=high): 70th

Calhoun County

[BATTLE CREEK] **LAKEVIEW S.D.**

15 ARBOR STREET ● BATTLE CREEK MI 49015 ● (616) 965-3080

Grade Span: KG-12 **Schools**: *Regular* 7 ● *Spec Ed* 0 ● *Alt* 0 **Students**: 3,366 **Total Teachers**: 219 **Student/Classroom Teacher Ratio**: 21.2	**Expenditures/Student**: $6,011 **Librarians**: 3.0 1,122 students/librarian **Guidance Counselors**: 8.0 421 students/counselor	**% Amer Indian**: 1.3 **% Asian**: 4.4 **% Black**: 3.4 **% Hispanic**: 1.4 **% White**: 89.5	National ***Socio-Economic Status*** indicator percentile (100=high): 82nd

Calhoun County

MARSHALL S.D.

100 EAST GREEN STREET ● MARSHALL MI 49068 ● (616) 781-1256

Grade Span: KG-12 **Schools**: *Regular* 6 ● *Spec Ed* 0 ● *Alt* 0 **Students**: 2,588 **Total Teachers**: 131 **Student/Classroom Teacher Ratio**: 21.3	**Expenditures/Student**: $5,738 **Librarians**: 3.0 863 students/librarian **Guidance Counselors**: 6.0 431 students/counselor	**% Amer Indian**: 0.3 **% Asian**: 0.8 **% Black**: 0.2 **% Hispanic**: 2.9 **% White**: 95.8	National ***Socio-Economic Status*** indicator percentile (100=high): 79th

Cass County

DOWAGIAC UNION S.D.

206 MAIN STREET ● DOWAGIAC MI 49047 ● (616) 782-4400 ● http://www.remc11.k12.mi.us/dowagiac

Grade Span: KG-12 **Schools**: *Regular* 8 ● *Spec Ed* 0 ● *Alt* 1 **Students**: 3,120 **Total Teachers**: 168 **Student/Classroom Teacher Ratio**: 18.6	**Expenditures/Student**: $5,099 **Librarians**: 2.0 1,560 students/librarian **Guidance Counselors**: 7.0 446 students/counselor	**% Amer Indian**: 0.7 **% Asian**: 0.3 **% Black**: 11.1 **% Hispanic**: 10.5 **% White**: 77.3	National ***Socio-Economic Status*** indicator percentile (100=high): 38th

Chippewa County

SAULT STE. MARIE AREA S.D.

460 WEST SPRUCE STREET ● SAULT STE. MARIE MI 49783 ● (906) 635-6609 ● http://www.eup.k12.mi.us/sault

Grade Span: KG-12	**Expenditures/Student**: $5,450	**% Amer Indian**: 25.8	
Schools: *Regular* 9 ● *Spec Ed* 0 ● *Alt* 1	**Librarians**: 2.0	**% Asian**: 0.1	National ***Socio-Economic***
Students: 3,022	1,511 students/librarian	**% Black**: 0.4	***Status*** indicator percentile
Total Teachers: 173	**Guidance Counselors**: 4.0	**% Hispanic**: 0.2	(100=high): 51st
Student/Classroom Teacher Ratio: 17.7	756 students/counselor	**% White**: 73.5	

Clinton County

ST. JOHNS S.D.

P.O. BOX 230 ● ST. JOHNS MI 48879 ● (517) 224-9352

Grade Span: KG-12	**Expenditures/Student**: $5,727	**% Amer Indian**: 0.8	
Schools: *Regular* 8 ● *Spec Ed* 0 ● *Alt* 1	**Librarians**: 2.0	**% Asian**: 0.8	National ***Socio-Economic***
Students: 3,248	1,624 students/librarian	**% Black**: 0.5	***Status*** indicator percentile
Total Teachers: 165	**Guidance Counselors**: 9.0	**% Hispanic**: 2.7	(100=high): 86th
Student/Classroom Teacher Ratio: 20.2	361 students/counselor	**% White**: 95.3	

Delta County

ESCANABA AREA S.D.

111 NORTH 5TH STREET ● ESCANABA MI 49829 ● (906) 786-5411 ● http://www.grfn.org/~tbushey

Grade Span: KG-12	**Expenditures/Student**: $5,079	**% Amer Indian**: 4.0	
Schools: *Regular* 10 ● *Spec Ed* 0 ● *Alt* 0	**Librarians**: 2.0	**% Asian**: 0.4	National ***Socio-Economic***
Students: 3,834	1,917 students/librarian	**% Black**: 0.3	***Status*** indicator percentile
Total Teachers: 182	**Guidance Counselors**: 3.0	**% Hispanic**: 0.3	(100=high): 59th
Student/Classroom Teacher Ratio: 20.4	1,278 students/counselor	**% White**: 95.0	

Eaton County

CHARLOTTE S.D.

378 STATE STREET ● CHARLOTTE MI 48813 ● (517) 543-2810 ● http://scnc.cps.k12.mi.us

Grade Span: KG-12	**Expenditures/Student**: $5,532	**% Amer Indian**: 0.2	
Schools: *Regular* 6 ● *Spec Ed* 0 ● *Alt* 0	**Librarians**: 4.0	**% Asian**: 0.6	National ***Socio-Economic***
Students: 3,412	853 students/librarian	**% Black**: 0.4	***Status*** indicator percentile
Total Teachers: 167	**Guidance Counselors**: 9.0	**% Hispanic**: 2.8	(100=high): 77th
Student/Classroom Teacher Ratio: 21.2	379 students/counselor	**% White**: 95.9	

Eaton County

EATON RAPIDS S.D.

501 KING STREET ● EATON RAPIDS MI 48827 ● (517) 663-8155

Grade Span: KG-12	**Expenditures/Student**: $5,417	**% Amer Indian**: 0.1	
Schools: *Regular* 5 ● *Spec Ed* 0 ● *Alt* 0	**Librarians**: 2.0	**% Asian**: 0.4	National ***Socio-Economic***
Students: 3,115	1,558 students/librarian	**% Black**: 0.5	***Status*** indicator percentile
Total Teachers: 165	**Guidance Counselors**: 6.0	**% Hispanic**: 2.0	(100=high): 81st
Student/Classroom Teacher Ratio: 19.3	519 students/counselor	**% White**: 97.1	

Eaton County

GRAND LEDGE S.D.

220 LAMSON STREET ● GRAND LEDGE MI 48837 ● (517) 627-3241 ● http://scnc.glps.k12.mi.us

Grade Span: PK-12	**Expenditures/Student**: $5,967	**% Amer Indian**: 0.2	
Schools: *Regular* 11 ● *Spec Ed* 0 ● *Alt* 0	**Librarians**: 4.0	**% Asian**: 1.3	National ***Socio-Economic***
Students: 5,086	1,272 students/librarian	**% Black**: 1.6	***Status*** indicator percentile
Total Teachers: 267	**Guidance Counselors**: 6.0	**% Hispanic**: 1.8	(100=high): 89th
Student/Classroom Teacher Ratio: 19.7	848 students/counselor	**% White**: 95.0	

Emmet County

[PETOSKEY] **S.D. OF PETOSKEY**

P.O. BOX 247 ● PETOSKEY MI 49770 ● (616) 348-0160

Grade Span: PK-12 **Schools**: *Regular* 6 ● *Spec Ed* 0 ● *Alt* 0 **Students**: 2,825 **Total Teachers**: 137 **Student/Classroom Teacher Ratio**: na	**Expenditures/Student**: $5,303 **Librarians**: 3.0 942 students/librarian **Guidance Counselors**: 5.0 565 students/counselor	**% Amer Indian**: 2.6 **% Asian**: 0.7 **% Black**: 0.4 **% Hispanic**: 0.8 **% White**: 95.6	National ***Socio-Economic Status*** indicator percentile (100=high): 72nd

Genesee County

CLIO AREA S.D.

430 NORTH MILL STREET ● CLIO MI 48420 ● (810) 686-0500

Grade Span: KG-12 **Schools**: *Regular* 5 ● *Spec Ed* 0 ● *Alt* 1 **Students**: 3,674 **Total Teachers**: 175 **Student/Classroom Teacher Ratio**: 22.4	**Expenditures/Student**: $5,676 **Librarians**: 1.0 3,674 students/librarian **Guidance Counselors**: 5.0 735 students/counselor	**% Amer Indian**: 0.4 **% Asian**: 0.5 **% Black**: 1.2 **% Hispanic**: 1.6 **% White**: 96.3	National ***Socio-Economic Status*** indicator percentile (100=high): 69th

Genesee County

DAVISON COMMUNITY S.D.

615 EAST CLARK STREET ● DAVISON MI 48423 ● (810) 653-3531 ● http://www.davison.k12.mi.us

Grade Span: KG-12 **Schools**: *Regular* 7 ● *Spec Ed* 0 ● *Alt* 2 **Students**: 4,890 **Total Teachers**: 219 **Student/Classroom Teacher Ratio**: 24.5	**Expenditures/Student**: $5,346 **Librarians**: 3.0 1,630 students/librarian **Guidance Counselors**: 9.0 543 students/counselor	**% Amer Indian**: 2.9 **% Asian**: 1.0 **% Black**: 0.8 **% Hispanic**: 1.1 **% White**: 94.2	National ***Socio-Economic Status*** indicator percentile (100=high): 79th

Genesee County

FENTON AREA S.D.

3100 OWEN ROAD ● FENTON MI 48430 ● (810) 629-2268

Grade Span: PK-12 **Schools**: *Regular* 5 ● *Spec Ed* 0 ● *Alt* 0 **Students**: 3,116 **Total Teachers**: 144 **Student/Classroom Teacher Ratio**: 22.4	**Expenditures/Student**: $6,112 **Librarians**: 2.0 1,558 students/librarian **Guidance Counselors**: 5.0 623 students/counselor	**% Amer Indian**: 0.1 **% Asian**: 0.9 **% Black**: 0.3 **% Hispanic**: 0.7 **% White**: 98.0	National ***Socio-Economic Status*** indicator percentile (100=high): 80th

Genesee County

[FLINT] **BEECHER COMMUNITY S.D.**

1020 WEST COLDWATER ROAD ● FLINT MI 48505 ● (810) 785-4731

Grade Span: PK-12 **Schools**: *Regular* 7 ● *Spec Ed* 0 ● *Alt* 2 **Students**: 2,785 **Total Teachers**: 192 **Student/Classroom Teacher Ratio**: 17.8	**Expenditures/Student**: $8,539 **Librarians**: 1.0 2,785 students/librarian **Guidance Counselors**: 2.0 1,393 students/counselor	**% Amer Indian**: 0.5 **% Asian**: 0.0 **% Black**: 78.0 **% Hispanic**: 2.5 **% White**: 19.0	National ***Socio-Economic Status*** indicator percentile (100=high): 5th

Genesee County

[FLINT] **CARMAN-AINSWORTH S.D.**

G-3475 WEST COURT STREET ● FLINT MI 48532 ● (810) 230-3200

Grade Span: KG-12 **Schools**: *Regular* 9 ● *Spec Ed* 0 ● *Alt* 0 **Students**: 5,198 **Total Teachers**: 271 **Student/Classroom Teacher Ratio**: 19.9	**Expenditures/Student**: $7,132 **Librarians**: 6.0 866 students/librarian **Guidance Counselors**: 12.0 433 students/counselor	**% Amer Indian**: 9.1 **% Asian**: 3.9 **% Black**: 14.1 **% Hispanic**: 1.6 **% White**: 71.3	National ***Socio-Economic Status*** indicator percentile (100=high): 58th

Genesee County
FLINT CITY S.D.
923 EAST KEARSLEY STREET ● FLINT MI 48502 ● (810) 760-1000

Grade Span: PK-12 **Schools**: *Regular* 46 ● *Spec Ed* 0 ● *Alt* 2 **Students**: 26,390 **Total Teachers**: 1,264 **Student/Classroom Teacher Ratio**: 22.8	**Expenditures/Student**: $8,182 **Librarians**: 9.0 2,932 students/librarian **Guidance Counselors**: 35.0 754 students/counselor	**% Amer Indian**: 2.6 **% Asian**: 0.5 **% Black**: 69.1 **% Hispanic**: 2.2 **% White**: 25.7	National ***Socio-Economic Status*** indicator percentile (100=high): 9th

Genesee County
[FLINT] **KEARSLEY COMMUNITY S.D.**
4396 UNDERHILL DRIVE ● FLINT MI 48506 ● (810) 736-8000

Grade Span: KG-12 **Schools**: *Regular* 6 ● *Spec Ed* 1 ● *Alt* 0 **Students**: 3,498 **Total Teachers**: 166 **Student/Classroom Teacher Ratio**: 21.7	**Expenditures/Student**: $5,771 **Librarians**: 2.0 1,749 students/librarian **Guidance Counselors**: 8.0 437 students/counselor	**% Amer Indian**: 0.3 **% Asian**: 0.6 **% Black**: 1.3 **% Hispanic**: 1.8 **% White**: 96.0	National ***Socio-Economic Status*** indicator percentile (100=high): 70th

Genesee County
FLUSHING COMMUNITY S.D.
522 NORTH MCKINLEY ROAD ● FLUSHING MI 48433 ● (810) 659-0600

Grade Span: PK-12 **Schools**: *Regular* 6 ● *Spec Ed* 0 ● *Alt* 0 **Students**: 4,175 **Total Teachers**: 187 **Student/Classroom Teacher Ratio**: 22.5	**Expenditures/Student**: $5,365 **Librarians**: 2.0 2,088 students/librarian **Guidance Counselors**: 4.0 1,044 students/counselor	**% Amer Indian**: 0.2 **% Asian**: 1.2 **% Black**: 1.2 **% Hispanic**: 1.3 **% White**: 96.1	National ***Socio-Economic Status*** indicator percentile (100=high): 89th

Genesee County
GRAND BLANC S.D.
G-11920 SOUTH SAGINAW STREET ● GRAND BLANC MI 48439 ● (810) 694-8211

Grade Span: KG-12 **Schools**: *Regular* 8 ● *Spec Ed* 1 ● *Alt* 0 **Students**: 5,702 **Total Teachers**: 266 **Student/Classroom Teacher Ratio**: 22.3	**Expenditures/Student**: $5,916 **Librarians**: 4.0 1,426 students/librarian **Guidance Counselors**: 12.0 475 students/counselor	**% Amer Indian**: 0.0 **% Asian**: 3.1 **% Black**: 7.3 **% Hispanic**: 1.3 **% White**: 88.3	National ***Socio-Economic Status*** indicator percentile (100=high): 91st

Genesee County
LINDEN COMMUNITY S.D.
P.O. BOX 67 ● LINDEN MI 48451 ● (810) 735-7821

Grade Span: KG-12 **Schools**: *Regular* 5 ● *Spec Ed* 0 ● *Alt* 0 **Students**: 2,678 **Total Teachers**: 118 **Student/Classroom Teacher Ratio**: 24.6	**Expenditures/Student**: $5,561 **Librarians**: 0.0 *** students/librarian **Guidance Counselors**: 3.0 893 students/counselor	**% Amer Indian**: 0.4 **% Asian**: 0.6 **% Black**: 0.1 **% Hispanic**: 1.1 **% White**: 97.9	National ***Socio-Economic Status*** indicator percentile (100=high): 87th

Genesee County
MOUNT MORRIS CONSOLIDATED S.D.
12356 WALTER STREET ● MOUNT MORRIS MI 48458 ● (810) 686-8760

Grade Span: KG-12 **Schools**: *Regular* 6 ● *Spec Ed* 0 ● *Alt* 1 **Students**: 3,143 **Total Teachers**: 167 **Student/Classroom Teacher Ratio**: 21.7	**Expenditures/Student**: $5,645 **Librarians**: 1.0 3,143 students/librarian **Guidance Counselors**: 5.0 629 students/counselor	**% Amer Indian**: 13.8 **% Asian**: 0.4 **% Black**: 3.1 **% Hispanic**: 1.9 **% White**: 80.8	National ***Socio-Economic Status*** indicator percentile (100=high): 47th

Genesee County

SWARTZ CREEK COMMUNITY S.D.

8354 CAPPY LANE ● SWARTZ CREEK MI 48473 ● (810) 635-4441

Grade Span: KG-12 **Schools**: *Regular* 7 ● *Spec Ed* 0 ● *Alt* 0 **Students**: 4,000 **Total Teachers**: 217 **Student/Classroom Teacher Ratio**: 18.8	**Expenditures/Student**: $6,074 **Librarians**: 3.0 1,333 students/librarian **Guidance Counselors**: 6.0 667 students/counselor	**% Amer Indian**: 4.0 **% Asian**: 1.0 **% Black**: 1.5 **% Hispanic**: 1.4 **% White**: 92.0	National ***Socio-Economic Status*** indicator percentile (100=high): 78th

Grand Traverse County

TRAVERSE CITY AREA S.D.

P.O. BOX 32 ● TRAVERSE CITY MI 49685 ● (616) 922-6450

Grade Span: KG-12 **Schools**: *Regular* 22 ● *Spec Ed* 0 ● *Alt* 0 **Students**: 11,123 **Total Teachers**: 573 **Student/Classroom Teacher Ratio**: 18.9	**Expenditures/Student**: $5,298 **Librarians**: 4.0 2,781 students/librarian **Guidance Counselors**: 13.0 856 students/counselor	**% Amer Indian**: 1.8 **% Asian**: 0.8 **% Black**: 0.5 **% Hispanic**: 1.2 **% White**: 95.7	National ***Socio-Economic Status*** indicator percentile (100=high): 67th

Gratiot County

ALMA S.D.

1500 NORTH PINE AVENUE ● ALMA MI 48801 ● (517) 463-3111

Grade Span: PK-12 **Schools**: *Regular* 5 ● *Spec Ed* 0 ● *Alt* 0 **Students**: 2,740 **Total Teachers**: 149 **Student/Classroom Teacher Ratio**: 20.4	**Expenditures/Student**: $5,879 **Librarians**: 2.0 1,370 students/librarian **Guidance Counselors**: 3.0 913 students/counselor	**% Amer Indian**: 0.9 **% Asian**: 0.8 **% Black**: 0.7 **% Hispanic**: 6.4 **% White**: 91.1	National ***Socio-Economic Status*** indicator percentile (100=high): 47th

Ingham County

EAST LANSING S.D.

509 BURCHAM DRIVE ● EAST LANSING MI 48823 ● (517) 333-7420 ● http://scnc.elps.k12.mi.us

Grade Span: PK-12 **Schools**: *Regular* 11 ● *Spec Ed* 0 ● *Alt* 0 **Students**: 3,916 **Total Teachers**: 251 **Student/Classroom Teacher Ratio**: 15.3	**Expenditures/Student**: $7,501 **Librarians**: 2.0 1,958 students/librarian **Guidance Counselors**: 7.0 559 students/counselor	**% Amer Indian**: 0.5 **% Asian**: 13.2 **% Black**: 12.6 **% Hispanic**: 4.6 **% White**: 69.0	National ***Socio-Economic Status*** indicator percentile (100=high): 67th

Ingham County

HASLETT S.D.

5593 FRANKLIN STREET ● HASLETT MI 48840 ● (517) 339-8242 ● http://scnc.haslett.k12.mi.us

Grade Span: PK-12 **Schools**: *Regular* 5 ● *Spec Ed* 0 ● *Alt* 1 **Students**: 2,543 **Total Teachers**: 129 **Student/Classroom Teacher Ratio**: 19.8	**Expenditures/Student**: $6,255 **Librarians**: 3.0 848 students/librarian **Guidance Counselors**: 4.0 636 students/counselor	**% Amer Indian**: 0.2 **% Asian**: 1.9 **% Black**: 2.6 **% Hispanic**: 2.0 **% White**: 93.4	National ***Socio-Economic Status*** indicator percentile (100=high): 94th

Ingham County

HOLT S.D.

4610 SPAHR AVENUE ● HOLT MI 48842 ● (517) 694-0401 ● http://scnc.holt.k12.mi.us

Grade Span: PK-12 **Schools**: *Regular* 10 ● *Spec Ed* 0 ● *Alt* 1 **Students**: 5,255 **Total Teachers**: 267 **Student/Classroom Teacher Ratio**: 20.0	**Expenditures/Student**: $6,717 **Librarians**: 4.0 1,314 students/librarian **Guidance Counselors**: 10.0 526 students/counselor	**% Amer Indian**: 0.4 **% Asian**: 1.3 **% Black**: 2.8 **% Hispanic**: 3.7 **% White**: 91.7	National ***Socio-Economic Status*** indicator percentile (100=high): 83rd

Ingham County

LANSING S.D.

519 WEST KALAMAZOO STREET ● LANSING MI 48933 ● (517) 325-6006 ● http://scnc.lsd.k12.mi.us/~bmorrow/index.html

Grade Span: PK-12 **Schools**: *Regular* 41 ● *Spec Ed* 1 ● *Alt* 3 **Students**: 20,103 **Total Teachers**: 1,057 **Student/Classroom Teacher Ratio**: 19.8	**Expenditures/Student**: $7,850 **Librarians**: 35.0 574 students/librarian **Guidance Counselors**: 38.0 529 students/counselor	**% Amer Indian**: 1.1 **% Asian**: 5.0 **% Black**: 33.3 **% Hispanic**: 12.0 **% White**: 48.5	National ***Socio-Economic Status*** indicator percentile (100=high): 21st

Ingham County

[LANSING] **WAVERLY COMMUNITY S.D.**

515 SNOW ROAD ● LANSING MI 48917 ● (517) 321-7265

Grade Span: PK-12 **Schools**: *Regular* 6 ● *Spec Ed* 0 ● *Alt* 1 **Students**: 3,204 **Total Teachers**: 193 **Student/Classroom Teacher Ratio**: 17.9	**Expenditures/Student**: $8,029 **Librarians**: 2.0 1,602 students/librarian **Guidance Counselors**: 9.0 356 students/counselor	**% Amer Indian**: 0.2 **% Asian**: 2.6 **% Black**: 11.7 **% Hispanic**: 5.3 **% White**: 80.3	National ***Socio-Economic Status*** indicator percentile (100=high): 82nd

Ingham County

MASON S.D.

118 WEST OAK STREET ● MASON MI 48854 ● (517) 676-2484

Grade Span: PK-12 **Schools**: *Regular* 6 ● *Spec Ed* 0 ● *Alt* 1 **Students**: 3,380 **Total Teachers**: 172 **Student/Classroom Teacher Ratio**: 20.8	**Expenditures/Student**: $5,954 **Librarians**: 2.0 1,690 students/librarian **Guidance Counselors**: 4.0 845 students/counselor	**% Amer Indian**: 0.3 **% Asian**: 1.0 **% Black**: 0.9 **% Hispanic**: 2.8 **% White**: 95.1	National ***Socio-Economic Status*** indicator percentile (100=high): 83rd

Ingham County

OKEMOS S.D.

4406 NORTH OKEMOS ROAD ● OKEMOS MI 48864 ● (517) 349-9460 ● http://okemos.k12.mi.us

Grade Span: KG-12 **Schools**: *Regular* 9 ● *Spec Ed* 0 ● *Alt* 0 **Students**: 4,323 **Total Teachers**: 237 **Student/Classroom Teacher Ratio**: 18.3	**Expenditures/Student**: $7,230 **Librarians**: 4.0 1,081 students/librarian **Guidance Counselors**: 14.0 309 students/counselor	**% Amer Indian**: 0.6 **% Asian**: 7.6 **% Black**: 6.1 **% Hispanic**: 1.9 **% White**: 83.8	National ***Socio-Economic Status*** indicator percentile (100=high): 90th

Ionia County

BELDING AREA S.D.

321 WILSON STREET ● BELDING MI 48809 ● (616) 794-1960

Grade Span: PK-12 **Schools**: *Regular* 6 ● *Spec Ed* 0 ● *Alt* 1 **Students**: 2,508 **Total Teachers**: 132 **Student/Classroom Teacher Ratio**: 19.1	**Expenditures/Student**: $4,943 **Librarians**: 2.0 1,254 students/librarian **Guidance Counselors**: 5.0 502 students/counselor	**% Amer Indian**: 0.4 **% Asian**: 0.1 **% Black**: 0.2 **% Hispanic**: 2.5 **% White**: 96.7	National ***Socio-Economic Status*** indicator percentile (100=high): 58th

Ionia County

IONIA S.D.

250 EAST TUTTLE ROAD ● IONIA MI 48846 ● (616) 527-9280 ● http://www.remc8.k12.mi.us/ioniaisd

Grade Span: PK-12 **Schools**: *Regular* 6 ● *Spec Ed* 0 ● *Alt* 2 **Students**: 3,542 **Total Teachers**: 193 **Student/Classroom Teacher Ratio**: 18.7	**Expenditures/Student**: $5,611 **Librarians**: 1.0 3,542 students/librarian **Guidance Counselors**: 6.0 590 students/counselor	**% Amer Indian**: 0.1 **% Asian**: 0.5 **% Black**: 0.7 **% Hispanic**: 3.5 **% White**: 95.2	National ***Socio-Economic Status*** indicator percentile (100=high): 47th

Ionia County

[LAKE ODESSA] **LAKEWOOD S.D.**

639 JORDAN LAKE STREET ● LAKE ODESSA MI 48849 ● (616) 374-8043

Grade Span: PK-12 **Schools**: *Regular* 7 ● *Spec Ed* 0 ● *Alt* 0 **Students**: 2,801 **Total Teachers**: 141 **Student/Classroom Teacher Ratio**: 20.0	**Expenditures/Student**: $5,410 **Librarians**: 1.0 2,801 students/librarian **Guidance Counselors**: 3.0 934 students/counselor	**% Amer Indian**: 0.6 **% Asian**: 0.4 **% Black**: 0.6 **% Hispanic**: 3.0 **% White**: 95.3	National ***Socio-Economic Status*** indicator percentile (100=high): 73rd

Isabella County

MOUNT PLEASANT CITY S.D.

201 SOUTH UNIVERSITY STREET ● MOUNT PLEASANT MI 48858 ● (517) 773-5500 ● http://remcen.ehhs.cmich.edu/~mpps/newindex.html

Grade Span: PK-12 **Schools**: *Regular* 10 ● *Spec Ed* 1 ● *Alt* 1 **Students**: 4,216 **Total Teachers**: 249 **Student/Classroom Teacher Ratio**: 18.6	**Expenditures/Student**: $6,804 **Librarians**: 3.0 1,405 students/librarian **Guidance Counselors**: 8.0 527 students/counselor	**% Amer Indian**: 5.0 **% Asian**: 2.2 **% Black**: 2.5 **% Hispanic**: 2.0 **% White**: 88.4	National ***Socio-Economic Status*** indicator percentile (100=high): 59th

Jackson County

JACKSON S.D.

1400 WEST MONROE STREET ● JACKSON MI 49202 ● (517) 789-8144 ● http://scnc.jps.k12.mi.us

Grade Span: KG-12 **Schools**: *Regular* 12 ● *Spec Ed* 0 ● *Alt* 1 **Students**: 7,518 **Total Teachers**: 401 **Student/Classroom Teacher Ratio**: 19.9	**Expenditures/Student**: $6,949 **Librarians**: 3.0 2,506 students/librarian **Guidance Counselors**: 9.0 835 students/counselor	**% Amer Indian**: 2.0 **% Asian**: 1.2 **% Black**: 28.3 **% Hispanic**: 2.4 **% White**: 66.1	National ***Socio-Economic Status*** indicator percentile (100=high): 16th

Jackson County

[JACKSON] **NORTHWEST S.D.**

4000 VAN HORN ROAD ● JACKSON MI 49201 ● (517) 569-2247 ● http://nsd.k12.mi.us

Grade Span: KG-12 **Schools**: *Regular* 4 ● *Spec Ed* 0 ● *Alt* 1 **Students**: 3,539 **Total Teachers**: 167 **Student/Classroom Teacher Ratio**: 19.8	**Expenditures/Student**: $5,337 **Librarians**: 3.0 1,180 students/librarian **Guidance Counselors**: 8.0 442 students/counselor	**% Amer Indian**: 0.3 **% Asian**: 0.8 **% Black**: 1.5 **% Hispanic**: 0.9 **% White**: 96.5	National ***Socio-Economic Status*** indicator percentile (100=high): 73rd

Kalamazoo County

COMSTOCK S.D.

301 NORTH 26TH STREET ● COMSTOCK MI 49041 ● (616) 388-9461 ● http://www.remc12.k12.mi.us/comstock

Grade Span: KG-12 **Schools**: *Regular* 6 ● *Spec Ed* 0 ● *Alt* 1 **Students**: 2,852 **Total Teachers**: 167 **Student/Classroom Teacher Ratio**: 17.9	**Expenditures/Student**: $6,239 **Librarians**: 5.0 570 students/librarian **Guidance Counselors**: 6.0 475 students/counselor	**% Amer Indian**: 0.7 **% Asian**: 1.3 **% Black**: 7.6 **% Hispanic**: 2.1 **% White**: 88.4	National ***Socio-Economic Status*** indicator percentile (100=high): 45th

Kalamazoo County

KALAMAZOO S.D.

1220 HOWARD STREET ● KALAMAZOO MI 49008 ● (616) 337-0123 ● http://www.kalamazoo.k12.mi.us

Grade Span: KG-12 **Schools**: *Regular* 24 ● *Spec Ed* 2 ● *Alt* 3 **Students**: 11,997 **Total Teachers**: 735 **Student/Classroom Teacher Ratio**: 17.5	**Expenditures/Student**: $6,939 **Librarians**: 16.0 750 students/librarian **Guidance Counselors**: 17.0 706 students/counselor	**% Amer Indian**: 1.0 **% Asian**: 1.1 **% Black**: 39.9 **% Hispanic**: 4.6 **% White**: 53.3	National ***Socio-Economic Status*** indicator percentile (100=high): 21st

Kalamazoo County
PORTAGE S.D.
8111 SOUTH WESTNEDGE AVENUE ● PORTAGE MI 49002 ● (616) 329-7400 ● http://portage.k12.mi.us

Grade Span: KG-12 **Schools**: *Regular* 13 ● *Spec Ed* 0 ● *Alt* 1 **Students**: 8,469 **Total Teachers**: 468 **Student/Classroom Teacher Ratio**: 19.4	**Expenditures/Student**: $5,596 **Librarians**: 14.0 605 students/librarian **Guidance Counselors**: 19.0 446 students/counselor	**% Amer Indian**: 0.4 **% Asian**: 3.3 **% Black**: 4.0 **% Hispanic**: 2.0 **% White**: 90.3	National ***Socio-Economic Status*** indicator percentile (100=high): 89th

Kalamazoo County
[RICHLAND] GULL LAKE COMMUNITY S.D.
11775 EAST D AVENUE ● RICHLAND MI 49083 ● (616) 629-5880

Grade Span: PK-12 **Schools**: *Regular* 6 ● *Spec Ed* 0 ● *Alt* 0 **Students**: 2,859 **Total Teachers**: 150 **Student/Classroom Teacher Ratio**: 19.2	**Expenditures/Student**: $5,211 **Librarians**: 3.0 953 students/librarian **Guidance Counselors**: 6.0 477 students/counselor	**% Amer Indian**: 0.1 **% Asian**: 0.6 **% Black**: 1.0 **% Hispanic**: 0.6 **% White**: 97.8	National ***Socio-Economic Status*** indicator percentile (100=high): 91st

Kalamazoo County
VICKSBURG COMMUNITY S.D.
301 SOUTH KALAMAZOO AVENUE ● VICKSBURG MI 49097 ● (616) 649-0550

Grade Span: PK-12 **Schools**: *Regular* 5 ● *Spec Ed* 0 ● *Alt* 0 **Students**: 2,621 **Total Teachers**: 136 **Student/Classroom Teacher Ratio**: 19.5	**Expenditures/Student**: $5,373 **Librarians**: 4.0 655 students/librarian **Guidance Counselors**: 6.0 437 students/counselor	**% Amer Indian**: 0.0 **% Asian**: 1.0 **% Black**: 1.0 **% Hispanic**: 0.6 **% White**: 97.4	National ***Socio-Economic Status*** indicator percentile (100=high): 82nd

Kent County
CALEDONIA COMMUNITY S.D.
203 EAST MAIN STREET ● CALEDONIA MI 49316 ● (616) 891-8185 ● http://www.caledonia.k12.mi.us

Grade Span: PK-12 **Schools**: *Regular* 5 ● *Spec Ed* 0 ● *Alt* 0 **Students**: 2,697 **Total Teachers**: 154 **Student/Classroom Teacher Ratio**: 18.5	**Expenditures/Student**: $6,571 **Librarians**: 1.0 2,697 students/librarian **Guidance Counselors**: 4.0 674 students/counselor	**% Amer Indian**: 0.3 **% Asian**: 1.3 **% Black**: 0.6 **% Hispanic**: 1.6 **% White**: 96.3	National ***Socio-Economic Status*** indicator percentile (100=high): 90th

Kent County
CEDAR SPRINGS S.D.
204 EAST MUSKEGON STREET ● CEDAR SPRINGS MI 49319 ● (616) 696-1204

Grade Span: KG-12 **Schools**: *Regular* 5 ● *Spec Ed* 0 ● *Alt* 0 **Students**: 2,856 **Total Teachers**: 148 **Student/Classroom Teacher Ratio**: 19.8	**Expenditures/Student**: $5,147 **Librarians**: 0.0 *** students/librarian **Guidance Counselors**: 6.0 476 students/counselor	**% Amer Indian**: 0.6 **% Asian**: 0.3 **% Black**: 0.6 **% Hispanic**: 1.4 **% White**: 97.0	National ***Socio-Economic Status*** indicator percentile (100=high): 60th

Kent County
EAST GRAND RAPIDS S.D.
2915 HALL STREET, S.E. ● EAST GRAND RAPIDS MI 49506 ● (616) 235-3535 ● http://remc8.k12.mi.us/eastgr/egrps.html

Grade Span: KG-12 **Schools**: *Regular* 5 ● *Spec Ed* 0 ● *Alt* 0 **Students**: 2,613 **Total Teachers**: 148 **Student/Classroom Teacher Ratio**: 17.6	**Expenditures/Student**: $6,836 **Librarians**: 5.0 523 students/librarian **Guidance Counselors**: 5.0 523 students/counselor	**% Amer Indian**: 0.1 **% Asian**: 1.8 **% Black**: 1.3 **% Hispanic**: 0.6 **% White**: 96.2	National ***Socio-Economic Status*** indicator percentile (100=high): 100th

Kent County

[GRAND RAPIDS] **FOREST HILLS S.D.**

6590 CASCADE ROAD, S.E. ● GRAND RAPIDS MI 49546 ● (616) 285-8800

Grade Span: KG-12 **Schools**: *Regular* 10 ● *Spec Ed* 0 ● *Alt* 0 **Students**: 6,902 **Total Teachers**: 402 **Student/Classroom Teacher Ratio**: 17.2	**Expenditures/Student**: $6,538 **Librarians**: 4.0 1,726 students/librarian **Guidance Counselors**: 16.0 431 students/counselor	**% Amer Indian**: 0.2 **% Asian**: 3.4 **% Black**: 1.4 **% Hispanic**: 1.0 **% White**: 94.0	National ***Socio-Economic Status*** indicator percentile (100=high): 98th

Kent County

GRAND RAPIDS CITY S.D.

P.O. BOX 117 ● GRAND RAPIDS MI 49501 ● (616) 771-2000 ● http://www.grps.k12.mi.us

Grade Span: PK-12 **Schools**: *Regular* 79 ● *Spec Ed* 8 ● *Alt* 7 **Students**: 27,087 **Total Teachers**: 1,342 **Student/Classroom Teacher Ratio**: 27.2	**Expenditures/Student**: $7,613 **Librarians**: 11.0 2,462 students/librarian **Guidance Counselors**: 39.0 695 students/counselor	**% Amer Indian**: 1.4 **% Asian**: 2.2 **% Black**: 41.6 **% Hispanic**: 12.2 **% White**: 42.5	National ***Socio-Economic Status*** indicator percentile (100=high): 19th

Kent County

[GRAND RAPIDS] **KENOWA HILLS S.D.**

2325 FOUR MILE ROAD, N.W. ● GRAND RAPIDS MI 49544 ● (616) 784-2511

Grade Span: KG-12 **Schools**: *Regular* 6 ● *Spec Ed* 1 ● *Alt* 0 **Students**: 3,041 **Total Teachers**: 156 **Student/Classroom Teacher Ratio**: 20.8	**Expenditures/Student**: $5,955 **Librarians**: 2.0 1,521 students/librarian **Guidance Counselors**: 5.0 608 students/counselor	**% Amer Indian**: 0.5 **% Asian**: 0.9 **% Black**: 1.3 **% Hispanic**: 1.7 **% White**: 95.6	National ***Socio-Economic Status*** indicator percentile (100=high): 66th

Kent County

[GRAND RAPIDS] **NORTHVIEW S.D.**

4365 HUNSBERGER DRIVE, N.E. ● GRAND RAPIDS MI 49505 ● (616) 363-6861

Grade Span: PK-12 **Schools**: *Regular* 6 ● *Spec Ed* 0 ● *Alt* 1 **Students**: 3,164 **Total Teachers**: 162 **Student/Classroom Teacher Ratio**: 19.2	**Expenditures/Student**: $5,781 **Librarians**: 2.0 1,582 students/librarian **Guidance Counselors**: 6.0 527 students/counselor	**% Amer Indian**: 0.1 **% Asian**: 0.6 **% Black**: 1.4 **% Hispanic**: 1.0 **% White**: 96.9	National ***Socio-Economic Status*** indicator percentile (100=high): 87th

Kent County

GRANDVILLE S.D.

3131 BARRETT STREET ● GRANDVILLE MI 49418 ● (616) 530-1600 ● http://www.remc8.k12.mi.us/grandvil

Grade Span: KG-12 **Schools**: *Regular* 10 ● *Spec Ed* 0 ● *Alt* 0 **Students**: 5,215 **Total Teachers**: 248 **Student/Classroom Teacher Ratio**: 21.3	**Expenditures/Student**: $5,367 **Librarians**: 3.0 1,738 students/librarian **Guidance Counselors**: 6.0 869 students/counselor	**% Amer Indian**: 0.2 **% Asian**: 1.9 **% Black**: 1.7 **% Hispanic**: 1.8 **% White**: 94.3	National ***Socio-Economic Status*** indicator percentile (100=high): 92nd

Kent County

KENTWOOD S.D.

5820 EASTERN AVENUE, S.E. ● KENTWOOD MI 49508 ● (616) 455-4400 ● http://www.remc8.k12.mi.us/kentwood/kentwood.htm

Grade Span: PK-12 **Schools**: *Regular* 16 ● *Spec Ed* 1 ● *Alt* 0 **Students**: 8,124 **Total Teachers**: 402 **Student/Classroom Teacher Ratio**: 20.8	**Expenditures/Student**: $6,228 **Librarians**: 5.0 1,625 students/librarian **Guidance Counselors**: 18.0 451 students/counselor	**% Amer Indian**: 0.5 **% Asian**: 4.7 **% Black**: 11.7 **% Hispanic**: 3.2 **% White**: 79.8	National ***Socio-Economic Status*** indicator percentile (100=high): 69th

Kent County

LOWELL AREA S.D.

12685 FOREMAN ROAD ● LOWELL MI 49331 ● (616) 897-8415 ● http://remc8.k12.mi.us/lowell

Grade Span: KG-12 **Schools**: *Regular* 6 ● *Spec Ed* 0 ● *Alt* 0 **Students**: 3,356 **Total Teachers**: 167 **Student/Classroom Teacher Ratio**: 21.3	**Expenditures/Student**: $5,533 **Librarians**: 2.0 1,678 students/librarian **Guidance Counselors**: 5.0 671 students/counselor	**% Amer Indian**: 0.4 **% Asian**: 1.0 **% Black**: 0.5 **% Hispanic**: 1.7 **% White**: 96.4	National ***Socio-Economic Status*** indicator percentile (100=high): 88th

Kent County

ROCKFORD S.D.

350 MAIN STREET ● ROCKFORD MI 49341 ● (616) 866-1597

Grade Span: KG-12 **Schools**: *Regular* 10 ● *Spec Ed* 0 ● *Alt* 0 **Students**: 6,498 **Total Teachers**: 303 **Student/Classroom Teacher Ratio**: 21.4	**Expenditures/Student**: $5,324 **Librarians**: 2.0 3,249 students/librarian **Guidance Counselors**: 6.0 1,083 students/counselor	**% Amer Indian**: 0.2 **% Asian**: 0.8 **% Black**: 0.6 **% Hispanic**: 0.9 **% White**: 97.4	National ***Socio-Economic Status*** indicator percentile (100=high): 94th

Kent County

SPARTA AREA S.D.

480 SOUTH STATE STREET ● SPARTA MI 49345 ● (616) 887-8253

Grade Span: KG-12 **Schools**: *Regular* 6 ● *Spec Ed* 0 ● *Alt* 0 **Students**: 2,904 **Total Teachers**: 150 **Student/Classroom Teacher Ratio**: 17.7	**Expenditures/Student**: $5,779 **Librarians**: 2.0 1,452 students/librarian **Guidance Counselors**: 6.0 484 students/counselor	**% Amer Indian**: 0.0 **% Asian**: 0.5 **% Black**: 0.7 **% Hispanic**: 1.3 **% White**: 97.6	National ***Socio-Economic Status*** indicator percentile (100=high): 57th

Kent County

WYOMING S.D.

3575 GLADIOLA STREET, S.W. ● WYOMING MI 49509 ● (616) 530-7550 ● http://www.remc8.k12.mi.us/wyoming

Grade Span: PK-12 **Schools**: *Regular* 12 ● *Spec Ed* 0 ● *Alt* 1 **Students**: 5,668 **Total Teachers**: 297 **Student/Classroom Teacher Ratio**: 20.4	**Expenditures/Student**: $6,935 **Librarians**: 6.0 945 students/librarian **Guidance Counselors**: 11.0 515 students/counselor	**% Amer Indian**: 0.6 **% Asian**: 3.4 **% Black**: 5.2 **% Hispanic**: 5.6 **% White**: 85.1	National ***Socio-Economic Status*** indicator percentile (100=high): 63rd

Lapeer County

LAPEER COMMUNITY S.D.

1025 WEST NEPESSING STREET ● LAPEER MI 48446 ● (810) 667-2401 ● http://www.lapeer.lib.mi.us/Education/Schools/Index.html

Grade Span: PK-12 **Schools**: *Regular* 16 ● *Spec Ed* 0 ● *Alt* 1 **Students**: 7,811 **Total Teachers**: 339 **Student/Classroom Teacher Ratio**: 26.1	**Expenditures/Student**: $5,394 **Librarians**: 3.0 2,604 students/librarian **Guidance Counselors**: 8.0 976 students/counselor	**% Amer Indian**: 0.3 **% Asian**: 0.9 **% Black**: 0.4 **% Hispanic**: 1.7 **% White**: 96.7	National ***Socio-Economic Status*** indicator percentile (100=high): 76th

Lenawee County

ADRIAN CITY S.D.

227 NORTH WINTER STREET ● ADRIAN MI 49221 ● (517) 263-2115 ● http://webserv.adrian.k12.mi.us/apshome.html

Grade Span: KG-12 **Schools**: *Regular* 11 ● *Spec Ed* 0 ● *Alt* 2 **Students**: 5,057 **Total Teachers**: 246 **Student/Classroom Teacher Ratio**: 20.1	**Expenditures/Student**: $6,319 **Librarians**: 4.0 1,264 students/librarian **Guidance Counselors**: 7.0 722 students/counselor	**% Amer Indian**: 0.1 **% Asian**: 0.8 **% Black**: 5.1 **% Hispanic**: 18.3 **% White**: 75.8	National ***Socio-Economic Status*** indicator percentile (100=high): 50th

Lenawee County

TECUMSEH S.D.

304 WEST CHICAGO BOULEVARD ● TECUMSEH MI 49286 ● (517) 423-2167 ● http://scnc.tps.k12.mi.us/%7Eths

Grade Span: KG-12 **Schools**: *Regular* 6 ● *Spec Ed* 0 ● *Alt* 0 **Students**: 3,096 **Total Teachers**: 94 **Student/Classroom Teacher Ratio**: na	**Expenditures/Student**: $5,762 **Librarians**: 2.0 1,548 students/librarian **Guidance Counselors**: 7.0 442 students/counselor	**% Amer Indian**: 0.3 **% Asian**: 1.0 **% Black**: 0.3 **% Hispanic**: 4.9 **% White**: 93.5	National ***Socio-Economic Status*** indicator percentile (100=high): 86th

Livingston County

BRIGHTON AREA S.D.

4740 BAUER ROAD ● BRIGHTON MI 48116 ● (810) 229-1450

Grade Span: KG-12 **Schools**: *Regular* 9 ● *Spec Ed* 0 ● *Alt* 1 **Students**: 6,457 **Total Teachers**: 311 **Student/Classroom Teacher Ratio**: 22.9	**Expenditures/Student**: $6,954 **Librarians**: 5.0 1,291 students/librarian **Guidance Counselors**: 8.0 807 students/counselor	**% Amer Indian**: 2.5 **% Asian**: 1.1 **% Black**: 0.2 **% Hispanic**: 0.6 **% White**: 95.6	National ***Socio-Economic Status*** indicator percentile (100=high): 97th

Livingston County

FOWLERVILLE COMMUNITY S.D.

4861 FOWLERVILLE ROAD ● FOWLERVILLE MI 48836 ● (517) 223-8459

Grade Span: KG-12 **Schools**: *Regular* 4 ● *Spec Ed* 0 ● *Alt* 0 **Students**: 2,609 **Total Teachers**: 134 **Student/Classroom Teacher Ratio**: 20.4	**Expenditures/Student**: $5,343 **Librarians**: 3.0 870 students/librarian **Guidance Counselors**: 5.0 522 students/counselor	**% Amer Indian**: 5.7 **% Asian**: 0.0 **% Black**: 0.0 **% Hispanic**: 0.1 **% White**: 94.1	National ***Socio-Economic Status*** indicator percentile (100=high): 79th

Livingston County

HARTLAND CONSOLIDATED S.D.

P.O. BOX 900 ● HARTLAND MI 48353 ● (810) 632-7481

Grade Span: PK-12 **Schools**: *Regular* 5 ● *Spec Ed* 0 ● *Alt* 1 **Students**: 3,685 **Total Teachers**: 172 **Student/Classroom Teacher Ratio**: 21.9	**Expenditures/Student**: $6,066 **Librarians**: 3.0 1,228 students/librarian **Guidance Counselors**: 4.0 921 students/counselor	**% Amer Indian**: 0.2 **% Asian**: 0.7 **% Black**: 0.4 **% Hispanic**: 0.8 **% White**: 98.0	National ***Socio-Economic Status*** indicator percentile (100=high): 96th

Livingston County

HOWELL S.D.

411 N. HIGHLANDER WAY ● HOWELL MI 48843 ● (517) 548-6234

Grade Span: KG-12 **Schools**: *Regular* 8 ● *Spec Ed* 0 ● *Alt* 1 **Students**: 6,252 **Total Teachers**: 286 **Student/Classroom Teacher Ratio**: 23.0	**Expenditures/Student**: $5,478 **Librarians**: 4.0 1,563 students/librarian **Guidance Counselors**: 10.0 625 students/counselor	**% Amer Indian**: 2.2 **% Asian**: 0.5 **% Black**: 0.2 **% Hispanic**: 0.4 **% White**: 96.7	National ***Socio-Economic Status*** indicator percentile (100=high): 89th

Livingston County

PINCKNEY COMMUNITY S.D.

P.O. BOX 9 ● PINCKNEY MI 48169 ● (734) 878-3115

Grade Span: PK-12 **Schools**: *Regular* 7 ● *Spec Ed* 0 ● *Alt* 0 **Students**: 4,142 **Total Teachers**: 193 **Student/Classroom Teacher Ratio**: 22.5	**Expenditures/Student**: $5,273 **Librarians**: 2.0 2,071 students/librarian **Guidance Counselors**: 4.0 1,036 students/counselor	**% Amer Indian**: 0.2 **% Asian**: 0.3 **% Black**: 0.2 **% Hispanic**: 0.2 **% White**: 99.2	National ***Socio-Economic Status*** indicator percentile (100=high): 93rd

Macomb County
CENTER LINE S.D.
ADMINISTRATION BUILDING ● CENTER LINE MI 48015 ● (810) 757-7000 ● http://www.macomb.k12.mi.us/centerl/schcent.htm

Grade Span: KG-12 **Schools**: *Regular* 7 ● *Spec Ed* 0 ● *Alt* 0 **Students**: 2,675 **Total Teachers**: 154 **Student/Classroom Teacher Ratio**: 18.4	**Expenditures/Student**: $8,275 **Librarians**: 2.0 1,338 students/librarian **Guidance Counselors**: 9.0 297 students/counselor	**% Amer Indian**: 1.8 **% Asian**: 2.7 **% Black**: 1.5 **% Hispanic**: 0.8 **% White**: 93.2	National ***Socio-Economic Status*** indicator percentile (100=high): 56th

Macomb County
[CLINTON TOWNSHIP] CHIPPEWA VALLEY S.D.
19120 CASS AVENUE ● CLINTON TOWNSHIP MI 48038 ● (810) 228-5500 ● http://www.macomb.k12.mi.us/Chippewa/Home.htm

Grade Span: PK-12 **Schools**: *Regular* 15 ● *Spec Ed* 0 ● *Alt* 0 **Students**: 9,947 **Total Teachers**: 417 **Student/Classroom Teacher Ratio**: 24.0	**Expenditures/Student**: $5,735 **Librarians**: 6.0 1,658 students/librarian **Guidance Counselors**: 17.0 585 students/counselor	**% Amer Indian**: 0.2 **% Asian**: 1.0 **% Black**: 1.0 **% Hispanic**: 0.4 **% White**: 97.5	National ***Socio-Economic Status*** indicator percentile (100=high): 94th

Macomb County
[CLINTON TOWNSHIP] CLINTONDALE COMMUNITY S.D.
35100 LITTLE MACK AVENUE ● CLINTON TOWNSHIP MI 48035 ● (810) 791-6300 ● http://www.clintondale.k12.mi.us

Grade Span: KG-12 **Schools**: *Regular* 5 ● *Spec Ed* 0 ● *Alt* 1 **Students**: 2,502 **Total Teachers**: 140 **Student/Classroom Teacher Ratio**: 21.6	**Expenditures/Student**: $11,597 **Librarians**: 5.0 500 students/librarian **Guidance Counselors**: 7.0 357 students/counselor	**% Amer Indian**: 1.6 **% Asian**: 2.3 **% Black**: 20.0 **% Hispanic**: 1.2 **% White**: 75.0	National ***Socio-Economic Status*** indicator percentile (100=high): 50th

Macomb County
[EASTPOINTE] EAST DETROIT S.D.
15115 DEERFIELD ● EASTPOINTE MI 48021 ● (810) 445-4410 ● http://www.macomb.k12.mi.us/eastdet/scheast.htm

Grade Span: PK-12 **Schools**: *Regular* 11 ● *Spec Ed* 0 ● *Alt* 4 **Students**: 6,766 **Total Teachers**: 343 **Student/Classroom Teacher Ratio**: 21.1	**Expenditures/Student**: $6,687 **Librarians**: 11.0 615 students/librarian **Guidance Counselors**: 11.0 615 students/counselor	**% Amer Indian**: 1.8 **% Asian**: 1.4 **% Black**: 1.5 **% Hispanic**: 0.3 **% White**: 95.0	National ***Socio-Economic Status*** indicator percentile (100=high): 61st

Macomb County
FRASER S.D.
33466 GARFIELD ROAD ● FRASER MI 48026 ● (810) 293-5100 ● http://www.macomb.k12.mi.us/fraser/schfras.htm

Grade Span: KG-12 **Schools**: *Regular* 9 ● *Spec Ed* 0 ● *Alt* 0 **Students**: 4,779 **Total Teachers**: 239 **Student/Classroom Teacher Ratio**: 22.4	**Expenditures/Student**: $6,986 **Librarians**: 2.0 2,390 students/librarian **Guidance Counselors**: 6.0 797 students/counselor	**% Amer Indian**: 1.1 **% Asian**: 1.9 **% Black**: 1.3 **% Hispanic**: 0.6 **% White**: 95.0	National ***Socio-Economic Status*** indicator percentile (100=high): 78th

Macomb County
[HARRISON TOWNSHIP] L ANSE CREUSE S.D.
36727 JEFFERSON AVENUE ● HARRISON TOWNSHIP MI 48045 ● (810) 763-6300 ● http://www.lansecreuse.k12.mi.us

Grade Span: PK-12 **Schools**: *Regular* 15 ● *Spec Ed* 1 ● *Alt* 3 **Students**: 9,172 **Total Teachers**: 419 **Student/Classroom Teacher Ratio**: 24.9	**Expenditures/Student**: $6,682 **Librarians**: 10.0 917 students/librarian **Guidance Counselors**: 28.0 328 students/counselor	**% Amer Indian**: 0.3 **% Asian**: 0.9 **% Black**: 2.6 **% Hispanic**: 1.0 **% White**: 95.2	National ***Socio-Economic Status*** indicator percentile (100=high): 82nd

Macomb County
MOUNT CLEMENS COMMUNITY S.D.
167 CASS AVENUE ● MOUNT CLEMENS MI 48043 ● (810) 469-6100 ● http://www.mtclemens.k12.mi.us

Grade Span: PK-12 **Schools**: *Regular* 7 ● *Spec Ed* 0 ● *Alt* 0 **Students**: 3,162 **Total Teachers**: 153 **Student/Classroom Teacher Ratio**: 26.6	**Expenditures/Student**: $8,099 **Librarians**: 3.0 1,054 students/librarian **Guidance Counselors**: 6.0 527 students/counselor	**% Amer Indian**: 0.2 **% Asian**: 2.1 **% Black**: 36.9 **% Hispanic**: 1.9 **% White**: 58.8	National ***Socio-Economic Status*** indicator percentile (100=high): 42nd

Macomb County
[NEW BALTIMORE] ANCHOR BAY S.D.
52801 ASHLEY STREET ● NEW BALTIMORE MI 48047 ● (810) 725-2861 ● http://www.macomb.k12.mi.us/anchor/schanch.htm

Grade Span: PK-12 **Schools**: *Regular* 7 ● *Spec Ed* 0 ● *Alt* 0 **Students**: 4,445 **Total Teachers**: 219 **Student/Classroom Teacher Ratio**: 20.7	**Expenditures/Student**: $5,764 **Librarians**: 1.0 4,445 students/librarian **Guidance Counselors**: 6.0 741 students/counselor	**% Amer Indian**: 1.4 **% Asian**: 0.8 **% Black**: 2.9 **% Hispanic**: 1.0 **% White**: 93.9	National ***Socio-Economic Status*** indicator percentile (100=high): 80th

Macomb County
ROMEO S.D.
316 NORTH MAIN STREET ● ROMEO MI 48065 ● (810) 752-0200 ● http://www.macomb.k12.mi.us/romeo/schrome.htm

Grade Span: PK-12 **Schools**: *Regular* 8 ● *Spec Ed* 0 ● *Alt* 0 **Students**: 4,685 **Total Teachers**: 235 **Student/Classroom Teacher Ratio**: na	**Expenditures/Student**: $6,314 **Librarians**: 4.0 1,171 students/librarian **Guidance Counselors**: 7.0 669 students/counselor	**% Amer Indian**: 0.1 **% Asian**: 0.7 **% Black**: 1.4 **% Hispanic**: 0.9 **% White**: 96.9	National ***Socio-Economic Status*** indicator percentile (100=high): 90th

Macomb County
ROSEVILLE COMMUNITY S.D.
18975 CHURCH STREET ● ROSEVILLE MI 48066 ● (810) 445-5505 ● http://www.macomb.k12.mi.us/rosevil/schrose.htm

Grade Span: PK-12 **Schools**: *Regular* 13 ● *Spec Ed* 0 ● *Alt* 0 **Students**: 6,239 **Total Teachers**: 315 **Student/Classroom Teacher Ratio**: 20.8	**Expenditures/Student**: $6,622 **Librarians**: 3.0 2,080 students/librarian **Guidance Counselors**: 8.0 780 students/counselor	**% Amer Indian**: 2.5 **% Asian**: 1.9 **% Black**: 2.3 **% Hispanic**: 1.3 **% White**: 92.0	National ***Socio-Economic Status*** indicator percentile (100=high): 61st

Macomb County
[ST. CLAIR SHORES] LAKE SHORE S.D.
28850 HARPER ● ST. CLAIR SHORES MI 48081 ● (810) 296-8205 ● http://www.macomb.k12.mi.us/lakesho/Admin/lake_adm.htm

Grade Span: KG-12 **Schools**: *Regular* 6 ● *Spec Ed* 0 ● *Alt* 1 **Students**: 3,135 **Total Teachers**: 179 **Student/Classroom Teacher Ratio**: 22.6	**Expenditures/Student**: $9,082 **Librarians**: 3.0 1,045 students/librarian **Guidance Counselors**: 9.0 348 students/counselor	**% Amer Indian**: 3.8 **% Asian**: 1.1 **% Black**: 0.6 **% Hispanic**: 1.0 **% White**: 93.5	National ***Socio-Economic Status*** indicator percentile (100=high): 89th

Macomb County
[ST. CLAIR SHORES] LAKEVIEW S.D.
20300 STATLER STREET ● ST. CLAIR SHORES MI 48081 ● (810) 445-4015 ● http://www.macomb.k12.mi.us/lakeview/home.htm

Grade Span: KG-12 **Schools**: *Regular* 6 ● *Spec Ed* 0 ● *Alt* 0 **Students**: 2,806 **Total Teachers**: 141 **Student/Classroom Teacher Ratio**: 31.9	**Expenditures/Student**: $6,835 **Librarians**: 2.0 1,403 students/librarian **Guidance Counselors**: 7.0 401 students/counselor	**% Amer Indian**: 2.6 **% Asian**: 0.9 **% Black**: 0.1 **% Hispanic**: 0.4 **% White**: 96.0	National ***Socio-Economic Status*** indicator percentile (100=high): 91st

Macomb County

[STERLING HEIGHTS] **UTICA COMMUNITY S.D.**

11303 GREENDALE ● STERLING HEIGHTS MI 48312-2925 ● (810) 795-2300 ● http://www.macomb.k12.mi.us/utica/schutic.htm

Grade Span: PK-12 **Schools**: *Regular* 38 ● *Spec Ed* 0 ● *Alt* 1 **Students**: 24,949 **Total Teachers**: 1,207 **Student/Classroom Teacher Ratio**: 20.9	**Expenditures/Student**: $6,338 **Librarians**: 14.0 1,782 students/librarian **Guidance Counselors**: 29.0 860 students/counselor	**% Amer Indian**: 0.2 **% Asian**: 2.4 **% Black**: 0.9 **% Hispanic**: 0.6 **% White**: 95.8	National ***Socio-Economic Status*** indicator percentile (100=high): 93rd

Macomb County

[WARREN] **FITZGERALD S.D.**

23200 RYAN ROAD ● WARREN MI 48091 ● (810) 757-1750 ● http://www.fitz.k12.mi.us

Grade Span: PK-12 **Schools**: *Regular* 6 ● *Spec Ed* 0 ● *Alt* 0 **Students**: 3,058 **Total Teachers**: 150 **Student/Classroom Teacher Ratio**: 20.6	**Expenditures/Student**: $7,070 **Librarians**: 3.0 1,019 students/librarian **Guidance Counselors**: 5.0 612 students/counselor	**% Amer Indian**: 0.3 **% Asian**: 4.2 **% Black**: 2.6 **% Hispanic**: 1.1 **% White**: 91.8	National ***Socio-Economic Status*** indicator percentile (100=high): 51st

Macomb County

[WARREN] **VAN DYKE S.D.**

22100 FEDERAL AVENUE ● WARREN MI 48089 ● (810) 758-8333 ● http://www.macomb.k12.mi.us/vandyke/schvand.htm

Grade Span: PK-12 **Schools**: *Regular* 10 ● *Spec Ed* 0 ● *Alt* 0 **Students**: 4,341 **Total Teachers**: 256 **Student/Classroom Teacher Ratio**: 21.5	**Expenditures/Student**: $7,221 **Librarians**: 7.0 620 students/librarian **Guidance Counselors**: 5.0 868 students/counselor	**% Amer Indian**: 1.9 **% Asian**: 2.5 **% Black**: 1.0 **% Hispanic**: 1.6 **% White**: 93.0	National ***Socio-Economic Status*** indicator percentile (100=high): 26th

Macomb County

WARREN CONSOLIDATED S.D.

31300 ANITA STREET ● WARREN MI 48093 ● (810) 825-2410 ● http://www.wcs.k12.mi.us

Grade Span: KG-12 **Schools**: *Regular* 25 ● *Spec Ed* 0 ● *Alt* 2 **Students**: 14,063 **Total Teachers**: 689 **Student/Classroom Teacher Ratio**: 21.3	**Expenditures/Student**: $8,047 **Librarians**: 26.0 541 students/librarian **Guidance Counselors**: 28.0 502 students/counselor	**% Amer Indian**: 0.1 **% Asian**: 2.8 **% Black**: 1.4 **% Hispanic**: 0.5 **% White**: 95.2	National ***Socio-Economic Status*** indicator percentile (100=high): 81st

Macomb County

WARREN WOODS S.D.

27100 SCHOENHERR ROAD ● WARREN MI 48093 ● (810) 445-6300 ● http://www.macomb.k12.mi.us/warrenw/wwd.htm

Grade Span: PK-12 **Schools**: *Regular* 5 ● *Spec Ed* 0 ● *Alt* 1 **Students**: 2,737 **Total Teachers**: 138 **Student/Classroom Teacher Ratio**: 21.7	**Expenditures/Student**: $8,322 **Librarians**: 2.0 1,369 students/librarian **Guidance Counselors**: 4.0 684 students/counselor	**% Amer Indian**: 0.7 **% Asian**: 2.3 **% Black**: 0.7 **% Hispanic**: 1.1 **% White**: 95.2	National ***Socio-Economic Status*** indicator percentile (100=high): 87th

Marquette County

MARQUETTE AREA S.D.

1201 WEST FAIR AVENUE ● MARQUETTE MI 49855 ● (906) 225-4200 ● http://www.up.net/~jolove/lovetoteach.html

Grade Span: KG-12 **Schools**: *Regular* 10 ● *Spec Ed* 0 ● *Alt* 0 **Students**: 4,740 **Total Teachers**: 232 **Student/Classroom Teacher Ratio**: 19.9	**Expenditures/Student**: $4,779 **Librarians**: 2.0 2,370 students/librarian **Guidance Counselors**: 10.0 474 students/counselor	**% Amer Indian**: 4.1 **% Asian**: 0.9 **% Black**: 1.0 **% Hispanic**: 0.3 **% White**: 93.7	National ***Socio-Economic Status*** indicator percentile (100=high): 69th

Mason County

LUDINGTON AREA S.D.

809 EAST TINKHAM AVENUE ● LUDINGTON MI 49431 ● (616) 845-7303

Grade Span: KG-12 **Schools**: *Regular* 7 ● *Spec Ed* 0 ● *Alt* 0 **Students**: 2,759 **Total Teachers**: 163 **Student/Classroom Teacher Ratio**: 17.3	**Expenditures/Student**: $5,555 **Librarians**: 1.0 2,759 students/librarian **Guidance Counselors**: 4.0 690 students/counselor	**% Amer Indian**: 0.5 **% Asian**: 0.8 **% Black**: 0.9 **% Hispanic**: 2.8 **% White**: 95.0	National ***Socio-Economic Status*** indicator percentile (100=high): 55th

Mecosta County

[REMUS] **CHIPPEWA HILLS S.D.**

3226 ARTHUR ROAD ● REMUS MI 49340 ● (517) 967-3614 ● http://www.chippewa-hills.k12.mi.us

Grade Span: PK-12 **Schools**: *Regular* 5 ● *Spec Ed* 0 ● *Alt* 0 **Students**: 2,569 **Total Teachers**: 133 **Student/Classroom Teacher Ratio**: 19.2	**Expenditures/Student**: $5,242 **Librarians**: 2.0 1,285 students/librarian **Guidance Counselors**: 3.0 856 students/counselor	**% Amer Indian**: 16.0 **% Asian**: 0.2 **% Black**: 0.6 **% Hispanic**: 0.5 **% White**: 82.8	National ***Socio-Economic Status*** indicator percentile (100=high): 33rd

Midland County

MIDLAND S.D.

600 EAST CARPENTER STREET ● MIDLAND MI 48640 ● (517) 839-2401 ● http://www.mps.k12.mi.us

Grade Span: KG-12 **Schools**: *Regular* 17 ● *Spec Ed* 2 ● *Alt* 1 **Students**: 9,395 **Total Teachers**: 503 **Student/Classroom Teacher Ratio**: 19.0	**Expenditures/Student**: $7,034 **Librarians**: 18.0 522 students/librarian **Guidance Counselors**: 21.0 447 students/counselor	**% Amer Indian**: 0.6 **% Asian**: 2.6 **% Black**: 2.2 **% Hispanic**: 1.9 **% White**: 92.7	National ***Socio-Economic Status*** indicator percentile (100=high): 79th

Monroe County

[CARLETON] **AIRPORT COMMUNITY S.D.**

11270 GRAFTON ROAD ● CARLETON MI 48117 ● (734) 654-2414 ● http://airport.k12.mi.us

Grade Span: PK-12 **Schools**: *Regular* 6 ● *Spec Ed* 0 ● *Alt* 0 **Students**: 2,760 **Total Teachers**: 125 **Student/Classroom Teacher Ratio**: 22.6	**Expenditures/Student**: $6,137 **Librarians**: 2.0 1,380 students/librarian **Guidance Counselors**: 4.0 690 students/counselor	**% Amer Indian**: 0.5 **% Asian**: 0.3 **% Black**: 4.0 **% Hispanic**: 1.1 **% White**: 94.1	National ***Socio-Economic Status*** indicator percentile (100=high): 69th

Monroe County

[MONROE] **JEFFERSON S.D.**

2400 NORTH DIXIE HIGHWAY ● MONROE MI 48161 ● (734) 289-5550

Grade Span: PK-12 **Schools**: *Regular* 5 ● *Spec Ed* 0 ● *Alt* 0 **Students**: 2,825 **Total Teachers**: 147 **Student/Classroom Teacher Ratio**: 21.2	**Expenditures/Student**: $8,093 **Librarians**: 5.0 565 students/librarian **Guidance Counselors**: 5.0 565 students/counselor	**% Amer Indian**: 0.6 **% Asian**: 0.1 **% Black**: 0.4 **% Hispanic**: 2.1 **% White**: 96.8	National ***Socio-Economic Status*** indicator percentile (100=high): 72nd

Monroe County

MONROE S.D.

1275 NORTH MACOMB STREET ● MONROE MI 48161 ● (734) 241-0330 ● http://www.monroe.k12.mi.us

Grade Span: KG-12 **Schools**: *Regular* 13 ● *Spec Ed* 0 ● *Alt* 1 **Students**: 7,143 **Total Teachers**: 347 **Student/Classroom Teacher Ratio**: 22.1	**Expenditures/Student**: $5,871 **Librarians**: 5.0 1,429 students/librarian **Guidance Counselors**: 17.0 420 students/counselor	**% Amer Indian**: 0.0 **% Asian**: 0.9 **% Black**: 5.2 **% Hispanic**: 1.5 **% White**: 92.4	National ***Socio-Economic Status*** indicator percentile (100=high): 55th

Monroe County

[TEMPERANCE] BEDFORD S.D.

1623 WEST STERNS ROAD ● TEMPERANCE MI 48182 ● (734) 847-6736

Grade Span: KG-12 **Schools**: *Regular* 6 ● *Spec Ed* 0 ● *Alt* 0 **Students**: 5,361 **Total Teachers**: 225 **Student/Classroom Teacher Ratio**: 25.5	**Expenditures/Student**: $5,343 **Librarians**: 4.0 1,340 students/librarian **Guidance Counselors**: 8.0 670 students/counselor	**% Amer Indian**: 0.1 **% Asian**: 0.5 **% Black**: 0.4 **% Hispanic**: 0.8 **% White**: 98.1	National ***Socio-Economic Status*** indicator percentile (100=high): 90th

Montcalm County

GREENVILLE S.D.

516 WEST CASS STREET ● GREENVILLE MI 48838 ● (616) 754-3686

Grade Span: KG-12 **Schools**: *Regular* 7 ● *Spec Ed* 0 ● *Alt* 1 **Students**: 3,938 **Total Teachers**: 217 **Student/Classroom Teacher Ratio**: 22.0	**Expenditures/Student**: $5,222 **Librarians**: 2.0 1,969 students/librarian **Guidance Counselors**: 9.0 438 students/counselor	**% Amer Indian**: 0.0 **% Asian**: 0.4 **% Black**: 0.2 **% Hispanic**: 2.1 **% White**: 97.2	National ***Socio-Economic Status*** indicator percentile (100=high): 61st

Muskegon County

FRUITPORT COMMUNITY S.D.

3255 PONTALUNA ROAD ● FRUITPORT MI 49415 ● (616) 865-3154 ● http://remc4.k12.mi.us/fport/home.htm

Grade Span: KG-12 **Schools**: *Regular* 5 ● *Spec Ed* 0 ● *Alt* 1 **Students**: 3,382 **Total Teachers**: 172 **Student/Classroom Teacher Ratio**: 19.6	**Expenditures/Student**: $6,318 **Librarians**: 2.0 1,691 students/librarian **Guidance Counselors**: 7.0 483 students/counselor	**% Amer Indian**: 0.8 **% Asian**: 0.5 **% Black**: 0.4 **% Hispanic**: 1.4 **% White**: 96.9	National ***Socio-Economic Status*** indicator percentile (100=high): 73rd

Muskegon County

MUSKEGON CITY S.D.

349 WEST WEBSTER ● MUSKEGON MI 49440 ● (616) 722-1602

Grade Span: PK-12 **Schools**: *Regular* 14 ● *Spec Ed* 4 ● *Alt* 3 **Students**: 6,851 **Total Teachers**: 404 **Student/Classroom Teacher Ratio**: 19.1	**Expenditures/Student**: $8,048 **Librarians**: 3.0 2,284 students/librarian **Guidance Counselors**: 15.0 457 students/counselor	**% Amer Indian**: 1.6 **% Asian**: 0.4 **% Black**: 45.2 **% Hispanic**: 5.0 **% White**: 47.8	National ***Socio-Economic Status*** indicator percentile (100=high): 11th

Muskegon County

[MUSKEGON] ORCHARD VIEW S.D.

2310 MARQUETTE AVENUE ● MUSKEGON MI 49442 ● (616) 760-1300

Grade Span: KG-12 **Schools**: *Regular* 5 ● *Spec Ed* 0 ● *Alt* 0 **Students**: 2,514 **Total Teachers**: 140 **Student/Classroom Teacher Ratio**: 21.4	**Expenditures/Student**: $7,690 **Librarians**: 3.0 838 students/librarian **Guidance Counselors**: 8.0 314 students/counselor	**% Amer Indian**: 1.0 **% Asian**: 0.5 **% Black**: 4.0 **% Hispanic**: 3.6 **% White**: 90.9	National ***Socio-Economic Status*** indicator percentile (100=high): 40th

Muskegon County

[MUSKEGON] REETHS PUFFER S.D.

991 WEST GILES ROAD ● MUSKEGON MI 49445 ● (616) 744-4736

Grade Span: PK-12 **Schools**: *Regular* 9 ● *Spec Ed* 0 ● *Alt* 0 **Students**: 4,431 **Total Teachers**: 247 **Student/Classroom Teacher Ratio**: 18.3	**Expenditures/Student**: $5,778 **Librarians**: 2.0 2,216 students/librarian **Guidance Counselors**: 4.0 1,108 students/counselor	**% Amer Indian**: 0.9 **% Asian**: 0.5 **% Black**: 4.4 **% Hispanic**: 1.0 **% White**: 93.1	National ***Socio-Economic Status*** indicator percentile (100=high): 69th

Muskegon County
MUSKEGON HEIGHTS S.D.
2603 LEAHY STREET ● MUSKEGON HEIGHTS MI 49444 ● (616) 739-9302

Grade Span: KG-12	**Expenditures/Student**: $7,546	**% Amer Indian**: 0.3	
Schools: *Regular* 8 ● *Spec Ed* 0 ● *Alt* 0	**Librarians**: 2.0	**% Asian**: 0.0	National ***Socio-Economic***
Students: 2,612	1,306 students/librarian	**% Black**: 92.3	***Status*** indicator percentile
Total Teachers: 142	**Guidance Counselors**: 3.0	**% Hispanic**: 1.1	(100=high): 1st
Student/Classroom Teacher Ratio: 18.7	871 students/counselor	**% White**: 6.3	

Muskegon County
[NORTON SHORES] **MONA SHORES S.D.**
3374 MCCRACKEN AVENUE ● NORTON SHORES MI 49441 ● (616) 780-4751 ● http://www.remc4.k12.mi.us/mona-shores

Grade Span: PK-12	**Expenditures/Student**: $5,189	**% Amer Indian**: 0.2	
Schools: *Regular* 6 ● *Spec Ed* 0 ● *Alt* 1	**Librarians**: 2.0	**% Asian**: 0.7	National ***Socio-Economic***
Students: 3,963	1,982 students/librarian	**% Black**: 1.7	***Status*** indicator percentile
Total Teachers: 167	**Guidance Counselors**: 5.0	**% Hispanic**: 0.9	(100=high): 88th
Student/Classroom Teacher Ratio: 22.9	793 students/counselor	**% White**: 96.5	

Newaygo County
FREMONT S.D.
220 WEST PINE STREET ● FREMONT MI 49412 ● (616) 924-2350

Grade Span: KG-12	**Expenditures/Student**: $5,453	**% Amer Indian**: 0.1	
Schools: *Regular* 5 ● *Spec Ed* 1 ● *Alt* 0	**Librarians**: 2.0	**% Asian**: 0.5	National ***Socio-Economic***
Students: 2,600	1,300 students/librarian	**% Black**: 0.5	***Status*** indicator percentile
Total Teachers: 135	**Guidance Counselors**: 5.0	**% Hispanic**: 3.9	(100=high): 54th
Student/Classroom Teacher Ratio: 20.2	520 students/counselor	**% White**: 95.0	

Oakland County
[AUBURN HILLS] **AVONDALE S.D.**
260 SOUTH SQUIRREL ROAD ● AUBURN HILLS MI 48326 ● (248) 852-4411 ● http://www.avondale.k12.mi.us

Grade Span: KG-12	**Expenditures/Student**: $7,386	**% Amer Indian**: 1.2	
Schools: *Regular* 8 ● *Spec Ed* 0 ● *Alt* 0	**Librarians**: 4.0	**% Asian**: 3.0	National ***Socio-Economic***
Students: 3,504	876 students/librarian	**% Black**: 8.8	***Status*** indicator percentile
Total Teachers: 185	**Guidance Counselors**: 6.0	**% Hispanic**: 2.2	(100=high): 86th
Student/Classroom Teacher Ratio: 18.4	584 students/counselor	**% White**: 84.8	

Oakland County
BERKLEY S.D.
2211 OAKSHIRE STREET ● BERKLEY MI 48072 ● (248) 544-5800 ● http://www.berkley.k12.mi.us

Grade Span: PK-12	**Expenditures/Student**: $7,198	**% Amer Indian**: 0.9	
Schools: *Regular* 8 ● *Spec Ed* 1 ● *Alt* 0	**Librarians**: 4.0	**% Asian**: 1.6	National ***Socio-Economic***
Students: 4,295	1,074 students/librarian	**% Black**: 3.2	***Status*** indicator percentile
Total Teachers: 237	**Guidance Counselors**: 6.0	**% Hispanic**: 0.5	(100=high): 82nd
Student/Classroom Teacher Ratio: 22.3	716 students/counselor	**% White**: 93.8	

Oakland County
BIRMINGHAM CITY S.D.
550 WEST MERRILL STREET ● BIRMINGHAM MI 48009 ● (248) 644-9300 ● http://www.birmingham.k12.mi.us

Grade Span: PK-12	**Expenditures/Student**: $10,316	**% Amer Indian**: 0.1	
Schools: *Regular* 16 ● *Spec Ed* 0 ● *Alt* 0	**Librarians**: 15.0	**% Asian**: 4.0	National ***Socio-Economic***
Students: 7,498	500 students/librarian	**% Black**: 3.8	***Status*** indicator percentile
Total Teachers: 479	**Guidance Counselors**: 25.0	**% Hispanic**: 1.0	(100=high): 98th
Student/Classroom Teacher Ratio: 32.0	300 students/counselor	**% White**: 91.1	

Oakland County
BLOOMFIELD HILLS S.D.
4175 ANDOVER ROAD ● BLOOMFIELD HILLS MI 48302 ● (248) 645-4500 ● http://www.bloomfield.k12.mi.us/bhsd/bhsd.html

Grade Span: PK-12	**Expenditures/Student**: $12,296	**% Amer Indian**: 0.0	
Schools: *Regular* 15 ● *Spec Ed* 4 ● *Alt* 0	**Librarians**: 11.0	**% Asian**: 10.7	National ***Socio-Economic***
Students: 5,804	528 students/librarian	**% Black**: 5.5	***Status*** indicator percentile
Total Teachers: 400	**Guidance Counselors**: 12.0	**% Hispanic**: 1.0	(100=high): 100th
Student/Classroom Teacher Ratio: 15.9	484 students/counselor	**% White**: 82.8	

Oakland County
CLARKSTON COMMUNITY S.D.
6389 CLARKSTON RD, POB 1050 ● CLARKSTON MI 48347-1050 ● (248) 625-4402 ● http://www.clarkston.k12.mi.us

Grade Span: PK-12	**Expenditures/Student**: $7,160	**% Amer Indian**: 0.4	
Schools: *Regular* 10 ● *Spec Ed* 1 ● *Alt* 1	**Librarians**: 9.0	**% Asian**: 0.8	National ***Socio-Economic***
Students: 6,497	722 students/librarian	**% Black**: 0.9	***Status*** indicator percentile
Total Teachers: 354	**Guidance Counselors**: 12.0	**% Hispanic**: 1.3	(100=high): 95th
Student/Classroom Teacher Ratio: 20.3	541 students/counselor	**% White**: 96.6	

Oakland County
FARMINGTON S.D.
32500 SHIAWASSEE STREET ● FARMINGTON MI 48336-2363 ● (248) 489-3300 ● http://www.farmington.k12.mi.us

Grade Span: KG-12	**Expenditures/Student**: $9,036	**% Amer Indian**: 0.1	
Schools: *Regular* 23 ● *Spec Ed* 4 ● *Alt* 2	**Librarians**: 20.0	**% Asian**: 4.3	National ***Socio-Economic***
Students: 11,609	580 students/librarian	**% Black**: 5.4	***Status*** indicator percentile
Total Teachers: 683	**Guidance Counselors**: 20.0	**% Hispanic**: 0.5	(100=high): 94th
Student/Classroom Teacher Ratio: 16.9	580 students/counselor	**% White**: 89.7	

Oakland County
FERNDALE CITY S.D.
725 PINECREST STREET ● FERNDALE MI 48220 ● (810) 547-2202

Grade Span: PK-12	**Expenditures/Student**: $9,907	**% Amer Indian**: 0.2	
Schools: *Regular* 11 ● *Spec Ed* 0 ● *Alt* 0	**Librarians**: 2.0	**% Asian**: 2.0	National ***Socio-Economic***
Students: 4,741	2,371 students/librarian	**% Black**: 20.6	***Status*** indicator percentile
Total Teachers: 241	**Guidance Counselors**: 19.0	**% Hispanic**: 0.9	(100=high): 42nd
Student/Classroom Teacher Ratio: 18.1	250 students/counselor	**% White**: 76.4	

Oakland County
HAZEL PARK CITY S.D.
23136 HUGHES STREET ● HAZEL PARK MI 48030 ● (248) 542-3910

Grade Span: PK-12	**Expenditures/Student**: $8,053	**% Amer Indian**: 7.5	
Schools: *Regular* 11 ● *Spec Ed* 0 ● *Alt* 1	**Librarians**: 2.0	**% Asian**: 2.4	National ***Socio-Economic***
Students: 5,165	2,583 students/librarian	**% Black**: 1.7	***Status*** indicator percentile
Total Teachers: 256	**Guidance Counselors**: 12.0	**% Hispanic**: 1.2	(100=high): 31st
Student/Classroom Teacher Ratio: 21.0	430 students/counselor	**% White**: 87.4	

Oakland County
[HIGHLAND] **HURON VALLEY S.D.**
2390 SOUTH MILFORD ROAD ● HIGHLAND MI 48357 ● (248) 684-8000 ● http://www.huronvalley.k12.mi.us

Grade Span: PK-12	**Expenditures/Student**: $5,839	**% Amer Indian**: 2.3	
Schools: *Regular* 16 ● *Spec Ed* 0 ● *Alt* 3	**Librarians**: 7.0	**% Asian**: 0.5	National ***Socio-Economic***
Students: 10,189	1,456 students/librarian	**% Black**: 0.3	***Status*** indicator percentile
Total Teachers: 470	**Guidance Counselors**: 13.0	**% Hispanic**: 0.8	(100=high): 89th
Student/Classroom Teacher Ratio: 21.7	784 students/counselor	**% White**: 96.1	

Oakland County
HOLLY AREA S.D.
111 COLLEGE STREET ● HOLLY MI 48442 ● (248) 634-4431

Grade Span: PK-12 **Schools**: *Regular* 5 ● *Spec Ed* 0 ● *Alt* 1 **Students**: 4,123 **Total Teachers**: 205 **Student/Classroom Teacher Ratio**: 20.3	**Expenditures/Student**: $5,633 **Librarians**: 2.0 2,062 students/librarian **Guidance Counselors**: 5.0 825 students/counselor	**% Amer Indian**: 0.4 **% Asian**: 0.6 **% Black**: 2.0 **% Hispanic**: 1.7 **% White**: 95.4	National ***Socio-Economic Status*** indicator percentile (100=high): 77th

Oakland County
LAKE ORION COMMUNITY S.D.
315 NORTH LAPEER STREET ● LAKE ORION MI 48362 ● (248) 693-5413 ● http://www.lakeorion.k12.mi.us

Grade Span: PK-12 **Schools**: *Regular* 10 ● *Spec Ed* 0 ● *Alt* 1 **Students**: 5,312 **Total Teachers**: 265 **Student/Classroom Teacher Ratio**: 20.6	**Expenditures/Student**: $6,862 **Librarians**: 8.0 664 students/librarian **Guidance Counselors**: 7.0 759 students/counselor	**% Amer Indian**: 0.2 **% Asian**: 0.9 **% Black**: 0.7 **% Hispanic**: 1.0 **% White**: 97.3	National ***Socio-Economic Status*** indicator percentile (100=high): 92nd

Oakland County
NOVI COMMUNITY S.D.
25345 TAFT ROAD ● NOVI MI 48374 ● (248) 449-1200 ● http://www.novi.k12.mi.us

Grade Span: PK-12 **Schools**: *Regular* 7 ● *Spec Ed* 0 ● *Alt* 0 **Students**: 4,913 **Total Teachers**: 244 **Student/Classroom Teacher Ratio**: 21.0	**Expenditures/Student**: $7,655 **Librarians**: 7.0 702 students/librarian **Guidance Counselors**: 8.0 614 students/counselor	**% Amer Indian**: 0.0 **% Asian**: 7.6 **% Black**: 1.4 **% Hispanic**: 0.8 **% White**: 90.2	National ***Socio-Economic Status*** indicator percentile (100=high): 99th

Oakland County
OAK PARK CITY S.D.
13900 GRANZON STREET ● OAK PARK MI 48237 ● (248) 691-8400

Grade Span: KG-12 **Schools**: *Regular* 7 ● *Spec Ed* 0 ● *Alt* 0 **Students**: 3,394 **Total Teachers**: 151 **Student/Classroom Teacher Ratio**: 25.6	**Expenditures/Student**: $7,844 **Librarians**: 2.0 1,697 students/librarian **Guidance Counselors**: 4.0 849 students/counselor	**% Amer Indian**: 0.1 **% Asian**: 1.6 **% Black**: 72.1 **% Hispanic**: 0.3 **% White**: 26.0	National ***Socio-Economic Status*** indicator percentile (100=high): 33rd

Oakland County
[ORTONVILLE] **BRANDON S.D.**
1025 ORTONVILLE ROAD ● ORTONVILLE MI 48462 ● (248) 627-4981

Grade Span: KG-12 **Schools**: *Regular* 6 ● *Spec Ed* 0 ● *Alt* 0 **Students**: 3,125 **Total Teachers**: 138 **Student/Classroom Teacher Ratio**: 23.0	**Expenditures/Student**: $6,674 **Librarians**: 1.0 3,125 students/librarian **Guidance Counselors**: 4.0 781 students/counselor	**% Amer Indian**: 0.1 **% Asian**: 0.5 **% Black**: 0.6 **% Hispanic**: 0.6 **% White**: 98.1	National ***Socio-Economic Status*** indicator percentile (100=high): 90th

Oakland County
OXFORD AREA COMMUNITY S.D.
105 PONTIAC STREET ● OXFORD MI 48371 ● (248) 628-2591

Grade Span: KG-12 **Schools**: *Regular* 6 ● *Spec Ed* 1 ● *Alt* 1 **Students**: 3,099 **Total Teachers**: 159 **Student/Classroom Teacher Ratio**: 20.0	**Expenditures/Student**: $6,050 **Librarians**: 3.0 1,033 students/librarian **Guidance Counselors**: 7.0 443 students/counselor	**% Amer Indian**: 0.4 **% Asian**: 0.5 **% Black**: 0.4 **% Hispanic**: 1.1 **% White**: 97.5	National ***Socio-Economic Status*** indicator percentile (100=high): 85th

Oakland County
PONTIAC CITY S.D.
350 EAST WIDETRACK DRIVE ● PONTIAC MI 48342 ● (248) 857-8123

Grade Span: KG-12 **Schools**: *Regular* 21 ● *Spec Ed* 5 ● *Alt* 0 **Students**: 12,649 **Total Teachers**: 588 **Student/Classroom Teacher Ratio**: 22.7	**Expenditures/Student**: $7,131 **Librarians**: 11.0 1,150 students/librarian **Guidance Counselors**: 11.0 1,150 students/counselor	**% Amer Indian**: 0.6 **% Asian**: 3.2 **% Black**: 58.6 **% Hispanic**: 9.9 **% White**: 27.7	National ***Socio-Economic Status*** indicator percentile (100=high): 10th

Oakland County
ROCHESTER COMMUNITY S.D.
501 WEST UNIVERSITY DRIVE ● ROCHESTER MI 48307 ● (248) 651-6210 ● http://www.rochester.k12.mi.us

Grade Span: KG-12 **Schools**: *Regular* 19 ● *Spec Ed* 0 ● *Alt* 0 **Students**: 12,437 **Total Teachers**: 627 **Student/Classroom Teacher Ratio**: 19.7	**Expenditures/Student**: $6,892 **Librarians**: 15.0 829 students/librarian **Guidance Counselors**: 25.0 497 students/counselor	**% Amer Indian**: 0.3 **% Asian**: 5.5 **% Black**: 2.0 **% Hispanic**: 1.1 **% White**: 91.1	National ***Socio-Economic Status*** indicator percentile (100=high): 98th

Oakland County
[ROYAL OAK] **CITY S.D. OF ROYAL OAK**
1123 LEXINGTON BOULEVARD ● ROYAL OAK MI 48073 ● (248) 435-8400

Grade Span: PK-12 **Schools**: *Regular* 18 ● *Spec Ed* 0 ● *Alt* 1 **Students**: 7,329 **Total Teachers**: 436 **Student/Classroom Teacher Ratio**: 18.0	**Expenditures/Student**: $8,806 **Librarians**: 5.0 1,466 students/librarian **Guidance Counselors**: 15.0 489 students/counselor	**% Amer Indian**: 0.0 **% Asian**: 0.9 **% Black**: 1.8 **% Hispanic**: 0.4 **% White**: 96.8	National ***Socio-Economic Status*** indicator percentile (100=high): 83rd

Oakland County
SOUTH LYON COMMUNITY S.D.
235 WEST LIBERTY STREET ● SOUTH LYON MI 48178 ● (248) 437-8111

Grade Span: KG-12 **Schools**: *Regular* 7 ● *Spec Ed* 0 ● *Alt* 0 **Students**: 5,001 **Total Teachers**: 218 **Student/Classroom Teacher Ratio**: 23.4	**Expenditures/Student**: $5,680 **Librarians**: 7.0 714 students/librarian **Guidance Counselors**: 6.0 834 students/counselor	**% Amer Indian**: 0.6 **% Asian**: 0.7 **% Black**: 0.5 **% Hispanic**: 1.1 **% White**: 97.1	National ***Socio-Economic Status*** indicator percentile (100=high): 84th

Oakland County
SOUTHFIELD S.D.
24661 LAHSER ROAD ● SOUTHFIELD MI 48034 ● (248) 746-8500

Grade Span: PK-12 **Schools**: *Regular* 17 ● *Spec Ed* 0 ● *Alt* 0 **Students**: 9,378 **Total Teachers**: 561 **Student/Classroom Teacher Ratio**: 16.6	**Expenditures/Student**: $9,902 **Librarians**: 17.0 552 students/librarian **Guidance Counselors**: 17.0 552 students/counselor	**% Amer Indian**: 0.2 **% Asian**: 2.1 **% Black**: 66.7 **% Hispanic**: 0.7 **% White**: 30.3	National ***Socio-Economic Status*** indicator percentile (100=high): 63rd

Oakland County
TROY S.D.
4400 LIVERNOIS AVENUE ● TROY MI 48098 ● (248) 689-0600 ● http://www.troy.k12.mi.us

Grade Span: PK-12 **Schools**: *Regular* 18 ● *Spec Ed* 0 ● *Alt* 1 **Students**: 11,951 **Total Teachers**: 618 **Student/Classroom Teacher Ratio**: 19.8	**Expenditures/Student**: $7,859 **Librarians**: 20.0 598 students/librarian **Guidance Counselors**: 19.0 629 students/counselor	**% Amer Indian**: 0.1 **% Asian**: 10.6 **% Black**: 2.2 **% Hispanic**: 0.8 **% White**: 86.3	National ***Socio-Economic Status*** indicator percentile (100=high): 97th

Oakland County

WALLED LAKE CONSOLIDATED S.D.

850 NORTH LADD ROAD ● WALLED LAKE MI 48390 ● (248) 960-8300 ● http://www.walledlake.k12.mi.us

Grade Span: PK-12 **Schools**: *Regular* 18 ● *Spec Ed* 0 ● *Alt* 1 **Students**: 12,091 **Total Teachers**: 679 **Student/Classroom Teacher Ratio**: 18.7	**Expenditures/Student**: $7,644 **Librarians**: 12.0 1,008 students/librarian **Guidance Counselors**: 34.0 356 students/counselor	**% Amer Indian**: 1.4 **% Asian**: 2.6 **% Black**: 1.0 **% Hispanic**: 0.8 **% White**: 94.2	National ***Socio-Economic Status*** indicator percentile (100=high): 89th

Oakland County

WATERFORD S.D.

6020 PONTIAC LAKE ● WATERFORD MI 48327 ● (248) 666-4000 ● http://www.waterford.k12.mi.us

Grade Span: KG-12 **Schools**: *Regular* 24 ● *Spec Ed* 5 ● *Alt* 1 **Students**: 11,083 **Total Teachers**: 531 **Student/Classroom Teacher Ratio**: 24.3	**Expenditures/Student**: $7,477 **Librarians**: 5.0 2,217 students/librarian **Guidance Counselors**: 22.0 504 students/counselor	**% Amer Indian**: 0.2 **% Asian**: 1.2 **% Black**: 1.8 **% Hispanic**: 2.0 **% White**: 94.8	National ***Socio-Economic Status*** indicator percentile (100=high): 73rd

Oakland County

WEST BLOOMFIELD S.D.

5810 COMMERCE ROAD ● WEST BLOOMFIELD MI 48324 ● (248) 738-3555 ● http://www.westbloomfield.org/opening.html

Grade Span: PK-12 **Schools**: *Regular* 9 ● *Spec Ed* 0 ● *Alt* 0 **Students**: 5,590 **Total Teachers**: 299 **Student/Classroom Teacher Ratio**: 19.3	**Expenditures/Student**: $10,331 **Librarians**: 10.0 559 students/librarian **Guidance Counselors**: 10.0 559 students/counselor	**% Amer Indian**: 0.4 **% Asian**: 6.1 **% Black**: 4.8 **% Hispanic**: 1.2 **% White**: 87.5	National ***Socio-Economic Status*** indicator percentile (100=high): 97th

Ogemaw County

WEST BRANCH-ROSE CITY AREA S.D.

960 SOUTH M-33, P.O. BOX 308 ● WEST BRANCH MI 48661 ● (517) 345-5320

Grade Span: KG-12 **Schools**: *Regular* 4 ● *Spec Ed* 0 ● *Alt* 1 **Students**: 2,898 **Total Teachers**: 148 **Student/Classroom Teacher Ratio**: 19.5	**Expenditures/Student**: $4,969 **Librarians**: 3.0 966 students/librarian **Guidance Counselors**: 8.0 362 students/counselor	**% Amer Indian**: 0.3 **% Asian**: 0.1 **% Black**: 0.2 **% Hispanic**: 0.7 **% White**: 98.6	National ***Socio-Economic Status*** indicator percentile (100=high): 39th

Otsego County

GAYLORD COMMUNITY S.D.

615 SOUTH ELM STREET ● GAYLORD MI 49735 ● (517) 732-6402

Grade Span: KG-12 **Schools**: *Regular* 6 ● *Spec Ed* 1 ● *Alt* 0 **Students**: 3,338 **Total Teachers**: 173 **Student/Classroom Teacher Ratio**: 19.0	**Expenditures/Student**: $5,188 **Librarians**: 3.0 1,113 students/librarian **Guidance Counselors**: 5.0 668 students/counselor	**% Amer Indian**: 1.0 **% Asian**: 0.6 **% Black**: 0.4 **% Hispanic**: 0.4 **% White**: 97.7	National ***Socio-Economic Status*** indicator percentile (100=high): 68th

Ottawa County

GRAND HAVEN CITY S.D.

1415 BEECH TREE STREET ● GRAND HAVEN MI 49417 ● (616) 847-4614

Grade Span: PK-12 **Schools**: *Regular* 11 ● *Spec Ed* 0 ● *Alt* 1 **Students**: 5,883 **Total Teachers**: 316 **Student/Classroom Teacher Ratio**: 19.0	**Expenditures/Student**: $6,124 **Librarians**: 8.0 735 students/librarian **Guidance Counselors**: 14.0 420 students/counselor	**% Amer Indian**: 0.9 **% Asian**: 1.1 **% Black**: 0.5 **% Hispanic**: 2.3 **% White**: 95.2	National ***Socio-Economic Status*** indicator percentile (100=high): 78th

Ottawa County
HOLLAND COMMUNITY S.D.
372 RIVER AVENUE ● HOLLAND MI 49423 ● (616) 393-7501

Grade Span: PK-12 **Schools**: *Regular* 13 ● *Spec Ed* 0 ● *Alt* 0 **Students**: 5,873 **Total Teachers**: 328 **Student/Classroom Teacher Ratio**: 17.1	**Expenditures/Student**: $7,117 **Librarians**: 7.0 839 students/librarian **Guidance Counselors**: 8.0 734 students/counselor	**% Amer Indian**: 0.5 **% Asian**: 4.9 **% Black**: 4.3 **% Hispanic**: 28.1 **% White**: 62.2	National ***Socio-Economic Status*** indicator percentile (100=high): 54th

Ottawa County
[HOLLAND] **WEST OTTAWA S.D.**
294 WEST LAKEWOOD BOULEVARD ● HOLLAND MI 49424 ● (616) 395-2300

Grade Span: PK-12 **Schools**: *Regular* 10 ● *Spec Ed* 0 ● *Alt* 0 **Students**: 6,248 **Total Teachers**: 321 **Student/Classroom Teacher Ratio**: 19.0	**Expenditures/Student**: $5,436 **Librarians**: 8.0 781 students/librarian **Guidance Counselors**: 12.0 521 students/counselor	**% Amer Indian**: 0.3 **% Asian**: 6.7 **% Black**: 1.6 **% Hispanic**: 7.7 **% White**: 83.7	National ***Socio-Economic Status*** indicator percentile (100=high): 82nd

Ottawa County
HUDSONVILLE S.D.
3886 VAN BUREN STREET ● HUDSONVILLE MI 49426 ● (616) 669-1740

Grade Span: PK-12 **Schools**: *Regular* 9 ● *Spec Ed* 0 ● *Alt* 0 **Students**: 3,887 **Total Teachers**: 173 **Student/Classroom Teacher Ratio**: 22.9	**Expenditures/Student**: $4,009 **Librarians**: 1.0 3,887 students/librarian **Guidance Counselors**: 4.0 972 students/counselor	**% Amer Indian**: 0.1 **% Asian**: 0.7 **% Black**: 0.2 **% Hispanic**: 0.9 **% White**: 98.0	National ***Socio-Economic Status*** indicator percentile (100=high): 93rd

Ottawa County
[JENISON] **JENNISON S.D.**
8375 20TH AVENUE ● JENISON MI 49428 ● (616) 457-1400

Grade Span: PK-12 **Schools**: *Regular* 7 ● *Spec Ed* 0 ● *Alt* 0 **Students**: 4,730 **Total Teachers**: 227 **Student/Classroom Teacher Ratio**: 21.2	**Expenditures/Student**: $5,598 **Librarians**: 7.0 676 students/librarian **Guidance Counselors**: 9.0 526 students/counselor	**% Amer Indian**: 0.1 **% Asian**: 1.4 **% Black**: 0.6 **% Hispanic**: 1.7 **% White**: 96.1	National ***Socio-Economic Status*** indicator percentile (100=high): 97th

Ottawa County
ZEELAND S.D.
P.O. BOX 110 ● ZEELAND MI 49464 ● (616) 772-7380 ● http://www.macatawa.org/~zps

Grade Span: PK-12 **Schools**: *Regular* 7 ● *Spec Ed* 1 ● *Alt* 0 **Students**: 3,786 **Total Teachers**: 199 **Student/Classroom Teacher Ratio**: 18.2	**Expenditures/Student**: $5,440 **Librarians**: 2.0 1,893 students/librarian **Guidance Counselors**: 5.0 757 students/counselor	**% Amer Indian**: 0.1 **% Asian**: 1.8 **% Black**: 0.3 **% Hispanic**: 5.1 **% White**: 92.6	National ***Socio-Economic Status*** indicator percentile (100=high): na

Saginaw County
BRIDGEPORT-SPAULDING CONSOLIDATED S.D.
3878 SHERMAN ● BRIDGEPORT MI 48722 ● (517) 777-1770

Grade Span: KG-12 **Schools**: *Regular* 6 ● *Spec Ed* 0 ● *Alt* 0 **Students**: 2,575 **Total Teachers**: 133 **Student/Classroom Teacher Ratio**: 19.1	**Expenditures/Student**: $6,566 **Librarians**: 1.0 2,575 students/librarian **Guidance Counselors**: 4.0 644 students/counselor	**% Amer Indian**: 0.3 **% Asian**: 0.6 **% Black**: 25.7 **% Hispanic**: 12.5 **% White**: 61.0	National ***Socio-Economic Status*** indicator percentile (100=high): 28th

Saginaw County
SAGINAW CITY S.D.
550 MILLARD STREET ● SAGINAW MI 48607 ● (517) 759-2200 ● http://www.saginaw-city.k12.mi.us

Grade Span: PK-12 **Schools**: *Regular* 30 ● *Spec Ed* 0 ● *Alt* 3 **Students**: 13,998 **Total Teachers**: 755 **Student/Classroom Teacher Ratio**: 19.7	**Expenditures/Student**: $6,865 **Librarians**: 7.0 2,000 students/librarian **Guidance Counselors**: 24.0 583 students/counselor	**% Amer Indian**: 0.3 **% Asian**: 1.0 **% Black**: 56.9 **% Hispanic**: 13.1 **% White**: 28.8	National ***Socio-Economic Status*** indicator percentile (100=high): 10th

Saginaw County
SAGINAW TOWNSHIP COMMUNITY S.D.
P.O. BOX 6278 ● SAGINAW MI 48608 ● (517) 797-1800

Grade Span: PK-12 **Schools**: *Regular* 8 ● *Spec Ed* 3 ● *Alt* 0 **Students**: 4,770 **Total Teachers**: 231 **Student/Classroom Teacher Ratio**: 21.2	**Expenditures/Student**: $5,824 **Librarians**: 3.0 1,590 students/librarian **Guidance Counselors**: 10.0 477 students/counselor	**% Amer Indian**: 0.3 **% Asian**: 3.4 **% Black**: 5.6 **% Hispanic**: 5.7 **% White**: 85.0	National ***Socio-Economic Status*** indicator percentile (100=high): 84th

St. Clair County
ALGONAC COMMUNITY S.D.
1216 ST CLAIR BOULEVARD ● ALGONAC MI 48001 ● (810) 794-9364

Grade Span: KG-12 **Schools**: *Regular* 7 ● *Spec Ed* 0 ● *Alt* 0 **Students**: 2,544 **Total Teachers**: 125 **Student/Classroom Teacher Ratio**: 20.8	**Expenditures/Student**: $5,453 **Librarians**: 3.0 848 students/librarian **Guidance Counselors**: 3.0 848 students/counselor	**% Amer Indian**: 1.7 **% Asian**: 0.3 **% Black**: 0.3 **% Hispanic**: 0.2 **% White**: 97.6	National ***Socio-Economic Status*** indicator percentile (100=high): 72nd

St. Clair County
EAST CHINA S.D.
1585 MEISNER ROAD ● EAST CHINA MI 48054-4143 ● (810) 765-8817 ● http://www.east-china.k12.mi.us

Grade Span: PK-12 **Schools**: *Regular* 10 ● *Spec Ed* 0 ● *Alt* 1 **Students**: 5,097 **Total Teachers**: 272 **Student/Classroom Teacher Ratio**: 19.1	**Expenditures/Student**: $6,216 **Librarians**: 4.0 1,274 students/librarian **Guidance Counselors**: 8.0 637 students/counselor	**% Amer Indian**: 0.4 **% Asian**: 0.2 **% Black**: 0.1 **% Hispanic**: 0.5 **% White**: 98.8	National ***Socio-Economic Status*** indicator percentile (100=high): 87th

St. Clair County
PORT HURON AREA S.D.
P.O. BOX 5013 ● PORT HURON MI 48061-5013 ● (810) 984-3101 ● http://husky.port-huron.k12.mi.us

Grade Span: PK-12 **Schools**: *Regular* 20 ● *Spec Ed* 0 ● *Alt* 1 **Students**: 12,195 **Total Teachers**: 638 **Student/Classroom Teacher Ratio**: 19.5	**Expenditures/Student**: $5,869 **Librarians**: 9.0 1,355 students/librarian **Guidance Counselors**: 21.0 581 students/counselor	**% Amer Indian**: 1.8 **% Asian**: 0.9 **% Black**: 6.0 **% Hispanic**: 2.4 **% White**: 88.9	National ***Socio-Economic Status*** indicator percentile (100=high): 43rd

St. Joseph County
STURGIS S.D.
216 VINEWOOD ● STURGIS MI 49091 ● (616) 659-1500

Grade Span: KG-12 **Schools**: *Regular* 9 ● *Spec Ed* 0 ● *Alt* 0 **Students**: 3,022 **Total Teachers**: 157 **Student/Classroom Teacher Ratio**: 22.6	**Expenditures/Student**: $5,441 **Librarians**: 3.0 1,007 students/librarian **Guidance Counselors**: 8.0 378 students/counselor	**% Amer Indian**: 0.0 **% Asian**: 0.9 **% Black**: 0.8 **% Hispanic**: 3.5 **% White**: 94.8	National ***Socio-Economic Status*** indicator percentile (100=high): 59th

St. Joseph County
THREE RIVERS COMMUNITY S.D.
1008 8TH STREET ● THREE RIVERS MI 49093 ● (616) 279-1100

Grade Span: PK-12 **Schools**: *Regular* 8 ● *Spec Ed* 1 ● *Alt* 0 **Students**: 2,863 **Total Teachers**: 153 **Student/Classroom Teacher Ratio**: 21.9	**Expenditures/Student**: $5,347 **Librarians**: 3.0 954 students/librarian **Guidance Counselors**: 7.0 409 students/counselor	**% Amer Indian**: 0.0 **% Asian**: 0.9 **% Black**: 12.5 **% Hispanic**: 0.9 **% White**: 85.7	National ***Socio-Economic Status*** indicator percentile (100=high): 55th

Shiawassee County
OWOSSO S.D.
P.O. BOX 340 ● OWOSSO MI 48867 ● (517) 723-8131

Grade Span: KG-12 **Schools**: *Regular* 8 ● *Spec Ed* 0 ● *Alt* 1 **Students**: 4,560 **Total Teachers**: 230 **Student/Classroom Teacher Ratio**: 21.5	**Expenditures/Student**: $5,030 **Librarians**: 3.0 1,520 students/librarian **Guidance Counselors**: 6.0 760 students/counselor	**% Amer Indian**: 0.2 **% Asian**: 0.8 **% Black**: 0.5 **% Hispanic**: 2.0 **% White**: 96.6	National ***Socio-Economic Status*** indicator percentile (100=high): 61st

Van Buren County
MATTAWAN CONSOLIDATED S.D.
56720 MURRAY STREET ● MATTAWAN MI 49071 ● (616) 668-3361

Grade Span: KG-12 **Schools**: *Regular* 4 ● *Spec Ed* 0 ● *Alt* 0 **Students**: 2,966 **Total Teachers**: 136 **Student/Classroom Teacher Ratio**: 21.9	**Expenditures/Student**: $4,436 **Librarians**: 2.0 1,483 students/librarian **Guidance Counselors**: 3.0 989 students/counselor	**% Amer Indian**: 0.9 **% Asian**: 1.3 **% Black**: 2.1 **% Hispanic**: 1.4 **% White**: 94.2	National ***Socio-Economic Status*** indicator percentile (100=high): 92nd

Van Buren County
SOUTH HAVEN S.D.
554 GREEN STREET ● SOUTH HAVEN MI 49090 ● (616) 637-0520

Grade Span: PK-12 **Schools**: *Regular* 7 ● *Spec Ed* 0 ● *Alt* 0 **Students**: 2,704 **Total Teachers**: 146 **Student/Classroom Teacher Ratio**: 20.4	**Expenditures/Student**: $5,727 **Librarians**: 1.0 2,704 students/librarian **Guidance Counselors**: 5.0 541 students/counselor	**% Amer Indian**: 0.7 **% Asian**: 0.3 **% Black**: 16.4 **% Hispanic**: 5.6 **% White**: 77.0	National ***Socio-Economic Status*** indicator percentile (100=high): 33rd

Washtenaw County
ANN ARBOR S.D.
2555 SOUTH STATE ROAD ● ANN ARBOR MI 48104 ● (734) 994-2230

Grade Span: PK-12 **Schools**: *Regular* 32 ● *Spec Ed* 1 ● *Alt* 0 **Students**: 15,255 **Total Teachers**: 846 **Student/Classroom Teacher Ratio**: 18.6	**Expenditures/Student**: $8,104 **Librarians**: 33.0 462 students/librarian **Guidance Counselors**: 26.0 587 students/counselor	**% Amer Indian**: 0.4 **% Asian**: 8.6 **% Black**: 17.4 **% Hispanic**: 2.1 **% White**: 71.6	National ***Socio-Economic Status*** indicator percentile (100=high): 74th

Washtenaw County
CHELSEA S.D.
500 EAST WASHINGTON STREET ● CHELSEA MI 48118 ● (734) 475-9131

Grade Span: KG-12 **Schools**: *Regular* 4 ● *Spec Ed* 0 ● *Alt* 0 **Students**: 2,711 **Total Teachers**: 123 **Student/Classroom Teacher Ratio**: 22.3	**Expenditures/Student**: $6,067 **Librarians**: 4.0 678 students/librarian **Guidance Counselors**: 5.0 542 students/counselor	**% Amer Indian**: 0.1 **% Asian**: 0.7 **% Black**: 0.5 **% Hispanic**: 0.4 **% White**: 98.2	National ***Socio-Economic Status*** indicator percentile (100=high): 98th

Washtenaw County

DEXTER COMMUNITY S.D.

2615 BAKER ROAD ● DEXTER MI 48130 ● (734) 426-4623 ● http://web.dexter.k12.mi.us/schools/district.html

Grade Span: KG-12 **Schools**: *Regular* 6 ● *Spec Ed* 0 ● *Alt* 0 **Students**: 2,581 **Total Teachers**: 149 **Student/Classroom Teacher Ratio**: 20.7	**Expenditures/Student**: $6,611 **Librarians**: 6.0 430 students/librarian **Guidance Counselors**: 4.0 645 students/counselor	**% Amer Indian**: 0.3 **% Asian**: 0.9 **% Black**: 0.2 **% Hispanic**: 0.6 **% White**: 98.1	National ***Socio-Economic Status*** indicator percentile (100=high): 96th

Washtenaw County

SALINE AREA S.D.

7190 MAPLE ROAD ● SALINE MI 48176 ● (734) 429-5454

Grade Span: PK-12 **Schools**: *Regular* 5 ● *Spec Ed* 0 ● *Alt* 0 **Students**: 4,084 **Total Teachers**: 184 **Student/Classroom Teacher Ratio**: 23.4	**Expenditures/Student**: $6,132 **Librarians**: 4.0 1,021 students/librarian **Guidance Counselors**: 7.0 583 students/counselor	**% Amer Indian**: 0.3 **% Asian**: 1.8 **% Black**: 0.4 **% Hispanic**: 1.0 **% White**: 96.4	National ***Socio-Economic Status*** indicator percentile (100=high): 96th

Washtenaw County

[YPSILANTI] **LINCOLN CONSOLIDATED S.D.**

8970 WHITTAKER ROAD ● YPSILANTI MI 48197 ● (734) 484-7001 ● http://lincoln.k12.mi.us

Grade Span: PK-12 **Schools**: *Regular* 5 ● *Spec Ed* 0 ● *Alt* 0 **Students**: 3,845 **Total Teachers**: 162 **Student/Classroom Teacher Ratio**: 28.9	**Expenditures/Student**: $5,687 **Librarians**: 4.0 961 students/librarian **Guidance Counselors**: 6.0 641 students/counselor	**% Amer Indian**: 0.3 **% Asian**: 1.0 **% Black**: 16.1 **% Hispanic**: 1.0 **% White**: 81.6	National ***Socio-Economic Status*** indicator percentile (100=high): 74th

Washtenaw County

[YPSILANTI] **S.D. OF YPSILANTI**

1885 PACKARD ROAD ● YPSILANTI MI 48197 ● (734) 482-9388

Grade Span: KG-12 **Schools**: *Regular* 11 ● *Spec Ed* 1 ● *Alt* 2 **Students**: 4,751 **Total Teachers**: 267 **Student/Classroom Teacher Ratio**: 18.2	**Expenditures/Student**: $7,960 **Librarians**: 8.0 594 students/librarian **Guidance Counselors**: 11.0 432 students/counselor	**% Amer Indian**: 0.2 **% Asian**: 2.0 **% Black**: 43.2 **% Hispanic**: 1.4 **% White**: 53.2	National ***Socio-Economic Status*** indicator percentile (100=high): 26th

Washtenaw County

[YPSILANTI] **WILLOW RUN COMMUNITY S.D.**

2171 EAST MICHIGAN AVENUE ● YPSILANTI MI 48198 ● (734) 481-8200 ● http://scnc.wrcs.k12.mi.us/~wrcshp

Grade Span: PK-12 **Schools**: *Regular* 8 ● *Spec Ed* 0 ● *Alt* 0 **Students**: 3,087 **Total Teachers**: 159 **Student/Classroom Teacher Ratio**: 19.5	**Expenditures/Student**: $8,235 **Librarians**: 2.0 1,544 students/librarian **Guidance Counselors**: 4.0 772 students/counselor	**% Amer Indian**: 0.6 **% Asian**: 1.3 **% Black**: 44.2 **% Hispanic**: 0.9 **% White**: 53.1	National ***Socio-Economic Status*** indicator percentile (100=high): 16th

Wayne County

ALLEN PARK S.D.

19001 CHAMPAIGN ● ALLEN PARK MI 48101 ● (313) 928-4667 ● http://www.wcresa.k12.mi.us/allenpark

Grade Span: KG-12 **Schools**: *Regular* 5 ● *Spec Ed* 0 ● *Alt* 0 **Students**: 3,120 **Total Teachers**: 154 **Student/Classroom Teacher Ratio**: 21.3	**Expenditures/Student**: $6,016 **Librarians**: 4.0 780 students/librarian **Guidance Counselors**: 5.0 624 students/counselor	**% Amer Indian**: 0.2 **% Asian**: 0.9 **% Black**: 0.1 **% Hispanic**: 3.3 **% White**: 95.6	National ***Socio-Economic Status*** indicator percentile (100=high): 92nd

Wayne County
[BELLEVILLE] **VAN BUREN S.D.**
555 W COLUMBIA AVENUE ● BELLEVILLE MI 48111 ● (313) 697-9123 ● http://www.wcresa.k12.mi.us/vanburen

Grade Span: PK-12 **Schools**: *Regular* 9 ● *Spec Ed* 0 ● *Alt* 0 **Students**: 6,041 **Total Teachers**: 303 **Student/Classroom Teacher Ratio**: 20.5	**Expenditures/Student**: $6,609 **Librarians**: 8.0 755 students/librarian **Guidance Counselors**: 7.0 863 students/counselor	**% Amer Indian**: 0.2 **% Asian**: 0.6 **% Black**: 18.5 **% Hispanic**: 1.0 **% White**: 79.7	National ***Socio-Economic Status*** indicator percentile (100=high): 60th

Wayne County
DEARBORN CITY S.D.
18700 AUDETTE ● DEARBORN MI 48124 ● (313) 730-3242 ● http://www.dearbornschools.org

Grade Span: PK-12 **Schools**: *Regular* 28 ● *Spec Ed* 1 ● *Alt* 1 **Students**: 15,549 **Total Teachers**: 821 **Student/Classroom Teacher Ratio**: 22.1	**Expenditures/Student**: $7,254 **Librarians**: 0.0 *** students/librarian **Guidance Counselors**: 0.0 *** students/counselor	**% Amer Indian**: 0.3 **% Asian**: 0.9 **% Black**: 1.1 **% Hispanic**: 2.0 **% White**: 95.6	National ***Socio-Economic Status*** indicator percentile (100=high): 45th

Wayne County
[DEARBORN HEIGHTS] **CRESTWOOD S.D.**
1501 N BEECH DALY ● DEARBORN HEIGHTS MI 48127 ● (313) 278-0903 ● http://csdm.k12.mi.us

Grade Span: PK-12 **Schools**: *Regular* 5 ● *Spec Ed* 0 ● *Alt* 0 **Students**: 2,887 **Total Teachers**: 134 **Student/Classroom Teacher Ratio**: 23.6	**Expenditures/Student**: $6,166 **Librarians**: 3.0 962 students/librarian **Guidance Counselors**: 5.0 577 students/counselor	**% Amer Indian**: 0.1 **% Asian**: 1.8 **% Black**: 0.6 **% Hispanic**: 1.1 **% White**: 96.4	National ***Socio-Economic Status*** indicator percentile (100=high): 84th

Wayne County
DETROIT CITY S.D.
5057 WOODWARD ● DETROIT MI 48202 ● (313) 494-1075 ● http://dpsnet.detpub.k12.mi.us.

Grade Span: PK-12 **Schools**: *Regular* 243 ● *Spec Ed* 15 ● *Alt* 10 **Students**: 173,750 **Total Teachers**: 7,687 **Student/Classroom Teacher Ratio**: 27.9	**Expenditures/Student**: $7,235 **Librarians**: 125.0 1,390 students/librarian **Guidance Counselors**: 346.0 502 students/counselor	**% Amer Indian**: 0.3 **% Asian**: 1.0 **% Black**: 90.2 **% Hispanic**: 2.9 **% White**: 5.7	National ***Socio-Economic Status*** indicator percentile (100=high): 7th

Wayne County
[FLAT ROCK] **WOODHAVEN S.D.**
24975 VAN HORN ROAD ● FLAT ROCK MI 48134 ● (734) 783-3300 ● http://www.wcresa.k12.mi.us/woodhaven

Grade Span: KG-12 **Schools**: *Regular* 7 ● *Spec Ed* 0 ● *Alt* 1 **Students**: 4,626 **Total Teachers**: 249 **Student/Classroom Teacher Ratio**: 19.8	**Expenditures/Student**: $6,759 **Librarians**: 2.0 2,313 students/librarian **Guidance Counselors**: 6.0 771 students/counselor	**% Amer Indian**: 1.5 **% Asian**: 4.1 **% Black**: 2.9 **% Hispanic**: 3.4 **% White**: 88.1	National ***Socio-Economic Status*** indicator percentile (100=high): 67th

Wayne County
GARDEN CITY S.D.
1333 RADCLIFF ● GARDEN CITY MI 48135 ● (734) 425-4900 ● http://www.wcresa.k12.mi.us/gardencity

Grade Span: KG-12 **Schools**: *Regular* 8 ● *Spec Ed* 1 ● *Alt* 1 **Students**: 5,202 **Total Teachers**: 267 **Student/Classroom Teacher Ratio**: na	**Expenditures/Student**: $8,552 **Librarians**: 2.0 2,601 students/librarian **Guidance Counselors**: 6.0 867 students/counselor	**% Amer Indian**: 0.5 **% Asian**: 0.6 **% Black**: 0.8 **% Hispanic**: 0.5 **% White**: 97.6	National ***Socio-Economic Status*** indicator percentile (100=high): 80th

Wayne County
GROSSE POINTE S.D.
389 ST CLAIR AVENUE ● GROSSE POINTE MI 48230 ● (313) 343-2000 ● http://boe.gp.k12.mi.us

Grade Span: PK-12 **Schools**: *Regular* 14 ● *Spec Ed* 1 ● *Alt* 0 **Students**: 8,158 **Total Teachers**: 464 **Student/Classroom Teacher Ratio**: 18.3	**Expenditures/Student**: $8,380 **Librarians**: 13.0 628 students/librarian **Guidance Counselors**: 16.0 510 students/counselor	**% Amer Indian**: 0.1 **% Asian**: 2.0 **% Black**: 1.7 **% Hispanic**: 0.6 **% White**: 95.5	National ***Socio-Economic Status*** indicator percentile (100=high): 99th

Wayne County
HAMTRAMCK S.D.
P.O. BOX 12012 ● HAMTRAMCK MI 48212 ● (313) 892-4980 ● http://www.wcresa.k12.mi.us/hamtramck

Grade Span: KG-12 **Schools**: *Regular* 5 ● *Spec Ed* 0 ● *Alt* 0 **Students**: 3,195 **Total Teachers**: 138 **Student/Classroom Teacher Ratio**: 21.7	**Expenditures/Student**: $7,034 **Librarians**: 1.0 3,195 students/librarian **Guidance Counselors**: 4.0 799 students/counselor	**% Amer Indian**: 0.3 **% Asian**: 0.3 **% Black**: 20.6 **% Hispanic**: 0.4 **% White**: 78.3	National ***Socio-Economic Status*** indicator percentile (100=high): 6th

Wayne County
HIGHLAND PARK CITY S.D.
20 BARTLETT ● HIGHLAND PARK MI 48203 ● (313) 252-0440 ● http://www.wcresa.k12.mi.us/highlandpark

Grade Span: KG-12 **Schools**: *Regular* 6 ● *Spec Ed* 0 ● *Alt* 1 **Students**: 3,342 **Total Teachers**: 163 **Student/Classroom Teacher Ratio**: 20.8	**Expenditures/Student**: $10,014 **Librarians**: 4.0 836 students/librarian **Guidance Counselors**: 8.0 418 students/counselor	**% Amer Indian**: 0.0 **% Asian**: 0.0 **% Black**: 99.9 **% Hispanic**: 0.0 **% White**: 0.1	National ***Socio-Economic Status*** indicator percentile (100=high): 13th

Wayne County
LINCOLN PARK S.D.
1545 SOUTHFIELD ROAD ● LINCOLN PARK MI 48146 ● (313) 389-0200 ● http://www.wcresa.k12.mi.us/lincolnpark

Grade Span: PK-12 **Schools**: *Regular* 10 ● *Spec Ed* 0 ● *Alt* 0 **Students**: 5,602 **Total Teachers**: 253 **Student/Classroom Teacher Ratio**: 23.1	**Expenditures/Student**: $5,865 **Librarians**: 1.0 5,602 students/librarian **Guidance Counselors**: 7.0 800 students/counselor	**% Amer Indian**: 0.4 **% Asian**: 0.5 **% Black**: 1.2 **% Hispanic**: 3.9 **% White**: 94.0	National ***Socio-Economic Status*** indicator percentile (100=high): 53rd

Wayne County
LIVONIA S.D.
15125 FARMINGTON ROAD ● LIVONIA MI 48154 ● (734) 523-8800 ● http://www.wcresa.k12.mi.us/livonia

Grade Span: PK-12 **Schools**: *Regular* 31 ● *Spec Ed* 1 ● *Alt* 2 **Students**: 17,750 **Total Teachers**: 867 **Student/Classroom Teacher Ratio**: 22.3	**Expenditures/Student**: $7,521 **Librarians**: 32.0 555 students/librarian **Guidance Counselors**: 50.0 355 students/counselor	**% Amer Indian**: 0.4 **% Asian**: 1.6 **% Black**: 1.4 **% Hispanic**: 0.9 **% White**: 95.8	National ***Socio-Economic Status*** indicator percentile (100=high): 95th

Wayne County
NORTHVILLE S.D.
501 WEST MAIN STREET ● NORTHVILLE MI 48167 ● (248) 349-3400 ● http://www.northville.k12.mi.us

Grade Span: KG-12 **Schools**: *Regular* 8 ● *Spec Ed* 3 ● *Alt* 0 **Students**: 4,725 **Total Teachers**: 265 **Student/Classroom Teacher Ratio**: 19.8	**Expenditures/Student**: $8,450 **Librarians**: 8.0 591 students/librarian **Guidance Counselors**: 7.0 675 students/counselor	**% Amer Indian**: 0.0 **% Asian**: 5.4 **% Black**: 0.7 **% Hispanic**: 0.8 **% White**: 93.1	National ***Socio-Economic Status*** indicator percentile (100=high): 99th

Wayne County
PLYMOUTH CANTON COMMUNITY S.D.
454 SOUTH HARVEY ● PLYMOUTH MI 48170 ● (734) 416-2700

Grade Span: PK-12 **Schools**: *Regular* 21 ● *Spec Ed* 1 ● *Alt* 0 **Students**: 15,362 **Total Teachers**: 704 **Student/Classroom Teacher Ratio**: 22.6	**Expenditures/Student**: $6,266 **Librarians**: 21.0 732 students/librarian **Guidance Counselors**: 25.0 614 students/counselor	**% Amer Indian**: 0.5 **% Asian**: 4.4 **% Black**: 2.3 **% Hispanic**: 1.0 **% White**: 91.8	National ***Socio-Economic Status*** indicator percentile (100=high): 91st

Wayne County
REDFORD UNION S.D.
18499 BEECH DALY ROAD ● REDFORD MI 48240 ● (313) 592-3300 ● http://www.redfordu.k12.mi.us

Grade Span: PK-12 **Schools**: *Regular* 9 ● *Spec Ed* 2 ● *Alt* 0 **Students**: 5,060 **Total Teachers**: 247 **Student/Classroom Teacher Ratio**: 25.8	**Expenditures/Student**: $7,232 **Librarians**: 3.0 1,687 students/librarian **Guidance Counselors**: 6.0 843 students/counselor	**% Amer Indian**: 0.7 **% Asian**: 1.0 **% Black**: 1.8 **% Hispanic**: 1.2 **% White**: 95.3	National ***Socio-Economic Status*** indicator percentile (100=high): 67th

Wayne County
[REDFORD] SOUTH REDFORD S.D.
26141 SCHOOLCRAFT ● REDFORD MI 48239 ● (313) 535-4000 ● http://www.wcresa.k12.mi.us/southredford

Grade Span: KG-12 **Schools**: *Regular* 6 ● *Spec Ed* 0 ● *Alt* 0 **Students**: 3,383 **Total Teachers**: 151 **Student/Classroom Teacher Ratio**: 23.7	**Expenditures/Student**: $6,437 **Librarians**: 4.0 846 students/librarian **Guidance Counselors**: 5.0 677 students/counselor	**% Amer Indian**: 0.1 **% Asian**: 0.8 **% Black**: 5.4 **% Hispanic**: 1.1 **% White**: 92.5	National ***Socio-Economic Status*** indicator percentile (100=high): 88th

Wayne County
ROMULUS COMMUNITY S.D.
36540 GRANT ROAD ● ROMULUS MI 48174 ● (313) 941-1600 ● http://www.wcresa.k12.mi.us/romulus

Grade Span: KG-12 **Schools**: *Regular* 7 ● *Spec Ed* 0 ● *Alt* 0 **Students**: 3,840 **Total Teachers**: 166 **Student/Classroom Teacher Ratio**: 24.7	**Expenditures/Student**: $7,869 **Librarians**: 0.0 *** students/librarian **Guidance Counselors**: 0.0 *** students/counselor	**% Amer Indian**: 1.1 **% Asian**: 0.3 **% Black**: 38.2 **% Hispanic**: 1.3 **% White**: 59.0	National ***Socio-Economic Status*** indicator percentile (100=high): 33rd

Wayne County
SOUTHGATE COMMUNITY S.D.
13201 TRENTON ROAD ● SOUTHGATE MI 48195 ● (734) 246-4600

Grade Span: PK-12 **Schools**: *Regular* 8 ● *Spec Ed* 0 ● *Alt* 0 **Students**: 4,189 **Total Teachers**: 194 **Student/Classroom Teacher Ratio**: 22.7	**Expenditures/Student**: $6,075 **Librarians**: 2.0 2,095 students/librarian **Guidance Counselors**: 11.0 381 students/counselor	**% Amer Indian**: 1.7 **% Asian**: 1.1 **% Black**: 1.0 **% Hispanic**: 2.5 **% White**: 93.7	National ***Socio-Economic Status*** indicator percentile (100=high): 55th

Wayne County
TAYLOR S.D.
23033 NORTHLINE ROAD ● TAYLOR MI 48180 ● (313) 374-1200 ● http://www.wcresa.k12.mi.us/taylor/index.htm

Grade Span: KG-12 **Schools**: *Regular* 21 ● *Spec Ed* 1 ● *Alt* 2 **Students**: 11,655 **Total Teachers**: 592 **Student/Classroom Teacher Ratio**: 20.8	**Expenditures/Student**: $6,704 **Librarians**: 0.0 *** students/librarian **Guidance Counselors**: 19.0 613 students/counselor	**% Amer Indian**: 1.0 **% Asian**: 1.3 **% Black**: 10.3 **% Hispanic**: 1.4 **% White**: 86.0	National ***Socio-Economic Status*** indicator percentile (100=high): 41st

Wayne County

TRENTON S.D.

2603 CHARLTON ● TRENTON MI 48183 ● (734) 676-8600

Grade Span: KG-12 **Schools**: *Regular* 6 ● *Spec Ed* 0 ● *Alt* 0 **Students**: 3,209 **Total Teachers**: 166 **Student/Classroom Teacher Ratio**: 20.1	**Expenditures/Student**: $7,601 **Librarians**: 5.0 642 students/librarian **Guidance Counselors**: 6.0 535 students/counselor	**% Amer Indian**: 0.1 **% Asian**: 1.6 **% Black**: 0.3 **% Hispanic**: 1.1 **% White**: 96.9	National ***Socio-Economic Status*** indicator percentile (100=high): 91st

Wayne County

[WESTLAND] **WAYNE-WESTLAND COMMUNITY S.D.**

36745 MARQUETTE ● WESTLAND MI 48185 ● (313) 595-2000 ● http://www.wcresa.k12.mi.us/wayne-westland

Grade Span: KG-12 **Schools**: *Regular* 22 ● *Spec Ed* 2 ● *Alt* 2 **Students**: 14,831 **Total Teachers**: 704 **Student/Classroom Teacher Ratio**: 22.3	**Expenditures/Student**: $6,924 **Librarians**: 2.0 7,416 students/librarian **Guidance Counselors**: 27.0 549 students/counselor	**% Amer Indian**: 1.4 **% Asian**: 1.0 **% Black**: 11.3 **% Hispanic**: 1.6 **% White**: 84.7	National ***Socio-Economic Status*** indicator percentile (100=high): 64th

Wayne County

[WOODHAVEN] **GIBRALTAR S.D.**

19370 VREELAND ● WOODHAVEN MI 48183 ● (734) 692-4002 ● http://www.wcresa.k12.mi.us/gibraltar

Grade Span: KG-12 **Schools**: *Regular* 7 ● *Spec Ed* 0 ● *Alt* 0 **Students**: 2,636 **Total Teachers**: 125 **Student/Classroom Teacher Ratio**: 22.2	**Expenditures/Student**: $6,267 **Librarians**: 2.0 1,318 students/librarian **Guidance Counselors**: 4.0 659 students/counselor	**% Amer Indian**: 8.2 **% Asian**: 0.9 **% Black**: 0.9 **% Hispanic**: 2.3 **% White**: 87.7	National ***Socio-Economic Status*** indicator percentile (100=high): 83rd

Wayne County

WYANDOTTE CITY S.D.

P.O. BOX 130 ● WYANDOTTE MI 48192 ● (734) 246-1000 ● http://www.gatecom.com/~wpsgesad

Grade Span: PK-12 **Schools**: *Regular* 7 ● *Spec Ed* 2 ● *Alt* 1 **Students**: 4,756 **Total Teachers**: 233 **Student/Classroom Teacher Ratio**: 24.9	**Expenditures/Student**: $6,924 **Librarians**: 2.0 2,378 students/librarian **Guidance Counselors**: 5.0 951 students/counselor	**% Amer Indian**: 0.3 **% Asian**: 0.5 **% Black**: 0.3 **% Hispanic**: 1.8 **% White**: 97.1	National ***Socio-Economic Status*** indicator percentile (100=high): 68th

Wexford County

CADILLAC AREA S.D.

115 SOUTH STREET ● CADILLAC MI 49601 ● (616) 779-9300

Grade Span: KG-12 **Schools**: *Regular* 7 ● *Spec Ed* 1 ● *Alt* 0 **Students**: 3,912 **Total Teachers**: 187 **Student/Classroom Teacher Ratio**: 22.5	**Expenditures/Student**: $5,153 **Librarians**: 1.0 3,912 students/librarian **Guidance Counselors**: 9.0 435 students/counselor	**% Amer Indian**: 0.7 **% Asian**: 0.6 **% Black**: 0.5 **% Hispanic**: 0.4 **% White**: 97.7	National ***Socio-Economic Status*** indicator percentile (100=high): 50th

Anoka County
[CIRCLE PINES] **CENTENNIAL S.D.**
4707 NORTH RD. ● CIRCLE PINES MN 55014-1898 ● (612) 780-7610 ● http://www.centennial.k12.mn.us

Grade Span: PK-12 **Schools**: *Regular* 6 ● *Spec Ed* 0 ● *Alt* 2 **Students**: 6,038 **Total Teachers**: na **Student/Classroom Teacher Ratio**: na	**Expenditures/Student**: $5,366 **Librarians**: na *** students/librarian **Guidance Counselors**: na *** students/counselor	**% Amer Indian**: 1.8 **% Asian**: 1.6 **% Black**: 0.5 **% Hispanic**: 1.0 **% White**: 95.1	National ***Socio-Economic Status*** indicator percentile (100=high): 89th

Anoka County
COLUMBIA HEIGHTS S.D.
1400 49TH AVE. N.E. ● COLUMBIA HEIGHTS MN 55421-1992 ● (612) 586-4505 ● http://www.colheights.k12.mn.us

Grade Span: PK-12 **Schools**: *Regular* 5 ● *Spec Ed* 0 ● *Alt* 2 **Students**: 3,016 **Total Teachers**: na **Student/Classroom Teacher Ratio**: 16.4	**Expenditures/Student**: $7,959 **Librarians**: na *** students/librarian **Guidance Counselors**: na *** students/counselor	**% Amer Indian**: 3.0 **% Asian**: 3.5 **% Black**: 5.3 **% Hispanic**: 3.4 **% White**: 84.8	National ***Socio-Economic Status*** indicator percentile (100=high): 50th

Anoka County
[COON RAPIDS] **ANOKA-HENNEPIN S.D.**
11299 HANSON BLVD. N.W. ● COON RAPIDS MN 55433-3799 ● (612) 422-5500 ● http://www.anoka.k12.mn.us

Grade Span: PK-12 **Schools**: *Regular* 38 ● *Spec Ed* 1 ● *Alt* 11 **Students**: 39,152 **Total Teachers**: na **Student/Classroom Teacher Ratio**: na	**Expenditures/Student**: $5,966 **Librarians**: na *** students/librarian **Guidance Counselors**: na *** students/counselor	**% Amer Indian**: 1.2 **% Asian**: 2.3 **% Black**: 2.0 **% Hispanic**: 1.1 **% White**: 93.5	National ***Socio-Economic Status*** indicator percentile (100=high): 82nd

Anoka County
FRIDLEY S.D.
6000 W. MOORE LAKE DR. ● FRIDLEY MN 55432-5698 ● (612) 571-6000

Grade Span: PK-12 **Schools**: *Regular* 4 ● *Spec Ed* 0 ● *Alt* 0 **Students**: 2,634 **Total Teachers**: na **Student/Classroom Teacher Ratio**: 18.4	**Expenditures/Student**: $7,561 **Librarians**: na *** students/librarian **Guidance Counselors**: na *** students/counselor	**% Amer Indian**: 2.4 **% Asian**: 3.0 **% Black**: 3.6 **% Hispanic**: 1.4 **% White**: 89.6	National ***Socio-Economic Status*** indicator percentile (100=high): 64th

Anoka County
SPRING LAKE PARK S.D.
8000 HWY. 65 N.E. ● SPRING LAKE PARK MN 55432-2071 ● (612) 786-5570

Grade Span: PK-12 **Schools**: *Regular* 6 ● *Spec Ed* 0 ● *Alt* 2 **Students**: 4,216 **Total Teachers**: na **Student/Classroom Teacher Ratio**: 19.5	**Expenditures/Student**: $6,435 **Librarians**: na *** students/librarian **Guidance Counselors**: na *** students/counselor	**% Amer Indian**: 1.2 **% Asian**: 2.8 **% Black**: 1.1 **% Hispanic**: 0.7 **% White**: 94.2	National ***Socio-Economic Status*** indicator percentile (100=high): 71st

Anoka County
ST. FRANCIS S.D.
3325 BRIDGE ST. ● ST. FRANCIS MN 55070-9732 ● (612) 753-7048 ● http://www.stfrancis.k12.mn.us

Grade Span: PK-12 **Schools**: *Regular* 7 ● *Spec Ed* 0 ● *Alt* 10 **Students**: 5,474 **Total Teachers**: na **Student/Classroom Teacher Ratio**: 19.9	**Expenditures/Student**: $5,807 **Librarians**: na *** students/librarian **Guidance Counselors**: na *** students/counselor	**% Amer Indian**: 1.2 **% Asian**: 0.9 **% Black**: 0.6 **% Hispanic**: 0.8 **% White**: 96.6	National ***Socio-Economic Status*** indicator percentile (100=high): 77th

Becker County

DETROIT LAKES S.D.

BOX 766, 702 LAKE AVE. ● DETROIT LAKES MN 56501 ● (218) 847-9271

Grade Span: PK-12 **Schools**: *Regular* 7 ● *Spec Ed* 0 ● *Alt* 1 **Students**: 3,024 **Total Teachers**: na **Student/Classroom Teacher Ratio**: 16.2	**Expenditures/Student**: $5,733 **Librarians**: na *** students/librarian **Guidance Counselors**: na *** students/counselor	**% Amer Indian**: 11.2 **% Asian**: 0.7 **% Black**: 0.3 **% Hispanic**: 0.8 **% White**: 87.0	National ***Socio-Economic Status*** indicator percentile (100=high): 44th

Beltrami County

BEMIDJI S.D.

201 15TH ST. N.W. ● BEMIDJI MN 56601-3865 ● (218) 759-3110

Grade Span: PK-12 **Schools**: *Regular* 10 ● *Spec Ed* 2 ● *Alt* 3 **Students**: 5,913 **Total Teachers**: na **Student/Classroom Teacher Ratio**: 17.6	**Expenditures/Student**: $6,134 **Librarians**: na *** students/librarian **Guidance Counselors**: na *** students/counselor	**% Amer Indian**: 13.0 **% Asian**: 1.0 **% Black**: 0.5 **% Hispanic**: 0.8 **% White**: 84.7	National ***Socio-Economic Status*** indicator percentile (100=high): 43rd

Benton County

SAUK RAPIDS S.D.

BOX 520 ● SAUK RAPIDS MN 56379-0520 ● (320) 253-4703 ● http://www.isd47.org

Grade Span: PK-12 **Schools**: *Regular* 5 ● *Spec Ed* 0 ● *Alt* 1 **Students**: 3,289 **Total Teachers**: na **Student/Classroom Teacher Ratio**: 17.9	**Expenditures/Student**: $5,643 **Librarians**: na *** students/librarian **Guidance Counselors**: na *** students/counselor	**% Amer Indian**: 0.1 **% Asian**: 0.5 **% Black**: 0.2 **% Hispanic**: 0.3 **% White**: 98.8	National ***Socio-Economic Status*** indicator percentile (100=high): 72nd

Blue Earth County

MANKATO S.D.

BOX 8741 ● MANKATO MN 56002-8741 ● (507) 387-1868 ● http://www.isd77.k12.mn.us

Grade Span: PK-12 **Schools**: *Regular* 13 ● *Spec Ed* 0 ● *Alt* 3 **Students**: 7,530 **Total Teachers**: na **Student/Classroom Teacher Ratio**: 18.5	**Expenditures/Student**: $5,344 **Librarians**: na *** students/librarian **Guidance Counselors**: na *** students/counselor	**% Amer Indian**: 0.3 **% Asian**: 2.8 **% Black**: 1.3 **% Hispanic**: 1.8 **% White**: 93.8	National ***Socio-Economic Status*** indicator percentile (100=high): 66th

Brown County

NEW ULM S.D.

400 S. PAYNE ● NEW ULM MN 56073-3296 ● (507) 359-8401 ● http://www.newulm.k12.mn.us

Grade Span: PK-12 **Schools**: *Regular* 6 ● *Spec Ed* 0 ● *Alt* 1 **Students**: 2,977 **Total Teachers**: na **Student/Classroom Teacher Ratio**: 16.8	**Expenditures/Student**: $5,750 **Librarians**: na *** students/librarian **Guidance Counselors**: na *** students/counselor	**% Amer Indian**: 0.2 **% Asian**: 0.8 **% Black**: 0.9 **% Hispanic**: 1.2 **% White**: 96.8	National ***Socio-Economic Status*** indicator percentile (100=high): 74th

Carlton County

CLOQUET S.D.

509 CARLTON AVE. ● CLOQUET MN 55720-1757 ● (218) 879-6721

Grade Span: PK-12 **Schools**: *Regular* 4 ● *Spec Ed* 0 ● *Alt* 1 **Students**: 2,521 **Total Teachers**: na **Student/Classroom Teacher Ratio**: 17.9	**Expenditures/Student**: $6,326 **Librarians**: na *** students/librarian **Guidance Counselors**: na *** students/counselor	**% Amer Indian**: 13.6 **% Asian**: 0.5 **% Black**: 0.4 **% Hispanic**: 0.6 **% White**: 84.9	National ***Socio-Economic Status*** indicator percentile (100=high): 49th

Carver County

CHASKA S.D.

110600 VILLAGE RD. ● CHASKA MN 55318-1394 ● (612) 368-3601 ● http://www.chaska.k12.mn.us

Grade Span: PK-12 **Schools**: *Regular* 7 ● *Spec Ed* 0 ● *Alt* 3 **Students**: 5,747 **Total Teachers**: na **Student/Classroom Teacher Ratio**: 17.9	**Expenditures/Student**: $6,098 **Librarians**: na *** students/librarian **Guidance Counselors**: na *** students/counselor	**% Amer Indian**: 0.1 **% Asian**: 2.6 **% Black**: 0.2 **% Hispanic**: 2.0 **% White**: 95.1	National ***Socio-Economic Status*** indicator percentile (100=high): 90th

Chisago County

[LINDSTROM] **CHISAGO LAKES S.D.**

13750 LAKE BLVD. ● LINDSTROM MN 55045-0187 ● (612) 257-5600

Grade Span: PK-12 **Schools**: *Regular* 5 ● *Spec Ed* 0 ● *Alt* 1 **Students**: 3,365 **Total Teachers**: na **Student/Classroom Teacher Ratio**: 23.1	**Expenditures/Student**: $4,929 **Librarians**: na *** students/librarian **Guidance Counselors**: na *** students/counselor	**% Amer Indian**: 0.1 **% Asian**: 0.5 **% Black**: 0.8 **% Hispanic**: 0.4 **% White**: 98.2	National ***Socio-Economic Status*** indicator percentile (100=high): 81st

Chisago County

NORTH BRANCH S.D.

BOX 370, 320 MAIN ST. ● NORTH BRANCH MN 55056-0370 ● (612) 674-5210

Grade Span: PK-12 **Schools**: *Regular* 4 ● *Spec Ed* 0 ● *Alt* 2 **Students**: 2,999 **Total Teachers**: na **Student/Classroom Teacher Ratio**: 19.3	**Expenditures/Student**: $5,593 **Librarians**: na *** students/librarian **Guidance Counselors**: na *** students/counselor	**% Amer Indian**: 0.2 **% Asian**: 1.0 **% Black**: 0.1 **% Hispanic**: 0.5 **% White**: 98.2	National ***Socio-Economic Status*** indicator percentile (100=high): 66th

Clay County

MOORHEAD S.D.

810 4TH AVE. S. ● MOORHEAD MN 56560 ● (218) 236-6400

Grade Span: PK-12 **Schools**: *Regular* 8 ● *Spec Ed* 0 ● *Alt* 3 **Students**: 6,130 **Total Teachers**: na **Student/Classroom Teacher Ratio**: na	**Expenditures/Student**: $5,968 **Librarians**: na *** students/librarian **Guidance Counselors**: na *** students/counselor	**% Amer Indian**: 3.0 **% Asian**: 1.7 **% Black**: 0.8 **% Hispanic**: 9.3 **% White**: 85.1	National ***Socio-Economic Status*** indicator percentile (100=high): 53rd

Crow Wing County

BRAINERD S.D.

300 QUINCE ST. ● BRAINERD MN 56401-4095 ● (218) 828-5300

Grade Span: PK-12 **Schools**: *Regular* 11 ● *Spec Ed* 0 ● *Alt* 4 **Students**: 7,263 **Total Teachers**: na **Student/Classroom Teacher Ratio**: na	**Expenditures/Student**: $6,034 **Librarians**: na *** students/librarian **Guidance Counselors**: na *** students/counselor	**% Amer Indian**: 0.9 **% Asian**: 0.7 **% Black**: 0.6 **% Hispanic**: 0.4 **% White**: 97.5	National ***Socio-Economic Status*** indicator percentile (100=high): 57th

Dakota County

BURNSVILLE S.D.

100 RIVER RIDGE COURT ● BURNSVILLE MN 55337 ● (612) 707-2000 ● http://www.burnsville.org/education/edu.html

Grade Span: PK-12 **Schools**: *Regular* 12 ● *Spec Ed* 0 ● *Alt* 6 **Students**: 11,329 **Total Teachers**: na **Student/Classroom Teacher Ratio**: 18.0	**Expenditures/Student**: $6,899 **Librarians**: na *** students/librarian **Guidance Counselors**: na *** students/counselor	**% Amer Indian**: 0.4 **% Asian**: 5.9 **% Black**: 4.3 **% Hispanic**: 1.4 **% White**: 88.0	National ***Socio-Economic Status*** indicator percentile (100=high): 81st

Dakota County
FARMINGTON S.D.
510 WALNUT ST. ● FARMINGTON MN 55024-1389 ● (612) 463-6400 ● http://www.farmington.k12.mn.us/schools.htm

Grade Span: PK-12 **Schools**: *Regular* 4 ● *Spec Ed* 0 ● *Alt* 1 **Students**: 3,457 **Total Teachers**: na **Student/Classroom Teacher Ratio**: na	**Expenditures/Student**: $5,760 **Librarians**: na *** students/librarian **Guidance Counselors**: na *** students/counselor	**% Amer Indian**: 0.3 **% Asian**: 0.6 **% Black**: 0.2 **% Hispanic**: 0.5 **% White**: 98.4	National ***Socio-Economic Status*** indicator percentile (100=high): 82nd

Dakota County
HASTINGS S.D.
9TH & VERMILLION ST. ● HASTINGS MN 55033-2116 ● (612) 437-6111 ● http://www.hastings.k12.mn.us

Grade Span: PK-12 **Schools**: *Regular* 7 ● *Spec Ed* 0 ● *Alt* 3 **Students**: 5,178 **Total Teachers**: na **Student/Classroom Teacher Ratio**: 18.4	**Expenditures/Student**: $5,804 **Librarians**: na *** students/librarian **Guidance Counselors**: na *** students/counselor	**% Amer Indian**: 0.2 **% Asian**: 0.9 **% Black**: 0.5 **% Hispanic**: 0.9 **% White**: 97.5	National ***Socio-Economic Status*** indicator percentile (100=high): 86th

Dakota County
[INVER GROVE HEIGHTS] INVER GROVE S.D.
2990 80TH ST. E. ● INVER GROVE HEIGHTS MN 55076-3235 ● (612) 457-7210

Grade Span: PK-12 **Schools**: *Regular* 7 ● *Spec Ed* 0 ● *Alt* 2 **Students**: 4,044 **Total Teachers**: na **Student/Classroom Teacher Ratio**: 18.4	**Expenditures/Student**: $6,267 **Librarians**: na *** students/librarian **Guidance Counselors**: na *** students/counselor	**% Amer Indian**: 0.5 **% Asian**: 1.5 **% Black**: 2.8 **% Hispanic**: 4.1 **% White**: 91.1	National ***Socio-Economic Status*** indicator percentile (100=high): 74th

Dakota County
LAKEVILLE S.D.
8670 210TH ST. W. ● LAKEVILLE MN 55044-8501 ● (612) 469-7100 ● http://www.isd194.k12.mn.us

Grade Span: PK-12 **Schools**: *Regular* 10 ● *Spec Ed* 0 ● *Alt* 0 **Students**: 7,388 **Total Teachers**: na **Student/Classroom Teacher Ratio**: 17.6	**Expenditures/Student**: $5,621 **Librarians**: na *** students/librarian **Guidance Counselors**: na *** students/counselor	**% Amer Indian**: 0.1 **% Asian**: 1.2 **% Black**: 0.7 **% Hispanic**: 0.5 **% White**: 97.4	National ***Socio-Economic Status*** indicator percentile (100=high): 96th

Dakota County
ROSEMOUNT-APPLE VALLEY-EAGAN S.D.
14445 DIAMOND PATH WEST ● ROSEMOUNT MN 55068-4199 ● (612) 423-7700 ● http://www.isd196.k12.mn.us/isd196.html

Grade Span: PK-12 **Schools**: *Regular* 26 ● *Spec Ed* 0 ● *Alt* 10 **Students**: 25,816 **Total Teachers**: na **Student/Classroom Teacher Ratio**: 19.2	**Expenditures/Student**: $5,036 **Librarians**: na *** students/librarian **Guidance Counselors**: na *** students/counselor	**% Amer Indian**: 0.4 **% Asian**: 4.0 **% Black**: 2.8 **% Hispanic**: 1.1 **% White**: 91.7	National ***Socio-Economic Status*** indicator percentile (100=high): 88th

Dakota County
SOUTH ST. PAUL S.D.
700 N. 2ND ST. ● SOUTH ST. PAUL MN 55075-2062 ● (612) 457-9400 ● http://www.sostpaul.k12.mn.us

Grade Span: PK-12 **Schools**: *Regular* 3 ● *Spec Ed* 0 ● *Alt* 1 **Students**: 3,606 **Total Teachers**: na **Student/Classroom Teacher Ratio**: na	**Expenditures/Student**: $6,454 **Librarians**: na *** students/librarian **Guidance Counselors**: na *** students/counselor	**% Amer Indian**: 0.6 **% Asian**: 1.2 **% Black**: 1.8 **% Hispanic**: 5.3 **% White**: 91.0	National ***Socio-Economic Status*** indicator percentile (100=high): 64th

Dakota County

WEST ST. PAUL-MENDOTA HEIGHTS-EAGAN S.D.

1897 DELAWARE AVE. ● WEST ST. PAUL MN 55118 ● (612) 681-2300

Grade Span: PK-12 **Schools**: *Regular* 7 ● *Spec Ed* 0 ● *Alt* 1 **Students**: 4,869 **Total Teachers**: na **Student/Classroom Teacher Ratio**: 17.4	**Expenditures/Student**: $6,373 **Librarians**: na *** students/librarian **Guidance Counselors**: na *** students/counselor	**% Amer Indian**: 0.6 **% Asian**: 4.0 **% Black**: 4.7 **% Hispanic**: 6.4 **% White**: 84.2	National ***Socio-Economic Status*** indicator percentile (100=high): 76th

Douglas County

ALEXANDRIA S.D.

BOX 308 ● ALEXANDRIA MN 56308-0308 ● (320) 762-2141

Grade Span: PK-12 **Schools**: *Regular* 8 ● *Spec Ed* 0 ● *Alt* 0 **Students**: 4,395 **Total Teachers**: na **Student/Classroom Teacher Ratio**: 20.0	**Expenditures/Student**: $5,424 **Librarians**: na *** students/librarian **Guidance Counselors**: na *** students/counselor	**% Amer Indian**: 0.1 **% Asian**: 0.6 **% Black**: 0.2 **% Hispanic**: 0.3 **% White**: 98.8	National ***Socio-Economic Status*** indicator percentile (100=high): 71st

Freeborn County

ALBERT LEA S.D.

109 WEST AVE. ● ALBERT LEA MN 56007-2477 ● (507) 377-5800 ● http://albertlea.k12.mn.us

Grade Span: PK-12 **Schools**: *Regular* 7 ● *Spec Ed* 0 ● *Alt* 1 **Students**: 4,267 **Total Teachers**: na **Student/Classroom Teacher Ratio**: 18.2	**Expenditures/Student**: $5,647 **Librarians**: na *** students/librarian **Guidance Counselors**: na *** students/counselor	**% Amer Indian**: 0.0 **% Asian**: 0.8 **% Black**: 0.2 **% Hispanic**: 6.5 **% White**: 92.5	National ***Socio-Economic Status*** indicator percentile (100=high): 56th

Goodhue County

RED WING S.D.

2451 EAGLE RIDGE DRIVE ● RED WING MN 55066 ● (612) 385-4500 ● http://www.redwing.k12.mn.us

Grade Span: PK-12 **Schools**: *Regular* 6 ● *Spec Ed* 0 ● *Alt* 2 **Students**: 3,536 **Total Teachers**: na **Student/Classroom Teacher Ratio**: 18.0	**Expenditures/Student**: $6,195 **Librarians**: na *** students/librarian **Guidance Counselors**: na *** students/counselor	**% Amer Indian**: 2.3 **% Asian**: 1.5 **% Black**: 1.3 **% Hispanic**: 0.5 **% White**: 94.5	National ***Socio-Economic Status*** indicator percentile (100=high): 77th

Hennepin County

BLOOMINGTON S.D.

8900 PORTLAND AVE. S. ● BLOOMINGTON MN 55420-2994 ● (612) 885-8450 ● http://www.bloomington.k12.mn.us

Grade Span: KG-12 **Schools**: *Regular* 15 ● *Spec Ed* 0 ● *Alt* 1 **Students**: 11,474 **Total Teachers**: na **Student/Classroom Teacher Ratio**: 21.0	**Expenditures/Student**: $6,854 **Librarians**: na *** students/librarian **Guidance Counselors**: na *** students/counselor	**% Amer Indian**: 0.5 **% Asian**: 7.7 **% Black**: 5.9 **% Hispanic**: 1.7 **% White**: 84.1	National ***Socio-Economic Status*** indicator percentile (100=high): 78th

Hennepin County

EDEN PRAIRIE S.D.

8100 SCHOOL RD. ● EDEN PRAIRIE MN 55344-2292 ● (612) 975-7000 ● http://www.edenpr.k12.mn.us

Grade Span: PK-12 **Schools**: *Regular* 8 ● *Spec Ed* 0 ● *Alt* 3 **Students**: 9,287 **Total Teachers**: na **Student/Classroom Teacher Ratio**: na	**Expenditures/Student**: $5,914 **Librarians**: na *** students/librarian **Guidance Counselors**: na *** students/counselor	**% Amer Indian**: 0.2 **% Asian**: 3.4 **% Black**: 1.5 **% Hispanic**: 0.9 **% White**: 94.1	National ***Socio-Economic Status*** indicator percentile (100=high): 96th

Hennepin County
EDINA S.D.
5701 NORMANDALE RD. ● EDINA MN 55424-1599 ● (612) 928-2500 ● http://www.edina.k12.mn.us

Grade Span: PK-12 **Schools**: *Regular* 9 ● *Spec Ed* 0 ● *Alt* 2 **Students**: 6,247 **Total Teachers**: na **Student/Classroom Teacher Ratio**: 26.9	**Expenditures/Student**: $6,933 **Librarians**: na *** students/librarian **Guidance Counselors**: na *** students/counselor	**% Amer Indian**: 0.2 **% Asian**: 3.2 **% Black**: 1.0 **% Hispanic**: 0.8 **% White**: 94.8	National ***Socio-Economic Status*** indicator percentile (100=high): 98th

Hennepin County
[EXCELSIOR] **MINNETONKA S.D.**
261 SCHOOL AVE. ● EXCELSIOR MN 55331-1987 ● (612) 470-3400 ● http://www.minnetonka.k12.mn.us

Grade Span: PK-12 **Schools**: *Regular* 9 ● *Spec Ed* 0 ● *Alt* 3 **Students**: 7,290 **Total Teachers**: na **Student/Classroom Teacher Ratio**: na	**Expenditures/Student**: $7,598 **Librarians**: na *** students/librarian **Guidance Counselors**: na *** students/counselor	**% Amer Indian**: 0.1 **% Asian**: 2.7 **% Black**: 1.1 **% Hispanic**: 1.2 **% White**: 94.9	National ***Socio-Economic Status*** indicator percentile (100=high): 97th

Hennepin County
HOPKINS S.D.
1001 HWY. 7 ● HOPKINS MN 55305-7294 ● (612) 988-4000 ● http://www.hopkins.k12.mn.us

Grade Span: KG-12 **Schools**: *Regular* 10 ● *Spec Ed* 0 ● *Alt* 4 **Students**: 8,097 **Total Teachers**: na **Student/Classroom Teacher Ratio**: 16.4	**Expenditures/Student**: $7,999 **Librarians**: na *** students/librarian **Guidance Counselors**: na *** students/counselor	**% Amer Indian**: 0.4 **% Asian**: 3.0 **% Black**: 3.0 **% Hispanic**: 1.7 **% White**: 91.9	National ***Socio-Economic Status*** indicator percentile (100=high): 85th

Hennepin County
[LONG LAKE] **ORONO S.D.**
BOX 46, 685 OLD CRYSTAL BAY ● LONG LAKE MN 55356-0046 ● (612) 449-8300

Grade Span: PK-12 **Schools**: *Regular* 4 ● *Spec Ed* 0 ● *Alt* 1 **Students**: 2,589 **Total Teachers**: na **Student/Classroom Teacher Ratio**: 18.3	**Expenditures/Student**: $6,617 **Librarians**: na *** students/librarian **Guidance Counselors**: na *** students/counselor	**% Amer Indian**: 0.3 **% Asian**: 1.2 **% Black**: 0.7 **% Hispanic**: 0.5 **% White**: 97.3	National ***Socio-Economic Status*** indicator percentile (100=high): 97th

Hennepin County
[MAPLE GROVE] **OSSEO S.D.**
11200 93RD AVE. N. ● MAPLE GROVE MN 55369-6605 ● (612) 391-7000 ● http://www.osseo.k12.mn.us

Grade Span: PK-12 **Schools**: *Regular* 26 ● *Spec Ed* 0 ● *Alt* 5 **Students**: 21,479 **Total Teachers**: na **Student/Classroom Teacher Ratio**: 19.6	**Expenditures/Student**: $6,102 **Librarians**: na *** students/librarian **Guidance Counselors**: na *** students/counselor	**% Amer Indian**: 0.5 **% Asian**: 5.0 **% Black**: 8.1 **% Hispanic**: 1.1 **% White**: 85.2	National ***Socio-Economic Status*** indicator percentile (100=high): 80th

Hennepin County
MINNEAPOLIS S.D.
807 N.E. BROADWAY ● MINNEAPOLIS MN 55413-2398 ● (612) 627-2050 ● http://www.mpls.k12.mn.us

Grade Span: PK-12 **Schools**: *Regular* 70 ● *Spec Ed* 4 ● *Alt* 70 **Students**: 46,612 **Total Teachers**: na **Student/Classroom Teacher Ratio**: na	**Expenditures/Student**: $8,350 **Librarians**: na *** students/librarian **Guidance Counselors**: na *** students/counselor	**% Amer Indian**: 5.8 **% Asian**: 13.0 **% Black**: 39.6 **% Hispanic**: 4.5 **% White**: 37.1	National ***Socio-Economic Status*** indicator percentile (100=high): 12th

Hennepin County

[NEW HOPE] **ROBBINSDALE S.D.**

4148 WINNETKA AVE. N. ● NEW HOPE MN 55427-1288 ● (612) 533-2781

Grade Span: PK-12 **Schools**: *Regular* 19 ● *Spec Ed* 1 ● *Alt* 8 **Students**: 13,595 **Total Teachers**: na **Student/Classroom Teacher Ratio**: 19.5	**Expenditures/Student**: $7,061 **Librarians**: na *** students/librarian **Guidance Counselors**: na *** students/counselor	**% Amer Indian**: 1.5 **% Asian**: 4.6 **% Black**: 7.0 **% Hispanic**: 1.8 **% White**: 85.1	National ***Socio-Economic Status*** indicator percentile (100=high): 67th

Hennepin County

RICHFIELD S.D.

7001 HARRIET AVE. S. ● RICHFIELD MN 55423-3000 ● (612) 798-6000 ● http://www.richfield.k12.mn.us

Grade Span: PK-12 **Schools**: *Regular* 6 ● *Spec Ed* 1 ● *Alt* 1 **Students**: 4,393 **Total Teachers**: na **Student/Classroom Teacher Ratio**: 17.8	**Expenditures/Student**: $7,447 **Librarians**: na *** students/librarian **Guidance Counselors**: na *** students/counselor	**% Amer Indian**: 1.3 **% Asian**: 6.6 **% Black**: 11.4 **% Hispanic**: 3.2 **% White**: 77.4	National ***Socio-Economic Status*** indicator percentile (100=high): 66th

Hennepin County

ST. LOUIS PARK S.D.

6425 W. 33RD ST. ● ST. LOUIS PARK MN 55426-3498 ● (612) 928-6001

Grade Span: PK-12 **Schools**: *Regular* 6 ● *Spec Ed* 0 ● *Alt* 2 **Students**: 4,301 **Total Teachers**: na **Student/Classroom Teacher Ratio**: 17.8	**Expenditures/Student**: $9,018 **Librarians**: na *** students/librarian **Guidance Counselors**: na *** students/counselor	**% Amer Indian**: 0.6 **% Asian**: 3.4 **% Black**: 7.5 **% Hispanic**: 1.7 **% White**: 86.9	National ***Socio-Economic Status*** indicator percentile (100=high): 66th

Hennepin County

WAYZATA S.D.

BOX 660 ● WAYZATA MN 55391-9990 ● (612) 476-3100 ● http://www.wayzata.k12.mn.us

Grade Span: PK-12 **Schools**: *Regular* 10 ● *Spec Ed* 0 ● *Alt* 0 **Students**: 8,098 **Total Teachers**: na **Student/Classroom Teacher Ratio**: 20.5	**Expenditures/Student**: $6,535 **Librarians**: na *** students/librarian **Guidance Counselors**: na *** students/counselor	**% Amer Indian**: 0.5 **% Asian**: 3.0 **% Black**: 1.5 **% Hispanic**: 1.1 **% White**: 93.8	National ***Socio-Economic Status*** indicator percentile (100=high): 93rd

Isanti County

CAMBRIDGE-ISANTI S.D.

315 7TH LANE N.E. ● CAMBRIDGE MN 55008-1269 ● (612) 689-4988

Grade Span: PK-12 **Schools**: *Regular* 5 ● *Spec Ed* 0 ● *Alt* 0 **Students**: 4,657 **Total Teachers**: na **Student/Classroom Teacher Ratio**: 20.0	**Expenditures/Student**: $5,588 **Librarians**: na *** students/librarian **Guidance Counselors**: na *** students/counselor	**% Amer Indian**: 0.7 **% Asian**: 1.0 **% Black**: 0.4 **% Hispanic**: 0.7 **% White**: 97.1	National ***Socio-Economic Status*** indicator percentile (100=high): 65th

Itasca County

GRAND RAPIDS S.D.

820 N. POKEGAMA AVE. ● GRAND RAPIDS MN 55744-2687 ● (218) 327-2261

Grade Span: PK-12 **Schools**: *Regular* 11 ● *Spec Ed* 0 ● *Alt* 6 **Students**: 5,056 **Total Teachers**: na **Student/Classroom Teacher Ratio**: na	**Expenditures/Student**: $6,601 **Librarians**: na *** students/librarian **Guidance Counselors**: na *** students/counselor	**% Amer Indian**: 3.7 **% Asian**: 0.5 **% Black**: 0.1 **% Hispanic**: 0.6 **% White**: 95.1	National ***Socio-Economic Status*** indicator percentile (100=high): 58th

Kandiyohi County

WILLMAR S.D.

611 S.W. 5TH ST. • WILLMAR MN 56201-3297 • (320) 231-1100

Grade Span: PK-12 **Schools**: *Regular* 7 • *Spec Ed* 0 • *Alt* 5 **Students**: 4,923 **Total Teachers**: na **Student/Classroom Teacher Ratio**: 15.5	**Expenditures/Student**: $6,573 **Librarians**: na *** students/librarian **Guidance Counselors**: na *** students/counselor	**% Amer Indian**: 0.5 **% Asian**: 0.7 **% Black**: 0.7 **% Hispanic**: 16.4 **% White**: 81.7	National ***Socio-Economic Status*** indicator percentile (100=high): 44th

McLeod County

HUTCHINSON S.D.

30 GLEN ST. N. • HUTCHINSON MN 55350-1696 • (320) 587-2860

Grade Span: PK-12 **Schools**: *Regular* 4 • *Spec Ed* 0 • *Alt* 1 **Students**: 3,214 **Total Teachers**: na **Student/Classroom Teacher Ratio**: 20.2	**Expenditures/Student**: $5,632 **Librarians**: na *** students/librarian **Guidance Counselors**: na *** students/counselor	**% Amer Indian**: 0.2 **% Asian**: 0.7 **% Black**: 0.4 **% Hispanic**: 1.6 **% White**: 97.1	National ***Socio-Economic Status*** indicator percentile (100=high): 95th

Mille Lacs County

PRINCETON S.D.

706 1ST ST. • PRINCETON MN 55371 • (612) 389-6901

Grade Span: PK-12 **Schools**: *Regular* 4 • *Spec Ed* 0 • *Alt* 0 **Students**: 3,012 **Total Teachers**: na **Student/Classroom Teacher Ratio**: 19.2	**Expenditures/Student**: $5,496 **Librarians**: na *** students/librarian **Guidance Counselors**: na *** students/counselor	**% Amer Indian**: 1.2 **% Asian**: 0.8 **% Black**: 0.3 **% Hispanic**: 0.8 **% White**: 96.8	National ***Socio-Economic Status*** indicator percentile (100=high): 72nd

Morrison County

LITTLE FALLS S.D.

1001 S.E. 5TH AVE. • LITTLE FALLS MN 56345-3398 • (320) 632-5709 • http://www.lfalls.k12.mn.us

Grade Span: KG-12 **Schools**: *Regular* 5 • *Spec Ed* 0 • *Alt* 0 **Students**: 3,618 **Total Teachers**: na **Student/Classroom Teacher Ratio**: 17.6	**Expenditures/Student**: $5,999 **Librarians**: na *** students/librarian **Guidance Counselors**: na *** students/counselor	**% Amer Indian**: 0.5 **% Asian**: 0.6 **% Black**: 0.5 **% Hispanic**: 0.4 **% White**: 98.0	National ***Socio-Economic Status*** indicator percentile (100=high): 42nd

Mower County

AUSTIN S.D.

202 4TH AVE. N.E. • AUSTIN MN 55912 • (507) 433-0966

Grade Span: PK-12 **Schools**: *Regular* 6 • *Spec Ed* 0 • *Alt* 4 **Students**: 4,336 **Total Teachers**: na **Student/Classroom Teacher Ratio**: 18.2	**Expenditures/Student**: $6,632 **Librarians**: na *** students/librarian **Guidance Counselors**: na *** students/counselor	**% Amer Indian**: 0.1 **% Asian**: 2.0 **% Black**: 0.5 **% Hispanic**: 2.1 **% White**: 95.3	National ***Socio-Economic Status*** indicator percentile (100=high): 60th

Nobles County

WORTHINGTON S.D.

BOX 878, 1117 MARINE AVE. • WORTHINGTON MN 56187-0878 • (507) 372-2172

Grade Span: PK-12 **Schools**: *Regular* 4 • *Spec Ed* 1 • *Alt* 2 **Students**: 2,522 **Total Teachers**: na **Student/Classroom Teacher Ratio**: na	**Expenditures/Student**: $6,728 **Librarians**: na *** students/librarian **Guidance Counselors**: na *** students/counselor	**% Amer Indian**: 0.3 **% Asian**: 9.6 **% Black**: 1.3 **% Hispanic**: 7.8 **% White**: 81.0	National ***Socio-Economic Status*** indicator percentile (100=high): 49th

Olmsted County

ROCHESTER S.D.

615 S.W. 7TH ST. ● ROCHESTER MN 55902 ● (507) 285-8551

Grade Span: PK-12	**Expenditures/Student**: $6,216	**% Amer Indian**: 0.2	
Schools: *Regular* 22 ● *Spec Ed* 1 ● *Alt* 6	**Librarians**: na	**% Asian**: 8.1	National ***Socio-Economic***
Students: 15,247	*** students/librarian	**% Black**: 3.2	***Status*** indicator percentile
Total Teachers: na	**Guidance Counselors**: na	**% Hispanic**: 1.7	(100=high): 69th
Student/Classroom Teacher Ratio: 18.7	*** students/counselor	**% White**: 86.8	

Otter Tail County

FERGUS FALLS S.D.

4B EAST DR. ● FERGUS FALLS MN 56537-4104 ● (218) 736-7576

Grade Span: KG-12	**Expenditures/Student**: $5,533	**% Amer Indian**: 0.7	
Schools: *Regular* 6 ● *Spec Ed* 0 ● *Alt* 1	**Librarians**: na	**% Asian**: 1.0	National ***Socio-Economic***
Students: 3,411	*** students/librarian	**% Black**: 0.3	***Status*** indicator percentile
Total Teachers: na	**Guidance Counselors**: na	**% Hispanic**: 0.6	(100=high): 69th
Student/Classroom Teacher Ratio: 19.1	*** students/counselor	**% White**: 97.5	

Ramsey County

[MAPLEWOOD] **NORTH ST. PAUL-MAPLEWOOD S.D.**

1801 BEEBE RD. ● MAPLEWOOD MN 55109 ● (612) 770-4601 ● http://www.metro2.k12.mn.us/~Wnstpaul/dist622.html

Grade Span: PK-12	**Expenditures/Student**: $6,259	**% Amer Indian**: 0.5	
Schools: *Regular* 14 ● *Spec Ed* 0 ● *Alt* 2	**Librarians**: na	**% Asian**: 3.1	National ***Socio-Economic***
Students: 10,725	*** students/librarian	**% Black**: 2.2	***Status*** indicator percentile
Total Teachers: na	**Guidance Counselors**: na	**% Hispanic**: 1.6	(100=high): 77th
Student/Classroom Teacher Ratio: 33.3	*** students/counselor	**% White**: 92.7	

Ramsey County

ROSEVILLE S.D.

1251 W. COUNTY RD. B-2 ● ROSEVILLE MN 55113-3299 ● (612) 635-1600 ● http://www.roseville.k12.mn.us

Grade Span: PK-12	**Expenditures/Student**: $7,362	**% Amer Indian**: 0.7	
Schools: *Regular* 9 ● *Spec Ed* 0 ● *Alt* 1	**Librarians**: na	**% Asian**: 7.5	National ***Socio-Economic***
Students: 6,829	*** students/librarian	**% Black**: 4.3	***Status*** indicator percentile
Total Teachers: na	**Guidance Counselors**: na	**% Hispanic**: 1.9	(100=high): 74th
Student/Classroom Teacher Ratio: 18.6	*** students/counselor	**% White**: 85.7	

Ramsey County

[ST. PAUL] **MOUNDS VIEW S.D.**

2959 HAMLINE AVE. N. ● ST. PAUL MN 55113-1664 ● (612) 636-3650 ● http://district.moundsview.k12.mn.us

Grade Span: PK-12	**Expenditures/Student**: $6,362	**% Amer Indian**: 0.9	
Schools: *Regular* 13 ● *Spec Ed* 1 ● *Alt* 8	**Librarians**: na	**% Asian**: 5.3	National ***Socio-Economic***
Students: 12,148	*** students/librarian	**% Black**: 1.7	***Status*** indicator percentile
Total Teachers: na	**Guidance Counselors**: na	**% Hispanic**: 1.3	(100=high): 88th
Student/Classroom Teacher Ratio: na	*** students/counselor	**% White**: 90.9	

Ramsey County

ST. PAUL S.D.

360 COLBORNE ST. ● ST. PAUL MN 55102 ● (612) 293-5100 ● http://www.stpaul.k12.mn.us

Grade Span: PK-12	**Expenditures/Student**: $7,116	**% Amer Indian**: 1.3	
Schools: *Regular* 55 ● *Spec Ed* 2 ● *Alt* 85	**Librarians**: na	**% Asian**: 25.1	National ***Socio-Economic***
Students: 42,520	*** students/librarian	**% Black**: 21.1	***Status*** indicator percentile
Total Teachers: na	**Guidance Counselors**: na	**% Hispanic**: 6.8	(100=high): 15th
Student/Classroom Teacher Ratio: na	*** students/counselor	**% White**: 45.7	

Ramsey County

WHITE BEAR LAKE S.D.

3554 WHITE BEAR AVE. ● WHITE BEAR LAKE MN 55110-5418 ● (612) 773-6101 ● http://wblwww.whitebear.k12.mn.us

Grade Span: PK-12 **Schools**: *Regular* 13 ● *Spec Ed* 0 ● *Alt* 3 **Students**: 9,700 **Total Teachers**: na **Student/Classroom Teacher Ratio**: 21.8	**Expenditures/Student**: $6,096 **Librarians**: na *** students/librarian **Guidance Counselors**: na *** students/counselor	**% Amer Indian**: 0.2 **% Asian**: 2.0 **% Black**: 0.8 **% Hispanic**: 0.7 **% White**: 96.4	National ***Socio-Economic Status*** indicator percentile (100=high): 87th

Rice County

FARIBAULT S.D.

BOX 618, 2855 N.W. 1ST AVE. ● FARIBAULT MN 55021-0618 ● (507) 334-2291 ● http://www.faribault.k12.mn.us

Grade Span: PK-12 **Schools**: *Regular* 8 ● *Spec Ed* 0 ● *Alt* 2 **Students**: 4,320 **Total Teachers**: na **Student/Classroom Teacher Ratio**: na	**Expenditures/Student**: $6,724 **Librarians**: na *** students/librarian **Guidance Counselors**: na *** students/counselor	**% Amer Indian**: 0.4 **% Asian**: 2.6 **% Black**: 0.5 **% Hispanic**: 3.4 **% White**: 93.2	National ***Socio-Economic Status*** indicator percentile (100=high): 65th

Rice County

NORTHFIELD S.D.

1400 DIVISION ST. S. ● NORTHFIELD MN 55057 ● (507) 663-0629 ● http://www.nfld.k12.mn.us

Grade Span: PK-12 **Schools**: *Regular* 5 ● *Spec Ed* 0 ● *Alt* 2 **Students**: 3,575 **Total Teachers**: na **Student/Classroom Teacher Ratio**: 15.8	**Expenditures/Student**: $6,074 **Librarians**: na *** students/librarian **Guidance Counselors**: na *** students/counselor	**% Amer Indian**: 0.3 **% Asian**: 1.7 **% Black**: 0.3 **% Hispanic**: 1.8 **% White**: 95.9	National ***Socio-Economic Status*** indicator percentile (100=high): 83rd

St. Louis County

DULUTH S.D.

215 NO. 1ST AVE. E. ● DULUTH MN 55802-2069 ● (218) 723-4150 ● http://www.duluth.k12.mn.us

Grade Span: PK-12 **Schools**: *Regular* 20 ● *Spec Ed* 0 ● *Alt* 19 **Students**: 14,017 **Total Teachers**: na **Student/Classroom Teacher Ratio**: 20.0	**Expenditures/Student**: $6,580 **Librarians**: na *** students/librarian **Guidance Counselors**: na *** students/counselor	**% Amer Indian**: 4.1 **% Asian**: 1.9 **% Black**: 2.4 **% Hispanic**: 0.9 **% White**: 90.8	National ***Socio-Economic Status*** indicator percentile (100=high): 54th

St. Louis County

HIBBING S.D.

8TH AVE. E. & 21ST ST. ● HIBBING MN 55746-1803 ● (218) 263-4850

Grade Span: PK-12 **Schools**: *Regular* 6 ● *Spec Ed* 0 ● *Alt* 3 **Students**: 3,471 **Total Teachers**: na **Student/Classroom Teacher Ratio**: 20.7	**Expenditures/Student**: $5,999 **Librarians**: na *** students/librarian **Guidance Counselors**: na *** students/counselor	**% Amer Indian**: 1.0 **% Asian**: 0.4 **% Black**: 0.2 **% Hispanic**: 0.3 **% White**: 98.1	National ***Socio-Economic Status*** indicator percentile (100=high): 62nd

St. Louis County

[VIRGINIA] **ST. LOUIS COUNTY S.D.**

731 3RD ST. S. ● VIRGINIA MN 55792-3099 ● (218) 749-8130

Grade Span: PK-12 **Schools**: *Regular* 14 ● *Spec Ed* 1 ● *Alt* 0 **Students**: 3,082 **Total Teachers**: na **Student/Classroom Teacher Ratio**: 14.5	**Expenditures/Student**: $7,045 **Librarians**: na *** students/librarian **Guidance Counselors**: na *** students/counselor	**% Amer Indian**: 9.7 **% Asian**: 0.4 **% Black**: 0.3 **% Hispanic**: 0.5 **% White**: 89.1	National ***Socio-Economic Status*** indicator percentile (100=high): 43rd

Scott County

PRIOR LAKE S.D.

BOX 539 ● PRIOR LAKE MN 55372 ● (612) 447-2185

Grade Span: PK-12 **Schools**: *Regular* 6 ● *Spec Ed* 0 ● *Alt* 1 **Students**: 3,872 **Total Teachers**: na **Student/Classroom Teacher Ratio**: 21.0	**Expenditures/Student**: $5,621 **Librarians**: na *** students/librarian **Guidance Counselors**: na *** students/counselor	**% Amer Indian**: 0.6 **% Asian**: 0.5 **% Black**: 0.2 **% Hispanic**: 0.5 **% White**: 98.2	National ***Socio-Economic Status*** indicator percentile (100=high): 92nd

Scott County

SHAKOPEE S.D.

505 HOLMES ST. S. ● SHAKOPEE MN 55379-1384 ● (612) 496-5000

Grade Span: PK-12 **Schools**: *Regular* 5 ● *Spec Ed* 0 ● *Alt* 0 **Students**: 3,057 **Total Teachers**: na **Student/Classroom Teacher Ratio**: 17.2	**Expenditures/Student**: $6,875 **Librarians**: na *** students/librarian **Guidance Counselors**: na *** students/counselor	**% Amer Indian**: 2.5 **% Asian**: 1.7 **% Black**: 0.8 **% Hispanic**: 2.1 **% White**: 92.9	National ***Socio-Economic Status*** indicator percentile (100=high): 84th

Sherburne County

ELK RIVER S.D.

400 SCHOOL ST. ● ELK RIVER MN 55330-1391 ● (612) 241-3400 ● http://www.elkriver.k12.mn.us

Grade Span: PK-12 **Schools**: *Regular* 10 ● *Spec Ed* 0 ● *Alt* 1 **Students**: 7,813 **Total Teachers**: na **Student/Classroom Teacher Ratio**: 20.5	**Expenditures/Student**: $5,724 **Librarians**: na *** students/librarian **Guidance Counselors**: na *** students/counselor	**% Amer Indian**: 1.4 **% Asian**: 0.7 **% Black**: 0.3 **% Hispanic**: 0.6 **% White**: 97.0	National ***Socio-Economic Status*** indicator percentile (100=high): 86th

Stearns County

ST. CLOUD S.D.

628 ROOSEVELT RD. ● ST. CLOUD MN 56301-4898 ● (320) 253-9333

Grade Span: PK-12 **Schools**: *Regular* 15 ● *Spec Ed* 1 ● *Alt* 4 **Students**: 11,690 **Total Teachers**: na **Student/Classroom Teacher Ratio**: na	**Expenditures/Student**: $5,655 **Librarians**: na *** students/librarian **Guidance Counselors**: na *** students/counselor	**% Amer Indian**: 0.5 **% Asian**: 2.5 **% Black**: 1.0 **% Hispanic**: 0.5 **% White**: 95.6	National ***Socio-Economic Status*** indicator percentile (100=high): 64th

Steele County

OWATONNA S.D.

515 W. BRIDGE ST. ● OWATONNA MN 55060-2816 ● (507) 455-8612

Grade Span: PK-12 **Schools**: *Regular* 7 ● *Spec Ed* 0 ● *Alt* 1 **Students**: 4,827 **Total Teachers**: na **Student/Classroom Teacher Ratio**: na	**Expenditures/Student**: $5,476 **Librarians**: na *** students/librarian **Guidance Counselors**: na *** students/counselor	**% Amer Indian**: 0.1 **% Asian**: 2.0 **% Black**: 0.5 **% Hispanic**: 2.2 **% White**: 95.3	National ***Socio-Economic Status*** indicator percentile (100=high): 73rd

Washington County

[COTTAGE GROVE] **SOUTH WASHINGTON COUNTY S.D.**

7362 E. POINT DOUGLAS RD. S ● COTTAGE GROVE MN 55016-3025 ● (612) 458-6300 ● http://www.sowashco.k12.mn.us

Grade Span: PK-12 **Schools**: *Regular* 17 ● *Spec Ed* 0 ● *Alt* 3 **Students**: 13,978 **Total Teachers**: na **Student/Classroom Teacher Ratio**: 21.5	**Expenditures/Student**: $5,167 **Librarians**: na *** students/librarian **Guidance Counselors**: na *** students/counselor	**% Amer Indian**: 0.4 **% Asian**: 2.4 **% Black**: 1.9 **% Hispanic**: 1.7 **% White**: 93.6	National ***Socio-Economic Status*** indicator percentile (100=high): 86th

Washington County
FOREST LAKE S.D.
6100 210TH ST. N. ● FOREST LAKE MN 55025-9796 ● (612) 464-9100 ● http://www.forestlake.k12.mn.us

Grade Span: PK-12 **Schools**: *Regular* 10 ● *Spec Ed* 1 ● *Alt* 3 **Students**: 7,931 **Total Teachers**: na **Student/Classroom Teacher Ratio**: 19.8	**Expenditures/Student**: $5,404 **Librarians**: na *** students/librarian **Guidance Counselors**: na *** students/counselor	**% Amer Indian**: 0.6 **% Asian**: 1.2 **% Black**: 0.4 **% Hispanic**: 0.5 **% White**: 97.3	National ***Socio-Economic Status*** indicator percentile (100=high): 82nd

Washington County
MAHTOMEDI S.D.
1520 MAHTOMEDI AVE. ● MAHTOMEDI MN 55115-1900 ● (612) 426-3224

Grade Span: PK-12 **Schools**: *Regular* 4 ● *Spec Ed* 0 ● *Alt* 1 **Students**: 2,699 **Total Teachers**: na **Student/Classroom Teacher Ratio**: 19.5	**Expenditures/Student**: $5,621 **Librarians**: na *** students/librarian **Guidance Counselors**: na *** students/counselor	**% Amer Indian**: 0.0 **% Asian**: 1.1 **% Black**: 0.4 **% Hispanic**: 1.2 **% White**: 97.2	National ***Socio-Economic Status*** indicator percentile (100=high): 94th

Washington County
STILLWATER S.D.
1875 GREELEY ST. S. ● STILLWATER MN 55082-6094 ● (612) 351-8301 ● http://galileo.stillwater.k12.mn.us/isd834

Grade Span: PK-12 **Schools**: *Regular* 12 ● *Spec Ed* 0 ● *Alt* 5 **Students**: 9,129 **Total Teachers**: na **Student/Classroom Teacher Ratio**: 20.9	**Expenditures/Student**: $5,970 **Librarians**: na *** students/librarian **Guidance Counselors**: na *** students/counselor	**% Amer Indian**: 0.2 **% Asian**: 1.3 **% Black**: 0.5 **% Hispanic**: 0.5 **% White**: 97.4	National ***Socio-Economic Status*** indicator percentile (100=high): 93rd

Winona County
WINONA S.D.
654 HUFF ● WINONA MN 55987-3320 ● (507) 454-9461 ● http://www.winonanet.com/schools/isd861.html

Grade Span: PK-12 **Schools**: *Regular* 10 ● *Spec Ed* 1 ● *Alt* 4 **Students**: 4,691 **Total Teachers**: na **Student/Classroom Teacher Ratio**: 15.1	**Expenditures/Student**: $6,049 **Librarians**: na *** students/librarian **Guidance Counselors**: na *** students/counselor	**% Amer Indian**: 0.1 **% Asian**: 3.4 **% Black**: 1.4 **% Hispanic**: 0.7 **% White**: 94.3	National ***Socio-Economic Status*** indicator percentile (100=high): 64th

Wright County
BUFFALO S.D.
214 N.E. 1ST AVE. ● BUFFALO MN 55313-1697 ● (612) 682-5200 ● http://www.buffalo.k12.mn.us/district/default.shtml

Grade Span: PK-12 **Schools**: *Regular* 6 ● *Spec Ed* 0 ● *Alt* 0 **Students**: 4,591 **Total Teachers**: na **Student/Classroom Teacher Ratio**: 18.1	**Expenditures/Student**: $5,531 **Librarians**: na *** students/librarian **Guidance Counselors**: na *** students/counselor	**% Amer Indian**: 0.1 **% Asian**: 0.8 **% Black**: 0.3 **% Hispanic**: 0.5 **% White**: 98.3	National ***Socio-Economic Status*** indicator percentile (100=high): 80th

Wright County
MONTICELLO S.D.
BOX 897 ● MONTICELLO MN 55362 ● (612) 295-5184 ● http://www.montitimes.com/school

Grade Span: PK-12 **Schools**: *Regular* 4 ● *Spec Ed* 0 ● *Alt* 1 **Students**: 3,494 **Total Teachers**: na **Student/Classroom Teacher Ratio**: 16.5	**Expenditures/Student**: $6,475 **Librarians**: na *** students/librarian **Guidance Counselors**: na *** students/counselor	**% Amer Indian**: 0.2 **% Asian**: 1.3 **% Black**: 0.5 **% Hispanic**: 0.7 **% White**: 97.4	National ***Socio-Economic Status*** indicator percentile (100=high): 76th

Adams County

NATCHEZ ADAMS S.D.

10 HOMOCHITTO ST ● NATCHEZ MS 39121-1188 ● (601) 445-2800

Grade Span: PK-12 **Schools**: *Regular* 6 ● *Spec Ed* 0 ● *Alt* 2 **Students**: 5,658 **Total Teachers**: 297 **Student/Classroom Teacher Ratio**: 20.6	**Expenditures/Student**: $4,103 **Librarians**: 8.0 707 students/librarian **Guidance Counselors**: 12.4 456 students/counselor	**% Amer Indian**: 0.0 **% Asian**: 0.0 **% Black**: 77.1 **% Hispanic**: 0.0 **% White**: 22.9	National ***Socio-Economic Status*** indicator percentile (100=high): 4th

Alcorn County

[CORINTH] ALCORN S.D.

P O BOX 1420 ● CORINTH MS 38834 ● (601) 286-5591

Grade Span: KG-12 **Schools**: *Regular* 9 ● *Spec Ed* 0 ● *Alt* 2 **Students**: 3,803 **Total Teachers**: 251 **Student/Classroom Teacher Ratio**: 15.6	**Expenditures/Student**: $4,020 **Librarians**: 6.0 634 students/librarian **Guidance Counselors**: 5.4 704 students/counselor	**% Amer Indian**: 0.0 **% Asian**: 0.2 **% Black**: 5.0 **% Hispanic**: 0.2 **% White**: 94.5	National ***Socio-Economic Status*** indicator percentile (100=high): 37th

Bolivar County

CLEVELAND S.D.

305 MERRITT DRIVE ● CLEVELAND MS 38732 ● (601) 843-3529

Grade Span: KG-12 **Schools**: *Regular* 10 ● *Spec Ed* 0 ● *Alt* 1 **Students**: 4,460 **Total Teachers**: 250 **Student/Classroom Teacher Ratio**: 18.3	**Expenditures/Student**: $3,624 **Librarians**: 6.7 666 students/librarian **Guidance Counselors**: 8.8 507 students/counselor	**% Amer Indian**: 0.0 **% Asian**: 0.4 **% Black**: 71.6 **% Hispanic**: 0.5 **% White**: 27.6	National ***Socio-Economic Status*** indicator percentile (100=high): 8th

Calhoun County

[PITTSBORO] CALHOUN COUNTY S.D.

CALHOUN COUNTY COURTHOUSE ● PITTSBORO MS 38951 ● (601) 983-3152

Grade Span: KG-12 **Schools**: *Regular* 8 ● *Spec Ed* 0 ● *Alt* 0 **Students**: 2,725 **Total Teachers**: 158 **Student/Classroom Teacher Ratio**: 17.2	**Expenditures/Student**: $3,907 **Librarians**: 5.0 545 students/librarian **Guidance Counselors**: 6.0 454 students/counselor	**% Amer Indian**: 0.0 **% Asian**: 0.1 **% Black**: 42.3 **% Hispanic**: 0.9 **% White**: 56.7	National ***Socio-Economic Status*** indicator percentile (100=high): 13th

Clarke County

QUITMAN S.D.

312 E FRANKLIN STREET ● QUITMAN MS 39355 ● (601) 776-2186

Grade Span: KG-12 **Schools**: *Regular* 4 ● *Spec Ed* 0 ● *Alt* 1 **Students**: 2,702 **Total Teachers**: 146 **Student/Classroom Teacher Ratio**: 19.3	**Expenditures/Student**: $3,456 **Librarians**: 4.0 676 students/librarian **Guidance Counselors**: 2.9 932 students/counselor	**% Amer Indian**: 0.0 **% Asian**: 0.0 **% Black**: 55.3 **% Hispanic**: 0.1 **% White**: 44.6	National ***Socio-Economic Status*** indicator percentile (100=high): 10th

Clay County

WEST POINT S.D.

429 COMMERCE STREET ● WEST POINT MS 39773 ● (601) 494-4242

Grade Span: PK-12 **Schools**: *Regular* 7 ● *Spec Ed* 0 ● *Alt* 1 **Students**: 3,843 **Total Teachers**: 213 **Student/Classroom Teacher Ratio**: 18.6	**Expenditures/Student**: $3,464 **Librarians**: 4.0 961 students/librarian **Guidance Counselors**: 7.0 549 students/counselor	**% Amer Indian**: 0.0 **% Asian**: 0.1 **% Black**: 76.3 **% Hispanic**: 0.2 **% White**: 23.4	National ***Socio-Economic Status*** indicator percentile (100=high): 5th

Coahoma County

CLARKSDALE SEPARATE S.D.

101 MCGUIRE STREET ● CLARKSDALE MS 38614 ● (601) 627-8500 ● http://www.tilc.com/~dakota/cps

Grade Span: KG-12 **Schools**: *Regular* 11 ● *Spec Ed* 0 ● *Alt* 1 **Students**: 4,383 **Total Teachers**: 237 **Student/Classroom Teacher Ratio**: 19.2	**Expenditures/Student**: $3,404 **Librarians**: 9.0 487 students/librarian **Guidance Counselors**: 4.0 1,096 students/counselor	**% Amer Indian**: 0.0 **% Asian**: 0.3 **% Black**: 78.3 **% Hispanic**: 0.2 **% White**: 21.2	National ***Socio-Economic Status*** indicator percentile (100=high): 3rd

Copiah County

[HAZLEHURST] **COPIAH COUNTY S.D.**

254 W GALLATIN STREET ● HAZLEHURST MS 39083 ● (601) 894-1341

Grade Span: KG-12 **Schools**: *Regular* 5 ● *Spec Ed* 0 ● *Alt* 0 **Students**: 3,331 **Total Teachers**: 183 **Student/Classroom Teacher Ratio**: 17.9	**Expenditures/Student**: $3,664 **Librarians**: 4.0 833 students/librarian **Guidance Counselors**: 3.6 925 students/counselor	**% Amer Indian**: 0.1 **% Asian**: 0.1 **% Black**: 61.9 **% Hispanic**: 0.2 **% White**: 37.7	National ***Socio-Economic Status*** indicator percentile (100=high): 6th

Covington County

[COLLINS] **COVINGTON COUNTY S.D.**

P O BOX 1269 ● COLLINS MS 39428 ● (601) 765-8247

Grade Span: KG-12 **Schools**: *Regular* 6 ● *Spec Ed* 0 ● *Alt* 1 **Students**: 3,650 **Total Teachers**: 218 **Student/Classroom Teacher Ratio**: 17.3	**Expenditures/Student**: $3,575 **Librarians**: 6.0 608 students/librarian **Guidance Counselors**: 7.9 462 students/counselor	**% Amer Indian**: 0.0 **% Asian**: 0.0 **% Black**: 50.4 **% Hispanic**: 0.0 **% White**: 49.6	National ***Socio-Economic Status*** indicator percentile (100=high): 9th

DeSoto County

[HERNANDO] **DESOTO COUNTY S.D.**

425 E COMMERCE STREET ● HERNANDO MS 38632 ● (601) 429-5271

Grade Span: KG-12 **Schools**: *Regular* 17 ● *Spec Ed* 0 ● *Alt* 2 **Students**: 15,907 **Total Teachers**: 822 **Student/Classroom Teacher Ratio**: 19.4	**Expenditures/Student**: $3,085 **Librarians**: 18.7 851 students/librarian **Guidance Counselors**: 30.0 530 students/counselor	**% Amer Indian**: 0.1 **% Asian**: 0.3 **% Black**: 16.6 **% Hispanic**: 0.5 **% White**: 82.5	National ***Socio-Economic Status*** indicator percentile (100=high): 56th

Forrest County

[HATTIESBURG] **FORREST COUNTY S.D.**

P O BOX 1977 ● HATTIESBURG MS 39403-1977 ● (601) 545-6055

Grade Span: KG-12 **Schools**: *Regular* 6 ● *Spec Ed* 0 ● *Alt* 0 **Students**: 2,561 **Total Teachers**: 181 **Student/Classroom Teacher Ratio**: 14.3	**Expenditures/Student**: $4,029 **Librarians**: 4.3 596 students/librarian **Guidance Counselors**: 1.0 2,561 students/counselor	**% Amer Indian**: 0.0 **% Asian**: 0.1 **% Black**: 36.9 **% Hispanic**: 0.0 **% White**: 63.1	National ***Socio-Economic Status*** indicator percentile (100=high): 17th

Forrest County

HATTIESBURG PUBLIC S.D.

P O BOX 1569 301 MAMIE STREET ● HATTIESBURG MS 39403-1569 ● (601) 584-6283 ● http://www2.mdek12.state.ms.us/1820

Grade Span: KG-12 **Schools**: *Regular* 8 ● *Spec Ed* 0 ● *Alt* 0 **Students**: 5,355 **Total Teachers**: 340 **Student/Classroom Teacher Ratio**: 16.1	**Expenditures/Student**: $4,539 **Librarians**: 9.0 595 students/librarian **Guidance Counselors**: 11.0 487 students/counselor	**% Amer Indian**: 0.0 **% Asian**: 0.8 **% Black**: 77.1 **% Hispanic**: 0.2 **% White**: 21.9	National ***Socio-Economic Status*** indicator percentile (100=high): 4th

Forrest County

PETAL S.D.

CENTRAL AVENUE ● PETAL MS 39465 ● (601) 545-3002 ● http://www.Petalschools.com

Grade Span: KG-12 **Schools**: *Regular* 4 ● *Spec Ed* 0 ● *Alt* 0 **Students**: 3,493 **Total Teachers**: 208 **Student/Classroom Teacher Ratio**: 17.0	**Expenditures/Student**: $3,719 **Librarians**: 3.9 896 students/librarian **Guidance Counselors**: 3.6 970 students/counselor	**% Amer Indian**: 0.1 **% Asian**: 0.3 **% Black**: 8.5 **% Hispanic**: 0.1 **% White**: 91.1	National ***Socio-Economic Status*** indicator percentile (100=high): 38th

George County

[LUCEDALE] GEORGE COUNTY S.D.

5152 MAIN STREET ● LUCEDALE MS 39452 ● (601) 947-6993

Grade Span: KG-12 **Schools**: *Regular* 7 ● *Spec Ed* 0 ● *Alt* 0 **Students**: 3,851 **Total Teachers**: 210 **Student/Classroom Teacher Ratio**: 18.9	**Expenditures/Student**: $3,163 **Librarians**: 4.6 837 students/librarian **Guidance Counselors**: 3.0 1,284 students/counselor	**% Amer Indian**: 0.0 **% Asian**: 0.2 **% Black**: 13.2 **% Hispanic**: 0.1 **% White**: 86.6	National ***Socio-Economic Status*** indicator percentile (100=high): 27th

Grenada County

GRENADA S.D.

1855 JACKSON AVENUE ● GRENADA MS 38901 ● (601) 226-1606 ● http://www.network-one.com/~gsd

Grade Span: KG-12 **Schools**: *Regular* 5 ● *Spec Ed* 0 ● *Alt* 1 **Students**: 4,399 **Total Teachers**: 241 **Student/Classroom Teacher Ratio**: 17.7	**Expenditures/Student**: $3,726 **Librarians**: 6.0 733 students/librarian **Guidance Counselors**: 8.0 550 students/counselor	**% Amer Indian**: 0.0 **% Asian**: 0.1 **% Black**: 55.7 **% Hispanic**: 0.0 **% White**: 44.1	National ***Socio-Economic Status*** indicator percentile (100=high): 14th

Hancock County

[WAVELAND] HANCOCK COUNTY S.D.

451 HIGHWAY 90 ● WAVELAND MS 39576 ● (228) 467-4466 ● http://www2.mdek12.state.ms.us/2300

Grade Span: PK-12 **Schools**: *Regular* 4 ● *Spec Ed* 0 ● *Alt* 2 **Students**: 3,451 **Total Teachers**: 187 **Student/Classroom Teacher Ratio**: 19.4	**Expenditures/Student**: $3,739 **Librarians**: 2.0 1,726 students/librarian **Guidance Counselors**: 6.0 575 students/counselor	**% Amer Indian**: 0.3 **% Asian**: 0.2 **% Black**: 5.4 **% Hispanic**: 1.0 **% White**: 93.1	National ***Socio-Economic Status*** indicator percentile (100=high): 12th

Harrison County

BILOXI PUBLIC S.D.

160 ST PETERS AVENUE ● BILOXI MS 39531 ● (228) 374-1810

Grade Span: KG-12 **Schools**: *Regular* 11 ● *Spec Ed* 0 ● *Alt* 1 **Students**: 6,399 **Total Teachers**: 378 **Student/Classroom Teacher Ratio**: 17.8	**Expenditures/Student**: $4,507 **Librarians**: 13.0 492 students/librarian **Guidance Counselors**: 11.0 582 students/counselor	**% Amer Indian**: 0.1 **% Asian**: 11.0 **% Black**: 31.4 **% Hispanic**: 1.6 **% White**: 55.9	National ***Socio-Economic Status*** indicator percentile (100=high): 16th

Harrison County

GULFPORT S.D.

2010 15TH STREET ● GULFPORT MS 39502 ● (228) 865-4600

Grade Span: KG-12 **Schools**: *Regular* 11 ● *Spec Ed* 0 ● *Alt* 2 **Students**: 6,362 **Total Teachers**: 382 **Student/Classroom Teacher Ratio**: 17.7	**Expenditures/Student**: $4,603 **Librarians**: 12.0 530 students/librarian **Guidance Counselors**: 12.5 509 students/counselor	**% Amer Indian**: 0.3 **% Asian**: 1.1 **% Black**: 47.6 **% Hispanic**: 0.8 **% White**: 50.2	National ***Socio-Economic Status*** indicator percentile (100=high): 11th

Harrison County
[GULFPORT] **HARRISON COUNTY S.D.**
1801 23RD AVENUE ● GULFPORT MS 39502 ● (228) 865-4052

Grade Span: KG-12 **Schools**: *Regular* 16 ● *Spec Ed* 0 ● *Alt* 1 **Students**: 11,915 **Total Teachers**: 638 **Student/Classroom Teacher Ratio**: 18.7	**Expenditures/Student**: $3,621 **Librarians**: 15.0 794 students/librarian **Guidance Counselors**: 8.0 1,489 students/counselor	**% Amer Indian**: 0.2 **% Asian**: 2.3 **% Black**: 22.4 **% Hispanic**: 0.6 **% White**: 74.5	National ***Socio-Economic Status*** indicator percentile (100=high): 27th

Harrison County
LONG BEACH S.D.
111 QUARLES STREET ● LONG BEACH MS 39560 ● (228) 864-1146

Grade Span: KG-12 **Schools**: *Regular* 5 ● *Spec Ed* 0 ● *Alt* 0 **Students**: 3,675 **Total Teachers**: 199 **Student/Classroom Teacher Ratio**: 18.9	**Expenditures/Student**: $3,623 **Librarians**: 5.0 735 students/librarian **Guidance Counselors**: 5.9 623 students/counselor	**% Amer Indian**: 0.1 **% Asian**: 3.1 **% Black**: 9.6 **% Hispanic**: 0.6 **% White**: 86.6	National ***Socio-Economic Status*** indicator percentile (100=high): 61st

Hinds County
CLINTON PUBLIC S.D.
203 EASTHAVEN DRIVE ● CLINTON MS 39060 ● (601) 924-7533 ● http://www2.mdek12.state.ms.us/2521

Grade Span: KG-12 **Schools**: *Regular* 7 ● *Spec Ed* 0 ● *Alt* 1 **Students**: 5,204 **Total Teachers**: 277 **Student/Classroom Teacher Ratio**: 19.5	**Expenditures/Student**: $3,353 **Librarians**: 8.0 651 students/librarian **Guidance Counselors**: 11.0 473 students/counselor	**% Amer Indian**: 0.1 **% Asian**: 1.4 **% Black**: 34.2 **% Hispanic**: 0.1 **% White**: 64.2	National ***Socio-Economic Status*** indicator percentile (100=high): 52nd

Hinds County
JACKSON PUBLIC S.D.
662 S PRESIDENT STREET ● JACKSON MS 39225-2338 ● (601) 960-8725 ● http://www.jackson.k12.ms.us

Grade Span: PK-12 **Schools**: *Regular* 56 ● *Spec Ed* 0 ● *Alt* 2 **Students**: 32,719 **Total Teachers**: 1,778 **Student/Classroom Teacher Ratio**: 19.0	**Expenditures/Student**: $4,394 **Librarians**: 59.0 555 students/librarian **Guidance Counselors**: 68.2 480 students/counselor	**% Amer Indian**: 0.1 **% Asian**: 0.3 **% Black**: 86.6 **% Hispanic**: 0.2 **% White**: 12.9	National ***Socio-Economic Status*** indicator percentile (100=high): 6th

Hinds County
[RAYMOND] **HINDS COUNTY S.D.**
13192 HIGHWAY 18 ● RAYMOND MS 39154-0100 ● (601) 857-5222

Grade Span: KG-12 **Schools**: *Regular* 8 ● *Spec Ed* 0 ● *Alt* 2 **Students**: 5,521 **Total Teachers**: 306 **Student/Classroom Teacher Ratio**: 18.4	**Expenditures/Student**: $3,582 **Librarians**: 6.0 920 students/librarian **Guidance Counselors**: 10.5 526 students/counselor	**% Amer Indian**: 0.0 **% Asian**: 0.2 **% Black**: 59.5 **% Hispanic**: 0.0 **% White**: 40.3	National ***Socio-Economic Status*** indicator percentile (100=high): 15th

Holmes County
[LEXINGTON] **HOLMES COUNTY S.D.**
P O BOX 630 ● LEXINGTON MS 39095 ● (601) 834-2175

Grade Span: KG-12 **Schools**: *Regular* 8 ● *Spec Ed* 0 ● *Alt* 1 **Students**: 4,137 **Total Teachers**: 209 **Student/Classroom Teacher Ratio**: 20.3	**Expenditures/Student**: $3,717 **Librarians**: 3.9 1,061 students/librarian **Guidance Counselors**: 3.5 1,182 students/counselor	**% Amer Indian**: 0.0 **% Asian**: 0.0 **% Black**: 99.9 **% Hispanic**: 0.1 **% White**: 0.0	National ***Socio-Economic Status*** indicator percentile (100=high): 0th

Humphreys County

[BELZONI] **HUMPHREYS COUNTY S.D.**

401 FOURTH STREET P O BOX 678 ● BELZONI MS 39038 ● (601) 247-3586

Grade Span: KG-12 **Schools**: *Regular* 3 ● *Spec Ed* 0 ● *Alt* 1 **Students**: 2,578 **Total Teachers**: 127 **Student/Classroom Teacher Ratio**: 21.7	**Expenditures/Student**: $3,753 **Librarians**: 2.8 921 students/librarian **Guidance Counselors**: 4.0 645 students/counselor	**% Amer Indian**: 0.0 **% Asian**: 0.0 **% Black**: 95.1 **% Hispanic**: 0.0 **% White**: 4.8	National ***Socio-Economic Status*** indicator percentile (100=high): 0th

Itawamba County

[FULTON] **ITAWAMBA COUNTY S.D.**

304 W WIYGUL STREET ● FULTON MS 38843 ● (601) 862-2159 ● http://www2.mdek12.state.ms.us/2900

Grade Span: KG-12 **Schools**: *Regular* 6 ● *Spec Ed* 0 ● *Alt* 1 **Students**: 3,210 **Total Teachers**: 194 **Student/Classroom Teacher Ratio**: 16.6	**Expenditures/Student**: $3,643 **Librarians**: 3.2 1,003 students/librarian **Guidance Counselors**: 4.9 655 students/counselor	**% Amer Indian**: 0.0 **% Asian**: 0.1 **% Black**: 7.9 **% Hispanic**: 0.3 **% White**: 91.6	National ***Socio-Economic Status*** indicator percentile (100=high): 32nd

Jackson County

MOSS POINT SEPARATE S.D.

4924 CHURCH STREET ● MOSS POINT MS 39563 ● (228) 475-1533 ● http://www.mphs.edu

Grade Span: KG-12 **Schools**: *Regular* 9 ● *Spec Ed* 0 ● *Alt* 2 **Students**: 5,123 **Total Teachers**: 298 **Student/Classroom Teacher Ratio**: 18.3	**Expenditures/Student**: $4,030 **Librarians**: 8.0 640 students/librarian **Guidance Counselors**: 4.1 1,250 students/counselor	**% Amer Indian**: 0.0 **% Asian**: 0.3 **% Black**: 63.4 **% Hispanic**: 0.1 **% White**: 36.2	National ***Socio-Economic Status*** indicator percentile (100=high): 11th

Jackson County

OCEAN SPRINGS S.D.

1600 GOVERNMENT STREET ● OCEAN SPRINGS MS 39564-7002 ● (228) 875-7706

Grade Span: KG-12 **Schools**: *Regular* 6 ● *Spec Ed* 0 ● *Alt* 1 **Students**: 4,631 **Total Teachers**: 254 **Student/Classroom Teacher Ratio**: 18.5	**Expenditures/Student**: $3,484 **Librarians**: 7.0 662 students/librarian **Guidance Counselors**: 9.5 487 students/counselor	**% Amer Indian**: 0.2 **% Asian**: 2.2 **% Black**: 6.3 **% Hispanic**: 0.5 **% White**: 90.9	National ***Socio-Economic Status*** indicator percentile (100=high): 69th

Jackson County

PASCAGOULA SEPARATE S.D.

1006 COMMUNY AVENUE ● PASCAGOULA MS 39568-0250 ● (228) 938-6495

Grade Span: KG-12 **Schools**: *Regular* 18 ● *Spec Ed* 0 ● *Alt* 2 **Students**: 7,717 **Total Teachers**: 451 **Student/Classroom Teacher Ratio**: 17.8	**Expenditures/Student**: $4,427 **Librarians**: 15.1 511 students/librarian **Guidance Counselors**: 14.1 547 students/counselor	**% Amer Indian**: 0.3 **% Asian**: 1.5 **% Black**: 35.2 **% Hispanic**: 0.8 **% White**: 62.2	National ***Socio-Economic Status*** indicator percentile (100=high): 25th

Jackson County

[VANCLEAVE] **JACKSON COUNTY S.D.**

12210 COLONEL VICKREY ROAD ● VANCLEAVE MS 39565-5069 ● (228) 826-1757

Grade Span: KG-12 **Schools**: *Regular* 11 ● *Spec Ed* 0 ● *Alt* 2 **Students**: 7,572 **Total Teachers**: 416 **Student/Classroom Teacher Ratio**: 18.8	**Expenditures/Student**: $3,504 **Librarians**: 11.0 688 students/librarian **Guidance Counselors**: 15.8 479 students/counselor	**% Amer Indian**: 0.1 **% Asian**: 2.1 **% Black**: 7.1 **% Hispanic**: 0.1 **% White**: 90.6	National ***Socio-Economic Status*** indicator percentile (100=high): 49th

Jefferson Davis County

[PRENTISS] **JEFFERSON DAVIS COUNTY S.D.**

1025 THIRD STREET P O BOX 119 ● PRENTISS MS 39474 ● (601) 792-4267

Grade Span: KG-12 **Schools**: *Regular* 4 ● *Spec Ed* 0 ● *Alt* 1 **Students**: 2,702 **Total Teachers**: 177 **Student/Classroom Teacher Ratio**: 16.3	**Expenditures/Student**: $4,131 **Librarians**: 4.0 676 students/librarian **Guidance Counselors**: 5.5 491 students/counselor	**% Amer Indian**: 0.0 **% Asian**: 0.0 **% Black**: 81.3 **% Hispanic**: 0.0 **% White**: 18.7	National ***Socio-Economic Status*** indicator percentile (100=high): 0th

Jones County

[ELLISVILLE] **JONES COUNTY S.D.**

5204 HIGHWAY 11 NORTH ● ELLISVILLE MS 39437 ● (601) 649-5201

Grade Span: KG-12 **Schools**: *Regular* 16 ● *Spec Ed* 0 ● *Alt* 2 **Students**: 8,325 **Total Teachers**: 498 **Student/Classroom Teacher Ratio**: 17.6	**Expenditures/Student**: $3,776 **Librarians**: 13.0 640 students/librarian **Guidance Counselors**: 15.0 555 students/counselor	**% Amer Indian**: 0.7 **% Asian**: 0.2 **% Black**: 21.7 **% Hispanic**: 3.7 **% White**: 73.6	National ***Socio-Economic Status*** indicator percentile (100=high): 24th

Jones County

LAUREL S.D.

600 S 16TH AVENUE ● LAUREL MS 39441-0288 ● (601) 649-6391

Grade Span: PK-12 **Schools**: *Regular* 7 ● *Spec Ed* 0 ● *Alt* 2 **Students**: 3,506 **Total Teachers**: 226 **Student/Classroom Teacher Ratio**: 16.3	**Expenditures/Student**: $4,549 **Librarians**: 6.8 516 students/librarian **Guidance Counselors**: 7.0 501 students/counselor	**% Amer Indian**: 0.0 **% Asian**: 0.1 **% Black**: 74.9 **% Hispanic**: 0.1 **% White**: 24.9	National ***Socio-Economic Status*** indicator percentile (100=high): 4th

Lafayette County

OXFORD S.D.

224 BRAMLETT BOULEVARD ● OXFORD MS 38655 ● (601) 234-3541 ● http://www.ci.oxford.ms.us/group2/education/cischool.html

Grade Span: KG-12 **Schools**: *Regular* 5 ● *Spec Ed* 0 ● *Alt* 2 **Students**: 2,897 **Total Teachers**: 183 **Student/Classroom Teacher Ratio**: 15.2	**Expenditures/Student**: $4,233 **Librarians**: 4.0 724 students/librarian **Guidance Counselors**: 6.5 446 students/counselor	**% Amer Indian**: 0.1 **% Asian**: 3.0 **% Black**: 45.6 **% Hispanic**: 0.2 **% White**: 51.0	National ***Socio-Economic Status*** indicator percentile (100=high): 19th

Lamar County

[PURVIS] **LAMAR COUNTY S.D.**

300 NORTH STREET ● PURVIS MS 39475 ● (601) 794-1030

Grade Span: KG-12 **Schools**: *Regular* 5 ● *Spec Ed* 0 ● *Alt* 1 **Students**: 6,229 **Total Teachers**: 361 **Student/Classroom Teacher Ratio**: 15.2	**Expenditures/Student**: $3,249 **Librarians**: 7.0 890 students/librarian **Guidance Counselors**: 6.5 958 students/counselor	**% Amer Indian**: 0.0 **% Asian**: 0.4 **% Black**: 8.7 **% Hispanic**: 0.3 **% White**: 90.5	National ***Socio-Economic Status*** indicator percentile (100=high): 51st

Lauderdale County

[MERIDIAN] **LAUDERDALE COUNTY S.D.**

P O BOX 5498 ● MERIDIAN MS 39302-5498 ● (601) 693-1683

Grade Span: KG-12 **Schools**: *Regular* 7 ● *Spec Ed* 0 ● *Alt* 1 **Students**: 6,793 **Total Teachers**: 390 **Student/Classroom Teacher Ratio**: 17.4	**Expenditures/Student**: $3,471 **Librarians**: 10.0 679 students/librarian **Guidance Counselors**: 8.0 849 students/counselor	**% Amer Indian**: 0.1 **% Asian**: 0.2 **% Black**: 30.4 **% Hispanic**: 0.5 **% White**: 68.9	National ***Socio-Economic Status*** indicator percentile (100=high): 34th

Lauderdale County

MERIDIAN PUBLIC S.D.

1015 25TH AVENUE ● MERIDIAN MS 39301 ● (601) 483-6271 ● http://ETV.STATE.MS.US/meridian/MPS/HOMEPAGE.HTML

Grade Span: KG-12 **Schools**: *Regular* 13 ● *Spec Ed* 0 ● *Alt* 2 **Students**: 7,363 **Total Teachers**: 461 **Student/Classroom Teacher Ratio**: 16.9	**Expenditures/Student**: $4,216 **Librarians**: 11.0 669 students/librarian **Guidance Counselors**: 12.3 599 students/counselor	**% Amer Indian**: 0.0 **% Asian**: 0.3 **% Black**: 69.2 **% Hispanic**: 0.3 **% White**: 30.2	National ***Socio-Economic Status*** indicator percentile (100=high): 9th

Lawrence County

[MONTICELLO] LAWRENCE COUNTY S.D.

130 BROOKHAVEN STREET ● MONTICELLO MS 39654 ● (601) 587-2506

Grade Span: KG-12 **Schools**: *Regular* 5 ● *Spec Ed* 0 ● *Alt* 1 **Students**: 2,552 **Total Teachers**: 156 **Student/Classroom Teacher Ratio**: 17.3	**Expenditures/Student**: $3,778 **Librarians**: 4.0 638 students/librarian **Guidance Counselors**: 3.8 672 students/counselor	**% Amer Indian**: 0.0 **% Asian**: 0.0 **% Black**: 44.4 **% Hispanic**: 0.1 **% White**: 55.4	National ***Socio-Economic Status*** indicator percentile (100=high): 10th

Leake County

[CARTHAGE] LEAKE COUNTY S.D.

MAIN ST COURTHOUSE ● CARTHAGE MS 39051 ● (601) 267-4579

Grade Span: KG-12 **Schools**: *Regular* 7 ● *Spec Ed* 0 ● *Alt* 1 **Students**: 3,142 **Total Teachers**: 184 **Student/Classroom Teacher Ratio**: 17.5	**Expenditures/Student**: $3,654 **Librarians**: 4.4 714 students/librarian **Guidance Counselors**: 5.0 628 students/counselor	**% Amer Indian**: 1.4 **% Asian**: 0.1 **% Black**: 60.6 **% Hispanic**: 0.2 **% White**: 37.8	National ***Socio-Economic Status*** indicator percentile (100=high): 5th

Lee County

[TUPELO] LEE COUNTY S.D.

311 EAST MAIN STREET ● TUPELO MS 38802-0832 ● (601) 841-9144

Grade Span: KG-12 **Schools**: *Regular* 8 ● *Spec Ed* 0 ● *Alt* 0 **Students**: 5,703 **Total Teachers**: 314 **Student/Classroom Teacher Ratio**: 18.6	**Expenditures/Student**: $3,570 **Librarians**: 7.0 815 students/librarian **Guidance Counselors**: 9.5 600 students/counselor	**% Amer Indian**: 0.0 **% Asian**: 0.6 **% Black**: 28.8 **% Hispanic**: 0.2 **% White**: 70.4	National ***Socio-Economic Status*** indicator percentile (100=high): 22nd

Lee County

TUPELO PUBLIC S.D.

201 S GREEN STREET ● TUPELO MS 38801-0557 ● (601) 841-8850

Grade Span: PK-12 **Schools**: *Regular* 12 ● *Spec Ed* 0 ● *Alt* 1 **Students**: 7,257 **Total Teachers**: 432 **Student/Classroom Teacher Ratio**: 16.0	**Expenditures/Student**: $4,184 **Librarians**: 12.0 605 students/librarian **Guidance Counselors**: 14.2 511 students/counselor	**% Amer Indian**: 0.0 **% Asian**: 0.5 **% Black**: 35.3 **% Hispanic**: 0.3 **% White**: 63.8	National ***Socio-Economic Status*** indicator percentile (100=high): 38th

Leflore County

GREENWOOD PUBLIC S.D.

401 HOWARD STREET ● GREENWOOD MS 38935-1497 ● (601) 453-4231

Grade Span: KG-12 **Schools**: *Regular* 7 ● *Spec Ed* 0 ● *Alt* 1 **Students**: 4,261 **Total Teachers**: 241 **Student/Classroom Teacher Ratio**: 18.3	**Expenditures/Student**: $3,936 **Librarians**: 7.5 568 students/librarian **Guidance Counselors**: 8.0 533 students/counselor	**% Amer Indian**: 0.0 **% Asian**: 0.2 **% Black**: 83.6 **% Hispanic**: 0.2 **% White**: 15.9	National ***Socio-Economic Status*** indicator percentile (100=high): 1st

Leflore County

[GREENWOOD] **LEFLORE COUNTY S.D.**

1901 HIGHWAY 82 WEST ● GREENWOOD MS 38930 ● (601) 459-7231

Grade Span: KG-12 **Schools**: *Regular* 7 ● *Spec Ed* 0 ● *Alt* 1 **Students**: 3,227 **Total Teachers**: 195 **Student/Classroom Teacher Ratio**: 17.6	**Expenditures/Student**: $4,239 **Librarians**: 5.0 645 students/librarian **Guidance Counselors**: 6.0 538 students/counselor	**% Amer Indian**: 0.0 **% Asian**: 0.0 **% Black**: 95.6 **% Hispanic**: 0.1 **% White**: 4.3	National ***Socio-Economic Status*** indicator percentile (100=high): 1st

Lincoln County

BROOKHAVEN S.D.

326 COURT STREET ● BROOKHAVEN MS 39601 ● (601) 833-6661 ● http://www.telapex.com/~bschool/index.html

Grade Span: KG-12 **Schools**: *Regular* 6 ● *Spec Ed* 0 ● *Alt* 1 **Students**: 3,298 **Total Teachers**: 203 **Student/Classroom Teacher Ratio**: 17.2	**Expenditures/Student**: $4,189 **Librarians**: 6.0 550 students/librarian **Guidance Counselors**: 8.6 383 students/counselor	**% Amer Indian**: 0.0 **% Asian**: 0.1 **% Black**: 58.2 **% Hispanic**: 0.0 **% White**: 41.7	National ***Socio-Economic Status*** indicator percentile (100=high): 11th

Lincoln County

[BROOKHAVEN] **LINCOLN COUNTY S.D.**

S 1ST STREET CITY COUNTY GOV BLDG ● BROOKHAVEN MS 39601 ● (601) 835-3448

Grade Span: KG-12 **Schools**: *Regular* 5 ● *Spec Ed* 0 ● *Alt* 0 **Students**: 2,654 **Total Teachers**: 143 **Student/Classroom Teacher Ratio**: 18.7	**Expenditures/Student**: $3,519 **Librarians**: 3.9 681 students/librarian **Guidance Counselors**: 2.0 1,327 students/counselor	**% Amer Indian**: 0.0 **% Asian**: 0.0 **% Black**: 20.0 **% Hispanic**: 0.1 **% White**: 79.9	National ***Socio-Economic Status*** indicator percentile (100=high): 23rd

Lowndes County

COLUMBUS MUNICIPAL S.D.

320 SEVENTH STREET N ● COLUMBUS MS 39703 ● (601) 328-2598

Grade Span: KG-12 **Schools**: *Regular* 14 ● *Spec Ed* 0 ● *Alt* 2 **Students**: 5,709 **Total Teachers**: 350 **Student/Classroom Teacher Ratio**: 16.9	**Expenditures/Student**: $4,308 **Librarians**: 13.0 439 students/librarian **Guidance Counselors**: 13.8 414 students/counselor	**% Amer Indian**: 0.0 **% Asian**: 0.1 **% Black**: 74.1 **% Hispanic**: 0.2 **% White**: 25.5	National ***Socio-Economic Status*** indicator percentile (100=high): 8th

Lowndes County

[COLUMBUS] **LOWNDES COUNTY S.D.**

P O DRAWER 8480 ● COLUMBUS MS 39705-8480 ● (601) 329-5775

Grade Span: KG-12 **Schools**: *Regular* 9 ● *Spec Ed* 0 ● *Alt* 1 **Students**: 5,548 **Total Teachers**: 299 **Student/Classroom Teacher Ratio**: 18.4	**Expenditures/Student**: $3,439 **Librarians**: 8.0 694 students/librarian **Guidance Counselors**: 8.3 668 students/counselor	**% Amer Indian**: 0.1 **% Asian**: 0.3 **% Black**: 40.1 **% Hispanic**: 0.4 **% White**: 59.2	National ***Socio-Economic Status*** indicator percentile (100=high): 26th

Madison County

CANTON PUBLIC S.D.

403 E LINCOLN STREET ● CANTON MS 39046 ● (601) 859-4110

Grade Span: KG-12 **Schools**: *Regular* 4 ● *Spec Ed* 0 ● *Alt* 1 **Students**: 3,727 **Total Teachers**: 186 **Student/Classroom Teacher Ratio**: 21.2	**Expenditures/Student**: $3,491 **Librarians**: 4.0 932 students/librarian **Guidance Counselors**: 6.0 621 students/counselor	**% Amer Indian**: 0.0 **% Asian**: 0.0 **% Black**: 98.8 **% Hispanic**: 0.1 **% White**: 1.1	National ***Socio-Economic Status*** indicator percentile (100=high): 1st

Madison County

[CANTON] **MADISON COUNTY S.D.**

1633 W PEACE STREET ● CANTON MS 39046 ● (601) 355-7412 ● http://www2.mdek12.state.ms.us/4500

Grade Span: KG-12	**Expenditures/Student**: $3,330	**% Amer Indian**: 0.0	
Schools: *Regular* 9 ● *Spec Ed* 0 ● *Alt* 1	**Librarians**: 8.0	**% Asian**: 0.9	National ***Socio-Economic***
Students: 7,554	944 students/librarian	**% Black**: 40.2	***Status*** indicator percentile
Total Teachers: 397	**Guidance Counselors**: 8.8	**% Hispanic**: 0.2	(100=high): 35th
Student/Classroom Teacher Ratio: 18.7	858 students/counselor	**% White**: 58.6	

Marion County

[COLUMBIA] **MARION COUNTY S.D.**

600 BROAD STREET ● COLUMBIA MS 39429 ● (601) 736-7193

Grade Span: KG-12	**Expenditures/Student**: $3,740	**% Amer Indian**: 0.0	
Schools: *Regular* 3 ● *Spec Ed* 0 ● *Alt* 1	**Librarians**: 4.0	**% Asian**: 0.0	National ***Socio-Economic***
Students: 2,980	745 students/librarian	**% Black**: 44.5	***Status*** indicator percentile
Total Teachers: 192	**Guidance Counselors**: 3.0	**% Hispanic**: 0.0	(100=high): 4th
Student/Classroom Teacher Ratio: 16.7	993 students/counselor	**% White**: 55.5	

Marshall County

[HOLLY SPRINGS] **MARSHALL COUNTY S.D.**

158 VAN DORN AVENUE ● HOLLY SPRINGS MS 38635 ● (601) 252-4271

Grade Span: KG-12	**Expenditures/Student**: $3,652	**% Amer Indian**: 0.0	
Schools: *Regular* 6 ● *Spec Ed* 0 ● *Alt* 0	**Librarians**: 2.8	**% Asian**: 0.0	National ***Socio-Economic***
Students: 3,387	1,210 students/librarian	**% Black**: 63.8	***Status*** indicator percentile
Total Teachers: 183	**Guidance Counselors**: 4.5	**% Hispanic**: 0.4	(100=high): 2nd
Student/Classroom Teacher Ratio: 18.0	753 students/counselor	**% White**: 35.8	

Monroe County

[ABERDEEN] **MONROE COUNTY S.D.**

COMMERCE STREET ● ABERDEEN MS 39730 ● (601) 369-2022 ● http://www2.mdek12.state.ms.us/4800

Grade Span: KG-12	**Expenditures/Student**: $3,621	**% Amer Indian**: 0.0	
Schools: *Regular* 5 ● *Spec Ed* 0 ● *Alt* 1	**Librarians**: 3.0	**% Asian**: 0.0	National ***Socio-Economic***
Students: 2,524	841 students/librarian	**% Black**: 12.7	***Status*** indicator percentile
Total Teachers: 148	**Guidance Counselors**: 4.6	**% Hispanic**: 0.7	(100=high): 40th
Student/Classroom Teacher Ratio: 18.0	549 students/counselor	**% White**: 86.5	

Neshoba County

[PHILADELPHIA] **NESHOBA COUNTY S.D.**

COURTHOUSE P O BOX 338 ● PHILADELPHIA MS 39350 ● (601) 656-3752

Grade Span: KG-12	**Expenditures/Student**: $3,312	**% Amer Indian**: 7.8	
Schools: *Regular* 2 ● *Spec Ed* 0 ● *Alt* 0	**Librarians**: 2.0	**% Asian**: 0.1	National ***Socio-Economic***
Students: 2,890	1,445 students/librarian	**% Black**: 20.7	***Status*** indicator percentile
Total Teachers: 167	**Guidance Counselors**: 3.0	**% Hispanic**: 0.0	(100=high): 27th
Student/Classroom Teacher Ratio: 17.6	963 students/counselor	**% White**: 71.4	

Oktibbeha County

STARKVILLE S.D.

401 GREENSBORO STREET ● STARKVILLE MS 39759 ● (601) 324-4050

Grade Span: KG-12	**Expenditures/Student**: $4,542	**% Amer Indian**: 0.0	
Schools: *Regular* 8 ● *Spec Ed* 0 ● *Alt* 2	**Librarians**: 7.0	**% Asian**: 3.6	National ***Socio-Economic***
Students: 4,152	593 students/librarian	**% Black**: 62.9	***Status*** indicator percentile
Total Teachers: 263	**Guidance Counselors**: 10.3	**% Hispanic**: 0.3	(100=high): 13th
Student/Classroom Teacher Ratio: 16.5	403 students/counselor	**% White**: 33.1	

Panola County

[BATESVILLE] **SOUTH PANOLA S.D.**

209 BOOTHE STREET ● BATESVILLE MS 38606 ● (601) 563-9361

Grade Span: KG-12 **Schools**: *Regular* 5 ● *Spec Ed* 0 ● *Alt* 1 **Students**: 4,425 **Total Teachers**: 232 **Student/Classroom Teacher Ratio**: 19.4	**Expenditures/Student**: $3,569 **Librarians**: 5.0 885 students/librarian **Guidance Counselors**: 9.0 492 students/counselor	**% Amer Indian**: 0.1 **% Asian**: 0.2 **% Black**: 54.8 **% Hispanic**: 0.2 **% White**: 44.7	National ***Socio-Economic Status*** indicator percentile (100=high): 8th

Pearl River County

PICAYUNE S.D.

706 GOODYEAR BOULEVARD ● PICAYUNE MS 39466 ● (601) 798-3230 ● http://picayuneschools.datastar.net

Grade Span: KG-12 **Schools**: *Regular* 8 ● *Spec Ed* 0 ● *Alt* 2 **Students**: 3,994 **Total Teachers**: 230 **Student/Classroom Teacher Ratio**: 18.3	**Expenditures/Student**: $3,572 **Librarians**: 6.0 666 students/librarian **Guidance Counselors**: 5.0 799 students/counselor	**% Amer Indian**: 0.1 **% Asian**: 0.2 **% Black**: 28.2 **% Hispanic**: 0.4 **% White**: 71.2	National ***Socio-Economic Status*** indicator percentile (100=high): 16th

Pike County

[MAGNOLIA] **SOUTH PIKE S.D.**

250 W BAY STREET ● MAGNOLIA MS 39652 ● (601) 783-3742

Grade Span: KG-12 **Schools**: *Regular* 6 ● *Spec Ed* 0 ● *Alt* 2 **Students**: 2,768 **Total Teachers**: 152 **Student/Classroom Teacher Ratio**: 18.8	**Expenditures/Student**: $3,603 **Librarians**: 5.0 554 students/librarian **Guidance Counselors**: 3.0 923 students/counselor	**% Amer Indian**: 0.0 **% Asian**: 0.1 **% Black**: 71.4 **% Hispanic**: 0.1 **% White**: 28.4	National ***Socio-Economic Status*** indicator percentile (100=high): 2nd

Pike County

MCCOMB S.D.

695 MINNESOTA AVENUE P O BOX 8 ● MCCOMB MS 39648 ● (601) 684-4661

Grade Span: KG-12 **Schools**: *Regular* 5 ● *Spec Ed* 0 ● *Alt* 2 **Students**: 3,131 **Total Teachers**: 201 **Student/Classroom Teacher Ratio**: 16.6	**Expenditures/Student**: $4,070 **Librarians**: 5.0 626 students/librarian **Guidance Counselors**: 7.0 447 students/counselor	**% Amer Indian**: 0.0 **% Asian**: 0.1 **% Black**: 69.5 **% Hispanic**: 0.0 **% White**: 30.3	National ***Socio-Economic Status*** indicator percentile (100=high): 5th

Pontotoc County

[PONTOTOC] **PONTOTOC COUNTY S.D.**

285 HIGHWAY 15 BYPASS S ● PONTOTOC MS 38863 ● (601) 489-3932

Grade Span: KG-12 **Schools**: *Regular* 2 ● *Spec Ed* 0 ● *Alt* 1 **Students**: 2,732 **Total Teachers**: 147 **Student/Classroom Teacher Ratio**: 20.6	**Expenditures/Student**: $3,438 **Librarians**: 2.0 1,366 students/librarian **Guidance Counselors**: 4.0 683 students/counselor	**% Amer Indian**: 0.1 **% Asian**: 0.1 **% Black**: 10.6 **% Hispanic**: 0.3 **% White**: 88.9	National ***Socio-Economic Status*** indicator percentile (100=high): 41st

Prentiss County

[BOONEVILLE] **PRENTISS COUNTY S.D.**

105 N COLLEGE STREET ● BOONEVILLE MS 38829 ● (601) 728-4911

Grade Span: KG-12 **Schools**: *Regular* 6 ● *Spec Ed* 0 ● *Alt* 1 **Students**: 2,626 **Total Teachers**: 184 **Student/Classroom Teacher Ratio**: 15.3	**Expenditures/Student**: $4,081 **Librarians**: 4.6 571 students/librarian **Guidance Counselors**: 4.2 625 students/counselor	**% Amer Indian**: 0.0 **% Asian**: 0.1 **% Black**: 9.1 **% Hispanic**: 0.1 **% White**: 90.7	National ***Socio-Economic Status*** indicator percentile (100=high): 24th

Rankin County

[BRANDON] **RANKIN COUNTY S.D.**

1220 APPLE PARK PLACE ● BRANDON MS 39043 ● (601) 825-5590

Grade Span: KG-12 **Schools**: *Regular* 21 ● *Spec Ed* 0 ● *Alt* 1 **Students**: 14,156 **Total Teachers**: 723 **Student/Classroom Teacher Ratio**: 19.4	**Expenditures/Student**: $3,263 **Librarians**: 22.0 643 students/librarian **Guidance Counselors**: 20.0 708 students/counselor	**% Amer Indian**: 0.0 **% Asian**: 0.4 **% Black**: 20.2 **% Hispanic**: 0.2 **% White**: 79.0	National ***Socio-Economic Status*** indicator percentile (100=high): 47th

Rankin County

PEARL PUBLIC S.D.

3375 HWY 80 EAST ● PEARL MS 39208 ● (601) 932-7916

Grade Span: KG-12 **Schools**: *Regular* 5 ● *Spec Ed* 0 ● *Alt* 1 **Students**: 3,964 **Total Teachers**: 207 **Student/Classroom Teacher Ratio**: 19.5	**Expenditures/Student**: $3,302 **Librarians**: 5.1 777 students/librarian **Guidance Counselors**: 6.9 574 students/counselor	**% Amer Indian**: 0.0 **% Asian**: 0.5 **% Black**: 22.4 **% Hispanic**: 0.5 **% White**: 76.6	National ***Socio-Economic Status*** indicator percentile (100=high): 41st

Scott County

[FOREST] **SCOTT COUNTY S.D.**

100 E FIRST ST ● FOREST MS 39074 ● (601) 469-3861

Grade Span: KG-12 **Schools**: *Regular* 7 ● *Spec Ed* 0 ● *Alt* 1 **Students**: 3,952 **Total Teachers**: 211 **Student/Classroom Teacher Ratio**: 19.9	**Expenditures/Student**: $3,542 **Librarians**: 6.0 659 students/librarian **Guidance Counselors**: 6.9 573 students/counselor	**% Amer Indian**: 0.5 **% Asian**: 0.0 **% Black**: 41.7 **% Hispanic**: 3.3 **% White**: 54.5	National ***Socio-Economic Status*** indicator percentile (100=high): 8th

Simpson County

[MENDENHALL] **SIMPSON COUNTY S.D.**

101 COURT STREET ● MENDENHALL MS 39114 ● (601) 847-1562

Grade Span: KG-12 **Schools**: *Regular* 7 ● *Spec Ed* 0 ● *Alt* 1 **Students**: 4,340 **Total Teachers**: 231 **Student/Classroom Teacher Ratio**: 19.4	**Expenditures/Student**: $3,343 **Librarians**: 6.7 648 students/librarian **Guidance Counselors**: 7.8 556 students/counselor	**% Amer Indian**: 0.0 **% Asian**: 0.0 **% Black**: 50.2 **% Hispanic**: 0.2 **% White**: 49.6	National ***Socio-Economic Status*** indicator percentile (100=high): 8th

Smith County

[RALEIGH] **SMITH COUNTY S.D.**

COUNTY OFFICE BLDG HIGHWAY 18 ● RALEIGH MS 39153 ● (601) 782-4296

Grade Span: KG-12 **Schools**: *Regular* 4 ● *Spec Ed* 0 ● *Alt* 2 **Students**: 3,092 **Total Teachers**: 180 **Student/Classroom Teacher Ratio**: 18.2	**Expenditures/Student**: $3,580 **Librarians**: 1.0 3,092 students/librarian **Guidance Counselors**: 3.6 859 students/counselor	**% Amer Indian**: 0.0 **% Asian**: 0.0 **% Black**: 31.0 **% Hispanic**: 0.0 **% White**: 69.0	National ***Socio-Economic Status*** indicator percentile (100=high): 19th

Stone County

[WIGGINS] **STONE COUNTY S.D.**

214 CRITZ STREET ● WIGGINS MS 39577 ● (601) 928-7247

Grade Span: KG-12 **Schools**: *Regular* 4 ● *Spec Ed* 0 ● *Alt* 0 **Students**: 2,583 **Total Teachers**: 153 **Student/Classroom Teacher Ratio**: 17.1	**Expenditures/Student**: $3,503 **Librarians**: 4.0 646 students/librarian **Guidance Counselors**: 3.0 861 students/counselor	**% Amer Indian**: 0.1 **% Asian**: 0.0 **% Black**: 26.2 **% Hispanic**: 0.1 **% White**: 73.6	National ***Socio-Economic Status*** indicator percentile (100=high): 18th

Sunflower County

INDIANOLA S.D.

HIGHWAY 82 E ● INDIANOLA MS 38751 ● (601) 887-2654

Grade Span: KG-12 **Schools**: *Regular* 5 ● *Spec Ed* 0 ● *Alt* 0 **Students**: 3,450 **Total Teachers**: 185 **Student/Classroom Teacher Ratio**: 18.0	**Expenditures/Student**: $3,107 **Librarians**: 4.7 734 students/librarian **Guidance Counselors**: 4.4 784 students/counselor	**% Amer Indian**: 0.0 **% Asian**: 0.0 **% Black**: 93.0 **% Hispanic**: 0.2 **% White**: 6.7	National ***Socio-Economic Status*** indicator percentile (100=high): 1st

Tate County

[SENATOBIA] TATE COUNTY S.D.

302 COURT ● SENATOBIA MS 38668 ● (601) 562-5861

Grade Span: KG-12 **Schools**: *Regular* 5 ● *Spec Ed* 0 ● *Alt* 1 **Students**: 2,955 **Total Teachers**: 162 **Student/Classroom Teacher Ratio**: 19.0	**Expenditures/Student**: $3,540 **Librarians**: 3.9 758 students/librarian **Guidance Counselors**: 3.0 985 students/counselor	**% Amer Indian**: 0.1 **% Asian**: 0.1 **% Black**: 53.0 **% Hispanic**: 0.1 **% White**: 46.7	National ***Socio-Economic Status*** indicator percentile (100=high): 10th

Tippah County

[RIPLEY] SOUTH TIPPAH S.D.

402 GREENLEE STREET ● RIPLEY MS 38663 ● (601) 837-7156 ● http://ww2.dixie-net.com/Ripley-HS

Grade Span: KG-12 **Schools**: *Regular* 5 ● *Spec Ed* 0 ● *Alt* 1 **Students**: 2,860 **Total Teachers**: 154 **Student/Classroom Teacher Ratio**: 19.5	**Expenditures/Student**: $3,392 **Librarians**: 4.0 715 students/librarian **Guidance Counselors**: 4.9 584 students/counselor	**% Amer Indian**: 0.0 **% Asian**: 0.3 **% Black**: 26.0 **% Hispanic**: 0.1 **% White**: 73.5	National ***Socio-Economic Status*** indicator percentile (100=high): 24th

Tishomingo County

[IUKA] TISHOMINGO COUNTY SEPARATE MUNICIPAL S.D.

507 W QUITMAN STREET ● IUKA MS 38852 ● (601) 423-3206

Grade Span: PK-12 **Schools**: *Regular* 6 ● *Spec Ed* 0 ● *Alt* 2 **Students**: 3,181 **Total Teachers**: 194 **Student/Classroom Teacher Ratio**: 17.3	**Expenditures/Student**: $3,740 **Librarians**: 5.5 578 students/librarian **Guidance Counselors**: 6.0 530 students/counselor	**% Amer Indian**: 0.0 **% Asian**: 0.0 **% Black**: 4.4 **% Hispanic**: 0.2 **% White**: 95.4	National ***Socio-Economic Status*** indicator percentile (100=high): 31st

Walthall County

[TYLERTOWN] WALTHALL COUNTY S.D.

814 A MORSE AVENUE ● TYLERTOWN MS 39667 ● (601) 876-3401

Grade Span: KG-12 **Schools**: *Regular* 5 ● *Spec Ed* 0 ● *Alt* 0 **Students**: 2,968 **Total Teachers**: 180 **Student/Classroom Teacher Ratio**: 17.6	**Expenditures/Student**: $3,667 **Librarians**: 3.9 761 students/librarian **Guidance Counselors**: 3.0 989 students/counselor	**% Amer Indian**: 0.0 **% Asian**: 0.1 **% Black**: 63.3 **% Hispanic**: 0.1 **% White**: 36.5	National ***Socio-Economic Status*** indicator percentile (100=high): 3rd

Warren County

VICKSBURG WARREN S.D.

1500 MISSION 66 ● VICKSBURG MS 39182 ● (601) 638-5122

Grade Span: KG-12 **Schools**: *Regular* 14 ● *Spec Ed* 0 ● *Alt* 2 **Students**: 9,587 **Total Teachers**: 558 **Student/Classroom Teacher Ratio**: 17.3	**Expenditures/Student**: $4,020 **Librarians**: 15.0 639 students/librarian **Guidance Counselors**: 20.9 459 students/counselor	**% Amer Indian**: 0.1 **% Asian**: 0.5 **% Black**: 56.0 **% Hispanic**: 0.3 **% White**: 43.2	National ***Socio-Economic Status*** indicator percentile (100=high): 15th

Washington County

GREENVILLE PUBLIC S.D.

412 S MAIN STREET ● GREENVILLE MS 38701-4747 ● (601) 334-7000 ● http://www2.mdek12.state.ms.us/7620

Grade Span: KG-12 **Schools**: *Regular* 15 ● *Spec Ed* 0 ● *Alt* 2 **Students**: 8,258 **Total Teachers**: 438 **Student/Classroom Teacher Ratio**: 19.8	**Expenditures/Student**: $3,775 **Librarians**: 10.0 826 students/librarian **Guidance Counselors**: 10.0 826 students/counselor	**% Amer Indian**: 0.0 **% Asian**: 0.1 **% Black**: 93.3 **% Hispanic**: 0.0 **% White**: 6.5	National ***Socio-Economic Status*** indicator percentile (100=high): 2nd

Wayne County

[WAYNESBORO] **WAYNE COUNTY S.D.**

COURTHOUSE ● WAYNESBORO MS 39367-2692 ● (601) 735-4871

Grade Span: KG-12 **Schools**: *Regular* 6 ● *Spec Ed* 0 ● *Alt* 1 **Students**: 4,171 **Total Teachers**: 246 **Student/Classroom Teacher Ratio**: 17.6	**Expenditures/Student**: $3,666 **Librarians**: 5.1 818 students/librarian **Guidance Counselors**: 3.8 1,098 students/counselor	**% Amer Indian**: 0.0 **% Asian**: 0.2 **% Black**: 50.4 **% Hispanic**: 0.0 **% White**: 49.3	National ***Socio-Economic Status*** indicator percentile (100=high): 8th

Winston County

LOUISVILLE MUNICIPAL S.D.

112 S COLUMBUS AVENUE ● LOUISVILLE MS 39339 ● (601) 773-3411

Grade Span: KG-12 **Schools**: *Regular* 6 ● *Spec Ed* 0 ● *Alt* 1 **Students**: 3,737 **Total Teachers**: 225 **Student/Classroom Teacher Ratio**: 17.4	**Expenditures/Student**: $3,960 **Librarians**: 6.0 623 students/librarian **Guidance Counselors**: 6.6 566 students/counselor	**% Amer Indian**: 1.0 **% Asian**: 0.1 **% Black**: 62.9 **% Hispanic**: 0.2 **% White**: 35.9	National ***Socio-Economic Status*** indicator percentile (100=high): 8th

Yazoo County

YAZOO CITY MUNICIPAL S.D.

1133 CALHOUN AVENUE ● YAZOO CITY MS 39194 ● (601) 746-2125

Grade Span: KG-12 **Schools**: *Regular* 5 ● *Spec Ed* 0 ● *Alt* 1 **Students**: 3,461 **Total Teachers**: 208 **Student/Classroom Teacher Ratio**: 17.1	**Expenditures/Student**: $3,714 **Librarians**: 4.0 865 students/librarian **Guidance Counselors**: 4.5 769 students/counselor	**% Amer Indian**: 0.0 **% Asian**: 0.1 **% Black**: 87.1 **% Hispanic**: 0.0 **% White**: 12.8	National ***Socio-Economic Status*** indicator percentile (100=high): 1st

Audrain County

MEXICO S.D. 59

920 S JEFFERSON ● MEXICO MO 65265-2563 ● (573) 581-3773

Grade Span: KG-12 **Schools**: *Regular* 5 ● *Spec Ed* 0 ● *Alt* 1 **Students**: 2,620 **Total Teachers**: 175 **Student/Classroom Teacher Ratio**: 16.0	**Expenditures/Student**: $4,299 **Librarians**: 4.5 582 students/librarian **Guidance Counselors**: 10.0 262 students/counselor	**% Amer Indian**: 0.3 **% Asian**: 0.3 **% Black**: 11.0 **% Hispanic**: 0.2 **% White**: 88.2	National ***Socio-Economic Status*** indicator percentile (100=high): 33rd

Boone County

COLUMBIA S.D. 93

1818 W WORLEY ST ● COLUMBIA MO 65203-1038 ● (573) 886-2100 ● http://www.ims.columbia.k12.mo.us

Grade Span: KG-12 **Schools**: *Regular* 27 ● *Spec Ed* 0 ● *Alt* 2 **Students**: 15,146 **Total Teachers**: 1,008 **Student/Classroom Teacher Ratio**: 15.2	**Expenditures/Student**: $5,090 **Librarians**: 24.6 616 students/librarian **Guidance Counselors**: 42.6 356 students/counselor	**% Amer Indian**: 0.4 **% Asian**: 3.8 **% Black**: 16.2 **% Hispanic**: 1.2 **% White**: 78.4	National ***Socio-Economic Status*** indicator percentile (100=high): 55th

Buchanan County

ST. JOSEPH S.D.

925 FELIX ● ST. JOSEPH MO 64501-2706 ● (816) 233-1301 ● http://www.sjsd.k12.mo.us

Grade Span: KG-12 **Schools**: *Regular* 27 ● *Spec Ed* 1 ● *Alt* 1 **Students**: 12,155 **Total Teachers**: 773 **Student/Classroom Teacher Ratio**: 15.4	**Expenditures/Student**: $4,340 **Librarians**: 9.0 1,351 students/librarian **Guidance Counselors**: 30.5 399 students/counselor	**% Amer Indian**: 0.0 **% Asian**: 0.0 **% Black**: 0.0 **% Hispanic**: 0.0 **% White**: 100.0	National ***Socio-Economic Status*** indicator percentile (100=high): 25th

Butler County

POPLAR BLUFF REORGANIZED S.D. 1

PO BOX 47 ● POPLAR BLUFF MO 63902-0047 ● (573) 785-7751

Grade Span: KG-12 **Schools**: *Regular* 10 ● *Spec Ed* 0 ● *Alt* 2 **Students**: 4,950 **Total Teachers**: 303 **Student/Classroom Teacher Ratio**: 17.2	**Expenditures/Student**: $3,811 **Librarians**: 6.9 717 students/librarian **Guidance Counselors**: 14.0 354 students/counselor	**% Amer Indian**: 0.3 **% Asian**: 0.2 **% Black**: 10.0 **% Hispanic**: 0.5 **% White**: 88.9	National ***Socio-Economic Status*** indicator percentile (100=high): 20th

Camden County

CAMDENTON REORGANIZED S.D. 3

PO BOX 1409 ● CAMDENTON MO 65020-1409 ● (573) 346-5651 ● http://www.oseda.missouri.edu/camdenton.k12.mo.us

Grade Span: KG-12 **Schools**: *Regular* 6 ● *Spec Ed* 0 ● *Alt* 1 **Students**: 3,688 **Total Teachers**: 230 **Student/Classroom Teacher Ratio**: 16.3	**Expenditures/Student**: $4,102 **Librarians**: 4.0 922 students/librarian **Guidance Counselors**: 10.8 341 students/counselor	**% Amer Indian**: 0.4 **% Asian**: 0.3 **% Black**: 0.4 **% Hispanic**: 0.4 **% White**: 98.5	National ***Socio-Economic Status*** indicator percentile (100=high): 47th

Cape Girardeau County

CAPE GIRARDEAU S.D. 63

61 N CLARK ● CAPE GIRARDEAU MO 63701-5101 ● (573) 335-6654

Grade Span: KG-12 **Schools**: *Regular* 9 ● *Spec Ed* 0 ● *Alt* 1 **Students**: 4,414 **Total Teachers**: 307 **Student/Classroom Teacher Ratio**: 14.9	**Expenditures/Student**: $4,664 **Librarians**: 6.0 736 students/librarian **Guidance Counselors**: 13.4 329 students/counselor	**% Amer Indian**: 0.1 **% Asian**: 1.2 **% Black**: 18.1 **% Hispanic**: 0.4 **% White**: 80.2	National ***Socio-Economic Status*** indicator percentile (100=high): 42nd

Cape Girardeau County
JACKSON REORGANIZED S.D. 2
221 S OKLAHOMA ● JACKSON MO 63755-2038 ● (573) 243-3579

Grade Span: KG-12 **Schools**: *Regular* 9 ● *Spec Ed* 0 ● *Alt* 0 **Students**: 3,995 **Total Teachers**: 213 **Student/Classroom Teacher Ratio**: 19.8	**Expenditures/Student**: $3,230 **Librarians**: 4.7 850 students/librarian **Guidance Counselors**: 6.8 588 students/counselor	**% Amer Indian**: 0.1 **% Asian**: 0.3 **% Black**: 1.1 **% Hispanic**: 0.1 **% White**: 98.4	National ***Socio-Economic Status*** indicator percentile (100=high): 69th

Cass County
BELTON S.D. 124
110 W WALNUT ● BELTON MO 64012-4808 ● (816) 348-1000 ● http://beltonschools.k12.mo.us

Grade Span: KG-12 **Schools**: *Regular* 6 ● *Spec Ed* 1 ● *Alt* 0 **Students**: 4,307 **Total Teachers**: 261 **Student/Classroom Teacher Ratio**: 16.5	**Expenditures/Student**: $4,073 **Librarians**: 6.0 718 students/librarian **Guidance Counselors**: 8.5 507 students/counselor	**% Amer Indian**: 0.6 **% Asian**: 0.9 **% Black**: 3.1 **% Hispanic**: 2.2 **% White**: 93.1	National ***Socio-Economic Status*** indicator percentile (100=high): 58th

Cass County
[PECULIAR] **RAYMORE-PECULIAR REORGANIZED S.D. 2**
PO BOX 366 ● PECULIAR MO 64078-0366 ● (816) 779-5191 ● http://www.raypec.k12.mo.us

Grade Span: KG-12 **Schools**: *Regular* 5 ● *Spec Ed* 0 ● *Alt* 0 **Students**: 3,501 **Total Teachers**: 194 **Student/Classroom Teacher Ratio**: 17.9	**Expenditures/Student**: $3,682 **Librarians**: 2.9 1,207 students/librarian **Guidance Counselors**: 7.0 500 students/counselor	**% Amer Indian**: 0.2 **% Asian**: 0.5 **% Black**: 1.3 **% Hispanic**: 0.8 **% White**: 97.2	National ***Socio-Economic Status*** indicator percentile (100=high): 82nd

Christian County
NIXA REORGANIZED S.D. 2
205 NORTH ST ● NIXA MO 65714-8663 ● (417) 725-7400 ● http://www.nixa.k12.mo.us

Grade Span: KG-12 **Schools**: *Regular* 5 ● *Spec Ed* 0 ● *Alt* 0 **Students**: 2,796 **Total Teachers**: 161 **Student/Classroom Teacher Ratio**: 17.4	**Expenditures/Student**: $3,314 **Librarians**: 5.0 559 students/librarian **Guidance Counselors**: 6.6 424 students/counselor	**% Amer Indian**: 0.4 **% Asian**: 0.5 **% Black**: 0.2 **% Hispanic**: 0.4 **% White**: 98.5	National ***Socio-Economic Status*** indicator percentile (100=high): 65th

Christian County
OZARK REORGANIZED S.D. 6
PO BOX 166 ● OZARK MO 65721-0166 ● (417) 581-7694 ● http://www.orion.org/ed/pubschls/Ozark/index.htm

Grade Span: KG-12 **Schools**: *Regular* 6 ● *Spec Ed* 0 ● *Alt* 0 **Students**: 2,989 **Total Teachers**: 192 **Student/Classroom Teacher Ratio**: 15.6	**Expenditures/Student**: $3,462 **Librarians**: 5.2 575 students/librarian **Guidance Counselors**: 6.8 440 students/counselor	**% Amer Indian**: 0.3 **% Asian**: 0.2 **% Black**: 0.3 **% Hispanic**: 0.5 **% White**: 98.6	National ***Socio-Economic Status*** indicator percentile (100=high): 64th

Clay County
EXCELSIOR SPRINGS S.D. 40
PO BOX 248 ● EXCELSIOR SPRINGS MO 64024-0248 ● (816) 630-9200

Grade Span: KG-12 **Schools**: *Regular* 7 ● *Spec Ed* 0 ● *Alt* 1 **Students**: 3,406 **Total Teachers**: 196 **Student/Classroom Teacher Ratio**: 17.6	**Expenditures/Student**: $3,844 **Librarians**: 2.9 1,174 students/librarian **Guidance Counselors**: 8.0 426 students/counselor	**% Amer Indian**: 0.2 **% Asian**: 0.7 **% Black**: 5.2 **% Hispanic**: 0.8 **% White**: 93.0	National ***Socio-Economic Status*** indicator percentile (100=high): 54th

Clay County

[KANSAS CITY] NORTH KANSAS CITY S.D. 74

2000 NE 46TH ST ● KANSAS CITY MO 64116-2042 ● (816) 453-5050 ● http://www.nkcsd.k12.mo.us

Grade Span: KG-12	**Expenditures/Student**: $4,915	**% Amer Indian**: 0.4	
Schools: *Regular* 27 ● *Spec Ed* 0 ● *Alt* 1	**Librarians**: 22.0	**% Asian**: 1.5	National ***Socio-Economic***
Students: 16,569	753 students/librarian	**% Black**: 3.5	***Status*** indicator percentile
Total Teachers: 1,049	**Guidance Counselors**: 37.6	**% Hispanic**: 2.8	(100=high): 62nd
Student/Classroom Teacher Ratio: 16.3	441 students/counselor	**% White**: 91.7	

Clay County

KEARNEY REORGANIZED S.D. 1

1002 S JEFFERSON ● KEARNEY MO 64060-8520 ● (816) 628-4116

Grade Span: KG-12	**Expenditures/Student**: $3,617	**% Amer Indian**: 0.4	
Schools: *Regular* 6 ● *Spec Ed* 0 ● *Alt* 0	**Librarians**: 4.0	**% Asian**: 0.1	National ***Socio-Economic***
Students: 2,563	641 students/librarian	**% Black**: 0.4	***Status*** indicator percentile
Total Teachers: 134	**Guidance Counselors**: 6.0	**% Hispanic**: 0.7	(100=high): 91st
Student/Classroom Teacher Ratio: 19.1	427 students/counselor	**% White**: 98.4	

Clay County

LIBERTY S.D. 53

14 S MAIN ● LIBERTY MO 64068-2323 ● (816) 781-4541 ● http://liberty.k12.mo.us

Grade Span: KG-12	**Expenditures/Student**: $4,331	**% Amer Indian**: 0.2	
Schools: *Regular* 9 ● *Spec Ed* 0 ● *Alt* 2	**Librarians**: 8.5	**% Asian**: 0.6	National ***Socio-Economic***
Students: 5,300	624 students/librarian	**% Black**: 3.8	***Status*** indicator percentile
Total Teachers: 309	**Guidance Counselors**: 13.0	**% Hispanic**: 1.4	(100=high): 73rd
Student/Classroom Teacher Ratio: 16.5	408 students/counselor	**% White**: 94.1	

Cole County

JEFFERSON CITY S.D.

315 E DUNKLIN ST ● JEFFERSON CITY MO 65101-3197 ● (573) 659-3000 ● http://www.oseda.missouri.edu/mupartners/JeffersonCity/index.html

Grade Span: KG-12	**Expenditures/Student**: $4,680	**% Amer Indian**: 0.3	
Schools: *Regular* 15 ● *Spec Ed* 0 ● *Alt* 2	**Librarians**: 16.4	**% Asian**: 0.6	National ***Socio-Economic***
Students: 8,679	529 students/librarian	**% Black**: 9.2	***Status*** indicator percentile
Total Teachers: 557	**Guidance Counselors**: 28.6	**% Hispanic**: 0.7	(100=high): 53rd
Student/Classroom Teacher Ratio: 15.7	303 students/counselor	**% White**: 89.2	

Franklin County

[PACIFIC] MERAMEC VALLEY REORGANIZED S.D. 3

126 N PAYNE ST ● PACIFIC MO 63069-1224 ● (314) 271-1400

Grade Span: KG-12	**Expenditures/Student**: $3,990	**% Amer Indian**: 0.4	
Schools: *Regular* 10 ● *Spec Ed* 0 ● *Alt* 0	**Librarians**: 4.0	**% Asian**: 0.5	National ***Socio-Economic***
Students: 3,681	920 students/librarian	**% Black**: 2.0	***Status*** indicator percentile
Total Teachers: 226	**Guidance Counselors**: 9.0	**% Hispanic**: 0.3	(100=high): 51st
Student/Classroom Teacher Ratio: 16.2	409 students/counselor	**% White**: 96.8	

Franklin County

UNION REORGANIZED S.D. 11

PO BOX 440 ● UNION MO 63084-0440 ● (314) 583-8626

Grade Span: KG-12	**Expenditures/Student**: $3,784	**% Amer Indian**: 0.0	
Schools: *Regular* 5 ● *Spec Ed* 0 ● *Alt* 0	**Librarians**: 2.9	**% Asian**: 0.2	National ***Socio-Economic***
Students: 2,998	1,034 students/librarian	**% Black**: 0.9	***Status*** indicator percentile
Total Teachers: 174	**Guidance Counselors**: 6.5	**% Hispanic**: 0.3	(100=high): 41st
Student/Classroom Teacher Ratio: 17.0	461 students/counselor	**% White**: 98.5	

Franklin County

WASHINGTON S.D.

PO BOX 357 ● WASHINGTON MO 63090-0357 ● (314) 239-2727

Grade Span: KG-12 **Schools**: *Regular* 10 ● *Spec Ed* 0 ● *Alt* 1 **Students**: 3,648 **Total Teachers**: 216 **Student/Classroom Teacher Ratio**: 16.2	**Expenditures/Student**: $4,706 **Librarians**: 2.7 1,351 students/librarian **Guidance Counselors**: 8.4 434 students/counselor	**% Amer Indian**: 0.0 **% Asian**: 0.2 **% Black**: 0.7 **% Hispanic**: 0.1 **% White**: 99.0	National ***Socio-Economic Status*** indicator percentile (100=high): na

Greene County

REPUBLIC REORGANIZED S.D. 3

518 N HAMPTON ● REPUBLIC MO 65738-1323 ● (417) 732-1812 ● http://www.republic.k12.mo.us

Grade Span: KG-12 **Schools**: *Regular* 5 ● *Spec Ed* 0 ● *Alt* 0 **Students**: 2,694 **Total Teachers**: 149 **Student/Classroom Teacher Ratio**: 18.2	**Expenditures/Student**: $3,188 **Librarians**: 5.0 539 students/librarian **Guidance Counselors**: 7.0 385 students/counselor	**% Amer Indian**: 0.2 **% Asian**: 0.9 **% Black**: 4.1 **% Hispanic**: 0.4 **% White**: 94.4	National ***Socio-Economic Status*** indicator percentile (100=high): na

Greene County

SPRINGFIELD REORGANIZED S.D. 12

940 N JEFFERSON ● SPRINGFIELD MO 65802-3718 ● (417) 864-3800 ● http://sps.k12.mo.us

Grade Span: KG-12 **Schools**: *Regular* 55 ● *Spec Ed* 0 ● *Alt* 2 **Students**: 24,740 **Total Teachers**: 1,475 **Student/Classroom Teacher Ratio**: 17.3	**Expenditures/Student**: $4,294 **Librarians**: 42.0 589 students/librarian **Guidance Counselors**: 58.8 421 students/counselor	**% Amer Indian**: 0.5 **% Asian**: 1.7 **% Black**: 3.8 **% Hispanic**: 1.2 **% White**: 92.8	National ***Socio-Economic Status*** indicator percentile (100=high): 50th

Greene County

WILLARD REORGANIZED S.D. 2

PO BOX 98 ● WILLARD MO 65781-0098 ● (417) 742-2584 ● http://www.willard.k12.mo.us

Grade Span: KG-12 **Schools**: *Regular* 4 ● *Spec Ed* 0 ● *Alt* 0 **Students**: 2,747 **Total Teachers**: 157 **Student/Classroom Teacher Ratio**: 17.5	**Expenditures/Student**: $3,283 **Librarians**: 4.0 687 students/librarian **Guidance Counselors**: 4.3 639 students/counselor	**% Amer Indian**: 0.1 **% Asian**: 0.3 **% Black**: 0.2 **% Hispanic**: 0.3 **% White**: 99.1	National ***Socio-Economic Status*** indicator percentile (100=high): 60th

Howell County

WEST PLAINS REORGANIZED S.D. 7

613 W FIRST ST ● WEST PLAINS MO 65775-2617 ● (417) 256-6150 ● http://wphs.k12.mo.us

Grade Span: KG-12 **Schools**: *Regular* 4 ● *Spec Ed* 0 ● *Alt* 1 **Students**: 2,722 **Total Teachers**: 165 **Student/Classroom Teacher Ratio**: 17.7	**Expenditures/Student**: $4,302 **Librarians**: 3.0 907 students/librarian **Guidance Counselors**: 9.0 302 students/counselor	**% Amer Indian**: 0.6 **% Asian**: 0.9 **% Black**: 1.0 **% Hispanic**: 0.6 **% White**: 96.9	National ***Socio-Economic Status*** indicator percentile (100=high): 32nd

Jackson County

BLUE SPRINGS REORGAINIZED S.D. 4

1801 W VESPER ● BLUE SPRINGS MO 64015-3219 ● (816) 224-1300

Grade Span: KG-12 **Schools**: *Regular* 17 ● *Spec Ed* 1 ● *Alt* 0 **Students**: 12,198 **Total Teachers**: 686 **Student/Classroom Teacher Ratio**: 17.2	**Expenditures/Student**: $4,443 **Librarians**: 6.0 2,033 students/librarian **Guidance Counselors**: 22.0 554 students/counselor	**% Amer Indian**: 0.2 **% Asian**: 1.2 **% Black**: 3.5 **% Hispanic**: 2.1 **% White**: 93.0	National ***Socio-Economic Status*** indicator percentile (100=high): 90th

Jackson County

GRANDVIEW CONSOLIDATED S.D. 4

724 MAIN ST ● GRANDVIEW MO 64030-2329 ● (816) 761-7486

Grade Span: KG-12 **Schools**: *Regular* 9 ● *Spec Ed* 0 ● *Alt* 1 **Students**: 4,294 **Total Teachers**: 283 **Student/Classroom Teacher Ratio**: 14.5	**Expenditures/Student**: $5,325 **Librarians**: 8.3 517 students/librarian **Guidance Counselors**: 13.0 330 students/counselor	**% Amer Indian**: 0.5 **% Asian**: 1.2 **% Black**: 34.0 **% Hispanic**: 1.7 **% White**: 62.6	National ***Socio-Economic Status*** indicator percentile (100=high): 40th

Jackson County

[INDEPENDENCE] **FORT OSAGE REORGANIZED S.D. 1**

2101 N TWYMAN RD ● INDEPENDENCE MO 64058-3200 ● (816) 650-6131 ● http://www.oseda.missouri.edu/fortosage.mo.us

Grade Span: KG-12 **Schools**: *Regular* 8 ● *Spec Ed* 0 ● *Alt* 1 **Students**: 4,902 **Total Teachers**: 301 **Student/Classroom Teacher Ratio**: 15.9	**Expenditures/Student**: $4,553 **Librarians**: 4.9 1,000 students/librarian **Guidance Counselors**: 13.0 377 students/counselor	**% Amer Indian**: 0.3 **% Asian**: 1.2 **% Black**: 2.4 **% Hispanic**: 1.3 **% White**: 94.7	National ***Socio-Economic Status*** indicator percentile (100=high): 59th

Jackson County

INDEPENDENCE S.D. 30

1231 S WINDSOR ● INDEPENDENCE MO 64055-1151 ● (816) 521-2700 ● http://www.indep.k12.mo.us

Grade Span: KG-12 **Schools**: *Regular* 20 ● *Spec Ed* 0 ● *Alt* 1 **Students**: 11,438 **Total Teachers**: 706 **Student/Classroom Teacher Ratio**: 15.4	**Expenditures/Student**: $5,283 **Librarians**: 12.6 908 students/librarian **Guidance Counselors**: 31.0 369 students/counselor	**% Amer Indian**: 0.3 **% Asian**: 2.4 **% Black**: 3.1 **% Hispanic**: 2.6 **% White**: 91.5	National ***Socio-Economic Status*** indicator percentile (100=high): 44th

Jackson County

[KANSAS CITY] **CENTER S.D. 58**

8701 HOLMES RD ● KANSAS CITY MO 64131-2802 ● (816) 363-6060

Grade Span: KG-12 **Schools**: *Regular* 6 ● *Spec Ed* 0 ● *Alt* 1 **Students**: 2,645 **Total Teachers**: 178 **Student/Classroom Teacher Ratio**: 15.4	**Expenditures/Student**: $6,433 **Librarians**: 5.0 529 students/librarian **Guidance Counselors**: 8.2 323 students/counselor	**% Amer Indian**: 0.3 **% Asian**: 2.4 **% Black**: 41.1 **% Hispanic**: 1.9 **% White**: 54.3	National ***Socio-Economic Status*** indicator percentile (100=high): 28th

Jackson County

[KANSAS CITY] **HICKMAN MILLS CONSOLIDATED S.D. 1**

9000 OLD SANTA FE RD ● KANSAS CITY MO 64138-3913 ● (816) 761-6111

Grade Span: KG-12 **Schools**: *Regular* 13 ● *Spec Ed* 0 ● *Alt* 1 **Students**: 7,084 **Total Teachers**: 450 **Student/Classroom Teacher Ratio**: 15.1	**Expenditures/Student**: $5,573 **Librarians**: 11.0 644 students/librarian **Guidance Counselors**: 18.5 383 students/counselor	**% Amer Indian**: 0.4 **% Asian**: 0.8 **% Black**: 53.3 **% Hispanic**: 1.9 **% White**: 43.5	National ***Socio-Economic Status*** indicator percentile (100=high): 36th

Jackson County

KANSAS CITY S.D. 33

1211 MCGEE ● KANSAS CITY MO 64106-2416 ● (816) 418-7000 ● http://www.kcmsd.k12.mo.us

Grade Span: KG-12 **Schools**: *Regular* 77 ● *Spec Ed* 1 ● *Alt* 5 **Students**: 36,515 **Total Teachers**: 2,840 **Student/Classroom Teacher Ratio**: 13.5	**Expenditures/Student**: $9,549 **Librarians**: 62.4 585 students/librarian **Guidance Counselors**: 92.4 395 students/counselor	**% Amer Indian**: 0.3 **% Asian**: 2.0 **% Black**: 69.8 **% Hispanic**: 5.5 **% White**: 22.3	National ***Socio-Economic Status*** indicator percentile (100=high): 14th

Jackson County

LEE'S SUMMIT REORGANIZED S.D. 7

600 SE MILLER ● LEE'S SUMMIT MO 64063-4261 ● (816) 524-3368

Grade Span: KG-12 **Schools**: *Regular* 16 ● *Spec Ed* 0 ● *Alt* 1 **Students**: 11,726 **Total Teachers**: 604 **Student/Classroom Teacher Ratio**: 19.5	**Expenditures/Student**: $4,449 **Librarians**: 13.0 902 students/librarian **Guidance Counselors**: 24.0 489 students/counselor	**% Amer Indian**: 0.1 **% Asian**: 0.9 **% Black**: 2.5 **% Hispanic**: 1.1 **% White**: 95.4	National ***Socio-Economic Status*** indicator percentile (100=high): 83rd

Jackson County

RAYTOWN CONSOLIDATED S.D. 2

10500 E 60TH TERR ● RAYTOWN MO 64133-3902 ● (816) 737-6200

Grade Span: KG-12 **Schools**: *Regular* 14 ● *Spec Ed* 0 ● *Alt* 2 **Students**: 8,252 **Total Teachers**: 503 **Student/Classroom Teacher Ratio**: 16.6	**Expenditures/Student**: $5,000 **Librarians**: 6.0 1,375 students/librarian **Guidance Counselors**: 20.8 397 students/counselor	**% Amer Indian**: 0.5 **% Asian**: 1.1 **% Black**: 17.5 **% Hispanic**: 1.9 **% White**: 79.0	National ***Socio-Economic Status*** indicator percentile (100=high): 65th

Jasper County

CARTHAGE REORGANIZED S.D. 9

714 S MAIN ST ● CARTHAGE MO 64836-1651 ● (417) 359-7000

Grade Span: KG-12 **Schools**: *Regular* 8 ● *Spec Ed* 0 ● *Alt* 1 **Students**: 3,471 **Total Teachers**: 209 **Student/Classroom Teacher Ratio**: 16.5	**Expenditures/Student**: $3,898 **Librarians**: 2.8 1,240 students/librarian **Guidance Counselors**: 9.3 373 students/counselor	**% Amer Indian**: 0.5 **% Asian**: 0.7 **% Black**: 2.0 **% Hispanic**: 2.0 **% White**: 94.8	National ***Socio-Economic Status*** indicator percentile (100=high): 46th

Jasper County

JOPLIN REORGANIZED S.D. 8

PO BOX 128 ● JOPLIN MO 64802-0128 ● (417) 625-5200 ● http://www.joplin.k12.mo.us

Grade Span: KG-12 **Schools**: *Regular* 18 ● *Spec Ed* 0 ● *Alt* 4 **Students**: 7,314 **Total Teachers**: 484 **Student/Classroom Teacher Ratio**: 15.7	**Expenditures/Student**: $4,378 **Librarians**: 11.4 642 students/librarian **Guidance Counselors**: 23.4 313 students/counselor	**% Amer Indian**: 0.9 **% Asian**: 1.1 **% Black**: 4.0 **% Hispanic**: 1.5 **% White**: 92.5	National ***Socio-Economic Status*** indicator percentile (100=high): 33rd

Jasper County

WEBB CITY REORGANIZED S.D. 7

411 N MADISON ● WEBB CITY MO 64870-1238 ● (417) 673-6000

Grade Span: KG-12 **Schools**: *Regular* 8 ● *Spec Ed* 0 ● *Alt* 0 **Students**: 3,228 **Total Teachers**: 180 **Student/Classroom Teacher Ratio**: 19.1	**Expenditures/Student**: $3,402 **Librarians**: 4.0 807 students/librarian **Guidance Counselors**: 7.8 414 students/counselor	**% Amer Indian**: 0.6 **% Asian**: 0.3 **% Black**: 0.4 **% Hispanic**: 0.7 **% White**: 98.0	National ***Socio-Economic Status*** indicator percentile (100=high): 38th

Jefferson County

[ARNOLD] **FOX CONSOLIDATED S.D. 6**

745 JEFFCO BLVD ● ARNOLD MO 63010-1432 ● (314) 296-8000 ● http://www.fox.k12.mo.us

Grade Span: KG-12 **Schools**: *Regular* 13 ● *Spec Ed* 0 ● *Alt* 0 **Students**: 10,416 **Total Teachers**: 548 **Student/Classroom Teacher Ratio**: 18.8	**Expenditures/Student**: $3,899 **Librarians**: 10.0 1,042 students/librarian **Guidance Counselors**: 21.0 496 students/counselor	**% Amer Indian**: 0.0 **% Asian**: 0.4 **% Black**: 0.3 **% Hispanic**: 0.4 **% White**: 98.8	National ***Socio-Economic Status*** indicator percentile (100=high): 58th

Jefferson County
DESOTO S.D. 73
PO BOX 579 ● DESOTO MO 63020-0579 ● (314) 586-8811 ● http://www.desoto.k12.mo.us

Grade Span: KG-12 **Schools**: *Regular* 4 ● *Spec Ed* 0 ● *Alt* 0 **Students**: 3,184 **Total Teachers**: 181 **Student/Classroom Teacher Ratio**: 17.5	**Expenditures/Student**: $3,667 **Librarians**: 4.0 796 students/librarian **Guidance Counselors**: 5.6 569 students/counselor	**% Amer Indian**: 0.0 **% Asian**: 0.1 **% Black**: 0.8 **% Hispanic**: 0.1 **% White**: 99.0	National ***Socio-Economic Status*** indicator percentile (100=high): 39th

Jefferson County
HILLSBORO REORGANIZED S.D. 3
20 HAWK DR ● HILLSBORO MO 63050-5080 ● (314) 789-3378

Grade Span: KG-12 **Schools**: *Regular* 6 ● *Spec Ed* 0 ● *Alt* 1 **Students**: 3,657 **Total Teachers**: 224 **Student/Classroom Teacher Ratio**: 15.6	**Expenditures/Student**: $3,523 **Librarians**: 5.0 731 students/librarian **Guidance Counselors**: 4.8 762 students/counselor	**% Amer Indian**: 0.2 **% Asian**: 0.2 **% Black**: 0.2 **% Hispanic**: 0.2 **% White**: 99.0	National ***Socio-Economic Status*** indicator percentile (100=high): na

Jefferson County
[HOUSE SPRINGS] NORTHWEST REORGANIZED S.D. 1
PO BOX 500 ● HOUSE SPRINGS MO 63051-0500 ● (314) 677-3473

Grade Span: KG-12 **Schools**: *Regular* 10 ● *Spec Ed* 0 ● *Alt* 0 **Students**: 7,797 **Total Teachers**: 425 **Student/Classroom Teacher Ratio**: 17.9	**Expenditures/Student**: $3,588 **Librarians**: 11.0 709 students/librarian **Guidance Counselors**: 17.0 459 students/counselor	**% Amer Indian**: 0.1 **% Asian**: 0.4 **% Black**: 0.2 **% Hispanic**: 0.3 **% White**: 99.0	National ***Socio-Economic Status*** indicator percentile (100=high): 54th

Jefferson County
[IMPERIAL] WINDSOR CONSOLIDATED S.D. 1
6208 HWY 61-67 ● IMPERIAL MO 63052-2311 ● (314) 464-4400 ● http://www.windsor.k12.mo.us

Grade Span: KG-12 **Schools**: *Regular* 4 ● *Spec Ed* 0 ● *Alt* 0 **Students**: 2,924 **Total Teachers**: 152 **Student/Classroom Teacher Ratio**: 19.2	**Expenditures/Student**: $3,458 **Librarians**: 4.0 731 students/librarian **Guidance Counselors**: 6.0 487 students/counselor	**% Amer Indian**: 0.1 **% Asian**: 0.2 **% Black**: 0.3 **% Hispanic**: 0.4 **% White**: 98.9	National ***Socio-Economic Status*** indicator percentile (100=high): 89th

Johnson County
WARRENSBURG REORGANIZED S.D. 6
PO BOX 638 ● WARRENSBURG MO 64093-0638 ● (660) 747-7823 ● http://oseda.missouri.edu/warrensburg.k12.mo.us

Grade Span: KG-12 **Schools**: *Regular* 7 ● *Spec Ed* 0 ● *Alt* 2 **Students**: 3,086 **Total Teachers**: 195 **Student/Classroom Teacher Ratio**: 17.0	**Expenditures/Student**: $4,119 **Librarians**: 4.0 772 students/librarian **Guidance Counselors**: 9.2 335 students/counselor	**% Amer Indian**: 0.2 **% Asian**: 2.1 **% Black**: 8.1 **% Hispanic**: 1.5 **% White**: 88.1	National ***Socio-Economic Status*** indicator percentile (100=high): na

Laclede County
LEBANON REORGANIZED S.D. 3
321 S JEFFERSON ● LEBANON MO 65536-3260 ● (417) 532-9141 ● http://www.llion.org/schools

Grade Span: KG-12 **Schools**: *Regular* 6 ● *Spec Ed* 0 ● *Alt* 1 **Students**: 3,975 **Total Teachers**: 234 **Student/Classroom Teacher Ratio**: 18.1	**Expenditures/Student**: $3,767 **Librarians**: 5.8 685 students/librarian **Guidance Counselors**: 10.0 398 students/counselor	**% Amer Indian**: 0.2 **% Asian**: 0.3 **% Black**: 0.7 **% Hispanic**: 0.6 **% White**: 98.3	National ***Socio-Economic Status*** indicator percentile (100=high): na

Lincoln County

TROY REORGANIZED S.D. 3

951 W COLLEGE ● TROY MO 63379-1112 ● (314) 462-6098 ● http://www.oseda.missouri.edu/troy.k12.mo.us

Grade Span: KG-12	**Expenditures/Student**: $3,392	**% Amer Indian**: 0.1	
Schools: *Regular* 6 ● *Spec Ed* 0 ● *Alt* 0	**Librarians**: 2.8	**% Asian**: 0.1	National ***Socio-Economic***
Students: 3,592	1,283 students/librarian	**% Black**: 2.0	***Status*** indicator percentile
Total Teachers: 176	**Guidance Counselors**: 5.4	**% Hispanic**: 0.4	(100=high): 60th
Student/Classroom Teacher Ratio: 20.3	665 students/counselor	**% White**: 97.3	

McDonald County

[ANDERSON] MCDONALD COUNTY REORGANIZED S.D. 1

PO BOX 378 ● ANDERSON MO 64831-0378 ● (417) 845-3321

Grade Span: KG-12	**Expenditures/Student**: $3,225	**% Amer Indian**: 1.5	
Schools: *Regular* 7 ● *Spec Ed* 0 ● *Alt* 0	**Librarians**: 2.9	**% Asian**: 0.3	National ***Socio-Economic***
Students: 3,079	1,062 students/librarian	**% Black**: 0.1	***Status*** indicator percentile
Total Teachers: 181	**Guidance Counselors**: 6.0	**% Hispanic**: 3.7	(100=high): 16th
Student/Classroom Teacher Ratio: 16.8	513 students/counselor	**% White**: 94.4	

Marion County

HANNIBAL S.D. 60

4650 MCMASTERS AVE ● HANNIBAL MO 63401-2244 ● (573) 221-1258 ● http://www.oseda.missouri.edu/mupartners/Hannibal60

Grade Span: KG-12	**Expenditures/Student**: $4,127	**% Amer Indian**: 0.2	
Schools: *Regular* 8 ● *Spec Ed* 0 ● *Alt* 1	**Librarians**: 3.2	**% Asian**: 0.6	National ***Socio-Economic***
Students: 3,881	1,213 students/librarian	**% Black**: 8.3	***Status*** indicator percentile
Total Teachers: 263	**Guidance Counselors**: 14.0	**% Hispanic**: 0.3	(100=high): 40th
Student/Classroom Teacher Ratio: 14.8	277 students/counselor	**% White**: 90.6	

Newton County

NEOSHO REORGANIZED S.D. 5

511 NEOSHO BLVD ● NEOSHO MO 64850-2049 ● (417) 451-8600 ● http://www.neosho.k12.mo.us

Grade Span: KG-12	**Expenditures/Student**: $3,246	**% Amer Indian**: 1.7	
Schools: *Regular* 8 ● *Spec Ed* 0 ● *Alt* 0	**Librarians**: 4.7	**% Asian**: 0.9	National ***Socio-Economic***
Students: 3,808	810 students/librarian	**% Black**: 1.1	***Status*** indicator percentile
Total Teachers: 198	**Guidance Counselors**: 8.0	**% Hispanic**: 1.4	(100=high): 33rd
Student/Classroom Teacher Ratio: 19.1	476 students/counselor	**% White**: 95.0	

Pettis County

SEDALIA S.D. 200

400 W FOURTH ST ● SEDALIA MO 65301-4296 ● (660) 826-1054

Grade Span: KG-12	**Expenditures/Student**: $4,097	**% Amer Indian**: 0.2	
Schools: *Regular* 8 ● *Spec Ed* 0 ● *Alt* 1	**Librarians**: 6.0	**% Asian**: 0.6	National ***Socio-Economic***
Students: 4,296	716 students/librarian	**% Black**: 7.8	***Status*** indicator percentile
Total Teachers: 271	**Guidance Counselors**: 11.0	**% Hispanic**: 1.0	(100=high): 23rd
Student/Classroom Teacher Ratio: 15.9	391 students/counselor	**% White**: 90.4	

Phelps County

ROLLA S.D. 31

SIXTH AND MAIN ST ● ROLLA MO 65401-3099 ● (573) 364-1329

Grade Span: KG-12	**Expenditures/Student**: $4,683	**% Amer Indian**: 0.2	
Schools: *Regular* 6 ● *Spec Ed* 0 ● *Alt* 1	**Librarians**: 6.0	**% Asian**: 2.1	National ***Socio-Economic***
Students: 4,005	668 students/librarian	**% Black**: 2.5	***Status*** indicator percentile
Total Teachers: 238	**Guidance Counselors**: 13.3	**% Hispanic**: 0.5	(100=high): 43rd
Student/Classroom Teacher Ratio: 18.8	301 students/counselor	**% White**: 94.7	

Platte County

[KANSAS CITY] **PARK HILL S.D.**

7703 NW BARRY RD ● KANSAS CITY MO 64153-1731 ● (816) 741-1521 ● http://www.parkhill.k12.mo.us

Grade Span: KG-12 **Schools**: *Regular* 11 ● *Spec Ed* 0 ● *Alt* 0 **Students**: 8,220 **Total Teachers**: 477 **Student/Classroom Teacher Ratio**: 16.1	**Expenditures/Student**: $5,063 **Librarians**: 12.0 685 students/librarian **Guidance Counselors**: 18.0 457 students/counselor	**% Amer Indian**: 0.2 **% Asian**: 1.8 **% Black**: 4.2 **% Hispanic**: 2.4 **% White**: 91.5	National ***Socio-Economic Status*** indicator percentile (100=high): 76th

Pulaski County

WAYNESVILLE REORGANIZED S.D. 6

399 SCHOOL ST ● WAYNESVILLE MO 65583-2545 ● (573) 774-6497 ● http://waynesville.k12.mo.us

Grade Span: KG-12 **Schools**: *Regular* 10 ● *Spec Ed* 0 ● *Alt* 1 **Students**: 4,592 **Total Teachers**: 314 **Student/Classroom Teacher Ratio**: 14.2	**Expenditures/Student**: $4,830 **Librarians**: 12.0 383 students/librarian **Guidance Counselors**: 18.5 248 students/counselor	**% Amer Indian**: 0.5 **% Asian**: 5.0 **% Black**: 22.6 **% Hispanic**: 6.3 **% White**: 65.6	National ***Socio-Economic Status*** indicator percentile (100=high): 21st

St. Charles County

[O'FALLON] **FORT ZUMWALT REORGANIZED S.D. 2**

110 VIRGIL ST ● O'FALLON MO 63366-2637 ● (314) 272-6620

Grade Span: KG-12 **Schools**: *Regular* 14 ● *Spec Ed* 0 ● *Alt* 0 **Students**: 13,149 **Total Teachers**: 721 **Student/Classroom Teacher Ratio**: 18.5	**Expenditures/Student**: $4,081 **Librarians**: 12.3 1,069 students/librarian **Guidance Counselors**: 27.0 487 students/counselor	**% Amer Indian**: 0.1 **% Asian**: 0.7 **% Black**: 2.4 **% Hispanic**: 0.7 **% White**: 96.1	National ***Socio-Economic Status*** indicator percentile (100=high): 77th

St. Charles County

[ST. CHARLES] **FRANCIS HOWELL REORGANIZED S.D. 3**

4545 CENTRAL SCHOOL RD ● ST. CHARLES MO 63304-7113 ● (314) 441-0088 ● http://www.fhsd.k12.mo.us

Grade Span: KG-12 **Schools**: *Regular* 14 ● *Spec Ed* 0 ● *Alt* 0 **Students**: 17,251 **Total Teachers**: 1,025 **Student/Classroom Teacher Ratio**: 16.6	**Expenditures/Student**: $4,488 **Librarians**: 15.0 1,150 students/librarian **Guidance Counselors**: 32.4 532 students/counselor	**% Amer Indian**: 0.2 **% Asian**: 0.6 **% Black**: 2.8 **% Hispanic**: 0.6 **% White**: 95.8	National ***Socio-Economic Status*** indicator percentile (100=high): 90th

St. Charles County

ST. CHARLES REORGANIZED S.D. 6

1025 COUNTRY CLUB RD ● ST. CHARLES MO 63303-3346 ● (314) 724-5840

Grade Span: KG-12 **Schools**: *Regular* 11 ● *Spec Ed* 0 ● *Alt* 1 **Students**: 6,516 **Total Teachers**: 413 **Student/Classroom Teacher Ratio**: 16.2	**Expenditures/Student**: $5,588 **Librarians**: 6.0 1,086 students/librarian **Guidance Counselors**: 22.1 295 students/counselor	**% Amer Indian**: 0.2 **% Asian**: 1.0 **% Black**: 5.6 **% Hispanic**: 1.0 **% White**: 92.3	National ***Socio-Economic Status*** indicator percentile (100=high): 58th

St. Charles County

WENTZVILLE REORGANIZED S.D. 4

ONE CAMPUS DR ● WENTZVILLE MO 63385-3415 ● (314) 327-3800 ● http://www.oseda.missouri.edu/mupartners/Wentzville

Grade Span: KG-12 **Schools**: *Regular* 6 ● *Spec Ed* 0 ● *Alt* 0 **Students**: 4,977 **Total Teachers**: 299 **Student/Classroom Teacher Ratio**: 16.6	**Expenditures/Student**: $4,435 **Librarians**: 4.0 1,244 students/librarian **Guidance Counselors**: 10.6 470 students/counselor	**% Amer Indian**: 0.2 **% Asian**: 0.7 **% Black**: 8.9 **% Hispanic**: 1.0 **% White**: 89.2	National ***Socio-Economic Status*** indicator percentile (100=high): 58th

St. Francois County

[BONNE TERRE] **NORTH ST. FRANCOIS COUNTY REORGANIZED S.D. 1**

300 BERRY RD ● BONNE TERRE MO 63628-4388 ● (573) 358-2247

Grade Span: KG-12 **Schools**: *Regular* 6 ● *Spec Ed* 0 ● *Alt* 1 **Students**: 3,067 **Total Teachers**: 189 **Student/Classroom Teacher Ratio**: 17.9	**Expenditures/Student**: $3,948 **Librarians**: 4.0 767 students/librarian **Guidance Counselors**: 7.5 409 students/counselor	**% Amer Indian**: 0.0 **% Asian**: 0.1 **% Black**: 0.5 **% Hispanic**: 0.3 **% White**: 99.2	National ***Socio-Economic Status*** indicator percentile (100=high): 53rd

St. Francois County

FARMINGTON REORGANIZED S.D. 7

PO BOX 570 ● FARMINGTON MO 63640-0570 ● (573) 701-1300

Grade Span: KG-12 **Schools**: *Regular* 7 ● *Spec Ed* 0 ● *Alt* 0 **Students**: 3,526 **Total Teachers**: 207 **Student/Classroom Teacher Ratio**: 15.7	**Expenditures/Student**: $3,869 **Librarians**: 3.9 904 students/librarian **Guidance Counselors**: 8.7 405 students/counselor	**% Amer Indian**: 0.1 **% Asian**: 0.5 **% Black**: 1.1 **% Hispanic**: 0.5 **% White**: 97.8	National ***Socio-Economic Status*** indicator percentile (100=high): 32nd

St. Louis County

[CHESTERFIELD] **PARKWAY CONSOLIDATED S.D. 2**

455 N WOODS MILL RD ● CHESTERFIELD MO 63017-3327 ● (314) 415-8100 ● http://info.csd.org/schools/parkway

Grade Span: KG-12 **Schools**: *Regular* 28 ● *Spec Ed* 0 ● *Alt* 0 **Students**: 21,841 **Total Teachers**: 1,281 **Student/Classroom Teacher Ratio**: 16.7	**Expenditures/Student**: $5,832 **Librarians**: 31.0 705 students/librarian **Guidance Counselors**: 60.5 361 students/counselor	**% Amer Indian**: 0.1 **% Asian**: 6.0 **% Black**: 18.3 **% Hispanic**: 0.9 **% White**: 74.7	National ***Socio-Economic Status*** indicator percentile (100=high): 97th

St. Louis County

[EUREKA] **ROCKWOOD REORGANIZED S.D. 6**

111 E NORTH ST ● EUREKA MO 63025-1229 ● (314) 938-5225 ● http://www.rockwood.k12.mo.us

Grade Span: KG-12 **Schools**: *Regular* 25 ● *Spec Ed* 0 ● *Alt* 1 **Students**: 19,610 **Total Teachers**: 1,053 **Student/Classroom Teacher Ratio**: 19.1	**Expenditures/Student**: $4,965 **Librarians**: 22.0 891 students/librarian **Guidance Counselors**: 52.0 377 students/counselor	**% Amer Indian**: 0.1 **% Asian**: 1.8 **% Black**: 14.9 **% Hispanic**: 0.5 **% White**: 82.7	National ***Socio-Economic Status*** indicator percentile (100=high): 83rd

St. Louis County

[FLORISSANT] **FERGUSON-FLORISSANT REORGANIZED S.D. 2**

1005 WATERFORD DR ● FLORISSANT MO 63033-3694 ● (314) 831-4411 ● http://www.fergflor.k12.mo.us

Grade Span: KG-12 **Schools**: *Regular* 23 ● *Spec Ed* 0 ● *Alt* 1 **Students**: 10,985 **Total Teachers**: 703 **Student/Classroom Teacher Ratio**: 16.0	**Expenditures/Student**: $5,935 **Librarians**: 25.0 439 students/librarian **Guidance Counselors**: 35.5 309 students/counselor	**% Amer Indian**: 0.1 **% Asian**: 0.6 **% Black**: 50.7 **% Hispanic**: 0.4 **% White**: 48.2	National ***Socio-Economic Status*** indicator percentile (100=high): 30th

St. Louis County

[FLORISSANT] **HAZELWOOD S.D.**

15955 NEW HALLS FERRY RD ● FLORISSANT MO 63031-1227 ● (314) 839-9400 ● http://www.hazelwood.k12.mo.us/index.html

Grade Span: KG-12 **Schools**: *Regular* 24 ● *Spec Ed* 1 ● *Alt* 0 **Students**: 18,156 **Total Teachers**: 1,023 **Student/Classroom Teacher Ratio**: 18.3	**Expenditures/Student**: $4,949 **Librarians**: 20.3 894 students/librarian **Guidance Counselors**: 47.7 381 students/counselor	**% Amer Indian**: 0.1 **% Asian**: 1.0 **% Black**: 35.0 **% Hispanic**: 0.7 **% White**: 63.2	National ***Socio-Economic Status*** indicator percentile (100=high): 68th

St. Louis County
JENNINGS S.D.
8888 CLIFTON AVE ● JENNINGS MO 63136-3804 ● (314) 867-8900 ● http://www.jennings.k12.mo.us

Grade Span: KG-12 **Schools**: *Regular* 5 ● *Spec Ed* 0 ● *Alt* 0 **Students**: 2,641 **Total Teachers**: 132 **Student/Classroom Teacher Ratio**: 20.0	**Expenditures/Student**: $3,651 **Librarians**: 1.0 2,641 students/librarian **Guidance Counselors**: 6.0 440 students/counselor	**% Amer Indian**: 0.0 **% Asian**: 0.5 **% Black**: 86.2 **% Hispanic**: 0.4 **% White**: 12.9	National ***Socio-Economic Status*** indicator percentile (100=high): 9th

St. Louis County
KIRKWOOD REORGANIZED S.D. 7
11289 MANCHESTER RD ● KIRKWOOD MO 63122-1122 ● (314) 965-9570 ● http://www.kirkwood.k12.mo.us/asc/ksdhome.htm

Grade Span: KG-12 **Schools**: *Regular* 8 ● *Spec Ed* 0 ● *Alt* 0 **Students**: 5,138 **Total Teachers**: 311 **Student/Classroom Teacher Ratio**: 16.6	**Expenditures/Student**: $5,599 **Librarians**: 9.0 571 students/librarian **Guidance Counselors**: 16.0 321 students/counselor	**% Amer Indian**: 0.0 **% Asian**: 0.9 **% Black**: 25.1 **% Hispanic**: 0.4 **% White**: 73.6	National ***Socio-Economic Status*** indicator percentile (100=high): 64th

St. Louis County
[ST. ANN] PATTONVILLE REORGANIZED S.D. 3
11097 ST. CHARLES ROCK RD ● ST. ANN MO 63074-1509 ● (314) 213-8005 ● http://info.csd.org:80/WWW/schools/pattonville/home.html

Grade Span: KG-12 **Schools**: *Regular* 12 ● *Spec Ed* 0 ● *Alt* 0 **Students**: 6,872 **Total Teachers**: 462 **Student/Classroom Teacher Ratio**: 15.5	**Expenditures/Student**: $7,195 **Librarians**: 13.0 529 students/librarian **Guidance Counselors**: 25.0 275 students/counselor	**% Amer Indian**: 0.0 **% Asian**: 1.0 **% Black**: 24.7 **% Hispanic**: 0.5 **% White**: 73.8	National ***Socio-Economic Status*** indicator percentile (100=high): na

St. Louis County
[ST. LOUIS] AFFTON S.D. 101
8701 MACKENZIE RD ● ST. LOUIS MO 63123-3436 ● (314) 638-8770 ● http://info.csd.org/affton.htm

Grade Span: KG-12 **Schools**: *Regular* 4 ● *Spec Ed* 0 ● *Alt* 0 **Students**: 2,563 **Total Teachers**: 149 **Student/Classroom Teacher Ratio**: 17.3	**Expenditures/Student**: $6,129 **Librarians**: 4.0 641 students/librarian **Guidance Counselors**: 7.7 333 students/counselor	**% Amer Indian**: 0.0 **% Asian**: 2.3 **% Black**: 15.2 **% Hispanic**: 0.5 **% White**: 82.1	National ***Socio-Economic Status*** indicator percentile (100=high): na

St. Louis County
[ST. LOUIS] LADUE S.D.
9703 CONWAY RD ● ST. LOUIS MO 63124-1646 ● (314) 994-7080 ● http://www.ladue.k12.mo.us

Grade Span: KG-12 **Schools**: *Regular* 6 ● *Spec Ed* 0 ● *Alt* 0 **Students**: 3,356 **Total Teachers**: 245 **Student/Classroom Teacher Ratio**: 14.3	**Expenditures/Student**: $8,361 **Librarians**: 10.0 336 students/librarian **Guidance Counselors**: 12.9 260 students/counselor	**% Amer Indian**: 0.1 **% Asian**: 4.0 **% Black**: 24.4 **% Hispanic**: 1.2 **% White**: 70.3	National ***Socio-Economic Status*** indicator percentile (100=high): na

St. Louis County
[ST. LOUIS] LINDBERGH REORGANIZED S.D. 8
4900 S LINDBERGH BLVD ● ST. LOUIS MO 63126-3235 ● (314) 842-3800 ● http://www.lindbergh.k12.mo.us

Grade Span: KG-12 **Schools**: *Regular* 7 ● *Spec Ed* 0 ● *Alt* 0 **Students**: 5,227 **Total Teachers**: 312 **Student/Classroom Teacher Ratio**: 16.5	**Expenditures/Student**: $5,494 **Librarians**: 7.0 747 students/librarian **Guidance Counselors**: 13.5 387 students/counselor	**% Amer Indian**: 0.0 **% Asian**: 1.1 **% Black**: 19.7 **% Hispanic**: 0.5 **% White**: 78.6	National ***Socio-Economic Status*** indicator percentile (100=high): 94th

St. Louis County

[ST. LOUIS] **MEHLVILLE REORGANIZED S.D. 9**

3120 LEMAY FERRY RD ● ST. LOUIS MO 63125-4416 ● (314) 892-5000

Grade Span: KG-12 **Schools**: *Regular* 16 ● *Spec Ed* 0 ● *Alt* 0 **Students**: 12,010 **Total Teachers**: 621 **Student/Classroom Teacher Ratio**: 19.7	**Expenditures/Student**: $4,393 **Librarians**: 11.5 1,044 students/librarian **Guidance Counselors**: 28.5 421 students/counselor	**% Amer Indian**: 0.1 **% Asian**: 0.8 **% Black**: 12.9 **% Hispanic**: 0.5 **% White**: 85.7	National ***Socio-Economic Status*** indicator percentile (100=high): 63rd

St. Louis County

[ST. LOUIS] **NORMANDY S.D.**

7837 NATURAL BRIDGE RD ● ST. LOUIS MO 63121-4625 ● (314) 389-8005

Grade Span: KG-12 **Schools**: *Regular* 13 ● *Spec Ed* 0 ● *Alt* 0 **Students**: 5,968 **Total Teachers**: 313 **Student/Classroom Teacher Ratio**: 18.5	**Expenditures/Student**: $5,181 **Librarians**: 6.0 995 students/librarian **Guidance Counselors**: 21.0 284 students/counselor	**% Amer Indian**: 0.1 **% Asian**: 0.2 **% Black**: 97.0 **% Hispanic**: 0.2 **% White**: 2.5	National ***Socio-Economic Status*** indicator percentile (100=high): 8th

St. Louis County

[ST. LOUIS] **RITENOUR S.D.**

2420 WOODSON RD ● ST. LOUIS MO 63114-5423 ● (314) 429-3500 ● http://info.csd.org/ritenour.html

Grade Span: KG-12 **Schools**: *Regular* 9 ● *Spec Ed* 0 ● *Alt* 0 **Students**: 6,582 **Total Teachers**: 340 **Student/Classroom Teacher Ratio**: 19.1	**Expenditures/Student**: $4,516 **Librarians**: 7.6 866 students/librarian **Guidance Counselors**: 15.0 439 students/counselor	**% Amer Indian**: 0.0 **% Asian**: 1.5 **% Black**: 28.7 **% Hispanic**: 0.9 **% White**: 68.9	National ***Socio-Economic Status*** indicator percentile (100=high): 36th

St. Louis County

[ST. LOUIS] **RIVERVIEW GARDENS S.D.**

1370 NORTHUMBERLAND ● ST. LOUIS MO 63137-1413 ● (314) 869-2505 ● http://www.rgsd.org

Grade Span: KG-12 **Schools**: *Regular* 11 ● *Spec Ed* 0 ● *Alt* 0 **Students**: 5,646 **Total Teachers**: 304 **Student/Classroom Teacher Ratio**: 19.1	**Expenditures/Student**: $4,513 **Librarians**: 8.0 706 students/librarian **Guidance Counselors**: 17.0 332 students/counselor	**% Amer Indian**: 0.0 **% Asian**: 0.3 **% Black**: 72.5 **% Hispanic**: 0.1 **% White**: 27.2	National ***Socio-Economic Status*** indicator percentile (100=high): 21st

St. Louis County

UNIVERSITY CITY S.D.

8346 DELCREST DR ● UNIVERSITY CITY MO 63124-2167 ● (314) 872-1900

Grade Span: KG-12 **Schools**: *Regular* 9 ● *Spec Ed* 0 ● *Alt* 0 **Students**: 4,481 **Total Teachers**: 292 **Student/Classroom Teacher Ratio**: 15.5	**Expenditures/Student**: $5,766 **Librarians**: 7.0 640 students/librarian **Guidance Counselors**: 15.0 299 students/counselor	**% Amer Indian**: 0.1 **% Asian**: 0.6 **% Black**: 83.7 **% Hispanic**: 0.6 **% White**: 15.1	National ***Socio-Economic Status*** indicator percentile (100=high): 23rd

St. Louis County

WEBSTER GROVES S.D.

400 E LOCKWOOD AVE ● WEBSTER GROVES MO 63119-3125 ● (314) 961-1233 ● http://www.webster.k12.mo.us

Grade Span: KG-12 **Schools**: *Regular* 10 ● *Spec Ed* 0 ● *Alt* 0 **Students**: 4,384 **Total Teachers**: 273 **Student/Classroom Teacher Ratio**: 16.2	**Expenditures/Student**: $5,137 **Librarians**: 4.0 1,096 students/librarian **Guidance Counselors**: 14.0 313 students/counselor	**% Amer Indian**: 0.1 **% Asian**: 1.0 **% Black**: 25.4 **% Hispanic**: 0.5 **% White**: 73.0	National ***Socio-Economic Status*** indicator percentile (100=high): 56th

St. Louis Independent City

ST. LOUIS CITY S.D.

911 LOCUST ST ● ST. LOUIS MO 63101-1401 ● (314) 231-3720 ● http://dtd1.slps.k12.mo.us

Grade Span: KG-12	**Expenditures/Student**: $7,918	**% Amer Indian**: 0.0	
Schools: *Regular* 105 ● *Spec Ed* 0 ● *Alt* 4	**Librarians**: 70.0	**% Asian**: 1.6	National ***Socio-Economic***
Students: 41,720	596 students/librarian	**% Black**: 79.2	***Status*** indicator percentile
Total Teachers: 3,153	**Guidance Counselors**: 114.0	**% Hispanic**: 0.7	(100=high): 2nd
Student/Classroom Teacher Ratio: 13.0	366 students/counselor	**% White**: 18.5	

Saline County

MARSHALL S.D.

468 S JEFFERSON ● MARSHALL MO 65340-2139 ● (660) 886-7414 ● http://www.mhsowls.k12.mo.us

Grade Span: KG-12	**Expenditures/Student**: $4,305	**% Amer Indian**: 0.0	
Schools: *Regular* 6 ● *Spec Ed* 0 ● *Alt* 1	**Librarians**: 2.8	**% Asian**: 0.6	National ***Socio-Economic***
Students: 2,516	899 students/librarian	**% Black**: 9.7	***Status*** indicator percentile
Total Teachers: 171	**Guidance Counselors**: 6.1	**% Hispanic**: 1.4	(100=high): 24th
Student/Classroom Teacher Ratio: 15.3	412 students/counselor	**% White**: 88.3	

Scott County

SIKESTON REORGANIZED S.D. 6

1002 VIRGINIA ● SIKESTON MO 63801-3347 ● (573) 472-2581 ● http://www.sikeston.k12.mo.us

Grade Span: KG-12	**Expenditures/Student**: $3,711	**% Amer Indian**: 0.2	
Schools: *Regular* 9 ● *Spec Ed* 0 ● *Alt* 1	**Librarians**: 5.5	**% Asian**: 0.4	National ***Socio-Economic***
Students: 4,129	751 students/librarian	**% Black**: 25.7	***Status*** indicator percentile
Total Teachers: 249	**Guidance Counselors**: 14.0	**% Hispanic**: 0.4	(100=high): 27th
Student/Classroom Teacher Ratio: 17.2	295 students/counselor	**% White**: 73.3	

Taney County

BRANSON REORGANIZED S.D. 4

400 CEDAR RIDGE DR ● BRANSON MO 65616-8143 ● (417) 334-6541 ● http://www.branson.k12.mo.us

Grade Span: KG-12	**Expenditures/Student**: $4,134	**% Amer Indian**: 0.6	
Schools: *Regular* 4 ● *Spec Ed* 0 ● *Alt* 0	**Librarians**: 2.0	**% Asian**: 1.0	National ***Socio-Economic***
Students: 2,523	1,262 students/librarian	**% Black**: 0.0	***Status*** indicator percentile
Total Teachers: 157	**Guidance Counselors**: 5.9	**% Hispanic**: 1.5	(100=high): na
Student/Classroom Teacher Ratio: 16.1	428 students/counselor	**% White**: 96.8	

Vernon County

NEVADA REORGANIZED S.D. 5

800 W HICKORY ● NEVADA MO 64772-2059 ● (417) 448-2000

Grade Span: KG-12	**Expenditures/Student**: $4,444	**% Amer Indian**: 0.6	
Schools: *Regular* 5 ● *Spec Ed* 0 ● *Alt* 1	**Librarians**: 3.0	**% Asian**: 0.3	National ***Socio-Economic***
Students: 2,682	894 students/librarian	**% Black**: 0.2	***Status*** indicator percentile
Total Teachers: 161	**Guidance Counselors**: 6.8	**% Hispanic**: 0.3	(100=high): na
Student/Classroom Teacher Ratio: 17.5	394 students/counselor	**% White**: 98.6	

Washington County

POTOSI REORGANIZED S.D. 3

400 N MINE ● POTOSI MO 63664-1734 ● (573) 438-5485 ● http://www.potosi.k12.mo.us

Grade Span: KG-12	**Expenditures/Student**: $3,672	**% Amer Indian**: 0.1	
Schools: *Regular* 5 ● *Spec Ed* 0 ● *Alt* 0	**Librarians**: 3.0	**% Asian**: 0.1	National ***Socio-Economic***
Students: 2,651	884 students/librarian	**% Black**: 1.4	***Status*** indicator percentile
Total Teachers: 157	**Guidance Counselors**: 5.8	**% Hispanic**: 0.3	(100=high): 25th
Student/Classroom Teacher Ratio: 18.2	457 students/counselor	**% White**: 98.1	

Cascade County

GREAT FALLS ELEMENTARY S.D.

PO BOX 2429 ● GREAT FALLS MT 59403 ● (406) 791-2350 ● http://www.gfps.k12.mt.us

Grade Span: PK-08 **Schools**: *Regular* 18 ● *Spec Ed* 0 ● *Alt* 0 **Students**: 9,337 **Total Teachers**: 502 **Student/Classroom Teacher Ratio**: 18.9	**Expenditures/Student**: $4,058 **Librarians**: 13.0 718 students/librarian **Guidance Counselors**: 17.0 549 students/counselor	**% Amer Indian**: 8.8 **% Asian**: 1.7 **% Black**: 2.2 **% Hispanic**: 1.4 **% White**: 85.9	National ***Socio-Economic Status*** indicator percentile (100=high): 46th

Cascade County

GREAT FALLS HIGH S.D.

PO BOX 2429 ● GREAT FALLS MT 59403 ● (406) 791-2350 ● http://www.gfps.k12.mt.us

Grade Span: 09-12 **Schools**: *Regular* 2 ● *Spec Ed* 0 ● *Alt* 0 **Students**: 3,829 **Total Teachers**: 210 **Student/Classroom Teacher Ratio**: 18.3	**Expenditures/Student**: $5,286 **Librarians**: 5.0 766 students/librarian **Guidance Counselors**: 13.3 288 students/counselor	**% Amer Indian**: 6.7 **% Asian**: 1.3 **% Black**: 1.1 **% Hispanic**: 0.8 **% White**: 90.1	National ***Socio-Economic Status*** indicator percentile (100=high): 74th

Flathead County

KALISPELL ELEMENTARY S.D.

233 FIRST AVENUE EAST ● KALISPELL MT 59901 ● (406) 755-5015

Grade Span: PK-08 **Schools**: *Regular* 7 ● *Spec Ed* 0 ● *Alt* 0 **Students**: 2,636 **Total Teachers**: 135 **Student/Classroom Teacher Ratio**: 20.1	**Expenditures/Student**: $4,439 **Librarians**: 8.0 330 students/librarian **Guidance Counselors**: 7.3 361 students/counselor	**% Amer Indian**: 2.0 **% Asian**: 1.1 **% Black**: 0.5 **% Hispanic**: 0.4 **% White**: 96.0	National ***Socio-Economic Status*** indicator percentile (100=high): 58th

Gallatin County

BOZEMAN ELEMENTARY S.D.

PO BOX 520 ● BOZEMAN MT 59715 ● (406) 585-1501 ● http://www.bps.montana.edu/index2.ssi

Grade Span: PK-08 **Schools**: *Regular* 8 ● *Spec Ed* 0 ● *Alt* 0 **Students**: 3,410 **Total Teachers**: 197 **Student/Classroom Teacher Ratio**: 17.7	**Expenditures/Student**: $3,914 **Librarians**: 7.1 480 students/librarian **Guidance Counselors**: 3.0 1,137 students/counselor	**% Amer Indian**: 2.1 **% Asian**: 1.8 **% Black**: 0.2 **% Hispanic**: 1.4 **% White**: 94.5	National ***Socio-Economic Status*** indicator percentile (100=high): 77th

Lewis and Clark County

HELENA ELEMENTARY S.D.

PO BOX 5417 ● HELENA MT 59604 ● (406) 442-5773 ● http://compaq.mthimc.mtlib.org

Grade Span: KG-08 **Schools**: *Regular* 14 ● *Spec Ed* 0 ● *Alt* 0 **Students**: 5,505 **Total Teachers**: 310 **Student/Classroom Teacher Ratio**: 18.6	**Expenditures/Student**: $4,299 **Librarians**: 11.8 467 students/librarian **Guidance Counselors**: 5.5 1,001 students/counselor	**% Amer Indian**: 3.7 **% Asian**: 0.9 **% Black**: 0.4 **% Hispanic**: 1.1 **% White**: 93.9	National ***Socio-Economic Status*** indicator percentile (100=high): 65th

Lewis and Clark County

HELENA HIGH S.D.

PO BOX 5417 ● HELENA MT 59604 ● (406) 442-5773 ● http://compaq.mthimc.mtlib.org

Grade Span: 09-12 **Schools**: *Regular* 2 ● *Spec Ed* 0 ● *Alt* 0 **Students**: 2,994 **Total Teachers**: 153 **Student/Classroom Teacher Ratio**: 19.8	**Expenditures/Student**: $5,200 **Librarians**: 4.0 749 students/librarian **Guidance Counselors**: 8.0 374 students/counselor	**% Amer Indian**: 3.5 **% Asian**: 0.6 **% Black**: 0.1 **% Hispanic**: 1.5 **% White**: 94.3	National ***Socio-Economic Status*** indicator percentile (100=high): 92nd

Missoula County
MISSOULA ELEMENTARY S.D.
215 SOUTH 6TH WEST • MISSOULA MT 59801 • (406) 728-4000 • http://www.mcps.k12.mt.us

Grade Span: KG-08 **Schools**: *Regular* 16 • *Spec Ed* 0 • *Alt* 0 **Students**: 5,941 **Total Teachers**: 325 **Student/Classroom Teacher Ratio**: 18.8	**Expenditures/Student**: $4,611 **Librarians**: 14.5 410 students/librarian **Guidance Counselors**: 8.0 743 students/counselor	**% Amer Indian**: 4.1 **% Asian**: 1.8 **% Black**: 0.7 **% Hispanic**: 0.8 **% White**: 92.7	National ***Socio-Economic Status*** indicator percentile (100=high): 49th

Missoula County
MISSOULA HIGH S.D.
915 SOUTH AVENUE WEST • MISSOULA MT 59801 • (406) 728-2400 • http://www.mcps.k12.mt.us

Grade Span: 09-12 **Schools**: *Regular* 4 • *Spec Ed* 0 • *Alt* 0 **Students**: 3,788 **Total Teachers**: 234 **Student/Classroom Teacher Ratio**: 15.5	**Expenditures/Student**: $5,925 **Librarians**: 3.5 1,082 students/librarian **Guidance Counselors**: 15.0 253 students/counselor	**% Amer Indian**: 2.1 **% Asian**: 1.5 **% Black**: 0.3 **% Hispanic**: 0.8 **% White**: 95.2	National ***Socio-Economic Status*** indicator percentile (100=high): 73rd

Silver Bow County
BUTTE ELEMENTARY S.D.
111 NORTH MONTANA • BUTTE MT 59701 • (406) 782-8315

Grade Span: PK-08 **Schools**: *Regular* 9 • *Spec Ed* 0 • *Alt* 0 **Students**: 4,025 **Total Teachers**: 194 **Student/Classroom Teacher Ratio**: 21.3	**Expenditures/Student**: $4,700 **Librarians**: 1.9 2,118 students/librarian **Guidance Counselors**: 8.0 503 students/counselor	**% Amer Indian**: 4.0 **% Asian**: 1.0 **% Black**: 0.3 **% Hispanic**: 2.7 **% White**: 91.9	National ***Socio-Economic Status*** indicator percentile (100=high): 44th

Yellowstone County
BILLINGS ELEMENTARY S.D.
415 NORTH 30TH STREET • BILLINGS MT 59101 • (406) 248-3500 • http://www.billings.k12.mt.us/About.html

Grade Span: PK-08 **Schools**: *Regular* 28 • *Spec Ed* 0 • *Alt* 0 **Students**: 10,971 **Total Teachers**: 587 **Student/Classroom Teacher Ratio**: 18.9	**Expenditures/Student**: $4,340 **Librarians**: 29.3 374 students/librarian **Guidance Counselors**: 19.1 574 students/counselor	**% Amer Indian**: 5.7 **% Asian**: 1.3 **% Black**: 0.9 **% Hispanic**: 4.5 **% White**: 87.6	National ***Socio-Economic Status*** indicator percentile (100=high): 51st

Yellowstone County
BILLINGS HIGH S.D.
415 NORTH 30TH STREET • BILLINGS MT 59101 • (406) 248-3500 • http://www.billings.k12.mt.us

Grade Span: 09-12 **Schools**: *Regular* 3 • *Spec Ed* 0 • *Alt* 0 **Students**: 5,234 **Total Teachers**: 273 **Student/Classroom Teacher Ratio**: 19.4	**Expenditures/Student**: $5,973 **Librarians**: 6.5 805 students/librarian **Guidance Counselors**: 20.0 262 students/counselor	**% Amer Indian**: 3.8 **% Asian**: 0.8 **% Black**: 0.7 **% Hispanic**: 3.6 **% White**: 91.0	National ***Socio-Economic Status*** indicator percentile (100=high): 83rd

Adams County

HASTINGS S.D.

714 W 5TH ● HASTINGS NE 68901 ● (402) 461-7500 ● http://esu9.esu9.k12.ne.us/~hastings

Grade Span: PK-12 **Schools**: *Regular* 8 ● *Spec Ed* 0 ● *Alt* 0 **Students**: 3,426 **Total Teachers**: 210 **Student/Classroom Teacher Ratio**: 16.2	**Expenditures/Student**: $4,746 **Librarians**: 5.0 685 students/librarian **Guidance Counselors**: 9.0 381 students/counselor	**% Amer Indian**: 0.8 **% Asian**: 2.0 **% Black**: 0.9 **% Hispanic**: 4.1 **% White**: 92.2	National ***Socio-Economic Status*** indicator percentile (100=high): 60th

Buffalo County

KEARNEY S.D.

310 W 24TH ST ● KEARNEY NE 68847 ● (308) 237-6000 ● http://www.esu10.k12.ne.us/~kearney/kps_home.html

Grade Span: PK-12 **Schools**: *Regular* 11 ● *Spec Ed* 1 ● *Alt* 0 **Students**: 4,648 **Total Teachers**: 274 **Student/Classroom Teacher Ratio**: 17.4	**Expenditures/Student**: $4,386 **Librarians**: 5.8 801 students/librarian **Guidance Counselors**: 10.2 456 students/counselor	**% Amer Indian**: 0.4 **% Asian**: 1.1 **% Black**: 0.5 **% Hispanic**: 4.9 **% White**: 93.2	National ***Socio-Economic Status*** indicator percentile (100=high): 62nd

Dakota County

SOUTH SIOUX CITY S.D.

820 EAST 29TH ST, BOX 158 ● SOUTH SIOUX CITY NE 68776-0158 ● (402) 494-2425

Grade Span: PK-12 **Schools**: *Regular* 8 ● *Spec Ed* 0 ● *Alt* 0 **Students**: 2,950 **Total Teachers**: 170 **Student/Classroom Teacher Ratio**: 17.5	**Expenditures/Student**: $4,074 **Librarians**: 3.6 819 students/librarian **Guidance Counselors**: 6.0 492 students/counselor	**% Amer Indian**: 2.9 **% Asian**: 4.8 **% Black**: 0.9 **% Hispanic**: 19.7 **% White**: 71.7	National ***Socio-Economic Status*** indicator percentile (100=high): 50th

Dodge County

FREMONT S.D.

957 N PIERCE ST ● FREMONT NE 68025-3949 ● (402) 727-3000

Grade Span: PK-12 **Schools**: *Regular* 13 ● *Spec Ed* 0 ● *Alt* 0 **Students**: 4,484 **Total Teachers**: 261 **Student/Classroom Teacher Ratio**: 16.8	**Expenditures/Student**: $4,762 **Librarians**: 6.0 747 students/librarian **Guidance Counselors**: 9.6 467 students/counselor	**% Amer Indian**: 0.4 **% Asian**: 0.7 **% Black**: 0.4 **% Hispanic**: 0.8 **% White**: 97.8	National ***Socio-Economic Status*** indicator percentile (100=high): 62nd

Douglas County

[OMAHA] **MILLARD S.D.**

5606 S 147TH ST ● OMAHA NE 68137 ● (402) 895-8200

Grade Span: PK-12 **Schools**: *Regular* 29 ● *Spec Ed* 1 ● *Alt* 0 **Students**: 18,288 **Total Teachers**: 1,059 **Student/Classroom Teacher Ratio**: 17.8	**Expenditures/Student**: $4,704 **Librarians**: 29.2 626 students/librarian **Guidance Counselors**: 39.6 462 students/counselor	**% Amer Indian**: 0.2 **% Asian**: 1.7 **% Black**: 1.0 **% Hispanic**: 1.2 **% White**: 95.9	National ***Socio-Economic Status*** indicator percentile (100=high): 95th

Douglas County

OMAHA S.D.

3215 CUMING ST ● OMAHA NE 68131 ● (402) 557-2222 ● http://www.ops.org

Grade Span: PK-12 **Schools**: *Regular* 80 ● *Spec Ed* 2 ● *Alt* 0 **Students**: 44,247 **Total Teachers**: 2,786 **Student/Classroom Teacher Ratio**: 16.3	**Expenditures/Student**: $5,248 **Librarians**: 85.6 517 students/librarian **Guidance Counselors**: 117.5 377 students/counselor	**% Amer Indian**: 1.5 **% Asian**: 1.3 **% Black**: 29.7 **% Hispanic**: 6.6 **% White**: 60.9	National ***Socio-Economic Status*** indicator percentile (100=high): 30th

Douglas County

[OMAHA] WESTSIDE COMMUNITY S.D.

909 S 76TH ST ● OMAHA NE 68114 ● (402) 390-2100 ● http://www.wst.esu3.k12.ne.us

Grade Span: PK-12 **Schools**: *Regular* 12 ● *Spec Ed* 1 ● *Alt* 0 **Students**: 4,896 **Total Teachers**: 344 **Student/Classroom Teacher Ratio**: 13.8	**Expenditures/Student**: $7,454 **Librarians**: 8.4 583 students/librarian **Guidance Counselors**: 16.1 304 students/counselor	**% Amer Indian**: 0.3 **% Asian**: 1.8 **% Black**: 2.3 **% Hispanic**: 1.6 **% White**: 93.9	National ***Socio-Economic Status*** indicator percentile (100=high): 83rd

Douglas County

RALSTON S.D.

8545 PARK DR ● RALSTON NE 68127 ● (402) 331-4700

Grade Span: PK-12 **Schools**: *Regular* 8 ● *Spec Ed* 0 ● *Alt* 0 **Students**: 3,180 **Total Teachers**: 210 **Student/Classroom Teacher Ratio**: 15.4	**Expenditures/Student**: $6,602 **Librarians**: 5.0 636 students/librarian **Guidance Counselors**: 9.0 353 students/counselor	**% Amer Indian**: 0.7 **% Asian**: 2.2 **% Black**: 2.6 **% Hispanic**: 3.1 **% White**: 91.4	National ***Socio-Economic Status*** indicator percentile (100=high): 83rd

Hall County

GRAND ISLAND S.D.

615 N ELM ST ● GRAND ISLAND NE 68801 ● (308) 385-5900

Grade Span: PK-12 **Schools**: *Regular* 18 ● *Spec Ed* 1 ● *Alt* 0 **Students**: 7,317 **Total Teachers**: 427 **Student/Classroom Teacher Ratio**: 17.6	**Expenditures/Student**: $5,367 **Librarians**: 13.0 563 students/librarian **Guidance Counselors**: 16.1 454 students/counselor	**% Amer Indian**: 0.5 **% Asian**: 2.9 **% Black**: 0.8 **% Hispanic**: 11.5 **% White**: 84.2	National ***Socio-Economic Status*** indicator percentile (100=high): 48th

Lancaster County

LINCOLN S.D.

BOX 82889 ● LINCOLN NE 68501-2889 ● (402) 436-1000

Grade Span: PK-12 **Schools**: *Regular* 53 ● *Spec Ed* 0 ● *Alt* 0 **Students**: 30,693 **Total Teachers**: 2,096 **Student/Classroom Teacher Ratio**: 14.3	**Expenditures/Student**: $5,593 **Librarians**: 54.5 563 students/librarian **Guidance Counselors**: 88.6 346 students/counselor	**% Amer Indian**: 1.1 **% Asian**: 3.0 **% Black**: 5.2 **% Hispanic**: 2.4 **% White**: 88.3	National ***Socio-Economic Status*** indicator percentile (100=high): 62nd

Lincoln County

NORTH PLATTE S.D.

1101 W 1ST ST, BOX 1557 ● NORTH PLATTE NE 69103 ● (308) 535-7100

Grade Span: PK-12 **Schools**: *Regular* 12 ● *Spec Ed* 0 ● *Alt* 0 **Students**: 4,490 **Total Teachers**: 283 **Student/Classroom Teacher Ratio**: 15.3	**Expenditures/Student**: $4,604 **Librarians**: 5.0 898 students/librarian **Guidance Counselors**: 11.0 408 students/counselor	**% Amer Indian**: 0.7 **% Asian**: 0.7 **% Black**: 1.4 **% Hispanic**: 8.6 **% White**: 88.7	National ***Socio-Economic Status*** indicator percentile (100=high): 55th

Madison County

NORFOLK S.D.

512 PHILIP, BOX 139 ● NORFOLK NE 68701 ● (402) 644-2500 ● http://jrhigh.nps.esu8.k12.ne.us

Grade Span: PK-12 **Schools**: *Regular* 12 ● *Spec Ed* 2 ● *Alt* 0 **Students**: 4,384 **Total Teachers**: 263 **Student/Classroom Teacher Ratio**: 17.1	**Expenditures/Student**: $4,274 **Librarians**: 5.0 877 students/librarian **Guidance Counselors**: 9.0 487 students/counselor	**% Amer Indian**: 2.0 **% Asian**: 0.4 **% Black**: 1.7 **% Hispanic**: 6.1 **% White**: 89.9	National ***Socio-Economic Status*** indicator percentile (100=high): 66th

Platte County

COLUMBUS S.D.

2508 27TH ST, BOX 947 ● COLUMBUS NE 68602-0947 ● (402) 563-7000

Grade Span: PK-12 **Schools**: *Regular* 10 ● *Spec Ed* 1 ● *Alt* 0 **Students**: 3,612 **Total Teachers**: 214 **Student/Classroom Teacher Ratio**: 17.4	**Expenditures/Student**: $4,653 **Librarians**: 7.0 516 students/librarian **Guidance Counselors**: 10.0 361 students/counselor	**% Amer Indian**: 0.6 **% Asian**: 0.8 **% Black**: 0.6 **% Hispanic**: 4.0 **% White**: 94.0	National ***Socio-Economic Status*** indicator percentile (100=high): 69th

Sarpy County

BELLEVUE S.D.

2009 FRANKLIN ST ● BELLEVUE NE 68005 ● (402) 293-4000 ● http://www.esu3.k12.ne.us/districts/bellevue/bpshome.html

Grade Span: PK-12 **Schools**: *Regular* 17 ● *Spec Ed* 1 ● *Alt* 0 **Students**: 8,668 **Total Teachers**: 510 **Student/Classroom Teacher Ratio**: 17.6	**Expenditures/Student**: $6,546 **Librarians**: 13.5 642 students/librarian **Guidance Counselors**: 20.0 433 students/counselor	**% Amer Indian**: 0.5 **% Asian**: 2.9 **% Black**: 10.4 **% Hispanic**: 3.7 **% White**: 82.4	National ***Socio-Economic Status*** indicator percentile (100=high): 75th

Sarpy County

[LA VISTA] **PAPILLION-LA VISTA S.D.**

7552 S 84TH ● LA VISTA NE 68128 ● (402) 339-3411

Grade Span: PK-12 **Schools**: *Regular* 13 ● *Spec Ed* 0 ● *Alt* 0 **Students**: 7,114 **Total Teachers**: 391 **Student/Classroom Teacher Ratio**: 18.2	**Expenditures/Student**: $4,451 **Librarians**: 10.6 671 students/librarian **Guidance Counselors**: 15.5 459 students/counselor	**% Amer Indian**: 0.6 **% Asian**: 1.6 **% Black**: 3.5 **% Hispanic**: 2.2 **% White**: 92.2	National ***Socio-Economic Status*** indicator percentile (100=high): 85th

Scotts Bluff County

SCOTTSBLUFF S.D.

2601 BROADWAY ● SCOTTSBLUFF NE 69361-1609 ● (308) 635-6200

Grade Span: PK-12 **Schools**: *Regular* 6 ● *Spec Ed* 0 ● *Alt* 0 **Students**: 3,141 **Total Teachers**: 182 **Student/Classroom Teacher Ratio**: 17.3	**Expenditures/Student**: $4,660 **Librarians**: 4.0 785 students/librarian **Guidance Counselors**: 6.0 524 students/counselor	**% Amer Indian**: 6.8 **% Asian**: 0.8 **% Black**: 0.6 **% Hispanic**: 28.3 **% White**: 63.5	National ***Socio-Economic Status*** indicator percentile (100=high): 34th

Carson City Independent City

CARSON CITY S.D.

1402 WEST KING ● CARSON CITY NV 89701 ● (702) 885-6300

Grade Span: PK-12 **Schools**: *Regular* 9 ● *Spec Ed* 1 ● *Alt* 0 **Students**: 7,694 **Total Teachers**: 431 **Student/Classroom Teacher Ratio**: 17.7	**Expenditures/Student**: $5,278 **Librarians**: 3.0 2,565 students/librarian **Guidance Counselors**: 15.0 513 students/counselor	**% Amer Indian**: 4.1 **% Asian**: 2.5 **% Black**: 0.8 **% Hispanic**: 13.9 **% White**: 78.6	National ***Socio-Economic Status*** indicator percentile (100=high): 43rd

Churchill County

[FALLON] CHURCHILL COUNTY S.D.

545 EAST RICHARDS ● FALLON NV 89406 ● (702) 423-5184 ● http://www.churchill.k12.nv.us

Grade Span: PK-12 **Schools**: *Regular* 6 ● *Spec Ed* 1 ● *Alt* 1 **Students**: 4,470 **Total Teachers**: 248 **Student/Classroom Teacher Ratio**: 17.8	**Expenditures/Student**: $5,311 **Librarians**: 4.0 1,118 students/librarian **Guidance Counselors**: 8.0 559 students/counselor	**% Amer Indian**: 7.4 **% Asian**: 4.5 **% Black**: 2.0 **% Hispanic**: 7.0 **% White**: 79.1	National ***Socio-Economic Status*** indicator percentile (100=high): 35th

Clark County

[LAS VEGAS] CLARK COUNTY S.D.

2832 EAST FLAMINGO ● LAS VEGAS NV 89121 ● (702) 799-5310 ● http://www.ccsd.net

Grade Span: PK-12 **Schools**: *Regular* 175 ● *Spec Ed* 6 ● *Alt* 17 **Students**: 166,788 **Total Teachers**: 8,186 **Student/Classroom Teacher Ratio**: 20.0	**Expenditures/Student**: $4,608 **Librarians**: 173.0 964 students/librarian **Guidance Counselors**: 270.0 618 students/counselor	**% Amer Indian**: 0.8 **% Asian**: 5.3 **% Black**: 13.6 **% Hispanic**: 19.3 **% White**: 60.9	National ***Socio-Economic Status*** indicator percentile (100=high): 43rd

Douglas County

[MINDEN] DOUGLAS COUNTY S.D.

751 MONO AVENUE ● MINDEN NV 89423 ● (702) 782-5134

Grade Span: PK-12 **Schools**: *Regular* 10 ● *Spec Ed* 0 ● *Alt* 1 **Students**: 7,090 **Total Teachers**: 393 **Student/Classroom Teacher Ratio**: 18.2	**Expenditures/Student**: $5,098 **Librarians**: 5.0 1,418 students/librarian **Guidance Counselors**: 15.0 473 students/counselor	**% Amer Indian**: 2.8 **% Asian**: 2.7 **% Black**: 0.5 **% Hispanic**: 6.5 **% White**: 87.4	National ***Socio-Economic Status*** indicator percentile (100=high): 57th

Elko County

[ELKO] ELKO COUNTY S.D.

1092 BURNS ROAD ● ELKO NV 89801 ● (702) 738-5196 ● http://www.elko.k12.nv.us

Grade Span: PK-12 **Schools**: *Regular* 25 ● *Spec Ed* 1 ● *Alt* 0 **Students**: 9,861 **Total Teachers**: 563 **Student/Classroom Teacher Ratio**: 16.1	**Expenditures/Student**: $5,146 **Librarians**: 14.0 704 students/librarian **Guidance Counselors**: 21.5 459 students/counselor	**% Amer Indian**: 6.7 **% Asian**: 0.9 **% Black**: 0.4 **% Hispanic**: 17.3 **% White**: 74.7	National ***Socio-Economic Status*** indicator percentile (100=high): 53rd

Humboldt County

[WINNEMUCCA] HUMBOLDT COUNTY S.D.

EAST 4TH AND REINHART ● WINNEMUCCA NV 89445 ● (702) 623-8100

Grade Span: PK-12 **Schools**: *Regular* 14 ● *Spec Ed* 0 ● *Alt* 1 **Students**: 3,845 **Total Teachers**: 227 **Student/Classroom Teacher Ratio**: 14.2	**Expenditures/Student**: $5,102 **Librarians**: 3.0 1,282 students/librarian **Guidance Counselors**: 10.0 385 students/counselor	**% Amer Indian**: 4.1 **% Asian**: 0.4 **% Black**: 0.3 **% Hispanic**: 20.8 **% White**: 74.3	National ***Socio-Economic Status*** indicator percentile (100=high): 54th

Lyon County

[YERINGTON] **LYON COUNTY S.D.**

25 EAST GOLDFIELD ● YERINGTON NV 89447 ● (702) 463-2205

Grade Span: PK-12 **Schools**: *Regular* 14 ● *Spec Ed* 1 ● *Alt* 0 **Students**: 5,426 **Total Teachers**: 318 **Student/Classroom Teacher Ratio**: 17.3	**Expenditures/Student**: $5,440 **Librarians**: 8.0 678 students/librarian **Guidance Counselors**: 12.2 445 students/counselor	**% Amer Indian**: 4.6 **% Asian**: 1.0 **% Black**: 0.6 **% Hispanic**: 10.1 **% White**: 83.7	National ***Socio-Economic Status*** indicator percentile (100=high): 30th

Nye County

[TONOPAH] **NYE COUNTY S.D.**

MILITARY CIRCLE ● TONOPAH NV 89049 ● (702) 482-6258

Grade Span: PK-12 **Schools**: *Regular* 16 ● *Spec Ed* 0 ● *Alt* 0 **Students**: 4,528 **Total Teachers**: 296 **Student/Classroom Teacher Ratio**: 15.9	**Expenditures/Student**: $5,249 **Librarians**: 2.0 2,264 students/librarian **Guidance Counselors**: 9.0 503 students/counselor	**% Amer Indian**: 2.9 **% Asian**: 1.9 **% Black**: 1.0 **% Hispanic**: 10.5 **% White**: 83.7	National ***Socio-Economic Status*** indicator percentile (100=high): 29th

Washoe County

[RENO] **WASHOE COUNTY S.D.**

425 EAST NINTH ● RENO NV 89520 ● (702) 348-0200

Grade Span: PK-12 **Schools**: *Regular* 75 ● *Spec Ed* 1 ● *Alt* 5 **Students**: 47,572 **Total Teachers**: 2,697 **Student/Classroom Teacher Ratio**: 19.4	**Expenditures/Student**: $4,547 **Librarians**: 21.0 2,265 students/librarian **Guidance Counselors**: 119.0 400 students/counselor	**% Amer Indian**: 2.5 **% Asian**: 4.7 **% Black**: 3.7 **% Hispanic**: 14.7 **% White**: 74.3	National ***Socio-Economic Status*** indicator percentile (100=high): 46th

Carroll County

[WOLFEBORO] **GOVERNOR WENTWORTH REGIONAL S.D.**

HC 69 BOX 430 ● WOLFEBORO NH 03894-9211 ● (603) 569-1658

Grade Span: KG-12	**Expenditures/Student**: $6,626	**% Amer Indian**: 0.2	
Schools: *Regular* 7 ● *Spec Ed* 0 ● *Alt* 0	**Librarians**: 4.2	**% Asian**: 0.2	National ***Socio-Economic***
Students: 2,729	650 students/librarian	**% Black**: 0.3	***Status*** indicator percentile
Total Teachers: 181	**Guidance Counselors**: 8.0	**% Hispanic**: 0.1	(100=high): 60th
Student/Classroom Teacher Ratio: 15.6	341 students/counselor	**% White**: 99.2	

Cheshire County

[EAST SWANZEY] **MONADNOCK REGIONAL S.D.**

SWANZEY CENTER 600 OLD HOMES ● EAST SWANZEY NH 03466 ● (603) 352-6955

Grade Span: KG-12	**Expenditures/Student**: $5,320	**% Amer Indian**: 0.1	
Schools: *Regular* 9 ● *Spec Ed* 0 ● *Alt* 0	**Librarians**: 1.0	**% Asian**: 0.3	National ***Socio-Economic***
Students: 2,666	2,666 students/librarian	**% Black**: 0.3	***Status*** indicator percentile
Total Teachers: 160	**Guidance Counselors**: 7.7	**% Hispanic**: 0.5	(100=high): 74th
Student/Classroom Teacher Ratio: 15.8	346 students/counselor	**% White**: 98.8	

Cheshire County

KEENE S.D.

34 WEST STREET ● KEENE NH 03431 ● (603) 357-9002 ● http://www.keene.k12.nh.us/keene/keene.html

Grade Span: PK-12	**Expenditures/Student**: $6,976	**% Amer Indian**: 0.1	
Schools: *Regular* 7 ● *Spec Ed* 0 ● *Alt* 0	**Librarians**: 7.0	**% Asian**: 0.8	National ***Socio-Economic***
Students: 3,852	550 students/librarian	**% Black**: 0.4	***Status*** indicator percentile
Total Teachers: 285	**Guidance Counselors**: 26.0	**% Hispanic**: 0.5	(100=high): 75th
Student/Classroom Teacher Ratio: 14.6	148 students/counselor	**% White**: 98.2	

Hillsborough County

GOFFSTOWN S.D.

WHITE SCHOOL ● GOFFSTOWN NH 03045 ● (603) 497-4818 ● http://www.goffstown.k12.nh.us/sau/sau.htm

Grade Span: PK-12	**Expenditures/Student**: $5,012	**% Amer Indian**: 0.7	
Schools: *Regular* 4 ● *Spec Ed* 0 ● *Alt* 0	**Librarians**: 3.0	**% Asian**: 0.4	National ***Socio-Economic***
Students: 2,608	869 students/librarian	**% Black**: 0.2	***Status*** indicator percentile
Total Teachers: 161	**Guidance Counselors**: 9.0	**% Hispanic**: 0.8	(100=high): 88th
Student/Classroom Teacher Ratio: 16.4	290 students/counselor	**% White**: 97.9	

Hillsborough County

HUDSON S.D.

20 LIBRARY STREET ● HUDSON NH 03051 ● (603) 883-7765 ● http://www.seresc.k12.nh.us/~hudson/schools.html

Grade Span: PK-12	**Expenditures/Student**: $5,187	**% Amer Indian**: 0.3	
Schools: *Regular* 5 ● *Spec Ed* 0 ● *Alt* 0	**Librarians**: 4.0	**% Asian**: 1.1	National ***Socio-Economic***
Students: 4,082	1,021 students/librarian	**% Black**: 0.8	***Status*** indicator percentile
Total Teachers: 222	**Guidance Counselors**: 12.0	**% Hispanic**: 1.1	(100=high): 93rd
Student/Classroom Teacher Ratio: 19.5	340 students/counselor	**% White**: 96.8	

Hillsborough County

MANCHESTER S.D.

196 BRIDGE STREET ● MANCHESTER NH 03104-1684 ● (603) 624-6300

Grade Span: PK-12	**Expenditures/Student**: $4,745	**% Amer Indian**: 0.5	
Schools: *Regular* 21 ● *Spec Ed* 0 ● *Alt* 0	**Librarians**: 14.2	**% Asian**: 1.7	National ***Socio-Economic***
Students: 16,088	1,133 students/librarian	**% Black**: 2.3	***Status*** indicator percentile
Total Teachers: 880	**Guidance Counselors**: 39.1	**% Hispanic**: 3.7	(100=high): 62nd
Student/Classroom Teacher Ratio: 18.8	411 students/counselor	**% White**: 91.9	

Hillsborough County
MERRIMACK S.D.
36 MCELWAIN STREET ● MERRIMACK NH 03054 ● (603) 424-6200

Grade Span: PK-12 **Schools**: *Regular* 5 ● *Spec Ed* 0 ● *Alt* 0 **Students**: 4,675 **Total Teachers**: 300 **Student/Classroom Teacher Ratio**: 15.8	**Expenditures/Student**: $6,004 **Librarians**: 7.0 668 students/librarian **Guidance Counselors**: 16.9 277 students/counselor	**% Amer Indian**: 0.5 **% Asian**: 1.2 **% Black**: 1.1 **% Hispanic**: 0.8 **% White**: 96.5	National ***Socio-Economic Status*** indicator percentile (100=high): 97th

Hillsborough County
NASHUA S.D.
PO BOX 687 ● NASHUA NH 03061-0687 ● (603) 594-4300

Grade Span: PK-12 **Schools**: *Regular* 16 ● *Spec Ed* 0 ● *Alt* 0 **Students**: 12,705 **Total Teachers**: 726 **Student/Classroom Teacher Ratio**: 18.1	**Expenditures/Student**: $5,259 **Librarians**: 11.0 1,155 students/librarian **Guidance Counselors**: 32.2 395 students/counselor	**% Amer Indian**: 0.3 **% Asian**: 2.8 **% Black**: 2.4 **% Hispanic**: 5.9 **% White**: 88.6	National ***Socio-Economic Status*** indicator percentile (100=high): 69th

Hillsborough County
[PETERBOROUGH] **CONTOOCOOK VALLEY REGIONAL S.D.**
ROUTE 202 NORTH ● PETERBOROUGH NH 03458 ● (603) 924-3336 ● http://www.conval.edu

Grade Span: KG-12 **Schools**: *Regular* 11 ● *Spec Ed* 0 ● *Alt* 0 **Students**: 3,037 **Total Teachers**: 210 **Student/Classroom Teacher Ratio**: 16.1	**Expenditures/Student**: $6,361 **Librarians**: 4.0 759 students/librarian **Guidance Counselors**: 8.8 345 students/counselor	**% Amer Indian**: 0.1 **% Asian**: 0.9 **% Black**: 0.4 **% Hispanic**: 0.3 **% White**: 98.3	National ***Socio-Economic Status*** indicator percentile (100=high): 78th

Merrimack County
CONCORD S.D.
16 RUMFORD STREET ● CONCORD NH 03301 ● (603) 225-0811 ● http://www.concord.k12.nh.us

Grade Span: PK-12 **Schools**: *Regular* 11 ● *Spec Ed* 0 ● *Alt* 0 **Students**: 5,479 **Total Teachers**: 368 **Student/Classroom Teacher Ratio**: 15.4	**Expenditures/Student**: $6,174 **Librarians**: 2.9 1,889 students/librarian **Guidance Counselors**: 17.5 313 students/counselor	**% Amer Indian**: 0.2 **% Asian**: 1.1 **% Black**: 1.0 **% Hispanic**: 0.6 **% White**: 97.1	National ***Socio-Economic Status*** indicator percentile (100=high): 75th

Merrimack County
[PENACOOK] **MERRIMACK VALLEY S.D.**
105 CENTER STREET ● PENACOOK NH 03303 ● (603) 753-6561 ● http://www.mv.k12.nh.us

Grade Span: PK-12 **Schools**: *Regular* 7 ● *Spec Ed* 0 ● *Alt* 0 **Students**: 2,543 **Total Teachers**: 137 **Student/Classroom Teacher Ratio**: 18.0	**Expenditures/Student**: $4,677 **Librarians**: 2.0 1,272 students/librarian **Guidance Counselors**: 7.9 322 students/counselor	**% Amer Indian**: 0.1 **% Asian**: 0.4 **% Black**: 0.2 **% Hispanic**: 0.3 **% White**: 99.0	National ***Socio-Economic Status*** indicator percentile (100=high): 81st

Rockingham County
DERRY COOPERATIVE S.D.
18 SOUTH MAIN STREET ● DERRY NH 03038 ● (603) 432-1210 ● http://www.derry.k12.nh.us

Grade Span: 01-08 **Schools**: *Regular* 6 ● *Spec Ed* 0 ● *Alt* 0 **Students**: 4,281 **Total Teachers**: 231 **Student/Classroom Teacher Ratio**: 19.2	**Expenditures/Student**: $6,200 **Librarians**: 4.0 1,070 students/librarian **Guidance Counselors**: 9.0 476 students/counselor	**% Amer Indian**: 0.1 **% Asian**: 1.0 **% Black**: 1.1 **% Hispanic**: 1.1 **% White**: 96.8	National ***Socio-Economic Status*** indicator percentile (100=high): 77th

Rockingham County
[DERRY] PINKERTON ACADEMY S.D.
PINKERTON STREET ● DERRY NH 03038 ● (603) 432-2588 ● http://www.mv.com/ipusers/pinkerton

Grade Span: 09-12 **Schools**: *Regular* 1 ● *Spec Ed* 0 ● *Alt* 0 **Students**: 2,676 **Total Teachers**: 165 **Student/Classroom Teacher Ratio**: 16.2	**Expenditures/Student**: $na **Librarians**: 2.5 1,070 students/librarian **Guidance Counselors**: 16.7 160 students/counselor	**% Amer Indian**: 0.6 **% Asian**: 1.2 **% Black**: 0.9 **% Hispanic**: 1.5 **% White**: 95.9	National ***Socio-Economic Status*** indicator percentile (100=high): 96th

Rockingham County
EXETER S.D.
24 FRONT STREET ● EXETER NH 03833 ● (603) 778-7772 ● http://www.nh.ultranet.com/~gregkann

Grade Span: PK-12 **Schools**: *Regular* 4 ● *Spec Ed* 0 ● *Alt* 0 **Students**: 3,278 **Total Teachers**: 204 **Student/Classroom Teacher Ratio**: 16.0	**Expenditures/Student**: $6,443 **Librarians**: 3.0 1,093 students/librarian **Guidance Counselors**: 9.0 364 students/counselor	**% Amer Indian**: 0.2 **% Asian**: 0.6 **% Black**: 0.7 **% Hispanic**: 0.5 **% White**: 98.0	National ***Socio-Economic Status*** indicator percentile (100=high): 94th

Rockingham County
LONDONDERRY S.D.
268 MAMMOTH ROAD ● LONDONDERRY NH 03053 ● (603) 432-6920

Grade Span: PK-12 **Schools**: *Regular* 5 ● *Spec Ed* 0 ● *Alt* 0 **Students**: 4,707 **Total Teachers**: 294 **Student/Classroom Teacher Ratio**: 16.7	**Expenditures/Student**: $5,740 **Librarians**: 6.0 785 students/librarian **Guidance Counselors**: 16.0 294 students/counselor	**% Amer Indian**: 0.1 **% Asian**: 1.2 **% Black**: 0.5 **% Hispanic**: 1.0 **% White**: 97.2	National ***Socio-Economic Status*** indicator percentile (100=high): 97th

Rockingham County
[PLAISTOW] TIMBERLANE REGIONAL S.D.
30 GREENOUGH ROAD ● PLAISTOW NH 03865 ● (603) 382-6119

Grade Span: PK-12 **Schools**: *Regular* 6 ● *Spec Ed* 0 ● *Alt* 0 **Students**: 3,514 **Total Teachers**: 255 **Student/Classroom Teacher Ratio**: 14.4	**Expenditures/Student**: $5,387 **Librarians**: 4.0 879 students/librarian **Guidance Counselors**: 10.6 332 students/counselor	**% Amer Indian**: 0.1 **% Asian**: 0.5 **% Black**: 0.3 **% Hispanic**: 0.6 **% White**: 98.5	National ***Socio-Economic Status*** indicator percentile (100=high): 93rd

Rockingham County
PORTSMOUTH S.D.
CLOUGH DRIVE ● PORTSMOUTH NH 03801 ● (603) 436-7100

Grade Span: PK-12 **Schools**: *Regular* 5 ● *Spec Ed* 0 ● *Alt* 0 **Students**: 2,747 **Total Teachers**: 199 **Student/Classroom Teacher Ratio**: 15.1	**Expenditures/Student**: $8,090 **Librarians**: 3.0 916 students/librarian **Guidance Counselors**: 12.0 229 students/counselor	**% Amer Indian**: 0.2 **% Asian**: 2.0 **% Black**: 5.4 **% Hispanic**: 1.7 **% White**: 90.8	National ***Socio-Economic Status*** indicator percentile (100=high): 58th

Rockingham County
SALEM S.D.
MAIN STREET ● SALEM NH 03079 ● (603) 893-7040 ● http://www.salemschooldistrictnh.com

Grade Span: PK-12 **Schools**: *Regular* 8 ● *Spec Ed* 0 ● *Alt* 0 **Students**: 4,376 **Total Teachers**: 273 **Student/Classroom Teacher Ratio**: 17.7	**Expenditures/Student**: $5,474 **Librarians**: 4.0 1,094 students/librarian **Guidance Counselors**: 19.5 224 students/counselor	**% Amer Indian**: 0.1 **% Asian**: 1.9 **% Black**: 0.7 **% Hispanic**: 1.5 **% White**: 95.7	National ***Socio-Economic Status*** indicator percentile (100=high): 92nd

Strafford County

DOVER S.D.

MUNICIPAL BUILDING ● DOVER NH 03820 ● (603) 742-6400

Grade Span: PK-12 **Schools**: *Regular* 5 ● *Spec Ed* 0 ● *Alt* 0 **Students**: 3,382 **Total Teachers**: 210 **Student/Classroom Teacher Ratio**: 16.3	**Expenditures/Student**: $5,805 **Librarians**: 3.0 1,127 students/librarian **Guidance Counselors**: 10.2 332 students/counselor	**% Amer Indian**: 0.0 **% Asian**: 2.3 **% Black**: 2.2 **% Hispanic**: 1.0 **% White**: 94.5	National ***Socio-Economic Status*** indicator percentile (100=high): 62nd

Strafford County

ROCHESTER S.D.

62 SOUTH MAIN STREET ● ROCHESTER NH 03867 ● (603) 332-3678 ● http://www.rochesterschools.com

Grade Span: PK-12 **Schools**: *Regular* 10 ● *Spec Ed* 0 ● *Alt* 0 **Students**: 4,728 **Total Teachers**: 283 **Student/Classroom Teacher Ratio**: 18.2	**Expenditures/Student**: $4,512 **Librarians**: 4.0 1,182 students/librarian **Guidance Counselors**: 13.1 361 students/counselor	**% Amer Indian**: 0.2 **% Asian**: 0.5 **% Black**: 0.8 **% Hispanic**: 0.3 **% White**: 98.1	National ***Socio-Economic Status*** indicator percentile (100=high): 62nd

Atlantic County

[ABSECON] **GALLOWAY TOWNSHIP S.D.**

101 S. REEDS RD. ● ABSECON NJ 08201-2104 ● (609) 748-1250 ● http://www.gtps.k12.nj.us

Grade Span: KG-08 **Schools**: *Regular* 7 ● *Spec Ed* 0 ● *Alt* 0 **Students**: 3,474 **Total Teachers**: 230 **Student/Classroom Teacher Ratio**: 15.0	**Expenditures/Student**: $7,100 **Librarians**: 4.5 772 students/librarian **Guidance Counselors**: 6.0 579 students/counselor	**% Amer Indian**: 0.0 **% Asian**: 7.5 **% Black**: 11.5 **% Hispanic**: 5.2 **% White**: 75.8	National ***Socio-Economic Status*** indicator percentile (100=high): 71st

Atlantic County

ATLANTIC CITY S.D.

1809 PACIFIC AVENUE ● ATLANTIC CITY NJ 08401-6803 ● (609) 343-7200 ● http://pw2.netcom.com/~gbmoore1/acschools.html

Grade Span: PK-12 **Schools**: *Regular* 11 ● *Spec Ed* 0 ● *Alt* 0 **Students**: 6,965 **Total Teachers**: 467 **Student/Classroom Teacher Ratio**: 17.1	**Expenditures/Student**: $8,893 **Librarians**: 7.0 995 students/librarian **Guidance Counselors**: 18.0 387 students/counselor	**% Amer Indian**: 0.2 **% Asian**: 6.1 **% Black**: 59.5 **% Hispanic**: 24.9 **% White**: 9.3	National ***Socio-Economic Status*** indicator percentile (100=high): 6th

Atlantic County

PLEASANTVILLE CITY S.D.

115 WEST DECATUR AVENUE ● PLEASANTVILLE NJ 08232 ● (609) 383-6810

Grade Span: PK-12 **Schools**: *Regular* 5 ● *Spec Ed* 0 ● *Alt* 0 **Students**: 3,363 **Total Teachers**: 222 **Student/Classroom Teacher Ratio**: 16.8	**Expenditures/Student**: $8,447 **Librarians**: 6.0 561 students/librarian **Guidance Counselors**: 9.0 374 students/counselor	**% Amer Indian**: 0.3 **% Asian**: 1.5 **% Black**: 75.2 **% Hispanic**: 17.7 **% White**: 5.4	National ***Socio-Economic Status*** indicator percentile (100=high): 11th

Atlantic County

[WEST ATLANTIC CITY] **EGG HARBOR TOWNSHIP S.D.**

P.O. BOX 31 ● WEST ATLANTIC CITY NJ 08232-2928 ● (609) 646-7911

Grade Span: KG-12 **Schools**: *Regular* 6 ● *Spec Ed* 0 ● *Alt* 0 **Students**: 4,683 **Total Teachers**: 333 **Student/Classroom Teacher Ratio**: 16.1	**Expenditures/Student**: $8,230 **Librarians**: 5.0 937 students/librarian **Guidance Counselors**: 10.0 468 students/counselor	**% Amer Indian**: 0.3 **% Asian**: 4.1 **% Black**: 14.1 **% Hispanic**: 4.9 **% White**: 76.6	National ***Socio-Economic Status*** indicator percentile (100=high): 62nd

Bergen County

BERGENFIELD BOROUGH S.D.

100 S. PROSPECT AVENUE ● BERGENFIELD NJ 07621-1958 ● (201) 385-8202

Grade Span: KG-12 **Schools**: *Regular* 7 ● *Spec Ed* 0 ● *Alt* 0 **Students**: 3,181 **Total Teachers**: 228 **Student/Classroom Teacher Ratio**: 17.6	**Expenditures/Student**: $9,709 **Librarians**: 3.0 1,060 students/librarian **Guidance Counselors**: 7.4 430 students/counselor	**% Amer Indian**: 0.1 **% Asian**: 20.8 **% Black**: 8.5 **% Hispanic**: 15.6 **% White**: 55.0	National ***Socio-Economic Status*** indicator percentile (100=high): 79th

Bergen County

ENGLEWOOD CITY S.D.

12 TENAFLY ROAD ● ENGLEWOOD NJ 07631-2206 ● (201) 833-6060

Grade Span: PK-12 **Schools**: *Regular* 5 ● *Spec Ed* 0 ● *Alt* 0 **Students**: 2,508 **Total Teachers**: 171 **Student/Classroom Teacher Ratio**: 16.6	**Expenditures/Student**: $12,160 **Librarians**: 6.0 418 students/librarian **Guidance Counselors**: 8.0 314 students/counselor	**% Amer Indian**: 0.0 **% Asian**: 3.7 **% Black**: 65.9 **% Hispanic**: 26.1 **% White**: 4.2	National ***Socio-Economic Status*** indicator percentile (100=high): 26th

Bergen County
FAIR LAWN BOROUGH S.D.
35-01 MORLOT AVENUE ● FAIR LAWN NJ 07410-4919 ● (201) 794-5511

Grade Span: KG-12 **Schools**: *Regular* 9 ● *Spec Ed* 0 ● *Alt* 0 **Students**: 4,191 **Total Teachers**: 300 **Student/Classroom Teacher Ratio**: 17.2	**Expenditures/Student**: $9,905 **Librarians**: 9.0 466 students/librarian **Guidance Counselors**: 10.6 395 students/counselor	**% Amer Indian**: 0.0 **% Asian**: 5.5 **% Black**: 0.7 **% Hispanic**: 5.1 **% White**: 88.7	National ***Socio-Economic Status*** indicator percentile (100=high): 95th

Bergen County
FORT LEE BOROUGH S.D.
255 WHITEMAN STREET ● FORT LEE NJ 07024-5629 ● (201) 585-4612

Grade Span: KG-12 **Schools**: *Regular* 6 ● *Spec Ed* 0 ● *Alt* 0 **Students**: 3,379 **Total Teachers**: 222 **Student/Classroom Teacher Ratio**: 18.1	**Expenditures/Student**: $9,130 **Librarians**: 6.0 563 students/librarian **Guidance Counselors**: 9.2 367 students/counselor	**% Amer Indian**: 0.0 **% Asian**: 45.1 **% Black**: 1.6 **% Hispanic**: 8.9 **% White**: 44.4	National ***Socio-Economic Status*** indicator percentile (100=high): 88th

Bergen County
GARFIELD CITY S.D.
125 OUTWATER LANE ● GARFIELD NJ 07026-2637 ● (201) 340-5000

Grade Span: KG-12 **Schools**: *Regular* 7 ● *Spec Ed* 0 ● *Alt* 0 **Students**: 3,333 **Total Teachers**: 201 **Student/Classroom Teacher Ratio**: 18.0	**Expenditures/Student**: $7,873 **Librarians**: 1.0 3,333 students/librarian **Guidance Counselors**: 7.5 444 students/counselor	**% Amer Indian**: 0.4 **% Asian**: 2.6 **% Black**: 5.4 **% Hispanic**: 24.1 **% White**: 67.4	National ***Socio-Economic Status*** indicator percentile (100=high): 33rd

Bergen County
HACKENSACK CITY S.D.
355 STATE STREET ● HACKENSACK NJ 07601-5510 ● (201) 646-7830 ● http://members.aol.com/iseckeb/home.htm

Grade Span: PK-12 **Schools**: *Regular* 6 ● *Spec Ed* 0 ● *Alt* 0 **Students**: 4,308 **Total Teachers**: 313 **Student/Classroom Teacher Ratio**: 14.8	**Expenditures/Student**: $11,082 **Librarians**: 8.8 490 students/librarian **Guidance Counselors**: 11.0 392 students/counselor	**% Amer Indian**: 0.2 **% Asian**: 5.3 **% Black**: 35.2 **% Hispanic**: 31.7 **% White**: 27.6	National ***Socio-Economic Status*** indicator percentile (100=high): 39th

Bergen County
PARAMUS BOROUGH S.D.
145 SPRING VALLEY ROAD ● PARAMUS NJ 07652-5333 ● (201) 261-7800

Grade Span: KG-12 **Schools**: *Regular* 7 ● *Spec Ed* 0 ● *Alt* 0 **Students**: 3,584 **Total Teachers**: 272 **Student/Classroom Teacher Ratio**: 14.9	**Expenditures/Student**: $10,495 **Librarians**: 8.0 448 students/librarian **Guidance Counselors**: 9.0 398 students/counselor	**% Amer Indian**: 0.1 **% Asian**: 23.4 **% Black**: 1.0 **% Hispanic**: 4.5 **% White**: 70.9	National ***Socio-Economic Status*** indicator percentile (100=high): 99th

Bergen County
RIDGEWOOD VILLAGE S.D.
EDUCATION CENTER ● RIDGEWOOD NJ 07451 ● (201) 670-2700

Grade Span: KG-12 **Schools**: *Regular* 9 ● *Spec Ed* 0 ● *Alt* 0 **Students**: 4,886 **Total Teachers**: 330 **Student/Classroom Teacher Ratio**: 16.5	**Expenditures/Student**: $9,712 **Librarians**: 7.5 651 students/librarian **Guidance Counselors**: 14.7 332 students/counselor	**% Amer Indian**: 0.0 **% Asian**: 12.3 **% Black**: 2.0 **% Hispanic**: 2.5 **% White**: 83.1	National ***Socio-Economic Status*** indicator percentile (100=high): 99th

Bergen County

TEANECK TOWNSHIP S.D.

ONE MERRISON STREET ● TEANECK NJ 07666-4616 ● (201) 833-5510

Grade Span: PK-12 **Schools**: *Regular* 8 ● *Spec Ed* 0 ● *Alt* 0 **Students**: 4,326 **Total Teachers**: 335 **Student/Classroom Teacher Ratio**: 15.0	**Expenditures/Student**: $11,787 **Librarians**: 4.0 1,082 students/librarian **Guidance Counselors**: 17.0 254 students/counselor	**% Amer Indian**: 0.1 **% Asian**: 10.5 **% Black**: 41.0 **% Hispanic**: 11.7 **% White**: 36.8	National ***Socio-Economic Status*** indicator percentile (100=high): 78th

Burlington County

[BROWNS MILLS] **PEMBERTON TOWNSHIP S.D.**

BOX 98 ● BROWNS MILLS NJ 08015-0098 ● (609) 893-8141 ● http://www.globalinc.com/pemberton.edu

Grade Span: PK-12 **Schools**: *Regular* 12 ● *Spec Ed* 0 ● *Alt* 0 **Students**: 6,020 **Total Teachers**: 463 **Student/Classroom Teacher Ratio**: 14.4	**Expenditures/Student**: $9,346 **Librarians**: 12.0 502 students/librarian **Guidance Counselors**: 25.0 241 students/counselor	**% Amer Indian**: 0.2 **% Asian**: 3.2 **% Black**: 28.4 **% Hispanic**: 7.8 **% White**: 60.3	National ***Socio-Economic Status*** indicator percentile (100=high): 45th

Burlington County

[MARLTON] **EVESHAM TOWNSHIP S.D.**

25 SOUTH MAPLE AVE. ● MARLTON NJ 08053 ● (609) 983-1800 ● http://www.evesham.k12.nj.us

Grade Span: KG-08 **Schools**: *Regular* 9 ● *Spec Ed* 0 ● *Alt* 0 **Students**: 4,672 **Total Teachers**: 290 **Student/Classroom Teacher Ratio**: 17.3	**Expenditures/Student**: $6,503 **Librarians**: 8.4 556 students/librarian **Guidance Counselors**: 9.0 519 students/counselor	**% Amer Indian**: 0.0 **% Asian**: 4.6 **% Black**: 3.8 **% Hispanic**: 0.7 **% White**: 90.9	National ***Socio-Economic Status*** indicator percentile (100=high): 97th

Burlington County

MEDFORD TOWNSHIP S.D.

WESTMINSTER HOUSE ● MEDFORD NJ 08055 ● (609) 654-6416

Grade Span: KG-08 **Schools**: *Regular* 5 ● *Spec Ed* 0 ● *Alt* 0 **Students**: 2,630 **Total Teachers**: 161 **Student/Classroom Teacher Ratio**: 16.3	**Expenditures/Student**: $7,618 **Librarians**: 5.0 526 students/librarian **Guidance Counselors**: 5.0 526 students/counselor	**% Amer Indian**: 0.2 **% Asian**: 2.3 **% Black**: 0.4 **% Hispanic**: 0.5 **% White**: 96.7	National ***Socio-Economic Status*** indicator percentile (100=high): 97th

Burlington County

MOORESTOWN TOWNSHIP S.D.

803 N. STANWICK ROAD ● MOORESTOWN NJ 08057 ● (609) 778-6600 ● http://www.moorestown.com/mtps

Grade Span: KG-12 **Schools**: *Regular* 5 ● *Spec Ed* 0 ● *Alt* 0 **Students**: 2,837 **Total Teachers**: 199 **Student/Classroom Teacher Ratio**: 16.4	**Expenditures/Student**: $8,927 **Librarians**: 7.0 405 students/librarian **Guidance Counselors**: 7.6 373 students/counselor	**% Amer Indian**: 0.1 **% Asian**: 3.8 **% Black**: 7.2 **% Hispanic**: 1.4 **% White**: 87.5	National ***Socio-Economic Status*** indicator percentile (100=high): 93rd

Burlington County

MOUNT LAUREL TOWNSHIP S.D.

330 MOORESTOWN-MT. LAUREL ● MOUNT LAUREL NJ 08054-9521 ● (609) 235-3387

Grade Span: KG-08 **Schools**: *Regular* 6 ● *Spec Ed* 0 ● *Alt* 0 **Students**: 3,906 **Total Teachers**: 248 **Student/Classroom Teacher Ratio**: 16.4	**Expenditures/Student**: $6,966 **Librarians**: 7.0 558 students/librarian **Guidance Counselors**: 8.0 488 students/counselor	**% Amer Indian**: 0.0 **% Asian**: 4.3 **% Black**: 6.9 **% Hispanic**: 1.7 **% White**: 87.1	National ***Socio-Economic Status*** indicator percentile (100=high): 95th

Burlington County

[SHAMONG] **LENAPE REGIONAL S.D.**

93 WILLOW GROVE ROAD ● SHAMONG NJ 08088 ● (609) 268-2000 ● http://www.lr.k12.nj.us

Grade Span: 09-12 **Schools**: *Regular* 3 ● *Spec Ed* 0 ● *Alt* 0 **Students**: 5,607 **Total Teachers**: 405 **Student/Classroom Teacher Ratio**: 13.9	**Expenditures/Student**: $9,340 **Librarians**: 8.0 701 students/librarian **Guidance Counselors**: 29.0 193 students/counselor	**% Amer Indian**: 0.3 **% Asian**: 3.3 **% Black**: 3.8 **% Hispanic**: 1.0 **% White**: 91.6	National ***Socio-Economic Status*** indicator percentile (100=high): 99th

Burlington County

WILLINGBORO TOWNSHIP S.D.

LEVITT BUILDING ● WILLINGBORO NJ 08046 ● (609) 835-8600

Grade Span: KG-12 **Schools**: *Regular* 9 ● *Spec Ed* 0 ● *Alt* 0 **Students**: 5,518 **Total Teachers**: 427 **Student/Classroom Teacher Ratio**: 13.9	**Expenditures/Student**: $9,591 **Librarians**: 10.0 552 students/librarian **Guidance Counselors**: 18.0 307 students/counselor	**% Amer Indian**: 0.2 **% Asian**: 1.5 **% Black**: 84.3 **% Hispanic**: 4.9 **% White**: 9.1	National ***Socio-Economic Status*** indicator percentile (100=high): 44th

Camden County

[ATCO] **LOWER CAMDEN COUNTY REGIONAL S.D.**

200 COOPERS FOLLY ROAD ● ATCO NJ 08004 ● (609) 767-2850

Grade Span: 07-12 **Schools**: *Regular* 4 ● *Spec Ed* 1 ● *Alt* 0 **Students**: 5,098 **Total Teachers**: 384 **Student/Classroom Teacher Ratio**: 14.3	**Expenditures/Student**: $9,592 **Librarians**: 4.0 1,275 students/librarian **Guidance Counselors**: 20.0 255 students/counselor	**% Amer Indian**: 0.6 **% Asian**: 0.9 **% Black**: 26.9 **% Hispanic**: 2.9 **% White**: 68.7	National ***Socio-Economic Status*** indicator percentile (100=high): 67th

Camden County

[BLACKWOOD] **BLACK HORSE PIKE REGIONAL S.D.**

DISTRICT ADMINISTRATION O ● BLACKWOOD NJ 08012 ● (609) 227-4106

Grade Span: 09-12 **Schools**: *Regular* 2 ● *Spec Ed* 0 ● *Alt* 0 **Students**: 3,333 **Total Teachers**: 208 **Student/Classroom Teacher Ratio**: 16.3	**Expenditures/Student**: $9,141 **Librarians**: 6.0 556 students/librarian **Guidance Counselors**: 15.0 222 students/counselor	**% Amer Indian**: 0.5 **% Asian**: 3.1 **% Black**: 9.1 **% Hispanic**: 2.2 **% White**: 85.2	National ***Socio-Economic Status*** indicator percentile (100=high): 88th

Camden County

[BLACKWOOD] **GLOUCESTER TOWNSHIP S.D.**

17 ERIAL ROAD ● BLACKWOOD NJ 08012-3964 ● (609) 227-1400 ● http://www.jersey.net/~gtps

Grade Span: PK-08 **Schools**: *Regular* 10 ● *Spec Ed* 0 ● *Alt* 0 **Students**: 7,652 **Total Teachers**: 442 **Student/Classroom Teacher Ratio**: 20.6	**Expenditures/Student**: $6,481 **Librarians**: 8.0 957 students/librarian **Guidance Counselors**: 13.0 589 students/counselor	**% Amer Indian**: 0.2 **% Asian**: 2.6 **% Black**: 10.5 **% Hispanic**: 2.2 **% White**: 84.5	National ***Socio-Economic Status*** indicator percentile (100=high): 71st

Camden County

[BLUE ANCHOR] **WINSLOW TOWNSHIP S.D.**

113 CENTRAL AVENUE ● BLUE ANCHOR NJ 08037-9554 ● (609) 561-4102

Grade Span: KG-06 **Schools**: *Regular* 6 ● *Spec Ed* 0 ● *Alt* 0 **Students**: 3,296 **Total Teachers**: 220 **Student/Classroom Teacher Ratio**: 15.7	**Expenditures/Student**: $7,349 **Librarians**: 6.0 549 students/librarian **Guidance Counselors**: 0.0 *** students/counselor	**% Amer Indian**: 0.2 **% Asian**: 1.2 **% Black**: 35.1 **% Hispanic**: 2.9 **% White**: 60.6	National ***Socio-Economic Status*** indicator percentile (100=high): 50th

Camden County
CAMDEN CITY S.D.
201 NORTH FRONT STREET ● CAMDEN NJ 08102-1935 ● (609) 966-2040

Grade Span: PK-12	**Expenditures/Student**: $10,360	**% Amer Indian**: 0.1	
Schools: *Regular* 31 ● *Spec Ed* 2 ● *Alt* 0	**Librarians**: 19.0	**% Asian**: 2.3	National ***Socio-Economic***
Students: 19,841	1,044 students/librarian	**% Black**: 57.5	***Status*** indicator percentile
Total Teachers: 1,512	**Guidance Counselors**: 59.0	**% Hispanic**: 36.9	(100=high): 5th
Student/Classroom Teacher Ratio: 13.6	336 students/counselor	**% White**: 3.1	

Camden County
CHERRY HILL TOWNSHIP S.D.
ADMIN. AT HERITAGE SCHOOL ● CHERRY HILL NJ 08034-0391 ● (609) 429-5600 ● http://www.cherryhill.k12.nj.us

Grade Span: KG-12	**Expenditures/Student**: $9,316	**% Amer Indian**: 0.1	
Schools: *Regular* 16 ● *Spec Ed* 1 ● *Alt* 0	**Librarians**: 19.0	**% Asian**: 12.4	National ***Socio-Economic***
Students: 10,101	532 students/librarian	**% Black**: 5.0	***Status*** indicator percentile
Total Teachers: 654	**Guidance Counselors**: 34.5	**% Hispanic**: 1.8	(100=high): 92nd
Student/Classroom Teacher Ratio: 19.2	293 students/counselor	**% White**: 80.8	

Camden County
PENNSAUKEN TOWNSHIP S.D.
1695 HYLTON ROAD ● PENNSAUKEN NJ 08110 ● (609) 662-8505

Grade Span: PK-12	**Expenditures/Student**: $8,094	**% Amer Indian**: 0.3	
Schools: *Regular* 11 ● *Spec Ed* 0 ● *Alt* 0	**Librarians**: 4.0	**% Asian**: 3.4	National ***Socio-Economic***
Students: 5,763	1,441 students/librarian	**% Black**: 30.2	***Status*** indicator percentile
Total Teachers: 364	**Guidance Counselors**: 16.0	**% Hispanic**: 11.6	(100=high): 47th
Student/Classroom Teacher Ratio: 20.4	360 students/counselor	**% White**: 54.5	

Camden County
VOORHEES TOWNSHIP S.D.
ADMINISTRATION BUILDING ● VOORHEES NJ 08043 ● (609) 751-2435

Grade Span: PK-08	**Expenditures/Student**: $7,261	**% Amer Indian**: 0.0	
Schools: *Regular* 5 ● *Spec Ed* 0 ● *Alt* 0	**Librarians**: 5.0	**% Asian**: 11.5	National ***Socio-Economic***
Students: 3,361	672 students/librarian	**% Black**: 7.2	***Status*** indicator percentile
Total Teachers: 215	**Guidance Counselors**: 6.0	**% Hispanic**: 1.8	(100=high): 95th
Student/Classroom Teacher Ratio: 16.3	560 students/counselor	**% White**: 79.4	

Cape May County
[CAPE MAY COURT HOUSE] **MIDDLE TOWNSHIP S.D.**
216 SOUTH MAIN STREET ● CAPE MAY COURT HOUSE NJ 08210-2273 ● (609) 465-1800

Grade Span: KG-12	**Expenditures/Student**: $7,956	**% Amer Indian**: 0.1	
Schools: *Regular* 4 ● *Spec Ed* 0 ● *Alt* 0	**Librarians**: 1.0	**% Asian**: 1.6	National ***Socio-Economic***
Students: 2,796	2,796 students/librarian	**% Black**: 19.4	***Status*** indicator percentile
Total Teachers: 197	**Guidance Counselors**: 5.0	**% Hispanic**: 1.6	(100=high): 60th
Student/Classroom Teacher Ratio: 14.5	559 students/counselor	**% White**: 77.3	

Cape May County
OCEAN CITY S.D.
801 ASBURY AVENUE ● OCEAN CITY NJ 08226 ● (609) 399-5150 ● http://www.ocean.city.k12.nj.us

Grade Span: KG-12	**Expenditures/Student**: $9,343	**% Amer Indian**: 0.0	
Schools: *Regular* 3 ● *Spec Ed* 0 ● *Alt* 0	**Librarians**: 4.0	**% Asian**: 0.7	National ***Socio-Economic***
Students: 2,593	648 students/librarian	**% Black**: 8.6	***Status*** indicator percentile
Total Teachers: 205	**Guidance Counselors**: 9.0	**% Hispanic**: 1.8	(100=high): 70th
Student/Classroom Teacher Ratio: 13.2	288 students/counselor	**% White**: 88.9	

Cumberland County

BRIDGETON CITY S.D.

P.O. BOX 657 ● BRIDGETON NJ 08302-0482 ● (609) 453-3200

Grade Span: PK-12 **Schools**: *Regular* 7 ● *Spec Ed* 0 ● *Alt* 0 **Students**: 3,871 **Total Teachers**: 314 **Student/Classroom Teacher Ratio**: 21.9	**Expenditures/Student**: $9,420 **Librarians**: 6.0 645 students/librarian **Guidance Counselors**: 6.0 645 students/counselor	**% Amer Indian**: 0.7 **% Asian**: 0.6 **% Black**: 57.1 **% Hispanic**: 17.6 **% White**: 24.1	National ***Socio-Economic Status*** indicator percentile (100=high): 4th

Cumberland County

MILLVILLE CITY S.D.

P. O. BOX 5010 ● MILLVILLE NJ 08332-3829 ● (609) 327-6001 ● http://millville.org

Grade Span: PK-12 **Schools**: *Regular* 9 ● *Spec Ed* 0 ● *Alt* 0 **Students**: 5,542 **Total Teachers**: 376 **Student/Classroom Teacher Ratio**: 18.1	**Expenditures/Student**: $7,488 **Librarians**: 8.0 693 students/librarian **Guidance Counselors**: 14.0 396 students/counselor	**% Amer Indian**: 0.3 **% Asian**: 0.8 **% Black**: 20.7 **% Hispanic**: 12.5 **% White**: 65.7	National ***Socio-Economic Status*** indicator percentile (100=high): 31st

Cumberland County

VINELAND CITY S.D.

625 PLUM STREET ● VINELAND NJ 08360-3708 ● (609) 794-6700 ● http://www.vineland.org

Grade Span: KG-12 **Schools**: *Regular* 18 ● *Spec Ed* 0 ● *Alt* 0 **Students**: 9,138 **Total Teachers**: 631 **Student/Classroom Teacher Ratio**: 19.0	**Expenditures/Student**: $8,904 **Librarians**: 13.0 703 students/librarian **Guidance Counselors**: 29.0 315 students/counselor	**% Amer Indian**: 0.1 **% Asian**: 1.1 **% Black**: 18.8 **% Hispanic**: 38.7 **% White**: 41.3	National ***Socio-Economic Status*** indicator percentile (100=high): 22nd

Essex County

BELLEVILLE TOWN S.D.

100 PASSAIC AVENUE ● BELLEVILLE NJ 07109-3127 ● (973) 450-3507

Grade Span: KG-12 **Schools**: *Regular* 9 ● *Spec Ed* 0 ● *Alt* 0 **Students**: 4,081 **Total Teachers**: 288 **Student/Classroom Teacher Ratio**: 18.3	**Expenditures/Student**: $8,138 **Librarians**: 6.0 680 students/librarian **Guidance Counselors**: 11.0 371 students/counselor	**% Amer Indian**: 0.1 **% Asian**: 11.5 **% Black**: 6.0 **% Hispanic**: 25.2 **% White**: 57.2	National ***Socio-Economic Status*** indicator percentile (100=high): 55th

Essex County

BLOOMFIELD TOWNSHIP S.D.

155 BROAD STREET ● BLOOMFIELD NJ 07003-2629 ● (973) 680-8555

Grade Span: PK-12 **Schools**: *Regular* 10 ● *Spec Ed* 0 ● *Alt* 0 **Students**: 5,183 **Total Teachers**: 340 **Student/Classroom Teacher Ratio**: 18.6	**Expenditures/Student**: $7,981 **Librarians**: 6.8 762 students/librarian **Guidance Counselors**: 17.0 305 students/counselor	**% Amer Indian**: 0.2 **% Asian**: 9.9 **% Black**: 10.2 **% Hispanic**: 14.4 **% White**: 65.4	National ***Socio-Economic Status*** indicator percentile (100=high): 68th

Essex County

EAST ORANGE S.D.

715 PARK AVENUE ● EAST ORANGE NJ 07017-1004 ● (973) 266-5760

Grade Span: KG-12 **Schools**: *Regular* 16 ● *Spec Ed* 0 ● *Alt* 0 **Students**: 11,631 **Total Teachers**: 721 **Student/Classroom Teacher Ratio**: 18.4	**Expenditures/Student**: $9,266 **Librarians**: 16.0 727 students/librarian **Guidance Counselors**: 39.3 296 students/counselor	**% Amer Indian**: 0.1 **% Asian**: 0.2 **% Black**: 96.6 **% Hispanic**: 3.1 **% White**: 0.1	National ***Socio-Economic Status*** indicator percentile (100=high): 11th

Essex County

IRVINGTON TOWNSHIP S.D.

1150 SPRINGFIELD AVENUE ● IRVINGTON NJ 07111-2441 ● (973) 399-6801

Grade Span: KG-12 **Schools**: *Regular* 11 ● *Spec Ed* 0 ● *Alt* 0 **Students**: 8,653 **Total Teachers**: 583 **Student/Classroom Teacher Ratio**: 15.4	**Expenditures/Student**: $9,204 **Librarians**: 15.0 577 students/librarian **Guidance Counselors**: 27.0 320 students/counselor	**% Amer Indian**: 0.1 **% Asian**: 0.9 **% Black**: 89.4 **% Hispanic**: 8.7 **% White**: 0.9	National ***Socio-Economic Status*** indicator percentile (100=high): 10th

Essex County

LIVINGSTON TOWNSHIP S.D.

11 FOXCROFT DRIVE ● LIVINGSTON NJ 07039-2613 ● (973) 535-8010 ● http://www.livingston.org

Grade Span: PK-12 **Schools**: *Regular* 9 ● *Spec Ed* 0 ● *Alt* 0 **Students**: 4,182 **Total Teachers**: 334 **Student/Classroom Teacher Ratio**: 15.4	**Expenditures/Student**: $11,203 **Librarians**: 10.0 418 students/librarian **Guidance Counselors**: 15.0 279 students/counselor	**% Amer Indian**: 0.0 **% Asian**: 19.5 **% Black**: 1.1 **% Hispanic**: 2.0 **% White**: 77.3	National ***Socio-Economic Status*** indicator percentile (100=high): 100th

Essex County

[MAPLEWOOD] **SOUTH ORANGE-MAPLEWOOD S.D.**

525 ACADEMY STREET ● MAPLEWOOD NJ 07040-1311 ● (973) 378-9630 ● http://www.somsd.k12.nj.us

Grade Span: KG-12 **Schools**: *Regular* 9 ● *Spec Ed* 0 ● *Alt* 0 **Students**: 5,566 **Total Teachers**: 384 **Student/Classroom Teacher Ratio**: 15.4	**Expenditures/Student**: $8,877 **Librarians**: 13.4 415 students/librarian **Guidance Counselors**: 13.0 428 students/counselor	**% Amer Indian**: 0.5 **% Asian**: 4.0 **% Black**: 41.1 **% Hispanic**: 4.0 **% White**: 50.3	National ***Socio-Economic Status*** indicator percentile (100=high): 81st

Essex County

MILLBURN TOWNSHIP S.D.

434 MILLBURN AVENUE ● MILLBURN NJ 07041-1210 ● (973) 376-3600 ● http://www.millburn.org

Grade Span: PK-12 **Schools**: *Regular* 6 ● *Spec Ed* 0 ● *Alt* 0 **Students**: 2,772 **Total Teachers**: 212 **Student/Classroom Teacher Ratio**: 16.2	**Expenditures/Student**: $10,577 **Librarians**: 7.0 396 students/librarian **Guidance Counselors**: 7.0 396 students/counselor	**% Amer Indian**: 1.5 **% Asian**: 7.5 **% Black**: 1.8 **% Hispanic**: 1.4 **% White**: 87.8	National ***Socio-Economic Status*** indicator percentile (100=high): 100th

Essex County

MONTCLAIR TOWN S.D.

22 VALLEY ROAD ● MONTCLAIR NJ 07042-2709 ● (973) 509-4010

Grade Span: PK-12 **Schools**: *Regular* 10 ● *Spec Ed* 0 ● *Alt* 0 **Students**: 5,970 **Total Teachers**: 425 **Student/Classroom Teacher Ratio**: 15.6	**Expenditures/Student**: $9,105 **Librarians**: 7.0 853 students/librarian **Guidance Counselors**: 9.9 603 students/counselor	**% Amer Indian**: 0.1 **% Asian**: 3.6 **% Black**: 46.8 **% Hispanic**: 3.8 **% White**: 45.7	National ***Socio-Economic Status*** indicator percentile (100=high): 71st

Essex County

NEWARK CITY S.D.

2 CEDAR STREET ● NEWARK NJ 07102-3015 ● (973) 733-7333 ● http://hosting.injersey.com/schools/Newark

Grade Span: PK-12 **Schools**: *Regular* 75 ● *Spec Ed* 5 ● *Alt* 0 **Students**: 45,805 **Total Teachers**: 3,538 **Student/Classroom Teacher Ratio**: 14.7	**Expenditures/Student**: $11,320 **Librarians**: 64.0 716 students/librarian **Guidance Counselors**: 96.8 473 students/counselor	**% Amer Indian**: 0.0 **% Asian**: 0.8 **% Black**: 63.2 **% Hispanic**: 27.3 **% White**: 8.7	National ***Socio-Economic Status*** indicator percentile (100=high): 2nd

Essex County

NUTLEY TOWN S.D.

375 BLOOMFIELD AVENUE ● NUTLEY NJ 07110-2252 ● (973) 661-8798

Grade Span: KG-12 **Schools**: *Regular* 7 ● *Spec Ed* 0 ● *Alt* 0 **Students**: 3,751 **Total Teachers**: 240 **Student/Classroom Teacher Ratio**: 17.9	**Expenditures/Student**: $8,169 **Librarians**: 8.0 469 students/librarian **Guidance Counselors**: 8.0 469 students/counselor	**% Amer Indian**: 0.0 **% Asian**: 9.6 **% Black**: 1.7 **% Hispanic**: 6.0 **% White**: 82.8	National ***Socio-Economic Status*** indicator percentile (100=high): 92nd

Essex County

[ORANGE] **CITY OF ORANGE TOWNSHIP S.D.**

369 MAIN STREET ● ORANGE NJ 07050-2704 ● (973) 677-4040

Grade Span: KG-12 **Schools**: *Regular* 9 ● *Spec Ed* 0 ● *Alt* 0 **Students**: 3,979 **Total Teachers**: 286 **Student/Classroom Teacher Ratio**: 16.4	**Expenditures/Student**: $10,307 **Librarians**: 5.6 711 students/librarian **Guidance Counselors**: 10.0 398 students/counselor	**% Amer Indian**: 0.0 **% Asian**: 0.2 **% Black**: 91.1 **% Hispanic**: 7.7 **% White**: 1.0	National ***Socio-Economic Status*** indicator percentile (100=high): 6th

Essex County

WEST ORANGE TOWN S.D.

179 EAGLE ROCK AVE. ● WEST ORANGE NJ 07052-5007 ● (973) 669-5430 ● http://www.westorange.k12.nj.us

Grade Span: KG-12 **Schools**: *Regular* 9 ● *Spec Ed* 0 ● *Alt* 0 **Students**: 4,843 **Total Teachers**: 379 **Student/Classroom Teacher Ratio**: 14.7	**Expenditures/Student**: $10,947 **Librarians**: 10.0 484 students/librarian **Guidance Counselors**: 14.9 325 students/counselor	**% Amer Indian**: 0.0 **% Asian**: 10.6 **% Black**: 19.7 **% Hispanic**: 11.7 **% White**: 58.0	National ***Socio-Economic Status*** indicator percentile (100=high): 80th

Gloucester County

DEPTFORD TOWNSHIP S.D.

2022 GOOD INTENT ROAD ● DEPTFORD NJ 08096 ● (609) 232-2707

Grade Span: KG-12 **Schools**: *Regular* 8 ● *Spec Ed* 1 ● *Alt* 0 **Students**: 3,588 **Total Teachers**: 239 **Student/Classroom Teacher Ratio**: 17.7	**Expenditures/Student**: $7,928 **Librarians**: 8.6 417 students/librarian **Guidance Counselors**: 7.0 513 students/counselor	**% Amer Indian**: 0.4 **% Asian**: 1.3 **% Black**: 18.1 **% Hispanic**: 2.1 **% White**: 78.0	National ***Socio-Economic Status*** indicator percentile (100=high): 59th

Gloucester County

[SEWELL] **WASHINGTON TOWNSHIP S.D.**

206 EAST HOLLY AVE ● SEWELL NJ 08080-9231 ● (609) 589-6644

Grade Span: KG-12 **Schools**: *Regular* 11 ● *Spec Ed* 0 ● *Alt* 0 **Students**: 9,152 **Total Teachers**: 593 **Student/Classroom Teacher Ratio**: 17.6	**Expenditures/Student**: $7,035 **Librarians**: 11.5 796 students/librarian **Guidance Counselors**: 30.7 298 students/counselor	**% Amer Indian**: 0.0 **% Asian**: 2.5 **% Black**: 5.4 **% Hispanic**: 1.1 **% White**: 91.0	National ***Socio-Economic Status*** indicator percentile (100=high): 92nd

Gloucester County

WEST DEPTFORD TOWNSHIP S.D.

WEST DEPTFORD MIDDLE SCHO ● WEST DEPTFORD NJ 08066-1999 ● (609) 848-4300

Grade Span: KG-12 **Schools**: *Regular* 5 ● *Spec Ed* 0 ● *Alt* 0 **Students**: 3,043 **Total Teachers**: 210 **Student/Classroom Teacher Ratio**: 17.5	**Expenditures/Student**: $7,815 **Librarians**: 4.0 761 students/librarian **Guidance Counselors**: 9.0 338 students/counselor	**% Amer Indian**: 0.1 **% Asian**: 1.2 **% Black**: 5.8 **% Hispanic**: 1.6 **% White**: 91.3	National ***Socio-Economic Status*** indicator percentile (100=high): 78th

Gloucester County

[WILLIAMSTOWN] **MONROE TOWNSHIP S.D.**

MAPLE GROVE SCHOOL ● WILLIAMSTOWN NJ 08094 ● (609) 629-6400

Grade Span: KG-12	**Expenditures/Student**: $6,885	**% Amer Indian**: 0.3	National ***Socio-Economic Status*** indicator percentile (100=high): 65th
Schools: *Regular* 5 ● *Spec Ed* 0 ● *Alt* 0	**Librarians**: 5.0	**% Asian**: 1.7	
Students: 4,270	854 students/librarian	**% Black**: 13.3	
Total Teachers: 263	**Guidance Counselors**: 8.0	**% Hispanic**: 1.8	
Student/Classroom Teacher Ratio: 17.5	534 students/counselor	**% White**: 82.9	

Hudson County

BAYONNE CITY S.D.

AVENUE A AND 29TH STREET ● BAYONNE NJ 07002 ● (201) 858-5814

Grade Span: PK-12	**Expenditures/Student**: $7,515	**% Amer Indian**: 0.2	National ***Socio-Economic Status*** indicator percentile (100=high): 39th
Schools: *Regular* 11 ● *Spec Ed* 0 ● *Alt* 0	**Librarians**: 7.0	**% Asian**: 4.3	
Students: 7,716	1,102 students/librarian	**% Black**: 8.6	
Total Teachers: 558	**Guidance Counselors**: 13.0	**% Hispanic**: 21.5	
Student/Classroom Teacher Ratio: 15.7	594 students/counselor	**% White**: 65.3	

Hudson County

HOBOKEN CITY S.D.

1115 CLINTON STREET ● HOBOKEN NJ 07030-3201 ● (201) 420-2151

Grade Span: PK-12	**Expenditures/Student**: $12,192	**% Amer Indian**: 0.1	National ***Socio-Economic Status*** indicator percentile (100=high): 5th
Schools: *Regular* 6 ● *Spec Ed* 0 ● *Alt* 0	**Librarians**: 2.0	**% Asian**: 3.6	
Students: 2,722	1,361 students/librarian	**% Black**: 14.0	
Total Teachers: 261	**Guidance Counselors**: 11.6	**% Hispanic**: 65.0	
Student/Classroom Teacher Ratio: 10.8	235 students/counselor	**% White**: 17.4	

Hudson County

JERSEY CITY S.D.

346 CLAREMONT AVENUE ● JERSEY CITY NJ 07305-1634 ● (201) 915-6202 ● http://www.jerseycity.k12.nj.us

Grade Span: PK-12	**Expenditures/Student**: $8,796	**% Amer Indian**: 0.7	National ***Socio-Economic Status*** indicator percentile (100=high): 4th
Schools: *Regular* 35 ● *Spec Ed* 2 ● *Alt* 0	**Librarians**: 35.0	**% Asian**: 10.6	
Students: 31,666	905 students/librarian	**% Black**: 42.1	
Total Teachers: 2,133	**Guidance Counselors**: 65.5	**% Hispanic**: 37.4	
Student/Classroom Teacher Ratio: 15.6	483 students/counselor	**% White**: 9.2	

Hudson County

KEARNY TOWN S.D.

336 DEVON STREET ● KEARNY NJ 07032-2612 ● (201) 955-5021

Grade Span: KG-12	**Expenditures/Student**: $7,788	**% Amer Indian**: 0.4	National ***Socio-Economic Status*** indicator percentile (100=high): 72nd
Schools: *Regular* 7 ● *Spec Ed* 0 ● *Alt* 0	**Librarians**: 7.0	**% Asian**: 4.2	
Students: 5,174	739 students/librarian	**% Black**: 0.9	
Total Teachers: 349	**Guidance Counselors**: 10.0	**% Hispanic**: 29.1	
Student/Classroom Teacher Ratio: 15.9	517 students/counselor	**% White**: 65.4	

Hudson County

NORTH BERGEN TOWNSHIP S.D.

73L7 KENNEDY BOULEVARD ● NORTH BERGEN NJ 07047 ● (201) 295-2706

Grade Span: KG-12	**Expenditures/Student**: $7,496	**% Amer Indian**: 0.3	National ***Socio-Economic Status*** indicator percentile (100=high): 27th
Schools: *Regular* 7 ● *Spec Ed* 0 ● *Alt* 0	**Librarians**: 5.0	**% Asian**: 8.5	
Students: 6,578	1,316 students/librarian	**% Black**: 1.6	
Total Teachers: 394	**Guidance Counselors**: 16.0	**% Hispanic**: 65.5	
Student/Classroom Teacher Ratio: 17.0	411 students/counselor	**% White**: 24.0	

Hudson County

UNION CITY S.D.

3912 BERGEN TURNPIKE ● UNION CITY NJ 07087 ● (201) 348-5851 ● http://www.union-city.k12.nj.us

Grade Span: PK-12 **Schools**: *Regular* 10 ● *Spec Ed* 0 ● *Alt* 0 **Students**: 9,001 **Total Teachers**: 552 **Student/Classroom Teacher Ratio**: 16.7	**Expenditures/Student**: $8,466 **Librarians**: 4.2 2,143 students/librarian **Guidance Counselors**: 16.0 563 students/counselor	**% Amer Indian**: 0.0 **% Asian**: 1.4 **% Black**: 1.0 **% Hispanic**: 91.9 **% White**: 5.8	National ***Socio-Economic Status*** indicator percentile (100=high): 2nd

Hudson County

WEST NEW YORK TOWN S.D.

100 51ST STREET ● WEST NEW YORK NJ 07093-5223 ● (201) 902-1120

Grade Span: KG-12 **Schools**: *Regular* 7 ● *Spec Ed* 0 ● *Alt* 0 **Students**: 5,902 **Total Teachers**: 408 **Student/Classroom Teacher Ratio**: 16.8	**Expenditures/Student**: $8,019 **Librarians**: 9.0 656 students/librarian **Guidance Counselors**: 11.2 527 students/counselor	**% Amer Indian**: 0.1 **% Asian**: 1.6 **% Black**: 0.9 **% Hispanic**: 90.4 **% White**: 7.1	National ***Socio-Economic Status*** indicator percentile (100=high): 12th

Hunterdon County

FLEMINGTON-RARITAN REGIONAL S.D.

50 COURT STREET ● FLEMINGTON NJ 08822-1325 ● (908) 782-8074

Grade Span: KG-08 **Schools**: *Regular* 4 ● *Spec Ed* 0 ● *Alt* 0 **Students**: 3,015 **Total Teachers**: 212 **Student/Classroom Teacher Ratio**: 14.5	**Expenditures/Student**: $7,051 **Librarians**: 3.0 1,005 students/librarian **Guidance Counselors**: 6.0 503 students/counselor	**% Amer Indian**: 0.1 **% Asian**: 3.5 **% Black**: 2.0 **% Hispanic**: 2.8 **% White**: 91.6	National ***Socio-Economic Status*** indicator percentile (100=high): 94th

Mercer County

EWING TOWNSHIP S.D.

1331 LOWER FERRY ROAD ● EWING NJ 08618-1409 ● (609) 883-3388 ● http://www.ewing.k12.nj.us

Grade Span: KG-12 **Schools**: *Regular* 5 ● *Spec Ed* 0 ● *Alt* 0 **Students**: 3,564 **Total Teachers**: 269 **Student/Classroom Teacher Ratio**: 13.2	**Expenditures/Student**: $9,710 **Librarians**: 7.0 509 students/librarian **Guidance Counselors**: 14.0 255 students/counselor	**% Amer Indian**: 0.1 **% Asian**: 2.1 **% Black**: 34.7 **% Hispanic**: 3.4 **% White**: 59.8	National ***Socio-Economic Status*** indicator percentile (100=high): 75th

Mercer County

[HAMILTON SQUARE] **HAMILTON TOWNSHIP S.D.**

90 PARK AVENUE ● HAMILTON SQUARE NJ 08690 ● (609) 890-3723

Grade Span: KG-12 **Schools**: *Regular* 23 ● *Spec Ed* 0 ● *Alt* 0 **Students**: 11,996 **Total Teachers**: 834 **Student/Classroom Teacher Ratio**: 17.0	**Expenditures/Student**: $8,450 **Librarians**: 14.0 857 students/librarian **Guidance Counselors**: 49.0 245 students/counselor	**% Amer Indian**: 0.1 **% Asian**: 3.4 **% Black**: 10.7 **% Hispanic**: 4.1 **% White**: 81.7	National ***Socio-Economic Status*** indicator percentile (100=high): 82nd

Mercer County

[HIGHTSTOWN] **EAST WINDSOR REGIONAL S.D.**

384 STOCKTON STREET ● HIGHTSTOWN NJ 08520-4228 ● (609) 443-7704

Grade Span: KG-12 **Schools**: *Regular* 6 ● *Spec Ed* 0 ● *Alt* 0 **Students**: 3,914 **Total Teachers**: 317 **Student/Classroom Teacher Ratio**: 13.4	**Expenditures/Student**: $10,168 **Librarians**: 7.0 559 students/librarian **Guidance Counselors**: 12.0 326 students/counselor	**% Amer Indian**: 0.1 **% Asian**: 7.5 **% Black**: 12.3 **% Hispanic**: 9.9 **% White**: 70.2	National ***Socio-Economic Status*** indicator percentile (100=high): 77th

Mercer County

[LAWRENCEVILLE] **LAWRENCE TOWNSHIP S.D.**

2565 PRINCETON PIKE ● LAWRENCEVILLE NJ 08648-3631 ● (609) 530-8609

Grade Span: KG-12 **Schools**: *Regular* 7 ● *Spec Ed* 0 ● *Alt* 0 **Students**: 3,619 **Total Teachers**: 260 **Student/Classroom Teacher Ratio**: 15.3	**Expenditures/Student**: $9,357 **Librarians**: 4.0 905 students/librarian **Guidance Counselors**: 12.8 283 students/counselor	**% Amer Indian**: 0.0 **% Asian**: 8.6 **% Black**: 15.0 **% Hispanic**: 4.2 **% White**: 72.3	National ***Socio-Economic Status*** indicator percentile (100=high): 83rd

Mercer County

[PENNINGTON] **HOPEWELL VALLEY REGIONAL S.D.**

425 SOUTH MAIN STREET ● PENNINGTON NJ 08534-2716 ● (609) 737-0105 ● http://www.hvrsd.k12.nj.us

Grade Span: KG-12 **Schools**: *Regular* 5 ● *Spec Ed* 0 ● *Alt* 0 **Students**: 2,936 **Total Teachers**: 204 **Student/Classroom Teacher Ratio**: 15.9	**Expenditures/Student**: $8,701 **Librarians**: 7.0 419 students/librarian **Guidance Counselors**: 9.4 312 students/counselor	**% Amer Indian**: 0.0 **% Asian**: 2.1 **% Black**: 1.5 **% Hispanic**: 0.9 **% White**: 95.4	National ***Socio-Economic Status*** indicator percentile (100=high): 99th

Mercer County

PRINCETON REGIONAL S.D.

P.O. BOX 711 ● PRINCETON NJ 08542-0711 ● (609) 924-9322 ● http://www.prs.k12.nj.us

Grade Span: KG-12 **Schools**: *Regular* 6 ● *Spec Ed* 0 ● *Alt* 0 **Students**: 3,049 **Total Teachers**: 214 **Student/Classroom Teacher Ratio**: 14.8	**Expenditures/Student**: $11,084 **Librarians**: 6.0 508 students/librarian **Guidance Counselors**: 7.7 396 students/counselor	**% Amer Indian**: 0.5 **% Asian**: 8.4 **% Black**: 10.6 **% Hispanic**: 8.2 **% White**: 72.4	National ***Socio-Economic Status*** indicator percentile (100=high): 81st

Mercer County

[PRINCETON JUNCTION] **WEST WINDSOR-PLAINSBORO REGIONAL S.D.**

Y.O. BOX 248 ● PRINCETON JUNCTION NJ 08550 ● (609) 799-0200 ● http://www.njcc.com/~wwp

Grade Span: KG-12 **Schools**: *Regular* 6 ● *Spec Ed* 0 ● *Alt* 0 **Students**: 6,810 **Total Teachers**: 489 **Student/Classroom Teacher Ratio**: 15.2	**Expenditures/Student**: $8,648 **Librarians**: 7.0 973 students/librarian **Guidance Counselors**: 18.6 366 students/counselor	**% Amer Indian**: 0.2 **% Asian**: 24.1 **% Black**: 7.3 **% Hispanic**: 3.4 **% White**: 64.9	National ***Socio-Economic Status*** indicator percentile (100=high): 97th

Mercer County

TRENTON CITY S.D.

108 NORTH CLINTON AVENUE ● TRENTON NJ 08609-1014 ● (609) 989-2744

Grade Span: PK-12 **Schools**: *Regular* 22 ● *Spec Ed* 1 ● *Alt* 0 **Students**: 12,783 **Total Teachers**: 1,015 **Student/Classroom Teacher Ratio**: 13.8	**Expenditures/Student**: $10,843 **Librarians**: 21.5 595 students/librarian **Guidance Counselors**: 46.0 278 students/counselor	**% Amer Indian**: 0.1 **% Asian**: 0.7 **% Black**: 73.0 **% Hispanic**: 19.6 **% White**: 6.6	National ***Socio-Economic Status*** indicator percentile (100=high): 6th

Middlesex County

CARTERET BOROUGH S.D.

599 ROOSEVELT AVENUE ● CARTERET NJ 07008 ● (732) 541-8961

Grade Span: PK-12 **Schools**: *Regular* 6 ● *Spec Ed* 0 ● *Alt* 0 **Students**: 2,761 **Total Teachers**: 197 **Student/Classroom Teacher Ratio**: 18.0	**Expenditures/Student**: $8,686 **Librarians**: 3.0 920 students/librarian **Guidance Counselors**: 9.0 307 students/counselor	**% Amer Indian**: 0.0 **% Asian**: 10.2 **% Black**: 13.8 **% Hispanic**: 28.9 **% White**: 47.1	National ***Socio-Economic Status*** indicator percentile (100=high): 39th

Middlesex County

EAST BRUNSWICK TOWNSHIP S.D.

760 ROUTE #18 ● EAST BRUNSWICK NJ 08816-3068 ● (732) 613-6705 ● http://www.ebruns.k12.nj.us

Grade Span: KG-12 **Schools**: *Regular* 11 ● *Spec Ed* 0 ● *Alt* 0 **Students**: 7,256 **Total Teachers**: 516 **Student/Classroom Teacher Ratio**: 16.4	**Expenditures/Student**: $8,841 **Librarians**: 13.0 558 students/librarian **Guidance Counselors**: 23.0 315 students/counselor	**% Amer Indian**: 0.2 **% Asian**: 18.3 **% Black**: 2.5 **% Hispanic**: 2.8 **% White**: 76.1	National ***Socio-Economic Status*** indicator percentile (100=high): 94th

Middlesex County

EDISON TOWNSHIP S.D.

100 MUNICIPAL BOULEVARD ● EDISON NJ 08817-3353 ● (908) 287-4400

Grade Span: KG-12 **Schools**: *Regular* 17 ● *Spec Ed* 0 ● *Alt* 0 **Students**: 12,509 **Total Teachers**: 807 **Student/Classroom Teacher Ratio**: 17.6	**Expenditures/Student**: $8,169 **Librarians**: 9.4 1,331 students/librarian **Guidance Counselors**: 23.0 544 students/counselor	**% Amer Indian**: 0.1 **% Asian**: 28.6 **% Black**: 8.9 **% Hispanic**: 5.5 **% White**: 56.9	National ***Socio-Economic Status*** indicator percentile (100=high): 86th

Middlesex County

[JAMESBURG] **MONROE TOWNSHIP S.D.**

423 BUCKELEW AVENUE ● JAMESBURG NJ 08831-9802 ● (732) 521-2111 ● http://monroe.k12.nj.us

Grade Span: KG-12 **Schools**: *Regular* 6 ● *Spec Ed* 0 ● *Alt* 0 **Students**: 2,678 **Total Teachers**: 193 **Student/Classroom Teacher Ratio**: 15.5	**Expenditures/Student**: $8,755 **Librarians**: 1.0 2,678 students/librarian **Guidance Counselors**: 12.0 223 students/counselor	**% Amer Indian**: 0.1 **% Asian**: 3.7 **% Black**: 3.7 **% Hispanic**: 2.3 **% White**: 90.2	National ***Socio-Economic Status*** indicator percentile (100=high): 91st

Middlesex County

[MATAWAN] **OLD BRIDGE TOWNSHIP S.D.**

ADMINISTRATIVE BUILDING ● MATAWAN NJ 07747-9641 ● (732) 290-3976

Grade Span: KG-12 **Schools**: *Regular* 14 ● *Spec Ed* 0 ● *Alt* 0 **Students**: 8,923 **Total Teachers**: 614 **Student/Classroom Teacher Ratio**: 17.7	**Expenditures/Student**: $9,128 **Librarians**: 13.0 686 students/librarian **Guidance Counselors**: 15.0 595 students/counselor	**% Amer Indian**: 0.3 **% Asian**: 11.4 **% Black**: 6.0 **% Hispanic**: 6.2 **% White**: 76.1	National ***Socio-Economic Status*** indicator percentile (100=high): 83rd

Middlesex County

[MONMOUTH JUNCTION] **SOUTH BRUNSWICK TOWNSHIP S.D.**

P.O. BOX 181 ● MONMOUTH JUNCTION NJ 08852 ● (732) 297-7800

Grade Span: KG-12 **Schools**: *Regular* 10 ● *Spec Ed* 0 ● *Alt* 0 **Students**: 5,440 **Total Teachers**: 382 **Student/Classroom Teacher Ratio**: 14.5	**Expenditures/Student**: $8,577 **Librarians**: 10.0 544 students/librarian **Guidance Counselors**: 14.2 383 students/counselor	**% Amer Indian**: 0.2 **% Asian**: 15.6 **% Black**: 10.2 **% Hispanic**: 4.5 **% White**: 69.4	National ***Socio-Economic Status*** indicator percentile (100=high): 91st

Middlesex County

NEW BRUNSWICK CITY S.D.

24 BAYARD STREET ● NEW BRUNSWICK NJ 08901-1203 ● (732) 745-5414

Grade Span: PK-12 **Schools**: *Regular* 9 ● *Spec Ed* 1 ● *Alt* 0 **Students**: 4,554 **Total Teachers**: 334 **Student/Classroom Teacher Ratio**: 14.9	**Expenditures/Student**: $10,456 **Librarians**: 2.8 1,626 students/librarian **Guidance Counselors**: 7.0 651 students/counselor	**% Amer Indian**: 0.1 **% Asian**: 1.8 **% Black**: 47.5 **% Hispanic**: 46.1 **% White**: 4.5	National ***Socio-Economic Status*** indicator percentile (100=high): 3rd

Middlesex County
NORTH BRUNSWICK TOWNSHIP S.D.
P.O. BOX 6016 ● NORTH BRUNSWICK NJ 08902-0407 ● (732) 297-9000

Grade Span: KG-12	**Expenditures/Student**: $7,910	**% Amer Indian**: 0.0	
Schools: *Regular* 6 ● *Spec Ed* 0 ● *Alt* 0	**Librarians**: 6.0	**% Asian**: 14.4	National ***Socio-Economic***
Students: 4,412	735 students/librarian	**% Black**: 15.3	***Status*** indicator percentile
Total Teachers: 308	**Guidance Counselors**: 9.0	**% Hispanic**: 9.0	(100=high): 81st
Student/Classroom Teacher Ratio: 15.9	490 students/counselor	**% White**: 61.2	

Middlesex County
PERTH AMBOY CITY S.D.
178 BARRACKS STREET ● PERTH AMBOY NJ 08861-3402 ● (732) 826-3360 ● http://www.perthamboy.k12.nj.us

Grade Span: PK-12	**Expenditures/Student**: $8,597	**% Amer Indian**: 0.1	
Schools: *Regular* 10 ● *Spec Ed* 0 ● *Alt* 0	**Librarians**: 11.0	**% Asian**: 0.4	National ***Socio-Economic***
Students: 7,292	663 students/librarian	**% Black**: 9.1	***Status*** indicator percentile
Total Teachers: 498	**Guidance Counselors**: 16.5	**% Hispanic**: 83.3	(100=high): 4th
Student/Classroom Teacher Ratio: 15.9	442 students/counselor	**% White**: 7.1	

Middlesex County
PISCATAWAY TOWNSHIP S.D.
1515 STELTON ROAD ● PISCATAWAY NJ 08854-5997 ● (908) 572-2289

Grade Span: KG-12	**Expenditures/Student**: $9,797	**% Amer Indian**: 0.0	
Schools: *Regular* 10 ● *Spec Ed* 0 ● *Alt* 0	**Librarians**: 10.0	**% Asian**: 19.3	National ***Socio-Economic***
Students: 6,164	616 students/librarian	**% Black**: 29.8	***Status*** indicator percentile
Total Teachers: 422	**Guidance Counselors**: 19.8	**% Hispanic**: 7.2	(100=high): 79th
Student/Classroom Teacher Ratio: 14.9	311 students/counselor	**% White**: 43.7	

Middlesex County
SAYREVILLE BOROUGH S.D.
P.O. BOX 997 ● SAYREVILLE NJ 08872 ● (732) 525-5224 ● http://ourworld.compuserve.com/homepages/Sayreville_Schools

Grade Span: KG-12	**Expenditures/Student**: $6,774	**% Amer Indian**: 0.0	
Schools: *Regular* 6 ● *Spec Ed* 0 ● *Alt* 0	**Librarians**: 5.0	**% Asian**: 7.1	National ***Socio-Economic***
Students: 4,908	982 students/librarian	**% Black**: 10.1	***Status*** indicator percentile
Total Teachers: 301	**Guidance Counselors**: 11.0	**% Hispanic**: 6.9	(100=high): 77th
Student/Classroom Teacher Ratio: 17.6	446 students/counselor	**% White**: 75.8	

Middlesex County
SOUTH PLAINFIELD BOROUGH S.D.
305 CROMWELL PLACE ● SOUTH PLAINFIELD NJ 07080 ● (908) 754-4620

Grade Span: KG-12	**Expenditures/Student**: $9,537	**% Amer Indian**: 0.0	
Schools: *Regular* 6 ● *Spec Ed* 1 ● *Alt* 0	**Librarians**: 6.0	**% Asian**: 7.9	National ***Socio-Economic***
Students: 3,251	542 students/librarian	**% Black**: 9.8	***Status*** indicator percentile
Total Teachers: 239	**Guidance Counselors**: 10.0	**% Hispanic**: 7.5	(100=high): 87th
Student/Classroom Teacher Ratio: 14.4	325 students/counselor	**% White**: 74.8	

Middlesex County
WOODBRIDGE TOWNSHIP S.D.
P.O. BOX 428 ● WOODBRIDGE NJ 07095-0952 ● (732) 602-8549 ● http://members.home.net/woodbridgeschools/index.html

Grade Span: KG-12	**Expenditures/Student**: $9,629	**% Amer Indian**: 0.2	
Schools: *Regular* 24 ● *Spec Ed* 0 ● *Alt* 0	**Librarians**: 16.5	**% Asian**: 12.0	National ***Socio-Economic***
Students: 11,593	703 students/librarian	**% Black**: 8.8	***Status*** indicator percentile
Total Teachers: 867	**Guidance Counselors**: 36.3	**% Hispanic**: 7.9	(100=high): 82nd
Student/Classroom Teacher Ratio: 16.8	319 students/counselor	**% White**: 71.1	

Monmouth County
[ABERDEEN] **MATAWAN-ABERDEEN REGIONAL S.D.**
CAMBRIDGE PARK SCHOOL ● ABERDEEN NJ 07747-2286 ● (732) 290-2705

Grade Span: PK-12 **Schools**: *Regular* 6 ● *Spec Ed* 0 ● *Alt* 0 **Students**: 3,448 **Total Teachers**: 258 **Student/Classroom Teacher Ratio**: 15.0	**Expenditures/Student**: $10,719 **Librarians**: 6.0 575 students/librarian **Guidance Counselors**: 8.2 420 students/counselor	**% Amer Indian**: 0.0 **% Asian**: 5.8 **% Black**: 14.6 **% Hispanic**: 6.4 **% White**: 73.1	National ***Socio-Economic Status*** indicator percentile (100=high): 77th

Monmouth County
ASBURY PARK CITY S.D.
1506 PARK AVENUE ● ASBURY PARK NJ 07712-5493 ● (732) 776-2606

Grade Span: PK-12 **Schools**: *Regular* 6 ● *Spec Ed* 1 ● *Alt* 0 **Students**: 3,167 **Total Teachers**: 247 **Student/Classroom Teacher Ratio**: 14.9	**Expenditures/Student**: $9,923 **Librarians**: 4.0 792 students/librarian **Guidance Counselors**: 10.0 317 students/counselor	**% Amer Indian**: 0.0 **% Asian**: 0.1 **% Black**: 86.5 **% Hispanic**: 10.6 **% White**: 2.8	National ***Socio-Economic Status*** indicator percentile (100=high): 1st

Monmouth County
[ENGLISHTOWN] **FREEHOLD REGIONAL S.D.**
11 PINE STREET ● ENGLISHTOWN NJ 07726-1595 ● (732) 431-8538

Grade Span: 09-12 **Schools**: *Regular* 5 ● *Spec Ed* 1 ● *Alt* 0 **Students**: 7,354 **Total Teachers**: 513 **Student/Classroom Teacher Ratio**: 15.5	**Expenditures/Student**: $9,247 **Librarians**: 10.0 735 students/librarian **Guidance Counselors**: 29.0 254 students/counselor	**% Amer Indian**: 0.5 **% Asian**: 5.8 **% Black**: 4.5 **% Hispanic**: 3.9 **% White**: 85.3	National ***Socio-Economic Status*** indicator percentile (100=high): 94th

Monmouth County
[ENGLISHTOWN] **MANALAPAN-ENGLISHTOWN REGIONAL S.D.**
54 MAIN STREET ● ENGLISHTOWN NJ 07726-1599 ● (732) 446-5506

Grade Span: KG-08 **Schools**: *Regular* 6 ● *Spec Ed* 0 ● *Alt* 0 **Students**: 4,916 **Total Teachers**: 295 **Student/Classroom Teacher Ratio**: 18.0	**Expenditures/Student**: $7,037 **Librarians**: 6.7 734 students/librarian **Guidance Counselors**: 8.0 615 students/counselor	**% Amer Indian**: 0.0 **% Asian**: 4.5 **% Black**: 2.0 **% Hispanic**: 2.0 **% White**: 91.5	National ***Socio-Economic Status*** indicator percentile (100=high): 98th

Monmouth County
FREEHOLD TOWNSHIP S.D.
237 STONEHURST BOULEVARD ● FREEHOLD NJ 07728-3198 ● (732) 866-6815 ● http://www.freeholdtwp.k12.nj.us

Grade Span: KG-08 **Schools**: *Regular* 7 ● *Spec Ed* 0 ● *Alt* 0 **Students**: 3,135 **Total Teachers**: 230 **Student/Classroom Teacher Ratio**: 14.6	**Expenditures/Student**: $7,966 **Librarians**: 7.0 448 students/librarian **Guidance Counselors**: 2.0 1,568 students/counselor	**% Amer Indian**: 0.4 **% Asian**: 5.8 **% Black**: 4.3 **% Hispanic**: 3.7 **% White**: 85.8	National ***Socio-Economic Status*** indicator percentile (100=high): 94th

Monmouth County
HAZLET TOWNSHIP S.D.
ONE BETHANY ROAD, BLDG. 4 ● HAZLET NJ 07730-2342 ● (732) 264-8402

Grade Span: KG-12 **Schools**: *Regular* 8 ● *Spec Ed* 0 ● *Alt* 0 **Students**: 3,176 **Total Teachers**: 241 **Student/Classroom Teacher Ratio**: 13.8	**Expenditures/Student**: $8,851 **Librarians**: 4.7 676 students/librarian **Guidance Counselors**: 7.0 454 students/counselor	**% Amer Indian**: 0.1 **% Asian**: 3.9 **% Black**: 1.4 **% Hispanic**: 4.4 **% White**: 90.3	National ***Socio-Economic Status*** indicator percentile (100=high): 89th

Monmouth County
HOLMDEL TOWNSHIP S.D.
4 CRAWFORD'S CORNER ROAD ● HOLMDEL NJ 07733-0407 ● (732) 946-1800

Grade Span: KG-12 **Schools**: *Regular* 4 ● *Spec Ed* 0 ● *Alt* 0 **Students**: 2,773 **Total Teachers**: 182 **Student/Classroom Teacher Ratio**: 16.5	**Expenditures/Student**: $8,804 **Librarians**: 4.2 660 students/librarian **Guidance Counselors**: 8.0 347 students/counselor	**% Amer Indian**: 0.1 **% Asian**: 20.3 **% Black**: 0.9 **% Hispanic**: 1.9 **% White**: 76.7	National ***Socio-Economic Status*** indicator percentile (100=high): 100th

Monmouth County
HOWELL TOWNSHIP S.D.
449 ROUTE #524 ● HOWELL NJ 07731-0579 ● (732) 938-6995

Grade Span: KG-08 **Schools**: *Regular* 9 ● *Spec Ed* 0 ● *Alt* 0 **Students**: 6,605 **Total Teachers**: 392 **Student/Classroom Teacher Ratio**: 17.7	**Expenditures/Student**: $7,180 **Librarians**: 8.0 826 students/librarian **Guidance Counselors**: 10.0 661 students/counselor	**% Amer Indian**: 0.3 **% Asian**: 3.4 **% Black**: 4.3 **% Hispanic**: 3.4 **% White**: 88.6	National ***Socio-Economic Status*** indicator percentile (100=high): 84th

Monmouth County
LONG BRANCH CITY S.D.
6 WEST END COURT ● LONG BRANCH NJ 07740-5108 ● (732) 571-2868 ● http://www.longbranch.k12.nj.us

Grade Span: KG-12 **Schools**: *Regular* 8 ● *Spec Ed* 0 ● *Alt* 0 **Students**: 4,117 **Total Teachers**: 360 **Student/Classroom Teacher Ratio**: 14.2	**Expenditures/Student**: $10,754 **Librarians**: 5.0 823 students/librarian **Guidance Counselors**: 14.0 294 students/counselor	**% Amer Indian**: 0.3 **% Asian**: 0.9 **% Black**: 36.5 **% Hispanic**: 24.5 **% White**: 37.8	National ***Socio-Economic Status*** indicator percentile (100=high): 11th

Monmouth County
MARLBORO TOWNSHIP S.D.
1980 TOWNSHIP DRIVE ● MARLBORO NJ 07746-2298 ● (732) 972-2000

Grade Span: KG-08 **Schools**: *Regular* 6 ● *Spec Ed* 0 ● *Alt* 0 **Students**: 4,506 **Total Teachers**: 283 **Student/Classroom Teacher Ratio**: 16.8	**Expenditures/Student**: $7,000 **Librarians**: 6.5 693 students/librarian **Guidance Counselors**: 7.0 644 students/counselor	**% Amer Indian**: 0.1 **% Asian**: 11.1 **% Black**: 2.0 **% Hispanic**: 1.2 **% White**: 85.5	National ***Socio-Economic Status*** indicator percentile (100=high): 98th

Monmouth County
MIDDLETOWN TOWNSHIP S.D.
59 TINDALL ROAD ● MIDDLETOWN NJ 07748-2999 ● (732) 706-6002 ● http://www.middletownk12.com

Grade Span: KG-12 **Schools**: *Regular* 17 ● *Spec Ed* 0 ● *Alt* 0 **Students**: 9,984 **Total Teachers**: 697 **Student/Classroom Teacher Ratio**: 17.5	**Expenditures/Student**: $8,277 **Librarians**: 6.0 1,664 students/librarian **Guidance Counselors**: 25.0 399 students/counselor	**% Amer Indian**: 0.1 **% Asian**: 3.2 **% Black**: 2.0 **% Hispanic**: 2.3 **% White**: 92.4	National ***Socio-Economic Status*** indicator percentile (100=high): 90th

Monmouth County
NEPTUNE TOWNSHIP S.D.
2106 BANGS AVENUE ● NEPTUNE NJ 07753-4596 ● (732) 776-2001

Grade Span: PK-12 **Schools**: *Regular* 7 ● *Spec Ed* 0 ● *Alt* 0 **Students**: 3,494 **Total Teachers**: 265 **Student/Classroom Teacher Ratio**: 16.0	**Expenditures/Student**: $10,775 **Librarians**: 4.0 874 students/librarian **Guidance Counselors**: 15.5 225 students/counselor	**% Amer Indian**: 0.1 **% Asian**: 0.9 **% Black**: 59.8 **% Hispanic**: 5.9 **% White**: 33.4	National ***Socio-Economic Status*** indicator percentile (100=high): 31st

Monmouth County

[OAKHURST] **OCEAN TOWNSHIP S.D.**

163 MONMOUTH ROAD ● OAKHURST NJ 07755-1597 ● (732) 531-5600 ● http://www.ocean.k12.nj.us

Grade Span: KG-12 **Schools**: *Regular* 5 ● *Spec Ed* 0 ● *Alt* 0 **Students**: 4,143 **Total Teachers**: 280 **Student/Classroom Teacher Ratio**: 16.6	**Expenditures/Student**: $8,463 **Librarians**: 5.0 829 students/librarian **Guidance Counselors**: 9.5 436 students/counselor	**% Amer Indian**: 0.0 **% Asian**: 4.9 **% Black**: 7.9 **% Hispanic**: 3.9 **% White**: 83.2	National ***Socio-Economic Status*** indicator percentile (100=high): 84th

Monmouth County

WALL TOWNSHIP S.D.

P.O. BOX 1199 ● WALL NJ 07719-1199 ● (732) 681-7900

Grade Span: KG-12 **Schools**: *Regular* 7 ● *Spec Ed* 0 ● *Alt* 0 **Students**: 3,424 **Total Teachers**: 235 **Student/Classroom Teacher Ratio**: 16.7	**Expenditures/Student**: $7,856 **Librarians**: 2.7 1,268 students/librarian **Guidance Counselors**: 9.0 380 students/counselor	**% Amer Indian**: 0.1 **% Asian**: 0.7 **% Black**: 0.1 **% Hispanic**: 0.9 **% White**: 98.1	National ***Socio-Economic Status*** indicator percentile (100=high): 93rd

Morris County

[BUDD LAKE] **MOUNT OLIVE TOWNSHIP S.D.**

ROUTE 46 ● BUDD LAKE NJ 07828 ● (973) 691-4005

Grade Span: KG-12 **Schools**: *Regular* 5 ● *Spec Ed* 0 ● *Alt* 0 **Students**: 3,753 **Total Teachers**: 253 **Student/Classroom Teacher Ratio**: 16.4	**Expenditures/Student**: $9,385 **Librarians**: 5.0 751 students/librarian **Guidance Counselors**: 11.0 341 students/counselor	**% Amer Indian**: 0.0 **% Asian**: 3.8 **% Black**: 5.7 **% Hispanic**: 3.6 **% White**: 86.9	National ***Socio-Economic Status*** indicator percentile (100=high): 87th

Morris County

DOVER TOWN S.D.

100 GRACE STREET ● DOVER NJ 07801 ● (973) 989-2000

Grade Span: KG-12 **Schools**: *Regular* 5 ● *Spec Ed* 0 ● *Alt* 0 **Students**: 2,513 **Total Teachers**: 177 **Student/Classroom Teacher Ratio**: 16.4	**Expenditures/Student**: $8,558 **Librarians**: 4.5 558 students/librarian **Guidance Counselors**: 8.5 296 students/counselor	**% Amer Indian**: 0.1 **% Asian**: 3.1 **% Black**: 10.1 **% Hispanic**: 58.6 **% White**: 28.1	National ***Socio-Economic Status*** indicator percentile (100=high): 39th

Morris County

[HIBERNIA] **ROCKAWAY TOWNSHIP S.D.**

P.O. BOX 500 ● HIBERNIA NJ 07842 ● (973) 627-8200

Grade Span: KG-08 **Schools**: *Regular* 6 ● *Spec Ed* 0 ● *Alt* 0 **Students**: 2,527 **Total Teachers**: 176 **Student/Classroom Teacher Ratio**: 15.2	**Expenditures/Student**: $9,240 **Librarians**: 2.2 1,149 students/librarian **Guidance Counselors**: 4.0 632 students/counselor	**% Amer Indian**: 0.5 **% Asian**: 6.5 **% Black**: 3.4 **% Hispanic**: 4.0 **% White**: 85.6	National ***Socio-Economic Status*** indicator percentile (100=high): 97th

Morris County

[LAKE HOPATCONG] **JEFFERSON TOWNSHIP S.D.**

HEADQUARTERS PLAZA OF JEF ● LAKE HOPATCONG NJ 07849-2259 ● (973) 663-5780

Grade Span: KG-12 **Schools**: *Regular* 8 ● *Spec Ed* 0 ● *Alt* 0 **Students**: 3,186 **Total Teachers**: 215 **Student/Classroom Teacher Ratio**: 20.4	**Expenditures/Student**: $8,694 **Librarians**: 4.0 797 students/librarian **Guidance Counselors**: 7.0 455 students/counselor	**% Amer Indian**: 0.2 **% Asian**: 1.4 **% Black**: 3.0 **% Hispanic**: 2.2 **% White**: 93.2	National ***Socio-Economic Status*** indicator percentile (100=high): 89th

Morris County

MONTVILLE TOWNSHIP S.D.

221 CHANGEBRIDGE ROAD ● MONTVILLE NJ 07045 ● (973) 331-7117

Grade Span: KG-12 **Schools**: *Regular* 7 ● *Spec Ed* 0 ● *Alt* 0 **Students**: 2,928 **Total Teachers**: 229 **Student/Classroom Teacher Ratio**: 15.7	**Expenditures/Student**: $9,439 **Librarians**: 4.4 665 students/librarian **Guidance Counselors**: 9.0 325 students/counselor	**% Amer Indian**: 0.0 **% Asian**: 15.8 **% Black**: 1.1 **% Hispanic**: 1.7 **% White**: 81.4	National ***Socio-Economic Status*** indicator percentile (100=high): 99th

Morris County

[MORRISTOWN] **MORRIS S.D.**

NORMANDY PARKWAY ● MORRISTOWN NJ 07960 ● (973) 292-2010

Grade Span: KG-12 **Schools**: *Regular* 8 ● *Spec Ed* 1 ● *Alt* 0 **Students**: 4,124 **Total Teachers**: 327 **Student/Classroom Teacher Ratio**: 14.6	**Expenditures/Student**: $11,944 **Librarians**: 9.0 458 students/librarian **Guidance Counselors**: 8.9 463 students/counselor	**% Amer Indian**: 0.0 **% Asian**: 4.1 **% Black**: 20.6 **% Hispanic**: 13.0 **% White**: 62.3	National ***Socio-Economic Status*** indicator percentile (100=high): 65th

Morris County

PARSIPPANY-TROY HILLS TOWNSHIP S.D.

P.O. BOX 52 ● PARSIPPANY NJ 07054-0052 ● (973) 263-7250 ● http://www.pthsd.k12.nj.us

Grade Span: KG-12 **Schools**: *Regular* 12 ● *Spec Ed* 0 ● *Alt* 0 **Students**: 6,015 **Total Teachers**: 468 **Student/Classroom Teacher Ratio**: 16.1	**Expenditures/Student**: $11,230 **Librarians**: 14.2 424 students/librarian **Guidance Counselors**: 24.0 251 students/counselor	**% Amer Indian**: 0.0 **% Asian**: 20.3 **% Black**: 3.6 **% Hispanic**: 6.3 **% White**: 69.7	National ***Socio-Economic Status*** indicator percentile (100=high): 92nd

Morris County

RANDOLPH TOWNSHIP S.D.

SCHOOL HOUSE ROAD ● RANDOLPH NJ 07869-3199 ● (973) 328-2775

Grade Span: KG-12 **Schools**: *Regular* 6 ● *Spec Ed* 0 ● *Alt* 0 **Students**: 4,350 **Total Teachers**: 304 **Student/Classroom Teacher Ratio**: 16.0	**Expenditures/Student**: $9,117 **Librarians**: 7.5 580 students/librarian **Guidance Counselors**: 10.0 435 students/counselor	**% Amer Indian**: 0.1 **% Asian**: 7.5 **% Black**: 3.0 **% Hispanic**: 3.7 **% White**: 85.7	National ***Socio-Economic Status*** indicator percentile (100=high): 98th

Morris County

[SUCCASUNNA] **ROXBURY TOWNSHIP S.D.**

25 MEEKER STREET ● SUCCASUNNA NJ 07876-1418 ● (201) 584-6867

Grade Span: KG-12 **Schools**: *Regular* 7 ● *Spec Ed* 0 ● *Alt* 0 **Students**: 3,893 **Total Teachers**: 293 **Student/Classroom Teacher Ratio**: 16.2	**Expenditures/Student**: $9,125 **Librarians**: 8.0 487 students/librarian **Guidance Counselors**: 12.0 324 students/counselor	**% Amer Indian**: 0.0 **% Asian**: 4.3 **% Black**: 2.0 **% Hispanic**: 2.0 **% White**: 91.6	National ***Socio-Economic Status*** indicator percentile (100=high): 94th

Ocean County

BRICK TOWNSHIP S.D.

101 HENDRICKSON AVENUE ● BRICK TOWN NJ 08724-2505 ● (732) 477-2800 ● http://brickschools.baweb.com

Grade Span: KG-12 **Schools**: *Regular* 11 ● *Spec Ed* 0 ● *Alt* 0 **Students**: 10,210 **Total Teachers**: 630 **Student/Classroom Teacher Ratio**: 19.2	**Expenditures/Student**: $7,359 **Librarians**: 12.6 810 students/librarian **Guidance Counselors**: 15.0 681 students/counselor	**% Amer Indian**: 0.3 **% Asian**: 1.3 **% Black**: 2.0 **% Hispanic**: 3.2 **% White**: 93.1	National ***Socio-Economic Status*** indicator percentile (100=high): 82nd

Ocean County

JACKSON TOWNSHIP S.D.

DON CONNOR BLVD. ● JACKSON NJ 08527 ● (732) 928-1400 ● http://www.jacksonsd.k12.nj.us

Grade Span: KG-12 **Schools**: *Regular* 7 ● *Spec Ed* 0 ● *Alt* 0 **Students**: 6,367 **Total Teachers**: 427 **Student/Classroom Teacher Ratio**: 16.6	**Expenditures/Student**: $8,490 **Librarians**: 8.0 796 students/librarian **Guidance Counselors**: 17.0 375 students/counselor	**% Amer Indian**: 0.1 **% Asian**: 2.3 **% Black**: 4.0 **% Hispanic**: 3.7 **% White**: 89.9	National ***Socio-Economic Status*** indicator percentile (100=high): 87th

Ocean County

LAKEWOOD TOWNSHIP S.D.

655 PRINCETON AVENUE ● LAKEWOOD NJ 08701-3611 ● (732) 905-3633

Grade Span: KG-12 **Schools**: *Regular* 6 ● *Spec Ed* 0 ● *Alt* 0 **Students**: 5,042 **Total Teachers**: 380 **Student/Classroom Teacher Ratio**: 14.0	**Expenditures/Student**: $9,923 **Librarians**: 6.5 776 students/librarian **Guidance Counselors**: 15.0 336 students/counselor	**% Amer Indian**: 0.6 **% Asian**: 1.2 **% Black**: 34.7 **% Hispanic**: 25.7 **% White**: 37.8	National ***Socio-Economic Status*** indicator percentile (100=high): 19th

Ocean County

[LANOKA HARBOR] LACEY TOWNSHIP S.D.

200 WESTERN BLVD. ● LANOKA HARBOR NJ 08734 ● (609) 971-2002

Grade Span: KG-12 **Schools**: *Regular* 5 ● *Spec Ed* 0 ● *Alt* 0 **Students**: 4,437 **Total Teachers**: 290 **Student/Classroom Teacher Ratio**: 15.8	**Expenditures/Student**: $6,941 **Librarians**: 5.0 887 students/librarian **Guidance Counselors**: 12.0 370 students/counselor	**% Amer Indian**: 0.0 **% Asian**: 0.6 **% Black**: 0.4 **% Hispanic**: 0.8 **% White**: 98.2	National ***Socio-Economic Status*** indicator percentile (100=high): 76th

Ocean County

[MANAHAWKIN] SOUTHERN REGIONAL S.D.

105 CEDAR BRIDGE ROAD ● MANAHAWKIN NJ 08050-3056 ● (609) 597-9481 ● http://dune.srhs.k12.nj.us

Grade Span: 07-12 **Schools**: *Regular* 2 ● *Spec Ed* 0 ● *Alt* 0 **Students**: 2,648 **Total Teachers**: 218 **Student/Classroom Teacher Ratio**: 13.7	**Expenditures/Student**: $10,298 **Librarians**: 2.0 1,324 students/librarian **Guidance Counselors**: 11.0 241 students/counselor	**% Amer Indian**: 0.1 **% Asian**: 0.4 **% Black**: 0.6 **% Hispanic**: 1.6 **% White**: 97.3	National ***Socio-Economic Status*** indicator percentile (100=high): 78th

Ocean County

POINT PLEASANT BOROUGH S.D.

2100 PANTHER PATH ● POINT PLEASANT NJ 08742-3770 ● (732) 892-0265

Grade Span: KG-12 **Schools**: *Regular* 4 ● *Spec Ed* 0 ● *Alt* 0 **Students**: 2,797 **Total Teachers**: 187 **Student/Classroom Teacher Ratio**: 15.9	**Expenditures/Student**: $7,754 **Librarians**: 4.2 666 students/librarian **Guidance Counselors**: 7.0 400 students/counselor	**% Amer Indian**: 0.4 **% Asian**: 0.6 **% Black**: 0.2 **% Hispanic**: 1.9 **% White**: 97.0	National ***Socio-Economic Status*** indicator percentile (100=high): 91st

Ocean County

TOMS RIVER REGIONAL S.D.

1144 HOOPER AVENUE ● TOMS RIVER NJ 08753-7643 ● (973) 505-5506 ● http://www.tomsriver.k12.nj.us

Grade Span: KG-12 **Schools**: *Regular* 16 ● *Spec Ed* 0 ● *Alt* 0 **Students**: 16,854 **Total Teachers**: 1,058 **Student/Classroom Teacher Ratio**: 18.8	**Expenditures/Student**: $7,698 **Librarians**: 18.0 936 students/librarian **Guidance Counselors**: 40.0 421 students/counselor	**% Amer Indian**: 0.1 **% Asian**: 1.5 **% Black**: 2.1 **% Hispanic**: 2.2 **% White**: 94.1	National ***Socio-Economic Status*** indicator percentile (100=high): 81st

Ocean County

[WHITING] MANCHESTER TOWNSHIP S.D.

121 ROUTE 539, BOX 4100 ● WHITING NJ 08759-1237 ● (732) 350-5901 ● http://www.thecore.com/manchester

Grade Span: KG-12 **Schools**: *Regular* 5 ● *Spec Ed* 1 ● *Alt* 0 **Students**: 2,954 **Total Teachers**: 236 **Student/Classroom Teacher Ratio**: 13.2	**Expenditures/Student**: $7,868 **Librarians**: 5.0 591 students/librarian **Guidance Counselors**: 8.0 369 students/counselor	**% Amer Indian**: 0.0 **% Asian**: 2.2 **% Black**: 9.7 **% Hispanic**: 4.3 **% White**: 83.9	National ***Socio-Economic Status*** indicator percentile (100=high): 74th

Passaic County

CLIFTON CITY S.D.

745 CLIFTON AVENUE ● CLIFTON NJ 07015-2209 ● (973) 470-2260

Grade Span: KG-12 **Schools**: *Regular* 16 ● *Spec Ed* 0 ● *Alt* 0 **Students**: 8,398 **Total Teachers**: 567 **Student/Classroom Teacher Ratio**: 18.1	**Expenditures/Student**: $7,617 **Librarians**: 12.0 700 students/librarian **Guidance Counselors**: 18.0 467 students/counselor	**% Amer Indian**: 0.1 **% Asian**: 8.0 **% Black**: 2.9 **% Hispanic**: 21.6 **% White**: 67.5	National ***Socio-Economic Status*** indicator percentile (100=high): 57th

Passaic County

PASSAIC CITY S.D.

101 PASSAIC AVENUE ● PASSAIC NJ 07055-4828 ● (973) 470-5201

Grade Span: PK-12 **Schools**: *Regular* 12 ● *Spec Ed* 0 ● *Alt* 0 **Students**: 9,896 **Total Teachers**: 660 **Student/Classroom Teacher Ratio**: 16.9	**Expenditures/Student**: $8,619 **Librarians**: 6.0 1,649 students/librarian **Guidance Counselors**: 20.0 495 students/counselor	**% Amer Indian**: 0.3 **% Asian**: 5.6 **% Black**: 17.4 **% Hispanic**: 73.0 **% White**: 3.6	National ***Socio-Economic Status*** indicator percentile (100=high): 2nd

Passaic County

PATERSON CITY S.D.

33-35 CHURCH STREET ● PATERSON NJ 07505-1306 ● (973) 881-6213 ● http://www.paterson.k12.nj.us

Grade Span: PK-12 **Schools**: *Regular* 35 ● *Spec Ed* 0 ● *Alt* 0 **Students**: 23,408 **Total Teachers**: 1,666 **Student/Classroom Teacher Ratio**: 15.2	**Expenditures/Student**: $10,107 **Librarians**: 25.0 936 students/librarian **Guidance Counselors**: 61.0 384 students/counselor	**% Amer Indian**: 0.0 **% Asian**: 2.0 **% Black**: 41.3 **% Hispanic**: 50.1 **% White**: 6.6	National ***Socio-Economic Status*** indicator percentile (100=high): 3rd

Passaic County

WAYNE TOWNSHIP S.D.

50 NELLIS DRIVE ● WAYNE NJ 07470-3562 ● (973) 633-3032

Grade Span: KG-12 **Schools**: *Regular* 12 ● *Spec Ed* 0 ● *Alt* 0 **Students**: 6,855 **Total Teachers**: 488 **Student/Classroom Teacher Ratio**: 16.9	**Expenditures/Student**: $9,794 **Librarians**: 12.0 571 students/librarian **Guidance Counselors**: 18.6 369 students/counselor	**% Amer Indian**: 0.1 **% Asian**: 6.1 **% Black**: 0.9 **% Hispanic**: 3.5 **% White**: 89.4	National ***Socio-Economic Status*** indicator percentile (100=high): 95th

Passaic County

WEST MILFORD TOWNSHIP S.D.

46 HIGHLANDER DRIVE ● WEST MILFORD NJ 07480-1511 ● (973) 697-1700

Grade Span: PK-12 **Schools**: *Regular* 8 ● *Spec Ed* 0 ● *Alt* 0 **Students**: 4,380 **Total Teachers**: 293 **Student/Classroom Teacher Ratio**: 17.2	**Expenditures/Student**: $8,663 **Librarians**: 9.0 487 students/librarian **Guidance Counselors**: 10.0 438 students/counselor	**% Amer Indian**: 0.2 **% Asian**: 1.4 **% Black**: 2.9 **% Hispanic**: 1.5 **% White**: 93.9	National ***Socio-Economic Status*** indicator percentile (100=high): 88th

Somerset County

[BASKING RIDGE] **BERNARDS TOWNSHIP S.D.**

CEDAR HILL ANNEX ● BASKING RIDGE NJ 07920 ● (908) 204-2601

Grade Span: KG-12 **Schools**: *Regular* 5 ● *Spec Ed* 0 ● *Alt* 0 **Students**: 2,673 **Total Teachers**: 200 **Student/Classroom Teacher Ratio**: 15.4	**Expenditures/Student**: $8,579 **Librarians**: 5.0 535 students/librarian **Guidance Counselors**: 9.6 278 students/counselor	**% Amer Indian**: 0.3 **% Asian**: 6.1 **% Black**: 1.0 **% Hispanic**: 2.0 **% White**: 90.7	National ***Socio-Economic Status*** indicator percentile (100=high): 100th

Somerset County

BRIDGEWATER-RARITAN REGIONAL S.D.

836 NEWMANS LANE ● BRIDGEWATER NJ 08807-0030 ● (908) 563-1888 ● http://brrsd.k12.nj.us

Grade Span: PK-08 **Schools**: *Regular* 9 ● *Spec Ed* 0 ● *Alt* 0 **Students**: 6,149 **Total Teachers**: 427 **Student/Classroom Teacher Ratio**: 16.6	**Expenditures/Student**: $9,406 **Librarians**: 11.0 559 students/librarian **Guidance Counselors**: 18.0 342 students/counselor	**% Amer Indian**: 0.1 **% Asian**: 10.1 **% Black**: 2.9 **% Hispanic**: 4.7 **% White**: 82.3	National ***Socio-Economic Status*** indicator percentile (100=high): 90th

Somerset County

[NESHANIC STATION] **HILLSBOROUGH TOWNSHIP S.D.**

555 AMWELL ROAD ● NESHANIC STATION NJ 08853 ● (908) 369-0030 ● http://www.hillsborough.k12.nj.us

Grade Span: KG-12 **Schools**: *Regular* 8 ● *Spec Ed* 0 ● *Alt* 0 **Students**: 5,905 **Total Teachers**: 439 **Student/Classroom Teacher Ratio**: 15.1	**Expenditures/Student**: $7,560 **Librarians**: 7.0 844 students/librarian **Guidance Counselors**: 13.5 437 students/counselor	**% Amer Indian**: 0.1 **% Asian**: 6.6 **% Black**: 4.5 **% Hispanic**: 3.1 **% White**: 85.8	National ***Socio-Economic Status*** indicator percentile (100=high): 97th

Somerset County

NORTH PLAINFIELD BOROUGH S.D.

33 MOUNTAIN AVENUE ● NORTH PLAINFIELD NJ 07060-5336 ● (908) 769-6060

Grade Span: KG-12 **Schools**: *Regular* 6 ● *Spec Ed* 0 ● *Alt* 0 **Students**: 2,716 **Total Teachers**: 216 **Student/Classroom Teacher Ratio**: 16.9	**Expenditures/Student**: $8,866 **Librarians**: 4.8 566 students/librarian **Guidance Counselors**: 8.0 340 students/counselor	**% Amer Indian**: 0.0 **% Asian**: 4.6 **% Black**: 9.9 **% Hispanic**: 29.9 **% White**: 55.6	National ***Socio-Economic Status*** indicator percentile (100=high): 56th

Somerset County

[SOMERSET] **FRANKLIN TOWNSHIP S.D.**

1755 AMWELL ROAD ● SOMERSET NJ 08873-2793 ● (732) 873-2400

Grade Span: KG-12 **Schools**: *Regular* 9 ● *Spec Ed* 0 ● *Alt* 0 **Students**: 4,874 **Total Teachers**: 374 **Student/Classroom Teacher Ratio**: 14.7	**Expenditures/Student**: $9,463 **Librarians**: 7.0 696 students/librarian **Guidance Counselors**: 12.0 406 students/counselor	**% Amer Indian**: 0.1 **% Asian**: 11.0 **% Black**: 42.4 **% Hispanic**: 7.7 **% White**: 38.7	National ***Socio-Economic Status*** indicator percentile (100=high): 61st

Sussex County

HOPATCONG S.D.

P.O. BOX 1029 ● HOPATCONG NJ 07843 ● (973) 398-8801

Grade Span: PK-12 **Schools**: *Regular* 5 ● *Spec Ed* 0 ● *Alt* 0 **Students**: 2,692 **Total Teachers**: 171 **Student/Classroom Teacher Ratio**: 17.3	**Expenditures/Student**: $8,519 **Librarians**: 4.0 673 students/librarian **Guidance Counselors**: 8.7 309 students/counselor	**% Amer Indian**: 0.1 **% Asian**: 2.9 **% Black**: 2.0 **% Hispanic**: 3.3 **% White**: 91.8	National ***Socio-Economic Status*** indicator percentile (100=high): 85th

Sussex County
SPARTA TOWNSHIP S.D.
328 SPARTA AVENUE ● SPARTA NJ 07871 ● (973) 729-7886

Grade Span: KG-12 **Schools**: *Regular* 4 ● *Spec Ed* 0 ● *Alt* 0 **Students**: 3,047 **Total Teachers**: 187 **Student/Classroom Teacher Ratio**: 17.6	**Expenditures/Student**: $8,326 **Librarians**: 4.0 762 students/librarian **Guidance Counselors**: 8.6 354 students/counselor	**% Amer Indian**: 0.0 **% Asian**: 1.8 **% Black**: 0.4 **% Hispanic**: 1.7 **% White**: 96.1	National ***Socio-Economic Status*** indicator percentile (100=high): 99th

Sussex County
VERNON TOWNSHIP S.D.
P.O. BOX 99 ● VERNON NJ 07462-0099 ● (973) 764-4486 ● http://vernonschools.k12.nj.us

Grade Span: KG-12 **Schools**: *Regular* 6 ● *Spec Ed* 0 ● *Alt* 0 **Students**: 5,196 **Total Teachers**: 331 **Student/Classroom Teacher Ratio**: 17.2	**Expenditures/Student**: $7,620 **Librarians**: 7.0 742 students/librarian **Guidance Counselors**: 15.0 346 students/counselor	**% Amer Indian**: 0.1 **% Asian**: 0.8 **% Black**: 0.7 **% Hispanic**: 2.8 **% White**: 95.6	National ***Socio-Economic Status*** indicator percentile (100=high): 95th

Union County
CRANFORD TOWNSHIP S.D.
132 THOMAS STREET ● CRANFORD NJ 07016-3134 ● (908) 272-9100 ● http://www.cranfordschools.k12.nj.us.

Grade Span: KG-12 **Schools**: *Regular* 6 ● *Spec Ed* 0 ● *Alt* 0 **Students**: 3,153 **Total Teachers**: 255 **Student/Classroom Teacher Ratio**: 15.6	**Expenditures/Student**: $8,964 **Librarians**: 5.0 631 students/librarian **Guidance Counselors**: 6.0 526 students/counselor	**% Amer Indian**: 0.0 **% Asian**: 2.2 **% Black**: 3.4 **% Hispanic**: 2.3 **% White**: 92.0	National ***Socio-Economic Status*** indicator percentile (100=high): 98th

Union County
ELIZABETH CITY S.D.
MITCHELL BUILDING ● ELIZABETH NJ 07207 ● (908) 558-3025

Grade Span: PK-12 **Schools**: *Regular* 25 ● *Spec Ed* 0 ● *Alt* 0 **Students**: 17,056 **Total Teachers**: 1,247 **Student/Classroom Teacher Ratio**: 14.7	**Expenditures/Student**: $8,787 **Librarians**: 31.0 550 students/librarian **Guidance Counselors**: 47.0 363 students/counselor	**% Amer Indian**: 0.1 **% Asian**: 2.7 **% Black**: 28.7 **% Hispanic**: 51.9 **% White**: 16.6	National ***Socio-Economic Status*** indicator percentile (100=high): 4th

Union County
HILLSIDE TOWNSHIP S.D.
195 VIRGINIA STREET ● HILLSIDE NJ 07205-2742 ● (908) 352-2433

Grade Span: KG-12 **Schools**: *Regular* 6 ● *Spec Ed* 0 ● *Alt* 0 **Students**: 2,818 **Total Teachers**: 177 **Student/Classroom Teacher Ratio**: 18.8	**Expenditures/Student**: $8,012 **Librarians**: 4.6 613 students/librarian **Guidance Counselors**: 5.7 494 students/counselor	**% Amer Indian**: 0.1 **% Asian**: 4.5 **% Black**: 61.5 **% Hispanic**: 11.9 **% White**: 21.9	National ***Socio-Economic Status*** indicator percentile (100=high): 40th

Union County
LINDEN CITY S.D.
728 NORTH AVENUE ● LINDEN NJ 07036-4064 ● (908) 486-5818 ● http://linden.k12.nj.us

Grade Span: PK-12 **Schools**: *Regular* 11 ● *Spec Ed* 0 ● *Alt* 0 **Students**: 5,025 **Total Teachers**: 338 **Student/Classroom Teacher Ratio**: 18.3	**Expenditures/Student**: $8,713 **Librarians**: 5.0 1,005 students/librarian **Guidance Counselors**: 9.0 558 students/counselor	**% Amer Indian**: 0.0 **% Asian**: 2.5 **% Black**: 36.0 **% Hispanic**: 11.4 **% White**: 50.0	National ***Socio-Economic Status*** indicator percentile (100=high): 39th

Union County
PLAINFIELD CITY S.D.
504 MADISON AVENUE ● PLAINFIELD NJ 07060-1540 ● (908) 753-3155

Grade Span: PK-12 **Schools**: *Regular* 14 ● *Spec Ed* 1 ● *Alt* 0 **Students**: 6,926 **Total Teachers**: 500 **Student/Classroom Teacher Ratio**: 14.5	**Expenditures/Student**: $9,364 **Librarians**: 10.0 693 students/librarian **Guidance Counselors**: 23.2 299 students/counselor	**% Amer Indian**: 0.1 **% Asian**: 0.3 **% Black**: 82.1 **% Hispanic**: 16.2 **% White**: 1.3	National ***Socio-Economic Status*** indicator percentile (100=high): 9th

Union County
RAHWAY CITY S.D.
RAHWAY INTERMEDIATE SCHOO ● RAHWAY NJ 07065 ● (732) 396-1020

Grade Span: PK-12 **Schools**: *Regular* 6 ● *Spec Ed* 0 ● *Alt* 0 **Students**: 3,150 **Total Teachers**: 229 **Student/Classroom Teacher Ratio**: 15.0	**Expenditures/Student**: $8,835 **Librarians**: 4.0 788 students/librarian **Guidance Counselors**: 9.0 350 students/counselor	**% Amer Indian**: 0.1 **% Asian**: 3.6 **% Black**: 37.1 **% Hispanic**: 11.7 **% White**: 47.6	National ***Socio-Economic Status*** indicator percentile (100=high): 44th

Union County
SCOTCH PLAINS-FANWOOD REGIONAL S.D.
EVERGREEN AVENUE & CEDAR ● SCOTCH PLAINS NJ 07076-1955 ● (908) 232-6161 ● http://njcommunity.org/spfnet

Grade Span: PK-12 **Schools**: *Regular* 8 ● *Spec Ed* 0 ● *Alt* 0 **Students**: 4,014 **Total Teachers**: 297 **Student/Classroom Teacher Ratio**: 15.4	**Expenditures/Student**: $10,339 **Librarians**: 9.0 446 students/librarian **Guidance Counselors**: 8.0 502 students/counselor	**% Amer Indian**: 0.0 **% Asian**: 6.5 **% Black**: 13.9 **% Hispanic**: 3.1 **% White**: 76.5	National ***Socio-Economic Status*** indicator percentile (100=high): 96th

Union County
SUMMIT CITY S.D.
90 MAPLE STREET ● SUMMIT NJ 07901-2545 ● (908) 273-3023

Grade Span: KG-12 **Schools**: *Regular* 7 ● *Spec Ed* 0 ● *Alt* 0 **Students**: 2,680 **Total Teachers**: 204 **Student/Classroom Teacher Ratio**: 16.2	**Expenditures/Student**: $10,327 **Librarians**: 6.3 425 students/librarian **Guidance Counselors**: 6.0 447 students/counselor	**% Amer Indian**: 0.1 **% Asian**: 5.1 **% Black**: 7.5 **% Hispanic**: 9.9 **% White**: 77.5	National ***Socio-Economic Status*** indicator percentile (100=high): 86th

Union County
UNION TOWNSHIP S.D.
2369 MORRIS AVENUE ● UNION NJ 07083-5703 ● (908) 851-6420

Grade Span: PK-12 **Schools**: *Regular* 10 ● *Spec Ed* 0 ● *Alt* 0 **Students**: 7,008 **Total Teachers**: 429 **Student/Classroom Teacher Ratio**: 18.2	**Expenditures/Student**: $7,838 **Librarians**: 5.0 1,402 students/librarian **Guidance Counselors**: 11.0 637 students/counselor	**% Amer Indian**: 0.2 **% Asian**: 8.7 **% Black**: 18.2 **% Hispanic**: 6.5 **% White**: 66.3	National ***Socio-Economic Status*** indicator percentile (100=high): 80th

Union County
WESTFIELD TOWN S.D.
302 ELM STREET ● WESTFIELD NJ 07090-3104 ● (908) 789-4420

Grade Span: KG-12 **Schools**: *Regular* 9 ● *Spec Ed* 0 ● *Alt* 0 **Students**: 4,619 **Total Teachers**: 347 **Student/Classroom Teacher Ratio**: 15.4	**Expenditures/Student**: $9,774 **Librarians**: 11.0 420 students/librarian **Guidance Counselors**: 11.0 420 students/counselor	**% Amer Indian**: 0.0 **% Asian**: 4.9 **% Black**: 4.8 **% Hispanic**: 2.1 **% White**: 88.2	National ***Socio-Economic Status*** indicator percentile (100=high): 98th

Warren County

PHILLIPSBURG TOWN S.D.

575 ELDER AVENUE ● PHILLIPSBURG NJ 08865-1656 ● (908) 454-3400

Grade Span: PK-12 **Schools**: *Regular* 6 ● *Spec Ed* 0 ● *Alt* 0 **Students**: 3,301 **Total Teachers**: 256 **Student/Classroom Teacher Ratio**: 14.0	**Expenditures/Student**: $8,333 **Librarians**: 5.0 660 students/librarian **Guidance Counselors**: 9.0 367 students/counselor	**% Amer Indian**: 0.2 **% Asian**: 0.9 **% Black**: 4.2 **% Hispanic**: 5.1 **% White**: 89.6	National ***Socio-Economic Status*** indicator percentile (100=high): 41st

Bernalillo County

ALBUQUERQUE S.D.

PO BOX 25704 ● ALBUQUERQUE NM 87125 ● (505) 842-8211 ● http://www.aps.edu

Grade Span: PK-12 **Schools**: *Regular* 112 ● *Spec Ed* 1 ● *Alt* 9 **Students**: 89,019 **Total Teachers**: 5,526 **Student/Classroom Teacher Ratio**: 16.0	**Expenditures/Student**: $4,210 **Librarians**: 75.4 1,181 students/librarian **Guidance Counselors**: 182.9 487 students/counselor	**% Amer Indian**: 4.1 **% Asian**: 1.9 **% Black**: 3.6 **% Hispanic**: 45.5 **% White**: 44.8	National ***Socio-Economic Status*** indicator percentiles are not available for the state of New Mexico

Chaves County

ROSWELL INDEPENDENT S.D.

PO BOX 1437 ● ROSWELL NM 88201 ● (505) 625-8100

Grade Span: PK-12 **Schools**: *Regular* 21 ● *Spec Ed* 1 ● *Alt* 1 **Students**: 11,304 **Total Teachers**: 618 **Student/Classroom Teacher Ratio**: 18.4	**Expenditures/Student**: $3,739 **Librarians**: 8.0 1,413 students/librarian **Guidance Counselors**: 22.0 514 students/counselor	**% Amer Indian**: 0.5 **% Asian**: 0.4 **% Black**: 2.6 **% Hispanic**: 50.4 **% White**: 46.1	National ***Socio-Economic Status*** indicator percentiles are not available for the state of New Mexico

Cibola County

[GRANTS] **GRANTS-CIBOLA COUNTY S.D.**

PO BOX 8 ● GRANTS NM 87020 ● (505) 287-2961

Grade Span: PK-12 **Schools**: *Regular* 11 ● *Spec Ed* 0 ● *Alt* 0 **Students**: 3,999 **Total Teachers**: 230 **Student/Classroom Teacher Ratio**: 16.1	**Expenditures/Student**: $4,021 **Librarians**: 3.0 1,333 students/librarian **Guidance Counselors**: 9.5 421 students/counselor	**% Amer Indian**: 28.9 **% Asian**: 0.4 **% Black**: 0.9 **% Hispanic**: 43.4 **% White**: 26.5	National ***Socio-Economic Status*** indicator percentiles are not available for the state of New Mexico

Curry County

CLOVIS MUNICIPAL S.D.

P.O. BOX 19000 ● CLOVIS NM 88101-9000 ● (505) 769-4300

Grade Span: PK-12 **Schools**: *Regular* 17 ● *Spec Ed* 1 ● *Alt* 2 **Students**: 9,620 **Total Teachers**: 517 **Student/Classroom Teacher Ratio**: 18.2	**Expenditures/Student**: $3,538 **Librarians**: 5.0 1,924 students/librarian **Guidance Counselors**: 9.0 1,069 students/counselor	**% Amer Indian**: 0.8 **% Asian**: 1.7 **% Black**: 10.2 **% Hispanic**: 33.7 **% White**: 53.6	National ***Socio-Economic Status*** indicator percentiles are not available for the state of New Mexico

Dona Ana County

[ANTHONY] **GADSDEN INDEPENDENT S.D.**

PO DRAWER 70 ● ANTHONY NM 88021 ● (505) 882-3531

Grade Span: PK-12 **Schools**: *Regular* 18 ● *Spec Ed* 1 ● *Alt* 0 **Students**: 11,785 **Total Teachers**: 676 **Student/Classroom Teacher Ratio**: 17.3	**Expenditures/Student**: $3,899 **Librarians**: 7.0 1,684 students/librarian **Guidance Counselors**: 24.0 491 students/counselor	**% Amer Indian**: 3.7 **% Asian**: 0.1 **% Black**: 0.3 **% Hispanic**: 88.8 **% White**: 7.2	National ***Socio-Economic Status*** indicator percentiles are not available for the state of New Mexico

Dona Ana County

LAS CRUCES S.D.

505 S. MAINE, SUITE 249 ● LAS CRUCES NM 88001 ● (505) 527-5807

Grade Span: PK-12 **Schools**: *Regular* 29 ● *Spec Ed* 3 ● *Alt* 3 **Students**: 22,112 **Total Teachers**: 1,317 **Student/Classroom Teacher Ratio**: 17.3	**Expenditures/Student**: $4,018 **Librarians**: 13.0 1,701 students/librarian **Guidance Counselors**: 38.9 568 students/counselor	**% Amer Indian**: 0.9 **% Asian**: 1.1 **% Black**: 2.4 **% Hispanic**: 60.0 **% White**: 35.6	National ***Socio-Economic Status*** indicator percentiles are not available for the state of New Mexico

Eddy County
ARTESIA S.D.
1106 WEST QUAY ● ARTESIA NM 88210 ● (505) 746-3585 ● http://www.bulldogs.org

Grade Span: PK-12 **Schools**: *Regular* 10 ● *Spec Ed* 0 ● *Alt* 0 **Students**: 4,012 **Total Teachers**: 236 **Student/Classroom Teacher Ratio**: 16.9	**Expenditures/Student**: $3,818 **Librarians**: 2.0 2,006 students/librarian **Guidance Counselors**: 6.0 669 students/counselor	**% Amer Indian**: 0.4 **% Asian**: 0.0 **% Black**: 1.1 **% Hispanic**: 49.0 **% White**: 49.5	National ***Socio-Economic Status*** indicator percentiles are not available for the state of New Mexico

Eddy County
CARLSBAD MUNICIPAL S.D.
408 NORTH CANYON ● CARLSBAD NM 88220 ● (505) 887-2821

Grade Span: PK-12 **Schools**: *Regular* 14 ● *Spec Ed* 0 ● *Alt* 1 **Students**: 7,084 **Total Teachers**: 391 **Student/Classroom Teacher Ratio**: 17.7	**Expenditures/Student**: $3,913 **Librarians**: 3.0 2,361 students/librarian **Guidance Counselors**: 9.0 787 students/counselor	**% Amer Indian**: 0.7 **% Asian**: 0.7 **% Black**: 2.5 **% Hispanic**: 42.0 **% White**: 54.0	National ***Socio-Economic Status*** indicator percentiles are not available for the state of New Mexico

Grant County
SILVER CITY CONSOLIDATED S.D.
2810 NORTH SWAN STREET ● SILVER CITY NM 88061 ● (505) 388-1527

Grade Span: PK-12 **Schools**: *Regular* 8 ● *Spec Ed* 0 ● *Alt* 0 **Students**: 4,085 **Total Teachers**: 248 **Student/Classroom Teacher Ratio**: 16.1	**Expenditures/Student**: $4,140 **Librarians**: 2.5 1,634 students/librarian **Guidance Counselors**: 13.0 314 students/counselor	**% Amer Indian**: 0.3 **% Asian**: 0.3 **% Black**: 0.8 **% Hispanic**: 47.6 **% White**: 51.0	National ***Socio-Economic Status*** indicator percentiles are not available for the state of New Mexico

Lea County
HOBBS MUNICIPAL S.D.
PO BOX 1040 ● HOBBS NM 88240 ● (505) 393-9183 ● http://hobbsschools.leaco.net/index.html

Grade Span: PK-12 **Schools**: *Regular* 16 ● *Spec Ed* 2 ● *Alt* 1 **Students**: 8,487 **Total Teachers**: 432 **Student/Classroom Teacher Ratio**: 19.2	**Expenditures/Student**: $3,594 **Librarians**: 4.0 2,122 students/librarian **Guidance Counselors**: 11.0 772 students/counselor	**% Amer Indian**: 0.3 **% Asian**: 0.3 **% Black**: 8.5 **% Hispanic**: 43.0 **% White**: 48.0	National ***Socio-Economic Status*** indicator percentiles are not available for the state of New Mexico

Lea County
LOVINGTON S.D.
PO BOX 1537 ● LOVINGTON NM 88260 ● (505) 396-3020 ● http://lovschools.leaco.net

Grade Span: PK-12 **Schools**: *Regular* 8 ● *Spec Ed* 0 ● *Alt* 0 **Students**: 3,048 **Total Teachers**: 173 **Student/Classroom Teacher Ratio**: 19.0	**Expenditures/Student**: $3,777 **Librarians**: 0.9 3,387 students/librarian **Guidance Counselors**: 4.8 635 students/counselor	**% Amer Indian**: 0.2 **% Asian**: 0.0 **% Black**: 2.2 **% Hispanic**: 52.7 **% White**: 44.9	National ***Socio-Economic Status*** indicator percentiles are not available for the state of New Mexico

Los Alamos County
LOS ALAMOS S.D.
PO DRAWER 90 ● LOS ALAMOS NM 87544 ● (505) 662-4141

Grade Span: PK-12 **Schools**: *Regular* 7 ● *Spec Ed* 0 ● *Alt* 0 **Students**: 3,715 **Total Teachers**: 271 **Student/Classroom Teacher Ratio**: 14.0	**Expenditures/Student**: $6,204 **Librarians**: 7.5 495 students/librarian **Guidance Counselors**: 11.4 326 students/counselor	**% Amer Indian**: 0.4 **% Asian**: 2.4 **% Black**: 0.6 **% Hispanic**: 12.1 **% White**: 84.5	National ***Socio-Economic Status*** indicator percentiles are not available for the state of New Mexico

Luna County

DEMING S.D.

501 WEST FLORIDA ● DEMING NM 88030 ● (505) 546-8841

Grade Span: PK-12 **Schools**: *Regular* 10 ● *Spec Ed* 0 ● *Alt* 1 **Students**: 5,417 **Total Teachers**: 286 **Student/Classroom Teacher Ratio**: 19.7	**Expenditures/Student**: $3,477 **Librarians**: 3.0 1,806 students/librarian **Guidance Counselors**: 9.0 602 students/counselor	**% Amer Indian**: 0.4 **% Asian**: 0.3 **% Black**: 1.2 **% Hispanic**: 75.1 **% White**: 22.9	National ***Socio-Economic Status*** indicator percentiles are not available for the state of New Mexico

McKinley County

[GALLUP] GALLUP-MCKINLEY COUNTY S.D.

PO BOX 1318 ● GALLUP NM 87301 ● (505) 722-7711

Grade Span: PK-12 **Schools**: *Regular* 29 ● *Spec Ed* 1 ● *Alt* 1 **Students**: 14,294 **Total Teachers**: 812 **Student/Classroom Teacher Ratio**: 17.3	**Expenditures/Student**: $3,883 **Librarians**: 8.0 1,787 students/librarian **Guidance Counselors**: 45.0 318 students/counselor	**% Amer Indian**: 75.6 **% Asian**: 0.5 **% Black**: 0.5 **% Hispanic**: 12.4 **% White**: 11.0	National ***Socio-Economic Status*** indicator percentiles are not available for the state of New Mexico

Otero County

ALAMOGORDO S.D.

PO BOX 617 ● ALAMOGORDO NM 88310 ● (505) 439-3200

Grade Span: PK-12 **Schools**: *Regular* 14 ● *Spec Ed* 0 ● *Alt* 0 **Students**: 8,501 **Total Teachers**: 453 **Student/Classroom Teacher Ratio**: 18.6	**Expenditures/Student**: $3,589 **Librarians**: 3.0 2,834 students/librarian **Guidance Counselors**: 14.0 607 students/counselor	**% Amer Indian**: 1.4 **% Asian**: 3.3 **% Black**: 7.5 **% Hispanic**: 26.9 **% White**: 60.8	National ***Socio-Economic Status*** indicator percentiles are not available for the state of New Mexico

Rio Arriba County

ESPANOLA MUNICIPAL S.D.

714 DON DIEGO STREET ● ESPANOLA NM 87532 ● (505) 753-2254

Grade Span: PK-12 **Schools**: *Regular* 14 ● *Spec Ed* 0 ● *Alt* 0 **Students**: 5,413 **Total Teachers**: 300 **Student/Classroom Teacher Ratio**: 18.0	**Expenditures/Student**: $4,295 **Librarians**: 5.0 1,083 students/librarian **Guidance Counselors**: 10.2 531 students/counselor	**% Amer Indian**: 6.0 **% Asian**: 0.1 **% Black**: 0.2 **% Hispanic**: 87.7 **% White**: 6.1	National ***Socio-Economic Status*** indicator percentiles are not available for the state of New Mexico

Roosevelt County

PORTALES MUNICIPAL S.D.

501 SOUTH ABILENE STREET ● PORTALES NM 88130 ● (505) 356-6641

Grade Span: PK-12 **Schools**: *Regular* 7 ● *Spec Ed* 0 ● *Alt* 1 **Students**: 3,100 **Total Teachers**: 174 **Student/Classroom Teacher Ratio**: 17.9	**Expenditures/Student**: $3,957 **Librarians**: 2.0 1,550 students/librarian **Guidance Counselors**: 6.0 517 students/counselor	**% Amer Indian**: 0.6 **% Asian**: 0.6 **% Black**: 2.0 **% Hispanic**: 41.0 **% White**: 55.8	National ***Socio-Economic Status*** indicator percentiles are not available for the state of New Mexico

San Juan County

AZTEC MUNICIPAL S.D.

1118 WEST AZTEC BLVD. ● AZTEC NM 87410 ● (505) 334-9474

Grade Span: PK-12 **Schools**: *Regular* 5 ● *Spec Ed* 1 ● *Alt* 0 **Students**: 3,347 **Total Teachers**: 201 **Student/Classroom Teacher Ratio**: 16.7	**Expenditures/Student**: $3,729 **Librarians**: 2.0 1,674 students/librarian **Guidance Counselors**: 7.0 478 students/counselor	**% Amer Indian**: 9.4 **% Asian**: 0.4 **% Black**: 0.4 **% Hispanic**: 16.7 **% White**: 73.0	National ***Socio-Economic Status*** indicator percentiles are not available for the state of New Mexico

San Juan County

BLOOMFIELD MUNICIPAL S.D.

325 NORTH BERGIN LANE ● BLOOMFIELD NM 87413 ● (505) 632-3316

Grade Span: PK-12	**Expenditures/Student**: $4,134	**% Amer Indian**: 30.6	National ***Socio-Economic***
Schools: *Regular* 7 ● *Spec Ed* 0 ● *Alt* 0	**Librarians**: 5.0	**% Asian**: 0.2	***Status*** indicator percentiles
Students: 3,575	715 students/librarian	**% Black**: 0.1	are not available for the
Total Teachers: 209	**Guidance Counselors**: 6.0	**% Hispanic**: 28.0	state of New Mexico
Student/Classroom Teacher Ratio: 16.2	596 students/counselor	**% White**: 41.2	

San Juan County

FARMINGTON MUNICIPAL S.D.

PO BOX 5850 ● FARMINGTON NM 87499-5850 ● (505) 599-8615

Grade Span: PK-12	**Expenditures/Student**: $3,694	**% Amer Indian**: 22.4	National ***Socio-Economic***
Schools: *Regular* 16 ● *Spec Ed* 1 ● *Alt* 2	**Librarians**: 5.3	**% Asian**: 0.3	***Status*** indicator percentiles
Students: 10,493	1,980 students/librarian	**% Black**: 0.9	are not available for the
Total Teachers: 588	**Guidance Counselors**: 15.8	**% Hispanic**: 18.9	state of New Mexico
Student/Classroom Teacher Ratio: 17.5	664 students/counselor	**% White**: 57.4	

San Juan County

[SHIPROCK] CENTRAL CONSOLIDATED S.D.

PO BOX 1179 ● SHIPROCK NM 87420 ● (505) 368-4984 ● http://bird.kchs.k12.nm.us

Grade Span: PK-12	**Expenditures/Student**: $4,231	**% Amer Indian**: 86.0	National ***Socio-Economic***
Schools: *Regular* 15 ● *Spec Ed* 0 ● *Alt* 0	**Librarians**: 5.0	**% Asian**: 0.1	***Status*** indicator percentiles
Students: 7,456	1,491 students/librarian	**% Black**: 0.2	are not available for the
Total Teachers: 434	**Guidance Counselors**: 17.1	**% Hispanic**: 2.2	state of New Mexico
Student/Classroom Teacher Ratio: 16.9	436 students/counselor	**% White**: 11.5	

San Miguel County

LAS VEGAS CITY S.D.

901 DOUGLAS AVENUE ● LAS VEGAS NM 87701 ● (505) 425-1940

Grade Span: PK-12	**Expenditures/Student**: $4,098	**% Amer Indian**: 0.7	National ***Socio-Economic***
Schools: *Regular* 7 ● *Spec Ed* 0 ● *Alt* 0	**Librarians**: 3.0	**% Asian**: 0.6	***Status*** indicator percentiles
Students: 2,923	974 students/librarian	**% Black**: 0.4	are not available for the
Total Teachers: 156	**Guidance Counselors**: 5.8	**% Hispanic**: 83.8	state of New Mexico
Student/Classroom Teacher Ratio: 19.6	504 students/counselor	**% White**: 14.6	

Sandoval County

BERNALILLO S.D.

PO BOX 640 ● BERNALILLO NM 87004 ● (505) 867-2317

Grade Span: PK-12	**Expenditures/Student**: $4,346	**% Amer Indian**: 39.9	National ***Socio-Economic***
Schools: *Regular* 10 ● *Spec Ed* 0 ● *Alt* 0	**Librarians**: 5.0	**% Asian**: 0.6	***Status*** indicator percentiles
Students: 3,647	729 students/librarian	**% Black**: 0.8	are not available for the
Total Teachers: 204	**Guidance Counselors**: 10.5	**% Hispanic**: 46.5	state of New Mexico
Student/Classroom Teacher Ratio: 18.0	347 students/counselor	**% White**: 12.2	

Sandoval County

RIO RANCHO S.D.

2002 SOUTHERN SE ● RIO RANCHO NM 87124 ● (505) 896-0667

Grade Span: PK-08	**Expenditures/Student**: $3,807	**% Amer Indian**: 2.3	National ***Socio-Economic***
Schools: *Regular* 8 ● *Spec Ed* 0 ● *Alt* 0	**Librarians**: 8.0	**% Asian**: 1.5	***Status*** indicator percentiles
Students: 6,234	779 students/librarian	**% Black**: 2.7	are not available for the
Total Teachers: 350	**Guidance Counselors**: 8.0	**% Hispanic**: 25.2	state of New Mexico
Student/Classroom Teacher Ratio: 17.9	779 students/counselor	**% White**: 68.2	

Santa Fe County
SANTA FE S.D.
610 ALTA VISTA STREET ● SANTA FE NM 87501-4197 ● (505) 982-2631 ● http://www.sfps.k12.nm.us

Grade Span: PK-12	**Expenditures/Student**: $3,854	**% Amer Indian**: 2.3	National ***Socio-Economic Status*** indicator percentiles are not available for the state of New Mexico
Schools: *Regular* 26 ● *Spec Ed* 1 ● *Alt* 0	**Librarians**: 8.0	**% Asian**: 0.7	
Students: 13,280	1,660 students/librarian	**% Black**: 0.7	
Total Teachers: 749	**Guidance Counselors**: 26.0	**% Hispanic**: 61.1	
Student/Classroom Teacher Ratio: 17.8	511 students/counselor	**% White**: 35.2	

Taos County
TAOS MUNICIPAL S.D.
213 PASEO DEL CANON ● TAOS NM 87571 ● (505) 758-5201

Grade Span: PK-12	**Expenditures/Student**: $4,291	**% Amer Indian**: 5.7	National ***Socio-Economic Status*** indicator percentiles are not available for the state of New Mexico
Schools: *Regular* 8 ● *Spec Ed* 0 ● *Alt* 0	**Librarians**: 3.0	**% Asian**: 1.0	
Students: 3,417	1,139 students/librarian	**% Black**: 0.4	
Total Teachers: 177	**Guidance Counselors**: 7.9	**% Hispanic**: 69.4	
Student/Classroom Teacher Ratio: 19.5	433 students/counselor	**% White**: 23.6	

Torrance County
MORIARTY MUNCIPAL S.D.
PO DRAWER 20 ● MORIARTY NM 87035-2000 ● (505) 832-4471

Grade Span: PK-12	**Expenditures/Student**: $4,291	**% Amer Indian**: 1.5	National ***Socio-Economic Status*** indicator percentiles are not available for the state of New Mexico
Schools: *Regular* 6 ● *Spec Ed* 0 ● *Alt* 0	**Librarians**: 1.0	**% Asian**: 0.6	
Students: 4,491	4,491 students/librarian	**% Black**: 0.7	
Total Teachers: 248	**Guidance Counselors**: 3.0	**% Hispanic**: 27.8	
Student/Classroom Teacher Ratio: 18.1	1,497 students/counselor	**% White**: 69.4	

Valencia County
BELEN CONSOLIDATED S.D.
520 NORTH MAIN ● BELEN NM 87002 ● (505) 864-4466

Grade Span: PK-12	**Expenditures/Student**: $3,921	**% Amer Indian**: 0.8	National ***Socio-Economic Status*** indicator percentiles are not available for the state of New Mexico
Schools: *Regular* 8 ● *Spec Ed* 0 ● *Alt* 1	**Librarians**: 2.0	**% Asian**: 0.3	
Students: 4,854	2,427 students/librarian	**% Black**: 1.3	
Total Teachers: 268	**Guidance Counselors**: 10.0	**% Hispanic**: 60.9	
Student/Classroom Teacher Ratio: 18.6	485 students/counselor	**% White**: 36.7	

Valencia County
LOS LUNAS S.D.
PO DRAWER 1300 ● LOS LUNAS NM 87031 ● (505) 865-9636 ● http://www.loslunas.k12.nm.us

Grade Span: PK-12	**Expenditures/Student**: $3,655	**% Amer Indian**: 7.7	National ***Socio-Economic Status*** indicator percentiles are not available for the state of New Mexico
Schools: *Regular* 11 ● *Spec Ed* 0 ● *Alt* 0	**Librarians**: 7.0	**% Asian**: 0.5	
Students: 7,509	1,073 students/librarian	**% Black**: 0.8	
Total Teachers: 373	**Guidance Counselors**: 13.0	**% Hispanic**: 55.1	
Student/Classroom Teacher Ratio: 19.8	578 students/counselor	**% White**: 35.9	

Albany County
ALBANY CITY S.D.
ACADEMY PARK ● ALBANY NY 12207-1099 ● (518) 462-7200

Grade Span: PK-12 **Schools**: *Regular* 18 ● *Spec Ed* 0 ● *Alt* 0 **Students**: 9,708 **Total Teachers**: 657 **Student/Classroom Teacher Ratio**: 15.2	**Expenditures/Student**: $10,234 **Librarians**: 13.2 735 students/librarian **Guidance Counselors**: 13.5 719 students/counselor	**% Amer Indian**: 0.1 **% Asian**: 3.8 **% Black**: 56.1 **% Hispanic**: 6.0 **% White**: 34.0	National ***Socio-Economic Status*** indicator percentile (100=high): 12th

Albany County
[ALBANY] **SOUTH COLONIE CENTRAL S.D.**
102 LORALEE DR ● ALBANY NY 12205-2223 ● (518) 869-3576

Grade Span: KG-12 **Schools**: *Regular* 8 ● *Spec Ed* 0 ● *Alt* 0 **Students**: 5,621 **Total Teachers**: 362 **Student/Classroom Teacher Ratio**: 17.4	**Expenditures/Student**: $8,177 **Librarians**: 9.2 611 students/librarian **Guidance Counselors**: 8.0 703 students/counselor	**% Amer Indian**: 0.4 **% Asian**: 2.5 **% Black**: 4.7 **% Hispanic**: 0.7 **% White**: 91.8	National ***Socio-Economic Status*** indicator percentile (100=high): 84th

Albany County
[DELMAR] **BETHLEHEM CENTRAL S.D.**
90 ADAMS PL ● DELMAR NY 12054-3297 ● (518) 439-7098

Grade Span: KG-12 **Schools**: *Regular* 7 ● *Spec Ed* 0 ● *Alt* 0 **Students**: 4,540 **Total Teachers**: 284 **Student/Classroom Teacher Ratio**: 17.5	**Expenditures/Student**: $7,726 **Librarians**: 5.7 796 students/librarian **Guidance Counselors**: 11.0 413 students/counselor	**% Amer Indian**: 0.1 **% Asian**: 2.2 **% Black**: 1.4 **% Hispanic**: 0.6 **% White**: 95.7	National ***Socio-Economic Status*** indicator percentile (100=high): 96th

Albany County
GUILDERLAND CENTRAL S.D.
6094 STATE FARM RD ● GUILDERLAND NY 12084-9533 ● (518) 456-6200

Grade Span: KG-12 **Schools**: *Regular* 7 ● *Spec Ed* 0 ● *Alt* 0 **Students**: 5,330 **Total Teachers**: 340 **Student/Classroom Teacher Ratio**: 18.0	**Expenditures/Student**: $8,277 **Librarians**: 8.7 613 students/librarian **Guidance Counselors**: 9.0 592 students/counselor	**% Amer Indian**: 0.2 **% Asian**: 2.9 **% Black**: 3.0 **% Hispanic**: 1.3 **% White**: 92.6	National ***Socio-Economic Status*** indicator percentile (100=high): 94th

Albany County
[NEWTONVILLE] **NORTH COLONIE CENTRAL S.D.**
543 LOUDON RD ● NEWTONVILLE NY 12128-0708 ● (518) 785-8591 ● http://www.crisny.org/communities/colonie/schools/nccs/index.html

Grade Span: KG-12 **Schools**: *Regular* 8 ● *Spec Ed* 0 ● *Alt* 0 **Students**: 5,144 **Total Teachers**: 324 **Student/Classroom Teacher Ratio**: 19.9	**Expenditures/Student**: $7,296 **Librarians**: 9.7 530 students/librarian **Guidance Counselors**: 11.0 468 students/counselor	**% Amer Indian**: 0.1 **% Asian**: 5.4 **% Black**: 2.8 **% Hispanic**: 1.3 **% White**: 90.4	National ***Socio-Economic Status*** indicator percentile (100=high): 92nd

Albany County
[SELKIRK] **RAVENA-COEYMANS-SELKIRK CENTRAL S.D.**
26 THATCHER ST ● SELKIRK NY 12158-0097 ● (518) 767-2513

Grade Span: PK-12 **Schools**: *Regular* 4 ● *Spec Ed* 0 ● *Alt* 0 **Students**: 2,521 **Total Teachers**: 173 **Student/Classroom Teacher Ratio**: 15.2	**Expenditures/Student**: $8,994 **Librarians**: 3.5 720 students/librarian **Guidance Counselors**: 7.0 360 students/counselor	**% Amer Indian**: 0.2 **% Asian**: 0.6 **% Black**: 3.5 **% Hispanic**: 3.5 **% White**: 92.3	National ***Socio-Economic Status*** indicator percentile (100=high): 61st

Broome County

BINGHAMTON CITY S.D.

98 OAK ST ● BINGHAMTON NY 13902-2126 ● (607) 762-8131 ● http://www.bcsd.stier.org

Grade Span: PK-12 **Schools**: *Regular* 10 ● *Spec Ed* 0 ● *Alt* 0 **Students**: 6,382 **Total Teachers**: 466 **Student/Classroom Teacher Ratio**: 15.0	**Expenditures/Student**: $7,784 **Librarians**: 11.3 565 students/librarian **Guidance Counselors**: 14.0 456 students/counselor	**% Amer Indian**: 0.1 **% Asian**: 4.9 **% Black**: 15.1 **% Hispanic**: 4.3 **% White**: 75.5	National ***Socio-Economic Status*** indicator percentile (100=high): 11th

Broome County

[ENDICOTT] **UNION-ENDICOTT CENTRAL S.D.**

1401 BROAD ST ● ENDICOTT NY 13760-5499 ● (607) 757-2112

Grade Span: KG-12 **Schools**: *Regular* 8 ● *Spec Ed* 0 ● *Alt* 0 **Students**: 4,898 **Total Teachers**: 324 **Student/Classroom Teacher Ratio**: 17.7	**Expenditures/Student**: $7,634 **Librarians**: 7.2 680 students/librarian **Guidance Counselors**: 8.2 597 students/counselor	**% Amer Indian**: 0.2 **% Asian**: 2.6 **% Black**: 3.9 **% Hispanic**: 1.0 **% White**: 92.3	National ***Socio-Economic Status*** indicator percentile (100=high): 62nd

Broome County

[ENDWELL] **MAINE-ENDWELL CENTRAL S.D.**

712 FARM-TO-MARKET RD ● ENDWELL NY 13760-1199 ● (607) 754-1400

Grade Span: KG-12 **Schools**: *Regular* 4 ● *Spec Ed* 0 ● *Alt* 0 **Students**: 2,653 **Total Teachers**: 159 **Student/Classroom Teacher Ratio**: 16.9	**Expenditures/Student**: $7,667 **Librarians**: 3.5 758 students/librarian **Guidance Counselors**: 6.0 442 students/counselor	**% Amer Indian**: 0.0 **% Asian**: 2.1 **% Black**: 1.4 **% Hispanic**: 0.3 **% White**: 96.2	National ***Socio-Economic Status*** indicator percentile (100=high): 71st

Broome County

JOHNSON CITY CENTRAL S.D.

666 REYNOLDS RD ● JOHNSON CITY NY 13790-1398 ● (607) 763-1230 ● http://www.tier.net/jcschools

Grade Span: KG-12 **Schools**: *Regular* 4 ● *Spec Ed* 0 ● *Alt* 0 **Students**: 2,906 **Total Teachers**: 193 **Student/Classroom Teacher Ratio**: 15.2	**Expenditures/Student**: $8,049 **Librarians**: 2.7 1,076 students/librarian **Guidance Counselors**: 6.0 484 students/counselor	**% Amer Indian**: 0.0 **% Asian**: 6.0 **% Black**: 3.2 **% Hispanic**: 1.5 **% White**: 89.2	National ***Socio-Economic Status*** indicator percentile (100=high): 42nd

Broome County

VESTAL CENTRAL S.D.

201 MAIN ST ● VESTAL NY 13850-1599 ● (607) 757-2241 ● http://www.vestal.stier.org

Grade Span: KG-12 **Schools**: *Regular* 7 ● *Spec Ed* 0 ● *Alt* 0 **Students**: 4,346 **Total Teachers**: 281 **Student/Classroom Teacher Ratio**: 18.6	**Expenditures/Student**: $7,016 **Librarians**: 6.3 690 students/librarian **Guidance Counselors**: 9.4 462 students/counselor	**% Amer Indian**: 0.2 **% Asian**: 4.3 **% Black**: 2.4 **% Hispanic**: 0.9 **% White**: 92.3	National ***Socio-Economic Status*** indicator percentile (100=high): 90th

Cattaraugus County

OLEAN CITY S.D.

410 W SULLIVAN ST ● OLEAN NY 14760-2596 ● (716) 375-4417

Grade Span: KG-12 **Schools**: *Regular* 7 ● *Spec Ed* 0 ● *Alt* 0 **Students**: 2,681 **Total Teachers**: 187 **Student/Classroom Teacher Ratio**: 19.9	**Expenditures/Student**: $7,369 **Librarians**: 3.7 725 students/librarian **Guidance Counselors**: 5.0 536 students/counselor	**% Amer Indian**: 0.3 **% Asian**: 0.4 **% Black**: 6.3 **% Hispanic**: 1.4 **% White**: 91.5	National ***Socio-Economic Status*** indicator percentile (100=high): 45th

Cattaraugus County

YORKSHIRE-PIONEER CENTRAL S.D.

COUNTY LINE RD ● YORKSHIRE NY 14173-0579 ● (716) 492-1051

Grade Span: KG-12 **Schools**: *Regular* 4 ● *Spec Ed* 0 ● *Alt* 0 **Students**: 3,658 **Total Teachers**: 218 **Student/Classroom Teacher Ratio**: 17.2	**Expenditures/Student**: $7,125 **Librarians**: 3.4 1,076 students/librarian **Guidance Counselors**: 4.0 915 students/counselor	**% Amer Indian**: 0.7 **% Asian**: 0.7 **% Black**: 0.6 **% Hispanic**: 0.4 **% White**: 97.7	National ***Socio-Economic Status*** indicator percentile (100=high): 45th

Cayuga County

AUBURN CITY S.D.

78 THORNTON AVE ● AUBURN NY 13021-4698 ● (315) 255-5835 ● http://www.auburn.cnyric.org

Grade Span: KG-12 **Schools**: *Regular* 8 ● *Spec Ed* 0 ● *Alt* 0 **Students**: 5,454 **Total Teachers**: 319 **Student/Classroom Teacher Ratio**: 18.3	**Expenditures/Student**: $7,358 **Librarians**: 4.8 1,136 students/librarian **Guidance Counselors**: 8.0 682 students/counselor	**% Amer Indian**: 0.4 **% Asian**: 1.0 **% Black**: 7.5 **% Hispanic**: 1.3 **% White**: 89.7	National ***Socio-Economic Status*** indicator percentile (100=high): 57th

Chautauqua County

JAMESTOWN CITY S.D.

200 E FOURTH ST ● JAMESTOWN NY 14701-5397 ● (716) 483-4420 ● http://www.jamestown.wnyric.org

Grade Span: PK-12 **Schools**: *Regular* 10 ● *Spec Ed* 0 ● *Alt* 0 **Students**: 5,870 **Total Teachers**: 411 **Student/Classroom Teacher Ratio**: 15.3	**Expenditures/Student**: $7,120 **Librarians**: 7.7 762 students/librarian **Guidance Counselors**: 15.0 391 students/counselor	**% Amer Indian**: 0.5 **% Asian**: 0.6 **% Black**: 5.5 **% Hispanic**: 6.3 **% White**: 87.2	National ***Socio-Economic Status*** indicator percentile (100=high): 30th

Chemung County

ELMIRA CITY S.D.

951 HOFFMAN ST ● ELMIRA NY 14905-1715 ● (607) 735-3010

Grade Span: PK-12 **Schools**: *Regular* 13 ● *Spec Ed* 0 ● *Alt* 0 **Students**: 8,660 **Total Teachers**: 548 **Student/Classroom Teacher Ratio**: 17.0	**Expenditures/Student**: $7,807 **Librarians**: 11.7 740 students/librarian **Guidance Counselors**: 18.5 468 students/counselor	**% Amer Indian**: 0.4 **% Asian**: 0.7 **% Black**: 11.2 **% Hispanic**: 1.1 **% White**: 86.6	National ***Socio-Economic Status*** indicator percentile (100=high): 32nd

Chemung County

HORSEHEADS CENTRAL S.D.

ONE RAIDER LN ● HORSEHEADS NY 14845-2398 ● (607) 739-5601

Grade Span: PK-12 **Schools**: *Regular* 7 ● *Spec Ed* 0 ● *Alt* 0 **Students**: 4,814 **Total Teachers**: 271 **Student/Classroom Teacher Ratio**: 19.8	**Expenditures/Student**: $7,776 **Librarians**: 4.7 1,024 students/librarian **Guidance Counselors**: 8.0 602 students/counselor	**% Amer Indian**: 0.0 **% Asian**: 1.2 **% Black**: 1.0 **% Hispanic**: 0.2 **% White**: 97.5	National ***Socio-Economic Status*** indicator percentile (100=high): 77th

Cortland County

CORTLAND CITY S.D.

1 VALLEY VIEW DR ● CORTLAND NY 13045-3297 ● (607) 753-6061 ● http://www.cortland.cnyric.org

Grade Span: KG-12 **Schools**: *Regular* 6 ● *Spec Ed* 0 ● *Alt* 0 **Students**: 3,029 **Total Teachers**: 216 **Student/Classroom Teacher Ratio**: 15.9	**Expenditures/Student**: $7,764 **Librarians**: 4.5 673 students/librarian **Guidance Counselors**: 5.9 513 students/counselor	**% Amer Indian**: 0.3 **% Asian**: 1.0 **% Black**: 2.4 **% Hispanic**: 0.7 **% White**: 95.6	National ***Socio-Economic Status*** indicator percentile (100=high): 50th

Cortland County

HOMER CENTRAL S.D.

80 S WEST ST ● HOMER NY 13077-0500 ● (607) 749-7241

Grade Span: KG-12 **Schools**: *Regular* 4 ● *Spec Ed* 0 ● *Alt* 0 **Students**: 2,630 **Total Teachers**: 184 **Student/Classroom Teacher Ratio**: 14.5	**Expenditures/Student**: $7,107 **Librarians**: 3.6 731 students/librarian **Guidance Counselors**: 4.0 658 students/counselor	**% Amer Indian**: 0.0 **% Asian**: 0.5 **% Black**: 0.6 **% Hispanic**: 0.6 **% White**: 98.4	National ***Socio-Economic Status*** indicator percentile (100=high): 61st

Dutchess County

BEACON CITY S.D.

88 SARGENT AVE ● BEACON NY 12508-3994 ● (914) 838-6900

Grade Span: PK-12 **Schools**: *Regular* 6 ● *Spec Ed* 0 ● *Alt* 0 **Students**: 3,091 **Total Teachers**: 195 **Student/Classroom Teacher Ratio**: 16.9	**Expenditures/Student**: $7,868 **Librarians**: 1.0 3,091 students/librarian **Guidance Counselors**: 4.0 773 students/counselor	**% Amer Indian**: 0.2 **% Asian**: 1.5 **% Black**: 22.4 **% Hispanic**: 15.8 **% White**: 60.2	National ***Socio-Economic Status*** indicator percentile (100=high): 49th

Dutchess County

HYDE PARK CENTRAL S.D.

HAVILAND RD ● HYDE PARK NY 12538-0737 ● (914) 229-4000

Grade Span: KG-12 **Schools**: *Regular* 7 ● *Spec Ed* 0 ● *Alt* 0 **Students**: 4,489 **Total Teachers**: 298 **Student/Classroom Teacher Ratio**: 17.0	**Expenditures/Student**: $8,382 **Librarians**: 6.0 748 students/librarian **Guidance Counselors**: 6.9 651 students/counselor	**% Amer Indian**: 0.1 **% Asian**: 2.0 **% Black**: 8.8 **% Hispanic**: 2.0 **% White**: 87.1	National ***Socio-Economic Status*** indicator percentile (100=high): 65th

Dutchess County

[POUGHKEEPSIE] **ARLINGTON CENTRAL S.D.**

120 DUTCHESS TPKE ● POUGHKEEPSIE NY 12603 ● (914) 486-4460 ● http://www.academic.marist.edu/arlington

Grade Span: KG-12 **Schools**: *Regular* 10 ● *Spec Ed* 0 ● *Alt* 0 **Students**: 8,204 **Total Teachers**: 504 **Student/Classroom Teacher Ratio**: 16.5	**Expenditures/Student**: $7,448 **Librarians**: 9.7 846 students/librarian **Guidance Counselors**: 10.6 774 students/counselor	**% Amer Indian**: 0.0 **% Asian**: 2.7 **% Black**: 4.7 **% Hispanic**: 2.8 **% White**: 89.7	National ***Socio-Economic Status*** indicator percentile (100=high): 87th

Dutchess County

POUGHKEEPSIE CITY S.D.

11 COLLEGE AVE ● POUGHKEEPSIE NY 12603 ● (914) 451-4950

Grade Span: PK-12 **Schools**: *Regular* 8 ● *Spec Ed* 0 ● *Alt* 0 **Students**: 4,053 **Total Teachers**: 292 **Student/Classroom Teacher Ratio**: 16.3	**Expenditures/Student**: $10,292 **Librarians**: 8.0 507 students/librarian **Guidance Counselors**: 8.0 507 students/counselor	**% Amer Indian**: 0.1 **% Asian**: 1.2 **% Black**: 63.8 **% Hispanic**: 5.8 **% White**: 29.1	National ***Socio-Economic Status*** indicator percentile (100=high): 12th

Dutchess County

[WAPPINGERS FALLS] **WAPPINGERS CENTRAL S.D.**

15 MYERS CORNERS RD ● WAPPINGERS FALLS NY 12590-3296 ● (914) 298-5000 ● http://northernlight.net/~wcsd/default.htm

Grade Span: KG-12 **Schools**: *Regular* 14 ● *Spec Ed* 0 ● *Alt* 0 **Students**: 11,299 **Total Teachers**: 657 **Student/Classroom Teacher Ratio**: 17.3	**Expenditures/Student**: $8,569 **Librarians**: 13.7 825 students/librarian **Guidance Counselors**: 17.0 665 students/counselor	**% Amer Indian**: 0.1 **% Asian**: 4.5 **% Black**: 4.5 **% Hispanic**: 4.3 **% White**: 86.7	National ***Socio-Economic Status*** indicator percentile (100=high): 90th

Erie County
AMHERST CENTRAL S.D.
55 KINGS HWY ● AMHERST NY 14226-4398 ● (716) 836-3000 ● http://www.amherst.k12.ny.us

Grade Span: KG-12 **Schools**: *Regular* 4 ● *Spec Ed* 0 ● *Alt* 0 **Students**: 3,044 **Total Teachers**: 202 **Student/Classroom Teacher Ratio**: 15.7	**Expenditures/Student**: $9,016 **Librarians**: 3.5 870 students/librarian **Guidance Counselors**: 8.0 381 students/counselor	**% Amer Indian**: 0.6 **% Asian**: 3.4 **% Black**: 6.6 **% Hispanic**: 1.3 **% White**: 88.2	National ***Socio-Economic Status*** indicator percentile (100=high): 73rd

Erie County
[AMHERST] **SWEET HOME CENTRAL S.D.**
1901 SWEET HOME RD ● AMHERST NY 14228-3399 ● (716) 689-5201 ● http://www.shs.k12.ny.us

Grade Span: KG-12 **Schools**: *Regular* 6 ● *Spec Ed* 0 ● *Alt* 0 **Students**: 4,105 **Total Teachers**: 287 **Student/Classroom Teacher Ratio**: 15.2	**Expenditures/Student**: $9,202 **Librarians**: 5.5 746 students/librarian **Guidance Counselors**: 8.2 501 students/counselor	**% Amer Indian**: 0.2 **% Asian**: 4.8 **% Black**: 4.8 **% Hispanic**: 1.9 **% White**: 88.4	National ***Socio-Economic Status*** indicator percentile (100=high): 73rd

Erie County
[ANGOLA] **EVANS-BRANT CENTRAL S.D.**
8855 ERIE RD ● ANGOLA NY 14006-9624 ● (716) 549-2300

Grade Span: KG-12 **Schools**: *Regular* 7 ● *Spec Ed* 0 ● *Alt* 0 **Students**: 3,653 **Total Teachers**: 247 **Student/Classroom Teacher Ratio**: 17.1	**Expenditures/Student**: $8,201 **Librarians**: 4.9 746 students/librarian **Guidance Counselors**: 8.2 445 students/counselor	**% Amer Indian**: 4.6 **% Asian**: 0.5 **% Black**: 0.6 **% Hispanic**: 1.3 **% White**: 93.0	National ***Socio-Economic Status*** indicator percentile (100=high): 61st

Erie County
BUFFALO CITY S.D.
712 CITY HALL ● BUFFALO NY 14202-3375 ● (716) 851-3575 ● http://drew.buffalo.k12.ny.us/bps.html

Grade Span: PK-12 **Schools**: *Regular* 68 ● *Spec Ed* 1 ● *Alt* 6 **Students**: 48,540 **Total Teachers**: 3,279 **Student/Classroom Teacher Ratio**: 15.4	**Expenditures/Student**: $8,739 **Librarians**: 52.8 919 students/librarian **Guidance Counselors**: 89.3 544 students/counselor	**% Amer Indian**: 1.3 **% Asian**: 1.2 **% Black**: 53.8 **% Hispanic**: 10.4 **% White**: 33.4	National ***Socio-Economic Status*** indicator percentile (100=high): 6th

Erie County
[BUFFALO] **KENMORE-TONAWANDA UNION FREE S.D.**
1500 COLVIN BLVD ● BUFFALO NY 14223-1196 ● (716) 874-8400

Grade Span: KG-12 **Schools**: *Regular* 13 ● *Spec Ed* 0 ● *Alt* 0 **Students**: 9,178 **Total Teachers**: 596 **Student/Classroom Teacher Ratio**: 17.1	**Expenditures/Student**: $8,716 **Librarians**: 10.8 850 students/librarian **Guidance Counselors**: 18.9 486 students/counselor	**% Amer Indian**: 0.3 **% Asian**: 0.8 **% Black**: 1.5 **% Hispanic**: 0.8 **% White**: 96.5	National ***Socio-Economic Status*** indicator percentile (100=high): 70th

Erie County
CLARENCE CENTRAL S.D.
9625 MAIN ST ● CLARENCE NY 14031-2083 ● (716) 759-0102

Grade Span: KG-12 **Schools**: *Regular* 6 ● *Spec Ed* 0 ● *Alt* 0 **Students**: 3,888 **Total Teachers**: 269 **Student/Classroom Teacher Ratio**: 15.8	**Expenditures/Student**: $7,775 **Librarians**: 6.1 637 students/librarian **Guidance Counselors**: 7.0 555 students/counselor	**% Amer Indian**: 0.1 **% Asian**: 1.6 **% Black**: 0.5 **% Hispanic**: 0.2 **% White**: 97.6	National ***Socio-Economic Status*** indicator percentile (100=high): 95th

NEW YORK (Erie County)

Erie County

DEPEW UNION FREE S.D.

591 TERRACE BLVD ● DEPEW NY 14043-4535 ● (716) 686-2251

Grade Span: KG-12 **Schools**: *Regular* 3 ● *Spec Ed* 0 ● *Alt* 0 **Students**: 2,595 **Total Teachers**: 173 **Student/Classroom Teacher Ratio**: 16.1	**Expenditures/Student**: $8,758 **Librarians**: 2.8 927 students/librarian **Guidance Counselors**: 6.0 433 students/counselor	**% Amer Indian**: 0.3 **% Asian**: 0.3 **% Black**: 0.5 **% Hispanic**: 0.3 **% White**: 98.5	National ***Socio-Economic Status*** indicator percentile (100=high): 65th

Erie County

[ELMA] **IROQUOIS CENTRAL S.D.**

GIRDLE RD ● ELMA NY 14059-0032 ● (716) 652-3000

Grade Span: KG-12 **Schools**: *Regular* 6 ● *Spec Ed* 0 ● *Alt* 0 **Students**: 2,789 **Total Teachers**: 170 **Student/Classroom Teacher Ratio**: 19.0	**Expenditures/Student**: $7,588 **Librarians**: 2.8 996 students/librarian **Guidance Counselors**: 3.5 797 students/counselor	**% Amer Indian**: 0.0 **% Asian**: 0.2 **% Black**: 0.2 **% Hispanic**: 0.1 **% White**: 99.5	National ***Socio-Economic Status*** indicator percentile (100=high): 88th

Erie County

GRAND ISLAND CENTRAL S.D.

1100 RANSOM RD ● GRAND ISLAND NY 14072-1460 ● (716) 773-8800 ● http://www.grandisland-cs.k12.ny.us

Grade Span: KG-12 **Schools**: *Regular* 5 ● *Spec Ed* 0 ● *Alt* 0 **Students**: 3,173 **Total Teachers**: 214 **Student/Classroom Teacher Ratio**: 15.5	**Expenditures/Student**: $7,888 **Librarians**: 4.4 721 students/librarian **Guidance Counselors**: 7.0 453 students/counselor	**% Amer Indian**: 0.1 **% Asian**: 1.9 **% Black**: 2.2 **% Hispanic**: 0.5 **% White**: 95.3	National ***Socio-Economic Status*** indicator percentile (100=high): 92nd

Erie County

[HAMBURG] **FRONTIER CENTRAL S.D.**

S 5120 ORCHARD AVE ● HAMBURG NY 14075-5657 ● (716) 627-1060 ● http://members.aol.com/frontiersc

Grade Span: KG-12 **Schools**: *Regular* 6 ● *Spec Ed* 0 ● *Alt* 0 **Students**: 5,452 **Total Teachers**: 338 **Student/Classroom Teacher Ratio**: 17.7	**Expenditures/Student**: $7,504 **Librarians**: 5.8 940 students/librarian **Guidance Counselors**: 9.0 606 students/counselor	**% Amer Indian**: 0.1 **% Asian**: 0.4 **% Black**: 0.5 **% Hispanic**: 0.8 **% White**: 98.3	National ***Socio-Economic Status*** indicator percentile (100=high): 69th

Erie County

HAMBURG CENTRAL S.D.

5305 ABBOTT RD ● HAMBURG NY 14075-1699 ● (716) 646-3220

Grade Span: PK-12 **Schools**: *Regular* 6 ● *Spec Ed* 0 ● *Alt* 0 **Students**: 4,199 **Total Teachers**: 275 **Student/Classroom Teacher Ratio**: 17.3	**Expenditures/Student**: $7,830 **Librarians**: 4.6 913 students/librarian **Guidance Counselors**: 10.0 420 students/counselor	**% Amer Indian**: 0.2 **% Asian**: 0.6 **% Black**: 0.5 **% Hispanic**: 0.6 **% White**: 98.1	National ***Socio-Economic Status*** indicator percentile (100=high): 80th

Erie County

LANCASTER CENTRAL S.D.

177 CENTRAL AVE ● LANCASTER NY 14086-1897 ● (716) 686-3200

Grade Span: KG-12 **Schools**: *Regular* 7 ● *Spec Ed* 0 ● *Alt* 0 **Students**: 5,113 **Total Teachers**: 321 **Student/Classroom Teacher Ratio**: 16.6	**Expenditures/Student**: $7,813 **Librarians**: 6.5 787 students/librarian **Guidance Counselors**: 8.0 639 students/counselor	**% Amer Indian**: 0.1 **% Asian**: 0.7 **% Black**: 0.6 **% Hispanic**: 0.2 **% White**: 98.4	National ***Socio-Economic Status*** indicator percentile (100=high): 78th

Erie County
ORCHARD PARK CENTRAL S.D.
3330 BAKER RD ● ORCHARD PARK NY 14127-1472 ● (716) 662-6280

Grade Span: KG-12 **Schools**: *Regular* 6 ● *Spec Ed* 0 ● *Alt* 0 **Students**: 5,084 **Total Teachers**: 337 **Student/Classroom Teacher Ratio**: 15.5	**Expenditures/Student**: $8,019 **Librarians**: 8.1 628 students/librarian **Guidance Counselors**: 9.0 565 students/counselor	**% Amer Indian**: 1.0 **% Asian**: 1.4 **% Black**: 0.7 **% Hispanic**: 0.6 **% White**: 96.4	National ***Socio-Economic Status*** indicator percentile (100=high): 93rd

Erie County
TONAWANDA CITY S.D.
202 BROAD ST ● TONAWANDA NY 14150-2098 ● (716) 694-7784

Grade Span: KG-12 **Schools**: *Regular* 6 ● *Spec Ed* 0 ● *Alt* 0 **Students**: 2,665 **Total Teachers**: 164 **Student/Classroom Teacher Ratio**: 18.2	**Expenditures/Student**: $7,527 **Librarians**: 1.8 1,481 students/librarian **Guidance Counselors**: 4.0 666 students/counselor	**% Amer Indian**: 0.1 **% Asian**: 0.6 **% Black**: 0.5 **% Hispanic**: 0.5 **% White**: 98.3	National ***Socio-Economic Status*** indicator percentile (100=high): 62nd

Erie County
WEST SENECA CENTRAL S.D.
1397 ORCHARD PARK RD ● WEST SENECA NY 14224-4098 ● (716) 674-5300

Grade Span: KG-12 **Schools**: *Regular* 11 ● *Spec Ed* 0 ● *Alt* 0 **Students**: 7,748 **Total Teachers**: 479 **Student/Classroom Teacher Ratio**: 18.6	**Expenditures/Student**: $7,981 **Librarians**: 10.1 767 students/librarian **Guidance Counselors**: 13.0 596 students/counselor	**% Amer Indian**: 0.1 **% Asian**: 0.7 **% Black**: 0.8 **% Hispanic**: 0.5 **% White**: 97.9	National ***Socio-Economic Status*** indicator percentile (100=high): 79th

Erie County
WILLIAMSVILLE CENTRAL S.D.
415 LAWRENCE BELL DR ● WILLIAMSVILLE NY 14231-9070 ● (716) 626-7220 ● http://www.wmsvcsd.wnyric.org

Grade Span: KG-12 **Schools**: *Regular* 13 ● *Spec Ed* 0 ● *Alt* 0 **Students**: 10,549 **Total Teachers**: 762 **Student/Classroom Teacher Ratio**: 14.6	**Expenditures/Student**: $8,342 **Librarians**: 12.0 879 students/librarian **Guidance Counselors**: 26.0 406 students/counselor	**% Amer Indian**: 0.1 **% Asian**: 4.8 **% Black**: 2.5 **% Hispanic**: 0.7 **% White**: 92.0	National ***Socio-Economic Status*** indicator percentile (100=high): 93rd

Franklin County
MALONE CENTRAL S.D.
80 WEST ST ● MALONE NY 12953-1118 ● (518) 483-7800

Grade Span: PK-12 **Schools**: *Regular* 6 ● *Spec Ed* 0 ● *Alt* 0 **Students**: 2,839 **Total Teachers**: 194 **Student/Classroom Teacher Ratio**: 20.7	**Expenditures/Student**: $7,617 **Librarians**: 2.0 1,420 students/librarian **Guidance Counselors**: 7.0 406 students/counselor	**% Amer Indian**: 0.0 **% Asian**: 0.4 **% Black**: 0.4 **% Hispanic**: 0.4 **% White**: 98.9	National ***Socio-Economic Status*** indicator percentile (100=high): 36th

Fulton County
GLOVERSVILLE CITY S.D.
90 N MAIN ST ● GLOVERSVILLE NY 12078-0005 ● (518) 725-2612

Grade Span: PK-12 **Schools**: *Regular* 7 ● *Spec Ed* 0 ● *Alt* 0 **Students**: 3,552 **Total Teachers**: 263 **Student/Classroom Teacher Ratio**: 14.5	**Expenditures/Student**: $7,419 **Librarians**: 4.5 789 students/librarian **Guidance Counselors**: 9.0 395 students/counselor	**% Amer Indian**: 0.0 **% Asian**: 0.7 **% Black**: 3.3 **% Hispanic**: 1.3 **% White**: 94.7	National ***Socio-Economic Status*** indicator percentile (100=high): 35th

Genesee County

BATAVIA CITY S.D.

39 WASHINGTON AVE ● BATAVIA NY 14021-0677 ● (716) 344-8217

Grade Span: KG-12 **Schools**: *Regular* 5 ● *Spec Ed* 0 ● *Alt* 0 **Students**: 2,880 **Total Teachers**: 201 **Student/Classroom Teacher Ratio**: 15.4	**Expenditures/Student**: $8,626 **Librarians**: 5.0 576 students/librarian **Guidance Counselors**: 8.0 360 students/counselor	**% Amer Indian**: 0.1 **% Asian**: 1.0 **% Black**: 7.3 **% Hispanic**: 1.1 **% White**: 90.6	National ***Socio-Economic Status*** indicator percentile (100=high): 54th

Jefferson County

CARTHAGE CENTRAL S.D.

25059 COUNTY RT 197 ● CARTHAGE NY 13619-9527 ● (315) 493-0510

Grade Span: KG-12 **Schools**: *Regular* 5 ● *Spec Ed* 0 ● *Alt* 0 **Students**: 3,218 **Total Teachers**: 215 **Student/Classroom Teacher Ratio**: 16.3	**Expenditures/Student**: $7,799 **Librarians**: 4.5 715 students/librarian **Guidance Counselors**: 5.4 596 students/counselor	**% Amer Indian**: 0.2 **% Asian**: 2.2 **% Black**: 8.5 **% Hispanic**: 3.3 **% White**: 85.8	National ***Socio-Economic Status*** indicator percentile (100=high): 44th

Jefferson County

[PHILADELPHIA] **INDIAN RIVER CENTRAL S.D.**

COUNTY RT 29 FT DRUM ● PHILADELPHIA NY 13673-0308 ● (315) 642-3441

Grade Span: KG-12 **Schools**: *Regular* 7 ● *Spec Ed* 0 ● *Alt* 0 **Students**: 3,771 **Total Teachers**: 249 **Student/Classroom Teacher Ratio**: 17.0	**Expenditures/Student**: $7,563 **Librarians**: 6.2 608 students/librarian **Guidance Counselors**: 6.4 589 students/counselor	**% Amer Indian**: 0.4 **% Asian**: 3.0 **% Black**: 16.9 **% Hispanic**: 6.2 **% White**: 73.5	National ***Socio-Economic Status*** indicator percentile (100=high): 47th

Jefferson County

WATERTOWN CITY S.D.

376 BUTTERFIELD AVE ● WATERTOWN NY 13601-4593 ● (315) 785-3700

Grade Span: KG-12 **Schools**: *Regular* 8 ● *Spec Ed* 0 ● *Alt* 0 **Students**: 4,733 **Total Teachers**: 284 **Student/Classroom Teacher Ratio**: 19.2	**Expenditures/Student**: $6,843 **Librarians**: 3.9 1,214 students/librarian **Guidance Counselors**: 5.0 947 students/counselor	**% Amer Indian**: 0.5 **% Asian**: 1.9 **% Black**: 8.1 **% Hispanic**: 3.8 **% White**: 85.7	National ***Socio-Economic Status*** indicator percentile (100=high): 20th

Kings County

[BROOKLYN] **NEW YORK CITY S.D.**

110 LIVINGSTON ST ● BROOKLYN NY 11201 ● (718) 935-2800

Grade Span: PK-12 **Schools**: *Regular* 969 ● *Spec Ed* 60 ● *Alt* 79 **Students**: 1,049,039 **Total Teachers**: 55,538 **Student/Classroom Teacher Ratio**: 19.8	**Expenditures/Student**: $8,097 **Librarians**: 677.1 1,549 students/librarian **Guidance Counselors**: 1,752.5 599 students/counselor	**% Amer Indian**: 0.4 **% Asian**: 10.0 **% Black**: 35.5 **% Hispanic**: 37.0 **% White**: 17.1	National ***Socio-Economic Status*** indicator percentile (100=high): na

Madison County

CHITTENANGO CENTRAL S.D.

1732 FYLER RD ● CHITTENANGO NY 13037-9520 ● (315) 687-2669

Grade Span: KG-12 **Schools**: *Regular* 5 ● *Spec Ed* 0 ● *Alt* 0 **Students**: 2,812 **Total Teachers**: 174 **Student/Classroom Teacher Ratio**: 18.2	**Expenditures/Student**: $6,713 **Librarians**: 4.4 639 students/librarian **Guidance Counselors**: 5.9 477 students/counselor	**% Amer Indian**: 0.2 **% Asian**: 0.4 **% Black**: 0.4 **% Hispanic**: 0.5 **% White**: 98.4	National ***Socio-Economic Status*** indicator percentile (100=high): 73rd

Madison County

ONEIDA CITY S.D.

565 SAYLES ST ● ONEIDA NY 13421-0327 ● (315) 363-2550 ● http://www.oneidany.org

Grade Span: KG-12 **Schools**: *Regular* 8 ● *Spec Ed* 0 ● *Alt* 0 **Students**: 2,727 **Total Teachers**: 191 **Student/Classroom Teacher Ratio**: 16.8	**Expenditures/Student**: $7,871 **Librarians**: 7.2 379 students/librarian **Guidance Counselors**: 4.0 682 students/counselor	**% Amer Indian**: 1.7 **% Asian**: 0.4 **% Black**: 0.8 **% Hispanic**: 0.1 **% White**: 97.0	National ***Socio-Economic Status*** indicator percentile (100=high): 58th

Monroe County

BROCKPORT CENTRAL S.D.

40 ALLEN ST ● BROCKPORT NY 14420-2296 ● (716) 637-1810

Grade Span: KG-12 **Schools**: *Regular* 5 ● *Spec Ed* 0 ● *Alt* 0 **Students**: 4,770 **Total Teachers**: 287 **Student/Classroom Teacher Ratio**: 18.1	**Expenditures/Student**: $7,380 **Librarians**: 4.4 1,084 students/librarian **Guidance Counselors**: 11.2 426 students/counselor	**% Amer Indian**: 0.3 **% Asian**: 1.0 **% Black**: 4.7 **% Hispanic**: 2.0 **% White**: 92.0	National ***Socio-Economic Status*** indicator percentile (100=high): 65th

Monroe County

CHURCHVILLE-CHILI CENTRAL S.D.

139 FAIRBANKS RD ● CHURCHVILLE NY 14428-9797 ● (716) 293-1800

Grade Span: KG-12 **Schools**: *Regular* 5 ● *Spec Ed* 0 ● *Alt* 0 **Students**: 4,519 **Total Teachers**: 283 **Student/Classroom Teacher Ratio**: 16.8	**Expenditures/Student**: $7,371 **Librarians**: 5.1 886 students/librarian **Guidance Counselors**: 10.0 452 students/counselor	**% Amer Indian**: 0.2 **% Asian**: 1.5 **% Black**: 4.4 **% Hispanic**: 1.5 **% White**: 92.5	National ***Socio-Economic Status*** indicator percentile (100=high): 87th

Monroe County

FAIRPORT CENTRAL S.D.

38 W CHURCH ST ● FAIRPORT NY 14450-2130 ● (716) 421-2000

Grade Span: KG-12 **Schools**: *Regular* 8 ● *Spec Ed* 0 ● *Alt* 0 **Students**: 6,971 **Total Teachers**: 453 **Student/Classroom Teacher Ratio**: 17.2	**Expenditures/Student**: $7,698 **Librarians**: 10.1 690 students/librarian **Guidance Counselors**: 13.0 536 students/counselor	**% Amer Indian**: 0.3 **% Asian**: 4.1 **% Black**: 2.3 **% Hispanic**: 0.7 **% White**: 92.5	National ***Socio-Economic Status*** indicator percentile (100=high): 92nd

Monroe County

[HENRIETTA] **RUSH-HENRIETTA CENTRAL S.D.**

2034 LEHIGH STA RD ● HENRIETTA NY 14467-9692 ● (716) 359-5010 ● http://www.rh.monroe.edu

Grade Span: KG-12 **Schools**: *Regular* 8 ● *Spec Ed* 0 ● *Alt* 0 **Students**: 5,810 **Total Teachers**: 413 **Student/Classroom Teacher Ratio**: 15.2	**Expenditures/Student**: $10,210 **Librarians**: 9.2 632 students/librarian **Guidance Counselors**: 11.0 528 students/counselor	**% Amer Indian**: 0.9 **% Asian**: 5.5 **% Black**: 10.2 **% Hispanic**: 2.9 **% White**: 80.5	National ***Socio-Economic Status*** indicator percentile (100=high): 79th

Monroe County

HILTON CENTRAL S.D.

225 WEST AVE ● HILTON NY 14468-1283 ● (716) 392-3450 ● http://www.hilton.k12.ny.us

Grade Span: KG-12 **Schools**: *Regular* 5 ● *Spec Ed* 0 ● *Alt* 0 **Students**: 4,423 **Total Teachers**: 283 **Student/Classroom Teacher Ratio**: 16.8	**Expenditures/Student**: $7,555 **Librarians**: 4.4 1,005 students/librarian **Guidance Counselors**: 10.7 413 students/counselor	**% Amer Indian**: 0.2 **% Asian**: 1.0 **% Black**: 1.6 **% Hispanic**: 0.4 **% White**: 96.8	National ***Socio-Economic Status*** indicator percentile (100=high): 83rd

Monroe County
[NORTH GREECE] **GREECE CENTRAL S.D.**
P.O. BOX 300 ● NORTH GREECE NY 14515-0300 ● (716) 621-1000 ● http://www.greeceny.com/index.html

Grade Span: KG-12 **Schools**: *Regular* 21 ● *Spec Ed* 0 ● *Alt* 0 **Students**: 14,090 **Total Teachers**: 872 **Student/Classroom Teacher Ratio**: 17.8	**Expenditures/Student**: $7,879 **Librarians**: 13.2 1,067 students/librarian **Guidance Counselors**: 27.7 509 students/counselor	**% Amer Indian**: 0.3 **% Asian**: 2.1 **% Black**: 3.2 **% Hispanic**: 2.3 **% White**: 92.1	National ***Socio-Economic Status*** indicator percentile (100=high): 81st

Monroe County
PENFIELD CENTRAL S.D.
P.O. BOX 900 ● PENFIELD NY 14526-0900 ● (716) 248-3220

Grade Span: KG-12 **Schools**: *Regular* 6 ● *Spec Ed* 0 ● *Alt* 0 **Students**: 4,841 **Total Teachers**: 341 **Student/Classroom Teacher Ratio**: 15.6	**Expenditures/Student**: $8,858 **Librarians**: 6.3 768 students/librarian **Guidance Counselors**: 12.4 390 students/counselor	**% Amer Indian**: 0.2 **% Asian**: 4.0 **% Black**: 5.0 **% Hispanic**: 1.4 **% White**: 89.4	National ***Socio-Economic Status*** indicator percentile (100=high): 92nd

Monroe County
PITTSFORD CENTRAL S.D.
42 W JEFFERSON RD ● PITTSFORD NY 14534-1978 ● (716) 381-9940

Grade Span: PK-12 **Schools**: *Regular* 8 ● *Spec Ed* 0 ● *Alt* 0 **Students**: 5,286 **Total Teachers**: 359 **Student/Classroom Teacher Ratio**: 16.8	**Expenditures/Student**: $9,369 **Librarians**: 8.2 645 students/librarian **Guidance Counselors**: 16.2 326 students/counselor	**% Amer Indian**: 0.3 **% Asian**: 5.7 **% Black**: 4.4 **% Hispanic**: 0.9 **% White**: 88.7	National ***Socio-Economic Status*** indicator percentile (100=high): 98th

Monroe County
[ROCHESTER] **BRIGHTON CENTRAL S.D.**
2035 MONROE AVE ● ROCHESTER NY 14618-2027 ● (716) 461-9670

Grade Span: KG-12 **Schools**: *Regular* 4 ● *Spec Ed* 0 ● *Alt* 0 **Students**: 3,175 **Total Teachers**: 210 **Student/Classroom Teacher Ratio**: 16.7	**Expenditures/Student**: $9,858 **Librarians**: 3.6 882 students/librarian **Guidance Counselors**: 8.2 387 students/counselor	**% Amer Indian**: 0.3 **% Asian**: 7.1 **% Black**: 5.5 **% Hispanic**: 1.9 **% White**: 85.3	National ***Socio-Economic Status*** indicator percentile (100=high): 94th

Monroe County
[ROCHESTER] **EAST IRONDEQUOIT CENTRAL S.D.**
600 PARDEE RD ● ROCHESTER NY 14609-2898 ● (716) 336-7010

Grade Span: KG-12 **Schools**: *Regular* 6 ● *Spec Ed* 0 ● *Alt* 0 **Students**: 3,195 **Total Teachers**: 201 **Student/Classroom Teacher Ratio**: 17.0	**Expenditures/Student**: $9,172 **Librarians**: 3.8 841 students/librarian **Guidance Counselors**: 5.6 571 students/counselor	**% Amer Indian**: 0.1 **% Asian**: 1.0 **% Black**: 4.5 **% Hispanic**: 3.9 **% White**: 90.4	National ***Socio-Economic Status*** indicator percentile (100=high): 71st

Monroe County
[ROCHESTER] **GATES-CHILI CENTRAL S.D.**
910 WEGMAN RD ● ROCHESTER NY 14624-1492 ● (716) 247-5050 ● http://www.gateschili.org

Grade Span: KG-12 **Schools**: *Regular* 7 ● *Spec Ed* 0 ● *Alt* 0 **Students**: 5,327 **Total Teachers**: 334 **Student/Classroom Teacher Ratio**: 17.9	**Expenditures/Student**: $8,708 **Librarians**: 7.1 750 students/librarian **Guidance Counselors**: 12.0 444 students/counselor	**% Amer Indian**: 0.1 **% Asian**: 2.1 **% Black**: 7.9 **% Hispanic**: 2.0 **% White**: 87.9	National ***Socio-Economic Status*** indicator percentile (100=high): 76th

Monroe County
ROCHESTER CITY S.D.
131 W BROAD ST ● ROCHESTER NY 14614-1187 ● (716) 262-8378

Grade Span: PK-12 **Schools**: *Regular* 56 ● *Spec Ed* 0 ● *Alt* 1 **Students**: 36,962 **Total Teachers**: 2,533 **Student/Classroom Teacher Ratio**: 16.2	**Expenditures/Student**: $9,458 **Librarians**: 40.8 906 students/librarian **Guidance Counselors**: 63.7 580 students/counselor	**% Amer Indian**: 0.6 **% Asian**: 2.4 **% Black**: 59.0 **% Hispanic**: 17.5 **% White**: 20.4	National ***Socio-Economic Status*** indicator percentile (100=high): 7th

Monroe County
[ROCHESTER] **WEST IRONDEQUOIT CENTRAL S.D.**
370 COOPER RD ● ROCHESTER NY 14617-3093 ● (716) 342-5500

Grade Span: KG-12 **Schools**: *Regular* 10 ● *Spec Ed* 0 ● *Alt* 0 **Students**: 3,939 **Total Teachers**: 238 **Student/Classroom Teacher Ratio**: 20.9	**Expenditures/Student**: $7,961 **Librarians**: 5.8 679 students/librarian **Guidance Counselors**: 13.0 303 students/counselor	**% Amer Indian**: 0.3 **% Asian**: 1.9 **% Black**: 4.3 **% Hispanic**: 2.3 **% White**: 91.1	National ***Socio-Economic Status*** indicator percentile (100=high): 91st

Monroe County
SPENCERPORT CENTRAL S.D.
71 LYELL AVE ● SPENCERPORT NY 14559-1899 ● (716) 352-3421 ● http://www.spencerport.k12.ny.us

Grade Span: KG-12 **Schools**: *Regular* 5 ● *Spec Ed* 0 ● *Alt* 0 **Students**: 4,138 **Total Teachers**: 253 **Student/Classroom Teacher Ratio**: 17.6	**Expenditures/Student**: $7,567 **Librarians**: 4.7 880 students/librarian **Guidance Counselors**: 8.0 517 students/counselor	**% Amer Indian**: 0.4 **% Asian**: 2.7 **% Black**: 4.0 **% Hispanic**: 1.4 **% White**: 91.5	National ***Socio-Economic Status*** indicator percentile (100=high): 87th

Monroe County
WEBSTER CENTRAL S.D.
119 SOUTH AVE ● WEBSTER NY 14580-3594 ● (716) 265-3600

Grade Span: KG-12 **Schools**: *Regular* 10 ● *Spec Ed* 0 ● *Alt* 0 **Students**: 7,686 **Total Teachers**: 486 **Student/Classroom Teacher Ratio**: 16.9	**Expenditures/Student**: $7,991 **Librarians**: 8.8 873 students/librarian **Guidance Counselors**: 14.2 541 students/counselor	**% Amer Indian**: 0.0 **% Asian**: 1.9 **% Black**: 2.1 **% Hispanic**: 1.1 **% White**: 95.0	National ***Socio-Economic Status*** indicator percentile (100=high): 92nd

Montgomery County
AMSTERDAM CITY S.D.
11 LIBERTY ST ● AMSTERDAM NY 12010-0670 ● (518) 843-5217

Grade Span: PK-12 **Schools**: *Regular* 7 ● *Spec Ed* 0 ● *Alt* 0 **Students**: 3,756 **Total Teachers**: 287 **Student/Classroom Teacher Ratio**: 14.6	**Expenditures/Student**: $7,533 **Librarians**: 4.3 873 students/librarian **Guidance Counselors**: 9.0 417 students/counselor	**% Amer Indian**: 0.1 **% Asian**: 0.6 **% Black**: 2.3 **% Hispanic**: 21.2 **% White**: 75.8	National ***Socio-Economic Status*** indicator percentile (100=high): 40th

Nassau County
BALDWIN UNION FREE S.D.
960 HASTINGS ST ● BALDWIN NY 11510-4798 ● (516) 377-9271

Grade Span: KG-12 **Schools**: *Regular* 9 ● *Spec Ed* 0 ● *Alt* 0 **Students**: 5,035 **Total Teachers**: 332 **Student/Classroom Teacher Ratio**: 18.7	**Expenditures/Student**: $9,696 **Librarians**: 3.0 1,678 students/librarian **Guidance Counselors**: 10.4 484 students/counselor	**% Amer Indian**: 0.2 **% Asian**: 3.8 **% Black**: 17.1 **% Hispanic**: 6.9 **% White**: 72.0	National ***Socio-Economic Status*** indicator percentile (100=high): na

Nassau County

BETHPAGE UNION FREE S.D.

CHERRY AVE ● BETHPAGE NY 11714-1595 ● (516) 733-3700 ● http://www.bethpage.k12.ny.us

Grade Span: KG-12 **Schools**: *Regular* 5 ● *Spec Ed* 0 ● *Alt* 0 **Students**: 2,622 **Total Teachers**: 195 **Student/Classroom Teacher Ratio**: 15.8	**Expenditures/Student**: $12,133 **Librarians**: 5.1 514 students/librarian **Guidance Counselors**: 5.0 524 students/counselor	**% Amer Indian**: 0.0 **% Asian**: 4.5 **% Black**: 0.2 **% Hispanic**: 4.5 **% White**: 90.9	National ***Socio-Economic Status*** indicator percentile (100=high): 95th

Nassau County

EAST MEADOW UNION FREE S.D.

101 CARMAN AVE ● EAST MEADOW NY 11554-1156 ● (516) 228-5200

Grade Span: KG-12 **Schools**: *Regular* 9 ● *Spec Ed* 0 ● *Alt* 0 **Students**: 7,750 **Total Teachers**: 553 **Student/Classroom Teacher Ratio**: 15.9	**Expenditures/Student**: $10,102 **Librarians**: 11.9 651 students/librarian **Guidance Counselors**: 18.0 431 students/counselor	**% Amer Indian**: 0.1 **% Asian**: 7.7 **% Black**: 2.2 **% Hispanic**: 5.9 **% White**: 84.1	National ***Socio-Economic Status*** indicator percentile (100=high): 94th

Nassau County

ELMONT UNION FREE S.D.

135 ELMONT RD ● ELMONT NY 11003-1609 ● (516) 326-5500

Grade Span: PK-06 **Schools**: *Regular* 7 ● *Spec Ed* 0 ● *Alt* 0 **Students**: 3,714 **Total Teachers**: 231 **Student/Classroom Teacher Ratio**: 19.1	**Expenditures/Student**: $8,023 **Librarians**: 5.1 728 students/librarian **Guidance Counselors**: 0.0 *** students/counselor	**% Amer Indian**: 0.2 **% Asian**: 12.6 **% Black**: 36.5 **% Hispanic**: 14.6 **% White**: 36.0	National ***Socio-Economic Status*** indicator percentile (100=high): 62nd

Nassau County

[ELMONT] **SEWANHAKA CENTRAL HIGH S.D.**

555 RIDGE RD ● ELMONT NY 11003-3524 ● (516) 488-9800

Grade Span: 07-12 **Schools**: *Regular* 5 ● *Spec Ed* 0 ● *Alt* 0 **Students**: 7,016 **Total Teachers**: 446 **Student/Classroom Teacher Ratio**: 16.4	**Expenditures/Student**: $10,506 **Librarians**: 11.2 626 students/librarian **Guidance Counselors**: 34.0 206 students/counselor	**% Amer Indian**: 0.0 **% Asian**: 11.3 **% Black**: 17.2 **% Hispanic**: 9.7 **% White**: 61.8	National ***Socio-Economic Status*** indicator percentile (100=high): 86th

Nassau County

FARMINGDALE UNION FREE S.D.

50 VAN COTT AVE ● FARMINGDALE NY 11735-3742 ● (516) 752-6510

Grade Span: KG-12 **Schools**: *Regular* 6 ● *Spec Ed* 0 ● *Alt* 0 **Students**: 5,776 **Total Teachers**: 415 **Student/Classroom Teacher Ratio**: 14.7	**Expenditures/Student**: $10,780 **Librarians**: 9.2 628 students/librarian **Guidance Counselors**: 11.3 511 students/counselor	**% Amer Indian**: 0.2 **% Asian**: 3.4 **% Black**: 7.3 **% Hispanic**: 6.9 **% White**: 82.2	National ***Socio-Economic Status*** indicator percentile (100=high): 84th

Nassau County

FREEPORT UNION FREE S.D.

235 N OCEAN AVE ● FREEPORT NY 11520-0801 ● (516) 867-5205

Grade Span: PK-12 **Schools**: *Regular* 8 ● *Spec Ed* 0 ● *Alt* 0 **Students**: 7,103 **Total Teachers**: 418 **Student/Classroom Teacher Ratio**: 18.6	**Expenditures/Student**: $9,737 **Librarians**: 6.0 1,184 students/librarian **Guidance Counselors**: 10.8 658 students/counselor	**% Amer Indian**: 0.0 **% Asian**: 1.2 **% Black**: 38.6 **% Hispanic**: 35.7 **% White**: 24.5	National ***Socio-Economic Status*** indicator percentile (100=high): 43rd

Nassau County

GARDEN CITY UNION FREE S.D.

56 CATHEDRAL AVE ● GARDEN CITY NY 11530-0216 ● (516) 294-3004 ● http://WWW.gardencity.k12.ny.us

Grade Span: KG-12 **Schools**: *Regular* 7 ● *Spec Ed* 0 ● *Alt* 0 **Students**: 3,198 **Total Teachers**: 241 **Student/Classroom Teacher Ratio**: 16.1	**Expenditures/Student**: $11,988 **Librarians**: 3.7 864 students/librarian **Guidance Counselors**: 7.0 457 students/counselor	**% Amer Indian**: 0.0 **% Asian**: 3.1 **% Black**: 0.4 **% Hispanic**: 1.2 **% White**: 95.3	National ***Socio-Economic Status*** indicator percentile (100=high): na

Nassau County

GLEN COVE CITY S.D.

DOSORIS LN ● GLEN COVE NY 11542-1237 ● (516) 759-7217 ● http://www.glencove.k12.ny.us

Grade Span: PK-12 **Schools**: *Regular* 6 ● *Spec Ed* 0 ● *Alt* 0 **Students**: 3,069 **Total Teachers**: 222 **Student/Classroom Teacher Ratio**: 15.8	**Expenditures/Student**: $11,916 **Librarians**: 3.8 808 students/librarian **Guidance Counselors**: 9.0 341 students/counselor	**% Amer Indian**: 0.0 **% Asian**: 6.0 **% Black**: 15.7 **% Hispanic**: 23.0 **% White**: 55.3	National ***Socio-Economic Status*** indicator percentile (100=high): 46th

Nassau County

GREAT NECK UNION FREE S.D.

345 LAKEVILLE RD ● GREAT NECK NY 11020-1606 ● (516) 773-1405 ● http://www.greatneck.k12.ny.us

Grade Span: PK-12 **Schools**: *Regular* 9 ● *Spec Ed* 0 ● *Alt* 0 **Students**: 5,692 **Total Teachers**: 508 **Student/Classroom Teacher Ratio**: 13.3	**Expenditures/Student**: $15,890 **Librarians**: 10.3 553 students/librarian **Guidance Counselors**: 16.1 354 students/counselor	**% Amer Indian**: 0.0 **% Asian**: 10.2 **% Black**: 3.5 **% Hispanic**: 7.7 **% White**: 78.6	National ***Socio-Economic Status*** indicator percentile (100=high): 86th

Nassau County

HEMPSTEAD UNION FREE S.D.

185 PENINSULA BLVD ● HEMPSTEAD NY 11550 ● (516) 292-7001

Grade Span: PK-12 **Schools**: *Regular* 10 ● *Spec Ed* 0 ● *Alt* 0 **Students**: 6,063 **Total Teachers**: 340 **Student/Classroom Teacher Ratio**: 20.4	**Expenditures/Student**: $11,550 **Librarians**: 7.3 831 students/librarian **Guidance Counselors**: 7.6 798 students/counselor	**% Amer Indian**: 0.0 **% Asian**: 0.4 **% Black**: 70.9 **% Hispanic**: 28.0 **% White**: 0.7	National ***Socio-Economic Status*** indicator percentile (100=high): 9th

Nassau County

HICKSVILLE UNION FREE S.D.

200 DIVISION AVE ● HICKSVILLE NY 11801-4800 ● (516) 733-6600

Grade Span: PK-12 **Schools**: *Regular* 8 ● *Spec Ed* 0 ● *Alt* 0 **Students**: 4,613 **Total Teachers**: 329 **Student/Classroom Teacher Ratio**: 16.4	**Expenditures/Student**: $11,970 **Librarians**: 5.9 782 students/librarian **Guidance Counselors**: 10.0 461 students/counselor	**% Amer Indian**: 0.0 **% Asian**: 10.1 **% Black**: 2.2 **% Hispanic**: 9.9 **% White**: 77.7	National ***Socio-Economic Status*** indicator percentile (100=high): 87th

Nassau County

LAWRENCE UNION FREE S.D.

195 BROADWAY ● LAWRENCE NY 11559-0477 ● (516) 295-7030 ● http://www.lawrence.org

Grade Span: PK-12 **Schools**: *Regular* 7 ● *Spec Ed* 0 ● *Alt* 0 **Students**: 3,853 **Total Teachers**: 333 **Student/Classroom Teacher Ratio**: 13.0	**Expenditures/Student**: $15,243 **Librarians**: 6.9 558 students/librarian **Guidance Counselors**: 11.0 350 students/counselor	**% Amer Indian**: 0.8 **% Asian**: 2.9 **% Black**: 14.8 **% Hispanic**: 15.0 **% White**: 66.5	National ***Socio-Economic Status*** indicator percentile (100=high): 67th

Nassau County
LEVITTOWN UNION FREE S.D.
ABBEY LN ● LEVITTOWN NY 11756-4042 ● (516) 520-8300

Grade Span: KG-12 **Schools**: *Regular* 10 ● *Spec Ed* 0 ● *Alt* 0 **Students**: 6,995 **Total Teachers**: 487 **Student/Classroom Teacher Ratio**: 16.8	**Expenditures/Student**: $10,652 **Librarians**: 8.9 786 students/librarian **Guidance Counselors**: 13.4 522 students/counselor	**% Amer Indian**: 0.1 **% Asian**: 2.9 **% Black**: 0.5 **% Hispanic**: 3.9 **% White**: 92.6	National ***Socio-Economic Status*** indicator percentile (100=high): 95th

Nassau County
LONG BEACH CITY S.D.
235 LIDO BLVD ● LONG BEACH NY 11561-5093 ● (516) 897-2104

Grade Span: PK-12 **Schools**: *Regular* 7 ● *Spec Ed* 0 ● *Alt* 0 **Students**: 4,624 **Total Teachers**: 298 **Student/Classroom Teacher Ratio**: 18.8	**Expenditures/Student**: $12,029 **Librarians**: 5.0 925 students/librarian **Guidance Counselors**: 9.0 514 students/counselor	**% Amer Indian**: 0.0 **% Asian**: 3.4 **% Black**: 13.2 **% Hispanic**: 18.7 **% White**: 64.7	National ***Socio-Economic Status*** indicator percentile (100=high): 68th

Nassau County
LYNBROOK UNION FREE S.D.
111 ATLANTIC AVE ● LYNBROOK NY 11563-3437 ● (516) 887-0253 ● http://lynbrook.k12.ny.us

Grade Span: KG-12 **Schools**: *Regular* 7 ● *Spec Ed* 0 ● *Alt* 0 **Students**: 2,642 **Total Teachers**: 199 **Student/Classroom Teacher Ratio**: 17.9	**Expenditures/Student**: $11,892 **Librarians**: 5.8 456 students/librarian **Guidance Counselors**: 7.0 377 students/counselor	**% Amer Indian**: 0.0 **% Asian**: 3.3 **% Black**: 0.7 **% Hispanic**: 5.6 **% White**: 90.3	National ***Socio-Economic Status*** indicator percentile (100=high): na

Nassau County
MASSAPEQUA UNION FREE S.D.
4925 MERRICK RD ● MASSAPEQUA NY 11758-6298 ● (516) 797-6160 ● http://www.massapequa.k12.ny.us/msd/msd.htm

Grade Span: KG-12 **Schools**: *Regular* 8 ● *Spec Ed* 0 ● *Alt* 0 **Students**: 6,879 **Total Teachers**: 519 **Student/Classroom Teacher Ratio**: 15.0	**Expenditures/Student**: $10,214 **Librarians**: 11.6 593 students/librarian **Guidance Counselors**: 16.0 430 students/counselor	**% Amer Indian**: 0.1 **% Asian**: 1.0 **% Black**: 0.2 **% Hispanic**: 1.0 **% White**: 97.7	National ***Socio-Economic Status*** indicator percentile (100=high): 98th

Nassau County
MINEOLA UNION FREE S.D.
200 EMORY RD ● MINEOLA NY 11501-2361 ● (516) 741-5036

Grade Span: KG-12 **Schools**: *Regular* 5 ● *Spec Ed* 0 ● *Alt* 0 **Students**: 2,726 **Total Teachers**: 224 **Student/Classroom Teacher Ratio**: 13.0	**Expenditures/Student**: $14,380 **Librarians**: 5.0 545 students/librarian **Guidance Counselors**: 7.6 359 students/counselor	**% Amer Indian**: 0.0 **% Asian**: 5.7 **% Black**: 3.3 **% Hispanic**: 11.2 **% White**: 79.8	National ***Socio-Economic Status*** indicator percentile (100=high): 86th

Nassau County
[NEW HYDE PARK] **HERRICKS UNION FREE S.D.**
99 SHELTER ROCK RD ● NEW HYDE PARK NY 11040-1355 ● (516) 248-3105 ● http://www.herricks.org

Grade Span: KG-12 **Schools**: *Regular* 5 ● *Spec Ed* 0 ● *Alt* 0 **Students**: 3,531 **Total Teachers**: 269 **Student/Classroom Teacher Ratio**: 15.1	**Expenditures/Student**: $11,893 **Librarians**: 5.3 666 students/librarian **Guidance Counselors**: 8.5 415 students/counselor	**% Amer Indian**: 0.0 **% Asian**: 32.3 **% Black**: 0.5 **% Hispanic**: 3.5 **% White**: 63.7	National ***Socio-Economic Status*** indicator percentile (100=high): 99th

Nassau County
[NORTH MASSAPEQUA] **PLAINEDGE UNION FREE S.D.**
241 WYNGATE DR ● NORTH MASSAPEQUA NY 11758-0912 ● (516) 797-4410

Grade Span: PK-12 **Schools**: *Regular* 5 ● *Spec Ed* 0 ● *Alt* 0 **Students**: 3,031 **Total Teachers**: 185 **Student/Classroom Teacher Ratio**: 19.2	**Expenditures/Student**: $11,005 **Librarians**: 3.6 842 students/librarian **Guidance Counselors**: 6.0 505 students/counselor	**% Amer Indian**: 0.0 **% Asian**: 2.0 **% Black**: 0.1 **% Hispanic**: 2.4 **% White**: 95.5	National ***Socio-Economic Status*** indicator percentile (100=high): 95th

Nassau County
[NORTH MERRICK] **BELLMORE-MERRICK CENTRAL HIGH S.D.**
1260 MEADOWBROOK RD ● NORTH MERRICK NY 11566-9998 ● (516) 623-8900

Grade Span: 07-12 **Schools**: *Regular* 5 ● *Spec Ed* 0 ● *Alt* 0 **Students**: 4,788 **Total Teachers**: 307 **Student/Classroom Teacher Ratio**: 17.1	**Expenditures/Student**: $11,861 **Librarians**: 4.9 977 students/librarian **Guidance Counselors**: 18.7 256 students/counselor	**% Amer Indian**: 0.0 **% Asian**: 2.8 **% Black**: 1.4 **% Hispanic**: 2.4 **% White**: 93.4	National ***Socio-Economic Status*** indicator percentile (100=high): 99th

Nassau County
OCEANSIDE UNION FREE S.D.
145 MERLE AVE ● OCEANSIDE NY 11572-2206 ● (516) 678-1215

Grade Span: KG-12 **Schools**: *Regular* 8 ● *Spec Ed* 0 ● *Alt* 0 **Students**: 5,583 **Total Teachers**: 375 **Student/Classroom Teacher Ratio**: 17.5	**Expenditures/Student**: $10,215 **Librarians**: 7.5 744 students/librarian **Guidance Counselors**: 13.0 429 students/counselor	**% Amer Indian**: 0.0 **% Asian**: 2.3 **% Black**: 0.5 **% Hispanic**: 7.0 **% White**: 90.1	National ***Socio-Economic Status*** indicator percentile (100=high): 93rd

Nassau County
[OLD WESTBURY] **WESTBURY UNION FREE S.D.**
2 HITCHCOCK LN ● OLD WESTBURY NY 11568-1624 ● (516) 876-5016

Grade Span: PK-12 **Schools**: *Regular* 5 ● *Spec Ed* 0 ● *Alt* 0 **Students**: 3,184 **Total Teachers**: 222 **Student/Classroom Teacher Ratio**: 14.7	**Expenditures/Student**: $11,934 **Librarians**: 3.5 910 students/librarian **Guidance Counselors**: 9.2 346 students/counselor	**% Amer Indian**: 1.8 **% Asian**: 1.5 **% Black**: 57.9 **% Hispanic**: 29.2 **% White**: 9.7	National ***Socio-Economic Status*** indicator percentile (100=high): 18th

Nassau County
PLAINVIEW-OLD BETHPAGE CENTRAL S.D.
85 JAMAICA AVE ● PLAINVIEW NY 11803-3612 ● (516) 937-6301

Grade Span: KG-12 **Schools**: *Regular* 6 ● *Spec Ed* 0 ● *Alt* 0 **Students**: 4,375 **Total Teachers**: 335 **Student/Classroom Teacher Ratio**: 14.3	**Expenditures/Student**: $11,811 **Librarians**: 6.4 684 students/librarian **Guidance Counselors**: 13.0 337 students/counselor	**% Amer Indian**: 0.0 **% Asian**: 4.0 **% Black**: 0.3 **% Hispanic**: 1.4 **% White**: 94.3	National ***Socio-Economic Status*** indicator percentile (100=high): 99th

Nassau County
PORT WASHINGTON UNION FREE S.D.
100 CAMPUS DR ● PORT WASHINGTON NY 11050-3719 ● (516) 767-4326 ● http://www.portnet.k12.ny.us

Grade Span: KG-12 **Schools**: *Regular* 6 ● *Spec Ed* 0 ● *Alt* 0 **Students**: 3,908 **Total Teachers**: 332 **Student/Classroom Teacher Ratio**: 13.3	**Expenditures/Student**: $14,594 **Librarians**: 6.4 611 students/librarian **Guidance Counselors**: 13.2 296 students/counselor	**% Amer Indian**: 0.0 **% Asian**: 12.0 **% Black**: 2.7 **% Hispanic**: 14.5 **% White**: 70.8	National ***Socio-Economic Status*** indicator percentile (100=high): 85th

Nassau County

ROCKVILLE CENTRE UNION FREE S.D.

128 SHEPHERD ST ● ROCKVILLE CENTRE NY 11570-2298 ● (516) 255-8920

Grade Span: KG-12 **Schools**: *Regular* 7 ● *Spec Ed* 0 ● *Alt* 0 **Students**: 3,326 **Total Teachers**: 250 **Student/Classroom Teacher Ratio**: 15.2	**Expenditures/Student**: $11,075 **Librarians**: 3.0 1,109 students/librarian **Guidance Counselors**: 8.0 416 students/counselor	**% Amer Indian**: 0.1 **% Asian**: 2.2 **% Black**: 7.1 **% Hispanic**: 8.2 **% White**: 82.4	National ***Socio-Economic Status*** indicator percentile (100=high): 94th

Nassau County

ROOSEVELT UNION FREE S.D.

240 DENTON PL ● ROOSEVELT NY 11575 ● (516) 867-8616

Grade Span: PK-12 **Schools**: *Regular* 6 ● *Spec Ed* 0 ● *Alt* 0 **Students**: 2,928 **Total Teachers**: 186 **Student/Classroom Teacher Ratio**: 17.9	**Expenditures/Student**: $10,520 **Librarians**: 2.5 1,171 students/librarian **Guidance Counselors**: 4.0 732 students/counselor	**% Amer Indian**: 0.0 **% Asian**: 0.1 **% Black**: 90.4 **% Hispanic**: 9.3 **% White**: 0.3	National ***Socio-Economic Status*** indicator percentile (100=high): 13th

Nassau County

ROSLYN UNION FREE S.D.

HARBOR HILL RD ● ROSLYN NY 11576-1531 ● (516) 625-6303

Grade Span: PK-12 **Schools**: *Regular* 5 ● *Spec Ed* 0 ● *Alt* 0 **Students**: 2,670 **Total Teachers**: 207 **Student/Classroom Teacher Ratio**: 14.8	**Expenditures/Student**: $15,276 **Librarians**: 4.3 621 students/librarian **Guidance Counselors**: 9.0 297 students/counselor	**% Amer Indian**: 0.0 **% Asian**: 9.8 **% Black**: 6.4 **% Hispanic**: 3.4 **% White**: 80.4	National ***Socio-Economic Status*** indicator percentile (100=high): 91st

Nassau County

SYOSSET CENTRAL S.D.

99 PELL LN ● SYOSSET NY 11791-2998 ● (516) 364-5605 ● http://www.syosset.k12.ny.us

Grade Span: KG-12 **Schools**: *Regular* 10 ● *Spec Ed* 0 ● *Alt* 0 **Students**: 5,365 **Total Teachers**: 433 **Student/Classroom Teacher Ratio**: 14.5	**Expenditures/Student**: $12,631 **Librarians**: 10.8 497 students/librarian **Guidance Counselors**: 15.0 358 students/counselor	**% Amer Indian**: 0.0 **% Asian**: 13.3 **% Black**: 0.3 **% Hispanic**: 1.0 **% White**: 85.5	National ***Socio-Economic Status*** indicator percentile (100=high): na

Nassau County

UNIONDALE UNION FREE S.D.

933 GOODRICH ST ● UNIONDALE NY 11553-2499 ● (516) 560-8824

Grade Span: KG-12 **Schools**: *Regular* 8 ● *Spec Ed* 0 ● *Alt* 0 **Students**: 5,157 **Total Teachers**: 377 **Student/Classroom Teacher Ratio**: 14.2	**Expenditures/Student**: $12,722 **Librarians**: 7.4 697 students/librarian **Guidance Counselors**: 12.0 430 students/counselor	**% Amer Indian**: 0.0 **% Asian**: 1.6 **% Black**: 73.7 **% Hispanic**: 19.4 **% White**: 5.3	National ***Socio-Economic Status*** indicator percentile (100=high): 55th

Nassau County

VALLEY STREAM CENTRAL HIGH S.D.

ONE KENT RD ● VALLEY STREAM NY 11582-3007 ● (516) 872-5601

Grade Span: 07-12 **Schools**: *Regular* 4 ● *Spec Ed* 0 ● *Alt* 0 **Students**: 3,473 **Total Teachers**: 242 **Student/Classroom Teacher Ratio**: 15.8	**Expenditures/Student**: $12,277 **Librarians**: 4.0 868 students/librarian **Guidance Counselors**: 14.3 243 students/counselor	**% Amer Indian**: 0.0 **% Asian**: 8.6 **% Black**: 3.2 **% Hispanic**: 8.7 **% White**: 79.5	National ***Socio-Economic Status*** indicator percentile (100=high): 98th

Nassau County
WANTAGH UNION FREE S.D.
3301 BELTAGH AVE ● WANTAGH NY 11793-3395 ● (516) 679-6407

Grade Span: KG-12 **Schools**: *Regular* 5 ● *Spec Ed* 0 ● *Alt* 0 **Students**: 2,869 **Total Teachers**: 216 **Student/Classroom Teacher Ratio**: 16.3	**Expenditures/Student**: $10,319 **Librarians**: 5.4 531 students/librarian **Guidance Counselors**: 8.0 359 students/counselor	**% Amer Indian**: 0.0 **% Asian**: 2.0 **% Black**: 0.2 **% Hispanic**: 1.0 **% White**: 96.8	National ***Socio-Economic Status*** indicator percentile (100=high): 99th

Nassau County
[WOODMERE] **HEWLETT-WOODMERE UNION FREE S.D.**
1 JOHNSON PL ● WOODMERE NY 11598-1312 ● (516) 374-8100

Grade Span: PK-12 **Schools**: *Regular* 5 ● *Spec Ed* 0 ● *Alt* 0 **Students**: 3,206 **Total Teachers**: 232 **Student/Classroom Teacher Ratio**: 15.5	**Expenditures/Student**: $12,426 **Librarians**: 1.9 1,687 students/librarian **Guidance Counselors**: 8.5 377 students/counselor	**% Amer Indian**: 0.0 **% Asian**: 5.9 **% Black**: 0.8 **% Hispanic**: 5.1 **% White**: 88.2	National ***Socio-Economic Status*** indicator percentile (100=high): 94th

Niagara County
LOCKPORT CITY S.D.
130 BEATTIE AVE ● LOCKPORT NY 14094-5099 ● (716) 439-6411

Grade Span: PK-12 **Schools**: *Regular* 11 ● *Spec Ed* 0 ● *Alt* 0 **Students**: 6,456 **Total Teachers**: 421 **Student/Classroom Teacher Ratio**: 18.3	**Expenditures/Student**: $7,344 **Librarians**: 7.4 872 students/librarian **Guidance Counselors**: 12.0 538 students/counselor	**% Amer Indian**: 0.3 **% Asian**: 0.6 **% Black**: 9.3 **% Hispanic**: 1.9 **% White**: 87.9	National ***Socio-Economic Status*** indicator percentile (100=high): 57th

Niagara County
[LOCKPORT] **STARPOINT CENTRAL S.D.**
4363 MAPLETON RD ● LOCKPORT NY 14094-9623 ● (716) 625-7272

Grade Span: KG-12 **Schools**: *Regular* 3 ● *Spec Ed* 0 ● *Alt* 0 **Students**: 2,503 **Total Teachers**: 150 **Student/Classroom Teacher Ratio**: 18.9	**Expenditures/Student**: $7,407 **Librarians**: 2.7 927 students/librarian **Guidance Counselors**: 5.0 501 students/counselor	**% Amer Indian**: 0.2 **% Asian**: 0.7 **% Black**: 0.5 **% Hispanic**: 0.3 **% White**: 98.3	National ***Socio-Economic Status*** indicator percentile (100=high): 93rd

Niagara County
NIAGARA FALLS CITY S.D.
607 WALNUT AVE ● NIAGARA FALLS NY 14302-0399 ● (716) 286-4205 ● http://www.niagara.k12.ny.us

Grade Span: PK-12 **Schools**: *Regular* 14 ● *Spec Ed* 0 ● *Alt* 0 **Students**: 8,959 **Total Teachers**: 584 **Student/Classroom Teacher Ratio**: 17.7	**Expenditures/Student**: $8,954 **Librarians**: 8.2 1,093 students/librarian **Guidance Counselors**: 13.5 664 students/counselor	**% Amer Indian**: 3.1 **% Asian**: 0.6 **% Black**: 31.0 **% Hispanic**: 1.6 **% White**: 63.7	National ***Socio-Economic Status*** indicator percentile (100=high): 25th

Niagara County
NORTH TONAWANDA CITY S.D.
175 HUMPHREY ST ● NORTH TONAWANDA NY 14120-4097 ● (716) 694-3206

Grade Span: KG-12 **Schools**: *Regular* 9 ● *Spec Ed* 0 ● *Alt* 0 **Students**: 5,470 **Total Teachers**: 374 **Student/Classroom Teacher Ratio**: 15.4	**Expenditures/Student**: $8,185 **Librarians**: 7.5 729 students/librarian **Guidance Counselors**: 10.0 547 students/counselor	**% Amer Indian**: 0.0 **% Asian**: 0.2 **% Black**: 0.1 **% Hispanic**: 1.1 **% White**: 98.5	National ***Socio-Economic Status*** indicator percentile (100=high): 70th

Niagara County

[SANBORN] **NIAGARA-WHEATFIELD CENTRAL S.D.**

2794 SAUNDERS SETTLEM ● SANBORN NY 14132-9333 ● (716) 731-7342

Grade Span: PK-12 **Schools**: *Regular* 5 ● *Spec Ed* 0 ● *Alt* 0 **Students**: 3,942 **Total Teachers**: 251 **Student/Classroom Teacher Ratio**: 15.3	**Expenditures/Student**: $8,680 **Librarians**: 4.5 876 students/librarian **Guidance Counselors**: 9.0 438 students/counselor	**% Amer Indian**: 6.5 **% Asian**: 0.6 **% Black**: 1.8 **% Hispanic**: 0.3 **% White**: 90.7	National ***Socio-Economic Status*** indicator percentile (100=high): 69th

Niagara County

[YOUNGSTOWN] **LEWISTON-PORTER CENTRAL S.D.**

4061 CREEK RD ● YOUNGSTOWN NY 14174-9799 ● (716) 754-8281

Grade Span: KG-12 **Schools**: *Regular* 4 ● *Spec Ed* 0 ● *Alt* 0 **Students**: 2,656 **Total Teachers**: 181 **Student/Classroom Teacher Ratio**: 14.7	**Expenditures/Student**: $8,892 **Librarians**: 3.6 738 students/librarian **Guidance Counselors**: 5.2 511 students/counselor	**% Amer Indian**: 0.2 **% Asian**: 0.7 **% Black**: 0.4 **% Hispanic**: 0.9 **% White**: 97.9	National ***Socio-Economic Status*** indicator percentile (100=high): 88th

Oneida County

CAMDEN CENTRAL S.D.

51 THIRD ST ● CAMDEN NY 13316-1114 ● (315) 245-2500

Grade Span: KG-12 **Schools**: *Regular* 6 ● *Spec Ed* 0 ● *Alt* 0 **Students**: 2,961 **Total Teachers**: 200 **Student/Classroom Teacher Ratio**: 16.7	**Expenditures/Student**: $6,739 **Librarians**: 4.4 673 students/librarian **Guidance Counselors**: 7.0 423 students/counselor	**% Amer Indian**: 0.2 **% Asian**: 0.4 **% Black**: 1.0 **% Hispanic**: 0.7 **% White**: 97.7	National ***Socio-Economic Status*** indicator percentile (100=high): 37th

Oneida County

NEW HARTFORD CENTRAL S.D.

33 OXFORD RD ● NEW HARTFORD NY 13413-2699 ● (315) 738-9218

Grade Span: KG-12 **Schools**: *Regular* 5 ● *Spec Ed* 0 ● *Alt* 0 **Students**: 2,921 **Total Teachers**: 196 **Student/Classroom Teacher Ratio**: 16.9	**Expenditures/Student**: $7,879 **Librarians**: 4.7 621 students/librarian **Guidance Counselors**: 5.0 584 students/counselor	**% Amer Indian**: 0.0 **% Asian**: 3.9 **% Black**: 0.9 **% Hispanic**: 0.8 **% White**: 94.5	National ***Socio-Economic Status*** indicator percentile (100=high): 89th

Oneida County

ROME CITY S.D.

112 E THOMAS ST ● ROME NY 13440-5298 ● (315) 338-9100

Grade Span: PK-12 **Schools**: *Regular* 13 ● *Spec Ed* 0 ● *Alt* 0 **Students**: 6,636 **Total Teachers**: 515 **Student/Classroom Teacher Ratio**: 15.4	**Expenditures/Student**: $8,457 **Librarians**: 13.1 507 students/librarian **Guidance Counselors**: 19.2 346 students/counselor	**% Amer Indian**: 0.4 **% Asian**: 1.2 **% Black**: 5.7 **% Hispanic**: 2.5 **% White**: 90.2	National ***Socio-Economic Status*** indicator percentile (100=high): 41st

Oneida County

UTICA CITY S.D.

13 ELIZABETH ST ● UTICA NY 13501-2260 ● (315) 792-2222

Grade Span: KG-12 **Schools**: *Regular* 13 ● *Spec Ed* 0 ● *Alt* 0 **Students**: 8,151 **Total Teachers**: 566 **Student/Classroom Teacher Ratio**: 15.3	**Expenditures/Student**: $8,249 **Librarians**: 11.1 734 students/librarian **Guidance Counselors**: 14.0 582 students/counselor	**% Amer Indian**: 0.1 **% Asian**: 3.0 **% Black**: 26.4 **% Hispanic**: 8.9 **% White**: 61.8	National ***Socio-Economic Status*** indicator percentile (100=high): 10th

Oneida County

[VERONA] **SHERRILL CITY S.D.**

5275 STATE RT 31 ● VERONA NY 13478-0128 ● (315) 829-2520

Grade Span: KG-12 **Schools**: *Regular* 5 ● *Spec Ed* 0 ● *Alt* 0 **Students**: 2,551 **Total Teachers**: 165 **Student/Classroom Teacher Ratio**: 15.8	**Expenditures/Student**: $6,948 **Librarians**: 4.7 543 students/librarian **Guidance Counselors**: 4.0 638 students/counselor	**% Amer Indian**: 0.2 **% Asian**: 0.7 **% Black**: 0.4 **% Hispanic**: 0.2 **% White**: 98.6	National ***Socio-Economic Status*** indicator percentile (100=high): 64th

Oneida County

[YORKVILLE] **WHITESBORO CENTRAL S.D.**

67 WHITESBORO ST ● YORKVILLE NY 13495-0304 ● (315) 768-9700

Grade Span: KG-12 **Schools**: *Regular* 7 ● *Spec Ed* 0 ● *Alt* 0 **Students**: 3,972 **Total Teachers**: 271 **Student/Classroom Teacher Ratio**: 17.1	**Expenditures/Student**: $7,686 **Librarians**: 6.3 630 students/librarian **Guidance Counselors**: 7.0 567 students/counselor	**% Amer Indian**: 0.1 **% Asian**: 0.4 **% Black**: 0.6 **% Hispanic**: 0.2 **% White**: 98.8	National ***Socio-Economic Status*** indicator percentile (100=high): 87th

Onondaga County

BALDWINSVILLE CENTRAL S.D.

29 E ONEIDA ST ● BALDWINSVILLE NY 13027-2480 ● (315) 638-6043

Grade Span: KG-12 **Schools**: *Regular* 8 ● *Spec Ed* 0 ● *Alt* 0 **Students**: 5,833 **Total Teachers**: 371 **Student/Classroom Teacher Ratio**: 16.7	**Expenditures/Student**: $7,258 **Librarians**: 6.5 897 students/librarian **Guidance Counselors**: 12.0 486 students/counselor	**% Amer Indian**: 0.4 **% Asian**: 1.1 **% Black**: 1.4 **% Hispanic**: 0.3 **% White**: 96.7	National ***Socio-Economic Status*** indicator percentile (100=high): 83rd

Onondaga County

[CAMILLUS] **WEST GENESEE CENTRAL S.D.**

5525 IKE DIXON RD ● CAMILLUS NY 13031-9686 ● (315) 672-3120

Grade Span: KG-12 **Schools**: *Regular* 7 ● *Spec Ed* 0 ● *Alt* 0 **Students**: 5,042 **Total Teachers**: 312 **Student/Classroom Teacher Ratio**: 18.1	**Expenditures/Student**: $6,818 **Librarians**: 6.2 813 students/librarian **Guidance Counselors**: 11.0 458 students/counselor	**% Amer Indian**: 0.2 **% Asian**: 1.4 **% Black**: 1.1 **% Hispanic**: 0.2 **% White**: 97.2	National ***Socio-Economic Status*** indicator percentile (100=high): 88th

Onondaga County

[DEWITT] **JAMESVILLE-DEWITT CENTRAL S.D.**

EDINGER DR BOX 606 ● DEWITT NY 13214-0606 ● (315) 445-8304

Grade Span: KG-12 **Schools**: *Regular* 5 ● *Spec Ed* 0 ● *Alt* 0 **Students**: 2,504 **Total Teachers**: 192 **Student/Classroom Teacher Ratio**: 14.2	**Expenditures/Student**: $9,471 **Librarians**: 4.4 569 students/librarian **Guidance Counselors**: 5.0 501 students/counselor	**% Amer Indian**: 0.4 **% Asian**: 5.7 **% Black**: 7.4 **% Hispanic**: 0.5 **% White**: 85.9	National ***Socio-Economic Status*** indicator percentile (100=high): 83rd

Onondaga County

EAST SYRACUSE-MINOA CENTRAL S.D.

407 FREMONT RD ● EAST SYRACUSE NY 13057-2631 ● (315) 656-7201

Grade Span: PK-12 **Schools**: *Regular* 8 ● *Spec Ed* 0 ● *Alt* 0 **Students**: 4,223 **Total Teachers**: 295 **Student/Classroom Teacher Ratio**: 19.1	**Expenditures/Student**: $8,826 **Librarians**: 6.0 704 students/librarian **Guidance Counselors**: 9.5 445 students/counselor	**% Amer Indian**: 0.4 **% Asian**: 1.3 **% Black**: 1.3 **% Hispanic**: 0.4 **% White**: 96.5	National ***Socio-Economic Status*** indicator percentile (100=high): 69th

Onondaga County
LIVERPOOL CENTRAL S.D.
800 FOURTH ST ● LIVERPOOL NY 13088-4497 ● (315) 453-0225 ● http://www.liverpool.k12.ny.us

Grade Span: PK-12 **Schools**: *Regular* 16 ● *Spec Ed* 0 ● *Alt* 0 **Students**: 9,530 **Total Teachers**: 617 **Student/Classroom Teacher Ratio**: 16.0	**Expenditures/Student**: $7,617 **Librarians**: 12.9 739 students/librarian **Guidance Counselors**: 26.5 360 students/counselor	**% Amer Indian**: 0.4 **% Asian**: 2.5 **% Black**: 5.2 **% Hispanic**: 0.8 **% White**: 91.2	National ***Socio-Economic Status*** indicator percentile (100=high): 81st

Onondaga County
[MANLIUS] **FAYETTEVILLE-MANLIUS CENTRAL S.D.**
8199 E SENECA TPKE ● MANLIUS NY 13104-2140 ● (315) 682-1200

Grade Span: KG-12 **Schools**: *Regular* 6 ● *Spec Ed* 0 ● *Alt* 0 **Students**: 4,141 **Total Teachers**: 284 **Student/Classroom Teacher Ratio**: 16.5	**Expenditures/Student**: $7,720 **Librarians**: 6.4 647 students/librarian **Guidance Counselors**: 13.0 319 students/counselor	**% Amer Indian**: 0.1 **% Asian**: 4.1 **% Black**: 1.4 **% Hispanic**: 0.6 **% White**: 93.8	National ***Socio-Economic Status*** indicator percentile (100=high): 96th

Onondaga County
NORTH SYRACUSE CENTRAL S.D.
5355 W TAFT RD ● NORTH SYRACUSE NY 13212-2796 ● (315) 452-3128

Grade Span: PK-12 **Schools**: *Regular* 11 ● *Spec Ed* 0 ● *Alt* 0 **Students**: 10,037 **Total Teachers**: 672 **Student/Classroom Teacher Ratio**: 16.1	**Expenditures/Student**: $7,850 **Librarians**: 11.2 896 students/librarian **Guidance Counselors**: 15.9 631 students/counselor	**% Amer Indian**: 0.7 **% Asian**: 1.1 **% Black**: 1.8 **% Hispanic**: 0.6 **% White**: 95.8	National ***Socio-Economic Status*** indicator percentile (100=high): 80th

Onondaga County
SYRACUSE CITY S.D.
725 HARRISON ST ● SYRACUSE NY 13210-2325 ● (315) 435-4161 ● http://www.scsd.k12.ny.us

Grade Span: PK-12 **Schools**: *Regular* 35 ● *Spec Ed* 1 ● *Alt* 0 **Students**: 23,573 **Total Teachers**: 1,701 **Student/Classroom Teacher Ratio**: 14.5	**Expenditures/Student**: $8,645 **Librarians**: 28.9 816 students/librarian **Guidance Counselors**: 41.0 575 students/counselor	**% Amer Indian**: 1.1 **% Asian**: 1.9 **% Black**: 41.4 **% Hispanic**: 4.6 **% White**: 50.9	National ***Socio-Economic Status*** indicator percentile (100=high): 9th

Ontario County
CANANDAIGUA CITY S.D.
143 N PEARL ST ● CANANDAIGUA NY 14424-1496 ● (716) 396-3700

Grade Span: KG-12 **Schools**: *Regular* 4 ● *Spec Ed* 0 ● *Alt* 0 **Students**: 4,194 **Total Teachers**: 294 **Student/Classroom Teacher Ratio**: 14.8	**Expenditures/Student**: $7,439 **Librarians**: 3.8 1,104 students/librarian **Guidance Counselors**: 9.6 437 students/counselor	**% Amer Indian**: 0.4 **% Asian**: 1.1 **% Black**: 1.5 **% Hispanic**: 0.8 **% White**: 96.2	National ***Socio-Economic Status*** indicator percentile (100=high): 76th

Ontario County
VICTOR CENTRAL S.D.
953 HIGH ST ● VICTOR NY 14564-1167 ● (716) 924-3252 ● http://www.victor.k12.ny.us

Grade Span: PK-12 **Schools**: *Regular* 4 ● *Spec Ed* 0 ● *Alt* 0 **Students**: 3,102 **Total Teachers**: 216 **Student/Classroom Teacher Ratio**: 14.3	**Expenditures/Student**: $7,926 **Librarians**: 3.8 816 students/librarian **Guidance Counselors**: 7.0 443 students/counselor	**% Amer Indian**: 0.1 **% Asian**: 1.7 **% Black**: 1.1 **% Hispanic**: 0.9 **% White**: 96.1	National ***Socio-Economic Status*** indicator percentile (100=high): 87th

Orange County

[CENTRAL VALLEY] **MONROE-WOODBURY CENTRAL S.D.**

EDUCATION CTR RT 32 ● CENTRAL VALLEY NY 10917-1001 ● (914) 928-2321 ● http://mw.k12.ny.us

Grade Span: KG-12	**Expenditures/Student**: $9,752	**% Amer Indian**: 0.3	
Schools: *Regular* 8 ● *Spec Ed* 0 ● *Alt* 0	**Librarians**: 7.9	**% Asian**: 3.0	National ***Socio-Economic***
Students: 5,806	735 students/librarian	**% Black**: 2.1	***Status*** indicator percentile
Total Teachers: 382	**Guidance Counselors**: 9.5	**% Hispanic**: 6.3	(100=high): 91st
Student/Classroom Teacher Ratio: 17.4	611 students/counselor	**% White**: 88.4	

Orange County

CORNWALL CENTRAL S.D.

130 MAIN ST ● CORNWALL NY 12518-1531 ● (914) 534-8009

Grade Span: KG-12	**Expenditures/Student**: $7,346	**% Amer Indian**: 0.1	
Schools: *Regular* 4 ● *Spec Ed* 0 ● *Alt* 0	**Librarians**: 3.8	**% Asian**: 1.2	National ***Socio-Economic***
Students: 2,596	683 students/librarian	**% Black**: 1.5	***Status*** indicator percentile
Total Teachers: 155	**Guidance Counselors**: 4.0	**% Hispanic**: 4.4	(100=high): 90th
Student/Classroom Teacher Ratio: 17.8	649 students/counselor	**% White**: 92.9	

Orange County

MIDDLETOWN CITY S.D.

223 WISNER AVE EXT ● MIDDLETOWN NY 10940-3240 ● (914) 341-5690

Grade Span: KG-12	**Expenditures/Student**: $9,008	**% Amer Indian**: 0.2	
Schools: *Regular* 10 ● *Spec Ed* 0 ● *Alt* 0	**Librarians**: 3.7	**% Asian**: 2.2	National ***Socio-Economic***
Students: 5,716	1,545 students/librarian	**% Black**: 19.4	***Status*** indicator percentile
Total Teachers: 356	**Guidance Counselors**: 9.0	**% Hispanic**: 21.5	(100=high): 26th
Student/Classroom Teacher Ratio: 18.7	635 students/counselor	**% White**: 56.7	

Orange County

[MONTGOMERY] **VALLEY CENTRAL S.D.**

944 RT 17K ● MONTGOMERY NY 12549-2240 ● (914) 457-3030

Grade Span: KG-12	**Expenditures/Student**: $6,874	**% Amer Indian**: 0.6	
Schools: *Regular* 7 ● *Spec Ed* 0 ● *Alt* 0	**Librarians**: 5.4	**% Asian**: 1.1	National ***Socio-Economic***
Students: 4,689	868 students/librarian	**% Black**: 3.8	***Status*** indicator percentile
Total Teachers: 295	**Guidance Counselors**: 9.0	**% Hispanic**: 5.5	(100=high): 63rd
Student/Classroom Teacher Ratio: 17.4	521 students/counselor	**% White**: 89.1	

Orange County

NEWBURGH CITY S.D.

124 GRAND ST ● NEWBURGH NY 12550-4600 ● (914) 563-7221

Grade Span: PK-12	**Expenditures/Student**: $8,240	**% Amer Indian**: 0.0	
Schools: *Regular* 15 ● *Spec Ed* 0 ● *Alt* 0	**Librarians**: 12.0	**% Asian**: 1.7	National ***Socio-Economic***
Students: 11,731	978 students/librarian	**% Black**: 28.8	***Status*** indicator percentile
Total Teachers: 792	**Guidance Counselors**: 18.0	**% Hispanic**: 23.7	(100=high): 24th
Student/Classroom Teacher Ratio: 15.7	652 students/counselor	**% White**: 45.9	

Orange County

PINE BUSH CENTRAL S.D.

RT 302 ● PINE BUSH NY 12566-0700 ● (914) 744-2031

Grade Span: KG-12	**Expenditures/Student**: $7,484	**% Amer Indian**: 0.2	
Schools: *Regular* 7 ● *Spec Ed* 0 ● *Alt* 0	**Librarians**: 6.4	**% Asian**: 1.6	National ***Socio-Economic***
Students: 5,674	887 students/librarian	**% Black**: 4.7	***Status*** indicator percentile
Total Teachers: 358	**Guidance Counselors**: 10.0	**% Hispanic**: 5.0	(100=high): 70th
Student/Classroom Teacher Ratio: 16.1	567 students/counselor	**% White**: 88.6	

Orange County
PORT JERVIS CITY S.D.
9 THOMPSON ST ● PORT JERVIS NY 12771-3058 ● (914) 858-3175 ● http://www.portjerviscsd.k12.ny.us

Grade Span: KG-12	**Expenditures/Student**: $6,841	**% Amer Indian**: 0.3	
Schools: *Regular* 5 ● *Spec Ed* 0 ● *Alt* 0	**Librarians**: 4.3	**% Asian**: 0.9	National ***Socio-Economic***
Students: 3,528	820 students/librarian	**% Black**: 3.6	***Status*** indicator percentile
Total Teachers: 198	**Guidance Counselors**: 2.0	**% Hispanic**: 4.4	(100=high): 41st
Student/Classroom Teacher Ratio: 19.2	1,764 students/counselor	**% White**: 90.8	

Orange County
[SLATE HILL] MINISINK VALLEY CENTRAL S.D.
RT 6 ● SLATE HILL NY 10973-0217 ● (914) 355-5110

Grade Span: KG-12	**Expenditures/Student**: $7,384	**% Amer Indian**: 0.2	
Schools: *Regular* 5 ● *Spec Ed* 0 ● *Alt* 0	**Librarians**: 3.6	**% Asian**: 0.7	National ***Socio-Economic***
Students: 3,808	1,058 students/librarian	**% Black**: 2.2	***Status*** indicator percentile
Total Teachers: 230	**Guidance Counselors**: 5.0	**% Hispanic**: 3.9	(100=high): 76th
Student/Classroom Teacher Ratio: 17.9	762 students/counselor	**% White**: 93.0	

Orange County
WARWICK VALLEY CENTRAL S.D.
P.O. BOX 595 ● WARWICK NY 10990-0595 ● (914) 987-3010 ● http://www.warwickvalleyschools.com

Grade Span: KG-12	**Expenditures/Student**: $7,718	**% Amer Indian**: 0.1	
Schools: *Regular* 5 ● *Spec Ed* 0 ● *Alt* 0	**Librarians**: 4.4	**% Asian**: 1.2	National ***Socio-Economic***
Students: 3,765	856 students/librarian	**% Black**: 4.4	***Status*** indicator percentile
Total Teachers: 237	**Guidance Counselors**: 6.0	**% Hispanic**: 5.4	(100=high): 90th
Student/Classroom Teacher Ratio: 17.4	628 students/counselor	**% White**: 88.8	

Orange County
WASHINGTONVILLE CENTRAL S.D.
52 W MAIN ST ● WASHINGTONVILLE NY 10992-1492 ● (914) 496-2221 ● http://www.wcsd.mhrcc.org

Grade Span: KG-12	**Expenditures/Student**: $7,269	**% Amer Indian**: 0.3	
Schools: *Regular* 5 ● *Spec Ed* 0 ● *Alt* 0	**Librarians**: 5.0	**% Asian**: 1.4	National ***Socio-Economic***
Students: 4,701	940 students/librarian	**% Black**: 5.2	***Status*** indicator percentile
Total Teachers: 275	**Guidance Counselors**: 11.0	**% Hispanic**: 4.9	(100=high): 88th
Student/Classroom Teacher Ratio: 18.7	427 students/counselor	**% White**: 88.2	

Orleans County
ALBION CENTRAL S.D.
324 EAST AVE ● ALBION NY 14411-1697 ● (716) 589-6656 ● http://www.albion.wnyric.org

Grade Span: KG-12	**Expenditures/Student**: $6,731	**% Amer Indian**: 0.7	
Schools: *Regular* 3 ● *Spec Ed* 0 ● *Alt* 0	**Librarians**: 2.8	**% Asian**: 0.5	National ***Socio-Economic***
Students: 2,764	987 students/librarian	**% Black**: 7.3	***Status*** indicator percentile
Total Teachers: 178	**Guidance Counselors**: 6.0	**% Hispanic**: 2.7	(100=high): 45th
Student/Classroom Teacher Ratio: 15.9	461 students/counselor	**% White**: 88.6	

Oswego County
CENTRAL SQUARE CENTRAL S.D.
642 S MAIN ST ● CENTRAL SQUARE NY 13036-9785 ● (315) 668-4220 ● http://www.centralsquareschools.org

Grade Span: KG-12	**Expenditures/Student**: $7,471	**% Amer Indian**: 0.3	
Schools: *Regular* 8 ● *Spec Ed* 0 ● *Alt* 0	**Librarians**: 6.1	**% Asian**: 0.2	National ***Socio-Economic***
Students: 4,905	804 students/librarian	**% Black**: 0.4	***Status*** indicator percentile
Total Teachers: 278	**Guidance Counselors**: 8.0	**% Hispanic**: 0.2	(100=high): 61st
Student/Classroom Teacher Ratio: 19.5	613 students/counselor	**% White**: 98.9	

Oswego County
FULTON CITY S.D.
167 S FOURTH ST ● FULTON NY 13069-1859 ● (315) 593-5510

Grade Span: KG-12 **Schools**: *Regular* 6 ● *Spec Ed* 0 ● *Alt* 0 **Students**: 4,171 **Total Teachers**: 270 **Student/Classroom Teacher Ratio**: 16.3	**Expenditures/Student**: $7,616 **Librarians**: 6.0 695 students/librarian **Guidance Counselors**: 6.0 695 students/counselor	**% Amer Indian**: 0.2 **% Asian**: 0.5 **% Black**: 0.8 **% Hispanic**: 1.5 **% White**: 97.0	National ***Socio-Economic Status*** indicator percentile (100=high): 46th

Oswego County
MEXICO CENTRAL S.D.
40 ACADEMY ST ● MEXICO NY 13114 ● (315) 963-7831

Grade Span: KG-12 **Schools**: *Regular* 5 ● *Spec Ed* 0 ● *Alt* 0 **Students**: 2,781 **Total Teachers**: 177 **Student/Classroom Teacher Ratio**: 17.1	**Expenditures/Student**: $6,996 **Librarians**: 2.0 1,391 students/librarian **Guidance Counselors**: 5.0 556 students/counselor	**% Amer Indian**: 0.5 **% Asian**: 0.6 **% Black**: 0.4 **% Hispanic**: 0.6 **% White**: 97.9	National ***Socio-Economic Status*** indicator percentile (100=high): 59th

Oswego County
OSWEGO CITY S.D.
120 E 1ST ST ● OSWEGO NY 13126-2114 ● (315) 341-5885 ● http://oswego.org

Grade Span: KG-12 **Schools**: *Regular* 8 ● *Spec Ed* 0 ● *Alt* 0 **Students**: 5,298 **Total Teachers**: 365 **Student/Classroom Teacher Ratio**: 15.2	**Expenditures/Student**: $9,423 **Librarians**: 7.4 716 students/librarian **Guidance Counselors**: 10.5 505 students/counselor	**% Amer Indian**: 0.1 **% Asian**: 1.0 **% Black**: 0.7 **% Hispanic**: 2.5 **% White**: 95.6	National ***Socio-Economic Status*** indicator percentile (100=high): 60th

Oswego County
PHOENIX CENTRAL S.D.
400 VOLNEY ST ● PHOENIX NY 13135-9778 ● (315) 695-1511

Grade Span: KG-12 **Schools**: *Regular* 4 ● *Spec Ed* 0 ● *Alt* 0 **Students**: 2,705 **Total Teachers**: 175 **Student/Classroom Teacher Ratio**: 14.3	**Expenditures/Student**: $7,361 **Librarians**: 3.6 751 students/librarian **Guidance Counselors**: 6.0 451 students/counselor	**% Amer Indian**: 0.4 **% Asian**: 0.5 **% Black**: 0.4 **% Hispanic**: 0.6 **% White**: 98.1	National ***Socio-Economic Status*** indicator percentile (100=high): 66th

Putnam County
BREWSTER CENTRAL S.D.
FARM-TO-MARKET RD ● BREWSTER NY 10509-9806 ● (914) 279-8000

Grade Span: KG-12 **Schools**: *Regular* 4 ● *Spec Ed* 0 ● *Alt* 0 **Students**: 3,051 **Total Teachers**: 214 **Student/Classroom Teacher Ratio**: 15.5	**Expenditures/Student**: $10,609 **Librarians**: 3.7 825 students/librarian **Guidance Counselors**: 7.0 436 students/counselor	**% Amer Indian**: 0.0 **% Asian**: 0.9 **% Black**: 2.7 **% Hispanic**: 4.1 **% White**: 92.3	National ***Socio-Economic Status*** indicator percentile (100=high): 85th

Putnam County
MAHOPAC CENTRAL S.D.
179 EAST LAKE BLVD ● MAHOPAC NY 10541-1601 ● (914) 628-3415

Grade Span: KG-12 **Schools**: *Regular* 5 ● *Spec Ed* 0 ● *Alt* 0 **Students**: 4,388 **Total Teachers**: 295 **Student/Classroom Teacher Ratio**: 16.0	**Expenditures/Student**: $10,206 **Librarians**: 2.0 2,194 students/librarian **Guidance Counselors**: 8.0 549 students/counselor	**% Amer Indian**: 0.0 **% Asian**: 1.5 **% Black**: 0.8 **% Hispanic**: 2.7 **% White**: 94.9	National ***Socio-Economic Status*** indicator percentile (100=high): 97th

Putnam County

[PATTERSON] **CARMEL CENTRAL S.D.**

SOUTH ST ● PATTERSON NY 12563-0296 ● (914) 878-2094

Grade Span: KG-12	**Expenditures/Student**: $10,215	**% Amer Indian**: 0.1	
Schools: *Regular* 5 ● *Spec Ed* 0 ● *Alt* 0	**Librarians**: 2.1	**% Asian**: 0.7	National ***Socio-Economic***
Students: 4,486	2,136 students/librarian	**% Black**: 1.4	***Status*** indicator percentile
Total Teachers: 294	**Guidance Counselors**: 6.6	**% Hispanic**: 2.9	(100=high): 92nd
Student/Classroom Teacher Ratio: 16.4	680 students/counselor	**% White**: 94.8	

Rensselaer County

AVERILL PARK CENTRAL S.D.

146 GETTLE RD ● AVERILL PARK NY 12018-9798 ● (518) 674-3816

Grade Span: KG-12	**Expenditures/Student**: $na	**% Amer Indian**: 0.0	
Schools: *Regular* 6 ● *Spec Ed* 0 ● *Alt* 0	**Librarians**: 4.3	**% Asian**: 0.5	National ***Socio-Economic***
Students: 3,327	774 students/librarian	**% Black**: 0.5	***Status*** indicator percentile
Total Teachers: 204	**Guidance Counselors**: 6.5	**% Hispanic**: 0.0	(100=high): 83rd
Student/Classroom Teacher Ratio: 17.6	512 students/counselor	**% White**: 99.0	

Rensselaer County

EAST GREENBUSH CENTRAL S.D.

673 COLUMBIA TPKE ● EAST GREENBUSH NY 12061-2213 ● (518) 477-2755

Grade Span: KG-12	**Expenditures/Student**: $8,159	**% Amer Indian**: 0.1	
Schools: *Regular* 7 ● *Spec Ed* 0 ● *Alt* 0	**Librarians**: 4.9	**% Asian**: 1.2	National ***Socio-Economic***
Students: 4,547	928 students/librarian	**% Black**: 2.3	***Status*** indicator percentile
Total Teachers: 285	**Guidance Counselors**: 7.0	**% Hispanic**: 0.8	(100=high): 87th
Student/Classroom Teacher Ratio: 16.9	650 students/counselor	**% White**: 95.6	

Rensselaer County

TROY CITY S.D.

1728 TIBBITS AVE ● TROY NY 12180-7013 ● (518) 271-5210

Grade Span: PK-12	**Expenditures/Student**: $9,618	**% Amer Indian**: 0.1	
Schools: *Regular* 8 ● *Spec Ed* 0 ● *Alt* 1	**Librarians**: 6.1	**% Asian**: 2.8	National ***Socio-Economic***
Students: 5,050	828 students/librarian	**% Black**: 19.6	***Status*** indicator percentile
Total Teachers: 370	**Guidance Counselors**: 14.0	**% Hispanic**: 4.3	(100=high): 19th
Student/Classroom Teacher Ratio: 16.2	361 students/counselor	**% White**: 73.1	

Rockland County

[BLAUVELT] **SOUTH ORANGETOWN CENTRAL S.D.**

160 VAN WYCK RD ● BLAUVELT NY 10913-1299 ● (914) 365-4200

Grade Span: KG-12	**Expenditures/Student**: $13,800	**% Amer Indian**: 0.0	
Schools: *Regular* 5 ● *Spec Ed* 0 ● *Alt* 0	**Librarians**: 3.7	**% Asian**: 15.2	National ***Socio-Economic***
Students: 2,603	704 students/librarian	**% Black**: 2.3	***Status*** indicator percentile
Total Teachers: 218	**Guidance Counselors**: 5.0	**% Hispanic**: 5.7	(100=high): 95th
Student/Classroom Teacher Ratio: 13.9	521 students/counselor	**% White**: 76.8	

Rockland County

[GARNERVILLE] **HAVERSTRAW-STONY POINT CENTRAL S.D.**

65 CHAPEL ST ● GARNERVILLE NY 10923-1280 ● (914) 942-3001

Grade Span: PK-12	**Expenditures/Student**: $11,733	**% Amer Indian**: 0.2	
Schools: *Regular* 8 ● *Spec Ed* 0 ● *Alt* 0	**Librarians**: 7.3	**% Asian**: 2.6	National ***Socio-Economic***
Students: 7,398	1,013 students/librarian	**% Black**: 9.0	***Status*** indicator percentile
Total Teachers: 479	**Guidance Counselors**: 12.0	**% Hispanic**: 30.3	(100=high): 56th
Student/Classroom Teacher Ratio: 17.5	617 students/counselor	**% White**: 58.0	

Rockland County

[HILLBURN] **RAMAPO CENTRAL S.D.**

45 MOUNTAIN AVE ● HILLBURN NY 10931-0935 ● (914) 357-7783

Grade Span: KG-12 **Schools**: *Regular* 7 ● *Spec Ed* 0 ● *Alt* 0 **Students**: 3,998 **Total Teachers**: 293 **Student/Classroom Teacher Ratio**: 15.4	**Expenditures/Student**: $12,431 **Librarians**: 6.8 588 students/librarian **Guidance Counselors**: 5.8 689 students/counselor	**% Amer Indian**: 1.8 **% Asian**: 2.9 **% Black**: 5.4 **% Hispanic**: 6.7 **% White**: 83.2	National ***Socio-Economic Status*** indicator percentile (100=high): 89th

Rockland County

NYACK UNION FREE S.D.

13A DICKINSON AVE ● NYACK NY 10960-2914 ● (914) 353-7010

Grade Span: KG-12 **Schools**: *Regular* 5 ● *Spec Ed* 0 ● *Alt* 0 **Students**: 3,082 **Total Teachers**: 209 **Student/Classroom Teacher Ratio**: 17.0	**Expenditures/Student**: $11,990 **Librarians**: 3.8 811 students/librarian **Guidance Counselors**: 8.2 376 students/counselor	**% Amer Indian**: 0.0 **% Asian**: 5.8 **% Black**: 30.6 **% Hispanic**: 4.6 **% White**: 59.0	National ***Socio-Economic Status*** indicator percentile (100=high): 62nd

Rockland County

[SPRING VALLEY] **EAST RAMAPO CENTRAL S.D.**

105 S MADISON AVE ● SPRING VALLEY NY 10977-5400 ● (914) 577-6011

Grade Span: KG-12 **Schools**: *Regular* 15 ● *Spec Ed* 0 ● *Alt* 0 **Students**: 8,883 **Total Teachers**: 617 **Student/Classroom Teacher Ratio**: 16.6	**Expenditures/Student**: $13,046 **Librarians**: 4.9 1,813 students/librarian **Guidance Counselors**: 18.0 494 students/counselor	**% Amer Indian**: 0.2 **% Asian**: 9.4 **% Black**: 48.2 **% Hispanic**: 8.3 **% White**: 33.9	National ***Socio-Economic Status*** indicator percentile (100=high): 50th

Rockland County

[WEST NYACK] **CLARKSTOWN CENTRAL S.D.**

30 PARROTT RD ● WEST NYACK NY 10994-1045 ● (914) 639-6418 ● http://www.ccsd.edu

Grade Span: KG-12 **Schools**: *Regular* 13 ● *Spec Ed* 1 ● *Alt* 0 **Students**: 8,475 **Total Teachers**: 610 **Student/Classroom Teacher Ratio**: 16.7	**Expenditures/Student**: $9,792 **Librarians**: 12.6 673 students/librarian **Guidance Counselors**: 18.5 458 students/counselor	**% Amer Indian**: 0.1 **% Asian**: 8.1 **% Black**: 2.6 **% Hispanic**: 4.6 **% White**: 84.6	National ***Socio-Economic Status*** indicator percentile (100=high): 97th

St. Lawrence County

MASSENA CENTRAL S.D.

290 MAIN ST ● MASSENA NY 13662-1999 ● (315) 769-2471

Grade Span: KG-12 **Schools**: *Regular* 6 ● *Spec Ed* 0 ● *Alt* 0 **Students**: 3,033 **Total Teachers**: 196 **Student/Classroom Teacher Ratio**: 17.7	**Expenditures/Student**: $7,117 **Librarians**: 2.8 1,083 students/librarian **Guidance Counselors**: 8.7 349 students/counselor	**% Amer Indian**: 4.0 **% Asian**: 0.5 **% Black**: 0.2 **% Hispanic**: 0.4 **% White**: 94.9	National ***Socio-Economic Status*** indicator percentile (100=high): 50th

Saratoga County

BALLSTON SPA CENTRAL S.D.

70 MALTA AVE ● BALLSTON SPA NY 12020-1599 ● (518) 884-7110

Grade Span: KG-12 **Schools**: *Regular* 5 ● *Spec Ed* 0 ● *Alt* 0 **Students**: 3,930 **Total Teachers**: 241 **Student/Classroom Teacher Ratio**: 17.6	**Expenditures/Student**: $9,035 **Librarians**: 4.6 854 students/librarian **Guidance Counselors**: 7.0 561 students/counselor	**% Amer Indian**: 0.2 **% Asian**: 0.7 **% Black**: 1.0 **% Hispanic**: 0.7 **% White**: 97.5	National ***Socio-Economic Status*** indicator percentile (100=high): 71st

Saratoga County

[CLIFTON PARK] **SHENENDEHOWA CENTRAL S.D.**

ONE FAIRCHILD SQ ● CLIFTON PARK NY 12065-1254 ● (518) 877-6251

Grade Span: KG-12 **Schools**: *Regular* 11 ● *Spec Ed* 0 ● *Alt* 0 **Students**: 8,961 **Total Teachers**: 551 **Student/Classroom Teacher Ratio**: 17.7	**Expenditures/Student**: $7,851 **Librarians**: 11.8 759 students/librarian **Guidance Counselors**: 22.0 407 students/counselor	**% Amer Indian**: 0.0 **% Asian**: 2.5 **% Black**: 1.7 **% Hispanic**: 0.6 **% White**: 95.2	National ***Socio-Economic Status*** indicator percentile (100=high): 93rd

Saratoga County

SARATOGA SPRINGS CITY S.D.

5-7 WELLS ST ● SARATOGA SPRINGS NY 12866 ● (518) 583-4708

Grade Span: KG-12 **Schools**: *Regular* 9 ● *Spec Ed* 0 ● *Alt* 0 **Students**: 6,883 **Total Teachers**: 470 **Student/Classroom Teacher Ratio**: 15.4	**Expenditures/Student**: $7,827 **Librarians**: 7.7 894 students/librarian **Guidance Counselors**: 8.0 860 students/counselor	**% Amer Indian**: 0.0 **% Asian**: 0.9 **% Black**: 3.5 **% Hispanic**: 0.9 **% White**: 94.6	National ***Socio-Economic Status*** indicator percentile (100=high): 79th

Saratoga County

[SCOTIA] **BURNT HILLS-BALLSTON LAKE CENTRAL S.D.**

50 CYPRESS DR ● SCOTIA NY 12302-4398 ● (518) 399-6407 ● http://www.crisny.org/communities/burnt.hills/schools/bhbl

Grade Span: KG-12 **Schools**: *Regular* 5 ● *Spec Ed* 0 ● *Alt* 0 **Students**: 3,361 **Total Teachers**: 203 **Student/Classroom Teacher Ratio**: 18.5	**Expenditures/Student**: $7,626 **Librarians**: 5.3 634 students/librarian **Guidance Counselors**: 6.0 560 students/counselor	**% Amer Indian**: 0.5 **% Asian**: 0.6 **% Black**: 0.6 **% Hispanic**: 0.5 **% White**: 97.8	National ***Socio-Economic Status*** indicator percentile (100=high): 96th

Saratoga County

SOUTH GLENS FALLS CENTRAL S.D.

6 BLUEBIRD RD ● SOUTH GLENS FALLS NY 12803-5704 ● (518) 793-9617

Grade Span: KG-12 **Schools**: *Regular* 6 ● *Spec Ed* 0 ● *Alt* 0 **Students**: 2,976 **Total Teachers**: 190 **Student/Classroom Teacher Ratio**: 17.5	**Expenditures/Student**: $7,803 **Librarians**: 2.8 1,063 students/librarian **Guidance Counselors**: 4.0 744 students/counselor	**% Amer Indian**: 0.2 **% Asian**: 0.3 **% Black**: 0.7 **% Hispanic**: 0.3 **% White**: 98.5	National ***Socio-Economic Status*** indicator percentile (100=high): 67th

Schenectady County

[SCHENECTADY] **NISKAYUNA CENTRAL S.D.**

1239 VAN ANTWERP RD ● SCHENECTADY NY 12309-5317 ● (518) 377-4666 ● http://www.wizvax.net/nisk_hs/district

Grade Span: KG-12 **Schools**: *Regular* 8 ● *Spec Ed* 0 ● *Alt* 0 **Students**: 3,996 **Total Teachers**: 264 **Student/Classroom Teacher Ratio**: 17.2	**Expenditures/Student**: $8,188 **Librarians**: 8.6 465 students/librarian **Guidance Counselors**: 7.0 571 students/counselor	**% Amer Indian**: 0.1 **% Asian**: 5.9 **% Black**: 1.5 **% Hispanic**: 0.9 **% White**: 91.7	National ***Socio-Economic Status*** indicator percentile (100=high): 99th

Schenectady County

[SCHENECTADY] **ROTTERDAM-MOHONASEN CENTRAL S.D.**

2072 CURRY RD ● SCHENECTADY NY 12303-4400 ● (518) 356-5063

Grade Span: KG-12 **Schools**: *Regular* 4 ● *Spec Ed* 0 ● *Alt* 0 **Students**: 3,031 **Total Teachers**: 169 **Student/Classroom Teacher Ratio**: 19.7	**Expenditures/Student**: $7,466 **Librarians**: 3.9 777 students/librarian **Guidance Counselors**: 6.0 505 students/counselor	**% Amer Indian**: 0.0 **% Asian**: 0.7 **% Black**: 1.1 **% Hispanic**: 0.6 **% White**: 97.6	National ***Socio-Economic Status*** indicator percentile (100=high): 84th

Schenectady County

SCHENECTADY CITY S.D.

108 EDUCATION DR ● SCHENECTADY NY 12303-3442 ● (518) 370-8100 ● http://www.global2000.net/school/scsd

Grade Span: PK-12 **Schools**: *Regular* 15 ● *Spec Ed* 0 ● *Alt* 0 **Students**: 8,184 **Total Teachers**: 588 **Student/Classroom Teacher Ratio**: 15.2	**Expenditures/Student**: $8,718 **Librarians**: 9.8 835 students/librarian **Guidance Counselors**: 17.5 468 students/counselor	**% Amer Indian**: 0.2 **% Asian**: 3.5 **% Black**: 24.2 **% Hispanic**: 7.7 **% White**: 64.4	National ***Socio-Economic Status*** indicator percentile (100=high): 19th

Schenectady County

SCOTIA-GLENVILLE CENTRAL S.D.

900 PREDDICE PKY ● SCOTIA NY 12302 ● (518) 382-1215

Grade Span: KG-12 **Schools**: *Regular* 6 ● *Spec Ed* 0 ● *Alt* 0 **Students**: 3,120 **Total Teachers**: 181 **Student/Classroom Teacher Ratio**: 20.9	**Expenditures/Student**: $7,457 **Librarians**: 4.2 743 students/librarian **Guidance Counselors**: 6.0 520 students/counselor	**% Amer Indian**: 0.1 **% Asian**: 1.2 **% Black**: 1.1 **% Hispanic**: 0.7 **% White**: 97.0	National ***Socio-Economic Status*** indicator percentile (100=high): 86th

Steuben County

[PAINTED POST] **CORNING CITY S.D.**

165 CHARLES ST ● PAINTED POST NY 14870-1199 ● (607) 936-3704

Grade Span: PK-12 **Schools**: *Regular* 13 ● *Spec Ed* 0 ● *Alt* 0 **Students**: 5,683 **Total Teachers**: 380 **Student/Classroom Teacher Ratio**: 17.0	**Expenditures/Student**: $8,076 **Librarians**: 8.5 669 students/librarian **Guidance Counselors**: 12.0 474 students/counselor	**% Amer Indian**: 0.1 **% Asian**: 1.1 **% Black**: 2.1 **% Hispanic**: 0.5 **% White**: 96.2	National ***Socio-Economic Status*** indicator percentile (100=high): 57th

Suffolk County

AMITYVILLE UNION FREE S.D.

150 PARK AVE ● AMITYVILLE NY 11701-3195 ● (516) 598-6507

Grade Span: PK-12 **Schools**: *Regular* 5 ● *Spec Ed* 0 ● *Alt* 0 **Students**: 2,959 **Total Teachers**: 217 **Student/Classroom Teacher Ratio**: 15.9	**Expenditures/Student**: $12,113 **Librarians**: 3.3 897 students/librarian **Guidance Counselors**: 6.0 493 students/counselor	**% Amer Indian**: 0.0 **% Asian**: 1.6 **% Black**: 64.7 **% Hispanic**: 12.8 **% White**: 21.0	National ***Socio-Economic Status*** indicator percentile (100=high): 15th

Suffolk County

BAY SHORE UNION FREE S.D.

75 W PERKAL ST ● BAY SHORE NY 11706-6642 ● (516) 968-1117 ● http://www.bayshore.k12.ny.us

Grade Span: KG-12 **Schools**: *Regular* 7 ● *Spec Ed* 0 ● *Alt* 0 **Students**: 4,940 **Total Teachers**: 339 **Student/Classroom Teacher Ratio**: 15.9	**Expenditures/Student**: $12,350 **Librarians**: 7.0 706 students/librarian **Guidance Counselors**: 8.0 618 students/counselor	**% Amer Indian**: 0.1 **% Asian**: 1.8 **% Black**: 22.2 **% Hispanic**: 18.5 **% White**: 57.4	National ***Socio-Economic Status*** indicator percentile (100=high): 44th

Suffolk County

[BOHEMIA] **CONNETQUOT CENTRAL S.D.**

780 OCEAN AVE ● BOHEMIA NY 11716-3629 ● (516) 244-2211 ● http://connetquot.k12.ny.us

Grade Span: PK-12 **Schools**: *Regular* 10 ● *Spec Ed* 0 ● *Alt* 0 **Students**: 6,681 **Total Teachers**: 480 **Student/Classroom Teacher Ratio**: 15.9	**Expenditures/Student**: $12,117 **Librarians**: 8.8 759 students/librarian **Guidance Counselors**: 11.1 602 students/counselor	**% Amer Indian**: 0.0 **% Asian**: 1.2 **% Black**: 0.7 **% Hispanic**: 2.8 **% White**: 95.3	National ***Socio-Economic Status*** indicator percentile (100=high): na

Suffolk County
BRENTWOOD UNION FREE S.D.
51 THIRD AVE ● BRENTWOOD NY 11717-6198 ● (516) 434-2325

Grade Span: PK-12 **Schools**: *Regular* 17 ● *Spec Ed* 0 ● *Alt* 0 **Students**: 13,045 **Total Teachers**: 795 **Student/Classroom Teacher Ratio**: 17.5	**Expenditures/Student**: $10,995 **Librarians**: 7.9 1,651 students/librarian **Guidance Counselors**: 27.0 483 students/counselor	**% Amer Indian**: 0.4 **% Asian**: 1.4 **% Black**: 18.9 **% Hispanic**: 47.5 **% White**: 31.8	National ***Socio-Economic Status*** indicator percentile (100=high): 13th

Suffolk County
[CENTEREACH] **MIDDLE COUNTRY CENTRAL S.D.**
8 43RD ST ● CENTEREACH NY 11720-2325 ● (516) 468-5514 ● http://www.middlecountry.k12.ny.us

Grade Span: PK-12 **Schools**: *Regular* 12 ● *Spec Ed* 1 ● *Alt* 0 **Students**: 10,871 **Total Teachers**: 641 **Student/Classroom Teacher Ratio**: 18.8	**Expenditures/Student**: $9,293 **Librarians**: 11.1 979 students/librarian **Guidance Counselors**: 16.0 679 students/counselor	**% Amer Indian**: 0.2 **% Asian**: 1.8 **% Black**: 2.6 **% Hispanic**: 5.6 **% White**: 89.9	National ***Socio-Economic Status*** indicator percentile (100=high): 83rd

Suffolk County
CENTRAL ISLIP UNION FREE S.D.
WHEELER RD ● CENTRAL ISLIP NY 11722-9027 ● (516) 348-5001

Grade Span: PK-12 **Schools**: *Regular* 7 ● *Spec Ed* 0 ● *Alt* 0 **Students**: 5,239 **Total Teachers**: 354 **Student/Classroom Teacher Ratio**: 17.8	**Expenditures/Student**: $13,031 **Librarians**: 5.1 1,027 students/librarian **Guidance Counselors**: 9.0 582 students/counselor	**% Amer Indian**: 0.5 **% Asian**: 2.2 **% Black**: 34.3 **% Hispanic**: 36.4 **% White**: 26.6	National ***Socio-Economic Status*** indicator percentile (100=high): 19th

Suffolk County
COMMACK UNION FREE S.D.
P.O. BOX 150 ● COMMACK NY 11725-0150 ● (516) 754-7210 ● http://www.longisland.com/commackufsd

Grade Span: KG-12 **Schools**: *Regular* 8 ● *Spec Ed* 0 ● *Alt* 0 **Students**: 5,784 **Total Teachers**: 389 **Student/Classroom Teacher Ratio**: 18.8	**Expenditures/Student**: $11,303 **Librarians**: 6.2 933 students/librarian **Guidance Counselors**: 11.2 516 students/counselor	**% Amer Indian**: 0.1 **% Asian**: 5.1 **% Black**: 0.8 **% Hispanic**: 1.9 **% White**: 92.0	National ***Socio-Economic Status*** indicator percentile (100=high): 99th

Suffolk County
COPIAGUE UNION FREE S.D.
2650 GREAT NECK RD ● COPIAGUE NY 11726-1699 ● (516) 842-4000

Grade Span: KG-12 **Schools**: *Regular* 5 ● *Spec Ed* 0 ● *Alt* 0 **Students**: 4,138 **Total Teachers**: 249 **Student/Classroom Teacher Ratio**: 19.0	**Expenditures/Student**: $9,881 **Librarians**: 3.7 1,118 students/librarian **Guidance Counselors**: 8.0 517 students/counselor	**% Amer Indian**: 0.0 **% Asian**: 1.5 **% Black**: 34.9 **% Hispanic**: 18.5 **% White**: 45.1	National ***Socio-Economic Status*** indicator percentile (100=high): 29th

Suffolk County
DEER PARK UNION FREE S.D.
1881 DEER PARK AVE ● DEER PARK NY 11729-4326 ● (516) 242-6505

Grade Span: PK-12 **Schools**: *Regular* 5 ● *Spec Ed* 0 ● *Alt* 0 **Students**: 3,733 **Total Teachers**: 262 **Student/Classroom Teacher Ratio**: 15.8	**Expenditures/Student**: $11,137 **Librarians**: 6.4 583 students/librarian **Guidance Counselors**: 6.0 622 students/counselor	**% Amer Indian**: 0.1 **% Asian**: 3.6 **% Black**: 14.7 **% Hispanic**: 5.5 **% White**: 76.3	National ***Socio-Economic Status*** indicator percentile (100=high): 75th

Suffolk County
[DIX HILLS] **HALF HOLLOW HILLS CENTRAL S.D.**
525 HALF HOLLOW RD ● DIX HILLS NY 11746-5899 ● (516) 421-6408 ● http://www.halfhollowhills.k12.ny.us

Grade Span: KG-12 **Schools**: *Regular* 10 ● *Spec Ed* 0 ● *Alt* 0 **Students**: 7,110 **Total Teachers**: 524 **Student/Classroom Teacher Ratio**: 15.2	**Expenditures/Student**: $12,928 **Librarians**: 8.6 827 students/librarian **Guidance Counselors**: 23.4 304 students/counselor	**% Amer Indian**: 0.0 **% Asian**: 7.6 **% Black**: 12.0 **% Hispanic**: 3.9 **% White**: 76.5	National ***Socio-Economic Status*** indicator percentile (100=high): 89th

Suffolk County
[EAST PATCHOGUE] **SOUTH COUNTRY CENTRAL S.D.**
189 N DUNTON AVE ● EAST PATCHOGUE NY 11772-5598 ● (516) 286-4310

Grade Span: PK-12 **Schools**: *Regular* 6 ● *Spec Ed* 0 ● *Alt* 0 **Students**: 4,518 **Total Teachers**: 309 **Student/Classroom Teacher Ratio**: 16.3	**Expenditures/Student**: $11,999 **Librarians**: 5.0 904 students/librarian **Guidance Counselors**: 8.0 565 students/counselor	**% Amer Indian**: 0.2 **% Asian**: 2.3 **% Black**: 23.5 **% Hispanic**: 10.2 **% White**: 63.8	National ***Socio-Economic Status*** indicator percentile (100=high): 51st

Suffolk County
[EAST SETAUKET] **THREE VILLAGE CENTRAL S.D.**
200 NICOLL RD ● EAST SETAUKET NY 11733-9050 ● (516) 474-7514

Grade Span: KG-12 **Schools**: *Regular* 8 ● *Spec Ed* 0 ● *Alt* 0 **Students**: 6,623 **Total Teachers**: 461 **Student/Classroom Teacher Ratio**: 15.4	**Expenditures/Student**: $11,377 **Librarians**: 7.4 895 students/librarian **Guidance Counselors**: 15.0 442 students/counselor	**% Amer Indian**: 0.0 **% Asian**: 5.5 **% Black**: 1.4 **% Hispanic**: 1.4 **% White**: 91.6	National ***Socio-Economic Status*** indicator percentile (100=high): 97th

Suffolk County
[GREENLAWN] **HARBORFIELDS CENTRAL S.D.**
2 OLDFIELD RD ● GREENLAWN NY 11740-1200 ● (516) 754-5320

Grade Span: KG-12 **Schools**: *Regular* 4 ● *Spec Ed* 0 ● *Alt* 0 **Students**: 2,699 **Total Teachers**: 172 **Student/Classroom Teacher Ratio**: 21.3	**Expenditures/Student**: $11,167 **Librarians**: 3.9 692 students/librarian **Guidance Counselors**: 6.0 450 students/counselor	**% Amer Indian**: 0.1 **% Asian**: 3.6 **% Black**: 7.3 **% Hispanic**: 3.3 **% White**: 85.7	National ***Socio-Economic Status*** indicator percentile (100=high): 93rd

Suffolk County
HAUPPAUGE UNION FREE S.D.
600 TOWN LINE RD ● HAUPPAUGE NY 11788 ● (516) 265-3630

Grade Span: PK-12 **Schools**: *Regular* 5 ● *Spec Ed* 0 ● *Alt* 0 **Students**: 3,496 **Total Teachers**: 253 **Student/Classroom Teacher Ratio**: 15.7	**Expenditures/Student**: $12,948 **Librarians**: 6.4 546 students/librarian **Guidance Counselors**: 10.0 350 students/counselor	**% Amer Indian**: 0.0 **% Asian**: 2.1 **% Black**: 1.3 **% Hispanic**: 2.2 **% White**: 94.3	National ***Socio-Economic Status*** indicator percentile (100=high): 92nd

Suffolk County
[HOLBROOK] **SACHEM CENTRAL S.D.**
245 UNION AVE ● HOLBROOK NY 11741 ● (516) 467-8202 ● http://www.sachem.k12.ny.us

Grade Span: KG-12 **Schools**: *Regular* 15 ● *Spec Ed* 0 ● *Alt* 0 **Students**: 14,348 **Total Teachers**: 985 **Student/Classroom Teacher Ratio**: 15.4	**Expenditures/Student**: $10,137 **Librarians**: 17.3 829 students/librarian **Guidance Counselors**: 27.0 531 students/counselor	**% Amer Indian**: 0.1 **% Asian**: 2.0 **% Black**: 1.0 **% Hispanic**: 3.3 **% White**: 93.5	National ***Socio-Economic Status*** indicator percentile (100=high): 83rd

Suffolk County

HUNTINGTON UNION FREE S.D.

140 WOODHULL RD ● HUNTINGTON NY 11743-1500 ● (516) 673-2038

Grade Span: KG-12 **Schools**: *Regular* 8 ● *Spec Ed* 0 ● *Alt* 0 **Students**: 3,990 **Total Teachers**: 288 **Student/Classroom Teacher Ratio**: 17.3	**Expenditures/Student**: $12,836 **Librarians**: 5.9 676 students/librarian **Guidance Counselors**: 9.0 443 students/counselor	**% Amer Indian**: 0.0 **% Asian**: 1.3 **% Black**: 15.6 **% Hispanic**: 16.1 **% White**: 67.0	National ***Socio-Economic Status*** indicator percentile (100=high): 46th

Suffolk County

[HUNTINGTON STATION] SOUTH HUNTINGTON UNION FREE S.D.

60 WESTON ST ● HUNTINGTON STATION NY 11746-4098 ● (516) 673-1610

Grade Span: PK-12 **Schools**: *Regular* 7 ● *Spec Ed* 0 ● *Alt* 0 **Students**: 5,508 **Total Teachers**: 385 **Student/Classroom Teacher Ratio**: 14.8	**Expenditures/Student**: $11,311 **Librarians**: 3.6 1,530 students/librarian **Guidance Counselors**: 12.0 459 students/counselor	**% Amer Indian**: 0.1 **% Asian**: 3.0 **% Black**: 11.6 **% Hispanic**: 7.4 **% White**: 77.9	National ***Socio-Economic Status*** indicator percentile (100=high): 70th

Suffolk County

ISLIP UNION FREE S.D.

215 MAIN ST ● ISLIP NY 11751-3435 ● (516) 581-2560

Grade Span: KG-12 **Schools**: *Regular* 5 ● *Spec Ed* 0 ● *Alt* 0 **Students**: 2,936 **Total Teachers**: 190 **Student/Classroom Teacher Ratio**: 19.2	**Expenditures/Student**: $10,982 **Librarians**: 2.0 1,468 students/librarian **Guidance Counselors**: 5.0 587 students/counselor	**% Amer Indian**: 0.0 **% Asian**: 1.1 **% Black**: 3.7 **% Hispanic**: 7.6 **% White**: 87.6	National ***Socio-Economic Status*** indicator percentile (100=high): 81st

Suffolk County

[ISLIP TERRACE] EAST ISLIP UNION FREE S.D.

ONE C B GARIEPY AVE ● ISLIP TERRACE NY 11752-2820 ● (516) 581-1600 ● http://sricboces.org/e.islip

Grade Span: PK-12 **Schools**: *Regular* 7 ● *Spec Ed* 0 ● *Alt* 0 **Students**: 4,665 **Total Teachers**: 289 **Student/Classroom Teacher Ratio**: 19.7	**Expenditures/Student**: $11,340 **Librarians**: 2.9 1,609 students/librarian **Guidance Counselors**: 7.0 666 students/counselor	**% Amer Indian**: 0.1 **% Asian**: 1.9 **% Black**: 0.9 **% Hispanic**: 4.4 **% White**: 92.8	National ***Socio-Economic Status*** indicator percentile (100=high): 85th

Suffolk County

KINGS PARK CENTRAL S.D.

101 CHURCH ST ● KINGS PARK NY 11754-1769 ● (516) 269-3210

Grade Span: PK-12 **Schools**: *Regular* 5 ● *Spec Ed* 0 ● *Alt* 0 **Students**: 3,354 **Total Teachers**: 223 **Student/Classroom Teacher Ratio**: 18.6	**Expenditures/Student**: $11,271 **Librarians**: 4.0 839 students/librarian **Guidance Counselors**: 6.5 516 students/counselor	**% Amer Indian**: 0.0 **% Asian**: 2.3 **% Black**: 0.4 **% Hispanic**: 1.8 **% White**: 95.5	National ***Socio-Economic Status*** indicator percentile (100=high): 97th

Suffolk County

LINDENHURST UNION FREE S.D.

350 DANIEL ST ● LINDENHURST NY 11757-0621 ● (516) 226-6511 ● http://lhs.lindy.k12.ny.us

Grade Span: KG-12 **Schools**: *Regular* 9 ● *Spec Ed* 0 ● *Alt* 0 **Students**: 6,817 **Total Teachers**: 411 **Student/Classroom Teacher Ratio**: 18.8	**Expenditures/Student**: $9,252 **Librarians**: 8.1 842 students/librarian **Guidance Counselors**: 9.0 757 students/counselor	**% Amer Indian**: 0.1 **% Asian**: 1.7 **% Black**: 1.1 **% Hispanic**: 5.4 **% White**: 91.6	National ***Socio-Economic Status*** indicator percentile (100=high): 80th

Suffolk County
[MASTIC BEACH] **WILLIAM FLOYD UNION FREE S.D.**
240 MASTIC BEACH RD ● MASTIC BEACH NY 11951-1099 ● (516) 874-1201 ● http://www.wfsd.k12.ny.us

Grade Span: KG-12 **Schools**: *Regular* 7 ● *Spec Ed* 0 ● *Alt* 0 **Students**: 9,536 **Total Teachers**: 509 **Student/Classroom Teacher Ratio**: 20.7	**Expenditures/Student**: $9,001 **Librarians**: 9.2 1,037 students/librarian **Guidance Counselors**: 16.0 596 students/counselor	**% Amer Indian**: 0.1 **% Asian**: 1.1 **% Black**: 5.9 **% Hispanic**: 9.3 **% White**: 83.6	National ***Socio-Economic Status*** indicator percentile (100=high): 36th

Suffolk County
[MIDDLE ISLAND] **LONGWOOD CENTRAL S.D.**
35 YAPHNK-MID ISL RD ● MIDDLE ISLAND NY 11953-2369 ● (516) 345-2172

Grade Span: KG-12 **Schools**: *Regular* 7 ● *Spec Ed* 0 ● *Alt* 0 **Students**: 9,256 **Total Teachers**: 544 **Student/Classroom Teacher Ratio**: 17.7	**Expenditures/Student**: $10,529 **Librarians**: 8.1 1,143 students/librarian **Guidance Counselors**: 15.2 609 students/counselor	**% Amer Indian**: 0.3 **% Asian**: 2.3 **% Black**: 14.8 **% Hispanic**: 7.5 **% White**: 75.1	National ***Socio-Economic Status*** indicator percentile (100=high): 64th

Suffolk County
MILLER PLACE UNION FREE S.D.
191 N COUNTRY RD ● MILLER PLACE NY 11764-2036 ● (516) 474-2700

Grade Span: KG-12 **Schools**: *Regular* 4 ● *Spec Ed* 0 ● *Alt* 0 **Students**: 2,708 **Total Teachers**: 169 **Student/Classroom Teacher Ratio**: 18.1	**Expenditures/Student**: $9,071 **Librarians**: 3.7 732 students/librarian **Guidance Counselors**: 4.9 553 students/counselor	**% Amer Indian**: 0.0 **% Asian**: 0.8 **% Black**: 0.7 **% Hispanic**: 0.9 **% White**: 97.6	National ***Socio-Economic Status*** indicator percentile (100=high): 94th

Suffolk County
NORTH BABYLON UNION FREE S.D.
5 JARDINE PL ● NORTH BABYLON NY 11703-4203 ● (516) 321-3226

Grade Span: KG-12 **Schools**: *Regular* 7 ● *Spec Ed* 0 ● *Alt* 0 **Students**: 4,546 **Total Teachers**: 283 **Student/Classroom Teacher Ratio**: 16.7	**Expenditures/Student**: $11,072 **Librarians**: 2.8 1,624 students/librarian **Guidance Counselors**: 6.2 733 students/counselor	**% Amer Indian**: 0.2 **% Asian**: 1.5 **% Black**: 18.1 **% Hispanic**: 6.4 **% White**: 73.8	National ***Socio-Economic Status*** indicator percentile (100=high): 73rd

Suffolk County
NORTHPORT-EAST NORTHPORT UNION FREE S.D.
110 ELWOOD RD ● NORTHPORT NY 11768-3455 ● (516) 262-6600 ● http://northport.k12.ny.us

Grade Span: PK-12 **Schools**: *Regular* 9 ● *Spec Ed* 0 ● *Alt* 0 **Students**: 5,356 **Total Teachers**: 449 **Student/Classroom Teacher Ratio**: 13.8	**Expenditures/Student**: $12,401 **Librarians**: 8.9 602 students/librarian **Guidance Counselors**: 21.0 255 students/counselor	**% Amer Indian**: 0.0 **% Asian**: 2.6 **% Black**: 1.0 **% Hispanic**: 2.0 **% White**: 94.5	National ***Socio-Economic Status*** indicator percentile (100=high): 94th

Suffolk County
PATCHOGUE-MEDFORD UNION FREE S.D.
241 S OCEAN AVE ● PATCHOGUE NY 11772-3787 ● (516) 758-1017 ● http://www.pat-med.k12.ny.us

Grade Span: PK-12 **Schools**: *Regular* 11 ● *Spec Ed* 0 ● *Alt* 0 **Students**: 8,637 **Total Teachers**: 553 **Student/Classroom Teacher Ratio**: 17.5	**Expenditures/Student**: $10,019 **Librarians**: 9.7 890 students/librarian **Guidance Counselors**: 14.5 596 students/counselor	**% Amer Indian**: 0.2 **% Asian**: 1.5 **% Black**: 4.7 **% Hispanic**: 9.9 **% White**: 83.8	National ***Socio-Economic Status*** indicator percentile (100=high): 59th

Suffolk County

[PORT JEFFERSON STATION] **BROOKHAVEN-COMSEWOGUE UNION FREE S.D.**

290 NORWOOD AVE ● PORT JEFFERSON STATION NY 11776-2999 ● (516) 474-8105

Grade Span: KG-12 **Schools**: *Regular* 5 ● *Spec Ed* 0 ● *Alt* 0 **Students**: 3,331 **Total Teachers**: 214 **Student/Classroom Teacher Ratio**: 16.3	**Expenditures/Student**: $11,758 **Librarians**: 3.8 877 students/librarian **Guidance Counselors**: 6.1 546 students/counselor	**% Amer Indian**: 0.2 **% Asian**: 2.7 **% Black**: 2.5 **% Hispanic**: 10.1 **% White**: 84.5	National ***Socio-Economic Status*** indicator percentile (100=high): 76th

Suffolk County

RIVERHEAD CENTRAL S.D.

700 OSBORNE AVE ● RIVERHEAD NY 11901-2996 ● (516) 369-6716

Grade Span: KG-12 **Schools**: *Regular* 7 ● *Spec Ed* 0 ● *Alt* 0 **Students**: 4,297 **Total Teachers**: 273 **Student/Classroom Teacher Ratio**: 17.7	**Expenditures/Student**: $10,976 **Librarians**: 4.5 955 students/librarian **Guidance Counselors**: 6.0 716 students/counselor	**% Amer Indian**: 0.3 **% Asian**: 0.7 **% Black**: 32.5 **% Hispanic**: 3.6 **% White**: 62.9	National ***Socio-Economic Status*** indicator percentile (100=high): 44th

Suffolk County

ROCKY POINT UNION FREE S.D.

ROCKY PT-YAPHANK RD ● ROCKY POINT NY 11778-8401 ● (516) 744-1600

Grade Span: KG-12 **Schools**: *Regular* 3 ● *Spec Ed* 0 ● *Alt* 0 **Students**: 2,862 **Total Teachers**: 160 **Student/Classroom Teacher Ratio**: 20.3	**Expenditures/Student**: $9,267 **Librarians**: 1.6 1,789 students/librarian **Guidance Counselors**: 4.0 716 students/counselor	**% Amer Indian**: 0.1 **% Asian**: 0.6 **% Black**: 0.4 **% Hispanic**: 1.1 **% White**: 97.8	National ***Socio-Economic Status*** indicator percentile (100=high): 85th

Suffolk County

SAYVILLE UNION FREE S.D.

99 GREELEY AVE ● SAYVILLE NY 11782-2698 ● (516) 244-6510

Grade Span: KG-12 **Schools**: *Regular* 5 ● *Spec Ed* 0 ● *Alt* 0 **Students**: 3,289 **Total Teachers**: 236 **Student/Classroom Teacher Ratio**: 15.9	**Expenditures/Student**: $11,540 **Librarians**: 3.6 914 students/librarian **Guidance Counselors**: 6.3 522 students/counselor	**% Amer Indian**: 0.1 **% Asian**: 2.3 **% Black**: 0.8 **% Hispanic**: 1.5 **% White**: 95.3	National ***Socio-Economic Status*** indicator percentile (100=high): 95th

Suffolk County

SMITHTOWN CENTRAL S.D.

26 NEW YORK AVE ● SMITHTOWN NY 11787-3435 ● (516) 361-2206 ● http://www.smithtown.k12.ny.us

Grade Span: PK-12 **Schools**: *Regular* 11 ● *Spec Ed* 0 ● *Alt* 0 **Students**: 7,775 **Total Teachers**: 551 **Student/Classroom Teacher Ratio**: 17.6	**Expenditures/Student**: $11,733 **Librarians**: 11.6 670 students/librarian **Guidance Counselors**: 18.0 432 students/counselor	**% Amer Indian**: 0.0 **% Asian**: 2.2 **% Black**: 0.6 **% Hispanic**: 1.9 **% White**: 95.3	National ***Socio-Economic Status*** indicator percentile (100=high): 96th

Suffolk County

WEST BABYLON UNION FREE S.D.

10 FARMINGDALE RD ● WEST BABYLON NY 11704-6289 ● (516) 321-3142 ● http://www.westbabylon.k12.ny.us/public/default.htm

Grade Span: KG-12 **Schools**: *Regular* 7 ● *Spec Ed* 0 ● *Alt* 0 **Students**: 4,442 **Total Teachers**: 290 **Student/Classroom Teacher Ratio**: 17.6	**Expenditures/Student**: $10,715 **Librarians**: 6.4 694 students/librarian **Guidance Counselors**: 7.0 635 students/counselor	**% Amer Indian**: 0.0 **% Asian**: 1.9 **% Black**: 4.5 **% Hispanic**: 4.9 **% White**: 88.7	National ***Socio-Economic Status*** indicator percentile (100=high): 79th

Suffolk County

WEST ISLIP UNION FREE S.D.

100 SHERMAN AVE ● WEST ISLIP NY 11795 ● (516) 422-1560

Grade Span: KG-12 **Schools**: *Regular* 8 ● *Spec Ed* 0 ● *Alt* 0 **Students**: 4,910 **Total Teachers**: 340 **Student/Classroom Teacher Ratio**: 17.6	**Expenditures/Student**: $10,292 **Librarians**: 5.4 909 students/librarian **Guidance Counselors**: 10.0 491 students/counselor	**% Amer Indian**: 0.0 **% Asian**: 1.1 **% Black**: 0.4 **% Hispanic**: 1.7 **% White**: 96.8	National ***Socio-Economic Status*** indicator percentile (100=high): 90th

Sullivan County

MONTICELLO CENTRAL S.D.

295 FORESTBURGH RD ● MONTICELLO NY 12701 ● (914) 794-7700

Grade Span: KG-12 **Schools**: *Regular* 6 ● *Spec Ed* 0 ● *Alt* 0 **Students**: 3,607 **Total Teachers**: 250 **Student/Classroom Teacher Ratio**: 16.8	**Expenditures/Student**: $8,507 **Librarians**: 2.5 1,443 students/librarian **Guidance Counselors**: 6.9 523 students/counselor	**% Amer Indian**: 0.0 **% Asian**: 1.6 **% Black**: 18.4 **% Hispanic**: 13.5 **% White**: 66.5	National ***Socio-Economic Status*** indicator percentile (100=high): 22nd

Tioga County

OWEGO-APALACHIN CENTRAL S.D.

36 TALCOTT ST ● OWEGO NY 13827-1096 ● (607) 687-6224 ● http://do.oacsd.k12.ny.us

Grade Span: KG-12 **Schools**: *Regular* 4 ● *Spec Ed* 0 ● *Alt* 0 **Students**: 2,723 **Total Teachers**: 180 **Student/Classroom Teacher Ratio**: 16.0	**Expenditures/Student**: $7,302 **Librarians**: 3.6 756 students/librarian **Guidance Counselors**: 5.0 545 students/counselor	**% Amer Indian**: 0.2 **% Asian**: 1.0 **% Black**: 1.4 **% Hispanic**: 0.3 **% White**: 97.1	National ***Socio-Economic Status*** indicator percentile (100=high): 63rd

Tompkins County

ITHACA CITY S.D.

400 LAKE ST ● ITHACA NY 14851-0549 ● (607) 274-2101 ● http://www.icsd.k12.ny.us

Grade Span: PK-12 **Schools**: *Regular* 11 ● *Spec Ed* 0 ● *Alt* 1 **Students**: 6,306 **Total Teachers**: 462 **Student/Classroom Teacher Ratio**: 14.8	**Expenditures/Student**: $8,584 **Librarians**: 9.2 685 students/librarian **Guidance Counselors**: 12.0 526 students/counselor	**% Amer Indian**: 0.3 **% Asian**: 7.5 **% Black**: 8.9 **% Hispanic**: 2.7 **% White**: 80.6	National ***Socio-Economic Status*** indicator percentile (100=high): 59th

Ulster County

[ACCORD] **RONDOUT VALLEY CENTRAL S.D.**

P.O. BOX 9 ● ACCORD NY 12404-0009 ● (914) 334-8680 ● http://int11.mhrcc.org/rvcsd

Grade Span: KG-12 **Schools**: *Regular* 6 ● *Spec Ed* 0 ● *Alt* 0 **Students**: 2,845 **Total Teachers**: 199 **Student/Classroom Teacher Ratio**: 16.9	**Expenditures/Student**: $9,034 **Librarians**: 3.6 790 students/librarian **Guidance Counselors**: 7.0 406 students/counselor	**% Amer Indian**: 0.0 **% Asian**: 0.5 **% Black**: 2.8 **% Hispanic**: 2.1 **% White**: 94.6	National ***Socio-Economic Status*** indicator percentile (100=high): 60th

Ulster County

KINGSTON CITY S.D.

61 CROWN ST ● KINGSTON NY 12401-3879 ● (914) 339-3000

Grade Span: PK-12 **Schools**: *Regular* 13 ● *Spec Ed* 0 ● *Alt* 0 **Students**: 7,807 **Total Teachers**: 516 **Student/Classroom Teacher Ratio**: 16.7	**Expenditures/Student**: $9,181 **Librarians**: 12.3 635 students/librarian **Guidance Counselors**: 15.0 520 students/counselor	**% Amer Indian**: 0.1 **% Asian**: 1.8 **% Black**: 11.9 **% Hispanic**: 2.4 **% White**: 83.8	National ***Socio-Economic Status*** indicator percentile (100=high): 47th

Ulster County

SAUGERTIES CENTRAL S.D.

WASHINGTON AVE EXT ● SAUGERTIES NY 12477-0577 ● (914) 246-4934

Grade Span: KG-12 **Schools**: *Regular* 5 ● *Spec Ed* 0 ● *Alt* 0 **Students**: 3,390 **Total Teachers**: 205 **Student/Classroom Teacher Ratio**: 18.5	**Expenditures/Student**: $7,010 **Librarians**: 4.0 848 students/librarian **Guidance Counselors**: 4.0 848 students/counselor	**% Amer Indian**: 0.1 **% Asian**: 1.0 **% Black**: 2.2 **% Hispanic**: 1.5 **% White**: 95.2	National ***Socio-Economic Status*** indicator percentile (100=high): 68th

Ulster County

WALLKILL CENTRAL S.D.

19 MAIN ST ● WALLKILL NY 12589-0310 ● (914) 895-3301

Grade Span: KG-12 **Schools**: *Regular* 5 ● *Spec Ed* 0 ● *Alt* 0 **Students**: 3,250 **Total Teachers**: 195 **Student/Classroom Teacher Ratio**: 17.7	**Expenditures/Student**: $8,154 **Librarians**: 2.0 1,625 students/librarian **Guidance Counselors**: 6.0 542 students/counselor	**% Amer Indian**: 0.2 **% Asian**: 0.5 **% Black**: 4.2 **% Hispanic**: 11.6 **% White**: 83.4	National ***Socio-Economic Status*** indicator percentile (100=high): 68th

Warren County

GLENS FALLS CITY S.D.

15 QUADE ST ● GLENS FALLS NY 12801-2724 ● (518) 792-1212

Grade Span: KG-12 **Schools**: *Regular* 6 ● *Spec Ed* 0 ● *Alt* 0 **Students**: 2,887 **Total Teachers**: 201 **Student/Classroom Teacher Ratio**: 17.7	**Expenditures/Student**: $7,394 **Librarians**: 3.8 760 students/librarian **Guidance Counselors**: 6.8 425 students/counselor	**% Amer Indian**: 0.0 **% Asian**: 0.7 **% Black**: 1.7 **% Hispanic**: 0.8 **% White**: 96.8	National ***Socio-Economic Status*** indicator percentile (100=high): 58th

Warren County

QUEENSBURY UNION FREE S.D.

431 AVIATION RD ● QUEENSBURY NY 12804-2914 ● (518) 793-8811

Grade Span: KG-12 **Schools**: *Regular* 3 ● *Spec Ed* 0 ● *Alt* 0 **Students**: 3,505 **Total Teachers**: 203 **Student/Classroom Teacher Ratio**: 17.6	**Expenditures/Student**: $7,025 **Librarians**: 2.8 1,252 students/librarian **Guidance Counselors**: 7.0 501 students/counselor	**% Amer Indian**: 0.0 **% Asian**: 0.5 **% Black**: 0.7 **% Hispanic**: 0.2 **% White**: 98.6	National ***Socio-Economic Status*** indicator percentile (100=high): 80th

Washington County

HUDSON FALLS CENTRAL S.D.

85 NOTRE DAME ST ● HUDSON FALLS NY 12839-1594 ● (518) 747-2121 ● http://www.hudsonfalls.k12.ny.us

Grade Span: KG-12 **Schools**: *Regular* 6 ● *Spec Ed* 0 ● *Alt* 0 **Students**: 2,503 **Total Teachers**: 156 **Student/Classroom Teacher Ratio**: 19.1	**Expenditures/Student**: $7,196 **Librarians**: 2.9 863 students/librarian **Guidance Counselors**: 4.0 626 students/counselor	**% Amer Indian**: 0.1 **% Asian**: 0.6 **% Black**: 0.6 **% Hispanic**: 0.1 **% White**: 98.6	National ***Socio-Economic Status*** indicator percentile (100=high): 55th

Wayne County

NEWARK CENTRAL S.D.

100 E MILLER ST ● NEWARK NY 14513-1599 ● (315) 331-2260

Grade Span: KG-12 **Schools**: *Regular* 5 ● *Spec Ed* 0 ● *Alt* 0 **Students**: 2,933 **Total Teachers**: 206 **Student/Classroom Teacher Ratio**: 14.6	**Expenditures/Student**: $7,498 **Librarians**: 3.6 815 students/librarian **Guidance Counselors**: 4.9 599 students/counselor	**% Amer Indian**: 0.1 **% Asian**: 1.0 **% Black**: 5.8 **% Hispanic**: 8.7 **% White**: 84.5	National ***Socio-Economic Status*** indicator percentile (100=high): 59th

Wayne County

[ONTARIO CENTER] **WAYNE CENTRAL S.D.**

6200 ONTARIO CENTER R ● ONTARIO CENTER NY 14520-0155 ● (315) 524-0201

Grade Span: KG-12 **Schools**: *Regular* 5 ● *Spec Ed* 0 ● *Alt* 0 **Students**: 2,845 **Total Teachers**: 200 **Student/Classroom Teacher Ratio**: 15.4	**Expenditures/Student**: $7,173 **Librarians**: 4.4 647 students/librarian **Guidance Counselors**: 9.2 309 students/counselor	**% Amer Indian**: 0.5 **% Asian**: 0.8 **% Black**: 1.5 **% Hispanic**: 0.8 **% White**: 96.4	National ***Socio-Economic Status*** indicator percentile (100=high): 82nd

Westchester County

CHAPPAQUA CENTRAL S.D.

66 ROARING BROOK RD ● CHAPPAQUA NY 10514-1703 ● (914) 238-7200 ● http://www.chappaqua.k12.ny.us

Grade Span: KG-12 **Schools**: *Regular* 5 ● *Spec Ed* 0 ● *Alt* 0 **Students**: 3,201 **Total Teachers**: 237 **Student/Classroom Teacher Ratio**: 15.3	**Expenditures/Student**: $12,812 **Librarians**: 5.4 593 students/librarian **Guidance Counselors**: 8.0 400 students/counselor	**% Amer Indian**: 0.0 **% Asian**: 8.1 **% Black**: 1.2 **% Hispanic**: 1.5 **% White**: 89.2	National ***Socio-Economic Status*** indicator percentile (100=high): 100th

Westchester County

HARRISON CENTRAL S.D.

50 UNION AVE ● HARRISON NY 10528-2032 ● (914) 835-3300

Grade Span: KG-12 **Schools**: *Regular* 6 ● *Spec Ed* 0 ● *Alt* 0 **Students**: 2,713 **Total Teachers**: 214 **Student/Classroom Teacher Ratio**: 13.4	**Expenditures/Student**: $13,156 **Librarians**: 2.6 1,043 students/librarian **Guidance Counselors**: 6.2 438 students/counselor	**% Amer Indian**: 0.1 **% Asian**: 5.1 **% Black**: 0.7 **% Hispanic**: 6.7 **% White**: 87.4	National ***Socio-Economic Status*** indicator percentile (100=high): 95th

Westchester County

MAMARONECK UNION FREE S.D.

1000 W BOSTON POST RD ● MAMARONECK NY 10543-3399 ● (914) 698-9000 ● http://www.mamkschools.org

Grade Span: PK-12 **Schools**: *Regular* 7 ● *Spec Ed* 0 ● *Alt* 0 **Students**: 4,096 **Total Teachers**: 308 **Student/Classroom Teacher Ratio**: 14.9	**Expenditures/Student**: $12,624 **Librarians**: 5.7 719 students/librarian **Guidance Counselors**: 11.0 372 students/counselor	**% Amer Indian**: 0.1 **% Asian**: 3.1 **% Black**: 5.0 **% Hispanic**: 11.2 **% White**: 80.6	National ***Socio-Economic Status*** indicator percentile (100=high): 94th

Westchester County

[MOUNT KISCO] **BEDFORD CENTRAL S.D.**

FOX LN CAMPUS ● MOUNT KISCO NY 10549-0180 ● (914) 241-6000

Grade Span: KG-12 **Schools**: *Regular* 7 ● *Spec Ed* 0 ● *Alt* 0 **Students**: 3,248 **Total Teachers**: 265 **Student/Classroom Teacher Ratio**: 14.3	**Expenditures/Student**: $15,233 **Librarians**: 7.1 457 students/librarian **Guidance Counselors**: 7.5 433 students/counselor	**% Amer Indian**: 0.0 **% Asian**: 3.4 **% Black**: 8.1 **% Hispanic**: 11.8 **% White**: 76.7	National ***Socio-Economic Status*** indicator percentile (100=high): 79th

Westchester County

MOUNT VERNON CITY S.D.

165 NO COLUMBUS AVE ● MOUNT VERNON NY 10553 ● (914) 665-5201

Grade Span: PK-12 **Schools**: *Regular* 16 ● *Spec Ed* 0 ● *Alt* 0 **Students**: 10,055 **Total Teachers**: 649 **Student/Classroom Teacher Ratio**: 16.2	**Expenditures/Student**: $9,482 **Librarians**: 9.9 1,016 students/librarian **Guidance Counselors**: 20.9 481 students/counselor	**% Amer Indian**: 0.2 **% Asian**: 1.6 **% Black**: 76.1 **% Hispanic**: 9.5 **% White**: 12.7	National ***Socio-Economic Status*** indicator percentile (100=high): 34th

Westchester County
NEW ROCHELLE CITY S.D.
515 NORTH AVE ● NEW ROCHELLE NY 10801-3416 ● (914) 576-4200

Grade Span: PK-12 **Schools**: *Regular* 10 ● *Spec Ed* 0 ● *Alt* 0 **Students**: 8,905 **Total Teachers**: 558 **Student/Classroom Teacher Ratio**: 17.0	**Expenditures/Student**: $10,823 **Librarians**: 8.4 1,060 students/librarian **Guidance Counselors**: 16.0 557 students/counselor	**% Amer Indian**: 0.1 **% Asian**: 3.8 **% Black**: 30.1 **% Hispanic**: 21.6 **% White**: 44.5	National ***Socio-Economic Status*** indicator percentile (100=high): 45th

Westchester County
OSSINING UNION FREE S.D.
190 CROTON AVE ● OSSINING NY 10562-4599 ● (914) 941-7700

Grade Span: PK-12 **Schools**: *Regular* 5 ● *Spec Ed* 1 ● *Alt* 0 **Students**: 3,483 **Total Teachers**: 235 **Student/Classroom Teacher Ratio**: 17.1	**Expenditures/Student**: $11,533 **Librarians**: 3.6 968 students/librarian **Guidance Counselors**: 8.0 435 students/counselor	**% Amer Indian**: 0.0 **% Asian**: 3.8 **% Black**: 23.7 **% Hispanic**: 18.4 **% White**: 54.1	National ***Socio-Economic Status*** indicator percentile (100=high): 53rd

Westchester County
PEEKSKILL CITY S.D.
1031 ELM ST ● PEEKSKILL NY 10566-3499 ● (914) 737-3300

Grade Span: PK-12 **Schools**: *Regular* 7 ● *Spec Ed* 0 ● *Alt* 0 **Students**: 2,743 **Total Teachers**: 210 **Student/Classroom Teacher Ratio**: 17.4	**Expenditures/Student**: $12,679 **Librarians**: 4.5 610 students/librarian **Guidance Counselors**: 5.0 549 students/counselor	**% Amer Indian**: 0.2 **% Asian**: 1.4 **% Black**: 43.2 **% Hispanic**: 14.8 **% White**: 40.3	National ***Socio-Economic Status*** indicator percentile (100=high): 31st

Westchester County
PORT CHESTER-RYE UNION FREE S.D.
BOWMAN AVE ● PORT CHESTER NY 10573-2851 ● (914) 934-7901

Grade Span: KG-12 **Schools**: *Regular* 7 ● *Spec Ed* 0 ● *Alt* 0 **Students**: 3,164 **Total Teachers**: 222 **Student/Classroom Teacher Ratio**: 15.9	**Expenditures/Student**: $9,948 **Librarians**: 2.8 1,130 students/librarian **Guidance Counselors**: 8.0 396 students/counselor	**% Amer Indian**: 0.1 **% Asian**: 1.2 **% Black**: 14.2 **% Hispanic**: 50.0 **% White**: 34.5	National ***Socio-Economic Status*** indicator percentile (100=high): 36th

Westchester County
SCARSDALE UNION FREE S.D.
2 BREWSTER RD ● SCARSDALE NY 10583-3049 ● (914) 721-2410 ● http://www.shs.scarsdale.k12.ny.us

Grade Span: KG-12 **Schools**: *Regular* 7 ● *Spec Ed* 0 ● *Alt* 0 **Students**: 3,863 **Total Teachers**: 292 **Student/Classroom Teacher Ratio**: 15.1	**Expenditures/Student**: $12,310 **Librarians**: 7.5 515 students/librarian **Guidance Counselors**: 9.9 390 students/counselor	**% Amer Indian**: 0.0 **% Asian**: 16.6 **% Black**: 1.9 **% Hispanic**: 2.4 **% White**: 79.0	National ***Socio-Economic Status*** indicator percentile (100=high): na

Westchester County
[SHRUB OAK] LAKELAND CENTRAL S.D.
1086 MAIN ST ● SHRUB OAK NY 10588-1507 ● (914) 245-1700 ● http://www.townlink.net/ny/schools/lakeland

Grade Span: KG-12 **Schools**: *Regular* 8 ● *Spec Ed* 0 ● *Alt* 1 **Students**: 5,636 **Total Teachers**: 376 **Student/Classroom Teacher Ratio**: 16.4	**Expenditures/Student**: $11,565 **Librarians**: 7.5 751 students/librarian **Guidance Counselors**: 12.0 470 students/counselor	**% Amer Indian**: 0.0 **% Asian**: 2.1 **% Black**: 5.2 **% Hispanic**: 5.7 **% White**: 87.0	National ***Socio-Economic Status*** indicator percentile (100=high): 93rd

Westchester County
[SOUTH SALEM] **KATONAH-LEWISBORO UNION FREE S.D.**
1 SHADY LN RT 123 ● SOUTH SALEM NY 10536-9998 ● (914) 763-5000 ● http://www.k-lschools.org

Grade Span: KG-12 **Schools**: *Regular* 6 ● *Spec Ed* 0 ● *Alt* 0 **Students**: 3,285 **Total Teachers**: 239 **Student/Classroom Teacher Ratio**: 15.7	**Expenditures/Student**: $11,611 **Librarians**: 5.3 620 students/librarian **Guidance Counselors**: 8.0 411 students/counselor	**% Amer Indian**: 0.0 **% Asian**: 2.1 **% Black**: 1.2 **% Hispanic**: 1.0 **% White**: 95.7	National ***Socio-Economic Status*** indicator percentile (100=high): 100th

Westchester County
WHITE PLAINS CITY S.D.
5 HOMESIDE LN ● WHITE PLAINS NY 10605-4299 ● (914) 422-2019

Grade Span: PK-12 **Schools**: *Regular* 7 ● *Spec Ed* 1 ● *Alt* 0 **Students**: 5,945 **Total Teachers**: 425 **Student/Classroom Teacher Ratio**: 15.7	**Expenditures/Student**: $14,482 **Librarians**: 5.5 1,081 students/librarian **Guidance Counselors**: 15.0 396 students/counselor	**% Amer Indian**: 0.1 **% Asian**: 2.6 **% Black**: 25.7 **% Hispanic**: 28.3 **% White**: 43.3	National ***Socio-Economic Status*** indicator percentile (100=high): 42nd

Westchester County
YONKERS CITY S.D.
145 PALMER RD ● YONKERS NY 10701 ● (914) 376-8100 ● http://www.yonkerspublicschools.org

Grade Span: PK-12 **Schools**: *Regular* 34 ● *Spec Ed* 0 ● *Alt* 1 **Students**: 22,741 **Total Teachers**: 1,457 **Student/Classroom Teacher Ratio**: 17.2	**Expenditures/Student**: $10,443 **Librarians**: 21.5 1,058 students/librarian **Guidance Counselors**: 49.0 464 students/counselor	**% Amer Indian**: 0.1 **% Asian**: 4.2 **% Black**: 30.9 **% Hispanic**: 39.6 **% White**: 25.3	National ***Socio-Economic Status*** indicator percentile (100=high): 11th

Westchester County
[YORKTOWN HEIGHTS] **YORKTOWN CENTRAL S.D.**
2723 CROMPOND RD ● YORKTOWN HEIGHTS NY 10598-3197 ● (914) 243-8000

Grade Span: KG-12 **Schools**: *Regular* 6 ● *Spec Ed* 0 ● *Alt* 0 **Students**: 3,635 **Total Teachers**: 237 **Student/Classroom Teacher Ratio**: 17.5	**Expenditures/Student**: $10,789 **Librarians**: 4.3 845 students/librarian **Guidance Counselors**: 7.5 485 students/counselor	**% Amer Indian**: 0.2 **% Asian**: 4.3 **% Black**: 2.3 **% Hispanic**: 3.2 **% White**: 89.9	National ***Socio-Economic Status*** indicator percentile (100=high): 98th

Alamance County

BURLINGTON CITY S.D.

PO BOX 938 ● BURLINGTON NC 27216-0938 ● (336) 570-6060 ● http://www.abss.k12.nc.us

Grade Span: PK-12 **Schools**: *Regular* 10 ● *Spec Ed* 0 ● *Alt* 1 **Students**: 6,723 **Total Teachers**: 397 **Student/Classroom Teacher Ratio**: 17.2	**Expenditures/Student**: $4,635 **Librarians**: 11.0 611 students/librarian **Guidance Counselors**: 16.0 420 students/counselor	**% Amer Indian**: 0.1 **% Asian**: 1.8 **% Black**: 39.0 **% Hispanic**: 2.6 **% White**: 56.4	National ***Socio-Economic Status*** indicator percentile (100=high): 38th

Alamance County

[GRAHAM] **ALAMANCE COUNTY S.D.**

PO BOX 358 ● GRAHAM NC 27253-0358 ● (336) 570-6611 ● http://www.abss.k12.nc.us

Grade Span: PK-12 **Schools**: *Regular* 20 ● *Spec Ed* 0 ● *Alt* 0 **Students**: 11,738 **Total Teachers**: 702 **Student/Classroom Teacher Ratio**: 16.3	**Expenditures/Student**: $4,389 **Librarians**: 19.0 618 students/librarian **Guidance Counselors**: 30.0 391 students/counselor	**% Amer Indian**: 0.2 **% Asian**: 0.4 **% Black**: 19.5 **% Hispanic**: 2.4 **% White**: 77.6	National ***Socio-Economic Status*** indicator percentile (100=high): 57th

Alexander County

[TAYLORSVILLE] **ALEXANDER COUNTY S.D.**

PO BOX 128 ● TAYLORSVILLE NC 28681-0128 ● (828) 632-7001

Grade Span: PK-12 **Schools**: *Regular* 10 ● *Spec Ed* 0 ● *Alt* 0 **Students**: 4,978 **Total Teachers**: 276 **Student/Classroom Teacher Ratio**: 18.4	**Expenditures/Student**: $4,353 **Librarians**: 11.0 453 students/librarian **Guidance Counselors**: 12.0 415 students/counselor	**% Amer Indian**: 0.1 **% Asian**: 1.4 **% Black**: 7.1 **% Hispanic**: 0.9 **% White**: 90.6	National ***Socio-Economic Status*** indicator percentile (100=high): 65th

Anson County

[WADESBORO] **ANSON COUNTY S.D.**

PO BOX 719 ● WADESBORO NC 28170-0719 ● (704) 694-4417

Grade Span: PK-12 **Schools**: *Regular* 8 ● *Spec Ed* 0 ● *Alt* 0 **Students**: 4,461 **Total Teachers**: 293 **Student/Classroom Teacher Ratio**: 13.2	**Expenditures/Student**: $4,946 **Librarians**: 8.0 558 students/librarian **Guidance Counselors**: 10.0 446 students/counselor	**% Amer Indian**: 0.2 **% Asian**: 0.4 **% Black**: 62.5 **% Hispanic**: 0.1 **% White**: 36.7	National ***Socio-Economic Status*** indicator percentile (100=high): 15th

Ashe County

[JEFFERSON] **ASHE COUNTY S.D.**

PO BOX 604 ● JEFFERSON NC 28640-0604 ● (910) 246-7175

Grade Span: PK-12 **Schools**: *Regular* 7 ● *Spec Ed* 0 ● *Alt* 1 **Students**: 3,504 **Total Teachers**: 230 **Student/Classroom Teacher Ratio**: 15.6	**Expenditures/Student**: $5,074 **Librarians**: 7.0 501 students/librarian **Guidance Counselors**: 10.0 350 students/counselor	**% Amer Indian**: 0.0 **% Asian**: 0.1 **% Black**: 0.6 **% Hispanic**: 0.5 **% White**: 98.8	National ***Socio-Economic Status*** indicator percentile (100=high): 38th

Beaufort County

[WASHINGTON] **BEAUFORT COUNTY S.D.**

321 SMAW RD ● WASHINGTON NC 27889-3937 ● (252) 946-6593

Grade Span: PK-12 **Schools**: *Regular* 14 ● *Spec Ed* 0 ● *Alt* 1 **Students**: 7,806 **Total Teachers**: 501 **Student/Classroom Teacher Ratio**: 14.6	**Expenditures/Student**: $4,889 **Librarians**: 15.0 520 students/librarian **Guidance Counselors**: 19.0 411 students/counselor	**% Amer Indian**: 0.0 **% Asian**: 0.3 **% Black**: 43.1 **% Hispanic**: 0.9 **% White**: 55.7	National ***Socio-Economic Status*** indicator percentile (100=high): 28th

Bertie County

[WINDSOR] BERTIE COUNTY S.D.

PO BOX 10 ● WINDSOR NC 27983-0010 ● (252) 794-3173

Grade Span: PK-12 **Schools**: *Regular* 9 ● *Spec Ed* 0 ● *Alt* 0 **Students**: 4,003 **Total Teachers**: 256 **Student/Classroom Teacher Ratio**: 15.8	**Expenditures/Student**: $4,998 **Librarians**: 7.0 572 students/librarian **Guidance Counselors**: 9.0 445 students/counselor	**% Amer Indian**: 0.1 **% Asian**: 0.0 **% Black**: 79.4 **% Hispanic**: 0.3 **% White**: 20.2	National ***Socio-Economic Status*** indicator percentile (100=high): 8th

Bladen County

[ELIZABETHTOWN] BLADEN COUNTY S.D.

PO BOX 37 ● ELIZABETHTOWN NC 28337-0037 ● (910) 862-4136

Grade Span: PK-12 **Schools**: *Regular* 13 ● *Spec Ed* 0 ● *Alt* 1 **Students**: 5,674 **Total Teachers**: 429 **Student/Classroom Teacher Ratio**: 15.4	**Expenditures/Student**: $5,115 **Librarians**: 12.0 473 students/librarian **Guidance Counselors**: 11.0 516 students/counselor	**% Amer Indian**: 0.4 **% Asian**: 0.2 **% Black**: 50.2 **% Hispanic**: 0.8 **% White**: 48.4	National ***Socio-Economic Status*** indicator percentile (100=high): 17th

Brunswick County

[SOUTHPORT] BRUNSWICK COUNTY S.D.

8360 RIVER RD SE ● SOUTHPORT NC 28461-9604 ● (910) 457-5241

Grade Span: PK-12 **Schools**: *Regular* 12 ● *Spec Ed* 0 ● *Alt* 1 **Students**: 9,294 **Total Teachers**: 570 **Student/Classroom Teacher Ratio**: 15.7	**Expenditures/Student**: $4,822 **Librarians**: 14.0 664 students/librarian **Guidance Counselors**: 22.0 422 students/counselor	**% Amer Indian**: 0.8 **% Asian**: 0.2 **% Black**: 25.0 **% Hispanic**: 1.1 **% White**: 73.0	National ***Socio-Economic Status*** indicator percentile (100=high): 28th

Buncombe County

ASHEVILLE CITY S.D.

PO BOX 7347 ● ASHEVILLE NC 28802-7347 ● (828) 255-5304 ● http://www.ashevillecityschools.edu

Grade Span: KG-12 **Schools**: *Regular* 7 ● *Spec Ed* 0 ● *Alt* 2 **Students**: 4,887 **Total Teachers**: 350 **Student/Classroom Teacher Ratio**: 14.4	**Expenditures/Student**: $6,305 **Librarians**: 10.0 489 students/librarian **Guidance Counselors**: 15.0 326 students/counselor	**% Amer Indian**: 0.4 **% Asian**: 0.6 **% Black**: 41.8 **% Hispanic**: 1.6 **% White**: 55.6	National ***Socio-Economic Status*** indicator percentile (100=high): 29th

Buncombe County

[ASHEVILLE] BUNCOMBE COUNTY S.D.

175 BINGHAM RD ● ASHEVILLE NC 28806-3800 ● (828) 255-5921 ● http://eclipse.co.buncombe.k12.nc.us/public

Grade Span: PK-12 **Schools**: *Regular* 33 ● *Spec Ed* 0 ● *Alt* 2 **Students**: 24,207 **Total Teachers**: 1,401 **Student/Classroom Teacher Ratio**: 17.1	**Expenditures/Student**: $4,806 **Librarians**: 47.0 515 students/librarian **Guidance Counselors**: 85.0 285 students/counselor	**% Amer Indian**: 0.4 **% Asian**: 0.8 **% Black**: 5.5 **% Hispanic**: 1.1 **% White**: 92.2	National ***Socio-Economic Status*** indicator percentile (100=high): 51st

Burke County

[MORGANTON] BURKE COUNTY S.D.

PO DRAWER 989 ● MORGANTON NC 28680-0989 ● (828) 439-4321

Grade Span: PK-12 **Schools**: *Regular* 20 ● *Spec Ed* 1 ● *Alt* 1 **Students**: 13,237 **Total Teachers**: 847 **Student/Classroom Teacher Ratio**: 15.2	**Expenditures/Student**: $4,693 **Librarians**: 25.0 529 students/librarian **Guidance Counselors**: 27.0 490 students/counselor	**% Amer Indian**: 0.1 **% Asian**: 6.2 **% Black**: 7.5 **% Hispanic**: 1.4 **% White**: 84.8	National ***Socio-Economic Status*** indicator percentile (100=high): 55th

Cabarrus County

[CONCORD] **CABARRUS COUNTY S.D.**

PO BOX 388 ● CONCORD NC 28026-0388 ● (704) 786-6191 ● http://www.cabarrus.k12.nc.us

Grade Span: PK-12	**Expenditures/Student**: $4,497	**% Amer Indian**: 0.3	
Schools: *Regular* 19 ● *Spec Ed* 1 ● *Alt* 0	**Librarians**: 22.0	**% Asian**: 0.6	National ***Socio-Economic***
Students: 15,803	718 students/librarian	**% Black**: 13.2	***Status*** indicator percentile
Total Teachers: 956	**Guidance Counselors**: 44.0	**% Hispanic**: 1.6	(100=high): 68th
Student/Classroom Teacher Ratio: 16.3	359 students/counselor	**% White**: 84.3	

Cabarrus County

KANNAPOLIS CITY S.D.

PO BOX 1268 ● KANNAPOLIS NC 28082-1268 ● (704) 938-1131 ● http://www.gen.com/kannapolis/school/index.html

Grade Span: PK-12	**Expenditures/Student**: $4,763	**% Amer Indian**: 0.0	
Schools: *Regular* 8 ● *Spec Ed* 0 ● *Alt* 0	**Librarians**: 8.0	**% Asian**: 0.8	National ***Socio-Economic***
Students: 4,025	503 students/librarian	**% Black**: 30.9	***Status*** indicator percentile
Total Teachers: 247	**Guidance Counselors**: 11.0	**% Hispanic**: 2.2	(100=high): 29th
Student/Classroom Teacher Ratio: 17.4	366 students/counselor	**% White**: 66.1	

Caldwell County

[LENOIR] **CALDWELL COUNTY S.D.**

1914 HICKORY BLVD SW ● LENOIR NC 28645-1590 ● (828) 728-8407

Grade Span: PK-12	**Expenditures/Student**: $4,553	**% Amer Indian**: 0.0	
Schools: *Regular* 22 ● *Spec Ed* 0 ● *Alt* 1	**Librarians**: 29.0	**% Asian**: 0.3	National ***Socio-Economic***
Students: 11,849	409 students/librarian	**% Black**: 7.7	***Status*** indicator percentile
Total Teachers: 721	**Guidance Counselors**: 30.0	**% Hispanic**: 0.3	(100=high): 48th
Student/Classroom Teacher Ratio: 16.3	395 students/counselor	**% White**: 91.6	

Carteret County

[BEAUFORT] **CARTERET COUNTY S.D.**

PO DRAWER 600 ● BEAUFORT NC 28516-0600 ● (252) 728-4583

Grade Span: PK-12	**Expenditures/Student**: $4,707	**% Amer Indian**: 0.3	
Schools: *Regular* 13 ● *Spec Ed* 0 ● *Alt* 1	**Librarians**: 14.0	**% Asian**: 0.6	National ***Socio-Economic***
Students: 8,345	596 students/librarian	**% Black**: 12.5	***Status*** indicator percentile
Total Teachers: 532	**Guidance Counselors**: 26.0	**% Hispanic**: 1.1	(100=high): 42nd
Student/Classroom Teacher Ratio: 15.4	321 students/counselor	**% White**: 85.5	

Caswell County

[YANCEYVILLE] **CASWELL COUNTY S.D.**

PO BOX 160 ● YANCEYVILLE NC 27379-0160 ● (910) 694-4116

Grade Span: PK-12	**Expenditures/Student**: $4,962	**% Amer Indian**: 0.0	
Schools: *Regular* 6 ● *Spec Ed* 0 ● *Alt* 0	**Librarians**: 6.0	**% Asian**: 0.0	National ***Socio-Economic***
Students: 3,451	575 students/librarian	**% Black**: 46.3	***Status*** indicator percentile
Total Teachers: 233	**Guidance Counselors**: 8.0	**% Hispanic**: 0.7	(100=high): 34th
Student/Classroom Teacher Ratio: 15.9	431 students/counselor	**% White**: 53.0	

Catawba County

HICKORY CITY S.D.

432 4TH AVE SW ● HICKORY NC 28602-2805 ● (828) 322-2855 ● http://www.hickory.k12.nc.us

Grade Span: PK-12	**Expenditures/Student**: $4,896	**% Amer Indian**: 0.0	
Schools: *Regular* 8 ● *Spec Ed* 0 ● *Alt* 2	**Librarians**: 9.0	**% Asian**: 4.8	National ***Socio-Economic***
Students: 4,287	476 students/librarian	**% Black**: 27.4	***Status*** indicator percentile
Total Teachers: 270	**Guidance Counselors**: 15.0	**% Hispanic**: 2.2	(100=high): 39th
Student/Classroom Teacher Ratio: 16.1	286 students/counselor	**% White**: 65.5	

Catawba County

[NEWTON] **CATAWBA COUNTY S.D.**

PO BOX 1000 ● NEWTON NC 28658-1000 ● (828) 464-8333 ● http://www.catawba.k12.nc.us

Grade Span: PK-12 **Schools**: *Regular* 22 ● *Spec Ed* 0 ● *Alt* 1 **Students**: 14,107 **Total Teachers**: 841 **Student/Classroom Teacher Ratio**: 17.0	**Expenditures/Student**: $4,462 **Librarians**: 24.0 588 students/librarian **Guidance Counselors**: 31.0 455 students/counselor	**% Amer Indian**: 0.1 **% Asian**: 3.3 **% Black**: 6.9 **% Hispanic**: 1.4 **% White**: 88.2	National ***Socio-Economic Status*** indicator percentile (100=high): 71st

Catawba County

NEWTON-CONOVER CITY S.D.

605 NORTH ASHE AVE ● NEWTON NC 28658-3120 ● (828) 464-3191

Grade Span: PK-12 **Schools**: *Regular* 5 ● *Spec Ed* 1 ● *Alt* 0 **Students**: 2,749 **Total Teachers**: 178 **Student/Classroom Teacher Ratio**: 16.2	**Expenditures/Student**: $5,423 **Librarians**: 5.0 550 students/librarian **Guidance Counselors**: 8.0 344 students/counselor	**% Amer Indian**: 0.2 **% Asian**: 3.9 **% Black**: 18.2 **% Hispanic**: 3.9 **% White**: 73.8	National ***Socio-Economic Status*** indicator percentile (100=high): 46th

Chatham County

[PITTSBORO] **CHATHAM COUNTY S.D.**

PO BOX 128 ● PITTSBORO NC 27312-0128 ● (919) 542-3626 ● http://chatham.k12.nc.us

Grade Span: PK-12 **Schools**: *Regular* 13 ● *Spec Ed* 0 ● *Alt* 0 **Students**: 6,651 **Total Teachers**: 395 **Student/Classroom Teacher Ratio**: 17.1	**Expenditures/Student**: $4,864 **Librarians**: 13.0 512 students/librarian **Guidance Counselors**: 19.0 350 students/counselor	**% Amer Indian**: 0.3 **% Asian**: 0.3 **% Black**: 27.7 **% Hispanic**: 5.1 **% White**: 66.6	National ***Socio-Economic Status*** indicator percentile (100=high): 50th

Cherokee County

[MURPHY] **CHEROKEE COUNTY S.D.**

101 HIGH SCHOOL CIRCLE ● MURPHY NC 28906-0710 ● (828) 837-2722

Grade Span: PK-12 **Schools**: *Regular* 10 ● *Spec Ed* 0 ● *Alt* 0 **Students**: 3,473 **Total Teachers**: 227 **Student/Classroom Teacher Ratio**: 15.2	**Expenditures/Student**: $4,840 **Librarians**: 8.0 434 students/librarian **Guidance Counselors**: 7.0 496 students/counselor	**% Amer Indian**: 2.1 **% Asian**: 0.4 **% Black**: 2.4 **% Hispanic**: 0.7 **% White**: 94.4	National ***Socio-Economic Status*** indicator percentile (100=high): 27th

Chowan County

EDENTON-CHOWAN S.D.

PO BOX 206 ● EDENTON NC 27932-0206 ● (252) 482-4436

Grade Span: PK-12 **Schools**: *Regular* 4 ● *Spec Ed* 0 ● *Alt* 0 **Students**: 2,608 **Total Teachers**: 167 **Student/Classroom Teacher Ratio**: 15.6	**Expenditures/Student**: $5,155 **Librarians**: 4.0 652 students/librarian **Guidance Counselors**: 6.0 435 students/counselor	**% Amer Indian**: 0.0 **% Asian**: 0.2 **% Black**: 52.3 **% Hispanic**: 0.3 **% White**: 47.2	National ***Socio-Economic Status*** indicator percentile (100=high): 19th

Cleveland County

KINGS MOUNTAIN S.D.

105 E RIDGE ST ● KINGS MOUNTAIN NC 28086-0279 ● (704) 734-5637

Grade Span: PK-12 **Schools**: *Regular* 7 ● *Spec Ed* 0 ● *Alt* 1 **Students**: 4,101 **Total Teachers**: 316 **Student/Classroom Teacher Ratio**: 16.2	**Expenditures/Student**: $5,220 **Librarians**: 8.0 513 students/librarian **Guidance Counselors**: 14.0 293 students/counselor	**% Amer Indian**: 0.1 **% Asian**: 2.1 **% Black**: 24.6 **% Hispanic**: 0.5 **% White**: 72.7	National ***Socio-Economic Status*** indicator percentile (100=high): 49th

Cleveland County

[SHELBY] **CLEVELAND COUNTY S.D.**

130 S POST RD ● SHELBY NC 28152-6297 ● (704) 487-8581

Grade Span: PK-12 **Schools**: *Regular* 11 ● *Spec Ed* 0 ● *Alt* 0 **Students**: 8,698 **Total Teachers**: 513 **Student/Classroom Teacher Ratio**: 16.5	**Expenditures/Student**: $4,449 **Librarians**: 12.0 725 students/librarian **Guidance Counselors**: 19.0 458 students/counselor	**% Amer Indian**: 0.1 **% Asian**: 0.2 **% Black**: 23.9 **% Hispanic**: 0.6 **% White**: 75.3	National ***Socio-Economic Status*** indicator percentile (100=high): 44th

Cleveland County

SHELBY CITY S.D.

315 PATTON DR ● SHELBY NC 28150-5499 ● (704) 487-6367 ● http://www.blueridge.net/scs/scs.htm

Grade Span: PK-12 **Schools**: *Regular* 6 ● *Spec Ed* 1 ● *Alt* 0 **Students**: 3,418 **Total Teachers**: 226 **Student/Classroom Teacher Ratio**: 15.5	**Expenditures/Student**: $5,258 **Librarians**: 6.0 570 students/librarian **Guidance Counselors**: 6.0 570 students/counselor	**% Amer Indian**: 0.0 **% Asian**: 0.6 **% Black**: 53.4 **% Hispanic**: 0.5 **% White**: 45.4	National ***Socio-Economic Status*** indicator percentile (100=high): 28th

Columbus County

[WHITEVILLE] **COLUMBUS COUNTY S.D.**

PO BOX 729 ● WHITEVILLE NC 28472-0729 ● (910) 642-5168

Grade Span: PK-12 **Schools**: *Regular* 17 ● *Spec Ed* 0 ● *Alt* 2 **Students**: 7,624 **Total Teachers**: 482 **Student/Classroom Teacher Ratio**: 16.2	**Expenditures/Student**: $4,774 **Librarians**: 17.0 448 students/librarian **Guidance Counselors**: 24.0 318 students/counselor	**% Amer Indian**: 5.6 **% Asian**: 0.0 **% Black**: 42.9 **% Hispanic**: 0.8 **% White**: 50.8	National ***Socio-Economic Status*** indicator percentile (100=high): 10th

Columbus County

WHITEVILLE CITY S.D.

P O BOX 609 ● WHITEVILLE NC 28472-0609 ● (910) 642-4116

Grade Span: PK-12 **Schools**: *Regular* 4 ● *Spec Ed* 0 ● *Alt* 0 **Students**: 2,819 **Total Teachers**: 183 **Student/Classroom Teacher Ratio**: 15.5	**Expenditures/Student**: $4,573 **Librarians**: 4.0 705 students/librarian **Guidance Counselors**: 7.0 403 students/counselor	**% Amer Indian**: 0.5 **% Asian**: 0.5 **% Black**: 43.4 **% Hispanic**: 0.4 **% White**: 55.3	National ***Socio-Economic Status*** indicator percentile (100=high): 19th

Craven County

[NEW BERN] **CRAVEN COUNTY S.D.**

3600 TRENT RD ● NEW BERN NC 28562-2224 ● (252) 514-6300 ● http://www2.coastalnet.com/~cn2545

Grade Span: PK-12 **Schools**: *Regular* 21 ● *Spec Ed* 0 ● *Alt* 0 **Students**: 14,793 **Total Teachers**: 918 **Student/Classroom Teacher Ratio**: 16.3	**Expenditures/Student**: $4,593 **Librarians**: 24.0 616 students/librarian **Guidance Counselors**: 32.0 462 students/counselor	**% Amer Indian**: 0.2 **% Asian**: 0.7 **% Black**: 36.2 **% Hispanic**: 1.8 **% White**: 61.1	National ***Socio-Economic Status*** indicator percentile (100=high): 35th

Cumberland County

[FAYETTEVILLE] **CUMBERLAND COUNTY S.D.**

PO BOX 2357 ● FAYETTEVILLE NC 28302-2357 ● (910) 678-2300 ● http://www.ccs.k12.nc.us

Grade Span: PK-12 **Schools**: *Regular* 70 ● *Spec Ed* 1 ● *Alt* 1 **Students**: 51,148 **Total Teachers**: 2,868 **Student/Classroom Teacher Ratio**: 16.7	**Expenditures/Student**: $4,423 **Librarians**: 94.0 544 students/librarian **Guidance Counselors**: 120.0 426 students/counselor	**% Amer Indian**: 1.6 **% Asian**: 1.7 **% Black**: 44.6 **% Hispanic**: 4.5 **% White**: 47.6	National ***Socio-Economic Status*** indicator percentile (100=high): 30th

Currituck County

[CURRITUCK] **CURRITUCK COUNTY S.D.**

PO BOX 40 ● CURRITUCK NC 27929-0040 ● (252) 232-2223 ● http://schools.eastnet.ecu.edu/curritu c/curr.htm

Grade Span: PK-12 **Schools**: *Regular* 6 ● *Spec Ed* 0 ● *Alt* 0 **Students**: 2,979 **Total Teachers**: 209 **Student/Classroom Teacher Ratio**: 13.4	**Expenditures/Student**: $5,418 **Librarians**: 8.0 372 students/librarian **Guidance Counselors**: 11.0 271 students/counselor	**% Amer Indian**: 0.3 **% Asian**: 0.3 **% Black**: 12.3 **% Hispanic**: 0.8 **% White**: 86.3	National ***Socio-Economic Status*** indicator percentile (100=high): 50th

Dare County

[MANTEO] **DARE COUNTY S.D.**

PO BOX 640 ● MANTEO NC 27954-0640 ● (252) 473-1151 ● http://www.outer-banks.nc.us/dcs

Grade Span: PK-12 **Schools**: *Regular* 7 ● *Spec Ed* 0 ● *Alt* 1 **Students**: 4,192 **Total Teachers**: 280 **Student/Classroom Teacher Ratio**: 14.2	**Expenditures/Student**: $5,464 **Librarians**: 7.0 599 students/librarian **Guidance Counselors**: 11.0 381 students/counselor	**% Amer Indian**: 0.1 **% Asian**: 0.4 **% Black**: 4.7 **% Hispanic**: 1.2 **% White**: 93.6	National ***Socio-Economic Status*** indicator percentile (100=high): 66th

Davidson County

[LEXINGTON] **DAVIDSON COUNTY S.D.**

PO BOX 2057 ● LEXINGTON NC 27293-2057 ● (336) 249-8182

Grade Span: PK-12 **Schools**: *Regular* 24 ● *Spec Ed* 1 ● *Alt* 1 **Students**: 17,757 **Total Teachers**: 998 **Student/Classroom Teacher Ratio**: 17.1	**Expenditures/Student**: $4,190 **Librarians**: 25.0 710 students/librarian **Guidance Counselors**: 43.0 413 students/counselor	**% Amer Indian**: 0.3 **% Asian**: 0.4 **% Black**: 2.2 **% Hispanic**: 0.4 **% White**: 96.7	National ***Socio-Economic Status*** indicator percentile (100=high): 73rd

Davidson County

LEXINGTON CITY S.D.

1010 FAIR ST ● LEXINGTON NC 27292-2468 ● (336) 242-1527

Grade Span: PK-12 **Schools**: *Regular* 6 ● *Spec Ed* 0 ● *Alt* 1 **Students**: 3,071 **Total Teachers**: 201 **Student/Classroom Teacher Ratio**: 16.0	**Expenditures/Student**: $5,256 **Librarians**: 6.0 512 students/librarian **Guidance Counselors**: 9.0 341 students/counselor	**% Amer Indian**: 0.2 **% Asian**: 4.4 **% Black**: 45.2 **% Hispanic**: 4.0 **% White**: 46.2	National ***Socio-Economic Status*** indicator percentile (100=high): 15th

Davie County

[MOCKSVILLE] **DAVIE COUNTY S.D.**

220 CHERRY ST ● MOCKSVILLE NC 27028-2206 ● (704) 634-5921

Grade Span: PK-12 **Schools**: *Regular* 9 ● *Spec Ed* 0 ● *Alt* 0 **Students**: 4,832 **Total Teachers**: 316 **Student/Classroom Teacher Ratio**: 16.0	**Expenditures/Student**: $4,776 **Librarians**: 11.0 439 students/librarian **Guidance Counselors**: 14.0 345 students/counselor	**% Amer Indian**: 0.3 **% Asian**: 0.4 **% Black**: 10.1 **% Hispanic**: 0.9 **% White**: 88.3	National ***Socio-Economic Status*** indicator percentile (100=high): 73rd

Duplin County

[KENANSVILLE] **DUPLIN COUNTY S.D.**

PO BOX 128 ● KENANSVILLE NC 28349-0128 ● (910) 296-1521

Grade Span: PK-12 **Schools**: *Regular* 15 ● *Spec Ed* 0 ● *Alt* 0 **Students**: 8,303 **Total Teachers**: 501 **Student/Classroom Teacher Ratio**: 15.2	**Expenditures/Student**: $4,310 **Librarians**: 15.0 554 students/librarian **Guidance Counselors**: 22.0 377 students/counselor	**% Amer Indian**: 0.1 **% Asian**: 0.1 **% Black**: 40.1 **% Hispanic**: 7.5 **% White**: 52.2	National ***Socio-Economic Status*** indicator percentile (100=high): 20th

Durham County

DURHAM S.D.

PO BOX 30002 ● DURHAM NC 27702-3002 ● (919) 560-2000 ● http://www.dps.durham.k12.nc.us/Web/index.html

Grade Span: PK-12	**Expenditures/Student**: $5,667	**% Amer Indian**: 0.3	
Schools: *Regular* 43 ● *Spec Ed* 0 ● *Alt* 2	**Librarians**: 48.0	**% Asian**: 1.9	National ***Socio-Economic Status*** indicator percentile (100=high): 35th
Students: 28,472	593 students/librarian	**% Black**: 56.2	
Total Teachers: 1,976	**Guidance Counselors**: 89.0	**% Hispanic**: 2.0	
Student/Classroom Teacher Ratio: 14.0	320 students/counselor	**% White**: 39.6	

Edgecombe County

[TARBORO] EDGECOMBE COUNTY S.D.

PO BOX 7128 ● TARBORO NC 27886-7128 ● (252) 641-2600 ● http://schools.eastnet.ecu.edu/edgecomb

Grade Span: PK-12	**Expenditures/Student**: $4,713	**% Amer Indian**: 0.0	
Schools: *Regular* 14 ● *Spec Ed* 0 ● *Alt* 1	**Librarians**: 15.0	**% Asian**: 0.2	National ***Socio-Economic Status*** indicator percentile (100=high): 20th
Students: 8,033	536 students/librarian	**% Black**: 59.0	
Total Teachers: 509	**Guidance Counselors**: 18.0	**% Hispanic**: 1.6	
Student/Classroom Teacher Ratio: 15.6	446 students/counselor	**% White**: 39.2	

Forsyth County

[WINSTON-SALEM] FORSYTH COUNTY S.D.

PO BOX 2513 ● WINSTON-SALEM NC 27102-2513 ● (336) 727-2816 ● http://mts.admin.wsfcs.k12.nc.us

Grade Span: PK-12	**Expenditures/Student**: $5,208	**% Amer Indian**: 0.2	
Schools: *Regular* 53 ● *Spec Ed* 3 ● *Alt* 2	**Librarians**: 60.0	**% Asian**: 1.0	National ***Socio-Economic Status*** indicator percentile (100=high): 46th
Students: 40,895	682 students/librarian	**% Black**: 37.4	
Total Teachers: 2,705	**Guidance Counselors**: 106.0	**% Hispanic**: 2.3	
Student/Classroom Teacher Ratio: 14.0	386 students/counselor	**% White**: 59.1	

Franklin County

[LOUISBURG] FRANKLIN COUNTY S.D.

PO BOX 449 ● LOUISBURG NC 27549-0449 ● (919) 496-4159 ● http://www.franklinco.k12.nc.us/Franklin

Grade Span: PK-12	**Expenditures/Student**: $4,562	**% Amer Indian**: 0.3	
Schools: *Regular* 10 ● *Spec Ed* 0 ● *Alt* 0	**Librarians**: 11.0	**% Asian**: 0.2	National ***Socio-Economic Status*** indicator percentile (100=high): 28th
Students: 6,767	615 students/librarian	**% Black**: 44.1	
Total Teachers: 431	**Guidance Counselors**: 13.0	**% Hispanic**: 1.2	
Student/Classroom Teacher Ratio: 15.7	521 students/counselor	**% White**: 54.2	

Gaston County

[GASTONIA] GASTON COUNTY S.D.

PO BOX 1397 ● GASTONIA NC 28053-1397 ● (704) 866-6100 ● http://gcs.gaston.k12.nc.us

Grade Span: PK-12	**Expenditures/Student**: $4,410	**% Amer Indian**: 0.1	
Schools: *Regular* 52 ● *Spec Ed* 1 ● *Alt* 0	**Librarians**: 54.0	**% Asian**: 1.3	National ***Socio-Economic Status*** indicator percentile (100=high): 50th
Students: 29,334	543 students/librarian	**% Black**: 19.2	
Total Teachers: 1,740	**Guidance Counselors**: 67.0	**% Hispanic**: 0.5	
Student/Classroom Teacher Ratio: 16.6	438 students/counselor	**% White**: 78.7	

Granville County

[OXFORD] GRANVILLE COUNTY S.D.

P O BOX 927 ● OXFORD NC 27565-0927 ● (919) 693-4613 ● http://eclipse.gcs.k12.nc.us/public

Grade Span: PK-12	**Expenditures/Student**: $4,694	**% Amer Indian**: 0.2	
Schools: *Regular* 12 ● *Spec Ed* 0 ● *Alt* 0	**Librarians**: 11.0	**% Asian**: 0.2	National ***Socio-Economic Status*** indicator percentile (100=high): 36th
Students: 7,141	649 students/librarian	**% Black**: 42.4	
Total Teachers: 438	**Guidance Counselors**: 20.0	**% Hispanic**: 1.2	
Student/Classroom Teacher Ratio: 16.5	357 students/counselor	**% White**: 56.1	

Greene County

[SNOW HILL] **GREENE COUNTY S.D.**

301 KINGOLD BLVD ● SNOW HILL NC 28580-1393 ● (252) 747-3425 ● http://schools.eastnet.ecu.edu/greene/greene.htm

Grade Span: PK-12 **Schools**: *Regular* 4 ● *Spec Ed* 0 ● *Alt* 0 **Students**: 2,862 **Total Teachers**: 188 **Student/Classroom Teacher Ratio**: 15.3	**Expenditures/Student**: $5,271 **Librarians**: 4.0 716 students/librarian **Guidance Counselors**: 9.0 318 students/counselor	**% Amer Indian**: 0.0 **% Asian**: 0.1 **% Black**: 55.7 **% Hispanic**: 5.0 **% White**: 39.3	National ***Socio-Economic Status*** indicator percentile (100=high): 16th

Guilford County

[GREENSBORO] **GUILFORD COUNTY S.D.**

PO BOX 880 ● GREENSBORO NC 27402-0880 ● (336) 370-8100 ● http://www.guilford.k12.nc.us

Grade Span: PK-12 **Schools**: *Regular* 89 ● *Spec Ed* 2 ● *Alt* 2 **Students**: 57,211 **Total Teachers**: 3,574 **Student/Classroom Teacher Ratio**: 16.4	**Expenditures/Student**: $5,355 **Librarians**: 108.0 530 students/librarian **Guidance Counselors**: 179.0 320 students/counselor	**% Amer Indian**: 0.7 **% Asian**: 2.7 **% Black**: 38.1 **% Hispanic**: 1.3 **% White**: 57.3	National ***Socio-Economic Status*** indicator percentile (100=high): 45th

Halifax County

[HALIFAX] **HALIFAX COUNTY S.D.**

PO BOX 468 ● HALIFAX NC 27839-0468 ● (919) 583-5111

Grade Span: PK-12 **Schools**: *Regular* 15 ● *Spec Ed* 0 ● *Alt* 0 **Students**: 6,542 **Total Teachers**: 386 **Student/Classroom Teacher Ratio**: 15.8	**Expenditures/Student**: $4,798 **Librarians**: 11.0 595 students/librarian **Guidance Counselors**: 13.0 503 students/counselor	**% Amer Indian**: 6.3 **% Asian**: 0.0 **% Black**: 86.3 **% Hispanic**: 0.3 **% White**: 7.0	National ***Socio-Economic Status*** indicator percentile (100=high): 5th

Halifax County

ROANOKE RAPIDS CITY S.D.

536 HAMILTON ST ● ROANOKE RAPIDS NC 27870-9990 ● (252) 535-3111 ● http://www.schoollink.net/rrapids

Grade Span: PK-12 **Schools**: *Regular* 5 ● *Spec Ed* 0 ● *Alt* 0 **Students**: 3,164 **Total Teachers**: 200 **Student/Classroom Teacher Ratio**: 16.9	**Expenditures/Student**: $4,965 **Librarians**: 5.0 633 students/librarian **Guidance Counselors**: 10.0 316 students/counselor	**% Amer Indian**: 0.6 **% Asian**: 1.7 **% Black**: 19.6 **% Hispanic**: 0.7 **% White**: 77.4	National ***Socio-Economic Status*** indicator percentile (100=high): 42nd

Harnett County

[LILLINGTON] **HARNETT COUNTY S.D.**

PO BOX 1029 ● LILLINGTON NC 27546-1029 ● (910) 893-8151 ● http://www.intrstar.net/~hcss

Grade Span: PK-12 **Schools**: *Regular* 22 ● *Spec Ed* 0 ● *Alt* 0 **Students**: 13,887 **Total Teachers**: 810 **Student/Classroom Teacher Ratio**: 17.5	**Expenditures/Student**: $4,296 **Librarians**: 27.0 514 students/librarian **Guidance Counselors**: 30.0 463 students/counselor	**% Amer Indian**: 1.1 **% Asian**: 0.5 **% Black**: 30.1 **% Hispanic**: 3.2 **% White**: 65.2	National ***Socio-Economic Status*** indicator percentile (100=high): 33rd

Haywood County

[WAYNESVILLE] **HAYWOOD COUNTY S.D.**

1615 N MAIN ST ● WAYNESVILLE NC 28786-3461 ● (828) 456-2400 ● http://www.haywood.k12.nc.us

Grade Span: PK-12 **Schools**: *Regular* 15 ● *Spec Ed* 0 ● *Alt* 0 **Students**: 7,401 **Total Teachers**: 474 **Student/Classroom Teacher Ratio**: 14.9	**Expenditures/Student**: $5,124 **Librarians**: 16.0 463 students/librarian **Guidance Counselors**: 20.0 370 students/counselor	**% Amer Indian**: 0.4 **% Asian**: 0.1 **% Black**: 1.6 **% Hispanic**: 0.9 **% White**: 96.9	National ***Socio-Economic Status*** indicator percentile (100=high): 48th

Henderson County

[HENDERSONVILLE] **HENDERSON COUNTY S.D.**

414 4TH AVE W ● HENDERSONVILLE NC 28739-4261 ● (828) 697-4733

Grade Span: PK-12 **Schools**: *Regular* 19 ● *Spec Ed* 0 ● *Alt* 1 **Students**: 10,931 **Total Teachers**: 683 **Student/Classroom Teacher Ratio**: 16.6	**Expenditures/Student**: $4,629 **Librarians**: 19.0 575 students/librarian **Guidance Counselors**: 27.0 405 students/counselor	**% Amer Indian**: 0.2 **% Asian**: 0.7 **% Black**: 5.3 **% Hispanic**: 4.0 **% White**: 89.8	National ***Socio-Economic Status*** indicator percentile (100=high): 51st

Hertford County

[WINTON] **HERTFORD COUNTY S.D.**

PO BOX 158 ● WINTON NC 27986-0158 ● (252) 358-1761 ● http://www.schoollink.net/hertco

Grade Span: PK-12 **Schools**: *Regular* 6 ● *Spec Ed* 0 ● *Alt* 0 **Students**: 4,382 **Total Teachers**: 278 **Student/Classroom Teacher Ratio**: 16.3	**Expenditures/Student**: $4,711 **Librarians**: 7.0 626 students/librarian **Guidance Counselors**: 11.0 398 students/counselor	**% Amer Indian**: 0.7 **% Asian**: 0.1 **% Black**: 74.7 **% Hispanic**: 0.2 **% White**: 24.3	National ***Socio-Economic Status*** indicator percentile (100=high): 8th

Hoke County

[RAEFORD] **HOKE COUNTY S.D.**

PO BOX 370 ● RAEFORD NC 28376-0370 ● (910) 875-4106

Grade Span: PK-12 **Schools**: *Regular* 10 ● *Spec Ed* 0 ● *Alt* 0 **Students**: 5,809 **Total Teachers**: 337 **Student/Classroom Teacher Ratio**: 15.6	**Expenditures/Student**: $4,431 **Librarians**: 11.0 528 students/librarian **Guidance Counselors**: 16.0 363 students/counselor	**% Amer Indian**: 14.8 **% Asian**: 0.6 **% Black**: 50.5 **% Hispanic**: 2.4 **% White**: 31.6	National ***Socio-Economic Status*** indicator percentile (100=high): 16th

Iredell County

MOORESVILLE CITY S.D.

305 N MAIN ● MOORESVILLE NC 28115-0119 ● (704) 664-5553 ● http://www.mgsd.k12.nc.us

Grade Span: PK-12 **Schools**: *Regular* 4 ● *Spec Ed* 0 ● *Alt* 1 **Students**: 3,312 **Total Teachers**: 191 **Student/Classroom Teacher Ratio**: 18.1	**Expenditures/Student**: $4,589 **Librarians**: 4.0 828 students/librarian **Guidance Counselors**: 6.0 552 students/counselor	**% Amer Indian**: 0.2 **% Asian**: 2.3 **% Black**: 19.6 **% Hispanic**: 0.7 **% White**: 77.2	National ***Socio-Economic Status*** indicator percentile (100=high): 61st

Iredell County

[STATESVILLE] **IREDELL-STATESVILLE S.D.**

PO BOX 911 ● STATESVILLE NC 28687-0911 ● (704) 872-8931 ● http://www.iss.k12.nc.us

Grade Span: PK-12 **Schools**: *Regular* 28 ● *Spec Ed* 0 ● *Alt* 0 **Students**: 14,171 **Total Teachers**: 859 **Student/Classroom Teacher Ratio**: 16.7	**Expenditures/Student**: $4,735 **Librarians**: 34.0 417 students/librarian **Guidance Counselors**: 42.0 337 students/counselor	**% Amer Indian**: 0.2 **% Asian**: 0.8 **% Black**: 22.1 **% Hispanic**: 1.5 **% White**: 75.5	National ***Socio-Economic Status*** indicator percentile (100=high): 54th

Jackson County

[SYLVA] **JACKSON COUNTY S.D.**

43 HOSPITAL RD ● SYLVA NC 28779-2732 ● (828) 586-2311

Grade Span: PK-12 **Schools**: *Regular* 6 ● *Spec Ed* 0 ● *Alt* 0 **Students**: 3,586 **Total Teachers**: 237 **Student/Classroom Teacher Ratio**: 14.7	**Expenditures/Student**: $5,197 **Librarians**: 6.0 598 students/librarian **Guidance Counselors**: 9.0 398 students/counselor	**% Amer Indian**: 8.0 **% Asian**: 0.3 **% Black**: 1.1 **% Hispanic**: 0.5 **% White**: 90.1	National ***Socio-Economic Status*** indicator percentile (100=high): 42nd

Johnston County

[SMITHFIELD] **JOHNSTON COUNTY S.D.**

PO BOX 1336 ● SMITHFIELD NC 27577-1336 ● (919) 934-6031

Grade Span: PK-12 **Schools**: *Regular* 26 ● *Spec Ed* 0 ● *Alt* 1 **Students**: 16,809 **Total Teachers**: 1,075 **Student/Classroom Teacher Ratio**: 15.9	**Expenditures/Student**: $4,520 **Librarians**: 27.0 623 students/librarian **Guidance Counselors**: 38.0 442 students/counselor	**% Amer Indian**: 0.3 **% Asian**: 0.3 **% Black**: 22.8 **% Hispanic**: 3.9 **% White**: 72.8	National ***Socio-Economic Status*** indicator percentile (100=high): 45th

Lee County

[SANFORD] **LEE COUNTY S.D.**

PO BOX 1010 ● SANFORD NC 27331-1010 ● (919) 774-6226 ● http://www.lee.k12.nc.us

Grade Span: PK-12 **Schools**: *Regular* 11 ● *Spec Ed* 1 ● *Alt* 1 **Students**: 8,242 **Total Teachers**: 490 **Student/Classroom Teacher Ratio**: 17.4	**Expenditures/Student**: $4,530 **Librarians**: 12.0 687 students/librarian **Guidance Counselors**: 17.0 485 students/counselor	**% Amer Indian**: 0.5 **% Asian**: 0.5 **% Black**: 30.2 **% Hispanic**: 7.1 **% White**: 61.8	National ***Socio-Economic Status*** indicator percentile (100=high): 43rd

Lenoir County

[KINSTON] **LENOIR COUNTY S.D.**

PO BOX 729 ● KINSTON NC 28502-0729 ● (252) 527-1109

Grade Span: PK-12 **Schools**: *Regular* 18 ● *Spec Ed* 0 ● *Alt* 1 **Students**: 10,451 **Total Teachers**: 673 **Student/Classroom Teacher Ratio**: 16.0	**Expenditures/Student**: $4,811 **Librarians**: 21.0 498 students/librarian **Guidance Counselors**: 26.0 402 students/counselor	**% Amer Indian**: 0.2 **% Asian**: 0.3 **% Black**: 52.2 **% Hispanic**: 1.7 **% White**: 45.6	National ***Socio-Economic Status*** indicator percentile (100=high): 26th

Lincoln County

[LINCOLNTON] **LINCOLN COUNTY S.D.**

PO BOX 400 ● LINCOLNTON NC 28093-0400 ● (704) 732-2261 ● http://www.lincoln.k12.nc.us

Grade Span: PK-12 **Schools**: *Regular* 16 ● *Spec Ed* 0 ● *Alt* 1 **Students**: 9,558 **Total Teachers**: 554 **Student/Classroom Teacher Ratio**: 17.5	**Expenditures/Student**: $4,478 **Librarians**: 17.0 562 students/librarian **Guidance Counselors**: 24.0 398 students/counselor	**% Amer Indian**: 0.3 **% Asian**: 0.3 **% Black**: 10.7 **% Hispanic**: 2.6 **% White**: 86.2	National ***Socio-Economic Status*** indicator percentile (100=high): 58th

McDowell County

[MARION] **MCDOWELL COUNTY S.D.**

PO BOX 130 ● MARION NC 28752-0130 ● (828) 652-4535

Grade Span: PK-12 **Schools**: *Regular* 11 ● *Spec Ed* 0 ● *Alt* 0 **Students**: 6,151 **Total Teachers**: 360 **Student/Classroom Teacher Ratio**: 17.4	**Expenditures/Student**: $4,594 **Librarians**: 12.0 513 students/librarian **Guidance Counselors**: 16.0 384 students/counselor	**% Amer Indian**: 0.0 **% Asian**: 1.0 **% Black**: 4.9 **% Hispanic**: 0.5 **% White**: 93.5	National ***Socio-Economic Status*** indicator percentile (100=high): 53rd

Macon County

[FRANKLIN] **MACON COUNTY S.D.**

PO BOX 1029 ● FRANKLIN NC 28734-1029 ● (828) 524-3314

Grade Span: KG-12 **Schools**: *Regular* 11 ● *Spec Ed* 0 ● *Alt* 0 **Students**: 3,755 **Total Teachers**: 245 **Student/Classroom Teacher Ratio**: 14.2	**Expenditures/Student**: $5,022 **Librarians**: 9.0 417 students/librarian **Guidance Counselors**: 9.0 417 students/counselor	**% Amer Indian**: 0.1 **% Asian**: 0.5 **% Black**: 1.2 **% Hispanic**: 0.7 **% White**: 97.4	National ***Socio-Economic Status*** indicator percentile (100=high): 46th

Madison County

[MARSHALL] **MADISON COUNTY S.D.**

2 BLANNAHASSETT ISLAND RD ● MARSHALL NC 28753-9006 ● (828) 649-9276

Grade Span: PK-12 **Schools**: *Regular* 8 ● *Spec Ed* 0 ● *Alt* 0 **Students**: 2,552 **Total Teachers**: 168 **Student/Classroom Teacher Ratio**: 12.5	**Expenditures/Student**: $5,255 **Librarians**: 9.0 284 students/librarian **Guidance Counselors**: 5.0 510 students/counselor	**% Amer Indian**: 0.1 **% Asian**: 0.1 **% Black**: 0.2 **% Hispanic**: 0.5 **% White**: 99.2	National ***Socio-Economic Status*** indicator percentile (100=high): 29th

Martin County

[WILLIAMSTON] **MARTIN COUNTY S.D.**

300 N WATTS ST ● WILLIAMSTON NC 27892-2099 ● (252) 792-1575

Grade Span: PK-12 **Schools**: *Regular* 13 ● *Spec Ed* 0 ● *Alt* 0 **Students**: 5,027 **Total Teachers**: 358 **Student/Classroom Teacher Ratio**: 13.3	**Expenditures/Student**: $5,233 **Librarians**: 13.0 387 students/librarian **Guidance Counselors**: 12.0 419 students/counselor	**% Amer Indian**: 0.2 **% Asian**: 0.3 **% Black**: 56.8 **% Hispanic**: 0.5 **% White**: 42.2	National ***Socio-Economic Status*** indicator percentile (100=high): 21st

Mecklenburg County

CHARLOTTE-MECKLENBURG S.D.

PO BOX 30035 ● CHARLOTTE NC 28230-0035 ● (704) 379-7000 ● http://www.cms.k12.nc.us

Grade Span: PK-12 **Schools**: *Regular* 118 ● *Spec Ed* 2 ● *Alt* 6 **Students**: 89,544 **Total Teachers**: 5,356 **Student/Classroom Teacher Ratio**: 17.2	**Expenditures/Student**: $5,251 **Librarians**: 152.0 589 students/librarian **Guidance Counselors**: 213.0 420 students/counselor	**% Amer Indian**: 0.4 **% Asian**: 3.6 **% Black**: 40.3 **% Hispanic**: 2.0 **% White**: 53.7	National ***Socio-Economic Status*** indicator percentile (100=high): 41st

Montgomery County

[TROY] **MONTGOMERY COUNTY S.D.**

PO BOX 427 ● TROY NC 27371-0427 ● (910) 576-6511 ● http://www.ac.net/~mont1

Grade Span: PK-12 **Schools**: *Regular* 8 ● *Spec Ed* 0 ● *Alt* 0 **Students**: 4,278 **Total Teachers**: 265 **Student/Classroom Teacher Ratio**: 15.7	**Expenditures/Student**: $4,692 **Librarians**: 8.0 535 students/librarian **Guidance Counselors**: 10.0 428 students/counselor	**% Amer Indian**: 0.0 **% Asian**: 2.5 **% Black**: 32.6 **% Hispanic**: 7.5 **% White**: 57.4	National ***Socio-Economic Status*** indicator percentile (100=high): 27th

Moore County

[CARTHAGE] **MOORE COUNTY S.D.**

PO BOX 1180 ● CARTHAGE NC 28327-1180 ● (910) 947-2976 ● http://www.sandhills.org/schools/public.htm

Grade Span: PK-12 **Schools**: *Regular* 18 ● *Spec Ed* 0 ● *Alt* 0 **Students**: 10,329 **Total Teachers**: 638 **Student/Classroom Teacher Ratio**: 16.1	**Expenditures/Student**: $4,774 **Librarians**: 19.0 544 students/librarian **Guidance Counselors**: 22.0 470 students/counselor	**% Amer Indian**: 1.1 **% Asian**: 0.4 **% Black**: 27.2 **% Hispanic**: 2.2 **% White**: 69.2	National ***Socio-Economic Status*** indicator percentile (100=high): 40th

Nash County

[NASHVILLE] **NASH-ROCKY MOUNT SCHOOL ADMINISTRATIVE UNIT**

930 EASTERN AVE ● NASHVILLE NC 27856-1716 ● (252) 459-5220

Grade Span: PK-12 **Schools**: *Regular* 26 ● *Spec Ed* 0 ● *Alt* 1 **Students**: 17,867 **Total Teachers**: 1,096 **Student/Classroom Teacher Ratio**: 16.2	**Expenditures/Student**: $4,582 **Librarians**: 31.0 576 students/librarian **Guidance Counselors**: 58.0 308 students/counselor	**% Amer Indian**: 0.3 **% Asian**: 0.8 **% Black**: 54.0 **% Hispanic**: 2.7 **% White**: 42.2	National ***Socio-Economic Status*** indicator percentile (100=high): 26th

New Hanover County

[WILMINGTON] NEW HANOVER COUNTY S.D.

1802 S 15TH ST ● WILMINGTON NC 28401-6479 ● (910) 763-5431

Grade Span: PK-12 **Schools**: *Regular* 30 ● *Spec Ed* 0 ● *Alt* 0 **Students**: 21,180 **Total Teachers**: 1,296 **Student/Classroom Teacher Ratio**: 15.2	**Expenditures/Student**: $4,716 **Librarians**: 29.0 730 students/librarian **Guidance Counselors**: 46.0 460 students/counselor	**% Amer Indian**: 0.3 **% Asian**: 0.9 **% Black**: 29.7 **% Hispanic**: 0.7 **% White**: 68.3	National ***Socio-Economic Status*** indicator percentile (100=high): 45th

Northampton County

[JACKSON] NORTHAMPTON COUNTY S.D.

PO BOX 158 ● JACKSON NC 27845-0158 ● (252) 534-1371 ● http://www.northampton.k12.nc.us

Grade Span: PK-12 **Schools**: *Regular* 10 ● *Spec Ed* 0 ● *Alt* 0 **Students**: 3,941 **Total Teachers**: 231 **Student/Classroom Teacher Ratio**: 16.1	**Expenditures/Student**: $4,733 **Librarians**: 9.0 438 students/librarian **Guidance Counselors**: 10.0 394 students/counselor	**% Amer Indian**: 0.2 **% Asian**: 0.0 **% Black**: 79.9 **% Hispanic**: 0.2 **% White**: 19.7	National ***Socio-Economic Status*** indicator percentile (100=high): 8th

Onslow County

[JACKSONVILLE] ONSLOW COUNTY S.D.

PO BOX 99 ● JACKSONVILLE NC 28541-0099 ● (910) 455-2211

Grade Span: PK-12 **Schools**: *Regular* 28 ● *Spec Ed* 0 ● *Alt* 0 **Students**: 20,489 **Total Teachers**: 1,148 **Student/Classroom Teacher Ratio**: 17.4	**Expenditures/Student**: $3,962 **Librarians**: 38.0 539 students/librarian **Guidance Counselors**: 48.0 427 students/counselor	**% Amer Indian**: 0.6 **% Asian**: 2.2 **% Black**: 25.1 **% Hispanic**: 3.5 **% White**: 68.6	National ***Socio-Economic Status*** indicator percentile (100=high): 41st

Orange County

CHAPEL HILL-CARRBORO S.D.

750 S MERRITT MILL RD ● CHAPEL HILL NC 27516-2878 ● (919) 967-8211

Grade Span: PK-12 **Schools**: *Regular* 10 ● *Spec Ed* 0 ● *Alt* 1 **Students**: 7,926 **Total Teachers**: 528 **Student/Classroom Teacher Ratio**: 14.3	**Expenditures/Student**: $5,658 **Librarians**: 15.0 528 students/librarian **Guidance Counselors**: 23.0 345 students/counselor	**% Amer Indian**: 0.2 **% Asian**: 6.1 **% Black**: 19.7 **% Hispanic**: 1.4 **% White**: 72.6	National ***Socio-Economic Status*** indicator percentile (100=high): 73rd

Orange County

[HILLSBOROUGH] ORANGE COUNTY S.D.

200 E KING ST ● HILLSBOROUGH NC 27278-2570 ● (919) 732-8126

Grade Span: PK-12 **Schools**: *Regular* 8 ● *Spec Ed* 0 ● *Alt* 0 **Students**: 5,701 **Total Teachers**: 365 **Student/Classroom Teacher Ratio**: 15.2	**Expenditures/Student**: $5,227 **Librarians**: 9.0 633 students/librarian **Guidance Counselors**: 13.0 439 students/counselor	**% Amer Indian**: 0.3 **% Asian**: 0.5 **% Black**: 23.5 **% Hispanic**: 2.0 **% White**: 73.7	National ***Socio-Economic Status*** indicator percentile (100=high): 57th

Pasquotank County

[ELIZABETH CITY] PASQUOTANK COUNTY S.D.

PO BOX 2247 ● ELIZABETH CITY NC 27906-2247 ● (252) 335-2981

Grade Span: PK-12 **Schools**: *Regular* 10 ● *Spec Ed* 0 ● *Alt* 0 **Students**: 6,275 **Total Teachers**: 374 **Student/Classroom Teacher Ratio**: 16.6	**Expenditures/Student**: $4,629 **Librarians**: 11.0 570 students/librarian **Guidance Counselors**: 14.0 448 students/counselor	**% Amer Indian**: 0.1 **% Asian**: 0.7 **% Black**: 48.6 **% Hispanic**: 0.7 **% White**: 49.9	National ***Socio-Economic Status*** indicator percentile (100=high): 20th

Pender County

[BURGAW] **PENDER COUNTY S.D.**

PO BOX 1239 ● BURGAW NC 28425-1239 ● (910) 259-2187 ● http://localsonly.wilmington.net/pender

Grade Span: PK-12 **Schools**: *Regular* 10 ● *Spec Ed* 0 ● *Alt* 1 **Students**: 5,730 **Total Teachers**: 345 **Student/Classroom Teacher Ratio**: 16.4	**Expenditures/Student**: $4,751 **Librarians**: 11.0 521 students/librarian **Guidance Counselors**: 12.0 478 students/counselor	**% Amer Indian**: 0.1 **% Asian**: 0.1 **% Black**: 37.2 **% Hispanic**: 1.5 **% White**: 61.2	National ***Socio-Economic Status*** indicator percentile (100=high): 27th

Person County

[ROXBORO] **PERSON COUNTY S.D.**

ROOM 25 304 S MORGAN ST ● ROXBORO NC 27573-5245 ● (910) 599-2191

Grade Span: PK-12 **Schools**: *Regular* 11 ● *Spec Ed* 0 ● *Alt* 0 **Students**: 5,523 **Total Teachers**: 365 **Student/Classroom Teacher Ratio**: 15.2	**Expenditures/Student**: $4,884 **Librarians**: 13.0 425 students/librarian **Guidance Counselors**: 17.0 325 students/counselor	**% Amer Indian**: 0.4 **% Asian**: 0.2 **% Black**: 36.4 **% Hispanic**: 1.6 **% White**: 61.5	National ***Socio-Economic Status*** indicator percentile (100=high): 38th

Pitt County

[GREENVILLE] **PITT COUNTY S.D.**

1717 W 5TH ST ● GREENVILLE NC 27834-1698 ● (252) 830-4200 ● http://schools.eastnet.ecu.edu/pitt/pitt.htm

Grade Span: PK-12 **Schools**: *Regular* 29 ● *Spec Ed* 0 ● *Alt* 1 **Students**: 19,298 **Total Teachers**: 1,243 **Student/Classroom Teacher Ratio**: 16.4	**Expenditures/Student**: $4,576 **Librarians**: 34.0 568 students/librarian **Guidance Counselors**: 45.0 429 students/counselor	**% Amer Indian**: 0.1 **% Asian**: 0.8 **% Black**: 49.5 **% Hispanic**: 1.1 **% White**: 48.5	National ***Socio-Economic Status*** indicator percentile (100=high): 30th

Randolph County

ASHEBORO CITY S.D.

PO BOX 1103 ● ASHEBORO NC 27204-1103 ● (910) 625-5104

Grade Span: PK-12 **Schools**: *Regular* 8 ● *Spec Ed* 0 ● *Alt* 0 **Students**: 4,021 **Total Teachers**: 244 **Student/Classroom Teacher Ratio**: 16.2	**Expenditures/Student**: $5,034 **Librarians**: 15.0 268 students/librarian **Guidance Counselors**: 7.0 574 students/counselor	**% Amer Indian**: 0.2 **% Asian**: 1.4 **% Black**: 18.5 **% Hispanic**: 6.7 **% White**: 73.2	National ***Socio-Economic Status*** indicator percentile (100=high): 44th

Randolph County

[ASHEBORO] **RANDOLPH COUNTY S.D.**

2222-C S FAYETTEVILLE ST ● ASHEBORO NC 27203-7397 ● (910) 318-6100 ● http://www.randolph.org

Grade Span: PK-12 **Schools**: *Regular* 22 ● *Spec Ed* 0 ● *Alt* 0 **Students**: 15,187 **Total Teachers**: 878 **Student/Classroom Teacher Ratio**: 17.3	**Expenditures/Student**: $4,151 **Librarians**: 27.0 562 students/librarian **Guidance Counselors**: 37.0 410 students/counselor	**% Amer Indian**: 0.4 **% Asian**: 0.4 **% Black**: 4.8 **% Hispanic**: 1.7 **% White**: 92.7	National ***Socio-Economic Status*** indicator percentile (100=high): 64th

Richmond County

[HAMLET] **RICHMOND COUNTY S.D.**

PO DRAWER 1259 ● HAMLET NC 28345-1259 ● (910) 582-5860

Grade Span: PK-12 **Schools**: *Regular* 15 ● *Spec Ed* 1 ● *Alt* 1 **Students**: 8,299 **Total Teachers**: 500 **Student/Classroom Teacher Ratio**: 16.6	**Expenditures/Student**: $4,508 **Librarians**: 16.0 519 students/librarian **Guidance Counselors**: 26.0 319 students/counselor	**% Amer Indian**: 1.2 **% Asian**: 0.7 **% Black**: 40.6 **% Hispanic**: 1.0 **% White**: 56.4	National ***Socio-Economic Status*** indicator percentile (100=high): 22nd

Robeson County

[LUMBERTON] **PUBLIC S.D. OF ROBESON COUNTY**

PO BOX 2909 ● LUMBERTON NC 28359-2909 ● (910) 738-4841

Grade Span: PK-12 **Schools**: *Regular* 40 ● *Spec Ed* 0 ● *Alt* 1 **Students**: 23,482 **Total Teachers**: 1,523 **Student/Classroom Teacher Ratio**: 16.3	**Expenditures/Student**: $4,512 **Librarians**: 44.0 534 students/librarian **Guidance Counselors**: 51.0 460 students/counselor	**% Amer Indian**: 44.5 **% Asian**: 0.2 **% Black**: 31.0 **% Hispanic**: 0.9 **% White**: 23.4	National ***Socio-Economic Status*** indicator percentile (100=high): 9th

Rockingham County

[EDEN] **ROCKINGHAM COUNTY CONSOLIDATED S.D.**

511 HARRINGTON HWY ● EDEN NC 27288-7547 ● (910) 627-2600

Grade Span: PK-12 **Schools**: *Regular* 25 ● *Spec Ed* 0 ● *Alt* 0 **Students**: 14,343 **Total Teachers**: 857 **Student/Classroom Teacher Ratio**: 16.5	**Expenditures/Student**: $4,589 **Librarians**: 28.0 512 students/librarian **Guidance Counselors**: 33.0 435 students/counselor	**% Amer Indian**: 0.2 **% Asian**: 0.3 **% Black**: 25.4 **% Hispanic**: 1.6 **% White**: 72.5	National ***Socio-Economic Status*** indicator percentile (100=high): 48th

Rowan County

[SALISBURY] **ROWAN-SALISBURY S.D.**

PO BOX 2349 ● SALISBURY NC 28145-2349 ● (704) 636-7500

Grade Span: PK-12 **Schools**: *Regular* 28 ● *Spec Ed* 0 ● *Alt* 0 **Students**: 18,808 **Total Teachers**: 1,049 **Student/Classroom Teacher Ratio**: 16.8	**Expenditures/Student**: $4,502 **Librarians**: 31.0 607 students/librarian **Guidance Counselors**: 52.0 362 students/counselor	**% Amer Indian**: 0.3 **% Asian**: 1.0 **% Black**: 22.4 **% Hispanic**: 1.3 **% White**: 75.0	National ***Socio-Economic Status*** indicator percentile (100=high): 52nd

Rutherford County

[SPINDALE] **RUTHERFORD COUNTY S.D.**

219 FAIRGROUND RD ● SPINDALE NC 28160-2294 ● (828) 286-2757

Grade Span: PK-12 **Schools**: *Regular* 22 ● *Spec Ed* 1 ● *Alt* 0 **Students**: 10,049 **Total Teachers**: 620 **Student/Classroom Teacher Ratio**: 16.7	**Expenditures/Student**: $4,746 **Librarians**: 25.0 402 students/librarian **Guidance Counselors**: 24.0 419 students/counselor	**% Amer Indian**: 0.0 **% Asian**: 0.2 **% Black**: 15.7 **% Hispanic**: 0.8 **% White**: 83.2	National ***Socio-Economic Status*** indicator percentile (100=high): 41st

Sampson County

CLINTON CITY S.D.

PO BOX 646 ● CLINTON NC 28328-0646 ● (910) 592-3132

Grade Span: PK-12 **Schools**: *Regular* 4 ● *Spec Ed* 0 ● *Alt* 0 **Students**: 2,588 **Total Teachers**: 170 **Student/Classroom Teacher Ratio**: 15.3	**Expenditures/Student**: $4,947 **Librarians**: 4.0 647 students/librarian **Guidance Counselors**: 6.0 431 students/counselor	**% Amer Indian**: 4.7 **% Asian**: 0.2 **% Black**: 49.5 **% Hispanic**: 3.3 **% White**: 42.3	National ***Socio-Economic Status*** indicator percentile (100=high): 25th

Sampson County

[CLINTON] **SAMPSON COUNTY S.D.**

PO BOX 439 ● CLINTON NC 28328-0439 ● (910) 592-1401 ● http://sampson.k12.nc.us

Grade Span: PK-12 **Schools**: *Regular* 15 ● *Spec Ed* 0 ● *Alt* 1 **Students**: 7,127 **Total Teachers**: 435 **Student/Classroom Teacher Ratio**: 16.7	**Expenditures/Student**: $4,658 **Librarians**: 16.0 445 students/librarian **Guidance Counselors**: 15.0 475 students/counselor	**% Amer Indian**: 1.0 **% Asian**: 0.2 **% Black**: 35.0 **% Hispanic**: 6.9 **% White**: 56.9	National ***Socio-Economic Status*** indicator percentile (100=high): 24th

Scotland County

[LAURINBURG] **SCOTLAND COUNTY S.D.**

322 S MAIN ST ● LAURINBURG NC 28352-3855 ● (910) 276-1138

Grade Span: PK-12 **Schools**: *Regular* 13 ● *Spec Ed* 1 ● *Alt* 0 **Students**: 7,399 **Total Teachers**: 516 **Student/Classroom Teacher Ratio**: 14.1	**Expenditures/Student**: $4,926 **Librarians**: 14.0 529 students/librarian **Guidance Counselors**: 20.0 370 students/counselor	**% Amer Indian**: 9.7 **% Asian**: 0.3 **% Black**: 45.6 **% Hispanic**: 0.2 **% White**: 44.2	National ***Socio-Economic Status*** indicator percentile (100=high): 19th

Stanly County

[ALBEMARLE] **STANLY COUNTY S.D.**

PO BOX 1399 ● ALBEMARLE NC 28002-1399 ● (704) 983-5151 ● http://www.scs.k12.nc.us

Grade Span: PK-12 **Schools**: *Regular* 14 ● *Spec Ed* 0 ● *Alt* 0 **Students**: 7,225 **Total Teachers**: 436 **Student/Classroom Teacher Ratio**: 17.7	**Expenditures/Student**: $4,392 **Librarians**: 14.0 516 students/librarian **Guidance Counselors**: 21.0 344 students/counselor	**% Amer Indian**: 0.2 **% Asian**: 1.9 **% Black**: 10.3 **% Hispanic**: 1.1 **% White**: 86.6	National ***Socio-Economic Status*** indicator percentile (100=high): 59th

Stokes County

[DANBURY] **STOKES COUNTY S.D.**

PO BOX 50 ● DANBURY NC 27016-0050 ● (910) 593-8146

Grade Span: PK-12 **Schools**: *Regular* 15 ● *Spec Ed* 0 ● *Alt* 0 **Students**: 6,707 **Total Teachers**: 435 **Student/Classroom Teacher Ratio**: 15.5	**Expenditures/Student**: $4,712 **Librarians**: 16.0 419 students/librarian **Guidance Counselors**: 20.0 335 students/counselor	**% Amer Indian**: 0.2 **% Asian**: 0.2 **% Black**: 5.8 **% Hispanic**: 1.3 **% White**: 92.5	National ***Socio-Economic Status*** indicator percentile (100=high): 60th

Surry County

[DOBSON] **SURRY COUNTY S.D.**

PO BOX 364 ● DOBSON NC 27017-0364 ● (910) 386-8211

Grade Span: PK-12 **Schools**: *Regular* 15 ● *Spec Ed* 0 ● *Alt* 0 **Students**: 7,743 **Total Teachers**: 478 **Student/Classroom Teacher Ratio**: 16.4	**Expenditures/Student**: $4,487 **Librarians**: 16.0 484 students/librarian **Guidance Counselors**: 16.0 484 students/counselor	**% Amer Indian**: 0.1 **% Asian**: 0.1 **% Black**: 4.1 **% Hispanic**: 3.6 **% White**: 92.0	National ***Socio-Economic Status*** indicator percentile (100=high): 57th

Transylvania County

[BREVARD] **TRANSYLVANIA COUNTY S.D.**

400 ROSENWALD LN ● BREVARD NC 28712-3239 ● (828) 884-6173

Grade Span: PK-12 **Schools**: *Regular* 7 ● *Spec Ed* 0 ● *Alt* 0 **Students**: 3,911 **Total Teachers**: 233 **Student/Classroom Teacher Ratio**: 15.1	**Expenditures/Student**: $4,727 **Librarians**: 7.0 559 students/librarian **Guidance Counselors**: 8.0 489 students/counselor	**% Amer Indian**: 0.2 **% Asian**: 0.2 **% Black**: 6.7 **% Hispanic**: 0.3 **% White**: 92.6	National ***Socio-Economic Status*** indicator percentile (100=high): 55th

Union County

[MONROE] **UNION COUNTY S.D.**

500 N MAIN ST SUITE 700 ● MONROE NC 28112-4730 ● (704) 283-3733

Grade Span: PK-12 **Schools**: *Regular* 26 ● *Spec Ed* 2 ● *Alt* 2 **Students**: 18,303 **Total Teachers**: 1,035 **Student/Classroom Teacher Ratio**: 17.4	**Expenditures/Student**: $4,517 **Librarians**: 29.0 631 students/librarian **Guidance Counselors**: 46.0 398 students/counselor	**% Amer Indian**: 0.3 **% Asian**: 0.5 **% Black**: 20.5 **% Hispanic**: 1.4 **% White**: 77.3	National ***Socio-Economic Status*** indicator percentile (100=high): 52nd

Vance County

[HENDERSON] **VANCE COUNTY S.D.**

PO BOX 7001 ● HENDERSON NC 27536-7001 ● (252) 492-2127

Grade Span: PK-12 **Schools**: *Regular* 14 ● *Spec Ed* 0 ● *Alt* 0 **Students**: 7,519 **Total Teachers**: 449 **Student/Classroom Teacher Ratio**: 16.7	**Expenditures/Student**: $4,774 **Librarians**: 16.0 470 students/librarian **Guidance Counselors**: 17.0 442 students/counselor	**% Amer Indian**: 0.0 **% Asian**: 0.2 **% Black**: 63.8 **% Hispanic**: 1.1 **% White**: 34.9	National ***Socio-Economic Status*** indicator percentile (100=high): 14th

Wake County

[RALEIGH] **WAKE COUNTY S.D.**

PO BOX 28041 ● RALEIGH NC 27611-8041 ● (919) 850-1600

Grade Span: PK-12 **Schools**: *Regular* 94 ● *Spec Ed* 1 ● *Alt* 3 **Students**: 81,438 **Total Teachers**: 4,953 **Student/Classroom Teacher Ratio**: 15.8	**Expenditures/Student**: $4,708 **Librarians**: 125.0 652 students/librarian **Guidance Counselors**: 165.0 494 students/counselor	**% Amer Indian**: 0.2 **% Asian**: 2.9 **% Black**: 26.3 **% Hispanic**: 1.9 **% White**: 68.7	National ***Socio-Economic Status*** indicator percentile (100=high): 66th

Warren County

[WARRENTON] **WARREN COUNTY S.D.**

P O BOX 110 ● WARRENTON NC 27589-0110 ● (252) 257-3184

Grade Span: PK-12 **Schools**: *Regular* 7 ● *Spec Ed* 0 ● *Alt* 1 **Students**: 3,184 **Total Teachers**: 195 **Student/Classroom Teacher Ratio**: 15.4	**Expenditures/Student**: $5,214 **Librarians**: 6.0 531 students/librarian **Guidance Counselors**: 8.0 398 students/counselor	**% Amer Indian**: 5.4 **% Asian**: 0.0 **% Black**: 74.0 **% Hispanic**: 0.8 **% White**: 19.8	National ***Socio-Economic Status*** indicator percentile (100=high): 10th

Washington County

[PLYMOUTH] **WASHINGTON COUNTY S.D.**

PO BOX 747 ● PLYMOUTH NC 27962-0747 ● (252) 793-5171

Grade Span: PK-12 **Schools**: *Regular* 4 ● *Spec Ed* 0 ● *Alt* 0 **Students**: 2,721 **Total Teachers**: 197 **Student/Classroom Teacher Ratio**: 14.1	**Expenditures/Student**: $5,142 **Librarians**: 4.0 680 students/librarian **Guidance Counselors**: 6.0 454 students/counselor	**% Amer Indian**: 0.0 **% Asian**: 0.1 **% Black**: 67.3 **% Hispanic**: 0.8 **% White**: 31.8	National ***Socio-Economic Status*** indicator percentile (100=high): 14th

Watauga County

[BOONE] **WATAUGA COUNTY S.D.**

PO BOX 1790 ● BOONE NC 28607-1790 ● (828) 264-7190

Grade Span: PK-12 **Schools**: *Regular* 9 ● *Spec Ed* 0 ● *Alt* 0 **Students**: 4,882 **Total Teachers**: 274 **Student/Classroom Teacher Ratio**: 14.4	**Expenditures/Student**: $4,814 **Librarians**: 10.0 488 students/librarian **Guidance Counselors**: 13.0 376 students/counselor	**% Amer Indian**: 0.1 **% Asian**: 0.5 **% Black**: 1.6 **% Hispanic**: 0.5 **% White**: 97.4	National ***Socio-Economic Status*** indicator percentile (100=high): 60th

Wayne County

[GOLDSBORO] **WAYNE COUNTY S.D.**

PO BOX 1797 ● GOLDSBORO NC 27533-1797 ● (919) 731-5900 ● http://www.waynecountyschools.org

Grade Span: PK-12 **Schools**: *Regular* 25 ● *Spec Ed* 1 ● *Alt* 1 **Students**: 18,908 **Total Teachers**: 1,094 **Student/Classroom Teacher Ratio**: 16.4	**Expenditures/Student**: $4,475 **Librarians**: 33.0 573 students/librarian **Guidance Counselors**: 39.0 485 students/counselor	**% Amer Indian**: 0.1 **% Asian**: 0.9 **% Black**: 41.5 **% Hispanic**: 2.4 **% White**: 55.1	National ***Socio-Economic Status*** indicator percentile (100=high): 33rd

Wilkes County

[WILKESBORO] WILKES COUNTY S.D.

201 W MAIN ST ● WILKESBORO NC 28697-2424 ● (910) 667-1121

Grade Span: PK-12 **Schools**: *Regular* 21 ● *Spec Ed* 0 ● *Alt* 1 **Students**: 9,942 **Total Teachers**: 623 **Student/Classroom Teacher Ratio**: 16.4	**Expenditures/Student**: $4,721 **Librarians**: 22.0 452 students/librarian **Guidance Counselors**: 29.0 343 students/counselor	**% Amer Indian**: 0.1 **% Asian**: 0.2 **% Black**: 5.4 **% Hispanic**: 1.8 **% White**: 92.5	National ***Socio-Economic Status*** indicator percentile (100=high): 46th

Wilson County

[WILSON] WILSON COUNTY S.D.

PO BOX 2048 ● WILSON NC 27894-2048 ● (252) 399-7700 ● http://schools.eastnet.ecu.edu/wilson

Grade Span: PK-12 **Schools**: *Regular* 23 ● *Spec Ed* 0 ● *Alt* 0 **Students**: 12,174 **Total Teachers**: 769 **Student/Classroom Teacher Ratio**: 15.8	**Expenditures/Student**: $4,686 **Librarians**: 26.0 468 students/librarian **Guidance Counselors**: 33.0 369 students/counselor	**% Amer Indian**: 0.1 **% Asian**: 0.5 **% Black**: 53.5 **% Hispanic**: 3.3 **% White**: 42.6	National ***Socio-Economic Status*** indicator percentile (100=high): 24th

Yadkin County

[YADKINVILLE] YADKIN COUNTY S.D.

121 WASHINGTON ST ● YADKINVILLE NC 27055-9806 ● (910) 679-2051 ● http://www.cuacs.ncsu.edu/k12/yadkin

Grade Span: PK-12 **Schools**: *Regular* 10 ● *Spec Ed* 0 ● *Alt* 0 **Students**: 5,296 **Total Teachers**: 312 **Student/Classroom Teacher Ratio**: 17.3	**Expenditures/Student**: $4,744 **Librarians**: 13.0 407 students/librarian **Guidance Counselors**: 13.0 407 students/counselor	**% Amer Indian**: 0.1 **% Asian**: 0.2 **% Black**: 4.8 **% Hispanic**: 5.4 **% White**: 89.6	National ***Socio-Economic Status*** indicator percentile (100=high): 62nd

Burleigh County
BISMARCK S.D. 1
400 E AVENUE E ● BISMARCK ND 58501-3955 ● (701) 221-3706 ● http://www.bismarck.k12.nd.us

Grade Span: PK-12 **Schools**: *Regular* 24 ● *Spec Ed* 0 ● *Alt* 0 **Students**: 10,958 **Total Teachers**: 559 **Student/Classroom Teacher Ratio**: 19.4	**Expenditures/Student**: $4,061 **Librarians**: 5.0 2,192 students/librarian **Guidance Counselors**: 16.5 664 students/counselor	**% Amer Indian**: 4.6 **% Asian**: 0.6 **% Black**: 0.3 **% Hispanic**: 0.4 **% White**: 94.1	National ***Socio-Economic Status*** indicator percentile (100=high): 75th

Cass County
FARGO S.D. 1
415 N 4TH ST ● FARGO ND 58102-4514 ● (701) 241-4801 ● http://www.fargo.k12.nd.us

Grade Span: PK-12 **Schools**: *Regular* 22 ● *Spec Ed* 0 ● *Alt* 0 **Students**: 11,270 **Total Teachers**: 619 **Student/Classroom Teacher Ratio**: 18.1	**Expenditures/Student**: $4,714 **Librarians**: 14.6 772 students/librarian **Guidance Counselors**: 21.1 534 students/counselor	**% Amer Indian**: 2.5 **% Asian**: 2.1 **% Black**: 0.8 **% Hispanic**: 1.0 **% White**: 93.6	National ***Socio-Economic Status*** indicator percentile (100=high): 76th

Cass County
WEST FARGO S.D. 6
207 MAIN AVE W ● WEST FARGO ND 58078-1793 ● (701) 282-3387 ● http://www.west-fargo.k12.nd.us

Grade Span: PK-12 **Schools**: *Regular* 9 ● *Spec Ed* 0 ● *Alt* 0 **Students**: 4,822 **Total Teachers**: 255 **Student/Classroom Teacher Ratio**: 21.2	**Expenditures/Student**: $3,802 **Librarians**: 3.0 1,607 students/librarian **Guidance Counselors**: 9.0 536 students/counselor	**% Amer Indian**: 1.8 **% Asian**: 0.6 **% Black**: 0.6 **% Hispanic**: 1.1 **% White**: 95.9	National ***Socio-Economic Status*** indicator percentile (100=high): 76th

Grand Forks County
GRAND FORKS S.D. 1
PO BOX 6000 ● GRAND FORKS ND 58206-6000 ● (701) 746-2200 ● http://www.grand-forks.k12.nd.us

Grade Span: PK-12 **Schools**: *Regular* 20 ● *Spec Ed* 0 ● *Alt* 0 **Students**: 9,911 **Total Teachers**: 579 **Student/Classroom Teacher Ratio**: 17.7	**Expenditures/Student**: $3,984 **Librarians**: 13.3 745 students/librarian **Guidance Counselors**: 17.1 580 students/counselor	**% Amer Indian**: 3.7 **% Asian**: 1.6 **% Black**: 3.0 **% Hispanic**: 2.0 **% White**: 89.8	National ***Socio-Economic Status*** indicator percentile (100=high): 66th

Morton County
MANDAN S.D. 1
309 COLLINS AVE ● MANDAN ND 58554-3000 ● (701) 663-9531

Grade Span: PK-12 **Schools**: *Regular* 7 ● *Spec Ed* 0 ● *Alt* 0 **Students**: 3,833 **Total Teachers**: 168 **Student/Classroom Teacher Ratio**: 22.7	**Expenditures/Student**: $3,593 **Librarians**: 4.0 958 students/librarian **Guidance Counselors**: 5.8 661 students/counselor	**% Amer Indian**: 3.4 **% Asian**: 0.3 **% Black**: 0.1 **% Hispanic**: 0.3 **% White**: 95.9	National ***Socio-Economic Status*** indicator percentile (100=high): 67th

Stark County
DICKINSON S.D. 1
PO BOX 1057 ● DICKINSON ND 58602-1057 ● (701) 225-1550 ● http://www.dickinson.k12.nd.us

Grade Span: PK-12 **Schools**: *Regular* 8 ● *Spec Ed* 0 ● *Alt* 0 **Students**: 3,097 **Total Teachers**: 143 **Student/Classroom Teacher Ratio**: 21.4	**Expenditures/Student**: $3,931 **Librarians**: 3.0 1,032 students/librarian **Guidance Counselors**: 4.9 632 students/counselor	**% Amer Indian**: 0.8 **% Asian**: 0.9 **% Black**: 0.3 **% Hispanic**: 0.7 **% White**: 97.2	National ***Socio-Economic Status*** indicator percentile (100=high): 56th

Stutsman County

JAMESTOWN S.D. 1

PO BOX 269 ● JAMESTOWN ND 58402-0269 ● (701) 252-1950 ● http://www.jamestown.k12.nd.us

Grade Span: PK-12	**Expenditures/Student**: $3,922	**% Amer Indian**: 1.5	
Schools: *Regular* 9 ● *Spec Ed* 0 ● *Alt* 0	**Librarians**: 3.0	**% Asian**: 0.8	National ***Socio-Economic***
Students: 2,920	973 students/librarian	**% Black**: 0.6	***Status*** indicator percentile
Total Teachers: 166	**Guidance Counselors**: 5.4	**% Hispanic**: 0.4	(100=high): 65th
Student/Classroom Teacher Ratio: 15.5	541 students/counselor	**% White**: 96.6	

Ward County

MINOT S.D. 1

215 2ND ST SE ● MINOT ND 58701-3985 ● (701) 857-4422 ● http://www.minot.com/~mps

Grade Span: PK-12	**Expenditures/Student**: $4,210	**% Amer Indian**: 2.7	
Schools: *Regular* 19 ● *Spec Ed* 0 ● *Alt* 0	**Librarians**: 5.5	**% Asian**: 1.5	National ***Socio-Economic***
Students: 7,948	1,445 students/librarian	**% Black**: 4.3	***Status*** indicator percentile
Total Teachers: 471	**Guidance Counselors**: 18.5	**% Hispanic**: 1.9	(100=high): 62nd
Student/Classroom Teacher Ratio: 16.4	430 students/counselor	**% White**: 89.7	

Williams County

WILLISTON S.D. 1

PO BOX 1407 ● WILLISTON ND 58802-1407 ● (701) 572-1580

Grade Span: PK-12	**Expenditures/Student**: $3,813	**% Amer Indian**: 8.0	
Schools: *Regular* 7 ● *Spec Ed* 0 ● *Alt* 0	**Librarians**: 2.0	**% Asian**: 0.2	National ***Socio-Economic***
Students: 2,942	1,471 students/librarian	**% Black**: 0.1	***Status*** indicator percentile
Total Teachers: 154	**Guidance Counselors**: 6.0	**% Hispanic**: 1.1	(100=high): 68th
Student/Classroom Teacher Ratio: 18.4	490 students/counselor	**% White**: 90.6	

Adams County

[WEST UNION] **ADAMS COUNTY-OHIO VALLEY LOCAL S.D.**

141 LLOYD RD ● WEST UNION OH 45693 ● (937) 544-5586

Grade Span: PK-12 **Schools**: *Regular* 9 ● *Spec Ed* 0 ● *Alt* 1 **Students**: 5,461 **Total Teachers**: 348 **Student/Classroom Teacher Ratio**: 16.3	**Expenditures/Student**: $4,666 **Librarians**: 4.0 1,365 students/librarian **Guidance Counselors**: 9.0 607 students/counselor	**% Amer Indian**: 0.1 **% Asian**: 0.2 **% Black**: 0.2 **% Hispanic**: 0.4 **% White**: 99.2	National ***Socio-Economic Status*** indicator percentile (100=high): na

Allen County

ELIDA LOCAL S.D.

101 E NORTH ST ● ELIDA OH 45807 ● (419) 331-4155

Grade Span: PK-12 **Schools**: *Regular* 4 ● *Spec Ed* 0 ● *Alt* 0 **Students**: 3,278 **Total Teachers**: 156 **Student/Classroom Teacher Ratio**: 20.9	**Expenditures/Student**: $4,034 **Librarians**: 1.0 3,278 students/librarian **Guidance Counselors**: 5.0 656 students/counselor	**% Amer Indian**: 0.0 **% Asian**: 1.1 **% Black**: 9.6 **% Hispanic**: 1.1 **% White**: 88.2	National ***Socio-Economic Status*** indicator percentile (100=high): na

Allen County

LIMA CITY S.D.

515 S CALUMET AVE ● LIMA OH 45804 ● (419) 998-2400

Grade Span: PK-12 **Schools**: *Regular* 14 ● *Spec Ed* 1 ● *Alt* 0 **Students**: 6,017 **Total Teachers**: 363 **Student/Classroom Teacher Ratio**: 18.9	**Expenditures/Student**: $5,850 **Librarians**: 3.0 2,006 students/librarian **Guidance Counselors**: 11.0 547 students/counselor	**% Amer Indian**: 0.0 **% Asian**: 0.5 **% Black**: 41.8 **% Hispanic**: 1.0 **% White**: 56.6	National ***Socio-Economic Status*** indicator percentile (100=high): 13th

Allen County

[LIMA] **SHAWNEE LOCAL S.D.**

3255 ZURMEHLY RD ● LIMA OH 45806 ● (419) 998-8031

Grade Span: PK-12 **Schools**: *Regular* 4 ● *Spec Ed* 0 ● *Alt* 0 **Students**: 2,596 **Total Teachers**: 135 **Student/Classroom Teacher Ratio**: 19.0	**Expenditures/Student**: $5,133 **Librarians**: 1.0 2,596 students/librarian **Guidance Counselors**: 8.0 325 students/counselor	**% Amer Indian**: 0.2 **% Asian**: 2.3 **% Black**: 9.7 **% Hispanic**: 1.3 **% White**: 86.5	National ***Socio-Economic Status*** indicator percentile (100=high): 92nd

Ashland County

ASHLAND CITY S.D.

416 ARTHUR ST ● ASHLAND OH 44805 ● (419) 289-1117 ● http://ashland-city.k12.oh.us/index.html

Grade Span: PK-12 **Schools**: *Regular* 10 ● *Spec Ed* 0 ● *Alt* 0 **Students**: 4,220 **Total Teachers**: 231 **Student/Classroom Teacher Ratio**: 20.4	**Expenditures/Student**: $4,944 **Librarians**: 2.0 2,110 students/librarian **Guidance Counselors**: 7.0 603 students/counselor	**% Amer Indian**: 0.2 **% Asian**: 0.6 **% Black**: 1.4 **% Hispanic**: 0.2 **% White**: 97.5	National ***Socio-Economic Status*** indicator percentile (100=high): 66th

Ashtabula County

ASHTABULA AREA CITY S.D.

401 W 44TH ST, PO BOX 290 ● ASHTABULA OH 44005 ● (440) 993-2500

Grade Span: PK-12 **Schools**: *Regular* 12 ● *Spec Ed* 0 ● *Alt* 0 **Students**: 5,274 **Total Teachers**: 311 **Student/Classroom Teacher Ratio**: 18.5	**Expenditures/Student**: $4,863 **Librarians**: 1.0 5,274 students/librarian **Guidance Counselors**: 10.0 527 students/counselor	**% Amer Indian**: 0.0 **% Asian**: 0.4 **% Black**: 12.5 **% Hispanic**: 4.4 **% White**: 82.7	National ***Socio-Economic Status*** indicator percentile (100=high): 29th

Ashtabula County

CONNEAUT AREA CITY S.D.

263 LIBERTY ST ● CONNEAUT OH 44030 ● (440) 593-7200

Grade Span: PK-12 **Schools**: *Regular* 6 ● *Spec Ed* 0 ● *Alt* 0 **Students**: 2,570 **Total Teachers**: 129 **Student/Classroom Teacher Ratio**: 20.7	**Expenditures/Student**: $4,689 **Librarians**: 2.0 1,285 students/librarian **Guidance Counselors**: 4.0 643 students/counselor	**% Amer Indian**: 0.0 **% Asian**: 0.1 **% Black**: 1.4 **% Hispanic**: 0.4 **% White**: 98.1	National ***Socio-Economic Status*** indicator percentile (100=high): 40th

Ashtabula County

GENEVA AREA CITY S.D.

135 S EAGLE ST ● GENEVA OH 44041 ● (440) 466-4831

Grade Span: PK-12 **Schools**: *Regular* 7 ● *Spec Ed* 0 ● *Alt* 0 **Students**: 3,331 **Total Teachers**: 160 **Student/Classroom Teacher Ratio**: 22.3	**Expenditures/Student**: $4,383 **Librarians**: 1.0 3,331 students/librarian **Guidance Counselors**: 6.0 555 students/counselor	**% Amer Indian**: 0.0 **% Asian**: 0.0 **% Black**: 1.2 **% Hispanic**: 2.9 **% White**: 95.9	National ***Socio-Economic Status*** indicator percentile (100=high): 47th

Athens County

[THE PLAINS] **ATHENS CITY S.D.**

25 S PLAINS RD, PO BOX 68 ● THE PLAINS OH 45780 ● (614) 797-4544

Grade Span: PK-12 **Schools**: *Regular* 7 ● *Spec Ed* 0 ● *Alt* 0 **Students**: 3,358 **Total Teachers**: 204 **Student/Classroom Teacher Ratio**: 16.7	**Expenditures/Student**: $5,383 **Librarians**: 1.0 3,358 students/librarian **Guidance Counselors**: 5.0 672 students/counselor	**% Amer Indian**: 0.1 **% Asian**: 4.3 **% Black**: 2.5 **% Hispanic**: 0.9 **% White**: 92.1	National ***Socio-Economic Status*** indicator percentile (100=high): na

Auglaize County

ST. MARYS CITY S.D.

101 W SOUTH ST ● ST. MARYS OH 45885 ● (419) 394-4312

Grade Span: PK-12 **Schools**: *Regular* 7 ● *Spec Ed* 0 ● *Alt* 0 **Students**: 2,790 **Total Teachers**: 140 **Student/Classroom Teacher Ratio**: 25.7	**Expenditures/Student**: $4,337 **Librarians**: 2.0 1,395 students/librarian **Guidance Counselors**: 4.0 698 students/counselor	**% Amer Indian**: 0.1 **% Asian**: 0.6 **% Black**: 0.4 **% Hispanic**: 0.4 **% White**: 98.5	National ***Socio-Economic Status*** indicator percentile (100=high): 82nd

Auglaize County

WAPAKONETA CITY S.D.

3 N PINE ST ● WAPAKONETA OH 45895 ● (419) 738-2315

Grade Span: PK-12 **Schools**: *Regular* 6 ● *Spec Ed* 0 ● *Alt* 0 **Students**: 3,703 **Total Teachers**: 169 **Student/Classroom Teacher Ratio**: 23.6	**Expenditures/Student**: $3,851 **Librarians**: 2.0 1,852 students/librarian **Guidance Counselors**: 5.0 741 students/counselor	**% Amer Indian**: 0.0 **% Asian**: 0.5 **% Black**: 0.3 **% Hispanic**: 0.8 **% White**: 98.4	National ***Socio-Economic Status*** indicator percentile (100=high): 77th

Brown County

[MOUNT ORAB] **WESTERN BROWN LOCAL S.D.**

211 S HIGH ST, PO BOX 455 ● MOUNT ORAB OH 45154 ● (937) 444-2044

Grade Span: PK-12 **Schools**: *Regular* 4 ● *Spec Ed* 0 ● *Alt* 0 **Students**: 3,139 **Total Teachers**: 156 **Student/Classroom Teacher Ratio**: 20.5	**Expenditures/Student**: $3,701 **Librarians**: 4.0 785 students/librarian **Guidance Counselors**: 10.0 314 students/counselor	**% Amer Indian**: 0.1 **% Asian**: 0.0 **% Black**: 0.3 **% Hispanic**: 0.1 **% White**: 99.6	National ***Socio-Economic Status*** indicator percentile (100=high): 55th

Butler County
FAIRFIELD CITY S.D.
211 DONALD DR ● FAIRFIELD OH 45014 ● (513) 829-6300 ● http://www.iac.net/~fairfld

Grade Span: PK-12 **Schools**: *Regular* 9 ● *Spec Ed* 0 ● *Alt* 0 **Students**: 8,757 **Total Teachers**: 437 **Student/Classroom Teacher Ratio**: 22.5	**Expenditures/Student**: $4,756 **Librarians**: 15.0 584 students/librarian **Guidance Counselors**: 25.0 350 students/counselor	**% Amer Indian**: 0.2 **% Asian**: 1.5 **% Black**: 4.6 **% Hispanic**: 0.7 **% White**: 93.0	National ***Socio-Economic Status*** indicator percentile (100=high): 87th

Butler County
HAMILTON CITY S.D.
332 DAYTON ST, PO BOX 627 ● HAMILTON OH 45012 ● (513) 887-5000 ● http://SWOCAI.SWOCA.OHIO.GOV/~hamilton

Grade Span: PK-12 **Schools**: *Regular* 19 ● *Spec Ed* 0 ● *Alt* 0 **Students**: 10,517 **Total Teachers**: 643 **Student/Classroom Teacher Ratio**: 19.1	**Expenditures/Student**: $4,891 **Librarians**: 4.0 2,629 students/librarian **Guidance Counselors**: 23.0 457 students/counselor	**% Amer Indian**: 0.1 **% Asian**: 0.4 **% Black**: 10.8 **% Hispanic**: 0.6 **% White**: 88.1	National ***Socio-Economic Status*** indicator percentile (100=high): 34th

Butler County
[HAMILTON] ROSS LOCAL S.D.
3371 HAMILTON CLEVES RD ● HAMILTON OH 45013 ● (513) 863-1253

Grade Span: KG-12 **Schools**: *Regular* 4 ● *Spec Ed* 0 ● *Alt* 0 **Students**: 2,725 **Total Teachers**: 133 **Student/Classroom Teacher Ratio**: 20.9	**Expenditures/Student**: $4,269 **Librarians**: 2.0 1,363 students/librarian **Guidance Counselors**: 6.0 454 students/counselor	**% Amer Indian**: 0.0 **% Asian**: 0.1 **% Black**: 0.1 **% Hispanic**: 0.1 **% White**: 99.6	National ***Socio-Economic Status*** indicator percentile (100=high): 82nd

Butler County
MIDDLETOWN CITY S.D.
1515 GIRARD AVE ● MIDDLETOWN OH 45044 ● (513) 423-0781

Grade Span: KG-12 **Schools**: *Regular* 18 ● *Spec Ed* 1 ● *Alt* 1 **Students**: 9,780 **Total Teachers**: 525 **Student/Classroom Teacher Ratio**: 18.9	**Expenditures/Student**: $5,553 **Librarians**: 4.0 2,445 students/librarian **Guidance Counselors**: 13.0 752 students/counselor	**% Amer Indian**: 0.1 **% Asian**: 0.4 **% Black**: 13.3 **% Hispanic**: 0.4 **% White**: 85.9	National ***Socio-Economic Status*** indicator percentile (100=high): 47th

Butler County
[OXFORD] TALAWANDA CITY S.D.
131 W CHESTNUT ● OXFORD OH 45056 ● (513) 523-4716 ● http://www.tcs.k12.oh.us

Grade Span: KG-12 **Schools**: *Regular* 5 ● *Spec Ed* 0 ● *Alt* 0 **Students**: 3,611 **Total Teachers**: 195 **Student/Classroom Teacher Ratio**: 18.9	**Expenditures/Student**: $4,547 **Librarians**: 3.0 1,204 students/librarian **Guidance Counselors**: 11.0 328 students/counselor	**% Amer Indian**: 0.1 **% Asian**: 1.1 **% Black**: 2.7 **% Hispanic**: 0.2 **% White**: 95.8	National ***Socio-Economic Status*** indicator percentile (100=high): 77th

Butler County
[TRENTON] EDGEWOOD CITY S.D.
5005 ST RT 73 ● TRENTON OH 45067 ● (513) 863-4692

Grade Span: PK-12 **Schools**: *Regular* 6 ● *Spec Ed* 0 ● *Alt* 0 **Students**: 2,713 **Total Teachers**: 137 **Student/Classroom Teacher Ratio**: 25.1	**Expenditures/Student**: $4,329 **Librarians**: 4.0 678 students/librarian **Guidance Counselors**: 5.0 543 students/counselor	**% Amer Indian**: 0.0 **% Asian**: 0.1 **% Black**: 0.5 **% Hispanic**: 0.2 **% White**: 99.2	National ***Socio-Economic Status*** indicator percentile (100=high): 86th

Butler County

[WEST CHESTER] **LAKOTA LOCAL S.D.**

5030 TYLERSVILLE RD • WEST CHESTER OH 45069 • (513) 874-5505 • http://www.lakotaonline.com

Grade Span: PK-12 **Schools**: *Regular* 15 • *Spec Ed* 0 • *Alt* 0 **Students**: 12,746 **Total Teachers**: 660 **Student/Classroom Teacher Ratio**: 19.4	**Expenditures/Student**: $4,422 **Librarians**: 28.0 455 students/librarian **Guidance Counselors**: 42.0 303 students/counselor	**% Amer Indian**: 0.1 **% Asian**: 3.1 **% Black**: 2.3 **% Hispanic**: 0.6 **% White**: 94.0	National ***Socio-Economic Status*** indicator percentile (100=high): na

Carroll County

CARROLLTON EXEMPTED VILLAGE S.D.

252 THIRD ST NE • CARROLLTON OH 44615 • (330) 627-2181

Grade Span: PK-12 **Schools**: *Regular* 8 • *Spec Ed* 0 • *Alt* 0 **Students**: 3,006 **Total Teachers**: 137 **Student/Classroom Teacher Ratio**: 22.0	**Expenditures/Student**: $3,948 **Librarians**: 2.0 1,503 students/librarian **Guidance Counselors**: 5.0 601 students/counselor	**% Amer Indian**: 0.1 **% Asian**: 0.1 **% Black**: 0.1 **% Hispanic**: 0.4 **% White**: 99.4	National ***Socio-Economic Status*** indicator percentile (100=high): 52nd

Champaign County

URBANA CITY S.D.

711 WOOD ST • URBANA OH 43078 • (937) 653-1402 • http://www.urbana.k12.oh.us

Grade Span: PK-12 **Schools**: *Regular* 6 • *Spec Ed* 0 • *Alt* 0 **Students**: 2,502 **Total Teachers**: 140 **Student/Classroom Teacher Ratio**: 19.9	**Expenditures/Student**: $4,640 **Librarians**: 1.0 2,502 students/librarian **Guidance Counselors**: 6.0 417 students/counselor	**% Amer Indian**: 0.2 **% Asian**: 0.3 **% Black**: 8.1 **% Hispanic**: 1.2 **% White**: 90.2	National ***Socio-Economic Status*** indicator percentile (100=high): 68th

Clark County

[NEW CARLISLE] **TECUMSEH LOCAL S.D.**

9760 W NATIONAL RD • NEW CARLISLE OH 45344 • (937) 845-3576

Grade Span: PK-12 **Schools**: *Regular* 8 • *Spec Ed* 0 • *Alt* 0 **Students**: 3,879 **Total Teachers**: 207 **Student/Classroom Teacher Ratio**: 21.6	**Expenditures/Student**: $4,550 **Librarians**: 2.0 1,940 students/librarian **Guidance Counselors**: 6.0 647 students/counselor	**% Amer Indian**: 0.3 **% Asian**: 0.4 **% Black**: 0.4 **% Hispanic**: 1.1 **% White**: 97.8	National ***Socio-Economic Status*** indicator percentile (100=high): 63rd

Clark County

[SPRINGFIELD] **NORTHEASTERN LOCAL S.D.**

1414 BOWMAN RD • SPRINGFIELD OH 45502 • (937) 325-7615

Grade Span: PK-12 **Schools**: *Regular* 5 • *Spec Ed* 0 • *Alt* 0 **Students**: 3,483 **Total Teachers**: 178 **Student/Classroom Teacher Ratio**: 19.5	**Expenditures/Student**: $4,584 **Librarians**: 4.0 871 students/librarian **Guidance Counselors**: 7.0 498 students/counselor	**% Amer Indian**: 0.4 **% Asian**: 0.5 **% Black**: 1.7 **% Hispanic**: 0.5 **% White**: 97.0	National ***Socio-Economic Status*** indicator percentile (100=high): 90th

Clark County

SPRINGFIELD CITY S.D.

49 E COLLEGE AVE • SPRINGFIELD OH 45504 • (937) 328-2000

Grade Span: PK-12 **Schools**: *Regular* 22 • *Spec Ed* 1 • *Alt* 0 **Students**: 11,072 **Total Teachers**: 592 **Student/Classroom Teacher Ratio**: 19.0	**Expenditures/Student**: $4,957 **Librarians**: 8.0 1,384 students/librarian **Guidance Counselors**: 26.0 426 students/counselor	**% Amer Indian**: 0.2 **% Asian**: 0.4 **% Black**: 25.7 **% Hispanic**: 0.6 **% White**: 73.1	National ***Socio-Economic Status*** indicator percentile (100=high): 24th

Clermont County
[CINCINNATI] WEST CLERMONT LOCAL S.D.
4578 E TECH DR, SUITE 101 ● CINCINNATI OH 45245 ● (513) 528-0664 ● http://www.westcler.k12.oh.us

Grade Span: PK-12 **Schools**: *Regular* 13 ● *Spec Ed* 0 ● *Alt* 1 **Students**: 9,160 **Total Teachers**: 477 **Student/Classroom Teacher Ratio**: 18.5	**Expenditures/Student**: $4,019 **Librarians**: 5.0 1,832 students/librarian **Guidance Counselors**: 20.0 458 students/counselor	**% Amer Indian**: 0.1 **% Asian**: 0.5 **% Black**: 0.8 **% Hispanic**: 0.4 **% White**: 98.2	National ***Socio-Economic Status*** indicator percentile (100=high): 80th

Clermont County
GOSHEN LOCAL S.D.
6785 GOSHEN RD ● GOSHEN OH 45122 ● (513) 722-2222

Grade Span: KG-12 **Schools**: *Regular* 5 ● *Spec Ed* 0 ● *Alt* 0 **Students**: 2,770 **Total Teachers**: 145 **Student/Classroom Teacher Ratio**: 20.1	**Expenditures/Student**: $4,249 **Librarians**: 3.0 923 students/librarian **Guidance Counselors**: 5.0 554 students/counselor	**% Amer Indian**: 0.1 **% Asian**: 0.2 **% Black**: 0.2 **% Hispanic**: 0.1 **% White**: 99.3	National ***Socio-Economic Status*** indicator percentile (100=high): 70th

Clermont County
MILFORD EXEMPTED VILLAGE S.D.
525 LILA AVE ● MILFORD OH 45150 ● (513) 831-5100

Grade Span: PK-12 **Schools**: *Regular* 8 ● *Spec Ed* 0 ● *Alt* 0 **Students**: 5,758 **Total Teachers**: 273 **Student/Classroom Teacher Ratio**: 19.3	**Expenditures/Student**: $4,590 **Librarians**: 3.0 1,919 students/librarian **Guidance Counselors**: 7.0 823 students/counselor	**% Amer Indian**: 0.1 **% Asian**: 0.5 **% Black**: 2.1 **% Hispanic**: 0.4 **% White**: 96.9	National ***Socio-Economic Status*** indicator percentile (100=high): 88th

Clermont County
NEW RICHMOND EXEMPTED VILLAGE S.D.
212 MARKET ST, 3RD FLOOR ● NEW RICHMOND OH 45157 ● (513) 553-2616

Grade Span: PK-12 **Schools**: *Regular* 5 ● *Spec Ed* 0 ● *Alt* 0 **Students**: 2,898 **Total Teachers**: 164 **Student/Classroom Teacher Ratio**: 17.8	**Expenditures/Student**: $5,965 **Librarians**: 10.0 290 students/librarian **Guidance Counselors**: 19.0 153 students/counselor	**% Amer Indian**: 0.2 **% Asian**: 0.3 **% Black**: 0.6 **% Hispanic**: 0.4 **% White**: 98.5	National ***Socio-Economic Status*** indicator percentile (100=high): 50th

Clinton County
WILMINGTON CITY S.D.
341 S NELSON AVE ● WILMINGTON OH 45177 ● (937) 382-1641

Grade Span: PK-12 **Schools**: *Regular* 6 ● *Spec Ed* 0 ● *Alt* 0 **Students**: 3,384 **Total Teachers**: 173 **Student/Classroom Teacher Ratio**: 20.8	**Expenditures/Student**: $4,183 **Librarians**: 2.0 1,692 students/librarian **Guidance Counselors**: 4.0 846 students/counselor	**% Amer Indian**: 0.2 **% Asian**: 0.9 **% Black**: 4.7 **% Hispanic**: 0.2 **% White**: 94.0	National ***Socio-Economic Status*** indicator percentile (100=high): 67th

Columbiana County
EAST LIVERPOOL CITY S.D.
202 MAPLEWOOD AVE ● EAST LIVERPOOL OH 43920 ● (330) 385-7132

Grade Span: PK-12 **Schools**: *Regular* 6 ● *Spec Ed* 0 ● *Alt* 0 **Students**: 3,461 **Total Teachers**: 224 **Student/Classroom Teacher Ratio**: 18.6	**Expenditures/Student**: $5,675 **Librarians**: 4.0 865 students/librarian **Guidance Counselors**: 8.0 433 students/counselor	**% Amer Indian**: 0.0 **% Asian**: 0.1 **% Black**: 4.9 **% Hispanic**: 0.2 **% White**: 94.7	National ***Socio-Economic Status*** indicator percentile (100=high): na

Columbiana County

SALEM CITY S.D.

1226 EAST STATE ST ● SALEM OH 44460 ● (330) 332-0316 ● http://www.access-k12.org/sale/sale.htm

Grade Span: PK-12 **Schools**: *Regular* 6 ● *Spec Ed* 0 ● *Alt* 0 **Students**: 2,897 **Total Teachers**: 150 **Student/Classroom Teacher Ratio**: 21.9	**Expenditures/Student**: $5,361 **Librarians**: 3.0 966 students/librarian **Guidance Counselors**: 6.0 483 students/counselor	**% Amer Indian**: 0.0 **% Asian**: 0.4 **% Black**: 0.4 **% Hispanic**: 0.2 **% White**: 98.9	National ***Socio-Economic Status*** indicator percentile (100=high): 53rd

Coshocton County

[WARSAW] **RIVER VIEW LOCAL S.D.**

26496 ST RT 60 N ● WARSAW OH 43844 ● (614) 824-3521

Grade Span: PK-12 **Schools**: *Regular* 7 ● *Spec Ed* 0 ● *Alt* 0 **Students**: 2,839 **Total Teachers**: 134 **Student/Classroom Teacher Ratio**: 31.1	**Expenditures/Student**: $4,868 **Librarians**: 1.0 2,839 students/librarian **Guidance Counselors**: 2.0 1,420 students/counselor	**% Amer Indian**: 0.0 **% Asian**: 0.1 **% Black**: 1.8 **% Hispanic**: 0.1 **% White**: 98.0	National ***Socio-Economic Status*** indicator percentile (100=high): 67th

Crawford County

GALION CITY S.D.

200 W CHURCH ST ● GALION OH 44833 ● (419) 468-3432

Grade Span: PK-12 **Schools**: *Regular* 6 ● *Spec Ed* 0 ● *Alt* 0 **Students**: 2,521 **Total Teachers**: 159 **Student/Classroom Teacher Ratio**: 18.2	**Expenditures/Student**: $5,008 **Librarians**: 2.0 1,261 students/librarian **Guidance Counselors**: 5.0 504 students/counselor	**% Amer Indian**: 0.4 **% Asian**: 0.2 **% Black**: 0.2 **% Hispanic**: 0.5 **% White**: 98.7	National ***Socio-Economic Status*** indicator percentile (100=high): 63rd

Cuyahoga County

BEDFORD CITY S.D.

475 NORTHFIELD RD ● BEDFORD OH 44146 ● (216) 439-1500 ● http://www.lnoca.ohio.gov/~bedford

Grade Span: PK-12 **Schools**: *Regular* 8 ● *Spec Ed* 0 ● *Alt* 0 **Students**: 4,141 **Total Teachers**: 254 **Student/Classroom Teacher Ratio**: 15.8	**Expenditures/Student**: $7,696 **Librarians**: 4.0 1,035 students/librarian **Guidance Counselors**: 10.0 414 students/counselor	**% Amer Indian**: 0.0 **% Asian**: 0.9 **% Black**: 52.7 **% Hispanic**: 0.7 **% White**: 45.7	National ***Socio-Economic Status*** indicator percentile (100=high): 62nd

Cuyahoga County

BEREA CITY S.D.

390 FAIR ST ● BEREA OH 44017 ● (440) 243-6000

Grade Span: PK-12 **Schools**: *Regular* 12 ● *Spec Ed* 1 ● *Alt* 0 **Students**: 8,529 **Total Teachers**: 438 **Student/Classroom Teacher Ratio**: 20.3	**Expenditures/Student**: $6,464 **Librarians**: 9.0 948 students/librarian **Guidance Counselors**: 18.0 474 students/counselor	**% Amer Indian**: 0.2 **% Asian**: 1.2 **% Black**: 3.7 **% Hispanic**: 1.6 **% White**: 93.3	National ***Socio-Economic Status*** indicator percentile (100=high): 86th

Cuyahoga County

BRECKSVILLE-BROADVIEW HEIGHTS CITY S.D.

6638 MILL RD ● BRECKSVILLE OH 44141 ● (440) 526-4370

Grade Span: PK-12 **Schools**: *Regular* 6 ● *Spec Ed* 0 ● *Alt* 0 **Students**: 3,705 **Total Teachers**: 209 **Student/Classroom Teacher Ratio**: 18.0	**Expenditures/Student**: $6,417 **Librarians**: 4.0 926 students/librarian **Guidance Counselors**: 6.0 618 students/counselor	**% Amer Indian**: 0.0 **% Asian**: 2.6 **% Black**: 0.5 **% Hispanic**: 0.4 **% White**: 96.6	National ***Socio-Economic Status*** indicator percentile (100=high): na

Cuyahoga County
CLEVELAND CITY S.D.
1380 E 6TH ST ● CLEVELAND OH 44114 ● (216) 574-8000 ● http://cps.cleveland.k12.oh.us

Grade Span: PK-12 **Schools**: *Regular* 124 ● *Spec Ed* 2 ● *Alt* 5 **Students**: 74,380 **Total Teachers**: 4,323 **Student/Classroom Teacher Ratio**: 17.8	**Expenditures/Student**: $6,658 **Librarians**: 100.0 744 students/librarian **Guidance Counselors**: 105.0 708 students/counselor	**% Amer Indian**: 0.2 **% Asian**: 1.1 **% Black**: 70.5 **% Hispanic**: 7.5 **% White**: 20.7	National ***Socio-Economic Status*** indicator percentile (100=high): na

Cuyahoga County
EAST CLEVELAND CITY S.D.
15305 TERRACE RD ● EAST CLEVELAND OH 44112 ● (216) 268-6570

Grade Span: PK-12 **Schools**: *Regular* 9 ● *Spec Ed* 0 ● *Alt* 0 **Students**: 7,309 **Total Teachers**: 381 **Student/Classroom Teacher Ratio**: 19.9	**Expenditures/Student**: $5,907 **Librarians**: 6.0 1,218 students/librarian **Guidance Counselors**: 10.0 731 students/counselor	**% Amer Indian**: 0.1 **% Asian**: 0.0 **% Black**: 99.9 **% Hispanic**: 0.0 **% White**: 0.0	National ***Socio-Economic Status*** indicator percentile (100=high): 15th

Cuyahoga County
EUCLID CITY S.D.
651 E 222 ST ● EUCLID OH 44123 ● (216) 261-2900

Grade Span: PK-12 **Schools**: *Regular* 9 ● *Spec Ed* 0 ● *Alt* 0 **Students**: 6,039 **Total Teachers**: 329 **Student/Classroom Teacher Ratio**: 19.9	**Expenditures/Student**: $6,884 **Librarians**: 9.0 671 students/librarian **Guidance Counselors**: 14.0 431 students/counselor	**% Amer Indian**: 0.0 **% Asian**: 0.8 **% Black**: 43.1 **% Hispanic**: 0.5 **% White**: 55.6	National ***Socio-Economic Status*** indicator percentile (100=high): 53rd

Cuyahoga County
GARFIELD HEIGHTS CITY S.D.
5640 BRIARCLIFF DR ● GARFIELD HEIGHTS OH 44125 ● (216) 475-8100

Grade Span: PK-12 **Schools**: *Regular* 4 ● *Spec Ed* 0 ● *Alt* 0 **Students**: 3,218 **Total Teachers**: 163 **Student/Classroom Teacher Ratio**: 20.3	**Expenditures/Student**: $5,942 **Librarians**: 3.0 1,073 students/librarian **Guidance Counselors**: 5.0 644 students/counselor	**% Amer Indian**: 0.2 **% Asian**: 0.7 **% Black**: 13.5 **% Hispanic**: 1.1 **% White**: 84.4	National ***Socio-Economic Status*** indicator percentile (100=high): 62nd

Cuyahoga County
LAKEWOOD CITY S.D.
1470 WARREN RD ● LAKEWOOD OH 44107 ● (216) 529-4092

Grade Span: PK-12 **Schools**: *Regular* 15 ● *Spec Ed* 0 ● *Alt* 0 **Students**: 7,984 **Total Teachers**: 497 **Student/Classroom Teacher Ratio**: 15.6	**Expenditures/Student**: $6,826 **Librarians**: 9.0 887 students/librarian **Guidance Counselors**: 14.0 570 students/counselor	**% Amer Indian**: 0.3 **% Asian**: 1.4 **% Black**: 2.0 **% Hispanic**: 1.8 **% White**: 94.6	National ***Socio-Economic Status*** indicator percentile (100=high): na

Cuyahoga County
[LYNDHURST] **SOUTH EUCLID-LYNDHURST CITY S.D.**
5044 MAYFIELD RD ● LYNDHURST OH 44124 ● (216) 691-2000

Grade Span: PK-12 **Schools**: *Regular* 10 ● *Spec Ed* 0 ● *Alt* 0 **Students**: 4,413 **Total Teachers**: 301 **Student/Classroom Teacher Ratio**: 18.0	**Expenditures/Student**: $7,565 **Librarians**: 6.0 736 students/librarian **Guidance Counselors**: 9.0 490 students/counselor	**% Amer Indian**: 0.0 **% Asian**: 2.0 **% Black**: 15.5 **% Hispanic**: 0.3 **% White**: 82.2	National ***Socio-Economic Status*** indicator percentile (100=high): 88th

Cuyahoga County
MAPLE HEIGHTS CITY S.D.
5500 CLEMENT DR ● MAPLE HEIGHTS OH 44137 ● (216) 587-3200

Grade Span: PK-12 **Schools**: *Regular* 7 ● *Spec Ed* 0 ● *Alt* 0 **Students**: 3,769 **Total Teachers**: 211 **Student/Classroom Teacher Ratio**: 16.8	**Expenditures/Student**: $5,730 **Librarians**: 2.0 1,885 students/librarian **Guidance Counselors**: 7.0 538 students/counselor	**% Amer Indian**: 0.2 **% Asian**: 2.4 **% Black**: 56.0 **% Hispanic**: 1.0 **% White**: 40.4	National ***Socio-Economic Status*** indicator percentile (100=high): 56th

Cuyahoga County
MAYFIELD CITY S.D.
784 SOM CENTER RD ● MAYFIELD OH 44143 ● (440) 442-2200

Grade Span: PK-12 **Schools**: *Regular* 6 ● *Spec Ed* 1 ● *Alt* 0 **Students**: 4,141 **Total Teachers**: 270 **Student/Classroom Teacher Ratio**: 18.0	**Expenditures/Student**: $8,629 **Librarians**: 3.0 1,380 students/librarian **Guidance Counselors**: 10.0 414 students/counselor	**% Amer Indian**: 0.3 **% Asian**: 4.4 **% Black**: 4.1 **% Hispanic**: 0.5 **% White**: 90.7	National ***Socio-Economic Status*** indicator percentile (100=high): 87th

Cuyahoga County
NORTH OLMSTED CITY S.D.
24100 PALM DR ● NORTH OLMSTED OH 44070 ● (440) 779-3549 ● http://www.nocs.leeca.esu.k12.oh.us/index.htm

Grade Span: PK-12 **Schools**: *Regular* 9 ● *Spec Ed* 0 ● *Alt* 0 **Students**: 5,059 **Total Teachers**: 317 **Student/Classroom Teacher Ratio**: 17.0	**Expenditures/Student**: $6,243 **Librarians**: 4.0 1,265 students/librarian **Guidance Counselors**: 22.0 230 students/counselor	**% Amer Indian**: 0.0 **% Asian**: 2.6 **% Black**: 1.0 **% Hispanic**: 1.1 **% White**: 95.3	National ***Socio-Economic Status*** indicator percentile (100=high): na

Cuyahoga County
NORTH ROYALTON CITY S.D.
6579 ROYALTON RD ● NORTH ROYALTON OH 44133 ● (440) 237-8800

Grade Span: PK-12 **Schools**: *Regular* 5 ● *Spec Ed* 0 ● *Alt* 0 **Students**: 4,082 **Total Teachers**: 197 **Student/Classroom Teacher Ratio**: 21.1	**Expenditures/Student**: $6,057 **Librarians**: 4.0 1,021 students/librarian **Guidance Counselors**: 7.0 583 students/counselor	**% Amer Indian**: 0.0 **% Asian**: 2.0 **% Black**: 0.4 **% Hispanic**: 0.2 **% White**: 97.4	National ***Socio-Economic Status*** indicator percentile (100=high): 91st

Cuyahoga County
OLMSTED FALLS CITY S.D.
7918 MAPLEWAY DR, PO BOX 38010 ● OLMSTED FALLS OH 44138 ● (440) 235-7979

Grade Span: PK-12 **Schools**: *Regular* 5 ● *Spec Ed* 0 ● *Alt* 0 **Students**: 2,866 **Total Teachers**: 151 **Student/Classroom Teacher Ratio**: 16.3	**Expenditures/Student**: $5,672 **Librarians**: 6.0 478 students/librarian **Guidance Counselors**: 12.0 239 students/counselor	**% Amer Indian**: 0.0 **% Asian**: 0.5 **% Black**: 1.1 **% Hispanic**: 0.9 **% White**: 97.5	National ***Socio-Economic Status*** indicator percentile (100=high): 93rd

Cuyahoga County
PARMA CITY S.D.
6726 RIDGE RD ● PARMA OH 44129 ● (216) 842-5300

Grade Span: PK-12 **Schools**: *Regular* 22 ● *Spec Ed* 1 ● *Alt* 0 **Students**: 13,131 **Total Teachers**: 825 **Student/Classroom Teacher Ratio**: 16.0	**Expenditures/Student**: $6,337 **Librarians**: 15.0 875 students/librarian **Guidance Counselors**: 21.0 625 students/counselor	**% Amer Indian**: 0.1 **% Asian**: 2.0 **% Black**: 1.7 **% Hispanic**: 0.9 **% White**: 95.3	National ***Socio-Economic Status*** indicator percentile (100=high): 78th

Cuyahoga County
SHAKER HEIGHTS CITY S.D.
15600 PARKLAND DR ● SHAKER HEIGHTS OH 44120 ● (216) 295-1400 ● http://www.shaker.k12.oh.us

Grade Span: PK-12 **Schools**: *Regular* 9 ● *Spec Ed* 0 ● *Alt* 0 **Students**: 5,485 **Total Teachers**: 383 **Student/Classroom Teacher Ratio**: 14.7	**Expenditures/Student**: $9,407 **Librarians**: 9.0 609 students/librarian **Guidance Counselors**: 9.0 609 students/counselor	**% Amer Indian**: 0.0 **% Asian**: 2.6 **% Black**: 50.5 **% Hispanic**: 0.7 **% White**: 46.2	National ***Socio-Economic Status*** indicator percentile (100=high): 89th

Cuyahoga County
SOLON CITY S.D.
33425 ARTHUR RD ● SOLON OH 44139 ● (440) 248-1600

Grade Span: PK-12 **Schools**: *Regular* 7 ● *Spec Ed* 0 ● *Alt* 0 **Students**: 4,466 **Total Teachers**: 306 **Student/Classroom Teacher Ratio**: 16.7	**Expenditures/Student**: $7,674 **Librarians**: 7.0 638 students/librarian **Guidance Counselors**: 11.0 406 students/counselor	**% Amer Indian**: 0.1 **% Asian**: 4.9 **% Black**: 5.0 **% Hispanic**: 0.3 **% White**: 89.7	National ***Socio-Economic Status*** indicator percentile (100=high): 99th

Cuyahoga County
STRONGSVILLE CITY S.D.
13200 PEARL RD ● STRONGSVILLE OH 44136 ● (440) 572-7000

Grade Span: PK-12 **Schools**: *Regular* 11 ● *Spec Ed* 0 ● *Alt* 0 **Students**: 6,610 **Total Teachers**: 551 **Student/Classroom Teacher Ratio**: 12.8	**Expenditures/Student**: $5,722 **Librarians**: 11.0 601 students/librarian **Guidance Counselors**: 38.0 174 students/counselor	**% Amer Indian**: 0.0 **% Asian**: 3.2 **% Black**: 1.0 **% Hispanic**: 1.1 **% White**: 94.7	National ***Socio-Economic Status*** indicator percentile (100=high): 97th

Cuyahoga County
[UNIVERSITY HEIGHTS] CLEVELAND HEIGHTS-UNIVERSITY HEIGHTS CITY S.D.
2155 MIRAMAR BLVD ● UNIVERSITY HEIGHTS OH 44118 ● (216) 371-7171 ● http://tiger.chuh.cleveland-heights.k12.oh.us

Grade Span: PK-12 **Schools**: *Regular* 13 ● *Spec Ed* 1 ● *Alt* 0 **Students**: 7,710 **Total Teachers**: 494 **Student/Classroom Teacher Ratio**: 16.3	**Expenditures/Student**: $8,360 **Librarians**: 11.0 701 students/librarian **Guidance Counselors**: 23.0 335 students/counselor	**% Amer Indian**: 0.1 **% Asian**: 1.6 **% Black**: 68.6 **% Hispanic**: 0.9 **% White**: 28.9	National ***Socio-Economic Status*** indicator percentile (100=high): na

Cuyahoga County
WARRENSVILLE HEIGHTS CITY S.D.
4500 WARRENSVILLE CENTER ● WARRENSVILLE HEIGHTS OH 44128 ● (216) 663-2770

Grade Span: PK-12 **Schools**: *Regular* 7 ● *Spec Ed* 0 ● *Alt* 0 **Students**: 3,247 **Total Teachers**: 180 **Student/Classroom Teacher Ratio**: 17.3	**Expenditures/Student**: $7,555 **Librarians**: 5.0 649 students/librarian **Guidance Counselors**: 9.0 361 students/counselor	**% Amer Indian**: 0.0 **% Asian**: 0.1 **% Black**: 99.8 **% Hispanic**: 0.0 **% White**: 0.2	National ***Socio-Economic Status*** indicator percentile (100=high): na

Cuyahoga County
WESTLAKE CITY S.D.
2260 DOVER RD ● WESTLAKE OH 44145 ● (440) 871-7300

Grade Span: PK-12 **Schools**: *Regular* 8 ● *Spec Ed* 0 ● *Alt* 0 **Students**: 4,082 **Total Teachers**: 252 **Student/Classroom Teacher Ratio**: 17.6	**Expenditures/Student**: $7,150 **Librarians**: 10.0 408 students/librarian **Guidance Counselors**: 18.0 227 students/counselor	**% Amer Indian**: 0.0 **% Asian**: 3.3 **% Black**: 0.8 **% Hispanic**: 0.7 **% White**: 95.2	National ***Socio-Economic Status*** indicator percentile (100=high): na

Darke County

GREENVILLE CITY S.D.

MEMORIAL HALL, 215 W FOURTH ST ● GREENVILLE OH 45331 ● (937) 548-3185

Grade Span: PK-12 **Schools**: *Regular* 8 ● *Spec Ed* 0 ● *Alt* 0 **Students**: 3,706 **Total Teachers**: 213 **Student/Classroom Teacher Ratio**: 17.8	**Expenditures/Student**: $4,516 **Librarians**: 2.0 1,853 students/librarian **Guidance Counselors**: 5.0 741 students/counselor	**% Amer Indian**: 0.1 **% Asian**: 0.5 **% Black**: 0.7 **% Hispanic**: 0.4 **% White**: 98.3	National ***Socio-Economic Status*** indicator percentile (100=high): 74th

Defiance County

DEFIANCE CITY S.D.

629 ARABELLA ST ● DEFIANCE OH 43512 ● (419) 782-0070

Grade Span: PK-12 **Schools**: *Regular* 7 ● *Spec Ed* 0 ● *Alt* 0 **Students**: 3,193 **Total Teachers**: 177 **Student/Classroom Teacher Ratio**: 17.9	**Expenditures/Student**: $4,594 **Librarians**: 3.0 1,064 students/librarian **Guidance Counselors**: 8.0 399 students/counselor	**% Amer Indian**: 0.0 **% Asian**: 0.6 **% Black**: 4.6 **% Hispanic**: 16.3 **% White**: 78.4	National ***Socio-Economic Status*** indicator percentile (100=high): 75th

Delaware County

DELAWARE CITY S.D.

248 N WASHINGTON ST ● DELAWARE OH 43015 ● (614) 363-1188

Grade Span: PK-12 **Schools**: *Regular* 7 ● *Spec Ed* 0 ● *Alt* 0 **Students**: 3,977 **Total Teachers**: 221 **Student/Classroom Teacher Ratio**: 18.4	**Expenditures/Student**: $5,388 **Librarians**: 2.0 1,989 students/librarian **Guidance Counselors**: 9.0 442 students/counselor	**% Amer Indian**: 0.0 **% Asian**: 0.3 **% Black**: 5.1 **% Hispanic**: 0.6 **% White**: 94.1	National ***Socio-Economic Status*** indicator percentile (100=high): 75th

Delaware County

[GALENA] **BIG WALNUT LOCAL S.D.**

70 WALNUT, PO BOX 218 ● GALENA OH 43021 ● (614) 965-2706

Grade Span: PK-12 **Schools**: *Regular* 5 ● *Spec Ed* 0 ● *Alt* 0 **Students**: 2,669 **Total Teachers**: 148 **Student/Classroom Teacher Ratio**: 19.1	**Expenditures/Student**: $4,410 **Librarians**: 3.0 890 students/librarian **Guidance Counselors**: 6.0 445 students/counselor	**% Amer Indian**: 0.0 **% Asian**: 0.1 **% Black**: 0.7 **% Hispanic**: 0.3 **% White**: 98.9	National ***Socio-Economic Status*** indicator percentile (100=high): 85th

Delaware County

[LEWIS CENTER] **OLENTANGY LOCAL S.D.**

814 SHANAHAN RD ● LEWIS CENTER OH 43035 ● (614) 548-6111

Grade Span: PK-12 **Schools**: *Regular* 4 ● *Spec Ed* 0 ● *Alt* 0 **Students**: 3,463 **Total Teachers**: 206 **Student/Classroom Teacher Ratio**: 16.2	**Expenditures/Student**: $5,237 **Librarians**: 7.0 495 students/librarian **Guidance Counselors**: 15.0 231 students/counselor	**% Amer Indian**: 0.1 **% Asian**: 0.9 **% Black**: 0.6 **% Hispanic**: 0.3 **% White**: 98.1	National ***Socio-Economic Status*** indicator percentile (100=high): 94th

Erie County

SANDUSKY CITY S.D.

407 DECATUR ST ● SANDUSKY OH 44870 ● (419) 626-6940

Grade Span: PK-12 **Schools**: *Regular* 12 ● *Spec Ed* 0 ● *Alt* 0 **Students**: 4,745 **Total Teachers**: 284 **Student/Classroom Teacher Ratio**: 19.1	**Expenditures/Student**: $6,102 **Librarians**: 3.0 1,582 students/librarian **Guidance Counselors**: 8.0 593 students/counselor	**% Amer Indian**: 0.1 **% Asian**: 0.3 **% Black**: 37.3 **% Hispanic**: 2.5 **% White**: 59.8	National ***Socio-Economic Status*** indicator percentile (100=high): 22nd

Erie County

VERMILION LOCAL S.D.

1230 BEECHVIEW DR ● VERMILION OH 44089 ● (440) 967-5210

Grade Span: PK-12 **Schools**: *Regular* 4 ● *Spec Ed* 0 ● *Alt* 0 **Students**: 2,792 **Total Teachers**: 163 **Student/Classroom Teacher Ratio**: 17.6	**Expenditures/Student**: $6,262 **Librarians**: 3.0 931 students/librarian **Guidance Counselors**: 5.0 558 students/counselor	**% Amer Indian**: 0.1 **% Asian**: 0.2 **% Black**: 0.1 **% Hispanic**: 1.1 **% White**: 98.5	National ***Socio-Economic Status*** indicator percentile (100=high): 83rd

Fairfield County

LANCASTER CITY S.D.

111 S BROAD ST ● LANCASTER OH 43130 ● (614) 687-7300

Grade Span: PK-12 **Schools**: *Regular* 14 ● *Spec Ed* 0 ● *Alt* 0 **Students**: 6,634 **Total Teachers**: 375 **Student/Classroom Teacher Ratio**: 19.3	**Expenditures/Student**: $5,635 **Librarians**: 9.0 737 students/librarian **Guidance Counselors**: 7.0 948 students/counselor	**% Amer Indian**: 0.0 **% Asian**: 0.2 **% Black**: 0.4 **% Hispanic**: 0.3 **% White**: 99.0	National ***Socio-Economic Status*** indicator percentile (100=high): 52nd

Fairfield County

PICKERINGTON LOCAL S.D.

777 LONG RD ● PICKERINGTON OH 43147 ● (614) 833-2110

Grade Span: PK-12 **Schools**: *Regular* 6 ● *Spec Ed* 0 ● *Alt* 0 **Students**: 6,232 **Total Teachers**: 328 **Student/Classroom Teacher Ratio**: 19.6	**Expenditures/Student**: $4,944 **Librarians**: 4.0 1,558 students/librarian **Guidance Counselors**: 12.0 519 students/counselor	**% Amer Indian**: 0.0 **% Asian**: 1.3 **% Black**: 4.0 **% Hispanic**: 0.5 **% White**: 94.2	National ***Socio-Economic Status*** indicator percentile (100=high): na

Fayette County

[WASHINGTON COURT HOUSE] **MIAMI TRACE LOCAL S.D.**

1400 US RT 22 NW ● WASHINGTON COURT HOUSE OH 43160 ● (614) 335-3010 ● http://oak-web.washington-ch.oh.us/mt

Grade Span: PK-12 **Schools**: *Regular* 10 ● *Spec Ed* 0 ● *Alt* 0 **Students**: 3,080 **Total Teachers**: 168 **Student/Classroom Teacher Ratio**: 19.2	**Expenditures/Student**: $4,320 **Librarians**: 2.0 1,540 students/librarian **Guidance Counselors**: 6.0 513 students/counselor	**% Amer Indian**: 0.0 **% Asian**: 0.0 **% Black**: 0.6 **% Hispanic**: 0.2 **% White**: 99.1	National ***Socio-Economic Status*** indicator percentile (100=high): na

Franklin County

COLUMBUS CITY S.D.

270 E STATE ST ● COLUMBUS OH 43215 ● (614) 365-5000 ● http://www.columbus.k12.oh.us

Grade Span: PK-12 **Schools**: *Regular* 137 ● *Spec Ed* 3 ● *Alt* 4 **Students**: 63,082 **Total Teachers**: 4,018 **Student/Classroom Teacher Ratio**: 18.7	**Expenditures/Student**: $6,279 **Librarians**: 64.0 986 students/librarian **Guidance Counselors**: 62.0 1,017 students/counselor	**% Amer Indian**: 0.2 **% Asian**: 2.4 **% Black**: 54.0 **% Hispanic**: 0.8 **% White**: 42.6	National ***Socio-Economic Status*** indicator percentile (100=high): na

Franklin County

[COLUMBUS] **HAMILTON LOCAL S.D.**

4999 LOCKBOURNE RD ● COLUMBUS OH 43207 ● (614) 491-8044

Grade Span: PK-12 **Schools**: *Regular* 4 ● *Spec Ed* 0 ● *Alt* 0 **Students**: 2,522 **Total Teachers**: 137 **Student/Classroom Teacher Ratio**: 18.7	**Expenditures/Student**: $4,574 **Librarians**: 3.0 841 students/librarian **Guidance Counselors**: 5.0 504 students/counselor	**% Amer Indian**: 0.3 **% Asian**: 1.0 **% Black**: 6.1 **% Hispanic**: 1.0 **% White**: 91.6	National ***Socio-Economic Status*** indicator percentile (100=high): 63rd

Franklin County
DUBLIN CITY S.D.
7030 COFFMAN RD ● DUBLIN OH 43017 ● (614) 764-5913

Grade Span: PK-12 **Schools**: *Regular* 13 ● *Spec Ed* 0 ● *Alt* 0 **Students**: 9,854 **Total Teachers**: 618 **Student/Classroom Teacher Ratio**: 16.7	**Expenditures/Student**: $5,515 **Librarians**: 15.0 657 students/librarian **Guidance Counselors**: 24.0 411 students/counselor	**% Amer Indian**: 0.1 **% Asian**: 7.0 **% Black**: 2.0 **% Hispanic**: 0.6 **% White**: 90.2	National ***Socio-Economic Status*** indicator percentile (100=high): na

Franklin County
GAHANNA-JEFFERSON CITY S.D.
160 HAMILTON RD ● GAHANNA OH 43230 ● (614) 471-7065 ● http://www.gahanna.k12.oh.us

Grade Span: KG-12 **Schools**: *Regular* 12 ● *Spec Ed* 0 ● *Alt* 0 **Students**: 6,884 **Total Teachers**: 406 **Student/Classroom Teacher Ratio**: 17.2	**Expenditures/Student**: $5,635 **Librarians**: 12.0 574 students/librarian **Guidance Counselors**: 12.0 574 students/counselor	**% Amer Indian**: 0.2 **% Asian**: 1.9 **% Black**: 7.7 **% Hispanic**: 0.9 **% White**: 89.3	National ***Socio-Economic Status*** indicator percentile (100=high): 93rd

Franklin County
[GROVE CITY] SOUTH-WESTERN CITY S.D.
2975 KINGSTON AVE ● GROVE CITY OH 43123 ● (614) 875-2318

Grade Span: PK-12 **Schools**: *Regular* 24 ● *Spec Ed* 2 ● *Alt* 1 **Students**: 18,498 **Total Teachers**: 994 **Student/Classroom Teacher Ratio**: 22.3	**Expenditures/Student**: $5,186 **Librarians**: 5.0 3,700 students/librarian **Guidance Counselors**: 25.0 740 students/counselor	**% Amer Indian**: 0.1 **% Asian**: 1.2 **% Black**: 6.5 **% Hispanic**: 0.6 **% White**: 91.7	National ***Socio-Economic Status*** indicator percentile (100=high): 61st

Franklin County
GROVEPORT MADISON LOCAL S.D.
5055 S HAMILTON RD ● GROVEPORT OH 43125 ● (614) 836-5371

Grade Span: PK-12 **Schools**: *Regular* 10 ● *Spec Ed* 0 ● *Alt* 0 **Students**: 6,119 **Total Teachers**: 311 **Student/Classroom Teacher Ratio**: 20.8	**Expenditures/Student**: $5,096 **Librarians**: 13.0 471 students/librarian **Guidance Counselors**: 15.0 408 students/counselor	**% Amer Indian**: 0.3 **% Asian**: 1.1 **% Black**: 9.4 **% Hispanic**: 0.7 **% White**: 88.5	National ***Socio-Economic Status*** indicator percentile (100=high): 80th

Franklin County
HILLIARD CITY S.D.
5323 CEMETERY RD ● HILLIARD OH 43026 ● (614) 771-4273 ● http://WWW.Hilliard.K12.Oh.US

Grade Span: PK-12 **Schools**: *Regular* 13 ● *Spec Ed* 0 ● *Alt* 0 **Students**: 10,041 **Total Teachers**: 539 **Student/Classroom Teacher Ratio**: 18.6	**Expenditures/Student**: $4,911 **Librarians**: 6.0 1,674 students/librarian **Guidance Counselors**: 17.0 591 students/counselor	**% Amer Indian**: 0.1 **% Asian**: 2.2 **% Black**: 2.3 **% Hispanic**: 1.0 **% White**: 94.4	National ***Socio-Economic Status*** indicator percentile (100=high): 92nd

Franklin County
REYNOLDSBURG CITY S.D.
6549 E LIVINGSTON AVE ● REYNOLDSBURG OH 43068 ● (614) 866-2815

Grade Span: PK-12 **Schools**: *Regular* 9 ● *Spec Ed* 0 ● *Alt* 0 **Students**: 5,300 **Total Teachers**: 281 **Student/Classroom Teacher Ratio**: 19.3	**Expenditures/Student**: $5,024 **Librarians**: 3.0 1,767 students/librarian **Guidance Counselors**: 10.0 530 students/counselor	**% Amer Indian**: 0.2 **% Asian**: 1.4 **% Black**: 7.9 **% Hispanic**: 0.8 **% White**: 89.8	National ***Socio-Economic Status*** indicator percentile (100=high): na

Franklin County
UPPER ARLINGTON CITY S.D.
1950 N MALLWAY ● UPPER ARLINGTON OH 43221 ● (614) 487-5000 ● http://www.upper-arlington.k12.oh.us/schools

Grade Span: PK-12 **Schools**: *Regular* 9 ● *Spec Ed* 0 ● *Alt* 0 **Students**: 5,637 **Total Teachers**: 359 **Student/Classroom Teacher Ratio**: 16.3	**Expenditures/Student**: $6,962 **Librarians**: 9.0 626 students/librarian **Guidance Counselors**: 17.0 332 students/counselor	**% Amer Indian**: 0.1 **% Asian**: 3.2 **% Black**: 0.7 **% Hispanic**: 0.6 **% White**: 95.4	National ***Socio-Economic Status*** indicator percentile (100=high): na

Franklin County
WESTERVILLE CITY S.D.
336 S OTTERBEIN AVE ● WESTERVILLE OH 43081 ● (614) 895-6080

Grade Span: PK-12 **Schools**: *Regular* 19 ● *Spec Ed* 0 ● *Alt* 0 **Students**: 12,806 **Total Teachers**: 679 **Student/Classroom Teacher Ratio**: 21.5	**Expenditures/Student**: $5,381 **Librarians**: 14.0 915 students/librarian **Guidance Counselors**: 23.0 557 students/counselor	**% Amer Indian**: 0.5 **% Asian**: 1.7 **% Black**: 8.1 **% Hispanic**: 0.7 **% White**: 89.0	National ***Socio-Economic Status*** indicator percentile (100=high): 91st

Franklin County
WHITEHALL CITY S.D.
625 S YEARLING ● WHITEHALL OH 43213 ● (614) 235-2385

Grade Span: PK-12 **Schools**: *Regular* 5 ● *Spec Ed* 0 ● *Alt* 1 **Students**: 2,984 **Total Teachers**: 189 **Student/Classroom Teacher Ratio**: 20.9	**Expenditures/Student**: $5,724 **Librarians**: 4.0 746 students/librarian **Guidance Counselors**: 8.0 373 students/counselor	**% Amer Indian**: 0.9 **% Asian**: 2.3 **% Black**: 12.8 **% Hispanic**: 0.6 **% White**: 83.4	National ***Socio-Economic Status*** indicator percentile (100=high): 48th

Franklin County
WORTHINGTON CITY S.D.
752 HIGH ST ● WORTHINGTON OH 43085 ● (614) 431-6500

Grade Span: PK-12 **Schools**: *Regular* 19 ● *Spec Ed* 0 ● *Alt* 0 **Students**: 10,805 **Total Teachers**: 660 **Student/Classroom Teacher Ratio**: 16.4	**Expenditures/Student**: $6,300 **Librarians**: 20.0 540 students/librarian **Guidance Counselors**: 23.0 470 students/counselor	**% Amer Indian**: 0.1 **% Asian**: 6.1 **% Black**: 4.5 **% Hispanic**: 0.7 **% White**: 88.5	National ***Socio-Economic Status*** indicator percentile (100=high): 97th

Gallia County
[GALLIPOLIS] GALLIA COUNTY LOCAL S.D.
230 SHAWNEE LN ● GALLIPOLIS OH 45631 ● (614) 446-7917

Grade Span: PK-12 **Schools**: *Regular* 7 ● *Spec Ed* 0 ● *Alt* 0 **Students**: 3,085 **Total Teachers**: 187 **Student/Classroom Teacher Ratio**: 18.8	**Expenditures/Student**: $4,464 **Librarians**: 2.0 1,543 students/librarian **Guidance Counselors**: 4.0 771 students/counselor	**% Amer Indian**: 0.1 **% Asian**: 0.1 **% Black**: 2.3 **% Hispanic**: 0.2 **% White**: 97.3	National ***Socio-Economic Status*** indicator percentile (100=high): 30th

Gallia County
GALLIPOLIS CITY S.D.
61 STATE ST ● GALLIPOLIS OH 45631 ● (614) 446-3211

Grade Span: PK-12 **Schools**: *Regular* 4 ● *Spec Ed* 0 ● *Alt* 0 **Students**: 2,679 **Total Teachers**: 133 **Student/Classroom Teacher Ratio**: 19.9	**Expenditures/Student**: $4,183 **Librarians**: 2.0 1,340 students/librarian **Guidance Counselors**: 3.0 893 students/counselor	**% Amer Indian**: 0.6 **% Asian**: 0.2 **% Black**: 4.5 **% Hispanic**: 0.7 **% White**: 93.9	National ***Socio-Economic Status*** indicator percentile (100=high): 45th

Geauga County
[CHAGRIN FALLS] **KENSTON LOCAL S.D.**
17419 SNYDER RD ● CHAGRIN FALLS OH 44023 ● (440) 543-9677

Grade Span: PK-12 **Schools**: *Regular* 6 ● *Spec Ed* 0 ● *Alt* 0 **Students**: 2,789 **Total Teachers**: 158 **Student/Classroom Teacher Ratio**: 17.1	**Expenditures/Student**: $6,034 **Librarians**: 1.0 2,789 students/librarian **Guidance Counselors**: 3.0 930 students/counselor	**% Amer Indian**: 0.0 **% Asian**: 0.7 **% Black**: 6.2 **% Hispanic**: 0.7 **% White**: 92.4	National ***Socio-Economic Status*** indicator percentile (100=high): 94th

Geauga County
CHARDON LOCAL S.D.
428 NORTH ST ● CHARDON OH 44024 ● (216) 285-4052

Grade Span: PK-12 **Schools**: *Regular* 7 ● *Spec Ed* 0 ● *Alt* 0 **Students**: 3,000 **Total Teachers**: 163 **Student/Classroom Teacher Ratio**: 17.5	**Expenditures/Student**: $5,903 **Librarians**: 4.0 750 students/librarian **Guidance Counselors**: 4.0 750 students/counselor	**% Amer Indian**: 0.1 **% Asian**: 0.6 **% Black**: 0.7 **% Hispanic**: 0.3 **% White**: 98.4	National ***Socio-Economic Status*** indicator percentile (100=high): 91st

Greene County
BEAVERCREEK LOCAL S.D.
2940 DAYTON-XENIA RD ● BEAVERCREEK OH 45434 ● (937) 426-1522

Grade Span: PK-12 **Schools**: *Regular* 9 ● *Spec Ed* 0 ● *Alt* 0 **Students**: 6,783 **Total Teachers**: 367 **Student/Classroom Teacher Ratio**: 17.4	**Expenditures/Student**: $5,332 **Librarians**: 4.0 1,696 students/librarian **Guidance Counselors**: 18.0 377 students/counselor	**% Amer Indian**: 0.2 **% Asian**: 3.9 **% Black**: 0.8 **% Hispanic**: 0.7 **% White**: 94.4	National ***Socio-Economic Status*** indicator percentile (100=high): 97th

Greene County
FAIRBORN CITY S.D.
306 E WHITTIER ● FAIRBORN OH 45324 ● (937) 878-3961

Grade Span: PK-12 **Schools**: *Regular* 8 ● *Spec Ed* 0 ● *Alt* 0 **Students**: 6,325 **Total Teachers**: 325 **Student/Classroom Teacher Ratio**: 19.8	**Expenditures/Student**: $4,472 **Librarians**: 2.0 3,163 students/librarian **Guidance Counselors**: 8.0 791 students/counselor	**% Amer Indian**: 0.2 **% Asian**: 3.4 **% Black**: 6.5 **% Hispanic**: 1.2 **% White**: 88.6	National ***Socio-Economic Status*** indicator percentile (100=high): 68th

Greene County
XENIA CITY S.D.
578 E MARKET ST ● XENIA OH 45385 ● (937) 376-2961

Grade Span: PK-12 **Schools**: *Regular* 10 ● *Spec Ed* 0 ● *Alt* 0 **Students**: 5,734 **Total Teachers**: 313 **Student/Classroom Teacher Ratio**: 20.0	**Expenditures/Student**: $4,925 **Librarians**: 7.0 819 students/librarian **Guidance Counselors**: 17.0 337 students/counselor	**% Amer Indian**: 0.2 **% Asian**: 0.6 **% Black**: 15.6 **% Hispanic**: 1.0 **% White**: 82.5	National ***Socio-Economic Status*** indicator percentile (100=high): 51st

Guernsey County
CAMBRIDGE CITY S.D.
152 HIGHLAND AVE ● CAMBRIDGE OH 43725 ● (614) 439-5021

Grade Span: KG-12 **Schools**: *Regular* 8 ● *Spec Ed* 0 ● *Alt* 0 **Students**: 2,982 **Total Teachers**: 195 **Student/Classroom Teacher Ratio**: 16.6	**Expenditures/Student**: $4,453 **Librarians**: 2.0 1,491 students/librarian **Guidance Counselors**: 7.0 426 students/counselor	**% Amer Indian**: 0.1 **% Asian**: 0.7 **% Black**: 5.3 **% Hispanic**: 0.2 **% White**: 93.7	National ***Socio-Economic Status*** indicator percentile (100=high): na

Hamilton County
CINCINNATI CITY S.D.
2651 BURNET AVE, PO BOX 5381 ● CINCINNATI OH 45201 ● (513) 475-7000 ● http://www.cpsboe.k12.oh.us

Grade Span: PK-12 **Schools**: *Regular* 80 ● *Spec Ed* 2 ● *Alt* 0 **Students**: 52,172 **Total Teachers**: 3,082 **Student/Classroom Teacher Ratio**: 20.3	**Expenditures/Student**: $6,469 **Librarians**: 64.0 815 students/librarian **Guidance Counselors**: 19.0 2,746 students/counselor	**% Amer Indian**: 0.1 **% Asian**: 0.9 **% Black**: 67.8 **% Hispanic**: 0.3 **% White**: 31.0	National ***Socio-Economic Status*** indicator percentile (100=high): na

Hamilton County
[CINCINNATI] **FOREST HILLS LOCAL S.D.**
7550 FOREST RD ● CINCINNATI OH 45255 ● (513) 231-3600

Grade Span: PK-12 **Schools**: *Regular* 8 ● *Spec Ed* 0 ● *Alt* 0 **Students**: 8,174 **Total Teachers**: 401 **Student/Classroom Teacher Ratio**: 20.5	**Expenditures/Student**: $4,543 **Librarians**: 8.0 1,022 students/librarian **Guidance Counselors**: 17.0 481 students/counselor	**% Amer Indian**: 0.0 **% Asian**: 1.4 **% Black**: 0.6 **% Hispanic**: 0.7 **% White**: 97.3	National ***Socio-Economic Status*** indicator percentile (100=high): 96th

Hamilton County
[CINCINNATI] **MOUNT HEALTHY CITY S.D.**
7615 HARRISON AVE ● CINCINNATI OH 45231 ● (513) 729-0077 ● http://home.fuse.net/MtHealthy

Grade Span: PK-12 **Schools**: *Regular* 9 ● *Spec Ed* 0 ● *Alt* 1 **Students**: 4,027 **Total Teachers**: 232 **Student/Classroom Teacher Ratio**: 15.9	**Expenditures/Student**: $5,352 **Librarians**: 3.0 1,342 students/librarian **Guidance Counselors**: 10.0 403 students/counselor	**% Amer Indian**: 0.0 **% Asian**: 0.6 **% Black**: 51.4 **% Hispanic**: 0.2 **% White**: 47.9	National ***Socio-Economic Status*** indicator percentile (100=high): 37th

Hamilton County
[CINCINNATI] **NORTHWEST LOCAL S.D.**
3240 BANNING RD ● CINCINNATI OH 45239 ● (513) 923-1000 ● http://www.nwlsd.org

Grade Span: PK-12 **Schools**: *Regular* 14 ● *Spec Ed* 0 ● *Alt* 0 **Students**: 10,720 **Total Teachers**: 560 **Student/Classroom Teacher Ratio**: 19.7	**Expenditures/Student**: $4,639 **Librarians**: 6.0 1,787 students/librarian **Guidance Counselors**: 19.0 564 students/counselor	**% Amer Indian**: 0.2 **% Asian**: 0.9 **% Black**: 9.9 **% Hispanic**: 0.6 **% White**: 88.4	National ***Socio-Economic Status*** indicator percentile (100=high): 73rd

Hamilton County
[CINCINNATI] **OAK HILLS LOCAL S.D.**
6479 BRIDGETOWN RD ● CINCINNATI OH 45248 ● (513) 574-3200 ● http://www.oakhills.k12.oh.us

Grade Span: PK-12 **Schools**: *Regular* 8 ● *Spec Ed* 0 ● *Alt* 0 **Students**: 8,357 **Total Teachers**: 405 **Student/Classroom Teacher Ratio**: 21.4	**Expenditures/Student**: $4,291 **Librarians**: 4.0 2,089 students/librarian **Guidance Counselors**: 18.0 464 students/counselor	**% Amer Indian**: 0.2 **% Asian**: 0.6 **% Black**: 0.4 **% Hispanic**: 0.2 **% White**: 98.6	National ***Socio-Economic Status*** indicator percentile (100=high): na

Hamilton County
[CINCINNATI] **PRINCETON CITY S.D.**
25 W SHARON AVE ● CINCINNATI OH 45246 ● (513) 771-8560 ● http://www.phs.princeton.k12.oh.us

Grade Span: PK-12 **Schools**: *Regular* 11 ● *Spec Ed* 0 ● *Alt* 0 **Students**: 6,917 **Total Teachers**: 521 **Student/Classroom Teacher Ratio**: 13.8	**Expenditures/Student**: $7,768 **Librarians**: 10.0 692 students/librarian **Guidance Counselors**: 15.0 461 students/counselor	**% Amer Indian**: 0.2 **% Asian**: 2.8 **% Black**: 39.9 **% Hispanic**: 0.7 **% White**: 56.5	National ***Socio-Economic Status*** indicator percentile (100=high): na

Hamilton County
[CINCINNATI] **SYCAMORE COMMUNITY CITY S.D.**
4881 COOPER RD ● CINCINNATI OH 45242 ● (513) 791-4848

Grade Span: PK-12 **Schools**: *Regular* 8 ● *Spec Ed* 0 ● *Alt* 0 **Students**: 6,161 **Total Teachers**: 381 **Student/Classroom Teacher Ratio**: 16.1	**Expenditures/Student**: $7,187 **Librarians**: 7.0 880 students/librarian **Guidance Counselors**: 13.0 474 students/counselor	**% Amer Indian**: 0.1 **% Asian**: 5.6 **% Black**: 4.5 **% Hispanic**: 1.0 **% White**: 88.8	National ***Socio-Economic Status*** indicator percentile (100=high): na

Hamilton County
[CINCINNATI] **WINTON WOODS CITY S.D.**
1215 W KEMPER RD ● CINCINNATI OH 45240 ● (513) 825-5700

Grade Span: PK-12 **Schools**: *Regular* 8 ● *Spec Ed* 0 ● *Alt* 0 **Students**: 4,527 **Total Teachers**: 282 **Student/Classroom Teacher Ratio**: 16.2	**Expenditures/Student**: $5,683 **Librarians**: 4.0 1,132 students/librarian **Guidance Counselors**: 8.0 566 students/counselor	**% Amer Indian**: 0.0 **% Asian**: 2.0 **% Black**: 55.3 **% Hispanic**: 0.6 **% White**: 42.1	National ***Socio-Economic Status*** indicator percentile (100=high): 67th

Hamilton County
[HARRISON] **SOUTHWEST LOCAL S.D.**
230 S ELM ST ● HARRISON OH 45030 ● (513) 367-4139 ● http://www.slsd.k12.oh.us

Grade Span: PK-12 **Schools**: *Regular* 8 ● *Spec Ed* 0 ● *Alt* 0 **Students**: 4,106 **Total Teachers**: 217 **Student/Classroom Teacher Ratio**: 18.8	**Expenditures/Student**: $4,525 **Librarians**: 3.0 1,369 students/librarian **Guidance Counselors**: 8.0 513 students/counselor	**% Amer Indian**: 0.0 **% Asian**: 0.1 **% Black**: 0.1 **% Hispanic**: 0.2 **% White**: 99.5	National ***Socio-Economic Status*** indicator percentile (100=high): 78th

Hamilton County
LOVELAND CITY S.D.
757 S LEBANON RD ● LOVELAND OH 45140 ● (513) 683-5600

Grade Span: PK-12 **Schools**: *Regular* 5 ● *Spec Ed* 0 ● *Alt* 0 **Students**: 3,524 **Total Teachers**: 185 **Student/Classroom Teacher Ratio**: 19.5	**Expenditures/Student**: $4,759 **Librarians**: 2.0 1,762 students/librarian **Guidance Counselors**: 5.0 705 students/counselor	**% Amer Indian**: 0.0 **% Asian**: 0.6 **% Black**: 2.1 **% Hispanic**: 0.5 **% White**: 96.7	National ***Socio-Economic Status*** indicator percentile (100=high): 91st

Hamilton County
NORWOOD CITY S.D.
2132 WILLIAMS AVE ● NORWOOD OH 45212 ● (513) 396-5521

Grade Span: PK-12 **Schools**: *Regular* 6 ● *Spec Ed* 0 ● *Alt* 0 **Students**: 3,421 **Total Teachers**: 172 **Student/Classroom Teacher Ratio**: 20.0	**Expenditures/Student**: $5,414 **Librarians**: 1.0 3,421 students/librarian **Guidance Counselors**: 7.0 489 students/counselor	**% Amer Indian**: 0.1 **% Asian**: 0.6 **% Black**: 1.5 **% Hispanic**: 0.6 **% White**: 97.2	National ***Socio-Economic Status*** indicator percentile (100=high): 39th

Hancock County
FINDLAY CITY S.D.
227 S WEST ST ● FINDLAY OH 45840 ● (419) 425-8213

Grade Span: PK-12 **Schools**: *Regular* 13 ● *Spec Ed* 1 ● *Alt* 0 **Students**: 6,203 **Total Teachers**: 405 **Student/Classroom Teacher Ratio**: 17.0	**Expenditures/Student**: $5,757 **Librarians**: 5.0 1,241 students/librarian **Guidance Counselors**: 12.0 517 students/counselor	**% Amer Indian**: 0.0 **% Asian**: 1.7 **% Black**: 2.2 **% Hispanic**: 4.0 **% White**: 92.1	National ***Socio-Economic Status*** indicator percentile (100=high): 73rd

Highland County

HILLSBORO CITY S.D.

338 W MAIN ST ● HILLSBORO OH 45133 ● (937) 393-3475 ● http://balboa.mveca.ohio.gov/~hillsboro

Grade Span: PK-12 **Schools**: *Regular* 5 ● *Spec Ed* 0 ● *Alt* 0 **Students**: 2,798 **Total Teachers**: 149 **Student/Classroom Teacher Ratio**: 20.9	**Expenditures/Student**: $4,275 **Librarians**: 3.0 933 students/librarian **Guidance Counselors**: 4.0 700 students/counselor	**% Amer Indian**: 0.0 **% Asian**: 0.3 **% Black**: 3.8 **% Hispanic**: 0.3 **% White**: 95.6	National ***Socio-Economic Status*** indicator percentile (100=high): 62nd

Hocking County

LOGAN-HOCKING LOCAL S.D.

57 S WALNUT ● LOGAN OH 43138 ● (614) 385-8517

Grade Span: PK-12 **Schools**: *Regular* 11 ● *Spec Ed* 0 ● *Alt* 0 **Students**: 4,188 **Total Teachers**: 190 **Student/Classroom Teacher Ratio**: 24.5	**Expenditures/Student**: $4,077 **Librarians**: 3.0 1,396 students/librarian **Guidance Counselors**: 7.0 598 students/counselor	**% Amer Indian**: 0.0 **% Asian**: 0.1 **% Black**: 0.8 **% Hispanic**: 0.1 **% White**: 98.9	National ***Socio-Economic Status*** indicator percentile (100=high): 53rd

Holmes County

[MILLERSBURG] WEST HOLMES LOCAL S.D.

10901 ST RT 39 ● MILLERSBURG OH 44654 ● (330) 674-3546

Grade Span: PK-12 **Schools**: *Regular* 7 ● *Spec Ed* 0 ● *Alt* 0 **Students**: 2,788 **Total Teachers**: 159 **Student/Classroom Teacher Ratio**: 19.0	**Expenditures/Student**: $3,918 **Librarians**: 1.0 2,788 students/librarian **Guidance Counselors**: 5.0 558 students/counselor	**% Amer Indian**: 0.0 **% Asian**: 0.3 **% Black**: 0.1 **% Hispanic**: 0.5 **% White**: 99.1	National ***Socio-Economic Status*** indicator percentile (100=high): 66th

Huron County

NORWALK CITY S.D.

134 BENEDICT AVE ● NORWALK OH 44857 ● (419) 668-2779 ● http://www.norwalk-city.k12.oh.us

Grade Span: PK-12 **Schools**: *Regular* 6 ● *Spec Ed* 0 ● *Alt* 0 **Students**: 2,713 **Total Teachers**: 135 **Student/Classroom Teacher Ratio**: 20.6	**Expenditures/Student**: $4,312 **Librarians**: 3.0 904 students/librarian **Guidance Counselors**: 5.0 543 students/counselor	**% Amer Indian**: 0.1 **% Asian**: 0.3 **% Black**: 3.2 **% Hispanic**: 2.3 **% White**: 94.1	National ***Socio-Economic Status*** indicator percentile (100=high): 65th

Jackson County

JACKSON CITY S.D.

379 E SOUTH ST ● JACKSON OH 45640 ● (614) 286-6442

Grade Span: PK-12 **Schools**: *Regular* 8 ● *Spec Ed* 0 ● *Alt* 0 **Students**: 2,838 **Total Teachers**: 137 **Student/Classroom Teacher Ratio**: 21.8	**Expenditures/Student**: $4,567 **Librarians**: 2.0 1,419 students/librarian **Guidance Counselors**: 3.0 946 students/counselor	**% Amer Indian**: 0.2 **% Asian**: 0.1 **% Black**: 0.9 **% Hispanic**: 0.1 **% White**: 98.7	National ***Socio-Economic Status*** indicator percentile (100=high): na

Jefferson County

[HAMMONDSVILLE] EDISON LOCAL S.D.

PO BOX 158 ● HAMMONDSVILLE OH 43930 ● (330) 532-1594

Grade Span: PK-12 **Schools**: *Regular* 8 ● *Spec Ed* 0 ● *Alt* 0 **Students**: 3,031 **Total Teachers**: 181 **Student/Classroom Teacher Ratio**: 18.4	**Expenditures/Student**: $5,302 **Librarians**: 2.0 1,516 students/librarian **Guidance Counselors**: 4.0 758 students/counselor	**% Amer Indian**: 0.0 **% Asian**: 0.2 **% Black**: 0.8 **% Hispanic**: 0.3 **% White**: 98.8	National ***Socio-Economic Status*** indicator percentile (100=high): 47th

Jefferson County
[RAYLAND] **BUCKEYE LOCAL S.D.**
198 MAIN, PO BOX 300 ● RAYLAND OH 43943 ● (614) 859-2114

Grade Span: PK-12 **Schools**: *Regular* 7 ● *Spec Ed* 0 ● *Alt* 0 **Students**: 2,890 **Total Teachers**: 156 **Student/Classroom Teacher Ratio**: 19.7	**Expenditures/Student**: $4,443 **Librarians**: 2.0 1,445 students/librarian **Guidance Counselors**: 3.0 963 students/counselor	**% Amer Indian**: 0.0 **% Asian**: 0.2 **% Black**: 1.8 **% Hispanic**: 0.1 **% White**: 98.0	National ***Socio-Economic Status*** indicator percentile (100=high): na

Jefferson County
STEUBENVILLE CITY S.D.
932 N 5TH ST, PO BOX 189 ● STEUBENVILLE OH 43952 ● (614) 283-3767 ● http://www.weir.net/~pbasil

Grade Span: PK-12 **Schools**: *Regular* 8 ● *Spec Ed* 0 ● *Alt* 0 **Students**: 2,888 **Total Teachers**: 161 **Student/Classroom Teacher Ratio**: 19.4	**Expenditures/Student**: $4,823 **Librarians**: 1.0 2,888 students/librarian **Guidance Counselors**: 6.0 481 students/counselor	**% Amer Indian**: 0.1 **% Asian**: 0.6 **% Black**: 30.6 **% Hispanic**: 0.3 **% White**: 68.3	National ***Socio-Economic Status*** indicator percentile (100=high): 21st

Jefferson County
[WINTERSVILLE] **INDIAN CREEK LOCAL S.D.**
RD #2 BANTAM RIDGE RD ● WINTERSVILLE OH 43952 ● (614) 264-3502

Grade Span: PK-12 **Schools**: *Regular* 7 ● *Spec Ed* 0 ● *Alt* 0 **Students**: 2,512 **Total Teachers**: 152 **Student/Classroom Teacher Ratio**: 16.9	**Expenditures/Student**: $4,972 **Librarians**: 2.0 1,256 students/librarian **Guidance Counselors**: 9.0 279 students/counselor	**% Amer Indian**: 0.1 **% Asian**: 0.3 **% Black**: 3.8 **% Hispanic**: 0.2 **% White**: 95.7	National ***Socio-Economic Status*** indicator percentile (100=high): 50th

Knox County
MOUNT VERNON CITY S.D.
302 MARTINSBURG RD ● MOUNT VERNON OH 43050 ● (614) 397-7422

Grade Span: PK-12 **Schools**: *Regular* 9 ● *Spec Ed* 0 ● *Alt* 0 **Students**: 4,282 **Total Teachers**: 212 **Student/Classroom Teacher Ratio**: 21.6	**Expenditures/Student**: $4,409 **Librarians**: 3.0 1,427 students/librarian **Guidance Counselors**: 5.0 856 students/counselor	**% Amer Indian**: 0.1 **% Asian**: 0.7 **% Black**: 1.1 **% Hispanic**: 0.3 **% White**: 97.8	National ***Socio-Economic Status*** indicator percentile (100=high): 64th

Lake County
MADISON LOCAL S.D.
6741 N RIDGE RD ● MADISON OH 44057 ● (216) 428-2166

Grade Span: PK-12 **Schools**: *Regular* 5 ● *Spec Ed* 0 ● *Alt* 0 **Students**: 3,668 **Total Teachers**: 184 **Student/Classroom Teacher Ratio**: 21.1	**Expenditures/Student**: $4,953 **Librarians**: 1.0 3,668 students/librarian **Guidance Counselors**: 6.0 611 students/counselor	**% Amer Indian**: 0.1 **% Asian**: 0.2 **% Black**: 0.3 **% Hispanic**: 0.2 **% White**: 99.3	National ***Socio-Economic Status*** indicator percentile (100=high): 73rd

Lake County
MENTOR EXEMPTED VILLAGE S.D.
6451 CENTER ST ● MENTOR OH 44060 ● (440) 255-4444 ● http://www.lcol.net/mentorschools

Grade Span: PK-12 **Schools**: *Regular* 17 ● *Spec Ed* 0 ● *Alt* 0 **Students**: 11,263 **Total Teachers**: 600 **Student/Classroom Teacher Ratio**: 21.0	**Expenditures/Student**: $5,782 **Librarians**: 16.0 704 students/librarian **Guidance Counselors**: 15.0 751 students/counselor	**% Amer Indian**: 0.1 **% Asian**: 0.8 **% Black**: 0.6 **% Hispanic**: 0.3 **% White**: 98.3	National ***Socio-Economic Status*** indicator percentile (100=high): 89th

Lake County
PAINESVILLE TOWNSHIP LOCAL S.D.
585 RIVERSIDE DR ● PAINESVILLE OH 44077 ● (440) 352-0668

Grade Span: PK-12 **Schools**: *Regular* 10 ● *Spec Ed* 0 ● *Alt* 0 **Students**: 3,884 **Total Teachers**: 184 **Student/Classroom Teacher Ratio**: 21.1	**Expenditures/Student**: $5,544 **Librarians**: 2.0 1,942 students/librarian **Guidance Counselors**: 7.0 555 students/counselor	**% Amer Indian**: 0.1 **% Asian**: 0.5 **% Black**: 1.1 **% Hispanic**: 0.2 **% White**: 98.2	National ***Socio-Economic Status*** indicator percentile (100=high): 88th

Lake County
WILLOUGHBY-EASTLAKE CITY S.D.
37047 RIDGE RD ● WILLOUGHBY OH 44094 ● (440) 946-5000 ● http://www.willoughby-eastlake.k12.oh.us

Grade Span: PK-12 **Schools**: *Regular* 14 ● *Spec Ed* 0 ● *Alt* 1 **Students**: 9,076 **Total Teachers**: 489 **Student/Classroom Teacher Ratio**: 17.8	**Expenditures/Student**: $6,476 **Librarians**: 5.0 1,815 students/librarian **Guidance Counselors**: 14.0 648 students/counselor	**% Amer Indian**: 0.0 **% Asian**: 0.8 **% Black**: 1.4 **% Hispanic**: 0.2 **% White**: 97.5	National ***Socio-Economic Status*** indicator percentile (100=high): na

Licking County
[KIRKERSVILLE] **SOUTHWEST LICKING LOCAL S.D.**
PO BOX 400 ● KIRKERSVILLE OH 43033 ● (614) 927-3941

Grade Span: PK-12 **Schools**: *Regular* 5 ● *Spec Ed* 0 ● *Alt* 0 **Students**: 3,087 **Total Teachers**: 164 **Student/Classroom Teacher Ratio**: 19.7	**Expenditures/Student**: $4,424 **Librarians**: 2.0 1,544 students/librarian **Guidance Counselors**: 5.0 617 students/counselor	**% Amer Indian**: 0.4 **% Asian**: 0.4 **% Black**: 0.7 **% Hispanic**: 0.6 **% White**: 97.9	National ***Socio-Economic Status*** indicator percentile (100=high): 84th

Licking County
NEWARK CITY S.D.
85 E MAIN ST ● NEWARK OH 43055 ● (614) 345-9891

Grade Span: PK-12 **Schools**: *Regular* 17 ● *Spec Ed* 0 ● *Alt* 0 **Students**: 7,879 **Total Teachers**: 458 **Student/Classroom Teacher Ratio**: 17.3	**Expenditures/Student**: $4,738 **Librarians**: 4.0 1,970 students/librarian **Guidance Counselors**: 12.0 657 students/counselor	**% Amer Indian**: 0.1 **% Asian**: 0.4 **% Black**: 3.9 **% Hispanic**: 0.3 **% White**: 95.3	National ***Socio-Economic Status*** indicator percentile (100=high): 52nd

Logan County
BELLEFONTAINE CITY S.D.
820 LUDLOW RD ● BELLEFONTAINE OH 43311 ● (937) 593-9060

Grade Span: PK-12 **Schools**: *Regular* 7 ● *Spec Ed* 0 ● *Alt* 0 **Students**: 3,013 **Total Teachers**: 168 **Student/Classroom Teacher Ratio**: 17.9	**Expenditures/Student**: $4,623 **Librarians**: 2.0 1,507 students/librarian **Guidance Counselors**: 7.0 430 students/counselor	**% Amer Indian**: 0.4 **% Asian**: 0.9 **% Black**: 6.6 **% Hispanic**: 0.6 **% White**: 91.5	National ***Socio-Economic Status*** indicator percentile (100=high): 59th

Lorain County
AMHERST EXEMPTED VILLAGE S.D.
185 FOREST ST ● AMHERST OH 44001 ● (440) 988-4406 ● http://leeca8.leeca.ohio.gov/amherst/amherst.html

Grade Span: PK-12 **Schools**: *Regular* 6 ● *Spec Ed* 0 ● *Alt* 0 **Students**: 3,591 **Total Teachers**: 181 **Student/Classroom Teacher Ratio**: 16.8	**Expenditures/Student**: $4,862 **Librarians**: 2.0 1,796 students/librarian **Guidance Counselors**: 6.0 599 students/counselor	**% Amer Indian**: 0.1 **% Asian**: 0.6 **% Black**: 0.6 **% Hispanic**: 3.7 **% White**: 95.0	National ***Socio-Economic Status*** indicator percentile (100=high): 92nd

Lorain County

AVON LAKE CITY S.D.

175 AVON BELDEN RD ● AVON LAKE OH 44012 ● (440) 933-6210

Grade Span: PK-12 **Schools**: *Regular* 8 ● *Spec Ed* 0 ● *Alt* 0 **Students**: 2,975 **Total Teachers**: 179 **Student/Classroom Teacher Ratio**: 18.0	**Expenditures/Student**: $5,784 **Librarians**: 3.0 992 students/librarian **Guidance Counselors**: 9.0 331 students/counselor	**% Amer Indian**: 0.0 **% Asian**: 0.6 **% Black**: 0.1 **% Hispanic**: 0.4 **% White**: 98.9	National ***Socio-Economic Status*** indicator percentile (100=high): 95th

Lorain County

ELYRIA CITY S.D.

42101 GRISWOLD RD ● ELYRIA OH 44035 ● (440) 284-8000

Grade Span: PK-12 **Schools**: *Regular* 19 ● *Spec Ed* 0 ● *Alt* 0 **Students**: 9,323 **Total Teachers**: 590 **Student/Classroom Teacher Ratio**: 17.2	**Expenditures/Student**: $5,664 **Librarians**: 10.0 932 students/librarian **Guidance Counselors**: 20.0 466 students/counselor	**% Amer Indian**: 0.1 **% Asian**: 0.8 **% Black**: 21.1 **% Hispanic**: 1.9 **% White**: 76.2	National ***Socio-Economic Status*** indicator percentile (100=high): 46th

Lorain County

[GRAFTON] **MIDVIEW LOCAL S.D.**

1097 ELM ST ● GRAFTON OH 44044 ● (440) 926-3737

Grade Span: PK-12 **Schools**: *Regular* 6 ● *Spec Ed* 0 ● *Alt* 0 **Students**: 3,254 **Total Teachers**: 171 **Student/Classroom Teacher Ratio**: 19.8	**Expenditures/Student**: $4,533 **Librarians**: 3.0 1,085 students/librarian **Guidance Counselors**: 6.0 542 students/counselor	**% Amer Indian**: 0.1 **% Asian**: 0.2 **% Black**: 3.0 **% Hispanic**: 0.4 **% White**: 96.3	National ***Socio-Economic Status*** indicator percentile (100=high): 77th

Lorain County

LORAIN CITY S.D.

2350 POLE AVE ● LORAIN OH 44052 ● (440) 233-2230

Grade Span: PK-12 **Schools**: *Regular* 17 ● *Spec Ed* 0 ● *Alt* 0 **Students**: 10,629 **Total Teachers**: 627 **Student/Classroom Teacher Ratio**: 18.8	**Expenditures/Student**: $6,622 **Librarians**: 5.0 2,126 students/librarian **Guidance Counselors**: 20.0 531 students/counselor	**% Amer Indian**: 0.6 **% Asian**: 0.2 **% Black**: 24.8 **% Hispanic**: 25.6 **% White**: 48.8	National ***Socio-Economic Status*** indicator percentile (100=high): 17th

Lorain County

NORTH RIDGEVILLE CITY S.D.

5490 MILLS CREEK LA ● NORTH RIDGEVILLE OH 44039 ● (440) 327-4444

Grade Span: PK-12 **Schools**: *Regular* 7 ● *Spec Ed* 0 ● *Alt* 0 **Students**: 3,565 **Total Teachers**: 194 **Student/Classroom Teacher Ratio**: 18.0	**Expenditures/Student**: $5,394 **Librarians**: 2.0 1,783 students/librarian **Guidance Counselors**: 6.0 594 students/counselor	**% Amer Indian**: 0.1 **% Asian**: 0.6 **% Black**: 0.6 **% Hispanic**: 0.8 **% White**: 98.0	National ***Socio-Economic Status*** indicator percentile (100=high): 86th

Lucas County

[HOLLAND] **SPRINGFIELD LOCAL S.D.**

6900 HALL ST ● HOLLAND OH 43528 ● (419) 867-5600

Grade Span: PK-12 **Schools**: *Regular* 6 ● *Spec Ed* 0 ● *Alt* 0 **Students**: 3,704 **Total Teachers**: 212 **Student/Classroom Teacher Ratio**: 17.9	**Expenditures/Student**: $5,391 **Librarians**: 1.0 3,704 students/librarian **Guidance Counselors**: 9.0 412 students/counselor	**% Amer Indian**: 0.2 **% Asian**: 1.6 **% Black**: 11.3 **% Hispanic**: 2.4 **% White**: 84.5	National ***Socio-Economic Status*** indicator percentile (100=high): 56th

Lucas County
MAUMEE CITY S.D.
2345 DETROIT AVE ● MAUMEE OH 43537 ● (419) 893-3200

Grade Span: PK-12 **Schools**: *Regular* 6 ● *Spec Ed* 0 ● *Alt* 0 **Students**: 3,123 **Total Teachers**: 195 **Student/Classroom Teacher Ratio**: 16.7	**Expenditures/Student**: $5,892 **Librarians**: 3.0 1,041 students/librarian **Guidance Counselors**: 8.0 390 students/counselor	**% Amer Indian**: 0.1 **% Asian**: 0.9 **% Black**: 2.7 **% Hispanic**: 1.0 **% White**: 95.4	National ***Socio-Economic Status*** indicator percentile (100=high): 91st

Lucas County
OREGON CITY S.D.
5721 SEAMAN RD ● OREGON OH 43616 ● (419) 693-0661

Grade Span: PK-12 **Schools**: *Regular* 7 ● *Spec Ed* 0 ● *Alt* 0 **Students**: 3,808 **Total Teachers**: 240 **Student/Classroom Teacher Ratio**: 17.8	**Expenditures/Student**: $6,052 **Librarians**: 2.0 1,904 students/librarian **Guidance Counselors**: 8.0 476 students/counselor	**% Amer Indian**: 0.0 **% Asian**: 0.7 **% Black**: 0.7 **% Hispanic**: 3.8 **% White**: 94.8	National ***Socio-Economic Status*** indicator percentile (100=high): 75th

Lucas County
SYLVANIA CITY S.D.
6850 MONROE ST, PO BOX 608 ● SYLVANIA OH 43560 ● (419) 885-7900 ● http://www.sylvania.k12.oh.us

Grade Span: PK-12 **Schools**: *Regular* 12 ● *Spec Ed* 1 ● *Alt* 0 **Students**: 7,734 **Total Teachers**: 462 **Student/Classroom Teacher Ratio**: 16.8	**Expenditures/Student**: $5,750 **Librarians**: 4.0 1,934 students/librarian **Guidance Counselors**: 14.0 552 students/counselor	**% Amer Indian**: 0.1 **% Asian**: 2.6 **% Black**: 2.2 **% Hispanic**: 1.5 **% White**: 93.7	National ***Socio-Economic Status*** indicator percentile (100=high): na

Lucas County
TOLEDO CITY S.D.
420 E MANHATTAN ● TOLEDO OH 43608 ● (419) 729-8200 ● http://tps.toledo.k12.oh.us

Grade Span: PK-12 **Schools**: *Regular* 61 ● *Spec Ed* 1 ● *Alt* 2 **Students**: 39,193 **Total Teachers**: 2,514 **Student/Classroom Teacher Ratio**: 17.1	**Expenditures/Student**: $6,138 **Librarians**: 28.0 1,400 students/librarian **Guidance Counselors**: 65.0 603 students/counselor	**% Amer Indian**: 0.1 **% Asian**: 0.8 **% Black**: 42.4 **% Hispanic**: 6.0 **% White**: 50.7	National ***Socio-Economic Status*** indicator percentile (100=high): 13th

Lucas County
[TOLEDO] **WASHINGTON LOCAL S.D.**
3505 W LINCOLNSHIRE BLVD ● TOLEDO OH 43606 ● (419) 531-9066

Grade Span: PK-12 **Schools**: *Regular* 13 ● *Spec Ed* 1 ● *Alt* 0 **Students**: 7,499 **Total Teachers**: 418 **Student/Classroom Teacher Ratio**: 19.2	**Expenditures/Student**: $5,649 **Librarians**: 3.0 2,500 students/librarian **Guidance Counselors**: 17.0 441 students/counselor	**% Amer Indian**: 0.3 **% Asian**: 0.6 **% Black**: 7.2 **% Hispanic**: 2.8 **% White**: 89.2	National ***Socio-Economic Status*** indicator percentile (100=high): 62nd

Lucas County
[WHITEHOUSE] **ANTHONY WAYNE LOCAL S.D.**
11012 SHEPLER PO BOX 2487 ● WHITEHOUSE OH 43571 ● (419) 877-5377

Grade Span: PK-12 **Schools**: *Regular* 5 ● *Spec Ed* 0 ● *Alt* 0 **Students**: 3,318 **Total Teachers**: 174 **Student/Classroom Teacher Ratio**: 20.7	**Expenditures/Student**: $5,037 **Librarians**: 3.0 1,106 students/librarian **Guidance Counselors**: 7.0 474 students/counselor	**% Amer Indian**: 0.1 **% Asian**: 0.4 **% Black**: 0.4 **% Hispanic**: 1.3 **% White**: 97.8	National ***Socio-Economic Status*** indicator percentile (100=high): 95th

Mahoning County

[BELOIT] **WEST BRANCH LOCAL S.D.**

14277 MAIN ST ● BELOIT OH 44609 ● (330) 938-9324

Grade Span: PK-12	**Expenditures/Student**: $4,635	**% Amer Indian**: 0.2	
Schools: *Regular* 7 ● *Spec Ed* 0 ● *Alt* 0	**Librarians**: 1.0	**% Asian**: 0.2	National ***Socio-Economic***
Students: 2,551	2,551 students/librarian	**% Black**: 0.4	***Status*** indicator percentile
Total Teachers: 132	**Guidance Counselors**: 6.0	**% Hispanic**: 0.2	(100=high): 66th
Student/Classroom Teacher Ratio: 21.9	425 students/counselor	**% White**: 99.0	

Mahoning County

CANFIELD LOCAL S.D.

100 WADSWORTH ST ● CANFIELD OH 44406 ● (330) 533-3303

Grade Span: PK-12	**Expenditures/Student**: $4,615	**% Amer Indian**: 0.0	
Schools: *Regular* 5 ● *Spec Ed* 0 ● *Alt* 0	**Librarians**: 3.0	**% Asian**: 1.7	National ***Socio-Economic***
Students: 2,784	928 students/librarian	**% Black**: 0.3	***Status*** indicator percentile
Total Teachers: 139	**Guidance Counselors**: 3.0	**% Hispanic**: 0.5	(100=high): 99th
Student/Classroom Teacher Ratio: 23.5	928 students/counselor	**% White**: 97.5	

Mahoning County

POLAND LOCAL S.D.

30 RIVERSIDE DR ● POLAND OH 44514 ● (330) 757-7000

Grade Span: PK-12	**Expenditures/Student**: $4,692	**% Amer Indian**: 0.4	
Schools: *Regular* 5 ● *Spec Ed* 1 ● *Alt* 0	**Librarians**: 4.0	**% Asian**: 0.6	National ***Socio-Economic***
Students: 2,531	633 students/librarian	**% Black**: 0.2	***Status*** indicator percentile
Total Teachers: 120	**Guidance Counselors**: 6.0	**% Hispanic**: 0.5	(100=high): 96th
Student/Classroom Teacher Ratio: 22.2	422 students/counselor	**% White**: 98.3	

Mahoning County

[YOUNGSTOWN] **AUSTINTOWN LOCAL S.D.**

225 IDAHO RD ● YOUNGSTOWN OH 44515 ● (330) 797-3911 ● http://www.cisnet.com/fitch

Grade Span: PK-12	**Expenditures/Student**: $4,984	**% Amer Indian**: 0.1	
Schools: *Regular* 8 ● *Spec Ed* 0 ● *Alt* 0	**Librarians**: 3.0	**% Asian**: 0.6	National ***Socio-Economic***
Students: 5,282	1,761 students/librarian	**% Black**: 4.3	***Status*** indicator percentile
Total Teachers: 261	**Guidance Counselors**: 11.0	**% Hispanic**: 1.1	(100=high): 63rd
Student/Classroom Teacher Ratio: 22.5	480 students/counselor	**% White**: 93.8	

Mahoning County

[YOUNGSTOWN] **BOARDMAN LOCAL S.D.**

7410 MARKET ST ● YOUNGSTOWN OH 44512 ● (330) 726-3404

Grade Span: PK-12	**Expenditures/Student**: $5,247	**% Amer Indian**: 0.0	
Schools: *Regular* 7 ● *Spec Ed* 0 ● *Alt* 0	**Librarians**: 3.0	**% Asian**: 1.1	National ***Socio-Economic***
Students: 5,286	1,762 students/librarian	**% Black**: 2.1	***Status*** indicator percentile
Total Teachers: 283	**Guidance Counselors**: 11.0	**% Hispanic**: 0.6	(100=high): 85th
Student/Classroom Teacher Ratio: 20.1	481 students/counselor	**% White**: 96.2	

Mahoning County

YOUNGSTOWN CITY S.D.

20 W WOOD ST, PO BOX 550 ● YOUNGSTOWN OH 44501 ● (330) 744-6900

Grade Span: PK-12	**Expenditures/Student**: $6,977	**% Amer Indian**: 0.0	
Schools: *Regular* 29 ● *Spec Ed* 1 ● *Alt* 3	**Librarians**: 9.0	**% Asian**: 0.2	National ***Socio-Economic***
Students: 12,965	1,441 students/librarian	**% Black**: 63.8	***Status*** indicator percentile
Total Teachers: 854	**Guidance Counselors**: 26.0	**% Hispanic**: 5.7	(100=high): 6th
Student/Classroom Teacher Ratio: 15.5	499 students/counselor	**% White**: 30.3	

Marion County

MARION CITY S.D.

910 E CHURCH ST ● MARION OH 43302 ● (614) 387-3300 ● http://www.treca.ohio.gov/schools/marcit/mcs.html

Grade Span: PK-12 **Schools**: *Regular* 15 ● *Spec Ed* 0 ● *Alt* 0 **Students**: 6,224 **Total Teachers**: 350 **Student/Classroom Teacher Ratio**: 18.6	**Expenditures/Student**: $4,486 **Librarians**: 2.0 3,112 students/librarian **Guidance Counselors**: 10.0 622 students/counselor	**% Amer Indian**: 0.0 **% Asian**: 0.5 **% Black**: 7.9 **% Hispanic**: 1.2 **% White**: 90.4	National ***Socio-Economic Status*** indicator percentile (100=high): na

Medina County

BRUNSWICK CITY S.D.

3643 CENTER RD ● BRUNSWICK OH 44212 ● (330) 225-7731

Grade Span: PK-12 **Schools**: *Regular* 10 ● *Spec Ed* 0 ● *Alt* 0 **Students**: 6,802 **Total Teachers**: 372 **Student/Classroom Teacher Ratio**: 19.2	**Expenditures/Student**: $4,893 **Librarians**: 3.0 2,267 students/librarian **Guidance Counselors**: 9.0 756 students/counselor	**% Amer Indian**: 0.2 **% Asian**: 0.7 **% Black**: 0.5 **% Hispanic**: 0.6 **% White**: 98.0	National ***Socio-Economic Status*** indicator percentile (100=high): 89th

Medina County

[LODI] **CLOVERLEAF LOCAL S.D.**

8525 FRIENDSVILLE RD ● LODI OH 44254 ● (330) 948-2500

Grade Span: PK-12 **Schools**: *Regular* 8 ● *Spec Ed* 0 ● *Alt* 0 **Students**: 3,856 **Total Teachers**: 181 **Student/Classroom Teacher Ratio**: 20.8	**Expenditures/Student**: $4,497 **Librarians**: 3.0 1,285 students/librarian **Guidance Counselors**: 6.0 643 students/counselor	**% Amer Indian**: 0.0 **% Asian**: 0.0 **% Black**: 0.0 **% Hispanic**: 0.1 **% White**: 99.8	National ***Socio-Economic Status*** indicator percentile (100=high): 85th

Medina County

MEDINA CITY S.D.

120 W WASHINGTON ● MEDINA OH 44256 ● (330) 725-9201

Grade Span: PK-12 **Schools**: *Regular* 8 ● *Spec Ed* 0 ● *Alt* 0 **Students**: 5,938 **Total Teachers**: 337 **Student/Classroom Teacher Ratio**: 20.2	**Expenditures/Student**: $6,056 **Librarians**: 4.0 1,485 students/librarian **Guidance Counselors**: 11.0 540 students/counselor	**% Amer Indian**: 0.1 **% Asian**: 0.8 **% Black**: 1.9 **% Hispanic**: 0.4 **% White**: 96.9	National ***Socio-Economic Status*** indicator percentile (100=high): 92nd

Medina County

WADSWORTH CITY S.D.

360 COLLEGE ST ● WADSWORTH OH 44281 ● (330) 336-3571

Grade Span: PK-12 **Schools**: *Regular* 7 ● *Spec Ed* 0 ● *Alt* 0 **Students**: 4,047 **Total Teachers**: 236 **Student/Classroom Teacher Ratio**: 21.2	**Expenditures/Student**: $4,906 **Librarians**: 2.0 2,024 students/librarian **Guidance Counselors**: 6.0 675 students/counselor	**% Amer Indian**: 0.1 **% Asian**: 0.7 **% Black**: 0.5 **% Hispanic**: 0.3 **% White**: 98.3	National ***Socio-Economic Status*** indicator percentile (100=high): 85th

Mercer County

CELINA CITY S.D.

585 E LIVINGSTON ● CELINA OH 45822 ● (419) 586-8300

Grade Span: PK-12 **Schools**: *Regular* 7 ● *Spec Ed* 0 ● *Alt* 0 **Students**: 3,951 **Total Teachers**: 194 **Student/Classroom Teacher Ratio**: 20.9	**Expenditures/Student**: $4,716 **Librarians**: 2.0 1,976 students/librarian **Guidance Counselors**: 7.0 564 students/counselor	**% Amer Indian**: 0.3 **% Asian**: 0.4 **% Black**: 0.2 **% Hispanic**: 1.1 **% White**: 98.0	National ***Socio-Economic Status*** indicator percentile (100=high): na

Miami County
PIQUA CITY S.D.
719 EAST ASH ST ● PIQUA OH 45356 ● (937) 773-4321

Grade Span: PK-12 **Schools**: *Regular* 9 ● *Spec Ed* 0 ● *Alt* 0 **Students**: 4,084 **Total Teachers**: 203 **Student/Classroom Teacher Ratio**: 22.1	**Expenditures/Student**: $4,263 **Librarians**: 2.0 2,042 students/librarian **Guidance Counselors**: 7.0 583 students/counselor	**% Amer Indian**: 0.4 **% Asian**: 0.5 **% Black**: 5.0 **% Hispanic**: 0.4 **% White**: 93.8	National ***Socio-Economic Status*** indicator percentile (100=high): 54th

Miami County
TIPP CITY EXEMPTED VILLAGE S.D.
90 S TIPPECANOE DR ● TIPP CITY OH 45371 ● (937) 667-8444

Grade Span: PK-12 **Schools**: *Regular* 6 ● *Spec Ed* 0 ● *Alt* 0 **Students**: 2,552 **Total Teachers**: 135 **Student/Classroom Teacher Ratio**: 18.1	**Expenditures/Student**: $4,126 **Librarians**: 2.0 1,276 students/librarian **Guidance Counselors**: 5.0 510 students/counselor	**% Amer Indian**: 0.2 **% Asian**: 0.7 **% Black**: 0.2 **% Hispanic**: 1.1 **% White**: 97.9	National ***Socio-Economic Status*** indicator percentile (100=high): 93rd

Miami County
TROY CITY S.D.
500 N MARKET ST ● TROY OH 45373 ● (937) 332-6700 ● http://www.TDN-Net.com/troyschools

Grade Span: PK-12 **Schools**: *Regular* 9 ● *Spec Ed* 0 ● *Alt* 0 **Students**: 4,762 **Total Teachers**: 246 **Student/Classroom Teacher Ratio**: 22.7	**Expenditures/Student**: $5,157 **Librarians**: 3.0 1,587 students/librarian **Guidance Counselors**: 6.0 794 students/counselor	**% Amer Indian**: 0.3 **% Asian**: 2.4 **% Black**: 4.5 **% Hispanic**: 0.6 **% White**: 92.2	National ***Socio-Economic Status*** indicator percentile (100=high): 75th

Monroe County
[WOODSFIELD] SWITZERLAND OF OHIO LOCAL S.D.
304 MILL ST ● WOODSFIELD OH 43793 ● (614) 472-5801

Grade Span: PK-12 **Schools**: *Regular* 9 ● *Spec Ed* 0 ● *Alt* 1 **Students**: 3,137 **Total Teachers**: 189 **Student/Classroom Teacher Ratio**: 19.1	**Expenditures/Student**: $5,518 **Librarians**: 3.0 1,046 students/librarian **Guidance Counselors**: 4.0 784 students/counselor	**% Amer Indian**: 0.0 **% Asian**: 0.0 **% Black**: 0.1 **% Hispanic**: 0.0 **% White**: 99.8	National ***Socio-Economic Status*** indicator percentile (100=high): 34th

Montgomery County
CENTERVILLE CITY S.D.
111 VIRGINIA AVE ● CENTERVILLE OH 45458 ● (937) 433-8841 ● http://www.centerville.k12.oh.us

Grade Span: PK-12 **Schools**: *Regular* 12 ● *Spec Ed* 0 ● *Alt* 0 **Students**: 7,355 **Total Teachers**: 404 **Student/Classroom Teacher Ratio**: 17.8	**Expenditures/Student**: $5,735 **Librarians**: 13.0 566 students/librarian **Guidance Counselors**: 15.0 490 students/counselor	**% Amer Indian**: 0.1 **% Asian**: 4.9 **% Black**: 2.1 **% Hispanic**: 0.7 **% White**: 92.2	National ***Socio-Economic Status*** indicator percentile (100=high): 97th

Montgomery County
DAYTON CITY S.D.
348 W FIRST ST ● DAYTON OH 45402 ● (937) 461-3000

Grade Span: PK-12 **Schools**: *Regular* 48 ● *Spec Ed* 1 ● *Alt* 1 **Students**: 27,942 **Total Teachers**: 1,750 **Student/Classroom Teacher Ratio**: 17.1	**Expenditures/Student**: $6,669 **Librarians**: 14.0 1,996 students/librarian **Guidance Counselors**: 28.0 998 students/counselor	**% Amer Indian**: 0.1 **% Asian**: 0.5 **% Black**: 66.4 **% Hispanic**: 0.4 **% White**: 32.7	National ***Socio-Economic Status*** indicator percentile (100=high): na

Montgomery County
[DAYTON] **MAD RIVER LOCAL S.D.**
801 HARSHMAN RD ● DAYTON OH 45431 ● (937) 259-6606

Grade Span: KG-12 **Schools**: *Regular* 8 ● *Spec Ed* 0 ● *Alt* 0 **Students**: 3,877 **Total Teachers**: 227 **Student/Classroom Teacher Ratio**: 18.2	**Expenditures/Student**: $5,527 **Librarians**: 2.0 1,939 students/librarian **Guidance Counselors**: 9.0 431 students/counselor	**% Amer Indian**: 0.3 **% Asian**: 1.7 **% Black**: 7.1 **% Hispanic**: 1.9 **% White**: 89.0	National ***Socio-Economic Status*** indicator percentile (100=high): 58th

Montgomery County
[ENGLEWOOD] **NORTHMONT CITY S.D.**
4001 OLD SALEM RD ● ENGLEWOOD OH 45322 ● (937) 836-2601

Grade Span: KG-12 **Schools**: *Regular* 9 ● *Spec Ed* 0 ● *Alt* 0 **Students**: 5,922 **Total Teachers**: 305 **Student/Classroom Teacher Ratio**: 20.9	**Expenditures/Student**: $4,776 **Librarians**: 2.0 2,961 students/librarian **Guidance Counselors**: 11.0 538 students/counselor	**% Amer Indian**: 0.0 **% Asian**: 1.1 **% Black**: 3.1 **% Hispanic**: 0.3 **% White**: 95.5	National ***Socio-Economic Status*** indicator percentile (100=high): 89th

Montgomery County
HUBER HEIGHTS CITY S.D.
5954 LONGFORD RD ● HUBER HEIGHTS OH 45424 ● (937) 237-6300

Grade Span: PK-12 **Schools**: *Regular* 11 ● *Spec Ed* 0 ● *Alt* 0 **Students**: 7,612 **Total Teachers**: 416 **Student/Classroom Teacher Ratio**: 19.0	**Expenditures/Student**: $4,623 **Librarians**: 3.0 2,537 students/librarian **Guidance Counselors**: 14.0 544 students/counselor	**% Amer Indian**: 0.1 **% Asian**: 2.3 **% Black**: 12.5 **% Hispanic**: 1.0 **% White**: 84.1	National ***Socio-Economic Status*** indicator percentile (100=high): 75th

Montgomery County
KETTERING CITY S.D.
3750 FAR HILLS AVE ● KETTERING OH 45429 ● (937) 296-7600 ● http://www.kettering.k12.oh.us

Grade Span: KG-12 **Schools**: *Regular* 13 ● *Spec Ed* 0 ● *Alt* 0 **Students**: 7,991 **Total Teachers**: 411 **Student/Classroom Teacher Ratio**: 19.5	**Expenditures/Student**: $5,802 **Librarians**: 4.0 1,998 students/librarian **Guidance Counselors**: 24.0 333 students/counselor	**% Amer Indian**: 0.1 **% Asian**: 1.5 **% Black**: 1.3 **% Hispanic**: 0.6 **% White**: 96.6	National ***Socio-Economic Status*** indicator percentile (100=high): 81st

Montgomery County
MIAMISBURG CITY S.D.
540 E PARK AVE ● MIAMISBURG OH 45342 ● (937) 866-3381 ● http://www.mvcc.net/Miamisburg/mbschools.htm

Grade Span: PK-12 **Schools**: *Regular* 9 ● *Spec Ed* 0 ● *Alt* 0 **Students**: 4,552 **Total Teachers**: 243 **Student/Classroom Teacher Ratio**: 18.8	**Expenditures/Student**: $5,172 **Librarians**: 1.0 4,552 students/librarian **Guidance Counselors**: 9.0 506 students/counselor	**% Amer Indian**: 0.1 **% Asian**: 1.7 **% Black**: 2.5 **% Hispanic**: 0.6 **% White**: 95.1	National ***Socio-Economic Status*** indicator percentile (100=high): 78th

Montgomery County
TROTWOOD-MADISON CITY S.D.
444 S BROADWAY ● TROTWOOD OH 45426 ● (937) 854-3050

Grade Span: KG-12 **Schools**: *Regular* 8 ● *Spec Ed* 0 ● *Alt* 0 **Students**: 4,461 **Total Teachers**: 223 **Student/Classroom Teacher Ratio**: 20.5	**Expenditures/Student**: $4,973 **Librarians**: 2.0 2,231 students/librarian **Guidance Counselors**: 5.0 892 students/counselor	**% Amer Indian**: 0.1 **% Asian**: 0.3 **% Black**: 70.4 **% Hispanic**: 0.2 **% White**: 29.1	National ***Socio-Economic Status*** indicator percentile (100=high): 24th

Montgomery County
VANDALIA-BUTLER CITY S.D.
306 SOUTH DIXIE DR ● VANDALIA OH 45377 ● (937) 898-4618

Grade Span: PK-12 **Schools**: *Regular* 6 ● *Spec Ed* 0 ● *Alt* 0 **Students**: 3,570 **Total Teachers**: 222 **Student/Classroom Teacher Ratio**: 17.1	**Expenditures/Student**: $5,472 **Librarians**: 1.0 3,570 students/librarian **Guidance Counselors**: 7.0 510 students/counselor	**% Amer Indian**: 0.1 **% Asian**: 0.9 **% Black**: 1.5 **% Hispanic**: 0.6 **% White**: 96.8	National ***Socio-Economic Status*** indicator percentile (100=high): 91st

Montgomery County
WEST CARROLLTON CITY S.D.
430 E PEASE AVE ● WEST CARROLLTON OH 45449 ● (937) 859-5121

Grade Span: PK-12 **Schools**: *Regular* 7 ● *Spec Ed* 0 ● *Alt* 0 **Students**: 4,246 **Total Teachers**: 230 **Student/Classroom Teacher Ratio**: 19.9	**Expenditures/Student**: $4,720 **Librarians**: 2.0 2,123 students/librarian **Guidance Counselors**: 6.0 708 students/counselor	**% Amer Indian**: 0.1 **% Asian**: 2.1 **% Black**: 3.7 **% Hispanic**: 0.6 **% White**: 93.5	National ***Socio-Economic Status*** indicator percentile (100=high): na

Morgan County
[MCCONNELSVILLE] **MORGAN LOCAL S.D.**
PO BOX 509 ● MCCONNELSVILLE OH 43756 ● (614) 962-2782

Grade Span: PK-12 **Schools**: *Regular* 8 ● *Spec Ed* 0 ● *Alt* 0 **Students**: 2,702 **Total Teachers**: 162 **Student/Classroom Teacher Ratio**: 18.3	**Expenditures/Student**: $4,862 **Librarians**: 3.0 901 students/librarian **Guidance Counselors**: 2.0 1,351 students/counselor	**% Amer Indian**: 0.0 **% Asian**: 0.2 **% Black**: 5.4 **% Hispanic**: 0.2 **% White**: 94.2	National ***Socio-Economic Status*** indicator percentile (100=high): 35th

Muskingum County
[DRESDEN] **TRI-VALLEY LOCAL S.D.**
36 E MUSKINGUM AVE, BOX 125 ● DRESDEN OH 43821 ● (614) 754-1572

Grade Span: PK-12 **Schools**: *Regular* 7 ● *Spec Ed* 0 ● *Alt* 0 **Students**: 2,938 **Total Teachers**: 150 **Student/Classroom Teacher Ratio**: 24.3	**Expenditures/Student**: $4,302 **Librarians**: 2.0 1,469 students/librarian **Guidance Counselors**: 4.0 735 students/counselor	**% Amer Indian**: 0.1 **% Asian**: 0.1 **% Black**: 0.9 **% Hispanic**: 0.1 **% White**: 98.8	National ***Socio-Economic Status*** indicator percentile (100=high): na

Muskingum County
[DUNCAN FALLS] **FRANKLIN LOCAL S.D.**
360 CEDAR ST, PO BOX 428 ● DUNCAN FALLS OH 43734 ● (614) 674-5203

Grade Span: PK-12 **Schools**: *Regular* 6 ● *Spec Ed* 0 ● *Alt* 0 **Students**: 2,533 **Total Teachers**: 131 **Student/Classroom Teacher Ratio**: 20.9	**Expenditures/Student**: $4,016 **Librarians**: 1.0 2,533 students/librarian **Guidance Counselors**: 3.0 844 students/counselor	**% Amer Indian**: 0.0 **% Asian**: 0.1 **% Black**: 0.4 **% Hispanic**: 0.2 **% White**: 99.2	National ***Socio-Economic Status*** indicator percentile (100=high): 52nd

Muskingum County
ZANESVILLE CITY S.D.
160 N 4TH ST ● ZANESVILLE OH 43701 ● (614) 454-9751 ● http://www.zanesville.k12.oh.us

Grade Span: PK-12 **Schools**: *Regular* 11 ● *Spec Ed* 0 ● *Alt* 0 **Students**: 4,676 **Total Teachers**: 321 **Student/Classroom Teacher Ratio**: 15.4	**Expenditures/Student**: $5,337 **Librarians**: 3.0 1,559 students/librarian **Guidance Counselors**: 9.0 520 students/counselor	**% Amer Indian**: 0.0 **% Asian**: 0.2 **% Black**: 15.4 **% Hispanic**: 0.1 **% White**: 84.3	National ***Socio-Economic Status*** indicator percentile (100=high): na

Pickaway County

[ASHVILLE] **TEAYS VALLEY LOCAL S.D.**

385 CIRCLEVILLE AVE ● ASHVILLE OH 43103 ● (614) 983-4111

Grade Span: PK-12 **Schools**: *Regular* 5 ● *Spec Ed* 0 ● *Alt* 0 **Students**: 2,778 **Total Teachers**: 152 **Student/Classroom Teacher Ratio**: 18.5	**Expenditures/Student**: $4,275 **Librarians**: 2.0 1,389 students/librarian **Guidance Counselors**: 3.0 926 students/counselor	**% Amer Indian**: 0.0 **% Asian**: 0.4 **% Black**: 0.0 **% Hispanic**: 0.0 **% White**: 99.5	National ***Socio-Economic Status*** indicator percentile (100=high): 61st

Pickaway County

CIRCLEVILLE CITY S.D.

388 CLARK DR ● CIRCLEVILLE OH 43113 ● (614) 474-4340

Grade Span: PK-12 **Schools**: *Regular* 6 ● *Spec Ed* 0 ● *Alt* 0 **Students**: 2,524 **Total Teachers**: 140 **Student/Classroom Teacher Ratio**: 20.5	**Expenditures/Student**: $4,675 **Librarians**: 4.0 631 students/librarian **Guidance Counselors**: 5.0 505 students/counselor	**% Amer Indian**: 0.0 **% Asian**: 0.6 **% Black**: 1.3 **% Hispanic**: 0.2 **% White**: 97.8	National ***Socio-Economic Status*** indicator percentile (100=high): 55th

Portage County

KENT CITY S.D.

321 N DEPEYSTER ST ● KENT OH 44240 ● (330) 673-6515

Grade Span: PK-12 **Schools**: *Regular* 7 ● *Spec Ed* 0 ● *Alt* 0 **Students**: 4,173 **Total Teachers**: 292 **Student/Classroom Teacher Ratio**: 14.7	**Expenditures/Student**: $6,431 **Librarians**: 4.0 1,043 students/librarian **Guidance Counselors**: 8.0 522 students/counselor	**% Amer Indian**: 0.0 **% Asian**: 1.9 **% Black**: 9.9 **% Hispanic**: 0.4 **% White**: 87.8	National ***Socio-Economic Status*** indicator percentile (100=high): 61st

Portage County

[MANTUA] **CRESTWOOD LOCAL S.D.**

4565 W PROSPECT ● MANTUA OH 44255 ● (330) 274-8511

Grade Span: PK-12 **Schools**: *Regular* 6 ● *Spec Ed* 1 ● *Alt* 0 **Students**: 2,728 **Total Teachers**: 144 **Student/Classroom Teacher Ratio**: 21.9	**Expenditures/Student**: $4,519 **Librarians**: 3.0 909 students/librarian **Guidance Counselors**: 4.0 682 students/counselor	**% Amer Indian**: 0.0 **% Asian**: 0.3 **% Black**: 0.2 **% Hispanic**: 0.3 **% White**: 99.2	National ***Socio-Economic Status*** indicator percentile (100=high): 81st

Portage County

RAVENNA CITY S.D.

507 E MAIN ST ● RAVENNA OH 44266 ● (330) 296-9679

Grade Span: PK-12 **Schools**: *Regular* 7 ● *Spec Ed* 1 ● *Alt* 0 **Students**: 3,457 **Total Teachers**: 206 **Student/Classroom Teacher Ratio**: 19.1	**Expenditures/Student**: $5,136 **Librarians**: 2.0 1,729 students/librarian **Guidance Counselors**: 7.0 494 students/counselor	**% Amer Indian**: 0.1 **% Asian**: 0.2 **% Black**: 6.5 **% Hispanic**: 0.2 **% White**: 93.0	National ***Socio-Economic Status*** indicator percentile (100=high): 46th

Richland County

LEXINGTON LOCAL S.D.

103 CLEVER LA ● LEXINGTON OH 44904 ● (419) 884-2132

Grade Span: KG-12 **Schools**: *Regular* 5 ● *Spec Ed* 0 ● *Alt* 0 **Students**: 2,964 **Total Teachers**: 155 **Student/Classroom Teacher Ratio**: 19.3	**Expenditures/Student**: $4,263 **Librarians**: 3.0 988 students/librarian **Guidance Counselors**: 4.0 741 students/counselor	**% Amer Indian**: 0.0 **% Asian**: 1.7 **% Black**: 1.6 **% Hispanic**: 0.3 **% White**: 96.5	National ***Socio-Economic Status*** indicator percentile (100=high): 90th

Richland County

[MANSFIELD] **MADISON LOCAL S.D.**

1379 GRACE ST ● MANSFIELD OH 44905 ● (419) 589-2600

Grade Span: PK-12 **Schools**: *Regular* 7 ● *Spec Ed* 0 ● *Alt* 0 **Students**: 4,348 **Total Teachers**: 259 **Student/Classroom Teacher Ratio**: 22.8	**Expenditures/Student**: $5,359 **Librarians**: 2.0 2,174 students/librarian **Guidance Counselors**: 7.0 621 students/counselor	**% Amer Indian**: 0.0 **% Asian**: 0.9 **% Black**: 4.9 **% Hispanic**: 0.5 **% White**: 93.7	National ***Socio-Economic Status*** indicator percentile (100=high): na

Richland County

MANSFIELD CITY S.D.

PO BOX 1448 ● MANSFIELD OH 44901 ● (419) 525-6400

Grade Span: PK-12 **Schools**: *Regular* 15 ● *Spec Ed* 0 ● *Alt* 0 **Students**: 6,376 **Total Teachers**: 450 **Student/Classroom Teacher Ratio**: 16.3	**Expenditures/Student**: $6,184 **Librarians**: 4.0 1,594 students/librarian **Guidance Counselors**: 13.0 490 students/counselor	**% Amer Indian**: 0.0 **% Asian**: 0.3 **% Black**: 33.6 **% Hispanic**: 0.5 **% White**: 65.6	National ***Socio-Economic Status*** indicator percentile (100=high): na

Ross County

CHILLICOTHE CITY S.D.

235 CHERRY ST ● CHILLICOTHE OH 45601 ● (614) 775-4250 ● http://gsn.scoca.ohio.gov/Chillicothe/default.htm

Grade Span: KG-12 **Schools**: *Regular* 10 ● *Spec Ed* 0 ● *Alt* 0 **Students**: 4,040 **Total Teachers**: 199 **Student/Classroom Teacher Ratio**: 21.9	**Expenditures/Student**: $5,397 **Librarians**: 3.0 1,347 students/librarian **Guidance Counselors**: 9.0 449 students/counselor	**% Amer Indian**: 0.2 **% Asian**: 0.9 **% Black**: 8.1 **% Hispanic**: 0.5 **% White**: 90.4	National ***Socio-Economic Status*** indicator percentile (100=high): 47th

Sandusky County

FREMONT CITY S.D.

1220 CEDAR ST, SUITE A ● FREMONT OH 43420 ● (419) 332-6454

Grade Span: PK-12 **Schools**: *Regular* 10 ● *Spec Ed* 0 ● *Alt* 0 **Students**: 5,361 **Total Teachers**: 286 **Student/Classroom Teacher Ratio**: 20.5	**Expenditures/Student**: $4,597 **Librarians**: 6.0 894 students/librarian **Guidance Counselors**: 14.0 383 students/counselor	**% Amer Indian**: 0.1 **% Asian**: 0.4 **% Black**: 9.6 **% Hispanic**: 11.4 **% White**: 78.4	National ***Socio-Economic Status*** indicator percentile (100=high): 51st

Scioto County

PORTSMOUTH CITY S.D.

1149 GALLIA ST ● PORTSMOUTH OH 45662 ● (614) 354-5663 ● http://portsweb.scoca.ohio.gov

Grade Span: PK-12 **Schools**: *Regular* 10 ● *Spec Ed* 0 ● *Alt* 0 **Students**: 3,406 **Total Teachers**: 206 **Student/Classroom Teacher Ratio**: 18.1	**Expenditures/Student**: $5,373 **Librarians**: 2.0 1,703 students/librarian **Guidance Counselors**: 6.0 568 students/counselor	**% Amer Indian**: 0.1 **% Asian**: 0.4 **% Black**: 8.2 **% Hispanic**: 0.3 **% White**: 91.0	National ***Socio-Economic Status*** indicator percentile (100=high): 13th

Seneca County

FOSTORIA CITY S.D.

ADM BLDG 114 W HIGH ST ● FOSTORIA OH 44830 ● (419) 435-8163

Grade Span: PK-12 **Schools**: *Regular* 6 ● *Spec Ed* 0 ● *Alt* 0 **Students**: 2,794 **Total Teachers**: 148 **Student/Classroom Teacher Ratio**: 21.0	**Expenditures/Student**: $5,171 **Librarians**: 2.0 1,397 students/librarian **Guidance Counselors**: 6.0 466 students/counselor	**% Amer Indian**: 0.0 **% Asian**: 0.3 **% Black**: 8.5 **% Hispanic**: 9.2 **% White**: 82.0	National ***Socio-Economic Status*** indicator percentile (100=high): 37th

Seneca County
TIFFIN CITY S.D.
244 S MONROE ST ● TIFFIN OH 44883 ● (419) 447-2515

Grade Span: PK-12 **Schools**: *Regular* 9 ● *Spec Ed* 0 ● *Alt* 0 **Students**: 3,832 **Total Teachers**: 194 **Student/Classroom Teacher Ratio**: 20.3	**Expenditures/Student**: $4,561 **Librarians**: 2.0 1,916 students/librarian **Guidance Counselors**: 9.0 426 students/counselor	**% Amer Indian**: 0.3 **% Asian**: 0.5 **% Black**: 1.1 **% Hispanic**: 1.2 **% White**: 96.9	National ***Socio-Economic Status*** indicator percentile (100=high): 68th

Shelby County
SIDNEY CITY S.D.
232 N MIAMI AVE ● SIDNEY OH 45365 ● (937) 497-2200

Grade Span: KG-12 **Schools**: *Regular* 10 ● *Spec Ed* 0 ● *Alt* 0 **Students**: 4,030 **Total Teachers**: 204 **Student/Classroom Teacher Ratio**: 19.7	**Expenditures/Student**: $4,402 **Librarians**: 2.0 2,015 students/librarian **Guidance Counselors**: 9.0 448 students/counselor	**% Amer Indian**: 0.1 **% Asian**: 2.4 **% Black**: 3.8 **% Hispanic**: 0.4 **% White**: 93.3	National ***Socio-Economic Status*** indicator percentile (100=high): 64th

Stark County
ALLIANCE CITY S.D.
200 GLAMORGAN ST ● ALLIANCE OH 44601 ● (330) 821-2100

Grade Span: PK-12 **Schools**: *Regular* 9 ● *Spec Ed* 0 ● *Alt* 0 **Students**: 3,915 **Total Teachers**: 283 **Student/Classroom Teacher Ratio**: 16.9	**Expenditures/Student**: $5,400 **Librarians**: 6.0 653 students/librarian **Guidance Counselors**: 16.0 245 students/counselor	**% Amer Indian**: 0.0 **% Asian**: 0.2 **% Black**: 18.2 **% Hispanic**: 1.2 **% White**: 80.4	National ***Socio-Economic Status*** indicator percentile (100=high): na

Stark County
[ALLIANCE] MARLINGTON LOCAL S.D.
10320 MOULIN AVE NE ● ALLIANCE OH 44601 ● (330) 823-7458 ● http://dukes.stark.k12.oh.us

Grade Span: PK-12 **Schools**: *Regular* 5 ● *Spec Ed* 0 ● *Alt* 0 **Students**: 2,799 **Total Teachers**: 153 **Student/Classroom Teacher Ratio**: 19.0	**Expenditures/Student**: $4,844 **Librarians**: 1.0 2,799 students/librarian **Guidance Counselors**: 7.0 400 students/counselor	**% Amer Indian**: 0.0 **% Asian**: 0.8 **% Black**: 3.5 **% Hispanic**: 0.6 **% White**: 95.1	National ***Socio-Economic Status*** indicator percentile (100=high): 63rd

Stark County
CANTON CITY S.D.
617 MCKINLEY AVE SW ● CANTON OH 44707 ● (330) 438-2500 ● http://www.canton-ohio.com/schools/schools_ns.html

Grade Span: PK-12 **Schools**: *Regular* 26 ● *Spec Ed* 2 ● *Alt* 0 **Students**: 13,223 **Total Teachers**: 831 **Student/Classroom Teacher Ratio**: 17.3	**Expenditures/Student**: $5,747 **Librarians**: 4.0 3,306 students/librarian **Guidance Counselors**: 22.0 601 students/counselor	**% Amer Indian**: 0.3 **% Asian**: 0.3 **% Black**: 33.3 **% Hispanic**: 0.6 **% White**: 65.5	National ***Socio-Economic Status*** indicator percentile (100=high): 17th

Stark County
CANTON LOCAL S.D.
4526 RIDGE AVE SE ● CANTON OH 44707 ● (330) 484-8010 ● http://maccat.stark.k12.oh.us

Grade Span: PK-12 **Schools**: *Regular* 5 ● *Spec Ed* 0 ● *Alt* 0 **Students**: 2,568 **Total Teachers**: 142 **Student/Classroom Teacher Ratio**: 19.9	**Expenditures/Student**: $6,228 **Librarians**: 1.0 2,568 students/librarian **Guidance Counselors**: 6.0 428 students/counselor	**% Amer Indian**: 0.0 **% Asian**: 0.2 **% Black**: 5.1 **% Hispanic**: 0.0 **% White**: 94.7	National ***Socio-Economic Status*** indicator percentile (100=high): na

Stark County
[CANTON] **PLAIN LOCAL S.D.**
901 44TH ST NW ● CANTON OH 44709 ● (330) 492-3500 ● http://www.eagle.stark.k12.oh.us

Grade Span: PK-12	**Expenditures/Student**: $4,809	**% Amer Indian**: 0.0	National ***Socio-Economic Status*** indicator percentile (100=high): na
Schools: *Regular* 10 ● *Spec Ed* 0 ● *Alt* 0	**Librarians**: 8.0	**% Asian**: 0.8	
Students: 6,411	801 students/librarian	**% Black**: 9.7	
Total Teachers: 371	**Guidance Counselors**: 23.0	**% Hispanic**: 0.2	
Student/Classroom Teacher Ratio: 18.9	279 students/counselor	**% White**: 89.3	

Stark County
[HARTVILLE] **LAKE LOCAL S.D.**
12077 LISA AVE NW ● HARTVILLE OH 44632 ● (330) 877-9383

Grade Span: PK-12	**Expenditures/Student**: $4,424	**% Amer Indian**: 0.0	National ***Socio-Economic Status*** indicator percentile (100=high): 92nd
Schools: *Regular* 5 ● *Spec Ed* 0 ● *Alt* 0	**Librarians**: 2.0	**% Asian**: 0.5	
Students: 3,193	1,597 students/librarian	**% Black**: 0.3	
Total Teachers: 173	**Guidance Counselors**: 7.0	**% Hispanic**: 0.4	
Student/Classroom Teacher Ratio: 20.1	456 students/counselor	**% White**: 98.9	

Stark County
LOUISVILLE CITY S.D.
418 E MAIN ● LOUISVILLE OH 44641 ● (330) 875-1666

Grade Span: PK-12	**Expenditures/Student**: $4,813	**% Amer Indian**: 0.0	National ***Socio-Economic Status*** indicator percentile (100=high): na
Schools: *Regular* 6 ● *Spec Ed* 0 ● *Alt* 0	**Librarians**: 2.0	**% Asian**: 0.3	
Students: 3,046	1,523 students/librarian	**% Black**: 0.0	
Total Teachers: 151	**Guidance Counselors**: 6.0	**% Hispanic**: 0.1	
Student/Classroom Teacher Ratio: 21.4	508 students/counselor	**% White**: 99.5	

Stark County
[MASSILLON] **JACKSON LOCAL S.D.**
7984 FULTON DR NW ● MASSILLON OH 44646 ● (330) 830-8000 ● http://jackson.stark.k12.oh.us

Grade Span: PK-12	**Expenditures/Student**: $4,985	**% Amer Indian**: 0.0	National ***Socio-Economic Status*** indicator percentile (100=high): 96th
Schools: *Regular* 5 ● *Spec Ed* 0 ● *Alt* 0	**Librarians**: 2.0	**% Asian**: 1.5	
Students: 5,171	2,586 students/librarian	**% Black**: 1.9	
Total Teachers: 259	**Guidance Counselors**: 9.0	**% Hispanic**: 0.4	
Student/Classroom Teacher Ratio: 21.1	575 students/counselor	**% White**: 96.2	

Stark County
MASSILLON CITY S.D.
207 OAK AVE, NE ● MASSILLON OH 44646 ● (330) 830-1810 ● http://tigerweb.stark.k12.oh.us

Grade Span: PK-12	**Expenditures/Student**: $5,632	**% Amer Indian**: 0.0	National ***Socio-Economic Status*** indicator percentile (100=high): 40th
Schools: *Regular* 10 ● *Spec Ed* 0 ● *Alt* 0	**Librarians**: 4.0	**% Asian**: 0.1	
Students: 4,874	1,219 students/librarian	**% Black**: 13.3	
Total Teachers: 338	**Guidance Counselors**: 18.0	**% Hispanic**: 0.3	
Student/Classroom Teacher Ratio: 17.3	271 students/counselor	**% White**: 86.3	

Stark County
[MASSILLON] **PERRY LOCAL S.D.**
4201 HARSH AVE SW ● MASSILLON OH 44646 ● (330) 477-8121 ● http://www.perryschools.lgca.ohio.gov

Grade Span: PK-12	**Expenditures/Student**: $5,351	**% Amer Indian**: 0.0	National ***Socio-Economic Status*** indicator percentile (100=high): 78th
Schools: *Regular* 10 ● *Spec Ed* 0 ● *Alt* 0	**Librarians**: 3.0	**% Asian**: 0.4	
Students: 5,097	1,699 students/librarian	**% Black**: 3.7	
Total Teachers: 273	**Guidance Counselors**: 14.0	**% Hispanic**: 0.2	
Student/Classroom Teacher Ratio: 20.2	364 students/counselor	**% White**: 95.7	

Stark County
NORTH CANTON CITY S.D.
525 7TH ST NE ● NORTH CANTON OH 44720 ● (330) 497-5600 ● http://viking.stark.k12.oh.us

Grade Span: PK-12 **Schools**: *Regular* 7 ● *Spec Ed* 0 ● *Alt* 0 **Students**: 4,278 **Total Teachers**: 241 **Student/Classroom Teacher Ratio**: 20.4	**Expenditures/Student**: $5,099 **Librarians**: 1.0 4,278 students/librarian **Guidance Counselors**: 8.0 535 students/counselor	**% Amer Indian**: 0.2 **% Asian**: 1.1 **% Black**: 0.9 **% Hispanic**: 0.4 **% White**: 97.4	National ***Socio-Economic Status*** indicator percentile (100=high): 93rd

Summit County
AKRON CITY S.D.
70 N BROADWAY ● AKRON OH 44308 ● (330) 434-1661

Grade Span: PK-12 **Schools**: *Regular* 59 ● *Spec Ed* 0 ● *Alt* 1 **Students**: 32,095 **Total Teachers**: 2,145 **Student/Classroom Teacher Ratio**: 17.6	**Expenditures/Student**: $5,563 **Librarians**: 17.0 1,888 students/librarian **Guidance Counselors**: 56.0 573 students/counselor	**% Amer Indian**: 0.1 **% Asian**: 1.9 **% Black**: 44.5 **% Hispanic**: 0.5 **% White**: 53.1	National ***Socio-Economic Status*** indicator percentile (100=high): 20th

Summit County
[AKRON] COVENTRY LOCAL S.D.
3257 CORMANY RD ● AKRON OH 44319 ● (330) 644-8489 ● http://www.summit.k12.oh.us/coventry/coventry.htm

Grade Span: PK-12 **Schools**: *Regular* 6 ● *Spec Ed* 0 ● *Alt* 0 **Students**: 2,579 **Total Teachers**: 143 **Student/Classroom Teacher Ratio**: 24.6	**Expenditures/Student**: $5,168 **Librarians**: 3.0 860 students/librarian **Guidance Counselors**: 5.0 516 students/counselor	**% Amer Indian**: 0.1 **% Asian**: 0.2 **% Black**: 0.7 **% Hispanic**: 0.1 **% White**: 98.8	National ***Socio-Economic Status*** indicator percentile (100=high): 71st

Summit County
[AKRON] SPRINGFIELD LOCAL S.D.
2960 SANITARIUM RD ● AKRON OH 44312 ● (330) 784-0421

Grade Span: PK-12 **Schools**: *Regular* 8 ● *Spec Ed* 0 ● *Alt* 0 **Students**: 3,405 **Total Teachers**: 193 **Student/Classroom Teacher Ratio**: 18.3	**Expenditures/Student**: $5,023 **Librarians**: 3.0 1,135 students/librarian **Guidance Counselors**: 7.0 486 students/counselor	**% Amer Indian**: 0.2 **% Asian**: 0.6 **% Black**: 1.3 **% Hispanic**: 0.4 **% White**: 97.6	National ***Socio-Economic Status*** indicator percentile (100=high): 56th

Summit County
BARBERTON CITY S.D.
479 NORTON AVE ● BARBERTON OH 44203 ● (330) 753-1025

Grade Span: PK-12 **Schools**: *Regular* 9 ● *Spec Ed* 1 ● *Alt* 1 **Students**: 4,500 **Total Teachers**: 267 **Student/Classroom Teacher Ratio**: 16.1	**Expenditures/Student**: $6,446 **Librarians**: 3.0 1,500 students/librarian **Guidance Counselors**: 8.0 563 students/counselor	**% Amer Indian**: 0.0 **% Asian**: 0.3 **% Black**: 10.8 **% Hispanic**: 0.2 **% White**: 88.6	National ***Socio-Economic Status*** indicator percentile (100=high): na

Summit County
[BATH] REVERE LOCAL S.D.
3496 EVERETT RD, PO 340 ● BATH OH 44210 ● (330) 762-9491

Grade Span: PK-12 **Schools**: *Regular* 5 ● *Spec Ed* 0 ● *Alt* 0 **Students**: 2,788 **Total Teachers**: 168 **Student/Classroom Teacher Ratio**: 18.0	**Expenditures/Student**: $5,749 **Librarians**: 4.0 697 students/librarian **Guidance Counselors**: 7.0 398 students/counselor	**% Amer Indian**: 0.0 **% Asian**: 1.4 **% Black**: 0.6 **% Hispanic**: 0.1 **% White**: 97.8	National ***Socio-Economic Status*** indicator percentile (100=high): 96th

Summit County
COPLEY-FAIRLAWN CITY S.D.
3797 RIDGEWOOD RD ● COPLEY OH 44321 ● (330) 668-3200

Grade Span: PK-12 **Schools**: *Regular* 5 ● *Spec Ed* 0 ● *Alt* 0 **Students**: 2,548 **Total Teachers**: 148 **Student/Classroom Teacher Ratio**: 19.5	**Expenditures/Student**: $6,242 **Librarians**: 2.0 1,274 students/librarian **Guidance Counselors**: 8.0 319 students/counselor	**% Amer Indian**: 0.4 **% Asian**: 1.8 **% Black**: 9.2 **% Hispanic**: 0.5 **% White**: 88.0	National ***Socio-Economic Status*** indicator percentile (100=high): 91st

Summit County
CUYAHOGA FALLS CITY S.D.
431 STOW AVE, PO BOX 396 ● CUYAHOGA FALLS OH 44222 ● (330) 929-0581

Grade Span: PK-12 **Schools**: *Regular* 11 ● *Spec Ed* 0 ● *Alt* 0 **Students**: 5,906 **Total Teachers**: 342 **Student/Classroom Teacher Ratio**: 17.7	**Expenditures/Student**: $5,647 **Librarians**: 6.0 984 students/librarian **Guidance Counselors**: 11.0 537 students/counselor	**% Amer Indian**: 0.1 **% Asian**: 0.7 **% Black**: 1.0 **% Hispanic**: 0.2 **% White**: 98.0	National ***Socio-Economic Status*** indicator percentile (100=high): 80th

Summit County
GREEN LOCAL S.D.
1900 GREENSBURG RD, PO BOX 218 ● GREEN OH 44232 ● (330) 896-7500

Grade Span: KG-12 **Schools**: *Regular* 4 ● *Spec Ed* 0 ● *Alt* 0 **Students**: 3,581 **Total Teachers**: 178 **Student/Classroom Teacher Ratio**: 20.3	**Expenditures/Student**: $4,473 **Librarians**: 2.0 1,791 students/librarian **Guidance Counselors**: 7.0 512 students/counselor	**% Amer Indian**: 0.0 **% Asian**: 0.9 **% Black**: 0.3 **% Hispanic**: 0.2 **% White**: 98.6	National ***Socio-Economic Status*** indicator percentile (100=high): 84th

Summit County
HUDSON LOCAL S.D.
2400 HUDSON-AURORA RD ● HUDSON OH 44236 ● (216) 653-1200

Grade Span: PK-12 **Schools**: *Regular* 6 ● *Spec Ed* 0 ● *Alt* 0 **Students**: 5,365 **Total Teachers**: 298 **Student/Classroom Teacher Ratio**: 18.5	**Expenditures/Student**: $5,692 **Librarians**: 6.0 894 students/librarian **Guidance Counselors**: 11.0 488 students/counselor	**% Amer Indian**: 0.1 **% Asian**: 1.6 **% Black**: 0.7 **% Hispanic**: 0.3 **% White**: 97.2	National ***Socio-Economic Status*** indicator percentile (100=high): 100th

Summit County
[NORTHFIELD] NORDONIA HILLS CITY S.D.
9370 OLDE EIGHT RD ● NORTHFIELD OH 44067 ● (216) 467-0580

Grade Span: PK-12 **Schools**: *Regular* 6 ● *Spec Ed* 0 ● *Alt* 0 **Students**: 3,277 **Total Teachers**: 195 **Student/Classroom Teacher Ratio**: 17.0	**Expenditures/Student**: $6,259 **Librarians**: 2.0 1,639 students/librarian **Guidance Counselors**: 7.0 468 students/counselor	**% Amer Indian**: 0.2 **% Asian**: 1.3 **% Black**: 3.1 **% Hispanic**: 0.5 **% White**: 94.8	National ***Socio-Economic Status*** indicator percentile (100=high): 85th

Summit County
NORTON CITY S.D.
4128 CLEVELAND-MASSILLON RD ● NORTON OH 44203 ● (330) 825-0863

Grade Span: PK-12 **Schools**: *Regular* 7 ● *Spec Ed* 0 ● *Alt* 0 **Students**: 2,548 **Total Teachers**: 146 **Student/Classroom Teacher Ratio**: 18.2	**Expenditures/Student**: $4,659 **Librarians**: 1.0 2,548 students/librarian **Guidance Counselors**: 4.0 637 students/counselor	**% Amer Indian**: 0.0 **% Asian**: 0.2 **% Black**: 1.1 **% Hispanic**: 0.1 **% White**: 98.7	National ***Socio-Economic Status*** indicator percentile (100=high): 84th

Summit County

STOW CITY S.D.

1819 GRAHAM RD ● STOW OH 44224 ● (330) 688-8266 ● http://www.stow.summit.k12.oh.us

Grade Span: PK-12 **Schools**: *Regular* 9 ● *Spec Ed* 0 ● *Alt* 0 **Students**: 6,055 **Total Teachers**: 318 **Student/Classroom Teacher Ratio**: 22.3	**Expenditures/Student**: $4,765 **Librarians**: 5.0 1,211 students/librarian **Guidance Counselors**: 10.0 606 students/counselor	**% Amer Indian**: 0.0 **% Asian**: 1.6 **% Black**: 1.1 **% Hispanic**: 0.1 **% White**: 97.2	National ***Socio-Economic Status*** indicator percentile (100=high): 94th

Summit County

TALLMADGE CITY S.D.

486 EAST AVE ● TALLMADGE OH 44278 ● (330) 633-3291

Grade Span: PK-12 **Schools**: *Regular* 5 ● *Spec Ed* 0 ● *Alt* 0 **Students**: 2,672 **Total Teachers**: 150 **Student/Classroom Teacher Ratio**: 23.7	**Expenditures/Student**: $5,271 **Librarians**: 3.0 891 students/librarian **Guidance Counselors**: 5.0 534 students/counselor	**% Amer Indian**: 0.1 **% Asian**: 0.7 **% Black**: 1.8 **% Hispanic**: 0.4 **% White**: 97.0	National ***Socio-Economic Status*** indicator percentile (100=high): na

Summit County

TWINSBURG CITY S.D.

11136 RAVENNA RD ● TWINSBURG OH 44087 ● (216) 963-8300

Grade Span: PK-12 **Schools**: *Regular* 4 ● *Spec Ed* 0 ● *Alt* 0 **Students**: 2,858 **Total Teachers**: 163 **Student/Classroom Teacher Ratio**: 18.5	**Expenditures/Student**: $6,098 **Librarians**: 2.0 1,429 students/librarian **Guidance Counselors**: 7.0 408 students/counselor	**% Amer Indian**: 0.0 **% Asian**: 1.7 **% Black**: 19.9 **% Hispanic**: 0.2 **% White**: 78.1	National ***Socio-Economic Status*** indicator percentile (100=high): 79th

Trumbull County

NILES CITY S.D.

345 WARREN AVE ● NILES OH 44446 ● (330) 652-2509

Grade Span: PK-12 **Schools**: *Regular* 7 ● *Spec Ed* 0 ● *Alt* 0 **Students**: 3,025 **Total Teachers**: 153 **Student/Classroom Teacher Ratio**: 20.1	**Expenditures/Student**: $4,935 **Librarians**: 3.0 1,008 students/librarian **Guidance Counselors**: 5.0 605 students/counselor	**% Amer Indian**: 0.0 **% Asian**: 0.2 **% Black**: 1.4 **% Hispanic**: 0.3 **% White**: 98.1	National ***Socio-Economic Status*** indicator percentile (100=high): 60th

Trumbull County

[WARREN] HOWLAND LOCAL S.D.

8200 SOUTH ST SE ● WARREN OH 44484 ● (330) 856-8200

Grade Span: PK-12 **Schools**: *Regular* 6 ● *Spec Ed* 0 ● *Alt* 0 **Students**: 3,519 **Total Teachers**: 186 **Student/Classroom Teacher Ratio**: 20.2	**Expenditures/Student**: $5,862 **Librarians**: 2.0 1,760 students/librarian **Guidance Counselors**: 7.0 503 students/counselor	**% Amer Indian**: 0.1 **% Asian**: 2.6 **% Black**: 3.3 **% Hispanic**: 0.5 **% White**: 93.5	National ***Socio-Economic Status*** indicator percentile (100=high): 81st

Trumbull County

WARREN CITY S.D.

261 MONROE ST NW ● WARREN OH 44483 ● (330) 841-2321

Grade Span: PK-12 **Schools**: *Regular* 18 ● *Spec Ed* 0 ● *Alt* 0 **Students**: 7,212 **Total Teachers**: 454 **Student/Classroom Teacher Ratio**: 17.0	**Expenditures/Student**: $6,439 **Librarians**: 3.0 2,404 students/librarian **Guidance Counselors**: 10.0 721 students/counselor	**% Amer Indian**: 0.0 **% Asian**: 0.2 **% Black**: 41.1 **% Hispanic**: 0.5 **% White**: 58.1	National ***Socio-Economic Status*** indicator percentile (100=high): 20th

Tuscarawas County
DOVER CITY S.D.
219 W 6TH ST ● DOVER OH 44622 ● (330) 364-1906

Grade Span: PK-12 **Schools**: *Regular* 6 ● *Spec Ed* 0 ● *Alt* 0 **Students**: 2,892 **Total Teachers**: 159 **Student/Classroom Teacher Ratio**: 19.3	**Expenditures/Student**: $4,476 **Librarians**: 2.0 1,446 students/librarian **Guidance Counselors**: 5.0 578 students/counselor	**% Amer Indian**: 0.0 **% Asian**: 0.6 **% Black**: 1.3 **% Hispanic**: 0.0 **% White**: 98.1	National ***Socio-Economic Status*** indicator percentile (100=high): 88th

Tuscarawas County
NEW PHILADELPHIA CITY S.D.
303 FOURTH ST NW ● NEW PHILADELPHIA OH 44663 ● (330) 364-0600 ● http://web.tusco.net/npschool

Grade Span: PK-12 **Schools**: *Regular* 8 ● *Spec Ed* 0 ● *Alt* 0 **Students**: 3,446 **Total Teachers**: 198 **Student/Classroom Teacher Ratio**: 21.4	**Expenditures/Student**: $4,286 **Librarians**: 1.0 3,446 students/librarian **Guidance Counselors**: 4.0 862 students/counselor	**% Amer Indian**: 0.1 **% Asian**: 0.3 **% Black**: 1.1 **% Hispanic**: 0.3 **% White**: 98.3	National ***Socio-Economic Status*** indicator percentile (100=high): 77th

Union County
MARYSVILLE EXEMPTED VILLAGE S.D.
1000 EDGEWOOD DR ● MARYSVILLE OH 43040 ● (937) 644-8105

Grade Span: KG-12 **Schools**: *Regular* 6 ● *Spec Ed* 0 ● *Alt* 0 **Students**: 3,245 **Total Teachers**: 180 **Student/Classroom Teacher Ratio**: 15.7	**Expenditures/Student**: $5,447 **Librarians**: 2.0 1,623 students/librarian **Guidance Counselors**: 6.0 541 students/counselor	**% Amer Indian**: 0.0 **% Asian**: 0.6 **% Black**: 0.4 **% Hispanic**: 0.3 **% White**: 98.7	National ***Socio-Economic Status*** indicator percentile (100=high): na

Van Wert County
VAN WERT CITY S.D.
205 W CRAWFORD ST ● VAN WERT OH 45891 ● (419) 238-0648

Grade Span: PK-12 **Schools**: *Regular* 9 ● *Spec Ed* 0 ● *Alt* 0 **Students**: 2,580 **Total Teachers**: 139 **Student/Classroom Teacher Ratio**: 17.9	**Expenditures/Student**: $4,251 **Librarians**: 2.0 1,290 students/librarian **Guidance Counselors**: 5.0 516 students/counselor	**% Amer Indian**: 0.1 **% Asian**: 0.5 **% Black**: 2.0 **% Hispanic**: 1.9 **% White**: 95.5	National ***Socio-Economic Status*** indicator percentile (100=high): 71st

Warren County
FRANKLIN CITY S.D.
150 E SIXTH ST ● FRANKLIN OH 45005 ● (513) 746-1699

Grade Span: KG-12 **Schools**: *Regular* 8 ● *Spec Ed* 0 ● *Alt* 0 **Students**: 3,097 **Total Teachers**: 166 **Student/Classroom Teacher Ratio**: 19.8	**Expenditures/Student**: $4,742 **Librarians**: 3.0 1,032 students/librarian **Guidance Counselors**: 6.0 516 students/counselor	**% Amer Indian**: 0.0 **% Asian**: 0.2 **% Black**: 0.3 **% Hispanic**: 0.2 **% White**: 99.3	National ***Socio-Economic Status*** indicator percentile (100=high): 63rd

Warren County
[KINGS MILLS] **KINGS LOCAL S.D.**
5620 COLUMBIA RD ● KINGS MILLS OH 45034 ● (513) 398-3776

Grade Span: PK-12 **Schools**: *Regular* 5 ● *Spec Ed* 0 ● *Alt* 0 **Students**: 3,357 **Total Teachers**: 176 **Student/Classroom Teacher Ratio**: 19.5	**Expenditures/Student**: $4,408 **Librarians**: 6.0 560 students/librarian **Guidance Counselors**: 8.0 420 students/counselor	**% Amer Indian**: 0.0 **% Asian**: 1.5 **% Black**: 0.4 **% Hispanic**: 0.2 **% White**: 98.0	National ***Socio-Economic Status*** indicator percentile (100=high): 93rd

Warren County
LEBANON CITY S.D.
25 OAKWOOD AVE ● LEBANON OH 45036 ● (513) 932-0999

Grade Span: PK-12 **Schools**: *Regular* 7 ● *Spec Ed* 0 ● *Alt* 0 **Students**: 3,988 **Total Teachers**: 206 **Student/Classroom Teacher Ratio**: 21.8	**Expenditures/Student**: $4,035 **Librarians**: 7.0 570 students/librarian **Guidance Counselors**: 8.0 499 students/counselor	**% Amer Indian**: 0.1 **% Asian**: 0.4 **% Black**: 2.3 **% Hispanic**: 0.3 **% White**: 97.0	National ***Socio-Economic Status*** indicator percentile (100=high): 77th

Warren County
MASON CITY S.D.
211 N EAST ST ● MASON OH 45040 ● (513) 398-0474

Grade Span: PK-12 **Schools**: *Regular* 5 ● *Spec Ed* 0 ● *Alt* 0 **Students**: 3,845 **Total Teachers**: 197 **Student/Classroom Teacher Ratio**: 24.1	**Expenditures/Student**: $4,615 **Librarians**: 3.0 1,282 students/librarian **Guidance Counselors**: 9.0 427 students/counselor	**% Amer Indian**: 0.2 **% Asian**: 1.2 **% Black**: 0.5 **% Hispanic**: 0.7 **% White**: 97.4	National ***Socio-Economic Status*** indicator percentile (100=high): 98th

Warren County
SPRINGBORO COMMUNITY CITY S.D.
270 W CENTRAL AVE ● SPRINGBORO OH 45066 ● (513) 748-3960

Grade Span: KG-12 **Schools**: *Regular* 4 ● *Spec Ed* 0 ● *Alt* 0 **Students**: 2,729 **Total Teachers**: 175 **Student/Classroom Teacher Ratio**: 16.1	**Expenditures/Student**: $4,361 **Librarians**: 2.0 1,365 students/librarian **Guidance Counselors**: 4.0 682 students/counselor	**% Amer Indian**: 0.1 **% Asian**: 0.7 **% Black**: 0.5 **% Hispanic**: 0.3 **% White**: 98.4	National ***Socio-Economic Status*** indicator percentile (100=high): 98th

Washington County
MARIETTA CITY S.D.
701 3RD ST ● MARIETTA OH 45750 ● (614) 374-6500

Grade Span: PK-12 **Schools**: *Regular* 8 ● *Spec Ed* 0 ● *Alt* 0 **Students**: 3,955 **Total Teachers**: 224 **Student/Classroom Teacher Ratio**: 18.8	**Expenditures/Student**: $4,527 **Librarians**: 3.0 1,318 students/librarian **Guidance Counselors**: 6.0 659 students/counselor	**% Amer Indian**: 0.1 **% Asian**: 0.5 **% Black**: 0.6 **% Hispanic**: 0.3 **% White**: 98.5	National ***Socio-Economic Status*** indicator percentile (100=high): na

Washington County
[VINCENT] **WARREN LOCAL S.D.**
RT 1, BOX 1 ● VINCENT OH 45784 ● (614) 678-2366

Grade Span: PK-12 **Schools**: *Regular* 6 ● *Spec Ed* 1 ● *Alt* 0 **Students**: 2,813 **Total Teachers**: 138 **Student/Classroom Teacher Ratio**: 21.4	**Expenditures/Student**: $3,996 **Librarians**: 1.0 2,813 students/librarian **Guidance Counselors**: 2.0 1,407 students/counselor	**% Amer Indian**: 0.1 **% Asian**: 0.2 **% Black**: 1.4 **% Hispanic**: 0.2 **% White**: 98.1	National ***Socio-Economic Status*** indicator percentile (100=high): 67th

Wayne County
WOOSTER CITY S.D.
144 N MARKET ST ● WOOSTER OH 44691 ● (330) 264-0869 ● http://www.wooster.k12.oh.us

Grade Span: KG-12 **Schools**: *Regular* 10 ● *Spec Ed* 1 ● *Alt* 0 **Students**: 4,529 **Total Teachers**: 266 **Student/Classroom Teacher Ratio**: 20.0	**Expenditures/Student**: $5,494 **Librarians**: 3.0 1,510 students/librarian **Guidance Counselors**: 10.0 453 students/counselor	**% Amer Indian**: 0.2 **% Asian**: 0.9 **% Black**: 5.8 **% Hispanic**: 0.9 **% White**: 92.2	National ***Socio-Economic Status*** indicator percentile (100=high): 61st

Wood County
BOWLING GREEN CITY S.D.
140 S GROVE ● BOWLING GREEN OH 43402 ● (419) 352-3576 ● http://www.wcnet.org/~bgschool

Grade Span: PK-12 **Schools**: *Regular* 8 ● *Spec Ed* 0 ● *Alt* 0 **Students**: 3,604 **Total Teachers**: 197 **Student/Classroom Teacher Ratio**: 17.8	**Expenditures/Student**: $5,392 **Librarians**: 3.0 1,201 students/librarian **Guidance Counselors**: 7.0 515 students/counselor	**% Amer Indian**: 0.1 **% Asian**: 1.8 **% Black**: 1.1 **% Hispanic**: 4.4 **% White**: 92.5	National ***Socio-Economic Status*** indicator percentile (100=high): 76th

Wood County
PERRYSBURG EXEMPTED VILLAGE S.D.
140 E INDIANA AVE ● PERRYSBURG OH 43551 ● (419) 874-9131

Grade Span: PK-12 **Schools**: *Regular* 6 ● *Spec Ed* 0 ● *Alt* 0 **Students**: 4,058 **Total Teachers**: 208 **Student/Classroom Teacher Ratio**: 20.1	**Expenditures/Student**: $5,210 **Librarians**: 2.0 2,029 students/librarian **Guidance Counselors**: 11.0 369 students/counselor	**% Amer Indian**: 0.0 **% Asian**: 1.4 **% Black**: 0.7 **% Hispanic**: 2.6 **% White**: 95.3	National ***Socio-Economic Status*** indicator percentile (100=high): 96th

Bryan County

DURANT INDEPENDENT S.D.

P O DRAWER 1160 ● DURANT OK 74702-1160 ● (580) 924-1276

Grade Span: KG-12 **Schools**: *Regular* 6 ● *Spec Ed* 0 ● *Alt* 0 **Students**: 2,966 **Total Teachers**: 192 **Student/Classroom Teacher Ratio**: 15.1	**Expenditures/Student**: $4,460 **Librarians**: 5.0 593 students/librarian **Guidance Counselors**: 10.0 297 students/counselor	**% Amer Indian**: 23.1 **% Asian**: 0.8 **% Black**: 1.3 **% Hispanic**: 1.3 **% White**: 73.4	National ***Socio-Economic Status*** indicator percentile (100=high): 20th

Canadian County

EL RENO INDEPENDENT S.D.

P O BOX 580 ● EL RENO OK 73036-0580 ● (405) 262-1703

Grade Span: KG-12 **Schools**: *Regular* 6 ● *Spec Ed* 0 ● *Alt* 0 **Students**: 2,722 **Total Teachers**: 157 **Student/Classroom Teacher Ratio**: 15.8	**Expenditures/Student**: $4,257 **Librarians**: 4.0 681 students/librarian **Guidance Counselors**: 4.0 681 students/counselor	**% Amer Indian**: 12.7 **% Asian**: 0.6 **% Black**: 9.1 **% Hispanic**: 3.9 **% White**: 73.8	National ***Socio-Economic Status*** indicator percentile (100=high): 28th

Canadian County

MUSTANG INDEPENDENT S.D.

906 S HEIGHTS DR ● MUSTANG OK 73064-3599 ● (405) 376-2461

Grade Span: KG-12 **Schools**: *Regular* 8 ● *Spec Ed* 0 ● *Alt* 0 **Students**: 6,255 **Total Teachers**: 340 **Student/Classroom Teacher Ratio**: 17.7	**Expenditures/Student**: $3,576 **Librarians**: 9.0 695 students/librarian **Guidance Counselors**: 16.0 391 students/counselor	**% Amer Indian**: 3.3 **% Asian**: 3.9 **% Black**: 1.1 **% Hispanic**: 1.9 **% White**: 89.9	National ***Socio-Economic Status*** indicator percentile (100=high): 84th

Canadian County

YUKON INDEPENDENT S.D.

600 MAPLE AVE ● YUKON OK 73099-2533 ● (405) 354-2587

Grade Span: KG-12 **Schools**: *Regular* 10 ● *Spec Ed* 0 ● *Alt* 0 **Students**: 5,894 **Total Teachers**: 316 **Student/Classroom Teacher Ratio**: 17.6	**Expenditures/Student**: $3,623 **Librarians**: 8.0 737 students/librarian **Guidance Counselors**: 14.8 398 students/counselor	**% Amer Indian**: 3.0 **% Asian**: 2.1 **% Black**: 1.1 **% Hispanic**: 2.3 **% White**: 91.6	National ***Socio-Economic Status*** indicator percentile (100=high): 84th

Carter County

ARDMORE INDEPENDENT S.D.

P O BOX 1709 ● ARDMORE OK 73402-1709 ● (580) 223-2483

Grade Span: KG-12 **Schools**: *Regular* 8 ● *Spec Ed* 1 ● *Alt* 0 **Students**: 3,462 **Total Teachers**: 226 **Student/Classroom Teacher Ratio**: 14.8	**Expenditures/Student**: $5,079 **Librarians**: 5.0 692 students/librarian **Guidance Counselors**: 12.0 289 students/counselor	**% Amer Indian**: 13.7 **% Asian**: 1.0 **% Black**: 21.7 **% Hispanic**: 2.7 **% White**: 61.1	National ***Socio-Economic Status*** indicator percentile (100=high): 19th

Cherokee County

TAHLEQUAH INDEPENDENT S.D.

P O BOX 517 ● TAHLEQUAH OK 74465-0517 ● (918) 458-4100 ● http://www.tahlequah.k12.ok.us

Grade Span: KG-12 **Schools**: *Regular* 7 ● *Spec Ed* 0 ● *Alt* 0 **Students**: 3,464 **Total Teachers**: 221 **Student/Classroom Teacher Ratio**: 15.7	**Expenditures/Student**: $4,480 **Librarians**: 6.0 577 students/librarian **Guidance Counselors**: 10.0 346 students/counselor	**% Amer Indian**: 51.2 **% Asian**: 0.1 **% Black**: 4.9 **% Hispanic**: 1.6 **% White**: 42.1	National ***Socio-Economic Status*** indicator percentile (100=high): 19th

Cleveland County
MOORE INDEPENDENT S.D.
1500 S E 4TH ST ● MOORE OK 73160-8283 ● (405) 793-3032 ● http://www.telepath.com/mps

Grade Span: KG-12 **Schools**: *Regular* 27 ● *Spec Ed* 0 ● *Alt* 0 **Students**: 18,083 **Total Teachers**: 1,109 **Student/Classroom Teacher Ratio**: 15.9	**Expenditures/Student**: $4,000 **Librarians**: 29.0 624 students/librarian **Guidance Counselors**: 50.0 362 students/counselor	**% Amer Indian**: 12.7 **% Asian**: 3.2 **% Black**: 3.7 **% Hispanic**: 3.7 **% White**: 76.7	National ***Socio-Economic Status*** indicator percentile (100=high): 70th

Cleveland County
NOBLE INDEPENDENT S.D.
P O BOX 499 ● NOBLE OK 73068-0499 ● (405) 872-3452

Grade Span: KG-12 **Schools**: *Regular* 5 ● *Spec Ed* 0 ● *Alt* 0 **Students**: 2,553 **Total Teachers**: 151 **Student/Classroom Teacher Ratio**: 16.5	**Expenditures/Student**: $3,760 **Librarians**: 4.8 532 students/librarian **Guidance Counselors**: 7.0 365 students/counselor	**% Amer Indian**: 5.9 **% Asian**: 0.3 **% Black**: 0.3 **% Hispanic**: 2.4 **% White**: 91.0	National ***Socio-Economic Status*** indicator percentile (100=high): 42nd

Cleveland County
NORMAN INDEPENDENT S.D.
131 SOUTH FLOOD ● NORMAN OK 73069-5499 ● (405) 321-5014 ● http://www.norman.k12.ok.us/nps

Grade Span: KG-12 **Schools**: *Regular* 21 ● *Spec Ed* 4 ● *Alt* 0 **Students**: 12,459 **Total Teachers**: 780 **Student/Classroom Teacher Ratio**: 15.8	**Expenditures/Student**: $4,133 **Librarians**: 22.3 559 students/librarian **Guidance Counselors**: 31.6 394 students/counselor	**% Amer Indian**: 6.2 **% Asian**: 2.9 **% Black**: 5.3 **% Hispanic**: 2.8 **% White**: 82.8	National ***Socio-Economic Status*** indicator percentile (100=high): 52nd

Comanche County
LAWTON INDEPENDENT S.D.
P O BOX 1009 ● LAWTON OK 73501-1009 ● (580) 357-6900 ● http://www.lawtonps.k12.ok.us

Grade Span: PK-12 **Schools**: *Regular* 42 ● *Spec Ed* 0 ● *Alt* 0 **Students**: 19,122 **Total Teachers**: 1,067 **Student/Classroom Teacher Ratio**: 16.7	**Expenditures/Student**: $4,363 **Librarians**: 16.0 1,195 students/librarian **Guidance Counselors**: 43.7 438 students/counselor	**% Amer Indian**: 5.3 **% Asian**: 2.7 **% Black**: 29.7 **% Hispanic**: 7.4 **% White**: 54.9	National ***Socio-Economic Status*** indicator percentile (100=high): 32nd

Creek County
SAPULPA INDEPENDENT S.D.
1 S MISSION ST ● SAPULPA OK 74066-4699 ● (918) 224-3400

Grade Span: PK-12 **Schools**: *Regular* 10 ● *Spec Ed* 0 ● *Alt* 0 **Students**: 4,203 **Total Teachers**: 239 **Student/Classroom Teacher Ratio**: 25.0	**Expenditures/Student**: $4,164 **Librarians**: 6.0 701 students/librarian **Guidance Counselors**: 12.0 350 students/counselor	**% Amer Indian**: 14.8 **% Asian**: 0.2 **% Black**: 4.5 **% Hispanic**: 1.6 **% White**: 78.8	National ***Socio-Economic Status*** indicator percentile (100=high): 38th

Garfield County
ENID INDEPENDENT S.D.
500 S INDEPENDENCE ST ● ENID OK 73701-5632 ● (580) 234-5270 ● http://www.enid.org/enidschools

Grade Span: KG-12 **Schools**: *Regular* 16 ● *Spec Ed* 0 ● *Alt* 0 **Students**: 7,042 **Total Teachers**: 464 **Student/Classroom Teacher Ratio**: 15.5	**Expenditures/Student**: $4,171 **Librarians**: 13.5 522 students/librarian **Guidance Counselors**: 22.8 309 students/counselor	**% Amer Indian**: 6.3 **% Asian**: 2.8 **% Black**: 7.7 **% Hispanic**: 3.9 **% White**: 79.3	National ***Socio-Economic Status*** indicator percentile (100=high): 34th

Grady County

CHICKASHA INDEPENDENT S.D.

900 W CHOCTAW AVE ● CHICKASHA OK 73018-2213 ● (405) 222-6500

Grade Span: KG-12 **Schools**: *Regular* 7 ● *Spec Ed* 0 ● *Alt* 0 **Students**: 3,024 **Total Teachers**: 186 **Student/Classroom Teacher Ratio**: 16.2	**Expenditures/Student**: $4,108 **Librarians**: 5.0 605 students/librarian **Guidance Counselors**: 6.0 504 students/counselor	**% Amer Indian**: 4.7 **% Asian**: 1.0 **% Black**: 13.2 **% Hispanic**: 3.7 **% White**: 77.5	National ***Socio-Economic Status*** indicator percentile (100=high): 34th

Jackson County

ALTUS INDEPENDENT S.D.

P O BOX 558 ● ALTUS OK 73522-0558 ● (580) 481-2100

Grade Span: KG-12 **Schools**: *Regular* 9 ● *Spec Ed* 0 ● *Alt* 0 **Students**: 4,824 **Total Teachers**: 289 **Student/Classroom Teacher Ratio**: 16.9	**Expenditures/Student**: $4,384 **Librarians**: 4.0 1,206 students/librarian **Guidance Counselors**: 8.0 603 students/counselor	**% Amer Indian**: 1.6 **% Asian**: 1.5 **% Black**: 14.9 **% Hispanic**: 18.0 **% White**: 64.0	National ***Socio-Economic Status*** indicator percentile (100=high): 36th

Kay County

PONCA CITY INDEPENDENT S.D.

P O BOX 271 ● PONCA CITY OK 74602-0271 ● (580) 767-8000

Grade Span: KG-12 **Schools**: *Regular* 12 ● *Spec Ed* 0 ● *Alt* 0 **Students**: 5,644 **Total Teachers**: 338 **Student/Classroom Teacher Ratio**: 17.9	**Expenditures/Student**: $4,220 **Librarians**: 12.0 470 students/librarian **Guidance Counselors**: 15.5 364 students/counselor	**% Amer Indian**: 12.1 **% Asian**: 1.1 **% Black**: 4.4 **% Hispanic**: 3.1 **% White**: 79.3	National ***Socio-Economic Status*** indicator percentile (100=high): 37th

Logan County

GUTHRIE INDEPENDENT S.D.

802 E VILAS ● GUTHRIE OK 73044-5228 ● (405) 282-8900

Grade Span: KG-12 **Schools**: *Regular* 6 ● *Spec Ed* 0 ● *Alt* 0 **Students**: 3,290 **Total Teachers**: 210 **Student/Classroom Teacher Ratio**: 15.4	**Expenditures/Student**: $4,418 **Librarians**: 2.0 1,645 students/librarian **Guidance Counselors**: 6.0 548 students/counselor	**% Amer Indian**: 5.4 **% Asian**: 0.3 **% Black**: 13.2 **% Hispanic**: 3.0 **% White**: 78.1	National ***Socio-Economic Status*** indicator percentile (100=high): 25th

Muskogee County

MUSKOGEE INDEPENDENT S.D.

570 N 6TH ST ● MUSKOGEE OK 74401-6009 ● (918) 684-3700 ● http://www.azalea.net/mpsbest/mpsbest.html

Grade Span: KG-12 **Schools**: *Regular* 13 ● *Spec Ed* 0 ● *Alt* 0 **Students**: 6,717 **Total Teachers**: 417 **Student/Classroom Teacher Ratio**: 15.0	**Expenditures/Student**: $4,356 **Librarians**: 12.0 560 students/librarian **Guidance Counselors**: 17.0 395 students/counselor	**% Amer Indian**: 24.3 **% Asian**: 0.6 **% Black**: 27.8 **% Hispanic**: 1.6 **% White**: 45.7	National ***Socio-Economic Status*** indicator percentile (100=high): 16th

Oklahoma County

CHOCTAW-NICOMA PARK INDEPENDENT S.D.

12880 NE 10TH ST ● CHOCTAW OK 73020-9726 ● (405) 769-4859 ● http://www.ionet.net/~choctaw/cnpindex.html

Grade Span: KG-12 **Schools**: *Regular* 9 ● *Spec Ed* 0 ● *Alt* 0 **Students**: 4,678 **Total Teachers**: 273 **Student/Classroom Teacher Ratio**: 16.7	**Expenditures/Student**: $3,797 **Librarians**: 8.0 585 students/librarian **Guidance Counselors**: 10.4 450 students/counselor	**% Amer Indian**: 7.7 **% Asian**: 1.1 **% Black**: 3.5 **% Hispanic**: 1.8 **% White**: 86.0	National ***Socio-Economic Status*** indicator percentile (100=high): 65th

Oklahoma County
EDMOND INDEPENDENT S.D.
1001 W DANFORTH ● EDMOND OK 73003-4801 ● (405) 340-2800 ● http://www.tkb.com/edmond/schools/index.html

Grade Span: KG-12 **Schools**: *Regular* 20 ● *Spec Ed* 1 ● *Alt* 0 **Students**: 15,637 **Total Teachers**: 890 **Student/Classroom Teacher Ratio**: 17.5	**Expenditures/Student**: $3,819 **Librarians**: 22.0 711 students/librarian **Guidance Counselors**: 39.5 396 students/counselor	**% Amer Indian**: 2.7 **% Asian**: 1.9 **% Black**: 4.8 **% Hispanic**: 1.3 **% White**: 89.3	National ***Socio-Economic Status*** indicator percentile (100=high): 86th

Oklahoma County
MIDWEST CITY-DEL CITY INDEPENDENT S.D.
7217 SE 15TH ● MIDWEST CITY OK 73110-5236 ● (405) 737-4461

Grade Span: PK-12 **Schools**: *Regular* 25 ● *Spec Ed* 1 ● *Alt* 0 **Students**: 15,843 **Total Teachers**: 930 **Student/Classroom Teacher Ratio**: 16.9	**Expenditures/Student**: $4,226 **Librarians**: 26.0 609 students/librarian **Guidance Counselors**: 37.0 428 students/counselor	**% Amer Indian**: 5.4 **% Asian**: 2.5 **% Black**: 21.5 **% Hispanic**: 3.0 **% White**: 67.8	National ***Socio-Economic Status*** indicator percentile (100=high): 38th

Oklahoma County
OKLAHOMA CITY INDEPENDENT S.D.
900 N KLEIN ST ● OKLAHOMA CITY OK 73106-7098 ● (405) 297-6522

Grade Span: PK-12 **Schools**: *Regular* 85 ● *Spec Ed* 1 ● *Alt* 0 **Students**: 39,829 **Total Teachers**: 2,377 **Student/Classroom Teacher Ratio**: 16.3	**Expenditures/Student**: $4,676 **Librarians**: 40.3 988 students/librarian **Guidance Counselors**: 72.9 546 students/counselor	**% Amer Indian**: 5.2 **% Asian**: 2.8 **% Black**: 39.9 **% Hispanic**: 14.2 **% White**: 38.0	National ***Socio-Economic Status*** indicator percentile (100=high): 5th

Oklahoma County
[OKLAHOMA CITY] **PUTNAM CITY INDEPENDENT S.D.**
5401 NW 40TH ST ● OKLAHOMA CITY OK 73122-3398 ● (405) 495-5200

Grade Span: PK-12 **Schools**: *Regular* 27 ● *Spec Ed* 0 ● *Alt* 0 **Students**: 19,035 **Total Teachers**: 1,143 **Student/Classroom Teacher Ratio**: 16.3	**Expenditures/Student**: $3,983 **Librarians**: 28.0 680 students/librarian **Guidance Counselors**: 39.9 477 students/counselor	**% Amer Indian**: 3.2 **% Asian**: 3.9 **% Black**: 11.6 **% Hispanic**: 3.7 **% White**: 77.6	National ***Socio-Economic Status*** indicator percentile (100=high): 59th

Oklahoma County
[OKLAHOMA CITY] **WESTERN HEIGHGTS INDEPENDENT S.D.**
8401 SW 44TH ● OKLAHOMA CITY OK 73179-4010 ● (405) 745-6300

Grade Span: KG-12 **Schools**: *Regular* 6 ● *Spec Ed* 0 ● *Alt* 0 **Students**: 2,945 **Total Teachers**: 191 **Student/Classroom Teacher Ratio**: 15.2	**Expenditures/Student**: $4,692 **Librarians**: 2.0 1,473 students/librarian **Guidance Counselors**: 6.8 433 students/counselor	**% Amer Indian**: 8.8 **% Asian**: 6.9 **% Black**: 17.7 **% Hispanic**: 5.6 **% White**: 60.9	National ***Socio-Economic Status*** indicator percentile (100=high): 14th

Payne County
STILLWATER INDEPENDENT S.D.
P O BOX 879 ● STILLWATER OK 74076-0879 ● (405) 743-6300 ● http://www.stillwater.k12.ok.us

Grade Span: KG-12 **Schools**: *Regular* 9 ● *Spec Ed* 0 ● *Alt* 0 **Students**: 5,546 **Total Teachers**: 318 **Student/Classroom Teacher Ratio**: 17.0	**Expenditures/Student**: $4,089 **Librarians**: 8.0 693 students/librarian **Guidance Counselors**: 14.0 396 students/counselor	**% Amer Indian**: 6.8 **% Asian**: 3.0 **% Black**: 6.6 **% Hispanic**: 2.1 **% White**: 81.4	National ***Socio-Economic Status*** indicator percentile (100=high): 49th

Pittsburg County

MCALESTER INDEPENDENT S.D.

P O BOX 1027 ● MCALESTER OK 74502-1027 ● (918) 423-4771

Grade Span: KG-12 **Schools**: *Regular* 10 ● *Spec Ed* 1 ● *Alt* 0 **Students**: 2,929 **Total Teachers**: 182 **Student/Classroom Teacher Ratio**: 14.7	**Expenditures/Student**: $4,371 **Librarians**: 5.0 586 students/librarian **Guidance Counselors**: 9.0 325 students/counselor	**% Amer Indian**: 15.0 **% Asian**: 0.6 **% Black**: 9.9 **% Hispanic**: 2.2 **% White**: 72.3	National ***Socio-Economic Status*** indicator percentile (100=high): 27th

Pontotoc County

ADA INDEPENDENT S.D.

P O BOX 1359 ● ADA OK 74821-1359 ● (580) 332-0255

Grade Span: KG-12 **Schools**: *Regular* 6 ● *Spec Ed* 0 ● *Alt* 0 **Students**: 2,793 **Total Teachers**: 183 **Student/Classroom Teacher Ratio**: 14.2	**Expenditures/Student**: $4,018 **Librarians**: 2.0 1,397 students/librarian **Guidance Counselors**: 6.0 466 students/counselor	**% Amer Indian**: 22.4 **% Asian**: 0.6 **% Black**: 4.8 **% Hispanic**: 1.6 **% White**: 70.7	National ***Socio-Economic Status*** indicator percentile (100=high): 27th

Pottawatomie County

SHAWNEE INDEPENDENT S.D.

326 N UNION ST ● SHAWNEE OK 74801-7053 ● (405) 273-0653

Grade Span: KG-12 **Schools**: *Regular* 8 ● *Spec Ed* 0 ● *Alt* 0 **Students**: 3,980 **Total Teachers**: 234 **Student/Classroom Teacher Ratio**: 17.2	**Expenditures/Student**: $4,421 **Librarians**: 5.0 796 students/librarian **Guidance Counselors**: 9.0 442 students/counselor	**% Amer Indian**: 20.9 **% Asian**: 1.0 **% Black**: 6.8 **% Hispanic**: 2.1 **% White**: 69.2	National ***Socio-Economic Status*** indicator percentile (100=high): 23rd

Rogers County

CLAREMORE INDEPENDENT S.D.

P O BOX 907 ● CLAREMORE OK 74018-0907 ● (918) 341-2213 ● http://www.claremore.k12.ok.us

Grade Span: KG-12 **Schools**: *Regular* 7 ● *Spec Ed* 0 ● *Alt* 0 **Students**: 3,666 **Total Teachers**: 225 **Student/Classroom Teacher Ratio**: 18.5	**Expenditures/Student**: $4,096 **Librarians**: 6.0 611 students/librarian **Guidance Counselors**: 10.0 367 students/counselor	**% Amer Indian**: 22.9 **% Asian**: 0.7 **% Black**: 2.7 **% Hispanic**: 2.3 **% White**: 71.4	National ***Socio-Economic Status*** indicator percentile (100=high): 57th

Stephens County

DUNCAN INDEPENDENT S.D.

P O BOX 1548 ● DUNCAN OK 73534-1548 ● (580) 255-0686

Grade Span: KG-12 **Schools**: *Regular* 10 ● *Spec Ed* 0 ● *Alt* 0 **Students**: 3,966 **Total Teachers**: 230 **Student/Classroom Teacher Ratio**: 16.4	**Expenditures/Student**: $4,104 **Librarians**: 3.0 1,322 students/librarian **Guidance Counselors**: 10.0 397 students/counselor	**% Amer Indian**: 2.4 **% Asian**: 0.7 **% Black**: 7.2 **% Hispanic**: 7.6 **% White**: 82.1	National ***Socio-Economic Status*** indicator percentile (100=high): 37th

Tulsa County

BIXBY INDEPENDENT S.D.

P O BOX 160 ● BIXBY OK 74008-0160 ● (918) 366-4421

Grade Span: KG-12 **Schools**: *Regular* 6 ● *Spec Ed* 0 ● *Alt* 0 **Students**: 2,996 **Total Teachers**: 159 **Student/Classroom Teacher Ratio**: 19.0	**Expenditures/Student**: $3,549 **Librarians**: 4.0 749 students/librarian **Guidance Counselors**: 6.0 499 students/counselor	**% Amer Indian**: 6.8 **% Asian**: 0.3 **% Black**: 1.6 **% Hispanic**: 3.9 **% White**: 87.4	National ***Socio-Economic Status*** indicator percentile (100=high): 64th

Tulsa County

BROKEN ARROW INDEPENDENT S.D.

601 S MAIN ST ● BROKEN ARROW OK 74012-4399 ● (918) 259-4300 ● http://www.ba.k12.ok.us

Grade Span: KG-12 **Schools**: *Regular* 23 ● *Spec Ed* 0 ● *Alt* 0 **Students**: 14,445 **Total Teachers**: 799 **Student/Classroom Teacher Ratio**: 18.3	**Expenditures/Student**: $3,899 **Librarians**: 22.0 657 students/librarian **Guidance Counselors**: 36.9 391 students/counselor	**% Amer Indian**: 6.9 **% Asian**: 0.9 **% Black**: 3.9 **% Hispanic**: 1.3 **% White**: 87.0	National ***Socio-Economic Status*** indicator percentile (100=high): 72nd

Tulsa County

JENKS INDEPENDENT S.D.

205 EAST B ST ● JENKS OK 74037-3905 ● (918) 299-4411 ● http://web.jenksusa.k12.ok.us

Grade Span: PK-12 **Schools**: *Regular* 7 ● *Spec Ed* 0 ● *Alt* 0 **Students**: 8,676 **Total Teachers**: 444 **Student/Classroom Teacher Ratio**: 18.9	**Expenditures/Student**: $4,289 **Librarians**: 10.0 868 students/librarian **Guidance Counselors**: 19.0 457 students/counselor	**% Amer Indian**: 3.6 **% Asian**: 2.4 **% Black**: 5.0 **% Hispanic**: 2.3 **% White**: 86.6	National ***Socio-Economic Status*** indicator percentile (100=high): 85th

Tulsa County

OWASSO INDEPENDENT S.D.

1501 N ASH ST ● OWASSO OK 74055-4998 ● (918) 272-5367

Grade Span: PK-12 **Schools**: *Regular* 10 ● *Spec Ed* 0 ● *Alt* 0 **Students**: 5,622 **Total Teachers**: 333 **Student/Classroom Teacher Ratio**: 16.5	**Expenditures/Student**: $3,656 **Librarians**: 11.0 511 students/librarian **Guidance Counselors**: 12.0 469 students/counselor	**% Amer Indian**: 6.7 **% Asian**: 0.6 **% Black**: 1.1 **% Hispanic**: 1.1 **% White**: 90.6	National ***Socio-Economic Status*** indicator percentile (100=high): 82nd

Tulsa County

SAND SPRINGS INDEPENDENT S.D.

P O BOX 970 ● SAND SPRINGS OK 74063-0970 ● (918) 245-3206

Grade Span: PK-12 **Schools**: *Regular* 10 ● *Spec Ed* 1 ● *Alt* 0 **Students**: 5,308 **Total Teachers**: 332 **Student/Classroom Teacher Ratio**: 14.4	**Expenditures/Student**: $4,284 **Librarians**: 6.0 885 students/librarian **Guidance Counselors**: 9.0 590 students/counselor	**% Amer Indian**: 17.5 **% Asian**: 0.7 **% Black**: 3.5 **% Hispanic**: 1.3 **% White**: 77.1	National ***Socio-Economic Status*** indicator percentile (100=high): 54th

Tulsa County

TULSA INDEPENDENT S.D.

P O BOX 470208 ● TULSA OK 74147-0208 ● (918) 745-6800 ● http://www.tulsaschools.org

Grade Span: PK-12 **Schools**: *Regular* 79 ● *Spec Ed* 1 ● *Alt* 0 **Students**: 41,125 **Total Teachers**: 2,437 **Student/Classroom Teacher Ratio**: 16.5	**Expenditures/Student**: $4,709 **Librarians**: 35.0 1,175 students/librarian **Guidance Counselors**: 111.0 370 students/counselor	**% Amer Indian**: 7.7 **% Asian**: 1.3 **% Black**: 32.8 **% Hispanic**: 4.4 **% White**: 53.7	National ***Socio-Economic Status*** indicator percentile (100=high): 17th

Tulsa County

[TULSA] **UNION INDEPENDENT S.D.**

5656 S 129TH E AVE ● TULSA OK 74134-6711 ● (918) 459-5432 ● http://www.unionps.org

Grade Span: KG-12 **Schools**: *Regular* 14 ● *Spec Ed* 0 ● *Alt* 0 **Students**: 11,611 **Total Teachers**: 613 **Student/Classroom Teacher Ratio**: 18.5	**Expenditures/Student**: $3,964 **Librarians**: 13.0 893 students/librarian **Guidance Counselors**: 21.0 553 students/counselor	**% Amer Indian**: 4.3 **% Asian**: 3.9 **% Black**: 7.7 **% Hispanic**: 4.0 **% White**: 80.1	National ***Socio-Economic Status*** indicator percentile (100=high): 77th

Washington County

BARTLESVILLE INDEPENDENT S.D.

P O BOX 1357 ● BARTLESVILLE OK 74005-1357 ● (918) 336-8600 ● http://www.edumaster.net/schools/bartles/index.html

Grade Span: KG-12 **Schools**: *Regular* 12 ● *Spec Ed* 0 ● *Alt* 0 **Students**: 6,512 **Total Teachers**: 391 **Student/Classroom Teacher Ratio**: 16.4	**Expenditures/Student**: $4,312 **Librarians**: 11.0 592 students/librarian **Guidance Counselors**: 18.0 362 students/counselor	**% Amer Indian**: 8.2 **% Asian**: 1.1 **% Black**: 5.8 **% Hispanic**: 1.9 **% White**: 82.9	National ***Socio-Economic Status*** indicator percentile (100=high): 46th

Woodward County

WOODWARD INDEPENDENT S.D.

P O BOX 668 ● WOODWARD OK 73802-0668 ● (580) 256-6063

Grade Span: KG-12 **Schools**: *Regular* 10 ● *Spec Ed* 0 ● *Alt* 0 **Students**: 2,927 **Total Teachers**: 195 **Student/Classroom Teacher Ratio**: 15.3	**Expenditures/Student**: $4,211 **Librarians**: 6.0 488 students/librarian **Guidance Counselors**: 8.5 344 students/counselor	**% Amer Indian**: 2.6 **% Asian**: 0.3 **% Black**: 0.1 **% Hispanic**: 4.6 **% White**: 92.3	National ***Socio-Economic Status*** indicator percentile (100=high): 49th

Benton County

CORVALLIS S.D. 509J

PO BOX 3509J ● CORVALLIS OR 97333-1198 ● (541) 757-5811 ● http://www.corvallis.k12.or.us

Grade Span: KG-12 **Schools**: *Regular* 16 ● *Spec Ed* 0 ● *Alt* 1 **Students**: 7,590 **Total Teachers**: 345 **Student/Classroom Teacher Ratio**: 22.3	**Expenditures/Student**: $5,290 **Librarians**: 6.0 1,265 students/librarian **Guidance Counselors**: 12.7 598 students/counselor	**% Amer Indian**: 0.5 **% Asian**: 3.9 **% Black**: 1.4 **% Hispanic**: 3.2 **% White**: 91.0	National ***Socio-Economic Status*** indicator percentile (100=high): 80th

Clackamas County

CANBY S.D. 86

811 SW 5TH AVE ● CANBY OR 97013-3999 ● (503) 266-7861

Grade Span: KG-12 **Schools**: *Regular* 7 ● *Spec Ed* 0 ● *Alt* 0 **Students**: 4,865 **Total Teachers**: 259 **Student/Classroom Teacher Ratio**: 20.0	**Expenditures/Student**: $5,470 **Librarians**: 7.0 695 students/librarian **Guidance Counselors**: 13.0 374 students/counselor	**% Amer Indian**: 0.3 **% Asian**: 1.2 **% Black**: 0.5 **% Hispanic**: 6.7 **% White**: 91.3	National ***Socio-Economic Status*** indicator percentile (100=high): 70th

Clackamas County

LAKE OSWEGO S.D. 7J

PO BOX 70 ● LAKE OSWEGO OR 97034-0070 ● (503) 636-7691 ● http://www.loswego.k12.or.us

Grade Span: KG-12 **Schools**: *Regular* 13 ● *Spec Ed* 0 ● *Alt* 0 **Students**: 7,029 **Total Teachers**: 328 **Student/Classroom Teacher Ratio**: 21.9	**Expenditures/Student**: $5,774 **Librarians**: 11.1 633 students/librarian **Guidance Counselors**: 15.4 456 students/counselor	**% Amer Indian**: 0.1 **% Asian**: 5.7 **% Black**: 0.9 **% Hispanic**: 1.5 **% White**: 91.7	National ***Socio-Economic Status*** indicator percentile (100=high): 99th

Clackamas County

[MILWAUKIE] NORTH CLACKAMAS S.D. 12

4444 SE LAKE RD ● MILWAUKIE OR 97222-4799 ● (503) 653-3600 ● http://www.nclack.k12.or.us

Grade Span: PK-12 **Schools**: *Regular* 25 ● *Spec Ed* 0 ● *Alt* 0 **Students**: 13,887 **Total Teachers**: 673 **Student/Classroom Teacher Ratio**: 21.6	**Expenditures/Student**: $5,236 **Librarians**: 21.2 655 students/librarian **Guidance Counselors**: 19.5 712 students/counselor	**% Amer Indian**: 1.1 **% Asian**: 4.7 **% Black**: 1.4 **% Hispanic**: 3.8 **% White**: 88.9	National ***Socio-Economic Status*** indicator percentile (100=high): 72nd

Clackamas County

MOLALLA RIVER S.D. 35

PO BOX 188 ● MOLALLA OR 97038-0188 ● (503) 829-2350

Grade Span: KG-12 **Schools**: *Regular* 9 ● *Spec Ed* 0 ● *Alt* 0 **Students**: 2,856 **Total Teachers**: 140 **Student/Classroom Teacher Ratio**: 20.4	**Expenditures/Student**: $5,608 **Librarians**: 4.0 714 students/librarian **Guidance Counselors**: 7.4 386 students/counselor	**% Amer Indian**: 0.7 **% Asian**: 1.2 **% Black**: 0.6 **% Hispanic**: 5.4 **% White**: 92.2	National ***Socio-Economic Status*** indicator percentile (100=high): 60th

Clackamas County

OREGON CITY S.D. 62

PO BOX 591 ● OREGON CITY OR 97045-0032 ● (503) 656-4283 ● http://www.orecity.k12.or.us

Grade Span: KG-12 **Schools**: *Regular* 14 ● *Spec Ed* 0 ● *Alt* 0 **Students**: 6,949 **Total Teachers**: 280 **Student/Classroom Teacher Ratio**: 23.4	**Expenditures/Student**: $5,144 **Librarians**: 1.8 3,861 students/librarian **Guidance Counselors**: 17.0 409 students/counselor	**% Amer Indian**: 1.2 **% Asian**: 1.3 **% Black**: 0.5 **% Hispanic**: 3.4 **% White**: 93.6	National ***Socio-Economic Status*** indicator percentile (100=high): 68th

Clackamas County

WEST LINN S.D. 3J

ADMINISTRATION BUILDING ● WEST LINN OR 97068-0100 ● (503) 638-9869

Grade Span: KG-12 **Schools**: *Regular* 11 ● *Spec Ed* 0 ● *Alt* 0 **Students**: 6,938 **Total Teachers**: 308 **Student/Classroom Teacher Ratio**: 22.7	**Expenditures/Student**: $5,243 **Librarians**: 11.0 631 students/librarian **Guidance Counselors**: 14.2 489 students/counselor	**% Amer Indian**: 0.2 **% Asian**: 3.1 **% Black**: 0.5 **% Hispanic**: 2.2 **% White**: 94.0	National ***Socio-Economic Status*** indicator percentile (100=high): 94th

Columbia County

ST. HELENS S.D. 502

474 N 16TH ST ● ST. HELENS OR 97051-1340 ● (503) 397-3085

Grade Span: KG-12 **Schools**: *Regular* 7 ● *Spec Ed* 0 ● *Alt* 0 **Students**: 2,852 **Total Teachers**: 155 **Student/Classroom Teacher Ratio**: 19.2	**Expenditures/Student**: $4,952 **Librarians**: 3.0 951 students/librarian **Guidance Counselors**: 7.0 407 students/counselor	**% Amer Indian**: 2.3 **% Asian**: 2.1 **% Black**: 0.3 **% Hispanic**: 3.2 **% White**: 92.1	National ***Socio-Economic Status*** indicator percentile (100=high): 64th

Coos County

COOS BAY S.D. 9

PO BOX 509 ● COOS BAY OR 97420-0102 ● (541) 267-3104 ● http://www.coos-bay.k12.or.us

Grade Span: KG-12 **Schools**: *Regular* 9 ● *Spec Ed* 0 ● *Alt* 0 **Students**: 4,373 **Total Teachers**: 202 **Student/Classroom Teacher Ratio**: 21.8	**Expenditures/Student**: $5,083 **Librarians**: 4.0 1,093 students/librarian **Guidance Counselors**: 8.8 497 students/counselor	**% Amer Indian**: 8.9 **% Asian**: 2.7 **% Black**: 0.5 **% Hispanic**: 3.4 **% White**: 84.6	National ***Socio-Economic Status*** indicator percentile (100=high): 29th

Coos County

NORTH BEND S.D. 13

1313 AIRPORT LN ● NORTH BEND OR 97459-2099 ● (541) 756-2521

Grade Span: KG-12 **Schools**: *Regular* 7 ● *Spec Ed* 1 ● *Alt* 0 **Students**: 2,929 **Total Teachers**: 145 **Student/Classroom Teacher Ratio**: 20.0	**Expenditures/Student**: $5,027 **Librarians**: 2.0 1,465 students/librarian **Guidance Counselors**: 5.0 586 students/counselor	**% Amer Indian**: 3.9 **% Asian**: 1.9 **% Black**: 0.6 **% Hispanic**: 2.3 **% White**: 91.2	National ***Socio-Economic Status*** indicator percentile (100=high): 50th

Crook County

[PRINEVILLE] **CROOK COUNTY S.D.**

1390 SE 2ND ST ● PRINEVILLE OR 97754-2498 ● (541) 447-5664 ● http://www.crookcounty.k12.or.us

Grade Span: KG-12 **Schools**: *Regular* 6 ● *Spec Ed* 0 ● *Alt* 0 **Students**: 3,007 **Total Teachers**: 154 **Student/Classroom Teacher Ratio**: 18.7	**Expenditures/Student**: $4,758 **Librarians**: 2.5 1,203 students/librarian **Guidance Counselors**: 5.0 601 students/counselor	**% Amer Indian**: 0.6 **% Asian**: 0.6 **% Black**: 0.2 **% Hispanic**: 4.0 **% White**: 94.6	National ***Socio-Economic Status*** indicator percentile (100=high): 57th

Deschutes County

BEND ADMINISTRATIVE S.D. 1

520 NW WALL ST ● BEND OR 97701-2699 ● (541) 385-5201

Grade Span: KG-12 **Schools**: *Regular* 19 ● *Spec Ed* 0 ● *Alt* 0 **Students**: 11,293 **Total Teachers**: 516 **Student/Classroom Teacher Ratio**: 22.6	**Expenditures/Student**: $5,279 **Librarians**: 12.4 911 students/librarian **Guidance Counselors**: 24.4 463 students/counselor	**% Amer Indian**: 0.5 **% Asian**: 0.9 **% Black**: 0.4 **% Hispanic**: 1.7 **% White**: 96.4	National ***Socio-Economic Status*** indicator percentile (100=high): 62nd

Deschutes County
REDMOND S.D. 2J
716 W EVERGREEN AVE ● REDMOND OR 97756-2294 ● (541) 923-5437 ● http://www.redmond.k12.or.us

Grade Span: KG-12 **Schools**: *Regular* 8 ● *Spec Ed* 0 ● *Alt* 0 **Students**: 4,864 **Total Teachers**: 228 **Student/Classroom Teacher Ratio**: 21.4	**Expenditures/Student**: $4,986 **Librarians**: 1.0 4,864 students/librarian **Guidance Counselors**: 11.7 416 students/counselor	**% Amer Indian**: 0.8 **% Asian**: 1.0 **% Black**: 0.2 **% Hispanic**: 2.9 **% White**: 95.2	National ***Socio-Economic Status*** indicator percentile (100=high): 61st

Douglas County
ROSEBURG S.D. 4
1419 NW VALLEY VIEW DR ● ROSEBURG OR 97470-1798 ● (541) 440-4015

Grade Span: KG-12 **Schools**: *Regular* 12 ● *Spec Ed* 0 ● *Alt* 0 **Students**: 6,819 **Total Teachers**: 332 **Student/Classroom Teacher Ratio**: 20.7	**Expenditures/Student**: $4,777 **Librarians**: 3.0 2,273 students/librarian **Guidance Counselors**: 18.5 369 students/counselor	**% Amer Indian**: 1.3 **% Asian**: 1.5 **% Black**: 0.4 **% Hispanic**: 2.6 **% White**: 94.2	National ***Socio-Economic Status*** indicator percentile (100=high): 35th

Hood River County
[HOOD RIVER] HOOD RIVER COUNTY S.D. 1
PO BOX 920 ● HOOD RIVER OR 97031-0030 ● (541) 386-2511

Grade Span: KG-12 **Schools**: *Regular* 9 ● *Spec Ed* 0 ● *Alt* 0 **Students**: 3,601 **Total Teachers**: 207 **Student/Classroom Teacher Ratio**: 16.9	**Expenditures/Student**: $5,904 **Librarians**: 4.0 900 students/librarian **Guidance Counselors**: 5.5 655 students/counselor	**% Amer Indian**: 0.6 **% Asian**: 1.4 **% Black**: 0.5 **% Hispanic**: 28.3 **% White**: 69.3	National ***Socio-Economic Status*** indicator percentile (100=high): 37th

Jackson County
ASHLAND S.D. 5
885 SISKIYOU BLVD ● ASHLAND OR 97520 ● (541) 482-2811 ● http://www.ashland.k12.or.us

Grade Span: KG-12 **Schools**: *Regular* 7 ● *Spec Ed* 1 ● *Alt* 0 **Students**: 3,451 **Total Teachers**: 180 **Student/Classroom Teacher Ratio**: 19.2	**Expenditures/Student**: $5,441 **Librarians**: 4.5 767 students/librarian **Guidance Counselors**: 8.5 406 students/counselor	**% Amer Indian**: 1.5 **% Asian**: 1.9 **% Black**: 1.4 **% Hispanic**: 2.5 **% White**: 92.7	National ***Socio-Economic Status*** indicator percentile (100=high): 61st

Jackson County
CENTRAL POINT S.D. 6
451 N 2ND ST ● CENTRAL POINT OR 97502-1699 ● (541) 664-6611

Grade Span: KG-12 **Schools**: *Regular* 8 ● *Spec Ed* 0 ● *Alt* 0 **Students**: 4,354 **Total Teachers**: 210 **Student/Classroom Teacher Ratio**: 20.9	**Expenditures/Student**: $5,115 **Librarians**: 3.8 1,146 students/librarian **Guidance Counselors**: 7.0 622 students/counselor	**% Amer Indian**: 2.2 **% Asian**: 1.3 **% Black**: 0.5 **% Hispanic**: 4.6 **% White**: 91.4	National ***Socio-Economic Status*** indicator percentile (100=high): 47th

Jackson County
EAGLE POINT S.D. 9
PO BOX 548 ● EAGLE POINT OR 97524-0548 ● (541) 830-1200

Grade Span: KG-12 **Schools**: *Regular* 8 ● *Spec Ed* 0 ● *Alt* 0 **Students**: 3,957 **Total Teachers**: 178 **Student/Classroom Teacher Ratio**: 22.5	**Expenditures/Student**: $4,772 **Librarians**: 1.0 3,957 students/librarian **Guidance Counselors**: 10.0 396 students/counselor	**% Amer Indian**: 1.8 **% Asian**: 0.7 **% Black**: 0.4 **% Hispanic**: 6.4 **% White**: 90.7	National ***Socio-Economic Status*** indicator percentile (100=high): 41st

Jackson County
MEDFORD S.D. 549
500 MONROE ST ● MEDFORD OR 97501-3522 ● (541) 776-8600

Grade Span: KG-12 **Schools**: *Regular* 17 ● *Spec Ed* 0 ● *Alt* 0 **Students**: 11,658 **Total Teachers**: 556 **Student/Classroom Teacher Ratio**: 21.9	**Expenditures/Student**: $5,018 **Librarians**: 17.6 662 students/librarian **Guidance Counselors**: 28.1 415 students/counselor	**% Amer Indian**: 1.6 **% Asian**: 1.9 **% Black**: 0.6 **% Hispanic**: 7.9 **% White**: 88.0	National ***Socio-Economic Status*** indicator percentile (100=high): 56th

Jackson County
PHOENIX-TALENT S.D. 4
PO BOX 698 ● PHOENIX OR 97535-0698 ● (541) 535-1517

Grade Span: KG-12 **Schools**: *Regular* 5 ● *Spec Ed* 0 ● *Alt* 0 **Students**: 2,620 **Total Teachers**: 114 **Student/Classroom Teacher Ratio**: 22.7	**Expenditures/Student**: $5,105 **Librarians**: 2.0 1,310 students/librarian **Guidance Counselors**: 3.0 873 students/counselor	**% Amer Indian**: 2.6 **% Asian**: 1.5 **% Black**: 1.0 **% Hispanic**: 10.6 **% White**: 84.3	National ***Socio-Economic Status*** indicator percentile (100=high): 46th

Jefferson County
[MADRAS] **JEFFERSON COUNTY S.D. 509J**
1355 BUFF ST ● MADRAS OR 97741-1543 ● (541) 475-6192 ● http://www.whitebuffalos.net

Grade Span: KG-12 **Schools**: *Regular* 6 ● *Spec Ed* 0 ● *Alt* 0 **Students**: 2,959 **Total Teachers**: 167 **Student/Classroom Teacher Ratio**: 17.5	**Expenditures/Student**: $5,703 **Librarians**: 6.5 455 students/librarian **Guidance Counselors**: 9.0 329 students/counselor	**% Amer Indian**: 40.3 **% Asian**: 0.4 **% Black**: 0.1 **% Hispanic**: 16.2 **% White**: 42.9	National ***Socio-Economic Status*** indicator percentile (100=high): 20th

Josephine County
GRANTS PASS S.D. 7
610 NE A ST ● GRANTS PASS OR 97526-3133 ● (541) 474-5700

Grade Span: KG-12 **Schools**: *Regular* 8 ● *Spec Ed* 0 ● *Alt* 0 **Students**: 4,953 **Total Teachers**: 246 **Student/Classroom Teacher Ratio**: 21.2	**Expenditures/Student**: $4,705 **Librarians**: 4.0 1,238 students/librarian **Guidance Counselors**: 7.0 708 students/counselor	**% Amer Indian**: 1.6 **% Asian**: 1.2 **% Black**: 0.8 **% Hispanic**: 4.6 **% White**: 91.8	National ***Socio-Economic Status*** indicator percentile (100=high): 31st

Josephine County
[MURPHY] **THREE RIVERS S.D.**
PO BOX 160 ● MURPHY OR 97533 ● (541) 862-3111 ● http://www.threerivers.k12.or.us

Grade Span: KG-12 **Schools**: *Regular* 17 ● *Spec Ed* 0 ● *Alt* 1 **Students**: 6,646 **Total Teachers**: 354 **Student/Classroom Teacher Ratio**: 20.3	**Expenditures/Student**: $5,331 **Librarians**: 1.0 6,646 students/librarian **Guidance Counselors**: 10.0 665 students/counselor	**% Amer Indian**: 2.6 **% Asian**: 1.1 **% Black**: 0.8 **% Hispanic**: 3.4 **% White**: 92.0	National ***Socio-Economic Status*** indicator percentile (100=high): 20th

Klamath County
[KLAMATH FALLS] **KLAMATH COUNTY S.D.**
10501 WASHBURN WAY ● KLAMATH FALLS OR 97603-8626 ● (541) 883-5000

Grade Span: KG-12 **Schools**: *Regular* 19 ● *Spec Ed* 0 ● *Alt* 0 **Students**: 7,160 **Total Teachers**: 360 **Student/Classroom Teacher Ratio**: 19.0	**Expenditures/Student**: $5,214 **Librarians**: 0.0 *** students/librarian **Guidance Counselors**: 15.4 465 students/counselor	**% Amer Indian**: 7.0 **% Asian**: 1.3 **% Black**: 2.2 **% Hispanic**: 6.8 **% White**: 82.8	National ***Socio-Economic Status*** indicator percentile (100=high): 31st

Lane County

[COTTAGE GROVE] **SOUTH LANE S.D. 45J**

PO BOX 218 ● COTTAGE GROVE OR 97424-0218 ● (541) 942-3381

Grade Span: KG-12 **Schools**: *Regular* 8 ● *Spec Ed* 0 ● *Alt* 0 **Students**: 2,874 **Total Teachers**: 131 **Student/Classroom Teacher Ratio**: 22.9	**Expenditures/Student**: $5,094 **Librarians**: 2.0 1,437 students/librarian **Guidance Counselors**: 5.0 575 students/counselor	**% Amer Indian**: 1.7 **% Asian**: 2.0 **% Black**: 0.3 **% Hispanic**: 4.3 **% White**: 91.7	National ***Socio-Economic Status*** indicator percentile (100=high): 25th

Lane County

[EUGENE] **BETHEL S.D. 52**

4640 BARGER AVE ● EUGENE OR 97402 ● (541) 689-3280 ● http://www.bethel.k12.or.us

Grade Span: KG-12 **Schools**: *Regular* 8 ● *Spec Ed* 0 ● *Alt* 0 **Students**: 4,471 **Total Teachers**: 214 **Student/Classroom Teacher Ratio**: 21.0	**Expenditures/Student**: $5,105 **Librarians**: 0.5 8,942 students/librarian **Guidance Counselors**: 5.0 894 students/counselor	**% Amer Indian**: 0.9 **% Asian**: 1.9 **% Black**: 1.5 **% Hispanic**: 3.9 **% White**: 91.8	National ***Socio-Economic Status*** indicator percentile (100=high): 43rd

Lane County

EUGENE S.D. 4J

200 N MONROE ST ● EUGENE OR 97402-4295 ● (541) 687-3123 ● http://www.4j.lane.edu

Grade Span: KG-12 **Schools**: *Regular* 36 ● *Spec Ed* 0 ● *Alt* 9 **Students**: 18,371 **Total Teachers**: 833 **Student/Classroom Teacher Ratio**: 21.5	**Expenditures/Student**: $5,346 **Librarians**: 13.9 1,322 students/librarian **Guidance Counselors**: 17.2 1,068 students/counselor	**% Amer Indian**: 2.0 **% Asian**: 3.6 **% Black**: 2.3 **% Hispanic**: 3.5 **% White**: 88.6	National ***Socio-Economic Status*** indicator percentile (100=high): 63rd

Lane County

SPRINGFIELD S.D. 19

525 MILL ST ● SPRINGFIELD OR 97477-4598 ● (541) 747-3331 ● http://www.sps.lane.edu

Grade Span: PK-12 **Schools**: *Regular* 21 ● *Spec Ed* 1 ● *Alt* 0 **Students**: 11,270 **Total Teachers**: 557 **Student/Classroom Teacher Ratio**: 20.5	**Expenditures/Student**: $5,157 **Librarians**: 0.8 14,088 students/librarian **Guidance Counselors**: 27.8 405 students/counselor	**% Amer Indian**: 1.8 **% Asian**: 2.3 **% Black**: 1.1 **% Hispanic**: 3.5 **% White**: 91.3	National ***Socio-Economic Status*** indicator percentile (100=high): 45th

Lincoln County

[NEWPORT] **LINCOLN COUNTY S.D.**

PO BOX 1110 ● NEWPORT OR 97365-0088 ● (541) 265-9211 ● http://www.lincoln.k12.or.us

Grade Span: KG-12 **Schools**: *Regular* 17 ● *Spec Ed* 0 ● *Alt* 1 **Students**: 7,131 **Total Teachers**: 361 **Student/Classroom Teacher Ratio**: 20.1	**Expenditures/Student**: $5,801 **Librarians**: 15.0 475 students/librarian **Guidance Counselors**: 16.0 446 students/counselor	**% Amer Indian**: 7.2 **% Asian**: 1.6 **% Black**: 0.9 **% Hispanic**: 2.8 **% White**: 87.4	National ***Socio-Economic Status*** indicator percentile (100=high): 45th

Linn County

[ALBANY] **GREATER ALBANY S.D. 8J**

718 SW 7TH ST ● ALBANY OR 97321-2399 ● (541) 967-4501 ● http://www.albany.k12.or.us

Grade Span: KG-12 **Schools**: *Regular* 19 ● *Spec Ed* 0 ● *Alt* 0 **Students**: 7,707 **Total Teachers**: 362 **Student/Classroom Teacher Ratio**: 21.3	**Expenditures/Student**: $5,161 **Librarians**: 11.6 664 students/librarian **Guidance Counselors**: 21.9 352 students/counselor	**% Amer Indian**: 1.5 **% Asian**: 1.8 **% Black**: 0.6 **% Hispanic**: 4.2 **% White**: 91.9	National ***Socio-Economic Status*** indicator percentile (100=high): 54th

Linn County
LEBANON COMMUNITY S.D. 9
485 S FIFTH ST ● LEBANON OR 97355 ● (541) 451-1250 ● http://lcsd.skipnet.com

Grade Span: KG-12 **Schools**: *Regular* 14 ● *Spec Ed* 0 ● *Alt* 0 **Students**: 4,567 **Total Teachers**: 238 **Student/Classroom Teacher Ratio**: 18.8	**Expenditures/Student**: $5,716 **Librarians**: 5.5 830 students/librarian **Guidance Counselors**: 13.4 341 students/counselor	**% Amer Indian**: 0.9 **% Asian**: 0.9 **% Black**: 0.3 **% Hispanic**: 3.3 **% White**: 94.6	National ***Socio-Economic Status*** indicator percentile (100=high): 49th

Linn County
SWEET HOME S.D. 55
1920 LONG ST ● SWEET HOME OR 97386-2395 ● (541) 367-6111

Grade Span: KG-12 **Schools**: *Regular* 8 ● *Spec Ed* 0 ● *Alt* 0 **Students**: 2,528 **Total Teachers**: 121 **Student/Classroom Teacher Ratio**: 23.0	**Expenditures/Student**: $5,304 **Librarians**: 1.0 2,528 students/librarian **Guidance Counselors**: 6.0 421 students/counselor	**% Amer Indian**: 0.5 **% Asian**: 1.7 **% Black**: 0.2 **% Hispanic**: 2.5 **% White**: 95.1	National ***Socio-Economic Status*** indicator percentile (100=high): 41st

Malheur County
ONTARIO S.D. 8
195 SW 3RD AVE ● ONTARIO OR 97914-2786 ● (541) 889-5374 ● http://www.ontariosd.k12.or.us/index.html

Grade Span: KG-12 **Schools**: *Regular* 8 ● *Spec Ed* 0 ● *Alt* 0 **Students**: 2,797 **Total Teachers**: 158 **Student/Classroom Teacher Ratio**: 18.1	**Expenditures/Student**: $5,769 **Librarians**: 4.0 699 students/librarian **Guidance Counselors**: 7.0 400 students/counselor	**% Amer Indian**: 1.1 **% Asian**: 2.8 **% Black**: 1.0 **% Hispanic**: 34.2 **% White**: 61.0	National ***Socio-Economic Status*** indicator percentile (100=high): 27th

Marion County
SALEM-KEIZER S.D. 24J
PO BOX 12024 ● SALEM OR 97309-0024 ● (503) 399-3000 ● http://www.salkeiz.k12.or.us

Grade Span: KG-12 **Schools**: *Regular* 52 ● *Spec Ed* 0 ● *Alt* 0 **Students**: 31,364 **Total Teachers**: 1,353 **Student/Classroom Teacher Ratio**: 24.8	**Expenditures/Student**: $5,565 **Librarians**: 44.6 703 students/librarian **Guidance Counselors**: 75.5 415 students/counselor	**% Amer Indian**: 1.4 **% Asian**: 2.5 **% Black**: 1.2 **% Hispanic**: 10.7 **% White**: 84.1	National ***Socio-Economic Status*** indicator percentile (100=high): 61st

Marion County
WOODBURN S.D. 103
965 N BOONES FERRY RD ● WOODBURN OR 97071-9602 ● (503) 981-9555

Grade Span: KG-12 **Schools**: *Regular* 5 ● *Spec Ed* 0 ● *Alt* 0 **Students**: 3,289 **Total Teachers**: 194 **Student/Classroom Teacher Ratio**: 17.2	**Expenditures/Student**: $5,980 **Librarians**: 5.0 658 students/librarian **Guidance Counselors**: 8.0 411 students/counselor	**% Amer Indian**: 0.2 **% Asian**: 0.3 **% Black**: 0.4 **% Hispanic**: 55.1 **% White**: 44.0	National ***Socio-Economic Status*** indicator percentile (100=high): 5th

Multnomah County
GRESHAM-BARLOW S.D. 10J
1331 NW EASTMAN PKWY ● GRESHAM OR 97030-3825 ● (503) 661-3000 ● http://district.gresham.k12.or.us

Grade Span: KG-12 **Schools**: *Regular* 17 ● *Spec Ed* 0 ● *Alt* 0 **Students**: 10,991 **Total Teachers**: 510 **Student/Classroom Teacher Ratio**: 20.9	**Expenditures/Student**: $5,088 **Librarians**: 11.8 931 students/librarian **Guidance Counselors**: 26.9 409 students/counselor	**% Amer Indian**: 0.6 **% Asian**: 2.8 **% Black**: 1.4 **% Hispanic**: 3.3 **% White**: 92.0	National ***Socio-Economic Status*** indicator percentile (100=high): 74th

Multnomah County

[PORTLAND] **CENTENNIAL S.D. 28J**

18135 SE BROOKLYN ST ● PORTLAND OR 97236-1099 ● (503) 760-7990

Grade Span: KG-12 **Schools**: *Regular* 8 ● *Spec Ed* 0 ● *Alt* 0 **Students**: 5,583 **Total Teachers**: 283 **Student/Classroom Teacher Ratio**: 19.4	**Expenditures/Student**: $5,167 **Librarians**: 8.0 698 students/librarian **Guidance Counselors**: 13.8 405 students/counselor	**% Amer Indian**: 0.5 **% Asian**: 5.9 **% Black**: 1.8 **% Hispanic**: 3.5 **% White**: 88.3	National ***Socio-Economic Status*** indicator percentile (100=high): 57th

Multnomah County

[PORTLAND] **DAVID DOUGLAS S.D. 40**

1500 SE 130TH AVE ● PORTLAND OR 97233-1799 ● (503) 252-2900 ● http://www.ddouglas.k12.or.us

Grade Span: KG-12 **Schools**: *Regular* 11 ● *Spec Ed* 0 ● *Alt* 1 **Students**: 7,152 **Total Teachers**: 367 **Student/Classroom Teacher Ratio**: 20.5	**Expenditures/Student**: $5,380 **Librarians**: 11.0 650 students/librarian **Guidance Counselors**: 17.0 421 students/counselor	**% Amer Indian**: 1.7 **% Asian**: 7.0 **% Black**: 2.2 **% Hispanic**: 3.9 **% White**: 85.2	National ***Socio-Economic Status*** indicator percentile (100=high): 41st

Multnomah County

[PORTLAND] **PARKROSE S.D. 3**

10636 NE PRESCOTT ST ● PORTLAND OR 97220-2699 ● (503) 257-5200 ● http://www.parkrose.k12.or.us

Grade Span: KG-12 **Schools**: *Regular* 6 ● *Spec Ed* 0 ● *Alt* 0 **Students**: 3,285 **Total Teachers**: 148 **Student/Classroom Teacher Ratio**: 21.0	**Expenditures/Student**: $5,809 **Librarians**: 6.0 548 students/librarian **Guidance Counselors**: 10.6 310 students/counselor	**% Amer Indian**: 0.7 **% Asian**: 12.1 **% Black**: 5.1 **% Hispanic**: 3.6 **% White**: 78.4	National ***Socio-Economic Status*** indicator percentile (100=high): 60th

Multnomah County

PORTLAND S.D. 1J

PO BOX 3107 ● PORTLAND OR 97208-3107 ● (503) 249-2000 ● http://www.pps.k12.or.us

Grade Span: PK-12 **Schools**: *Regular* 89 ● *Spec Ed* 4 ● *Alt* 8 **Students**: 55,130 **Total Teachers**: 3,073 **Student/Classroom Teacher Ratio**: 20.1	**Expenditures/Student**: $6,288 **Librarians**: 45.6 1,209 students/librarian **Guidance Counselors**: 193.0 286 students/counselor	**% Amer Indian**: 2.2 **% Asian**: 8.9 **% Black**: 16.1 **% Hispanic**: 5.2 **% White**: 67.5	National ***Socio-Economic Status*** indicator percentile (100=high): na

Multnomah County

[TROUTDALE] **REYNOLDS S.D. 7**

1424 NE 201ST AVE ● TROUTDALE OR 97060-2499 ● (503) 661-7200 ● http://www.reynolds.k12.or.us

Grade Span: KG-12 **Schools**: *Regular* 12 ● *Spec Ed* 1 ● *Alt* 1 **Students**: 7,907 **Total Teachers**: 375 **Student/Classroom Teacher Ratio**: 21.8	**Expenditures/Student**: $5,236 **Librarians**: 12.0 659 students/librarian **Guidance Counselors**: 17.0 465 students/counselor	**% Amer Indian**: 0.7 **% Asian**: 3.3 **% Black**: 3.0 **% Hispanic**: 7.5 **% White**: 85.5	National ***Socio-Economic Status*** indicator percentile (100=high): 58th

Polk County

DALLAS S.D. 2

111 SW ASH ST ● DALLAS OR 97338-2299 ● (503) 623-5594

Grade Span: KG-12 **Schools**: *Regular* 9 ● *Spec Ed* 0 ● *Alt* 1 **Students**: 3,106 **Total Teachers**: 166 **Student/Classroom Teacher Ratio**: 19.5	**Expenditures/Student**: $5,062 **Librarians**: 5.0 621 students/librarian **Guidance Counselors**: 9.8 317 students/counselor	**% Amer Indian**: 2.1 **% Asian**: 1.6 **% Black**: 0.8 **% Hispanic**: 3.7 **% White**: 91.8	National ***Socio-Economic Status*** indicator percentile (100=high): 66th

Polk County
[INDEPENDENCE] **CENTRAL S.D. 13J**
1610 MONMOUTH ST ● INDEPENDENCE OR 97351-1096 ● (503) 838-0030

Grade Span: KG-12	**Expenditures/Student**: $5,444	**% Amer Indian**: 0.3	
Schools: *Regular* 6 ● *Spec Ed* 0 ● *Alt* 1	**Librarians**: 2.0	**% Asian**: 2.0	National ***Socio-Economic***
Students: 2,606	1,303 students/librarian	**% Black**: 1.0	***Status*** indicator percentile
Total Teachers: 134	**Guidance Counselors**: 7.0	**% Hispanic**: 24.0	(100=high): 33rd
Student/Classroom Teacher Ratio: 19.3	372 students/counselor	**% White**: 72.7	

Umatilla County
HERMISTON S.D. 8
341 NE 3RD ST ● HERMISTON OR 97838-1890 ● (541) 567-5574

Grade Span: KG-12	**Expenditures/Student**: $4,927	**% Amer Indian**: 0.6	
Schools: *Regular* 6 ● *Spec Ed* 0 ● *Alt* 0	**Librarians**: 7.0	**% Asian**: 1.4	National ***Socio-Economic***
Students: 3,730	533 students/librarian	**% Black**: 0.8	***Status*** indicator percentile
Total Teachers: 202	**Guidance Counselors**: 13.0	**% Hispanic**: 23.5	(100=high): 37th
Student/Classroom Teacher Ratio: 19.1	287 students/counselor	**% White**: 73.8	

Umatilla County
PENDLETON S.D. 16
1207 SW FRAZER ● PENDLETON OR 97801-2899 ● (541) 276-6711

Grade Span: KG-12	**Expenditures/Student**: $5,098	**% Amer Indian**: 9.9	
Schools: *Regular* 8 ● *Spec Ed* 0 ● *Alt* 0	**Librarians**: 5.5	**% Asian**: 1.0	National ***Socio-Economic***
Students: 3,659	665 students/librarian	**% Black**: 0.8	***Status*** indicator percentile
Total Teachers: 191	**Guidance Counselors**: 10.0	**% Hispanic**: 4.2	(100=high): 55th
Student/Classroom Teacher Ratio: 20.5	366 students/counselor	**% White**: 84.0	

Union County
LA GRANDE S.D. 1
2802 ADAMS AVE ● LA GRANDE OR 97850-2179 ● (541) 963-1902

Grade Span: KG-12	**Expenditures/Student**: $4,960	**% Amer Indian**: 0.5	
Schools: *Regular* 8 ● *Spec Ed* 1 ● *Alt* 0	**Librarians**: 4.0	**% Asian**: 1.7	National ***Socio-Economic***
Students: 2,775	694 students/librarian	**% Black**: 0.7	***Status*** indicator percentile
Total Teachers: 161	**Guidance Counselors**: 7.0	**% Hispanic**: 1.8	(100=high): 52nd
Student/Classroom Teacher Ratio: 17.0	396 students/counselor	**% White**: 95.4	

Washington County
[ALOHA] **REEDVILLE S.D. 29**
2425 SW 219TH AVE ● ALOHA OR 97123-6699 ● (503) 649-1622

Grade Span: KG-06	**Expenditures/Student**: $4,351	**% Amer Indian**: 0.2	
Schools: *Regular* 6 ● *Spec Ed* 0 ● *Alt* 0	**Librarians**: 3.0	**% Asian**: 8.8	National ***Socio-Economic***
Students: 2,505	835 students/librarian	**% Black**: 1.2	***Status*** indicator percentile
Total Teachers: 106	**Guidance Counselors**: 3.0	**% Hispanic**: 4.9	(100=high): 71st
Student/Classroom Teacher Ratio: 23.4	835 students/counselor	**% White**: 85.0	

Washington County
BEAVERTON S.D. 48J
16550 SW MERLO RD ● BEAVERTON OR 97075 ● (503) 591-8000 ● http://www.beavton.k12.or.us

Grade Span: KG-12	**Expenditures/Student**: $4,764	**% Amer Indian**: 0.7	
Schools: *Regular* 40 ● *Spec Ed* 0 ● *Alt* 2	**Librarians**: 41.3	**% Asian**: 9.8	National ***Socio-Economic***
Students: 29,025	703 students/librarian	**% Black**: 2.0	***Status*** indicator percentile
Total Teachers: 1,301	**Guidance Counselors**: 52.7	**% Hispanic**: 5.7	(100=high): 80th
Student/Classroom Teacher Ratio: 22.3	551 students/counselor	**% White**: 81.8	

Washington County

FOREST GROVE S.D. 15

1343 PACIFIC AVE ● FOREST GROVE OR 97116 ● (503) 357-6171

Grade Span: KG-12 **Schools**: *Regular* 9 ● *Spec Ed* 0 ● *Alt* 0 **Students**: 4,842 **Total Teachers**: 240 **Student/Classroom Teacher Ratio**: 21.0	**Expenditures/Student**: $5,516 **Librarians**: 3.0 1,614 students/librarian **Guidance Counselors**: 10.0 484 students/counselor	**% Amer Indian**: 0.2 **% Asian**: 1.8 **% Black**: 0.6 **% Hispanic**: 21.1 **% White**: 76.3	National ***Socio-Economic Status*** indicator percentile (100=high): 37th

Washington County

HILLSBORO S.D. 7

215 SE 6TH AVE ● HILLSBORO OR 97123-4108 ● (503) 648-1126 ● http://www.hsd.k12.or.us

Grade Span: KG-06 **Schools**: *Regular* 9 ● *Spec Ed* 0 ● *Alt* 0 **Students**: 4,710 **Total Teachers**: 216 **Student/Classroom Teacher Ratio**: 21.9	**Expenditures/Student**: $4,889 **Librarians**: 4.5 1,047 students/librarian **Guidance Counselors**: 9.0 523 students/counselor	**% Amer Indian**: 0.5 **% Asian**: 2.3 **% Black**: 1.2 **% Hispanic**: 22.9 **% White**: 73.1	National ***Socio-Economic Status*** indicator percentile (100=high): 41st

Washington County

HILLSBORO UNION HIGH S.D. 3J

759 SE WASHINGTON ● HILLSBORO OR 97123 ● (503) 640-4604

Grade Span: 07-12 **Schools**: *Regular* 6 ● *Spec Ed* 0 ● *Alt* 0 **Students**: 6,615 **Total Teachers**: 330 **Student/Classroom Teacher Ratio**: 20.5	**Expenditures/Student**: $6,059 **Librarians**: 6.0 1,103 students/librarian **Guidance Counselors**: 20.0 331 students/counselor	**% Amer Indian**: 0.9 **% Asian**: 4.4 **% Black**: 1.0 **% Hispanic**: 12.5 **% White**: 81.1	National ***Socio-Economic Status*** indicator percentile (100=high): 71st

Washington County

TIGARD-TUALATIN S.D. 23J

13137 SW PACIFIC HWY ● TIGARD OR 97223 ● (503) 620-1620 ● http://www.ttsd.k12.or.us

Grade Span: KG-12 **Schools**: *Regular* 14 ● *Spec Ed* 0 ● *Alt* 0 **Students**: 10,586 **Total Teachers**: 519 **Student/Classroom Teacher Ratio**: 20.6	**Expenditures/Student**: $5,223 **Librarians**: 13.0 814 students/librarian **Guidance Counselors**: 27.5 385 students/counselor	**% Amer Indian**: 0.3 **% Asian**: 4.7 **% Black**: 1.2 **% Hispanic**: 5.2 **% White**: 88.7	National ***Socio-Economic Status*** indicator percentile (100=high): 80th

Yamhill County

MCMINNVILLE S.D. 40

1500 N BAKER ST ● MCMINNVILLE OR 97128-3004 ● (503) 434-6551 ● http://www.teleport.com/~lsimmons

Grade Span: KG-12 **Schools**: *Regular* 9 ● *Spec Ed* 0 ● *Alt* 0 **Students**: 4,947 **Total Teachers**: 227 **Student/Classroom Teacher Ratio**: 20.8	**Expenditures/Student**: $4,822 **Librarians**: 7.5 660 students/librarian **Guidance Counselors**: 12.5 396 students/counselor	**% Amer Indian**: 0.3 **% Asian**: 1.4 **% Black**: 0.5 **% Hispanic**: 13.0 **% White**: 84.8	National ***Socio-Economic Status*** indicator percentile (100=high): 54th

Yamhill County

NEWBERG S.D. 29J

714 E SIXTH ST ● NEWBERG OR 97132-3406 ● (503) 538-8361

Grade Span: KG-12 **Schools**: *Regular* 6 ● *Spec Ed* 0 ● *Alt* 0 **Students**: 4,694 **Total Teachers**: 181 **Student/Classroom Teacher Ratio**: 21.3	**Expenditures/Student**: $4,863 **Librarians**: 6.0 782 students/librarian **Guidance Counselors**: 11.3 415 students/counselor	**% Amer Indian**: 0.6 **% Asian**: 1.1 **% Black**: 1.5 **% Hispanic**: 5.9 **% White**: 91.0	National ***Socio-Economic Status*** indicator percentile (100=high): 72nd

Adams County

GETTYSBURG AREA S.D.

900 BIGLERVILLE ROAD ● GETTYSBURG PA 17325-8007 ● (717) 334-6254

Grade Span: KG-12	**Expenditures/Student**: $5,796	**% Amer Indian**: 0.2	National ***Socio-Economic Status*** indicator percentiles are not available for the state of Pennsylvania
Schools: *Regular* 6 ● *Spec Ed* 0 ● *Alt* 0	**Librarians**: 4.0	**% Asian**: 1.4	
Students: 3,731	933 students/librarian	**% Black**: 4.8	
Total Teachers: 207	**Guidance Counselors**: 6.0	**% Hispanic**: 4.7	
Student/Classroom Teacher Ratio: 19.0	622 students/counselor	**% White**: 88.9	

Adams County

[NEW OXFORD] CONEWAGO VALLEY S.D.

130 BERLIN ROAD ● NEW OXFORD PA 17350-1298 ● (717) 624-2157

Grade Span: KG-12	**Expenditures/Student**: $5,184	**% Amer Indian**: 0.1	National ***Socio-Economic Status*** indicator percentiles are not available for the state of Pennsylvania
Schools: *Regular* 4 ● *Spec Ed* 0 ● *Alt* 0	**Librarians**: 4.0	**% Asian**: 0.3	
Students: 3,202	801 students/librarian	**% Black**: 0.5	
Total Teachers: 149	**Guidance Counselors**: 4.0	**% Hispanic**: 2.8	
Student/Classroom Teacher Ratio: 22.3	801 students/counselor	**% White**: 96.2	

Allegheny County

[ALLISON PARK] HAMPTON TOWNSHIP S.D.

4482 MOUNT ROYAL BOULEVARD ● ALLISON PARK PA 15101-2697 ● (412) 486-6000 ● http://www.htsd.k12.pa.us

Grade Span: KG-12	**Expenditures/Student**: $6,601	**% Amer Indian**: 0.0	National ***Socio-Economic Status*** indicator percentiles are not available for the state of Pennsylvania
Schools: *Regular* 5 ● *Spec Ed* 0 ● *Alt* 0	**Librarians**: 5.0	**% Asian**: 1.6	
Students: 3,120	624 students/librarian	**% Black**: 0.4	
Total Teachers: 179	**Guidance Counselors**: 6.0	**% Hispanic**: 0.4	
Student/Classroom Teacher Ratio: 17.6	520 students/counselor	**% White**: 97.7	

Allegheny County

BETHEL PARK S.D.

301 CHURCH ROAD ● BETHEL PARK PA 15102-1696 ● (412) 833-5000 ● http://bpsd.k12.pa.us

Grade Span: KG-12	**Expenditures/Student**: $7,410	**% Amer Indian**: 0.1	National ***Socio-Economic Status*** indicator percentiles are not available for the state of Pennsylvania
Schools: *Regular* 8 ● *Spec Ed* 0 ● *Alt* 0	**Librarians**: 7.0	**% Asian**: 1.4	
Students: 4,982	712 students/librarian	**% Black**: 1.5	
Total Teachers: 309	**Guidance Counselors**: 8.0	**% Hispanic**: 0.4	
Student/Classroom Teacher Ratio: 17.3	623 students/counselor	**% White**: 96.5	

Allegheny County

[CORAOPOLIS] MONTOUR S.D.

90 GRANT STREET ● CORAOPOLIS PA 15108-3610 ● (412) 778-1060

Grade Span: KG-12	**Expenditures/Student**: $8,607	**% Amer Indian**: 0.1	National ***Socio-Economic Status*** indicator percentiles are not available for the state of Pennsylvania
Schools: *Regular* 5 ● *Spec Ed* 0 ● *Alt* 0	**Librarians**: 5.0	**% Asian**: 0.6	
Students: 3,343	669 students/librarian	**% Black**: 0.9	
Total Teachers: 185	**Guidance Counselors**: 9.0	**% Hispanic**: 0.1	
Student/Classroom Teacher Ratio: 19.4	371 students/counselor	**% White**: 98.4	

Allegheny County

ELIZABETH FORWARD S.D.

401 ROCK RUN ROAD ● ELIZABETH PA 15037-2416 ● (412) 751-9413

Grade Span: KG-12	**Expenditures/Student**: $6,468	**% Amer Indian**: 0.0	National ***Socio-Economic Status*** indicator percentiles are not available for the state of Pennsylvania
Schools: *Regular* 6 ● *Spec Ed* 0 ● *Alt* 0	**Librarians**: 3.0	**% Asian**: 0.7	
Students: 3,015	1,005 students/librarian	**% Black**: 2.4	
Total Teachers: 155	**Guidance Counselors**: 3.0	**% Hispanic**: 0.2	
Student/Classroom Teacher Ratio: 21.4	1,005 students/counselor	**% White**: 96.7	

Allegheny County
[GIBSONIA] **PINE-RICHLAND S.D.**
4046 EWALT ROAD ● GIBSONIA PA 15044-9534 ● (412) 443-7276

Grade Span: KG-12 **Schools**: *Regular* 5 ● *Spec Ed* 0 ● *Alt* 0 **Students**: 2,699 **Total Teachers**: 157 **Student/Classroom Teacher Ratio**: 17.9	**Expenditures/Student**: $6,866 **Librarians**: 4.0 675 students/librarian **Guidance Counselors**: 5.0 540 students/counselor	**% Amer Indian**: 0.0 **% Asian**: 0.4 **% Black**: 0.7 **% Hispanic**: 0.4 **% White**: 98.5	National ***Socio-Economic Status*** indicator percentiles are not available for the state of Pennsylvania

Allegheny County
[GLENSHAW] **SHALER AREA S.D.**
1800 MT ROYAL BOULEVARD ● GLENSHAW PA 15116-2196 ● (412) 492-1202 ● http://sasd.k12.pa.us

Grade Span: KG-12 **Schools**: *Regular* 7 ● *Spec Ed* 0 ● *Alt* 0 **Students**: 5,337 **Total Teachers**: 328 **Student/Classroom Teacher Ratio**: 18.0	**Expenditures/Student**: $6,946 **Librarians**: 7.0 762 students/librarian **Guidance Counselors**: 7.0 762 students/counselor	**% Amer Indian**: 0.2 **% Asian**: 0.7 **% Black**: 0.6 **% Hispanic**: 0.1 **% White**: 98.4	National ***Socio-Economic Status*** indicator percentiles are not available for the state of Pennsylvania

Allegheny County
[IMPERIAL] **WEST ALLEGHENY S.D.**
BOX 55 ● IMPERIAL PA 15126-0055 ● (412) 695-3422 ● http://www.westallegheny.k12.pa.us

Grade Span: KG-12 **Schools**: *Regular* 4 ● *Spec Ed* 0 ● *Alt* 0 **Students**: 2,809 **Total Teachers**: 164 **Student/Classroom Teacher Ratio**: 17.3	**Expenditures/Student**: $6,631 **Librarians**: 4.0 702 students/librarian **Guidance Counselors**: 6.0 468 students/counselor	**% Amer Indian**: 0.2 **% Asian**: 0.8 **% Black**: 3.1 **% Hispanic**: 0.4 **% White**: 95.5	National ***Socio-Economic Status*** indicator percentiles are not available for the state of Pennsylvania

Allegheny County
MCKEESPORT AREA S.D.
2225 FIFTH AVENUE ● MCKEESPORT PA 15132-1100 ● (412) 664-3610

Grade Span: KG-12 **Schools**: *Regular* 6 ● *Spec Ed* 0 ● *Alt* 0 **Students**: 5,178 **Total Teachers**: 271 **Student/Classroom Teacher Ratio**: 20.2	**Expenditures/Student**: $6,172 **Librarians**: 7.0 740 students/librarian **Guidance Counselors**: 11.0 471 students/counselor	**% Amer Indian**: 0.3 **% Asian**: 0.2 **% Black**: 27.8 **% Hispanic**: 0.8 **% White**: 71.0	National ***Socio-Economic Status*** indicator percentiles are not available for the state of Pennsylvania

Allegheny County
[MONROEVILLE] **GATEWAY S.D.**
2609 MOSS SIDE BLVD ● MONROEVILLE PA 15146-3379 ● (412) 372-5300

Grade Span: KG-12 **Schools**: *Regular* 8 ● *Spec Ed* 0 ● *Alt* 0 **Students**: 4,442 **Total Teachers**: 289 **Student/Classroom Teacher Ratio**: 15.5	**Expenditures/Student**: $8,377 **Librarians**: 5.0 888 students/librarian **Guidance Counselors**: 9.0 494 students/counselor	**% Amer Indian**: 0.0 **% Asian**: 4.8 **% Black**: 9.2 **% Hispanic**: 0.4 **% White**: 85.6	National ***Socio-Economic Status*** indicator percentiles are not available for the state of Pennsylvania

Allegheny County
[MOON TOWNSHIP] **MOON AREA S.D.**
1407 BEERS SCHOOL ROAD ● MOON TOWNSHIP PA 15108-2597 ● (412) 264-9440

Grade Span: KG-12 **Schools**: *Regular* 6 ● *Spec Ed* 0 ● *Alt* 0 **Students**: 3,395 **Total Teachers**: 213 **Student/Classroom Teacher Ratio**: 16.8	**Expenditures/Student**: $7,937 **Librarians**: 3.0 1,132 students/librarian **Guidance Counselors**: 5.0 679 students/counselor	**% Amer Indian**: 0.0 **% Asian**: 2.2 **% Black**: 4.2 **% Hispanic**: 0.7 **% White**: 92.9	National ***Socio-Economic Status*** indicator percentiles are not available for the state of Pennsylvania

Allegheny County
[NATRONA HEIGHTS] **HIGHLANDS S.D.**
CALIFORNIA & 11TH AVE BOX 288 ● NATRONA HEIGHTS PA 15065-0288 ● (412) 226-2400

Grade Span: PK-12 **Schools**: *Regular* 6 ● *Spec Ed* 0 ● *Alt* 0 **Students**: 3,388 **Total Teachers**: 187 **Student/Classroom Teacher Ratio**: 19.2	**Expenditures/Student**: $6,433 **Librarians**: 3.0 1,129 students/librarian **Guidance Counselors**: 5.0 678 students/counselor	**% Amer Indian**: 0.2 **% Asian**: 0.5 **% Black**: 5.8 **% Hispanic**: 0.5 **% White**: 93.1	National ***Socio-Economic Status*** indicator percentiles are not available for the state of Pennsylvania

Allegheny County
[PITTSBURGH] **BALDWIN-WHITEHALL S.D.**
4900 CURRY ROAD ● PITTSBURGH PA 15236-1898 ● (412) 885-7810 ● http://www.baldwin.k12.pa.us

Grade Span: KG-12 **Schools**: *Regular* 5 ● *Spec Ed* 0 ● *Alt* 0 **Students**: 4,742 **Total Teachers**: 263 **Student/Classroom Teacher Ratio**: 18.4	**Expenditures/Student**: $7,050 **Librarians**: 5.5 862 students/librarian **Guidance Counselors**: 8.0 593 students/counselor	**% Amer Indian**: 0.2 **% Asian**: 0.6 **% Black**: 1.9 **% Hispanic**: 0.3 **% White**: 97.0	National ***Socio-Economic Status*** indicator percentiles are not available for the state of Pennsylvania

Allegheny County
[PITTSBURGH] **CHARTIERS VALLEY S.D.**
2030 SWALLOW HILL ROAD ● PITTSBURGH PA 15220-1699 ● (412) 429-2201 ● http://www.chartiersvalley.k12.pa.us

Grade Span: KG-12 **Schools**: *Regular* 9 ● *Spec Ed* 0 ● *Alt* 0 **Students**: 2,876 **Total Teachers**: 177 **Student/Classroom Teacher Ratio**: 18.8	**Expenditures/Student**: $8,456 **Librarians**: 5.0 575 students/librarian **Guidance Counselors**: 7.0 411 students/counselor	**% Amer Indian**: 0.1 **% Asian**: 1.3 **% Black**: 3.6 **% Hispanic**: 0.1 **% White**: 95.0	National ***Socio-Economic Status*** indicator percentiles are not available for the state of Pennsylvania

Allegheny County
[PITTSBURGH] **FOX CHAPEL AREA S.D.**
611 FIELD CLUB ROAD ● PITTSBURGH PA 15238-2406 ● (412) 963-9600 ● http://www.fcasd.edu

Grade Span: KG-12 **Schools**: *Regular* 6 ● *Spec Ed* 0 ● *Alt* 0 **Students**: 4,231 **Total Teachers**: 302 **Student/Classroom Teacher Ratio**: 14.7	**Expenditures/Student**: $8,921 **Librarians**: 7.0 604 students/librarian **Guidance Counselors**: 11.0 385 students/counselor	**% Amer Indian**: 0.1 **% Asian**: 1.6 **% Black**: 0.8 **% Hispanic**: 0.5 **% White**: 97.1	National ***Socio-Economic Status*** indicator percentiles are not available for the state of Pennsylvania

Allegheny County
[PITTSBURGH] **KEYSTONE OAKS S.D.**
1000 KELTON AVENUE ● PITTSBURGH PA 15216-2487 ● (412) 571-6000 ● http://www.kosd.org

Grade Span: PK-12 **Schools**: *Regular* 7 ● *Spec Ed* 0 ● *Alt* 0 **Students**: 2,904 **Total Teachers**: 181 **Student/Classroom Teacher Ratio**: 16.6	**Expenditures/Student**: $9,019 **Librarians**: 4.0 726 students/librarian **Guidance Counselors**: 7.0 415 students/counselor	**% Amer Indian**: 0.2 **% Asian**: 1.2 **% Black**: 1.5 **% Hispanic**: 0.2 **% White**: 96.8	National ***Socio-Economic Status*** indicator percentiles are not available for the state of Pennsylvania

Allegheny County
[PITTSBURGH] **MT. LEBANON S.D.**
7 HORSMAN DRIVE ● PITTSBURGH PA 15228-1107 ● (412) 344-2077 ● http://www.mtlebanon.k12.pa.us

Grade Span: KG-12 **Schools**: *Regular* 9 ● *Spec Ed* 0 ● *Alt* 0 **Students**: 5,411 **Total Teachers**: 334 **Student/Classroom Teacher Ratio**: 16.9	**Expenditures/Student**: $7,543 **Librarians**: 9.0 601 students/librarian **Guidance Counselors**: 9.0 601 students/counselor	**% Amer Indian**: 0.0 **% Asian**: 2.3 **% Black**: 0.8 **% Hispanic**: 0.5 **% White**: 96.4	National ***Socio-Economic Status*** indicator percentiles are not available for the state of Pennsylvania

Allegheny County
[PITTSBURGH] **NORTH ALLEGHENY S.D.**
200 HILLVUE LANE ● PITTSBURGH PA 15237-5391 ● (412) 366-2100

Grade Span: KG-12 **Schools**: *Regular* 13 ● *Spec Ed* 0 ● *Alt* 0 **Students**: 8,273 **Total Teachers**: 503 **Student/Classroom Teacher Ratio**: 16.7	**Expenditures/Student**: $7,393 **Librarians**: 13.0 636 students/librarian **Guidance Counselors**: 23.0 360 students/counselor	**% Amer Indian**: 0.1 **% Asian**: 2.5 **% Black**: 1.3 **% Hispanic**: 0.4 **% White**: 95.8	National ***Socio-Economic Status*** indicator percentiles are not available for the state of Pennsylvania

Allegheny County
[PITTSBURGH] **NORTH HILLS S.D.**
135 SIXTH AVENUE ● PITTSBURGH PA 15229-1291 ● (412) 367-6000 ● http://www.nhsd.k12.pa.us

Grade Span: KG-12 **Schools**: *Regular* 9 ● *Spec Ed* 0 ● *Alt* 0 **Students**: 4,977 **Total Teachers**: 295 **Student/Classroom Teacher Ratio**: 17.9	**Expenditures/Student**: $7,915 **Librarians**: 10.0 498 students/librarian **Guidance Counselors**: 11.5 433 students/counselor	**% Amer Indian**: 0.1 **% Asian**: 1.4 **% Black**: 1.4 **% Hispanic**: 0.4 **% White**: 96.8	National ***Socio-Economic Status*** indicator percentiles are not available for the state of Pennsylvania

Allegheny County
[PITTSBURGH] **PENN HILLS S.D.**
309 COLLINS DRIVE ● PITTSBURGH PA 15235-3899 ● (412) 793-7000

Grade Span: KG-12 **Schools**: *Regular* 8 ● *Spec Ed* 0 ● *Alt* 0 **Students**: 5,837 **Total Teachers**: 365 **Student/Classroom Teacher Ratio**: 18.0	**Expenditures/Student**: $7,324 **Librarians**: 8.0 730 students/librarian **Guidance Counselors**: 11.0 531 students/counselor	**% Amer Indian**: 0.1 **% Asian**: 0.3 **% Black**: 30.2 **% Hispanic**: 0.1 **% White**: 69.4	National ***Socio-Economic Status*** indicator percentiles are not available for the state of Pennsylvania

Allegheny County
PITTSBURGH S.D.
341 SOUTH BELLEFIELD AVENUE ● PITTSBURGH PA 15213-3585 ● (412) 622-3500 ● http://www.pps.pgh.pa.us/mainframe.html

Grade Span: KG-12 **Schools**: *Regular* 83 ● *Spec Ed* 3 ● *Alt* 0 **Students**: 39,761 **Total Teachers**: 2,674 **Student/Classroom Teacher Ratio**: 17.3	**Expenditures/Student**: $9,124 **Librarians**: 71.0 560 students/librarian **Guidance Counselors**: 75.0 530 students/counselor	**% Amer Indian**: 0.1 **% Asian**: 1.4 **% Black**: 55.2 **% Hispanic**: 0.4 **% White**: 42.9	National ***Socio-Economic Status*** indicator percentiles are not available for the state of Pennsylvania

Allegheny County
[PITTSBURGH] **PLUM BOROUGH S.D.**
200 SCHOOL ROAD ● PITTSBURGH PA 15239-1457 ● (412) 793-1352

Grade Span: KG-12 **Schools**: *Regular* 7 ● *Spec Ed* 0 ● *Alt* 0 **Students**: 4,358 **Total Teachers**: 232 **Student/Classroom Teacher Ratio**: 18.9	**Expenditures/Student**: $5,886 **Librarians**: 3.0 1,453 students/librarian **Guidance Counselors**: 6.0 726 students/counselor	**% Amer Indian**: 0.2 **% Asian**: 0.8 **% Black**: 2.8 **% Hispanic**: 0.2 **% White**: 96.0	National ***Socio-Economic Status*** indicator percentiles are not available for the state of Pennsylvania

Allegheny County
[PITTSBURGH] **UPPER ST. CLAIR S.D.**
1820 MCLUGHLN RN RD UPR ST CLR ● PITTSBURGH PA 15241-2396 ● (412) 833-1604 ● http://www.uscsd.k12.pa.us

Grade Span: KG-12 **Schools**: *Regular* 6 ● *Spec Ed* 0 ● *Alt* 0 **Students**: 3,929 **Total Teachers**: 228 **Student/Classroom Teacher Ratio**: 18.2	**Expenditures/Student**: $7,594 **Librarians**: 8.0 491 students/librarian **Guidance Counselors**: 12.0 327 students/counselor	**% Amer Indian**: 0.0 **% Asian**: 5.3 **% Black**: 1.0 **% Hispanic**: 0.7 **% White**: 93.0	National ***Socio-Economic Status*** indicator percentiles are not available for the state of Pennsylvania

Allegheny County

[PITTSBURGH] **WEST JEFFERSON HILLS S.D.**

PO BOX 18019 PLEASANT HILLS ● PITTSBURGH PA 15236-0019 ● (412) 655-8450

Grade Span: KG-12 **Schools**: *Regular* 5 ● *Spec Ed* 0 ● *Alt* 0 **Students**: 2,920 **Total Teachers**: 149 **Student/Classroom Teacher Ratio**: 19.9	**Expenditures/Student**: $7,084 **Librarians**: 4.0 730 students/librarian **Guidance Counselors**: 3.0 973 students/counselor	**% Amer Indian**: 0.1 **% Asian**: 0.9 **% Black**: 1.8 **% Hispanic**: 0.2 **% White**: 97.0	National ***Socio-Economic Status*** indicator percentiles are not available for the state of Pennsylvania

Allegheny County

[PITTSBURGH] **WOODLAND HILLS S.D.**

2430 GREENSBURG PIKE ● PITTSBURGH PA 15221-3666 ● (412) 731-1300 ● http://www.whsd.k12.pa.us

Grade Span: KG-12 **Schools**: *Regular* 9 ● *Spec Ed* 0 ● *Alt* 0 **Students**: 6,072 **Total Teachers**: 337 **Student/Classroom Teacher Ratio**: 22.0	**Expenditures/Student**: $8,100 **Librarians**: 8.0 759 students/librarian **Guidance Counselors**: 17.0 357 students/counselor	**% Amer Indian**: 0.0 **% Asian**: 0.7 **% Black**: 35.7 **% Hispanic**: 0.4 **% White**: 63.1	National ***Socio-Economic Status*** indicator percentiles are not available for the state of Pennsylvania

Allegheny County

WEST MIFFLIN AREA S.D.

515 CAMP HOLLOW ROAD ● WEST MIFFLIN PA 15122-2697 ● (412) 466-9131

Grade Span: KG-12 **Schools**: *Regular* 6 ● *Spec Ed* 0 ● *Alt* 0 **Students**: 3,007 **Total Teachers**: 158 **Student/Classroom Teacher Ratio**: 21.0	**Expenditures/Student**: $7,945 **Librarians**: 5.0 601 students/librarian **Guidance Counselors**: 5.0 601 students/counselor	**% Amer Indian**: 0.0 **% Asian**: 0.3 **% Black**: 13.3 **% Hispanic**: 0.3 **% White**: 86.1	National ***Socio-Economic Status*** indicator percentiles are not available for the state of Pennsylvania

Armstrong County

[FORD CITY] **ARMSTRONG S.D.**

410 MAIN STREET ● FORD CITY PA 16226-1698 ● (412) 763-7151

Grade Span: KG-12 **Schools**: *Regular* 15 ● *Spec Ed* 0 ● *Alt* 0 **Students**: 7,276 **Total Teachers**: 450 **Student/Classroom Teacher Ratio**: 16.3	**Expenditures/Student**: $6,932 **Librarians**: 14.0 520 students/librarian **Guidance Counselors**: 9.0 808 students/counselor	**% Amer Indian**: 0.0 **% Asian**: 0.1 **% Black**: 0.9 **% Hispanic**: 0.1 **% White**: 99.0	National ***Socio-Economic Status*** indicator percentiles are not available for the state of Pennsylvania

Beaver County

[ALIQUIPPA] **HOPEWELL AREA S.D.**

2121 BRODHEAD ROAD ● ALIQUIPPA PA 15001-4206 ● (412) 375-6691

Grade Span: KG-12 **Schools**: *Regular* 6 ● *Spec Ed* 0 ● *Alt* 0 **Students**: 3,173 **Total Teachers**: 176 **Student/Classroom Teacher Ratio**: 18.4	**Expenditures/Student**: $5,803 **Librarians**: 4.0 793 students/librarian **Guidance Counselors**: 7.0 453 students/counselor	**% Amer Indian**: 0.2 **% Asian**: 0.1 **% Black**: 2.7 **% Hispanic**: 0.1 **% White**: 96.9	National ***Socio-Economic Status*** indicator percentiles are not available for the state of Pennsylvania

Beaver County

AMBRIDGE AREA S.D.

740 PARK ROAD ● AMBRIDGE PA 15003-2513 ● (412) 266-8870

Grade Span: KG-12 **Schools**: *Regular* 7 ● *Spec Ed* 0 ● *Alt* 0 **Students**: 3,471 **Total Teachers**: 192 **Student/Classroom Teacher Ratio**: 18.5	**Expenditures/Student**: $6,284 **Librarians**: 4.0 868 students/librarian **Guidance Counselors**: 6.0 579 students/counselor	**% Amer Indian**: 0.0 **% Asian**: 0.3 **% Black**: 6.6 **% Hispanic**: 0.6 **% White**: 92.5	National ***Socio-Economic Status*** indicator percentiles are not available for the state of Pennsylvania

Beaver County

[BEAVER FALLS] **BLACKHAWK S.D.**

500 BLACKHAWK ROAD ● BEAVER FALLS PA 15010-1498 ● (412) 846-6600 ● http://www.ccia.com/~bhhs2/bhs1.html

Grade Span: KG-12 **Schools**: *Regular* 5 ● *Spec Ed* 0 ● *Alt* 0 **Students**: 3,053 **Total Teachers**: 161 **Student/Classroom Teacher Ratio**: 19.3	**Expenditures/Student**: $5,752 **Librarians**: 3.0 1,018 students/librarian **Guidance Counselors**: 5.0 611 students/counselor	**% Amer Indian**: 0.0 **% Asian**: 0.4 **% Black**: 0.9 **% Hispanic**: 0.2 **% White**: 98.4	National ***Socio-Economic Status*** indicator percentiles are not available for the state of Pennsylvania

Berks County

BOYERTOWN AREA S.D.

911 MONTGOMERY AVE RR 6 BOX 61 ● BOYERTOWN PA 19512-9607 ● (610) 367-6031

Grade Span: KG-12 **Schools**: *Regular* 10 ● *Spec Ed* 0 ● *Alt* 0 **Students**: 6,548 **Total Teachers**: 349 **Student/Classroom Teacher Ratio**: 19.7	**Expenditures/Student**: $5,797 **Librarians**: 9.8 668 students/librarian **Guidance Counselors**: 12.0 546 students/counselor	**% Amer Indian**: 0.1 **% Asian**: 0.7 **% Black**: 1.0 **% Hispanic**: 0.4 **% White**: 97.8	National ***Socio-Economic Status*** indicator percentiles are not available for the state of Pennsylvania

Berks County

[ELVERSON] **TWIN VALLEY S.D.**

RD 3 BOX 52 ● ELVERSON PA 19520-9310 ● (610) 286-8600 ● http://www.chesco.com/~tvms

Grade Span: KG-12 **Schools**: *Regular* 5 ● *Spec Ed* 0 ● *Alt* 0 **Students**: 2,865 **Total Teachers**: 177 **Student/Classroom Teacher Ratio**: 16.9	**Expenditures/Student**: $6,427 **Librarians**: 5.0 573 students/librarian **Guidance Counselors**: 7.6 377 students/counselor	**% Amer Indian**: 0.0 **% Asian**: 0.7 **% Black**: 0.7 **% Hispanic**: 0.4 **% White**: 98.2	National ***Socio-Economic Status*** indicator percentiles are not available for the state of Pennsylvania

Berks County

HAMBURG AREA S.D.

WINDSOR STREET ● HAMBURG PA 19526-0401 ● (610) 562-2241

Grade Span: KG-12 **Schools**: *Regular* 6 ● *Spec Ed* 0 ● *Alt* 0 **Students**: 2,669 **Total Teachers**: 133 **Student/Classroom Teacher Ratio**: 21.3	**Expenditures/Student**: $5,277 **Librarians**: 3.0 890 students/librarian **Guidance Counselors**: 5.0 534 students/counselor	**% Amer Indian**: 0.0 **% Asian**: 0.4 **% Black**: 0.4 **% Hispanic**: 0.7 **% White**: 98.4	National ***Socio-Economic Status*** indicator percentiles are not available for the state of Pennsylvania

Berks County

[READING] **EXETER TOWNSHIP S.D.**

3650 PERKIOMEN AVENUE ● READING PA 19606-2798 ● (610) 779-0700 ● http://www.exetersd.org

Grade Span: KG-12 **Schools**: *Regular* 5 ● *Spec Ed* 0 ● *Alt* 0 **Students**: 3,377 **Total Teachers**: 194 **Student/Classroom Teacher Ratio**: 17.8	**Expenditures/Student**: $6,139 **Librarians**: 5.0 675 students/librarian **Guidance Counselors**: 8.0 422 students/counselor	**% Amer Indian**: 0.2 **% Asian**: 1.2 **% Black**: 1.5 **% Hispanic**: 1.2 **% White**: 95.9	National ***Socio-Economic Status*** indicator percentiles are not available for the state of Pennsylvania

Berks County

[READING] **MUHLENBERG S.D.**

801 BELLEVUE AVENUE LAURELDALE ● READING PA 19605-1799 ● (610) 921-8000 ● http://www.muhlsd.berksiu.k12.pa.us

Grade Span: KG-12 **Schools**: *Regular* 4 ● *Spec Ed* 0 ● *Alt* 0 **Students**: 2,623 **Total Teachers**: 153 **Student/Classroom Teacher Ratio**: 17.6	**Expenditures/Student**: $7,166 **Librarians**: 3.0 874 students/librarian **Guidance Counselors**: 6.0 437 students/counselor	**% Amer Indian**: 0.0 **% Asian**: 0.7 **% Black**: 1.1 **% Hispanic**: 4.3 **% White**: 93.9	National ***Socio-Economic Status*** indicator percentiles are not available for the state of Pennsylvania

Berks County

READING S.D.

800 WASHINGTON STREET ● READING PA 19601-3691 ● (610) 371-5611

Grade Span: PK-12 **Schools**: *Regular* 18 ● *Spec Ed* 0 ● *Alt* 0 **Students**: 14,239 **Total Teachers**: 736 **Student/Classroom Teacher Ratio**: 22.3	**Expenditures/Student**: $6,226 **Librarians**: 17.0 838 students/librarian **Guidance Counselors**: 31.0 459 students/counselor	**% Amer Indian**: 0.0 **% Asian**: 1.4 **% Black**: 14.6 **% Hispanic**: 44.4 **% White**: 39.6	National ***Socio-Economic Status*** indicator percentiles are not available for the state of Pennsylvania

Berks County

[ROBESONIA] **CONRAD WEISER AREA S.D.**

347 EAST PENN AVENUE ● ROBESONIA PA 19551-8948 ● (610) 693-8545

Grade Span: KG-12 **Schools**: *Regular* 3 ● *Spec Ed* 0 ● *Alt* 0 **Students**: 2,550 **Total Teachers**: 148 **Student/Classroom Teacher Ratio**: 17.9	**Expenditures/Student**: $6,222 **Librarians**: 4.0 638 students/librarian **Guidance Counselors**: 6.0 425 students/counselor	**% Amer Indian**: 0.2 **% Asian**: 0.5 **% Black**: 1.5 **% Hispanic**: 0.7 **% White**: 97.1	National ***Socio-Economic Status*** indicator percentiles are not available for the state of Pennsylvania

Berks County

[SHILLINGTON] **GOVERNOR MIFFLIN S.D.**

10 SOUTH WAVERLY ST BOX C750 ● SHILLINGTON PA 19607-0075 ● (610) 775-1461 ● http://www.gmsd.k12.pa.us

Grade Span: KG-12 **Schools**: *Regular* 5 ● *Spec Ed* 0 ● *Alt* 0 **Students**: 4,163 **Total Teachers**: 234 **Student/Classroom Teacher Ratio**: 18.2	**Expenditures/Student**: $6,045 **Librarians**: 5.0 833 students/librarian **Guidance Counselors**: 10.0 416 students/counselor	**% Amer Indian**: 0.0 **% Asian**: 1.5 **% Black**: 1.6 **% Hispanic**: 1.3 **% White**: 95.6	National ***Socio-Economic Status*** indicator percentiles are not available for the state of Pennsylvania

Berks County

[WEST LAWN] **WILSON S.D.**

2601 GRANDVIEW BOULEVARD ● WEST LAWN PA 19609-1324 ● (610) 670-0180

Grade Span: KG-12 **Schools**: *Regular* 10 ● *Spec Ed* 0 ● *Alt* 0 **Students**: 4,317 **Total Teachers**: 240 **Student/Classroom Teacher Ratio**: 19.9	**Expenditures/Student**: $6,549 **Librarians**: 7.0 617 students/librarian **Guidance Counselors**: 12.0 360 students/counselor	**% Amer Indian**: 0.1 **% Asian**: 2.0 **% Black**: 1.8 **% Hispanic**: 2.2 **% White**: 93.8	National ***Socio-Economic Status*** indicator percentiles are not available for the state of Pennsylvania

Blair County

ALTOONA AREA S.D.

1415 SIXTH AVENUE ● ALTOONA PA 16602-3691 ● (814) 946-8211 ● http://cat99.altoona.k12.pa.us/AASD/AASD.HTM

Grade Span: PK-12 **Schools**: *Regular* 14 ● *Spec Ed* 0 ● *Alt* 0 **Students**: 9,567 **Total Teachers**: 470 **Student/Classroom Teacher Ratio**: 21.7	**Expenditures/Student**: $5,323 **Librarians**: 7.0 1,367 students/librarian **Guidance Counselors**: 15.0 638 students/counselor	**% Amer Indian**: 0.1 **% Asian**: 0.4 **% Black**: 3.8 **% Hispanic**: 0.4 **% White**: 95.4	National ***Socio-Economic Status*** indicator percentiles are not available for the state of Pennsylvania

Blair County

HOLLIDAYSBURG AREA S.D.

201-15 JACKSON STREET ● HOLLIDAYSBURG PA 16648-1698 ● (814) 695-8702

Grade Span: KG-12 **Schools**: *Regular* 6 ● *Spec Ed* 0 ● *Alt* 0 **Students**: 4,130 **Total Teachers**: 222 **Student/Classroom Teacher Ratio**: 18.9	**Expenditures/Student**: $5,586 **Librarians**: 4.0 1,033 students/librarian **Guidance Counselors**: 9.0 459 students/counselor	**% Amer Indian**: 0.0 **% Asian**: 1.0 **% Black**: 0.9 **% Hispanic**: 0.2 **% White**: 97.9	National ***Socio-Economic Status*** indicator percentiles are not available for the state of Pennsylvania

Bradford County

ATHENS AREA S.D.

204 WILLOW STREET ● ATHENS PA 18810-1298 ● (717) 888-7766 ● http://www.cyber-quest.com/aahs

Grade Span: KG-12 **Schools**: *Regular* 8 ● *Spec Ed* 0 ● *Alt* 0 **Students**: 2,697 **Total Teachers**: 175 **Student/Classroom Teacher Ratio**: 16.7	**Expenditures/Student**: $5,708 **Librarians**: 5.0 539 students/librarian **Guidance Counselors**: 4.0 674 students/counselor	**% Amer Indian**: 0.2 **% Asian**: 0.8 **% Black**: 0.7 **% Hispanic**: 0.4 **% White**: 97.9	National ***Socio-Economic Status*** indicator percentiles are not available for the state of Pennsylvania

Bucks County

BENSALEM TOWNSHIP S.D.

3000 DONALLEN DRIVE ● BENSALEM PA 19020-1898 ● (215) 750-2810 ● http://www.bciu.k12.pa.us/bensalem/bensalemhome.html

Grade Span: KG-12 **Schools**: *Regular* 10 ● *Spec Ed* 0 ● *Alt* 0 **Students**: 7,854 **Total Teachers**: 405 **Student/Classroom Teacher Ratio**: 19.8	**Expenditures/Student**: $7,741 **Librarians**: 10.0 785 students/librarian **Guidance Counselors**: 18.0 436 students/counselor	**% Amer Indian**: 0.2 **% Asian**: 6.2 **% Black**: 10.7 **% Hispanic**: 2.9 **% White**: 80.0	National ***Socio-Economic Status*** indicator percentiles are not available for the state of Pennsylvania

Bucks County

[DOYLESTOWN] **CENTRAL BUCKS S.D.**

16 WELDON DRIVE ● DOYLESTOWN PA 18901-2359 ● (215) 345-1400

Grade Span: KG-12 **Schools**: *Regular* 17 ● *Spec Ed* 0 ● *Alt* 0 **Students**: 13,284 **Total Teachers**: 615 **Student/Classroom Teacher Ratio**: 22.2	**Expenditures/Student**: $6,474 **Librarians**: 10.0 1,328 students/librarian **Guidance Counselors**: 28.0 474 students/counselor	**% Amer Indian**: 0.1 **% Asian**: 1.7 **% Black**: 1.7 **% Hispanic**: 0.7 **% White**: 95.8	National ***Socio-Economic Status*** indicator percentiles are not available for the state of Pennsylvania

Bucks County

[FALLSINGTON] **PENNSBURY S.D.**

134 YARDLEY AVENUE BOX 338 ● FALLSINGTON PA 19058-0338 ● (215) 428-4100

Grade Span: KG-12 **Schools**: *Regular* 14 ● *Spec Ed* 0 ● *Alt* 0 **Students**: 11,115 **Total Teachers**: 618 **Student/Classroom Teacher Ratio**: 18.5	**Expenditures/Student**: $7,771 **Librarians**: 13.0 855 students/librarian **Guidance Counselors**: 23.0 483 students/counselor	**% Amer Indian**: 0.4 **% Asian**: 2.0 **% Black**: 4.2 **% Hispanic**: 1.0 **% White**: 92.4	National ***Socio-Economic Status*** indicator percentiles are not available for the state of Pennsylvania

Bucks County

[LANGHORNE] **NESHAMINY S.D.**

2001 OLD LINCOLN HIGHWAY ● LANGHORNE PA 19047-3295 ● (215) 752-6300

Grade Span: KG-12 **Schools**: *Regular* 14 ● *Spec Ed* 0 ● *Alt* 0 **Students**: 10,178 **Total Teachers**: 616 **Student/Classroom Teacher Ratio**: 17.8	**Expenditures/Student**: $8,085 **Librarians**: 15.0 679 students/librarian **Guidance Counselors**: 23.0 443 students/counselor	**% Amer Indian**: 0.1 **% Asian**: 1.8 **% Black**: 2.5 **% Hispanic**: 0.6 **% White**: 95.0	National ***Socio-Economic Status*** indicator percentiles are not available for the state of Pennsylvania

Bucks County

[LEVITTOWN] **BRISTOL TOWNSHIP S.D.**

6401 MILL CREEK ROAD ● LEVITTOWN PA 19057-4014 ● (215) 943-3200 ● http://www.bciu.k12.pa.us/BRISTTWP/BRISTTWPHOME.HTML

Grade Span: KG-12 **Schools**: *Regular* 12 ● *Spec Ed* 0 ● *Alt* 0 **Students**: 7,965 **Total Teachers**: 456 **Student/Classroom Teacher Ratio**: 18.4	**Expenditures/Student**: $7,364 **Librarians**: 13.0 613 students/librarian **Guidance Counselors**: 11.0 724 students/counselor	**% Amer Indian**: 0.1 **% Asian**: 2.3 **% Black**: 13.6 **% Hispanic**: 3.5 **% White**: 80.5	National ***Socio-Economic Status*** indicator percentiles are not available for the state of Pennsylvania

Bucks County

[PERKASIE] **PENNRIDGE S.D.**

1506 NORTH 5TH STREET ● PERKASIE PA 18944-2295 ● (215) 257-5016

Grade Span: KG-12	**Expenditures/Student**: $6,789	**% Amer Indian**: 0.1	National ***Socio-Economic Status*** indicator percentiles are not available for the state of Pennsylvania
Schools: *Regular* 10 ● *Spec Ed* 0 ● *Alt* 0	**Librarians**: 10.0	**% Asian**: 0.8	
Students: 6,594	659 students/librarian	**% Black**: 1.5	
Total Teachers: 343	**Guidance Counselors**: 14.0	**% Hispanic**: 1.3	
Student/Classroom Teacher Ratio: 20.6	471 students/counselor	**% White**: 96.3	

Bucks County

QUAKERTOWN COMMUNITY S.D.

600 PARK AVENUE ● QUAKERTOWN PA 18951-1588 ● (215) 538-5010 ● http://www.qcsd.org

Grade Span: KG-12	**Expenditures/Student**: $7,230	**% Amer Indian**: 0.3	National ***Socio-Economic Status*** indicator percentiles are not available for the state of Pennsylvania
Schools: *Regular* 9 ● *Spec Ed* 0 ● *Alt* 0	**Librarians**: 6.0	**% Asian**: 0.8	
Students: 4,814	802 students/librarian	**% Black**: 0.9	
Total Teachers: 223	**Guidance Counselors**: 9.0	**% Hispanic**: 0.9	
Student/Classroom Teacher Ratio: 24.6	535 students/counselor	**% White**: 97.1	

Bucks County

[RICHBORO] **COUNCIL ROCK S.D.**

251 TWINING FORD ROAD ● RICHBORO PA 18954-1897 ● (215) 355-9901 ● http://www.cr.k12.pa.us

Grade Span: KG-12	**Expenditures/Student**: $7,571	**% Amer Indian**: 0.0	National ***Socio-Economic Status*** indicator percentiles are not available for the state of Pennsylvania
Schools: *Regular* 14 ● *Spec Ed* 0 ● *Alt* 0	**Librarians**: 16.0	**% Asian**: 2.3	
Students: 11,541	721 students/librarian	**% Black**: 0.7	
Total Teachers: 590	**Guidance Counselors**: 16.0	**% Hispanic**: 0.4	
Student/Classroom Teacher Ratio: 20.5	721 students/counselor	**% White**: 96.7	

Bucks County

[WARMINSTER] **CENTENNIAL S.D.**

433 CENTENNIAL ROAD ● WARMINSTER PA 18974-5448 ● (215) 441-6000

Grade Span: KG-12	**Expenditures/Student**: $7,646	**% Amer Indian**: 0.1	National ***Socio-Economic Status*** indicator percentiles are not available for the state of Pennsylvania
Schools: *Regular* 9 ● *Spec Ed* 0 ● *Alt* 0	**Librarians**: 10.0	**% Asian**: 2.6	
Students: 6,411	641 students/librarian	**% Black**: 4.4	
Total Teachers: 354	**Guidance Counselors**: 15.0	**% Hispanic**: 5.1	
Student/Classroom Teacher Ratio: 18.1	427 students/counselor	**% White**: 87.8	

Butler County

BUTLER AREA S.D.

167 NEW CASTLE ROAD ● BUTLER PA 16001-2693 ● (412) 287-8721 ● http://www.butler.k12.pa.us

Grade Span: KG-12	**Expenditures/Student**: $5,344	**% Amer Indian**: 0.2	National ***Socio-Economic Status*** indicator percentiles are not available for the state of Pennsylvania
Schools: *Regular* 14 ● *Spec Ed* 0 ● *Alt* 0	**Librarians**: 8.5	**% Asian**: 0.5	
Students: 8,707	1,024 students/librarian	**% Black**: 1.2	
Total Teachers: 471	**Guidance Counselors**: 11.0	**% Hispanic**: 0.4	
Student/Classroom Teacher Ratio: 21.2	792 students/counselor	**% White**: 97.6	

Butler County

[HARMONY] **SENECA VALLEY S.D.**

124 SENECA SCHOOL ROAD ● HARMONY PA 16037-9134 ● (412) 452-6040 ● http://www.seneca.k12.pa.us

Grade Span: KG-12	**Expenditures/Student**: $5,194	**% Amer Indian**: 0.0	National ***Socio-Economic Status*** indicator percentiles are not available for the state of Pennsylvania
Schools: *Regular* 7 ● *Spec Ed* 0 ● *Alt* 0	**Librarians**: 7.0	**% Asian**: 0.5	
Students: 6,872	982 students/librarian	**% Black**: 1.2	
Total Teachers: 375	**Guidance Counselors**: 10.0	**% Hispanic**: 0.3	
Student/Classroom Teacher Ratio: 18.6	687 students/counselor	**% White**: 97.9	

Butler County

[SAXONBURG] **SOUTH BUTLER COUNTY S.D.**

KNOCH RD BOX 657 ● SAXONBURG PA 16056-0657 ● (412) 352-1700 ● http://southbutler.k12.pa.us

Grade Span: KG-12 **Schools**: *Regular* 6 ● *Spec Ed* 0 ● *Alt* 0 **Students**: 2,911 **Total Teachers**: 148 **Student/Classroom Teacher Ratio**: 20.2	**Expenditures/Student**: $5,335 **Librarians**: 3.0 970 students/librarian **Guidance Counselors**: 3.0 970 students/counselor	**% Amer Indian**: 0.1 **% Asian**: 0.0 **% Black**: 0.3 **% Hispanic**: 0.2 **% White**: 99.4	National ***Socio-Economic Status*** indicator percentiles are not available for the state of Pennsylvania

Butler County

SLIPPERY ROCK AREA S.D.

201 KIESTER ROAD ● SLIPPERY ROCK PA 16057-1698 ● (412) 794-2960

Grade Span: KG-12 **Schools**: *Regular* 5 ● *Spec Ed* 0 ● *Alt* 0 **Students**: 2,603 **Total Teachers**: 142 **Student/Classroom Teacher Ratio**: 18.1	**Expenditures/Student**: $5,304 **Librarians**: 3.0 868 students/librarian **Guidance Counselors**: 3.5 744 students/counselor	**% Amer Indian**: 0.2 **% Asian**: 0.7 **% Black**: 0.8 **% Hispanic**: 0.2 **% White**: 98.0	National ***Socio-Economic Status*** indicator percentiles are not available for the state of Pennsylvania

Cambria County

[JOHNSTOWN] **GREATER JOHNSTOWN S.D.**

1091 BROAD STREET ● JOHNSTOWN PA 15906-2437 ● (814) 533-5651 ● http://www.pitt.edu/~bparkins/gjsd.html

Grade Span: KG-12 **Schools**: *Regular* 5 ● *Spec Ed* 0 ● *Alt* 0 **Students**: 3,582 **Total Teachers**: 243 **Student/Classroom Teacher Ratio**: 16.4	**Expenditures/Student**: $7,291 **Librarians**: 2.0 1,791 students/librarian **Guidance Counselors**: 8.0 448 students/counselor	**% Amer Indian**: 0.0 **% Asian**: 0.3 **% Black**: 16.2 **% Hispanic**: 0.8 **% White**: 82.8	National ***Socio-Economic Status*** indicator percentiles are not available for the state of Pennsylvania

Carbon County

LEHIGHTON AREA S.D.

200 BEAVER RUN ROAD ● LEHIGHTON PA 18235-1198 ● (610) 377-4490

Grade Span: KG-12 **Schools**: *Regular* 6 ● *Spec Ed* 0 ● *Alt* 0 **Students**: 2,548 **Total Teachers**: 154 **Student/Classroom Teacher Ratio**: 18.9	**Expenditures/Student**: $6,644 **Librarians**: 3.0 849 students/librarian **Guidance Counselors**: 6.0 425 students/counselor	**% Amer Indian**: 0.0 **% Asian**: 0.6 **% Black**: 0.4 **% Hispanic**: 0.5 **% White**: 98.5	National ***Socio-Economic Status*** indicator percentiles are not available for the state of Pennsylvania

Centre County

BELLEFONTE AREA S.D.

318 NORTH ALLEGHENY STREET ● BELLEFONTE PA 16823-1613 ● (814) 355-4814

Grade Span: KG-12 **Schools**: *Regular* 6 ● *Spec Ed* 0 ● *Alt* 0 **Students**: 2,977 **Total Teachers**: 174 **Student/Classroom Teacher Ratio**: 19.7	**Expenditures/Student**: $5,789 **Librarians**: 4.0 744 students/librarian **Guidance Counselors**: 7.0 425 students/counselor	**% Amer Indian**: 0.0 **% Asian**: 0.1 **% Black**: 0.7 **% Hispanic**: 0.4 **% White**: 98.8	National ***Socio-Economic Status*** indicator percentiles are not available for the state of Pennsylvania

Centre County

STATE COLLEGE AREA S.D.

131 WEST NITTANY AVENUE ● STATE COLLEGE PA 16801-4899 ● (814) 231-1011 ● http://www.scasd.k12.pa.us

Grade Span: KG-12 **Schools**: *Regular* 12 ● *Spec Ed* 0 ● *Alt* 0 **Students**: 7,114 **Total Teachers**: 453 **Student/Classroom Teacher Ratio**: 19.2	**Expenditures/Student**: $6,373 **Librarians**: 10.4 684 students/librarian **Guidance Counselors**: 18.6 382 students/counselor	**% Amer Indian**: 0.2 **% Asian**: 5.6 **% Black**: 3.5 **% Hispanic**: 1.3 **% White**: 89.5	National ***Socio-Economic Status*** indicator percentiles are not available for the state of Pennsylvania

Chester County
[ATGLEN] **OCTORARA AREA S.D.**
PO BOX 500 HIGHLAND ROAD ● ATGLEN PA 19310-0500 ● (610) 593-8293 ● http://www.octorara.k12.pa.us

Grade Span: KG-12 **Schools**: *Regular* 3 ● *Spec Ed* 0 ● *Alt* 0 **Students**: 2,511 **Total Teachers**: 147 **Student/Classroom Teacher Ratio**: 17.0	**Expenditures/Student**: $6,510 **Librarians**: 3.0 837 students/librarian **Guidance Counselors**: 5.0 502 students/counselor	**% Amer Indian**: 0.0 **% Asian**: 0.2 **% Black**: 5.5 **% Hispanic**: 1.6 **% White**: 92.8	National ***Socio-Economic Status*** indicator percentiles are not available for the state of Pennsylvania

Chester County
[BERWYN] **TREDYFFRIN-EASTTOWN S.D.**
738 FIRST AVENUE ● BERWYN PA 19312-1779 ● (610) 644-6600 ● http://www.tesd.k12.pa.us

Grade Span: KG-12 **Schools**: *Regular* 8 ● *Spec Ed* 0 ● *Alt* 0 **Students**: 4,543 **Total Teachers**: 279 **Student/Classroom Teacher Ratio**: 16.6	**Expenditures/Student**: $10,405 **Librarians**: 10.0 454 students/librarian **Guidance Counselors**: 18.0 252 students/counselor	**% Amer Indian**: 0.0 **% Asian**: 4.3 **% Black**: 4.0 **% Hispanic**: 0.8 **% White**: 91.0	National ***Socio-Economic Status*** indicator percentiles are not available for the state of Pennsylvania

Chester County
COATESVILLE AREA S.D.
1515 EAST LINCOLN HIGHWAY ● COATESVILLE PA 19320-2494 ● (610) 383-7900

Grade Span: KG-12 **Schools**: *Regular* 12 ● *Spec Ed* 0 ● *Alt* 0 **Students**: 8,132 **Total Teachers**: 441 **Student/Classroom Teacher Ratio**: 18.1	**Expenditures/Student**: $6,817 **Librarians**: 11.0 739 students/librarian **Guidance Counselors**: 20.0 407 students/counselor	**% Amer Indian**: 0.1 **% Asian**: 0.8 **% Black**: 29.1 **% Hispanic**: 3.8 **% White**: 66.2	National ***Socio-Economic Status*** indicator percentiles are not available for the state of Pennsylvania

Chester County
[DEVAULT] **GREAT VALLEY S.D.**
PO BOX 617 ● DEVAULT PA 19432-0617 ● (610) 889-2100 ● http://www.great-valley.k12.pa.us

Grade Span: KG-12 **Schools**: *Regular* 5 ● *Spec Ed* 0 ● *Alt* 0 **Students**: 3,186 **Total Teachers**: 205 **Student/Classroom Teacher Ratio**: 16.5	**Expenditures/Student**: $8,084 **Librarians**: 4.6 693 students/librarian **Guidance Counselors**: 10.0 319 students/counselor	**% Amer Indian**: 0.1 **% Asian**: 2.5 **% Black**: 3.9 **% Hispanic**: 0.7 **% White**: 92.8	National ***Socio-Economic Status*** indicator percentiles are not available for the state of Pennsylvania

Chester County
DOWNINGTOWN AREA S.D.
122 WALLACE AVENUE ● DOWNINGTOWN PA 19335-2600 ● (610) 269-8460

Grade Span: KG-12 **Schools**: *Regular* 12 ● *Spec Ed* 0 ● *Alt* 0 **Students**: 9,753 **Total Teachers**: 556 **Student/Classroom Teacher Ratio**: 18.5	**Expenditures/Student**: $6,032 **Librarians**: 12.7 768 students/librarian **Guidance Counselors**: 22.0 443 students/counselor	**% Amer Indian**: 0.1 **% Asian**: 1.7 **% Black**: 3.1 **% Hispanic**: 0.8 **% White**: 94.2	National ***Socio-Economic Status*** indicator percentiles are not available for the state of Pennsylvania

Chester County
[KENNETT SQUARE] **KENNETT CONSOLIDATED S.D.**
300 EAST SOUTH STREET ● KENNETT SQUARE PA 19348-3297 ● (610) 444-6600

Grade Span: KG-12 **Schools**: *Regular* 5 ● *Spec Ed* 0 ● *Alt* 0 **Students**: 3,023 **Total Teachers**: 168 **Student/Classroom Teacher Ratio**: 18.3	**Expenditures/Student**: $6,929 **Librarians**: 4.0 756 students/librarian **Guidance Counselors**: 6.0 504 students/counselor	**% Amer Indian**: 0.0 **% Asian**: 1.5 **% Black**: 7.6 **% Hispanic**: 15.7 **% White**: 75.2	National ***Socio-Economic Status*** indicator percentiles are not available for the state of Pennsylvania

Chester County

[KENNETT SQUARE] **UNIONVILLE-CHADDS FORD S.D.**

740 UNIONVILLE ROAD ● KENNETT SQUARE PA 19348-1531 ● (610) 347-0970 ● http://www.ucf.k12.pa.us

Grade Span: KG-12 **Schools**: *Regular* 5 ● *Spec Ed* 0 ● *Alt* 0 **Students**: 3,223 **Total Teachers**: 200 **Student/Classroom Teacher Ratio**: 17.1	**Expenditures/Student**: $7,908 **Librarians**: 3.8 848 students/librarian **Guidance Counselors**: 9.0 358 students/counselor	**% Amer Indian**: 0.1 **% Asian**: 1.9 **% Black**: 0.8 **% Hispanic**: 0.7 **% White**: 96.5	National ***Socio-Economic Status*** indicator percentiles are not available for the state of Pennsylvania

Chester County

OXFORD AREA S.D.

119 SOUTH FIFTH STREET ● OXFORD PA 19363-1797 ● (610) 932-6600

Grade Span: KG-12 **Schools**: *Regular* 5 ● *Spec Ed* 0 ● *Alt* 0 **Students**: 2,718 **Total Teachers**: 158 **Student/Classroom Teacher Ratio**: 18.1	**Expenditures/Student**: $5,847 **Librarians**: 4.0 680 students/librarian **Guidance Counselors**: 6.0 453 students/counselor	**% Amer Indian**: 0.0 **% Asian**: 0.5 **% Black**: 7.5 **% Hispanic**: 7.2 **% White**: 84.8	National ***Socio-Economic Status*** indicator percentiles are not available for the state of Pennsylvania

Chester County

PHOENIXVILLE AREA S.D.

1120 SOUTH GAY STREET ● PHOENIXVILLE PA 19460-4400 ● (610) 933-8861

Grade Span: KG-12 **Schools**: *Regular* 7 ● *Spec Ed* 0 ● *Alt* 0 **Students**: 3,240 **Total Teachers**: 186 **Student/Classroom Teacher Ratio**: 21.6	**Expenditures/Student**: $8,121 **Librarians**: 5.0 648 students/librarian **Guidance Counselors**: 8.5 381 students/counselor	**% Amer Indian**: 0.1 **% Asian**: 1.7 **% Black**: 8.3 **% Hispanic**: 1.4 **% White**: 88.5	National ***Socio-Economic Status*** indicator percentiles are not available for the state of Pennsylvania

Chester County

[POTTSTOWN] **OWEN J ROBERTS S.D.**

901 RIDGE ROAD ● POTTSTOWN PA 19465-9314 ● (610) 469-6261 ● http://www.ojr.k12.pa.us

Grade Span: KG-12 **Schools**: *Regular* 7 ● *Spec Ed* 0 ● *Alt* 0 **Students**: 3,698 **Total Teachers**: 208 **Student/Classroom Teacher Ratio**: 18.6	**Expenditures/Student**: $7,679 **Librarians**: 4.0 925 students/librarian **Guidance Counselors**: 8.5 435 students/counselor	**% Amer Indian**: 0.1 **% Asian**: 0.3 **% Black**: 2.8 **% Hispanic**: 0.2 **% White**: 96.6	National ***Socio-Economic Status*** indicator percentiles are not available for the state of Pennsylvania

Chester County

WEST CHESTER AREA S.D.

829 PAOLI PIKE ● WEST CHESTER PA 19380-4500 ● (610) 436-7000

Grade Span: KG-12 **Schools**: *Regular* 15 ● *Spec Ed* 0 ● *Alt* 0 **Students**: 11,012 **Total Teachers**: 610 **Student/Classroom Teacher Ratio**: 19.0	**Expenditures/Student**: $7,199 **Librarians**: 15.0 734 students/librarian **Guidance Counselors**: 20.9 527 students/counselor	**% Amer Indian**: 0.0 **% Asian**: 2.4 **% Black**: 9.6 **% Hispanic**: 3.4 **% White**: 84.6	National ***Socio-Economic Status*** indicator percentiles are not available for the state of Pennsylvania

Chester County

[WEST GROVE] **AVON GROVE S.D.**

375 KELTON JENNERSVILLE ROAD ● WEST GROVE PA 19390-9409 ● (610) 869-2441

Grade Span: KG-12 **Schools**: *Regular* 5 ● *Spec Ed* 0 ● *Alt* 0 **Students**: 3,904 **Total Teachers**: 202 **Student/Classroom Teacher Ratio**: 20.2	**Expenditures/Student**: $5,897 **Librarians**: 5.0 781 students/librarian **Guidance Counselors**: 9.0 434 students/counselor	**% Amer Indian**: 0.1 **% Asian**: 0.5 **% Black**: 4.8 **% Hispanic**: 5.5 **% White**: 89.1	National ***Socio-Economic Status*** indicator percentiles are not available for the state of Pennsylvania

Clearfield County

CLEARFIELD AREA S.D.

PO BOX 710 ● CLEARFIELD PA 16830-0710 ● (814) 765-5511

Grade Span: KG-12 **Schools**: *Regular* 8 ● *Spec Ed* 0 ● *Alt* 0 **Students**: 3,340 **Total Teachers**: 181 **Student/Classroom Teacher Ratio**: 21.5	**Expenditures/Student**: $5,577 **Librarians**: 3.0 1,113 students/librarian **Guidance Counselors**: 6.0 557 students/counselor	**% Amer Indian**: 0.1 **% Asian**: 0.4 **% Black**: 0.7 **% Hispanic**: 0.2 **% White**: 98.7	National ***Socio-Economic Status*** indicator percentiles are not available for the state of Pennsylvania

Clearfield County

DUBOIS AREA S.D.

500 LIBERTY BLVD ● DUBOIS PA 15801-2410 ● (814) 371-2700

Grade Span: KG-12 **Schools**: *Regular* 10 ● *Spec Ed* 0 ● *Alt* 0 **Students**: 4,871 **Total Teachers**: 282 **Student/Classroom Teacher Ratio**: 17.9	**Expenditures/Student**: $5,951 **Librarians**: 5.0 974 students/librarian **Guidance Counselors**: 11.0 443 students/counselor	**% Amer Indian**: 0.1 **% Asian**: 0.2 **% Black**: 0.4 **% Hispanic**: 0.2 **% White**: 99.1	National ***Socio-Economic Status*** indicator percentiles are not available for the state of Pennsylvania

Clinton County

[LOCK HAVEN] **KEYSTONE CENTRAL S.D.**

95 WEST FOURTH STREET ● LOCK HAVEN PA 17745-1100 ● (717) 893-4900 ● http://oak.kcsd.k12.pa.us

Grade Span: KG-12 **Schools**: *Regular* 15 ● *Spec Ed* 0 ● *Alt* 0 **Students**: 5,560 **Total Teachers**: 381 **Student/Classroom Teacher Ratio**: 15.4	**Expenditures/Student**: $6,635 **Librarians**: 13.0 428 students/librarian **Guidance Counselors**: 11.0 505 students/counselor	**% Amer Indian**: 0.0 **% Asian**: 0.3 **% Black**: 0.3 **% Hispanic**: 0.0 **% White**: 99.4	National ***Socio-Economic Status*** indicator percentiles are not available for the state of Pennsylvania

Columbia County

BERWICK AREA S.D.

500 MARKET STREET ● BERWICK PA 18603-3799 ● (717) 759-6400

Grade Span: KG-12 **Schools**: *Regular* 7 ● *Spec Ed* 0 ● *Alt* 0 **Students**: 3,768 **Total Teachers**: 225 **Student/Classroom Teacher Ratio**: 17.0	**Expenditures/Student**: $5,666 **Librarians**: 3.0 1,256 students/librarian **Guidance Counselors**: 6.0 628 students/counselor	**% Amer Indian**: 0.0 **% Asian**: 0.6 **% Black**: 1.2 **% Hispanic**: 0.6 **% White**: 97.6	National ***Socio-Economic Status*** indicator percentiles are not available for the state of Pennsylvania

Crawford County

[LINESVILLE] **CONNEAUT S.D.**

302 EAST ERIE ST RR 3 BOX 135C ● LINESVILLE PA 16424-9717 ● (814) 683-5900 ● http://connwww.trinet.k12.pa.us

Grade Span: KG-12 **Schools**: *Regular* 7 ● *Spec Ed* 0 ● *Alt* 0 **Students**: 3,175 **Total Teachers**: 185 **Student/Classroom Teacher Ratio**: 17.8	**Expenditures/Student**: $5,417 **Librarians**: 6.0 529 students/librarian **Guidance Counselors**: 6.0 529 students/counselor	**% Amer Indian**: 0.0 **% Asian**: 0.1 **% Black**: 0.8 **% Hispanic**: 0.2 **% White**: 98.9	National ***Socio-Economic Status*** indicator percentiles are not available for the state of Pennsylvania

Crawford County

[MEADVILLE] **CRAWFORD CENTRAL S.D.**

RR 9 BOX 462 ROUTE 102 ● MEADVILLE PA 16335-9504 ● (814) 724-3960

Grade Span: KG-12 **Schools**: *Regular* 9 ● *Spec Ed* 0 ● *Alt* 0 **Students**: 4,820 **Total Teachers**: 295 **Student/Classroom Teacher Ratio**: 16.3	**Expenditures/Student**: $5,954 **Librarians**: 7.0 689 students/librarian **Guidance Counselors**: 14.0 344 students/counselor	**% Amer Indian**: 0.2 **% Asian**: 0.7 **% Black**: 5.5 **% Hispanic**: 0.7 **% White**: 92.9	National ***Socio-Economic Status*** indicator percentiles are not available for the state of Pennsylvania

Crawford County

[SAEGERTOWN] **PENNCREST S.D.**

PO BOX 808 ● SAEGERTOWN PA 16433-0808 ● (814) 763-2323

Grade Span: KG-12 **Schools**: *Regular* 7 ● *Spec Ed* 0 ● *Alt* 0 **Students**: 4,359 **Total Teachers**: 245 **Student/Classroom Teacher Ratio**: 18.0	**Expenditures/Student**: $6,216 **Librarians**: 6.5 671 students/librarian **Guidance Counselors**: 9.0 484 students/counselor	**% Amer Indian**: 0.0 **% Asian**: 0.0 **% Black**: 0.2 **% Hispanic**: 0.3 **% White**: 99.5	National ***Socio-Economic Status*** indicator percentiles are not available for the state of Pennsylvania

Cumberland County

CARLISLE AREA S.D.

623 WEST PENN STREET ● CARLISLE PA 17013-2298 ● (717) 240-6800

Grade Span: KG-12 **Schools**: *Regular* 10 ● *Spec Ed* 0 ● *Alt* 0 **Students**: 5,136 **Total Teachers**: 322 **Student/Classroom Teacher Ratio**: 16.6	**Expenditures/Student**: $5,572 **Librarians**: 6.2 828 students/librarian **Guidance Counselors**: 14.5 354 students/counselor	**% Amer Indian**: 0.0 **% Asian**: 2.8 **% Black**: 8.0 **% Hispanic**: 1.0 **% White**: 88.2	National ***Socio-Economic Status*** indicator percentiles are not available for the state of Pennsylvania

Cumberland County

[ENOLA] **EAST PENNSBORO AREA S.D.**

890 VALLEY STREET ● ENOLA PA 17025-1599 ● (717) 732-3601 ● http://www.caiu.k12.pa.us/epasd/EastPenn.htm

Grade Span: KG-12 **Schools**: *Regular* 4 ● *Spec Ed* 0 ● *Alt* 0 **Students**: 2,589 **Total Teachers**: 161 **Student/Classroom Teacher Ratio**: 16.7	**Expenditures/Student**: $6,074 **Librarians**: 4.0 647 students/librarian **Guidance Counselors**: 7.0 370 students/counselor	**% Amer Indian**: 0.2 **% Asian**: 3.0 **% Black**: 1.7 **% Hispanic**: 1.5 **% White**: 93.6	National ***Socio-Economic Status*** indicator percentiles are not available for the state of Pennsylvania

Cumberland County

[MECHANICSBURG] **CUMBERLAND VALLEY S.D.**

6746 CARLISLE PIKE ● MECHANICSBURG PA 17055-1796 ● (717) 697-8261 ● http://www2.epix.net/~cvsd

Grade Span: KG-12 **Schools**: *Regular* 10 ● *Spec Ed* 0 ● *Alt* 0 **Students**: 7,290 **Total Teachers**: 431 **Student/Classroom Teacher Ratio**: 17.7	**Expenditures/Student**: $6,117 **Librarians**: 4.0 1,823 students/librarian **Guidance Counselors**: 20.0 365 students/counselor	**% Amer Indian**: 0.1 **% Asian**: 3.4 **% Black**: 0.8 **% Hispanic**: 0.7 **% White**: 95.1	National ***Socio-Economic Status*** indicator percentiles are not available for the state of Pennsylvania

Cumberland County

MECHANICSBURG AREA S.D.

500 SOUTH BROAD STREET ● MECHANICSBURG PA 17055-4199 ● (717) 691-4500 ● http://www.caiu.k12.pa.us/mbgsd/default.htm

Grade Span: KG-12 **Schools**: *Regular* 8 ● *Spec Ed* 0 ● *Alt* 0 **Students**: 3,314 **Total Teachers**: 215 **Student/Classroom Teacher Ratio**: 17.6	**Expenditures/Student**: $6,412 **Librarians**: 3.0 1,105 students/librarian **Guidance Counselors**: 9.0 368 students/counselor	**% Amer Indian**: 0.0 **% Asian**: 1.4 **% Black**: 0.5 **% Hispanic**: 0.4 **% White**: 97.7	National ***Socio-Economic Status*** indicator percentiles are not available for the state of Pennsylvania

Cumberland County

[NEW CUMBERLAND] **WEST SHORE S.D.**

PO BOX 803 ● NEW CUMBERLAND PA 17070-0803 ● (717) 938-9577 ● http://www.WSSD.k12.pa.us

Grade Span: KG-12 **Schools**: *Regular* 17 ● *Spec Ed* 0 ● *Alt* 0 **Students**: 7,974 **Total Teachers**: 463 **Student/Classroom Teacher Ratio**: 18.7	**Expenditures/Student**: $6,036 **Librarians**: 12.0 665 students/librarian **Guidance Counselors**: 19.0 420 students/counselor	**% Amer Indian**: 0.1 **% Asian**: 2.0 **% Black**: 1.6 **% Hispanic**: 1.0 **% White**: 95.2	National ***Socio-Economic Status*** indicator percentiles are not available for the state of Pennsylvania

Cumberland County

[NEWVILLE] **BIG SPRING S.D.**

45 MOUNT ROCK ROAD ● NEWVILLE PA 17241-9466 ● (717) 776-2000

Grade Span: KG-12 **Schools**: *Regular* 7 ● *Spec Ed* 0 ● *Alt* 0 **Students**: 3,237 **Total Teachers**: 191 **Student/Classroom Teacher Ratio**: 18.3	**Expenditures/Student**: $5,271 **Librarians**: 4.0 809 students/librarian **Guidance Counselors**: 7.0 462 students/counselor	**% Amer Indian**: 0.1 **% Asian**: 0.4 **% Black**: 0.9 **% Hispanic**: 0.5 **% White**: 98.2	National ***Socio-Economic Status*** indicator percentiles are not available for the state of Pennsylvania

Cumberland County

SHIPPENSBURG AREA S.D.

317 NORTH MORRIS STREET ● SHIPPENSBURG PA 17257-1654 ● (717) 530-2700

Grade Span: KG-12 **Schools**: *Regular* 5 ● *Spec Ed* 0 ● *Alt* 0 **Students**: 2,933 **Total Teachers**: 159 **Student/Classroom Teacher Ratio**: 21.0	**Expenditures/Student**: $5,819 **Librarians**: 4.0 733 students/librarian **Guidance Counselors**: 5.0 587 students/counselor	**% Amer Indian**: 0.1 **% Asian**: 1.1 **% Black**: 2.2 **% Hispanic**: 0.6 **% White**: 96.0	National ***Socio-Economic Status*** indicator percentiles are not available for the state of Pennsylvania

Dauphin County

[HARRISBURG] **CENTRAL DAUPHIN S.D.**

600 RUTHERFORD ROAD ● HARRISBURG PA 17109-5297 ● (717) 545-4703

Grade Span: KG-12 **Schools**: *Regular* 20 ● *Spec Ed* 0 ● *Alt* 0 **Students**: 10,495 **Total Teachers**: 683 **Student/Classroom Teacher Ratio**: 15.1	**Expenditures/Student**: $6,888 **Librarians**: 12.0 875 students/librarian **Guidance Counselors**: 24.0 437 students/counselor	**% Amer Indian**: 0.2 **% Asian**: 2.6 **% Black**: 10.7 **% Hispanic**: 2.0 **% White**: 84.5	National ***Socio-Economic Status*** indicator percentiles are not available for the state of Pennsylvania

Dauphin County

HARRISBURG CITY S.D.

1201 N SIXTH ST PO BOX 2645 ● HARRISBURG PA 17105-2645 ● (717) 255-2511

Grade Span: PK-12 **Schools**: *Regular* 15 ● *Spec Ed* 0 ● *Alt* 0 **Students**: 9,583 **Total Teachers**: 605 **Student/Classroom Teacher Ratio**: 17.0	**Expenditures/Student**: $7,081 **Librarians**: 5.0 1,917 students/librarian **Guidance Counselors**: 25.0 383 students/counselor	**% Amer Indian**: 0.1 **% Asian**: 2.6 **% Black**: 77.9 **% Hispanic**: 9.2 **% White**: 10.2	National ***Socio-Economic Status*** indicator percentiles are not available for the state of Pennsylvania

Dauphin County

[HARRISBURG] **SUSQUEHANNA TOWNSHIP S.D.**

3550 ELMERTON AVENUE ● HARRISBURG PA 17109-1198 ● (717) 657-5100 ● http://www.caiu.k12.pa.us/hannaweb/index.htm

Grade Span: KG-12 **Schools**: *Regular* 5 ● *Spec Ed* 0 ● *Alt* 0 **Students**: 2,681 **Total Teachers**: 157 **Student/Classroom Teacher Ratio**: 22.2	**Expenditures/Student**: $6,047 **Librarians**: 4.0 670 students/librarian **Guidance Counselors**: 7.0 383 students/counselor	**% Amer Indian**: 0.2 **% Asian**: 2.1 **% Black**: 25.4 **% Hispanic**: 1.6 **% White**: 70.8	National ***Socio-Economic Status*** indicator percentiles are not available for the state of Pennsylvania

Dauphin County

[HERSHEY] **DERRY TOWNSHIP S.D.**

PO BOX 898 ● HERSHEY PA 17033-0898 ● (717) 534-2501 ● http://www.emagic.com/pub/dtsd

Grade Span: KG-12 **Schools**: *Regular* 4 ● *Spec Ed* 0 ● *Alt* 0 **Students**: 2,806 **Total Teachers**: 170 **Student/Classroom Teacher Ratio**: 16.7	**Expenditures/Student**: $6,669 **Librarians**: 4.0 702 students/librarian **Guidance Counselors**: 7.0 401 students/counselor	**% Amer Indian**: 0.2 **% Asian**: 3.1 **% Black**: 1.1 **% Hispanic**: 0.4 **% White**: 95.2	National ***Socio-Economic Status*** indicator percentiles are not available for the state of Pennsylvania

Dauphin County

[HUMMELSTOWN] **LOWER DAUPHIN S.D.**

291 EAST MAIN STREET ● HUMMELSTOWN PA 17036-1799 ● (717) 566-5300

Grade Span: KG-12 **Schools**: *Regular* 7 ● *Spec Ed* 0 ● *Alt* 0 **Students**: 3,755 **Total Teachers**: 222 **Student/Classroom Teacher Ratio**: 17.5	**Expenditures/Student**: $6,123 **Librarians**: 4.0 939 students/librarian **Guidance Counselors**: 8.8 427 students/counselor	**% Amer Indian**: 0.1 **% Asian**: 0.8 **% Black**: 1.1 **% Hispanic**: 0.9 **% White**: 97.2	National ***Socio-Economic Status*** indicator percentiles are not available for the state of Pennsylvania

Dauphin County

MIDDLETOWN AREA S.D.

55 WEST WATER STREET ● MIDDLETOWN PA 17057-1467 ● (717) 948-3300 ● http://www.caiu.k12.pa.us/masd/masd.htm

Grade Span: PK-12 **Schools**: *Regular* 6 ● *Spec Ed* 0 ● *Alt* 0 **Students**: 2,856 **Total Teachers**: 163 **Student/Classroom Teacher Ratio**: 21.2	**Expenditures/Student**: $5,943 **Librarians**: 4.0 714 students/librarian **Guidance Counselors**: 6.0 476 students/counselor	**% Amer Indian**: 0.1 **% Asian**: 0.8 **% Black**: 8.2 **% Hispanic**: 1.9 **% White**: 89.0	National ***Socio-Economic Status*** indicator percentiles are not available for the state of Pennsylvania

Delaware County

[ASTON] **PENN-DELCO S.D.**

95 CONCORD ROAD ● ASTON PA 19014-2907 ● (610) 497-6310

Grade Span: KG-12 **Schools**: *Regular* 6 ● *Spec Ed* 0 ● *Alt* 0 **Students**: 3,261 **Total Teachers**: 169 **Student/Classroom Teacher Ratio**: 20.0	**Expenditures/Student**: $6,705 **Librarians**: 4.0 815 students/librarian **Guidance Counselors**: 8.0 408 students/counselor	**% Amer Indian**: 0.3 **% Asian**: 0.8 **% Black**: 0.8 **% Hispanic**: 0.4 **% White**: 97.6	National ***Socio-Economic Status*** indicator percentiles are not available for the state of Pennsylvania

Delaware County

[BOOTHWYN] **CHICHESTER S.D.**

PO BOX 2100 ● BOOTHWYN PA 19061-8100 ● (610) 485-6881 ● http://www.chichester.k12.pa.us

Grade Span: KG-12 **Schools**: *Regular* 6 ● *Spec Ed* 0 ● *Alt* 0 **Students**: 3,772 **Total Teachers**: 222 **Student/Classroom Teacher Ratio**: 17.0	**Expenditures/Student**: $7,080 **Librarians**: 3.0 1,257 students/librarian **Guidance Counselors**: 6.0 629 students/counselor	**% Amer Indian**: 0.0 **% Asian**: 0.4 **% Black**: 9.5 **% Hispanic**: 0.3 **% White**: 89.7	National ***Socio-Economic Status*** indicator percentiles are not available for the state of Pennsylvania

Delaware County

CHESTER-UPLAND S.D.

1720 MELROSE AVENUE ● CHESTER PA 19013-5897 ● (610) 447-3600

Grade Span: KG-12 **Schools**: *Regular* 11 ● *Spec Ed* 0 ● *Alt* 0 **Students**: 7,587 **Total Teachers**: 399 **Student/Classroom Teacher Ratio**: 19.6	**Expenditures/Student**: $6,393 **Librarians**: 8.0 948 students/librarian **Guidance Counselors**: 7.6 998 students/counselor	**% Amer Indian**: 0.0 **% Asian**: 0.1 **% Black**: 86.9 **% Hispanic**: 5.8 **% White**: 7.3	National ***Socio-Economic Status*** indicator percentiles are not available for the state of Pennsylvania

Delaware County

[DREXEL HILL] **UPPER DARBY S.D.**

4611 BOND AVENUE ● DREXEL HILL PA 19026-4592 ● (610) 789-7200

Grade Span: KG-12 **Schools**: *Regular* 11 ● *Spec Ed* 0 ● *Alt* 0 **Students**: 10,691 **Total Teachers**: 569 **Student/Classroom Teacher Ratio**: 19.9	**Expenditures/Student**: $6,449 **Librarians**: 10.6 1,009 students/librarian **Guidance Counselors**: 17.0 629 students/counselor	**% Amer Indian**: 0.0 **% Asian**: 9.7 **% Black**: 7.4 **% Hispanic**: 0.7 **% White**: 82.2	National ***Socio-Economic Status*** indicator percentiles are not available for the state of Pennsylvania

Delaware County
[FOLCROFT] **SOUTHEAST DELCO S.D.**
BOX 328 DELMAR DR & PRIMOS AVE ● FOLCROFT PA 19032-0328 ● (610) 522-4300

Grade Span: KG-12 **Schools**: *Regular* 6 ● *Spec Ed* 0 ● *Alt* 0 **Students**: 3,973 **Total Teachers**: 204 **Student/Classroom Teacher Ratio**: 19.5	**Expenditures/Student**: $7,080 **Librarians**: 5.0 795 students/librarian **Guidance Counselors**: 6.0 662 students/counselor	**% Amer Indian**: 0.0 **% Asian**: 0.8 **% Black**: 29.2 **% Hispanic**: 0.5 **% White**: 69.5	National ***Socio-Economic Status*** indicator percentiles are not available for the state of Pennsylvania

Delaware County
[FOLSOM] **RIDLEY S.D.**
1001 MORTON AVENUE ● FOLSOM PA 19033-2997 ● (610) 534-1900 ● http://www.ridleysd.k12.pa.us

Grade Span: KG-12 **Schools**: *Regular* 9 ● *Spec Ed* 0 ● *Alt* 0 **Students**: 5,574 **Total Teachers**: 314 **Student/Classroom Teacher Ratio**: 18.7	**Expenditures/Student**: $6,928 **Librarians**: 3.0 1,858 students/librarian **Guidance Counselors**: 8.0 697 students/counselor	**% Amer Indian**: 0.0 **% Asian**: 1.5 **% Black**: 5.5 **% Hispanic**: 0.3 **% White**: 92.7	National ***Socio-Economic Status*** indicator percentiles are not available for the state of Pennsylvania

Delaware County
[HAVERTOWN] **HAVERFORD TOWNSHIP S.D.**
1801 DARBY ROAD ● HAVERTOWN PA 19083-3796 ● (610) 853-5900

Grade Span: KG-12 **Schools**: *Regular* 7 ● *Spec Ed* 0 ● *Alt* 0 **Students**: 5,376 **Total Teachers**: 289 **Student/Classroom Teacher Ratio**: 18.6	**Expenditures/Student**: $7,046 **Librarians**: 7.0 768 students/librarian **Guidance Counselors**: 10.0 538 students/counselor	**% Amer Indian**: 0.2 **% Asian**: 3.6 **% Black**: 2.5 **% Hispanic**: 0.6 **% White**: 93.2	National ***Socio-Economic Status*** indicator percentiles are not available for the state of Pennsylvania

Delaware County
[LANSDOWNE] **WILLIAM PENN S.D.**
100 GREEN AVENUE ANNEX ● LANSDOWNE PA 19050-3896 ● (610) 284-8000

Grade Span: KG-12 **Schools**: *Regular* 10 ● *Spec Ed* 0 ● *Alt* 0 **Students**: 5,070 **Total Teachers**: 285 **Student/Classroom Teacher Ratio**: 18.8	**Expenditures/Student**: $7,717 **Librarians**: 7.5 676 students/librarian **Guidance Counselors**: 8.0 634 students/counselor	**% Amer Indian**: 0.0 **% Asian**: 1.2 **% Black**: 61.9 **% Hispanic**: 1.1 **% White**: 35.7	National ***Socio-Economic Status*** indicator percentiles are not available for the state of Pennsylvania

Delaware County
[MEDIA] **ROSE TREE MEDIA S.D.**
901 NORTH PROVIDENCE ROAD ● MEDIA PA 19063-1495 ● (610) 565-1200 ● http://forum.swarthmore.edu/~pete

Grade Span: KG-12 **Schools**: *Regular* 6 ● *Spec Ed* 0 ● *Alt* 0 **Students**: 3,822 **Total Teachers**: 235 **Student/Classroom Teacher Ratio**: 16.7	**Expenditures/Student**: $8,247 **Librarians**: 3.0 1,274 students/librarian **Guidance Counselors**: 11.0 347 students/counselor	**% Amer Indian**: 0.1 **% Asian**: 2.4 **% Black**: 7.5 **% Hispanic**: 1.0 **% White**: 89.0	National ***Socio-Economic Status*** indicator percentiles are not available for the state of Pennsylvania

Delaware County
[NEWTOWN SQUARE] **MARPLE NEWTOWN S.D.**
120 MEDIA LINE ROAD ● NEWTOWN SQUARE PA 19073-4696 ● (610) 359-4200

Grade Span: KG-12 **Schools**: *Regular* 6 ● *Spec Ed* 0 ● *Alt* 0 **Students**: 3,617 **Total Teachers**: 227 **Student/Classroom Teacher Ratio**: 16.5	**Expenditures/Student**: $8,096 **Librarians**: 2.0 1,809 students/librarian **Guidance Counselors**: 10.0 362 students/counselor	**% Amer Indian**: 0.5 **% Asian**: 7.1 **% Black**: 0.9 **% Hispanic**: 0.4 **% White**: 91.0	National ***Socio-Economic Status*** indicator percentiles are not available for the state of Pennsylvania

Delaware County

[PROSPECT PARK] **INTERBORO S.D.**

900 WASHINGTON AVENUE ● PROSPECT PARK PA 19076-1498 ● (610) 461-6700

Grade Span: KG-12 **Schools**: *Regular* 5 ● *Spec Ed* 0 ● *Alt* 0 **Students**: 3,696 **Total Teachers**: 196 **Student/Classroom Teacher Ratio**: 19.1	**Expenditures/Student**: $7,588 **Librarians**: 3.0 1,232 students/librarian **Guidance Counselors**: 7.0 528 students/counselor	**% Amer Indian**: 0.1 **% Asian**: 0.9 **% Black**: 1.0 **% Hispanic**: 0.5 **% White**: 97.5	National ***Socio-Economic Status*** indicator percentiles are not available for the state of Pennsylvania

Delaware County

SPRINGFIELD S.D.

111 WEST LEAMY AVENUE ● SPRINGFIELD PA 19064-2396 ● (610) 690-1781 ● http://springfieldsd-delco.org

Grade Span: KG-12 **Schools**: *Regular* 4 ● *Spec Ed* 0 ● *Alt* 0 **Students**: 3,381 **Total Teachers**: 190 **Student/Classroom Teacher Ratio**: 18.3	**Expenditures/Student**: $7,173 **Librarians**: 4.0 845 students/librarian **Guidance Counselors**: 7.0 483 students/counselor	**% Amer Indian**: 0.0 **% Asian**: 2.9 **% Black**: 4.9 **% Hispanic**: 0.4 **% White**: 91.7	National ***Socio-Economic Status*** indicator percentiles are not available for the state of Pennsylvania

Delaware County

WALLINGFORD-SWARTHMORE S.D.

200 SOUTH PROVIDENCE ROAD ● WALLINGFORD PA 19086-6334 ● (610) 892-3404

Grade Span: KG-12 **Schools**: *Regular* 6 ● *Spec Ed* 0 ● *Alt* 0 **Students**: 3,451 **Total Teachers**: 205 **Student/Classroom Teacher Ratio**: 21.8	**Expenditures/Student**: $7,690 **Librarians**: 4.0 863 students/librarian **Guidance Counselors**: 8.0 431 students/counselor	**% Amer Indian**: 0.1 **% Asian**: 2.3 **% Black**: 7.5 **% Hispanic**: 0.5 **% White**: 89.6	National ***Socio-Economic Status*** indicator percentiles are not available for the state of Pennsylvania

Delaware County

[WAYNE] **RADNOR TOWNSHIP S.D.**

135 SOUTH WAYNE AVENUE ● WAYNE PA 19087-4194 ● (610) 688-8100 ● http://www.radnor.com/schools/schools.html

Grade Span: KG-12 **Schools**: *Regular* 4 ● *Spec Ed* 0 ● *Alt* 0 **Students**: 2,841 **Total Teachers**: 214 **Student/Classroom Teacher Ratio**: 13.8	**Expenditures/Student**: $11,542 **Librarians**: 5.5 517 students/librarian **Guidance Counselors**: 9.0 316 students/counselor	**% Amer Indian**: 0.0 **% Asian**: 9.0 **% Black**: 4.1 **% Hispanic**: 1.3 **% White**: 85.6	National ***Socio-Economic Status*** indicator percentiles are not available for the state of Pennsylvania

Elk County

ST. MARYS AREA S.D.

977 SOUTH ST MARYS ROAD ● ST. MARYS PA 15857-2891 ● (814) 834-7831 ● http://dns.ncentral.com/~stmlib

Grade Span: KG-12 **Schools**: *Regular* 5 ● *Spec Ed* 0 ● *Alt* 0 **Students**: 2,509 **Total Teachers**: 149 **Student/Classroom Teacher Ratio**: 17.1	**Expenditures/Student**: $5,640 **Librarians**: 3.0 836 students/librarian **Guidance Counselors**: 6.0 418 students/counselor	**% Amer Indian**: 0.1 **% Asian**: 0.6 **% Black**: 0.2 **% Hispanic**: 0.4 **% White**: 98.7	National ***Socio-Economic Status*** indicator percentiles are not available for the state of Pennsylvania

Erie County

CORRY AREA S.D.

800 EAST SOUTH STREET ● CORRY PA 16407-2054 ● (814) 664-4677

Grade Span: KG-12 **Schools**: *Regular* 6 ● *Spec Ed* 0 ● *Alt* 0 **Students**: 2,732 **Total Teachers**: 156 **Student/Classroom Teacher Ratio**: 18.3	**Expenditures/Student**: $5,338 **Librarians**: 3.5 781 students/librarian **Guidance Counselors**: 5.0 546 students/counselor	**% Amer Indian**: 0.0 **% Asian**: 0.1 **% Black**: 0.0 **% Hispanic**: 0.0 **% White**: 99.8	National ***Socio-Economic Status*** indicator percentiles are not available for the state of Pennsylvania

Erie County
[EDINBORO] **GENERAL MCLANE S.D.**
11771 EDINBORO ROAD ● EDINBORO PA 16412-1025 ● (814) 734-1033

Grade Span: KG-12 **Schools**: *Regular* 5 ● *Spec Ed* 0 ● *Alt* 0 **Students**: 3,068 **Total Teachers**: 157 **Student/Classroom Teacher Ratio**: 19.1	**Expenditures/Student**: $4,492 **Librarians**: 4.0 767 students/librarian **Guidance Counselors**: 7.0 438 students/counselor	**% Amer Indian**: 0.2 **% Asian**: 0.4 **% Black**: 0.8 **% Hispanic**: 0.2 **% White**: 98.4	National ***Socio-Economic Status*** indicator percentiles are not available for the state of Pennsylvania

Erie County
ERIE CITY S.D.
1511 PEACH STREET ● ERIE PA 16501-2193 ● (814) 871-6200

Grade Span: KG-12 **Schools**: *Regular* 20 ● *Spec Ed* 0 ● *Alt* 0 **Students**: 12,034 **Total Teachers**: 735 **Student/Classroom Teacher Ratio**: 17.8	**Expenditures/Student**: $6,552 **Librarians**: 6.0 2,006 students/librarian **Guidance Counselors**: 30.0 401 students/counselor	**% Amer Indian**: 0.2 **% Asian**: 1.0 **% Black**: 29.7 **% Hispanic**: 7.0 **% White**: 62.2	National ***Socio-Economic Status*** indicator percentiles are not available for the state of Pennsylvania

Erie County
[ERIE] **MILLCREEK TOWNSHIP S.D.**
3740 WEST 26TH STREET ● ERIE PA 16506-2096 ● (814) 835-5300 ● http://www.mtsd.k12.pa.us

Grade Span: KG-12 **Schools**: *Regular* 12 ● *Spec Ed* 0 ● *Alt* 0 **Students**: 7,554 **Total Teachers**: 398 **Student/Classroom Teacher Ratio**: 20.5	**Expenditures/Student**: $5,561 **Librarians**: 7.5 1,007 students/librarian **Guidance Counselors**: 11.5 657 students/counselor	**% Amer Indian**: 0.2 **% Asian**: 1.7 **% Black**: 1.7 **% Hispanic**: 0.9 **% White**: 95.5	National ***Socio-Economic Status*** indicator percentiles are not available for the state of Pennsylvania

Erie County
[HARBORCREEK] **HARBOR CREEK S.D.**
6375 BUFFALO ROAD ● HARBORCREEK PA 16421-1606 ● (814) 898-5700

Grade Span: KG-12 **Schools**: *Regular* 4 ● *Spec Ed* 0 ● *Alt* 0 **Students**: 2,751 **Total Teachers**: 143 **Student/Classroom Teacher Ratio**: 20.2	**Expenditures/Student**: $5,523 **Librarians**: 2.0 1,376 students/librarian **Guidance Counselors**: 4.0 688 students/counselor	**% Amer Indian**: 0.0 **% Asian**: 0.4 **% Black**: 1.1 **% Hispanic**: 0.1 **% White**: 98.4	National ***Socio-Economic Status*** indicator percentiles are not available for the state of Pennsylvania

Fayette County
CONNELLSVILLE AREA S.D.
125 NORTH SEVENTH STREET ● CONNELLSVILLE PA 15425-2529 ● (412) 628-3300

Grade Span: KG-12 **Schools**: *Regular* 11 ● *Spec Ed* 0 ● *Alt* 0 **Students**: 6,138 **Total Teachers**: 298 **Student/Classroom Teacher Ratio**: 20.9	**Expenditures/Student**: $5,875 **Librarians**: 7.0 877 students/librarian **Guidance Counselors**: 11.0 558 students/counselor	**% Amer Indian**: 0.0 **% Asian**: 0.1 **% Black**: 2.2 **% Hispanic**: 0.1 **% White**: 97.7	National ***Socio-Economic Status*** indicator percentiles are not available for the state of Pennsylvania

Fayette County
[MASONTOWN] **ALBERT GALLATIN AREA S.D.**
10 WEST CHURCH STREET ● MASONTOWN PA 15461-1800 ● (412) 583-1654

Grade Span: KG-12 **Schools**: *Regular* 9 ● *Spec Ed* 0 ● *Alt* 0 **Students**: 4,347 **Total Teachers**: 213 **Student/Classroom Teacher Ratio**: 20.7	**Expenditures/Student**: $4,954 **Librarians**: 6.0 725 students/librarian **Guidance Counselors**: 6.0 725 students/counselor	**% Amer Indian**: 0.1 **% Asian**: 0.1 **% Black**: 3.8 **% Hispanic**: 0.1 **% White**: 95.9	National ***Socio-Economic Status*** indicator percentiles are not available for the state of Pennsylvania

Fayette County
[UNIONTOWN] LAUREL HIGHLANDS S.D.
304 BAILEY AVENUE ● UNIONTOWN PA 15401-2497 ● (412) 437-2821 ● http://www.hhs.net/lhsd

Grade Span: KG-12 **Schools**: *Regular* 7 ● *Spec Ed* 0 ● *Alt* 0 **Students**: 3,953 **Total Teachers**: 208 **Student/Classroom Teacher Ratio**: 20.4	**Expenditures/Student**: $5,814 **Librarians**: 5.0 791 students/librarian **Guidance Counselors**: 4.0 988 students/counselor	**% Amer Indian**: 0.0 **% Asian**: 0.3 **% Black**: 5.3 **% Hispanic**: 0.2 **% White**: 94.2	National ***Socio-Economic Status*** indicator percentiles are not available for the state of Pennsylvania

Fayette County
UNIONTOWN AREA S.D.
23 EAST CHURCH STREET ● UNIONTOWN PA 15401-3578 ● (412) 438-4501

Grade Span: KG-12 **Schools**: *Regular* 8 ● *Spec Ed* 0 ● *Alt* 0 **Students**: 3,724 **Total Teachers**: 184 **Student/Classroom Teacher Ratio**: 21.7	**Expenditures/Student**: $5,897 **Librarians**: 6.0 621 students/librarian **Guidance Counselors**: 8.0 466 students/counselor	**% Amer Indian**: 0.2 **% Asian**: 0.0 **% Black**: 10.9 **% Hispanic**: 0.1 **% White**: 88.7	National ***Socio-Economic Status*** indicator percentiles are not available for the state of Pennsylvania

Franklin County
CHAMBERSBURG AREA S.D.
511 SOUTH SIXTH STREET ● CHAMBERSBURG PA 17201-3405 ● (717) 263-9281

Grade Span: KG-12 **Schools**: *Regular* 22 ● *Spec Ed* 0 ● *Alt* 0 **Students**: 8,092 **Total Teachers**: 425 **Student/Classroom Teacher Ratio**: 20.4	**Expenditures/Student**: $5,347 **Librarians**: 12.0 674 students/librarian **Guidance Counselors**: 16.0 506 students/counselor	**% Amer Indian**: 0.1 **% Asian**: 0.9 **% Black**: 6.7 **% Hispanic**: 2.2 **% White**: 90.1	National ***Socio-Economic Status*** indicator percentiles are not available for the state of Pennsylvania

Franklin County
[MERCERSBURG] TUSCARORA S.D.
118 EAST SEMINARY STREET ● MERCERSBURG PA 17236-1698 ● (717) 328-3127

Grade Span: KG-12 **Schools**: *Regular* 6 ● *Spec Ed* 0 ● *Alt* 0 **Students**: 2,720 **Total Teachers**: 161 **Student/Classroom Teacher Ratio**: 18.0	**Expenditures/Student**: $6,345 **Librarians**: 3.0 907 students/librarian **Guidance Counselors**: 5.0 544 students/counselor	**% Amer Indian**: 0.2 **% Asian**: 0.3 **% Black**: 1.5 **% Hispanic**: 0.7 **% White**: 97.3	National ***Socio-Economic Status*** indicator percentiles are not available for the state of Pennsylvania

Franklin County
WAYNESBORO AREA S.D.
210 CLAYTON AVENUE PO BOX 72 ● WAYNESBORO PA 17268-0072 ● (717) 762-1191

Grade Span: KG-12 **Schools**: *Regular* 6 ● *Spec Ed* 0 ● *Alt* 0 **Students**: 4,218 **Total Teachers**: 245 **Student/Classroom Teacher Ratio**: 17.8	**Expenditures/Student**: $5,860 **Librarians**: 5.5 767 students/librarian **Guidance Counselors**: 5.0 844 students/counselor	**% Amer Indian**: 0.2 **% Asian**: 0.9 **% Black**: 2.7 **% Hispanic**: 1.2 **% White**: 95.0	National ***Socio-Economic Status*** indicator percentiles are not available for the state of Pennsylvania

Huntingdon County
HUNTINGDON AREA S.D.
2400 CASSADY AVENUE SUITE 2 ● HUNTINGDON PA 16652-2602 ● (814) 643-4140

Grade Span: KG-12 **Schools**: *Regular* 8 ● *Spec Ed* 0 ● *Alt* 0 **Students**: 2,500 **Total Teachers**: 170 **Student/Classroom Teacher Ratio**: 17.7	**Expenditures/Student**: $5,726 **Librarians**: 4.0 625 students/librarian **Guidance Counselors**: 4.0 625 students/counselor	**% Amer Indian**: 0.1 **% Asian**: 0.4 **% Black**: 1.6 **% Hispanic**: 0.3 **% White**: 97.6	National ***Socio-Economic Status*** indicator percentiles are not available for the state of Pennsylvania

Indiana County

INDIANA AREA S.D.

501 EAST PIKE ● INDIANA PA 15701-2298 ● (412) 463-8713

Grade Span: KG-12 **Schools**: *Regular* 6 ● *Spec Ed* 0 ● *Alt* 0 **Students**: 3,757 **Total Teachers**: 221 **Student/Classroom Teacher Ratio**: 17.6	**Expenditures/Student**: $6,296 **Librarians**: 6.0 626 students/librarian **Guidance Counselors**: 9.0 417 students/counselor	**% Amer Indian**: 0.1 **% Asian**: 1.5 **% Black**: 2.6 **% Hispanic**: 0.5 **% White**: 95.3	National ***Socio-Economic Status*** indicator percentiles are not available for the state of Pennsylvania

Jefferson County

PUNXSUTAWNEY AREA S.D.

PO BOX 478 ● PUNXSUTAWNEY PA 15767-0478 ● (814) 938-5110

Grade Span: KG-12 **Schools**: *Regular* 11 ● *Spec Ed* 0 ● *Alt* 0 **Students**: 3,418 **Total Teachers**: 201 **Student/Classroom Teacher Ratio**: 18.1	**Expenditures/Student**: $5,962 **Librarians**: 4.0 855 students/librarian **Guidance Counselors**: 8.0 427 students/counselor	**% Amer Indian**: 0.1 **% Asian**: 0.3 **% Black**: 0.3 **% Hispanic**: 0.1 **% White**: 99.2	National ***Socio-Economic Status*** indicator percentiles are not available for the state of Pennsylvania

Juniata County

[MIFFLINTOWN] **JUNIATA COUNTY S.D.**

SOUTH SEVENTH STREET ● MIFFLINTOWN PA 17059-0227 ● (717) 436-2111 ● http://dns.tiu.k12.pa.us:80/~rangle

Grade Span: KG-12 **Schools**: *Regular* 12 ● *Spec Ed* 0 ● *Alt* 0 **Students**: 3,432 **Total Teachers**: 172 **Student/Classroom Teacher Ratio**: 20.2	**Expenditures/Student**: $4,207 **Librarians**: 4.0 858 students/librarian **Guidance Counselors**: 4.0 858 students/counselor	**% Amer Indian**: 0.1 **% Asian**: 0.7 **% Black**: 0.2 **% Hispanic**: 0.3 **% White**: 98.7	National ***Socio-Economic Status*** indicator percentiles are not available for the state of Pennsylvania

Lackawanna County

[CLARKS SUMMIT] **ABINGTON HEIGHTS S.D.**

218 EAST GROVE STREET ● CLARKS SUMMIT PA 18411-1776 ● (717) 586-2511 ● http://ns.neiu.k12.pa.us/WWW/AHNC/AHNChome.html

Grade Span: KG-12 **Schools**: *Regular* 6 ● *Spec Ed* 0 ● *Alt* 0 **Students**: 3,629 **Total Teachers**: 204 **Student/Classroom Teacher Ratio**: 19.3	**Expenditures/Student**: $6,156 **Librarians**: 5.0 726 students/librarian **Guidance Counselors**: 10.0 363 students/counselor	**% Amer Indian**: 0.4 **% Asian**: 1.8 **% Black**: 0.7 **% Hispanic**: 0.3 **% White**: 96.9	National ***Socio-Economic Status*** indicator percentiles are not available for the state of Pennsylvania

Lackawanna County

[MOSCOW] **NORTH POCONO S.D.**

701 CHURCH STREET ● MOSCOW PA 18444-9392 ● (717) 842-7659 ● http://ns.neiu.k12.pa.us./WWW/NP

Grade Span: KG-12 **Schools**: *Regular* 5 ● *Spec Ed* 0 ● *Alt* 0 **Students**: 3,329 **Total Teachers**: 177 **Student/Classroom Teacher Ratio**: 20.4	**Expenditures/Student**: $5,759 **Librarians**: 3.0 1,110 students/librarian **Guidance Counselors**: 8.0 416 students/counselor	**% Amer Indian**: 0.0 **% Asian**: 0.4 **% Black**: 1.0 **% Hispanic**: 0.9 **% White**: 97.8	National ***Socio-Economic Status*** indicator percentiles are not available for the state of Pennsylvania

Lackawanna County

SCRANTON S.D.

425 NORTH WASHINGTON AVENUE ● SCRANTON PA 18503-1396 ● (717) 348-3400 ● http://scrantonsd.neiu.k12.pa.us

Grade Span: PK-12 **Schools**: *Regular* 18 ● *Spec Ed* 0 ● *Alt* 0 **Students**: 8,918 **Total Teachers**: 567 **Student/Classroom Teacher Ratio**: 18.2	**Expenditures/Student**: $7,029 **Librarians**: 12.0 743 students/librarian **Guidance Counselors**: 19.0 469 students/counselor	**% Amer Indian**: 0.1 **% Asian**: 1.9 **% Black**: 6.1 **% Hispanic**: 2.5 **% White**: 89.4	National ***Socio-Economic Status*** indicator percentiles are not available for the state of Pennsylvania

Lancaster County
[DENVER] **COCALICO S.D.**
800 SOUTH FOURTH STREET ● DENVER PA 17517-1199 ● (717) 336-1413

Grade Span: KG-12 **Schools**: *Regular* 6 ● *Spec Ed* 0 ● *Alt* 0 **Students**: 2,949 **Total Teachers**: 163 **Student/Classroom Teacher Ratio**: 19.1	**Expenditures/Student**: $5,799 **Librarians**: 5.0 590 students/librarian **Guidance Counselors**: 7.0 421 students/counselor	**% Amer Indian**: 0.0 **% Asian**: 2.4 **% Black**: 0.4 **% Hispanic**: 1.1 **% White**: 96.1	National ***Socio-Economic Status*** indicator percentiles are not available for the state of Pennsylvania

Lancaster County
ELIZABETHTOWN AREA S.D.
600 EAST HIGH STREET ● ELIZABETHTOWN PA 17022-1799 ● (717) 367-1521

Grade Span: KG-12 **Schools**: *Regular* 7 ● *Spec Ed* 0 ● *Alt* 0 **Students**: 3,803 **Total Teachers**: 192 **Student/Classroom Teacher Ratio**: 21.2	**Expenditures/Student**: $5,198 **Librarians**: 5.0 761 students/librarian **Guidance Counselors**: 7.6 500 students/counselor	**% Amer Indian**: 0.3 **% Asian**: 1.2 **% Black**: 0.8 **% Hispanic**: 1.0 **% White**: 96.7	National ***Socio-Economic Status*** indicator percentiles are not available for the state of Pennsylvania

Lancaster County
EPHRATA AREA S.D.
803 OAK BOULEVARD ● EPHRATA PA 17522-1998 ● (717) 733-1513

Grade Span: KG-12 **Schools**: *Regular* 9 ● *Spec Ed* 0 ● *Alt* 0 **Students**: 4,383 **Total Teachers**: 234 **Student/Classroom Teacher Ratio**: 20.1	**Expenditures/Student**: $5,321 **Librarians**: 6.5 674 students/librarian **Guidance Counselors**: 10.2 430 students/counselor	**% Amer Indian**: 0.0 **% Asian**: 2.4 **% Black**: 0.7 **% Hispanic**: 1.5 **% White**: 95.4	National ***Socio-Economic Status*** indicator percentiles are not available for the state of Pennsylvania

Lancaster County
LAMPETER-STRASBURG S.D.
BOX 428 ● LAMPETER PA 17537-0428 ● (717) 464-3311 ● http://www.iu13.k12.pa.us/lampstras/home.html

Grade Span: KG-12 **Schools**: *Regular* 5 ● *Spec Ed* 0 ● *Alt* 0 **Students**: 2,647 **Total Teachers**: 149 **Student/Classroom Teacher Ratio**: 20.2	**Expenditures/Student**: $5,732 **Librarians**: 3.0 882 students/librarian **Guidance Counselors**: 5.0 529 students/counselor	**% Amer Indian**: 0.0 **% Asian**: 0.6 **% Black**: 0.6 **% Hispanic**: 1.4 **% White**: 97.5	National ***Socio-Economic Status*** indicator percentiles are not available for the state of Pennsylvania

Lancaster County
[LANCASTER] **CONESTOGA VALLEY S.D.**
2110 HORSESHOE ROAD ● LANCASTER PA 17601-6099 ● (717) 397-2421 ● http://www.iu13.k12.pa.us/cvsd

Grade Span: KG-12 **Schools**: *Regular* 7 ● *Spec Ed* 0 ● *Alt* 0 **Students**: 3,545 **Total Teachers**: 211 **Student/Classroom Teacher Ratio**: 17.6	**Expenditures/Student**: $6,336 **Librarians**: 6.0 591 students/librarian **Guidance Counselors**: 10.0 355 students/counselor	**% Amer Indian**: 0.0 **% Asian**: 4.3 **% Black**: 1.8 **% Hispanic**: 3.9 **% White**: 89.9	National ***Socio-Economic Status*** indicator percentiles are not available for the state of Pennsylvania

Lancaster County
LANCASTER S.D.
1020 LEHIGH AVENUE PO BOX 150 ● LANCASTER PA 17603-0150 ● (717) 291-6121 ● http://www.lancaster.k12.pa.us/index.htm

Grade Span: KG-12 **Schools**: *Regular* 19 ● *Spec Ed* 0 ● *Alt* 0 **Students**: 10,737 **Total Teachers**: 621 **Student/Classroom Teacher Ratio**: 18.0	**Expenditures/Student**: $6,328 **Librarians**: 20.0 537 students/librarian **Guidance Counselors**: 26.0 413 students/counselor	**% Amer Indian**: 0.1 **% Asian**: 3.0 **% Black**: 21.1 **% Hispanic**: 39.7 **% White**: 36.0	National ***Socio-Economic Status*** indicator percentiles are not available for the state of Pennsylvania

Lancaster County
[LANCASTER] **MANHEIM TOWNSHIP S.D.**
SCHOOL ROAD PO BOX 5134 ● LANCASTER PA 17606-5134 ● (717) 569-8231 ● http://www.iu13.k12.pa.us/mtwp

Grade Span: KG-12 **Schools**: *Regular* 7 ● *Spec Ed* 0 ● *Alt* 0 **Students**: 4,672 **Total Teachers**: 273 **Student/Classroom Teacher Ratio**: 22.4	**Expenditures/Student**: $6,377 **Librarians**: 9.0 519 students/librarian **Guidance Counselors**: 13.0 359 students/counselor	**% Amer Indian**: 0.1 **% Asian**: 4.9 **% Black**: 2.3 **% Hispanic**: 3.2 **% White**: 89.6	National ***Socio-Economic Status*** indicator percentiles are not available for the state of Pennsylvania

Lancaster County
[LANDISVILLE] **HEMPFIELD S.D.**
200 CHURCH STREET ● LANDISVILLE PA 17538-1299 ● (717) 898-5560

Grade Span: KG-12 **Schools**: *Regular* 10 ● *Spec Ed* 0 ● *Alt* 0 **Students**: 6,961 **Total Teachers**: 391 **Student/Classroom Teacher Ratio**: 26.3	**Expenditures/Student**: $5,450 **Librarians**: 12.0 580 students/librarian **Guidance Counselors**: 12.0 580 students/counselor	**% Amer Indian**: 0.2 **% Asian**: 2.1 **% Black**: 2.0 **% Hispanic**: 4.2 **% White**: 91.6	National ***Socio-Economic Status*** indicator percentiles are not available for the state of Pennsylvania

Lancaster County
[LITITZ] **WARWICK S.D.**
301 WEST ORANGE STREET ● LITITZ PA 17543-1898 ● (717) 626-3734 ● http://www.warwick.k12.pa.us

Grade Span: KG-12 **Schools**: *Regular* 6 ● *Spec Ed* 0 ● *Alt* 0 **Students**: 4,230 **Total Teachers**: 236 **Student/Classroom Teacher Ratio**: 18.6	**Expenditures/Student**: $5,323 **Librarians**: 7.0 604 students/librarian **Guidance Counselors**: 8.2 516 students/counselor	**% Amer Indian**: 0.1 **% Asian**: 1.3 **% Black**: 0.7 **% Hispanic**: 1.4 **% White**: 96.5	National ***Socio-Economic Status*** indicator percentiles are not available for the state of Pennsylvania

Lancaster County
MANHEIM CENTRAL S.D.
71 NORTH HAZEL STREET ● MANHEIM PA 17545-1500 ● (717) 665-3422

Grade Span: KG-12 **Schools**: *Regular* 8 ● *Spec Ed* 0 ● *Alt* 0 **Students**: 3,251 **Total Teachers**: 173 **Student/Classroom Teacher Ratio**: 20.6	**Expenditures/Student**: $5,423 **Librarians**: 4.5 722 students/librarian **Guidance Counselors**: 8.5 382 students/counselor	**% Amer Indian**: 0.0 **% Asian**: 1.4 **% Black**: 0.8 **% Hispanic**: 0.8 **% White**: 97.0	National ***Socio-Economic Status*** indicator percentiles are not available for the state of Pennsylvania

Lancaster County
[MILLERSVILLE] **PENN MANOR S.D.**
PO BOX 1001 ● MILLERSVILLE PA 17551-0301 ● (717) 872-9500 ● http://www.iu13.k12.pa.us/pmsd

Grade Span: KG-12 **Schools**: *Regular* 10 ● *Spec Ed* 0 ● *Alt* 0 **Students**: 5,359 **Total Teachers**: 278 **Student/Classroom Teacher Ratio**: 19.7	**Expenditures/Student**: $5,105 **Librarians**: 5.0 1,072 students/librarian **Guidance Counselors**: 8.3 646 students/counselor	**% Amer Indian**: 0.1 **% Asian**: 1.2 **% Black**: 1.7 **% Hispanic**: 1.8 **% White**: 95.3	National ***Socio-Economic Status*** indicator percentiles are not available for the state of Pennsylvania

Lancaster County
[MOUNT JOY] **DONEGAL S.D.**
CALLER 304 ● MOUNT JOY PA 17552-0304 ● (717) 653-1447 ● http://www.donegal.k12.pa.us

Grade Span: KG-12 **Schools**: *Regular* 6 ● *Spec Ed* 0 ● *Alt* 0 **Students**: 2,561 **Total Teachers**: 136 **Student/Classroom Teacher Ratio**: 21.1	**Expenditures/Student**: $5,451 **Librarians**: 4.0 640 students/librarian **Guidance Counselors**: 5.6 457 students/counselor	**% Amer Indian**: 0.1 **% Asian**: 0.6 **% Black**: 1.8 **% Hispanic**: 1.3 **% White**: 96.1	National ***Socio-Economic Status*** indicator percentiles are not available for the state of Pennsylvania

Lancaster County
[NEW HOLLAND] EASTERN LANCASTER COUNTY S.D.
117-119 S CUSTER AV PO BOX 609 ● NEW HOLLAND PA 17557-0609 ● (717) 354-1500 ● http://www.iu13.k12.pa.us/elanco

Grade Span: KG-12	**Expenditures/Student**: $5,710	**% Amer Indian**: 0.1	National ***Socio-Economic***
Schools: *Regular* 7 ● *Spec Ed* 0 ● *Alt* 0	**Librarians**: 5.0	**% Asian**: 2.5	***Status*** indicator percentiles
Students: 3,501	700 students/librarian	**% Black**: 1.3	are not available for the
Total Teachers: 207	**Guidance Counselors**: 4.4	**% Hispanic**: 2.5	state of Pennsylvania
Student/Classroom Teacher Ratio: 17.4	796 students/counselor	**% White**: 93.6	

Lancaster County
[QUARRYVILLE] SOLANCO S.D.
121 SOUTH HESS STREET ● QUARRYVILLE PA 17566-1200 ● (717) 786-8401

Grade Span: KG-12	**Expenditures/Student**: $4,902	**% Amer Indian**: 0.0	National ***Socio-Economic***
Schools: *Regular* 8 ● *Spec Ed* 0 ● *Alt* 0	**Librarians**: 6.0	**% Asian**: 0.3	***Status*** indicator percentiles
Students: 4,262	710 students/librarian	**% Black**: 1.7	are not available for the
Total Teachers: 199	**Guidance Counselors**: 8.5	**% Hispanic**: 1.1	state of Pennsylvania
Student/Classroom Teacher Ratio: 23.2	501 students/counselor	**% White**: 96.8	

Lawrence County
NEW CASTLE AREA S.D.
420 FERN STREET ● NEW CASTLE PA 16101-2596 ● (412) 656-4756 ● http://www.newcastle.k12.pa.us

Grade Span: KG-12	**Expenditures/Student**: $6,107	**% Amer Indian**: 0.0	National ***Socio-Economic***
Schools: *Regular* 8 ● *Spec Ed* 0 ● *Alt* 0	**Librarians**: 6.0	**% Asian**: 0.1	***Status*** indicator percentiles
Students: 3,853	642 students/librarian	**% Black**: 18.0	are not available for the
Total Teachers: 225	**Guidance Counselors**: 5.0	**% Hispanic**: 0.2	state of Pennsylvania
Student/Classroom Teacher Ratio: 20.0	771 students/counselor	**% White**: 81.6	

Lebanon County
[LEBANON] CORNWALL-LEBANON S.D.
105 EAST EVERGREEN RD ● LEBANON PA 17042-7595 ● (717) 272-2031

Grade Span: KG-12	**Expenditures/Student**: $6,023	**% Amer Indian**: 0.4	National ***Socio-Economic***
Schools: *Regular* 6 ● *Spec Ed* 0 ● *Alt* 0	**Librarians**: 4.0	**% Asian**: 2.3	***Status*** indicator percentiles
Students: 4,442	1,111 students/librarian	**% Black**: 1.5	are not available for the
Total Teachers: 258	**Guidance Counselors**: 5.0	**% Hispanic**: 5.2	state of Pennsylvania
Student/Classroom Teacher Ratio: 17.1	888 students/counselor	**% White**: 90.6	

Lebanon County
LEBANON S.D.
1000 SOUTH EIGHTH STREET ● LEBANON PA 17042-6727 ● (717) 273-9391

Grade Span: PK-12	**Expenditures/Student**: $5,617	**% Amer Indian**: 0.0	National ***Socio-Economic***
Schools: *Regular* 7 ● *Spec Ed* 0 ● *Alt* 0	**Librarians**: 4.0	**% Asian**: 1.4	***Status*** indicator percentiles
Students: 4,101	1,025 students/librarian	**% Black**: 3.4	are not available for the
Total Teachers: 213	**Guidance Counselors**: 8.0	**% Hispanic**: 20.7	state of Pennsylvania
Student/Classroom Teacher Ratio: 23.0	513 students/counselor	**% White**: 74.4	

Lebanon County
PALMYRA AREA S.D.
1125 PARK DRIVE ● PALMYRA PA 17078-3499 ● (717) 838-3144

Grade Span: KG-12	**Expenditures/Student**: $4,875	**% Amer Indian**: 0.0	National ***Socio-Economic***
Schools: *Regular* 5 ● *Spec Ed* 0 ● *Alt* 0	**Librarians**: 4.0	**% Asian**: 1.1	***Status*** indicator percentiles
Students: 2,729	682 students/librarian	**% Black**: 1.2	are not available for the
Total Teachers: 144	**Guidance Counselors**: 5.0	**% Hispanic**: 0.4	state of Pennsylvania
Student/Classroom Teacher Ratio: 19.5	546 students/counselor	**% White**: 97.3	

Lehigh County
ALLENTOWN CITY S.D.
31 SOUTH PENN ST PO BOX 328 ● ALLENTOWN PA 18105-0328 ● (610) 821-2600

Grade Span: KG-12 **Schools**: *Regular* 23 ● *Spec Ed* 0 ● *Alt* 0 **Students**: 15,042 **Total Teachers**: 741 **Student/Classroom Teacher Ratio**: 23.0	**Expenditures/Student**: $6,345 **Librarians**: 16.8 895 students/librarian **Guidance Counselors**: 35.0 430 students/counselor	**% Amer Indian**: 0.1 **% Asian**: 2.4 **% Black**: 12.1 **% Hispanic**: 36.1 **% White**: 49.4	National ***Socio-Economic Status*** indicator percentiles are not available for the state of Pennsylvania

Lehigh County
[ALLENTOWN] **PARKLAND S.D.**
1210 SPRINGHOUSE ROAD ● ALLENTOWN PA 18104-2119 ● (610) 366-1910

Grade Span: KG-12 **Schools**: *Regular* 10 ● *Spec Ed* 0 ● *Alt* 0 **Students**: 6,830 **Total Teachers**: 373 **Student/Classroom Teacher Ratio**: 19.9	**Expenditures/Student**: $6,249 **Librarians**: 10.3 663 students/librarian **Guidance Counselors**: 16.0 427 students/counselor	**% Amer Indian**: 0.0 **% Asian**: 3.1 **% Black**: 1.2 **% Hispanic**: 1.2 **% White**: 94.5	National ***Socio-Economic Status*** indicator percentiles are not available for the state of Pennsylvania

Lehigh County
[EMMAUS] **EAST PENN S.D.**
640 MACUNGIE AVENUE ● EMMAUS PA 18049-2130 ● (610) 967-3101

Grade Span: KG-12 **Schools**: *Regular* 11 ● *Spec Ed* 0 ● *Alt* 0 **Students**: 6,583 **Total Teachers**: 351 **Student/Classroom Teacher Ratio**: 20.3	**Expenditures/Student**: $5,783 **Librarians**: 5.8 1,135 students/librarian **Guidance Counselors**: 14.0 470 students/counselor	**% Amer Indian**: 0.1 **% Asian**: 4.0 **% Black**: 1.0 **% Hispanic**: 1.0 **% White**: 93.9	National ***Socio-Economic Status*** indicator percentiles are not available for the state of Pennsylvania

Lehigh County
WHITEHALL-COPLAY S.D.
2940 MACARTHUR ROAD ● WHITEHALL PA 18052-3492 ● (610) 439-1431

Grade Span: KG-12 **Schools**: *Regular* 4 ● *Spec Ed* 0 ● *Alt* 0 **Students**: 3,515 **Total Teachers**: 179 **Student/Classroom Teacher Ratio**: 20.6	**Expenditures/Student**: $6,006 **Librarians**: 4.0 879 students/librarian **Guidance Counselors**: 7.8 451 students/counselor	**% Amer Indian**: 0.3 **% Asian**: 2.5 **% Black**: 3.5 **% Hispanic**: 3.2 **% White**: 90.5	National ***Socio-Economic Status*** indicator percentiles are not available for the state of Pennsylvania

Luzerne County
DALLAS S.D.
CHURCH STREET BOX 2000 ● DALLAS PA 18612-0720 ● (717) 675-5201

Grade Span: KG-12 **Schools**: *Regular* 4 ● *Spec Ed* 0 ● *Alt* 0 **Students**: 2,508 **Total Teachers**: 133 **Student/Classroom Teacher Ratio**: 19.2	**Expenditures/Student**: $5,980 **Librarians**: 3.0 836 students/librarian **Guidance Counselors**: 5.6 448 students/counselor	**% Amer Indian**: 0.0 **% Asian**: 1.0 **% Black**: 0.3 **% Hispanic**: 0.3 **% White**: 98.4	National ***Socio-Economic Status*** indicator percentiles are not available for the state of Pennsylvania

Luzerne County
[EXETER] **WYOMING AREA S.D.**
MEMORIAL STREET ● EXETER PA 18643-2698 ● (717) 655-3733

Grade Span: PK-12 **Schools**: *Regular* 5 ● *Spec Ed* 0 ● *Alt* 0 **Students**: 2,714 **Total Teachers**: 126 **Student/Classroom Teacher Ratio**: 23.3	**Expenditures/Student**: $5,488 **Librarians**: 3.0 905 students/librarian **Guidance Counselors**: 5.0 543 students/counselor	**% Amer Indian**: 0.0 **% Asian**: 0.1 **% Black**: 0.7 **% Hispanic**: 0.0 **% White**: 99.2	National ***Socio-Economic Status*** indicator percentiles are not available for the state of Pennsylvania

Luzerne County

HAZLETON AREA S.D.

101 SOUTH CHURCH STREET ● HAZLETON PA 18201-6292 ● (717) 459-3111

Grade Span: KG-12	**Expenditures/Student**: $7,006	**% Amer Indian**: 0.1	National ***Socio-Economic Status*** indicator percentiles are not available for the state of Pennsylvania
Schools: *Regular* 14 ● *Spec Ed* 0 ● *Alt* 0	**Librarians**: 4.0	**% Asian**: 0.3	
Students: 8,657	2,164 students/librarian	**% Black**: 0.4	
Total Teachers: 497	**Guidance Counselors**: 16.0	**% Hispanic**: 1.6	
Student/Classroom Teacher Ratio: 19.0	541 students/counselor	**% White**: 97.6	

Luzerne County

[KINGSTON] **WYOMING VALLEY WEST S.D.**

450 NORTH MAPLE AVENUE ● KINGSTON PA 18704-3683 ● (717) 288-6551 ● http://www.microserve.net/~liu8

Grade Span: KG-12	**Expenditures/Student**: $6,083	**% Amer Indian**: 0.2	National ***Socio-Economic Status*** indicator percentiles are not available for the state of Pennsylvania
Schools: *Regular* 9 ● *Spec Ed* 0 ● *Alt* 0	**Librarians**: 4.0	**% Asian**: 0.6	
Students: 5,411	1,353 students/librarian	**% Black**: 0.9	
Total Teachers: 308	**Guidance Counselors**: 10.0	**% Hispanic**: 0.4	
Student/Classroom Teacher Ratio: 17.7	541 students/counselor	**% White**: 97.9	

Luzerne County

[MOUNTAINTOP] **CRESTWOOD S.D.**

281 SOUTH MOUNTAIN BOULEVARD ● MOUNTAINTOP PA 18707-1994 ● (717) 474-6888

Grade Span: KG-12	**Expenditures/Student**: $5,348	**% Amer Indian**: 0.2	National ***Socio-Economic Status*** indicator percentiles are not available for the state of Pennsylvania
Schools: *Regular* 3 ● *Spec Ed* 0 ● *Alt* 0	**Librarians**: 2.0	**% Asian**: 0.9	
Students: 2,795	1,398 students/librarian	**% Black**: 0.9	
Total Teachers: 123	**Guidance Counselors**: 4.0	**% Hispanic**: 0.9	
Student/Classroom Teacher Ratio: 22.9	699 students/counselor	**% White**: 97.1	

Luzerne County

PITTSTON AREA S.D.

5 STOUT STREET ● PITTSTON PA 18640-3399 ● (717) 654-2271

Grade Span: KG-12	**Expenditures/Student**: $6,453	**% Amer Indian**: 0.0	National ***Socio-Economic Status*** indicator percentiles are not available for the state of Pennsylvania
Schools: *Regular* 5 ● *Spec Ed* 0 ● *Alt* 0	**Librarians**: 4.0	**% Asian**: 0.3	
Students: 3,252	813 students/librarian	**% Black**: 0.7	
Total Teachers: 163	**Guidance Counselors**: 5.0	**% Hispanic**: 0.2	
Student/Classroom Teacher Ratio: 20.2	650 students/counselor	**% White**: 98.7	

Luzerne County

WILKES-BARRE AREA S.D.

730 SOUTH MAIN STREET ● WILKES-BARRE PA 18711-0375 ● (717) 826-7111

Grade Span: KG-12	**Expenditures/Student**: $6,916	**% Amer Indian**: 0.3	National ***Socio-Economic Status*** indicator percentiles are not available for the state of Pennsylvania
Schools: *Regular* 12 ● *Spec Ed* 0 ● *Alt* 0	**Librarians**: 7.0	**% Asian**: 1.2	
Students: 7,525	1,075 students/librarian	**% Black**: 6.6	
Total Teachers: 438	**Guidance Counselors**: 14.0	**% Hispanic**: 0.7	
Student/Classroom Teacher Ratio: 18.4	538 students/counselor	**% White**: 91.2	

Lycoming County

JERSEY SHORE AREA S.D.

201 SOUTH BROAD STREET ● JERSEY SHORE PA 17740-1898 ● (717) 398-1561

Grade Span: KG-12	**Expenditures/Student**: $5,397	**% Amer Indian**: 0.1	National ***Socio-Economic Status*** indicator percentiles are not available for the state of Pennsylvania
Schools: *Regular* 6 ● *Spec Ed* 0 ● *Alt* 0	**Librarians**: 4.0	**% Asian**: 0.4	
Students: 3,372	843 students/librarian	**% Black**: 0.4	
Total Teachers: 175	**Guidance Counselors**: 6.0	**% Hispanic**: 0.1	
Student/Classroom Teacher Ratio: 20.2	562 students/counselor	**% White**: 99.0	

Lycoming County
MONTOURSVILLE AREA S.D.
50 NORTH ARCH STREET ● MONTOURSVILLE PA 17754-1900 ● (717) 368-2491

Grade Span: KG-12 **Schools**: *Regular* 4 ● *Spec Ed* 0 ● *Alt* 0 **Students**: 2,542 **Total Teachers**: 137 **Student/Classroom Teacher Ratio**: 19.5	**Expenditures/Student**: $5,024 **Librarians**: 2.0 1,271 students/librarian **Guidance Counselors**: 5.0 508 students/counselor	**% Amer Indian**: 0.0 **% Asian**: 0.4 **% Black**: 0.1 **% Hispanic**: 0.1 **% White**: 99.3	National ***Socio-Economic Status*** indicator percentiles are not available for the state of Pennsylvania

Lycoming County
WILLIAMSPORT AREA S.D.
201 WEST THIRD STREET ● WILLIAMSPORT PA 17701-6463 ● (717) 327-5500 ● http://www.wasd.org

Grade Span: KG-12 **Schools**: *Regular* 12 ● *Spec Ed* 0 ● *Alt* 0 **Students**: 7,029 **Total Teachers**: 410 **Student/Classroom Teacher Ratio**: 18.1	**Expenditures/Student**: $6,183 **Librarians**: 5.0 1,406 students/librarian **Guidance Counselors**: 17.0 413 students/counselor	**% Amer Indian**: 0.1 **% Asian**: 0.7 **% Black**: 15.3 **% Hispanic**: 0.5 **% White**: 83.4	National ***Socio-Economic Status*** indicator percentiles are not available for the state of Pennsylvania

McKean County
BRADFORD AREA S.D.
50 CONGRESS STREET ● BRADFORD PA 16701-0375 ● (814) 362-3841 ● http://www.penn.com/basd/bahs

Grade Span: KG-12 **Schools**: *Regular* 6 ● *Spec Ed* 0 ● *Alt* 0 **Students**: 3,140 **Total Teachers**: 178 **Student/Classroom Teacher Ratio**: 17.5	**Expenditures/Student**: $6,342 **Librarians**: 7.0 449 students/librarian **Guidance Counselors**: 6.0 523 students/counselor	**% Amer Indian**: 0.5 **% Asian**: 1.0 **% Black**: 0.6 **% Hispanic**: 0.4 **% White**: 97.6	National ***Socio-Economic Status*** indicator percentiles are not available for the state of Pennsylvania

Mercer County
GROVE CITY AREA S.D.
511 HIGHLAND AVENUE ● GROVE CITY PA 16127-1190 ● (412) 458-6733

Grade Span: KG-12 **Schools**: *Regular* 7 ● *Spec Ed* 0 ● *Alt* 0 **Students**: 2,757 **Total Teachers**: 162 **Student/Classroom Teacher Ratio**: 19.4	**Expenditures/Student**: $5,307 **Librarians**: 4.0 689 students/librarian **Guidance Counselors**: 5.0 551 students/counselor	**% Amer Indian**: 0.3 **% Asian**: 0.8 **% Black**: 7.1 **% Hispanic**: 0.9 **% White**: 90.9	National ***Socio-Economic Status*** indicator percentiles are not available for the state of Pennsylvania

Mercer County
SHARON CITY S.D.
215 FORKER BOULEVARD ● SHARON PA 16146-3699 ● (412) 983-4000

Grade Span: KG-12 **Schools**: *Regular* 4 ● *Spec Ed* 0 ● *Alt* 0 **Students**: 2,614 **Total Teachers**: 151 **Student/Classroom Teacher Ratio**: 17.6	**Expenditures/Student**: $5,257 **Librarians**: 2.0 1,307 students/librarian **Guidance Counselors**: 5.0 523 students/counselor	**% Amer Indian**: 0.2 **% Asian**: 0.8 **% Black**: 17.3 **% Hispanic**: 0.5 **% White**: 81.3	National ***Socio-Economic Status*** indicator percentiles are not available for the state of Pennsylvania

Mifflin County
[LEWISTOWN] **MIFFLIN COUNTY S.D.**
201 EIGHTH STREET ● LEWISTOWN PA 17044-1197 ● (717) 248-0148

Grade Span: KG-12 **Schools**: *Regular* 14 ● *Spec Ed* 0 ● *Alt* 0 **Students**: 6,362 **Total Teachers**: 384 **Student/Classroom Teacher Ratio**: 17.3	**Expenditures/Student**: $5,650 **Librarians**: 7.0 909 students/librarian **Guidance Counselors**: 8.0 795 students/counselor	**% Amer Indian**: 0.1 **% Asian**: 0.7 **% Black**: 0.9 **% Hispanic**: 0.2 **% White**: 98.0	National ***Socio-Economic Status*** indicator percentiles are not available for the state of Pennsylvania

Monroe County
[BRODHEADSVILLE] **PLEASANT VALLEY S.D.**
ROUTE 115 ● BRODHEADSVILLE PA 18322-2002 ● (717) 992-5711

Grade Span: KG-12	**Expenditures/Student**: $5,044	**% Amer Indian**: 0.1	National ***Socio-Economic Status*** indicator percentiles are not available for the state of Pennsylvania
Schools: *Regular* 6 ● *Spec Ed* 0 ● *Alt* 0	**Librarians**: 5.0	**% Asian**: 0.6	
Students: 5,114	1,023 students/librarian	**% Black**: 2.0	
Total Teachers: 254	**Guidance Counselors**: 10.0	**% Hispanic**: 3.7	
Student/Classroom Teacher Ratio: 21.3	511 students/counselor	**% White**: 93.6	

Monroe County
EAST STROUDSBURG AREA S.D.
321 N COURTLAND ST PO BOX 298 ● EAST STROUDSBURG PA 18301-0298 ● (717) 424-8500

Grade Span: KG-12	**Expenditures/Student**: $5,647	**% Amer Indian**: 0.2	National ***Socio-Economic Status*** indicator percentiles are not available for the state of Pennsylvania
Schools: *Regular* 7 ● *Spec Ed* 0 ● *Alt* 0	**Librarians**: 6.6	**% Asian**: 1.6	
Students: 5,690	862 students/librarian	**% Black**: 7.0	
Total Teachers: 326	**Guidance Counselors**: 12.0	**% Hispanic**: 6.0	
Student/Classroom Teacher Ratio: 17.9	474 students/counselor	**% White**: 85.2	

Monroe County
STROUDSBURG AREA S.D.
123 LINDEN STREET ● STROUDSBURG PA 18360-1399 ● (717) 421-1990

Grade Span: KG-12	**Expenditures/Student**: $6,762	**% Amer Indian**: 0.1	National ***Socio-Economic Status*** indicator percentiles are not available for the state of Pennsylvania
Schools: *Regular* 7 ● *Spec Ed* 0 ● *Alt* 0	**Librarians**: 4.6	**% Asian**: 1.0	
Students: 3,881	844 students/librarian	**% Black**: 4.1	
Total Teachers: 231	**Guidance Counselors**: 10.0	**% Hispanic**: 3.2	
Student/Classroom Teacher Ratio: 16.7	388 students/counselor	**% White**: 91.7	

Monroe County
[SWIFTWATER] **POCONO MOUNTAIN S.D.**
PO BOX 200 ● SWIFTWATER PA 18370-0200 ● (717) 839-7121

Grade Span: KG-12	**Expenditures/Student**: $5,341	**% Amer Indian**: 0.4	National ***Socio-Economic Status*** indicator percentiles are not available for the state of Pennsylvania
Schools: *Regular* 10 ● *Spec Ed* 0 ● *Alt* 0	**Librarians**: 7.0	**% Asian**: 0.9	
Students: 8,945	1,278 students/librarian	**% Black**: 6.7	
Total Teachers: 457	**Guidance Counselors**: 21.0	**% Hispanic**: 6.1	
Student/Classroom Teacher Ratio: 22.1	426 students/counselor	**% White**: 85.9	

Montgomery County
ABINGTON S.D.
970 HIGHLAND AVENUE ● ABINGTON PA 19001-4532 ● (215) 884-4700

Grade Span: KG-12	**Expenditures/Student**: $8,358	**% Amer Indian**: 0.1	National ***Socio-Economic Status*** indicator percentiles are not available for the state of Pennsylvania
Schools: *Regular* 10 ● *Spec Ed* 0 ● *Alt* 0	**Librarians**: 11.5	**% Asian**: 4.8	
Students: 6,840	595 students/librarian	**% Black**: 15.5	
Total Teachers: 411	**Guidance Counselors**: 13.0	**% Hispanic**: 0.9	
Student/Classroom Teacher Ratio: 19.7	526 students/counselor	**% White**: 78.8	

Montgomery County
[AMBLER] **WISSAHICKON S.D.**
601 KNIGHT ROAD ● AMBLER PA 19002-3496 ● (215) 628-1600 ● http://mciunix.mciu.k12.pa.us/~wsdweb

Grade Span: KG-12	**Expenditures/Student**: $9,125	**% Amer Indian**: 0.1	National ***Socio-Economic Status*** indicator percentiles are not available for the state of Pennsylvania
Schools: *Regular* 6 ● *Spec Ed* 0 ● *Alt* 0	**Librarians**: 5.6	**% Asian**: 9.1	
Students: 4,148	741 students/librarian	**% Black**: 12.2	
Total Teachers: 263	**Guidance Counselors**: 11.6	**% Hispanic**: 1.0	
Student/Classroom Teacher Ratio: 16.6	358 students/counselor	**% White**: 77.6	

Montgomery County
[ARDMORE] **LOWER MERION S.D.**
301 EAST MONTGOMERY AVENUE ● ARDMORE PA 19003-3399 ● (610) 645-1930 ● http://www.lmsd.k12.pa.us

Grade Span: KG-12 **Schools**: *Regular* 9 ● *Spec Ed* 0 ● *Alt* 0 **Students**: 5,922 **Total Teachers**: 414 **Student/Classroom Teacher Ratio**: 14.7	**Expenditures/Student**: $10,461 **Librarians**: 9.0 658 students/librarian **Guidance Counselors**: 17.6 336 students/counselor	**% Amer Indian**: 0.3 **% Asian**: 3.5 **% Black**: 7.4 **% Hispanic**: 1.0 **% White**: 87.8	National ***Socio-Economic Status*** indicator percentiles are not available for the state of Pennsylvania

Montgomery County
[COLLEGEVILLE] **PERKIOMEN VALLEY S.D.**
3 IRON BRIDGE DRIVE ● COLLEGEVILLE PA 19426-2035 ● (610) 489-8506 ● http://mciunix.mciu.k12.pa.us:80/~pvweb

Grade Span: KG-12 **Schools**: *Regular* 4 ● *Spec Ed* 0 ● *Alt* 0 **Students**: 3,099 **Total Teachers**: 179 **Student/Classroom Teacher Ratio**: 18.3	**Expenditures/Student**: $7,185 **Librarians**: 3.0 1,033 students/librarian **Guidance Counselors**: 8.0 387 students/counselor	**% Amer Indian**: 0.1 **% Asian**: 1.7 **% Black**: 2.2 **% Hispanic**: 0.7 **% White**: 95.4	National ***Socio-Economic Status*** indicator percentiles are not available for the state of Pennsylvania

Montgomery County
[COLLEGEVILLE] **SPRING-FORD AREA S.D.**
199 BECHTEL ROAD ● COLLEGEVILLE PA 19426-2852 ● (610) 489-1666

Grade Span: KG-12 **Schools**: *Regular* 6 ● *Spec Ed* 0 ● *Alt* 0 **Students**: 4,344 **Total Teachers**: 248 **Student/Classroom Teacher Ratio**: 17.6	**Expenditures/Student**: $6,452 **Librarians**: 5.7 762 students/librarian **Guidance Counselors**: 10.5 414 students/counselor	**% Amer Indian**: 0.1 **% Asian**: 1.0 **% Black**: 2.1 **% Hispanic**: 0.6 **% White**: 96.1	National ***Socio-Economic Status*** indicator percentiles are not available for the state of Pennsylvania

Montgomery County
[DRESHER] **UPPER DUBLIN S.D.**
530 TWINING ROAD ● DRESHER PA 19025-1999 ● (215) 576-3293 ● http://mciunix.mciu.k12.pa.us:80/~udsdweb

Grade Span: KG-12 **Schools**: *Regular* 5 ● *Spec Ed* 0 ● *Alt* 0 **Students**: 4,035 **Total Teachers**: 223 **Student/Classroom Teacher Ratio**: 18.6	**Expenditures/Student**: $7,824 **Librarians**: 5.0 807 students/librarian **Guidance Counselors**: 9.0 448 students/counselor	**% Amer Indian**: 0.0 **% Asian**: 7.4 **% Black**: 7.8 **% Hispanic**: 0.4 **% White**: 84.3	National ***Socio-Economic Status*** indicator percentiles are not available for the state of Pennsylvania

Montgomery County
[EAST GREENVILLE] **UPPER PERKIOMEN S.D.**
201 WEST FIFTH STREET ● EAST GREENVILLE PA 18041-1598 ● (215) 679-7961

Grade Span: KG-12 **Schools**: *Regular* 4 ● *Spec Ed* 0 ● *Alt* 0 **Students**: 3,453 **Total Teachers**: 171 **Student/Classroom Teacher Ratio**: 20.7	**Expenditures/Student**: $6,520 **Librarians**: 4.0 863 students/librarian **Guidance Counselors**: 7.0 493 students/counselor	**% Amer Indian**: 0.1 **% Asian**: 0.5 **% Black**: 1.2 **% Hispanic**: 1.4 **% White**: 96.7	National ***Socio-Economic Status*** indicator percentiles are not available for the state of Pennsylvania

Montgomery County
[ELKINS PARK] **CHELTENHAM TOWNSHIP S.D.**
1000 ASHBOURNE ROAD ● ELKINS PARK PA 19027-1097 ● (215) 886-9500

Grade Span: KG-12 **Schools**: *Regular* 7 ● *Spec Ed* 0 ● *Alt* 0 **Students**: 4,864 **Total Teachers**: 293 **Student/Classroom Teacher Ratio**: 17.0	**Expenditures/Student**: $8,391 **Librarians**: 8.0 608 students/librarian **Guidance Counselors**: 10.0 486 students/counselor	**% Amer Indian**: 0.2 **% Asian**: 8.5 **% Black**: 29.0 **% Hispanic**: 1.1 **% White**: 61.2	National ***Socio-Economic Status*** indicator percentiles are not available for the state of Pennsylvania

Montgomery County
[HORSHAM] **HATBORO-HORSHAM S.D.**
229 MEETINGHOUSE ROAD ● HORSHAM PA 19044-2192 ● (215) 672-5660

Grade Span: KG-12 **Schools**: *Regular* 7 ● *Spec Ed* 0 ● *Alt* 0 **Students**: 4,513 **Total Teachers**: 268 **Student/Classroom Teacher Ratio**: 18.0	**Expenditures/Student**: $8,079 **Librarians**: 7.5 602 students/librarian **Guidance Counselors**: 11.5 392 students/counselor	**% Amer Indian**: 0.1 **% Asian**: 4.1 **% Black**: 4.1 **% Hispanic**: 1.7 **% White**: 90.0	National ***Socio-Economic Status*** indicator percentiles are not available for the state of Pennsylvania

Montgomery County
[KING OF PRUSSIA] **UPPER MERION AREA S.D.**
435 CROSSFIELD ROAD ● KING OF PRUSSIA PA 19406-2300 ● (610) 337-6006 ● http://upper-merion.k12.pa.us

Grade Span: KG-12 **Schools**: *Regular* 6 ● *Spec Ed* 0 ● *Alt* 0 **Students**: 3,179 **Total Teachers**: 223 **Student/Classroom Teacher Ratio**: 17.6	**Expenditures/Student**: $10,907 **Librarians**: 7.0 454 students/librarian **Guidance Counselors**: 9.0 353 students/counselor	**% Amer Indian**: 0.0 **% Asian**: 6.5 **% Black**: 6.1 **% Hispanic**: 1.2 **% White**: 86.2	National ***Socio-Economic Status*** indicator percentiles are not available for the state of Pennsylvania

Montgomery County
[LANSDALE] **NORTH PENN S.D.**
401 EAST HANCOCK STREET ● LANSDALE PA 19446-3807 ● (215) 368-0400

Grade Span: KG-12 **Schools**: *Regular* 17 ● *Spec Ed* 0 ● *Alt* 0 **Students**: 12,513 **Total Teachers**: 726 **Student/Classroom Teacher Ratio**: 17.7	**Expenditures/Student**: $6,722 **Librarians**: 18.0 695 students/librarian **Guidance Counselors**: 27.6 453 students/counselor	**% Amer Indian**: 0.0 **% Asian**: 7.9 **% Black**: 3.9 **% Hispanic**: 1.5 **% White**: 86.7	National ***Socio-Economic Status*** indicator percentiles are not available for the state of Pennsylvania

Montgomery County
[NORRISTOWN] **METHACTON S.D.**
1001 KRIEBEL MILL ROAD ● NORRISTOWN PA 19408-2011 ● (610) 489-5000 ● http://www.methacton.k12.pa.us

Grade Span: KG-12 **Schools**: *Regular* 6 ● *Spec Ed* 0 ● *Alt* 0 **Students**: 3,954 **Total Teachers**: 261 **Student/Classroom Teacher Ratio**: 16.1	**Expenditures/Student**: $7,975 **Librarians**: 7.0 565 students/librarian **Guidance Counselors**: 12.0 330 students/counselor	**% Amer Indian**: 0.0 **% Asian**: 3.4 **% Black**: 2.3 **% Hispanic**: 0.5 **% White**: 93.8	National ***Socio-Economic Status*** indicator percentiles are not available for the state of Pennsylvania

Montgomery County
NORRISTOWN AREA S.D.
401 NORTH WHITEHALL ROAD ● NORRISTOWN PA 19403-2799 ● (610) 630-5000 ● http://www.nasd.k12.pa.us

Grade Span: KG-12 **Schools**: *Regular* 12 ● *Spec Ed* 0 ● *Alt* 0 **Students**: 6,429 **Total Teachers**: 442 **Student/Classroom Teacher Ratio**: 14.5	**Expenditures/Student**: $8,118 **Librarians**: 11.0 584 students/librarian **Guidance Counselors**: 16.0 402 students/counselor	**% Amer Indian**: 0.1 **% Asian**: 2.8 **% Black**: 42.3 **% Hispanic**: 4.5 **% White**: 50.3	National ***Socio-Economic Status*** indicator percentiles are not available for the state of Pennsylvania

Montgomery County
[PLYMOUTH MEETING] **COLONIAL S.D.**
230 FLOURTOWN ROAD ● PLYMOUTH MEETING PA 19462-1291 ● (610) 834-1670 ● http://mciunix.mciu.k12.pa.us:80/~csdhp

Grade Span: KG-12 **Schools**: *Regular* 7 ● *Spec Ed* 0 ● *Alt* 0 **Students**: 4,374 **Total Teachers**: 266 **Student/Classroom Teacher Ratio**: 17.5	**Expenditures/Student**: $9,107 **Librarians**: 5.9 741 students/librarian **Guidance Counselors**: 14.0 312 students/counselor	**% Amer Indian**: 0.2 **% Asian**: 4.4 **% Black**: 8.8 **% Hispanic**: 1.4 **% White**: 85.2	National ***Socio-Economic Status*** indicator percentiles are not available for the state of Pennsylvania

Montgomery County
[POTTSTOWN] **POTTSGROVE S.D.**
1301 KAUFFMAN ROAD ● POTTSTOWN PA 19464-2398 ● (610) 327-2277

Grade Span: KG-12 **Schools**: *Regular* 5 ● *Spec Ed* 0 ● *Alt* 0 **Students**: 3,161 **Total Teachers**: 171 **Student/Classroom Teacher Ratio**: 19.9	**Expenditures/Student**: $6,765 **Librarians**: 4.0 790 students/librarian **Guidance Counselors**: 8.0 395 students/counselor	**% Amer Indian**: 0.2 **% Asian**: 0.5 **% Black**: 10.9 **% Hispanic**: 0.9 **% White**: 87.4	National ***Socio-Economic Status*** indicator percentiles are not available for the state of Pennsylvania

Montgomery County
POTTSTOWN S.D.
BEECH & PENN STREETS ● POTTSTOWN PA 19464-0779 ● (610) 323-8200

Grade Span: PK-12 **Schools**: *Regular* 7 ● *Spec Ed* 0 ● *Alt* 0 **Students**: 3,278 **Total Teachers**: 188 **Student/Classroom Teacher Ratio**: 21.2	**Expenditures/Student**: $7,175 **Librarians**: 4.0 820 students/librarian **Guidance Counselors**: 7.0 468 students/counselor	**% Amer Indian**: 0.2 **% Asian**: 0.6 **% Black**: 27.6 **% Hispanic**: 6.2 **% White**: 65.5	National ***Socio-Economic Status*** indicator percentiles are not available for the state of Pennsylvania

Montgomery County
SOUDERTON AREA S.D.
139 HARLEYSVILLE PIKE ● SOUDERTON PA 18964-2094 ● (215) 723-6061 ● http://mciunix.mciu.k12.pa.us/~sasdhp/SASD.html

Grade Span: KG-12 **Schools**: *Regular* 9 ● *Spec Ed* 0 ● *Alt* 0 **Students**: 5,786 **Total Teachers**: 327 **Student/Classroom Teacher Ratio**: 19.9	**Expenditures/Student**: $6,826 **Librarians**: 8.0 723 students/librarian **Guidance Counselors**: 13.0 445 students/counselor	**% Amer Indian**: 0.1 **% Asian**: 2.6 **% Black**: 2.0 **% Hispanic**: 1.9 **% White**: 93.4	National ***Socio-Economic Status*** indicator percentiles are not available for the state of Pennsylvania

Montgomery County
[WILLOW GROVE] **UPPER MORELAND TOWNSHIP S.D.**
2900 TERWOOD ROAD ● WILLOW GROVE PA 19090-1489 ● (215) 659-6800 ● http://www.libertynet.org/umsd-hs

Grade Span: KG-12 **Schools**: *Regular* 4 ● *Spec Ed* 0 ● *Alt* 0 **Students**: 3,104 **Total Teachers**: 157 **Student/Classroom Teacher Ratio**: 20.3	**Expenditures/Student**: $7,480 **Librarians**: 4.0 776 students/librarian **Guidance Counselors**: 6.0 517 students/counselor	**% Amer Indian**: 0.0 **% Asian**: 2.7 **% Black**: 5.2 **% Hispanic**: 0.9 **% White**: 91.1	National ***Socio-Economic Status*** indicator percentiles are not available for the state of Pennsylvania

Montour County
DANVILLE AREA S.D.
600 WALNUT STREET ● DANVILLE PA 17821-9102 ● (717) 275-7575

Grade Span: KG-12 **Schools**: *Regular* 6 ● *Spec Ed* 0 ● *Alt* 0 **Students**: 2,817 **Total Teachers**: 165 **Student/Classroom Teacher Ratio**: 18.1	**Expenditures/Student**: $6,539 **Librarians**: 4.0 704 students/librarian **Guidance Counselors**: 7.0 402 students/counselor	**% Amer Indian**: 0.8 **% Asian**: 1.2 **% Black**: 0.9 **% Hispanic**: 1.0 **% White**: 96.1	National ***Socio-Economic Status*** indicator percentiles are not available for the state of Pennsylvania

Northampton County
BANGOR AREA S.D.
44 SOUTH THIRD STREET ● BANGOR PA 18013-2594 ● (610) 588-2163 ● http://www.bangor.k12.pa.us

Grade Span: KG-12 **Schools**: *Regular* 5 ● *Spec Ed* 0 ● *Alt* 0 **Students**: 3,159 **Total Teachers**: 173 **Student/Classroom Teacher Ratio**: 19.9	**Expenditures/Student**: $5,585 **Librarians**: 4.0 790 students/librarian **Guidance Counselors**: 7.0 451 students/counselor	**% Amer Indian**: 0.0 **% Asian**: 0.6 **% Black**: 0.6 **% Hispanic**: 0.8 **% White**: 97.9	National ***Socio-Economic Status*** indicator percentiles are not available for the state of Pennsylvania

Northampton County

BETHLEHEM AREA S.D.

1516 SYCAMORE STREET ● BETHLEHEM PA 18017-6099 ● (610) 861-0500 ● http://www.beth.k12.pa.us

Grade Span: KG-12 **Schools**: *Regular* 22 ● *Spec Ed* 0 ● *Alt* 0 **Students**: 13,418 **Total Teachers**: 723 **Student/Classroom Teacher Ratio**: 19.1	**Expenditures/Student**: $6,643 **Librarians**: 14.9 901 students/librarian **Guidance Counselors**: 36.8 365 students/counselor	**% Amer Indian**: 0.1 **% Asian**: 1.8 **% Black**: 4.7 **% Hispanic**: 23.8 **% White**: 69.7	National ***Socio-Economic Status*** indicator percentiles are not available for the state of Pennsylvania

Northampton County

EASTON AREA S.D.

811 NORTHAMPTON STREET ● EASTON PA 18042-4298 ● (610) 250-2400

Grade Span: KG-12 **Schools**: *Regular* 9 ● *Spec Ed* 0 ● *Alt* 0 **Students**: 7,451 **Total Teachers**: 408 **Student/Classroom Teacher Ratio**: 18.8	**Expenditures/Student**: $5,981 **Librarians**: 7.0 1,064 students/librarian **Guidance Counselors**: 14.0 532 students/counselor	**% Amer Indian**: 0.2 **% Asian**: 1.9 **% Black**: 12.0 **% Hispanic**: 5.0 **% White**: 80.9	National ***Socio-Economic Status*** indicator percentiles are not available for the state of Pennsylvania

Northampton County

NAZARETH AREA S.D.

8 CENTER SQUARE ● NAZARETH PA 18064-2042 ● (610) 759-1170

Grade Span: KG-12 **Schools**: *Regular* 5 ● *Spec Ed* 0 ● *Alt* 0 **Students**: 3,774 **Total Teachers**: 191 **Student/Classroom Teacher Ratio**: 20.0	**Expenditures/Student**: $6,178 **Librarians**: 3.0 1,258 students/librarian **Guidance Counselors**: 5.0 755 students/counselor	**% Amer Indian**: 0.0 **% Asian**: 1.2 **% Black**: 0.6 **% Hispanic**: 0.6 **% White**: 97.6	National ***Socio-Economic Status*** indicator percentiles are not available for the state of Pennsylvania

Northampton County

NORTHAMPTON AREA S.D.

1617 LAUBACH AVENUE BOX 118 ● NORTHAMPTON PA 18067-0118 ● (610) 262-7811

Grade Span: KG-12 **Schools**: *Regular* 6 ● *Spec Ed* 0 ● *Alt* 0 **Students**: 5,712 **Total Teachers**: 305 **Student/Classroom Teacher Ratio**: 18.9	**Expenditures/Student**: $6,176 **Librarians**: 6.0 952 students/librarian **Guidance Counselors**: 11.0 519 students/counselor	**% Amer Indian**: 0.0 **% Asian**: 0.7 **% Black**: 0.6 **% Hispanic**: 1.1 **% White**: 97.5	National ***Socio-Economic Status*** indicator percentiles are not available for the state of Pennsylvania

Northumberland County

MILTON AREA S.D.

700 MAHONING STREET ● MILTON PA 17847-2200 ● (717) 742-7614 ● http://www.sunlink.net/~masd

Grade Span: KG-12 **Schools**: *Regular* 5 ● *Spec Ed* 0 ● *Alt* 0 **Students**: 2,752 **Total Teachers**: 170 **Student/Classroom Teacher Ratio**: 16.2	**Expenditures/Student**: $5,622 **Librarians**: 3.0 917 students/librarian **Guidance Counselors**: 6.0 459 students/counselor	**% Amer Indian**: 0.0 **% Asian**: 0.7 **% Black**: 2.7 **% Hispanic**: 1.2 **% White**: 95.4	National ***Socio-Economic Status*** indicator percentiles are not available for the state of Pennsylvania

Northumberland County

SHAMOKIN AREA S.D.

2000 WEST STATE STREET ● SHAMOKIN PA 17872-2899 ● (717) 648-5752

Grade Span: KG-12 **Schools**: *Regular* 3 ● *Spec Ed* 0 ● *Alt* 0 **Students**: 2,602 **Total Teachers**: 129 **Student/Classroom Teacher Ratio**: 19.8	**Expenditures/Student**: $4,935 **Librarians**: 3.0 867 students/librarian **Guidance Counselors**: 3.0 867 students/counselor	**% Amer Indian**: 0.0 **% Asian**: 0.0 **% Black**: 0.3 **% Hispanic**: 0.4 **% White**: 99.3	National ***Socio-Economic Status*** indicator percentiles are not available for the state of Pennsylvania

Northumberland County

[SUNBURY] **SHIKELLAMY S.D.**

350 ISLAND BOULEVARD ● SUNBURY PA 17801-1030 ● (717) 286-3720

Grade Span: KG-12	**Expenditures/Student**: $5,302	**% Amer Indian**: 0.0	National ***Socio-Economic***
Schools: *Regular* 11 ● *Spec Ed* 0 ● *Alt* 0	**Librarians**: 5.0	**% Asian**: 0.6	***Status*** indicator percentiles
Students: 3,728	746 students/librarian	**% Black**: 0.5	are not available for the
Total Teachers: 206	**Guidance Counselors**: 7.0	**% Hispanic**: 2.7	state of Pennsylvania
Student/Classroom Teacher Ratio: 20.4	533 students/counselor	**% White**: 96.2	

Perry County

[DUNCANNON] **SUSQUENITA S.D.**

1725 SCHOOLHOUSE ROAD ● DUNCANNON PA 17020-9540 ● (717) 957-2303

Grade Span: KG-12	**Expenditures/Student**: $5,704	**% Amer Indian**: 0.2	National ***Socio-Economic***
Schools: *Regular* 3 ● *Spec Ed* 0 ● *Alt* 0	**Librarians**: 2.0	**% Asian**: 0.3	***Status*** indicator percentiles
Students: 2,551	1,276 students/librarian	**% Black**: 0.5	are not available for the
Total Teachers: 136	**Guidance Counselors**: 5.0	**% Hispanic**: 0.6	state of Pennsylvania
Student/Classroom Teacher Ratio: 18.8	510 students/counselor	**% White**: 98.4	

Perry County

[ELLIOTTSBURG] **WEST PERRY S.D.**

RD 1 BOX 7A ● ELLIOTTSBURG PA 17024-9706 ● (717) 789-3934

Grade Span: KG-12	**Expenditures/Student**: $5,582	**% Amer Indian**: 0.1	National ***Socio-Economic***
Schools: *Regular* 5 ● *Spec Ed* 0 ● *Alt* 0	**Librarians**: 3.0	**% Asian**: 0.3	***Status*** indicator percentiles
Students: 2,929	976 students/librarian	**% Black**: 0.8	are not available for the
Total Teachers: 183	**Guidance Counselors**: 6.5	**% Hispanic**: 0.5	state of Pennsylvania
Student/Classroom Teacher Ratio: 17.1	451 students/counselor	**% White**: 98.3	

Philadelphia County

PHILADELPHIA CITY S.D.

PARKWAY AT 21ST STREET ● PHILADELPHIA PA 19103-1099 ● (215) 299-7000 ● http://www.philsch.k12.pa.us

Grade Span: KG-12	**Expenditures/Student**: $6,113	**% Amer Indian**: 0.2	National ***Socio-Economic***
Schools: *Regular* 247 ● *Spec Ed* 5 ● *Alt* 6	**Librarians**: 142.0	**% Asian**: 4.8	***Status*** indicator percentiles
Students: 210,503	1,482 students/librarian	**% Black**: 63.4	are not available for the
Total Teachers: 11,105	**Guidance Counselors**: 318.0	**% Hispanic**: 11.3	state of Pennsylvania
Student/Classroom Teacher Ratio: 19.2	662 students/counselor	**% White**: 20.4	

Pike County

[MILFORD] **DELAWARE VALLEY S.D.**

HC 77 BOX 379A ● MILFORD PA 18337-1499 ● (717) 296-6431 ● http://dvasdweb.dvasd.k12.pa.us

Grade Span: KG-12	**Expenditures/Student**: $6,283	**% Amer Indian**: 0.2	National ***Socio-Economic***
Schools: *Regular* 6 ● *Spec Ed* 0 ● *Alt* 0	**Librarians**: 5.5	**% Asian**: 0.4	***Status*** indicator percentiles
Students: 4,079	742 students/librarian	**% Black**: 1.4	are not available for the
Total Teachers: 234	**Guidance Counselors**: 9.0	**% Hispanic**: 2.2	state of Pennsylvania
Student/Classroom Teacher Ratio: 17.6	453 students/counselor	**% White**: 95.9	

Schuylkill County

[ORWIGSBURG] **BLUE MOUNTAIN S.D.**

PO BOX 279 ● ORWIGSBURG PA 17961-0279 ● (717) 366-0515

Grade Span: KG-12	**Expenditures/Student**: $5,512	**% Amer Indian**: 0.1	National ***Socio-Economic***
Schools: *Regular* 5 ● *Spec Ed* 0 ● *Alt* 0	**Librarians**: 4.0	**% Asian**: 1.6	***Status*** indicator percentiles
Students: 2,985	746 students/librarian	**% Black**: 0.4	are not available for the
Total Teachers: 157	**Guidance Counselors**: 7.0	**% Hispanic**: 0.3	state of Pennsylvania
Student/Classroom Teacher Ratio: 20.0	426 students/counselor	**% White**: 97.6	

Schuylkill County

POTTSVILLE AREA S.D.

1501 WEST LAUREL BOULEVARD ● POTTSVILLE PA 17901-1498 ● (717) 621-2900 ● http://www.pottsville.com/pasd

Grade Span: KG-12 **Schools**: *Regular* 3 ● *Spec Ed* 0 ● *Alt* 0 **Students**: 3,418 **Total Teachers**: 162 **Student/Classroom Teacher Ratio**: 21.3	**Expenditures/Student**: $5,453 **Librarians**: 3.0 1,139 students/librarian **Guidance Counselors**: 6.0 570 students/counselor	**% Amer Indian**: 0.1 **% Asian**: 0.8 **% Black**: 2.4 **% Hispanic**: 1.1 **% White**: 95.6	National ***Socio-Economic Status*** indicator percentiles are not available for the state of Pennsylvania

Snyder County

[MIDDLEBURG] **MIDD-WEST S.D.**

568 EAST MAIN STREET ● MIDDLEBURG PA 17842-1295 ● (717) 837-0046

Grade Span: KG-12 **Schools**: *Regular* 7 ● *Spec Ed* 0 ● *Alt* 0 **Students**: 2,710 **Total Teachers**: 168 **Student/Classroom Teacher Ratio**: 16.7	**Expenditures/Student**: $5,505 **Librarians**: 3.0 903 students/librarian **Guidance Counselors**: 6.0 452 students/counselor	**% Amer Indian**: 0.0 **% Asian**: 0.0 **% Black**: 0.3 **% Hispanic**: 0.3 **% White**: 99.3	National ***Socio-Economic Status*** indicator percentiles are not available for the state of Pennsylvania

Snyder County

SELINSGROVE AREA S.D.

401 NORTH 18TH STREET ● SELINSGROVE PA 17870-1198 ● (717) 374-1144

Grade Span: KG-12 **Schools**: *Regular* 7 ● *Spec Ed* 0 ● *Alt* 0 **Students**: 2,942 **Total Teachers**: 166 **Student/Classroom Teacher Ratio**: 20.3	**Expenditures/Student**: $5,819 **Librarians**: 4.0 736 students/librarian **Guidance Counselors**: 8.0 368 students/counselor	**% Amer Indian**: 0.2 **% Asian**: 1.0 **% Black**: 0.6 **% Hispanic**: 2.2 **% White**: 96.1	National ***Socio-Economic Status*** indicator percentiles are not available for the state of Pennsylvania

Somerset County

SOMERSET AREA S.D.

821 SOUTH COLUMBIA AVENUE ● SOMERSET PA 15501-2513 ● (814) 445-9714

Grade Span: KG-12 **Schools**: *Regular* 6 ● *Spec Ed* 0 ● *Alt* 0 **Students**: 3,080 **Total Teachers**: 167 **Student/Classroom Teacher Ratio**: 21.6	**Expenditures/Student**: $5,256 **Librarians**: 2.0 1,540 students/librarian **Guidance Counselors**: 3.5 880 students/counselor	**% Amer Indian**: 0.1 **% Asian**: 0.8 **% Black**: 0.8 **% Hispanic**: 0.5 **% White**: 97.8	National ***Socio-Economic Status*** indicator percentiles are not available for the state of Pennsylvania

Tioga County

[ELKLAND] **NORTHERN TIOGA S.D.**

117 COATES AVENUE ● ELKLAND PA 16920-1398 ● (814) 258-5642

Grade Span: KG-12 **Schools**: *Regular* 6 ● *Spec Ed* 0 ● *Alt* 0 **Students**: 2,727 **Total Teachers**: 185 **Student/Classroom Teacher Ratio**: 14.9	**Expenditures/Student**: $5,579 **Librarians**: 4.0 682 students/librarian **Guidance Counselors**: 3.0 909 students/counselor	**% Amer Indian**: 0.0 **% Asian**: 0.1 **% Black**: 0.7 **% Hispanic**: 0.1 **% White**: 99.0	National ***Socio-Economic Status*** indicator percentiles are not available for the state of Pennsylvania

Union County

MIFFLINBURG AREA S.D.

178 MAPLE STREET BOX 285 ● MIFFLINBURG PA 17844-0285 ● (717) 966-1553

Grade Span: KG-12 **Schools**: *Regular* 6 ● *Spec Ed* 0 ● *Alt* 0 **Students**: 2,575 **Total Teachers**: 139 **Student/Classroom Teacher Ratio**: 22.9	**Expenditures/Student**: $5,027 **Librarians**: 3.0 858 students/librarian **Guidance Counselors**: 4.0 644 students/counselor	**% Amer Indian**: 0.2 **% Asian**: 0.3 **% Black**: 0.3 **% Hispanic**: 0.6 **% White**: 98.6	National ***Socio-Economic Status*** indicator percentiles are not available for the state of Pennsylvania

Venango County
FRANKLIN AREA S.D.
417 13TH ST ● FRANKLIN PA 16323-1380 ● (814) 432-8917

Grade Span: KG-12	**Expenditures/Student**: $6,418	**% Amer Indian**: 0.0	National ***Socio-Economic***
Schools: *Regular* 8 ● *Spec Ed* 0 ● *Alt* 0	**Librarians**: 3.0	**% Asian**: 0.5	***Status*** indicator percentiles
Students: 2,792	931 students/librarian	**% Black**: 3.3	are not available for the
Total Teachers: 163	**Guidance Counselors**: 4.0	**% Hispanic**: 0.6	state of Pennsylvania
Student/Classroom Teacher Ratio: 17.7	698 students/counselor	**% White**: 95.5	

Venango County
OIL CITY AREA S.D.
825 GRANDVIEW ROAD PO BOX 929 ● OIL CITY PA 16301-0929 ● (814) 676-1867

Grade Span: KG-12	**Expenditures/Student**: $5,619	**% Amer Indian**: 0.3	National ***Socio-Economic***
Schools: *Regular* 6 ● *Spec Ed* 0 ● *Alt* 0	**Librarians**: 3.0	**% Asian**: 0.4	***Status*** indicator percentiles
Students: 2,740	913 students/librarian	**% Black**: 1.0	are not available for the
Total Teachers: 157	**Guidance Counselors**: 4.0	**% Hispanic**: 0.5	state of Pennsylvania
Student/Classroom Teacher Ratio: 19.2	685 students/counselor	**% White**: 97.8	

Venango County
TITUSVILLE AREA S.D.
221 NORTH WASHINGTON STREET ● TITUSVILLE PA 16354-1785 ● (814) 827-2715

Grade Span: PK-12	**Expenditures/Student**: $4,960	**% Amer Indian**: 0.0	National ***Socio-Economic***
Schools: *Regular* 7 ● *Spec Ed* 0 ● *Alt* 0	**Librarians**: 3.0	**% Asian**: 0.2	***Status*** indicator percentiles
Students: 2,813	938 students/librarian	**% Black**: 0.2	are not available for the
Total Teachers: 150	**Guidance Counselors**: 3.0	**% Hispanic**: 0.0	state of Pennsylvania
Student/Classroom Teacher Ratio: 20.6	938 students/counselor	**% White**: 99.6	

Warren County
[WARREN] **WARREN COUNTY S.D.**
185 HOSPITAL DRIVE ● WARREN PA 16365-4885 ● (814) 723-6900

Grade Span: KG-12	**Expenditures/Student**: $5,531	**% Amer Indian**: 0.0	National ***Socio-Economic***
Schools: *Regular* 21 ● *Spec Ed* 0 ● *Alt* 0	**Librarians**: 10.0	**% Asian**: 0.5	***Status*** indicator percentiles
Students: 7,201	720 students/librarian	**% Black**: 0.2	are not available for the
Total Teachers: 413	**Guidance Counselors**: 17.5	**% Hispanic**: 0.2	state of Pennsylvania
Student/Classroom Teacher Ratio: 17.6	411 students/counselor	**% White**: 99.1	

Washington County
[CANONSBURG] **CANON-MCMILLAN S.D.**
ONE NORTH JEFFERSON AVENUE ● CANONSBURG PA 15317-1305 ● (412) 746-2940

Grade Span: KG-12	**Expenditures/Student**: $6,472	**% Amer Indian**: 0.0	National ***Socio-Economic***
Schools: *Regular* 10 ● *Spec Ed* 0 ● *Alt* 0	**Librarians**: 5.0	**% Asian**: 0.3	***Status*** indicator percentiles
Students: 3,868	774 students/librarian	**% Black**: 5.9	are not available for the
Total Teachers: 238	**Guidance Counselors**: 9.0	**% Hispanic**: 0.1	state of Pennsylvania
Student/Classroom Teacher Ratio: 16.7	430 students/counselor	**% White**: 93.7	

Washington County
[CLAYSVILLE] **MCGUFFEY S.D.**
BOX 431 ● CLAYSVILLE PA 15323-0431 ● (412) 663-7745

Grade Span: KG-12	**Expenditures/Student**: $5,726	**% Amer Indian**: 0.0	National ***Socio-Economic***
Schools: *Regular* 8 ● *Spec Ed* 0 ● *Alt* 0	**Librarians**: 2.0	**% Asian**: 0.0	***Status*** indicator percentiles
Students: 2,767	1,384 students/librarian	**% Black**: 0.3	are not available for the
Total Teachers: 165	**Guidance Counselors**: 4.0	**% Hispanic**: 0.1	state of Pennsylvania
Student/Classroom Teacher Ratio: 19.0	692 students/counselor	**% White**: 99.6	

Washington County
[MCMURRAY] **PETERS TOWNSHIP S.D.**
631 EAST MCMURRAY ROAD ● MCMURRAY PA 15317-3498 ● (412) 941-6251 ● http://www.sgi.net/ptsd

Grade Span: KG-12	**Expenditures/Student**: $5,767	**% Amer Indian**: 0.0	National ***Socio-Economic***
Schools: *Regular* 4 ● *Spec Ed* 0 ● *Alt* 0	**Librarians**: 4.0	**% Asian**: 1.1	***Status*** indicator percentiles
Students: 3,138	785 students/librarian	**% Black**: 0.8	are not available for the
Total Teachers: 158	**Guidance Counselors**: 5.0	**% Hispanic**: 0.6	state of Pennsylvania
Student/Classroom Teacher Ratio: 20.4	628 students/counselor	**% White**: 97.6	

Washington County
[NEW EAGLE] **RINGGOLD S.D.**
400 MAIN STREET ● NEW EAGLE PA 15067-1108 ● (412) 258-9329

Grade Span: KG-12	**Expenditures/Student**: $5,592	**% Amer Indian**: 0.1	National ***Socio-Economic***
Schools: *Regular* 6 ● *Spec Ed* 0 ● *Alt* 0	**Librarians**: 5.0	**% Asian**: 0.4	***Status*** indicator percentiles
Students: 3,691	738 students/librarian	**% Black**: 7.7	are not available for the
Total Teachers: 216	**Guidance Counselors**: 5.0	**% Hispanic**: 0.4	state of Pennsylvania
Student/Classroom Teacher Ratio: 16.9	738 students/counselor	**% White**: 91.4	

Washington County
[WASHINGTON] **TRINITY AREA S.D.**
231 PARK AVENUE ● WASHINGTON PA 15301-5799 ● (412) 225-9880

Grade Span: KG-12	**Expenditures/Student**: $6,089	**% Amer Indian**: 0.1	National ***Socio-Economic***
Schools: *Regular* 6 ● *Spec Ed* 0 ● *Alt* 0	**Librarians**: 6.0	**% Asian**: 0.5	***Status*** indicator percentiles
Students: 4,034	672 students/librarian	**% Black**: 3.1	are not available for the
Total Teachers: 241	**Guidance Counselors**: 8.0	**% Hispanic**: 0.1	state of Pennsylvania
Student/Classroom Teacher Ratio: 17.5	504 students/counselor	**% White**: 96.1	

Wayne County
[HAWLEY] **WALLENPAUPACK AREA S.D.**
HC 6 BOX 6075 ● HAWLEY PA 18428-9045 ● (717) 226-4557 ● http://www.paupack.ptd.net

Grade Span: PK-12	**Expenditures/Student**: $6,984	**% Amer Indian**: 0.1	National ***Socio-Economic***
Schools: *Regular* 5 ● *Spec Ed* 0 ● *Alt* 0	**Librarians**: 5.0	**% Asian**: 0.4	***Status*** indicator percentiles
Students: 3,234	647 students/librarian	**% Black**: 2.2	are not available for the
Total Teachers: 180	**Guidance Counselors**: 6.0	**% Hispanic**: 1.5	state of Pennsylvania
Student/Classroom Teacher Ratio: 21.3	539 students/counselor	**% White**: 95.8	

Wayne County
[HONESDALE] **WAYNE HIGHLANDS S.D.**
474 GROVE STREET ● HONESDALE PA 18431-1099 ● (717) 253-4661 ● http://ns.neiu.k12.pa.us/WWW/WH/WayneHighlandsHome.html

Grade Span: KG-12	**Expenditures/Student**: $6,594	**% Amer Indian**: 0.0	National ***Socio-Economic***
Schools: *Regular* 6 ● *Spec Ed* 0 ● *Alt* 0	**Librarians**: 4.0	**% Asian**: 0.7	***Status*** indicator percentiles
Students: 3,363	841 students/librarian	**% Black**: 0.5	are not available for the
Total Teachers: 177	**Guidance Counselors**: 8.5	**% Hispanic**: 0.2	state of Pennsylvania
Student/Classroom Teacher Ratio: 19.7	396 students/counselor	**% White**: 98.7	

Westmoreland County
BELLE VERNON AREA S.D.
RD 2 CREST AVENUE ● BELLE VERNON PA 15012-9625 ● (412) 929-5262

Grade Span: KG-12	**Expenditures/Student**: $5,461	**% Amer Indian**: 0.2	National ***Socio-Economic***
Schools: *Regular* 5 ● *Spec Ed* 0 ● *Alt* 0	**Librarians**: 5.0	**% Asian**: 0.4	***Status*** indicator percentiles
Students: 2,978	596 students/librarian	**% Black**: 2.6	are not available for the
Total Teachers: 140	**Guidance Counselors**: 7.0	**% Hispanic**: 0.3	state of Pennsylvania
Student/Classroom Teacher Ratio: 21.9	425 students/counselor	**% White**: 96.5	

Westmoreland County
DERRY AREA S.D.
RD 1 BOX 169 ● DERRY PA 15627-9703 ● (412) 694-8383 ● http://wiu.k12.pa.us/derry

Grade Span: PK-12 **Schools**: *Regular* 6 ● *Spec Ed* 0 ● *Alt* 0 **Students**: 3,092 **Total Teachers**: 162 **Student/Classroom Teacher Ratio**: 21.7	**Expenditures/Student**: $5,618 **Librarians**: 3.0 1,031 students/librarian **Guidance Counselors**: 6.0 515 students/counselor	**% Amer Indian**: 0.5 **% Asian**: 0.2 **% Black**: 1.8 **% Hispanic**: 0.3 **% White**: 97.2	National ***Socio-Economic Status*** indicator percentiles are not available for the state of Pennsylvania

Westmoreland County
GREENSBURG SALEM S.D.
11 PARK STREET ● GREENSBURG PA 15601-1839 ● (412) 832-2901 ● http://wiu.k12.pa.us/gbgsalem

Grade Span: KG-12 **Schools**: *Regular* 5 ● *Spec Ed* 0 ● *Alt* 0 **Students**: 3,784 **Total Teachers**: 188 **Student/Classroom Teacher Ratio**: 20.8	**Expenditures/Student**: $5,542 **Librarians**: 5.0 757 students/librarian **Guidance Counselors**: 7.0 541 students/counselor	**% Amer Indian**: 0.4 **% Asian**: 0.9 **% Black**: 5.6 **% Hispanic**: 0.5 **% White**: 92.6	National ***Socio-Economic Status*** indicator percentiles are not available for the state of Pennsylvania

Westmoreland County
[GREENSBURG] **HEMPFIELD AREA S.D.**
RD 6 BOX 76 ● GREENSBURG PA 15601-9315 ● (412) 834-2590

Grade Span: KG-12 **Schools**: *Regular* 11 ● *Spec Ed* 0 ● *Alt* 0 **Students**: 7,236 **Total Teachers**: 377 **Student/Classroom Teacher Ratio**: 19.9	**Expenditures/Student**: $5,784 **Librarians**: 11.0 658 students/librarian **Guidance Counselors**: 17.0 426 students/counselor	**% Amer Indian**: 0.3 **% Asian**: 1.3 **% Black**: 1.1 **% Hispanic**: 0.3 **% White**: 97.0	National ***Socio-Economic Status*** indicator percentiles are not available for the state of Pennsylvania

Westmoreland County
[HARRISON CITY] **PENN-TRAFFORD S.D.**
ADMINISTRATION BLDG ● HARRISON CITY PA 15636-0366 ● (412) 744-4496

Grade Span: KG-12 **Schools**: *Regular* 8 ● *Spec Ed* 0 ● *Alt* 0 **Students**: 4,327 **Total Teachers**: 210 **Student/Classroom Teacher Ratio**: 20.3	**Expenditures/Student**: $4,954 **Librarians**: 4.0 1,082 students/librarian **Guidance Counselors**: 6.0 721 students/counselor	**% Amer Indian**: 0.0 **% Asian**: 0.5 **% Black**: 0.5 **% Hispanic**: 0.1 **% White**: 98.8	National ***Socio-Economic Status*** indicator percentiles are not available for the state of Pennsylvania

Westmoreland County
[HERMINIE] **YOUGH S.D.**
99 LOWBER ROAD ● HERMINIE PA 15637-1299 ● (412) 446-7272

Grade Span: KG-12 **Schools**: *Regular* 5 ● *Spec Ed* 0 ● *Alt* 0 **Students**: 2,764 **Total Teachers**: 156 **Student/Classroom Teacher Ratio**: 18.1	**Expenditures/Student**: $5,662 **Librarians**: 5.0 553 students/librarian **Guidance Counselors**: 6.0 461 students/counselor	**% Amer Indian**: 0.3 **% Asian**: 0.3 **% Black**: 1.1 **% Hispanic**: 0.0 **% White**: 98.3	National ***Socio-Economic Status*** indicator percentiles are not available for the state of Pennsylvania

Westmoreland County
[LATROBE] **GREATER LATROBE S.D.**
410 MAIN STREET ● LATROBE PA 15650-1598 ● (412) 539-4200

Grade Span: KG-12 **Schools**: *Regular* 5 ● *Spec Ed* 0 ● *Alt* 0 **Students**: 3,995 **Total Teachers**: 218 **Student/Classroom Teacher Ratio**: 18.9	**Expenditures/Student**: $6,388 **Librarians**: 5.0 799 students/librarian **Guidance Counselors**: 8.0 499 students/counselor	**% Amer Indian**: 0.0 **% Asian**: 0.6 **% Black**: 0.5 **% Hispanic**: 0.1 **% White**: 98.7	National ***Socio-Economic Status*** indicator percentiles are not available for the state of Pennsylvania

Westmoreland County

LIGONIER VALLEY S.D.

120 EAST MAIN STREET • LIGONIER PA 15658-1295 • (412) 238-5696

Grade Span: KG-12 **Schools**: *Regular* 5 • *Spec Ed* 0 • *Alt* 0 **Students**: 2,525 **Total Teachers**: 137 **Student/Classroom Teacher Ratio**: 18.5	**Expenditures/Student**: $5,982 **Librarians**: 5.0 505 students/librarian **Guidance Counselors**: 5.0 505 students/counselor	**% Amer Indian**: 0.0 **% Asian**: 0.3 **% Black**: 0.3 **% Hispanic**: 0.1 **% White**: 99.3	National ***Socio-Economic Status*** indicator percentiles are not available for the state of Pennsylvania

Westmoreland County

MOUNT PLEASANT AREA S.D.

RD 4 BOX 2222 • MOUNT PLEASANT PA 15666-9041 • (412) 547-5706

Grade Span: KG-12 **Schools**: *Regular* 5 • *Spec Ed* 0 • *Alt* 0 **Students**: 2,817 **Total Teachers**: 133 **Student/Classroom Teacher Ratio**: 23.3	**Expenditures/Student**: $5,411 **Librarians**: 3.0 939 students/librarian **Guidance Counselors**: 6.0 470 students/counselor	**% Amer Indian**: 0.0 **% Asian**: 0.2 **% Black**: 0.7 **% Hispanic**: 0.2 **% White**: 98.9	National ***Socio-Economic Status*** indicator percentiles are not available for the state of Pennsylvania

Westmoreland County

[MURRYSVILLE] **FRANKLIN REGIONAL S.D.**

3210 SCHOOL ROAD • MURRYSVILLE PA 15668-1553 • (412) 327-5456 • http://fr-www.nb.net

Grade Span: KG-12 **Schools**: *Regular* 5 • *Spec Ed* 0 • *Alt* 0 **Students**: 3,745 **Total Teachers**: 207 **Student/Classroom Teacher Ratio**: 18.6	**Expenditures/Student**: $5,998 **Librarians**: 5.0 749 students/librarian **Guidance Counselors**: 9.0 416 students/counselor	**% Amer Indian**: 0.1 **% Asian**: 4.3 **% Black**: 0.8 **% Hispanic**: 0.4 **% White**: 94.4	National ***Socio-Economic Status*** indicator percentiles are not available for the state of Pennsylvania

Westmoreland County

NEW KENSINGTON-ARNOLD S.D.

701 STEVENSON BOULEVARD • NEW KENSINGTON PA 15068-5356 • (412) 335-8581 • http://nkasd.wiu.k12.pa.us

Grade Span: PK-12 **Schools**: *Regular* 7 • *Spec Ed* 0 • *Alt* 0 **Students**: 2,738 **Total Teachers**: 153 **Student/Classroom Teacher Ratio**: 19.3	**Expenditures/Student**: $5,748 **Librarians**: 3.0 913 students/librarian **Guidance Counselors**: 4.0 685 students/counselor	**% Amer Indian**: 0.2 **% Asian**: 0.3 **% Black**: 24.2 **% Hispanic**: 0.4 **% White**: 74.8	National ***Socio-Economic Status*** indicator percentiles are not available for the state of Pennsylvania

Westmoreland County

[NORTH HUNTINGDON] **NORWIN S.D.**

281 MCMAHON DRIVE • NORTH HUNTINGDON PA 15642-2491 • (412) 863-5052

Grade Span: KG-12 **Schools**: *Regular* 9 • *Spec Ed* 0 • *Alt* 0 **Students**: 5,168 **Total Teachers**: 250 **Student/Classroom Teacher Ratio**: 23.6	**Expenditures/Student**: $5,821 **Librarians**: 5.0 1,034 students/librarian **Guidance Counselors**: 8.0 646 students/counselor	**% Amer Indian**: 0.0 **% Asian**: 0.7 **% Black**: 0.6 **% Hispanic**: 0.1 **% White**: 98.6	National ***Socio-Economic Status*** indicator percentiles are not available for the state of Pennsylvania

Westmoreland County

[VANDERGRIFT] **KISKI AREA S.D.**

200 POPLAR STREET • VANDERGRIFT PA 15690-1491 • (412) 845-2022

Grade Span: KG-12 **Schools**: *Regular* 10 • *Spec Ed* 0 • *Alt* 0 **Students**: 4,839 **Total Teachers**: 215 **Student/Classroom Teacher Ratio**: 23.3	**Expenditures/Student**: $5,710 **Librarians**: 3.0 1,613 students/librarian **Guidance Counselors**: 7.0 691 students/counselor	**% Amer Indian**: 0.1 **% Asian**: 0.2 **% Black**: 3.3 **% Hispanic**: 0.2 **% White**: 96.2	National ***Socio-Economic Status*** indicator percentiles are not available for the state of Pennsylvania

Wyoming County

TUNKHANNOCK AREA S.D.

200 FRANKLIN AVENUE ● TUNKHANNOCK PA 18657-1299 ● (717) 836-3111

Grade Span: KG-12 **Schools**: *Regular* 6 ● *Spec Ed* 0 ● *Alt* 0 **Students**: 3,624 **Total Teachers**: 201 **Student/Classroom Teacher Ratio**: 19.2	**Expenditures/Student**: $6,121 **Librarians**: 4.0 906 students/librarian **Guidance Counselors**: 7.0 518 students/counselor	**% Amer Indian**: 0.0 **% Asian**: 0.1 **% Black**: 0.6 **% Hispanic**: 0.4 **% White**: 99.0	National ***Socio-Economic Status*** indicator percentiles are not available for the state of Pennsylvania

York County

DALLASTOWN AREA S.D.

700 NEW SCHOOL LANE ● DALLASTOWN PA 17313-9780 ● (717) 244-4021

Grade Span: KG-12 **Schools**: *Regular* 7 ● *Spec Ed* 0 ● *Alt* 0 **Students**: 4,789 **Total Teachers**: 269 **Student/Classroom Teacher Ratio**: 18.8	**Expenditures/Student**: $5,683 **Librarians**: 5.6 855 students/librarian **Guidance Counselors**: 9.0 532 students/counselor	**% Amer Indian**: 0.0 **% Asian**: 1.8 **% Black**: 1.0 **% Hispanic**: 1.0 **% White**: 96.2	National ***Socio-Economic Status*** indicator percentiles are not available for the state of Pennsylvania

York County

[DILLSBURG] **NORTHERN YORK COUNTY S.D.**

149 SOUTH BALTIMORE STREET ● DILLSBURG PA 17019-1032 ● (717) 432-8691

Grade Span: KG-12 **Schools**: *Regular* 5 ● *Spec Ed* 0 ● *Alt* 0 **Students**: 3,052 **Total Teachers**: 163 **Student/Classroom Teacher Ratio**: 19.9	**Expenditures/Student**: $5,250 **Librarians**: 3.0 1,017 students/librarian **Guidance Counselors**: 6.0 509 students/counselor	**% Amer Indian**: 0.0 **% Asian**: 1.2 **% Black**: 0.5 **% Hispanic**: 0.5 **% White**: 97.8	National ***Socio-Economic Status*** indicator percentiles are not available for the state of Pennsylvania

York County

DOVER AREA S.D.

SCHOOL LANE ● DOVER PA 17315-1498 ● (717) 292-3671 ● http://www.dover.k12.pa.us

Grade Span: KG-12 **Schools**: *Regular* 6 ● *Spec Ed* 0 ● *Alt* 0 **Students**: 3,555 **Total Teachers**: 192 **Student/Classroom Teacher Ratio**: 18.8	**Expenditures/Student**: $5,480 **Librarians**: 4.0 889 students/librarian **Guidance Counselors**: 8.0 444 students/counselor	**% Amer Indian**: 0.1 **% Asian**: 0.6 **% Black**: 1.0 **% Hispanic**: 0.6 **% White**: 97.7	National ***Socio-Economic Status*** indicator percentiles are not available for the state of Pennsylvania

York County

[FAWN GROVE] **SOUTH EASTERN S.D.**

PO BOX 217 104 EAST MAIN ST ● FAWN GROVE PA 17321-0217 ● (717) 382-4843

Grade Span: KG-12 **Schools**: *Regular* 5 ● *Spec Ed* 0 ● *Alt* 0 **Students**: 2,867 **Total Teachers**: 153 **Student/Classroom Teacher Ratio**: 19.2	**Expenditures/Student**: $5,358 **Librarians**: 3.0 956 students/librarian **Guidance Counselors**: 5.0 573 students/counselor	**% Amer Indian**: 0.1 **% Asian**: 0.9 **% Black**: 1.1 **% Hispanic**: 0.5 **% White**: 97.4	National ***Socio-Economic Status*** indicator percentiles are not available for the state of Pennsylvania

York County

[GLEN ROCK] **SOUTHERN YORK COUNTY S.D.**

PO BOX 128 ● GLEN ROCK PA 17327-0128 ● (717) 235-4811 ● http://www.syc.k12.pa.us

Grade Span: KG-12 **Schools**: *Regular* 4 ● *Spec Ed* 0 ● *Alt* 0 **Students**: 3,248 **Total Teachers**: 176 **Student/Classroom Teacher Ratio**: 18.9	**Expenditures/Student**: $5,377 **Librarians**: 4.0 812 students/librarian **Guidance Counselors**: 7.0 464 students/counselor	**% Amer Indian**: 0.0 **% Asian**: 0.9 **% Black**: 0.8 **% Hispanic**: 0.2 **% White**: 98.1	National ***Socio-Economic Status*** indicator percentiles are not available for the state of Pennsylvania

York County
[HANOVER] **SOUTH WESTERN S.D.**
225 BOWMAN ROAD ● HANOVER PA 17331-4297 ● (717) 632-2500 ● http://www.swsd.k12.pa.us

Grade Span: KG-12 **Schools**: *Regular* 6 ● *Spec Ed* 0 ● *Alt* 0 **Students**: 3,891 **Total Teachers**: 216 **Student/Classroom Teacher Ratio**: 19.8	**Expenditures/Student**: $5,625 **Librarians**: 4.0 973 students/librarian **Guidance Counselors**: 8.0 486 students/counselor	**% Amer Indian**: 0.1 **% Asian**: 0.7 **% Black**: 0.5 **% Hispanic**: 0.7 **% White**: 97.9	National ***Socio-Economic Status*** indicator percentiles are not available for the state of Pennsylvania

York County
[MANCHESTER] **NORTHEASTERN YORK S.D.**
41 HARDING STREET ● MANCHESTER PA 17345-1119 ● (717) 266-3667 ● http://www.cyberia.com/nesd

Grade Span: KG-12 **Schools**: *Regular* 6 ● *Spec Ed* 0 ● *Alt* 0 **Students**: 2,735 **Total Teachers**: 151 **Student/Classroom Teacher Ratio**: 21.1	**Expenditures/Student**: $5,910 **Librarians**: 5.0 547 students/librarian **Guidance Counselors**: 5.0 547 students/counselor	**% Amer Indian**: 0.0 **% Asian**: 0.5 **% Black**: 1.3 **% Hispanic**: 0.7 **% White**: 97.6	National ***Socio-Economic Status*** indicator percentiles are not available for the state of Pennsylvania

York County
RED LION AREA S.D.
696 DELTA ROAD ● RED LION PA 17356-9107 ● (717) 244-4518

Grade Span: KG-12 **Schools**: *Regular* 10 ● *Spec Ed* 0 ● *Alt* 0 **Students**: 4,888 **Total Teachers**: 258 **Student/Classroom Teacher Ratio**: 20.5	**Expenditures/Student**: $5,239 **Librarians**: 4.5 1,086 students/librarian **Guidance Counselors**: 9.0 543 students/counselor	**% Amer Indian**: 0.0 **% Asian**: 0.7 **% Black**: 0.7 **% Hispanic**: 0.3 **% White**: 98.3	National ***Socio-Economic Status*** indicator percentiles are not available for the state of Pennsylvania

York County
SPRING GROVE AREA S.D.
220 WEST JACKSON STREET ● SPRING GROVE PA 17362-1198 ● (717) 225-4731

Grade Span: KG-12 **Schools**: *Regular* 10 ● *Spec Ed* 0 ● *Alt* 0 **Students**: 4,041 **Total Teachers**: 203 **Student/Classroom Teacher Ratio**: 23.7	**Expenditures/Student**: $5,276 **Librarians**: 5.0 808 students/librarian **Guidance Counselors**: 7.0 577 students/counselor	**% Amer Indian**: 0.4 **% Asian**: 0.5 **% Black**: 0.4 **% Hispanic**: 0.3 **% White**: 98.4	National ***Socio-Economic Status*** indicator percentiles are not available for the state of Pennsylvania

York County
[WRIGHTSVILLE] **EASTERN YORK S.D.**
COOL CREEK ROAD PO BOX 150 ● WRIGHTSVILLE PA 17368-0150 ● (717) 252-1555

Grade Span: KG-12 **Schools**: *Regular* 5 ● *Spec Ed* 0 ● *Alt* 0 **Students**: 2,697 **Total Teachers**: 156 **Student/Classroom Teacher Ratio**: 17.9	**Expenditures/Student**: $5,542 **Librarians**: 3.0 899 students/librarian **Guidance Counselors**: 4.3 627 students/counselor	**% Amer Indian**: 0.0 **% Asian**: 0.6 **% Black**: 0.7 **% Hispanic**: 1.1 **% White**: 97.6	National ***Socio-Economic Status*** indicator percentiles are not available for the state of Pennsylvania

York County
[YORK] **CENTRAL YORK S.D.**
775 MARION ROAD ● YORK PA 17402-1555 ● (717) 846-6789

Grade Span: KG-12 **Schools**: *Regular* 6 ● *Spec Ed* 0 ● *Alt* 0 **Students**: 3,653 **Total Teachers**: 192 **Student/Classroom Teacher Ratio**: 21.2	**Expenditures/Student**: $5,516 **Librarians**: 5.0 731 students/librarian **Guidance Counselors**: 7.0 522 students/counselor	**% Amer Indian**: 0.1 **% Asian**: 3.0 **% Black**: 4.2 **% Hispanic**: 1.8 **% White**: 91.0	National ***Socio-Economic Status*** indicator percentiles are not available for the state of Pennsylvania

York County

[YORK] **WEST YORK AREA S.D.**

2605 WEST MARKET STREET ● YORK PA 17404-5585 ● (717) 792-3067 ● http://www.cyberia.com/westyork

Grade Span: KG-12 **Schools**: *Regular* 6 ● *Spec Ed* 0 ● *Alt* 0 **Students**: 2,695 **Total Teachers**: 145 **Student/Classroom Teacher Ratio**: 22.1	**Expenditures/Student**: $5,357 **Librarians**: 4.0 674 students/librarian **Guidance Counselors**: 5.0 539 students/counselor	**% Amer Indian**: 0.0 **% Asian**: 2.3 **% Black**: 2.3 **% Hispanic**: 1.6 **% White**: 93.8	National ***Socio-Economic Status*** indicator percentiles are not available for the state of Pennsylvania

York County

YORK CITY S.D.

PO BOX 1927 329 S LINDBRGH AVE ● YORK PA 17405-1927 ● (717) 845-3571 ● http://www.lincnet-liu.k12.pa.us/ycs/index.html

Grade Span: KG-12 **Schools**: *Regular* 10 ● *Spec Ed* 0 ● *Alt* 0 **Students**: 7,443 **Total Teachers**: 357 **Student/Classroom Teacher Ratio**: 22.0	**Expenditures/Student**: $5,845 **Librarians**: 6.0 1,241 students/librarian **Guidance Counselors**: 4.5 1,654 students/counselor	**% Amer Indian**: 0.1 **% Asian**: 1.6 **% Black**: 40.5 **% Hispanic**: 20.5 **% White**: 37.3	National ***Socio-Economic Status*** indicator percentiles are not available for the state of Pennsylvania

Bristol County

BARRINGTON S.D.

283 COUNTY RD ● BARRINGTON RI 02806 ● (401) 245-5000

Grade Span: PK-12	**Expenditures/Student**: $6,435	**% Amer Indian**: 0.1	
Schools: *Regular* 6 ● *Spec Ed* 0 ● *Alt* 0	**Librarians**: 3.0	**% Asian**: 1.4	National ***Socio-Economic***
Students: 2,879	960 students/librarian	**% Black**: 0.4	***Status*** indicator percentile
Total Teachers: 209	**Guidance Counselors**: 8.0	**% Hispanic**: 0.5	(100=high): 98th
Student/Classroom Teacher Ratio: 14.3	360 students/counselor	**% White**: 97.6	

Bristol County

BRISTOL-WARREN REGIONAL S.D.

151 STATE ST ● BRISTOL RI 02809 ● (401) 253-4000 ● http://ride.ri.net/schools/Burrillville

Grade Span: KG-12	**Expenditures/Student**: $7,561	**% Amer Indian**: 0.0	
Schools: *Regular* 12 ● *Spec Ed* 0 ● *Alt* 0	**Librarians**: 1.0	**% Asian**: 0.1	National ***Socio-Economic***
Students: 4,006	4,006 students/librarian	**% Black**: 0.9	***Status*** indicator percentile
Total Teachers: 323	**Guidance Counselors**: 8.0	**% Hispanic**: 0.9	(100=high): 63rd
Student/Classroom Teacher Ratio: 13.0	501 students/counselor	**% White**: 98.1	

Kent County

COVENTRY S.D.

WOOD ST ● COVENTRY RI 02816 ● (401) 821-4300

Grade Span: PK-12	**Expenditures/Student**: $6,407	**% Amer Indian**: 0.6	
Schools: *Regular* 8 ● *Spec Ed* 0 ● *Alt* 0	**Librarians**: 3.0	**% Asian**: 0.6	National ***Socio-Economic***
Students: 5,478	1,826 students/librarian	**% Black**: 1.0	***Status*** indicator percentile
Total Teachers: 371	**Guidance Counselors**: 8.0	**% Hispanic**: 0.9	(100=high): 78th
Student/Classroom Teacher Ratio: 15.0	685 students/counselor	**% White**: 96.9	

Kent County

WARWICK S.D.

34 WARWICK LAKE AVE ● WARWICK RI 02889 ● (401) 737-3300 ● http://users.ids.net/~tollgate

Grade Span: PK-12	**Expenditures/Student**: $7,752	**% Amer Indian**: 0.2	
Schools: *Regular* 26 ● *Spec Ed* 0 ● *Alt* 0	**Librarians**: 8.0	**% Asian**: 1.3	National ***Socio-Economic***
Students: 11,931	1,491 students/librarian	**% Black**: 1.2	***Status*** indicator percentile
Total Teachers: 923	**Guidance Counselors**: 27.9	**% Hispanic**: 1.1	(100=high): 71st
Student/Classroom Teacher Ratio: 14.3	428 students/counselor	**% White**: 96.2	

Kent County

WEST WARWICK S.D.

10 HARRIS AVE ● WEST WARWICK RI 02893 ● (401) 821-1180 ● http://horgan.ww.k12.ri.us

Grade Span: PK-12	**Expenditures/Student**: $7,452	**% Amer Indian**: 0.4	
Schools: *Regular* 7 ● *Spec Ed* 0 ● *Alt* 0	**Librarians**: 2.0	**% Asian**: 1.7	National ***Socio-Economic***
Students: 3,906	1,953 students/librarian	**% Black**: 2.0	***Status*** indicator percentile
Total Teachers: 296	**Guidance Counselors**: 6.0	**% Hispanic**: 3.4	(100=high): 53rd
Student/Classroom Teacher Ratio: 13.1	651 students/counselor	**% White**: 92.6	

Newport County

MIDDLETOWN S.D.

WEST MAIN RD ● MIDDLETOWN RI 02840 ● (401) 849-2122

Grade Span: KG-12	**Expenditures/Student**: $7,894	**% Amer Indian**: 0.4	
Schools: *Regular* 6 ● *Spec Ed* 0 ● *Alt* 0	**Librarians**: 1.0	**% Asian**: 3.1	National ***Socio-Economic***
Students: 2,740	2,740 students/librarian	**% Black**: 6.8	***Status*** indicator percentile
Total Teachers: 226	**Guidance Counselors**: 10.0	**% Hispanic**: 2.5	(100=high): 73rd
Student/Classroom Teacher Ratio: 12.8	274 students/counselor	**% White**: 87.2	

Newport County
NEWPORT S.D.
437 BROADWAY ● NEWPORT RI 02840 ● (401) 847-2100

Grade Span: PK-12 **Schools**: *Regular* 9 ● *Spec Ed* 0 ● *Alt* 0 **Students**: 3,115 **Total Teachers**: 256 **Student/Classroom Teacher Ratio**: 13.3	**Expenditures/Student**: $9,518 **Librarians**: 2.0 1,558 students/librarian **Guidance Counselors**: 11.0 283 students/counselor	**% Amer Indian**: 1.0 **% Asian**: 1.5 **% Black**: 19.1 **% Hispanic**: 5.7 **% White**: 72.6	National ***Socio-Economic Status*** indicator percentile (100=high): 35th

Newport County
PORTSMOUTH S.D.
29 MIDDLE RD ● PORTSMOUTH RI 02871 ● (401) 683-1039 ● http://www3.edgenet.net/~patriots

Grade Span: KG-12 **Schools**: *Regular* 6 ● *Spec Ed* 0 ● *Alt* 0 **Students**: 2,730 **Total Teachers**: 197 **Student/Classroom Teacher Ratio**: 15.1	**Expenditures/Student**: $7,400 **Librarians**: 2.0 1,365 students/librarian **Guidance Counselors**: 8.4 325 students/counselor	**% Amer Indian**: 0.0 **% Asian**: 1.6 **% Black**: 1.3 **% Hispanic**: 0.8 **% White**: 96.2	National ***Socio-Economic Status*** indicator percentile (100=high): 92nd

Providence County
[ASHTON] **CUMBERLAND S.D.**
2602 MENDON RD ● ASHTON RI 02864 ● (401) 658-1600

Grade Span: KG-12 **Schools**: *Regular* 9 ● *Spec Ed* 0 ● *Alt* 0 **Students**: 4,750 **Total Teachers**: 352 **Student/Classroom Teacher Ratio**: 14.0	**Expenditures/Student**: $6,476 **Librarians**: 3.0 1,583 students/librarian **Guidance Counselors**: 17.0 279 students/counselor	**% Amer Indian**: 0.2 **% Asian**: 0.5 **% Black**: 0.7 **% Hispanic**: 1.7 **% White**: 97.0	National ***Socio-Economic Status*** indicator percentile (100=high): 84th

Providence County
CENTRAL FALLS S.D.
21 HEDLEY AVE ● CENTRAL FALLS RI 02863 ● (401) 727-7700

Grade Span: PK-12 **Schools**: *Regular* 7 ● *Spec Ed* 0 ● *Alt* 0 **Students**: 3,013 **Total Teachers**: 197 **Student/Classroom Teacher Ratio**: 16.8	**Expenditures/Student**: $7,209 **Librarians**: 1.0 3,013 students/librarian **Guidance Counselors**: 4.0 753 students/counselor	**% Amer Indian**: 0.3 **% Asian**: 0.5 **% Black**: 9.5 **% Hispanic**: 50.7 **% White**: 39.0	National ***Socio-Economic Status*** indicator percentile (100=high): 1st

Providence County
CRANSTON S.D.
845 PARK AVE ● CRANSTON RI 02910 ● (401) 785-0400

Grade Span: PK-12 **Schools**: *Regular* 23 ● *Spec Ed* 0 ● *Alt* 0 **Students**: 10,364 **Total Teachers**: 715 **Student/Classroom Teacher Ratio**: 16.0	**Expenditures/Student**: $6,930 **Librarians**: 4.0 2,591 students/librarian **Guidance Counselors**: 29.0 357 students/counselor	**% Amer Indian**: 0.1 **% Asian**: 5.2 **% Black**: 2.8 **% Hispanic**: 3.8 **% White**: 88.1	National ***Socio-Economic Status*** indicator percentile (100=high): 64th

Providence County
EAST PROVIDENCE S.D.
80 BURNSIDE AVE ● EAST PROVIDENCE RI 02915 ● (401) 437-0750

Grade Span: PK-12 **Schools**: *Regular* 15 ● *Spec Ed* 0 ● *Alt* 0 **Students**: 6,822 **Total Teachers**: 453 **Student/Classroom Teacher Ratio**: 17.3	**Expenditures/Student**: $6,623 **Librarians**: 6.7 1,018 students/librarian **Guidance Counselors**: 10.2 669 students/counselor	**% Amer Indian**: 0.4 **% Asian**: 0.7 **% Black**: 11.1 **% Hispanic**: 1.5 **% White**: 86.3	National ***Socio-Economic Status*** indicator percentile (100=high): 55th

Providence County
[ESMOND] SMITHFIELD S.D.
49 FARNUM PIKE ● ESMOND RI 02917 ● (401) 231-6606

Grade Span: PK-12 **Schools**: *Regular* 6 ● *Spec Ed* 0 ● *Alt* 0 **Students**: 2,702 **Total Teachers**: 172 **Student/Classroom Teacher Ratio**: 16.2	**Expenditures/Student**: $5,517 **Librarians**: 1.0 2,702 students/librarian **Guidance Counselors**: 4.2 643 students/counselor	**% Amer Indian**: 0.0 **% Asian**: 1.0 **% Black**: 0.4 **% Hispanic**: 0.1 **% White**: 98.4	National ***Socio-Economic Status*** indicator percentile (100=high): 91st

Providence County
[HARRISVILLE] BURRILLVILLE S.D.
425 EAST AVE ● HARRISVILLE RI 02830 ● (401) 568-6261

Grade Span: PK-12 **Schools**: *Regular* 5 ● *Spec Ed* 0 ● *Alt* 0 **Students**: 2,966 **Total Teachers**: 206 **Student/Classroom Teacher Ratio**: 14.5	**Expenditures/Student**: $6,444 **Librarians**: 1.0 2,966 students/librarian **Guidance Counselors**: 5.5 539 students/counselor	**% Amer Indian**: 0.0 **% Asian**: 0.3 **% Black**: 0.3 **% Hispanic**: 0.5 **% White**: 98.9	National ***Socio-Economic Status*** indicator percentile (100=high): 73rd

Providence County
JOHNSTON S.D.
345 CHERRY HILL RD ● JOHNSTON RI 02919 ● (401) 231-8780 ● http://users.ids.net/JohnstonSchool

Grade Span: PK-12 **Schools**: *Regular* 8 ● *Spec Ed* 0 ● *Alt* 0 **Students**: 3,352 **Total Teachers**: 228 **Student/Classroom Teacher Ratio**: 15.3	**Expenditures/Student**: $6,999 **Librarians**: 1.0 3,352 students/librarian **Guidance Counselors**: 6.0 559 students/counselor	**% Amer Indian**: 0.5 **% Asian**: 1.3 **% Black**: 1.3 **% Hispanic**: 2.2 **% White**: 94.6	National ***Socio-Economic Status*** indicator percentile (100=high): 76th

Providence County
LINCOLN S.D.
1624 LONSDALE AVE ● LINCOLN RI 02865 ● (401) 726-2150

Grade Span: PK-12 **Schools**: *Regular* 9 ● *Spec Ed* 0 ● *Alt* 0 **Students**: 3,331 **Total Teachers**: 219 **Student/Classroom Teacher Ratio**: 16.0	**Expenditures/Student**: $6,188 **Librarians**: 3.0 1,110 students/librarian **Guidance Counselors**: 9.0 370 students/counselor	**% Amer Indian**: 0.1 **% Asian**: 1.5 **% Black**: 1.3 **% Hispanic**: 1.5 **% White**: 95.6	National ***Socio-Economic Status*** indicator percentile (100=high): 84th

Providence County
NORTH PROVIDENCE S.D.
9 GEORGE ST ● NORTH PROVIDENCE RI 02911 ● (401) 232-0840

Grade Span: PK-12 **Schools**: *Regular* 9 ● *Spec Ed* 0 ● *Alt* 0 **Students**: 3,571 **Total Teachers**: 288 **Student/Classroom Teacher Ratio**: 12.7	**Expenditures/Student**: $7,212 **Librarians**: 1.0 3,571 students/librarian **Guidance Counselors**: 6.0 595 students/counselor	**% Amer Indian**: 0.0 **% Asian**: 1.9 **% Black**: 2.8 **% Hispanic**: 5.0 **% White**: 90.3	National ***Socio-Economic Status*** indicator percentile (100=high): 71st

Providence County
PAWTUCKET S.D.
PARK PLACE ● PAWTUCKET RI 02860 ● (401) 728-2120 ● http://www.pa.k12.ri.us

Grade Span: KG-12 **Schools**: *Regular* 15 ● *Spec Ed* 0 ● *Alt* 0 **Students**: 9,550 **Total Teachers**: 623 **Student/Classroom Teacher Ratio**: 15.6	**Expenditures/Student**: $6,469 **Librarians**: 3.0 3,183 students/librarian **Guidance Counselors**: 13.0 735 students/counselor	**% Amer Indian**: 1.1 **% Asian**: 0.8 **% Black**: 13.0 **% Hispanic**: 17.7 **% White**: 67.5	National ***Socio-Economic Status*** indicator percentile (100=high): 19th

Providence County
PROVIDENCE S.D.
797 WESTMINSTER ST ● PROVIDENCE RI 02903 ● (401) 456-9211

Grade Span: KG-12 **Schools**: *Regular* 35 ● *Spec Ed* 3 ● *Alt* 4 **Students**: 24,069 **Total Teachers**: 1,377 **Student/Classroom Teacher Ratio**: 19.8	**Expenditures/Student**: $6,904 **Librarians**: 6.0 4,012 students/librarian **Guidance Counselors**: 43.0 560 students/counselor	**% Amer Indian**: 0.6 **% Asian**: 11.1 **% Black**: 23.0 **% Hispanic**: 40.6 **% White**: 24.6	National ***Socio-Economic Status*** indicator percentile (100=high): 5th

Providence County
WOONSOCKET S.D.
108 HIGH ST ● WOONSOCKET RI 02895 ● (401) 762-4440 ● http://www.woonsockethigh.org

Grade Span: KG-12 **Schools**: *Regular* 14 ● *Spec Ed* 0 ● *Alt* 0 **Students**: 6,595 **Total Teachers**: 448 **Student/Classroom Teacher Ratio**: 14.8	**Expenditures/Student**: $5,886 **Librarians**: 3.0 2,198 students/librarian **Guidance Counselors**: 19.0 347 students/counselor	**% Amer Indian**: 0.5 **% Asian**: 7.8 **% Black**: 7.6 **% Hispanic**: 10.5 **% White**: 73.7	National ***Socio-Economic Status*** indicator percentile (100=high): 20th

Washington County
NORTH KINGSTOWN S.D.
100 FAIRWAY BOX 356 ● NORTH KINGSTOWN RI 02852 ● (401) 294-4581

Grade Span: KG-12 **Schools**: *Regular* 10 ● *Spec Ed* 0 ● *Alt* 0 **Students**: 4,441 **Total Teachers**: 304 **Student/Classroom Teacher Ratio**: 15.1	**Expenditures/Student**: $7,217 **Librarians**: 4.0 1,110 students/librarian **Guidance Counselors**: 7.0 634 students/counselor	**% Amer Indian**: 0.9 **% Asian**: 0.8 **% Black**: 2.3 **% Hispanic**: 1.3 **% White**: 94.7	National ***Socio-Economic Status*** indicator percentile (100=high): 80th

Washington County
[WAKEFIELD] SOUTH KINGSTOWN S.D.
307 CURTIS CORNER RD ● WAKEFIELD RI 02879 ● (401) 792-9681

Grade Span: PK-12 **Schools**: *Regular* 7 ● *Spec Ed* 0 ● *Alt* 0 **Students**: 3,968 **Total Teachers**: 267 **Student/Classroom Teacher Ratio**: 15.1	**Expenditures/Student**: $6,757 **Librarians**: 2.0 1,984 students/librarian **Guidance Counselors**: 5.0 794 students/counselor	**% Amer Indian**: 2.0 **% Asian**: 2.3 **% Black**: 3.5 **% Hispanic**: 1.1 **% White**: 91.1	National ***Socio-Economic Status*** indicator percentile (100=high): 82nd

Washington County
WESTERLY S.D.
28 CHESTNUT ST ● WESTERLY RI 02891 ● (401) 596-0315

Grade Span: PK-12 **Schools**: *Regular* 6 ● *Spec Ed* 0 ● *Alt* 0 **Students**: 3,431 **Total Teachers**: 250 **Student/Classroom Teacher Ratio**: 14.1	**Expenditures/Student**: $7,403 **Librarians**: 2.0 1,716 students/librarian **Guidance Counselors**: 2.0 1,716 students/counselor	**% Amer Indian**: 0.3 **% Asian**: 2.1 **% Black**: 1.2 **% Hispanic**: 0.7 **% White**: 95.7	National ***Socio-Economic Status*** indicator percentile (100=high): 71st

Washington County
[WOOD RIVER JUNCTION] CHARIHO REGIONAL S.D.
SWITCH RD ● WOOD RIVER JUNCTION RI 02894 ● (401) 364-7575 ● http://www.chariho.k12.ri.us

Grade Span: PK-12 **Schools**: *Regular* 6 ● *Spec Ed* 0 ● *Alt* 0 **Students**: 3,801 **Total Teachers**: 302 **Student/Classroom Teacher Ratio**: 13.4	**Expenditures/Student**: $7,722 **Librarians**: 2.0 1,901 students/librarian **Guidance Counselors**: 10.0 380 students/counselor	**% Amer Indian**: 1.6 **% Asian**: 0.6 **% Black**: 0.5 **% Hispanic**: 0.9 **% White**: 96.5	National ***Socio-Economic Status*** indicator percentile (100=high): 81st

Abbeville County

[ABBEVILLE] **ABBEVILLE COUNTY S.D.**

500 CHESTNUT STREET ● ABBEVILLE SC 29620 ● (864) 459-5427

Grade Span: KG-12 **Schools**: *Regular* 9 ● *Spec Ed* 0 ● *Alt* 1 **Students**: 3,803 **Total Teachers**: 252 **Student/Classroom Teacher Ratio**: 15.7	**Expenditures/Student**: $4,697 **Librarians**: 8.5 447 students/librarian **Guidance Counselors**: 8.0 475 students/counselor	**% Amer Indian**: 0.0 **% Asian**: 0.1 **% Black**: 45.9 **% Hispanic**: 0.0 **% White**: 54.0	National ***Socio-Economic Status*** indicator percentile (100=high): 22nd

Aiken County

[AIKEN] **AIKEN COUNTY S.D.**

DRAWER 1137, 843 EDGEFIELD AVE ● AIKEN SC 29802-1137 ● (803) 641-2700 ● http://www.aiken.k12.sc.us

Grade Span: KG-12 **Schools**: *Regular* 36 ● *Spec Ed* 0 ● *Alt* 1 **Students**: 24,367 **Total Teachers**: 1,316 **Student/Classroom Teacher Ratio**: 18.4	**Expenditures/Student**: $4,024 **Librarians**: 39.0 625 students/librarian **Guidance Counselors**: 60.7 401 students/counselor	**% Amer Indian**: 0.1 **% Asian**: 0.5 **% Black**: 33.5 **% Hispanic**: 0.8 **% White**: 65.0	National ***Socio-Economic Status*** indicator percentile (100=high): 34th

Anderson County

ANDERSON S.D. 5

PO BOX 439, 400 PEARMAN DAIRY ● ANDERSON SC 29622 ● (864) 260-5000

Grade Span: KG-12 **Schools**: *Regular* 16 ● *Spec Ed* 0 ● *Alt* 0 **Students**: 10,876 **Total Teachers**: 651 **Student/Classroom Teacher Ratio**: 15.8	**Expenditures/Student**: $4,502 **Librarians**: 17.0 640 students/librarian **Guidance Counselors**: 25.0 435 students/counselor	**% Amer Indian**: 0.0 **% Asian**: 0.5 **% Black**: 32.6 **% Hispanic**: 0.2 **% White**: 66.7	National ***Socio-Economic Status*** indicator percentile (100=high): 43rd

Anderson County

[HONEA PATH] **ANDERSON S.D. 2**

PO BOX 266, HWY 76 ● HONEA PATH SC 29654 ● (864) 369-7364 ● http://www.anderson1234.k12.sc.us

Grade Span: KG-12 **Schools**: *Regular* 7 ● *Spec Ed* 0 ● *Alt* 0 **Students**: 3,437 **Total Teachers**: 208 **Student/Classroom Teacher Ratio**: 16.9	**Expenditures/Student**: $4,149 **Librarians**: 7.3 471 students/librarian **Guidance Counselors**: 7.0 491 students/counselor	**% Amer Indian**: 0.0 **% Asian**: 0.1 **% Black**: 20.5 **% Hispanic**: 0.3 **% White**: 79.2	National ***Socio-Economic Status*** indicator percentile (100=high): 45th

Anderson County

[WILLIAMSTON] **ANDERSON S.D. 1**

PO BOX 99, 861 HAMILTON ST ● WILLIAMSTON SC 29697 ● (864) 847-7344 ● http://www.anderson1234.k12.sc.us

Grade Span: KG-12 **Schools**: *Regular* 13 ● *Spec Ed* 0 ● *Alt* 1 **Students**: 6,689 **Total Teachers**: 366 **Student/Classroom Teacher Ratio**: 17.2	**Expenditures/Student**: $3,977 **Librarians**: 12.0 557 students/librarian **Guidance Counselors**: 13.5 495 students/counselor	**% Amer Indian**: 0.0 **% Asian**: 0.0 **% Black**: 6.4 **% Hispanic**: 0.1 **% White**: 93.4	National ***Socio-Economic Status*** indicator percentile (100=high): 67th

Barnwell County

BARNWELL S.D. 45

2008 HAGOOD AVENUE ● BARNWELL SC 29812 ● (803) 541-1300

Grade Span: KG-12 **Schools**: *Regular* 3 ● *Spec Ed* 0 ● *Alt* 0 **Students**: 2,712 **Total Teachers**: 166 **Student/Classroom Teacher Ratio**: 16.2	**Expenditures/Student**: $4,339 **Librarians**: 4.0 678 students/librarian **Guidance Counselors**: 5.0 542 students/counselor	**% Amer Indian**: 0.1 **% Asian**: 0.2 **% Black**: 39.5 **% Hispanic**: 0.7 **% White**: 59.5	National ***Socio-Economic Status*** indicator percentile (100=high): 22nd

Beaufort County

[BEAUFORT] BEAUFORT COUNTY S.D.

PO BOX 309, 1300 KING STREET ● BEAUFORT SC 29901 ● (803) 525-4200 ● http://www.hhisland.com/learning/beaufort.htm

Grade Span: KG-12	**Expenditures/Student**: $4,817	**% Amer Indian**: 0.2	
Schools: *Regular* 19 ● *Spec Ed* 1 ● *Alt* 1	**Librarians**: 23.5	**% Asian**: 0.6	National ***Socio-Economic***
Students: 14,180	603 students/librarian	**% Black**: 47.1	***Status*** indicator percentile
Total Teachers: 889	**Guidance Counselors**: 34.5	**% Hispanic**: 2.0	(100=high): 25th
Student/Classroom Teacher Ratio: 15.5	411 students/counselor	**% White**: 50.0	

Berkeley County

[MONCKS CORNER] BERKELEY COUNTY S.D.

PO BOX 608, MAIN STREET ● MONCKS CORNER SC 29461 ● (843) 761-8600 ● http://www.berkeley.k12.sc.us

Grade Span: KG-12	**Expenditures/Student**: $3,979	**% Amer Indian**: 0.4	
Schools: *Regular* 35 ● *Spec Ed* 0 ● *Alt* 2	**Librarians**: 36.0	**% Asian**: 1.9	National ***Socio-Economic***
Students: 26,062	724 students/librarian	**% Black**: 33.7	***Status*** indicator percentile
Total Teachers: 1,453	**Guidance Counselors**: 60.5	**% Hispanic**: 1.2	(100=high): 30th
Student/Classroom Teacher Ratio: 17.6	431 students/counselor	**% White**: 62.8	

Charleston County

[CHARLESTON] CHARLESTON COUNTY S.D.

75 CALHOUN STREET ● CHARLESTON SC 29403 ● (843) 724-7716

Grade Span: KG-12	**Expenditures/Student**: $4,501	**% Amer Indian**: 0.1	
Schools: *Regular* 71 ● *Spec Ed* 0 ● *Alt* 0	**Librarians**: 74.0	**% Asian**: 1.0	National ***Socio-Economic***
Students: 43,480	588 students/librarian	**% Black**: 58.4	***Status*** indicator percentile
Total Teachers: 2,694	**Guidance Counselors**: 101.2	**% Hispanic**: 0.8	(100=high): 18th
Student/Classroom Teacher Ratio: 15.9	430 students/counselor	**% White**: 39.6	

Cherokee County

[GAFFNEY] CHEROKEE COUNTY S.D.

PO BOX 460, 115 MADISON AVE ● GAFFNEY SC 29342 ● (864) 489-0261

Grade Span: KG-12	**Expenditures/Student**: $4,721	**% Amer Indian**: 0.0	
Schools: *Regular* 18 ● *Spec Ed* 0 ● *Alt* 1	**Librarians**: 17.0	**% Asian**: 0.4	National ***Socio-Economic***
Students: 8,353	491 students/librarian	**% Black**: 29.6	***Status*** indicator percentile
Total Teachers: 532	**Guidance Counselors**: 21.0	**% Hispanic**: 0.8	(100=high): 31st
Student/Classroom Teacher Ratio: 17.0	398 students/counselor	**% White**: 69.1	

Chester County

[CHESTER] CHESTER COUNTY S.D.

109 HINTON STREET ● CHESTER SC 29706 ● (803) 385-6122 ● http://www.chester.k12.sc.us

Grade Span: KG-12	**Expenditures/Student**: $4,565	**% Amer Indian**: 0.1	
Schools: *Regular* 9 ● *Spec Ed* 0 ● *Alt* 1	**Librarians**: 11.0	**% Asian**: 0.1	National ***Socio-Economic***
Students: 6,569	597 students/librarian	**% Black**: 51.9	***Status*** indicator percentile
Total Teachers: 429	**Guidance Counselors**: 12.7	**% Hispanic**: 0.0	(100=high): 18th
Student/Classroom Teacher Ratio: 15.7	517 students/counselor	**% White**: 48.0	

Chesterfield County

[CHESTERFIELD] CHESTERFIELD COUNTY S.D.

401 WEST BOULEVARD ● CHESTERFIELD SC 29709 ● (843) 623-2175 ● http://www.chesterfield.k12.sc.us

Grade Span: KG-12	**Expenditures/Student**: $4,512	**% Amer Indian**: 0.2	
Schools: *Regular* 16 ● *Spec Ed* 0 ● *Alt* 0	**Librarians**: 15.5	**% Asian**: 0.2	National ***Socio-Economic***
Students: 7,853	507 students/librarian	**% Black**: 42.7	***Status*** indicator percentile
Total Teachers: 487	**Guidance Counselors**: 15.8	**% Hispanic**: 0.2	(100=high): 17th
Student/Classroom Teacher Ratio: 16.0	497 students/counselor	**% White**: 56.7	

Clarendon County

[MANNING] CLARENDON S.D. 2

PO BOX 1252, 15 MAJOR DRIVE ● MANNING SC 29102 ● (803) 435-4435

Grade Span: KG-12 **Schools**: *Regular* 5 ● *Spec Ed* 0 ● *Alt* 1 **Students**: 3,635 **Total Teachers**: 202 **Student/Classroom Teacher Ratio**: 18.1	**Expenditures/Student**: $3,840 **Librarians**: 5.0 727 students/librarian **Guidance Counselors**: 6.0 606 students/counselor	**% Amer Indian**: 0.1 **% Asian**: 0.3 **% Black**: 66.5 **% Hispanic**: 0.7 **% White**: 32.5	National ***Socio-Economic Status*** indicator percentile (100=high): 6th

Colleton County

[WALTERBORO] COLLETON COUNTY S.D.

PO BOX 290, 213 JEFFRIES BLVD ● WALTERBORO SC 29488 ● (843) 549-5715

Grade Span: KG-12 **Schools**: *Regular* 13 ● *Spec Ed* 0 ● *Alt* 1 **Students**: 6,947 **Total Teachers**: 475 **Student/Classroom Teacher Ratio**: 14.0	**Expenditures/Student**: $4,757 **Librarians**: 13.0 534 students/librarian **Guidance Counselors**: 17.0 409 students/counselor	**% Amer Indian**: 0.5 **% Asian**: 0.2 **% Black**: 56.3 **% Hispanic**: 0.2 **% White**: 42.8	National ***Socio-Economic Status*** indicator percentile (100=high): 11th

Darlington County

[DARLINGTON] DARLINGTON COUNTY S.D.

PO BOX 493, 304 COURTHOUSE ● DARLINGTON SC 29532 ● (843) 398-5200 ● http://www.darlington.k12.sc.us

Grade Span: KG-12 **Schools**: *Regular* 21 ● *Spec Ed* 0 ● *Alt* 0 **Students**: 11,030 **Total Teachers**: 772 **Student/Classroom Teacher Ratio**: 14.5	**Expenditures/Student**: $4,928 **Librarians**: 24.0 460 students/librarian **Guidance Counselors**: 33.0 334 students/counselor	**% Amer Indian**: 0.1 **% Asian**: 0.1 **% Black**: 53.2 **% Hispanic**: 0.4 **% White**: 46.2	National ***Socio-Economic Status*** indicator percentile (100=high): 13th

Dillon County

DILLON S.D. 2

401 WASHINGTON STREET WEST ● DILLON SC 29536-2898 ● (843) 774-1200 ● http://www.dillon2.k12.sc.us

Grade Span: KG-12 **Schools**: *Regular* 6 ● *Spec Ed* 0 ● *Alt* 1 **Students**: 3,996 **Total Teachers**: 233 **Student/Classroom Teacher Ratio**: 16.8	**Expenditures/Student**: $4,195 **Librarians**: 7.0 571 students/librarian **Guidance Counselors**: 9.0 444 students/counselor	**% Amer Indian**: 2.6 **% Asian**: 0.5 **% Black**: 61.8 **% Hispanic**: 0.2 **% White**: 35.0	National ***Socio-Economic Status*** indicator percentile (100=high): 6th

Dorchester County

[SUMMERVILLE] DORCHESTER S.D. 2

102 GREENWAVE BLVD. ● SUMMERVILLE SC 29483 ● (843) 873-2901

Grade Span: KG-12 **Schools**: *Regular* 16 ● *Spec Ed* 0 ● *Alt* 0 **Students**: 15,188 **Total Teachers**: 841 **Student/Classroom Teacher Ratio**: 17.9	**Expenditures/Student**: $3,987 **Librarians**: 15.0 1,013 students/librarian **Guidance Counselors**: 29.3 518 students/counselor	**% Amer Indian**: 0.4 **% Asian**: 1.0 **% Black**: 23.6 **% Hispanic**: 0.7 **% White**: 74.3	National ***Socio-Economic Status*** indicator percentile (100=high): 58th

Edgefield County

[EDGEFIELD] EDGEFIELD COUNTY S.D.

PO BOX 608, SC 23 ● EDGEFIELD SC 29824 ● (803) 275-4601

Grade Span: KG-12 **Schools**: *Regular* 7 ● *Spec Ed* 0 ● *Alt* 1 **Students**: 4,044 **Total Teachers**: 283 **Student/Classroom Teacher Ratio**: 15.1	**Expenditures/Student**: $4,617 **Librarians**: 8.0 506 students/librarian **Guidance Counselors**: 13.0 311 students/counselor	**% Amer Indian**: 0.0 **% Asian**: 0.2 **% Black**: 56.8 **% Hispanic**: 0.4 **% White**: 42.6	National ***Socio-Economic Status*** indicator percentile (100=high): 14th

Fairfield County

[WINNSBORO] **FAIRFIELD COUNTY S.D.**

DRAWER 622, OLD CAMDEN ROAD ● WINNSBORO SC 29180 ● (803) 635-4607

Grade Span: KG-12 **Schools**: *Regular* 7 ● *Spec Ed* 0 ● *Alt* 1 **Students**: 3,663 **Total Teachers**: 305 **Student/Classroom Teacher Ratio**: 12.5	**Expenditures/Student**: $6,325 **Librarians**: 8.0 458 students/librarian **Guidance Counselors**: 12.0 305 students/counselor	**% Amer Indian**: 0.0 **% Asian**: 0.0 **% Black**: 81.4 **% Hispanic**: 0.3 **% White**: 18.3	National ***Socio-Economic Status*** indicator percentile (100=high): 10th

Florence County

FLORENCE S.D. 1

319 S. DARGAN STREET ● FLORENCE SC 29506 ● (803) 669-4141 ● http://www.fsd1.com

Grade Span: KG-12 **Schools**: *Regular* 19 ● *Spec Ed* 0 ● *Alt* 1 **Students**: 14,644 **Total Teachers**: 876 **Student/Classroom Teacher Ratio**: 17.0	**Expenditures/Student**: $4,114 **Librarians**: 21.0 697 students/librarian **Guidance Counselors**: 26.0 563 students/counselor	**% Amer Indian**: 0.1 **% Asian**: 0.5 **% Black**: 48.3 **% Hispanic**: 0.4 **% White**: 50.7	National ***Socio-Economic Status*** indicator percentile (100=high): 23rd

Florence County

[LAKE CITY] **FLORENCE S.D. 3**

DRAWER 1389, 140 WESTOVER ● LAKE CITY SC 29560 ● (843) 394-8652

Grade Span: KG-12 **Schools**: *Regular* 8 ● *Spec Ed* 0 ● *Alt* 0 **Students**: 4,520 **Total Teachers**: 263 **Student/Classroom Teacher Ratio**: 17.0	**Expenditures/Student**: $4,244 **Librarians**: 6.2 729 students/librarian **Guidance Counselors**: 7.5 603 students/counselor	**% Amer Indian**: 0.0 **% Asian**: 0.4 **% Black**: 64.4 **% Hispanic**: 0.2 **% White**: 35.0	National ***Socio-Economic Status*** indicator percentile (100=high): 6th

Georgetown County

[GEORGETOWN] **GEORGETOWN COUNTY S.D.**

624 FRONT STREET ● GEORGETOWN SC 29440 ● (843) 546-2561 ● http://www.gcsd.k12.sc.us/default.htm

Grade Span: KG-12 **Schools**: *Regular* 18 ● *Spec Ed* 0 ● *Alt* 1 **Students**: 10,703 **Total Teachers**: 755 **Student/Classroom Teacher Ratio**: 14.6	**Expenditures/Student**: $5,069 **Librarians**: 18.0 595 students/librarian **Guidance Counselors**: 32.5 329 students/counselor	**% Amer Indian**: 0.0 **% Asian**: 0.1 **% Black**: 57.5 **% Hispanic**: 0.2 **% White**: 42.1	National ***Socio-Economic Status*** indicator percentile (100=high): 16th

Greenville County

[GREENVILLE] **GREENVILLE COUNTY S.D.**

PO BOX 2848/301 CAMPERDOWN WAY ● GREENVILLE SC 29602 ● (864) 241-3457 ● http://www.greenville.k12.sc.us

Grade Span: KG-12 **Schools**: *Regular* 85 ● *Spec Ed* 3 ● *Alt* 4 **Students**: 54,619 **Total Teachers**: 3,265 **Student/Classroom Teacher Ratio**: 16.8	**Expenditures/Student**: $4,362 **Librarians**: 103.8 526 students/librarian **Guidance Counselors**: 116.6 468 students/counselor	**% Amer Indian**: 0.0 **% Asian**: 1.0 **% Black**: 26.8 **% Hispanic**: 1.0 **% White**: 71.2	National ***Socio-Economic Status*** indicator percentile (100=high): 50th

Greenwood County

GREENWOOD S.D. 50

PO BOX 248, 1855 CALHOUN RD ● GREENWOOD SC 29648 ● (864) 223-4348 ● http://www.gwd50.k12.sc.us

Grade Span: KG-12 **Schools**: *Regular* 14 ● *Spec Ed* 0 ● *Alt* 1 **Students**: 8,602 **Total Teachers**: 559 **Student/Classroom Teacher Ratio**: 15.0	**Expenditures/Student**: $4,736 **Librarians**: 15.0 573 students/librarian **Guidance Counselors**: 23.0 374 students/counselor	**% Amer Indian**: 0.0 **% Asian**: 0.9 **% Black**: 44.8 **% Hispanic**: 0.6 **% White**: 53.6	National ***Socio-Economic Status*** indicator percentile (100=high): 27th

Hampton County

HAMPTON S.D. 1

BOX 177, 410 PINE STREET ● HAMPTON SC 29924 ● (803) 943-4576

Grade Span: KG-12 **Schools**: *Regular* 7 ● *Spec Ed* 0 ● *Alt* 0 **Students**: 2,777 **Total Teachers**: 206 **Student/Classroom Teacher Ratio**: 13.7	**Expenditures/Student**: $4,750 **Librarians**: 5.0 555 students/librarian **Guidance Counselors**: 8.4 331 students/counselor	**% Amer Indian**: 0.0 **% Asian**: 0.0 **% Black**: 56.8 **% Hispanic**: 0.0 **% White**: 43.2	National ***Socio-Economic Status*** indicator percentile (100=high): 11th

Horry County

[CONWAY] HORRY COUNTY S.D.

1600 NINTH AVENUE ● CONWAY SC 29526 ● (843) 248-2206 ● http://www.hcs.k12.sc.us

Grade Span: KG-12 **Schools**: *Regular* 33 ● *Spec Ed* 0 ● *Alt* 3 **Students**: 25,470 **Total Teachers**: 1,688 **Student/Classroom Teacher Ratio**: 15.6	**Expenditures/Student**: $4,935 **Librarians**: 37.0 688 students/librarian **Guidance Counselors**: 59.8 426 students/counselor	**% Amer Indian**: 0.2 **% Asian**: 0.8 **% Black**: 28.8 **% Hispanic**: 0.5 **% White**: 69.7	National ***Socio-Economic Status*** indicator percentile (100=high): 21st

Jasper County

[RIDGELAND] JASPER COUNTY S.D.

212 JACOB SMARK BLVD ● RIDGELAND SC 29936 ● (843) 726-7200

Grade Span: KG-12 **Schools**: *Regular* 4 ● *Spec Ed* 0 ● *Alt* 0 **Students**: 2,954 **Total Teachers**: 192 **Student/Classroom Teacher Ratio**: 16.0	**Expenditures/Student**: $4,481 **Librarians**: 4.0 739 students/librarian **Guidance Counselors**: 8.1 365 students/counselor	**% Amer Indian**: 0.1 **% Asian**: 0.1 **% Black**: 81.0 **% Hispanic**: 0.4 **% White**: 18.3	National ***Socio-Economic Status*** indicator percentile (100=high): 3rd

Kershaw County

[CAMDEN] KERSHAW COUNTY S.D.

1301 DUBOSE COURT ● CAMDEN SC 29020 ● (803) 432-8416

Grade Span: KG-12 **Schools**: *Regular* 16 ● *Spec Ed* 0 ● *Alt* 1 **Students**: 9,296 **Total Teachers**: 539 **Student/Classroom Teacher Ratio**: 17.9	**Expenditures/Student**: $4,443 **Librarians**: 16.5 563 students/librarian **Guidance Counselors**: 21.0 443 students/counselor	**% Amer Indian**: 0.1 **% Asian**: 0.2 **% Black**: 35.0 **% Hispanic**: 0.6 **% White**: 64.1	National ***Socio-Economic Status*** indicator percentile (100=high): 35th

Lancaster County

[LANCASTER] LANCASTER COUNTY S.D.

PO DRAWER 130/300 S CATAWBA ST ● LANCASTER SC 29720 ● (803) 286-6972

Grade Span: KG-12 **Schools**: *Regular* 17 ● *Spec Ed* 0 ● *Alt* 1 **Students**: 10,623 **Total Teachers**: 662 **Student/Classroom Teacher Ratio**: 16.6	**Expenditures/Student**: $4,323 **Librarians**: 17.8 597 students/librarian **Guidance Counselors**: 23.0 462 students/counselor	**% Amer Indian**: 0.1 **% Asian**: 0.2 **% Black**: 34.8 **% Hispanic**: 0.2 **% White**: 64.7	National ***Socio-Economic Status*** indicator percentile (100=high): 35th

Laurens County

[CLINTON] LAURENS S.D. 56

DRAWER 484, 600 E FLORIDA ST ● CLINTON SC 29325 ● (864) 833-0800 ● http://www.laurens56.k12.sc.us

Grade Span: KG-12 **Schools**: *Regular* 7 ● *Spec Ed* 0 ● *Alt* 0 **Students**: 3,461 **Total Teachers**: 209 **Student/Classroom Teacher Ratio**: 16.6	**Expenditures/Student**: $4,282 **Librarians**: 8.0 433 students/librarian **Guidance Counselors**: 8.0 433 students/counselor	**% Amer Indian**: 0.0 **% Asian**: 0.3 **% Black**: 41.6 **% Hispanic**: 0.1 **% White**: 58.1	National ***Socio-Economic Status*** indicator percentile (100=high): 23rd

Laurens County
LAURENS S.D. 55
PO BOX 388,1029 W MAIN STREET ● LAURENS SC 29360 ● (864) 984-3568 ● http://www.laurens55.k12.sc.us

Grade Span: KG-12 **Schools**: *Regular* 9 ● *Spec Ed* 0 ● *Alt* 0 **Students**: 5,580 **Total Teachers**: 306 **Student/Classroom Teacher Ratio**: 18.4	**Expenditures/Student**: $4,124 **Librarians**: 10.0 558 students/librarian **Guidance Counselors**: 13.4 416 students/counselor	**% Amer Indian**: 0.0 **% Asian**: 0.2 **% Black**: 37.1 **% Hispanic**: 0.3 **% White**: 62.4	National ***Socio-Economic Status*** indicator percentile (100=high): 27th

Lee County
[BISHOPVILLE] LEE COUNTY S.D.
PO BOX 507, 521 PARK STREET ● BISHOPVILLE SC 29010 ● (803) 484-5327

Grade Span: KG-12 **Schools**: *Regular* 7 ● *Spec Ed* 0 ● *Alt* 1 **Students**: 3,377 **Total Teachers**: 194 **Student/Classroom Teacher Ratio**: 18.6	**Expenditures/Student**: $4,628 **Librarians**: 4.0 844 students/librarian **Guidance Counselors**: 9.5 355 students/counselor	**% Amer Indian**: 0.0 **% Asian**: 0.1 **% Black**: 89.6 **% Hispanic**: 0.4 **% White**: 9.9	National ***Socio-Economic Status*** indicator percentile (100=high): 2nd

Lexington County
[BALLENTINE] LEXINGTON S.D. 5
PO BOX 938, 1020 DUTCH FORD RD ● BALLENTINE SC 29002 ● (803) 732-8000 ● http://www.lex5.k12.sc.us

Grade Span: KG-12 **Schools**: *Regular* 14 ● *Spec Ed* 0 ● *Alt* 1 **Students**: 13,038 **Total Teachers**: 844 **Student/Classroom Teacher Ratio**: 15.9	**Expenditures/Student**: $4,967 **Librarians**: 16.0 815 students/librarian **Guidance Counselors**: 32.0 407 students/counselor	**% Amer Indian**: 0.0 **% Asian**: 1.8 **% Black**: 14.6 **% Hispanic**: 0.7 **% White**: 82.9	National ***Socio-Economic Status*** indicator percentile (100=high): 86th

Lexington County
LEXINGTON S.D. 1
PO BOX 1869/100 TARRAR SPRINGS ● LEXINGTON SC 29072 ● (803) 359-4178 ● http://www.lex1.k12.state.sc.us

Grade Span: KG-12 **Schools**: *Regular* 15 ● *Spec Ed* 0 ● *Alt* 1 **Students**: 13,734 **Total Teachers**: 847 **Student/Classroom Teacher Ratio**: 16.6	**Expenditures/Student**: $4,458 **Librarians**: 16.0 858 students/librarian **Guidance Counselors**: 34.3 400 students/counselor	**% Amer Indian**: 0.0 **% Asian**: 0.4 **% Black**: 5.8 **% Hispanic**: 0.6 **% White**: 93.1	National ***Socio-Economic Status*** indicator percentile (100=high): 66th

Lexington County
[WEST COLUMBIA] LEXINGTON S.D. 2
715 NINTH STREET ● WEST COLUMBIA SC 29169 ● (803) 739-4017 ● http://www.lex2.k12.sc.us

Grade Span: KG-12 **Schools**: *Regular* 15 ● *Spec Ed* 0 ● *Alt* 0 **Students**: 9,256 **Total Teachers**: 605 **Student/Classroom Teacher Ratio**: 15.9	**Expenditures/Student**: $4,984 **Librarians**: 19.5 475 students/librarian **Guidance Counselors**: 24.7 375 students/counselor	**% Amer Indian**: 0.1 **% Asian**: 1.2 **% Black**: 25.0 **% Hispanic**: 0.7 **% White**: 73.0	National ***Socio-Economic Status*** indicator percentile (100=high): 34th

Marion County
MARION S.D. 1
616 NORTHSIDE AVENUE ● MARION SC 29571 ● (843) 423-1811

Grade Span: KG-12 **Schools**: *Regular* 4 ● *Spec Ed* 0 ● *Alt* 1 **Students**: 3,373 **Total Teachers**: 203 **Student/Classroom Teacher Ratio**: 16.6	**Expenditures/Student**: $4,178 **Librarians**: 5.0 675 students/librarian **Guidance Counselors**: 7.2 468 students/counselor	**% Amer Indian**: 0.0 **% Asian**: 0.3 **% Black**: 68.5 **% Hispanic**: 0.1 **% White**: 31.0	National ***Socio-Economic Status*** indicator percentile (100=high): 12th

Marion County

[MULLINS] **MARION S.D. 2**

PO BOX 689, 514 MULLINS ST ● MULLINS SC 29574 ● (843) 464-3700

Grade Span: KG-12 **Schools**: *Regular* 6 ● *Spec Ed* 0 ● *Alt* 0 **Students**: 2,626 **Total Teachers**: 166 **Student/Classroom Teacher Ratio**: 15.5	**Expenditures/Student**: $4,518 **Librarians**: 6.0 438 students/librarian **Guidance Counselors**: 6.5 404 students/counselor	**% Amer Indian**: 0.5 **% Asian**: 0.1 **% Black**: 67.8 **% Hispanic**: 0.2 **% White**: 31.4	National ***Socio-Economic Status*** indicator percentile (100=high): 7th

Marlboro County

[BENNETTSVILLE] **MARLBORO COUNTY S.D.**

PO BOX 947, 122 BROAD STREET ● BENNETTSVILLE SC 29512 ● (803) 479-4016

Grade Span: KG-12 **Schools**: *Regular* 8 ● *Spec Ed* 0 ● *Alt* 0 **Students**: 5,693 **Total Teachers**: 376 **Student/Classroom Teacher Ratio**: 14.7	**Expenditures/Student**: $4,534 **Librarians**: 9.0 633 students/librarian **Guidance Counselors**: 12.0 474 students/counselor	**% Amer Indian**: 2.4 **% Asian**: 0.1 **% Black**: 62.2 **% Hispanic**: 0.1 **% White**: 35.3	National ***Socio-Economic Status*** indicator percentile (100=high): 7th

Newberry County

[NEWBERRY] **NEWBERRY COUNTY S.D.**

PO BOX 718, 1539 MARTIN ST ● NEWBERRY SC 29108 ● (803) 321-2600

Grade Span: KG-12 **Schools**: *Regular* 15 ● *Spec Ed* 0 ● *Alt* 1 **Students**: 5,755 **Total Teachers**: 378 **Student/Classroom Teacher Ratio**: 16.3	**Expenditures/Student**: $4,888 **Librarians**: 11.0 523 students/librarian **Guidance Counselors**: 19.0 303 students/counselor	**% Amer Indian**: 0.1 **% Asian**: 0.5 **% Black**: 48.4 **% Hispanic**: 0.2 **% White**: 50.8	National ***Socio-Economic Status*** indicator percentile (100=high): 22nd

Oconee County

[WALHALLA] **OCONEE COUNTY S.D.**

PO BOX 649, 1101 E N BROAD ST ● WALHALLA SC 29691 ● (803) 638-4029

Grade Span: KG-12 **Schools**: *Regular* 21 ● *Spec Ed* 0 ● *Alt* 1 **Students**: 9,868 **Total Teachers**: 663 **Student/Classroom Teacher Ratio**: 15.2	**Expenditures/Student**: $5,290 **Librarians**: 19.0 519 students/librarian **Guidance Counselors**: 27.8 355 students/counselor	**% Amer Indian**: 0.0 **% Asian**: 0.4 **% Black**: 11.9 **% Hispanic**: 1.1 **% White**: 86.6	National ***Socio-Economic Status*** indicator percentile (100=high): 42nd

Orangeburg County

[HOLLY HILL] **ORANGEBURG S.D. 3**

PO BOX 98, 1515 BRAND AVENUE ● HOLLY HILL SC 29059 ● (803) 496-3288

Grade Span: KG-12 **Schools**: *Regular* 6 ● *Spec Ed* 0 ● *Alt* 0 **Students**: 3,294 **Total Teachers**: 208 **Student/Classroom Teacher Ratio**: 16.1	**Expenditures/Student**: $4,758 **Librarians**: 4.0 824 students/librarian **Guidance Counselors**: 6.5 507 students/counselor	**% Amer Indian**: 0.2 **% Asian**: 0.0 **% Black**: 86.4 **% Hispanic**: 0.1 **% White**: 13.3	National ***Socio-Economic Status*** indicator percentile (100=high): 2nd

Orangeburg County

ORANGEBURG S.D. 5

578 ELLIS AVENUE ● ORANGEBURG SC 29115 ● (803) 534-5454 ● http://WWW.ORANGEBURG5.K12.SC.US/TITLE1.HTM

Grade Span: KG-12 **Schools**: *Regular* 10 ● *Spec Ed* 0 ● *Alt* 1 **Students**: 6,474 **Total Teachers**: 423 **Student/Classroom Teacher Ratio**: 14.5	**Expenditures/Student**: $5,210 **Librarians**: 11.0 589 students/librarian **Guidance Counselors**: 16.0 405 students/counselor	**% Amer Indian**: 0.0 **% Asian**: 0.8 **% Black**: 83.1 **% Hispanic**: 0.1 **% White**: 16.1	National ***Socio-Economic Status*** indicator percentile (100=high): 4th

Pickens County

[EASLEY] **PICKENS COUNTY S.D.**

1348 GRIFFIN MILL ROAD ● EASLEY SC 29640 ● (864) 855-8150 ● http://www.pickens.k12.sc.us

Grade Span: KG-12 **Schools**: *Regular* 24 ● *Spec Ed* 0 ● *Alt* 1 **Students**: 15,299 **Total Teachers**: 901 **Student/Classroom Teacher Ratio**: 17.4	**Expenditures/Student**: $4,160 **Librarians**: 24.0 637 students/librarian **Guidance Counselors**: 29.0 528 students/counselor	**% Amer Indian**: 0.1 **% Asian**: 0.8 **% Black**: 8.9 **% Hispanic**: 0.5 **% White**: 89.8	National ***Socio-Economic Status*** indicator percentile (100=high): 59th

Richland County

[COLUMBIA] **RICHLAND S.D. 1**

1616 RICHLAND STREET ● COLUMBIA SC 29201 ● (803) 733-6041 ● http://www.richlandone.org

Grade Span: KG-12 **Schools**: *Regular* 45 ● *Spec Ed* 5 ● *Alt* 1 **Students**: 27,139 **Total Teachers**: 1,876 **Student/Classroom Teacher Ratio**: 14.2	**Expenditures/Student**: $5,474 **Librarians**: 53.8 504 students/librarian **Guidance Counselors**: 71.8 378 students/counselor	**% Amer Indian**: 0.1 **% Asian**: 0.6 **% Black**: 76.2 **% Hispanic**: 0.9 **% White**: 22.1	National ***Socio-Economic Status*** indicator percentile (100=high): 12th

Richland County

[COLUMBIA] **RICHLAND S.D. 2**

6831 BROOKFIELD ROAD ● COLUMBIA SC 29206 ● (803) 787-1910 ● http://www.richland2.k12.sc.us

Grade Span: KG-12 **Schools**: *Regular* 16 ● *Spec Ed* 0 ● *Alt* 0 **Students**: 14,866 **Total Teachers**: 910 **Student/Classroom Teacher Ratio**: 15.4	**Expenditures/Student**: $4,866 **Librarians**: 17.0 874 students/librarian **Guidance Counselors**: 37.5 396 students/counselor	**% Amer Indian**: 0.2 **% Asian**: 2.4 **% Black**: 43.5 **% Hispanic**: 2.8 **% White**: 51.1	National ***Socio-Economic Status*** indicator percentile (100=high): 54th

Spartanburg County

[CAMPOBELLO] **SPARTANBURG S.D. 1**

PO BOX 218, 121 WHEELER ST. ● CAMPOBELLO SC 29322 ● (864) 468-4542 ● http://www.spartanburg1.k12.sc.us

Grade Span: KG-12 **Schools**: *Regular* 9 ● *Spec Ed* 0 ● *Alt* 1 **Students**: 3,891 **Total Teachers**: 252 **Student/Classroom Teacher Ratio**: 15.4	**Expenditures/Student**: $4,687 **Librarians**: 8.0 486 students/librarian **Guidance Counselors**: 8.4 463 students/counselor	**% Amer Indian**: 0.0 **% Asian**: 1.1 **% Black**: 14.3 **% Hispanic**: 1.0 **% White**: 83.6	National ***Socio-Economic Status*** indicator percentile (100=high): 54th

Spartanburg County

[DUNCAN] **SPARTANBURG S.D. 5**

BOX 307, 100 N. DANTZLER RD ● DUNCAN SC 29334 ● (864) 949-2350

Grade Span: KG-12 **Schools**: *Regular* 7 ● *Spec Ed* 0 ● *Alt* 0 **Students**: 4,663 **Total Teachers**: 275 **Student/Classroom Teacher Ratio**: 16.7	**Expenditures/Student**: $4,477 **Librarians**: 9.0 518 students/librarian **Guidance Counselors**: 13.0 359 students/counselor	**% Amer Indian**: 0.0 **% Asian**: 0.2 **% Black**: 20.7 **% Hispanic**: 0.6 **% White**: 78.4	National ***Socio-Economic Status*** indicator percentile (100=high): 45th

Spartanburg County

[GLENDALE] **SPARTANBURG S.D. 3**

BOX 267, 3535 CLIFTON GLENDALE ● GLENDALE SC 29346 ● (864) 579-8000 ● http://www.spa3.k12.sc.us

Grade Span: KG-12 **Schools**: *Regular* 7 ● *Spec Ed* 0 ● *Alt* 0 **Students**: 3,142 **Total Teachers**: 206 **Student/Classroom Teacher Ratio**: 14.9	**Expenditures/Student**: $5,624 **Librarians**: 6.0 524 students/librarian **Guidance Counselors**: 8.0 393 students/counselor	**% Amer Indian**: 0.0 **% Asian**: 0.4 **% Black**: 20.2 **% Hispanic**: 0.6 **% White**: 78.9	National ***Socio-Economic Status*** indicator percentile (100=high): 40th

Spartanburg County
SPARTANBURG S.D. 2
3655A BOILING SPRINGS ROAD ● SPARTANBURG SC 29303 ● (864) 578-0128 ● http://www.spartanburg2.k12.sc.us

Grade Span: KG-12 **Schools**: *Regular* 11 ● *Spec Ed* 0 ● *Alt* 0 **Students**: 6,848 **Total Teachers**: 373 **Student/Classroom Teacher Ratio**: 18.2	**Expenditures/Student**: $4,146 **Librarians**: 12.0 571 students/librarian **Guidance Counselors**: 13.3 515 students/counselor	**% Amer Indian**: 0.0 **% Asian**: 1.7 **% Black**: 10.8 **% Hispanic**: 0.8 **% White**: 86.7	National ***Socio-Economic Status*** indicator percentile (100=high): 59th

Spartanburg County
SPARTANBURG S.D. 6
1493 W. O. EZELL BLVD. ● SPARTANBURG SC 29301 ● (864) 576-4212

Grade Span: KG-12 **Schools**: *Regular* 12 ● *Spec Ed* 0 ● *Alt* 1 **Students**: 8,437 **Total Teachers**: 515 **Student/Classroom Teacher Ratio**: 15.9	**Expenditures/Student**: $4,283 **Librarians**: 13.4 630 students/librarian **Guidance Counselors**: 23.0 367 students/counselor	**% Amer Indian**: 0.2 **% Asian**: 2.3 **% Black**: 22.4 **% Hispanic**: 1.0 **% White**: 74.2	National ***Socio-Economic Status*** indicator percentile (100=high): 48th

Spartanburg County
SPARTANBURG S.D. 7
PO BOX 970, 610 DUPRE DRIVE ● SPARTANBURG SC 29304 ● (864) 594-4400

Grade Span: KG-12 **Schools**: *Regular* 13 ● *Spec Ed* 1 ● *Alt* 1 **Students**: 9,447 **Total Teachers**: 669 **Student/Classroom Teacher Ratio**: 13.6	**Expenditures/Student**: $5,594 **Librarians**: 15.0 630 students/librarian **Guidance Counselors**: 20.0 472 students/counselor	**% Amer Indian**: 0.0 **% Asian**: 2.7 **% Black**: 55.5 **% Hispanic**: 0.6 **% White**: 41.2	National ***Socio-Economic Status*** indicator percentile (100=high): 16th

Spartanburg County
[WOODRUFF] **SPARTANBURG S.D. 4**
PO BOX 669, MCEDCO ROAD ● WOODRUFF SC 29388 ● (864) 476-3186

Grade Span: KG-12 **Schools**: *Regular* 4 ● *Spec Ed* 0 ● *Alt* 0 **Students**: 2,586 **Total Teachers**: 145 **Student/Classroom Teacher Ratio**: 17.7	**Expenditures/Student**: $3,831 **Librarians**: 4.0 647 students/librarian **Guidance Counselors**: 4.0 647 students/counselor	**% Amer Indian**: 0.0 **% Asian**: 0.0 **% Black**: 22.4 **% Hispanic**: 0.7 **% White**: 76.9	National ***Socio-Economic Status*** indicator percentile (100=high): 47th

Sumter County
SUMTER S.D. 17
DRAWER 1180, 1109 N PIKE WEST ● SUMTER SC 29150-1180 ● (803) 469-8536

Grade Span: KG-12 **Schools**: *Regular* 10 ● *Spec Ed* 0 ● *Alt* 1 **Students**: 9,252 **Total Teachers**: 549 **Student/Classroom Teacher Ratio**: 15.9	**Expenditures/Student**: $4,296 **Librarians**: 12.0 771 students/librarian **Guidance Counselors**: 21.0 441 students/counselor	**% Amer Indian**: 0.1 **% Asian**: 0.9 **% Black**: 60.3 **% Hispanic**: 0.5 **% White**: 38.3	National ***Socio-Economic Status*** indicator percentile (100=high): 18th

Sumter County
SUMTER S.D. 2
PO BOX 2425, 1345 WILSON HALL ● SUMTER SC 29151 ● (803) 469-6900

Grade Span: KG-12 **Schools**: *Regular* 15 ● *Spec Ed* 0 ● *Alt* 0 **Students**: 9,838 **Total Teachers**: 549 **Student/Classroom Teacher Ratio**: 17.8	**Expenditures/Student**: $4,033 **Librarians**: 14.0 703 students/librarian **Guidance Counselors**: 20.0 492 students/counselor	**% Amer Indian**: 0.4 **% Asian**: 1.2 **% Black**: 57.1 **% Hispanic**: 1.0 **% White**: 40.3	National ***Socio-Economic Status*** indicator percentile (100=high): 11th

Union County

[UNION] **UNION COUNTY S.D.**

PO BOX 907, EAST MAIN STREET ● UNION SC 29379 ● (864) 429-1740

Grade Span: KG-12 **Schools**: *Regular* 10 ● *Spec Ed* 0 ● *Alt* 0 **Students**: 5,240 **Total Teachers**: 351 **Student/Classroom Teacher Ratio**: 15.0	**Expenditures/Student**: $4,517 **Librarians**: 9.0 582 students/librarian **Guidance Counselors**: 15.0 349 students/counselor	**% Amer Indian**: 0.1 **% Asian**: 0.2 **% Black**: 40.4 **% Hispanic**: 0.1 **% White**: 59.2	National ***Socio-Economic Status*** indicator percentile (100=high): 24th

Williamsburg County

[KINGSTREE] **WILLIAMSBURG COUNTY S.D.**

PO BOX 1067, 423 SCHOOL ST ● KINGSTREE SC 29556 ● (843) 354-5571

Grade Span: KG-12 **Schools**: *Regular* 13 ● *Spec Ed* 0 ● *Alt* 0 **Students**: 6,907 **Total Teachers**: 419 **Student/Classroom Teacher Ratio**: 16.6	**Expenditures/Student**: $4,574 **Librarians**: 14.0 493 students/librarian **Guidance Counselors**: 15.9 434 students/counselor	**% Amer Indian**: 0.0 **% Asian**: 0.0 **% Black**: 90.4 **% Hispanic**: 0.3 **% White**: 9.2	National ***Socio-Economic Status*** indicator percentile (100=high): 2nd

York County

[CLOVER] **YORK S.D. 2**

PO BOX 99, 604 BETHEL STREET ● CLOVER SC 29710 ● (803) 222-7191

Grade Span: KG-12 **Schools**: *Regular* 7 ● *Spec Ed* 0 ● *Alt* 0 **Students**: 3,719 **Total Teachers**: 276 **Student/Classroom Teacher Ratio**: 13.2	**Expenditures/Student**: $5,984 **Librarians**: 8.0 465 students/librarian **Guidance Counselors**: 10.6 351 students/counselor	**% Amer Indian**: 0.2 **% Asian**: 0.7 **% Black**: 12.7 **% Hispanic**: 0.4 **% White**: 86.1	National ***Socio-Economic Status*** indicator percentile (100=high): 53rd

York County

[FORT MILL] **YORK S.D. 4**

PO BOX 669, 120 E. ELLIOTT ST. ● FORT MILL SC 29715-0669 ● (803) 548-2527

Grade Span: KG-12 **Schools**: *Regular* 5 ● *Spec Ed* 0 ● *Alt* 0 **Students**: 3,663 **Total Teachers**: 202 **Student/Classroom Teacher Ratio**: 17.9	**Expenditures/Student**: $4,528 **Librarians**: 6.0 611 students/librarian **Guidance Counselors**: 7.0 523 students/counselor	**% Amer Indian**: 0.2 **% Asian**: 1.0 **% Black**: 8.1 **% Hispanic**: 0.5 **% White**: 90.2	National ***Socio-Economic Status*** indicator percentile (100=high): 75th

York County

[ROCK HILL] **YORK S.D. 3**

DRAWER 10072/660 N ANDERSON RD ● ROCK HILL SC 29731 ● (803) 324-5360

Grade Span: KG-12 **Schools**: *Regular* 19 ● *Spec Ed* 0 ● *Alt* 1 **Students**: 13,474 **Total Teachers**: 779 **Student/Classroom Teacher Ratio**: 17.2	**Expenditures/Student**: $4,436 **Librarians**: 21.0 642 students/librarian **Guidance Counselors**: 26.0 518 students/counselor	**% Amer Indian**: 1.0 **% Asian**: 1.3 **% Black**: 33.8 **% Hispanic**: 0.5 **% White**: 63.4	National ***Socio-Economic Status*** indicator percentile (100=high): 46th

York County

YORK S.D. 1

PO BOX 770, 18 SPRUCE STREET ● YORK SC 29745 ● (803) 684-9916 ● http://www.york.k12.sc.us

Grade Span: KG-12 **Schools**: *Regular* 6 ● *Spec Ed* 0 ● *Alt* 1 **Students**: 4,472 **Total Teachers**: 257 **Student/Classroom Teacher Ratio**: 18.3	**Expenditures/Student**: $4,309 **Librarians**: 6.0 745 students/librarian **Guidance Counselors**: 10.5 426 students/counselor	**% Amer Indian**: 0.1 **% Asian**: 0.2 **% Black**: 26.2 **% Hispanic**: 0.1 **% White**: 73.4	National ***Socio-Economic Status*** indicator percentile (100=high): 36th

Beadle County

HURON S.D. 2-2

P O BOX 949 ● HURON SD 57350-0949 ● (605) 352-8461 ● http://www.huron.tie.net

Grade Span: PK-12	**Expenditures/Student**: $4,573	**% Amer Indian**: 0.9	National ***Socio-Economic Status*** indicator percentiles are not available for the state of South Dakota
Schools: *Regular* 9 ● *Spec Ed* 2 ● *Alt* 0	**Librarians**: 3.0	**% Asian**: 0.7	
Students: 2,619	873 students/librarian	**% Black**: 0.9	
Total Teachers: 160	**Guidance Counselors**: 6.0	**% Hispanic**: 0.7	
Student/Classroom Teacher Ratio: 17.0	437 students/counselor	**% White**: 96.9	

Brookings County

BROOKINGS S.D. 5-1

2130 8TH ST S ● BROOKINGS SD 57006-3507 ● (605) 696-4700 ● http://www.bpsce.org/bsshp.htm

Grade Span: PK-12	**Expenditures/Student**: $4,179	**% Amer Indian**: 1.3	National ***Socio-Economic Status*** indicator percentiles are not available for the state of South Dakota
Schools: *Regular* 5 ● *Spec Ed* 0 ● *Alt* 0	**Librarians**: 4.5	**% Asian**: 2.2	
Students: 2,965	659 students/librarian	**% Black**: 1.3	
Total Teachers: 175	**Guidance Counselors**: 7.0	**% Hispanic**: 0.7	
Student/Classroom Teacher Ratio: 16.8	424 students/counselor	**% White**: 94.5	

Brown County

ABERDEEN S.D. 6-1

314 S MAIN ● ABERDEEN SD 57401-4146 ● (605) 626-7177 ● http://aberdeen.k12.sd.us/index.html

Grade Span: PK-12	**Expenditures/Student**: $4,613	**% Amer Indian**: 7.5	National ***Socio-Economic Status*** indicator percentiles are not available for the state of South Dakota
Schools: *Regular* 10 ● *Spec Ed* 0 ● *Alt* 0	**Librarians**: 5.0	**% Asian**: 1.0	
Students: 4,541	908 students/librarian	**% Black**: 0.4	
Total Teachers: 268	**Guidance Counselors**: 10.5	**% Hispanic**: 0.4	
Student/Classroom Teacher Ratio: 17.8	432 students/counselor	**% White**: 90.7	

Codington County

WATERTOWN S.D. 14-4

P O BOX 730 ● WATERTOWN SD 57201-0730 ● (605) 882-6312

Grade Span: KG-12	**Expenditures/Student**: $3,741	**% Amer Indian**: 2.1	National ***Socio-Economic Status*** indicator percentiles are not available for the state of South Dakota
Schools: *Regular* 8 ● *Spec Ed* 0 ● *Alt* 0	**Librarians**: 3.0	**% Asian**: 0.7	
Students: 4,272	1,424 students/librarian	**% Black**: 0.3	
Total Teachers: 230	**Guidance Counselors**: 9.5	**% Hispanic**: 0.5	
Student/Classroom Teacher Ratio: 19.2	450 students/counselor	**% White**: 96.4	

Davison County

MITCHELL S.D. 17-2

P O BOX 7760 ● MITCHELL SD 57301-7760 ● (605) 995-3010 ● http://www.santel.net/~bmastel/mhs.html

Grade Span: KG-12	**Expenditures/Student**: $4,747	**% Amer Indian**: 3.2	National ***Socio-Economic Status*** indicator percentiles are not available for the state of South Dakota
Schools: *Regular* 7 ● *Spec Ed* 0 ● *Alt* 1	**Librarians**: 3.0	**% Asian**: 1.0	
Students: 2,935	978 students/librarian	**% Black**: 0.3	
Total Teachers: 183	**Guidance Counselors**: 6.4	**% Hispanic**: 0.5	
Student/Classroom Teacher Ratio: 15.9	459 students/counselor	**% White**: 95.0	

Hughes County

PIERRE S.D. 32-2

211 S POPLAR AVE ● PIERRE SD 57501-1845 ● (605) 773-7300

Grade Span: PK-12	**Expenditures/Student**: $4,278	**% Amer Indian**: 9.6	National ***Socio-Economic Status*** indicator percentiles are not available for the state of South Dakota
Schools: *Regular* 7 ● *Spec Ed* 0 ● *Alt* 0	**Librarians**: 3.0	**% Asian**: 0.6	
Students: 2,952	984 students/librarian	**% Black**: 0.0	
Total Teachers: 165	**Guidance Counselors**: 8.6	**% Hispanic**: 0.6	
Student/Classroom Teacher Ratio: 16.2	343 students/counselor	**% White**: 89.2	

Meade County

[STURGIS] **MEADE S.D. 46-1**

1230 DOUGLAS ST ● STURGIS SD 57785-1869 ● (605) 347-2523

Grade Span: KG-12 **Schools**: *Regular* 16 ● *Spec Ed* 0 ● *Alt* 0 **Students**: 3,092 **Total Teachers**: 193 **Student/Classroom Teacher Ratio**: 12.0	**Expenditures/Student**: $3,998 **Librarians**: 2.0 1,546 students/librarian **Guidance Counselors**: 8.0 387 students/counselor	**% Amer Indian**: 3.5 **% Asian**: 0.5 **% Black**: 0.5 **% Hispanic**: 1.1 **% White**: 94.5	National ***Socio-Economic Status*** indicator percentiles are not available for the state of South Dakota

Minnehaha County

SIOUX FALLS S.D. 49-5

P O BOX 5051 ● SIOUX FALLS SD 57117-5051 ● (605) 367-7920 ● http://inst.augie.edu/~wellman/linhome.htm

Grade Span: PK-12 **Schools**: *Regular* 34 ● *Spec Ed* 3 ● *Alt* 0 **Students**: 18,303 **Total Teachers**: 1,070 **Student/Classroom Teacher Ratio**: 28.1	**Expenditures/Student**: $4,659 **Librarians**: 15.3 1,196 students/librarian **Guidance Counselors**: 43.4 422 students/counselor	**% Amer Indian**: 2.9 **% Asian**: 1.9 **% Black**: 2.7 **% Hispanic**: 1.1 **% White**: 91.4	National ***Socio-Economic Status*** indicator percentiles are not available for the state of South Dakota

Pennington County

[BOX ELDER] **DOUGLAS S.D. 51-1**

400 PATRIOT DR ● BOX ELDER SD 57719-2218 ● (605) 923-1431 ● http://www.dsdk12.net

Grade Span: PK-12 **Schools**: *Regular* 5 ● *Spec Ed* 0 ● *Alt* 0 **Students**: 2,809 **Total Teachers**: 168 **Student/Classroom Teacher Ratio**: 16.8	**Expenditures/Student**: $4,200 **Librarians**: 3.0 936 students/librarian **Guidance Counselors**: 6.0 468 students/counselor	**% Amer Indian**: 4.5 **% Asian**: 2.0 **% Black**: 5.9 **% Hispanic**: 3.4 **% White**: 84.2	National ***Socio-Economic Status*** indicator percentiles are not available for the state of South Dakota

Pennington County

RAPID CITY S.D. 51-4

300 6TH ST ● RAPID CITY SD 57701-2724 ● (605) 394-4031 ● http://rcas.tie.net

Grade Span: PK-12 **Schools**: *Regular* 26 ● *Spec Ed* 0 ● *Alt* 1 **Students**: 14,636 **Total Teachers**: 892 **Student/Classroom Teacher Ratio**: 16.3	**Expenditures/Student**: $4,296 **Librarians**: 17.9 818 students/librarian **Guidance Counselors**: 34.5 424 students/counselor	**% Amer Indian**: 13.7 **% Asian**: 1.2 **% Black**: 1.3 **% Hispanic**: 1.4 **% White**: 82.5	National ***Socio-Economic Status*** indicator percentiles are not available for the state of South Dakota

Yankton County

YANKTON S.D. 63-3

P O BOX 738 ● YANKTON SD 57078-0738 ● (605) 665-3998 ● http://scream.iw.net/~yanktnms//index2.html

Grade Span: PK-12 **Schools**: *Regular* 7 ● *Spec Ed* 0 ● *Alt* 0 **Students**: 3,216 **Total Teachers**: 166 **Student/Classroom Teacher Ratio**: 17.7	**Expenditures/Student**: $3,636 **Librarians**: 2.0 1,608 students/librarian **Guidance Counselors**: 6.0 536 students/counselor	**% Amer Indian**: 2.1 **% Asian**: 0.7 **% Black**: 0.7 **% Hispanic**: 0.4 **% White**: 96.1	National ***Socio-Economic Status*** indicator percentiles are not available for the state of South Dakota

Anderson County

[CLINTON] **ANDERSON COUNTY S.D.**

SUITE 500, 101 SOUTH MAIN ● CLINTON TN 37716 ● (423) 457-5400 ● http://www.acorns.k12.tn.us

Grade Span: PK-12 **Schools**: *Regular* 15 ● *Spec Ed* 0 ● *Alt* 1 **Students**: 6,878 **Total Teachers**: 413 **Student/Classroom Teacher Ratio**: 15.5	**Expenditures/Student**: $4,540 **Librarians**: 12.0 573 students/librarian **Guidance Counselors**: 15.0 459 students/counselor	**% Amer Indian**: 0.1 **% Asian**: 0.2 **% Black**: 1.5 **% Hispanic**: 0.1 **% White**: 98.1	National ***Socio-Economic Status*** indicator percentiles are not available for the state of Tennessee

Anderson County

OAK RIDGE CITY S.D.

NEW YORK AVENUE, PO BOX 6588 ● OAK RIDGE TN 37831-6588 ● (423) 482-6320

Grade Span: PK-12 **Schools**: *Regular* 8 ● *Spec Ed* 0 ● *Alt* 0 **Students**: 4,965 **Total Teachers**: 318 **Student/Classroom Teacher Ratio**: 14.0	**Expenditures/Student**: $5,863 **Librarians**: 8.0 621 students/librarian **Guidance Counselors**: 15.7 316 students/counselor	**% Amer Indian**: 0.1 **% Asian**: 2.9 **% Black**: 12.6 **% Hispanic**: 1.2 **% White**: 83.2	National ***Socio-Economic Status*** indicator percentiles are not available for the state of Tennessee

Bedford County

[SHELBYVILLE] **BEDFORD COUNTY S.D.**

500 MADISON STREET ● SHELBYVILLE TN 37160-3391 ● (931) 684-3284 ● http://volweb.utk.edu/school/bedford/bedford.htm

Grade Span: KG-12 **Schools**: *Regular* 10 ● *Spec Ed* 0 ● *Alt* 1 **Students**: 5,889 **Total Teachers**: 319 **Student/Classroom Teacher Ratio**: 17.2	**Expenditures/Student**: $3,443 **Librarians**: 10.0 589 students/librarian **Guidance Counselors**: 10.5 561 students/counselor	**% Amer Indian**: 0.2 **% Asian**: 0.7 **% Black**: 10.2 **% Hispanic**: 3.2 **% White**: 85.7	National ***Socio-Economic Status*** indicator percentiles are not available for the state of Tennessee

Benton County

[CAMDEN] **BENTON COUNTY S.D.**

197 BRIARWOOD STREET ● CAMDEN TN 38320 ● (901) 584-6111

Grade Span: KG-12 **Schools**: *Regular* 6 ● *Spec Ed* 0 ● *Alt* 1 **Students**: 2,571 **Total Teachers**: 151 **Student/Classroom Teacher Ratio**: 17.3	**Expenditures/Student**: $3,783 **Librarians**: 4.0 643 students/librarian **Guidance Counselors**: 5.5 467 students/counselor	**% Amer Indian**: 0.0 **% Asian**: 0.2 **% Black**: 2.4 **% Hispanic**: 0.4 **% White**: 96.9	National ***Socio-Economic Status*** indicator percentiles are not available for the state of Tennessee

Blount County

[MARYVILLE] **BLOUNT COUNTY S.D.**

831 GRANDVIEW DRIVE ● MARYVILLE TN 37803 ● (423) 984-1212

Grade Span: KG-12 **Schools**: *Regular* 16 ● *Spec Ed* 0 ● *Alt* 0 **Students**: 10,155 **Total Teachers**: 497 **Student/Classroom Teacher Ratio**: 16.4	**Expenditures/Student**: $3,880 **Librarians**: 14.0 725 students/librarian **Guidance Counselors**: 15.2 668 students/counselor	**% Amer Indian**: 0.2 **% Asian**: 0.7 **% Black**: 0.9 **% Hispanic**: 0.4 **% White**: 97.9	National ***Socio-Economic Status*** indicator percentiles are not available for the state of Tennessee

Blount County

MARYVILLE CITY S.D.

833 LAWRENCE AVENUE ● MARYVILLE TN 37801 ● (423) 982-7122 ● http://www.ci.maryville.tn.us/schools

Grade Span: KG-12 **Schools**: *Regular* 6 ● *Spec Ed* 0 ● *Alt* 0 **Students**: 3,882 **Total Teachers**: 213 **Student/Classroom Teacher Ratio**: 16.7	**Expenditures/Student**: $4,800 **Librarians**: 6.0 647 students/librarian **Guidance Counselors**: 6.0 647 students/counselor	**% Amer Indian**: 0.0 **% Asian**: 2.3 **% Black**: 3.0 **% Hispanic**: 0.5 **% White**: 94.2	National ***Socio-Economic Status*** indicator percentiles are not available for the state of Tennessee

Bradley County

[CLEVELAND] **BRADLEY COUNTY S.D.**

800 SOUTH LEE HIGHWAY ● CLEVELAND TN 37311-0399 ● (423) 476-0620 ● http://www.bradleyschools.org

Grade Span: PK-12	**Expenditures/Student**: $3,506	**% Amer Indian**: 0.1	National ***Socio-Economic***
Schools: *Regular* 15 ● *Spec Ed* 0 ● *Alt* 1	**Librarians**: 11.0	**% Asian**: 0.3	***Status*** indicator percentiles
Students: 8,853	805 students/librarian	**% Black**: 1.6	are not available for the
Total Teachers: 476	**Guidance Counselors**: 15.0	**% Hispanic**: 1.0	state of Tennessee
Student/Classroom Teacher Ratio: 20.5	590 students/counselor	**% White**: 97.1	

Bradley County

CLEVELAND CITY S.D.

4300 MOUSE CREEK ROAD NW ● CLEVELAND TN 37312 ● (423) 472-9571 ● http://www.clevelandschools.org/index.html

Grade Span: PK-12	**Expenditures/Student**: $4,349	**% Amer Indian**: 0.2	National ***Socio-Economic***
Schools: *Regular* 9 ● *Spec Ed* 0 ● *Alt* 0	**Librarians**: 10.0	**% Asian**: 0.9	***Status*** indicator percentiles
Students: 4,557	456 students/librarian	**% Black**: 12.3	are not available for the
Total Teachers: 266	**Guidance Counselors**: 10.0	**% Hispanic**: 2.1	state of Tennessee
Student/Classroom Teacher Ratio: 15.2	456 students/counselor	**% White**: 84.5	

Campbell County

[JACKSBORO] **CAMPBELL COUNTY S.D.**

PO BOX 445 ● JACKSBORO TN 37757 ● (423) 562-8377

Grade Span: PK-12	**Expenditures/Student**: $3,733	**% Amer Indian**: 0.2	National ***Socio-Economic***
Schools: *Regular* 18 ● *Spec Ed* 0 ● *Alt* 0	**Librarians**: 10.0	**% Asian**: 0.0	***Status*** indicator percentiles
Students: 6,494	649 students/librarian	**% Black**: 0.4	are not available for the
Total Teachers: 388	**Guidance Counselors**: 4.0	**% Hispanic**: 0.1	state of Tennessee
Student/Classroom Teacher Ratio: 14.8	1,624 students/counselor	**% White**: 99.3	

Carter County

[ELIZABETHTON] **CARTER COUNTY S.D.**

308 ACADEMY STREET ● ELIZABETHTON TN 37643 ● (423) 547-4000

Grade Span: PK-12	**Expenditures/Student**: $3,876	**% Amer Indian**: 0.0	National ***Socio-Economic***
Schools: *Regular* 15 ● *Spec Ed* 0 ● *Alt* 1	**Librarians**: 11.0	**% Asian**: 0.3	***Status*** indicator percentiles
Students: 6,160	560 students/librarian	**% Black**: 0.1	are not available for the
Total Teachers: 368	**Guidance Counselors**: 9.0	**% Hispanic**: 0.2	state of Tennessee
Student/Classroom Teacher Ratio: 16.1	684 students/counselor	**% White**: 99.3	

Cheatham County

[ASHLAND CITY] **CHEATHAM COUNTY S.D.**

102 ELIZABETH STREET ● ASHLAND CITY TN 37015 ● (615) 792-5664

Grade Span: PK-12	**Expenditures/Student**: $3,287	**% Amer Indian**: 0.2	National ***Socio-Economic***
Schools: *Regular* 11 ● *Spec Ed* 0 ● *Alt* 0	**Librarians**: 9.0	**% Asian**: 0.1	***Status*** indicator percentiles
Students: 6,366	707 students/librarian	**% Black**: 1.6	are not available for the
Total Teachers: 316	**Guidance Counselors**: 13.0	**% Hispanic**: 0.3	state of Tennessee
Student/Classroom Teacher Ratio: 16.8	490 students/counselor	**% White**: 97.7	

Claiborne County

[TAZEWELL] **CLAIBORNE COUNTY S.D.**

PO BOX 179 ● TAZEWELL TN 37879 ● (423) 626-3543

Grade Span: KG-12	**Expenditures/Student**: $3,919	**% Amer Indian**: 0.0	National ***Socio-Economic***
Schools: *Regular* 11 ● *Spec Ed* 0 ● *Alt* 0	**Librarians**: 6.0	**% Asian**: 0.1	***Status*** indicator percentiles
Students: 4,644	774 students/librarian	**% Black**: 0.9	are not available for the
Total Teachers: 295	**Guidance Counselors**: 6.0	**% Hispanic**: 0.1	state of Tennessee
Student/Classroom Teacher Ratio: 14.9	774 students/counselor	**% White**: 98.9	

Cocke County

[NEWPORT] **COCKE COUNTY S.D.**

305 HEDRICK DR ● NEWPORT TN 37821-9998 ● (423) 623-7821

Grade Span: KG-12 **Schools**: *Regular* 11 ● *Spec Ed* 0 ● *Alt* 0 **Students**: 4,496 **Total Teachers**: 272 **Student/Classroom Teacher Ratio**: 17.5	**Expenditures/Student**: $3,693 **Librarians**: 5.0 899 students/librarian **Guidance Counselors**: 7.0 642 students/counselor	**% Amer Indian**: 0.1 **% Asian**: 0.2 **% Black**: 1.9 **% Hispanic**: 1.2 **% White**: 96.4	National ***Socio-Economic Status*** indicator percentiles are not available for the state of Tennessee

Coffee County

[MANCHESTER] **COFFEE COUNTY S.D.**

300 HILLSBORO HIGHWAY BOX 5 ● MANCHESTER TN 37355 ● (931) 723-5150 ● http://edge.edge.net/~ccss

Grade Span: PK-12 **Schools**: *Regular* 8 ● *Spec Ed* 1 ● *Alt* 0 **Students**: 3,953 **Total Teachers**: 231 **Student/Classroom Teacher Ratio**: 13.7	**Expenditures/Student**: $3,987 **Librarians**: 6.0 659 students/librarian **Guidance Counselors**: 6.0 659 students/counselor	**% Amer Indian**: 0.0 **% Asian**: 0.4 **% Black**: 1.2 **% Hispanic**: 0.7 **% White**: 97.8	National ***Socio-Economic Status*** indicator percentiles are not available for the state of Tennessee

Coffee County

TULLAHOMA CITY S.D.

510 SOUTH JACKSON STREET ● TULLAHOMA TN 37388 ● (931) 454-2600

Grade Span: PK-12 **Schools**: *Regular* 7 ● *Spec Ed* 0 ● *Alt* 0 **Students**: 3,447 **Total Teachers**: 204 **Student/Classroom Teacher Ratio**: 14.6	**Expenditures/Student**: $4,476 **Librarians**: 8.0 431 students/librarian **Guidance Counselors**: 7.0 492 students/counselor	**% Amer Indian**: 0.0 **% Asian**: 0.9 **% Black**: 8.3 **% Hispanic**: 0.9 **% White**: 89.9	National ***Socio-Economic Status*** indicator percentiles are not available for the state of Tennessee

Cumberland County

[CROSSVILLE] **CUMBERLAND COUNTY S.D.**

STADIUM COMPLEX WEST STANLEY ● CROSSVILLE TN 38555 ● (931) 484-6135

Grade Span: KG-12 **Schools**: *Regular* 9 ● *Spec Ed* 0 ● *Alt* 0 **Students**: 6,264 **Total Teachers**: 338 **Student/Classroom Teacher Ratio**: 16.5	**Expenditures/Student**: $3,464 **Librarians**: 8.5 737 students/librarian **Guidance Counselors**: 9.0 696 students/counselor	**% Amer Indian**: 0.0 **% Asian**: 0.1 **% Black**: 0.1 **% Hispanic**: 0.3 **% White**: 99.5	National ***Socio-Economic Status*** indicator percentiles are not available for the state of Tennessee

Davidson County

[NASHVILLE] **NASHVILLE-DAVIDSON COUNTY S.D.**

2601 BRANSFORD AVENUE ● NASHVILLE TN 37204 ● (615) 259-8419

Grade Span: PK-12 **Schools**: *Regular* 117 ● *Spec Ed* 3 ● *Alt* 2 **Students**: 70,913 **Total Teachers**: 4,168 **Student/Classroom Teacher Ratio**: 22.9	**Expenditures/Student**: $4,808 **Librarians**: 109.5 648 students/librarian **Guidance Counselors**: 80.0 886 students/counselor	**% Amer Indian**: 1.2 **% Asian**: 3.1 **% Black**: 41.5 **% Hispanic**: 1.3 **% White**: 52.9	National ***Socio-Economic Status*** indicator percentiles are not available for the state of Tennessee

DeKalb County

[SMITHVILLE] **DEKALB COUNTY S.D.**

110 SOUTH PUBLIC SQUARE ● SMITHVILLE TN 37166 ● (615) 597-4084

Grade Span: PK-12 **Schools**: *Regular* 4 ● *Spec Ed* 0 ● *Alt* 0 **Students**: 2,694 **Total Teachers**: 143 **Student/Classroom Teacher Ratio**: 18.0	**Expenditures/Student**: $3,034 **Librarians**: 4.0 674 students/librarian **Guidance Counselors**: 4.0 674 students/counselor	**% Amer Indian**: 0.1 **% Asian**: 0.0 **% Black**: 1.7 **% Hispanic**: 0.9 **% White**: 97.2	National ***Socio-Economic Status*** indicator percentiles are not available for the state of Tennessee

Dickson County

[DICKSON] **DICKSON COUNTY S.D.**

817 NORTH CHARLOTTE STREET ● DICKSON TN 37055 ● (615) 446-7571

Grade Span: PK-12	**Expenditures/Student**: $3,509	**% Amer Indian**: 0.1	National ***Socio-Economic Status*** indicator percentiles are not available for the state of Tennessee
Schools: *Regular* 11 ● *Spec Ed* 0 ● *Alt* 0	**Librarians**: 11.0	**% Asian**: 0.5	
Students: 7,493	681 students/librarian	**% Black**: 6.2	
Total Teachers: 390	**Guidance Counselors**: 15.0	**% Hispanic**: 0.3	
Student/Classroom Teacher Ratio: 17.3	500 students/counselor	**% White**: 92.8	

Dyer County

[DYERSBURG] **DYER COUNTY S.D.**

159 EVERETT AVENUE ● DYERSBURG TN 38024 ● (901) 285-6712 ● http://www.dyer-lea.dyer.k12.tn.us

Grade Span: KG-12	**Expenditures/Student**: $4,162	**% Amer Indian**: 0.0	National ***Socio-Economic Status*** indicator percentiles are not available for the state of Tennessee
Schools: *Regular* 8 ● *Spec Ed* 0 ● *Alt* 0	**Librarians**: 3.8	**% Asian**: 0.1	
Students: 3,505	922 students/librarian	**% Black**: 10.3	
Total Teachers: 181	**Guidance Counselors**: 2.2	**% Hispanic**: 0.3	
Student/Classroom Teacher Ratio: 19.9	1,593 students/counselor	**% White**: 89.3	

Dyer County

DYERSBURG CITY S.D.

PO BOX 1507 ● DYERSBURG TN 38025-1507 ● (901) 286-3600

Grade Span: PK-12	**Expenditures/Student**: $4,277	**% Amer Indian**: 0.1	National ***Socio-Economic Status*** indicator percentiles are not available for the state of Tennessee
Schools: *Regular* 4 ● *Spec Ed* 0 ● *Alt* 0	**Librarians**: 5.0	**% Asian**: 0.5	
Students: 3,358	672 students/librarian	**% Black**: 21.4	
Total Teachers: 189	**Guidance Counselors**: 5.0	**% Hispanic**: 0.3	
Student/Classroom Teacher Ratio: 15.5	672 students/counselor	**% White**: 77.6	

Fayette County

[SOMERVILLE] **FAYETTE COUNTY S.D.**

PO BOX 9 ● SOMERVILLE TN 38068 ● (901) 465-5260

Grade Span: PK-12	**Expenditures/Student**: $3,592	**% Amer Indian**: 0.0	National ***Socio-Economic Status*** indicator percentiles are not available for the state of Tennessee
Schools: *Regular* 8 ● *Spec Ed* 0 ● *Alt* 0	**Librarians**: 9.0	**% Asian**: 0.1	
Students: 4,121	458 students/librarian	**% Black**: 63.2	
Total Teachers: 251	**Guidance Counselors**: 6.0	**% Hispanic**: 5.7	
Student/Classroom Teacher Ratio: 16.4	687 students/counselor	**% White**: 31.1	

Franklin County

[WINCHESTER] **FRANKLIN COUNTY S.D.**

215 SOUTH COLLEGE STREET ● WINCHESTER TN 37398 ● (931) 967-0626

Grade Span: KG-12	**Expenditures/Student**: $3,735	**% Amer Indian**: 0.1	National ***Socio-Economic Status*** indicator percentiles are not available for the state of Tennessee
Schools: *Regular* 12 ● *Spec Ed* 0 ● *Alt* 0	**Librarians**: 6.0	**% Asian**: 0.3	
Students: 5,930	988 students/librarian	**% Black**: 6.9	
Total Teachers: 353	**Guidance Counselors**: 5.0	**% Hispanic**: 0.7	
Student/Classroom Teacher Ratio: 15.8	1,186 students/counselor	**% White**: 92.1	

Giles County

[PULASKI] **GILES COUNTY S.D.**

720 WEST FLOWER STREET ● PULASKI TN 38478 ● (931) 363-4558

Grade Span: KG-12	**Expenditures/Student**: $3,764	**% Amer Indian**: 0.1	National ***Socio-Economic Status*** indicator percentiles are not available for the state of Tennessee
Schools: *Regular* 8 ● *Spec Ed* 0 ● *Alt* 0	**Librarians**: 9.0	**% Asian**: 0.3	
Students: 4,892	544 students/librarian	**% Black**: 14.8	
Total Teachers: 268	**Guidance Counselors**: 11.0	**% Hispanic**: 0.4	
Student/Classroom Teacher Ratio: 16.9	445 students/counselor	**% White**: 84.4	

Grainger County

[RUTLEDGE] **GRAINGER COUNTY S.D.**

PO BOX 38 ● RUTLEDGE TN 37861 ● (423) 828-3611

Grade Span: PK-12	**Expenditures/Student**: $3,420	**% Amer Indian**: 0.0	National ***Socio-Economic Status*** indicator percentiles are not available for the state of Tennessee
Schools: *Regular* 6 ● *Spec Ed* 0 ● *Alt* 0	**Librarians**: 5.0	**% Asian**: 0.0	
Students: 3,143	629 students/librarian	**% Black**: 0.2	
Total Teachers: 186	**Guidance Counselors**: 4.0	**% Hispanic**: 0.1	
Student/Classroom Teacher Ratio: 15.1	786 students/counselor	**% White**: 99.6	

Greene County

[GREENEVILLE] **GREENE COUNTY S.D.**

910 WEST SUMMER STREET ● GREENEVILLE TN 37743 ● (423) 639-4194 ● http://www.greene.xtn.net/~gcs

Grade Span: KG-12	**Expenditures/Student**: $3,542	**% Amer Indian**: 0.0	National ***Socio-Economic Status*** indicator percentiles are not available for the state of Tennessee
Schools: *Regular* 15 ● *Spec Ed* 0 ● *Alt* 0	**Librarians**: 8.0	**% Asian**: 0.2	
Students: 6,654	832 students/librarian	**% Black**: 0.9	
Total Teachers: 365	**Guidance Counselors**: 6.0	**% Hispanic**: 0.3	
Student/Classroom Teacher Ratio: 18.1	1,109 students/counselor	**% White**: 98.6	

Greene County

GREENEVILLE CITY S.D.

PO BOX 1420 ● GREENEVILLE TN 37744-1420 ● (423) 638-8138

Grade Span: KG-12	**Expenditures/Student**: $5,550	**% Amer Indian**: 0.0	National ***Socio-Economic Status*** indicator percentiles are not available for the state of Tennessee
Schools: *Regular* 6 ● *Spec Ed* 0 ● *Alt* 1	**Librarians**: 6.0	**% Asian**: 0.6	
Students: 2,529	422 students/librarian	**% Black**: 8.0	
Total Teachers: 183	**Guidance Counselors**: 8.0	**% Hispanic**: 4.9	
Student/Classroom Teacher Ratio: 14.0	316 students/counselor	**% White**: 86.5	

Hamblen County

[MORRISTOWN] **HAMBLEN COUNTY S.D.**

210 EAST MORRIS BOULEVARD ● MORRISTOWN TN 37813 ● (423) 586-7700

Grade Span: KG-12	**Expenditures/Student**: $4,062	**% Amer Indian**: 0.1	National ***Socio-Economic Status*** indicator percentiles are not available for the state of Tennessee
Schools: *Regular* 19 ● *Spec Ed* 1 ● *Alt* 1	**Librarians**: 20.0	**% Asian**: 0.4	
Students: 8,794	440 students/librarian	**% Black**: 5.5	
Total Teachers: 530	**Guidance Counselors**: 14.0	**% Hispanic**: 1.3	
Student/Classroom Teacher Ratio: 16.2	628 students/counselor	**% White**: 92.6	

Hamilton County

CHATTANOOGA CITY S.D.

1161 WEST 40TH STREET ● CHATTANOOGA TN 37409 ● (423) 825-7200

Grade Span: PK-12	**Expenditures/Student**: $4,595	**% Amer Indian**: 0.1	National ***Socio-Economic Status*** indicator percentiles are not available for the state of Tennessee
Schools: *Regular* 37 ● *Spec Ed* 0 ● *Alt* 0	**Librarians**: 38.0	**% Asian**: 1.6	
Students: 20,491	539 students/librarian	**% Black**: 61.8	
Total Teachers: 1,132	**Guidance Counselors**: 51.0	**% Hispanic**: 0.5	
Student/Classroom Teacher Ratio: 17.2	402 students/counselor	**% White**: 36.0	

Hamilton County

[CHATTANOOGA] **HAMILTON COUNTY S.D.**

201 BROAD STREET ● CHATTANOOGA TN 37402 ● (423) 209-8400

Grade Span: KG-12	**Expenditures/Student**: $4,045	**% Amer Indian**: 0.1	National ***Socio-Economic Status*** indicator percentiles are not available for the state of Tennessee
Schools: *Regular* 40 ● *Spec Ed* 1 ● *Alt* 2	**Librarians**: 34.0	**% Asian**: 1.0	
Students: 23,866	702 students/librarian	**% Black**: 3.5	
Total Teachers: 1,267	**Guidance Counselors**: 35.0	**% Hispanic**: 0.6	
Student/Classroom Teacher Ratio: 17.7	682 students/counselor	**% White**: 94.9	

Hardeman County

[BOLIVAR] **HARDEMAN COUNTY S.D.**

PO BOX 112 ● BOLIVAR TN 38008 ● (901) 658-5181

Grade Span: PK-12 **Schools**: *Regular* 9 ● *Spec Ed* 0 ● *Alt* 0 **Students**: 4,846 **Total Teachers**: 289 **Student/Classroom Teacher Ratio**: 15.5	**Expenditures/Student**: $3,446 **Librarians**: 7.0 692 students/librarian **Guidance Counselors**: 10.0 485 students/counselor	**% Amer Indian**: 0.0 **% Asian**: 0.4 **% Black**: 52.6 **% Hispanic**: 0.1 **% White**: 46.9	National ***Socio-Economic Status*** indicator percentiles are not available for the state of Tennessee

Hardin County

[SAVANNAH] **HARDIN COUNTY S.D.**

116 NORTH GUINN STREET ● SAVANNAH TN 38372 ● (901) 925-3943

Grade Span: KG-12 **Schools**: *Regular* 10 ● *Spec Ed* 0 ● *Alt* 0 **Students**: 4,128 **Total Teachers**: 238 **Student/Classroom Teacher Ratio**: 15.6	**Expenditures/Student**: $3,645 **Librarians**: 7.0 590 students/librarian **Guidance Counselors**: 10.0 413 students/counselor	**% Amer Indian**: 0.0 **% Asian**: 0.2 **% Black**: 5.7 **% Hispanic**: 0.3 **% White**: 93.7	National ***Socio-Economic Status*** indicator percentiles are not available for the state of Tennessee

Hawkins County

[ROGERSVILLE] **HAWKINS COUNTY S.D.**

200 NORTH DEPOT STREET ● ROGERSVILLE TN 37857-2699 ● (423) 272-7629

Grade Span: KG-12 **Schools**: *Regular* 16 ● *Spec Ed* 0 ● *Alt* 0 **Students**: 6,645 **Total Teachers**: 408 **Student/Classroom Teacher Ratio**: 15.3	**Expenditures/Student**: $3,953 **Librarians**: 14.0 475 students/librarian **Guidance Counselors**: 13.0 511 students/counselor	**% Amer Indian**: 0.0 **% Asian**: 0.1 **% Black**: 0.8 **% Hispanic**: 0.2 **% White**: 98.8	National ***Socio-Economic Status*** indicator percentiles are not available for the state of Tennessee

Haywood County

[BROWNSVILLE] **HAYWOOD COUNTY S.D.**

900 EAST MAIN STR ● BROWNSVILLE TN 38012 ● (901) 772-9613

Grade Span: PK-12 **Schools**: *Regular* 6 ● *Spec Ed* 0 ● *Alt* 0 **Students**: 3,978 **Total Teachers**: 249 **Student/Classroom Teacher Ratio**: 16.3	**Expenditures/Student**: $3,908 **Librarians**: 7.0 568 students/librarian **Guidance Counselors**: 7.0 568 students/counselor	**% Amer Indian**: 0.0 **% Asian**: 0.1 **% Black**: 63.8 **% Hispanic**: 1.0 **% White**: 35.0	National ***Socio-Economic Status*** indicator percentiles are not available for the state of Tennessee

Henderson County

[LEXINGTON] **HENDERSON COUNTY S.D.**

35 WILSON STREET PO BOX 190 ● LEXINGTON TN 38351 ● (901) 968-3661 ● http://voyager.rtd.utk.edu/volweb/school/hencty/index.htm

Grade Span: PK-12 **Schools**: *Regular* 8 ● *Spec Ed* 0 ● *Alt* 0 **Students**: 3,480 **Total Teachers**: 189 **Student/Classroom Teacher Ratio**: 17.4	**Expenditures/Student**: $3,294 **Librarians**: 4.0 870 students/librarian **Guidance Counselors**: 2.0 1,740 students/counselor	**% Amer Indian**: 0.0 **% Asian**: 0.0 **% Black**: 8.3 **% Hispanic**: 0.2 **% White**: 91.5	National ***Socio-Economic Status*** indicator percentiles are not available for the state of Tennessee

Henry County

[PARIS] **HENRY COUNTY S.D.**

217 GROVE BOULEVARD ● PARIS TN 38242 ● (901) 642-9733 ● http://paris.aeneas.net/hcs

Grade Span: PK-12 **Schools**: *Regular* 7 ● *Spec Ed* 0 ● *Alt* 0 **Students**: 3,427 **Total Teachers**: 193 **Student/Classroom Teacher Ratio**: 16.3	**Expenditures/Student**: $3,602 **Librarians**: 4.0 857 students/librarian **Guidance Counselors**: 8.0 428 students/counselor	**% Amer Indian**: 0.0 **% Asian**: 0.1 **% Black**: 9.0 **% Hispanic**: 0.3 **% White**: 90.6	National ***Socio-Economic Status*** indicator percentiles are not available for the state of Tennessee

Hickman County

[CENTERVILLE] **HICKMAN COUNTY S.D.**

108 COLLEGE AVENUE ● CENTERVILLE TN 37033 ● (931) 729-3391

Grade Span: PK-12 **Schools**: *Regular* 5 ● *Spec Ed* 0 ● *Alt* 0 **Students**: 3,305 **Total Teachers**: 195 **Student/Classroom Teacher Ratio**: 16.5	**Expenditures/Student**: $3,811 **Librarians**: 4.0 826 students/librarian **Guidance Counselors**: 4.0 826 students/counselor	**% Amer Indian**: 0.3 **% Asian**: 0.1 **% Black**: 2.5 **% Hispanic**: 0.2 **% White**: 96.9	National ***Socio-Economic Status*** indicator percentiles are not available for the state of Tennessee

Humphreys County

[WAVERLY] **HUMPHREYS COUNTY S.D.**

2443 HIGHWAY 70 EAST ● WAVERLY TN 37185 ● (931) 296-2568

Grade Span: KG-12 **Schools**: *Regular* 5 ● *Spec Ed* 0 ● *Alt* 1 **Students**: 3,003 **Total Teachers**: 170 **Student/Classroom Teacher Ratio**: 18.1	**Expenditures/Student**: $3,653 **Librarians**: 4.8 626 students/librarian **Guidance Counselors**: 3.0 1,001 students/counselor	**% Amer Indian**: 0.0 **% Asian**: 0.3 **% Black**: 4.4 **% Hispanic**: 0.3 **% White**: 95.0	National ***Socio-Economic Status*** indicator percentiles are not available for the state of Tennessee

Jefferson County

[DANDRIDGE] **JEFFERSON COUNTY S.D.**

PO BOX 190 ● DANDRIDGE TN 37725 ● (423) 397-3194

Grade Span: PK-12 **Schools**: *Regular* 10 ● *Spec Ed* 0 ● *Alt* 0 **Students**: 5,962 **Total Teachers**: 301 **Student/Classroom Teacher Ratio**: 18.0	**Expenditures/Student**: $3,597 **Librarians**: 8.0 745 students/librarian **Guidance Counselors**: 9.0 662 students/counselor	**% Amer Indian**: 0.0 **% Asian**: 0.2 **% Black**: 2.8 **% Hispanic**: 0.4 **% White**: 96.5	National ***Socio-Economic Status*** indicator percentiles are not available for the state of Tennessee

Knox County

[KNOXVILLE] **KNOX COUNTY S.D.**

PO BOX 2188 ● KNOXVILLE TN 37902-2188 ● (615) 594-1800 ● http://www.kornet.org/kcschool

Grade Span: PK-12 **Schools**: *Regular* 81 ● *Spec Ed* 2 ● *Alt* 3 **Students**: 52,627 **Total Teachers**: 2,958 **Student/Classroom Teacher Ratio**: 18.0	**Expenditures/Student**: $4,035 **Librarians**: 86.5 608 students/librarian **Guidance Counselors**: 77.6 678 students/counselor	**% Amer Indian**: 0.1 **% Asian**: 1.4 **% Black**: 13.2 **% Hispanic**: 0.6 **% White**: 84.6	National ***Socio-Economic Status*** indicator percentiles are not available for the state of Tennessee

Lauderdale County

[RIPLEY] **LAUDERDALE COUNTY S.D.**

P O BOX 350 ● RIPLEY TN 38063 ● (901) 635-2941

Grade Span: PK-12 **Schools**: *Regular* 6 ● *Spec Ed* 0 ● *Alt* 0 **Students**: 5,082 **Total Teachers**: 282 **Student/Classroom Teacher Ratio**: 16.7	**Expenditures/Student**: $3,219 **Librarians**: 5.0 1,016 students/librarian **Guidance Counselors**: 8.0 635 students/counselor	**% Amer Indian**: 0.8 **% Asian**: 0.1 **% Black**: 39.0 **% Hispanic**: 0.6 **% White**: 59.5	National ***Socio-Economic Status*** indicator percentiles are not available for the state of Tennessee

Lawrence County

[LAWRENCEBURG] **LAWRENCE COUNTY S.D.**

410 WEST GAINES STREET ● LAWRENCEBURG TN 38464 ● (931) 762-3581

Grade Span: PK-12 **Schools**: *Regular* 13 ● *Spec Ed* 0 ● *Alt* 1 **Students**: 6,859 **Total Teachers**: 377 **Student/Classroom Teacher Ratio**: 16.6	**Expenditures/Student**: $3,493 **Librarians**: 11.0 624 students/librarian **Guidance Counselors**: 10.5 653 students/counselor	**% Amer Indian**: 0.0 **% Asian**: 0.3 **% Black**: 1.9 **% Hispanic**: 0.4 **% White**: 97.3	National ***Socio-Economic Status*** indicator percentiles are not available for the state of Tennessee

Lincoln County

[FAYETTEVILLE] **LINCOLN COUNTY S.D.**

208 EAST DAVIDSON DRIVE ● FAYETTEVILLE TN 37334 ● (931) 433-3565

Grade Span: KG-12 **Schools**: *Regular* 9 ● *Spec Ed* 0 ● *Alt* 0 **Students**: 4,295 **Total Teachers**: 248 **Student/Classroom Teacher Ratio**: 16.7	**Expenditures/Student**: $3,376 **Librarians**: 10.0 430 students/librarian **Guidance Counselors**: 5.0 859 students/counselor	**% Amer Indian**: 0.0 **% Asian**: 0.0 **% Black**: 5.6 **% Hispanic**: 0.3 **% White**: 94.0	National ***Socio-Economic Status*** indicator percentiles are not available for thc state of Tennessee

Loudon County

[LOUDON] **LOUDON COUNTY S.D.**

100 RIVER ROAD BOX 113 ● LOUDON TN 37774-1042 ● (423) 458-5411

Grade Span: KG-12 **Schools**: *Regular* 10 ● *Spec Ed* 0 ● *Alt* 0 **Students**: 4,566 **Total Teachers**: 232 **Student/Classroom Teacher Ratio**: 19.6	**Expenditures/Student**: $3,675 **Librarians**: 8.0 571 students/librarian **Guidance Counselors**: 7.0 652 students/counselor	**% Amer Indian**: 0.0 **% Asian**: 0.3 **% Black**: 1.2 **% Hispanic**: 0.2 **% White**: 98.2	National ***Socio-Economic Status*** indicator percentiles are not available for the state of Tennessee

McMinn County

[ATHENS] **MCMINN COUNTY S.D.**

216 NORTH JACKSON ● ATHENS TN 37303 ● (423) 745-1612

Grade Span: KG-12 **Schools**: *Regular* 9 ● *Spec Ed* 0 ● *Alt* 0 **Students**: 5,906 **Total Teachers**: 323 **Student/Classroom Teacher Ratio**: 18.3	**Expenditures/Student**: $3,608 **Librarians**: 9.0 656 students/librarian **Guidance Counselors**: 4.0 1,477 students/counselor	**% Amer Indian**: 0.1 **% Asian**: 0.6 **% Black**: 4.6 **% Hispanic**: 0.6 **% White**: 94.1	National ***Socio-Economic Status*** indicator percentiles are not available for the state of Tennessee

McNairy County

[SELMER] **MCNAIRY COUNTY S.D.**

COURTHOUSE ROOM 107 ● SELMER TN 38375 ● (901) 645-3267

Grade Span: PK-12 **Schools**: *Regular* 8 ● *Spec Ed* 0 ● *Alt* 0 **Students**: 4,013 **Total Teachers**: 235 **Student/Classroom Teacher Ratio**: 16.2	**Expenditures/Student**: $3,528 **Librarians**: 8.0 502 students/librarian **Guidance Counselors**: 7.0 573 students/counselor	**% Amer Indian**: 0.0 **% Asian**: 0.0 **% Black**: 9.7 **% Hispanic**: 0.3 **% White**: 89.9	National ***Socio-Economic Status*** indicator percentiles are not available for the state of Tennessee

Macon County

[LAFAYETTE] **MACON COUNTY S.D.**

501 COLLEGE STREET ● LAFAYETTE TN 37083 ● (615) 666-2125

Grade Span: KG-12 **Schools**: *Regular* 6 ● *Spec Ed* 0 ● *Alt* 0 **Students**: 3,278 **Total Teachers**: 176 **Student/Classroom Teacher Ratio**: 19.9	**Expenditures/Student**: $3,174 **Librarians**: 7.0 468 students/librarian **Guidance Counselors**: 6.0 546 students/counselor	**% Amer Indian**: 0.0 **% Asian**: 0.2 **% Black**: 0.1 **% Hispanic**: 0.3 **% White**: 99.5	National ***Socio-Economic Status*** indicator percentiles are not available for the state of Tennessee

Madison County

JACKSON-MADISON CONSOLIDATED S.D.

310 NORTH PARKWAY ● JACKSON TN 38305-2799 ● (901) 664-2500

Grade Span: KG-12 **Schools**: *Regular* 23 ● *Spec Ed* 0 ● *Alt* 1 **Students**: 13,544 **Total Teachers**: 838 **Student/Classroom Teacher Ratio**: 15.6	**Expenditures/Student**: $4,815 **Librarians**: 24.0 564 students/librarian **Guidance Counselors**: 25.0 542 students/counselor	**% Amer Indian**: 0.0 **% Asian**: 0.4 **% Black**: 48.2 **% Hispanic**: 0.2 **% White**: 51.2	National ***Socio-Economic Status*** indicator percentiles are not available for the state of Tennessee

Marion County

[JASPER] **MARION COUNTY S.D.**

300 RIDLEY DRIVE ● JASPER TN 37347 ● (423) 942-3434

Grade Span: PK-12 **Schools**: *Regular* 11 ● *Spec Ed* 0 ● *Alt* 0 **Students**: 4,461 **Total Teachers**: 274 **Student/Classroom Teacher Ratio**: 16.8	**Expenditures/Student**: $3,585 **Librarians**: 7.0 637 students/librarian **Guidance Counselors**: 5.0 892 students/counselor	**% Amer Indian**: 0.0 **% Asian**: 0.0 **% Black**: 5.1 **% Hispanic**: 0.2 **% White**: 94.7	National ***Socio-Economic Status*** indicator percentiles are not available for the state of Tennessee

Marshall County

[LEWISBURG] **MARSHALL COUNTY S.D.**

700 JONES CIRCLE ● LEWISBURG TN 37091 ● (615) 359-1581

Grade Span: PK-12 **Schools**: *Regular* 6 ● *Spec Ed* 0 ● *Alt* 0 **Students**: 4,511 **Total Teachers**: 244 **Student/Classroom Teacher Ratio**: 18.2	**Expenditures/Student**: $3,735 **Librarians**: 5.0 902 students/librarian **Guidance Counselors**: 8.0 564 students/counselor	**% Amer Indian**: 0.1 **% Asian**: 0.6 **% Black**: 8.9 **% Hispanic**: 0.7 **% White**: 89.8	National ***Socio-Economic Status*** indicator percentiles are not available for the state of Tennessee

Maury County

[COLUMBIA] **MAURY COUNTY S.D.**

501 WEST EIGHT STREET ● COLUMBIA TN 38401 ● (931) 388-8403 ● http://www.maury-lea.maury.k12.tn.us

Grade Span: PK-12 **Schools**: *Regular* 15 ● *Spec Ed* 0 ● *Alt* 0 **Students**: 11,823 **Total Teachers**: 616 **Student/Classroom Teacher Ratio**: 17.2	**Expenditures/Student**: $3,385 **Librarians**: 15.0 788 students/librarian **Guidance Counselors**: 18.5 639 students/counselor	**% Amer Indian**: 0.1 **% Asian**: 0.4 **% Black**: 20.5 **% Hispanic**: 2.0 **% White**: 76.9	National ***Socio-Economic Status*** indicator percentiles are not available for the state of Tennessee

Monroe County

[MADISONVILLE] **MONROE COUNTY S.D.**

103 COLLEGE STREET SUITE 6 ● MADISONVILLE TN 37354 ● (423) 442-2373

Grade Span: PK-12 **Schools**: *Regular* 11 ● *Spec Ed* 0 ● *Alt* 0 **Students**: 4,849 **Total Teachers**: 256 **Student/Classroom Teacher Ratio**: 17.7	**Expenditures/Student**: $3,614 **Librarians**: 7.0 693 students/librarian **Guidance Counselors**: 6.0 808 students/counselor	**% Amer Indian**: 0.1 **% Asian**: 0.2 **% Black**: 1.7 **% Hispanic**: 0.4 **% White**: 97.5	National ***Socio-Economic Status*** indicator percentiles are not available for the state of Tennessee

Montgomery County

[CLARKSVILLE] **MONTGOMERY COUNTY S.D.**

PO BOX 867 ● CLARKSVILLE TN 37041-0867 ● (931) 648-5600

Grade Span: PK-12 **Schools**: *Regular* 25 ● *Spec Ed* 0 ● *Alt* 0 **Students**: 21,492 **Total Teachers**: 1,064 **Student/Classroom Teacher Ratio**: 17.2	**Expenditures/Student**: $3,462 **Librarians**: 26.0 827 students/librarian **Guidance Counselors**: 30.0 716 students/counselor	**% Amer Indian**: 0.3 **% Asian**: 2.1 **% Black**: 23.7 **% Hispanic**: 3.4 **% White**: 70.6	National ***Socio-Economic Status*** indicator percentiles are not available for the state of Tennessee

Morgan County

[WARTBURG] **MORGAN COUNTY S.D.**

PO BOX 348, 710 MAIN STR ● WARTBURG TN 37887 ● (423) 346-6214

Grade Span: KG-12 **Schools**: *Regular* 6 ● *Spec Ed* 0 ● *Alt* 1 **Students**: 3,325 **Total Teachers**: 203 **Student/Classroom Teacher Ratio**: 16.6	**Expenditures/Student**: $3,581 **Librarians**: 5.0 665 students/librarian **Guidance Counselors**: 5.0 665 students/counselor	**% Amer Indian**: 0.0 **% Asian**: 0.0 **% Black**: 0.2 **% Hispanic**: 0.2 **% White**: 99.7	National ***Socio-Economic Status*** indicator percentiles are not available for the state of Tennessee

Obion County

[UNION CITY] **OBION COUNTY S.D.**

PO BOX 747, 316 S THIRD STREET ● UNION CITY TN 38261 ● (901) 885-9743

Grade Span: PK-12 **Schools**: *Regular* 7 ● *Spec Ed* 0 ● *Alt* 1 **Students**: 4,058 **Total Teachers**: 242 **Student/Classroom Teacher Ratio**: 15.4	**Expenditures/Student**: $3,937 **Librarians**: 7.0 580 students/librarian **Guidance Counselors**: 6.0 676 students/counselor	**% Amer Indian**: 0.0 **% Asian**: 0.1 **% Black**: 6.0 **% Hispanic**: 0.4 **% White**: 93.4	National ***Socio-Economic Status*** indicator percentiles are not available for the state of Tennessee

Overton County

[LIVINGSTON] **OVERTON COUNTY S.D.**

112 BUSSELL STREET ● LIVINGSTON TN 38570 ● (931) 823-1287

Grade Span: KG-12 **Schools**: *Regular* 8 ● *Spec Ed* 0 ● *Alt* 0 **Students**: 2,994 **Total Teachers**: 179 **Student/Classroom Teacher Ratio**: 15.3	**Expenditures/Student**: $3,719 **Librarians**: 3.0 998 students/librarian **Guidance Counselors**: 4.0 749 students/counselor	**% Amer Indian**: 0.0 **% Asian**: 0.0 **% Black**: 0.2 **% Hispanic**: 0.0 **% White**: 99.8	National ***Socio-Economic Status*** indicator percentiles are not available for the state of Tennessee

Putnam County

[COOKEVILLE] **PUTNAM COUNTY S.D.**

1400 EAST SPRING STREET ● COOKEVILLE TN 38506 ● (931) 526-9777

Grade Span: KG-12 **Schools**: *Regular* 14 ● *Spec Ed* 0 ● *Alt* 2 **Students**: 9,117 **Total Teachers**: 458 **Student/Classroom Teacher Ratio**: 17.1	**Expenditures/Student**: $3,466 **Librarians**: 14.0 651 students/librarian **Guidance Counselors**: 18.0 507 students/counselor	**% Amer Indian**: 0.2 **% Asian**: 0.8 **% Black**: 1.4 **% Hispanic**: 0.6 **% White**: 97.0	National ***Socio-Economic Status*** indicator percentiles are not available for the state of Tennessee

Rhea County

[DAYTON] **RHEA COUNTY S.D.**

250 CALIFORNIA AVENUE ● DAYTON TN 37321 ● (423) 775-7813 ● http://mac.rhea-lea.rhea.k12.tn.us

Grade Span: KG-12 **Schools**: *Regular* 5 ● *Spec Ed* 0 ● *Alt* 0 **Students**: 4,046 **Total Teachers**: 209 **Student/Classroom Teacher Ratio**: 17.9	**Expenditures/Student**: $3,362 **Librarians**: 3.0 1,349 students/librarian **Guidance Counselors**: 4.0 1,012 students/counselor	**% Amer Indian**: 0.2 **% Asian**: 0.3 **% Black**: 1.7 **% Hispanic**: 1.1 **% White**: 96.7	National ***Socio-Economic Status*** indicator percentiles are not available for the state of Tennessee

Roane County

[KINGSTON] **ROANE COUNTY S.D.**

105 BLUFF ROAD ● KINGSTON TN 37763-9781 ● (423) 376-5592 ● http://www.roane-lea.roane.k12.tn.us

Grade Span: PK-12 **Schools**: *Regular* 12 ● *Spec Ed* 0 ● *Alt* 2 **Students**: 5,942 **Total Teachers**: 336 **Student/Classroom Teacher Ratio**: 16.4	**Expenditures/Student**: $4,111 **Librarians**: 11.0 540 students/librarian **Guidance Counselors**: 14.0 424 students/counselor	**% Amer Indian**: 0.1 **% Asian**: 0.4 **% Black**: 2.2 **% Hispanic**: 0.2 **% White**: 97.2	National ***Socio-Economic Status*** indicator percentiles are not available for the state of Tennessee

Robertson County

[SPRINGFIELD] **ROBERTSON COUNTY S.D.**

2121 WOODLAND ST PO BOX 130 ● SPRINGFIELD TN 37172 ● (615) 384-5588

Grade Span: PK-12 **Schools**: *Regular* 16 ● *Spec Ed* 0 ● *Alt* 1 **Students**: 9,481 **Total Teachers**: 487 **Student/Classroom Teacher Ratio**: 17.0	**Expenditures/Student**: $3,391 **Librarians**: 14.0 677 students/librarian **Guidance Counselors**: 5.0 1,896 students/counselor	**% Amer Indian**: 0.1 **% Asian**: 0.2 **% Black**: 11.5 **% Hispanic**: 0.4 **% White**: 87.9	National ***Socio-Economic Status*** indicator percentiles are not available for the state of Tennessee

Rutherford County
MURFREESBORO CITY ELEMENTARY S.D.
400 NORTH MAPLE ST, PO BOX 279 ● MURFREESBORO TN 37133-0279 ● (615) 893-2313

Grade Span: KG-08 **Schools**: *Regular* 9 ● *Spec Ed* 0 ● *Alt* 0 **Students**: 5,305 **Total Teachers**: 309 **Student/Classroom Teacher Ratio**: 15.0	**Expenditures/Student**: $4,399 **Librarians**: 9.0 589 students/librarian **Guidance Counselors**: 9.0 589 students/counselor	**% Amer Indian**: 0.2 **% Asian**: 3.7 **% Black**: 20.7 **% Hispanic**: 0.6 **% White**: 74.9	National ***Socio-Economic Status*** indicator percentiles are not available for the state of Tennessee

Rutherford County
[MURFREESBORO] **RUTHERFORD COUNTY S.D.**
502 MEMORIAL BOULEVARD ● MURFREESBORO TN 37129 ● (615) 893-5812

Grade Span: PK-12 **Schools**: *Regular* 26 ● *Spec Ed* 0 ● *Alt* 1 **Students**: 21,965 **Total Teachers**: 1,095 **Student/Classroom Teacher Ratio**: 20.2	**Expenditures/Student**: $3,796 **Librarians**: 29.0 757 students/librarian **Guidance Counselors**: 28.0 784 students/counselor	**% Amer Indian**: 0.2 **% Asian**: 1.8 **% Black**: 8.7 **% Hispanic**: 0.8 **% White**: 88.5	National ***Socio-Economic Status*** indicator percentiles are not available for the state of Tennessee

Scott County
[HUNTSVILLE] **SCOTT COUNTY S.D.**
PO BOX 37, 208 COURT STREET ● HUNTSVILLE TN 37756 ● (423) 663-2159 ● http://www.scottcounty.net

Grade Span: PK-12 **Schools**: *Regular* 7 ● *Spec Ed* 0 ● *Alt* 0 **Students**: 2,971 **Total Teachers**: 187 **Student/Classroom Teacher Ratio**: 15.3	**Expenditures/Student**: $3,759 **Librarians**: 4.0 743 students/librarian **Guidance Counselors**: 3.0 990 students/counselor	**% Amer Indian**: 0.0 **% Asian**: 0.0 **% Black**: 0.0 **% Hispanic**: 0.0 **% White**: 100.0	National ***Socio-Economic Status*** indicator percentiles are not available for the state of Tennessee

Sevier County
[SEVIERVILLE] **SEVIER COUNTY S.D.**
226 CEDAR STREET ● SEVIERVILLE TN 37862 ● (423) 453-4671 ● http://www.sevier.org

Grade Span: PK-12 **Schools**: *Regular* 18 ● *Spec Ed* 1 ● *Alt* 1 **Students**: 11,032 **Total Teachers**: 564 **Student/Classroom Teacher Ratio**: 18.4	**Expenditures/Student**: $3,829 **Librarians**: 15.5 712 students/librarian **Guidance Counselors**: 18.5 596 students/counselor	**% Amer Indian**: 0.2 **% Asian**: 0.5 **% Black**: 0.4 **% Hispanic**: 0.1 **% White**: 98.8	National ***Socio-Economic Status*** indicator percentiles are not available for the state of Tennessee

Shelby County
MEMPHIS CITY S.D.
2597 AVERY AVENUE ● MEMPHIS TN 38112 ● (901) 325-5300 ● http://www.memphis-schools.k12.tn.us

Grade Span: PK-12 **Schools**: *Regular* 151 ● *Spec Ed* 6 ● *Alt* 6 **Students**: 109,286 **Total Teachers**: 5,699 **Student/Classroom Teacher Ratio**: 19.3	**Expenditures/Student**: $4,439 **Librarians**: 168.0 651 students/librarian **Guidance Counselors**: 230.0 475 students/counselor	**% Amer Indian**: 1.3 **% Asian**: 0.8 **% Black**: 81.7 **% Hispanic**: 0.5 **% White**: 15.7	National ***Socio-Economic Status*** indicator percentiles are not available for the state of Tennessee

Shelby County
[MEMPHIS] **SHELBY COUNTY S.D.**
160 SOUTH HOLLYWOOD ● MEMPHIS TN 38112 ● (901) 325-7900 ● http://www.scs.k12.tn.us

Grade Span: KG-12 **Schools**: *Regular* 44 ● *Spec Ed* 0 ● *Alt* 0 **Students**: 45,686 **Total Teachers**: 2,118 **Student/Classroom Teacher Ratio**: 19.1	**Expenditures/Student**: $3,454 **Librarians**: 47.6 960 students/librarian **Guidance Counselors**: 56.0 816 students/counselor	**% Amer Indian**: 0.3 **% Asian**: 1.8 **% Black**: 19.3 **% Hispanic**: 1.0 **% White**: 77.6	National ***Socio-Economic Status*** indicator percentiles are not available for the state of Tennessee

Smith County

[CARTHAGE] **SMITH COUNTY S.D.**

PO BOX 155 ● CARTHAGE TN 37030 ● (615) 735-9625

Grade Span: PK-12	**Expenditures/Student**: $3,193	**% Amer Indian**: 0.1	National ***Socio-Economic Status*** indicator percentiles are not available for the state of Tennessee
Schools: *Regular* 8 ● *Spec Ed* 0 ● *Alt* 1	**Librarians**: 3.0	**% Asian**: 0.2	
Students: 3,030	1,010 students/librarian	**% Black**: 2.6	
Total Teachers: 155	**Guidance Counselors**: 4.0	**% Hispanic**: 0.3	
Student/Classroom Teacher Ratio: 19.0	758 students/counselor	**% White**: 96.8	

Sullivan County

[BLOUNTVILLE] **SULLIVAN COUNTY S.D.**

PO BOX 306 ● BLOUNTVILLE TN 37617 ● (423) 279-2300

Grade Span: KG-12	**Expenditures/Student**: $4,789	**% Amer Indian**: 0.0	National ***Socio-Economic Status*** indicator percentiles are not available for the state of Tennessee
Schools: *Regular* 30 ● *Spec Ed* 1 ● *Alt* 0	**Librarians**: 30.0	**% Asian**: 0.2	
Students: 13,514	450 students/librarian	**% Black**: 0.3	
Total Teachers: 833	**Guidance Counselors**: 31.0	**% Hispanic**: 0.2	
Student/Classroom Teacher Ratio: 16.6	436 students/counselor	**% White**: 99.3	

Sullivan County

BRISTOL CITY S.D.

615 EDGEMONT AVENUE ● BRISTOL TN 37620-2397 ● (423) 652-9451

Grade Span: KG-12	**Expenditures/Student**: $5,404	**% Amer Indian**: 0.1	National ***Socio-Economic Status*** indicator percentiles are not available for the state of Tennessee
Schools: *Regular* 8 ● *Spec Ed* 0 ● *Alt* 0	**Librarians**: 9.0	**% Asian**: 0.5	
Students: 3,682	409 students/librarian	**% Black**: 3.6	
Total Teachers: 237	**Guidance Counselors**: 8.0	**% Hispanic**: 0.4	
Student/Classroom Teacher Ratio: 16.3	460 students/counselor	**% White**: 95.4	

Sullivan County

KINGSPORT CITY S.D.

1701 EAST CENTER STREET ● KINGSPORT TN 37664 ● (423) 378-2100 ● http://www.kpt.k12.tn.us

Grade Span: PK-12	**Expenditures/Student**: $5,645	**% Amer Indian**: 0.1	National ***Socio-Economic Status*** indicator percentiles are not available for the state of Tennessee
Schools: *Regular* 10 ● *Spec Ed* 0 ● *Alt* 0	**Librarians**: 12.0	**% Asian**: 1.2	
Students: 6,039	503 students/librarian	**% Black**: 5.0	
Total Teachers: 386	**Guidance Counselors**: 15.0	**% Hispanic**: 0.6	
Student/Classroom Teacher Ratio: 15.6	403 students/counselor	**% White**: 93.0	

Sumner County

[GALLATIN] **SUMNER COUNTY S.D.**

PO BOX 1199, 225 E MAIN STREET ● GALLATIN TN 37066 ● (615) 451-5200 ● http://volweb.utk.edu/Schools/sumnercs

Grade Span: KG-12	**Expenditures/Student**: $3,706	**% Amer Indian**: 0.2	National ***Socio-Economic Status*** indicator percentiles are not available for the state of Tennessee
Schools: *Regular* 34 ● *Spec Ed* 0 ● *Alt* 0	**Librarians**: 35.0	**% Asian**: 0.5	
Students: 21,692	620 students/librarian	**% Black**: 6.9	
Total Teachers: 1,118	**Guidance Counselors**: 45.0	**% Hispanic**: 0.5	
Student/Classroom Teacher Ratio: 16.3	482 students/counselor	**% White**: 91.9	

Tipton County

[COVINGTON] **TIPTON COUNTY S.D.**

PO BOX 486, 1580 HIGHWAY 51S ● COVINGTON TN 38019 ● (901) 476-7148

Grade Span: KG-12	**Expenditures/Student**: $3,052	**% Amer Indian**: 0.1	National ***Socio-Economic Status*** indicator percentiles are not available for the state of Tennessee
Schools: *Regular* 8 ● *Spec Ed* 0 ● *Alt* 1	**Librarians**: 10.0	**% Asian**: 0.2	
Students: 9,150	915 students/librarian	**% Black**: 22.8	
Total Teachers: 436	**Guidance Counselors**: 8.0	**% Hispanic**: 0.3	
Student/Classroom Teacher Ratio: 20.5	1,144 students/counselor	**% White**: 76.6	

Unicoi County

[ERWIN] **UNICOI S.D.**

600 NORTH ELM AVENUE ● ERWIN TN 37650-1399 ● (423) 743-1600 ● http://www.unicoi-ms.unicoi.k12.tn.us

Grade Span: PK-12	**Expenditures/Student**: $3,701	**% Amer Indian**: 0.1	National ***Socio-Economic***
Schools: *Regular* 6 ● *Spec Ed* 0 ● *Alt* 0	**Librarians**: 3.0	**% Asian**: 0.0	***Status*** indicator percentiles
Students: 2,625	875 students/librarian	**% Black**: 0.0	are not available for the
Total Teachers: 151	**Guidance Counselors**: 3.0	**% Hispanic**: 3.6	state of Tennessee
Student/Classroom Teacher Ratio: 16.8	875 students/counselor	**% White**: 96.3	

Union County

[MAYNARDVILLE] **UNION COUNTY S.D.**

BOX 10, 635 MAIN STREET ● MAYNARDVILLE TN 37807 ● (423) 992-5466

Grade Span: PK-12	**Expenditures/Student**: $3,030	**% Amer Indian**: 0.2	National ***Socio-Economic***
Schools: *Regular* 5 ● *Spec Ed* 0 ● *Alt* 0	**Librarians**: 2.0	**% Asian**: 0.0	***Status*** indicator percentiles
Students: 2,826	1,413 students/librarian	**% Black**: 0.1	are not available for the
Total Teachers: 146	**Guidance Counselors**: 3.0	**% Hispanic**: 0.0	state of Tennessee
Student/Classroom Teacher Ratio: 17.4	942 students/counselor	**% White**: 99.7	

Warren County

[MCMINNVILLE] **WARREN COUNTY S.D.**

109 LYON STREET ● MCMINNVILLE TN 37110 ● (931) 473-2331

Grade Span: KG-12	**Expenditures/Student**: $3,592	**% Amer Indian**: 1.6	National ***Socio-Economic***
Schools: *Regular* 10 ● *Spec Ed* 0 ● *Alt* 1	**Librarians**: 12.0	**% Asian**: 0.5	***Status*** indicator percentiles
Students: 6,240	520 students/librarian	**% Black**: 4.3	are not available for the
Total Teachers: 358	**Guidance Counselors**: 12.0	**% Hispanic**: 1.5	state of Tennessee
Student/Classroom Teacher Ratio: 14.1	520 students/counselor	**% White**: 92.2	

Washington County

JOHNSON CITY S.D.

PO BOX 1517 ● JOHNSON CITY TN 37605-1517 ● (423) 434-5200

Grade Span: PK-12	**Expenditures/Student**: $4,622	**% Amer Indian**: 0.1	National ***Socio-Economic***
Schools: *Regular* 10 ● *Spec Ed* 0 ● *Alt* 0	**Librarians**: 12.0	**% Asian**: 1.2	***Status*** indicator percentiles
Students: 6,272	523 students/librarian	**% Black**: 8.3	are not available for the
Total Teachers: 347	**Guidance Counselors**: 15.0	**% Hispanic**: 3.5	state of Tennessee
Student/Classroom Teacher Ratio: 18.1	418 students/counselor	**% White**: 86.8	

Washington County

[JONESBOROUGH] **WASHINGTON COUNTY S.D.**

405 WEST COLLEGE STREET ● JONESBOROUGH TN 37659 ● (423) 753-1100 ● http://www.wcs.k12.tn.us

Grade Span: KG-12	**Expenditures/Student**: $3,602	**% Amer Indian**: 0.1	National ***Socio-Economic***
Schools: *Regular* 13 ● *Spec Ed* 0 ● *Alt* 0	**Librarians**: 26.0	**% Asian**: 0.2	***Status*** indicator percentiles
Students: 8,533	328 students/librarian	**% Black**: 1.1	are not available for the
Total Teachers: 444	**Guidance Counselors**: 16.0	**% Hispanic**: 0.4	state of Tennessee
Student/Classroom Teacher Ratio: 17.6	533 students/counselor	**% White**: 98.2	

Wayne County

[WAYNESBORO] **WAYNE COUNTY S.D.**

PO BOX 658 ● WAYNESBORO TN 38485 ● (931) 722-3548

Grade Span: PK-12	**Expenditures/Student**: $3,668	**% Amer Indian**: 0.0	National ***Socio-Economic***
Schools: *Regular* 7 ● *Spec Ed* 0 ● *Alt* 1	**Librarians**: 5.0	**% Asian**: 0.0	***Status*** indicator percentiles
Students: 2,694	539 students/librarian	**% Black**: 1.1	are not available for the
Total Teachers: 159	**Guidance Counselors**: 5.0	**% Hispanic**: 0.1	state of Tennessee
Student/Classroom Teacher Ratio: 15.6	539 students/counselor	**% White**: 98.7	

Weakley County

[DRESDEN] **WEAKLEY COUNTY S.D.**

ROOM 309 COURTHOUSE ● DRESDEN TN 38225 ● (901) 364-2247

Grade Span: KG-12	**Expenditures/Student**: $3,481	**% Amer Indian**: 0.1	National ***Socio-Economic***
Schools: *Regular* 11 ● *Spec Ed* 0 ● *Alt* 1	**Librarians**: 10.0	**% Asian**: 0.4	***Status*** indicator percentiles
Students: 5,141	514 students/librarian	**% Black**: 8.4	are not available for the
Total Teachers: 290	**Guidance Counselors**: 10.5	**% Hispanic**: 0.3	state of Tennessee
Student/Classroom Teacher Ratio: 17.2	490 students/counselor	**% White**: 90.8	

White County

[SPARTA] **WHITE COUNTY S.D.**

136 BAKER STREET ● SPARTA TN 38583 ● (931) 836-2229

Grade Span: PK-12	**Expenditures/Student**: $3,258	**% Amer Indian**: 0.1	National ***Socio-Economic***
Schools: *Regular* 8 ● *Spec Ed* 0 ● *Alt* 0	**Librarians**: 6.0	**% Asian**: 0.2	***Status*** indicator percentiles
Students: 3,778	630 students/librarian	**% Black**: 1.8	are not available for the
Total Teachers: 201	**Guidance Counselors**: 5.5	**% Hispanic**: 0.5	state of Tennessee
Student/Classroom Teacher Ratio: 17.2	687 students/counselor	**% White**: 97.5	

Williamson County

FRANKLIN CITY ELEMENTARY S.D.

507 NEW HIGHWAY 96 WEST ● FRANKLIN TN 37064 ● (615) 794-6624

Grade Span: PK-08	**Expenditures/Student**: $5,278	**% Amer Indian**: 0.1	National ***Socio-Economic***
Schools: *Regular* 6 ● *Spec Ed* 0 ● *Alt* 0	**Librarians**: 6.0	**% Asian**: 1.4	***Status*** indicator percentiles
Students: 3,526	588 students/librarian	**% Black**: 19.9	are not available for the
Total Teachers: 231	**Guidance Counselors**: 8.0	**% Hispanic**: 2.2	state of Tennessee
Student/Classroom Teacher Ratio: 14.8	441 students/counselor	**% White**: 76.4	

Williamson County

[FRANKLIN] **WILLIAMSON COUNTY S.D.**

1320 WEST MAIN SUITE 202 ● FRANKLIN TN 37064-3706 ● (615) 790-5850 ● http://www.wcs.edu

Grade Span: PK-12	**Expenditures/Student**: $3,978	**% Amer Indian**: 0.1	National ***Socio-Economic***
Schools: *Regular* 24 ● *Spec Ed* 0 ● *Alt* 0	**Librarians**: 23.5	**% Asian**: 1.1	***Status*** indicator percentiles
Students: 15,713	669 students/librarian	**% Black**: 4.7	are not available for the
Total Teachers: 812	**Guidance Counselors**: 35.5	**% Hispanic**: 0.9	state of Tennessee
Student/Classroom Teacher Ratio: 15.8	443 students/counselor	**% White**: 93.2	

Wilson County

LEBANON CITY ELEMENTARY S.D.

701 COLES FERRY PIKE ● LEBANON TN 37087 ● (615) 449-6060

Grade Span: KG-08	**Expenditures/Student**: $3,738	**% Amer Indian**: 0.3	National ***Socio-Economic***
Schools: *Regular* 4 ● *Spec Ed* 0 ● *Alt* 0	**Librarians**: 5.0	**% Asian**: 1.1	***Status*** indicator percentiles
Students: 2,555	511 students/librarian	**% Black**: 18.9	are not available for the
Total Teachers: 147	**Guidance Counselors**: 4.0	**% Hispanic**: 0.4	state of Tennessee
Student/Classroom Teacher Ratio: 16.3	639 students/counselor	**% White**: 79.4	

Wilson County

[LEBANON] **WILSON COUNTY S.D.**

501 B PARK AVENUE ● LEBANON TN 37087 ● (615) 444-3282

Grade Span: KG-12	**Expenditures/Student**: $3,382	**% Amer Indian**: 0.2	National ***Socio-Economic***
Schools: *Regular* 15 ● *Spec Ed* 0 ● *Alt* 1	**Librarians**: 17.0	**% Asian**: 0.3	***Status*** indicator percentiles
Students: 11,233	661 students/librarian	**% Black**: 4.5	are not available for the
Total Teachers: 525	**Guidance Counselors**: 22.0	**% Hispanic**: 0.3	state of Tennessee
Student/Classroom Teacher Ratio: 19.0	511 students/counselor	**% White**: 94.7	

Anderson County

PALESTINE INDEPENDENT S.D.

1600 SOUTH LOOP 256 ● PALESTINE TX 75801-5847 ● (903) 731-8000

Grade Span: PK-12 **Schools**: *Regular* 8 ● *Spec Ed* 0 ● *Alt* 1 **Students**: 3,808 **Total Teachers**: 275 **Student/Classroom Teacher Ratio**: 13.8	**Expenditures/Student**: $4,838 **Librarians**: 3.0 1,269 students/librarian **Guidance Counselors**: 7.0 544 students/counselor	**% Amer Indian**: 0.1 **% Asian**: 0.4 **% Black**: 32.3 **% Hispanic**: 16.1 **% White**: 51.1	National ***Socio-Economic Status*** indicator percentile (100=high): 22nd

Andrews County

ANDREWS INDEPENDENT S.D.

405 NORTHWEST 3RD. ST. ● ANDREWS TX 79714-5098 ● (915) 523-3640

Grade Span: PK-12 **Schools**: *Regular* 7 ● *Spec Ed* 0 ● *Alt* 0 **Students**: 3,638 **Total Teachers**: 249 **Student/Classroom Teacher Ratio**: 13.8	**Expenditures/Student**: $5,485 **Librarians**: 6.0 606 students/librarian **Guidance Counselors**: 5.5 661 students/counselor	**% Amer Indian**: 0.4 **% Asian**: 0.9 **% Black**: 1.8 **% Hispanic**: 46.3 **% White**: 50.7	National ***Socio-Economic Status*** indicator percentile (100=high): 30th

Angelina County

LUFKIN INDEPENDENT S.D.

P. O. BOX 1407 ● LUFKIN TX 75902-1407 ● (409) 634-6696 ● http://webmall.lcc.net/lufkin-isd

Grade Span: PK-12 **Schools**: *Regular* 13 ● *Spec Ed* 3 ● *Alt* 1 **Students**: 8,053 **Total Teachers**: 522 **Student/Classroom Teacher Ratio**: 15.4	**Expenditures/Student**: $4,246 **Librarians**: 11.0 732 students/librarian **Guidance Counselors**: 19.5 413 students/counselor	**% Amer Indian**: 0.2 **% Asian**: 1.0 **% Black**: 30.7 **% Hispanic**: 16.0 **% White**: 52.1	National ***Socio-Economic Status*** indicator percentile (100=high): 26th

Aransas County

[ROCKPORT] ARANSAS COUNTY INDEPENDENT S.D.

P. O. BOX 907 ● ROCKPORT TX 78381-0907 ● (512) 790-2210

Grade Span: PK-12 **Schools**: *Regular* 6 ● *Spec Ed* 0 ● *Alt* 0 **Students**: 3,320 **Total Teachers**: 237 **Student/Classroom Teacher Ratio**: 14.4	**Expenditures/Student**: $5,010 **Librarians**: 1.0 3,320 students/librarian **Guidance Counselors**: 10.0 332 students/counselor	**% Amer Indian**: 0.1 **% Asian**: 8.4 **% Black**: 2.2 **% Hispanic**: 28.3 **% White**: 61.1	National ***Socio-Economic Status*** indicator percentile (100=high): 20th

Atascosa County

PLEASANTON INDEPENDENT S.D.

831 STADIUM DR. ● PLEASANTON TX 78064-2499 ● (830) 569-2171

Grade Span: PK-12 **Schools**: *Regular* 7 ● *Spec Ed* 0 ● *Alt* 0 **Students**: 3,426 **Total Teachers**: 243 **Student/Classroom Teacher Ratio**: 13.2	**Expenditures/Student**: $4,533 **Librarians**: 3.0 1,142 students/librarian **Guidance Counselors**: 9.2 372 students/counselor	**% Amer Indian**: 0.1 **% Asian**: 0.2 **% Black**: 0.8 **% Hispanic**: 56.5 **% White**: 42.4	National ***Socio-Economic Status*** indicator percentile (100=high): 20th

Bastrop County

BASTROP INDEPENDENT S.D.

105 LOOP 150 WEST, SUITE J ● BASTROP TX 78602-3717 ● (512) 321-2292 ● http://www.bastrop.isd.tenet.edu

Grade Span: PK-12 **Schools**: *Regular* 6 ● *Spec Ed* 1 ● *Alt* 2 **Students**: 5,338 **Total Teachers**: 379 **Student/Classroom Teacher Ratio**: 14.8	**Expenditures/Student**: $4,557 **Librarians**: 5.0 1,068 students/librarian **Guidance Counselors**: 13.3 401 students/counselor	**% Amer Indian**: 0.8 **% Asian**: 0.4 **% Black**: 9.9 **% Hispanic**: 24.6 **% White**: 64.4	National ***Socio-Economic Status*** indicator percentile (100=high): 33rd

Bastrop County
ELGIN INDEPENDENT S.D.
P. O. BOX 351 ● ELGIN TX 78621-0351 ● (512) 281-3434

Grade Span: PK-12 **Schools**: *Regular* 4 ● *Spec Ed* 0 ● *Alt* 1 **Students**: 2,551 **Total Teachers**: 181 **Student/Classroom Teacher Ratio**: 14.0	**Expenditures/Student**: $4,506 **Librarians**: 4.0 638 students/librarian **Guidance Counselors**: 8.0 319 students/counselor	**% Amer Indian**: 0.3 **% Asian**: 0.6 **% Black**: 16.0 **% Hispanic**: 35.8 **% White**: 47.3	National ***Socio-Economic Status*** indicator percentile (100=high): 23rd

Bee County
BEEVILLE INDEPENDENT S.D.
2400 NORTH SAINT MARY'S ST. ● BEEVILLE TX 78102-2494 ● (512) 358-7111

Grade Span: PK-12 **Schools**: *Regular* 7 ● *Spec Ed* 0 ● *Alt* 1 **Students**: 4,305 **Total Teachers**: 262 **Student/Classroom Teacher Ratio**: 17.1	**Expenditures/Student**: $4,613 **Librarians**: 4.0 1,076 students/librarian **Guidance Counselors**: 13.0 331 students/counselor	**% Amer Indian**: 0.1 **% Asian**: 0.6 **% Black**: 3.5 **% Hispanic**: 68.0 **% White**: 27.8	National ***Socio-Economic Status*** indicator percentile (100=high): 12th

Bell County
BELTON INDEPENDENT S.D.
P. O. BOX 269 ● BELTON TX 76513-0269 ● (254) 939-1881 ● http://www.bisd.net

Grade Span: PK-12 **Schools**: *Regular* 10 ● *Spec Ed* 0 ● *Alt* 0 **Students**: 6,180 **Total Teachers**: 397 **Student/Classroom Teacher Ratio**: 15.8	**Expenditures/Student**: $4,311 **Librarians**: 5.0 1,236 students/librarian **Guidance Counselors**: 16.0 386 students/counselor	**% Amer Indian**: 0.5 **% Asian**: 0.5 **% Black**: 5.3 **% Hispanic**: 20.7 **% White**: 73.0	National ***Socio-Economic Status*** indicator percentile (100=high): 38th

Bell County
KILLEEN INDEPENDENT S.D.
P. O. BOX 967 ● KILLEEN TX 76540-0967 ● (254) 520-1309 ● http://www.killeen.isd.tenet.edu

Grade Span: PK-12 **Schools**: *Regular* 35 ● *Spec Ed* 1 ● *Alt* 4 **Students**: 27,892 **Total Teachers**: 1,728 **Student/Classroom Teacher Ratio**: 16.2	**Expenditures/Student**: $4,163 **Librarians**: 27.9 1,000 students/librarian **Guidance Counselors**: 57.9 482 students/counselor	**% Amer Indian**: 0.5 **% Asian**: 4.5 **% Black**: 37.1 **% Hispanic**: 15.7 **% White**: 42.1	National ***Socio-Economic Status*** indicator percentile (100=high): 38th

Bell County
TEMPLE INDEPENDENT S.D.
P. O. BOX 788 ● TEMPLE TX 76503-0788 ● (254) 778-6721 ● http://www-tenet.cc.utexas.edu/Pub/temple/main.html

Grade Span: PK-12 **Schools**: *Regular* 17 ● *Spec Ed* 1 ● *Alt* 1 **Students**: 8,852 **Total Teachers**: 615 **Student/Classroom Teacher Ratio**: 14.2	**Expenditures/Student**: $4,981 **Librarians**: 11.0 805 students/librarian **Guidance Counselors**: 19.5 454 students/counselor	**% Amer Indian**: 0.4 **% Asian**: 1.2 **% Black**: 26.0 **% Hispanic**: 20.2 **% White**: 52.3	National ***Socio-Economic Status*** indicator percentile (100=high): 34th

Bexar County
[CONVERSE] **JUDSON INDEPENDENT S.D.**
P. O. BOX 249 ● CONVERSE TX 78109-0249 ● (210) 659-9605

Grade Span: PK-12 **Schools**: *Regular* 16 ● *Spec Ed* 0 ● *Alt* 1 **Students**: 15,049 **Total Teachers**: 958 **Student/Classroom Teacher Ratio**: 15.5	**Expenditures/Student**: $4,375 **Librarians**: 14.6 1,031 students/librarian **Guidance Counselors**: 27.0 557 students/counselor	**% Amer Indian**: 0.2 **% Asian**: 2.8 **% Black**: 21.4 **% Hispanic**: 29.3 **% White**: 46.2	National ***Socio-Economic Status*** indicator percentile (100=high): 47th

Bexar County

[SAN ANTONIO] **ALAMO HEIGHTS INDEPENDENT S.D.**

7101 BROADWAY ST. ● SAN ANTONIO TX 78209-3797 ● (210) 824-2483 ● http://www.alamo-heights.k12.tx.us

Grade Span: PK-12 **Schools**: *Regular* 5 ● *Spec Ed* 0 ● *Alt* 0 **Students**: 4,054 **Total Teachers**: 266 **Student/Classroom Teacher Ratio**: 15.3	**Expenditures/Student**: $5,589 **Librarians**: 4.0 1,014 students/librarian **Guidance Counselors**: 8.8 461 students/counselor	**% Amer Indian**: 0.2 **% Asian**: 0.6 **% Black**: 2.3 **% Hispanic**: 23.8 **% White**: 73.1	National ***Socio-Economic Status*** indicator percentile (100=high): 71st

Bexar County

[SAN ANTONIO] **EAST CENTRAL INDEPENDENT S.D.**

6634 NEW SULPHUR SPRINGS RD. ● SAN ANTONIO TX 78263-9701 ● (210) 648-7861 ● http://www.east-central.k12.tx.us

Grade Span: PK-12 **Schools**: *Regular* 8 ● *Spec Ed* 0 ● *Alt* 0 **Students**: 6,673 **Total Teachers**: 408 **Student/Classroom Teacher Ratio**: 16.4	**Expenditures/Student**: $4,453 **Librarians**: 7.3 914 students/librarian **Guidance Counselors**: 14.0 477 students/counselor	**% Amer Indian**: 0.1 **% Asian**: 0.4 **% Black**: 12.4 **% Hispanic**: 37.9 **% White**: 49.2	National ***Socio-Economic Status*** indicator percentile (100=high): 32nd

Bexar County

[SAN ANTONIO] **EDGEWOOD INDEPENDENT S.D.**

5358 W. COMMERCE ST. ● SAN ANTONIO TX 78237-1399 ● (210) 433-2361

Grade Span: PK-12 **Schools**: *Regular* 22 ● *Spec Ed* 1 ● *Alt* 3 **Students**: 14,587 **Total Teachers**: 981 **Student/Classroom Teacher Ratio**: 15.1	**Expenditures/Student**: $5,693 **Librarians**: 19.7 740 students/librarian **Guidance Counselors**: 31.4 465 students/counselor	**% Amer Indian**: 0.1 **% Asian**: 0.1 **% Black**: 2.0 **% Hispanic**: 95.8 **% White**: 2.0	National ***Socio-Economic Status*** indicator percentile (100=high): 1st

Bexar County

[SAN ANTONIO] **HARLANDALE INDEPENDENT S.D.**

102 GENEVIEVE ST. ● SAN ANTONIO TX 78214-2997 ● (210) 921-4300 ● http://www.harlandale.k12.tx.us

Grade Span: PK-12 **Schools**: *Regular* 22 ● *Spec Ed* 1 ● *Alt* 3 **Students**: 14,847 **Total Teachers**: 947 **Student/Classroom Teacher Ratio**: 16.4	**Expenditures/Student**: $5,580 **Librarians**: 20.5 724 students/librarian **Guidance Counselors**: 33.9 438 students/counselor	**% Amer Indian**: 0.1 **% Asian**: 0.2 **% Black**: 0.4 **% Hispanic**: 92.0 **% White**: 7.4	National ***Socio-Economic Status*** indicator percentile (100=high): 4th

Bexar County

[SAN ANTONIO] **NORTH EAST INDEPENDENT S.D.**

8961 TESORO DR. ● SAN ANTONIO TX 78217-6225 ● (210) 804-7000 ● http://www.northeast.isd.tenet.edu

Grade Span: PK-12 **Schools**: *Regular* 46 ● *Spec Ed* 3 ● *Alt* 4 **Students**: 44,447 **Total Teachers**: 2,844 **Student/Classroom Teacher Ratio**: 15.6	**Expenditures/Student**: $4,764 **Librarians**: 46.1 964 students/librarian **Guidance Counselors**: 111.0 400 students/counselor	**% Amer Indian**: 0.1 **% Asian**: 2.3 **% Black**: 8.6 **% Hispanic**: 33.2 **% White**: 55.8	National ***Socio-Economic Status*** indicator percentile (100=high): 48th

Bexar County

[SAN ANTONIO] **NORTHSIDE INDEPENDENT S.D.**

5900 EVERS ROAD ● SAN ANTONIO TX 78238-1699 ● (210) 647-2100 ● http://www.northside.isd.tenet.edu

Grade Span: PK-12 **Schools**: *Regular* 56 ● *Spec Ed* 15 ● *Alt* 3 **Students**: 57,409 **Total Teachers**: 3,658 **Student/Classroom Teacher Ratio**: 15.7	**Expenditures/Student**: $4,412 **Librarians**: 56.0 1,025 students/librarian **Guidance Counselors**: 166.8 344 students/counselor	**% Amer Indian**: 0.2 **% Asian**: 2.0 **% Black**: 6.8 **% Hispanic**: 49.9 **% White**: 41.0	National ***Socio-Economic Status*** indicator percentile (100=high): 39th

Bexar County

SAN ANTONIO INDEPENDENT S.D.

141 LAVACA ST. ● SAN ANTONIO TX 78210-1039 ● (210) 299-5500 ● http://www.san-antonio.isd.tenet.edu

Grade Span: PK-12	**Expenditures/Student**: $5,656	**% Amer Indian**: 0.1	
Schools: *Regular* 93 ● *Spec Ed* 8 ● *Alt* 10	**Librarians**: 69.9	**% Asian**: 0.3	National ***Socio-Economic***
Students: 60,794	870 students/librarian	**% Black**: 10.9	***Status*** indicator percentile
Total Teachers: 3,692	**Guidance Counselors**: 152.5	**% Hispanic**: 83.3	(100=high): 1st
Student/Classroom Teacher Ratio: 16.4	399 students/counselor	**% White**: 5.5	

Bexar County

[SAN ANTONIO] **SOUTH SAN ANTONIO INDEPENDENT S.D.**

2515 SIOUX ST. ● SAN ANTONIO TX 78224-1298 ● (210) 924-8541

Grade Span: PK-12	**Expenditures/Student**: $5,371	**% Amer Indian**: 0.0	
Schools: *Regular* 15 ● *Spec Ed* 0 ● *Alt* 2	**Librarians**: 11.0	**% Asian**: 0.2	National ***Socio-Economic***
Students: 10,314	938 students/librarian	**% Black**: 1.9	***Status*** indicator percentile
Total Teachers: 698	**Guidance Counselors**: 26.9	**% Hispanic**: 92.6	(100=high): 2nd
Student/Classroom Teacher Ratio: 15.2	383 students/counselor	**% White**: 5.1	

Bexar County

[SAN ANTONIO] **SOUTHSIDE INDEPENDENT S.D.**

1610 MARTINEZ-LOSOYA RD. ● SAN ANTONIO TX 78221-9613 ● (210) 626-0600

Grade Span: PK-12	**Expenditures/Student**: $5,020	**% Amer Indian**: 0.2	
Schools: *Regular* 4 ● *Spec Ed* 0 ● *Alt* 0	**Librarians**: 3.4	**% Asian**: 0.1	National ***Socio-Economic***
Students: 3,400	1,000 students/librarian	**% Black**: 0.8	***Status*** indicator percentile
Total Teachers: 230	**Guidance Counselors**: 6.0	**% Hispanic**: 79.9	(100=high): 6th
Student/Classroom Teacher Ratio: 14.8	567 students/counselor	**% White**: 19.0	

Bexar County

[SAN ANTONIO] **SOUTHWEST INDEPENDENT S.D.**

11914 DRAGON LANE ● SAN ANTONIO TX 78252-2647 ● (210) 622-3488

Grade Span: PK-12	**Expenditures/Student**: $4,673	**% Amer Indian**: 0.1	
Schools: *Regular* 10 ● *Spec Ed* 0 ● *Alt* 2	**Librarians**: 6.0	**% Asian**: 0.5	National ***Socio-Economic***
Students: 9,036	1,506 students/librarian	**% Black**: 4.8	***Status*** indicator percentile
Total Teachers: 601	**Guidance Counselors**: 22.0	**% Hispanic**: 79.0	(100=high): 8th
Student/Classroom Teacher Ratio: 15.1	411 students/counselor	**% White**: 15.5	

Bowie County

[TEXARKANA] **LIBERTY-EYLAU INDEPENDENT S.D.**

2901 LEOPARD DRIVE ● TEXARKANA TX 75501-7817 ● (903) 832-1535 ● http://clover.cleaf.com/~nblain

Grade Span: PK-12	**Expenditures/Student**: $4,411	**% Amer Indian**: 0.2	
Schools: *Regular* 5 ● *Spec Ed* 0 ● *Alt* 1	**Librarians**: 3.0	**% Asian**: 0.4	National ***Socio-Economic***
Students: 2,712	904 students/librarian	**% Black**: 41.7	***Status*** indicator percentile
Total Teachers: 197	**Guidance Counselors**: 9.2	**% Hispanic**: 0.9	(100=high): 19th
Student/Classroom Teacher Ratio: 14.6	295 students/counselor	**% White**: 56.9	

Bowie County

TEXARKANA INDEPENDENT S.D.

4241 SUMMERHILL RD. ● TEXARKANA TX 75503-2733 ● (903) 794-3651 ● http://texarkana.isd.tenet.edu

Grade Span: PK-12	**Expenditures/Student**: $4,596	**% Amer Indian**: 0.4	
Schools: *Regular* 11 ● *Spec Ed* 0 ● *Alt* 1	**Librarians**: 5.9	**% Asian**: 0.7	National ***Socio-Economic***
Students: 5,535	938 students/librarian	**% Black**: 48.8	***Status*** indicator percentile
Total Teachers: 387	**Guidance Counselors**: 12.7	**% Hispanic**: 2.5	(100=high): 15th
Student/Classroom Teacher Ratio: 15.1	436 students/counselor	**% White**: 47.6	

Brazoria County
ALVIN INDEPENDENT S.D.
301 EAST HOUSE ST. ● ALVIN TX 77511-2702 ● (281) 388-1130

Grade Span: PK-12 **Schools**: *Regular* 13 ● *Spec Ed* 0 ● *Alt* 2 **Students**: 10,790 **Total Teachers**: 649 **Student/Classroom Teacher Ratio**: 17.2	**Expenditures/Student**: $4,510 **Librarians**: 12.0 899 students/librarian **Guidance Counselors**: 21.0 514 students/counselor	**% Amer Indian**: 0.2 **% Asian**: 1.5 **% Black**: 2.7 **% Hispanic**: 29.0 **% White**: 66.5	National ***Socio-Economic Status*** indicator percentile (100=high): 35th

Brazoria County
ANGLETON INDEPENDENT S.D.
1900 NORTH DOWNING RD. ● ANGLETON TX 77515-3799 ● (409) 849-8594 ● http://www.angleton.isd.tenet.edu

Grade Span: PK-12 **Schools**: *Regular* 9 ● *Spec Ed* 0 ● *Alt* 2 **Students**: 6,589 **Total Teachers**: 380 **Student/Classroom Teacher Ratio**: 18.7	**Expenditures/Student**: $3,966 **Librarians**: 8.0 824 students/librarian **Guidance Counselors**: 15.0 439 students/counselor	**% Amer Indian**: 0.2 **% Asian**: 0.9 **% Black**: 14.1 **% Hispanic**: 24.4 **% White**: 60.4	National ***Socio-Economic Status*** indicator percentile (100=high): 49th

Brazoria County
[FREEPORT] **BRAZOSPORT INDEPENDENT S.D.**
P. O. DRAWER Z ● FREEPORT TX 77541-1926 ● (409) 265-6181 ● http://www.brazosport.isd.tenet.edu

Grade Span: PK-12 **Schools**: *Regular* 18 ● *Spec Ed* 0 ● *Alt* 0 **Students**: 12,629 **Total Teachers**: 744 **Student/Classroom Teacher Ratio**: 17.1	**Expenditures/Student**: $4,811 **Librarians**: 19.0 665 students/librarian **Guidance Counselors**: 31.9 396 students/counselor	**% Amer Indian**: 0.2 **% Asian**: 1.3 **% Black**: 8.5 **% Hispanic**: 31.2 **% White**: 58.8	National ***Socio-Economic Status*** indicator percentile (100=high): 43rd

Brazoria County
PEARLAND INDEPENDENT S.D.
P. O. BOX 7 ● PEARLAND TX 77588-0007 ● (281) 485-3203

Grade Span: PK-12 **Schools**: *Regular* 10 ● *Spec Ed* 0 ● *Alt* 0 **Students**: 8,411 **Total Teachers**: 488 **Student/Classroom Teacher Ratio**: 17.1	**Expenditures/Student**: $4,309 **Librarians**: 10.9 772 students/librarian **Guidance Counselors**: 16.0 526 students/counselor	**% Amer Indian**: 0.1 **% Asian**: 3.8 **% Black**: 5.2 **% Hispanic**: 19.9 **% White**: 71.0	National ***Socio-Economic Status*** indicator percentile (100=high): 73rd

Brazoria County
[WEST COLUMBIA] **COLUMBIA-BRAZORIA INDEPENDENT S.D.**
P. O. BOX 158 ● WEST COLUMBIA TX 77486-0158 ● (409) 345-5147 ● http://www.columbia-brazoria.isd.tenet.edu

Grade Span: PK-12 **Schools**: *Regular* 8 ● *Spec Ed* 0 ● *Alt* 0 **Students**: 3,662 **Total Teachers**: 215 **Student/Classroom Teacher Ratio**: 18.7	**Expenditures/Student**: $4,268 **Librarians**: 6.0 610 students/librarian **Guidance Counselors**: 5.7 642 students/counselor	**% Amer Indian**: 0.1 **% Asian**: 0.2 **% Black**: 16.5 **% Hispanic**: 13.9 **% White**: 69.4	National ***Socio-Economic Status*** indicator percentile (100=high): 44th

Brazos County
BRYAN INDEPENDENT S.D.
101 NORTH TEXAS AVE. ● BRYAN TX 77803-5398 ● (409) 361-5200

Grade Span: PK-12 **Schools**: *Regular* 18 ● *Spec Ed* 0 ● *Alt* 2 **Students**: 12,969 **Total Teachers**: 892 **Student/Classroom Teacher Ratio**: 14.1	**Expenditures/Student**: $4,827 **Librarians**: 18.9 686 students/librarian **Guidance Counselors**: 36.0 360 students/counselor	**% Amer Indian**: 0.1 **% Asian**: 0.5 **% Black**: 23.3 **% Hispanic**: 28.6 **% White**: 47.6	National ***Socio-Economic Status*** indicator percentile (100=high): 25th

Brazos County

COLLEGE STATION INDEPENDENT S.D.

1812 WELSH ● COLLEGE STATION TX 77840-4851 ● (409) 764-5400 ● http://www.collegestation.isd.tenet.edu

Grade Span: PK-12 **Schools**: *Regular* 7 ● *Spec Ed* 2 ● *Alt* 1 **Students**: 6,545 **Total Teachers**: 403 **Student/Classroom Teacher Ratio**: 16.7	**Expenditures/Student**: $4,387 **Librarians**: 9.0 727 students/librarian **Guidance Counselors**: 12.9 507 students/counselor	**% Amer Indian**: 0.0 **% Asian**: 7.0 **% Black**: 11.9 **% Hispanic**: 8.3 **% White**: 72.8	National ***Socio-Economic Status*** indicator percentile (100=high): 81st

Brown County

BROWNWOOD INDEPENDENT S.D.

P. O. BOX 730 ● BROWNWOOD TX 76804-0730 ● (915) 643-5644

Grade Span: PK-12 **Schools**: *Regular* 8 ● *Spec Ed* 1 ● *Alt* 1 **Students**: 4,126 **Total Teachers**: 290 **Student/Classroom Teacher Ratio**: 14.5	**Expenditures/Student**: $4,609 **Librarians**: 1.1 3,751 students/librarian **Guidance Counselors**: 8.0 516 students/counselor	**% Amer Indian**: 0.2 **% Asian**: 0.4 **% Black**: 8.0 **% Hispanic**: 24.1 **% White**: 67.3	National ***Socio-Economic Status*** indicator percentile (100=high): 32nd

Burnet County

MARBLE FALLS INDEPENDENT S.D.

2001 BROADWAY ST. ● MARBLE FALLS TX 78654-4803 ● (830) 693-4357

Grade Span: PK-12 **Schools**: *Regular* 4 ● *Spec Ed* 0 ● *Alt* 0 **Students**: 3,211 **Total Teachers**: 222 **Student/Classroom Teacher Ratio**: 14.8	**Expenditures/Student**: $4,890 **Librarians**: 3.0 1,070 students/librarian **Guidance Counselors**: 6.0 535 students/counselor	**% Amer Indian**: 0.3 **% Asian**: 0.3 **% Black**: 2.1 **% Hispanic**: 21.9 **% White**: 75.3	National ***Socio-Economic Status*** indicator percentile (100=high): 32nd

Caldwell County

LOCKHART INDEPENDENT S.D.

P. O. BOX 120 ● LOCKHART TX 78644-2730 ● (512) 398-2371

Grade Span: PK-12 **Schools**: *Regular* 7 ● *Spec Ed* 2 ● *Alt* 1 **Students**: 3,972 **Total Teachers**: 240 **Student/Classroom Teacher Ratio**: 15.9	**Expenditures/Student**: $5,022 **Librarians**: 5.0 794 students/librarian **Guidance Counselors**: 9.0 441 students/counselor	**% Amer Indian**: 0.4 **% Asian**: 0.2 **% Black**: 8.7 **% Hispanic**: 44.5 **% White**: 46.1	National ***Socio-Economic Status*** indicator percentile (100=high): 22nd

Calhoun County

[PORT LAVACA] **CALHOUN COUNTY INDEPENDENT S.D.**

525 N. COMMERCE ST. ● PORT LAVACA TX 77979-0068 ● (512) 552-9728

Grade Span: PK-12 **Schools**: *Regular* 8 ● *Spec Ed* 0 ● *Alt* 1 **Students**: 4,269 **Total Teachers**: 263 **Student/Classroom Teacher Ratio**: 15.5	**Expenditures/Student**: $4,556 **Librarians**: 4.0 1,067 students/librarian **Guidance Counselors**: 10.0 427 students/counselor	**% Amer Indian**: 0.0 **% Asian**: 4.6 **% Black**: 3.1 **% Hispanic**: 47.0 **% White**: 45.3	National ***Socio-Economic Status*** indicator percentile (100=high): 28th

Cameron County

BROWNSVILLE INDEPENDENT S.D.

1900 PRICE ROAD ● BROWNSVILLE TX 78521-2417 ● (956) 548-8000 ● http://www.brownsville.isd.tenet.edu

Grade Span: PK-12 **Schools**: *Regular* 39 ● *Spec Ed* 0 ● *Alt* 3 **Students**: 40,270 **Total Teachers**: 2,684 **Student/Classroom Teacher Ratio**: 15.9	**Expenditures/Student**: $5,208 **Librarians**: 46.9 859 students/librarian **Guidance Counselors**: 112.3 359 students/counselor	**% Amer Indian**: 0.0 **% Asian**: 0.2 **% Black**: 0.1 **% Hispanic**: 96.7 **% White**: 2.9	National ***Socio-Economic Status*** indicator percentile (100=high): 35th

Cameron County
HARLINGEN CONSOLIDATED INDEPENDENT S.D.
1409 EAST HARRISON ST. ● HARLINGEN TX 78550-7129 ● (956) 427-3400 ● http://www.harlingen.isd.tenet.edu

Grade Span: PK-12 **Schools**: *Regular* 21 ● *Spec Ed* 0 ● *Alt* 1 **Students**: 15,801 **Total Teachers**: 955 **Student/Classroom Teacher Ratio**: 16.6	**Expenditures/Student**: $4,431 **Librarians**: 11.0 1,436 students/librarian **Guidance Counselors**: 36.0 439 students/counselor	**% Amer Indian**: 0.0 **% Asian**: 0.6 **% Black**: 0.6 **% Hispanic**: 84.4 **% White**: 14.4	National ***Socio-Economic Status*** indicator percentile (100=high): 9th

Cameron County
LA FERIA INDEPENDENT S.D.
P. O. BOX 1157 ● LA FERIA TX 78559-1157 ● (956) 797-2612

Grade Span: PK-12 **Schools**: *Regular* 5 ● *Spec Ed* 0 ● *Alt* 1 **Students**: 2,589 **Total Teachers**: 173 **Student/Classroom Teacher Ratio**: 15.4	**Expenditures/Student**: $4,774 **Librarians**: 2.0 1,295 students/librarian **Guidance Counselors**: 6.0 432 students/counselor	**% Amer Indian**: 0.0 **% Asian**: 0.2 **% Black**: 0.2 **% Hispanic**: 87.4 **% White**: 12.3	National ***Socio-Economic Status*** indicator percentile (100=high): 3rd

Cameron County
LOS FRESNOS CONSOLIDATED INDEPENDENT S.D.
P. O. BOX 309 ● LOS FRESNOS TX 78566-0309 ● (956) 233-4407

Grade Span: PK-12 **Schools**: *Regular* 8 ● *Spec Ed* 0 ● *Alt* 0 **Students**: 5,718 **Total Teachers**: 341 **Student/Classroom Teacher Ratio**: 16.9	**Expenditures/Student**: $4,890 **Librarians**: 7.0 817 students/librarian **Guidance Counselors**: 14.0 408 students/counselor	**% Amer Indian**: 0.3 **% Asian**: 0.2 **% Black**: 0.3 **% Hispanic**: 89.5 **% White**: 9.7	National ***Socio-Economic Status*** indicator percentile (100=high): 2nd

Cameron County
SAN BENITO CONSOLIDATED INDEPENDENT S.D.
195 WEST ADELE ST. ● SAN BENITO TX 78586-4501 ● (956) 361-1000 ● http://www.sanbenito.k12.tx.us

Grade Span: PK-12 **Schools**: *Regular* 14 ● *Spec Ed* 0 ● *Alt* 0 **Students**: 8,336 **Total Teachers**: 503 **Student/Classroom Teacher Ratio**: 18.2	**Expenditures/Student**: $4,785 **Librarians**: 6.0 1,389 students/librarian **Guidance Counselors**: 23.0 362 students/counselor	**% Amer Indian**: 0.0 **% Asian**: 0.1 **% Black**: 0.1 **% Hispanic**: 96.5 **% White**: 3.3	National ***Socio-Economic Status*** indicator percentile (100=high): 2nd

Cherokee County
JACKSONVILLE INDEPENDENT S.D.
P. O. BOX 631 ● JACKSONVILLE TX 75766-0631 ● (972) 586-6511

Grade Span: PK-12 **Schools**: *Regular* 6 ● *Spec Ed* 0 ● *Alt* 1 **Students**: 4,459 **Total Teachers**: 313 **Student/Classroom Teacher Ratio**: 14.6	**Expenditures/Student**: $4,617 **Librarians**: 5.0 892 students/librarian **Guidance Counselors**: 12.0 372 students/counselor	**% Amer Indian**: 0.2 **% Asian**: 0.3 **% Black**: 23.5 **% Hispanic**: 16.1 **% White**: 59.9	National ***Socio-Economic Status*** indicator percentile (100=high): 26th

Collin County
ALLEN INDEPENDENT S.D.
P. O. BOX 13 ● ALLEN TX 75002-0013 ● (972) 727-0511 ● http://aisd1.allen.k12.tx.us

Grade Span: PK-12 **Schools**: *Regular* 9 ● *Spec Ed* 0 ● *Alt* 0 **Students**: 7,452 **Total Teachers**: 452 **Student/Classroom Teacher Ratio**: 16.7	**Expenditures/Student**: $4,079 **Librarians**: 8.3 898 students/librarian **Guidance Counselors**: 13.8 540 students/counselor	**% Amer Indian**: 0.6 **% Asian**: 1.6 **% Black**: 4.0 **% Hispanic**: 5.2 **% White**: 88.5	National ***Socio-Economic Status*** indicator percentile (100=high): 97th

Collin County

FRISCO INDEPENDENT S.D.

P. O. BOX 910 ● FRISCO TX 75034-0910 ● (972) 335-6000 ● http://www.ednet10.net/frisco

Grade Span: PK-12 **Schools**: *Regular* 5 ● *Spec Ed* 0 ● *Alt* 0 **Students**: 2,692 **Total Teachers**: 170 **Student/Classroom Teacher Ratio**: 15.9	**Expenditures/Student**: $4,469 **Librarians**: 4.0 673 students/librarian **Guidance Counselors**: 5.1 528 students/counselor	**% Amer Indian**: 0.6 **% Asian**: 0.7 **% Black**: 2.7 **% Hispanic**: 21.9 **% White**: 74.1	National ***Socio-Economic Status*** indicator percentile (100=high): 65th

Collin County

MCKINNEY INDEPENDENT S.D.

DUVALL ST. # 1 ● MCKINNEY TX 75069-3211 ● (972) 569-6400 ● http://misd.deltos.com

Grade Span: PK-12 **Schools**: *Regular* 11 ● *Spec Ed* 0 ● *Alt* 1 **Students**: 7,086 **Total Teachers**: 434 **Student/Classroom Teacher Ratio**: 16.3	**Expenditures/Student**: $4,740 **Librarians**: 11.0 644 students/librarian **Guidance Counselors**: 16.5 429 students/counselor	**% Amer Indian**: 0.3 **% Asian**: 0.7 **% Black**: 10.1 **% Hispanic**: 19.2 **% White**: 69.6	National ***Socio-Economic Status*** indicator percentile (100=high): 48th

Collin County

PLANO INDEPENDENT S.D.

2700 W. 15TH. ● PLANO TX 75075-5898 ● (972) 519-8100 ● http://www.pisd.edu

Grade Span: PK-12 **Schools**: *Regular* 45 ● *Spec Ed* 1 ● *Alt* 0 **Students**: 38,429 **Total Teachers**: 2,433 **Student/Classroom Teacher Ratio**: 16.0	**Expenditures/Student**: $5,057 **Librarians**: 47.0 818 students/librarian **Guidance Counselors**: 90.1 427 students/counselor	**% Amer Indian**: 0.2 **% Asian**: 8.8 **% Black**: 5.4 **% Hispanic**: 7.0 **% White**: 78.6	National ***Socio-Economic Status*** indicator percentile (100=high): 87th

Collin County

WYLIE INDEPENDENT S.D.

P. O. BOX 490 ● WYLIE TX 75098-0490 ● (972) 442-5444 ● http://www.wylie.k12.tx.us/index.htm

Grade Span: PK-12 **Schools**: *Regular* 5 ● *Spec Ed* 0 ● *Alt* 0 **Students**: 3,407 **Total Teachers**: 212 **Student/Classroom Teacher Ratio**: 16.2	**Expenditures/Student**: $4,637 **Librarians**: 2.0 1,704 students/librarian **Guidance Counselors**: 5.0 681 students/counselor	**% Amer Indian**: 0.7 **% Asian**: 0.5 **% Black**: 1.2 **% Hispanic**: 7.4 **% White**: 90.3	National ***Socio-Economic Status*** indicator percentile (100=high): 79th

Comal County

[NEW BRAUNFELS] **COMAL INDEPENDENT S.D.**

1421 HIGHWAY 81 EAST ● NEW BRAUNFELS TX 78130-3240 ● (830) 625-8081

Grade Span: PK-12 **Schools**: *Regular* 11 ● *Spec Ed* 1 ● *Alt* 1 **Students**: 8,586 **Total Teachers**: 552 **Student/Classroom Teacher Ratio**: 15.8	**Expenditures/Student**: $4,460 **Librarians**: 10.1 850 students/librarian **Guidance Counselors**: 22.0 390 students/counselor	**% Amer Indian**: 0.1 **% Asian**: 0.4 **% Black**: 1.0 **% Hispanic**: 18.4 **% White**: 80.1	National ***Socio-Economic Status*** indicator percentile (100=high): 59th

Comal County

NEW BRAUNFELS INDEPENDENT S.D.

BOX 311688 ● NEW BRAUNFELS TX 78131-1688 ● (830) 620-6200

Grade Span: PK-12 **Schools**: *Regular* 8 ● *Spec Ed* 1 ● *Alt* 0 **Students**: 5,698 **Total Teachers**: 355 **Student/Classroom Teacher Ratio**: 15.9	**Expenditures/Student**: $4,303 **Librarians**: 6.0 950 students/librarian **Guidance Counselors**: 11.0 518 students/counselor	**% Amer Indian**: 0.1 **% Asian**: 0.4 **% Black**: 1.4 **% Hispanic**: 43.9 **% White**: 54.2	National ***Socio-Economic Status*** indicator percentile (100=high): 37th

Cooke County

GAINESVILLE INDEPENDENT S.D.

1201 SOUTH LINDSAY ST. ● GAINESVILLE TX 76240-5621 ● (940) 665-4362

Grade Span: PK-12 **Schools**: *Regular* 8 ● *Spec Ed* 0 ● *Alt* 1 **Students**: 2,724 **Total Teachers**: 191 **Student/Classroom Teacher Ratio**: 14.7	**Expenditures/Student**: $4,689 **Librarians**: 2.0 1,362 students/librarian **Guidance Counselors**: 6.1 447 students/counselor	**% Amer Indian**: 0.6 **% Asian**: 0.7 **% Black**: 10.6 **% Hispanic**: 16.9 **% White**: 71.1	National ***Socio-Economic Status*** indicator percentile (100=high): 25th

Coryell County

COPPERAS COVE INDEPENDENT S.D.

P. O. BOX 580 ● COPPERAS COVE TX 76522-0580 ● (254) 547-7076 ● http://www.ccisd.com

Grade Span: PK-12 **Schools**: *Regular* 11 ● *Spec Ed* 0 ● *Alt* 0 **Students**: 7,586 **Total Teachers**: 491 **Student/Classroom Teacher Ratio**: 15.3	**Expenditures/Student**: $4,650 **Librarians**: 14.0 542 students/librarian **Guidance Counselors**: 16.0 474 students/counselor	**% Amer Indian**: 0.7 **% Asian**: 4.0 **% Black**: 24.4 **% Hispanic**: 10.2 **% White**: 60.7	National ***Socio-Economic Status*** indicator percentile (100=high): 59th

Dallas County

CARROLLTON-FARMERS BRANCH INDEPENDENT S.D.

P. O. BOX 115186 ● CARROLLTON TX 75011-5186 ● (972) 323-5700 ● http://www.cfbisd.edu

Grade Span: PK-12 **Schools**: *Regular* 27 ● *Spec Ed* 1 ● *Alt* 1 **Students**: 20,343 **Total Teachers**: 1,282 **Student/Classroom Teacher Ratio**: 16.3	**Expenditures/Student**: $4,576 **Librarians**: 26.1 779 students/librarian **Guidance Counselors**: 47.2 431 students/counselor	**% Amer Indian**: 0.5 **% Asian**: 11.3 **% Black**: 7.5 **% Hispanic**: 24.0 **% White**: 56.7	National ***Socio-Economic Status*** indicator percentile (100=high): 55th

Dallas County

CEDAR HILL INDEPENDENT S.D.

270 S. HWY. 67 ● CEDAR HILL TX 75104-0248 ● (972) 291-1581

Grade Span: PK-12 **Schools**: *Regular* 9 ● *Spec Ed* 0 ● *Alt* 0 **Students**: 5,615 **Total Teachers**: 335 **Student/Classroom Teacher Ratio**: 17.0	**Expenditures/Student**: $4,015 **Librarians**: 9.0 624 students/librarian **Guidance Counselors**: 13.9 404 students/counselor	**% Amer Indian**: 0.7 **% Asian**: 2.1 **% Black**: 28.5 **% Hispanic**: 11.0 **% White**: 57.8	National ***Socio-Economic Status*** indicator percentile (100=high): 70th

Dallas County

COPPELL INDEPENDENT S.D.

200 S. DENTON TAP ROAD ● COPPELL TX 75019-3205 ● (972) 471-1111

Grade Span: PK-12 **Schools**: *Regular* 10 ● *Spec Ed* 0 ● *Alt* 0 **Students**: 6,357 **Total Teachers**: 410 **Student/Classroom Teacher Ratio**: 15.4	**Expenditures/Student**: $4,757 **Librarians**: 11.0 578 students/librarian **Guidance Counselors**: 14.0 454 students/counselor	**% Amer Indian**: 0.8 **% Asian**: 8.4 **% Black**: 2.6 **% Hispanic**: 6.7 **% White**: 81.5	National ***Socio-Economic Status*** indicator percentile (100=high): 99th

Dallas County

DALLAS INDEPENDENT S.D.

3700 ROSS AVENUE ● DALLAS TX 75204-5491 ● (214) 824-1620 ● http://www.dallas.isd.tenet.edu

Grade Span: PK-12 **Schools**: *Regular* 190 ● *Spec Ed* 2 ● *Alt* 11 **Students**: 148,839 **Total Teachers**: 8,922 **Student/Classroom Teacher Ratio**: 19.0	**Expenditures/Student**: $5,199 **Librarians**: 195.1 763 students/librarian **Guidance Counselors**: 291.0 511 students/counselor	**% Amer Indian**: 0.4 **% Asian**: 1.7 **% Black**: 42.4 **% Hispanic**: 43.6 **% White**: 11.8	National ***Socio-Economic Status*** indicator percentile (100=high): 6th

Dallas County
[DALLAS] **HIGHLAND PARK INDEPENDENT S.D.**
7015 WESTCHESTER DRIVE ● DALLAS TX 75205-1061 ● (214) 523-1600 ● http://www.highlandpark.k12.tx.us

Grade Span: PK-12 **Schools**: *Regular* 7 ● *Spec Ed* 0 ● *Alt* 0 **Students**: 5,222 **Total Teachers**: 355 **Student/Classroom Teacher Ratio**: 15.1	**Expenditures/Student**: $5,284 **Librarians**: 4.9 1,066 students/librarian **Guidance Counselors**: 14.5 360 students/counselor	**% Amer Indian**: 0.2 **% Asian**: 1.0 **% Black**: 0.1 **% Hispanic**: 1.3 **% White**: 97.5	National ***Socio-Economic Status*** indicator percentile (100=high): na

Dallas County
[DALLAS] **WILMER-HUTCHINS INDEPENDENT S.D.**
3820 EAST ILLINOIS AVE. ● DALLAS TX 75216-4140 ● (214) 376-7311

Grade Span: PK-12 **Schools**: *Regular* 8 ● *Spec Ed* 0 ● *Alt* 0 **Students**: 3,837 **Total Teachers**: 261 **Student/Classroom Teacher Ratio**: 15.3	**Expenditures/Student**: $5,256 **Librarians**: 4.0 959 students/librarian **Guidance Counselors**: 9.0 426 students/counselor	**% Amer Indian**: 0.3 **% Asian**: 0.1 **% Black**: 78.3 **% Hispanic**: 14.6 **% White**: 6.6	National ***Socio-Economic Status*** indicator percentile (100=high): 10th

Dallas County
DE SOTO INDEPENDENT S.D.
200 EAST BELT LINE ROAD ● DE SOTO TX 75115-5795 ● (972) 223-6666

Grade Span: PK-12 **Schools**: *Regular* 10 ● *Spec Ed* 0 ● *Alt* 0 **Students**: 6,558 **Total Teachers**: 420 **Student/Classroom Teacher Ratio**: 15.7	**Expenditures/Student**: $4,108 **Librarians**: 9.1 721 students/librarian **Guidance Counselors**: 13.1 501 students/counselor	**% Amer Indian**: 0.1 **% Asian**: 1.3 **% Black**: 37.6 **% Hispanic**: 7.5 **% White**: 53.5	National ***Socio-Economic Status*** indicator percentile (100=high): 72nd

Dallas County
DUNCANVILLE INDEPENDENT S.D.
802 SOUTH MAIN ST. ● DUNCANVILLE TX 75137-2316 ● (972) 296-4761 ● http://www.duncanville.k12.tx.us

Grade Span: PK-12 **Schools**: *Regular* 14 ● *Spec Ed* 0 ● *Alt* 1 **Students**: 10,126 **Total Teachers**: 629 **Student/Classroom Teacher Ratio**: 16.5	**Expenditures/Student**: $4,440 **Librarians**: 14.0 723 students/librarian **Guidance Counselors**: 26.4 384 students/counselor	**% Amer Indian**: 0.3 **% Asian**: 2.9 **% Black**: 31.6 **% Hispanic**: 12.5 **% White**: 52.7	National ***Socio-Economic Status*** indicator percentile (100=high): 61st

Dallas County
GARLAND INDEPENDENT S.D.
720 STADIUM DRIVE ● GARLAND TX 75040-4616 ● (972) 494-8201 ● http://www.gisd.ci.garland.tx.us

Grade Span: PK-12 **Schools**: *Regular* 56 ● *Spec Ed* 1 ● *Alt* 3 **Students**: 43,553 **Total Teachers**: 2,465 **Student/Classroom Teacher Ratio**: 17.5	**Expenditures/Student**: $3,986 **Librarians**: 59.0 738 students/librarian **Guidance Counselors**: 102.1 427 students/counselor	**% Amer Indian**: 0.6 **% Asian**: 5.4 **% Black**: 14.3 **% Hispanic**: 19.9 **% White**: 59.8	National ***Socio-Economic Status*** indicator percentile (100=high): 48th

Dallas County
GRAND PRAIRIE INDEPENDENT S.D.
BOX 531170 ● GRAND PRAIRIE TX 75053-1170 ● (972) 264-6141

Grade Span: PK-12 **Schools**: *Regular* 26 ● *Spec Ed* 0 ● *Alt* 1 **Students**: 17,934 **Total Teachers**: 1,033 **Student/Classroom Teacher Ratio**: 16.9	**Expenditures/Student**: $4,276 **Librarians**: 14.6 1,228 students/librarian **Guidance Counselors**: 38.2 469 students/counselor	**% Amer Indian**: 0.8 **% Asian**: 3.7 **% Black**: 12.6 **% Hispanic**: 37.7 **% White**: 45.3	National ***Socio-Economic Status*** indicator percentile (100=high): 31st

Dallas County
IRVING INDEPENDENT S.D.
BOX 152637 ● IRVING TX 75015-2637 ● (972) 259-4575 ● http://www.irving.isd.tenet.edu

Grade Span: PK-12 **Schools**: *Regular* 26 ● *Spec Ed* 3 ● *Alt* 1 **Students**: 26,459 **Total Teachers**: 1,575 **Student/Classroom Teacher Ratio**: 17.1	**Expenditures/Student**: $4,412 **Librarians**: 29.0 912 students/librarian **Guidance Counselors**: 63.1 419 students/counselor	**% Amer Indian**: 0.6 **% Asian**: 6.0 **% Black**: 13.8 **% Hispanic**: 33.2 **% White**: 46.4	National ***Socio-Economic Status*** indicator percentile (100=high): 27th

Dallas County
LANCASTER INDEPENDENT S.D.
P. O. BOX 400 ● LANCASTER TX 75146-0400 ● (972) 227-4141

Grade Span: PK-12 **Schools**: *Regular* 8 ● *Spec Ed* 0 ● *Alt* 0 **Students**: 4,042 **Total Teachers**: 263 **Student/Classroom Teacher Ratio**: 15.9	**Expenditures/Student**: $4,295 **Librarians**: 7.0 577 students/librarian **Guidance Counselors**: 6.3 642 students/counselor	**% Amer Indian**: 0.4 **% Asian**: 0.5 **% Black**: 52.9 **% Hispanic**: 11.5 **% White**: 34.8	National ***Socio-Economic Status*** indicator percentile (100=high): 93rd

Dallas County
MESQUITE INDEPENDENT S.D.
405 EAST DAVIS ST. ● MESQUITE TX 75149-4701 ● (972) 288-6411 ● http://www.mesquite.isd.tenet.edu/misdweb/index.html

Grade Span: PK-12 **Schools**: *Regular* 37 ● *Spec Ed* 0 ● *Alt* 1 **Students**: 29,242 **Total Teachers**: 1,628 **Student/Classroom Teacher Ratio**: 18.1	**Expenditures/Student**: $3,893 **Librarians**: 39.0 750 students/librarian **Guidance Counselors**: 49.2 594 students/counselor	**% Amer Indian**: 0.4 **% Asian**: 3.5 **% Black**: 10.8 **% Hispanic**: 12.6 **% White**: 72.7	National ***Socio-Economic Status*** indicator percentile (100=high): 60th

Dallas County
RICHARDSON INDEPENDENT S.D.
400 SOUTH GREENVILLE AVE. ● RICHARDSON TX 75081-1498 ● (972) 301-3333 ● http://www.richardson.k12.tx.us

Grade Span: PK-12 **Schools**: *Regular* 50 ● *Spec Ed* 0 ● *Alt* 2 **Students**: 33,984 **Total Teachers**: 2,100 **Student/Classroom Teacher Ratio**: 16.4	**Expenditures/Student**: $4,838 **Librarians**: 38.2 890 students/librarian **Guidance Counselors**: 89.0 382 students/counselor	**% Amer Indian**: 0.3 **% Asian**: 8.9 **% Black**: 18.8 **% Hispanic**: 11.3 **% White**: 60.6	National ***Socio-Economic Status*** indicator percentile (100=high): 60th

Dawson County
LAMESA INDEPENDENT S.D.
P. O. BOX 261 ● LAMESA TX 79331-0261 ● (806) 872-5461 ● http://www.lamesa.isd.tenet.edu

Grade Span: PK-12 **Schools**: *Regular* 6 ● *Spec Ed* 0 ● *Alt* 1 **Students**: 2,626 **Total Teachers**: 184 **Student/Classroom Teacher Ratio**: 13.3	**Expenditures/Student**: $4,609 **Librarians**: 2.0 1,313 students/librarian **Guidance Counselors**: 3.0 875 students/counselor	**% Amer Indian**: 0.0 **% Asian**: 0.0 **% Black**: 5.3 **% Hispanic**: 63.7 **% White**: 31.0	National ***Socio-Economic Status*** indicator percentile (100=high): 12th

Deaf Smith County
HEREFORD INDEPENDENT S.D.
601 N. 25 MILE AVE. ● HEREFORD TX 79045-4406 ● (806) 364-0606

Grade Span: PK-12 **Schools**: *Regular* 8 ● *Spec Ed* 1 ● *Alt* 0 **Students**: 4,501 **Total Teachers**: 327 **Student/Classroom Teacher Ratio**: 13.6	**Expenditures/Student**: $4,735 **Librarians**: 8.0 563 students/librarian **Guidance Counselors**: 14.0 322 students/counselor	**% Amer Indian**: 0.1 **% Asian**: 0.3 **% Black**: 2.4 **% Hispanic**: 70.0 **% White**: 27.2	National ***Socio-Economic Status*** indicator percentile (100=high): 12th

Denton County

DENTON INDEPENDENT S.D.

P. O. BOX 2387 ● DENTON TX 76202-2387 ● (940) 387-6151 ● http://www.denton.isd.tenet.edu

Grade Span: PK-12 **Schools**: *Regular* 14 ● *Spec Ed* 1 ● *Alt* 2 **Students**: 12,035 **Total Teachers**: 760 **Student/Classroom Teacher Ratio**: 16.0	**Expenditures/Student**: $4,548 **Librarians**: 13.0 926 students/librarian **Guidance Counselors**: 22.0 547 students/counselor	**% Amer Indian**: 0.4 **% Asian**: 1.5 **% Black**: 11.6 **% Hispanic**: 14.3 **% White**: 72.1	National ***Socio-Economic Status*** indicator percentile (100=high): 47th

Denton County

[JUSTIN] **NORTHWEST INDEPENDENT S.D.**

18501 ST. HWY. 114 ● JUSTIN TX 76247-9709 ● (940) 648-2611

Grade Span: PK-12 **Schools**: *Regular* 9 ● *Spec Ed* 0 ● *Alt* 1 **Students**: 4,265 **Total Teachers**: 311 **Student/Classroom Teacher Ratio**: 11.9	**Expenditures/Student**: $4,857 **Librarians**: 6.0 711 students/librarian **Guidance Counselors**: 10.8 395 students/counselor	**% Amer Indian**: 0.8 **% Asian**: 1.1 **% Black**: 0.5 **% Hispanic**: 6.5 **% White**: 91.0	National ***Socio-Economic Status*** indicator percentile (100=high): 64th

Denton County

LEWISVILLE INDEPENDENT S.D.

P. O. BOX 217 ● LEWISVILLE TX 75067-0217 ● (972) 539-1551 ● http://www.lewisville.isd.tenet.edu

Grade Span: PK-12 **Schools**: *Regular* 37 ● *Spec Ed* 0 ● *Alt* 1 **Students**: 28,320 **Total Teachers**: 1,867 **Student/Classroom Teacher Ratio**: 15.3	**Expenditures/Student**: $4,238 **Librarians**: 33.4 848 students/librarian **Guidance Counselors**: 73.9 383 students/counselor	**% Amer Indian**: 0.6 **% Asian**: 2.5 **% Black**: 5.2 **% Hispanic**: 8.3 **% White**: 83.4	National ***Socio-Economic Status*** indicator percentile (100=high): 87th

Ector County

[ODESSA] **ECTOR COUNTY INDEPENDENT S.D.**

P. O. BOX 3912 ● ODESSA TX 79760-3912 ● (915) 332-9151

Grade Span: PK-12 **Schools**: *Regular* 39 ● *Spec Ed* 1 ● *Alt* 4 **Students**: 28,528 **Total Teachers**: 1,684 **Student/Classroom Teacher Ratio**: 17.1	**Expenditures/Student**: $4,182 **Librarians**: 34.1 837 students/librarian **Guidance Counselors**: 46.0 620 students/counselor	**% Amer Indian**: 0.3 **% Asian**: 0.7 **% Black**: 5.1 **% Hispanic**: 48.4 **% White**: 45.5	National ***Socio-Economic Status*** indicator percentile (100=high): 11th

El Paso County

CANUTILLO INDEPENDENT S.D.

P. O. BOX 100 ● CANUTILLO TX 79835-0100 ● (915) 877-3726

Grade Span: PK-12 **Schools**: *Regular* 5 ● *Spec Ed* 0 ● *Alt* 1 **Students**: 4,206 **Total Teachers**: 283 **Student/Classroom Teacher Ratio**: 15.2	**Expenditures/Student**: $5,243 **Librarians**: 5.0 841 students/librarian **Guidance Counselors**: 10.0 421 students/counselor	**% Amer Indian**: 0.1 **% Asian**: 0.0 **% Black**: 0.5 **% Hispanic**: 92.0 **% White**: 7.3	National ***Socio-Economic Status*** indicator percentile (100=high): 0th

El Paso County

CLINT INDEPENDENT S.D.

P. O. BOX 779 ● CLINT TX 79836-0779 ● (915) 851-3368 ● http://www.cisd.org

Grade Span: PK-12 **Schools**: *Regular* 8 ● *Spec Ed* 0 ● *Alt* 1 **Students**: 6,064 **Total Teachers**: 402 **Student/Classroom Teacher Ratio**: 15.0	**Expenditures/Student**: $4,575 **Librarians**: 4.3 1,410 students/librarian **Guidance Counselors**: 14.1 430 students/counselor	**% Amer Indian**: 0.2 **% Asian**: 0.2 **% Black**: 0.6 **% Hispanic**: 90.6 **% White**: 8.4	National ***Socio-Economic Status*** indicator percentile (100=high): 3rd

El Paso County
EL PASO INDEPENDENT S.D.
P. O. BOX 20100 ● EL PASO TX 79998-0100 ● (915) 779-3781 ● http://www.elpaso.k12.tx.us

Grade Span: PK-12 **Schools**: *Regular* 74 ● *Spec Ed* 1 ● *Alt* 5 **Students**: 64,260 **Total Teachers**: 4,068 **Student/Classroom Teacher Ratio**: 15.9	**Expenditures/Student**: $4,586 **Librarians**: 88.0 730 students/librarian **Guidance Counselors**: 141.0 456 students/counselor	**% Amer Indian**: 0.1 **% Asian**: 1.0 **% Black**: 4.5 **% Hispanic**: 75.6 **% White**: 18.7	National ***Socio-Economic Status*** indicator percentile (100=high): 10th

El Paso County
[EL PASO] **SOCORRO INDEPENDENT S.D.**
P. O. BOX 27400 ● EL PASO TX 79926-7737 ● (915) 860-3400

Grade Span: PK-12 **Schools**: *Regular* 18 ● *Spec Ed* 0 ● *Alt* 1 **Students**: 20,115 **Total Teachers**: 1,194 **Student/Classroom Teacher Ratio**: 17.6	**Expenditures/Student**: $4,790 **Librarians**: 19.0 1,059 students/librarian **Guidance Counselors**: 47.2 426 students/counselor	**% Amer Indian**: 0.1 **% Asian**: 0.3 **% Black**: 1.3 **% Hispanic**: 88.3 **% White**: 10.0	National ***Socio-Economic Status*** indicator percentile (100=high): 7th

El Paso County
[EL PASO] **YSLETA INDEPENDENT S.D.**
9600 SIMS DRIVE ● EL PASO TX 79925-7225 ● (915) 595-5500 ● http://www.ysleta.isd.tenet.edu

Grade Span: PK-12 **Schools**: *Regular* 54 ● *Spec Ed* 2 ● *Alt* 11 **Students**: 47,144 **Total Teachers**: 2,944 **Student/Classroom Teacher Ratio**: 15.8	**Expenditures/Student**: $4,785 **Librarians**: 49.7 949 students/librarian **Guidance Counselors**: 97.5 484 students/counselor	**% Amer Indian**: 0.4 **% Asian**: 0.5 **% Black**: 2.7 **% Hispanic**: 84.6 **% White**: 11.7	National ***Socio-Economic Status*** indicator percentile (100=high): 9th

El Paso County
FABENS INDEPENDENT S.D.
P. O. BOX 697 ● FABENS TX 79838-0697 ● (915) 764-2025

Grade Span: PK-12 **Schools**: *Regular* 4 ● *Spec Ed* 0 ● *Alt* 0 **Students**: 2,681 **Total Teachers**: 180 **Student/Classroom Teacher Ratio**: 14.9	**Expenditures/Student**: $4,656 **Librarians**: 2.8 958 students/librarian **Guidance Counselors**: 5.0 536 students/counselor	**% Amer Indian**: 0.3 **% Asian**: 0.0 **% Black**: 0.1 **% Hispanic**: 96.7 **% White**: 2.8	National ***Socio-Economic Status*** indicator percentile (100=high): 8th

El Paso County
SAN ELIZARIO INDEPENDENT S.D.
P. O. BOX 920 ● SAN ELIZARIO TX 79849-0920 ● (915) 851-2780 ● http://www.san-elizario.k12.tx.us

Grade Span: PK-12 **Schools**: *Regular* 5 ● *Spec Ed* 0 ● *Alt* 1 **Students**: 3,315 **Total Teachers**: 209 **Student/Classroom Teacher Ratio**: 15.6	**Expenditures/Student**: $5,229 **Librarians**: 3.0 1,105 students/librarian **Guidance Counselors**: 5.0 663 students/counselor	**% Amer Indian**: 0.2 **% Asian**: 0.0 **% Black**: 0.0 **% Hispanic**: 99.0 **% White**: 0.9	National ***Socio-Economic Status*** indicator percentile (100=high): 0th

Ellis County
ENNIS INDEPENDENT S.D.
P. O. BOX 1420 ● ENNIS TX 75120-1420 ● (972) 875-9027

Grade Span: PK-12 **Schools**: *Regular* 6 ● *Spec Ed* 0 ● *Alt* 0 **Students**: 4,392 **Total Teachers**: 285 **Student/Classroom Teacher Ratio**: 15.5	**Expenditures/Student**: $4,334 **Librarians**: 3.0 1,464 students/librarian **Guidance Counselors**: 10.0 439 students/counselor	**% Amer Indian**: 0.2 **% Asian**: 0.3 **% Black**: 17.6 **% Hispanic**: 33.2 **% White**: 48.8	National ***Socio-Economic Status*** indicator percentile (100=high): 27th

Ellis County

MIDLOTHIAN INDEPENDENT S.D.

925 SOUTH 9TH. ST. ● MIDLOTHIAN TX 76065-3699 ● (972) 775-8296

Grade Span: PK-12 **Schools**: *Regular* 5 ● *Spec Ed* 0 ● *Alt* 0 **Students**: 3,427 **Total Teachers**: 226 **Student/Classroom Teacher Ratio**: 15.3	**Expenditures/Student**: $4,231 **Librarians**: 3.0 1,142 students/librarian **Guidance Counselors**: 7.0 490 students/counselor	**% Amer Indian**: 0.2 **% Asian**: 0.5 **% Black**: 2.5 **% Hispanic**: 9.8 **% White**: 87.0	National ***Socio-Economic Status*** indicator percentile (100=high): 68th

Ellis County

RED OAK INDEPENDENT S.D.

P. O. BOX 9000 ● RED OAK TX 75154-9000 ● (972) 617-2941

Grade Span: PK-12 **Schools**: *Regular* 7 ● *Spec Ed* 0 ● *Alt* 0 **Students**: 3,688 **Total Teachers**: 216 **Student/Classroom Teacher Ratio**: 16.9	**Expenditures/Student**: $3,799 **Librarians**: 0.0 *** students/librarian **Guidance Counselors**: 8.0 461 students/counselor	**% Amer Indian**: 0.4 **% Asian**: 0.3 **% Black**: 4.2 **% Hispanic**: 11.4 **% White**: 83.8	National ***Socio-Economic Status*** indicator percentile (100=high): 75th

Ellis County

WAXAHACHIE INDEPENDENT S.D.

411 GIBSON ST. ● WAXAHACHIE TX 75165-3007 ● (972) 923-4631 ● http://www.wisd.org

Grade Span: PK-12 **Schools**: *Regular* 8 ● *Spec Ed* 0 ● *Alt* 1 **Students**: 5,083 **Total Teachers**: 323 **Student/Classroom Teacher Ratio**: 16.2	**Expenditures/Student**: $4,318 **Librarians**: 2.0 2,542 students/librarian **Guidance Counselors**: 13.0 391 students/counselor	**% Amer Indian**: 0.1 **% Asian**: 0.2 **% Black**: 17.2 **% Hispanic**: 20.4 **% White**: 62.0	National ***Socio-Economic Status*** indicator percentile (100=high): 40th

Erath County

STEPHENVILLE INDEPENDENT S.D.

726 NORTH CLINTON ST. ● STEPHENVILLE TX 76401-3003 ● (254) 968-7990

Grade Span: PK-12 **Schools**: *Regular* 5 ● *Spec Ed* 0 ● *Alt* 1 **Students**: 3,353 **Total Teachers**: 202 **Student/Classroom Teacher Ratio**: 16.6	**Expenditures/Student**: $3,890 **Librarians**: 3.0 1,118 students/librarian **Guidance Counselors**: 5.0 671 students/counselor	**% Amer Indian**: 0.3 **% Asian**: 0.5 **% Black**: 1.0 **% Hispanic**: 13.8 **% White**: 84.4	National ***Socio-Economic Status*** indicator percentile (100=high): 60th

Fort Bend County

[ROSENBERG] LAMAR CONSOLIDATED INDEPENDENT S.D.

3911 AVENUE I ● ROSENBERG TX 77471-3960 ● (281) 341-3100

Grade Span: PK-12 **Schools**: *Regular* 19 ● *Spec Ed* 1 ● *Alt* 5 **Students**: 13,774 **Total Teachers**: 841 **Student/Classroom Teacher Ratio**: 16.2	**Expenditures/Student**: $5,098 **Librarians**: 17.0 810 students/librarian **Guidance Counselors**: 36.5 377 students/counselor	**% Amer Indian**: 0.1 **% Asian**: 0.8 **% Black**: 13.3 **% Hispanic**: 46.5 **% White**: 39.3	National ***Socio-Economic Status*** indicator percentile (100=high): 23rd

Fort Bend County

[SUGAR LAND] FORT BEND INDEPENDENT S.D.

P. O. BOX 1004 ● SUGAR LAND TX 77487-1004 ● (281) 980-1300 ● http://www.fortbend.k12.tx.us

Grade Span: PK-12 **Schools**: *Regular* 38 ● *Spec Ed* 0 ● *Alt* 0 **Students**: 40,223 **Total Teachers**: 2,319 **Student/Classroom Teacher Ratio**: 18.4	**Expenditures/Student**: $4,150 **Librarians**: 45.2 890 students/librarian **Guidance Counselors**: 75.9 530 students/counselor	**% Amer Indian**: 0.1 **% Asian**: 13.5 **% Black**: 27.2 **% Hispanic**: 14.6 **% White**: 44.6	National ***Socio-Economic Status*** indicator percentile (100=high): na

Galveston County
DICKINSON INDEPENDENT S.D.
P. O. BOX Z ● DICKINSON TX 77539-6899 ● (281) 534-3581

Grade Span: PK-12 **Schools**: *Regular* 7 ● *Spec Ed* 0 ● *Alt* 0 **Students**: 5,898 **Total Teachers**: 373 **Student/Classroom Teacher Ratio**: 15.8	**Expenditures/Student**: $4,848 **Librarians**: 6.0 983 students/librarian **Guidance Counselors**: 9.9 596 students/counselor	**% Amer Indian**: 0.2 **% Asian**: 4.1 **% Black**: 12.8 **% Hispanic**: 22.2 **% White**: 60.8	National ***Socio-Economic Status*** indicator percentile (100=high): 25th

Galveston County
FRIENDSWOOD INDEPENDENT S.D.
302 LAUREL DRIVE ● FRIENDSWOOD TX 77546-3923 ● (281) 482-1267 ● http://www.friendswood.isd.tenet.edu

Grade Span: PK-12 **Schools**: *Regular* 5 ● *Spec Ed* 0 ● *Alt* 0 **Students**: 4,306 **Total Teachers**: 260 **Student/Classroom Teacher Ratio**: 17.0	**Expenditures/Student**: $4,386 **Librarians**: 4.0 1,077 students/librarian **Guidance Counselors**: 9.0 478 students/counselor	**% Amer Indian**: 0.2 **% Asian**: 2.4 **% Black**: 1.1 **% Hispanic**: 4.5 **% White**: 91.8	National ***Socio-Economic Status*** indicator percentile (100=high): 97th

Galveston County
GALVESTON INDEPENDENT S.D.
P. O. BOX 660 ● GALVESTON TX 77553-0660 ● (409) 765-9366

Grade Span: PK-12 **Schools**: *Regular* 12 ● *Spec Ed* 1 ● *Alt* 0 **Students**: 9,910 **Total Teachers**: 652 **Student/Classroom Teacher Ratio**: 14.8	**Expenditures/Student**: $5,684 **Librarians**: 6.1 1,625 students/librarian **Guidance Counselors**: 14.2 698 students/counselor	**% Amer Indian**: 0.1 **% Asian**: 2.5 **% Black**: 38.6 **% Hispanic**: 29.7 **% White**: 29.1	National ***Socio-Economic Status*** indicator percentile (100=high): 16th

Galveston County
LA MARQUE INDEPENDENT S.D.
P. O. BOX 7 ● LA MARQUE TX 77568-0007 ● (409) 938-4251 ● http://www.la-marque.isd.tenet.edu/wan/LM.HTM

Grade Span: PK-12 **Schools**: *Regular* 7 ● *Spec Ed* 0 ● *Alt* 0 **Students**: 4,435 **Total Teachers**: 281 **Student/Classroom Teacher Ratio**: 16.6	**Expenditures/Student**: $4,980 **Librarians**: 10.0 444 students/librarian **Guidance Counselors**: 10.0 444 students/counselor	**% Amer Indian**: 0.0 **% Asian**: 0.6 **% Black**: 61.5 **% Hispanic**: 9.5 **% White**: 28.3	National ***Socio-Economic Status*** indicator percentile (100=high): 36th

Galveston County
[LEAGUE CITY] **CLEAR CREEK INDEPENDENT S.D.**
P. O. BOX 799 ● LEAGUE CITY TX 77574-0799 ● (281) 332-2828

Grade Span: PK-12 **Schools**: *Regular* 28 ● *Spec Ed* 0 ● *Alt* 2 **Students**: 26,563 **Total Teachers**: 1,562 **Student/Classroom Teacher Ratio**: 17.3	**Expenditures/Student**: $4,478 **Librarians**: 26.0 1,022 students/librarian **Guidance Counselors**: 63.8 416 students/counselor	**% Amer Indian**: 0.3 **% Asian**: 8.0 **% Black**: 6.6 **% Hispanic**: 10.6 **% White**: 74.5	National ***Socio-Economic Status*** indicator percentile (100=high): 84th

Galveston County
SANTA FE INDEPENDENT S.D.
P. O. BOX 370 ● SANTA FE TX 77510-0370 ● (281) 925-3526

Grade Span: PK-12 **Schools**: *Regular* 5 ● *Spec Ed* 0 ● *Alt* 0 **Students**: 4,349 **Total Teachers**: 244 **Student/Classroom Teacher Ratio**: 18.0	**Expenditures/Student**: $4,015 **Librarians**: 5.0 870 students/librarian **Guidance Counselors**: 8.0 544 students/counselor	**% Amer Indian**: 0.1 **% Asian**: 0.2 **% Black**: 0.1 **% Hispanic**: 10.4 **% White**: 89.1	National ***Socio-Economic Status*** indicator percentile (100=high): 62nd

Galveston County

TEXAS CITY INDEPENDENT S.D.

P. O. BOX 1150 ● TEXAS CITY TX 77592-1150 ● (409) 942-2713

Grade Span: PK-12 **Schools**: *Regular* 7 ● *Spec Ed* 0 ● *Alt* 1 **Students**: 5,906 **Total Teachers**: 389 **Student/Classroom Teacher Ratio**: 15.6	**Expenditures/Student**: $5,288 **Librarians**: 7.1 832 students/librarian **Guidance Counselors**: 16.0 369 students/counselor	**% Amer Indian**: 0.3 **% Asian**: 0.9 **% Black**: 17.6 **% Hispanic**: 23.9 **% White**: 57.2	National ***Socio-Economic Status*** indicator percentile (100=high): 72nd

Gillespie County

FREDERICKSBURG INDEPENDENT S.D.

300-B WEST MAIN ST. ● FREDERICKSBURG TX 78624-3853 ● (830) 997-9551

Grade Span: PK-12 **Schools**: *Regular* 5 ● *Spec Ed* 0 ● *Alt* 1 **Students**: 2,790 **Total Teachers**: 179 **Student/Classroom Teacher Ratio**: 15.3	**Expenditures/Student**: $4,567 **Librarians**: 2.1 1,329 students/librarian **Guidance Counselors**: 6.0 465 students/counselor	**% Amer Indian**: 0.2 **% Asian**: 0.5 **% Black**: 0.6 **% Hispanic**: 29.8 **% White**: 68.9	National ***Socio-Economic Status*** indicator percentile (100=high): 41st

Gonzales County

GONZALES INDEPENDENT S.D.

BOX 157 ● GONZALES TX 78629-0157 ● (830) 672-9551

Grade Span: PK-12 **Schools**: *Regular* 4 ● *Spec Ed* 0 ● *Alt* 1 **Students**: 2,648 **Total Teachers**: 176 **Student/Classroom Teacher Ratio**: 15.2	**Expenditures/Student**: $4,366 **Librarians**: 2.0 1,324 students/librarian **Guidance Counselors**: 5.0 530 students/counselor	**% Amer Indian**: 0.0 **% Asian**: 0.3 **% Black**: 13.8 **% Hispanic**: 44.2 **% White**: 41.8	National ***Socio-Economic Status*** indicator percentile (100=high): 17th

Gray County

PAMPA INDEPENDENT S.D.

321 WEST ALBERT ST. ● PAMPA TX 79065-7801 ● (806) 669-4700 ● http://www.pampa.isd.tenet.edu

Grade Span: PK-12 **Schools**: *Regular* 8 ● *Spec Ed* 0 ● *Alt* 1 **Students**: 3,990 **Total Teachers**: 282 **Student/Classroom Teacher Ratio**: 14.4	**Expenditures/Student**: $4,539 **Librarians**: 0.1 39,900 students/librarian **Guidance Counselors**: 7.5 532 students/counselor	**% Amer Indian**: 1.2 **% Asian**: 0.9 **% Black**: 4.7 **% Hispanic**: 16.1 **% White**: 77.1	National ***Socio-Economic Status*** indicator percentile (100=high): 41st

Grayson County

DENISON INDEPENDENT S.D.

1201 SOUTH RUSK AVE. ● DENISON TX 75020-6340 ● (903) 465-4244

Grade Span: PK-12 **Schools**: *Regular* 8 ● *Spec Ed* 1 ● *Alt* 0 **Students**: 4,632 **Total Teachers**: 286 **Student/Classroom Teacher Ratio**: 15.8	**Expenditures/Student**: $4,315 **Librarians**: 5.0 926 students/librarian **Guidance Counselors**: 11.7 396 students/counselor	**% Amer Indian**: 1.7 **% Asian**: 0.6 **% Black**: 9.1 **% Hispanic**: 3.1 **% White**: 85.4	National ***Socio-Economic Status*** indicator percentile (100=high): 31st

Grayson County

SHERMAN INDEPENDENT S.D.

P. O. BOX 1176 ● SHERMAN TX 75091-0210 ● (903) 892-9115 ● http://www.shermanisd.net

Grade Span: PK-12 **Schools**: *Regular* 10 ● *Spec Ed* 1 ● *Alt* 1 **Students**: 5,964 **Total Teachers**: 378 **Student/Classroom Teacher Ratio**: 15.6	**Expenditures/Student**: $4,778 **Librarians**: 4.1 1,455 students/librarian **Guidance Counselors**: 14.5 411 students/counselor	**% Amer Indian**: 0.9 **% Asian**: 0.9 **% Black**: 17.7 **% Hispanic**: 8.5 **% White**: 72.0	National ***Socio-Economic Status*** indicator percentile (100=high): 36th

Gregg County
KILGORE INDEPENDENT S.D.
711 NORTH LONGVIEW ST. ● KILGORE TX 75662-5499 ● (903) 984-2073

Grade Span: PK-12 **Schools**: *Regular* 5 ● *Spec Ed* 1 ● *Alt* 2 **Students**: 3,637 **Total Teachers**: 248 **Student/Classroom Teacher Ratio**: 14.8	**Expenditures/Student**: $4,227 **Librarians**: 2.4 1,515 students/librarian **Guidance Counselors**: 3.7 983 students/counselor	**% Amer Indian**: 0.2 **% Asian**: 0.3 **% Black**: 21.3 **% Hispanic**: 5.7 **% White**: 72.5	National ***Socio-Economic Status*** indicator percentile (100=high): 34th

Gregg County
LONGVIEW INDEPENDENT S.D.
P. O. BOX 3268 ● LONGVIEW TX 75606-3268 ● (903) 753-0206 ● http://www.etnet.net/lisd

Grade Span: PK-12 **Schools**: *Regular* 16 ● *Spec Ed* 1 ● *Alt* 1 **Students**: 8,261 **Total Teachers**: 588 **Student/Classroom Teacher Ratio**: 14.4	**Expenditures/Student**: $4,867 **Librarians**: 12.9 640 students/librarian **Guidance Counselors**: 23.0 359 students/counselor	**% Amer Indian**: 0.1 **% Asian**: 0.7 **% Black**: 50.7 **% Hispanic**: 8.7 **% White**: 39.8	National ***Socio-Economic Status*** indicator percentile (100=high): 16th

Gregg County
[LONGVIEW] PINE TREE INDEPENDENT S.D.
P. O. BOX 5878 ● LONGVIEW TX 75608-5878 ● (903) 295-5000 ● http://www.etnet.net/pinetree

Grade Span: PK-12 **Schools**: *Regular* 7 ● *Spec Ed* 0 ● *Alt* 0 **Students**: 5,030 **Total Teachers**: 319 **Student/Classroom Teacher Ratio**: 16.1	**Expenditures/Student**: $4,229 **Librarians**: 7.9 637 students/librarian **Guidance Counselors**: 8.6 585 students/counselor	**% Amer Indian**: 0.3 **% Asian**: 1.6 **% Black**: 6.3 **% Hispanic**: 9.5 **% White**: 82.4	National ***Socio-Economic Status*** indicator percentile (100=high): 54th

Grimes County
NAVASOTA INDEPENDENT S.D.
BOX 511 ● NAVASOTA TX 77868-0511 ● (409) 825-4200

Grade Span: PK-12 **Schools**: *Regular* 5 ● *Spec Ed* 0 ● *Alt* 0 **Students**: 3,036 **Total Teachers**: 198 **Student/Classroom Teacher Ratio**: 15.6	**Expenditures/Student**: $4,413 **Librarians**: 2.0 1,518 students/librarian **Guidance Counselors**: 7.0 434 students/counselor	**% Amer Indian**: 0.1 **% Asian**: 0.1 **% Black**: 29.0 **% Hispanic**: 24.6 **% White**: 46.2	National ***Socio-Economic Status*** indicator percentile (100=high): 18th

Guadalupe County
SCHERTZ-CIBOLO-UNIVERSAL CITY INDEPENDENT S.D.
1060 ELBEL ROAD ● SCHERTZ TX 78154-2099 ● (210) 658-3553

Grade Span: PK-12 **Schools**: *Regular* 6 ● *Spec Ed* 0 ● *Alt* 2 **Students**: 4,831 **Total Teachers**: 305 **Student/Classroom Teacher Ratio**: 15.9	**Expenditures/Student**: $4,669 **Librarians**: 5.2 929 students/librarian **Guidance Counselors**: 11.0 439 students/counselor	**% Amer Indian**: 0.2 **% Asian**: 1.3 **% Black**: 4.9 **% Hispanic**: 23.3 **% White**: 70.4	National ***Socio-Economic Status*** indicator percentile (100=high): 55th

Guadalupe County
SEGUIN INDEPENDENT S.D.
P. O. BOX 31 ● SEGUIN TX 78156-0031 ● (830) 372-5771

Grade Span: PK-12 **Schools**: *Regular* 13 ● *Spec Ed* 0 ● *Alt* 3 **Students**: 7,192 **Total Teachers**: 517 **Student/Classroom Teacher Ratio**: 14.3	**Expenditures/Student**: $5,129 **Librarians**: 11.0 654 students/librarian **Guidance Counselors**: 19.0 379 students/counselor	**% Amer Indian**: 0.1 **% Asian**: 0.6 **% Black**: 8.2 **% Hispanic**: 51.8 **% White**: 39.3	National ***Socio-Economic Status*** indicator percentile (100=high): 22nd

Hale County

PLAINVIEW INDEPENDENT S.D.

P. O. BOX 1540 ● PLAINVIEW TX 79073-1540 ● (806) 296-6392

Grade Span: PK-12 **Schools**: *Regular* 11 ● *Spec Ed* 0 ● *Alt* 1 **Students**: 6,265 **Total Teachers**: 409 **Student/Classroom Teacher Ratio**: 15.4	**Expenditures/Student**: $4,414 **Librarians**: 5.5 1,139 students/librarian **Guidance Counselors**: 14.5 432 students/counselor	**% Amer Indian**: 0.3 **% Asian**: 0.3 **% Black**: 6.8 **% Hispanic**: 59.8 **% White**: 32.9	National ***Socio-Economic Status*** indicator percentile (100=high): 17th

Hardin County

LUMBERTON INDEPENDENT S.D.

P. O. BOX 8123 ● LUMBERTON TX 77711-8123 ● (409) 755-4993

Grade Span: PK-12 **Schools**: *Regular* 5 ● *Spec Ed* 0 ● *Alt* 0 **Students**: 3,120 **Total Teachers**: 187 **Student/Classroom Teacher Ratio**: 16.7	**Expenditures/Student**: $3,774 **Librarians**: 4.0 780 students/librarian **Guidance Counselors**: 5.0 624 students/counselor	**% Amer Indian**: 0.1 **% Asian**: 0.3 **% Black**: 0.1 **% Hispanic**: 1.4 **% White**: 98.1	National ***Socio-Economic Status*** indicator percentile (100=high): 74th

Hardin County

SILSBEE INDEPENDENT S.D.

415 WEST AVENUE N ● SILSBEE TX 77656-4799 ● (409) 385-5288

Grade Span: PK-12 **Schools**: *Regular* 6 ● *Spec Ed* 1 ● *Alt* 0 **Students**: 3,639 **Total Teachers**: 249 **Student/Classroom Teacher Ratio**: 14.8	**Expenditures/Student**: $5,061 **Librarians**: 3.0 1,213 students/librarian **Guidance Counselors**: 8.0 455 students/counselor	**% Amer Indian**: 0.0 **% Asian**: 0.2 **% Black**: 21.1 **% Hispanic**: 1.1 **% White**: 77.6	National ***Socio-Economic Status*** indicator percentile (100=high): 34th

Harris County

ALIEF INDEPENDENT S.D.

P. O. BOX 68 ● ALIEF TX 77411-0068 ● (281) 498-8110 ● http://www.alief.isd.tenet.edu

Grade Span: PK-12 **Schools**: *Regular* 30 ● *Spec Ed* 1 ● *Alt* 1 **Students**: 36,587 **Total Teachers**: 2,219 **Student/Classroom Teacher Ratio**: 16.2	**Expenditures/Student**: $4,541 **Librarians**: 32.0 1,143 students/librarian **Guidance Counselors**: 65.5 559 students/counselor	**% Amer Indian**: 0.1 **% Asian**: 19.4 **% Black**: 32.5 **% Hispanic**: 27.6 **% White**: 20.4	National ***Socio-Economic Status*** indicator percentile (100=high): 29th

Harris County

[BAYTOWN] **GOOSE CREEK INDEPENDENT S.D.**

P. O. BOX 30 ● BAYTOWN TX 77522-0030 ● (281) 420-4800

Grade Span: PK-12 **Schools**: *Regular* 21 ● *Spec Ed* 1 ● *Alt* 2 **Students**: 17,876 **Total Teachers**: 1,087 **Student/Classroom Teacher Ratio**: 16.7	**Expenditures/Student**: $4,922 **Librarians**: 20.0 894 students/librarian **Guidance Counselors**: 36.1 495 students/counselor	**% Amer Indian**: 0.2 **% Asian**: 0.8 **% Black**: 17.0 **% Hispanic**: 34.0 **% White**: 48.1	National ***Socio-Economic Status*** indicator percentile (100=high): 27th

Harris County

CHANNELVIEW INDEPENDENT S.D.

1403 SHELDON ROAD ● CHANNELVIEW TX 77530-2603 ● (281) 452-8008

Grade Span: PK-12 **Schools**: *Regular* 7 ● *Spec Ed* 0 ● *Alt* 1 **Students**: 5,698 **Total Teachers**: 313 **Student/Classroom Teacher Ratio**: 17.9	**Expenditures/Student**: $4,620 **Librarians**: 5.0 1,140 students/librarian **Guidance Counselors**: 11.0 518 students/counselor	**% Amer Indian**: 0.1 **% Asian**: 2.0 **% Black**: 10.3 **% Hispanic**: 32.8 **% White**: 54.8	National ***Socio-Economic Status*** indicator percentile (100=high): 29th

Harris County
CROSBY INDEPENDENT S.D.
P. O. BOX 2009 ● CROSBY TX 77532-2009 ● (281) 328-9200

Grade Span: PK-12 **Schools**: *Regular* 5 ● *Spec Ed* 1 ● *Alt* 0 **Students**: 3,791 **Total Teachers**: 233 **Student/Classroom Teacher Ratio**: 16.0	**Expenditures/Student**: $4,754 **Librarians**: 5.0 758 students/librarian **Guidance Counselors**: 9.0 421 students/counselor	**% Amer Indian**: 0.3 **% Asian**: 0.5 **% Black**: 24.4 **% Hispanic**: 8.2 **% White**: 66.5	National ***Socio-Economic Status*** indicator percentile (100=high): 46th

Harris County
DEER PARK INDEPENDENT S.D.
203 IVY AVENUE ● DEER PARK TX 77536-2747 ● (281) 930-4600 ● http://internet.deer-park.isd.tenet.edu

Grade Span: PK-12 **Schools**: *Regular* 12 ● *Spec Ed* 0 ● *Alt* 1 **Students**: 11,352 **Total Teachers**: 706 **Student/Classroom Teacher Ratio**: 16.3	**Expenditures/Student**: $4,985 **Librarians**: 14.0 811 students/librarian **Guidance Counselors**: 25.1 452 students/counselor	**% Amer Indian**: 0.3 **% Asian**: 1.8 **% Black**: 1.1 **% Hispanic**: 20.7 **% White**: 76.2	National ***Socio-Economic Status*** indicator percentile (100=high): 68th

Harris County
GALENA PARK INDEPENDENT S.D.
P. O. BOX 565 ● GALENA PARK TX 77547-0565 ● (713) 672-7491 ● http://www.galena-park.isd.tenet.edu

Grade Span: PK-12 **Schools**: *Regular* 18 ● *Spec Ed* 0 ● *Alt* 1 **Students**: 17,439 **Total Teachers**: 977 **Student/Classroom Teacher Ratio**: 17.9	**Expenditures/Student**: $4,325 **Librarians**: 13.0 1,341 students/librarian **Guidance Counselors**: 33.0 528 students/counselor	**% Amer Indian**: 0.1 **% Asian**: 2.4 **% Black**: 20.0 **% Hispanic**: 50.1 **% White**: 27.4	National ***Socio-Economic Status*** indicator percentile (100=high): 14th

Harris County
[HOUSTON] **ALDINE INDEPENDENT S.D.**
14910 ALDINE WESTFIELD RD. ● HOUSTON TX 77032-3099 ● (713) 449-1011 ● http://www.aldine.k12.tx.us

Grade Span: PK-12 **Schools**: *Regular* 47 ● *Spec Ed* 1 ● *Alt* 0 **Students**: 45,139 **Total Teachers**: 2,975 **Student/Classroom Teacher Ratio**: 15.5	**Expenditures/Student**: $4,954 **Librarians**: 45.4 994 students/librarian **Guidance Counselors**: 104.7 431 students/counselor	**% Amer Indian**: 0.1 **% Asian**: 4.0 **% Black**: 35.4 **% Hispanic**: 40.4 **% White**: 20.2	National ***Socio-Economic Status*** indicator percentile (100=high): 13th

Harris County
[HOUSTON] **CYPRESS-FAIRBANKS INDEPENDENT S.D.**
BOX 692003 ● HOUSTON TX 77269-2003 ● (713) 897-4000 ● http://www.cy-fair.isd.tenet.edu

Grade Span: PK-12 **Schools**: *Regular* 45 ● *Spec Ed* 2 ● *Alt* 2 **Students**: 50,817 **Total Teachers**: 3,113 **Student/Classroom Teacher Ratio**: 16.7	**Expenditures/Student**: $4,746 **Librarians**: 56.6 898 students/librarian **Guidance Counselors**: 108.5 468 students/counselor	**% Amer Indian**: 0.2 **% Asian**: 7.3 **% Black**: 8.9 **% Hispanic**: 16.4 **% White**: 67.3	National ***Socio-Economic Status*** indicator percentile (100=high): 73rd

Harris County
HOUSTON INDEPENDENT S.D.
3830 RICHMOND AVENUE ● HOUSTON TX 77027-5838 ● (713) 892-6000 ● http://www.houston.isd.tenet.edu

Grade Span: PK-12 **Schools**: *Regular* 250 ● *Spec Ed* 3 ● *Alt* 19 **Students**: 206,704 **Total Teachers**: 11,935 **Student/Classroom Teacher Ratio**: 17.5	**Expenditures/Student**: $4,801 **Librarians**: 241.4 856 students/librarian **Guidance Counselors**: 354.6 583 students/counselor	**% Amer Indian**: 0.1 **% Asian**: 2.7 **% Black**: 34.7 **% Hispanic**: 51.2 **% White**: 11.3	National ***Socio-Economic Status*** indicator percentile (100=high): 8th

Harris County
[HOUSTON] **NORTH FOREST INDEPENDENT S.D.**
P. O. BOX 23278 ● HOUSTON TX 77228-3278 ● (713) 633-1600

Grade Span: PK-12 **Schools**: *Regular* 16 ● *Spec Ed* 0 ● *Alt* 0 **Students**: 13,450 **Total Teachers**: 843 **Student/Classroom Teacher Ratio**: 17.4	**Expenditures/Student**: $5,248 **Librarians**: 18.0 747 students/librarian **Guidance Counselors**: 36.0 374 students/counselor	**% Amer Indian**: 0.0 **% Asian**: 0.1 **% Black**: 85.6 **% Hispanic**: 13.2 **% White**: 1.1	National ***Socio-Economic Status*** indicator percentile (100=high): 5th

Harris County
[HOUSTON] **SHELDON INDEPENDENT S.D.**
8540 C. E. KING PARKWAY ● HOUSTON TX 77044-2002 ● (713) 459-7301

Grade Span: PK-12 **Schools**: *Regular* 6 ● *Spec Ed* 0 ● *Alt* 0 **Students**: 3,917 **Total Teachers**: 245 **Student/Classroom Teacher Ratio**: 16.0	**Expenditures/Student**: $5,087 **Librarians**: 5.0 783 students/librarian **Guidance Counselors**: 7.1 552 students/counselor	**% Amer Indian**: 0.1 **% Asian**: 1.4 **% Black**: 22.5 **% Hispanic**: 22.7 **% White**: 53.2	National ***Socio-Economic Status*** indicator percentile (100=high): 26th

Harris County
[HOUSTON] **SPRING BRANCH INDEPENDENT S.D.**
955 CAMPBELL ROAD ● HOUSTON TX 77024-2803 ● (713) 464-1511 ● http://www.spring-branch.isd.tenet.edu

Grade Span: PK-12 **Schools**: *Regular* 34 ● *Spec Ed* 1 ● *Alt* 1 **Students**: 29,543 **Total Teachers**: 1,885 **Student/Classroom Teacher Ratio**: 16.3	**Expenditures/Student**: $5,400 **Librarians**: 28.8 1,026 students/librarian **Guidance Counselors**: 63.8 463 students/counselor	**% Amer Indian**: 0.1 **% Asian**: 8.1 **% Black**: 7.3 **% Hispanic**: 42.9 **% White**: 41.6	National ***Socio-Economic Status*** indicator percentile (100=high): 21st

Harris County
[HOUSTON] **SPRING INDEPENDENT S.D.**
16717 ELLA BLVD. ● HOUSTON TX 77090-4213 ● (713) 586-1100 ● http://hiway.spring.isd.tenet.edu

Grade Span: PK-12 **Schools**: *Regular* 20 ● *Spec Ed* 1 ● *Alt* 1 **Students**: 20,246 **Total Teachers**: 1,254 **Student/Classroom Teacher Ratio**: 15.9	**Expenditures/Student**: $4,800 **Librarians**: 21.0 964 students/librarian **Guidance Counselors**: 48.2 420 students/counselor	**% Amer Indian**: 0.3 **% Asian**: 5.7 **% Black**: 19.7 **% Hispanic**: 18.1 **% White**: 56.1	National ***Socio-Economic Status*** indicator percentile (100=high): 58th

Harris County
HUMBLE INDEPENDENT S.D.
P. O. BOX 2000 ● HUMBLE TX 77347-2000 ● (281) 540-5000 ● http://www.humble.k12.tx.us

Grade Span: PK-12 **Schools**: *Regular* 26 ● *Spec Ed* 0 ● *Alt* 2 **Students**: 22,159 **Total Teachers**: 1,472 **Student/Classroom Teacher Ratio**: 15.0	**Expenditures/Student**: $4,560 **Librarians**: 22.9 968 students/librarian **Guidance Counselors**: 56.6 392 students/counselor	**% Amer Indian**: 0.2 **% Asian**: 2.6 **% Black**: 7.6 **% Hispanic**: 9.0 **% White**: 80.7	National ***Socio-Economic Status*** indicator percentile (100=high): 81st

Harris County
KATY INDEPENDENT S.D.
P. O. BOX 159 ● KATY TX 77492-0159 ● (281) 391-2184 ● http://www.katy.isd.tenet.edu

Grade Span: PK-12 **Schools**: *Regular* 22 ● *Spec Ed* 0 ● *Alt* 1 **Students**: 25,231 **Total Teachers**: 1,477 **Student/Classroom Teacher Ratio**: 17.1	**Expenditures/Student**: $4,361 **Librarians**: 25.2 1,001 students/librarian **Guidance Counselors**: 45.0 561 students/counselor	**% Amer Indian**: 0.1 **% Asian**: 4.1 **% Black**: 4.7 **% Hispanic**: 11.5 **% White**: 79.7	National ***Socio-Economic Status*** indicator percentile (100=high): 84th

Harris County

KLEIN INDEPENDENT S.D.

7200 SPRING-CYPRESS ROAD ● KLEIN TX 77379-3299 ● (281) 376-4180 ● http://www.klein.texas.schools.esc4.net

Grade Span: PK-12	**Expenditures/Student**: $4,761	**% Amer Indian**: 0.3	
Schools: *Regular* 27 ● *Spec Ed* 0 ● *Alt* 0	**Librarians**: 40.0	**% Asian**: 6.8	National ***Socio-Economic***
Students: 29,324	733 students/librarian	**% Black**: 11.3	***Status*** indicator percentile
Total Teachers: 1,802	**Guidance Counselors**: 69.1	**% Hispanic**: 12.8	(100=high): 76th
Student/Classroom Teacher Ratio: 16.3	424 students/counselor	**% White**: 68.8	

Harris County

LA PORTE INDEPENDENT S.D.

301 EAST FAIRMONT PARKWAY ● LA PORTE TX 77571-6496 ● (281) 842-2550 ● http://www.hti.net/~baker/lpisd.htm

Grade Span: PK-12	**Expenditures/Student**: $5,162	**% Amer Indian**: 0.3	
Schools: *Regular* 12 ● *Spec Ed* 0 ● *Alt* 1	**Librarians**: 10.0	**% Asian**: 1.2	National ***Socio-Economic***
Students: 7,444	744 students/librarian	**% Black**: 8.4	***Status*** indicator percentile
Total Teachers: 456	**Guidance Counselors**: 17.0	**% Hispanic**: 18.7	(100=high): 68th
Student/Classroom Teacher Ratio: 16.4	438 students/counselor	**% White**: 71.3	

Harris County

PASADENA INDEPENDENT S.D.

P. O. BOX 1799 ● PASADENA TX 77501-1799 ● (713) 920-6800

Grade Span: PK-12	**Expenditures/Student**: $4,605	**% Amer Indian**: 0.3	
Schools: *Regular* 49 ● *Spec Ed* 0 ● *Alt* 3	**Librarians**: 44.9	**% Asian**: 3.6	National ***Socio-Economic***
Students: 40,053	892 students/librarian	**% Black**: 5.4	***Status*** indicator percentile
Total Teachers: 2,326	**Guidance Counselors**: 71.0	**% Hispanic**: 51.3	(100=high): 21st
Student/Classroom Teacher Ratio: 17.2	564 students/counselor	**% White**: 39.4	

Harris County

TOMBALL INDEPENDENT S.D.

221 WEST MAIN ST. ● TOMBALL TX 77375-5529 ● (281) 357-3100

Grade Span: PK-12	**Expenditures/Student**: $4,646	**% Amer Indian**: 0.2	
Schools: *Regular* 7 ● *Spec Ed* 0 ● *Alt* 1	**Librarians**: 7.0	**% Asian**: 0.9	National ***Socio-Economic***
Students: 5,862	837 students/librarian	**% Black**: 3.4	***Status*** indicator percentile
Total Teachers: 362	**Guidance Counselors**: 12.2	**% Hispanic**: 8.0	(100=high): 82nd
Student/Classroom Teacher Ratio: 16.3	480 students/counselor	**% White**: 87.5	

Harrison County

HALLSVILLE INDEPENDENT S.D.

P. O. BOX 810 ● HALLSVILLE TX 75650-0810 ● (903) 660-4473

Grade Span: PK-12	**Expenditures/Student**: $4,502	**% Amer Indian**: 0.4	
Schools: *Regular* 6 ● *Spec Ed* 0 ● *Alt* 0	**Librarians**: 1.7	**% Asian**: 0.2	National ***Socio-Economic***
Students: 3,557	2,092 students/librarian	**% Black**: 6.1	***Status*** indicator percentile
Total Teachers: 229	**Guidance Counselors**: 7.0	**% Hispanic**: 2.2	(100=high): 66th
Student/Classroom Teacher Ratio: 15.7	508 students/counselor	**% White**: 91.1	

Harrison County

MARSHALL INDEPENDENT S.D.

P. O. BOX 879 ● MARSHALL TX 75671-0879 ● (903) 935-3914 ● http://marshall.isd.tenet.edu

Grade Span: PK-12	**Expenditures/Student**: $4,180	**% Amer Indian**: 0.1	
Schools: *Regular* 11 ● *Spec Ed* 0 ● *Alt* 1	**Librarians**: 6.5	**% Asian**: 0.3	National ***Socio-Economic***
Students: 6,299	969 students/librarian	**% Black**: 46.8	***Status*** indicator percentile
Total Teachers: 375	**Guidance Counselors**: 11.1	**% Hispanic**: 5.6	(100=high): 18th
Student/Classroom Teacher Ratio: 17.9	567 students/counselor	**% White**: 47.2	

Hays County

[KYLE] HAYS CONSOLIDATED INDEPENDENT S.D.

215100 IH 35 ● KYLE TX 78640-9530 ● (512) 268-2141 ● http://www.hays-cons.k12.tx.us

Grade Span: PK-12 **Schools**: *Regular* 7 ● *Spec Ed* 1 ● *Alt* 1 **Students**: 5,444 **Total Teachers**: 365 **Student/Classroom Teacher Ratio**: 15.1	**Expenditures/Student**: $5,013 **Librarians**: 9.0 605 students/librarian **Guidance Counselors**: 15.6 349 students/counselor	**% Amer Indian**: 0.1 **% Asian**: 0.3 **% Black**: 2.3 **% Hispanic**: 39.0 **% White**: 58.3	National ***Socio-Economic Status*** indicator percentile (100=high): 50th

Hays County

SAN MARCOS CONSOLIDATED INDEPENDENT S.D.

P. O. BOX 1087 ● SAN MARCOS TX 78667-1087 ● (512) 353-6700

Grade Span: PK-12 **Schools**: *Regular* 9 ● *Spec Ed* 0 ● *Alt* 1 **Students**: 6,649 **Total Teachers**: 457 **Student/Classroom Teacher Ratio**: 15.3	**Expenditures/Student**: $4,960 **Librarians**: 7.0 950 students/librarian **Guidance Counselors**: 19.0 350 students/counselor	**% Amer Indian**: 0.2 **% Asian**: 0.6 **% Black**: 4.3 **% Hispanic**: 61.6 **% White**: 33.4	National ***Socio-Economic Status*** indicator percentile (100=high): 16th

Henderson County

ATHENS INDEPENDENT S.D.

104 HAWN STREET ● ATHENS TX 75751-2423 ● (903) 677-6903

Grade Span: PK-12 **Schools**: *Regular* 6 ● *Spec Ed* 0 ● *Alt* 1 **Students**: 3,448 **Total Teachers**: 221 **Student/Classroom Teacher Ratio**: 15.5	**Expenditures/Student**: $4,220 **Librarians**: 3.0 1,149 students/librarian **Guidance Counselors**: 6.0 575 students/counselor	**% Amer Indian**: 0.1 **% Asian**: 0.3 **% Black**: 18.1 **% Hispanic**: 14.9 **% White**: 66.6	National ***Socio-Economic Status*** indicator percentile (100=high): 32nd

Hidalgo County

DONNA INDEPENDENT S.D.

116 NORTH 10TH. STREET ● DONNA TX 78537-2702 ● (956) 464-4461

Grade Span: PK-12 **Schools**: *Regular* 12 ● *Spec Ed* 0 ● *Alt* 0 **Students**: 9,391 **Total Teachers**: 594 **Student/Classroom Teacher Ratio**: 16.4	**Expenditures/Student**: $5,414 **Librarians**: 13.0 722 students/librarian **Guidance Counselors**: 25.9 363 students/counselor	**% Amer Indian**: 0.1 **% Asian**: 0.0 **% Black**: 0.1 **% Hispanic**: 98.2 **% White**: 1.6	National ***Socio-Economic Status*** indicator percentile (100=high): 9th

Hidalgo County

EDCOUCH-ELSA INDEPENDENT S.D.

P. O. BOX 127 ● EDCOUCH TX 78538-0127 ● (956) 262-2136

Grade Span: PK-12 **Schools**: *Regular* 6 ● *Spec Ed* 0 ● *Alt* 0 **Students**: 4,464 **Total Teachers**: 285 **Student/Classroom Teacher Ratio**: 16.2	**Expenditures/Student**: $5,312 **Librarians**: 5.0 893 students/librarian **Guidance Counselors**: 13.0 343 students/counselor	**% Amer Indian**: 0.1 **% Asian**: 0.0 **% Black**: 0.1 **% Hispanic**: 98.9 **% White**: 0.9	National ***Socio-Economic Status*** indicator percentile (100=high): 4th

Hidalgo County

EDINBURG CONSOLIDATED INDEPENDENT S.D.

P. O. BOX 990 ● EDINBURG TX 78540-0990 ● (956) 316-7200

Grade Span: PK-12 **Schools**: *Regular* 21 ● *Spec Ed* 0 ● *Alt* 2 **Students**: 18,710 **Total Teachers**: 1,144 **Student/Classroom Teacher Ratio**: 16.6	**Expenditures/Student**: $5,042 **Librarians**: 21.0 891 students/librarian **Guidance Counselors**: 52.8 354 students/counselor	**% Amer Indian**: 0.1 **% Asian**: 0.2 **% Black**: 0.1 **% Hispanic**: 95.0 **% White**: 4.5	National ***Socio-Economic Status*** indicator percentile (100=high): 2nd

Hidalgo County

HIDALGO INDEPENDENT S.D.

P. O. DRAWER D ● HIDALGO TX 78557-3004 ● (956) 843-3100 ● http://www.hidalgo.k12.tx.us

Grade Span: PK-12 **Schools**: *Regular* 4 ● *Spec Ed* 0 ● *Alt* 0 **Students**: 2,571 **Total Teachers**: 177 **Student/Classroom Teacher Ratio**: 14.8	**Expenditures/Student**: $5,820 **Librarians**: 3.0 857 students/librarian **Guidance Counselors**: 7.0 367 students/counselor	**% Amer Indian**: 0.0 **% Asian**: 0.0 **% Black**: 0.0 **% Hispanic**: 99.3 **% White**: 0.7	National ***Socio-Economic Status*** indicator percentile (100=high): 5th

Hidalgo County

LA JOYA INDEPENDENT S.D.

P. O. BOX J ● LA JOYA TX 78560-2009 ● (956) 580-5000

Grade Span: PK-12 **Schools**: *Regular* 13 ● *Spec Ed* 0 ● *Alt* 1 **Students**: 13,545 **Total Teachers**: 839 **Student/Classroom Teacher Ratio**: 16.5	**Expenditures/Student**: $5,070 **Librarians**: 13.0 1,042 students/librarian **Guidance Counselors**: 44.4 305 students/counselor	**% Amer Indian**: 0.0 **% Asian**: 0.0 **% Black**: 0.0 **% Hispanic**: 99.3 **% White**: 0.6	National ***Socio-Economic Status*** indicator percentile (100=high): 1st

Hidalgo County

MCALLEN INDEPENDENT S.D.

2000 NORTH 23RD. STREET ● MCALLEN TX 78501-6126 ● (956) 618-6000

Grade Span: PK-12 **Schools**: *Regular* 28 ● *Spec Ed* 1 ● *Alt* 2 **Students**: 21,830 **Total Teachers**: 1,419 **Student/Classroom Teacher Ratio**: 15.3	**Expenditures/Student**: $5,130 **Librarians**: 31.0 704 students/librarian **Guidance Counselors**: 79.5 275 students/counselor	**% Amer Indian**: 0.1 **% Asian**: 1.4 **% Black**: 0.4 **% Hispanic**: 86.7 **% White**: 11.5	National ***Socio-Economic Status*** indicator percentile (100=high): 11th

Hidalgo County

MERCEDES INDEPENDENT S.D.

P. O. BOX 419 ● MERCEDES TX 78570-0419 ● (956) 514-2000

Grade Span: PK-12 **Schools**: *Regular* 7 ● *Spec Ed* 0 ● *Alt* 1 **Students**: 5,103 **Total Teachers**: 293 **Student/Classroom Teacher Ratio**: 17.7	**Expenditures/Student**: $5,057 **Librarians**: 6.0 851 students/librarian **Guidance Counselors**: 13.0 393 students/counselor	**% Amer Indian**: 0.0 **% Asian**: 0.0 **% Black**: 0.1 **% Hispanic**: 98.2 **% White**: 1.6	National ***Socio-Economic Status*** indicator percentile (100=high): 4th

Hidalgo County

MISSION CONSOLIDATED INDEPENDENT S.D.

1201 BRYCE DRIVE ● MISSION TX 78572-4311 ● (956) 580-5500

Grade Span: PK-12 **Schools**: *Regular* 14 ● *Spec Ed* 0 ● *Alt* 0 **Students**: 11,746 **Total Teachers**: 763 **Student/Classroom Teacher Ratio**: 15.6	**Expenditures/Student**: $5,173 **Librarians**: 15.0 783 students/librarian **Guidance Counselors**: 35.0 336 students/counselor	**% Amer Indian**: 0.0 **% Asian**: 0.1 **% Black**: 0.1 **% Hispanic**: 95.7 **% White**: 4.1	National ***Socio-Economic Status*** indicator percentile (100=high): 1st

Hidalgo County

[MISSION] **SHARYLAND INDEPENDENT S.D.**

1106 NORTH SHARY ROAD ● MISSION TX 78572-4652 ● (956) 585-6701

Grade Span: PK-12 **Schools**: *Regular* 6 ● *Spec Ed* 1 ● *Alt* 0 **Students**: 4,298 **Total Teachers**: 261 **Student/Classroom Teacher Ratio**: 30.7	**Expenditures/Student**: $4,622 **Librarians**: 3.1 1,386 students/librarian **Guidance Counselors**: 10.0 430 students/counselor	**% Amer Indian**: 0.1 **% Asian**: 0.5 **% Black**: 0.1 **% Hispanic**: 77.2 **% White**: 22.0	National ***Socio-Economic Status*** indicator percentile (100=high): 19th

Hidalgo County

PHARR-SAN JUAN-ALAMO INDEPENDENT S.D.

P. O. BOX Y ● PHARR TX 78577-1225 ● (956) 702-5600 ● http://www.hiline.net/~psjaisd

Grade Span: PK-12 **Schools**: *Regular* 27 ● *Spec Ed* 0 ● *Alt* 2 **Students**: 20,299 **Total Teachers**: 1,243 **Student/Classroom Teacher Ratio**: 16.0	**Expenditures/Student**: $5,078 **Librarians**: 19.9 1,020 students/librarian **Guidance Counselors**: 55.2 368 students/counselor	**% Amer Indian**: 0.0 **% Asian**: 0.1 **% Black**: 0.1 **% Hispanic**: 98.0 **% White**: 1.8	National ***Socio-Economic Status*** indicator percentile (100=high): 5th

Hidalgo County

WESLACO INDEPENDENT S.D.

P. O. BOX 266 ● WESLACO TX 78596-0266 ● (956) 969-6500

Grade Span: PK-12 **Schools**: *Regular* 14 ● *Spec Ed* 1 ● *Alt* 1 **Students**: 12,814 **Total Teachers**: 790 **Student/Classroom Teacher Ratio**: 16.5	**Expenditures/Student**: $5,083 **Librarians**: 15.0 854 students/librarian **Guidance Counselors**: 42.9 299 students/counselor	**% Amer Indian**: 0.0 **% Asian**: 0.1 **% Black**: 0.1 **% Hispanic**: 96.3 **% White**: 3.5	National ***Socio-Economic Status*** indicator percentile (100=high): 1st

Hockley County

LEVELLAND INDEPENDENT S.D.

704 11TH. STREET ● LEVELLAND TX 79336-5499 ● (806) 894-9628

Grade Span: PK-12 **Schools**: *Regular* 9 ● *Spec Ed* 1 ● *Alt* 0 **Students**: 3,596 **Total Teachers**: 264 **Student/Classroom Teacher Ratio**: 14.6	**Expenditures/Student**: $5,242 **Librarians**: 7.0 514 students/librarian **Guidance Counselors**: 8.0 450 students/counselor	**% Amer Indian**: 0.2 **% Asian**: 0.1 **% Black**: 6.3 **% Hispanic**: 46.7 **% White**: 46.7	National ***Socio-Economic Status*** indicator percentile (100=high): 23rd

Hood County

GRANBURY INDEPENDENT S.D.

600 WEST PEARL ● GRANBURY TX 76048-2046 ● (817) 579-2200

Grade Span: PK-12 **Schools**: *Regular* 9 ● *Spec Ed* 0 ● *Alt* 1 **Students**: 5,816 **Total Teachers**: 366 **Student/Classroom Teacher Ratio**: 15.9	**Expenditures/Student**: $3,872 **Librarians**: 5.5 1,057 students/librarian **Guidance Counselors**: 13.0 447 students/counselor	**% Amer Indian**: 0.6 **% Asian**: 0.5 **% Black**: 0.6 **% Hispanic**: 7.8 **% White**: 90.5	National ***Socio-Economic Status*** indicator percentile (100=high): 53rd

Hopkins County

SULPHUR SPRINGS INDEPENDENT S.D.

631 CONNALLY ST. ● SULPHUR SPRINGS TX 75482-2401 ● (903) 885-2153

Grade Span: PK-12 **Schools**: *Regular* 8 ● *Spec Ed* 0 ● *Alt* 0 **Students**: 3,909 **Total Teachers**: 262 **Student/Classroom Teacher Ratio**: 14.9	**Expenditures/Student**: $4,426 **Librarians**: 2.3 1,700 students/librarian **Guidance Counselors**: 8.0 489 students/counselor	**% Amer Indian**: 0.1 **% Asian**: 0.5 **% Black**: 14.4 **% Hispanic**: 6.8 **% White**: 78.2	National ***Socio-Economic Status*** indicator percentile (100=high): 42nd

Howard County

BIG SPRING INDEPENDENT S.D.

708 ELEVENTH PLACE ● BIG SPRING TX 79720-0708 ● (915) 264-3600

Grade Span: PK-12 **Schools**: *Regular* 11 ● *Spec Ed* 0 ● *Alt* 1 **Students**: 4,480 **Total Teachers**: 300 **Student/Classroom Teacher Ratio**: 15.0	**Expenditures/Student**: $4,604 **Librarians**: 2.0 2,240 students/librarian **Guidance Counselors**: 9.0 498 students/counselor	**% Amer Indian**: 0.2 **% Asian**: 0.5 **% Black**: 6.0 **% Hispanic**: 45.9 **% White**: 47.5	National ***Socio-Economic Status*** indicator percentile (100=high): 20th

Hunt County
GREENVILLE INDEPENDENT S.D.
P. O. BOX 1022 ● GREENVILLE TX 75403-1022 ● (903) 457-2500 ● http://www.ednet10.net/greenville

Grade Span: PK-12 **Schools**: *Regular* 9 ● *Spec Ed* 0 ● *Alt* 1 **Students**: 5,372 **Total Teachers**: 369 **Student/Classroom Teacher Ratio**: 15.0	**Expenditures/Student**: $4,585 **Librarians**: 4.9 1,096 students/librarian **Guidance Counselors**: 10.7 502 students/counselor	**% Amer Indian**: 0.1 **% Asian**: 0.7 **% Black**: 26.5 **% Hispanic**: 12.1 **% White**: 60.6	National ***Socio-Economic Status*** indicator percentile (100=high): 25th

Hunt County
QUINLAN INDEPENDENT S.D.
P. O. BOX 466 ● QUINLAN TX 75474-0466 ● (903) 356-3293

Grade Span: PK-12 **Schools**: *Regular* 5 ● *Spec Ed* 0 ● *Alt* 0 **Students**: 2,649 **Total Teachers**: 171 **Student/Classroom Teacher Ratio**: 15.7	**Expenditures/Student**: $3,639 **Librarians**: 1.5 1,766 students/librarian **Guidance Counselors**: 4.1 646 students/counselor	**% Amer Indian**: 0.6 **% Asian**: 0.1 **% Black**: 0.3 **% Hispanic**: 5.9 **% White**: 93.1	National ***Socio-Economic Status*** indicator percentile (100=high): 30th

Hutchinson County
BORGER INDEPENDENT S.D.
200 EAST 9TH. ● BORGER TX 79007-3628 ● (806) 273-6481

Grade Span: PK-12 **Schools**: *Regular* 6 ● *Spec Ed* 0 ● *Alt* 0 **Students**: 3,318 **Total Teachers**: 218 **Student/Classroom Teacher Ratio**: 14.7	**Expenditures/Student**: $4,347 **Librarians**: 5.0 664 students/librarian **Guidance Counselors**: 5.0 664 students/counselor	**% Amer Indian**: 0.4 **% Asian**: 0.3 **% Black**: 4.2 **% Hispanic**: 22.4 **% White**: 72.6	National ***Socio-Economic Status*** indicator percentile (100=high): 52nd

Jasper County
JASPER INDEPENDENT S.D.
128 PARK STREET ● JASPER TX 75951-3499 ● (409) 384-2401

Grade Span: PK-12 **Schools**: *Regular* 4 ● *Spec Ed* 0 ● *Alt* 0 **Students**: 3,540 **Total Teachers**: 239 **Student/Classroom Teacher Ratio**: 15.0	**Expenditures/Student**: $4,823 **Librarians**: 4.0 885 students/librarian **Guidance Counselors**: 8.0 443 students/counselor	**% Amer Indian**: 0.1 **% Asian**: 0.3 **% Black**: 41.6 **% Hispanic**: 4.9 **% White**: 53.1	National ***Socio-Economic Status*** indicator percentile (100=high): 19th

Jefferson County
BEAUMONT INDEPENDENT S.D.
3395 HARRISON AVE. ● BEAUMONT TX 77706-5009 ● (409) 899-9972 ● http://www.esc05.k12.tx.us/beaumont/BISD.html

Grade Span: PK-12 **Schools**: *Regular* 31 ● *Spec Ed* 2 ● *Alt* 1 **Students**: 19,938 **Total Teachers**: 1,310 **Student/Classroom Teacher Ratio**: 15.2	**Expenditures/Student**: $5,205 **Librarians**: 19.0 1,049 students/librarian **Guidance Counselors**: 43.0 464 students/counselor	**% Amer Indian**: 0.1 **% Asian**: 2.5 **% Black**: 64.3 **% Hispanic**: 5.8 **% White**: 27.2	National ***Socio-Economic Status*** indicator percentile (100=high): 12th

Jefferson County
NEDERLAND INDEPENDENT S.D.
220 17TH. STREET ● NEDERLAND TX 77627-5098 ● (409) 724-2391 ● http://www.nederland.k12.tx.us

Grade Span: PK-12 **Schools**: *Regular* 7 ● *Spec Ed* 0 ● *Alt* 0 **Students**: 5,381 **Total Teachers**: 319 **Student/Classroom Teacher Ratio**: 17.0	**Expenditures/Student**: $4,396 **Librarians**: 7.0 769 students/librarian **Guidance Counselors**: 9.0 598 students/counselor	**% Amer Indian**: 0.0 **% Asian**: 2.2 **% Black**: 1.2 **% Hispanic**: 3.9 **% White**: 92.6	National ***Socio-Economic Status*** indicator percentile (100=high): 79th

Jefferson County
PORT ARTHUR INDEPENDENT S.D.
P. O. BOX 1388 ● PORT ARTHUR TX 77641-1388 ● (409) 989-6244 ● http://www.esc05.k12.tx.us/paisd/main.html

Grade Span: PK-12 **Schools**: *Regular* 15 ● *Spec Ed* 1 ● *Alt* 1 **Students**: 11,719 **Total Teachers**: 745 **Student/Classroom Teacher Ratio**: 15.8	**Expenditures/Student**: $5,433 **Librarians**: 15.0 781 students/librarian **Guidance Counselors**: 28.0 419 students/counselor	**% Amer Indian**: 0.1 **% Asian**: 9.2 **% Black**: 58.2 **% Hispanic**: 13.9 **% White**: 18.6	National ***Socio-Economic Status*** indicator percentile (100=high): 7th

Jefferson County
PORT NECHES-GROVES INDEPENDENT S.D.
620 AVENUE C ● PORT NECHES TX 77651-3798 ● (409) 722-3351 ● http://www.port-neches-groves.isd.tenet.edu

Grade Span: PK-12 **Schools**: *Regular* 9 ● *Spec Ed* 1 ● *Alt* 0 **Students**: 5,414 **Total Teachers**: 334 **Student/Classroom Teacher Ratio**: 16.4	**Expenditures/Student**: $4,318 **Librarians**: 10.0 541 students/librarian **Guidance Counselors**: 12.0 451 students/counselor	**% Amer Indian**: 0.1 **% Asian**: 1.3 **% Black**: 0.4 **% Hispanic**: 4.9 **% White**: 93.3	National ***Socio-Economic Status*** indicator percentile (100=high): 83rd

Jim Wells County
ALICE INDEPENDENT S.D.
1801 EAST MAIN STREET ● ALICE TX 78332-4140 ● (512) 664-0981

Grade Span: PK-12 **Schools**: *Regular* 11 ● *Spec Ed* 0 ● *Alt* 0 **Students**: 5,959 **Total Teachers**: 390 **Student/Classroom Teacher Ratio**: 15.6	**Expenditures/Student**: $4,846 **Librarians**: 9.2 648 students/librarian **Guidance Counselors**: 14.0 426 students/counselor	**% Amer Indian**: 0.1 **% Asian**: 0.4 **% Black**: 0.7 **% Hispanic**: 82.2 **% White**: 16.7	National ***Socio-Economic Status*** indicator percentile (100=high): 12th

Johnson County
ALVARADO INDEPENDENT S.D.
P. O. BOX 387 ● ALVARADO TX 76009-0387 ● (940) 783-2202 ● http://www.alvarado.isd.tenet.edu

Grade Span: PK-12 **Schools**: *Regular* 5 ● *Spec Ed* 0 ● *Alt* 0 **Students**: 2,637 **Total Teachers**: 160 **Student/Classroom Teacher Ratio**: 16.5	**Expenditures/Student**: $4,040 **Librarians**: 2.0 1,319 students/librarian **Guidance Counselors**: 6.0 440 students/counselor	**% Amer Indian**: 0.6 **% Asian**: 0.1 **% Black**: 4.6 **% Hispanic**: 11.5 **% White**: 83.2	National ***Socio-Economic Status*** indicator percentile (100=high): 35th

Johnson County
BURLESON INDEPENDENT S.D.
1160 SOUTH WEST WILSHIRE BLVD. ● BURLESON TX 76028-5719 ● (817) 447-5730

Grade Span: PK-12 **Schools**: *Regular* 7 ● *Spec Ed* 0 ● *Alt* 0 **Students**: 5,853 **Total Teachers**: 350 **Student/Classroom Teacher Ratio**: 17.3	**Expenditures/Student**: $4,241 **Librarians**: 5.0 1,171 students/librarian **Guidance Counselors**: 9.5 616 students/counselor	**% Amer Indian**: 0.2 **% Asian**: 0.5 **% Black**: 0.7 **% Hispanic**: 4.6 **% White**: 94.0	National ***Socio-Economic Status*** indicator percentile (100=high): 68th

Johnson County
CLEBURNE INDEPENDENT S.D.
103 SOUTH WALNUT ST. ● CLEBURNE TX 76031-5422 ● (817) 556-5600

Grade Span: PK-12 **Schools**: *Regular* 11 ● *Spec Ed* 2 ● *Alt* 1 **Students**: 5,720 **Total Teachers**: 338 **Student/Classroom Teacher Ratio**: 17.7	**Expenditures/Student**: $4,121 **Librarians**: 2.0 2,860 students/librarian **Guidance Counselors**: 12.9 443 students/counselor	**% Amer Indian**: 0.3 **% Asian**: 0.6 **% Black**: 5.8 **% Hispanic**: 17.6 **% White**: 75.7	National ***Socio-Economic Status*** indicator percentile (100=high): 32nd

Johnson County
JOSHUA INDEPENDENT S.D.
P. O. BOX 40 ● JOSHUA TX 76058-0040 ● (817) 558-3703

Grade Span: PK-12 **Schools**: *Regular* 4 ● *Spec Ed* 0 ● *Alt* 1 **Students**: 3,614 **Total Teachers**: 228 **Student/Classroom Teacher Ratio**: 15.9	**Expenditures/Student**: $3,996 **Librarians**: 2.0 1,807 students/librarian **Guidance Counselors**: 8.0 452 students/counselor	**% Amer Indian**: 0.2 **% Asian**: 0.1 **% Black**: 0.6 **% Hispanic**: 6.8 **% White**: 92.2	National ***Socio-Economic Status*** indicator percentile (100=high): 47th

Kaufman County
KAUFMAN INDEPENDENT S.D.
1000 SOUTH HOUSTON ST. ● KAUFMAN TX 75142-2298 ● (972) 932-2622

Grade Span: PK-12 **Schools**: *Regular* 5 ● *Spec Ed* 0 ● *Alt* 1 **Students**: 2,889 **Total Teachers**: 171 **Student/Classroom Teacher Ratio**: 17.0	**Expenditures/Student**: $3,626 **Librarians**: 2.0 1,445 students/librarian **Guidance Counselors**: 3.9 741 students/counselor	**% Amer Indian**: 0.1 **% Asian**: 0.2 **% Black**: 9.4 **% Hispanic**: 20.2 **% White**: 70.2	National ***Socio-Economic Status*** indicator percentile (100=high): 37th

Kaufman County
MABANK INDEPENDENT S.D.
124 E. MARKET ST. ● MABANK TX 75147-8377 ● (972) 887-9311

Grade Span: PK-12 **Schools**: *Regular* 4 ● *Spec Ed* 0 ● *Alt* 0 **Students**: 2,773 **Total Teachers**: 180 **Student/Classroom Teacher Ratio**: 15.6	**Expenditures/Student**: $4,341 **Librarians**: 4.0 693 students/librarian **Guidance Counselors**: 6.0 462 students/counselor	**% Amer Indian**: 0.4 **% Asian**: 0.2 **% Black**: 2.5 **% Hispanic**: 3.7 **% White**: 93.1	National ***Socio-Economic Status*** indicator percentile (100=high): 33rd

Kaufman County
TERRELL INDEPENDENT S.D.
212 WEST HIGH STREET ● TERRELL TX 75160-2613 ● (972) 563-7504

Grade Span: PK-12 **Schools**: *Regular* 7 ● *Spec Ed* 1 ● *Alt* 1 **Students**: 3,839 **Total Teachers**: 266 **Student/Classroom Teacher Ratio**: 15.1	**Expenditures/Student**: $4,678 **Librarians**: 4.6 835 students/librarian **Guidance Counselors**: 9.2 417 students/counselor	**% Amer Indian**: 0.1 **% Asian**: 1.1 **% Black**: 36.0 **% Hispanic**: 12.4 **% White**: 50.4	National ***Socio-Economic Status*** indicator percentile (100=high): 18th

Kendall County
BOERNE INDEPENDENT S.D.
123 WEST JOHNS ROAD ● BOERNE TX 78006-2023 ● (830) 249-2567 ● http://www.boerne.isd.tenet.edu

Grade Span: PK-12 **Schools**: *Regular* 5 ● *Spec Ed* 0 ● *Alt* 0 **Students**: 3,947 **Total Teachers**: 249 **Student/Classroom Teacher Ratio**: 16.2	**Expenditures/Student**: $4,137 **Librarians**: 4.0 987 students/librarian **Guidance Counselors**: 8.0 493 students/counselor	**% Amer Indian**: 0.1 **% Asian**: 0.3 **% Black**: 0.5 **% Hispanic**: 17.3 **% White**: 81.8	National ***Socio-Economic Status*** indicator percentile (100=high): 72nd

Kerr County
KERRVILLE INDEPENDENT S.D.
1009 BARNETT STREET ● KERRVILLE TX 78028-4614 ● (830) 257-2201 ● http://www.kerrvilleisd.com

Grade Span: PK-12 **Schools**: *Regular* 6 ● *Spec Ed* 0 ● *Alt* 2 **Students**: 4,637 **Total Teachers**: 299 **Student/Classroom Teacher Ratio**: 16.2	**Expenditures/Student**: $4,500 **Librarians**: 2.0 2,319 students/librarian **Guidance Counselors**: 11.6 400 students/counselor	**% Amer Indian**: 0.2 **% Asian**: 0.8 **% Black**: 3.5 **% Hispanic**: 32.4 **% White**: 63.0	National ***Socio-Economic Status*** indicator percentile (100=high): 33rd

Kleberg County
KINGSVILLE INDEPENDENT S.D.
P. O. BOX 871 ● KINGSVILLE TX 78364-0871 ● (512) 592-3387

Grade Span: PK-12	**Expenditures/Student**: $5,045	**% Amer Indian**: 0.2	
Schools: *Regular* 9 ● *Spec Ed* 1 ● *Alt* 2	**Librarians**: 6.0	**% Asian**: 1.2	National ***Socio-Economic***
Students: 5,136	856 students/librarian	**% Black**: 5.0	***Status*** indicator percentile
Total Teachers: 349	**Guidance Counselors**: 16.0	**% Hispanic**: 72.8	(100=high): 14th
Student/Classroom Teacher Ratio: 15.1	321 students/counselor	**% White**: 20.9	

Lamar County
[PARIS] NORTH LAMAR INDEPENDENT S.D.
3201 LEWIS LANE ● PARIS TX 75462-2092 ● (903) 737-2000

Grade Span: PK-12	**Expenditures/Student**: $4,257	**% Amer Indian**: 1.2	
Schools: *Regular* 5 ● *Spec Ed* 0 ● *Alt* 0	**Librarians**: 3.0	**% Asian**: 0.2	National ***Socio-Economic***
Students: 2,937	979 students/librarian	**% Black**: 5.1	***Status*** indicator percentile
Total Teachers: 193	**Guidance Counselors**: 6.0	**% Hispanic**: 0.8	(100=high): 60th
Student/Classroom Teacher Ratio: 15.3	490 students/counselor	**% White**: 92.7	

Lamar County
PARIS INDEPENDENT S.D.
1920 CLARKSVILLE ● PARIS TX 75460-1159 ● (903) 737-7473 ● http://www.neto.com/parisisd/top.htm

Grade Span: PK-12	**Expenditures/Student**: $5,201	**% Amer Indian**: 1.1	
Schools: *Regular* 6 ● *Spec Ed* 0 ● *Alt* 0	**Librarians**: 4.0	**% Asian**: 0.6	National ***Socio-Economic***
Students: 3,860	965 students/librarian	**% Black**: 39.1	***Status*** indicator percentile
Total Teachers: 282	**Guidance Counselors**: 12.5	**% Hispanic**: 2.2	(100=high): 15th
Student/Classroom Teacher Ratio: 14.0	309 students/counselor	**% White**: 57.1	

Lampasas County
LAMPASAS INDEPENDENT S.D.
207 WEST EIGHTH ST. ● LAMPASAS TX 76550-3125 ● (512) 556-6224

Grade Span: PK-12	**Expenditures/Student**: $4,135	**% Amer Indian**: 0.6	
Schools: *Regular* 4 ● *Spec Ed* 2 ● *Alt* 1	**Librarians**: 1.0	**% Asian**: 0.7	National ***Socio-Economic***
Students: 3,159	3,159 students/librarian	**% Black**: 3.6	***Status*** indicator percentile
Total Teachers: 199	**Guidance Counselors**: 5.9	**% Hispanic**: 15.8	(100=high): 31st
Student/Classroom Teacher Ratio: 15.9	535 students/counselor	**% White**: 79.3	

Liberty County
CLEVELAND INDEPENDENT S.D.
103 LEGION STREET ● CLEVELAND TX 77327-4709 ● (281) 592-8717

Grade Span: PK-12	**Expenditures/Student**: $4,647	**% Amer Indian**: 0.3	
Schools: *Regular* 4 ● *Spec Ed* 1 ● *Alt* 0	**Librarians**: 4.0	**% Asian**: 0.4	National ***Socio-Economic***
Students: 2,857	714 students/librarian	**% Black**: 21.3	***Status*** indicator percentile
Total Teachers: 186	**Guidance Counselors**: 7.0	**% Hispanic**: 16.7	(100=high): 17th
Student/Classroom Teacher Ratio: 15.2	408 students/counselor	**% White**: 61.3	

Liberty County
DAYTON INDEPENDENT S.D.
P. O. BOX 248 ● DAYTON TX 77535-0248 ● (409) 258-2667

Grade Span: PK-12	**Expenditures/Student**: $3,879	**% Amer Indian**: 0.1	
Schools: *Regular* 5 ● *Spec Ed* 0 ● *Alt* 0	**Librarians**: 4.0	**% Asian**: 0.3	National ***Socio-Economic***
Students: 3,947	987 students/librarian	**% Black**: 9.6	***Status*** indicator percentile
Total Teachers: 219	**Guidance Counselors**: 6.0	**% Hispanic**: 6.7	(100=high): 51st
Student/Classroom Teacher Ratio: 17.8	658 students/counselor	**% White**: 83.4	

Lubbock County

LUBBOCK INDEPENDENT S.D.

1628 19TH. STREET ● LUBBOCK TX 79401-4895 ● (806) 766-1000 ● http://www.lubbock.k12.tx.us

Grade Span: PK-12 **Schools**: *Regular* 55 ● *Spec Ed* 2 ● *Alt* 3 **Students**: 30,317 **Total Teachers**: 2,069 **Student/Classroom Teacher Ratio**: 14.1	**Expenditures/Student**: $4,922 **Librarians**: 34.0 892 students/librarian **Guidance Counselors**: 71.8 422 students/counselor	**% Amer Indian**: 0.2 **% Asian**: 1.1 **% Black**: 14.0 **% Hispanic**: 39.4 **% White**: 45.2	National ***Socio-Economic Status*** indicator percentile (100=high): 21st

Lubbock County

[WOLFFORTH] **FRENSHIP INDEPENDENT S.D.**

P. O. BOX 100 ● WOLFFORTH TX 79382-0100 ● (806) 866-9541

Grade Span: PK-12 **Schools**: *Regular* 8 ● *Spec Ed* 0 ● *Alt* 2 **Students**: 5,323 **Total Teachers**: 331 **Student/Classroom Teacher Ratio**: 16.0	**Expenditures/Student**: $3,962 **Librarians**: 4.0 1,331 students/librarian **Guidance Counselors**: 8.0 665 students/counselor	**% Amer Indian**: 0.1 **% Asian**: 1.0 **% Black**: 5.7 **% Hispanic**: 22.4 **% White**: 70.8	National ***Socio-Economic Status*** indicator percentile (100=high): 46th

McLennan County

[WACO] **CONNALLY INDEPENDENT S.D.**

715 NORTH RITA ● WACO TX 76705-1199 ● (254) 799-2426

Grade Span: PK-12 **Schools**: *Regular* 6 ● *Spec Ed* 0 ● *Alt* 0 **Students**: 2,510 **Total Teachers**: 170 **Student/Classroom Teacher Ratio**: 17.5	**Expenditures/Student**: $4,298 **Librarians**: 2.0 1,255 students/librarian **Guidance Counselors**: 4.0 628 students/counselor	**% Amer Indian**: 0.3 **% Asian**: 1.1 **% Black**: 12.6 **% Hispanic**: 13.1 **% White**: 72.8	National ***Socio-Economic Status*** indicator percentile (100=high): 34th

McLennan County

[WACO] **MIDWAY INDEPENDENT S.D.**

1205 FOUNDATION DRIVE ● WACO TX 76712-6899 ● (254) 666-7773

Grade Span: PK-12 **Schools**: *Regular* 8 ● *Spec Ed* 0 ● *Alt* 1 **Students**: 5,593 **Total Teachers**: 336 **Student/Classroom Teacher Ratio**: 16.6	**Expenditures/Student**: $4,107 **Librarians**: 8.0 699 students/librarian **Guidance Counselors**: 12.0 466 students/counselor	**% Amer Indian**: 0.4 **% Asian**: 2.1 **% Black**: 4.5 **% Hispanic**: 6.9 **% White**: 86.0	National ***Socio-Economic Status*** indicator percentile (100=high): 92nd

McLennan County

WACO INDEPENDENT S.D.

P. O. BOX 27 ● WACO TX 76703-0027 ● (254) 752-8341 ● http://www.waco.isd.tenet.edu

Grade Span: PK-12 **Schools**: *Regular* 24 ● *Spec Ed* 3 ● *Alt* 4 **Students**: 15,973 **Total Teachers**: 1,057 **Student/Classroom Teacher Ratio**: 14.8	**Expenditures/Student**: $5,166 **Librarians**: 18.0 887 students/librarian **Guidance Counselors**: 34.1 468 students/counselor	**% Amer Indian**: 0.0 **% Asian**: 0.5 **% Black**: 40.4 **% Hispanic**: 34.2 **% White**: 24.8	National ***Socio-Economic Status*** indicator percentile (100=high): 6th

Matagorda County

BAY CITY INDEPENDENT S.D.

1301 LIVE OAK, BOX 631 ● BAY CITY TX 77414-0631 ● (409) 245-5766

Grade Span: PK-12 **Schools**: *Regular* 7 ● *Spec Ed* 0 ● *Alt* 0 **Students**: 4,827 **Total Teachers**: 284 **Student/Classroom Teacher Ratio**: 17.2	**Expenditures/Student**: $4,508 **Librarians**: 6.0 805 students/librarian **Guidance Counselors**: 9.6 503 students/counselor	**% Amer Indian**: 0.1 **% Asian**: 0.9 **% Black**: 19.4 **% Hispanic**: 34.9 **% White**: 44.8	National ***Socio-Economic Status*** indicator percentile (100=high): 18th

Maverick County

EAGLE PASS INDEPENDENT S.D.

P. O. BOX 1409 ● EAGLE PASS TX 78853-1409 ● (830) 773-5181 ● http://www.eagle-pass.k12.tx.us

Grade Span: PK-12 **Schools**: *Regular* 13 ● *Spec Ed* 1 ● *Alt* 3 **Students**: 11,585 **Total Teachers**: 653 **Student/Classroom Teacher Ratio**: 17.3	**Expenditures/Student**: $4,454 **Librarians**: 2.1 5,517 students/librarian **Guidance Counselors**: 30.7 377 students/counselor	**% Amer Indian**: 0.9 **% Asian**: 0.4 **% Black**: 0.0 **% Hispanic**: 96.8 **% White**: 1.9	National ***Socio-Economic Status*** indicator percentile (100=high): 1st

Medina County

[CASTROVILLE] **MEDINA VALLEY INDEPENDENT S.D.**

8449 F. M. 471 S. ● CASTROVILLE TX 78009-9531 ● (830) 931-2243

Grade Span: PK-12 **Schools**: *Regular* 4 ● *Spec Ed* 0 ● *Alt* 1 **Students**: 2,544 **Total Teachers**: 137 **Student/Classroom Teacher Ratio**: 19.1	**Expenditures/Student**: $3,996 **Librarians**: 1.0 2,544 students/librarian **Guidance Counselors**: 4.0 636 students/counselor	**% Amer Indian**: 0.4 **% Asian**: 0.6 **% Black**: 0.5 **% Hispanic**: 44.5 **% White**: 54.0	National ***Socio-Economic Status*** indicator percentile (100=high): 35th

Midland County

MIDLAND INDEPENDENT S.D.

615 W. MISSOURI AVE. ● MIDLAND TX 79701-5017 ● (915) 689-1000

Grade Span: PK-12 **Schools**: *Regular* 32 ● *Spec Ed* 2 ● *Alt* 1 **Students**: 23,159 **Total Teachers**: 1,345 **Student/Classroom Teacher Ratio**: 17.8	**Expenditures/Student**: $4,352 **Librarians**: 24.9 930 students/librarian **Guidance Counselors**: 44.8 517 students/counselor	**% Amer Indian**: 0.3 **% Asian**: 1.0 **% Black**: 10.0 **% Hispanic**: 35.2 **% White**: 53.5	National ***Socio-Economic Status*** indicator percentile (100=high): 31st

Montgomery County

CONROE INDEPENDENT S.D.

702 NORTH THOMPSON ST. ● CONROE TX 77301-2557 ● (409) 756-7751 ● http://www.conroe.isd.tenet.edu

Grade Span: PK-12 **Schools**: *Regular* 31 ● *Spec Ed* 1 ● *Alt* 4 **Students**: 28,573 **Total Teachers**: 1,922 **Student/Classroom Teacher Ratio**: 15.2	**Expenditures/Student**: $5,345 **Librarians**: 33.5 853 students/librarian **Guidance Counselors**: 57.9 493 students/counselor	**% Amer Indian**: 0.1 **% Asian**: 1.4 **% Black**: 5.6 **% Hispanic**: 13.2 **% White**: 79.6	National ***Socio-Economic Status*** indicator percentile (100=high): 56th

Montgomery County

MAGNOLIA INDEPENDENT S.D.

P. O. BOX 88 ● MAGNOLIA TX 77355-0088 ● (281) 356-3570

Grade Span: PK-12 **Schools**: *Regular* 6 ● *Spec Ed* 0 ● *Alt* 0 **Students**: 4,599 **Total Teachers**: 281 **Student/Classroom Teacher Ratio**: 16.6	**Expenditures/Student**: $4,236 **Librarians**: 2.1 2,190 students/librarian **Guidance Counselors**: 8.9 517 students/counselor	**% Amer Indian**: 0.2 **% Asian**: 0.2 **% Black**: 2.4 **% Hispanic**: 10.6 **% White**: 86.7	National ***Socio-Economic Status*** indicator percentile (100=high): 51st

Montgomery County

MONTGOMERY INDEPENDENT S.D.

BOX 1475 ● MONTGOMERY TX 77356-1475 ● (409) 582-1333

Grade Span: PK-12 **Schools**: *Regular* 4 ● *Spec Ed* 0 ● *Alt* 0 **Students**: 2,658 **Total Teachers**: 176 **Student/Classroom Teacher Ratio**: 15.1	**Expenditures/Student**: $5,155 **Librarians**: 1.1 2,416 students/librarian **Guidance Counselors**: 5.0 532 students/counselor	**% Amer Indian**: 0.1 **% Asian**: 0.4 **% Black**: 8.9 **% Hispanic**: 4.9 **% White**: 85.7	National ***Socio-Economic Status*** indicator percentile (100=high): 58th

Montgomery County
NEW CANEY INDEPENDENT S.D.
RT. 4, BOX 89 ● NEW CANEY TX 77357-9804 ● (281) 354-1166

Grade Span: PK-12 **Schools**: *Regular* 6 ● *Spec Ed* 0 ● *Alt* 1 **Students**: 5,470 **Total Teachers**: 377 **Student/Classroom Teacher Ratio**: 14.9	**Expenditures/Student**: $4,898 **Librarians**: 6.9 793 students/librarian **Guidance Counselors**: 12.1 452 students/counselor	**% Amer Indian**: 0.1 **% Asian**: 0.3 **% Black**: 1.6 **% Hispanic**: 9.9 **% White**: 88.1	National ***Socio-Economic Status*** indicator percentile (100=high): 36th

Montgomery County
SPLENDORA INDEPENDENT S.D.
P. O. BOX 168 ● SPLENDORA TX 77372-0168 ● (281) 689-3128

Grade Span: PK-12 **Schools**: *Regular* 4 ● *Spec Ed* 0 ● *Alt* 0 **Students**: 2,556 **Total Teachers**: 166 **Student/Classroom Teacher Ratio**: 15.6	**Expenditures/Student**: $4,601 **Librarians**: 3.0 852 students/librarian **Guidance Counselors**: 6.0 426 students/counselor	**% Amer Indian**: 0.1 **% Asian**: 0.2 **% Black**: 0.3 **% Hispanic**: 6.8 **% White**: 92.7	National ***Socio-Economic Status*** indicator percentile (100=high): 25th

Montgomery County
WILLIS INDEPENDENT S.D.
204 WEST ROGERS STREET ● WILLIS TX 77378-9239 ● (409) 856-1200

Grade Span: PK-12 **Schools**: *Regular* 5 ● *Spec Ed* 0 ● *Alt* 1 **Students**: 3,785 **Total Teachers**: 253 **Student/Classroom Teacher Ratio**: 15.5	**Expenditures/Student**: $4,814 **Librarians**: 4.1 923 students/librarian **Guidance Counselors**: 8.1 467 students/counselor	**% Amer Indian**: 0.3 **% Asian**: 0.2 **% Black**: 9.4 **% Hispanic**: 11.2 **% White**: 79.0	National ***Socio-Economic Status*** indicator percentile (100=high): 36th

Moore County
DUMAS INDEPENDENT S.D.
P. O. BOX 615 ● DUMAS TX 79029-0615 ● (806) 935-6461

Grade Span: PK-12 **Schools**: *Regular* 8 ● *Spec Ed* 0 ● *Alt* 0 **Students**: 3,954 **Total Teachers**: 264 **Student/Classroom Teacher Ratio**: 15.1	**Expenditures/Student**: $4,464 **Librarians**: 7.0 565 students/librarian **Guidance Counselors**: 7.0 565 students/counselor	**% Amer Indian**: 0.3 **% Asian**: 1.5 **% Black**: 0.5 **% Hispanic**: 52.9 **% White**: 44.9	National ***Socio-Economic Status*** indicator percentile (100=high): 29th

Nacogdoches County
NACOGDOCHES INDEPENDENT S.D.
DRAWER 631521 ● NACOGDOCHES TX 75963-1521 ● (409) 569-5000

Grade Span: PK-12 **Schools**: *Regular* 8 ● *Spec Ed* 1 ● *Alt* 1 **Students**: 6,134 **Total Teachers**: 399 **Student/Classroom Teacher Ratio**: 17.3	**Expenditures/Student**: $4,756 **Librarians**: 8.0 767 students/librarian **Guidance Counselors**: 13.1 468 students/counselor	**% Amer Indian**: 0.1 **% Asian**: 0.7 **% Black**: 32.1 **% Hispanic**: 17.5 **% White**: 49.7	National ***Socio-Economic Status*** indicator percentile (100=high): 22nd

Navarro County
CORSICANA INDEPENDENT S.D.
601 NORTH 13TH. STREET ● CORSICANA TX 75110-3298 ● (903) 874-7441

Grade Span: PK-12 **Schools**: *Regular* 9 ● *Spec Ed* 0 ● *Alt* 1 **Students**: 4,966 **Total Teachers**: 347 **Student/Classroom Teacher Ratio**: 14.8	**Expenditures/Student**: $4,481 **Librarians**: 3.6 1,379 students/librarian **Guidance Counselors**: 15.0 331 students/counselor	**% Amer Indian**: 0.2 **% Asian**: 0.8 **% Black**: 31.1 **% Hispanic**: 15.2 **% White**: 52.6	National ***Socio-Economic Status*** indicator percentile (100=high): 19th

Nolan County

SWEETWATER INDEPENDENT S.D.

207 MUSGROVE STREET ● SWEETWATER TX 79556-5321 ● (915) 235-8601

Grade Span: PK-12	**Expenditures/Student**: $5,195	**% Amer Indian**: 0.1	
Schools: *Regular* 6 ● *Spec Ed* 0 ● *Alt* 2	**Librarians**: 2.0	**% Asian**: 0.1	National ***Socio-Economic***
Students: 2,851	1,426 students/librarian	**% Black**: 8.4	***Status*** indicator percentile
Total Teachers: 220	**Guidance Counselors**: 6.5	**% Hispanic**: 38.1	(100=high): 23rd
Student/Classroom Teacher Ratio: 14.0	439 students/counselor	**% White**: 53.2	

Nueces County

[CORPUS CHRISTI] CALALLEN INDEPENDENT S.D.

4205 WILDCAT DRIVE ● CORPUS CHRISTI TX 78410-5198 ● (512) 241-9321

Grade Span: PK-12	**Expenditures/Student**: $4,261	**% Amer Indian**: 0.2	
Schools: *Regular* 6 ● *Spec Ed* 0 ● *Alt* 0	**Librarians**: 4.0	**% Asian**: 0.4	National ***Socio-Economic***
Students: 4,767	1,192 students/librarian	**% Black**: 1.7	***Status*** indicator percentile
Total Teachers: 303	**Guidance Counselors**: 12.0	**% Hispanic**: 30.6	(100=high): 57th
Student/Classroom Teacher Ratio: 15.7	397 students/counselor	**% White**: 67.0	

Nueces County

CORPUS CHRISTI INDEPENDENT S.D.

P. O. BOX 110 ● CORPUS CHRISTI TX 78403-0110 ● (512) 886-9002

Grade Span: PK-12	**Expenditures/Student**: $4,653	**% Amer Indian**: 0.4	
Schools: *Regular* 55 ● *Spec Ed* 3 ● *Alt* 4	**Librarians**: 49.0	**% Asian**: 0.8	National ***Socio-Economic***
Students: 41,624	849 students/librarian	**% Black**: 5.8	***Status*** indicator percentile
Total Teachers: 2,427	**Guidance Counselors**: 121.9	**% Hispanic**: 67.8	(100=high): 19th
Student/Classroom Teacher Ratio: 17.0	341 students/counselor	**% White**: 25.3	

Nueces County

[CORPUS CHRISTI] FLOUR BLUFF INDEPENDENT S.D.

2505 WALDRON ROAD ● CORPUS CHRISTI TX 78418-4706 ● (512) 937-2681

Grade Span: PK-12	**Expenditures/Student**: $4,472	**% Amer Indian**: 0.7	
Schools: *Regular* 5 ● *Spec Ed* 0 ● *Alt* 1	**Librarians**: 5.0	**% Asian**: 3.9	National ***Socio-Economic***
Students: 5,402	1,080 students/librarian	**% Black**: 5.1	***Status*** indicator percentile
Total Teachers: 345	**Guidance Counselors**: 13.0	**% Hispanic**: 20.2	(100=high): 40th
Student/Classroom Teacher Ratio: 15.9	416 students/counselor	**% White**: 70.1	

Nueces County

[CORPUS CHRISTI] TULOSO-MIDWAY INDEPENDENT S.D.

P. O. BOX 10900 ● CORPUS CHRISTI TX 78460-0900 ● (512) 241-3286

Grade Span: PK-12	**Expenditures/Student**: $5,382	**% Amer Indian**: 0.2	
Schools: *Regular* 4 ● *Spec Ed* 0 ● *Alt* 1	**Librarians**: 1.1	**% Asian**: 0.3	National ***Socio-Economic***
Students: 2,884	2,622 students/librarian	**% Black**: 1.3	***Status*** indicator percentile
Total Teachers: 217	**Guidance Counselors**: 8.8	**% Hispanic**: 51.9	(100=high): 30th
Student/Classroom Teacher Ratio: 14.2	328 students/counselor	**% White**: 46.3	

Nueces County

ROBSTOWN INDEPENDENT S.D.

801 NORTH 1ST. STREET ● ROBSTOWN TX 78380-2608 ● (512) 387-9402 ● http://www.caller.com/educate/robstown/RISD_Home.html

Grade Span: PK-12	**Expenditures/Student**: $5,494	**% Amer Indian**: 0.1	
Schools: *Regular* 7 ● *Spec Ed* 0 ● *Alt* 1	**Librarians**: 7.0	**% Asian**: 0.0	National ***Socio-Economic***
Students: 4,437	634 students/librarian	**% Black**: 1.1	***Status*** indicator percentile
Total Teachers: 298	**Guidance Counselors**: 16.0	**% Hispanic**: 97.7	(100=high): 1st
Student/Classroom Teacher Ratio: 15.4	277 students/counselor	**% White**: 1.2	

Orange County
BRIDGE CITY INDEPENDENT S.D.
P. O. BOX 847 ● BRIDGE CITY TX 77611-0847 ● (409) 735-1502

Grade Span: PK-12 **Schools**: *Regular* 4 ● *Spec Ed* 0 ● *Alt* 0 **Students**: 2,845 **Total Teachers**: 189 **Student/Classroom Teacher Ratio**: 15.3	**Expenditures/Student**: $4,399 **Librarians**: 3.0 948 students/librarian **Guidance Counselors**: 5.1 558 students/counselor	**% Amer Indian**: 0.3 **% Asian**: 2.5 **% Black**: 0.2 **% Hispanic**: 3.2 **% White**: 93.7	National ***Socio-Economic Status*** indicator percentile (100=high): 55th

Orange County
[ORANGE] **LITTLE CYPRESS-MAURICEVILLE INDEPENDENT S.D.**
7293 NORTH 16TH. STREET ● ORANGE TX 77630-9808 ● (409) 883-2232

Grade Span: PK-12 **Schools**: *Regular* 6 ● *Spec Ed* 0 ● *Alt* 0 **Students**: 3,714 **Total Teachers**: 227 **Student/Classroom Teacher Ratio**: 16.0	**Expenditures/Student**: $4,452 **Librarians**: 4.0 929 students/librarian **Guidance Counselors**: 10.0 371 students/counselor	**% Amer Indian**: 0.4 **% Asian**: 0.8 **% Black**: 4.8 **% Hispanic**: 3.3 **% White**: 90.8	National ***Socio-Economic Status*** indicator percentile (100=high): 63rd

Orange County
[ORANGE] **WEST ORANGE-COVE CONSOLIDATED INDEPENDENT S.D.**
P. O. BOX 1107 ● ORANGE TX 77630-1107 ● (409) 882-5500 ● http://www.pnx.com/woccisd/index.htm

Grade Span: PK-12 **Schools**: *Regular* 7 ● *Spec Ed* 0 ● *Alt* 0 **Students**: 3,703 **Total Teachers**: 256 **Student/Classroom Teacher Ratio**: 15.6	**Expenditures/Student**: $6,108 **Librarians**: 6.0 617 students/librarian **Guidance Counselors**: 13.1 283 students/counselor	**% Amer Indian**: 0.1 **% Asian**: 0.2 **% Black**: 47.0 **% Hispanic**: 2.7 **% White**: 50.0	National ***Socio-Economic Status*** indicator percentile (100=high): 12th

Orange County
VIDOR INDEPENDENT S.D.
120 EAST BOLIVAR ST. ● VIDOR TX 77662-4907 ● (409) 769-2143

Grade Span: PK-12 **Schools**: *Regular* 6 ● *Spec Ed* 0 ● *Alt* 1 **Students**: 5,709 **Total Teachers**: 382 **Student/Classroom Teacher Ratio**: 15.1	**Expenditures/Student**: $4,451 **Librarians**: 5.0 1,142 students/librarian **Guidance Counselors**: 10.8 529 students/counselor	**% Amer Indian**: 0.1 **% Asian**: 0.1 **% Black**: 0.4 **% Hispanic**: 2.1 **% White**: 97.3	National ***Socio-Economic Status*** indicator percentile (100=high): 40th

Palo Pinto County
MINERAL WELLS INDEPENDENT S.D.
906 S. W. 5TH. AVENUE ● MINERAL WELLS TX 76067-4895 ● (940) 325-6404 ● http://www.mineral-wells.isd.tenet.edu

Grade Span: PK-12 **Schools**: *Regular* 5 ● *Spec Ed* 0 ● *Alt* 0 **Students**: 3,553 **Total Teachers**: 247 **Student/Classroom Teacher Ratio**: 15.0	**Expenditures/Student**: $4,407 **Librarians**: 3.0 1,184 students/librarian **Guidance Counselors**: 7.0 508 students/counselor	**% Amer Indian**: 0.5 **% Asian**: 0.7 **% Black**: 5.1 **% Hispanic**: 17.1 **% White**: 76.6	National ***Socio-Economic Status*** indicator percentile (100=high): 25th

Panola County
CARTHAGE INDEPENDENT S.D.
1 BULLDOG DRIVE ● CARTHAGE TX 75633-2370 ● (903) 693-3806

Grade Span: PK-12 **Schools**: *Regular* 5 ● *Spec Ed* 0 ● *Alt* 0 **Students**: 3,366 **Total Teachers**: 243 **Student/Classroom Teacher Ratio**: 14.0	**Expenditures/Student**: $5,177 **Librarians**: 5.0 673 students/librarian **Guidance Counselors**: 8.5 396 students/counselor	**% Amer Indian**: 0.1 **% Asian**: 0.1 **% Black**: 27.1 **% Hispanic**: 3.4 **% White**: 69.3	National ***Socio-Economic Status*** indicator percentile (100=high): 41st

Parker County
SPRINGTOWN INDEPENDENT S.D.
101 EAST SECOND STREET ● SPRINGTOWN TX 76082-2566 ● (817) 523-7243

Grade Span: PK-12 **Schools**: *Regular* 6 ● *Spec Ed* 0 ● *Alt* 1 **Students**: 2,856 **Total Teachers**: 190 **Student/Classroom Teacher Ratio**: 15.6	**Expenditures/Student**: $4,723 **Librarians**: 4.9 583 students/librarian **Guidance Counselors**: 6.0 476 students/counselor	**% Amer Indian**: 0.4 **% Asian**: 0.2 **% Black**: 0.3 **% Hispanic**: 4.1 **% White**: 94.9	National ***Socio-Economic Status*** indicator percentile (100=high): 44th

Parker County
WEATHERFORD INDEPENDENT S.D.
P. O. BOX 439 ● WEATHERFORD TX 76086-0439 ● (817) 598-2808

Grade Span: PK-12 **Schools**: *Regular* 8 ● *Spec Ed* 0 ● *Alt* 0 **Students**: 6,069 **Total Teachers**: 369 **Student/Classroom Teacher Ratio**: 16.7	**Expenditures/Student**: $4,104 **Librarians**: 2.0 3,035 students/librarian **Guidance Counselors**: 13.0 467 students/counselor	**% Amer Indian**: 0.3 **% Asian**: 0.4 **% Black**: 2.0 **% Hispanic**: 9.6 **% White**: 87.6	National ***Socio-Economic Status*** indicator percentile (100=high): 52nd

Pecos County
[FORT STOCKTON] FT. STOCKTON INDEPENDENT S.D.
101 WEST DIVISION ST. ● FORT STOCKTON TX 79735-7107 ● (915) 336-8517

Grade Span: PK-12 **Schools**: *Regular* 6 ● *Spec Ed* 0 ● *Alt* 1 **Students**: 2,949 **Total Teachers**: 221 **Student/Classroom Teacher Ratio**: 13.4	**Expenditures/Student**: $5,553 **Librarians**: 6.0 492 students/librarian **Guidance Counselors**: 8.0 369 students/counselor	**% Amer Indian**: 0.1 **% Asian**: 0.4 **% Black**: 0.6 **% Hispanic**: 74.1 **% White**: 24.8	National ***Socio-Economic Status*** indicator percentile (100=high): 16th

Polk County
LIVINGSTON INDEPENDENT S.D.
P. O. BOX 1297 ● LIVINGSTON TX 77351-1297 ● (409) 327-4351

Grade Span: PK-12 **Schools**: *Regular* 5 ● *Spec Ed* 0 ● *Alt* 0 **Students**: 3,860 **Total Teachers**: 216 **Student/Classroom Teacher Ratio**: 17.9	**Expenditures/Student**: $4,266 **Librarians**: 3.0 1,287 students/librarian **Guidance Counselors**: 10.8 357 students/counselor	**% Amer Indian**: 0.8 **% Asian**: 0.3 **% Black**: 13.1 **% Hispanic**: 7.4 **% White**: 78.4	National ***Socio-Economic Status*** indicator percentile (100=high): 30th

Potter County
AMARILLO INDEPENDENT S.D.
7200 I-40 WEST ● AMARILLO TX 79106-2598 ● (806) 354-4200 ● http://www.amarillo.isd.tenet.edu

Grade Span: PK-12 **Schools**: *Regular* 47 ● *Spec Ed* 2 ● *Alt* 1 **Students**: 29,958 **Total Teachers**: 1,853 **Student/Classroom Teacher Ratio**: 16.0	**Expenditures/Student**: $4,269 **Librarians**: 35.9 834 students/librarian **Guidance Counselors**: 76.7 391 students/counselor	**% Amer Indian**: 0.4 **% Asian**: 2.9 **% Black**: 9.6 **% Hispanic**: 27.6 **% White**: 59.5	National ***Socio-Economic Status*** indicator percentile (100=high): 71st

Randall County
CANYON INDEPENDENT S.D.
P. O. BOX 899 ● CANYON TX 79015-0899 ● (806) 656-6100

Grade Span: PK-12 **Schools**: *Regular* 12 ● *Spec Ed* 0 ● *Alt* 1 **Students**: 6,874 **Total Teachers**: 407 **Student/Classroom Teacher Ratio**: 17.1	**Expenditures/Student**: $3,798 **Librarians**: 12.0 573 students/librarian **Guidance Counselors**: 12.0 573 students/counselor	**% Amer Indian**: 0.4 **% Asian**: 0.8 **% Black**: 1.2 **% Hispanic**: 9.4 **% White**: 88.1	National ***Socio-Economic Status*** indicator percentile (100=high): 73rd

Reeves County

PECOS-BARSTOW-TOYAH INDEPENDENT S.D.

P. O. BOX 869 ● PECOS TX 79772-0869 ● (915) 447-7201

Grade Span: PK-12 **Schools**: *Regular* 9 ● *Spec Ed* 0 ● *Alt* 1 **Students**: 3,205 **Total Teachers**: 229 **Student/Classroom Teacher Ratio**: 14.4	**Expenditures/Student**: $4,680 **Librarians**: 4.9 654 students/librarian **Guidance Counselors**: 6.6 486 students/counselor	**% Amer Indian**: 0.1 **% Asian**: 0.2 **% Black**: 2.1 **% Hispanic**: 84.3 **% White**: 13.3	National ***Socio-Economic Status*** indicator percentile (100=high): 11th

Rockwall County

ROCKWALL INDEPENDENT S.D.

801 EAST WASHINGTON ST. ● ROCKWALL TX 75087-3832 ● (972) 771-0605

Grade Span: PK-12 **Schools**: *Regular* 9 ● *Spec Ed* 0 ● *Alt* 0 **Students**: 6,007 **Total Teachers**: 362 **Student/Classroom Teacher Ratio**: 16.0	**Expenditures/Student**: $4,021 **Librarians**: 9.0 667 students/librarian **Guidance Counselors**: 13.0 462 students/counselor	**% Amer Indian**: 0.2 **% Asian**: 1.0 **% Black**: 3.5 **% Hispanic**: 7.6 **% White**: 87.5	National ***Socio-Economic Status*** indicator percentile (100=high): 79th

Rusk County

HENDERSON INDEPENDENT S.D.

P. O. BOX 728 ● HENDERSON TX 75653-0728 ● (903) 657-8511

Grade Span: PK-12 **Schools**: *Regular* 7 ● *Spec Ed* 0 ● *Alt* 1 **Students**: 3,718 **Total Teachers**: 267 **Student/Classroom Teacher Ratio**: 14.2	**Expenditures/Student**: $4,751 **Librarians**: 5.0 744 students/librarian **Guidance Counselors**: 9.0 413 students/counselor	**% Amer Indian**: 0.0 **% Asian**: 0.4 **% Black**: 25.3 **% Hispanic**: 7.4 **% White**: 66.9	National ***Socio-Economic Status*** indicator percentile (100=high): 26th

San Patricio County

GREGORY-PORTLAND INDEPENDENT S.D.

P. O. BOX 338 ● GREGORY TX 78359-0338 ● (512) 643-6566 ● http://www.interconnect.net/gregport

Grade Span: PK-12 **Schools**: *Regular* 7 ● *Spec Ed* 0 ● *Alt* 0 **Students**: 4,223 **Total Teachers**: 261 **Student/Classroom Teacher Ratio**: 16.1	**Expenditures/Student**: $3,995 **Librarians**: 3.0 1,408 students/librarian **Guidance Counselors**: 5.6 754 students/counselor	**% Amer Indian**: 0.2 **% Asian**: 1.0 **% Black**: 1.4 **% Hispanic**: 39.2 **% White**: 58.2	National ***Socio-Economic Status*** indicator percentile (100=high): 52nd

Scurry County

SNYDER INDEPENDENT S.D.

2901 37TH. STREET ● SNYDER TX 79549-5226 ● (915) 573-5401

Grade Span: PK-12 **Schools**: *Regular* 7 ● *Spec Ed* 0 ● *Alt* 1 **Students**: 3,398 **Total Teachers**: 231 **Student/Classroom Teacher Ratio**: 15.0	**Expenditures/Student**: $5,123 **Librarians**: 7.0 485 students/librarian **Guidance Counselors**: 4.0 850 students/counselor	**% Amer Indian**: 0.3 **% Asian**: 0.3 **% Black**: 4.6 **% Hispanic**: 36.3 **% White**: 58.6	National ***Socio-Economic Status*** indicator percentile (100=high): 30th

Smith County

[TYLER] CHAPEL HILL INDEPENDENT S.D.

11134 CR 2249 ● TYLER TX 75707-9752 ● (903) 566-2441 ● http://www.esc8.net/chisd

Grade Span: PK-12 **Schools**: *Regular* 5 ● *Spec Ed* 0 ● *Alt* 1 **Students**: 3,294 **Total Teachers**: 236 **Student/Classroom Teacher Ratio**: 14.2	**Expenditures/Student**: $4,481 **Librarians**: 5.0 659 students/librarian **Guidance Counselors**: 6.8 484 students/counselor	**% Amer Indian**: 0.5 **% Asian**: 0.4 **% Black**: 27.1 **% Hispanic**: 8.9 **% White**: 63.1	National ***Socio-Economic Status*** indicator percentile (100=high): 36th

Smith County

TYLER INDEPENDENT S.D.

P. O. BOX 2035 ● TYLER TX 75710-2035 ● (903) 531-3500 ● http://www.tyler.k12.tx.us

Grade Span: PK-12 **Schools**: *Regular* 25 ● *Spec Ed* 2 ● *Alt* 1 **Students**: 16,534 **Total Teachers**: 1,086 **Student/Classroom Teacher Ratio**: 15.5	**Expenditures/Student**: $4,596 **Librarians**: 23.0 719 students/librarian **Guidance Counselors**: 34.7 476 students/counselor	**% Amer Indian**: 0.1 **% Asian**: 0.8 **% Black**: 36.0 **% Hispanic**: 18.6 **% White**: 44.6	National ***Socio-Economic Status*** indicator percentile (100=high): 27th

Smith County

WHITEHOUSE INDEPENDENT S.D.

106 W. WILDCAT DRIVE ● WHITEHOUSE TX 75791-3130 ● (903) 839-5500

Grade Span: PK-12 **Schools**: *Regular* 5 ● *Spec Ed* 0 ● *Alt* 0 **Students**: 3,609 **Total Teachers**: 237 **Student/Classroom Teacher Ratio**: 15.4	**Expenditures/Student**: $4,049 **Librarians**: 5.0 722 students/librarian **Guidance Counselors**: 6.0 602 students/counselor	**% Amer Indian**: 0.2 **% Asian**: 0.9 **% Black**: 8.7 **% Hispanic**: 2.7 **% White**: 87.5	National ***Socio-Economic Status*** indicator percentile (100=high): 72nd

Starr County

RIO GRANDE CITY INDEPENDENT S.D.

FORT RINGGOLD ● RIO GRANDE CITY TX 78582-4799 ● (956) 487-5591

Grade Span: PK-12 **Schools**: *Regular* 10 ● *Spec Ed* 0 ● *Alt* 1 **Students**: 7,944 **Total Teachers**: 494 **Student/Classroom Teacher Ratio**: 16.1	**Expenditures/Student**: $5,670 **Librarians**: 9.0 883 students/librarian **Guidance Counselors**: 23.9 332 students/counselor	**% Amer Indian**: 0.0 **% Asian**: 0.1 **% Black**: 0.0 **% Hispanic**: 99.5 **% White**: 0.4	National ***Socio-Economic Status*** indicator percentile (100=high): 1st

Starr County

ROMA INDEPENDENT S.D.

P. O. BOX 187 ● ROMA TX 78584-0187 ● (956) 849-1377

Grade Span: PK-12 **Schools**: *Regular* 8 ● *Spec Ed* 0 ● *Alt* 1 **Students**: 5,917 **Total Teachers**: 435 **Student/Classroom Teacher Ratio**: 15.6	**Expenditures/Student**: $6,054 **Librarians**: 5.0 1,183 students/librarian **Guidance Counselors**: 13.8 429 students/counselor	**% Amer Indian**: 0.0 **% Asian**: 0.0 **% Black**: 0.1 **% Hispanic**: 99.7 **% White**: 0.2	National ***Socio-Economic Status*** indicator percentile (100=high): 3rd

Tarrant County

ARLINGTON INDEPENDENT S.D.

1203 WEST PIONEER PARKWAY ● ARLINGTON TX 76013-6246 ● (817) 460-4611 ● http://www.arlington.isd.tenet.edu

Grade Span: PK-12 **Schools**: *Regular* 55 ● *Spec Ed* 3 ● *Alt* 3 **Students**: 51,960 **Total Teachers**: 3,037 **Student/Classroom Teacher Ratio**: 17.6	**Expenditures/Student**: $3,764 **Librarians**: 54.6 952 students/librarian **Guidance Counselors**: 93.5 556 students/counselor	**% Amer Indian**: 0.6 **% Asian**: 6.4 **% Black**: 16.0 **% Hispanic**: 15.6 **% White**: 61.4	National ***Socio-Economic Status*** indicator percentile (100=high): 51st

Tarrant County

AZLE INDEPENDENT S.D.

300 ROE STREET ● AZLE TX 76020-3194 ● (817) 444-3235

Grade Span: PK-12 **Schools**: *Regular* 8 ● *Spec Ed* 0 ● *Alt* 0 **Students**: 5,591 **Total Teachers**: 320 **Student/Classroom Teacher Ratio**: 17.5	**Expenditures/Student**: $3,982 **Librarians**: 2.0 2,796 students/librarian **Guidance Counselors**: 9.8 571 students/counselor	**% Amer Indian**: 0.5 **% Asian**: 0.3 **% Black**: 0.8 **% Hispanic**: 4.0 **% White**: 94.4	National ***Socio-Economic Status*** indicator percentile (100=high): 56th

Tarrant County
[BEDFORD] **HURST-EULESS-BEDFORD INDEPENDENT S.D.**
1849 CENTRAL DRIVE ● BEDFORD TX 76022-6096 ● (817) 283-4461 ● http://www.heb.isd.tenet.edu

Grade Span: PK-12 **Schools**: *Regular* 25 ● *Spec Ed* 2 ● *Alt* 1 **Students**: 19,243 **Total Teachers**: 1,174 **Student/Classroom Teacher Ratio**: 16.7	**Expenditures/Student**: $4,398 **Librarians**: 25.0 770 students/librarian **Guidance Counselors**: 41.8 460 students/counselor	**% Amer Indian**: 0.8 **% Asian**: 6.1 **% Black**: 6.0 **% Hispanic**: 9.1 **% White**: 78.0	National ***Socio-Economic Status*** indicator percentile (100=high): 64th

Tarrant County
CROWLEY INDEPENDENT S.D.
P. O. BOX 688 ● CROWLEY TX 76036-0688 ● (817) 297-5800

Grade Span: PK-12 **Schools**: *Regular* 9 ● *Spec Ed* 0 ● *Alt* 0 **Students**: 7,149 **Total Teachers**: 482 **Student/Classroom Teacher Ratio**: 15.7	**Expenditures/Student**: $4,420 **Librarians**: 7.0 1,021 students/librarian **Guidance Counselors**: 13.0 550 students/counselor	**% Amer Indian**: 0.6 **% Asian**: 3.5 **% Black**: 12.5 **% Hispanic**: 9.7 **% White**: 73.6	National ***Socio-Economic Status*** indicator percentile (100=high): 79th

Tarrant County
EVERMAN INDEPENDENT S.D.
608 TOWNLEY DRIVE ● EVERMAN TX 76140-5206 ● (817) 568-3500

Grade Span: PK-12 **Schools**: *Regular* 6 ● *Spec Ed* 0 ● *Alt* 0 **Students**: 3,290 **Total Teachers**: 208 **Student/Classroom Teacher Ratio**: 17.1	**Expenditures/Student**: $4,649 **Librarians**: 3.0 1,097 students/librarian **Guidance Counselors**: 7.4 445 students/counselor	**% Amer Indian**: 0.3 **% Asian**: 1.0 **% Black**: 55.8 **% Hispanic**: 14.0 **% White**: 28.9	National ***Socio-Economic Status*** indicator percentile (100=high): 15th

Tarrant County
[FORT WORTH] **BIRDVILLE INDEPENDENT S.D.**
6125 EAST BELKNAP ST. ● FORT WORTH TX 76117-4204 ● (817) 831-5700 ● http://www.birdville.k12.tx.us

Grade Span: PK-12 **Schools**: *Regular* 30 ● *Spec Ed* 1 ● *Alt* 3 **Students**: 20,129 **Total Teachers**: 1,223 **Student/Classroom Teacher Ratio**: 16.1	**Expenditures/Student**: $4,481 **Librarians**: 23.0 875 students/librarian **Guidance Counselors**: 41.0 491 students/counselor	**% Amer Indian**: 0.2 **% Asian**: 4.9 **% Black**: 2.6 **% Hispanic**: 10.5 **% White**: 81.8	National ***Socio-Economic Status*** indicator percentile (100=high): 63rd

Tarrant County
[FORT WORTH] **CASTLEBERRY INDEPENDENT S.D.**
315 CHURCHILL ROAD ● FORT WORTH TX 76114-3729 ● (817) 737-7235

Grade Span: PK-12 **Schools**: *Regular* 5 ● *Spec Ed* 0 ● *Alt* 2 **Students**: 3,138 **Total Teachers**: 210 **Student/Classroom Teacher Ratio**: 15.7	**Expenditures/Student**: $4,591 **Librarians**: 3.0 1,046 students/librarian **Guidance Counselors**: 9.0 349 students/counselor	**% Amer Indian**: 0.2 **% Asian**: 1.1 **% Black**: 1.3 **% Hispanic**: 25.1 **% White**: 72.4	National ***Socio-Economic Status*** indicator percentile (100=high): 27th

Tarrant County
[FORT WORTH] **EAGLE MT.-SAGINAW INDEPENDENT S.D.**
P. O. BOX 79160 ● FORT WORTH TX 76179-9160 ● (817) 232-0880

Grade Span: PK-12 **Schools**: *Regular* 7 ● *Spec Ed* 0 ● *Alt* 1 **Students**: 5,468 **Total Teachers**: 304 **Student/Classroom Teacher Ratio**: 18.0	**Expenditures/Student**: $3,955 **Librarians**: 7.0 781 students/librarian **Guidance Counselors**: 11.5 475 students/counselor	**% Amer Indian**: 0.3 **% Asian**: 5.4 **% Black**: 1.9 **% Hispanic**: 13.0 **% White**: 79.4	National ***Socio-Economic Status*** indicator percentile (100=high): 66th

Tarrant County
FORT WORTH INDEPENDENT S.D.
100 NORTH UNIVERSITY DR. ● FORT WORTH TX 76107-3010 ● (817) 871-2000 ● http://ftworth.isd.tenet.edu

Grade Span: PK-12 **Schools**: *Regular* 101 ● *Spec Ed* 11 ● *Alt* 17 **Students**: 74,021 **Total Teachers**: 4,165 **Student/Classroom Teacher Ratio**: 18.2	**Expenditures/Student**: $4,835 **Librarians**: 83.0 892 students/librarian **Guidance Counselors**: 162.0 457 students/counselor	**% Amer Indian**: 0.2 **% Asian**: 2.5 **% Black**: 33.7 **% Hispanic**: 36.9 **% White**: 26.8	National ***Socio-Economic Status*** indicator percentile (100=high): 12th

Tarrant County
GRAPEVINE-COLLEYVILLE INDEPENDENT S.D.
3051 IRA E. WOODS AVE. ● GRAPEVINE TX 76051-3897 ● (817) 488-9588 ● http://www.gcisd-k12.org/index.html

Grade Span: PK-12 **Schools**: *Regular* 15 ● *Spec Ed* 1 ● *Alt* 3 **Students**: 11,623 **Total Teachers**: 769 **Student/Classroom Teacher Ratio**: 15.0	**Expenditures/Student**: $4,747 **Librarians**: 16.0 726 students/librarian **Guidance Counselors**: 25.0 465 students/counselor	**% Amer Indian**: 0.4 **% Asian**: 2.1 **% Black**: 2.0 **% Hispanic**: 5.7 **% White**: 89.8	National ***Socio-Economic Status*** indicator percentile (100=high): 91st

Tarrant County
KELLER INDEPENDENT S.D.
328 LORINE ● KELLER TX 76248-0050 ● (817) 431-1555

Grade Span: PK-12 **Schools**: *Regular* 13 ● *Spec Ed* 0 ● *Alt* 1 **Students**: 11,880 **Total Teachers**: 624 **Student/Classroom Teacher Ratio**: 19.0	**Expenditures/Student**: $3,568 **Librarians**: 11.5 1,033 students/librarian **Guidance Counselors**: 16.0 743 students/counselor	**% Amer Indian**: 0.3 **% Asian**: 3.8 **% Black**: 3.2 **% Hispanic**: 5.8 **% White**: 86.8	National ***Socio-Economic Status*** indicator percentile (100=high): 85th

Tarrant County
MANSFIELD INDEPENDENT S.D.
605 EAST BROAD STREET ● MANSFIELD TX 76063-1766 ● (817) 473-5600

Grade Span: PK-12 **Schools**: *Regular* 11 ● *Spec Ed* 0 ● *Alt* 1 **Students**: 10,202 **Total Teachers**: 609 **Student/Classroom Teacher Ratio**: 16.8	**Expenditures/Student**: $4,027 **Librarians**: 10.0 1,020 students/librarian **Guidance Counselors**: 17.0 600 students/counselor	**% Amer Indian**: 0.5 **% Asian**: 2.5 **% Black**: 7.3 **% Hispanic**: 10.1 **% White**: 79.6	National ***Socio-Economic Status*** indicator percentile (100=high): 71st

Tarrant County
[SOUTHLAKE] CARROLL INDEPENDENT S.D.
1201 NORTH CARROLL AVE. ● SOUTHLAKE TX 76092-9405 ● (817) 481-5775 ● http://www.southlakecarroll.edu/INDEX2.HTM

Grade Span: PK-12 **Schools**: *Regular* 6 ● *Spec Ed* 0 ● *Alt* 0 **Students**: 4,142 **Total Teachers**: 279 **Student/Classroom Teacher Ratio**: 14.9	**Expenditures/Student**: $4,770 **Librarians**: 5.8 714 students/librarian **Guidance Counselors**: 8.1 511 students/counselor	**% Amer Indian**: 0.2 **% Asian**: 0.9 **% Black**: 1.0 **% Hispanic**: 2.1 **% White**: 95.7	National ***Socio-Economic Status*** indicator percentile (100=high): 100th

Tarrant County
WHITE SETTLEMENT INDEPENDENT S.D.
401 SOUTH CHERRY LANE ● WHITE SETTLEMENT TX 76108-2521 ● (817) 367-1350

Grade Span: PK-12 **Schools**: *Regular* 6 ● *Spec Ed* 0 ● *Alt* 1 **Students**: 4,301 **Total Teachers**: 271 **Student/Classroom Teacher Ratio**: 15.8	**Expenditures/Student**: $3,950 **Librarians**: 2.5 1,720 students/librarian **Guidance Counselors**: 4.8 896 students/counselor	**% Amer Indian**: 0.6 **% Asian**: 2.5 **% Black**: 6.6 **% Hispanic**: 11.2 **% White**: 79.1	National ***Socio-Economic Status*** indicator percentile (100=high): 49th

Taylor County

ABILENE INDEPENDENT S.D.

P. O. BOX 981 ● ABILENE TX 79604-0981 ● (915) 677-1444

Grade Span: PK-12 **Schools**: *Regular* 31 ● *Spec Ed* 8 ● *Alt* 3 **Students**: 19,649 **Total Teachers**: 1,432 **Student/Classroom Teacher Ratio**: 14.6	**Expenditures/Student**: $4,870 **Librarians**: 32.0 614 students/librarian **Guidance Counselors**: 50.8 387 students/counselor	**% Amer Indian**: 0.4 **% Asian**: 1.6 **% Black**: 10.4 **% Hispanic**: 25.6 **% White**: 62.0	National ***Socio-Economic Status*** indicator percentile (100=high): 27th

Taylor County

[ABILENE] **WYLIE INDEPENDENT S.D.**

7049 BUFFALO GAP ROAD ● ABILENE TX 79606-5448 ● (915) 692-4353 ● http://www.abilene.com/wisd

Grade Span: PK-12 **Schools**: *Regular* 6 ● *Spec Ed* 0 ● *Alt* 0 **Students**: 2,562 **Total Teachers**: 155 **Student/Classroom Teacher Ratio**: 16.8	**Expenditures/Student**: $3,501 **Librarians**: 2.0 1,281 students/librarian **Guidance Counselors**: 6.4 400 students/counselor	**% Amer Indian**: 0.1 **% Asian**: 1.2 **% Black**: 1.5 **% Hispanic**: 3.5 **% White**: 93.8	National ***Socio-Economic Status*** indicator percentile (100=high): 89th

Titus County

MOUNT PLEASANT INDEPENDENT S.D.

P. O. BOX 1117 ● MOUNT PLEASANT TX 75456-1117 ● (903) 572-6686 ● http://www.esc8.net/mpisd

Grade Span: PK-12 **Schools**: *Regular* 7 ● *Spec Ed* 0 ● *Alt* 1 **Students**: 4,290 **Total Teachers**: 317 **Student/Classroom Teacher Ratio**: 14.1	**Expenditures/Student**: $4,584 **Librarians**: 3.0 1,430 students/librarian **Guidance Counselors**: 10.0 429 students/counselor	**% Amer Indian**: 0.4 **% Asian**: 0.2 **% Black**: 18.5 **% Hispanic**: 31.2 **% White**: 49.6	National ***Socio-Economic Status*** indicator percentile (100=high): 20th

Tom Green County

SAN ANGELO INDEPENDENT S.D.

1621 UNIVERSITY AVE. ● SAN ANGELO TX 76904-5164 ● (915) 947-3700

Grade Span: PK-12 **Schools**: *Regular* 27 ● *Spec Ed* 0 ● *Alt* 2 **Students**: 17,489 **Total Teachers**: 1,051 **Student/Classroom Teacher Ratio**: 16.8	**Expenditures/Student**: $4,182 **Librarians**: 16.9 1,035 students/librarian **Guidance Counselors**: 37.5 466 students/counselor	**% Amer Indian**: 0.1 **% Asian**: 1.0 **% Black**: 5.9 **% Hispanic**: 41.9 **% White**: 51.1	National ***Socio-Economic Status*** indicator percentile (100=high): 39th

Travis County

AUSTIN INDEPENDENT S.D.

1111 WEST 6TH ST. ● AUSTIN TX 78703-5399 ● (512) 499-1700 ● http://www.austin.isd.tenet.edu

Grade Span: PK-12 **Schools**: *Regular* 94 ● *Spec Ed* 6 ● *Alt* 3 **Students**: 74,772 **Total Teachers**: 4,537 **Student/Classroom Teacher Ratio**: 16.2	**Expenditures/Student**: $4,884 **Librarians**: 91.4 818 students/librarian **Guidance Counselors**: 164.7 454 students/counselor	**% Amer Indian**: 0.3 **% Asian**: 2.3 **% Black**: 18.2 **% Hispanic**: 40.4 **% White**: 38.9	National ***Socio-Economic Status*** indicator percentile (100=high): 23rd

Travis County

[AUSTIN] **EANES INDEPENDENT S.D.**

601 CAMP CRAFT ROAD ● AUSTIN TX 78746-6511 ● (512) 329-3626

Grade Span: PK-12 **Schools**: *Regular* 8 ● *Spec Ed* 0 ● *Alt* 0 **Students**: 6,865 **Total Teachers**: 481 **Student/Classroom Teacher Ratio**: 14.1	**Expenditures/Student**: $5,443 **Librarians**: 9.0 763 students/librarian **Guidance Counselors**: 15.0 458 students/counselor	**% Amer Indian**: 0.5 **% Asian**: 4.3 **% Black**: 0.5 **% Hispanic**: 3.7 **% White**: 90.9	National ***Socio-Economic Status*** indicator percentile (100=high): 99th

Travis County

[AUSTIN] **LAKE TRAVIS INDEPENDENT S.D.**

3322 RANCH ROAD 620 SOUTH ● AUSTIN TX 78734-6801 ● (512) 263-4400

Grade Span: PK-12 **Schools**: *Regular* 4 ● *Spec Ed* 0 ● *Alt* 0 **Students**: 2,649 **Total Teachers**: 195 **Student/Classroom Teacher Ratio**: 13.8	**Expenditures/Student**: $4,961 **Librarians**: 4.0 662 students/librarian **Guidance Counselors**: 7.0 378 students/counselor	**% Amer Indian**: 0.3 **% Asian**: 0.5 **% Black**: 0.3 **% Hispanic**: 9.3 **% White**: 89.6	National ***Socio-Economic Status*** indicator percentile (100=high): 78th

Travis County

DEL VALLE INDEPENDENT S.D.

2404 SHAPARD LANE ● DEL VALLE TX 78617-9404 ● (512) 385-0890

Grade Span: PK-12 **Schools**: *Regular* 7 ● *Spec Ed* 0 ● *Alt* 1 **Students**: 4,745 **Total Teachers**: 353 **Student/Classroom Teacher Ratio**: 13.5	**Expenditures/Student**: $6,086 **Librarians**: 6.0 791 students/librarian **Guidance Counselors**: 16.8 282 students/counselor	**% Amer Indian**: 0.7 **% Asian**: 1.3 **% Black**: 12.4 **% Hispanic**: 53.2 **% White**: 32.5	National ***Socio-Economic Status*** indicator percentile (100=high): 28th

Travis County

PFLUGERVILLE INDEPENDENT S.D.

1401 WEST PECAN STREET ● PFLUGERVILLE TX 78660-2518 ● (512) 251-4159

Grade Span: PK-12 **Schools**: *Regular* 13 ● *Spec Ed* 0 ● *Alt* 1 **Students**: 9,689 **Total Teachers**: 596 **Student/Classroom Teacher Ratio**: 15.6	**Expenditures/Student**: $4,011 **Librarians**: 8.2 1,182 students/librarian **Guidance Counselors**: 16.1 602 students/counselor	**% Amer Indian**: 0.5 **% Asian**: 6.3 **% Black**: 11.7 **% Hispanic**: 18.6 **% White**: 63.1	National ***Socio-Economic Status*** indicator percentile (100=high): 81st

Uvalde County

UVALDE CONSOLIDATED INDEPENDENT S.D.

P. O. BOX 1909 ● UVALDE TX 78802-1909 ● (830) 278-6655 ● http://www.uvalde-cons.k12.tx.us

Grade Span: PK-12 **Schools**: *Regular* 9 ● *Spec Ed* 0 ● *Alt* 1 **Students**: 5,371 **Total Teachers**: 373 **Student/Classroom Teacher Ratio**: 14.3	**Expenditures/Student**: $4,538 **Librarians**: 7.0 767 students/librarian **Guidance Counselors**: 16.0 336 students/counselor	**% Amer Indian**: 0.0 **% Asian**: 0.3 **% Black**: 0.3 **% Hispanic**: 78.0 **% White**: 21.4	National ***Socio-Economic Status*** indicator percentile (100=high): 7th

Val Verde County

[DEL RIO] **SAN FELIPE-DEL RIO CONSOLIDATED INDEPENDENT S.D.**

P. O. BOX 420128 ● DEL RIO TX 78840-0128 ● (830) 774-9200

Grade Span: PK-12 **Schools**: *Regular* 15 ● *Spec Ed* 0 ● *Alt* 0 **Students**: 10,202 **Total Teachers**: 615 **Student/Classroom Teacher Ratio**: 17.0	**Expenditures/Student**: $4,786 **Librarians**: 9.0 1,134 students/librarian **Guidance Counselors**: 19.0 537 students/counselor	**% Amer Indian**: 0.1 **% Asian**: 0.4 **% Black**: 1.2 **% Hispanic**: 84.2 **% White**: 14.1	National ***Socio-Economic Status*** indicator percentile (100=high): 7th

Victoria County

VICTORIA INDEPENDENT S.D.

P. O. BOX 1759 ● VICTORIA TX 77902-1759 ● (512) 576-3131 ● http://www.visd.com

Grade Span: PK-12 **Schools**: *Regular* 20 ● *Spec Ed* 2 ● *Alt* 1 **Students**: 14,668 **Total Teachers**: 901 **Student/Classroom Teacher Ratio**: 15.8	**Expenditures/Student**: $4,779 **Librarians**: 17.0 863 students/librarian **Guidance Counselors**: 37.5 391 students/counselor	**% Amer Indian**: 0.1 **% Asian**: 0.7 **% Black**: 8.0 **% Hispanic**: 47.5 **% White**: 43.8	National ***Socio-Economic Status*** indicator percentile (100=high): 26th

Walker County

HUNTSVILLE INDEPENDENT S.D.

441 F.M. 2821 EAST ● HUNTSVILLE TX 77340-9298 ● (409) 295-3421

Grade Span: PK-12 **Schools**: *Regular* 8 ● *Spec Ed* 0 ● *Alt* 2 **Students**: 6,848 **Total Teachers**: 452 **Student/Classroom Teacher Ratio**: 15.2	**Expenditures/Student**: $4,459 **Librarians**: 8.6 796 students/librarian **Guidance Counselors**: 13.0 527 students/counselor	**% Amer Indian**: 0.1 **% Asian**: 0.7 **% Black**: 27.6 **% Hispanic**: 14.7 **% White**: 57.0	National ***Socio-Economic Status*** indicator percentile (100=high): 32nd

Waller County

WALLER INDEPENDENT S.D.

1918 KEY STREET ● WALLER TX 77484-1918 ● (409) 931-3685 ● http://www.hern.org/~waller

Grade Span: PK-12 **Schools**: *Regular* 5 ● *Spec Ed* 0 ● *Alt* 0 **Students**: 3,321 **Total Teachers**: 220 **Student/Classroom Teacher Ratio**: 15.2	**Expenditures/Student**: $4,750 **Librarians**: 5.0 664 students/librarian **Guidance Counselors**: 7.0 474 students/counselor	**% Amer Indian**: 0.2 **% Asian**: 1.1 **% Black**: 19.7 **% Hispanic**: 17.5 **% White**: 61.5	National ***Socio-Economic Status*** indicator percentile (100=high): 36th

Ward County

MONAHANS-WICKETT-PYOTE INDEPENDENT S.D.

606 SOUTH BETTY STREET ● MONAHANS TX 79756-5018 ● (915) 943-6711

Grade Span: PK-12 **Schools**: *Regular* 7 ● *Spec Ed* 0 ● *Alt* 0 **Students**: 2,526 **Total Teachers**: 171 **Student/Classroom Teacher Ratio**: 15.6	**Expenditures/Student**: $5,171 **Librarians**: 0.5 5,052 students/librarian **Guidance Counselors**: 4.0 632 students/counselor	**% Amer Indian**: 0.0 **% Asian**: 0.5 **% Black**: 5.1 **% Hispanic**: 45.4 **% White**: 48.9	National ***Socio-Economic Status*** indicator percentile (100=high): 25th

Washington County

BRENHAM INDEPENDENT S.D.

P. O. BOX 1147 ● BRENHAM TX 77833-1147 ● (409) 277-6500

Grade Span: PK-12 **Schools**: *Regular* 5 ● *Spec Ed* 1 ● *Alt* 1 **Students**: 4,782 **Total Teachers**: 304 **Student/Classroom Teacher Ratio**: 16.2	**Expenditures/Student**: $4,419 **Librarians**: 3.6 1,328 students/librarian **Guidance Counselors**: 10.9 439 students/counselor	**% Amer Indian**: 0.0 **% Asian**: 1.8 **% Black**: 30.7 **% Hispanic**: 8.1 **% White**: 59.3	National ***Socio-Economic Status*** indicator percentile (100=high): 35th

Webb County

LAREDO INDEPENDENT S.D.

1702 HOUSTON STREET ● LAREDO TX 78040-4906 ● (956) 727-4401

Grade Span: PK-12 **Schools**: *Regular* 28 ● *Spec Ed* 0 ● *Alt* 0 **Students**: 23,434 **Total Teachers**: 1,391 **Student/Classroom Teacher Ratio**: 17.3	**Expenditures/Student**: $5,076 **Librarians**: 30.7 763 students/librarian **Guidance Counselors**: 40.5 579 students/counselor	**% Amer Indian**: 0.0 **% Asian**: 0.1 **% Black**: 0.1 **% Hispanic**: 98.1 **% White**: 1.7	National ***Socio-Economic Status*** indicator percentile (100=high): 2nd

Webb County

[LAREDO] **UNITED INDEPENDENT S.D.**

201 LINDENWOOD DRIVE ● LAREDO TX 78041-2499 ● (956) 722-3938 ● http://www.united.isd.tenet.edu

Grade Span: PK-12 **Schools**: *Regular* 26 ● *Spec Ed* 0 ● *Alt* 1 **Students**: 19,765 **Total Teachers**: 1,211 **Student/Classroom Teacher Ratio**: 19.6	**Expenditures/Student**: $4,684 **Librarians**: 22.6 875 students/librarian **Guidance Counselors**: 49.0 403 students/counselor	**% Amer Indian**: 0.1 **% Asian**: 0.6 **% Black**: 0.1 **% Hispanic**: 94.0 **% White**: 5.1	National ***Socio-Economic Status*** indicator percentile (100=high): 8th

Wharton County

EL CAMPO INDEPENDENT S.D.

700 WEST NORRIS STREET ● EL CAMPO TX 77437-2499 ● (409) 543-6771 ● http://www2.esc3.tenet.edu/dweb/isds/elcampo

Grade Span: PK-12 **Schools**: *Regular* 5 ● *Spec Ed* 0 ● *Alt* 0 **Students**: 3,629 **Total Teachers**: 233 **Student/Classroom Teacher Ratio**: 15.8	**Expenditures/Student**: $4,570 **Librarians**: 3.0 1,210 students/librarian **Guidance Counselors**: 9.8 370 students/counselor	**% Amer Indian**: 0.0 **% Asian**: 0.4 **% Black**: 14.5 **% Hispanic**: 42.0 **% White**: 43.1	National ***Socio-Economic Status*** indicator percentile (100=high): 29th

Wharton County

WHARTON INDEPENDENT S.D.

2100 N. FULTON ST. ● WHARTON TX 77488-3146 ● (409) 532-3612 ● http://www.wharton.isd.tenet.edu

Grade Span: PK-12 **Schools**: *Regular* 5 ● *Spec Ed* 0 ● *Alt* 0 **Students**: 2,793 **Total Teachers**: 191 **Student/Classroom Teacher Ratio**: 15.2	**Expenditures/Student**: $5,044 **Librarians**: 4.0 698 students/librarian **Guidance Counselors**: 7.0 399 students/counselor	**% Amer Indian**: 0.1 **% Asian**: 0.2 **% Black**: 32.9 **% Hispanic**: 33.4 **% White**: 33.4	National ***Socio-Economic Status*** indicator percentile (100=high): 16th

Wichita County

BURKBURNETT INDEPENDENT S.D.

416 GLENDALE STREET ● BURKBURNETT TX 76354-2425 ● (940) 569-3326 ● http://www.wf.net/~bisdadm/BISD.html

Grade Span: PK-12 **Schools**: *Regular* 5 ● *Spec Ed* 0 ● *Alt* 0 **Students**: 3,764 **Total Teachers**: 258 **Student/Classroom Teacher Ratio**: 15.1	**Expenditures/Student**: $4,188 **Librarians**: 5.0 753 students/librarian **Guidance Counselors**: 6.0 627 students/counselor	**% Amer Indian**: 0.4 **% Asian**: 1.5 **% Black**: 8.7 **% Hispanic**: 5.3 **% White**: 84.1	National ***Socio-Economic Status*** indicator percentile (100=high): 63rd

Wichita County

WICHITA FALLS INDEPENDENT S.D.

P. O. BOX 2570 ● WICHITA FALLS TX 76307-2570 ● (940) 720-3273 ● http://www.wichita-falls.isd.tenet.edu/wfhs/index.htm

Grade Span: PK-12 **Schools**: *Regular* 25 ● *Spec Ed* 2 ● *Alt* 1 **Students**: 15,805 **Total Teachers**: 1,082 **Student/Classroom Teacher Ratio**: 15.3	**Expenditures/Student**: $4,688 **Librarians**: 27.0 585 students/librarian **Guidance Counselors**: 18.0 878 students/counselor	**% Amer Indian**: 0.4 **% Asian**: 2.6 **% Black**: 16.5 **% Hispanic**: 16.3 **% White**: 64.2	National ***Socio-Economic Status*** indicator percentile (100=high): 32nd

Wilbarger County

VERNON INDEPENDENT S.D.

1713 WILBARGER ST. #203 ● VERNON TX 76384-4741 ● (940) 553-1900

Grade Span: PK-12 **Schools**: *Regular* 5 ● *Spec Ed* 1 ● *Alt* 0 **Students**: 2,690 **Total Teachers**: 180 **Student/Classroom Teacher Ratio**: 15.6	**Expenditures/Student**: $4,149 **Librarians**: 2.1 1,281 students/librarian **Guidance Counselors**: 5.0 538 students/counselor	**% Amer Indian**: 0.4 **% Asian**: 0.3 **% Black**: 10.1 **% Hispanic**: 27.9 **% White**: 61.3	National ***Socio-Economic Status*** indicator percentile (100=high): 26th

Willacy County

RAYMONDVILLE INDEPENDENT S.D.

ONE BEARKAT BLVD. ● RAYMONDVILLE TX 78580-3351 ● (956) 689-2471

Grade Span: PK-12 **Schools**: *Regular* 4 ● *Spec Ed* 0 ● *Alt* 0 **Students**: 2,925 **Total Teachers**: 199 **Student/Classroom Teacher Ratio**: 15.0	**Expenditures/Student**: $5,208 **Librarians**: 3.0 975 students/librarian **Guidance Counselors**: 8.0 366 students/counselor	**% Amer Indian**: 0.0 **% Asian**: 0.1 **% Black**: 0.6 **% Hispanic**: 93.7 **% White**: 5.5	National ***Socio-Economic Status*** indicator percentile (100=high): 2nd

Williamson County

GEORGETOWN INDEPENDENT S.D.

603 LAKEWAY DRIVE ● GEORGETOWN TX 78628-2843 ● (512) 863-6595

Grade Span: PK-12 **Schools**: *Regular* 9 ● *Spec Ed* 0 ● *Alt* 4 **Students**: 6,283 **Total Teachers**: 465 **Student/Classroom Teacher Ratio**: 13.6	**Expenditures/Student**: $4,780 **Librarians**: 8.0 785 students/librarian **Guidance Counselors**: 13.0 483 students/counselor	**% Amer Indian**: 0.3 **% Asian**: 0.4 **% Black**: 3.3 **% Hispanic**: 19.0 **% White**: 76.9	National ***Socio-Economic Status*** indicator percentile (100=high): 60th

Williamson County

LEANDER INDEPENDENT S.D.

P. O. BOX 218 ● LEANDER TX 78646-0218 ● (512) 259-6789

Grade Span: PK-12 **Schools**: *Regular* 8 ● *Spec Ed* 0 ● *Alt* 0 **Students**: 8,932 **Total Teachers**: 551 **Student/Classroom Teacher Ratio**: 16.5	**Expenditures/Student**: $4,565 **Librarians**: 8.0 1,117 students/librarian **Guidance Counselors**: 15.4 580 students/counselor	**% Amer Indian**: 0.4 **% Asian**: 1.6 **% Black**: 2.6 **% Hispanic**: 11.5 **% White**: 83.9	National ***Socio-Economic Status*** indicator percentile (100=high): 74th

Williamson County

ROUND ROCK INDEPENDENT S.D.

1311 ROUND ROCK AVE. ● ROUND ROCK TX 78681-4941 ● (512) 255-4431

Grade Span: PK-12 **Schools**: *Regular* 29 ● *Spec Ed* 1 ● *Alt* 1 **Students**: 25,087 **Total Teachers**: 1,674 **Student/Classroom Teacher Ratio**: 14.9	**Expenditures/Student**: $4,746 **Librarians**: 29.9 839 students/librarian **Guidance Counselors**: 55.3 454 students/counselor	**% Amer Indian**: 0.3 **% Asian**: 4.4 **% Black**: 5.9 **% Hispanic**: 14.3 **% White**: 75.2	National ***Socio-Economic Status*** indicator percentile (100=high): 74th

Williamson County

TAYLOR INDEPENDENT S.D.

602 WEST TWELFTH STREET ● TAYLOR TX 76574-2998 ● (512) 352-6361

Grade Span: PK-12 **Schools**: *Regular* 4 ● *Spec Ed* 0 ● *Alt* 0 **Students**: 2,702 **Total Teachers**: 191 **Student/Classroom Teacher Ratio**: 14.4	**Expenditures/Student**: $4,937 **Librarians**: 3.0 901 students/librarian **Guidance Counselors**: 6.9 392 students/counselor	**% Amer Indian**: 0.4 **% Asian**: 0.1 **% Black**: 19.6 **% Hispanic**: 38.2 **% White**: 41.7	National ***Socio-Economic Status*** indicator percentile (100=high): 25th

Wilson County

FLORESVILLE INDEPENDENT S.D.

1103 FOURTH STREET ● FLORESVILLE TX 78114-2014 ● (830) 393-5300 ● http://www.floresville.isd.tenet.edu/index.html

Grade Span: PK-12 **Schools**: *Regular* 4 ● *Spec Ed* 0 ● *Alt* 0 **Students**: 2,942 **Total Teachers**: 195 **Student/Classroom Teacher Ratio**: 15.6	**Expenditures/Student**: $4,274 **Librarians**: 3.0 981 students/librarian **Guidance Counselors**: 5.0 588 students/counselor	**% Amer Indian**: 0.0 **% Asian**: 0.1 **% Black**: 1.5 **% Hispanic**: 54.1 **% White**: 44.3	National ***Socio-Economic Status*** indicator percentile (100=high): 26th

Young County

GRAHAM INDEPENDENT S.D.

1000 KENTUCKY STREET ● GRAHAM TX 76450-3966 ● (940) 549-0595

Grade Span: PK-12 **Schools**: *Regular* 5 ● *Spec Ed* 0 ● *Alt* 1 **Students**: 2,637 **Total Teachers**: 169 **Student/Classroom Teacher Ratio**: 16.1	**Expenditures/Student**: $3,994 **Librarians**: 1.0 2,637 students/librarian **Guidance Counselors**: 3.0 879 students/counselor	**% Amer Indian**: 0.4 **% Asian**: 0.8 **% Black**: 1.7 **% Hispanic**: 12.3 **% White**: 84.8	National ***Socio-Economic Status*** indicator percentile (100=high): 44th

Zapata County

[ZAPATA] **ZAPATA COUNTY INDEPENDENT S.D.**

P. O. BOX 158 ● ZAPATA TX 78076-0158 ● (956) 765-6546

Grade Span: PK-12 **Schools**: *Regular* 6 ● *Spec Ed* 0 ● *Alt* 0 **Students**: 2,894 **Total Teachers**: 195 **Student/Classroom Teacher Ratio**: 15.0	**Expenditures/Student**: $5,108 **Librarians**: 3.0 965 students/librarian **Guidance Counselors**: 7.4 391 students/counselor	**% Amer Indian**: 0.1 **% Asian**: 0.0 **% Black**: 0.1 **% Hispanic**: 93.7 **% White**: 6.1	National ***Socio-Economic Status*** indicator percentile (100=high): 5th

Box Elder County

[BRIGHAM CITY] **BOX ELDER S.D.**

230 W 200 S ● BRIGHAM CITY UT 84302 ● (435) 734-4800 ● http://www.boxelder.k12.ut.us

Grade Span: KG-12 **Schools**: *Regular* 24 ● *Spec Ed* 0 ● *Alt* 1 **Students**: 11,239 **Total Teachers**: 494 **Student/Classroom Teacher Ratio**: 20.9	**Expenditures/Student**: $3,255 **Librarians**: 4.0 2,810 students/librarian **Guidance Counselors**: 14.0 803 students/counselor	**% Amer Indian**: 0.9 **% Asian**: 1.0 **% Black**: 0.1 **% Hispanic**: 5.0 **% White**: 92.9	National ***Socio-Economic Status*** indicator percentile (100=high): 63rd

Cache County

[LOGAN] **CACHE S.D.**

2063 N 1200 E ● LOGAN UT 84341 ● (435) 752-3925 ● http://www.cache.k12.ut.us

Grade Span: KG-12 **Schools**: *Regular* 19 ● *Spec Ed* 0 ● *Alt* 2 **Students**: 12,907 **Total Teachers**: 525 **Student/Classroom Teacher Ratio**: 21.5	**Expenditures/Student**: $3,483 **Librarians**: 20.0 645 students/librarian **Guidance Counselors**: 12.8 1,008 students/counselor	**% Amer Indian**: 0.3 **% Asian**: 0.8 **% Black**: 0.1 **% Hispanic**: 2.7 **% White**: 96.1	National ***Socio-Economic Status*** indicator percentile (100=high): 68th

Cache County

LOGAN S.D.

101 W CENTER ● LOGAN UT 84321 ● (435) 755-2300 ● http://www.lsd.logan.k12.ut.us

Grade Span: KG-12 **Schools**: *Regular* 7 ● *Spec Ed* 0 ● *Alt* 2 **Students**: 5,980 **Total Teachers**: 279 **Student/Classroom Teacher Ratio**: 20.6	**Expenditures/Student**: $3,232 **Librarians**: 5.6 1,068 students/librarian **Guidance Counselors**: 7.0 854 students/counselor	**% Amer Indian**: 0.8 **% Asian**: 3.4 **% Black**: 0.3 **% Hispanic**: 4.6 **% White**: 91.0	National ***Socio-Economic Status*** indicator percentile (100=high): 52nd

Carbon County

[PRICE] **CARBON S.D.**

P O BOX 1438 ● PRICE UT 84501 ● (435) 637-1732 ● http://www.carbon.k12.ut.us

Grade Span: KG-12 **Schools**: *Regular* 10 ● *Spec Ed* 1 ● *Alt* 1 **Students**: 5,069 **Total Teachers**: 232 **Student/Classroom Teacher Ratio**: 20.8	**Expenditures/Student**: $3,706 **Librarians**: 2.8 1,810 students/librarian **Guidance Counselors**: 4.8 1,056 students/counselor	**% Amer Indian**: 1.0 **% Asian**: 0.3 **% Black**: 0.3 **% Hispanic**: 10.7 **% White**: 87.6	National ***Socio-Economic Status*** indicator percentile (100=high): 38th

Davis County

[FARMINGTON] **DAVIS S.D.**

45 E STATE ST ● FARMINGTON UT 84025 ● (801) 451-1251

Grade Span: KG-12 **Schools**: *Regular* 68 ● *Spec Ed* 2 ● *Alt* 5 **Students**: 58,782 **Total Teachers**: 2,356 **Student/Classroom Teacher Ratio**: 23.4	**Expenditures/Student**: $3,153 **Librarians**: 20.3 2,896 students/librarian **Guidance Counselors**: 47.3 1,243 students/counselor	**% Amer Indian**: 0.3 **% Asian**: 1.5 **% Black**: 0.9 **% Hispanic**: 2.6 **% White**: 94.7	National ***Socio-Economic Status*** indicator percentile (100=high): 75th

Duchesne County

DUCHESNE S.D.

P O BOX 446 ● DUCHESNE UT 84021 ● (435) 738-2411

Grade Span: KG-12 **Schools**: *Regular* 12 ● *Spec Ed* 2 ● *Alt* 1 **Students**: 4,557 **Total Teachers**: 219 **Student/Classroom Teacher Ratio**: 18.4	**Expenditures/Student**: $3,628 **Librarians**: 5.5 829 students/librarian **Guidance Counselors**: 0.8 5,696 students/counselor	**% Amer Indian**: 8.0 **% Asian**: 0.2 **% Black**: 0.1 **% Hispanic**: 2.4 **% White**: 89.2	National ***Socio-Economic Status*** indicator percentile (100=high): 35th

Emery County

[HUNTINGTON] **EMERY S.D.**

130 N MAIN ● HUNTINGTON UT 84528 ● (435) 687-9846 ● http://www.maintenance.emery.k12.ut.us

Grade Span: KG-12 **Schools**: *Regular* 10 ● *Spec Ed* 0 ● *Alt* 0 **Students**: 3,364 **Total Teachers**: 168 **Student/Classroom Teacher Ratio**: 18.0	**Expenditures/Student**: $4,295 **Librarians**: 0.5 6,728 students/librarian **Guidance Counselors**: 1.0 3,364 students/counselor	**% Amer Indian**: 0.5 **% Asian**: 0.4 **% Black**: 0.1 **% Hispanic**: 2.6 **% White**: 96.4	National ***Socio-Economic Status*** indicator percentile (100=high): 54th

Iron County

[CEDAR CITY] **IRON S.D.**

75 N 300 W ● CEDAR CITY UT 84720 ● (435) 586-2804 ● http://www.iron.k12.ut.us

Grade Span: KG-12 **Schools**: *Regular* 11 ● *Spec Ed* 0 ● *Alt* 2 **Students**: 6,238 **Total Teachers**: 270 **Student/Classroom Teacher Ratio**: 22.0	**Expenditures/Student**: $3,433 **Librarians**: 2.0 3,119 students/librarian **Guidance Counselors**: 3.3 1,890 students/counselor	**% Amer Indian**: 2.6 **% Asian**: 1.1 **% Black**: 0.4 **% Hispanic**: 2.8 **% White**: 93.1	National ***Socio-Economic Status*** indicator percentile (100=high): 47th

Millard County

[DELTA] **MILLARD S.D.**

P O BOX 666 ● DELTA UT 84624 ● (435) 864-2764 ● http://www.millard.k12.ut.us

Grade Span: KG-12 **Schools**: *Regular* 8 ● *Spec Ed* 0 ● *Alt* 1 **Students**: 3,816 **Total Teachers**: 187 **Student/Classroom Teacher Ratio**: 18.1	**Expenditures/Student**: $4,202 **Librarians**: 6.4 596 students/librarian **Guidance Counselors**: 3.2 1,193 students/counselor	**% Amer Indian**: 1.2 **% Asian**: 1.1 **% Black**: 0.1 **% Hispanic**: 4.0 **% White**: 93.6	National ***Socio-Economic Status*** indicator percentile (100=high): 45th

Salt Lake County

MURRAY S.D.

147 E 5065 S ● MURRAY UT 84107 ● (801) 264-7400 ● http://www.mury.k12.ut.us

Grade Span: KG-12 **Schools**: *Regular* 10 ● *Spec Ed* 0 ● *Alt* 1 **Students**: 6,841 **Total Teachers**: 297 **Student/Classroom Teacher Ratio**: 21.2	**Expenditures/Student**: $3,399 **Librarians**: 4.0 1,710 students/librarian **Guidance Counselors**: 10.5 652 students/counselor	**% Amer Indian**: 0.8 **% Asian**: 2.0 **% Black**: 1.0 **% Hispanic**: 4.3 **% White**: 91.9	National ***Socio-Economic Status*** indicator percentile (100=high): 78th

Salt Lake County

[SALT LAKE CITY] **GRANITE S.D.**

340 E 3545 S ● SALT LAKE CITY UT 84115 ● (801) 263-6100 ● http://www.granite.k12.ut.us

Grade Span: PK-12 **Schools**: *Regular* 86 ● *Spec Ed* 3 ● *Alt* 8 **Students**: 77,106 **Total Teachers**: 3,206 **Student/Classroom Teacher Ratio**: 22.8	**Expenditures/Student**: $3,397 **Librarians**: 61.4 1,256 students/librarian **Guidance Counselors**: 122.7 628 students/counselor	**% Amer Indian**: 0.9 **% Asian**: 4.7 **% Black**: 0.9 **% Hispanic**: 6.5 **% White**: 87.1	National ***Socio-Economic Status*** indicator percentile (100=high): 59th

Salt Lake County

SALT LAKE CITY S.D.

440 E 100 S ● SALT LAKE CITY UT 84111 ● (801) 578-8599 ● http://www.slc.k12.ut.us

Grade Span: PK-12 **Schools**: *Regular* 36 ● *Spec Ed* 2 ● *Alt* 2 **Students**: 25,712 **Total Teachers**: 1,151 **Student/Classroom Teacher Ratio**: 20.3	**Expenditures/Student**: $4,307 **Librarians**: 38.0 677 students/librarian **Guidance Counselors**: 47.0 547 students/counselor	**% Amer Indian**: 2.7 **% Asian**: 8.3 **% Black**: 2.6 **% Hispanic**: 18.2 **% White**: 68.2	National ***Socio-Economic Status*** indicator percentile (100=high): 24th

Salt Lake County

[SANDY] **JORDAN S.D.**

9361 S 300 E ● SANDY UT 84070 ● (801) 567-8100 ● http://www.jordan.k12.ut.us

Grade Span: KG-12 **Schools**: *Regular* 68 ● *Spec Ed* 3 ● *Alt* 1 **Students**: 71,702 **Total Teachers**: 2,877 **Student/Classroom Teacher Ratio**: 23.3	**Expenditures/Student**: $3,401 **Librarians**: 22.0 3,259 students/librarian **Guidance Counselors**: 78.3 916 students/counselor	**% Amer Indian**: 0.3 **% Asian**: 1.6 **% Black**: 0.3 **% Hispanic**: 3.4 **% White**: 94.4	National ***Socio-Economic Status*** indicator percentile (100=high): 74th

San Juan County

[BLANDING] **SAN JUAN S.D.**

200 N MAIN STREET ● BLANDING UT 84511 ● (435) 678-1200 ● http://www.sanjuan.k12.ut.us

Grade Span: PK-12 **Schools**: *Regular* 12 ● *Spec Ed* 0 ● *Alt* 0 **Students**: 3,395 **Total Teachers**: 223 **Student/Classroom Teacher Ratio**: 14.4	**Expenditures/Student**: $5,946 **Librarians**: 8.0 424 students/librarian **Guidance Counselors**: 6.0 566 students/counselor	**% Amer Indian**: 50.5 **% Asian**: 0.2 **% Black**: 0.0 **% Hispanic**: 2.7 **% White**: 46.6	National ***Socio-Economic Status*** indicator percentile (100=high): 13th

Sanpete County

[MANTI] **SOUTH SANPETE S.D.**

39 S MAIN ● MANTI UT 84642 ● (435) 835-2261 ● http://www.ssanpete.k12.ut.us

Grade Span: PK-12 **Schools**: *Regular* 6 ● *Spec Ed* 0 ● *Alt* 0 **Students**: 3,024 **Total Teachers**: 147 **Student/Classroom Teacher Ratio**: 20.4	**Expenditures/Student**: $3,654 **Librarians**: 0.0 *** students/librarian **Guidance Counselors**: 1.9 1,592 students/counselor	**% Amer Indian**: 1.0 **% Asian**: 1.1 **% Black**: 0.0 **% Hispanic**: 6.2 **% White**: 91.7	National ***Socio-Economic Status*** indicator percentile (100=high): 37th

Sevier County

[RICHFIELD] **SEVIER S.D.**

195 E 500 N ● RICHFIELD UT 84701 ● (435) 896-8214

Grade Span: PK-12 **Schools**: *Regular* 11 ● *Spec Ed* 0 ● *Alt* 1 **Students**: 4,909 **Total Teachers**: 220 **Student/Classroom Teacher Ratio**: 21.3	**Expenditures/Student**: $3,701 **Librarians**: 0.0 *** students/librarian **Guidance Counselors**: 1.0 4,909 students/counselor	**% Amer Indian**: 3.1 **% Asian**: 0.4 **% Black**: 0.2 **% Hispanic**: 1.8 **% White**: 94.5	National ***Socio-Economic Status*** indicator percentile (100=high): 42nd

Summit County

PARK CITY S.D.

P O BOX 680310 ● PARK CITY UT 84068 ● (435) 645-5600 ● http://www.parkcity.k12.ut.us

Grade Span: KG-12 **Schools**: *Regular* 5 ● *Spec Ed* 0 ● *Alt* 0 **Students**: 3,163 **Total Teachers**: 143 **Student/Classroom Teacher Ratio**: 18.9	**Expenditures/Student**: $4,223 **Librarians**: 1.0 3,163 students/librarian **Guidance Counselors**: 4.5 703 students/counselor	**% Amer Indian**: 0.1 **% Asian**: 0.8 **% Black**: 0.2 **% Hispanic**: 2.1 **% White**: 96.9	National ***Socio-Economic Status*** indicator percentile (100=high): 95th

Tooele County

TOOELE S.D.

66 W VINE ● TOOELE UT 84074 ● (435) 833-1900 ● http://tcsd.tooele.k12.ut.us

Grade Span: KG-12 **Schools**: *Regular* 16 ● *Spec Ed* 1 ● *Alt* 1 **Students**: 7,495 **Total Teachers**: 343 **Student/Classroom Teacher Ratio**: 17.1	**Expenditures/Student**: $3,659 **Librarians**: 3.0 2,498 students/librarian **Guidance Counselors**: 10.0 750 students/counselor	**% Amer Indian**: 1.5 **% Asian**: 0.9 **% Black**: 0.6 **% Hispanic**: 10.7 **% White**: 86.3	National ***Socio-Economic Status*** indicator percentile (100=high): 52nd

Uintah County

[VERNAL] UINTAH S.D.

635 W 200 S ● VERNAL UT 84078 ● (435) 781-3100

Grade Span: KG-12	**Expenditures/Student**: $3,661	**% Amer Indian**: 9.4	
Schools: *Regular* 11 ● *Spec Ed* 1 ● *Alt* 1	**Librarians**: 3.0	**% Asian**: 0.2	National ***Socio-Economic***
Students: 6,699	2,233 students/librarian	**% Black**: 0.2	***Status*** indicator percentile
Total Teachers: 317	**Guidance Counselors**: 7.4	**% Hispanic**: 2.0	(100=high): 40th
Student/Classroom Teacher Ratio: 20.3	905 students/counselor	**% White**: 88.2	

Utah County

[AMERICAN FORK] ALPINE S.D.

575 N 100 E ● AMERICAN FORK UT 84003 ● (801) 756-8400 ● http://www.alpine.k12.ut.us

Grade Span: KG-12	**Expenditures/Student**: $3,270	**% Amer Indian**: 0.7	
Schools: *Regular* 44 ● *Spec Ed* 3 ● *Alt* 1	**Librarians**: 12.5	**% Asian**: 1.4	National ***Socio-Economic***
Students: 42,763	3,421 students/librarian	**% Black**: 0.3	***Status*** indicator percentile
Total Teachers: 1,693	**Guidance Counselors**: 55.7	**% Hispanic**: 2.7	(100=high): 70th
Student/Classroom Teacher Ratio: 22.3	768 students/counselor	**% White**: 95.0	

Utah County

PROVO S.D.

280 W 940 N ● PROVO UT 84604 ● (801) 374-4800 ● http://www.provo.k12.ut.us

Grade Span: KG-12	**Expenditures/Student**: $3,843	**% Amer Indian**: 1.5	
Schools: *Regular* 16 ● *Spec Ed* 3 ● *Alt* 5	**Librarians**: 11.5	**% Asian**: 4.0	National ***Socio-Economic***
Students: 13,552	1,178 students/librarian	**% Black**: 0.5	***Status*** indicator percentile
Total Teachers: 605	**Guidance Counselors**: 15.0	**% Hispanic**: 7.8	(100=high): 48th
Student/Classroom Teacher Ratio: 20.9	903 students/counselor	**% White**: 86.3	

Utah County

[SPANISH FORK] NEBO S.D.

350 S MAIN ● SPANISH FORK UT 84660 ● (801) 798-4000 ● http://www.nebo.edu

Grade Span: KG-12	**Expenditures/Student**: $3,299	**% Amer Indian**: 0.3	
Schools: *Regular* 25 ● *Spec Ed* 0 ● *Alt* 1	**Librarians**: 8.6	**% Asian**: 0.5	National ***Socio-Economic***
Students: 18,736	2,179 students/librarian	**% Black**: 0.1	***Status*** indicator percentile
Total Teachers: 729	**Guidance Counselors**: 26.1	**% Hispanic**: 2.6	(100=high): 65th
Student/Classroom Teacher Ratio: 22.3	718 students/counselor	**% White**: 96.6	

Wasatch County

[HEBER CITY] WASATCH S.D.

173 E 200 N ● HEBER CITY UT 84032 ● (435) 654-0280

Grade Span: KG-12	**Expenditures/Student**: $3,176	**% Amer Indian**: 0.1	
Schools: *Regular* 6 ● *Spec Ed* 0 ● *Alt* 1	**Librarians**: 2.0	**% Asian**: 0.5	National ***Socio-Economic***
Students: 3,389	1,695 students/librarian	**% Black**: 0.4	***Status*** indicator percentile
Total Teachers: 143	**Guidance Counselors**: 4.3	**% Hispanic**: 1.9	(100=high): 74th
Student/Classroom Teacher Ratio: 21.1	788 students/counselor	**% White**: 97.1	

Washington County

[ST. GEORGE] WASHINGTON S.D.

189 W TABERNACLE ● ST. GEORGE UT 84770 ● (435) 673-3553 ● http://www.infowest.com/sites/w/washcoed

Grade Span: KG-12	**Expenditures/Student**: $3,015	**% Amer Indian**: 1.8	
Schools: *Regular* 25 ● *Spec Ed* 0 ● *Alt* 1	**Librarians**: 10.0	**% Asian**: 0.7	National ***Socio-Economic***
Students: 17,418	1,742 students/librarian	**% Black**: 0.2	***Status*** indicator percentile
Total Teachers: 652	**Guidance Counselors**: 22.0	**% Hispanic**: 2.7	(100=high): 70th
Student/Classroom Teacher Ratio: 23.5	792 students/counselor	**% White**: 94.6	

Weber County
OGDEN S.D.
1950 MONROE BLVD ● OGDEN UT 84401 ● (801) 625-8700 ● http://www.ogden.k12.ut.us.

Grade Span: KG-12	**Expenditures/Student**: $4,012	**% Amer Indian**: 1.2	National ***Socio-Economic Status*** indicator percentile (100=high): 18th
Schools: *Regular* 22 ● *Spec Ed* 0 ● *Alt* 1	**Librarians**: 18.8	**% Asian**: 1.7	
Students: 13,011	692 students/librarian	**% Black**: 2.9	
Total Teachers: 616	**Guidance Counselors**: 22.6	**% Hispanic**: 22.8	
Student/Classroom Teacher Ratio: 19.1	576 students/counselor	**% White**: 71.3	

Weber County
[OGDEN] WEBER S.D.
5320 S ADAMS AVE ● OGDEN UT 84405 ● (801) 476-7800 ● http://www.weber.k12.ut.us

Grade Span: KG-12	**Expenditures/Student**: $3,327	**% Amer Indian**: 0.4	National ***Socio-Economic Status*** indicator percentile (100=high): 77th
Schools: *Regular* 37 ● *Spec Ed* 1 ● *Alt* 1	**Librarians**: 11.8	**% Asian**: 1.4	
Students: 27,731	2,350 students/librarian	**% Black**: 0.8	
Total Teachers: 1,142	**Guidance Counselors**: 40.8	**% Hispanic**: 3.6	
Student/Classroom Teacher Ratio: 22.8	680 students/counselor	**% White**: 93.8	

Chittenden County

BURLINGTON S.D.

150 COLCHESTER AVENUE ● BURLINGTON VT 05401 ● (802) 864-8461 ● http://www.state.vt.us/schools/ira/bsd.htm

Grade Span: PK-12 **Schools**: *Regular* 9 ● *Spec Ed* 1 ● *Alt* 1 **Students**: 3,840 **Total Teachers**: 243 **Student/Classroom Teacher Ratio**: 16.0	**Expenditures/Student**: $7,284 **Librarians**: 5.0 768 students/librarian **Guidance Counselors**: 10.9 352 students/counselor	**% Amer Indian**: 0.3 **% Asian**: 4.5 **% Black**: 3.8 **% Hispanic**: 0.9 **% White**: 90.5	National ***Socio-Economic Status*** indicator percentile (100=high): 29th

Rutland County

RUTLAND CITY S.D.

6 CHURCH STREET ● RUTLAND VT 05701 ● (802) 773-1900 ● http://rutlandhs.k12.vt.us

Grade Span: KG-12 **Schools**: *Regular* 5 ● *Spec Ed* 0 ● *Alt* 0 **Students**: 2,631 **Total Teachers**: 183 **Student/Classroom Teacher Ratio**: 15.3	**Expenditures/Student**: $6,611 **Librarians**: 2.3 1,144 students/librarian **Guidance Counselors**: 6.0 439 students/counselor	**% Amer Indian**: 0.2 **% Asian**: 0.7 **% Black**: 0.9 **% Hispanic**: 0.4 **% White**: 97.9	National ***Socio-Economic Status*** indicator percentile (100=high): 40th

Accomack County

[ACCOMAC] ACCOMACK COUNTY S.D.

PO BOX 330 ● ACCOMAC VA 23301 ● (757) 787-5754

Grade Span: KG-12 **Schools**: *Regular* 13 ● *Spec Ed* 0 ● *Alt* 2 **Students**: 5,538 **Total Teachers**: 425 **Student/Classroom Teacher Ratio**: na	**Expenditures/Student**: $4,837 **Librarians**: 11.9 465 students/librarian **Guidance Counselors**: 16.0 346 students/counselor	**% Amer Indian**: 0.1 **% Asian**: 0.3 **% Black**: 50.7 **% Hispanic**: 4.4 **% White**: 44.5	National ***Socio-Economic Status*** indicator percentile (100=high): 14th

Albemarle County

[CHARLOTTESVILLE] ALBEMARLE COUNTY S.D.

401 MCINTIRE RD ● CHARLOTTESVILLE VA 22902-4596 ● (804) 296-5829 ● http://pen.k12.va.us/Anthology/Div/Albemarle/Schools

Grade Span: KG-12 **Schools**: *Regular* 22 ● *Spec Ed* 0 ● *Alt* 1 **Students**: 11,123 **Total Teachers**: 707 **Student/Classroom Teacher Ratio**: na	**Expenditures/Student**: $5,775 **Librarians**: 23.8 467 students/librarian **Guidance Counselors**: 41.1 271 students/counselor	**% Amer Indian**: 0.0 **% Asian**: 2.3 **% Black**: 12.0 **% Hispanic**: 1.5 **% White**: 84.1	National ***Socio-Economic Status*** indicator percentile (100=high): 75th

Alexandria Independent City

ALEXANDRIA CITY S.D.

2000 N BEAUREGARD ST ● ALEXANDRIA VA 22311 ● (703) 824-6610 ● http://www.acps.k12.va.us/acps.htm

Grade Span: KG-12 **Schools**: *Regular* 16 ● *Spec Ed* 1 ● *Alt* 1 **Students**: 10,044 **Total Teachers**: 850 **Student/Classroom Teacher Ratio**: na	**Expenditures/Student**: $8,864 **Librarians**: 22.0 457 students/librarian **Guidance Counselors**: 31.3 321 students/counselor	**% Amer Indian**: 0.1 **% Asian**: 6.2 **% Black**: 48.3 **% Hispanic**: 19.6 **% White**: 25.8	National ***Socio-Economic Status*** indicator percentile (100=high): 24th

Alleghany County

[COVINGTON] ALLEGHANY HIGHLANDS S.D.

110 ROSEDALE AVE ● COVINGTON VA 24426-1296 ● (540) 965-1800 ● http://www.alleghany.k12.va.us

Grade Span: PK-12 **Schools**: *Regular* 8 ● *Spec Ed* 0 ● *Alt* 0 **Students**: 3,070 **Total Teachers**: 219 **Student/Classroom Teacher Ratio**: na	**Expenditures/Student**: $5,304 **Librarians**: 8.0 384 students/librarian **Guidance Counselors**: 10.1 304 students/counselor	**% Amer Indian**: 0.1 **% Asian**: 0.2 **% Black**: 7.3 **% Hispanic**: 0.2 **% White**: 92.1	National ***Socio-Economic Status*** indicator percentile (100=high): 50th

Amherst County

[AMHERST] AMHERST COUNTY S.D.

PO BOX 1257 ● AMHERST VA 24521 ● (804) 946-9386

Grade Span: KG-12 **Schools**: *Regular* 10 ● *Spec Ed* 0 ● *Alt* 0 **Students**: 4,723 **Total Teachers**: 300 **Student/Classroom Teacher Ratio**: na	**Expenditures/Student**: $4,352 **Librarians**: 11.0 429 students/librarian **Guidance Counselors**: 12.0 394 students/counselor	**% Amer Indian**: 0.4 **% Asian**: 0.2 **% Black**: 24.3 **% Hispanic**: 0.1 **% White**: 74.9	National ***Socio-Economic Status*** indicator percentile (100=high): 54th

Arlington County

[ARLINGTON] ARLINGTON COUNTY S.D.

1426 N QUINCY ST ● ARLINGTON VA 22207 ● (703) 358-6010

Grade Span: KG-12 **Schools**: *Regular* 29 ● *Spec Ed* 0 ● *Alt* 1 **Students**: 17,178 **Total Teachers**: 1,569 **Student/Classroom Teacher Ratio**: na	**Expenditures/Student**: $9,274 **Librarians**: 37.5 458 students/librarian **Guidance Counselors**: 59.2 290 students/counselor	**% Amer Indian**: 0.1 **% Asian**: 9.8 **% Black**: 17.5 **% Hispanic**: 30.2 **% White**: 42.4	National ***Socio-Economic Status*** indicator percentile (100=high): 31st

Augusta County

[FISHERSVILLE] **AUGUSTA COUNTY S.D.**

RT 1 BOX 252 ● FISHERSVILLE VA 22939 ● (540) 245-5100 ● http://www.augusta.k12.va.us

Grade Span: KG-12 **Schools**: *Regular* 21 ● *Spec Ed* 0 ● *Alt* 1 **Students**: 10,673 **Total Teachers**: 744 **Student/Classroom Teacher Ratio**: na	**Expenditures/Student**: $4,912 **Librarians**: 21.0 508 students/librarian **Guidance Counselors**: 27.4 390 students/counselor	**% Amer Indian**: 0.1 **% Asian**: 0.3 **% Black**: 2.6 **% Hispanic**: 0.5 **% White**: 96.4	National ***Socio-Economic Status*** indicator percentile (100=high): 69th

Bedford County

[BEDFORD] **BEDFORD COUNTY S.D.**

PO BOX 748 ● BEDFORD VA 24523 ● (540) 586-1045 ● http://www.cablenet-va.com/bedford-schools

Grade Span: KG-12 **Schools**: *Regular* 19 ● *Spec Ed* 0 ● *Alt* 1 **Students**: 9,956 **Total Teachers**: 687 **Student/Classroom Teacher Ratio**: na	**Expenditures/Student**: $3,899 **Librarians**: 15.1 659 students/librarian **Guidance Counselors**: 15.4 646 students/counselor	**% Amer Indian**: 0.1 **% Asian**: 0.7 **% Black**: 11.3 **% Hispanic**: 0.4 **% White**: 87.6	National ***Socio-Economic Status*** indicator percentile (100=high): 62nd

Botetourt County

[FINCASTLE] **BOTETOURT COUNTY S.D.**

PO BOX 309 ● FINCASTLE VA 24090 ● (540) 473-8263

Grade Span: PK-12 **Schools**: *Regular* 9 ● *Spec Ed* 0 ● *Alt* 1 **Students**: 4,514 **Total Teachers**: 304 **Student/Classroom Teacher Ratio**: na	**Expenditures/Student**: $4,464 **Librarians**: 9.0 502 students/librarian **Guidance Counselors**: 10.2 443 students/counselor	**% Amer Indian**: 0.0 **% Asian**: 0.6 **% Black**: 3.7 **% Hispanic**: 0.2 **% White**: 95.5	National ***Socio-Economic Status*** indicator percentile (100=high): 84th

Bristol Independent City

BRISTOL CITY S.D.

222 OAK ST ● BRISTOL VA 24201-4198 ● (540) 669-8181

Grade Span: KG-12 **Schools**: *Regular* 6 ● *Spec Ed* 0 ● *Alt* 0 **Students**: 2,533 **Total Teachers**: 214 **Student/Classroom Teacher Ratio**: na	**Expenditures/Student**: $5,778 **Librarians**: 7.0 362 students/librarian **Guidance Counselors**: 8.0 317 students/counselor	**% Amer Indian**: 0.1 **% Asian**: 0.3 **% Black**: 9.0 **% Hispanic**: 0.4 **% White**: 90.2	National ***Socio-Economic Status*** indicator percentile (100=high): 35th

Brunswick County

[LAWRENCEVILLE] **BRUNSWICK COUNTY S.D.**

PO BOX 309 ● LAWRENCEVILLE VA 23868 ● (804) 848-3138

Grade Span: KG-12 **Schools**: *Regular* 6 ● *Spec Ed* 0 ● *Alt* 0 **Students**: 2,570 **Total Teachers**: 206 **Student/Classroom Teacher Ratio**: na	**Expenditures/Student**: $5,326 **Librarians**: 6.0 428 students/librarian **Guidance Counselors**: 6.0 428 students/counselor	**% Amer Indian**: 0.0 **% Asian**: 0.2 **% Black**: 75.3 **% Hispanic**: 0.2 **% White**: 24.4	National ***Socio-Economic Status*** indicator percentile (100=high): 8th

Buchanan County

[GRUNDY] **BUCHANAN COUNTY S.D.**

PO BOX 833 ● GRUNDY VA 24614 ● (540) 935-2331

Grade Span: KG-12 **Schools**: *Regular* 17 ● *Spec Ed* 0 ● *Alt* 1 **Students**: 5,210 **Total Teachers**: 472 **Student/Classroom Teacher Ratio**: na	**Expenditures/Student**: $5,244 **Librarians**: 16.1 324 students/librarian **Guidance Counselors**: 19.2 271 students/counselor	**% Amer Indian**: 0.0 **% Asian**: 0.0 **% Black**: 0.0 **% Hispanic**: 0.0 **% White**: 100.0	National ***Socio-Economic Status*** indicator percentile (100=high): 19th

Campbell County

[RUSTBURG] CAMPBELL COUNTY S.D.

PO BOX 99 ● RUSTBURG VA 24588 ● (804) 332-5161

Grade Span: KG-12	**Expenditures/Student**: $4,365	**% Amer Indian**: 0.1	
Schools: *Regular* 15 ● *Spec Ed* 0 ● *Alt* 1	**Librarians**: 16.0	**% Asian**: 0.5	National ***Socio-Economic***
Students: 8,386	524 students/librarian	**% Black**: 18.6	***Status*** indicator percentile
Total Teachers: 563	**Guidance Counselors**: 20.5	**% Hispanic**: 0.2	(100=high): 56th
Student/Classroom Teacher Ratio: na	409 students/counselor	**% White**: 80.5	

Caroline County

[BOWLING GREEN] CAROLINE COUNTY S.D.

16221 RICHMOND TURNPIKE ● BOWLING GREEN VA 22427 ● (804) 633-5088

Grade Span: KG-12	**Expenditures/Student**: $4,839	**% Amer Indian**: 0.5	
Schools: *Regular* 6 ● *Spec Ed* 0 ● *Alt* 0	**Librarians**: 5.8	**% Asian**: 0.4	National ***Socio-Economic***
Students: 3,667	632 students/librarian	**% Black**: 42.2	***Status*** indicator percentile
Total Teachers: 250	**Guidance Counselors**: 7.7	**% Hispanic**: 3.0	(100=high): 41st
Student/Classroom Teacher Ratio: na	476 students/counselor	**% White**: 53.9	

Carroll County

[HILLSVILLE] CARROLL COUNTY S.D.

405 9 N MAIN ST ● HILLSVILLE VA 24343 ● (540) 728-3191

Grade Span: KG-12	**Expenditures/Student**: $4,742	**% Amer Indian**: 0.0	
Schools: *Regular* 10 ● *Spec Ed* 0 ● *Alt* 0	**Librarians**: 9.3	**% Asian**: 0.2	National ***Socio-Economic***
Students: 3,987	429 students/librarian	**% Black**: 0.4	***Status*** indicator percentile
Total Teachers: 288	**Guidance Counselors**: 10.9	**% Hispanic**: 1.6	(100=high): 42nd
Student/Classroom Teacher Ratio: na	366 students/counselor	**% White**: 97.8	

Charlottesville Independent City

CHARLOTTESVILLE CITY S.D.

1562 DAIRY RD ● CHARLOTTESVILLE VA 22903 ● (804) 979-9250 ● http://pen.k12.va.us/Anthology/Div/Charlottesville/Charlottesville.html

Grade Span: KG-12	**Expenditures/Student**: $7,975	**% Amer Indian**: 0.0	
Schools: *Regular* 9 ● *Spec Ed* 0 ● *Alt* 0	**Librarians**: 0.0	**% Asian**: 0.9	National ***Socio-Economic***
Students: 4,440	*** students/librarian	**% Black**: 49.0	***Status*** indicator percentile
Total Teachers: 328	**Guidance Counselors**: 14.0	**% Hispanic**: 0.7	(100=high): 24th
Student/Classroom Teacher Ratio: na	317 students/counselor	**% White**: 49.3	

Chesapeake Independent City

CHESAPEAKE CITY S.D.

PO BOX 15204 ● CHESAPEAKE VA 23328 ● (757) 547-0153 ● http://pen1.pen.k12.va.us:80/Anthology/Div/Chesapeake/CPS/index.html

Grade Span: KG-12	**Expenditures/Student**: $4,857	**% Amer Indian**: 0.2	
Schools: *Regular* 38 ● *Spec Ed* 1 ● *Alt* 2	**Librarians**: 48.5	**% Asian**: 1.6	National ***Socio-Economic***
Students: 34,980	721 students/librarian	**% Black**: 33.6	***Status*** indicator percentile
Total Teachers: 2,126	**Guidance Counselors**: 90.4	**% Hispanic**: 0.9	(100=high): 57th
Student/Classroom Teacher Ratio: na	387 students/counselor	**% White**: 63.7	

Chesterfield County

[CHESTERFIELD] CHESTERFIELD COUNTY S.D.

PO BOX 10 ● CHESTERFIELD VA 23832 ● (804) 748-1411 ● http://chesterfield.k12.va.us

Grade Span: KG-12	**Expenditures/Student**: $4,578	**% Amer Indian**: 0.1	
Schools: *Regular* 55 ● *Spec Ed* 0 ● *Alt* 1	**Librarians**: 72.8	**% Asian**: 2.6	National ***Socio-Economic***
Students: 49,057	674 students/librarian	**% Black**: 18.6	***Status*** indicator percentile
Total Teachers: 3,372	**Guidance Counselors**: 155.8	**% Hispanic**: 1.3	(100=high): 83rd
Student/Classroom Teacher Ratio: na	315 students/counselor	**% White**: 77.3	

Colonial Heights Independent City

COLONIAL HEIGHTS CITY S.D.

512 BOULEVARD ● COLONIAL HEIGHTS VA 23834-3798 ● (804) 526-0811

Grade Span: KG-12 **Schools**: *Regular* 5 ● *Spec Ed* 0 ● *Alt* 0 **Students**: 2,752 **Total Teachers**: 195 **Student/Classroom Teacher Ratio**: na	**Expenditures/Student**: $5,687 **Librarians**: 0.2 13,760 students/librarian **Guidance Counselors**: 7.5 367 students/counselor	**% Amer Indian**: 0.0 **% Asian**: 4.2 **% Black**: 3.1 **% Hispanic**: 1.3 **% White**: 91.4	National ***Socio-Economic Status*** indicator percentile (100=high): 81st

Culpeper County

[CULPEPER] CULPEPER COUNTY S.D.

1051 N MAIN ST EXT ● CULPEPER VA 22701 ● (540) 825-3677

Grade Span: KG-12 **Schools**: *Regular* 7 ● *Spec Ed* 0 ● *Alt* 0 **Students**: 5,166 **Total Teachers**: 384 **Student/Classroom Teacher Ratio**: na	**Expenditures/Student**: $5,029 **Librarians**: 9.0 574 students/librarian **Guidance Counselors**: 14.5 356 students/counselor	**% Amer Indian**: 0.1 **% Asian**: 0.8 **% Black**: 23.3 **% Hispanic**: 1.0 **% White**: 74.9	National ***Socio-Economic Status*** indicator percentile (100=high): 53rd

Danville Independent City

DANVILLE CITY S.D.

PO BOX 9600 ● DANVILLE VA 24543 ● (804) 799-6400

Grade Span: KG-12 **Schools**: *Regular* 16 ● *Spec Ed* 0 ● *Alt* 1 **Students**: 8,273 **Total Teachers**: 582 **Student/Classroom Teacher Ratio**: na	**Expenditures/Student**: $4,792 **Librarians**: 17.0 487 students/librarian **Guidance Counselors**: 22.7 364 students/counselor	**% Amer Indian**: 0.0 **% Asian**: 0.4 **% Black**: 59.4 **% Hispanic**: 0.4 **% White**: 39.8	National ***Socio-Economic Status*** indicator percentile (100=high): 22nd

Dickenson County

[CLINTWOOD] DICKENSON COUNTY S.D.

PO BOX 1127 ● CLINTWOOD VA 24228 ● (540) 926-4643

Grade Span: KG-12 **Schools**: *Regular* 8 ● *Spec Ed* 0 ● *Alt* 1 **Students**: 3,181 **Total Teachers**: 320 **Student/Classroom Teacher Ratio**: na	**Expenditures/Student**: $5,569 **Librarians**: 8.0 398 students/librarian **Guidance Counselors**: 9.5 335 students/counselor	**% Amer Indian**: 0.0 **% Asian**: 0.0 **% Black**: 0.4 **% Hispanic**: 0.1 **% White**: 99.5	National ***Socio-Economic Status*** indicator percentile (100=high): 17th

Dinwiddie County

[DINWIDDIE] DINWIDDIE COUNTY S.D.

PO BOX 7 ● DINWIDDIE VA 23841 ● (804) 469-4517

Grade Span: KG-12 **Schools**: *Regular* 7 ● *Spec Ed* 0 ● *Alt* 0 **Students**: 3,900 **Total Teachers**: 296 **Student/Classroom Teacher Ratio**: na	**Expenditures/Student**: $4,716 **Librarians**: 8.0 488 students/librarian **Guidance Counselors**: 10.0 390 students/counselor	**% Amer Indian**: 0.1 **% Asian**: 0.4 **% Black**: 39.8 **% Hispanic**: 0.4 **% White**: 59.2	National ***Socio-Economic Status*** indicator percentile (100=high): 41st

Fairfax County

[FAIRFAX] FAIRFAX COUNTY S.D.

10700 PAGE AVE ● FAIRFAX VA 22030 ● (703) 246-2631 ● http://www.fcps.k12.va.us

Grade Span: KG-12 **Schools**: *Regular* 177 ● *Spec Ed* 21 ● *Alt* 12 **Students**: 140,820 **Total Teachers**: 9,981 **Student/Classroom Teacher Ratio**: na	**Expenditures/Student**: $6,858 **Librarians**: 243.4 579 students/librarian **Guidance Counselors**: 439.1 321 students/counselor	**% Amer Indian**: 0.2 **% Asian**: 13.5 **% Black**: 11.1 **% Hispanic**: 9.0 **% White**: 66.1	National ***Socio-Economic Status*** indicator percentile (100=high): 74th

Fauquier County

[WARRENTON] **FAUQUIER COUNTY S.D.**

10 HOTEL ST ● WARRENTON VA 22186 ● (540) 347-8729

Grade Span: KG-12 **Schools**: *Regular* 16 ● *Spec Ed* 0 ● *Alt* 1 **Students**: 8,919 **Total Teachers**: 795 **Student/Classroom Teacher Ratio**: na	**Expenditures/Student**: $5,847 **Librarians**: 20.3 439 students/librarian **Guidance Counselors**: 21.1 423 students/counselor	**% Amer Indian**: 0.1 **% Asian**: 0.7 **% Black**: 11.2 **% Hispanic**: 1.0 **% White**: 86.9	National ***Socio-Economic Status*** indicator percentile (100=high): 76th

Fluvanna County

[PALMYRA] **FLUVANNA COUNTY S.D.**

PO BOX 419 ● PALMYRA VA 22963-0419 ● (804) 589-8208

Grade Span: KG-12 **Schools**: *Regular* 6 ● *Spec Ed* 0 ● *Alt* 0 **Students**: 2,605 **Total Teachers**: 185 **Student/Classroom Teacher Ratio**: na	**Expenditures/Student**: $4,832 **Librarians**: 5.0 521 students/librarian **Guidance Counselors**: 5.9 442 students/counselor	**% Amer Indian**: 0.0 **% Asian**: 0.3 **% Black**: 27.5 **% Hispanic**: 0.4 **% White**: 71.7	National ***Socio-Economic Status*** indicator percentile (100=high): 58th

Franklin County

[ROCKY MOUNT] **FRANKLIN COUNTY S.D.**

102 BERNARD RD ● ROCKY MOUNT VA 24151 ● (540) 483-5138 ● http://www.frco.k12.va.us/#contents

Grade Span: KG-12 **Schools**: *Regular* 14 ● *Spec Ed* 0 ● *Alt* 0 **Students**: 6,758 **Total Teachers**: 415 **Student/Classroom Teacher Ratio**: na	**Expenditures/Student**: $4,500 **Librarians**: 14.9 454 students/librarian **Guidance Counselors**: 18.1 373 students/counselor	**% Amer Indian**: 0.1 **% Asian**: 0.5 **% Black**: 13.3 **% Hispanic**: 0.4 **% White**: 85.6	National ***Socio-Economic Status*** indicator percentile (100=high): 49th

Frederick County

[WINCHESTER] **FREDERICK COUNTY S.D.**

PO BOX 3508 ● WINCHESTER VA 22604-2546 ● (540) 662-3888

Grade Span: KG-12 **Schools**: *Regular* 14 ● *Spec Ed* 1 ● *Alt* 0 **Students**: 9,605 **Total Teachers**: 622 **Student/Classroom Teacher Ratio**: na	**Expenditures/Student**: $4,700 **Librarians**: 16.0 600 students/librarian **Guidance Counselors**: 25.7 374 students/counselor	**% Amer Indian**: 0.1 **% Asian**: 0.7 **% Black**: 2.7 **% Hispanic**: 0.7 **% White**: 95.8	National ***Socio-Economic Status*** indicator percentile (100=high): 76th

Giles County

[PEARISBURG] **GILES COUNTY S.D.**

RT 1 BOX 52 ● PEARISBURG VA 24134 ● (540) 921-1421 ● http://admin.sbo.giles.k12.va.us

Grade Span: KG-12 **Schools**: *Regular* 5 ● *Spec Ed* 0 ● *Alt* 1 **Students**: 2,575 **Total Teachers**: 182 **Student/Classroom Teacher Ratio**: na	**Expenditures/Student**: $5,111 **Librarians**: 5.0 515 students/librarian **Guidance Counselors**: 5.9 436 students/counselor	**% Amer Indian**: 0.0 **% Asian**: 0.3 **% Black**: 1.2 **% Hispanic**: 0.2 **% White**: 98.3	National ***Socio-Economic Status*** indicator percentile (100=high): 53rd

Gloucester County

[GLOUCESTER] **GLOUCESTER COUNTY S.D.**

RT 5 BOX 243 ● GLOUCESTER VA 23061 ● (804) 693-1425 ● http://www.sbo.gc.k12.va.us

Grade Span: KG-12 **Schools**: *Regular* 8 ● *Spec Ed* 0 ● *Alt* 0 **Students**: 6,553 **Total Teachers**: 424 **Student/Classroom Teacher Ratio**: na	**Expenditures/Student**: $4,486 **Librarians**: 9.0 728 students/librarian **Guidance Counselors**: 18.1 362 students/counselor	**% Amer Indian**: 0.4 **% Asian**: 1.1 **% Black**: 11.3 **% Hispanic**: 0.9 **% White**: 86.3	National ***Socio-Economic Status*** indicator percentile (100=high): 71st

Greensville County

[EMPORIA] **GREENSVILLE COUNTY S.D.**

PO BOX 1156 ● EMPORIA VA 23847 ● (804) 634-3748

Grade Span: KG-12 **Schools**: *Regular* 6 ● *Spec Ed* 0 ● *Alt* 0 **Students**: 2,772 **Total Teachers**: 228 **Student/Classroom Teacher Ratio**: na	**Expenditures/Student**: $5,502 **Librarians**: 5.0 554 students/librarian **Guidance Counselors**: 9.3 298 students/counselor	**% Amer Indian**: 0.0 **% Asian**: 0.3 **% Black**: 70.3 **% Hispanic**: 0.4 **% White**: 29.0	National ***Socio-Economic Status*** indicator percentile (100=high): 15th

Halifax County

[HALIFAX] **HALIFAX COUNTY S.D.**

PO BOX 1849 ● HALIFAX VA 24558 ● (804) 476-2171

Grade Span: KG-12 **Schools**: *Regular* 17 ● *Spec Ed* 0 ● *Alt* 2 **Students**: 6,453 **Total Teachers**: 421 **Student/Classroom Teacher Ratio**: na	**Expenditures/Student**: $6,924 **Librarians**: 14.0 461 students/librarian **Guidance Counselors**: 14.1 458 students/counselor	**% Amer Indian**: 0.0 **% Asian**: 0.2 **% Black**: 46.8 **% Hispanic**: 1.0 **% White**: 51.9	National ***Socio-Economic Status*** indicator percentile (100=high): 32nd

Hampton Independent City

HAMPTON CITY S.D.

1819 NICKERSON BLVD ● HAMPTON VA 23663 ● (757) 850-5225 ● http://members.visi.net/~crabber/hcs

Grade Span: KG-12 **Schools**: *Regular* 33 ● *Spec Ed* 1 ● *Alt* 1 **Students**: 23,611 **Total Teachers**: 1,527 **Student/Classroom Teacher Ratio**: na	**Expenditures/Student**: $4,693 **Librarians**: 47.4 498 students/librarian **Guidance Counselors**: 72.1 327 students/counselor	**% Amer Indian**: 0.3 **% Asian**: 1.9 **% Black**: 52.7 **% Hispanic**: 1.7 **% White**: 43.5	National ***Socio-Economic Status*** indicator percentile (100=high): 37th

Hanover County

[ASHLAND] **HANOVER COUNTY S.D.**

200 BERKLEY ST ● ASHLAND VA 23005-1399 ● (804) 752-6000

Grade Span: KG-12 **Schools**: *Regular* 17 ● *Spec Ed* 0 ● *Alt* 0 **Students**: 14,014 **Total Teachers**: 983 **Student/Classroom Teacher Ratio**: na	**Expenditures/Student**: $4,405 **Librarians**: 27.2 515 students/librarian **Guidance Counselors**: 35.3 397 students/counselor	**% Amer Indian**: 0.1 **% Asian**: 0.7 **% Black**: 10.8 **% Hispanic**: 0.4 **% White**: 88.0	National ***Socio-Economic Status*** indicator percentile (100=high): 87th

Harrisonburg Independent City

HARRISONBURG CITY S.D.

317 S MAIN ST ● HARRISONBURG VA 22801-3606 ● (540) 434-9916 ● http://www.rica.net/harrisonburghs

Grade Span: KG-12 **Schools**: *Regular* 6 ● *Spec Ed* 0 ● *Alt* 0 **Students**: 3,529 **Total Teachers**: 286 **Student/Classroom Teacher Ratio**: na	**Expenditures/Student**: $5,633 **Librarians**: 6.0 588 students/librarian **Guidance Counselors**: 9.2 384 students/counselor	**% Amer Indian**: 0.0 **% Asian**: 3.7 **% Black**: 9.0 **% Hispanic**: 6.9 **% White**: 80.5	National ***Socio-Economic Status*** indicator percentile (100=high): 33rd

Henrico County

[RICHMOND] **HENRICO COUNTY S.D.**

PO BOX 23120 ● RICHMOND VA 23223-0420 ● (804) 226-3600 ● http://www.co.henrico.va.us/schools

Grade Span: KG-12 **Schools**: *Regular* 52 ● *Spec Ed* 1 ● *Alt* 4 **Students**: 37,112 **Total Teachers**: 2,374 **Student/Classroom Teacher Ratio**: na	**Expenditures/Student**: $5,135 **Librarians**: 72.3 513 students/librarian **Guidance Counselors**: 101.4 366 students/counselor	**% Amer Indian**: 0.1 **% Asian**: 3.3 **% Black**: 30.7 **% Hispanic**: 1.0 **% White**: 64.9	National ***Socio-Economic Status*** indicator percentile (100=high): 72nd

Henry County

[COLLINSVILLE] **HENRY COUNTY S.D.**

PO BOX 8958 ● COLLINSVILLE VA 24078 ● (540) 634-4712

Grade Span: KG-12 **Schools**: *Regular* 20 ● *Spec Ed* 0 ● *Alt* 0 **Students**: 9,167 **Total Teachers**: 686 **Student/Classroom Teacher Ratio**: na	**Expenditures/Student**: $4,695 **Librarians**: 23.2 395 students/librarian **Guidance Counselors**: 26.0 353 students/counselor	**% Amer Indian**: 0.1 **% Asian**: 0.2 **% Black**: 33.2 **% Hispanic**: 0.7 **% White**: 65.7	National ***Socio-Economic Status*** indicator percentile (100=high): 45th

Hopewell Independent City

HOPEWELL CITY S.D.

103 N 11TH ST ● HOPEWELL VA 23860 ● (804) 541-2365 ● http://www.hopewell.k12.va.us

Grade Span: KG-12 **Schools**: *Regular* 5 ● *Spec Ed* 0 ● *Alt* 1 **Students**: 4,060 **Total Teachers**: 301 **Student/Classroom Teacher Ratio**: na	**Expenditures/Student**: $5,583 **Librarians**: 7.0 580 students/librarian **Guidance Counselors**: 12.0 338 students/counselor	**% Amer Indian**: 0.1 **% Asian**: 0.6 **% Black**: 43.9 **% Hispanic**: 2.1 **% White**: 53.4	National ***Socio-Economic Status*** indicator percentile (100=high): 28th

Isle of Wight County

[ISLE OF WIGHT] **ISLE OF WIGHT COUNTY S.D.**

PO BOX 78 ● ISLE OF WIGHT VA 23397 ● (757) 357-4393

Grade Span: PK-12 **Schools**: *Regular* 8 ● *Spec Ed* 0 ● *Alt* 0 **Students**: 4,669 **Total Teachers**: 314 **Student/Classroom Teacher Ratio**: na	**Expenditures/Student**: $5,097 **Librarians**: 8.0 584 students/librarian **Guidance Counselors**: 11.4 410 students/counselor	**% Amer Indian**: 0.2 **% Asian**: 0.2 **% Black**: 37.5 **% Hispanic**: 0.1 **% White**: 62.0	National ***Socio-Economic Status*** indicator percentile (100=high): 43rd

James City County

WILLIAMSBURG CITY S.D.

PO BOX 8783 ● WILLIAMSBURG VA 23187-8783 ● (757) 253-6777 ● http://www.sbo.wjcc.k12.va.us

Grade Span: KG-12 **Schools**: *Regular* 10 ● *Spec Ed* 0 ● *Alt* 0 **Students**: 7,385 **Total Teachers**: 502 **Student/Classroom Teacher Ratio**: na	**Expenditures/Student**: $5,751 **Librarians**: 10.0 739 students/librarian **Guidance Counselors**: 18.5 399 students/counselor	**% Amer Indian**: 0.2 **% Asian**: 1.4 **% Black**: 25.8 **% Hispanic**: 1.2 **% White**: 71.3	National ***Socio-Economic Status*** indicator percentile (100=high): 66th

King George County

[KING GEORGE] **KING GEORGE COUNTY S.D.**

PO BOX 21 ● KING GEORGE VA 22485 ● (540) 775-5833

Grade Span: PK-12 **Schools**: *Regular* 4 ● *Spec Ed* 0 ● *Alt* 0 **Students**: 2,833 **Total Teachers**: 212 **Student/Classroom Teacher Ratio**: na	**Expenditures/Student**: $5,011 **Librarians**: 4.0 708 students/librarian **Guidance Counselors**: 10.6 267 students/counselor	**% Amer Indian**: 0.2 **% Asian**: 0.8 **% Black**: 26.6 **% Hispanic**: 0.8 **% White**: 71.5	National ***Socio-Economic Status*** indicator percentile (100=high): 54th

Lee County

[JONESVILLE] **LEE COUNTY S.D.**

5 PARK STREET ● JONESVILLE VA 24263 ● (540) 346-2107

Grade Span: KG-12 **Schools**: *Regular* 13 ● *Spec Ed* 0 ● *Alt* 1 **Students**: 4,283 **Total Teachers**: 362 **Student/Classroom Teacher Ratio**: na	**Expenditures/Student**: $5,378 **Librarians**: 10.5 408 students/librarian **Guidance Counselors**: 12.8 335 students/counselor	**% Amer Indian**: 0.1 **% Asian**: 0.0 **% Black**: 0.4 **% Hispanic**: 0.0 **% White**: 99.4	National ***Socio-Economic Status*** indicator percentile (100=high): 12th

Loudoun County

[LEESBURG] **LOUDOUN COUNTY S.D.**

102 NORTH ST NW ● LEESBURG VA 22075 ● (703) 771-6410

Grade Span: PK-12 **Schools**: *Regular* 35 ● *Spec Ed* 0 ● *Alt* 1 **Students**: 19,827 **Total Teachers**: 1,281 **Student/Classroom Teacher Ratio**: na	**Expenditures/Student**: $5,931 **Librarians**: 31.1 638 students/librarian **Guidance Counselors**: 54.5 364 students/counselor	**% Amer Indian**: 0.1 **% Asian**: 4.2 **% Black**: 8.6 **% Hispanic**: 3.6 **% White**: 83.6	National ***Socio-Economic Status*** indicator percentile (100=high): 88th

Louisa County

[MINERAL] **LOUISA COUNTY S.D.**

PO BOX 7 ● MINERAL VA 23117 ● (540) 894-5115

Grade Span: KG-12 **Schools**: *Regular* 5 ● *Spec Ed* 0 ● *Alt* 0 **Students**: 3,897 **Total Teachers**: 268 **Student/Classroom Teacher Ratio**: na	**Expenditures/Student**: $4,715 **Librarians**: 5.0 779 students/librarian **Guidance Counselors**: 9.0 433 students/counselor	**% Amer Indian**: 0.0 **% Asian**: 0.2 **% Black**: 29.2 **% Hispanic**: 0.2 **% White**: 70.4	National ***Socio-Economic Status*** indicator percentile (100=high): 40th

Lynchburg Independent City

LYNCHBURG CITY S.D.

PO BOX 1599 ● LYNCHBURG VA 24505-1599 ● (804) 522-3700

Grade Span: KG-12 **Schools**: *Regular* 17 ● *Spec Ed* 1 ● *Alt* 3 **Students**: 9,476 **Total Teachers**: 680 **Student/Classroom Teacher Ratio**: na	**Expenditures/Student**: $5,510 **Librarians**: 18.0 526 students/librarian **Guidance Counselors**: 45.8 207 students/counselor	**% Amer Indian**: 0.3 **% Asian**: 1.0 **% Black**: 45.7 **% Hispanic**: 0.5 **% White**: 52.6	National ***Socio-Economic Status*** indicator percentile (100=high): 31st

Manassas Independent City

MANASSAS CITY S.D.

9000 TUDOR LN ● MANASSAS VA 22110 ● (703) 361-0166 ● http://www.manassas.k12.va.us

Grade Span: KG-12 **Schools**: *Regular* 7 ● *Spec Ed* 0 ● *Alt* 1 **Students**: 5,685 **Total Teachers**: 396 **Student/Classroom Teacher Ratio**: na	**Expenditures/Student**: $5,476 **Librarians**: 9.0 632 students/librarian **Guidance Counselors**: 13.0 437 students/counselor	**% Amer Indian**: 0.2 **% Asian**: 4.0 **% Black**: 16.7 **% Hispanic**: 8.2 **% White**: 70.9	National ***Socio-Economic Status*** indicator percentile (100=high): 75th

Martinsville Independent City

MARTINSVILLE CITY S.D.

PO BOX 5548 ● MARTINSVILLE VA 24115 ● (540) 632-6313

Grade Span: KG-12 **Schools**: *Regular* 6 ● *Spec Ed* 0 ● *Alt* 0 **Students**: 2,836 **Total Teachers**: 213 **Student/Classroom Teacher Ratio**: na	**Expenditures/Student**: $5,222 **Librarians**: 6.0 473 students/librarian **Guidance Counselors**: 10.0 284 students/counselor	**% Amer Indian**: 0.0 **% Asian**: 0.5 **% Black**: 53.4 **% Hispanic**: 0.1 **% White**: 45.9	National ***Socio-Economic Status*** indicator percentile (100=high): 28th

Mecklenburg County

[BOYDTON] **MECKLENBURG COUNTY S.D.**

PO BOX 190 ● BOYDTON VA 23917 ● (804) 738-6111

Grade Span: KG-12 **Schools**: *Regular* 11 ● *Spec Ed* 0 ● *Alt* 1 **Students**: 5,047 **Total Teachers**: 386 **Student/Classroom Teacher Ratio**: na	**Expenditures/Student**: $4,549 **Librarians**: 11.1 455 students/librarian **Guidance Counselors**: 12.1 417 students/counselor	**% Amer Indian**: 0.0 **% Asian**: 0.1 **% Black**: 49.2 **% Hispanic**: 0.4 **% White**: 50.2	National ***Socio-Economic Status*** indicator percentile (100=high): 28th

Montgomery County

[CHRISTIANSBURG] **MONTGOMERY COUNTY S.D.**

200 JUNKIN ST ● CHRISTIANSBURG VA 24073-3098 ● (540) 382-5105 ● http://www.bev.net/education/schools

Grade Span: KG-12 **Schools**: *Regular* 19 ● *Spec Ed* 0 ● *Alt* 1 **Students**: 8,959 **Total Teachers**: 676 **Student/Classroom Teacher Ratio**: na	**Expenditures/Student**: $5,205 **Librarians**: 23.3 385 students/librarian **Guidance Counselors**: 31.1 288 students/counselor	**% Amer Indian**: 0.1 **% Asian**: 2.6 **% Black**: 4.5 **% Hispanic**: 0.6 **% White**: 92.1	National ***Socio-Economic Status*** indicator percentile (100=high): 53rd

Newport News Independent City

NEWPORT NEWS CITY S.D.

12465 WARWICK BLVD ● NEWPORT NEWS VA 23606-0130 ● (757) 591-4545 ● http://www.sbo.nn.k12.va.us

Grade Span: PK-12 **Schools**: *Regular* 37 ● *Spec Ed* 0 ● *Alt* 4 **Students**: 32,574 **Total Teachers**: 2,006 **Student/Classroom Teacher Ratio**: na	**Expenditures/Student**: $4,826 **Librarians**: 41.2 791 students/librarian **Guidance Counselors**: 88.7 367 students/counselor	**% Amer Indian**: 0.8 **% Asian**: 2.4 **% Black**: 50.6 **% Hispanic**: 3.1 **% White**: 43.1	National ***Socio-Economic Status*** indicator percentile (100=high): 30th

Norfolk Independent City

NORFOLK CITY S.D.

PO BOX 1357 ● NORFOLK VA 23501 ● (757) 441-2107 ● http://www.nps.k12.va.us

Grade Span: PK-12 **Schools**: *Regular* 50 ● *Spec Ed* 2 ● *Alt* 6 **Students**: 36,771 **Total Teachers**: 2,359 **Student/Classroom Teacher Ratio**: na	**Expenditures/Student**: $5,514 **Librarians**: 57.0 645 students/librarian **Guidance Counselors**: 127.1 289 students/counselor	**% Amer Indian**: 0.2 **% Asian**: 2.1 **% Black**: 64.1 **% Hispanic**: 1.6 **% White**: 32.0	National ***Socio-Economic Status*** indicator percentile (100=high): 12th

Northampton County

[MACHIPONGO] **NORTHAMPTON COUNTY S.D.**

7207 YOUNG ST ● MACHIPONGO VA 23405 ● (757) 678-5151 ● http://www.whro.org/nms

Grade Span: KG-12 **Schools**: *Regular* 4 ● *Spec Ed* 0 ● *Alt* 1 **Students**: 2,514 **Total Teachers**: 189 **Student/Classroom Teacher Ratio**: na	**Expenditures/Student**: $4,870 **Librarians**: 4.0 629 students/librarian **Guidance Counselors**: 6.0 419 students/counselor	**% Amer Indian**: 0.1 **% Asian**: 0.1 **% Black**: 56.8 **% Hispanic**: 3.9 **% White**: 39.1	National ***Socio-Economic Status*** indicator percentile (100=high): 12th

Orange County

[ORANGE] **ORANGE COUNTY S.D.**

PO BOX 349 ● ORANGE VA 22960 ● (703) 672-1390 ● http://www.gemlink.com/ocss

Grade Span: KG-12 **Schools**: *Regular* 7 ● *Spec Ed* 0 ● *Alt* 0 **Students**: 3,823 **Total Teachers**: 278 **Student/Classroom Teacher Ratio**: na	**Expenditures/Student**: $5,126 **Librarians**: 8.0 478 students/librarian **Guidance Counselors**: 10.0 382 students/counselor	**% Amer Indian**: 0.1 **% Asian**: 0.2 **% Black**: 20.2 **% Hispanic**: 0.3 **% White**: 79.2	National ***Socio-Economic Status*** indicator percentile (100=high): 53rd

Page County

[LURAY] **PAGE COUNTY S.D.**

735 W MAIN ST ● LURAY VA 22835 ● (540) 743-6533 ● http://www.pen.k12.va.us/Anthology/Div/Page/pchome.html

Grade Span: KG-12 **Schools**: *Regular* 7 ● *Spec Ed* 0 ● *Alt* 1 **Students**: 3,507 **Total Teachers**: 244 **Student/Classroom Teacher Ratio**: na	**Expenditures/Student**: $4,571 **Librarians**: 7.0 501 students/librarian **Guidance Counselors**: 8.0 438 students/counselor	**% Amer Indian**: 0.0 **% Asian**: 0.3 **% Black**: 2.7 **% Hispanic**: 0.4 **% White**: 96.5	National ***Socio-Economic Status*** indicator percentile (100=high): 48th

Patrick County

[STUART] **PATRICK COUNTY S.D.**

PO BOX 346 ● STUART VA 24171 ● (540) 694-3163

Grade Span: KG-12 **Schools**: *Regular* 7 ● *Spec Ed* 0 ● *Alt* 0 **Students**: 2,601 **Total Teachers**: 183 **Student/Classroom Teacher Ratio**: na	**Expenditures/Student**: $4,719 **Librarians**: 6.0 434 students/librarian **Guidance Counselors**: 6.0 434 students/counselor	**% Amer Indian**: 0.0 **% Asian**: 0.2 **% Black**: 9.5 **% Hispanic**: 2.0 **% White**: 88.4	National ***Socio-Economic Status*** indicator percentile (100=high): 46th

Petersburg Independent City

PETERSBURG CITY S.D.

141 E WYTHE ST ● PETERSBURG VA 23803 ● (804) 862-7038 ● http://www.ctg.net/pps

Grade Span: KG-12 **Schools**: *Regular* 9 ● *Spec Ed* 0 ● *Alt* 1 **Students**: 6,167 **Total Teachers**: 483 **Student/Classroom Teacher Ratio**: na	**Expenditures/Student**: $5,284 **Librarians**: 11.0 561 students/librarian **Guidance Counselors**: 17.2 359 students/counselor	**% Amer Indian**: 0.1 **% Asian**: 0.3 **% Black**: 95.8 **% Hispanic**: 0.4 **% White**: 3.4	National ***Socio-Economic Status*** indicator percentile (100=high): 7th

Pittsylvania County

[CHATHAM] **PITTSYLVANIA COUNTY S.D.**

PO BOX 232 ● CHATHAM VA 24531 ● (804) 432-2761

Grade Span: KG-12 **Schools**: *Regular* 20 ● *Spec Ed* 0 ● *Alt* 1 **Students**: 9,378 **Total Teachers**: 634 **Student/Classroom Teacher Ratio**: na	**Expenditures/Student**: $4,398 **Librarians**: 20.3 462 students/librarian **Guidance Counselors**: 22.6 415 students/counselor	**% Amer Indian**: 0.0 **% Asian**: 0.1 **% Black**: 32.9 **% Hispanic**: 0.5 **% White**: 66.5	National ***Socio-Economic Status*** indicator percentile (100=high): 45th

Portsmouth Independent City

PORTSMOUTH CITY S.D.

PO BOX 998 ● PORTSMOUTH VA 23705-0998 ● (757) 393-8742 ● http://pps.k12.va.us

Grade Span: KG-12 **Schools**: *Regular* 26 ● *Spec Ed* 1 ● *Alt* 1 **Students**: 17,891 **Total Teachers**: 1,252 **Student/Classroom Teacher Ratio**: na	**Expenditures/Student**: $5,283 **Librarians**: 26.3 680 students/librarian **Guidance Counselors**: 50.5 354 students/counselor	**% Amer Indian**: 0.1 **% Asian**: 0.5 **% Black**: 67.9 **% Hispanic**: 0.8 **% White**: 30.7	National ***Socio-Economic Status*** indicator percentile (100=high): 17th

Powhatan County

[POWHATAN] **POWHATAN COUNTY S.D.**

2320 SKAGGS RD ● POWHATAN VA 23139 ● (804) 598-5700

Grade Span: KG-12 **Schools**: *Regular* 3 ● *Spec Ed* 0 ● *Alt* 1 **Students**: 2,764 **Total Teachers**: 192 **Student/Classroom Teacher Ratio**: na	**Expenditures/Student**: $4,727 **Librarians**: 3.0 921 students/librarian **Guidance Counselors**: 6.2 446 students/counselor	**% Amer Indian**: 0.2 **% Asian**: 0.4 **% Black**: 12.5 **% Hispanic**: 0.2 **% White**: 86.6	National ***Socio-Economic Status*** indicator percentile (100=high): 74th

Prince Edward County

[FARMVILLE] **PRINCE EDWARD COUNTY S.D.**

RT 5 BOX 680 ● FARMVILLE VA 23901 ● (804) 392-8893

Grade Span: KG-12 **Schools**: *Regular* 3 ● *Spec Ed* 0 ● *Alt* 0 **Students**: 2,634 **Total Teachers**: 217 **Student/Classroom Teacher Ratio**: na	**Expenditures/Student**: $4,765 **Librarians**: 3.0 878 students/librarian **Guidance Counselors**: 5.0 527 students/counselor	**% Amer Indian**: 0.0 **% Asian**: 0.5 **% Black**: 59.1 **% Hispanic**: 0.5 **% White**: 39.9	National ***Socio-Economic Status*** indicator percentile (100=high): 17th

Prince George County

[PRINCE GEORGE] **PRINCE GEORGE COUNTY S.D.**

PO BOX 80 ● PRINCE GEORGE VA 23875 ● (804) 733-2700 ● http://pgs.k12.va.us

Grade Span: KG-12	**Expenditures/Student**: $4,719	**% Amer Indian**: 0.1	
Schools: *Regular* 10 ● *Spec Ed* 0 ● *Alt* 0	**Librarians**: 11.0	**% Asian**: 0.9	National ***Socio-Economic***
Students: 5,521	502 students/librarian	**% Black**: 36.2	***Status*** indicator percentile
Total Teachers: 328	**Guidance Counselors**: 17.3	**% Hispanic**: 3.1	(100=high): 72nd
Student/Classroom Teacher Ratio: na	319 students/counselor	**% White**: 59.7	

Prince William County

[MANASSAS] **PRINCE WILLIAM COUNTY S.D.**

PO BOX 389 ● MANASSAS VA 22110 ● (703) 791-8712

Grade Span: KG-12	**Expenditures/Student**: $5,650	**% Amer Indian**: 0.7	
Schools: *Regular* 60 ● *Spec Ed* 4 ● *Alt* 4	**Librarians**: 72.9	**% Asian**: 3.5	National ***Socio-Economic***
Students: 47,072	646 students/librarian	**% Black**: 20.7	***Status*** indicator percentile
Total Teachers: 2,928	**Guidance Counselors**: 147.4	**% Hispanic**: 6.0	(100=high): 70th
Student/Classroom Teacher Ratio: na	319 students/counselor	**% White**: 69.2	

Pulaski County

[PULASKI] **PULASKI COUNTY S.D.**

44 THIRD ST NW ● PULASKI VA 24301 ● (540) 980-2237

Grade Span: KG-12	**Expenditures/Student**: $4,792	**% Amer Indian**: 0.0	
Schools: *Regular* 11 ● *Spec Ed* 0 ● *Alt* 0	**Librarians**: 10.0	**% Asian**: 0.5	National ***Socio-Economic***
Students: 5,146	515 students/librarian	**% Black**: 7.2	***Status*** indicator percentile
Total Teachers: 342	**Guidance Counselors**: 14.5	**% Hispanic**: 0.1	(100=high): 47th
Student/Classroom Teacher Ratio: na	355 students/counselor	**% White**: 92.1	

Richmond Independent City

RICHMOND CITY S.D.

301 N 9TH ST ● RICHMOND VA 23219-3913 ● (804) 780-7700 ● http://richmond.k12.va.us

Grade Span: PK-12	**Expenditures/Student**: $7,119	**% Amer Indian**: 0.1	
Schools: *Regular* 49 ● *Spec Ed* 6 ● *Alt* 6	**Librarians**: 53.2	**% Asian**: 0.7	National ***Socio-Economic***
Students: 27,708	521 students/librarian	**% Black**: 90.1	***Status*** indicator percentile
Total Teachers: 1,982	**Guidance Counselors**: 93.6	**% Hispanic**: 0.7	(100=high): 6th
Student/Classroom Teacher Ratio: na	296 students/counselor	**% White**: 8.4	

Roanoke County

[ROANOKE] **ROANOKE COUNTY S.D.**

5937 COVE RD NW ● ROANOKE VA 24019-2403 ● (540) 562-3700 ● http://www.rcs.k12.va.us

Grade Span: KG-12	**Expenditures/Student**: $5,383	**% Amer Indian**: 0.1	
Schools: *Regular* 25 ● *Spec Ed* 0 ● *Alt* 2	**Librarians**: 29.8	**% Asian**: 1.5	National ***Socio-Economic***
Students: 13,753	462 students/librarian	**% Black**: 3.3	***Status*** indicator percentile
Total Teachers: 1,036	**Guidance Counselors**: 46.4	**% Hispanic**: 0.5	(100=high): 90th
Student/Classroom Teacher Ratio: na	296 students/counselor	**% White**: 94.7	

Roanoke Independent City

ROANOKE CITY S.D.

PO BOX 13145 ● ROANOKE VA 24031 ● (540) 981-2381 ● http://www.roanoke.k12.va.us

Grade Span: PK-12	**Expenditures/Student**: $5,905	**% Amer Indian**: 0.0	
Schools: *Regular* 29 ● *Spec Ed* 0 ● *Alt* 1	**Librarians**: 32.4	**% Asian**: 1.8	National ***Socio-Economic***
Students: 13,219	408 students/librarian	**% Black**: 40.0	***Status*** indicator percentile
Total Teachers: 1,013	**Guidance Counselors**: 56.6	**% Hispanic**: 0.7	(100=high): 21st
Student/Classroom Teacher Ratio: na	234 students/counselor	**% White**: 57.5	

Rockbridge County

[LEXINGTON] **ROCKBRIDGE COUNTY S.D.**

417 MORNINGSIDE DR ● LEXINGTON VA 24450 ● (540) 463-7386 ● http://www.rcs.rang.k12.va.us

Grade Span: KG-12 **Schools**: *Regular* 8 ● *Spec Ed* 0 ● *Alt* 0 **Students**: 3,187 **Total Teachers**: 245 **Student/Classroom Teacher Ratio**: na	**Expenditures/Student**: $4,688 **Librarians**: 9.0 354 students/librarian **Guidance Counselors**: 10.3 309 students/counselor	**% Amer Indian**: 0.1 **% Asian**: 0.3 **% Black**: 4.2 **% Hispanic**: 0.1 **% White**: 95.2	National ***Socio-Economic Status*** indicator percentile (100=high): 58th

Rockingham County

[HARRISONBURG] **ROCKINGHAM COUNTY S.D.**

404 COUNTY OFC BLDG ● HARRISONBURG VA 22801 ● (540) 564-3230 ● http://www.rockingham.k12.va.us

Grade Span: KG-12 **Schools**: *Regular* 19 ● *Spec Ed* 0 ● *Alt* 0 **Students**: 10,228 **Total Teachers**: 739 **Student/Classroom Teacher Ratio**: na	**Expenditures/Student**: $5,068 **Librarians**: 21.5 476 students/librarian **Guidance Counselors**: 29.5 347 students/counselor	**% Amer Indian**: 0.0 **% Asian**: 0.5 **% Black**: 1.9 **% Hispanic**: 2.3 **% White**: 95.2	National ***Socio-Economic Status*** indicator percentile (100=high): 67th

Russell County

[LEBANON] **RUSSELL COUNTY S.D.**

PO BOX 8 ● LEBANON VA 24266 ● (540) 889-6500

Grade Span: KG-12 **Schools**: *Regular* 14 ● *Spec Ed* 0 ● *Alt* 1 **Students**: 4,713 **Total Teachers**: 317 **Student/Classroom Teacher Ratio**: na	**Expenditures/Student**: $4,582 **Librarians**: 6.8 693 students/librarian **Guidance Counselors**: 10.3 458 students/counselor	**% Amer Indian**: 0.0 **% Asian**: 0.0 **% Black**: 0.7 **% Hispanic**: 0.1 **% White**: 99.1	National ***Socio-Economic Status*** indicator percentile (100=high): 32nd

Salem Independent City

SALEM CITY S.D.

19 N COLLEGE AVE ● SALEM VA 24153 ● (540) 387-6400

Grade Span: KG-12 **Schools**: *Regular* 6 ● *Spec Ed* 0 ● *Alt* 0 **Students**: 3,841 **Total Teachers**: 274 **Student/Classroom Teacher Ratio**: na	**Expenditures/Student**: $5,284 **Librarians**: 7.0 549 students/librarian **Guidance Counselors**: 11.0 349 students/counselor	**% Amer Indian**: 0.0 **% Asian**: 1.8 **% Black**: 5.8 **% Hispanic**: 0.3 **% White**: 92.0	National ***Socio-Economic Status*** indicator percentile (100=high): 75th

Scott County

[GATE CITY] **SCOTT COUNTY S.D.**

261 E JACKSON ST ● GATE CITY VA 24251 ● (540) 386-6118 ● http://www.mounet.com/~scottsch

Grade Span: KG-12 **Schools**: *Regular* 13 ● *Spec Ed* 0 ● *Alt* 1 **Students**: 3,863 **Total Teachers**: 282 **Student/Classroom Teacher Ratio**: na	**Expenditures/Student**: $4,780 **Librarians**: 11.0 351 students/librarian **Guidance Counselors**: 10.0 386 students/counselor	**% Amer Indian**: 0.0 **% Asian**: 0.0 **% Black**: 0.8 **% Hispanic**: 0.2 **% White**: 99.0	National ***Socio-Economic Status*** indicator percentile (100=high): 31st

Shenandoah County

[WOODSTOCK] **SHENANDOAH COUNTY S.D.**

PO BOX 488 ● WOODSTOCK VA 22664 ● (540) 459-4091

Grade Span: KG-12 **Schools**: *Regular* 9 ● *Spec Ed* 0 ● *Alt* 1 **Students**: 5,302 **Total Teachers**: 364 **Student/Classroom Teacher Ratio**: na	**Expenditures/Student**: $4,880 **Librarians**: 11.0 482 students/librarian **Guidance Counselors**: 15.0 353 students/counselor	**% Amer Indian**: 0.2 **% Asian**: 0.5 **% Black**: 1.4 **% Hispanic**: 1.9 **% White**: 96.0	National ***Socio-Economic Status*** indicator percentile (100=high): 67th

Smyth County

[MARION] **SMYTH COUNTY S.D.**

PO BOX 987 ● MARION VA 24354 ● (540) 783-3791

Grade Span: KG-12 **Schools**: *Regular* 11 ● *Spec Ed* 0 ● *Alt* 1 **Students**: 5,267 **Total Teachers**: 400 **Student/Classroom Teacher Ratio**: na	**Expenditures/Student**: $4,760 **Librarians**: 12.0 439 students/librarian **Guidance Counselors**: 14.2 371 students/counselor	**% Amer Indian**: 0.1 **% Asian**: 0.2 **% Black**: 2.0 **% Hispanic**: 0.4 **% White**: 97.3	National ***Socio-Economic Status*** indicator percentile (100=high): 48th

Southampton County

[COURTLAND] **SOUTHAMPTON COUNTY S.D.**

PO BOX 96 ● COURTLAND VA 23837-0096 ● (757) 653-2692

Grade Span: KG-12 **Schools**: *Regular* 7 ● *Spec Ed* 0 ● *Alt* 0 **Students**: 2,857 **Total Teachers**: 209 **Student/Classroom Teacher Ratio**: na	**Expenditures/Student**: $5,081 **Librarians**: 7.0 408 students/librarian **Guidance Counselors**: 6.0 476 students/counselor	**% Amer Indian**: 0.0 **% Asian**: 0.2 **% Black**: 53.9 **% Hispanic**: 0.2 **% White**: 45.7	National ***Socio-Economic Status*** indicator percentile (100=high): 26th

Spotsylvania County

[SPOTSYLVANIA] **SPOTSYLVANIA COUNTY S.D.**

6717 SMITH STATION RD ● SPOTSYLVANIA VA 22553 ● (540) 898-6032 ● http://www.spotsylvania.k12.va.us

Grade Span: KG-12 **Schools**: *Regular* 21 ● *Spec Ed* 0 ● *Alt* 2 **Students**: 15,279 **Total Teachers**: 900 **Student/Classroom Teacher Ratio**: na	**Expenditures/Student**: $4,623 **Librarians**: 28.5 536 students/librarian **Guidance Counselors**: 47.3 323 students/counselor	**% Amer Indian**: 0.2 **% Asian**: 1.0 **% Black**: 13.3 **% Hispanic**: 1.7 **% White**: 83.7	National ***Socio-Economic Status*** indicator percentile (100=high): 78th

Stafford County

[STAFFORD] **STAFFORD COUNTY S.D.**

1729 JEFFERSON DAVIS HWY ● STAFFORD VA 22554 ● (540) 659-3141 ● http://pen.k12.va.us/Anthology/Div/Stafford

Grade Span: KG-12 **Schools**: *Regular* 19 ● *Spec Ed* 0 ● *Alt* 0 **Students**: 16,520 **Total Teachers**: 1,034 **Student/Classroom Teacher Ratio**: na	**Expenditures/Student**: $4,821 **Librarians**: 26.2 631 students/librarian **Guidance Counselors**: 40.3 410 students/counselor	**% Amer Indian**: 0.3 **% Asian**: 1.7 **% Black**: 10.6 **% Hispanic**: 2.0 **% White**: 85.5	National ***Socio-Economic Status*** indicator percentile (100=high): 78th

Staunton Independent City

STAUNTON CITY S.D.

PO BOX 900 ● STAUNTON VA 24401-0900 ● (540) 332-3920

Grade Span: KG-12 **Schools**: *Regular* 6 ● *Spec Ed* 0 ● *Alt* 0 **Students**: 2,923 **Total Teachers**: 218 **Student/Classroom Teacher Ratio**: na	**Expenditures/Student**: $5,328 **Librarians**: 6.0 487 students/librarian **Guidance Counselors**: 8.2 356 students/counselor	**% Amer Indian**: 0.1 **% Asian**: 0.6 **% Black**: 22.3 **% Hispanic**: 0.4 **% White**: 76.5	National ***Socio-Economic Status*** indicator percentile (100=high): 48th

Suffolk Independent City

SUFFOLK CITY S.D.

PO BOX 1549 ● SUFFOLK VA 23434-1549 ● (757) 925-5500 ● http://pen.k12.va.us/Anthology/Div/Suffolk

Grade Span: KG-12 **Schools**: *Regular* 15 ● *Spec Ed* 0 ● *Alt* 1 **Students**: 10,024 **Total Teachers**: 667 **Student/Classroom Teacher Ratio**: na	**Expenditures/Student**: $4,857 **Librarians**: 18.0 557 students/librarian **Guidance Counselors**: 24.0 418 students/counselor	**% Amer Indian**: 0.2 **% Asian**: 0.6 **% Black**: 57.4 **% Hispanic**: 0.5 **% White**: 41.4	National ***Socio-Economic Status*** indicator percentile (100=high): 22nd

Tazewell County

[TAZEWELL] TAZEWELL COUNTY S.D.

209 W FINCASTLE TRNPK ● TAZEWELL VA 24651 ● (540) 988-5511 ● http://tazewell.k12.va.us

Grade Span: KG-12	**Expenditures/Student**: $4,435	**% Amer Indian**: 0.0	
Schools: *Regular* 17 ● *Spec Ed* 0 ● *Alt* 1	**Librarians**: 17.2	**% Asian**: 0.9	National ***Socio-Economic***
Students: 8,033	467 students/librarian	**% Black**: 2.9	***Status*** indicator percentile
Total Teachers: 546	**Guidance Counselors**: 19.1	**% Hispanic**: 0.0	(100=high): 35th
Student/Classroom Teacher Ratio: na	421 students/counselor	**% White**: 96.1	

Virginia Beach Independent City

VIRGINIA BEACH CITY S.D.

PO BOX 6038 ● VIRGINIA BEACH VA 23456 ● (757) 427-4326 ● http://pen.k12.va.us/Anthology/Div/VaBeach/VBCPS.shtml

Grade Span: KG-12	**Expenditures/Student**: $4,684	**% Amer Indian**: 0.1	
Schools: *Regular* 76 ● *Spec Ed* 2 ● *Alt* 4	**Librarians**: 120.1	**% Asian**: 5.3	National ***Socio-Economic***
Students: 76,508	637 students/librarian	**% Black**: 22.9	***Status*** indicator percentile
Total Teachers: 4,987	**Guidance Counselors**: 213.3	**% Hispanic**: 2.5	(100=high): 66th
Student/Classroom Teacher Ratio: na	359 students/counselor	**% White**: 69.1	

Warren County

[FRONT ROYAL] WARREN COUNTY S.D.

111 E CRISER RD ● FRONT ROYAL VA 22630 ● (540) 635-2171

Grade Span: KG-12	**Expenditures/Student**: $4,298	**% Amer Indian**: 0.1	
Schools: *Regular* 6 ● *Spec Ed* 0 ● *Alt* 0	**Librarians**: 8.6	**% Asian**: 0.6	National ***Socio-Economic***
Students: 4,606	536 students/librarian	**% Black**: 5.9	***Status*** indicator percentile
Total Teachers: 308	**Guidance Counselors**: 34.1	**% Hispanic**: 0.8	(100=high): 67th
Student/Classroom Teacher Ratio: na	135 students/counselor	**% White**: 92.6	

Washington County

[ABINGDON] WASHINGTON COUNTY S.D.

812 THOMPSON DR ● ABINGDON VA 24210 ● (540) 628-1826 ● http://www.wcs.k12.va.us

Grade Span: KG-12	**Expenditures/Student**: $4,736	**% Amer Indian**: 0.0	
Schools: *Regular* 15 ● *Spec Ed* 0 ● *Alt* 2	**Librarians**: 15.0	**% Asian**: 0.3	National ***Socio-Economic***
Students: 7,539	503 students/librarian	**% Black**: 1.8	***Status*** indicator percentile
Total Teachers: 544	**Guidance Counselors**: 18.2	**% Hispanic**: 0.2	(100=high): 48th
Student/Classroom Teacher Ratio: na	414 students/counselor	**% White**: 97.7	

Waynesboro Independent City

WAYNESBORO CITY S.D.

301 PINE AVE ● WAYNESBORO VA 22980 ● (540) 946-4600

Grade Span: KG-12	**Expenditures/Student**: $4,956	**% Amer Indian**: 0.1	
Schools: *Regular* 6 ● *Spec Ed* 0 ● *Alt* 0	**Librarians**: 5.1	**% Asian**: 0.4	National ***Socio-Economic***
Students: 3,019	592 students/librarian	**% Black**: 16.7	***Status*** indicator percentile
Total Teachers: 195	**Guidance Counselors**: 7.8	**% Hispanic**: 1.2	(100=high): 61st
Student/Classroom Teacher Ratio: na	387 students/counselor	**% White**: 81.5	

Winchester Independent City

WINCHESTER CITY S.D.

PO BOX 551 ● WINCHESTER VA 22604 ● (540) 667-4253 ● http://www.pen.k12.va.us/Anthology/Div/Winchester

Grade Span: KG-12	**Expenditures/Student**: $6,672	**% Amer Indian**: 0.1	
Schools: *Regular* 6 ● *Spec Ed* 0 ● *Alt* 1	**Librarians**: 7.6	**% Asian**: 1.7	National ***Socio-Economic***
Students: 3,297	434 students/librarian	**% Black**: 17.2	***Status*** indicator percentile
Total Teachers: 254	**Guidance Counselors**: 11.0	**% Hispanic**: 2.5	(100=high): 39th
Student/Classroom Teacher Ratio: na	300 students/counselor	**% White**: 78.6	

Wise County

[WISE] **WISE COUNTY S.D.**

PO BOX 1217 ● WISE VA 24293 ● (540) 328-9421

Grade Span: KG-12 **Schools**: *Regular* 15 ● *Spec Ed* 0 ● *Alt* 1 **Students**: 7,853 **Total Teachers**: 517 **Student/Classroom Teacher Ratio**: na	**Expenditures/Student**: $4,979 **Librarians**: 14.9 527 students/librarian **Guidance Counselors**: 20.1 391 students/counselor	**% Amer Indian**: 0.0 **% Asian**: 0.4 **% Black**: 1.6 **% Hispanic**: 0.2 **% White**: 97.8	National ***Socio-Economic Status*** indicator percentile (100=high): 33rd

Wythe County

[WYTHEVILLE] **WYTHE COUNTY S.D.**

1570 W RESERVOIR ST ● WYTHEVILLE VA 24382 ● (540) 228-5411

Grade Span: KG-12 **Schools**: *Regular* 10 ● *Spec Ed* 0 ● *Alt* 1 **Students**: 4,356 **Total Teachers**: 320 **Student/Classroom Teacher Ratio**: na	**Expenditures/Student**: $4,854 **Librarians**: 9.0 484 students/librarian **Guidance Counselors**: 11.0 396 students/counselor	**% Amer Indian**: 0.0 **% Asian**: 0.2 **% Black**: 3.9 **% Hispanic**: 0.2 **% White**: 95.7	National ***Socio-Economic Status*** indicator percentile (100=high): 50th

York County

[YORKTOWN] **YORK COUNTY S.D.**

302 DARE RD ● YORKTOWN VA 23692 ● (757) 898-0300

Grade Span: KG-12 **Schools**: *Regular* 16 ● *Spec Ed* 0 ● *Alt* 0 **Students**: 10,729 **Total Teachers**: 630 **Student/Classroom Teacher Ratio**: na	**Expenditures/Student**: $4,552 **Librarians**: 17.0 631 students/librarian **Guidance Counselors**: 29.5 364 students/counselor	**% Amer Indian**: 0.4 **% Asian**: 3.5 **% Black**: 17.1 **% Hispanic**: 2.3 **% White**: 76.7	National ***Socio-Economic Status*** indicator percentile (100=high): 84th

Adams County
OTHELLO S.D.
615 E JUNIPER ● OTHELLO WA 99344 ● (509) 488-2659

Grade Span: KG-12 **Schools**: *Regular* 6 ● *Spec Ed* 0 ● *Alt* 0 **Students**: 2,855 **Total Teachers**: 149 **Student/Classroom Teacher Ratio**: 19.4	**Expenditures/Student**: $5,331 **Librarians**: 5.0 571 students/librarian **Guidance Counselors**: 4.7 607 students/counselor	**% Amer Indian**: 0.1 **% Asian**: 0.7 **% Black**: 0.3 **% Hispanic**: 65.5 **% White**: 33.4	National ***Socio-Economic Status*** indicator percentiles are not available for the state of Washington

Asotin County
CLARKSTON S.D.
PO BOX 70 ● CLARKSTON WA 99403 ● (509) 758-2532 ● http://jawbone.clarkston.wednet.edu/Websites/DO/index.html

Grade Span: KG-12 **Schools**: *Regular* 7 ● *Spec Ed* 1 ● *Alt* 1 **Students**: 3,077 **Total Teachers**: 152 **Student/Classroom Teacher Ratio**: 20.5	**Expenditures/Student**: $5,049 **Librarians**: 4.6 669 students/librarian **Guidance Counselors**: 4.0 769 students/counselor	**% Amer Indian**: 1.6 **% Asian**: 0.7 **% Black**: 0.5 **% Hispanic**: 1.7 **% White**: 95.6	National ***Socio-Economic Status*** indicator percentiles are not available for the state of Washington

Benton County
KENNEWICK S.D.
200 S DAYTON ST ● KENNEWICK WA 99336 ● (509) 582-8233 ● http://www.ksd.org

Grade Span: PK-12 **Schools**: *Regular* 23 ● *Spec Ed* 0 ● *Alt* 1 **Students**: 12,635 **Total Teachers**: 660 **Student/Classroom Teacher Ratio**: 20.4	**Expenditures/Student**: $5,448 **Librarians**: 22.9 552 students/librarian **Guidance Counselors**: 32.5 389 students/counselor	**% Amer Indian**: 0.2 **% Asian**: 2.5 **% Black**: 1.7 **% Hispanic**: 11.4 **% White**: 84.2	National ***Socio-Economic Status*** indicator percentiles are not available for the state of Washington

Benton County
PROSSER S.D.
823 PARK AVE ● PROSSER WA 99350 ● (509) 786-3323

Grade Span: KG-12 **Schools**: *Regular* 5 ● *Spec Ed* 0 ● *Alt* 0 **Students**: 2,759 **Total Teachers**: 141 **Student/Classroom Teacher Ratio**: 19.4	**Expenditures/Student**: $5,443 **Librarians**: 4.5 613 students/librarian **Guidance Counselors**: 5.1 541 students/counselor	**% Amer Indian**: 0.3 **% Asian**: 0.8 **% Black**: 0.4 **% Hispanic**: 37.9 **% White**: 60.6	National ***Socio-Economic Status*** indicator percentiles are not available for the state of Washington

Benton County
RICHLAND S.D.
615 SNOW AVE ● RICHLAND WA 99352 ● (509) 946-6106

Grade Span: KG-12 **Schools**: *Regular* 11 ● *Spec Ed* 1 ● *Alt* 1 **Students**: 8,762 **Total Teachers**: 428 **Student/Classroom Teacher Ratio**: 20.0	**Expenditures/Student**: $4,947 **Librarians**: 13.1 669 students/librarian **Guidance Counselors**: 22.0 398 students/counselor	**% Amer Indian**: 0.6 **% Asian**: 4.4 **% Black**: 2.1 **% Hispanic**: 4.3 **% White**: 88.6	National ***Socio-Economic Status*** indicator percentiles are not available for the state of Washington

Chelan County
WENATCHEE S.D.
235 SUNSET AVENUE ● WENATCHEE WA 98807 ● (509) 663-8161 ● http://home.wsd.wednet.edu

Grade Span: PK-12 **Schools**: *Regular* 15 ● *Spec Ed* 0 ● *Alt* 0 **Students**: 6,810 **Total Teachers**: 326 **Student/Classroom Teacher Ratio**: 21.2	**Expenditures/Student**: $5,166 **Librarians**: 10.2 668 students/librarian **Guidance Counselors**: 18.0 378 students/counselor	**% Amer Indian**: 1.3 **% Asian**: 1.7 **% Black**: 0.3 **% Hispanic**: 21.7 **% White**: 75.1	National ***Socio-Economic Status*** indicator percentiles are not available for the state of Washington

Clallam County
PORT ANGELES S.D.
216 E 4TH ST ● PORT ANGELES WA 98362 ● (360) 457-8575 ● http://www.pasd.wednet.edu

Grade Span: PK-12 **Schools**: *Regular* 10 ● *Spec Ed* 0 ● *Alt* 1 **Students**: 5,323 **Total Teachers**: 269 **Student/Classroom Teacher Ratio**: 19.0	**Expenditures/Student**: $5,092 **Librarians**: 4.0 1,331 students/librarian **Guidance Counselors**: 6.0 887 students/counselor	**% Amer Indian**: 5.8 **% Asian**: 2.0 **% Black**: 0.9 **% Hispanic**: 1.9 **% White**: 89.4	National ***Socio-Economic Status*** indicator percentiles are not available for the state of Washington

Clallam County
SEQUIM S.D.
503 N SEQUIM AVE ● SEQUIM WA 98382 ● (360) 683-3336

Grade Span: PK-12 **Schools**: *Regular* 4 ● *Spec Ed* 0 ● *Alt* 0 **Students**: 2,828 **Total Teachers**: 136 **Student/Classroom Teacher Ratio**: 20.8	**Expenditures/Student**: $4,884 **Librarians**: 4.1 690 students/librarian **Guidance Counselors**: 6.8 416 students/counselor	**% Amer Indian**: 4.2 **% Asian**: 1.7 **% Black**: 0.6 **% Hispanic**: 2.8 **% White**: 90.7	National ***Socio-Economic Status*** indicator percentiles are not available for the state of Washington

Clark County
BATTLE GROUND S.D.
204 W MAIN ST ● BATTLE GROUND WA 98604 ● (360) 687-5171 ● http://bgsd.k12.wa.us

Grade Span: KG-12 **Schools**: *Regular* 16 ● *Spec Ed* 0 ● *Alt* 1 **Students**: 10,303 **Total Teachers**: 469 **Student/Classroom Teacher Ratio**: 21.3	**Expenditures/Student**: $5,303 **Librarians**: 13.2 781 students/librarian **Guidance Counselors**: 8.8 1,171 students/counselor	**% Amer Indian**: 0.8 **% Asian**: 1.9 **% Black**: 0.6 **% Hispanic**: 2.4 **% White**: 94.3	National ***Socio-Economic Status*** indicator percentiles are not available for the state of Washington

Clark County
CAMAS S.D.
2041 NE IONE ST ● CAMAS WA 98607 ● (360) 834-2811 ● http://www.camas.wednet.edu

Grade Span: PK-12 **Schools**: *Regular* 6 ● *Spec Ed* 0 ● *Alt* 0 **Students**: 2,962 **Total Teachers**: 141 **Student/Classroom Teacher Ratio**: 21.3	**Expenditures/Student**: $5,409 **Librarians**: 4.5 658 students/librarian **Guidance Counselors**: 5.6 529 students/counselor	**% Amer Indian**: 0.8 **% Asian**: 1.8 **% Black**: 0.5 **% Hispanic**: 2.1 **% White**: 94.8	National ***Socio-Economic Status*** indicator percentiles are not available for the state of Washington

Clark County
[VANCOUVER] **EVERGREEN S.D.**
13501 NE 28TH STREET ● VANCOUVER WA 98668 ● (360) 256-6000 ● http://www.egreen.wednet.edu

Grade Span: PK-12 **Schools**: *Regular* 23 ● *Spec Ed* 1 ● *Alt* 3 **Students**: 17,596 **Total Teachers**: 884 **Student/Classroom Teacher Ratio**: 20.2	**Expenditures/Student**: $5,451 **Librarians**: 23.3 755 students/librarian **Guidance Counselors**: 35.4 497 students/counselor	**% Amer Indian**: 0.9 **% Asian**: 5.8 **% Black**: 2.4 **% Hispanic**: 3.0 **% White**: 87.9	National ***Socio-Economic Status*** indicator percentiles are not available for the state of Washington

Clark County
VANCOUVER S.D.
605 N. DEVINE ROAD ● VANCOUVER WA 98668 ● (360) 696-7161 ● http://www.vannet.k12.wa.us

Grade Span: PK-12 **Schools**: *Regular* 32 ● *Spec Ed* 3 ● *Alt* 1 **Students**: 19,910 **Total Teachers**: 935 **Student/Classroom Teacher Ratio**: 21.2	**Expenditures/Student**: $5,513 **Librarians**: 27.3 729 students/librarian **Guidance Counselors**: 37.0 538 students/counselor	**% Amer Indian**: 2.1 **% Asian**: 4.7 **% Black**: 3.5 **% Hispanic**: 4.3 **% White**: 85.3	National ***Socio-Economic Status*** indicator percentiles are not available for the state of Washington

Clark County

WASHOUGAL S.D.

2349 B ST ● WASHOUGAL WA 98671 ● (360) 835-2191

Grade Span: KG-12 **Schools**: *Regular* 5 ● *Spec Ed* 0 ● *Alt* 1 **Students**: 2,597 **Total Teachers**: 117 **Student/Classroom Teacher Ratio**: 22.0	**Expenditures/Student**: $5,568 **Librarians**: 1.0 2,597 students/librarian **Guidance Counselors**: 3.4 764 students/counselor	**% Amer Indian**: 1.4 **% Asian**: 1.2 **% Black**: 0.4 **% Hispanic**: 1.1 **% White**: 95.8	National ***Socio-Economic Status*** indicator percentiles are not available for the state of Washington

Cowlitz County

KELSO S.D.

601 CRAWFORD ST ● KELSO WA 98626 ● (360) 577-2400

Grade Span: PK-12 **Schools**: *Regular* 11 ● *Spec Ed* 1 ● *Alt* 1 **Students**: 5,244 **Total Teachers**: 256 **Student/Classroom Teacher Ratio**: 20.4	**Expenditures/Student**: $5,436 **Librarians**: 0.0 *** students/librarian **Guidance Counselors**: 7.1 739 students/counselor	**% Amer Indian**: 2.6 **% Asian**: 1.3 **% Black**: 0.7 **% Hispanic**: 3.8 **% White**: 91.5	National ***Socio-Economic Status*** indicator percentiles are not available for the state of Washington

Cowlitz County

LONGVIEW S.D.

28TH AND LILAC ST ● LONGVIEW WA 98632 ● (360) 577-2706 ● http://www.teleport.com/~lps

Grade Span: PK-12 **Schools**: *Regular* 14 ● *Spec Ed* 2 ● *Alt* 0 **Students**: 7,692 **Total Teachers**: 392 **Student/Classroom Teacher Ratio**: 19.4	**Expenditures/Student**: $5,493 **Librarians**: 10.2 754 students/librarian **Guidance Counselors**: 16.3 472 students/counselor	**% Amer Indian**: 2.2 **% Asian**: 3.8 **% Black**: 0.9 **% Hispanic**: 4.3 **% White**: 88.8	National ***Socio-Economic Status*** indicator percentiles are not available for the state of Washington

Douglas County

[EAST WENATCHEE] EASTMONT S.D.

460 9TH ST NE ● EAST WENATCHEE WA 98802 ● (509) 884-7169

Grade Span: KG-12 **Schools**: *Regular* 9 ● *Spec Ed* 0 ● *Alt* 0 **Students**: 4,530 **Total Teachers**: 213 **Student/Classroom Teacher Ratio**: 21.6	**Expenditures/Student**: $5,134 **Librarians**: 7.6 596 students/librarian **Guidance Counselors**: 6.0 755 students/counselor	**% Amer Indian**: 0.6 **% Asian**: 0.9 **% Black**: 0.5 **% Hispanic**: 15.4 **% White**: 82.6	National ***Socio-Economic Status*** indicator percentiles are not available for the state of Washington

Franklin County

PASCO S.D.

1004 N 16TH AVE ● PASCO WA 99301 ● (509) 547-9531 ● http://www.pasco.wednet.edu

Grade Span: PK-12 **Schools**: *Regular* 13 ● *Spec Ed* 0 ● *Alt* 1 **Students**: 7,882 **Total Teachers**: 425 **Student/Classroom Teacher Ratio**: 17.2	**Expenditures/Student**: $5,395 **Librarians**: 9.2 857 students/librarian **Guidance Counselors**: 16.4 481 students/counselor	**% Amer Indian**: 0.5 **% Asian**: 2.0 **% Black**: 4.5 **% Hispanic**: 54.1 **% White**: 39.0	National ***Socio-Economic Status*** indicator percentiles are not available for the state of Washington

Grant County

MOSES LAKE S.D.

1318 W IVY AVE ● MOSES LAKE WA 98837 ● (509) 765-3485

Grade Span: PK-12 **Schools**: *Regular* 13 ● *Spec Ed* 0 ● *Alt* 1 **Students**: 6,092 **Total Teachers**: 281 **Student/Classroom Teacher Ratio**: 21.3	**Expenditures/Student**: $5,014 **Librarians**: 4.1 1,486 students/librarian **Guidance Counselors**: 6.3 967 students/counselor	**% Amer Indian**: 1.4 **% Asian**: 1.8 **% Black**: 2.7 **% Hispanic**: 24.5 **% White**: 69.6	National ***Socio-Economic Status*** indicator percentiles are not available for the state of Washington

Grays Harbor County
ABERDEEN S.D.
216 N G ST ● ABERDEEN WA 98520 ● (360) 532-7690 ● http://www.esd113.wednet.edu/esd113/Aberdeen/AberdeenSD.html

Grade Span: PK-12 **Schools**: *Regular* 11 ● *Spec Ed* 1 ● *Alt* 0 **Students**: 4,230 **Total Teachers**: 215 **Student/Classroom Teacher Ratio**: 21.3	**Expenditures/Student**: $5,380 **Librarians**: 2.0 2,115 students/librarian **Guidance Counselors**: 6.0 705 students/counselor	**% Amer Indian**: 5.0 **% Asian**: 3.6 **% Black**: 1.1 **% Hispanic**: 4.8 **% White**: 85.6	National ***Socio-Economic Status*** indicator percentiles are not available for the state of Washington

Island County
OAK HARBOR S.D.
1250 MIDWAY BLVD ● OAK HARBOR WA 98277 ● (360) 675-0702

Grade Span: PK-12 **Schools**: *Regular* 11 ● *Spec Ed* 0 ● *Alt* 1 **Students**: 6,372 **Total Teachers**: 274 **Student/Classroom Teacher Ratio**: 23.2	**Expenditures/Student**: $4,557 **Librarians**: 9.7 657 students/librarian **Guidance Counselors**: 10.6 601 students/counselor	**% Amer Indian**: 0.8 **% Asian**: 13.8 **% Black**: 5.3 **% Hispanic**: 3.9 **% White**: 76.2	National ***Socio-Economic Status*** indicator percentiles are not available for the state of Washington

King County
AUBURN S.D.
915 4TH ST NE ● AUBURN WA 98002 ● (253) 931-4914 ● http://www.auburn.wednet.edu

Grade Span: KG-12 **Schools**: *Regular* 19 ● *Spec Ed* 0 ● *Alt* 1 **Students**: 12,113 **Total Teachers**: 589 **Student/Classroom Teacher Ratio**: 20.5	**Expenditures/Student**: $5,115 **Librarians**: 18.0 673 students/librarian **Guidance Counselors**: 29.0 418 students/counselor	**% Amer Indian**: 3.6 **% Asian**: 4.7 **% Black**: 2.4 **% Hispanic**: 4.3 **% White**: 85.1	National ***Socio-Economic Status*** indicator percentiles are not available for the state of Washington

King County
BELLEVUE S.D.
12111 NE 1ST ST ● BELLEVUE WA 98009 ● (425) 455-6015 ● http://belnet.bellevue.k12.wa.us

Grade Span: PK-12 **Schools**: *Regular* 28 ● *Spec Ed* 1 ● *Alt* 3 **Students**: 15,391 **Total Teachers**: 754 **Student/Classroom Teacher Ratio**: 22.2	**Expenditures/Student**: $5,852 **Librarians**: 22.5 684 students/librarian **Guidance Counselors**: 31.7 486 students/counselor	**% Amer Indian**: 0.4 **% Asian**: 18.9 **% Black**: 4.3 **% Hispanic**: 5.2 **% White**: 71.2	National ***Socio-Economic Status*** indicator percentiles are not available for the state of Washington

King County
[BOTHELL] **NORTHSHORE S.D.**
18315 BOTHELL WAY NE ● BOTHELL WA 98011 ● (425) 485-0417 ● http://www.norshore.wednet.edu

Grade Span: PK-12 **Schools**: *Regular* 31 ● *Spec Ed* 0 ● *Alt* 1 **Students**: 19,226 **Total Teachers**: 930 **Student/Classroom Teacher Ratio**: 20.3	**Expenditures/Student**: $5,363 **Librarians**: 31.6 608 students/librarian **Guidance Counselors**: 27.0 712 students/counselor	**% Amer Indian**: 0.9 **% Asian**: 6.6 **% Black**: 1.3 **% Hispanic**: 2.6 **% White**: 88.6	National ***Socio-Economic Status*** indicator percentiles are not available for the state of Washington

King County
[CARNATION] **RIVERVIEW S.D.**
32240 NE 50TH ST ● CARNATION WA 98014 ● (425) 333-4115 ● http://www.riverview.wednet.edu

Grade Span: KG-12 **Schools**: *Regular* 6 ● *Spec Ed* 0 ● *Alt* 0 **Students**: 2,757 **Total Teachers**: 135 **Student/Classroom Teacher Ratio**: 20.6	**Expenditures/Student**: $5,356 **Librarians**: 5.0 551 students/librarian **Guidance Counselors**: 4.9 563 students/counselor	**% Amer Indian**: 1.7 **% Asian**: 2.5 **% Black**: 0.3 **% Hispanic**: 3.7 **% White**: 91.7	National ***Socio-Economic Status*** indicator percentiles are not available for the state of Washington

King County

ENUMCLAW S.D.

2929 MCDOUGALL AVE ● ENUMCLAW WA 98022 ● (360) 825-2588

Grade Span: PK-12 **Schools**: *Regular* 9 ● *Spec Ed* 1 ● *Alt* 0 **Students**: 5,044 **Total Teachers**: 248 **Student/Classroom Teacher Ratio**: 20.2	**Expenditures/Student**: $4,884 **Librarians**: 5.2 970 students/librarian **Guidance Counselors**: 6.6 764 students/counselor	**% Amer Indian**: 1.5 **% Asian**: 1.0 **% Black**: 0.7 **% Hispanic**: 2.2 **% White**: 94.7	National ***Socio-Economic Status*** indicator percentiles are not available for the state of Washington

King County

FEDERAL WAY S.D.

31405 18TH AVE S ● FEDERAL WAY WA 98003 ● (253) 941-0100 ● http://www.fwsd.wednet.edu

Grade Span: PK-12 **Schools**: *Regular* 33 ● *Spec Ed* 2 ● *Alt* 1 **Students**: 20,579 **Total Teachers**: 968 **Student/Classroom Teacher Ratio**: 21.6	**Expenditures/Student**: $5,121 **Librarians**: 31.6 651 students/librarian **Guidance Counselors**: 44.8 459 students/counselor	**% Amer Indian**: 1.3 **% Asian**: 11.6 **% Black**: 9.3 **% Hispanic**: 4.7 **% White**: 73.1	National ***Socio-Economic Status*** indicator percentiles are not available for the state of Washington

King County

ISSAQUAH S.D.

565 NW HOLLY ST ● ISSAQUAH WA 98027 ● (425) 392-0712 ● http://www.issaquah.wednet.edu

Grade Span: PK-12 **Schools**: *Regular* 17 ● *Spec Ed* 1 ● *Alt* 3 **Students**: 11,464 **Total Teachers**: 535 **Student/Classroom Teacher Ratio**: 22.3	**Expenditures/Student**: $5,249 **Librarians**: 16.4 699 students/librarian **Guidance Counselors**: 22.2 516 students/counselor	**% Amer Indian**: 0.5 **% Asian**: 6.9 **% Black**: 1.2 **% Hispanic**: 1.7 **% White**: 89.7	National ***Socio-Economic Status*** indicator percentiles are not available for the state of Washington

King County

KENT S.D.

12033 SE 256TH ST ● KENT WA 98031 ● (206) 852-9550 ● http://www.kent.wednet.edu

Grade Span: PK-12 **Schools**: *Regular* 36 ● *Spec Ed* 1 ● *Alt* 1 **Students**: 24,492 **Total Teachers**: 1,182 **Student/Classroom Teacher Ratio**: 21.2	**Expenditures/Student**: $5,225 **Librarians**: 24.3 1,008 students/librarian **Guidance Counselors**: 44.9 545 students/counselor	**% Amer Indian**: 1.3 **% Asian**: 8.7 **% Black**: 6.5 **% Hispanic**: 3.8 **% White**: 79.7	National ***Socio-Economic Status*** indicator percentiles are not available for the state of Washington

King County

[KIRKLAND] **LAKE WASHINGTON S.D.**

PO BOX 2909 ● KIRKLAND WA 98083 ● (425) 828-3257 ● http://www.lkwash.wednet.edu

Grade Span: PK-12 **Schools**: *Regular* 39 ● *Spec Ed* 2 ● *Alt* 4 **Students**: 24,332 **Total Teachers**: 1,126 **Student/Classroom Teacher Ratio**: 21.4	**Expenditures/Student**: $5,172 **Librarians**: 34.2 711 students/librarian **Guidance Counselors**: 41.6 585 students/counselor	**% Amer Indian**: 0.5 **% Asian**: 8.8 **% Black**: 2.1 **% Hispanic**: 3.1 **% White**: 85.5	National ***Socio-Economic Status*** indicator percentiles are not available for the state of Washington

King County

[MAPLE VALLEY] **TAHOMA S.D.**

25720 MAPLE VALLEY BLACK DIA ● MAPLE VALLEY WA 98038 ● (425) 432-4481 ● http://www.tahoma.wednet.edu

Grade Span: PK-12 **Schools**: *Regular* 9 ● *Spec Ed* 0 ● *Alt* 0 **Students**: 5,100 **Total Teachers**: 250 **Student/Classroom Teacher Ratio**: 20.2	**Expenditures/Student**: $5,265 **Librarians**: 0.0 *** students/librarian **Guidance Counselors**: 4.9 1,041 students/counselor	**% Amer Indian**: 0.8 **% Asian**: 2.0 **% Black**: 1.2 **% Hispanic**: 1.5 **% White**: 94.3	National ***Socio-Economic Status*** indicator percentiles are not available for the state of Washington

King County
MERCER ISLAND S.D.
4160 86TH AVE SE ● MERCER ISLAND WA 98040 ● (206) 232-1660

Grade Span: KG-12 **Schools**: *Regular* 6 ● *Spec Ed* 1 ● *Alt* 1 **Students**: 3,765 **Total Teachers**: 172 **Student/Classroom Teacher Ratio**: 22.3	**Expenditures/Student**: $5,765 **Librarians**: 2.9 1,298 students/librarian **Guidance Counselors**: 5.8 649 students/counselor	**% Amer Indian**: 0.1 **% Asian**: 13.6 **% Black**: 1.6 **% Hispanic**: 1.0 **% White**: 83.7	National ***Socio-Economic Status*** indicator percentiles are not available for the state of Washington

King County
RENTON S.D.
435 MAIN AVE S ● RENTON WA 98055 ● (425) 235-2340 ● http://www.renton.wednet.edu

Grade Span: KG-12 **Schools**: *Regular* 20 ● *Spec Ed* 2 ● *Alt* 4 **Students**: 12,173 **Total Teachers**: 576 **Student/Classroom Teacher Ratio**: 22.5	**Expenditures/Student**: $5,432 **Librarians**: 18.4 662 students/librarian **Guidance Counselors**: 21.5 566 students/counselor	**% Amer Indian**: 1.6 **% Asian**: 14.6 **% Black**: 17.3 **% Hispanic**: 3.9 **% White**: 62.5	National ***Socio-Economic Status*** indicator percentiles are not available for the state of Washington

King County
[SEATTLE] HIGHLINE S.D.
15675 AMBAUM BLDV SW ● SEATTLE WA 98166 ● (206) 433-2217 ● http://www.hsd401.org

Grade Span: KG-12 **Schools**: *Regular* 33 ● *Spec Ed* 0 ● *Alt* 5 **Students**: 18,209 **Total Teachers**: 853 **Student/Classroom Teacher Ratio**: 22.2	**Expenditures/Student**: $5,454 **Librarians**: 31.8 573 students/librarian **Guidance Counselors**: 40.2 453 students/counselor	**% Amer Indian**: 3.1 **% Asian**: 16.4 **% Black**: 9.0 **% Hispanic**: 7.2 **% White**: 64.3	National ***Socio-Economic Status*** indicator percentiles are not available for the state of Washington

King County
SEATTLE S.D.
815 4TH AVE N ● SEATTLE WA 98109 ● (206) 281-6100 ● http://sea-css.ssd.k12.wa.us

Grade Span: PK-12 **Schools**: *Regular* 91 ● *Spec Ed* 17 ● *Alt* 6 **Students**: 46,757 **Total Teachers**: 2,420 **Student/Classroom Teacher Ratio**: 19.3	**Expenditures/Student**: $6,681 **Librarians**: 83.8 558 students/librarian **Guidance Counselors**: 85.4 548 students/counselor	**% Amer Indian**: 2.7 **% Asian**: 25.7 **% Black**: 22.9 **% Hispanic**: 8.0 **% White**: 40.7	National ***Socio-Economic Status*** indicator percentiles are not available for the state of Washington

King County
[SEATTLE] SHORELINE S.D.
18560 1ST AVE NE ● SEATTLE WA 98155 ● (206) 367-6111 ● http://www.shorelin.wednet.edu

Grade Span: KG-12 **Schools**: *Regular* 16 ● *Spec Ed* 1 ● *Alt* 1 **Students**: 9,929 **Total Teachers**: 490 **Student/Classroom Teacher Ratio**: 21.4	**Expenditures/Student**: $5,818 **Librarians**: 16.0 621 students/librarian **Guidance Counselors**: 12.0 827 students/counselor	**% Amer Indian**: 1.0 **% Asian**: 15.3 **% Black**: 3.5 **% Hispanic**: 2.8 **% White**: 77.5	National ***Socio-Economic Status*** indicator percentiles are not available for the state of Washington

King County
SNOQUALMIE VALLEY S.D.
PO BOX 400 ● SNOQUALMIE WA 98065 ● (425) 888-2334 ● http://www.snoqualmie.wednet.edu

Grade Span: PK-12 **Schools**: *Regular* 8 ● *Spec Ed* 0 ● *Alt* 1 **Students**: 4,111 **Total Teachers**: 196 **Student/Classroom Teacher Ratio**: 20.8	**Expenditures/Student**: $5,032 **Librarians**: 6.0 685 students/librarian **Guidance Counselors**: 5.6 734 students/counselor	**% Amer Indian**: 1.5 **% Asian**: 1.7 **% Black**: 1.0 **% Hispanic**: 2.4 **% White**: 93.5	National ***Socio-Economic Status*** indicator percentiles are not available for the state of Washington

Kitsap County
[BAINBRIDGE ISLAND] **BAINBRIDGE S.D.**
8489 MADISON AVE NE ● BAINBRIDGE ISLAND WA 98110 ● (206) 842-4714 ● http://www.bainbridge.wednet.edu

Grade Span: PK-12 **Schools**: *Regular* 7 ● *Spec Ed* 0 ● *Alt* 0 **Students**: 3,457 **Total Teachers**: 160 **Student/Classroom Teacher Ratio**: 22.0	**Expenditures/Student**: $5,258 **Librarians**: 5.0 691 students/librarian **Guidance Counselors**: 7.8 443 students/counselor	**% Amer Indian**: 1.1 **% Asian**: 5.7 **% Black**: 0.9 **% Hispanic**: 2.1 **% White**: 90.3	National ***Socio-Economic Status*** indicator percentiles are not available for the state of Washington

Kitsap County
BREMERTON S.D.
300 N MONTGOMERY AVE ● BREMERTON WA 98312 ● (360) 478-5151 ● http://bhs1.bremerton.wednet.edu

Grade Span: PK-12 **Schools**: *Regular* 14 ● *Spec Ed* 1 ● *Alt* 2 **Students**: 6,033 **Total Teachers**: 322 **Student/Classroom Teacher Ratio**: 20.7	**Expenditures/Student**: $5,342 **Librarians**: 9.0 670 students/librarian **Guidance Counselors**: 6.9 874 students/counselor	**% Amer Indian**: 3.6 **% Asian**: 9.7 **% Black**: 10.2 **% Hispanic**: 4.0 **% White**: 72.6	National ***Socio-Economic Status*** indicator percentiles are not available for the state of Washington

Kitsap County
[PORT ORCHARD] **SOUTH KITSAP S.D.**
1962 HOOVER AVE SE ● PORT ORCHARD WA 98366 ● (360) 876-7344

Grade Span: PK-12 **Schools**: *Regular* 16 ● *Spec Ed* 0 ● *Alt* 2 **Students**: 11,635 **Total Teachers**: 529 **Student/Classroom Teacher Ratio**: 22.3	**Expenditures/Student**: $4,817 **Librarians**: 14.9 781 students/librarian **Guidance Counselors**: 22.1 526 students/counselor	**% Amer Indian**: 2.7 **% Asian**: 5.5 **% Black**: 2.6 **% Hispanic**: 2.6 **% White**: 86.6	National ***Socio-Economic Status*** indicator percentiles are not available for the state of Washington

Kitsap County
[POULSBO] **NORTH KITSAP S.D.**
18360 CALDART AVE NE ● POULSBO WA 98370 ● (360) 779-3971 ● http://poulsbo.net/schools

Grade Span: PK-12 **Schools**: *Regular* 11 ● *Spec Ed* 1 ● *Alt* 1 **Students**: 6,890 **Total Teachers**: 322 **Student/Classroom Teacher Ratio**: 21.7	**Expenditures/Student**: $5,272 **Librarians**: 9.5 725 students/librarian **Guidance Counselors**: 15.0 459 students/counselor	**% Amer Indian**: 6.0 **% Asian**: 3.6 **% Black**: 1.3 **% Hispanic**: 2.7 **% White**: 86.4	National ***Socio-Economic Status*** indicator percentiles are not available for the state of Washington

Kitsap County
[SILVERDALE] **CENTRAL KITSAP S.D.**
PO BOX 8 ● SILVERDALE WA 98383 ● (360) 692-3111 ● http://www.cksd.wednet.edu

Grade Span: KG-12 **Schools**: *Regular* 20 ● *Spec Ed* 0 ● *Alt* 1 **Students**: 13,134 **Total Teachers**: 637 **Student/Classroom Teacher Ratio**: 20.4	**Expenditures/Student**: $4,935 **Librarians**: 18.5 710 students/librarian **Guidance Counselors**: 14.9 881 students/counselor	**% Amer Indian**: 1.2 **% Asian**: 12.4 **% Black**: 5.2 **% Hispanic**: 3.3 **% White**: 77.9	National ***Socio-Economic Status*** indicator percentiles are not available for the state of Washington

Kittitas County
ELLENSBURG S.D.
506 N SPRAGUE ST ● ELLENSBURG WA 98926 ● (509) 925-5365 ● http://www.esd105.wednet.edu/Ellensburg

Grade Span: KG-12 **Schools**: *Regular* 6 ● *Spec Ed* 0 ● *Alt* 1 **Students**: 2,796 **Total Teachers**: 139 **Student/Classroom Teacher Ratio**: 20.6	**Expenditures/Student**: $5,371 **Librarians**: 5.1 548 students/librarian **Guidance Counselors**: 7.0 399 students/counselor	**% Amer Indian**: 1.4 **% Asian**: 2.0 **% Black**: 0.8 **% Hispanic**: 5.5 **% White**: 90.3	National ***Socio-Economic Status*** indicator percentiles are not available for the state of Washington

Lewis County

CENTRALIA S.D.

PO BOX 610 ● CENTRALIA WA 98531 ● (360) 736-9387 ● http://www.centralia.wednet.edu

Grade Span: KG-12 **Schools**: *Regular* 8 ● *Spec Ed* 0 ● *Alt* 0 **Students**: 3,480 **Total Teachers**: 173 **Student/Classroom Teacher Ratio**: 19.9	**Expenditures/Student**: $5,404 **Librarians**: 2.0 1,740 students/librarian **Guidance Counselors**: 10.0 348 students/counselor	**% Amer Indian**: 1.1 **% Asian**: 1.4 **% Black**: 0.5 **% Hispanic**: 6.0 **% White**: 91.0	National ***Socio-Economic Status*** indicator percentiles are not available for the state of Washington

Lewis County

CHEHALIS S.D.

310 SW 16TH ST ● CHEHALIS WA 98532 ● (360) 748-8681 ● http://www.localaccess.com/chehalisschool

Grade Span: PK-12 **Schools**: *Regular* 5 ● *Spec Ed* 1 ● *Alt* 0 **Students**: 2,958 **Total Teachers**: 153 **Student/Classroom Teacher Ratio**: 20.7	**Expenditures/Student**: $6,730 **Librarians**: 3.5 845 students/librarian **Guidance Counselors**: 5.8 510 students/counselor	**% Amer Indian**: 0.6 **% Asian**: 0.9 **% Black**: 0.6 **% Hispanic**: 4.1 **% White**: 93.8	National ***Socio-Economic Status*** indicator percentiles are not available for the state of Washington

Mason County

SHELTON S.D.

811 W PINE ST ● SHELTON WA 98584 ● (360) 426-1687

Grade Span: PK-12 **Schools**: *Regular* 6 ● *Spec Ed* 0 ● *Alt* 1 **Students**: 4,124 **Total Teachers**: 194 **Student/Classroom Teacher Ratio**: 21.0	**Expenditures/Student**: $5,410 **Librarians**: 3.4 1,213 students/librarian **Guidance Counselors**: 9.0 458 students/counselor	**% Amer Indian**: 8.4 **% Asian**: 2.1 **% Black**: 0.7 **% Hispanic**: 4.4 **% White**: 84.4	National ***Socio-Economic Status*** indicator percentiles are not available for the state of Washington

Okanogan County

OMAK S.D.

619 WEST BARTLETT ● OMAK WA 98841 ● (509) 826-0320

Grade Span: PK-12 **Schools**: *Regular* 6 ● *Spec Ed* 0 ● *Alt* 2 **Students**: 2,515 **Total Teachers**: 142 **Student/Classroom Teacher Ratio**: 13.3	**Expenditures/Student**: $5,363 **Librarians**: 1.7 1,479 students/librarian **Guidance Counselors**: 6.9 364 students/counselor	**% Amer Indian**: 29.2 **% Asian**: 0.9 **% Black**: 0.4 **% Hispanic**: 8.1 **% White**: 61.5	National ***Socio-Economic Status*** indicator percentiles are not available for the state of Washington

Pierce County

[BUCKLEY] **WHITE RIVER S.D.**

PO BOX G ● BUCKLEY WA 98321 ● (360) 829-0600

Grade Span: KG-12 **Schools**: *Regular* 7 ● *Spec Ed* 0 ● *Alt* 1 **Students**: 3,524 **Total Teachers**: 174 **Student/Classroom Teacher Ratio**: 20.2	**Expenditures/Student**: $5,331 **Librarians**: 5.7 618 students/librarian **Guidance Counselors**: 7.5 470 students/counselor	**% Amer Indian**: 1.7 **% Asian**: 1.2 **% Black**: 0.5 **% Hispanic**: 1.4 **% White**: 95.2	National ***Socio-Economic Status*** indicator percentiles are not available for the state of Washington

Pierce County

[GIG HARBOR] **PENINSULA S.D.**

14015 62ND AVE NW ● GIG HARBOR WA 98332 ● (253) 857-2141

Grade Span: KG-12 **Schools**: *Regular* 15 ● *Spec Ed* 0 ● *Alt* 3 **Students**: 9,331 **Total Teachers**: 400 **Student/Classroom Teacher Ratio**: 23.4	**Expenditures/Student**: $4,838 **Librarians**: 4.0 2,333 students/librarian **Guidance Counselors**: 21.1 442 students/counselor	**% Amer Indian**: 1.3 **% Asian**: 2.5 **% Black**: 1.1 **% Hispanic**: 2.0 **% White**: 93.1	National ***Socio-Economic Status*** indicator percentiles are not available for the state of Washington

Pierce County
PUYALLUP S.D.
109 E PIONEER ● PUYALLUP WA 98372 ● (253) 841-1301 ● http://www.puyallup.k12.wa.us

Grade Span: PK-12 **Schools**: *Regular* 29 ● *Spec Ed* 1 ● *Alt* 4 **Students**: 17,304 **Total Teachers**: 856 **Student/Classroom Teacher Ratio**: 20.4	**Expenditures/Student**: $5,280 **Librarians**: 23.0 752 students/librarian **Guidance Counselors**: 35.9 482 students/counselor	**% Amer Indian**: 1.7 **% Asian**: 4.6 **% Black**: 2.2 **% Hispanic**: 3.0 **% White**: 88.4	National ***Socio-Economic Status*** indicator percentiles are not available for the state of Washington

Pierce County
[SPANAWAY] BETHEL S.D.
516 176TH ST E ● SPANAWAY WA 98387 ● (253) 535-0950

Grade Span: PK-12 **Schools**: *Regular* 25 ● *Spec Ed* 0 ● *Alt* 2 **Students**: 14,326 **Total Teachers**: 650 **Student/Classroom Teacher Ratio**: 22.7	**Expenditures/Student**: $5,187 **Librarians**: 10.7 1,339 students/librarian **Guidance Counselors**: 18.3 783 students/counselor	**% Amer Indian**: 2.6 **% Asian**: 7.4 **% Black**: 7.2 **% Hispanic**: 4.2 **% White**: 78.7	National ***Socio-Economic Status*** indicator percentiles are not available for the state of Washington

Pierce County
SUMNER S.D.
1202 WOOD AVE ● SUMNER WA 98390 ● (253) 863-4441

Grade Span: PK-12 **Schools**: *Regular* 12 ● *Spec Ed* 0 ● *Alt* 0 **Students**: 7,138 **Total Teachers**: 347 **Student/Classroom Teacher Ratio**: 21.1	**Expenditures/Student**: $5,258 **Librarians**: 10.2 700 students/librarian **Guidance Counselors**: 9.0 793 students/counselor	**% Amer Indian**: 2.6 **% Asian**: 2.2 **% Black**: 0.9 **% Hispanic**: 3.4 **% White**: 90.9	National ***Socio-Economic Status*** indicator percentiles are not available for the state of Washington

Pierce County
[TACOMA] CLOVER PARK S.D.
10903 GRAVELLY LAKE DR SW ● TACOMA WA 98499 ● (253) 584-9411 ● http://cpsd.cloverpark.k12.wa.us

Grade Span: PK-12 **Schools**: *Regular* 28 ● *Spec Ed* 2 ● *Alt* 1 **Students**: 13,692 **Total Teachers**: 661 **Student/Classroom Teacher Ratio**: 20.6	**Expenditures/Student**: $5,490 **Librarians**: 23.9 573 students/librarian **Guidance Counselors**: 29.9 458 students/counselor	**% Amer Indian**: 2.2 **% Asian**: 10.9 **% Black**: 24.3 **% Hispanic**: 6.8 **% White**: 55.9	National ***Socio-Economic Status*** indicator percentiles are not available for the state of Washington

Pierce County
[TACOMA] FIFE S.D.
5802 20TH ST E ● TACOMA WA 98424 ● (253) 922-6697 ● http://www.fifeschools.com

Grade Span: KG-12 **Schools**: *Regular* 4 ● *Spec Ed* 0 ● *Alt* 0 **Students**: 2,589 **Total Teachers**: 120 **Student/Classroom Teacher Ratio**: 21.7	**Expenditures/Student**: $5,014 **Librarians**: 4.0 647 students/librarian **Guidance Counselors**: 3.0 863 students/counselor	**% Amer Indian**: 4.9 **% Asian**: 3.4 **% Black**: 2.6 **% Hispanic**: 5.9 **% White**: 83.1	National ***Socio-Economic Status*** indicator percentiles are not available for the state of Washington

Pierce County
[TACOMA] FRANKLIN PIERCE S.D.
315 129TH ST S ● TACOMA WA 98444 ● (253) 537-0211

Grade Span: PK-12 **Schools**: *Regular* 13 ● *Spec Ed* 0 ● *Alt* 1 **Students**: 6,655 **Total Teachers**: 324 **Student/Classroom Teacher Ratio**: na	**Expenditures/Student**: $5,593 **Librarians**: 2.0 3,328 students/librarian **Guidance Counselors**: 16.0 416 students/counselor	**% Amer Indian**: 2.2 **% Asian**: 7.1 **% Black**: 9.9 **% Hispanic**: 3.8 **% White**: 77.0	National ***Socio-Economic Status*** indicator percentiles are not available for the state of Washington

Pierce County

TACOMA S.D.

601 S 8TH (ZIP 98405) ● TACOMA WA 98401 ● (253) 596-1000 ● http://www.tacoma.k12.wa.us

Grade Span: KG-12 **Schools**: *Regular* 56 ● *Spec Ed* 3 ● *Alt* 12 **Students**: 31,596 **Total Teachers**: 1,708 **Student/Classroom Teacher Ratio**: 18.4	**Expenditures/Student**: $6,275 **Librarians**: 54.3 582 students/librarian **Guidance Counselors**: 73.6 429 students/counselor	**% Amer Indian**: 1.8 **% Asian**: 13.6 **% Black**: 19.1 **% Hispanic**: 4.8 **% White**: 60.7	National ***Socio-Economic Status*** indicator percentiles are not available for the state of Washington

Pierce County

[TACOMA] UNIVERSITY PLACE S.D.

8805 40TH ST W ● TACOMA WA 98466 ● (253) 564-1400 ● http://www.upsd.wednet.edu

Grade Span: KG-12 **Schools**: *Regular* 9 ● *Spec Ed* 0 ● *Alt* 0 **Students**: 5,070 **Total Teachers**: 255 **Student/Classroom Teacher Ratio**: 20.5	**Expenditures/Student**: $5,064 **Librarians**: 8.1 626 students/librarian **Guidance Counselors**: 9.0 563 students/counselor	**% Amer Indian**: 0.6 **% Asian**: 9.9 **% Black**: 12.9 **% Hispanic**: 3.3 **% White**: 73.4	National ***Socio-Economic Status*** indicator percentiles are not available for the state of Washington

Skagit County

ANACORTES S.D.

2200 M AVE ● ANACORTES WA 98221 ● (360) 293-3171 ● http://www.cnw.com/~deets

Grade Span: KG-12 **Schools**: *Regular* 7 ● *Spec Ed* 0 ● *Alt* 1 **Students**: 2,978 **Total Teachers**: 133 **Student/Classroom Teacher Ratio**: 22.2	**Expenditures/Student**: $5,123 **Librarians**: 4.5 662 students/librarian **Guidance Counselors**: 5.1 584 students/counselor	**% Amer Indian**: 1.1 **% Asian**: 3.5 **% Black**: 0.8 **% Hispanic**: 3.1 **% White**: 91.6	National ***Socio-Economic Status*** indicator percentiles are not available for the state of Washington

Skagit County

BURLINGTON EDISON S.D.

927 E FAIRHAVEN AVE ● BURLINGTON WA 98233 ● (360) 755-0231 ● http://www.be.wednet.edu

Grade Span: PK-12 **Schools**: *Regular* 8 ● *Spec Ed* 0 ● *Alt* 1 **Students**: 3,288 **Total Teachers**: 150 **Student/Classroom Teacher Ratio**: 22.2	**Expenditures/Student**: $5,122 **Librarians**: 5.8 567 students/librarian **Guidance Counselors**: 9.3 354 students/counselor	**% Amer Indian**: 1.1 **% Asian**: 2.4 **% Black**: 0.6 **% Hispanic**: 13.6 **% White**: 82.2	National ***Socio-Economic Status*** indicator percentiles are not available for the state of Washington

Skagit County

MOUNT VERNON S.D.

124 E LAWRENCE ST ● MOUNT VERNON WA 98273 ● (360) 336-6114 ● http://www.mtvernon.wednet.edu

Grade Span: KG-12 **Schools**: *Regular* 8 ● *Spec Ed* 1 ● *Alt* 0 **Students**: 5,069 **Total Teachers**: 238 **Student/Classroom Teacher Ratio**: 20.8	**Expenditures/Student**: $5,140 **Librarians**: 7.1 714 students/librarian **Guidance Counselors**: 10.5 483 students/counselor	**% Amer Indian**: 1.4 **% Asian**: 2.4 **% Black**: 0.7 **% Hispanic**: 24.8 **% White**: 70.7	National ***Socio-Economic Status*** indicator percentiles are not available for the state of Washington

Skagit County

SEDRO-WOOLLEY S.D.

2079 COOK RD ● SEDRO-WOOLLEY WA 98284 ● (360) 856-0831

Grade Span: PK-12 **Schools**: *Regular* 11 ● *Spec Ed* 0 ● *Alt* 1 **Students**: 3,932 **Total Teachers**: 196 **Student/Classroom Teacher Ratio**: 20.5	**Expenditures/Student**: $4,931 **Librarians**: 4.8 819 students/librarian **Guidance Counselors**: 8.3 474 students/counselor	**% Amer Indian**: 3.7 **% Asian**: 1.3 **% Black**: 0.3 **% Hispanic**: 5.8 **% White**: 88.9	National ***Socio-Economic Status*** indicator percentiles are not available for the state of Washington

Snohomish County

ARLINGTON S.D.

600 EAST 1ST STREET ● ARLINGTON WA 98223 ● (360) 435-2156 ● http://www.asd.wednet.edu

Grade Span: KG-12	**Expenditures/Student**: $5,156	**% Amer Indian**: 1.5	National ***Socio-Economic***
Schools: *Regular* 6 ● *Spec Ed* 0 ● *Alt* 2	**Librarians**: 5.0	**% Asian**: 1.6	***Status*** indicator percentiles
Students: 4,143	829 students/librarian	**% Black**: 0.4	are not available for the
Total Teachers: 206	**Guidance Counselors**: 8.4	**% Hispanic**: 2.2	state of Washington
Student/Classroom Teacher Ratio: 20.5	493 students/counselor	**% White**: 94.2	

Snohomish County

EVERETT S.D.

PO BOX 2098 ● EVERETT WA 98203 ● (425) 342-7413 ● http://www.everett.wednet.edu

Grade Span: PK-12	**Expenditures/Student**: $5,495	**% Amer Indian**: 1.7	National ***Socio-Economic***
Schools: *Regular* 24 ● *Spec Ed* 4 ● *Alt* 1	**Librarians**: 22.9	**% Asian**: 7.4	***Status*** indicator percentiles
Students: 17,136	748 students/librarian	**% Black**: 2.8	are not available for the
Total Teachers: 795	**Guidance Counselors**: 43.6	**% Hispanic**: 3.9	state of Washington
Student/Classroom Teacher Ratio: 21.5	393 students/counselor	**% White**: 84.2	

Snohomish County

[EVERETT] MUKILTEO S.D.

9401 SHARON DR ● EVERETT WA 98204 ● (425) 353-7977 ● http://www.mukilteo.wednet.edu

Grade Span: PK-12	**Expenditures/Student**: $5,247	**% Amer Indian**: 1.1	National ***Socio-Economic***
Schools: *Regular* 18 ● *Spec Ed* 1 ● *Alt* 2	**Librarians**: 17.2	**% Asian**: 9.6	***Status*** indicator percentiles
Students: 12,191	709 students/librarian	**% Black**: 3.9	are not available for the
Total Teachers: 568	**Guidance Counselors**: 16.8	**% Hispanic**: 3.5	state of Washington
Student/Classroom Teacher Ratio: 22.5	726 students/counselor	**% White**: 81.9	

Snohomish County

LAKE STEVENS S.D.

2202A 123RD AVE NE ● LAKE STEVENS WA 98258 ● (425) 334-4051

Grade Span: PK-12	**Expenditures/Student**: $4,990	**% Amer Indian**: 1.6	National ***Socio-Economic***
Schools: *Regular* 10 ● *Spec Ed* 1 ● *Alt* 0	**Librarians**: 4.9	**% Asian**: 2.2	***Status*** indicator percentiles
Students: 5,286	1,079 students/librarian	**% Black**: 0.6	are not available for the
Total Teachers: 240	**Guidance Counselors**: 8.8	**% Hispanic**: 2.3	state of Washington
Student/Classroom Teacher Ratio: 22.3	601 students/counselor	**% White**: 93.2	

Snohomish County

[LYNNWOOD] EDMONDS S.D.

20420 68TH AVE W ● LYNNWOOD WA 98036-7400 ● (425) 670-7000 ● http://www.edmonds.wednet.edu

Grade Span: PK-12	**Expenditures/Student**: $5,415	**% Amer Indian**: 2.0	National ***Socio-Economic***
Schools: *Regular* 34 ● *Spec Ed* 1 ● *Alt* 4	**Librarians**: 28.9	**% Asian**: 10.4	***Status*** indicator percentiles
Students: 20,868	722 students/librarian	**% Black**: 3.6	are not available for the
Total Teachers: 1,003	**Guidance Counselors**: 32.3	**% Hispanic**: 3.6	state of Washington
Student/Classroom Teacher Ratio: 20.6	646 students/counselor	**% White**: 80.4	

Snohomish County

MARYSVILLE S.D.

4220 80TH ST NE ● MARYSVILLE WA 98270 ● (360) 659-6261 ● http://www.msvl.wednet.edu/MsvlSchools/msdhome.html

Grade Span: PK-12	**Expenditures/Student**: $5,490	**% Amer Indian**: 7.0	National ***Socio-Economic***
Schools: *Regular* 16 ● *Spec Ed* 0 ● *Alt* 1	**Librarians**: 12.5	**% Asian**: 3.4	***Status*** indicator percentiles
Students: 9,947	796 students/librarian	**% Black**: 0.7	are not available for the
Total Teachers: 468	**Guidance Counselors**: 22.0	**% Hispanic**: 2.7	state of Washington
Student/Classroom Teacher Ratio: 21.5	452 students/counselor	**% White**: 86.3	

Snohomish County
MONROE S.D.
200 E FREMONT ST ● MONROE WA 98272 ● (360) 794-7777 ● http://www.monroe.wednet.edu

Grade Span: PK-12 **Schools**: *Regular* 8 ● *Spec Ed* 2 ● *Alt* 0 **Students**: 4,838 **Total Teachers**: 227 **Student/Classroom Teacher Ratio**: 21.0	**Expenditures/Student**: $4,904 **Librarians**: 6.6 733 students/librarian **Guidance Counselors**: 10.0 484 students/counselor	**% Amer Indian**: 1.4 **% Asian**: 2.0 **% Black**: 0.6 **% Hispanic**: 3.1 **% White**: 92.9	National ***Socio-Economic Status*** indicator percentiles are not available for the state of Washington

Snohomish County
SNOHOMISH S.D.
1601 AVENUE D ● SNOHOMISH WA 98290 ● (360) 568-3151

Grade Span: KG-12 **Schools**: *Regular* 16 ● *Spec Ed* 0 ● *Alt* 0 **Students**: 8,352 **Total Teachers**: 378 **Student/Classroom Teacher Ratio**: 22.2	**Expenditures/Student**: $4,871 **Librarians**: 12.1 690 students/librarian **Guidance Counselors**: 14.0 597 students/counselor	**% Amer Indian**: 0.8 **% Asian**: 2.4 **% Black**: 0.8 **% Hispanic**: 2.3 **% White**: 93.9	National ***Socio-Economic Status*** indicator percentiles are not available for the state of Washington

Snohomish County
STANWOOD S.D.
PO BOX 430 ● STANWOOD WA 98292 ● (360) 629-2766

Grade Span: KG-12 **Schools**: *Regular* 5 ● *Spec Ed* 0 ● *Alt* 0 **Students**: 4,138 **Total Teachers**: 201 **Student/Classroom Teacher Ratio**: 20.7	**Expenditures/Student**: $4,738 **Librarians**: 5.3 781 students/librarian **Guidance Counselors**: 5.5 752 students/counselor	**% Amer Indian**: 1.2 **% Asian**: 1.4 **% Black**: 0.5 **% Hispanic**: 2.5 **% White**: 94.5	National ***Socio-Economic Status*** indicator percentiles are not available for the state of Washington

Spokane County
CHENEY S.D.
520 4TH ST ● CHENEY WA 99004 ● (509) 235-6205 ● http://www.netschool.com/pages/cheney/default.html

Grade Span: PK-12 **Schools**: *Regular* 9 ● *Spec Ed* 1 ● *Alt* 0 **Students**: 3,627 **Total Teachers**: 183 **Student/Classroom Teacher Ratio**: 19.5	**Expenditures/Student**: $5,693 **Librarians**: 6.9 526 students/librarian **Guidance Counselors**: 9.5 382 students/counselor	**% Amer Indian**: 2.9 **% Asian**: 2.5 **% Black**: 2.4 **% Hispanic**: 3.4 **% White**: 88.7	National ***Socio-Economic Status*** indicator percentiles are not available for the state of Washington

Spokane County
[GREENACRES] **CENTRAL VALLEY S.D.**
19307 E CATALDO AVE ● GREENACRES WA 99016 ● (509) 922-6706

Grade Span: PK-12 **Schools**: *Regular* 22 ● *Spec Ed* 0 ● *Alt* 0 **Students**: 10,784 **Total Teachers**: 548 **Student/Classroom Teacher Ratio**: 20.0	**Expenditures/Student**: $5,373 **Librarians**: 20.2 534 students/librarian **Guidance Counselors**: 26.4 408 students/counselor	**% Amer Indian**: 1.8 **% Asian**: 1.8 **% Black**: 0.9 **% Hispanic**: 1.5 **% White**: 93.9	National ***Socio-Economic Status*** indicator percentiles are not available for the state of Washington

Spokane County
MEAD S.D.
N 12508 FREYA ● MEAD WA 99021 ● (509) 466-6800

Grade Span: KG-12 **Schools**: *Regular* 12 ● *Spec Ed* 0 ● *Alt* 0 **Students**: 7,727 **Total Teachers**: 372 **Student/Classroom Teacher Ratio**: 21.5	**Expenditures/Student**: $5,256 **Librarians**: 9.0 859 students/librarian **Guidance Counselors**: 9.2 840 students/counselor	**% Amer Indian**: 1.1 **% Asian**: 1.8 **% Black**: 1.0 **% Hispanic**: 1.4 **% White**: 94.7	National ***Socio-Economic Status*** indicator percentiles are not available for the state of Washington

Spokane County

[SPOKANE] EAST VALLEY S.D.

NORTH 3415 PINES ROAD ● SPOKANE WA 99206 ● (509) 924-1830

Grade Span: KG-12	**Expenditures/Student**: $5,420	**% Amer Indian**: 2.4	National ***Socio-Economic Status*** indicator percentiles are not available for the state of Washington
Schools: *Regular* 9 ● *Spec Ed* 0 ● *Alt* 0	**Librarians**: 8.0	**% Asian**: 2.1	
Students: 4,743	593 students/librarian	**% Black**: 0.8	
Total Teachers: 231	**Guidance Counselors**: 11.7	**% Hispanic**: 1.4	
Student/Classroom Teacher Ratio: 20.4	405 students/counselor	**% White**: 93.3	

Spokane County

SPOKANE S.D.

N 200 BERNARD STREET ● SPOKANE WA 99201 ● (509) 455-5242 ● http://www.sd81.k12.wa.us

Grade Span: PK-12	**Expenditures/Student**: $5,380	**% Amer Indian**: 3.8	National ***Socio-Economic Status*** indicator percentiles are not available for the state of Washington
Schools: *Regular* 48 ● *Spec Ed* 5 ● *Alt* 12	**Librarians**: 48.1	**% Asian**: 3.1	
Students: 32,341	672 students/librarian	**% Black**: 3.7	
Total Teachers: 1,595	**Guidance Counselors**: 67.9	**% Hispanic**: 2.1	
Student/Classroom Teacher Ratio: 22.5	476 students/counselor	**% White**: 87.3	

Spokane County

[SPOKANE] WEST VALLEY S.D.

N 2805 ARGONNE ROAD ● SPOKANE WA 99211 ● (509) 924-2150

Grade Span: PK-12	**Expenditures/Student**: $5,441	**% Amer Indian**: 3.0	National ***Socio-Economic Status*** indicator percentiles are not available for the state of Washington
Schools: *Regular* 8 ● *Spec Ed* 0 ● *Alt* 1	**Librarians**: 0.0	**% Asian**: 1.3	
Students: 3,524	*** students/librarian	**% Black**: 1.1	
Total Teachers: 168	**Guidance Counselors**: 8.6	**% Hispanic**: 2.0	
Student/Classroom Teacher Ratio: 19.1	410 students/counselor	**% White**: 92.6	

Stevens County

COLVILLE S.D.

430 E HAWTHORNE AVE ● COLVILLE WA 99114 ● (509) 684-2536

Grade Span: KG-12	**Expenditures/Student**: $4,627	**% Amer Indian**: 2.7	National ***Socio-Economic Status*** indicator percentiles are not available for the state of Washington
Schools: *Regular* 6 ● *Spec Ed* 0 ● *Alt* 1	**Librarians**: 2.0	**% Asian**: 0.7	
Students: 2,634	1,317 students/librarian	**% Black**: 0.4	
Total Teachers: 117	**Guidance Counselors**: 3.0	**% Hispanic**: 1.4	
Student/Classroom Teacher Ratio: 22.7	878 students/counselor	**% White**: 94.8	

Thurston County

[LACEY] NORTH THURSTON S.D.

305 COLLEGE ST NE ● LACEY WA 98516 ● (360) 491-4300 ● http://www.ntsd.wednet.edu

Grade Span: PK-12	**Expenditures/Student**: $4,910	**% Amer Indian**: 2.2	National ***Socio-Economic Status*** indicator percentiles are not available for the state of Washington
Schools: *Regular* 19 ● *Spec Ed* 0 ● *Alt* 2	**Librarians**: 18.4	**% Asian**: 12.6	
Students: 13,150	715 students/librarian	**% Black**: 8.2	
Total Teachers: 666	**Guidance Counselors**: 27.5	**% Hispanic**: 4.9	
Student/Classroom Teacher Ratio: 20.6	478 students/counselor	**% White**: 72.0	

Thurston County

OLYMPIA S.D.

1113 LEGION WAY SE ● OLYMPIA WA 98501 ● (360) 753-8850 ● http://kids.osd.wednet.edu

Grade Span: KG-12	**Expenditures/Student**: $5,739	**% Amer Indian**: 1.2	National ***Socio-Economic Status*** indicator percentiles are not available for the state of Washington
Schools: *Regular* 20 ● *Spec Ed* 0 ● *Alt* 0	**Librarians**: 12.2	**% Asian**: 7.7	
Students: 8,632	708 students/librarian	**% Black**: 2.4	
Total Teachers: 424	**Guidance Counselors**: 8.9	**% Hispanic**: 2.5	
Student/Classroom Teacher Ratio: 20.3	970 students/counselor	**% White**: 86.3	

Thurston County
TUMWATER S.D.
419 LINWOOD AVE SW ● TUMWATER WA 98512 ● (360) 943-2276 ● http://www.tumwater.k12.wa.us

Grade Span: KG-12 **Schools**: *Regular* 10 ● *Spec Ed* 1 ● *Alt* 1 **Students**: 6,242 **Total Teachers**: 291 **Student/Classroom Teacher Ratio**: 21.2	**Expenditures/Student**: $5,721 **Librarians**: 8.6 726 students/librarian **Guidance Counselors**: 8.2 761 students/counselor	**% Amer Indian**: 1.6 **% Asian**: 3.4 **% Black**: 1.8 **% Hispanic**: 2.5 **% White**: 90.7	National ***Socio-Economic Status*** indicator percentiles are not available for the state of Washington

Thurston County
YELM S.D.
404 YELM AVE W ● YELM WA 98597 ● (360) 458-5731 ● http://www.yelmtel.com/~ycs

Grade Span: PK-12 **Schools**: *Regular* 8 ● *Spec Ed* 0 ● *Alt* 1 **Students**: 4,172 **Total Teachers**: 203 **Student/Classroom Teacher Ratio**: 19.9	**Expenditures/Student**: $5,611 **Librarians**: 5.8 719 students/librarian **Guidance Counselors**: 9.4 444 students/counselor	**% Amer Indian**: 3.0 **% Asian**: 2.1 **% Black**: 1.6 **% Hispanic**: 3.4 **% White**: 89.9	National ***Socio-Economic Status*** indicator percentiles are not available for the state of Washington

Walla Walla County
WALLA WALLA S.D.
364 S PARK ST ● WALLA WALLA WA 99362 ● (509) 525-6042 ● http://wwsd.ww.wednet.edu

Grade Span: PK-12 **Schools**: *Regular* 10 ● *Spec Ed* 2 ● *Alt* 0 **Students**: 6,894 **Total Teachers**: 338 **Student/Classroom Teacher Ratio**: 18.8	**Expenditures/Student**: $5,263 **Librarians**: 9.0 766 students/librarian **Guidance Counselors**: 8.5 811 students/counselor	**% Amer Indian**: 0.6 **% Asian**: 1.8 **% Black**: 1.6 **% Hispanic**: 19.7 **% White**: 76.2	National ***Socio-Economic Status*** indicator percentiles are not available for the state of Washington

Whatcom County
BELLINGHAM S.D.
PO BOX 878 ● BELLINGHAM WA 98227 ● (360) 676-6400 ● http://www.bham.wednet.edu/default.htm

Grade Span: PK-12 **Schools**: *Regular* 20 ● *Spec Ed* 0 ● *Alt* 1 **Students**: 10,090 **Total Teachers**: 480 **Student/Classroom Teacher Ratio**: 20.9	**Expenditures/Student**: $5,233 **Librarians**: 17.7 570 students/librarian **Guidance Counselors**: 14.0 721 students/counselor	**% Amer Indian**: 2.3 **% Asian**: 5.1 **% Black**: 1.4 **% Hispanic**: 3.9 **% White**: 87.3	National ***Socio-Economic Status*** indicator percentiles are not available for the state of Washington

Whatcom County
FERNDALE S.D.
PO BOX 698 ● FERNDALE WA 98248 ● (360) 384-3551

Grade Span: PK-12 **Schools**: *Regular* 10 ● *Spec Ed* 0 ● *Alt* 0 **Students**: 4,482 **Total Teachers**: 219 **Student/Classroom Teacher Ratio**: 20.0	**Expenditures/Student**: $5,039 **Librarians**: 8.1 553 students/librarian **Guidance Counselors**: 10.0 448 students/counselor	**% Amer Indian**: 11.6 **% Asian**: 1.5 **% Black**: 0.7 **% Hispanic**: 5.7 **% White**: 80.4	National ***Socio-Economic Status*** indicator percentiles are not available for the state of Washington

Whatcom County
LYNDEN S.D.
1203 BRADLEY RD ● LYNDEN WA 98264 ● (360) 354-4401

Grade Span: KG-12 **Schools**: *Regular* 5 ● *Spec Ed* 0 ● *Alt* 0 **Students**: 2,581 **Total Teachers**: 117 **Student/Classroom Teacher Ratio**: 22.1	**Expenditures/Student**: $4,697 **Librarians**: 1.0 2,581 students/librarian **Guidance Counselors**: 4.3 600 students/counselor	**% Amer Indian**: 1.5 **% Asian**: 2.6 **% Black**: 1.1 **% Hispanic**: 12.1 **% White**: 82.6	National ***Socio-Economic Status*** indicator percentiles are not available for the state of Washington

Yakima County
GRANDVIEW S.D.
913 W 2ND ST ● GRANDVIEW WA 98930 ● (509) 882-2271

Grade Span: PK-12 **Schools**: *Regular* 5 ● *Spec Ed* 0 ● *Alt* 2 **Students**: 2,828 **Total Teachers**: 137 **Student/Classroom Teacher Ratio**: 20.7	**Expenditures/Student**: $4,921 **Librarians**: 4.8 589 students/librarian **Guidance Counselors**: 5.0 566 students/counselor	**% Amer Indian**: 0.3 **% Asian**: 0.8 **% Black**: 0.5 **% Hispanic**: 69.3 **% White**: 29.2	National ***Socio-Economic Status*** indicator percentiles are not available for the state of Washington

Yakima County
SELAH S.D.
105 W BARTLETT AVE ● SELAH WA 98942 ● (509) 697-7243 ● http://www.esd105.wednet.edu/Selah

Grade Span: PK-12 **Schools**: *Regular* 5 ● *Spec Ed* 2 ● *Alt* 1 **Students**: 3,694 **Total Teachers**: 177 **Student/Classroom Teacher Ratio**: 20.9	**Expenditures/Student**: $5,304 **Librarians**: 4.1 901 students/librarian **Guidance Counselors**: 6.0 616 students/counselor	**% Amer Indian**: 0.8 **% Asian**: 1.1 **% Black**: 0.6 **% Hispanic**: 10.2 **% White**: 87.3	National ***Socio-Economic Status*** indicator percentiles are not available for the state of Washington

Yakima County
SUNNYSIDE S.D.
1110 S 6TH ST ● SUNNYSIDE WA 98944 ● (509) 837-5851 ● http://www.sunnyside.wednet.edu/district.html

Grade Span: PK-12 **Schools**: *Regular* 7 ● *Spec Ed* 0 ● *Alt* 0 **Students**: 4,920 **Total Teachers**: 236 **Student/Classroom Teacher Ratio**: 23.8	**Expenditures/Student**: $5,031 **Librarians**: 4.9 1,004 students/librarian **Guidance Counselors**: 12.0 410 students/counselor	**% Amer Indian**: 0.1 **% Asian**: 0.5 **% Black**: 0.2 **% Hispanic**: 72.1 **% White**: 27.1	National ***Socio-Economic Status*** indicator percentiles are not available for the state of Washington

Yakima County
TOPPENISH S.D.
106 FRANKLIN AVE ● TOPPENISH WA 98948 ● (509) 865-4455 ● http://www.esd105.wednet.edu/Toppenish

Grade Span: KG-12 **Schools**: *Regular* 6 ● *Spec Ed* 0 ● *Alt* 2 **Students**: 3,422 **Total Teachers**: 173 **Student/Classroom Teacher Ratio**: 19.8	**Expenditures/Student**: $5,054 **Librarians**: 5.0 684 students/librarian **Guidance Counselors**: 4.5 760 students/counselor	**% Amer Indian**: 17.5 **% Asian**: 0.2 **% Black**: 0.3 **% Hispanic**: 70.8 **% White**: 11.3	National ***Socio-Economic Status*** indicator percentiles are not available for the state of Washington

Yakima County
WAPATO S.D.
PO BOX 38 ● WAPATO WA 98951 ● (509) 877-4181

Grade Span: PK-12 **Schools**: *Regular* 4 ● *Spec Ed* 0 ● *Alt* 1 **Students**: 3,426 **Total Teachers**: 152 **Student/Classroom Teacher Ratio**: 22.1	**Expenditures/Student**: $5,279 **Librarians**: 4.4 779 students/librarian **Guidance Counselors**: 10.1 339 students/counselor	**% Amer Indian**: 27.6 **% Asian**: 1.5 **% Black**: 0.4 **% Hispanic**: 56.5 **% White**: 14.0	National ***Socio-Economic Status*** indicator percentiles are not available for the state of Washington

Yakima County
[YAKIMA] WEST VALLEY S.D.
8902 ZIER RD ● YAKIMA WA 98908 ● (509) 965-2000

Grade Span: KG-12 **Schools**: *Regular* 8 ● *Spec Ed* 0 ● *Alt* 0 **Students**: 4,508 **Total Teachers**: 207 **Student/Classroom Teacher Ratio**: 21.5	**Expenditures/Student**: $4,968 **Librarians**: 2.0 2,254 students/librarian **Guidance Counselors**: 7.2 626 students/counselor	**% Amer Indian**: 1.5 **% Asian**: 2.0 **% Black**: 0.7 **% Hispanic**: 8.3 **% White**: 87.6	National ***Socio-Economic Status*** indicator percentiles are not available for the state of Washington

Yakima County

YAKIMA S.D.

104 N 4TH AVE ● YAKIMA WA 98902 ● (509) 575-3230 ● http://www.esd105.wednet.edu/Yakima

Grade Span: PK-12	**Expenditures/Student**: $5,860	**% Amer Indian**: 2.4	National ***Socio-Economic***
Schools: *Regular* 23 ● *Spec Ed* 0 ● *Alt* 2	**Librarians**: 15.9	**% Asian**: 1.6	***Status*** indicator percentiles
Students: 13,829	870 students/librarian	**% Black**: 3.6	are not available for the
Total Teachers: 718	**Guidance Counselors**: 29.0	**% Hispanic**: 38.5	state of Washington
Student/Classroom Teacher Ratio: 19.6	477 students/counselor	**% White**: 53.9	

Barbour County

[PHILIPPI] **BARBOUR COUNTY S.D.**

105 SOUTH RAILROAD STREET ● PHILIPPI WV 26416-1177 ● (304) 457-3030 ● http://www.wvonline.com/pbhs/pbhs.html

Grade Span: PK-12 **Schools**: *Regular* 9 ● *Spec Ed* 0 ● *Alt* 0 **Students**: 2,842 **Total Teachers**: 196 **Student/Classroom Teacher Ratio**: 14.0	**Expenditures/Student**: $5,646 **Librarians**: 5.0 568 students/librarian **Guidance Counselors**: 4.1 693 students/counselor	**% Amer Indian**: 0.6 **% Asian**: 0.2 **% Black**: 0.7 **% Hispanic**: 0.5 **% White**: 98.0	National ***Socio-Economic Status*** indicator percentile (100=high): 13th

Berkeley County

[MARTINSBURG] **BERKELEY COUNTY S.D.**

401 SOUTH QUEEN STREET ● MARTINSBURG WV 25401-3285 ● (304) 267-3500

Grade Span: PK-12 **Schools**: *Regular* 22 ● *Spec Ed* 3 ● *Alt* 2 **Students**: 11,666 **Total Teachers**: 759 **Student/Classroom Teacher Ratio**: 17.3	**Expenditures/Student**: $5,839 **Librarians**: 14.5 805 students/librarian **Guidance Counselors**: 23.8 490 students/counselor	**% Amer Indian**: 0.1 **% Asian**: 0.6 **% Black**: 5.0 **% Hispanic**: 1.1 **% White**: 93.3	National ***Socio-Economic Status*** indicator percentile (100=high): 44th

Boone County

[MADISON] **BOONE COUNTY S.D.**

69 AVENUE B ● MADISON WV 25130-1196 ● (304) 369-3131 ● http://www.citynet.net/boonecountyschools

Grade Span: PK-12 **Schools**: *Regular* 18 ● *Spec Ed* 0 ● *Alt* 1 **Students**: 4,880 **Total Teachers**: 368 **Student/Classroom Teacher Ratio**: 14.3	**Expenditures/Student**: $5,999 **Librarians**: 4.0 1,220 students/librarian **Guidance Counselors**: 8.0 610 students/counselor	**% Amer Indian**: 0.1 **% Asian**: 0.1 **% Black**: 0.9 **% Hispanic**: 0.2 **% White**: 98.7	National ***Socio-Economic Status*** indicator percentile (100=high): 21st

Braxton County

[SUTTON] **BRAXTON COUNTY S.D.**

411 NORTH HILL ROAD ● SUTTON WV 26601-1147 ● (304) 765-7101

Grade Span: PK-12 **Schools**: *Regular* 8 ● *Spec Ed* 0 ● *Alt* 0 **Students**: 2,672 **Total Teachers**: 189 **Student/Classroom Teacher Ratio**: 14.6	**Expenditures/Student**: $5,562 **Librarians**: 2.0 1,336 students/librarian **Guidance Counselors**: 7.0 382 students/counselor	**% Amer Indian**: 0.0 **% Asian**: 0.3 **% Black**: 0.3 **% Hispanic**: 0.2 **% White**: 99.2	National ***Socio-Economic Status*** indicator percentile (100=high): 15th

Brooke County

[WELLSBURG] **BROOKE COUNTY S.D.**

1201 PLEASANT AVENUE ● WELLSBURG WV 26070-1497 ● (304) 737-3481

Grade Span: PK-12 **Schools**: *Regular* 12 ● *Spec Ed* 0 ● *Alt* 1 **Students**: 4,050 **Total Teachers**: 280 **Student/Classroom Teacher Ratio**: 14.4	**Expenditures/Student**: $5,982 **Librarians**: 5.0 810 students/librarian **Guidance Counselors**: 8.0 506 students/counselor	**% Amer Indian**: 0.1 **% Asian**: 0.3 **% Black**: 1.2 **% Hispanic**: 0.3 **% White**: 98.1	National ***Socio-Economic Status*** indicator percentile (100=high): 44th

Cabell County

[HUNTINGTON] **CABELL COUNTY S.D.**

PO BOX 446 ● HUNTINGTON WV 25709-0446 ● (304) 528-5000 ● http://boe.cabe.k12.wv.us

Grade Span: PK-12 **Schools**: *Regular* 32 ● *Spec Ed* 0 ● *Alt* 1 **Students**: 14,065 **Total Teachers**: 1,027 **Student/Classroom Teacher Ratio**: 14.1	**Expenditures/Student**: $6,184 **Librarians**: 10.5 1,340 students/librarian **Guidance Counselors**: 33.5 420 students/counselor	**% Amer Indian**: 0.4 **% Asian**: 0.7 **% Black**: 6.0 **% Hispanic**: 0.3 **% White**: 92.7	National ***Socio-Economic Status*** indicator percentile (100=high): 29th

Fayette County

[FAYETTEVILLE] **FAYETTE COUNTY S.D.**

111 FAYETTE AVENUE ● FAYETTEVILLE WV 25840-1299 ● (304) 574-1176

Grade Span: PK-12 **Schools**: *Regular* 33 ● *Spec Ed* 1 ● *Alt* 1 **Students**: 8,544 **Total Teachers**: 587 **Student/Classroom Teacher Ratio**: 14.8	**Expenditures/Student**: $5,425 **Librarians**: 8.0 1,068 students/librarian **Guidance Counselors**: 14.0 610 students/counselor	**% Amer Indian**: 0.1 **% Asian**: 0.2 **% Black**: 7.5 **% Hispanic**: 0.3 **% White**: 92.0	National ***Socio-Economic Status*** indicator percentile (100=high): 17th

Greenbrier County

[LEWISBURG] **GREENBRIER COUNTY S.D.**

PO BOX 987 ● LEWISBURG WV 24901-0987 ● (304) 647-6470

Grade Span: PK-12 **Schools**: *Regular* 13 ● *Spec Ed* 0 ● *Alt* 0 **Students**: 6,045 **Total Teachers**: 377 **Student/Classroom Teacher Ratio**: 15.7	**Expenditures/Student**: $4,605 **Librarians**: 4.0 1,511 students/librarian **Guidance Counselors**: 9.0 672 students/counselor	**% Amer Indian**: 0.0 **% Asian**: 0.1 **% Black**: 3.5 **% Hispanic**: 0.5 **% White**: 95.8	National ***Socio-Economic Status*** indicator percentile (100=high): 27th

Hampshire County

[ROMNEY] **HAMPSHIRE COUNTY S.D.**

46 SOUTH HIGH STREET ● ROMNEY WV 26757-1832 ● (304) 822-3528

Grade Span: PK-12 **Schools**: *Regular* 10 ● *Spec Ed* 0 ● *Alt* 0 **Students**: 3,383 **Total Teachers**: 207 **Student/Classroom Teacher Ratio**: 16.1	**Expenditures/Student**: $5,010 **Librarians**: 3.0 1,128 students/librarian **Guidance Counselors**: 6.5 520 students/counselor	**% Amer Indian**: 0.0 **% Asian**: 0.0 **% Black**: 0.9 **% Hispanic**: 0.6 **% White**: 98.5	National ***Socio-Economic Status*** indicator percentile (100=high): 26th

Hancock County

[NEW CUMBERLAND] **HANCOCK COUNTY S.D.**

PO BOX 1300 ● NEW CUMBERLAND WV 26047-9521 ● (304) 564-3411

Grade Span: PK-12 **Schools**: *Regular* 12 ● *Spec Ed* 0 ● *Alt* 1 **Students**: 4,866 **Total Teachers**: 325 **Student/Classroom Teacher Ratio**: 15.7	**Expenditures/Student**: $5,804 **Librarians**: 3.8 1,281 students/librarian **Guidance Counselors**: 7.0 695 students/counselor	**% Amer Indian**: 0.0 **% Asian**: 0.2 **% Black**: 3.1 **% Hispanic**: 0.1 **% White**: 96.5	National ***Socio-Economic Status*** indicator percentile (100=high): 45th

Harrison County

[CLARKSBURG] **HARRISON COUNTY S.D.**

PO BOX 1370 ● CLARKSBURG WV 26302-1370 ● (304) 624-3300 ● http://www.wvonline.com/bhs

Grade Span: PK-12 **Schools**: *Regular* 24 ● *Spec Ed* 3 ● *Alt* 1 **Students**: 12,266 **Total Teachers**: 801 **Student/Classroom Teacher Ratio**: 16.2	**Expenditures/Student**: $5,896 **Librarians**: 21.0 584 students/librarian **Guidance Counselors**: 23.0 533 students/counselor	**% Amer Indian**: 0.2 **% Asian**: 0.3 **% Black**: 1.7 **% Hispanic**: 0.2 **% White**: 97.5	National ***Socio-Economic Status*** indicator percentile (100=high): 30th

Jackson County

[RIPLEY] **JACKSON COUNTY S.D.**

PO BOX 770 ● RIPLEY WV 25271-0770 ● (304) 372-7300

Grade Span: PK-12 **Schools**: *Regular* 12 ● *Spec Ed* 0 ● *Alt* 1 **Students**: 5,118 **Total Teachers**: 345 **Student/Classroom Teacher Ratio**: 15.6	**Expenditures/Student**: $6,029 **Librarians**: 4.0 1,280 students/librarian **Guidance Counselors**: 10.8 474 students/counselor	**% Amer Indian**: 0.0 **% Asian**: 0.2 **% Black**: 0.2 **% Hispanic**: 0.0 **% White**: 99.6	National ***Socio-Economic Status*** indicator percentile (100=high): 31st

Jefferson County

[CHARLES TOWN] **JEFFERSON COUNTY S.D.**

PO BOX 987 ● CHARLES TOWN WV 25414-0987 ● (304) 725-9741

Grade Span: PK-12 **Schools**: *Regular* 13 ● *Spec Ed* 0 ● *Alt* 0 **Students**: 6,668 **Total Teachers**: 424 **Student/Classroom Teacher Ratio**: 15.8	**Expenditures/Student**: $5,319 **Librarians**: 13.0 513 students/librarian **Guidance Counselors**: 10.0 667 students/counselor	**% Amer Indian**: 0.2 **% Asian**: 0.4 **% Black**: 8.6 **% Hispanic**: 1.4 **% White**: 89.4	National ***Socio-Economic Status*** indicator percentile (100=high): 45th

Kanawha County

[CHARLESTON] **KANAWHA COUNTY S.D.**

200 ELIZABETH STREET ● CHARLESTON WV 25311-2119 ● (304) 348-7770

Grade Span: PK-12 **Schools**: *Regular* 84 ● *Spec Ed* 1 ● *Alt* 3 **Students**: 32,026 **Total Teachers**: 2,221 **Student/Classroom Teacher Ratio**: 15.3	**Expenditures/Student**: $5,676 **Librarians**: 23.5 1,363 students/librarian **Guidance Counselors**: 78.0 411 students/counselor	**% Amer Indian**: 0.2 **% Asian**: 0.9 **% Black**: 9.6 **% Hispanic**: 0.3 **% White**: 89.1	National ***Socio-Economic Status*** indicator percentile (100=high): 39th

Lewis County

[WESTON] **LEWIS COUNTY S.D.**

322 E. THIRD STREET ● WESTON WV 26452-2002 ● (304) 269-8300

Grade Span: PK-12 **Schools**: *Regular* 9 ● *Spec Ed* 0 ● *Alt* 0 **Students**: 2,880 **Total Teachers**: 217 **Student/Classroom Teacher Ratio**: 13.7	**Expenditures/Student**: $6,039 **Librarians**: 3.5 823 students/librarian **Guidance Counselors**: 5.0 576 students/counselor	**% Amer Indian**: 0.1 **% Asian**: 0.4 **% Black**: 0.1 **% Hispanic**: 0.2 **% White**: 99.3	National ***Socio-Economic Status*** indicator percentile (100=high): 16th

Lincoln County

[HAMLIN] **LINCOLN COUNTY S.D.**

10 MARLAND AVENUE ● HAMLIN WV 25523-1025 ● (304) 824-3033 ● http://members.aol.com/SUNONE1030/GuyanValley.html

Grade Span: PK-12 **Schools**: *Regular* 16 ● *Spec Ed* 0 ● *Alt* 1 **Students**: 4,249 **Total Teachers**: 320 **Student/Classroom Teacher Ratio**: 13.7	**Expenditures/Student**: $5,946 **Librarians**: 4.0 1,062 students/librarian **Guidance Counselors**: 7.0 607 students/counselor	**% Amer Indian**: 0.0 **% Asian**: 0.0 **% Black**: 0.0 **% Hispanic**: 0.0 **% White**: 100.0	National ***Socio-Economic Status*** indicator percentile (100=high): 8th

Logan County

[LOGAN] **LOGAN COUNTY S.D.**

PO BOX 477 ● LOGAN WV 25601-0477 ● (304) 752-1550

Grade Span: PK-12 **Schools**: *Regular* 25 ● *Spec Ed* 1 ● *Alt* 1 **Students**: 7,464 **Total Teachers**: 545 **Student/Classroom Teacher Ratio**: 14.2	**Expenditures/Student**: $6,029 **Librarians**: 8.0 933 students/librarian **Guidance Counselors**: 9.5 786 students/counselor	**% Amer Indian**: 0.0 **% Asian**: 0.3 **% Black**: 3.5 **% Hispanic**: 0.1 **% White**: 96.1	National ***Socio-Economic Status*** indicator percentile (100=high): 20th

McDowell County

[WELCH] **MCDOWELL COUNTY S.D.**

30 CENTRAL AVENUE ● WELCH WV 24801-2099 ● (304) 436-8441

Grade Span: PK-12 **Schools**: *Regular* 19 ● *Spec Ed* 0 ● *Alt* 2 **Students**: 6,307 **Total Teachers**: 447 **Student/Classroom Teacher Ratio**: 14.6	**Expenditures/Student**: $6,290 **Librarians**: 3.0 2,102 students/librarian **Guidance Counselors**: 13.0 485 students/counselor	**% Amer Indian**: 0.0 **% Asian**: 0.2 **% Black**: 15.1 **% Hispanic**: 0.1 **% White**: 84.6	National ***Socio-Economic Status*** indicator percentile (100=high): 4th

Marion County

[FAIRMONT] **MARION COUNTY S.D.**

200 GASTON AVENUE ● FAIRMONT WV 26554-2778 ● (304) 367-2100

Grade Span: PK-12 **Schools**: *Regular* 21 ● *Spec Ed* 0 ● *Alt* 1 **Students**: 9,109 **Total Teachers**: 616 **Student/Classroom Teacher Ratio**: 15.5	**Expenditures/Student**: $5,950 **Librarians**: 17.8 512 students/librarian **Guidance Counselors**: 19.5 467 students/counselor	**% Amer Indian**: 0.2 **% Asian**: 0.5 **% Black**: 5.0 **% Hispanic**: 0.2 **% White**: 94.1	National ***Socio-Economic Status*** indicator percentile (100=high): 32nd

Marshall County

[MOUNDSVILLE] **MARSHALL COUNTY S.D.**

PO BOX 578 ● MOUNDSVILLE WV 26041-0578 ● (304) 845-5200

Grade Span: PK-12 **Schools**: *Regular* 16 ● *Spec Ed* 0 ● *Alt* 0 **Students**: 5,897 **Total Teachers**: 403 **Student/Classroom Teacher Ratio**: 15.1	**Expenditures/Student**: $6,205 **Librarians**: 5.0 1,179 students/librarian **Guidance Counselors**: 13.0 454 students/counselor	**% Amer Indian**: 0.1 **% Asian**: 0.3 **% Black**: 0.4 **% Hispanic**: 0.1 **% White**: 99.1	National ***Socio-Economic Status*** indicator percentile (100=high): 36th

Mason County

[POINT PLEASANT] **MASON COUNTY S.D.**

307 8TH STREET ● POINT PLEASANT WV 25550-1298 ● (304) 675-4540

Grade Span: PK-12 **Schools**: *Regular* 14 ● *Spec Ed* 0 ● *Alt* 2 **Students**: 4,645 **Total Teachers**: 345 **Student/Classroom Teacher Ratio**: 14.5	**Expenditures/Student**: $6,092 **Librarians**: 4.0 1,161 students/librarian **Guidance Counselors**: 7.0 664 students/counselor	**% Amer Indian**: 0.0 **% Asian**: 0.2 **% Black**: 0.6 **% Hispanic**: 0.2 **% White**: 98.9	National ***Socio-Economic Status*** indicator percentile (100=high): 27th

Mercer County

[PRINCETON] **MERCER COUNTY S.D.**

1403 HONAKER AVENUE ● PRINCETON WV 24740-3048 ● (304) 487-1551

Grade Span: PK-12 **Schools**: *Regular* 29 ● *Spec Ed* 0 ● *Alt* 1 **Students**: 10,252 **Total Teachers**: 704 **Student/Classroom Teacher Ratio**: 15.1	**Expenditures/Student**: $5,655 **Librarians**: 22.9 448 students/librarian **Guidance Counselors**: 22.0 466 students/counselor	**% Amer Indian**: 0.2 **% Asian**: 0.6 **% Black**: 8.8 **% Hispanic**: 0.2 **% White**: 90.2	National ***Socio-Economic Status*** indicator percentile (100=high): 23rd

Mineral County

[KEYSER] **MINERAL COUNTY S.D.**

ONE BAKER PLACE ● KEYSER WV 26726-2898 ● (304) 788-4200

Grade Span: PK-12 **Schools**: *Regular* 12 ● *Spec Ed* 0 ● *Alt* 2 **Students**: 4,841 **Total Teachers**: 318 **Student/Classroom Teacher Ratio**: 16.0	**Expenditures/Student**: $5,791 **Librarians**: 6.0 807 students/librarian **Guidance Counselors**: 10.8 448 students/counselor	**% Amer Indian**: 0.0 **% Asian**: 0.3 **% Black**: 3.6 **% Hispanic**: 0.2 **% White**: 95.9	National ***Socio-Economic Status*** indicator percentile (100=high): 31st

Mingo County

[WILLIAMSON] **MINGO COUNTY S.D.**

815 ALDERSON STREET ● WILLIAMSON WV 25661-3296 ● (304) 235-3333

Grade Span: PK-12 **Schools**: *Regular* 24 ● *Spec Ed* 0 ● *Alt* 1 **Students**: 6,551 **Total Teachers**: 485 **Student/Classroom Teacher Ratio**: 14.0	**Expenditures/Student**: $6,253 **Librarians**: 10.0 655 students/librarian **Guidance Counselors**: 13.0 504 students/counselor	**% Amer Indian**: 0.0 **% Asian**: 0.2 **% Black**: 2.9 **% Hispanic**: 0.1 **% White**: 96.9	National ***Socio-Economic Status*** indicator percentile (100=high): 15th

Monongalia County

[MORGANTOWN] MONONGALIA S.D.

13 SOUTH HIGH STREET ● MORGANTOWN WV 26505-7546 ● (304) 291-9210

Grade Span: PK-12 **Schools**: *Regular* 28 ● *Spec Ed* 1 ● *Alt* 1 **Students**: 10,280 **Total Teachers**: 654 **Student/Classroom Teacher Ratio**: 15.7	**Expenditures/Student**: $5,749 **Librarians**: 19.0 541 students/librarian **Guidance Counselors**: 20.5 501 students/counselor	**% Amer Indian**: 0.2 **% Asian**: 2.0 **% Black**: 3.4 **% Hispanic**: 0.4 **% White**: 94.1	National ***Socio-Economic Status*** indicator percentile (100=high): 43rd

Nicholas County

[SUMMERSVILLE] NICHOLAS COUNTY S.D.

400 OLD MAIN DRIVE ● SUMMERSVILLE WV 26651-1388 ● (304) 872-3611

Grade Span: PK-12 **Schools**: *Regular* 16 ● *Spec Ed* 0 ● *Alt* 1 **Students**: 5,091 **Total Teachers**: 364 **Student/Classroom Teacher Ratio**: 14.3	**Expenditures/Student**: $5,834 **Librarians**: 4.0 1,273 students/librarian **Guidance Counselors**: 8.0 636 students/counselor	**% Amer Indian**: 0.0 **% Asian**: 0.3 **% Black**: 0.1 **% Hispanic**: 0.0 **% White**: 99.6	National ***Socio-Economic Status*** indicator percentile (100=high): 19th

Ohio County

[WHEELING] OHIO COUNTY S.D.

2203 NATIONAL ROAD ● WHEELING WV 26003-5299 ● (304) 243-0300

Grade Span: PK-12 **Schools**: *Regular* 15 ● *Spec Ed* 0 ● *Alt* 0 **Students**: 6,393 **Total Teachers**: 408 **Student/Classroom Teacher Ratio**: 15.8	**Expenditures/Student**: $5,695 **Librarians**: 10.0 639 students/librarian **Guidance Counselors**: 12.0 533 students/counselor	**% Amer Indian**: 0.1 **% Asian**: 0.7 **% Black**: 6.6 **% Hispanic**: 0.3 **% White**: 92.2	National ***Socio-Economic Status*** indicator percentile (100=high): 40th

Preston County

[KINGWOOD] PRESTON COUNTY S.D.

PO BOX 566 ● KINGWOOD WV 26537-0566 ● (304) 329-0580

Grade Span: PK-12 **Schools**: *Regular* 13 ● *Spec Ed* 0 ● *Alt* 0 **Students**: 5,397 **Total Teachers**: 356 **Student/Classroom Teacher Ratio**: 15.2	**Expenditures/Student**: $5,304 **Librarians**: 6.3 857 students/librarian **Guidance Counselors**: 11.0 491 students/counselor	**% Amer Indian**: 0.1 **% Asian**: 0.2 **% Black**: 0.4 **% Hispanic**: 0.1 **% White**: 99.2	National ***Socio-Economic Status*** indicator percentile (100=high): 17th

Putnam County

[WINFIELD] PUTNAM COUNTY S.D.

PO BOX 47 ● WINFIELD WV 25213-0047 ● (304) 586-0500 ● http://www.citynet.net/putnam

Grade Span: PK-12 **Schools**: *Regular* 21 ● *Spec Ed* 0 ● *Alt* 1 **Students**: 8,625 **Total Teachers**: 569 **Student/Classroom Teacher Ratio**: 15.9	**Expenditures/Student**: $5,209 **Librarians**: 8.0 1,078 students/librarian **Guidance Counselors**: 19.0 454 students/counselor	**% Amer Indian**: 0.0 **% Asian**: 0.4 **% Black**: 0.3 **% Hispanic**: 0.1 **% White**: 99.2	National ***Socio-Economic Status*** indicator percentile (100=high): 49th

Raleigh County

[BECKLEY] RALEIGH COUNTY S.D.

105 ADAIR STREET ● BECKLEY WV 25801-3791 ● (304) 256-4505 ● http://members.xoom.com/IHS

Grade Span: PK-12 **Schools**: *Regular* 34 ● *Spec Ed* 0 ● *Alt* 2 **Students**: 13,422 **Total Teachers**: 852 **Student/Classroom Teacher Ratio**: 16.1	**Expenditures/Student**: $5,442 **Librarians**: 12.0 1,119 students/librarian **Guidance Counselors**: 31.0 433 students/counselor	**% Amer Indian**: 0.1 **% Asian**: 0.6 **% Black**: 9.9 **% Hispanic**: 0.2 **% White**: 89.3	National ***Socio-Economic Status*** indicator percentile (100=high): 26th

Randolph County

[ELKINS] **RANDOLPH COUNTY S.D.**

40 11TH STREET ● ELKINS WV 26241-3512 ● (304) 636-9150

Grade Span: PK-12 **Schools**: *Regular* 15 ● *Spec Ed* 0 ● *Alt* 1 **Students**: 4,956 **Total Teachers**: 355 **Student/Classroom Teacher Ratio**: 14.2	**Expenditures/Student**: $5,525 **Librarians**: 3.0 1,652 students/librarian **Guidance Counselors**: 11.5 431 students/counselor	**% Amer Indian**: 0.1 **% Asian**: 0.4 **% Black**: 0.4 **% Hispanic**: 0.2 **% White**: 98.8	National ***Socio-Economic Status*** indicator percentile (100=high): 19th

Roane County

[SPENCER] **ROANE COUNTY S.D.**

PO BOX 609 ● SPENCER WV 25276-0609 ● (304) 927-6400 ● http://boe.roan.k12.wv.us

Grade Span: PK-12 **Schools**: *Regular* 7 ● *Spec Ed* 0 ● *Alt* 0 **Students**: 2,980 **Total Teachers**: 212 **Student/Classroom Teacher Ratio**: 13.6	**Expenditures/Student**: $5,348 **Librarians**: 0.0 *** students/librarian **Guidance Counselors**: 7.3 408 students/counselor	**% Amer Indian**: 0.0 **% Asian**: 0.3 **% Black**: 0.1 **% Hispanic**: 0.3 **% White**: 99.2	National ***Socio-Economic Status*** indicator percentile (100=high): 11th

Taylor County

[GRAFTON] **TAYLOR COUNTY S.D.**

306 BEECH STREET ● GRAFTON WV 26354 ● (304) 265-2497

Grade Span: PK-12 **Schools**: *Regular* 6 ● *Spec Ed* 0 ● *Alt* 1 **Students**: 2,746 **Total Teachers**: 183 **Student/Classroom Teacher Ratio**: 16.8	**Expenditures/Student**: $5,587 **Librarians**: 4.0 687 students/librarian **Guidance Counselors**: 6.5 422 students/counselor	**% Amer Indian**: 0.1 **% Asian**: 0.1 **% Black**: 0.5 **% Hispanic**: 0.0 **% White**: 99.2	National ***Socio-Economic Status*** indicator percentile (100=high): 21st

Upshur County

[BUCKHANNON] **UPSHUR COUNTY S.D.**

102 SMITHFIELD STREET ● BUCKHANNON WV 26201-0580 ● (304) 472-5480

Grade Span: PK-12 **Schools**: *Regular* 13 ● *Spec Ed* 0 ● *Alt* 1 **Students**: 4,266 **Total Teachers**: 287 **Student/Classroom Teacher Ratio**: 17.2	**Expenditures/Student**: $5,434 **Librarians**: 2.0 2,133 students/librarian **Guidance Counselors**: 8.0 533 students/counselor	**% Amer Indian**: 0.2 **% Asian**: 0.3 **% Black**: 0.2 **% Hispanic**: 0.1 **% White**: 99.3	National ***Socio-Economic Status*** indicator percentile (100=high): 21st

Wayne County

[WAYNE] **WAYNE COUNTY S.D.**

PO BOX 70 ● WAYNE WV 25570-0070 ● (304) 272-5116

Grade Span: PK-12 **Schools**: *Regular* 23 ● *Spec Ed* 0 ● *Alt* 1 **Students**: 7,863 **Total Teachers**: 529 **Student/Classroom Teacher Ratio**: 15.9	**Expenditures/Student**: $5,406 **Librarians**: 11.0 715 students/librarian **Guidance Counselors**: 14.0 562 students/counselor	**% Amer Indian**: 0.1 **% Asian**: 0.1 **% Black**: 0.1 **% Hispanic**: 0.1 **% White**: 99.6	National ***Socio-Economic Status*** indicator percentile (100=high): 29th

Wetzel County

[NEW MARTINSVILLE] **WETZEL COUNTY S.D.**

333 FOUNDRY STREET ● NEW MARTINSVILLE WV 26155-1110 ● (304) 455-2441

Grade Span: PK-12 **Schools**: *Regular* 8 ● *Spec Ed* 0 ● *Alt* 1 **Students**: 3,798 **Total Teachers**: 263 **Student/Classroom Teacher Ratio**: 15.0	**Expenditures/Student**: $5,596 **Librarians**: 4.5 844 students/librarian **Guidance Counselors**: 6.5 584 students/counselor	**% Amer Indian**: 0.0 **% Asian**: 0.4 **% Black**: 0.1 **% Hispanic**: 0.0 **% White**: 99.4	National ***Socio-Economic Status*** indicator percentile (100=high): 29th

Wood County

[PARKERSBURG] **WOOD COUNTY S.D.**

1210 13TH STREET ● PARKERSBURG WV 26101-4198 ● (304) 420-9663

Grade Span: PK-12 **Schools**: *Regular* 28 ● *Spec Ed* 0 ● *Alt* 1 **Students**: 14,885 **Total Teachers**: 1,000 **Student/Classroom Teacher Ratio**: 15.4	**Expenditures/Student**: $5,568 **Librarians**: 27.0 551 students/librarian **Guidance Counselors**: 23.0 647 students/counselor	**% Amer Indian**: 0.1 **% Asian**: 0.3 **% Black**: 1.8 **% Hispanic**: 0.1 **% White**: 97.8	National ***Socio-Economic Status*** indicator percentile (100=high): 41st

Wyoming County

[PINEVILLE] **WYOMING COUNTY S.D.**

PO BOX 69 ● PINEVILLE WV 24874-0069 ● (304) 732-6262

Grade Span: PK-12 **Schools**: *Regular* 17 ● *Spec Ed* 1 ● *Alt* 1 **Students**: 5,446 **Total Teachers**: 409 **Student/Classroom Teacher Ratio**: 14.7	**Expenditures/Student**: $5,982 **Librarians**: 4.0 1,362 students/librarian **Guidance Counselors**: 8.5 641 students/counselor	**% Amer Indian**: 0.0 **% Asian**: 0.2 **% Black**: 1.1 **% Hispanic**: 0.1 **% White**: 98.5	National ***Socio-Economic Status*** indicator percentile (100=high): 15th

Barron County

RICE LAKE AREA S.D.

700 AUGUSTA ST ● RICE LAKE WI 54868 ● (715) 234-9007

Grade Span: PK-12 **Schools**: *Regular* 8 ● *Spec Ed* 1 ● *Alt* 0 **Students**: 2,886 **Total Teachers**: 173 **Student/Classroom Teacher Ratio**: 18.7	**Expenditures/Student**: $5,705 **Librarians**: 5.0 577 students/librarian **Guidance Counselors**: 8.5 340 students/counselor	**% Amer Indian**: 1.2 **% Asian**: 1.0 **% Black**: 0.4 **% Hispanic**: 0.4 **% White**: 96.9	National ***Socio-Economic Status*** indicator percentile (100=high): 63rd

Brown County

[GREEN BAY] **ASHWAUBENON S.D.**

1055 GRIFFITHS LN ● GREEN BAY WI 54304-5599 ● (920) 492-2900

Grade Span: KG-12 **Schools**: *Regular* 5 ● *Spec Ed* 0 ● *Alt* 0 **Students**: 3,110 **Total Teachers**: 186 **Student/Classroom Teacher Ratio**: 18.6	**Expenditures/Student**: $6,227 **Librarians**: 4.0 778 students/librarian **Guidance Counselors**: 9.0 346 students/counselor	**% Amer Indian**: 1.2 **% Asian**: 1.4 **% Black**: 0.5 **% Hispanic**: 0.8 **% White**: 96.1	National ***Socio-Economic Status*** indicator percentile (100=high): 91st

Brown County

GREEN BAY AREA S.D.

PO BOX 23387 ● GREEN BAY WI 54305 ● (920) 448-2101

Grade Span: PK-12 **Schools**: *Regular* 35 ● *Spec Ed* 0 ● *Alt* 0 **Students**: 19,618 **Total Teachers**: 1,216 **Student/Classroom Teacher Ratio**: 16.9	**Expenditures/Student**: $6,238 **Librarians**: 19.5 1,006 students/librarian **Guidance Counselors**: 37.0 530 students/counselor	**% Amer Indian**: 3.9 **% Asian**: 8.9 **% Black**: 1.7 **% Hispanic**: 2.9 **% White**: 82.5	National ***Socio-Economic Status*** indicator percentile (100=high): 49th

Brown County

[GREEN BAY] **HOWARD-SUAMICO S.D.**

2700 LINEVILLE RD ● GREEN BAY WI 54313 ● (920) 434-4018

Grade Span: PK-12 **Schools**: *Regular* 6 ● *Spec Ed* 0 ● *Alt* 0 **Students**: 3,582 **Total Teachers**: 211 **Student/Classroom Teacher Ratio**: 17.6	**Expenditures/Student**: $5,355 **Librarians**: 5.0 716 students/librarian **Guidance Counselors**: 7.6 471 students/counselor	**% Amer Indian**: 1.1 **% Asian**: 0.9 **% Black**: 0.6 **% Hispanic**: 0.4 **% White**: 97.0	National ***Socio-Economic Status*** indicator percentile (100=high): 92nd

Brown County

PULASKI COMMUNITY S.D.

PO BOX 36 ● PULASKI WI 54162 ● (920) 822-4200

Grade Span: PK-12 **Schools**: *Regular* 6 ● *Spec Ed* 0 ● *Alt* 0 **Students**: 3,050 **Total Teachers**: 190 **Student/Classroom Teacher Ratio**: 16.7	**Expenditures/Student**: $5,635 **Librarians**: 3.9 782 students/librarian **Guidance Counselors**: 7.0 436 students/counselor	**% Amer Indian**: 2.5 **% Asian**: 0.8 **% Black**: 0.3 **% Hispanic**: 0.4 **% White**: 96.1	National ***Socio-Economic Status*** indicator percentile (100=high): 84th

Chippewa County

CHIPPEWA FALLS AREA S.D.

1130 MILES ST ● CHIPPEWA FALLS WI 54729 ● (715) 726-2417

Grade Span: PK-12 **Schools**: *Regular* 8 ● *Spec Ed* 0 ● *Alt* 1 **Students**: 4,430 **Total Teachers**: 274 **Student/Classroom Teacher Ratio**: 16.8	**Expenditures/Student**: $5,905 **Librarians**: 5.0 886 students/librarian **Guidance Counselors**: 12.0 369 students/counselor	**% Amer Indian**: 0.7 **% Asian**: 0.7 **% Black**: 0.2 **% Hispanic**: 0.4 **% White**: 97.9	National ***Socio-Economic Status*** indicator percentile (100=high): 68th

Columbia County

PORTAGE COMMUNITY S.D.

904 DEWITT ST ● PORTAGE WI 53901 ● (608) 742-4879 ● http://www.palacenet.net/portageschools

Grade Span: PK-12 **Schools**: *Regular* 8 ● *Spec Ed* 0 ● *Alt* 0 **Students**: 2,657 **Total Teachers**: 174 **Student/Classroom Teacher Ratio**: 16.9	**Expenditures/Student**: $5,511 **Librarians**: 4.0 664 students/librarian **Guidance Counselors**: 7.9 336 students/counselor	**% Amer Indian**: 0.5 **% Asian**: 0.4 **% Black**: 0.4 **% Hispanic**: 2.0 **% White**: 96.7	National ***Socio-Economic Status*** indicator percentile (100=high): 77th

Dane County

DE FOREST AREA S.D.

520 E HOLUM ST ● DE FOREST WI 53532 ● (608) 846-6500

Grade Span: PK-12 **Schools**: *Regular* 8 ● *Spec Ed* 0 ● *Alt* 0 **Students**: 2,956 **Total Teachers**: 197 **Student/Classroom Teacher Ratio**: 16.7	**Expenditures/Student**: $6,383 **Librarians**: 5.6 528 students/librarian **Guidance Counselors**: 8.0 370 students/counselor	**% Amer Indian**: 0.8 **% Asian**: 1.2 **% Black**: 0.8 **% Hispanic**: 1.4 **% White**: 95.8	National ***Socio-Economic Status*** indicator percentile (100=high): 97th

Dane County

MADISON METROPOLITAN S.D.

545 W DAYTON ST ● MADISON WI 53703 ● (608) 266-6235 ● http://www.madison.k12.wi.us

Grade Span: PK-12 **Schools**: *Regular* 43 ● *Spec Ed* 1 ● *Alt* 7 **Students**: 25,046 **Total Teachers**: 1,824 **Student/Classroom Teacher Ratio**: 13.9	**Expenditures/Student**: $7,622 **Librarians**: 51.2 489 students/librarian **Guidance Counselors**: 37.7 664 students/counselor	**% Amer Indian**: 0.5 **% Asian**: 7.7 **% Black**: 16.2 **% Hispanic**: 3.8 **% White**: 71.8	National ***Socio-Economic Status*** indicator percentile (100=high): 55th

Dane County

MIDDLETON-CROSS PLAINS S.D.

7106 SOUTH AVE ● MIDDLETON WI 53562 ● (608) 828-1500 ● http://www.mcpasd.k12.wi.us

Grade Span: PK-12 **Schools**: *Regular* 8 ● *Spec Ed* 0 ● *Alt* 0 **Students**: 4,602 **Total Teachers**: 296 **Student/Classroom Teacher Ratio**: 16.3	**Expenditures/Student**: $6,031 **Librarians**: 8.6 535 students/librarian **Guidance Counselors**: 9.6 479 students/counselor	**% Amer Indian**: 0.4 **% Asian**: 2.0 **% Black**: 2.7 **% Hispanic**: 1.3 **% White**: 93.7	National ***Socio-Economic Status*** indicator percentile (100=high): 94th

Dane County

OREGON S.D.

200 N MAIN ST ● OREGON WI 53575 ● (608) 835-3161

Grade Span: PK-12 **Schools**: *Regular* 5 ● *Spec Ed* 0 ● *Alt* 0 **Students**: 3,106 **Total Teachers**: 205 **Student/Classroom Teacher Ratio**: 15.7	**Expenditures/Student**: $6,511 **Librarians**: 2.5 1,242 students/librarian **Guidance Counselors**: 7.3 425 students/counselor	**% Amer Indian**: 0.5 **% Asian**: 0.7 **% Black**: 0.5 **% Hispanic**: 0.5 **% White**: 97.7	National ***Socio-Economic Status*** indicator percentile (100=high): 93rd

Dane County

STOUGHTON AREA S.D.

PO BOX 189 ● STOUGHTON WI 53589 ● (608) 873-2660 ● http://www.stoughton.k12.wi.us

Grade Span: PK-12 **Schools**: *Regular* 5 ● *Spec Ed* 0 ● *Alt* 0 **Students**: 3,353 **Total Teachers**: 208 **Student/Classroom Teacher Ratio**: 16.2	**Expenditures/Student**: $5,898 **Librarians**: 6.0 559 students/librarian **Guidance Counselors**: 5.0 671 students/counselor	**% Amer Indian**: 0.9 **% Asian**: 1.3 **% Black**: 1.7 **% Hispanic**: 1.8 **% White**: 94.3	National ***Socio-Economic Status*** indicator percentile (100=high): 86th

Dane County

SUN PRAIRIE AREA S.D.

509 COMMERCIAL AVE ● SUN PRAIRIE WI 53590 ● (608) 837-2541

Grade Span: PK-12	**Expenditures/Student**: $6,283	**% Amer Indian**: 0.3	National ***Socio-Economic Status*** indicator percentile (100=high): 84th
Schools: *Regular* 7 ● *Spec Ed* 0 ● *Alt* 0	**Librarians**: 6.0	**% Asian**: 1.1	
Students: 4,423	737 students/librarian	**% Black**: 2.7	
Total Teachers: 286	**Guidance Counselors**: 10.9	**% Hispanic**: 1.7	
Student/Classroom Teacher Ratio: 16.5	406 students/counselor	**% White**: 94.1	

Dane County

VERONA AREA S.D.

700 N MAIN ST ● VERONA WI 53593 ● (608) 845-6451 ● http://www.verona.k12.wi.us

Grade Span: PK-12	**Expenditures/Student**: $5,911	**% Amer Indian**: 0.2	National ***Socio-Economic Status*** indicator percentile (100=high): 89th
Schools: *Regular* 6 ● *Spec Ed* 0 ● *Alt* 0	**Librarians**: 5.0	**% Asian**: 2.3	
Students: 3,664	733 students/librarian	**% Black**: 4.4	
Total Teachers: 241	**Guidance Counselors**: 9.8	**% Hispanic**: 1.7	
Student/Classroom Teacher Ratio: 19.1	374 students/counselor	**% White**: 91.4	

Dodge County

BEAVER DAM S.D.

705 MCKINLEY ST ● BEAVER DAM WI 53916 ● (920) 885-7300

Grade Span: PK-12	**Expenditures/Student**: $6,007	**% Amer Indian**: 0.7	National ***Socio-Economic Status*** indicator percentile (100=high): 80th
Schools: *Regular* 9 ● *Spec Ed* 0 ● *Alt* 1	**Librarians**: 5.3	**% Asian**: 1.5	
Students: 3,440	649 students/librarian	**% Black**: 0.8	
Total Teachers: 212	**Guidance Counselors**: 8.0	**% Hispanic**: 2.4	
Student/Classroom Teacher Ratio: 17.7	430 students/counselor	**% White**: 94.6	

Douglas County

SUPERIOR S.D.

3025 TOWER AVE ● SUPERIOR WI 54880 ● (715) 394-8710

Grade Span: PK-12	**Expenditures/Student**: $5,877	**% Amer Indian**: 4.2	National ***Socio-Economic Status*** indicator percentile (100=high): 40th
Schools: *Regular* 11 ● *Spec Ed* 0 ● *Alt* 0	**Librarians**: 8.0	**% Asian**: 2.5	
Students: 5,732	717 students/librarian	**% Black**: 0.8	
Total Teachers: 321	**Guidance Counselors**: 15.0	**% Hispanic**: 0.4	
Student/Classroom Teacher Ratio: 16.8	382 students/counselor	**% White**: 92.1	

Dunn County

MENOMONIE AREA S.D.

718 N BROADWAY ● MENOMONIE WI 54751 ● (715) 232-1642 ● http://msd.k12.wi.us

Grade Span: PK-12	**Expenditures/Student**: $6,169	**% Amer Indian**: 0.2	National ***Socio-Economic Status*** indicator percentile (100=high): 49th
Schools: *Regular* 9 ● *Spec Ed* 0 ● *Alt* 0	**Librarians**: 5.0	**% Asian**: 10.4	
Students: 3,417	683 students/librarian	**% Black**: 0.5	
Total Teachers: 193	**Guidance Counselors**: 8.5	**% Hispanic**: 0.6	
Student/Classroom Teacher Ratio: 19.4	402 students/counselor	**% White**: 88.3	

Eau Claire County

EAU CLAIRE AREA S.D.

500 MAIN ST ● EAU CLAIRE WI 54701-3770 ● (715) 833-3465 ● http://www.central.ecasd.k12.wi.us

Grade Span: PK-12	**Expenditures/Student**: $6,456	**% Amer Indian**: 0.7	National ***Socio-Economic Status*** indicator percentile (100=high): 58th
Schools: *Regular* 22 ● *Spec Ed* 0 ● *Alt* 0	**Librarians**: 23.0	**% Asian**: 9.0	
Students: 11,674	508 students/librarian	**% Black**: 0.7	
Total Teachers: 726	**Guidance Counselors**: 30.7	**% Hispanic**: 0.8	
Student/Classroom Teacher Ratio: 17.7	380 students/counselor	**% White**: 88.7	

Fond du Lac County
FOND DU LAC S.D.
72 S PORTLAND ST ● FOND DU LAC WI 54935 ● (920) 929-2760 ● http://www.fonddulac.k12.wi.us

Grade Span: PK-12 **Schools**: *Regular* 13 ● *Spec Ed* 1 ● *Alt* 0 **Students**: 7,531 **Total Teachers**: 430 **Student/Classroom Teacher Ratio**: 19.7	**Expenditures/Student**: $5,700 **Librarians**: 15.0 502 students/librarian **Guidance Counselors**: 15.0 502 students/counselor	**% Amer Indian**: 0.4 **% Asian**: 3.0 **% Black**: 1.2 **% Hispanic**: 2.2 **% White**: 93.1	National ***Socio-Economic Status*** indicator percentile (100=high): 73rd

Fond du Lac County
WAUPUN S.D.
950 WILCOX ST ● WAUPUN WI 53963 ● (920) 324-9341

Grade Span: KG-12 **Schools**: *Regular* 7 ● *Spec Ed* 0 ● *Alt* 0 **Students**: 2,510 **Total Teachers**: 173 **Student/Classroom Teacher Ratio**: 17.1	**Expenditures/Student**: $6,080 **Librarians**: 3.4 738 students/librarian **Guidance Counselors**: 6.0 418 students/counselor	**% Amer Indian**: 0.2 **% Asian**: 0.3 **% Black**: 0.2 **% Hispanic**: 2.7 **% White**: 96.6	National ***Socio-Economic Status*** indicator percentile (100=high): 78th

Green County
MONROE S.D.
1220 16TH AVE ● MONROE WI 53566 ● (608) 328-9147

Grade Span: PK-12 **Schools**: *Regular* 5 ● *Spec Ed* 0 ● *Alt* 0 **Students**: 2,734 **Total Teachers**: 184 **Student/Classroom Teacher Ratio**: 16.0	**Expenditures/Student**: $6,656 **Librarians**: 5.2 526 students/librarian **Guidance Counselors**: 6.1 448 students/counselor	**% Amer Indian**: 0.5 **% Asian**: 0.8 **% Black**: 0.5 **% Hispanic**: 0.3 **% White**: 97.9	National ***Socio-Economic Status*** indicator percentile (100=high): 78th

Jefferson County
FORT ATKINSON S.D.
317 S HIGH ST ● FORT ATKINSON WI 53538 ● (920) 563-7807 ● http://www.fortschools.org

Grade Span: PK-12 **Schools**: *Regular* 5 ● *Spec Ed* 0 ● *Alt* 0 **Students**: 2,649 **Total Teachers**: 170 **Student/Classroom Teacher Ratio**: 16.0	**Expenditures/Student**: $6,289 **Librarians**: 3.9 679 students/librarian **Guidance Counselors**: 5.0 530 students/counselor	**% Amer Indian**: 0.2 **% Asian**: 1.0 **% Black**: 0.2 **% Hispanic**: 1.7 **% White**: 96.9	National ***Socio-Economic Status*** indicator percentile (100=high): 85th

Jefferson County
WATERTOWN S.D.
111 DODGE ST ● WATERTOWN WI 53094 ● (920) 262-1460 ● http://www.watertown.k12.wi.us

Grade Span: PK-12 **Schools**: *Regular* 8 ● *Spec Ed* 0 ● *Alt* 0 **Students**: 3,608 **Total Teachers**: 217 **Student/Classroom Teacher Ratio**: 17.1	**Expenditures/Student**: $6,592 **Librarians**: 4.9 736 students/librarian **Guidance Counselors**: 8.0 451 students/counselor	**% Amer Indian**: 1.2 **% Asian**: 1.1 **% Black**: 0.1 **% Hispanic**: 4.5 **% White**: 93.1	National ***Socio-Economic Status*** indicator percentile (100=high): 76th

Kenosha County
KENOSHA S.D.
PO BOX 340 ● KENOSHA WI 53141 ● (414) 653-6323 ● http://www.kusd.edu

Grade Span: PK-12 **Schools**: *Regular* 32 ● *Spec Ed* 0 ● *Alt* 1 **Students**: 18,683 **Total Teachers**: 1,077 **Student/Classroom Teacher Ratio**: 19.0	**Expenditures/Student**: $6,168 **Librarians**: 45.2 413 students/librarian **Guidance Counselors**: 42.0 445 students/counselor	**% Amer Indian**: 0.4 **% Asian**: 1.1 **% Black**: 12.2 **% Hispanic**: 9.2 **% White**: 77.2	National ***Socio-Economic Status*** indicator percentile (100=high): 51st

La Crosse County
HOLMEN S.D.
500 N HOLMEN DR STE 508 ● HOLMEN WI 54636 ● (608) 526-6610 ● http://www.holmen.k12.wi.us

Grade Span: PK-12 **Schools**: *Regular* 5 ● *Spec Ed* 0 ● *Alt* 0 **Students**: 2,669 **Total Teachers**: 163 **Student/Classroom Teacher Ratio**: 16.8	**Expenditures/Student**: $5,877 **Librarians**: 4.7 568 students/librarian **Guidance Counselors**: 5.5 485 students/counselor	**% Amer Indian**: 0.4 **% Asian**: 1.7 **% Black**: 0.3 **% Hispanic**: 0.4 **% White**: 97.2	National ***Socio-Economic Status*** indicator percentile (100=high): 79th

La Crosse County
LA CROSSE S.D.
HOGAN ADMIN CENTER ● LA CROSSE WI 54601 ● (608) 789-7628 ● http://www.centuryinter.net/hogan

Grade Span: PK-12 **Schools**: *Regular* 16 ● *Spec Ed* 0 ● *Alt* 1 **Students**: 8,152 **Total Teachers**: 559 **Student/Classroom Teacher Ratio**: 15.0	**Expenditures/Student**: $6,967 **Librarians**: 20.2 404 students/librarian **Guidance Counselors**: 20.0 408 students/counselor	**% Amer Indian**: 1.7 **% Asian**: 13.8 **% Black**: 2.7 **% Hispanic**: 0.6 **% White**: 81.3	National ***Socio-Economic Status*** indicator percentile (100=high): 38th

La Crosse County
ONALASKA S.D.
PO BOX 429 ● ONALASKA WI 54650-0429 ● (608) 781-9704 ● http://www.onalaska.k12.wi.us

Grade Span: PK-12 **Schools**: *Regular* 5 ● *Spec Ed* 0 ● *Alt* 0 **Students**: 2,715 **Total Teachers**: 171 **Student/Classroom Teacher Ratio**: 18.4	**Expenditures/Student**: $5,628 **Librarians**: 5.5 494 students/librarian **Guidance Counselors**: 6.0 453 students/counselor	**% Amer Indian**: 0.4 **% Asian**: 4.8 **% Black**: 0.6 **% Hispanic**: 0.7 **% White**: 93.4	National ***Socio-Economic Status*** indicator percentile (100=high): 83rd

Langlade County
ANTIGO S.D.
120 S DORR ST ● ANTIGO WI 54409 ● (715) 627-4355

Grade Span: PK-12 **Schools**: *Regular* 13 ● *Spec Ed* 0 ● *Alt* 0 **Students**: 3,171 **Total Teachers**: 212 **Student/Classroom Teacher Ratio**: 15.2	**Expenditures/Student**: $6,405 **Librarians**: 7.5 423 students/librarian **Guidance Counselors**: 7.0 453 students/counselor	**% Amer Indian**: 3.2 **% Asian**: 0.5 **% Black**: 0.3 **% Hispanic**: 0.6 **% White**: 95.3	National ***Socio-Economic Status*** indicator percentile (100=high): 49th

Lincoln County
MERRILL AREA S.D.
1111 N SALES ST ● MERRILL WI 54452 ● (715) 536-4581

Grade Span: PK-12 **Schools**: *Regular* 11 ● *Spec Ed* 0 ● *Alt* 0 **Students**: 3,443 **Total Teachers**: 209 **Student/Classroom Teacher Ratio**: 17.0	**Expenditures/Student**: $5,952 **Librarians**: 4.2 820 students/librarian **Guidance Counselors**: 8.0 430 students/counselor	**% Amer Indian**: 0.6 **% Asian**: 0.7 **% Black**: 0.1 **% Hispanic**: 0.4 **% White**: 98.2	National ***Socio-Economic Status*** indicator percentile (100=high): 67th

Manitowoc County
MANITOWOC S.D.
PO BOX 1657 ● MANITOWOC WI 54221 ● (920) 683-4781

Grade Span: PK-12 **Schools**: *Regular* 10 ● *Spec Ed* 0 ● *Alt* 0 **Students**: 5,592 **Total Teachers**: 328 **Student/Classroom Teacher Ratio**: 19.2	**Expenditures/Student**: $5,448 **Librarians**: 5.4 1,036 students/librarian **Guidance Counselors**: 11.2 499 students/counselor	**% Amer Indian**: 0.7 **% Asian**: 9.0 **% Black**: 0.6 **% Hispanic**: 1.7 **% White**: 87.9	National ***Socio-Economic Status*** indicator percentile (100=high): na

Marathon County

[SCHOFIELD] D C EVEREST AREA S.D.

6300 ALDERSON ST ● SCHOFIELD WI 54476 ● (715) 359-4221

Grade Span: PK-12 **Schools**: *Regular* 9 ● *Spec Ed* 0 ● *Alt* 0 **Students**: 4,879 **Total Teachers**: 288 **Student/Classroom Teacher Ratio**: 17.0	**Expenditures/Student**: $5,652 **Librarians**: 7.0 697 students/librarian **Guidance Counselors**: 10.5 465 students/counselor	**% Amer Indian**: 0.5 **% Asian**: 3.2 **% Black**: 0.3 **% Hispanic**: 0.4 **% White**: 95.6	National ***Socio-Economic Status*** indicator percentile (100=high): 78th

Marathon County

WAUSAU S.D.

415 SEYMOUR ST ● WAUSAU WI 54402-0359 ● (715) 261-2561 ● http://www.wausau.k12.wi.us

Grade Span: PK-12 **Schools**: *Regular* 19 ● *Spec Ed* 0 ● *Alt* 0 **Students**: 9,109 **Total Teachers**: 606 **Student/Classroom Teacher Ratio**: 15.6	**Expenditures/Student**: $6,371 **Librarians**: 12.8 712 students/librarian **Guidance Counselors**: 23.9 381 students/counselor	**% Amer Indian**: 0.5 **% Asian**: 20.6 **% Black**: 0.3 **% Hispanic**: 0.5 **% White**: 78.0	National ***Socio-Economic Status*** indicator percentile (100=high): 47th

Marinette County

MARINETTE S.D.

1010 MAIN ST ● MARINETTE WI 54143 ● (715) 732-7905 ● http://www.mari.net/~mpsc

Grade Span: PK-12 **Schools**: *Regular* 8 ● *Spec Ed* 0 ● *Alt* 0 **Students**: 2,960 **Total Teachers**: 176 **Student/Classroom Teacher Ratio**: 18.6	**Expenditures/Student**: $5,363 **Librarians**: 3.0 987 students/librarian **Guidance Counselors**: 6.5 455 students/counselor	**% Amer Indian**: 0.5 **% Asian**: 0.5 **% Black**: 0.4 **% Hispanic**: 0.5 **% White**: 98.1	National ***Socio-Economic Status*** indicator percentile (100=high): 69th

Milwaukee County

CUDAHY S.D.

PO BOX 618 ● CUDAHY WI 53110 ● (414) 769-2300

Grade Span: PK-12 **Schools**: *Regular* 6 ● *Spec Ed* 0 ● *Alt* 0 **Students**: 2,948 **Total Teachers**: 207 **Student/Classroom Teacher Ratio**: 14.5	**Expenditures/Student**: $7,170 **Librarians**: 4.0 737 students/librarian **Guidance Counselors**: 9.0 328 students/counselor	**% Amer Indian**: 1.3 **% Asian**: 3.9 **% Black**: 5.0 **% Hispanic**: 6.6 **% White**: 83.2	National ***Socio-Economic Status*** indicator percentile (100=high): 57th

Milwaukee County

FRANKLIN PUBLIC S.D.

8255 W FOREST HILL AVE ● FRANKLIN WI 53132-9705 ● (414) 529-8233

Grade Span: PK-12 **Schools**: *Regular* 7 ● *Spec Ed* 0 ● *Alt* 0 **Students**: 3,610 **Total Teachers**: 236 **Student/Classroom Teacher Ratio**: 16.9	**Expenditures/Student**: $6,918 **Librarians**: 6.5 555 students/librarian **Guidance Counselors**: 8.6 420 students/counselor	**% Amer Indian**: 0.5 **% Asian**: 5.9 **% Black**: 5.1 **% Hispanic**: 3.0 **% White**: 85.5	National ***Socio-Economic Status*** indicator percentile (100=high): 82nd

Milwaukee County

GREENFIELD S.D.

8500 W CHAPMAN ● GREENFIELD WI 53228 ● (414) 529-9090

Grade Span: PK-12 **Schools**: *Regular* 6 ● *Spec Ed* 0 ● *Alt* 0 **Students**: 3,181 **Total Teachers**: 198 **Student/Classroom Teacher Ratio**: 17.4	**Expenditures/Student**: $6,684 **Librarians**: 5.8 548 students/librarian **Guidance Counselors**: 8.9 357 students/counselor	**% Amer Indian**: 1.2 **% Asian**: 3.7 **% Black**: 5.8 **% Hispanic**: 5.0 **% White**: 84.3	National ***Socio-Economic Status*** indicator percentile (100=high): 69th

Milwaukee County

[GREENFIELD] **WHITNALL S.D.**

5000 S 116TH ST ● GREENFIELD WI 53228 ● (414) 425-4000

Grade Span: PK-12 **Schools**: *Regular* 4 ● *Spec Ed* 0 ● *Alt* 0 **Students**: 2,567 **Total Teachers**: 150 **Student/Classroom Teacher Ratio**: 18.7	**Expenditures/Student**: $6,847 **Librarians**: 5.0 513 students/librarian **Guidance Counselors**: 7.1 362 students/counselor	**% Amer Indian**: 0.2 **% Asian**: 6.3 **% Black**: 4.7 **% Hispanic**: 1.9 **% White**: 86.9	National ***Socio-Economic Status*** indicator percentile (100=high): 85th

Milwaukee County

MILWAUKEE S.D.

PO BOX 2181 ● MILWAUKEE WI 53201-2181 ● (414) 475-8001 ● http://www.milwaukee.k12.wi.us

Grade Span: PK-12 **Schools**: *Regular* 152 ● *Spec Ed* 1 ● *Alt* 2 **Students**: 98,378 **Total Teachers**: 5,673 **Student/Classroom Teacher Ratio**: 18.5	**Expenditures/Student**: $7,040 **Librarians**: 83.1 1,184 students/librarian **Guidance Counselors**: 165.4 595 students/counselor	**% Amer Indian**: 1.0 **% Asian**: 3.5 **% Black**: 59.7 **% Hispanic**: 12.0 **% White**: 23.8	National ***Socio-Economic Status*** indicator percentile (100=high): 6th

Milwaukee County

OAK CREEK-FRANKLIN S.D.

7630 S 10TH ST ● OAK CREEK WI 53154 ● (414) 768-5886

Grade Span: PK-12 **Schools**: *Regular* 8 ● *Spec Ed* 0 ● *Alt* 0 **Students**: 4,565 **Total Teachers**: 268 **Student/Classroom Teacher Ratio**: 17.9	**Expenditures/Student**: $5,895 **Librarians**: 6.8 671 students/librarian **Guidance Counselors**: 12.6 362 students/counselor	**% Amer Indian**: 0.9 **% Asian**: 3.8 **% Black**: 2.9 **% Hispanic**: 4.8 **% White**: 87.6	National ***Socio-Economic Status*** indicator percentile (100=high): 83rd

Milwaukee County

SOUTH MILWAUKEE S.D.

1225 MEMORIAL DR ● SOUTH MILWAUKEE WI 53172 ● (414) 768-6300 ● http://www.sdsm.k12.wi.us

Grade Span: PK-12 **Schools**: *Regular* 6 ● *Spec Ed* 0 ● *Alt* 0 **Students**: 3,583 **Total Teachers**: 209 **Student/Classroom Teacher Ratio**: 18.2	**Expenditures/Student**: $5,751 **Librarians**: 4.0 896 students/librarian **Guidance Counselors**: 10.0 358 students/counselor	**% Amer Indian**: 0.7 **% Asian**: 3.6 **% Black**: 4.9 **% Hispanic**: 5.1 **% White**: 85.7	National ***Socio-Economic Status*** indicator percentile (100=high): 67th

Milwaukee County

WAUWATOSA S.D.

12121 W NORTH AVE ● WAUWATOSA WI 53226 ● (414) 259-4495 ● http://www.execpc.com/~tosaeduc

Grade Span: PK-12 **Schools**: *Regular* 16 ● *Spec Ed* 0 ● *Alt* 0 **Students**: 7,408 **Total Teachers**: 470 **Student/Classroom Teacher Ratio**: 15.6	**Expenditures/Student**: $6,335 **Librarians**: 14.0 529 students/librarian **Guidance Counselors**: 14.8 501 students/counselor	**% Amer Indian**: 0.6 **% Asian**: 4.2 **% Black**: 12.0 **% Hispanic**: 2.3 **% White**: 80.8	National ***Socio-Economic Status*** indicator percentile (100=high): 90th

Milwaukee County

WEST ALLIS S.D.

9333 W LINCOLN AVE ● WEST ALLIS WI 53227 ● (414) 546-5500 ● http://www.wawm.k12.wi.us

Grade Span: PK-12 **Schools**: *Regular* 17 ● *Spec Ed* 0 ● *Alt* 0 **Students**: 9,331 **Total Teachers**: 577 **Student/Classroom Teacher Ratio**: 17.0	**Expenditures/Student**: $6,655 **Librarians**: 19.0 491 students/librarian **Guidance Counselors**: 14.5 644 students/counselor	**% Amer Indian**: 1.1 **% Asian**: 1.7 **% Black**: 3.3 **% Hispanic**: 3.2 **% White**: 90.7	National ***Socio-Economic Status*** indicator percentile (100=high): 76th

Milwaukee County

WHITEFISH BAY S.D.

1200 E FAIRMOUNT AVE ● WHITEFISH BAY WI 53217 ● (414) 963-3921 ● http://www.wfbschools.com

Grade Span: PK-12 **Schools**: *Regular* 4 ● *Spec Ed* 0 ● *Alt* 0 **Students**: 2,814 **Total Teachers**: 171 **Student/Classroom Teacher Ratio**: 16.9	**Expenditures/Student**: $6,859 **Librarians**: 4.0 704 students/librarian **Guidance Counselors**: 8.5 331 students/counselor	**% Amer Indian**: 0.2 **% Asian**: 3.1 **% Black**: 13.6 **% Hispanic**: 2.3 **% White**: 80.8	National ***Socio-Economic Status*** indicator percentile (100=high): na

Monroe County

SPARTA AREA S.D.

506 N BLACK RIVER ST ● SPARTA WI 54656 ● (608) 269-3151 ● http://www.spartan.org/education.html

Grade Span: PK-12 **Schools**: *Regular* 8 ● *Spec Ed* 0 ● *Alt* 0 **Students**: 2,790 **Total Teachers**: 180 **Student/Classroom Teacher Ratio**: 16.0	**Expenditures/Student**: $5,580 **Librarians**: 5.7 489 students/librarian **Guidance Counselors**: 6.5 429 students/counselor	**% Amer Indian**: 0.4 **% Asian**: 1.0 **% Black**: 1.0 **% Hispanic**: 1.1 **% White**: 96.6	National ***Socio-Economic Status*** indicator percentile (100=high): 59th

Monroe County

TOMAH AREA S.D.

129 W CLIFTON ST ● TOMAH WI 54660-2507 ● (608) 374-7210

Grade Span: PK-12 **Schools**: *Regular* 9 ● *Spec Ed* 0 ● *Alt* 0 **Students**: 3,197 **Total Teachers**: 200 **Student/Classroom Teacher Ratio**: 16.1	**Expenditures/Student**: $5,058 **Librarians**: 5.9 542 students/librarian **Guidance Counselors**: 8.0 400 students/counselor	**% Amer Indian**: 3.2 **% Asian**: 0.7 **% Black**: 0.9 **% Hispanic**: 1.0 **% White**: 94.2	National ***Socio-Economic Status*** indicator percentile (100=high): 63rd

Oneida County

RHINELANDER S.D.

315 S ONEIDA AVE ● RHINELANDER WI 54501 ● (715) 362-3465

Grade Span: PK-12 **Schools**: *Regular* 10 ● *Spec Ed* 0 ● *Alt* 0 **Students**: 3,439 **Total Teachers**: 206 **Student/Classroom Teacher Ratio**: 19.4	**Expenditures/Student**: $6,088 **Librarians**: 3.0 1,146 students/librarian **Guidance Counselors**: 9.6 358 students/counselor	**% Amer Indian**: 1.6 **% Asian**: 0.8 **% Black**: 0.4 **% Hispanic**: 0.8 **% White**: 96.5	National ***Socio-Economic Status*** indicator percentile (100=high): 63rd

Outagamie County

APPLETON AREA S.D.

PO BOX 2019 ● APPLETON WI 54913 ● (920) 832-6126

Grade Span: PK-12 **Schools**: *Regular* 24 ● *Spec Ed* 0 ● *Alt* 0 **Students**: 14,082 **Total Teachers**: 816 **Student/Classroom Teacher Ratio**: 17.3	**Expenditures/Student**: $5,645 **Librarians**: 24.0 587 students/librarian **Guidance Counselors**: 30.0 469 students/counselor	**% Amer Indian**: 0.5 **% Asian**: 7.5 **% Black**: 0.9 **% Hispanic**: 1.2 **% White**: 89.9	National ***Socio-Economic Status*** indicator percentile (100=high): 77th

Outagamie County

KAUKAUNA AREA S.D.

112 MAIN AVE ● KAUKAUNA WI 54130 ● (920) 766-6100 ● http://www.athenet.net/~kaueq/district.html

Grade Span: PK-12 **Schools**: *Regular* 6 ● *Spec Ed* 0 ● *Alt* 0 **Students**: 3,477 **Total Teachers**: 207 **Student/Classroom Teacher Ratio**: 18.3	**Expenditures/Student**: $6,071 **Librarians**: 4.5 773 students/librarian **Guidance Counselors**: 8.0 435 students/counselor	**% Amer Indian**: 1.0 **% Asian**: 3.5 **% Black**: 0.4 **% Hispanic**: 0.3 **% White**: 94.7	National ***Socio-Economic Status*** indicator percentile (100=high): 90th

Ozaukee County

CEDARBURG S.D.

W68 N611 EVERGREEN BLVD ● CEDARBURG WI 53012 ● (414) 375-5208

Grade Span: PK-12 **Schools**: *Regular* 5 ● *Spec Ed* 0 ● *Alt* 0 **Students**: 2,688 **Total Teachers**: 165 **Student/Classroom Teacher Ratio**: 16.8	**Expenditures/Student**: $6,485 **Librarians**: 5.2 517 students/librarian **Guidance Counselors**: 9.6 280 students/counselor	**% Amer Indian**: 0.2 **% Asian**: 0.7 **% Black**: 0.3 **% Hispanic**: 0.6 **% White**: 98.2	National ***Socio-Economic Status*** indicator percentile (100=high): 100th

Ozaukee County

MEQUON-THIENSVILLE S.D.

5000 W MEQUON RD ● MEQUON WI 53092 ● (414) 242-2412

Grade Span: PK-12 **Schools**: *Regular* 7 ● *Spec Ed* 0 ● *Alt* 0 **Students**: 4,094 **Total Teachers**: 248 **Student/Classroom Teacher Ratio**: 16.7	**Expenditures/Student**: $6,719 **Librarians**: 5.4 758 students/librarian **Guidance Counselors**: 10.0 409 students/counselor	**% Amer Indian**: 0.6 **% Asian**: 3.1 **% Black**: 6.1 **% Hispanic**: 1.7 **% White**: 88.4	National ***Socio-Economic Status*** indicator percentile (100=high): 99th

Ozaukee County

PORT WASHINGTON-SAUKVILLE S.D.

100 W MONROE ST ● PORT WASHINGTON WI 53074 ● (414) 284-7700

Grade Span: PK-12 **Schools**: *Regular* 5 ● *Spec Ed* 0 ● *Alt* 0 **Students**: 2,782 **Total Teachers**: 175 **Student/Classroom Teacher Ratio**: 16.3	**Expenditures/Student**: $7,096 **Librarians**: 3.7 752 students/librarian **Guidance Counselors**: 9.0 309 students/counselor	**% Amer Indian**: 0.9 **% Asian**: 0.8 **% Black**: 0.7 **% Hispanic**: 0.9 **% White**: 96.7	National ***Socio-Economic Status*** indicator percentile (100=high): 90th

Pierce County

RIVER FALLS S.D.

852 E DIVISION ST ● RIVER FALLS WI 54022-2599 ● (715) 425-1800 ● http://www.rfsd.k12.wi.us

Grade Span: PK-12 **Schools**: *Regular* 5 ● *Spec Ed* 0 ● *Alt* 0 **Students**: 2,874 **Total Teachers**: 181 **Student/Classroom Teacher Ratio**: 16.3	**Expenditures/Student**: $6,163 **Librarians**: 5.0 575 students/librarian **Guidance Counselors**: 7.5 383 students/counselor	**% Amer Indian**: 0.4 **% Asian**: 1.4 **% Black**: 1.0 **% Hispanic**: 1.2 **% White**: 96.0	National ***Socio-Economic Status*** indicator percentile (100=high): 86th

Portage County

STEVENS POINT AREA S.D.

1900 POLK ST ● STEVENS POINT WI 54481 ● (715) 345-5444

Grade Span: PK-12 **Schools**: *Regular* 13 ● *Spec Ed* 0 ● *Alt* 0 **Students**: 8,533 **Total Teachers**: 531 **Student/Classroom Teacher Ratio**: 16.9	**Expenditures/Student**: $5,808 **Librarians**: 18.0 474 students/librarian **Guidance Counselors**: 7.5 1,138 students/counselor	**% Amer Indian**: 0.5 **% Asian**: 8.4 **% Black**: 0.9 **% Hispanic**: 1.5 **% White**: 88.7	National ***Socio-Economic Status*** indicator percentile (100=high): 66th

Racine County

BURLINGTON AREA S.D.

100 N KANE ST ● BURLINGTON WI 53105 ● (414) 763-0210

Grade Span: PK-12 **Schools**: *Regular* 7 ● *Spec Ed* 0 ● *Alt* 0 **Students**: 3,520 **Total Teachers**: 186 **Student/Classroom Teacher Ratio**: 21.9	**Expenditures/Student**: $5,409 **Librarians**: 5.2 677 students/librarian **Guidance Counselors**: 9.5 371 students/counselor	**% Amer Indian**: 0.2 **% Asian**: 0.8 **% Black**: 0.5 **% Hispanic**: 3.7 **% White**: 94.8	National ***Socio-Economic Status*** indicator percentile (100=high): 86th

Racine County

RACINE S.D.

2220 NORTHWESTERN AVE • RACINE WI 53404 • (414) 631-7064

Grade Span: PK-12 **Schools**: *Regular* 31 • *Spec Ed* 1 • *Alt* 5 **Students**: 22,303 **Total Teachers**: 1,420 **Student/Classroom Teacher Ratio**: 18.5	**Expenditures/Student**: $6,507 **Librarians**: 34.1 654 students/librarian **Guidance Counselors**: 50.0 446 students/counselor	**% Amer Indian**: 0.3 **% Asian**: 0.9 **% Black**: 24.2 **% Hispanic**: 10.7 **% White**: 63.9	National ***Socio-Economic Status*** indicator percentile (100=high): 44th

Rock County

BELOIT S.D.

ROOSEVELT ADMIN CENTER • BELOIT WI 53511 • (608) 364-6017

Grade Span: PK-12 **Schools**: *Regular* 16 • *Spec Ed* 0 • *Alt* 0 **Students**: 7,236 **Total Teachers**: 445 **Student/Classroom Teacher Ratio**: 17.0	**Expenditures/Student**: $6,906 **Librarians**: 8.0 905 students/librarian **Guidance Counselors**: 12.0 603 students/counselor	**% Amer Indian**: 0.3 **% Asian**: 1.4 **% Black**: 29.5 **% Hispanic**: 5.9 **% White**: 62.9	National ***Socio-Economic Status*** indicator percentile (100=high): 41st

Rock County

JANESVILLE S.D.

527 S FRANKLIN ST • JANESVILLE WI 53545 • (608) 758-6410 • http://mars.inwave.com/schools/jps

Grade Span: PK-12 **Schools**: *Regular* 16 • *Spec Ed* 0 • *Alt* 0 **Students**: 10,586 **Total Teachers**: 709 **Student/Classroom Teacher Ratio**: 15.8	**Expenditures/Student**: $6,007 **Librarians**: 18.0 588 students/librarian **Guidance Counselors**: 20.5 516 students/counselor	**% Amer Indian**: 0.4 **% Asian**: 1.8 **% Black**: 2.0 **% Hispanic**: 1.8 **% White**: 94.0	National ***Socio-Economic Status*** indicator percentile (100=high): 78th

Rock County

MILTON S.D.

430 E HIGH ST SUITE 2 • MILTON WI 53563 • (608) 868-9204 • http://www.milton.k12.wi.us

Grade Span: PK-12 **Schools**: *Regular* 6 • *Spec Ed* 0 • *Alt* 0 **Students**: 2,686 **Total Teachers**: 168 **Student/Classroom Teacher Ratio**: 16.2	**Expenditures/Student**: $5,850 **Librarians**: 3.5 767 students/librarian **Guidance Counselors**: 7.0 384 students/counselor	**% Amer Indian**: 0.3 **% Asian**: 0.6 **% Black**: 0.6 **% Hispanic**: 0.6 **% White**: 97.9	National ***Socio-Economic Status*** indicator percentile (100=high): 89th

St. Croix County

HUDSON S.D.

1401 VINE ST • HUDSON WI 54016 • (715) 386-4901

Grade Span: PK-12 **Schools**: *Regular* 6 • *Spec Ed* 0 • *Alt* 0 **Students**: 3,608 **Total Teachers**: 209 **Student/Classroom Teacher Ratio**: 17.8	**Expenditures/Student**: $5,760 **Librarians**: 5.5 656 students/librarian **Guidance Counselors**: 8.5 424 students/counselor	**% Amer Indian**: 0.3 **% Asian**: 1.0 **% Black**: 0.3 **% Hispanic**: 0.5 **% White**: 97.9	National ***Socio-Economic Status*** indicator percentile (100=high): 94th

Sauk County

BARABOO S.D.

101 2ND AVE • BARABOO WI 53913 • (608) 355-3950

Grade Span: PK-12 **Schools**: *Regular* 8 • *Spec Ed* 0 • *Alt* 0 **Students**: 3,017 **Total Teachers**: 188 **Student/Classroom Teacher Ratio**: 17.8	**Expenditures/Student**: $5,565 **Librarians**: 12.9 234 students/librarian **Guidance Counselors**: 7.0 431 students/counselor	**% Amer Indian**: 3.2 **% Asian**: 0.6 **% Black**: 0.4 **% Hispanic**: 0.8 **% White**: 95.0	National ***Socio-Economic Status*** indicator percentile (100=high): 70th

Shawano County
SHAWANO-GRESHAM S.D.
210 S FRANKLIN ST ● SHAWANO WI 54166 ● (715) 524-7004

Grade Span: PK-12 **Schools**: *Regular* 6 ● *Spec Ed* 0 ● *Alt* 0 **Students**: 2,808 **Total Teachers**: 163 **Student/Classroom Teacher Ratio**: 16.5	**Expenditures/Student**: $5,389 **Librarians**: 4.0 702 students/librarian **Guidance Counselors**: 4.5 624 students/counselor	**% Amer Indian**: 13.8 **% Asian**: 1.2 **% Black**: 0.5 **% Hispanic**: 1.5 **% White**: 82.9	National ***Socio-Economic Status*** indicator percentile (100=high): 67th

Sheboygan County
PLYMOUTH S.D.
HIGHLAND AVE ● PLYMOUTH WI 53073 ● (920) 892-2661

Grade Span: PK-12 **Schools**: *Regular* 7 ● *Spec Ed* 0 ● *Alt* 0 **Students**: 2,513 **Total Teachers**: 153 **Student/Classroom Teacher Ratio**: 18.2	**Expenditures/Student**: $5,840 **Librarians**: 4.6 546 students/librarian **Guidance Counselors**: 7.5 335 students/counselor	**% Amer Indian**: 1.2 **% Asian**: 0.5 **% Black**: 0.1 **% Hispanic**: 0.6 **% White**: 97.6	National ***Socio-Economic Status*** indicator percentile (100=high): 90th

Sheboygan County
SHEBOYGAN AREA S.D.
830 VIRGINIA AVE ● SHEBOYGAN WI 53081 ● (920) 459-3511 ● http://www.sheboygan.k12.wi.us

Grade Span: PK-12 **Schools**: *Regular* 18 ● *Spec Ed* 0 ● *Alt* 0 **Students**: 10,264 **Total Teachers**: 633 **Student/Classroom Teacher Ratio**: 18.7	**Expenditures/Student**: $6,298 **Librarians**: 18.0 570 students/librarian **Guidance Counselors**: 22.0 467 students/counselor	**% Amer Indian**: 0.6 **% Asian**: 13.2 **% Black**: 0.7 **% Hispanic**: 5.4 **% White**: 80.2	National ***Socio-Economic Status*** indicator percentile (100=high): 64th

Taylor County
MEDFORD AREA S.D.
124 W STATE ST ● MEDFORD WI 54451 ● (715) 748-4620

Grade Span: PK-12 **Schools**: *Regular* 4 ● *Spec Ed* 0 ● *Alt* 0 **Students**: 2,572 **Total Teachers**: 153 **Student/Classroom Teacher Ratio**: 17.3	**Expenditures/Student**: $5,205 **Librarians**: 3.0 857 students/librarian **Guidance Counselors**: 4.6 559 students/counselor	**% Amer Indian**: 0.2 **% Asian**: 0.4 **% Black**: 0.2 **% Hispanic**: 0.2 **% White**: 99.1	National ***Socio-Economic Status*** indicator percentile (100=high): 76th

Washington County
GERMANTOWN S.D.
N104 W13840 DONGES BAY RD ● GERMANTOWN WI 53022-4499 ● (414) 253-3904

Grade Span: PK-12 **Schools**: *Regular* 7 ● *Spec Ed* 0 ● *Alt* 0 **Students**: 3,479 **Total Teachers**: 210 **Student/Classroom Teacher Ratio**: 15.2	**Expenditures/Student**: $6,660 **Librarians**: 4.8 725 students/librarian **Guidance Counselors**: 7.0 497 students/counselor	**% Amer Indian**: 0.4 **% Asian**: 1.3 **% Black**: 1.4 **% Hispanic**: 1.2 **% White**: 95.6	National ***Socio-Economic Status*** indicator percentile (100=high): 96th

Washington County
WEST BEND S.D.
PO BOX 2000 ● WEST BEND WI 53095-2000 ● (414) 335-5435 ● http://www.west-bend.k12.wi.us

Grade Span: PK-12 **Schools**: *Regular* 11 ● *Spec Ed* 0 ● *Alt* 0 **Students**: 6,981 **Total Teachers**: 406 **Student/Classroom Teacher Ratio**: 17.8	**Expenditures/Student**: $5,798 **Librarians**: 11.0 635 students/librarian **Guidance Counselors**: 16.0 436 students/counselor	**% Amer Indian**: 0.7 **% Asian**: 0.6 **% Black**: 0.4 **% Hispanic**: 1.4 **% White**: 97.0	National ***Socio-Economic Status*** indicator percentile (100=high): 88th

Waukesha County
[BROOKFIELD] **ELMBROOK S.D.**
13780 W HOPE ST • BROOKFIELD WI 53005 • (414) 781-3030

Grade Span: PK-12 **Schools**: *Regular* 9 • *Spec Ed* 1 • *Alt* 0 **Students**: 7,128 **Total Teachers**: 470 **Student/Classroom Teacher Ratio**: 16.2	**Expenditures/Student**: $8,048 **Librarians**: 18.8 379 students/librarian **Guidance Counselors**: 11.0 648 students/counselor	**% Amer Indian**: 0.2 **% Asian**: 4.6 **% Black**: 4.5 **% Hispanic**: 1.1 **% White**: 89.6	National ***Socio-Economic Status*** indicator percentile (100=high): 95th

Waukesha County
MENOMONEE FALLS S.D.
N84 W16579 MENOMONEE AVE • MENOMONEE FALLS WI 53051 • (414) 255-8440 • http://www.execpc.com/MenomoneeFallsSchools

Grade Span: PK-12 **Schools**: *Regular* 7 • *Spec Ed* 0 • *Alt* 0 **Students**: 4,025 **Total Teachers**: 277 **Student/Classroom Teacher Ratio**: 15.0	**Expenditures/Student**: $7,293 **Librarians**: 7.5 537 students/librarian **Guidance Counselors**: 11.6 347 students/counselor	**% Amer Indian**: 0.7 **% Asian**: 1.9 **% Black**: 7.0 **% Hispanic**: 1.7 **% White**: 88.7	National ***Socio-Economic Status*** indicator percentile (100=high): 91st

Waukesha County
MUKWONAGO S.D.
423 DIVISION ST • MUKWONAGO WI 53149 • (414) 363-6304

Grade Span: PK-12 **Schools**: *Regular* 6 • *Spec Ed* 0 • *Alt* 0 **Students**: 5,105 **Total Teachers**: 312 **Student/Classroom Teacher Ratio**: 16.5	**Expenditures/Student**: $5,932 **Librarians**: 7.0 729 students/librarian **Guidance Counselors**: 9.0 567 students/counselor	**% Amer Indian**: 0.3 **% Asian**: 0.3 **% Black**: 0.4 **% Hispanic**: 1.2 **% White**: 97.8	National ***Socio-Economic Status*** indicator percentile (100=high): 99th

Waukesha County
MUSKEGO-NORWAY S.D.
S87 W18763 WOODS RD • MUSKEGO WI 53150-9374 • (414) 679-5400

Grade Span: KG-12 **Schools**: *Regular* 7 • *Spec Ed* 0 • *Alt* 0 **Students**: 4,220 **Total Teachers**: 241 **Student/Classroom Teacher Ratio**: 17.9	**Expenditures/Student**: $6,199 **Librarians**: 6.2 681 students/librarian **Guidance Counselors**: 10.4 406 students/counselor	**% Amer Indian**: 0.3 **% Asian**: 0.6 **% Black**: 0.2 **% Hispanic**: 1.0 **% White**: 97.9	National ***Socio-Economic Status*** indicator percentile (100=high): 97th

Waukesha County
NEW BERLIN S.D.
4333 S SUNNY SLOPE RD • NEW BERLIN WI 53151 • (414) 789-6220

Grade Span: PK-12 **Schools**: *Regular* 11 • *Spec Ed* 0 • *Alt* 0 **Students**: 4,759 **Total Teachers**: 315 **Student/Classroom Teacher Ratio**: 16.2	**Expenditures/Student**: $8,099 **Librarians**: 10.0 476 students/librarian **Guidance Counselors**: 10.0 476 students/counselor	**% Amer Indian**: 0.1 **% Asian**: 4.1 **% Black**: 0.8 **% Hispanic**: 1.2 **% White**: 93.7	National ***Socio-Economic Status*** indicator percentile (100=high): 96th

Waukesha County
OCONOMOWOC AREA S.D.
7077 BROWN ST • OCONOMOWOC WI 53066 • (414) 567-6632

Grade Span: PK-12 **Schools**: *Regular* 9 • *Spec Ed* 0 • *Alt* 0 **Students**: 4,238 **Total Teachers**: 271 **Student/Classroom Teacher Ratio**: 16.0	**Expenditures/Student**: $6,933 **Librarians**: 6.6 642 students/librarian **Guidance Counselors**: 10.0 424 students/counselor	**% Amer Indian**: 0.1 **% Asian**: 0.3 **% Black**: 0.3 **% Hispanic**: 0.3 **% White**: 98.9	National ***Socio-Economic Status*** indicator percentile (100=high): 93rd

Waukesha County

[SUSSEX] **HAMILTON S.D.**

W220 N6151 TOWN LINE RD ● SUSSEX WI 53089 ● (414) 246-1973 ● http://www.hamiltondist.k12.wi.us

Grade Span: PK-12 **Schools**: *Regular* 6 ● *Spec Ed* 0 ● *Alt* 0 **Students**: 3,280 **Total Teachers**: 201 **Student/Classroom Teacher Ratio**: 17.2	**Expenditures/Student**: $6,760 **Librarians**: 5.9 556 students/librarian **Guidance Counselors**: 7.0 469 students/counselor	**% Amer Indian**: 0.6 **% Asian**: 0.9 **% Black**: 1.5 **% Hispanic**: 1.5 **% White**: 95.5	National ***Socio-Economic Status*** indicator percentile (100=high): 96th

Waukesha County

[WALES] **KETTLE MORAINE S.D.**

PO BOX 901 ● WALES WI 53183-0901 ● (414) 968-6301 ● http://www.kmsd.edu

Grade Span: PK-12 **Schools**: *Regular* 6 ● *Spec Ed* 0 ● *Alt* 0 **Students**: 4,075 **Total Teachers**: 251 **Student/Classroom Teacher Ratio**: 16.5	**Expenditures/Student**: $6,442 **Librarians**: 5.9 691 students/librarian **Guidance Counselors**: 9.3 438 students/counselor	**% Amer Indian**: 0.1 **% Asian**: 0.9 **% Black**: 0.1 **% Hispanic**: 1.1 **% White**: 97.7	National ***Socio-Economic Status*** indicator percentile (100=high): 98th

Waukesha County

WAUKESHA S.D.

222 MAPLE AVE ● WAUKESHA WI 53186 ● (414) 521-8864

Grade Span: PK-12 **Schools**: *Regular* 23 ● *Spec Ed* 0 ● *Alt* 0 **Students**: 13,268 **Total Teachers**: 858 **Student/Classroom Teacher Ratio**: 16.2	**Expenditures/Student**: $6,266 **Librarians**: 14.3 928 students/librarian **Guidance Counselors**: 29.0 458 students/counselor	**% Amer Indian**: 0.7 **% Asian**: 1.4 **% Black**: 1.2 **% Hispanic**: 7.3 **% White**: 89.3	National ***Socio-Economic Status*** indicator percentile (100=high): 83rd

Waupaca County

NEW LONDON S.D.

901 W WASHINGTON ST ● NEW LONDON WI 54961 ● (920) 982-8530 ● http://www.newlondon.k12.wi.us

Grade Span: PK-12 **Schools**: *Regular* 6 ● *Spec Ed* 0 ● *Alt* 0 **Students**: 2,563 **Total Teachers**: 138 **Student/Classroom Teacher Ratio**: 19.1	**Expenditures/Student**: $5,693 **Librarians**: 4.0 641 students/librarian **Guidance Counselors**: 6.0 427 students/counselor	**% Amer Indian**: 0.4 **% Asian**: 0.9 **% Black**: 0.2 **% Hispanic**: 2.5 **% White**: 96.0	National ***Socio-Economic Status*** indicator percentile (100=high): 86th

Waupaca County

WAUPACA S.D.

515 SCHOOL ST ● WAUPACA WI 54981 ● (715) 258-4121 ● http://wsd.waupaca.k12.wi.us

Grade Span: PK-12 **Schools**: *Regular* 7 ● *Spec Ed* 0 ● *Alt* 0 **Students**: 2,626 **Total Teachers**: 163 **Student/Classroom Teacher Ratio**: 17.9	**Expenditures/Student**: $5,182 **Librarians**: 4.0 657 students/librarian **Guidance Counselors**: 4.0 657 students/counselor	**% Amer Indian**: 0.8 **% Asian**: 0.5 **% Black**: 0.5 **% Hispanic**: 2.1 **% White**: 96.2	National ***Socio-Economic Status*** indicator percentile (100=high): 71st

Winnebago County

MENASHA S.D.

PO BOX 360 ● MENASHA WI 54952-0360 ● (920) 751-5070

Grade Span: PK-12 **Schools**: *Regular* 8 ● *Spec Ed* 0 ● *Alt* 0 **Students**: 3,619 **Total Teachers**: 216 **Student/Classroom Teacher Ratio**: 16.5	**Expenditures/Student**: $5,768 **Librarians**: 3.9 928 students/librarian **Guidance Counselors**: 10.0 362 students/counselor	**% Amer Indian**: 1.0 **% Asian**: 3.5 **% Black**: 0.8 **% Hispanic**: 2.1 **% White**: 92.6	National ***Socio-Economic Status*** indicator percentile (100=high): 80th

Winnebago County
NEENAH S.D.
410 S COMMERCIAL ST ● NEENAH WI 54956 ● (920) 751-6808

Grade Span: PK-12 **Schools**: *Regular* 13 ● *Spec Ed* 0 ● *Alt* 0 **Students**: 6,537 **Total Teachers**: 382 **Student/Classroom Teacher Ratio**: 17.1	**Expenditures/Student**: $6,295 **Librarians**: 15.6 419 students/librarian **Guidance Counselors**: 15.0 436 students/counselor	**% Amer Indian**: 0.8 **% Asian**: 1.6 **% Black**: 0.5 **% Hispanic**: 1.3 **% White**: 95.8	National ***Socio-Economic Status*** indicator percentile (100=high): 88th

Winnebago County
OSHKOSH AREA S.D.
PO BOX 3048 ● OSHKOSH WI 54903 ● (920) 424-0160 ● http://www.athenet.net/~oasdcent/index.html

Grade Span: PK-12 **Schools**: *Regular* 22 ● *Spec Ed* 0 ● *Alt* 0 **Students**: 10,092 **Total Teachers**: 586 **Student/Classroom Teacher Ratio**: 18.0	**Expenditures/Student**: $5,688 **Librarians**: 14.8 682 students/librarian **Guidance Counselors**: 20.0 505 students/counselor	**% Amer Indian**: 0.5 **% Asian**: 7.3 **% Black**: 1.3 **% Hispanic**: 1.0 **% White**: 89.8	National ***Socio-Economic Status*** indicator percentile (100=high): 65th

Wood County
MARSHFIELD S.D.
1010 E 4TH ST ● MARSHFIELD WI 54449 ● (715) 387-1101 ● http://www.marshfield.k12.wi.us

Grade Span: PK-12 **Schools**: *Regular* 9 ● *Spec Ed* 0 ● *Alt* 0 **Students**: 4,317 **Total Teachers**: 264 **Student/Classroom Teacher Ratio**: 18.4	**Expenditures/Student**: $5,649 **Librarians**: 6.0 720 students/librarian **Guidance Counselors**: 8.0 540 students/counselor	**% Amer Indian**: 0.2 **% Asian**: 1.7 **% Black**: 0.4 **% Hispanic**: 0.9 **% White**: 96.8	National ***Socio-Economic Status*** indicator percentile (100=high): 83rd

Wood County
WISCONSIN RAPIDS S.D.
510 PEACH ST ● WISCONSIN RAPIDS WI 54494-4698 ● (715) 422-6003

Grade Span: PK-12 **Schools**: *Regular* 13 ● *Spec Ed* 0 ● *Alt* 0 **Students**: 6,112 **Total Teachers**: 372 **Student/Classroom Teacher Ratio**: 17.2	**Expenditures/Student**: $6,009 **Librarians**: 11.4 536 students/librarian **Guidance Counselors**: 15.2 402 students/counselor	**% Amer Indian**: 1.3 **% Asian**: 6.7 **% Black**: 0.4 **% Hispanic**: 0.7 **% White**: 90.8	National ***Socio-Economic Status*** indicator percentile (100=high): 70th

Albany County

[LARAMIE] **ALBANY COUNTY S.D. 1**

1948 GRAND AVENUE ● LARAMIE WY 82070 ● (307) 721-4400 ● http://www.union-tel.com/~rockriver/rrshomepage.shl

Grade Span: KG-12 **Schools**: *Regular* 18 ● *Spec Ed* 0 ● *Alt* 0 **Students**: 4,196 **Total Teachers**: 294 **Student/Classroom Teacher Ratio**: 10.4	**Expenditures/Student**: $5,564 **Librarians**: 6.0 699 students/librarian **Guidance Counselors**: 16.0 262 students/counselor	**% Amer Indian**: 1.3 **% Asian**: 2.3 **% Black**: 1.3 **% Hispanic**: 9.7 **% White**: 85.4	National ***Socio-Economic Status*** indicator percentile (100=high): 41st

Campbell County

[GILLETTE] **CAMPBELL COUNTY S.D. 1**

PO BOX 3033 ● GILLETTE WY 82717-3033 ● (307) 682-5171 ● http://web.ccsd.k12.wy.us

Grade Span: KG-12 **Schools**: *Regular* 22 ● *Spec Ed* 0 ● *Alt* 1 **Students**: 7,975 **Total Teachers**: 531 **Student/Classroom Teacher Ratio**: 20.3	**Expenditures/Student**: $6,002 **Librarians**: 11.0 725 students/librarian **Guidance Counselors**: 10.0 798 students/counselor	**% Amer Indian**: 0.9 **% Asian**: 0.5 **% Black**: 0.1 **% Hispanic**: 2.1 **% White**: 96.4	National ***Socio-Economic Status*** indicator percentile (100=high): 72nd

Fremont County

[RIVERTON] **FREMONT COUNTY S.D. 25**

121 NORTH FIFTH STREET WEST ● RIVERTON WY 82501 ● (307) 856-9407 ● http://www.fremont25.k12.wy.us

Grade Span: KG-12 **Schools**: *Regular* 6 ● *Spec Ed* 0 ● *Alt* 0 **Students**: 2,988 **Total Teachers**: 175 **Student/Classroom Teacher Ratio**: 17.7	**Expenditures/Student**: $5,479 **Librarians**: 2.0 1,494 students/librarian **Guidance Counselors**: 12.0 249 students/counselor	**% Amer Indian**: 7.2 **% Asian**: 0.7 **% Black**: 0.3 **% Hispanic**: 6.0 **% White**: 85.8	National ***Socio-Economic Status*** indicator percentile (100=high): 61st

Laramie County

[CHEYENNE] **LARAMIE COUNTY S.D. 1**

2810 HOUSE AVENUE ● CHEYENNE WY 82001 ● (307) 771-2100 ● http://easthigh.laramie1.k12.wy.us

Grade Span: KG-12 **Schools**: *Regular* 31 ● *Spec Ed* 0 ● *Alt* 1 **Students**: 13,920 **Total Teachers**: 839 **Student/Classroom Teacher Ratio**: 17.1	**Expenditures/Student**: $5,355 **Librarians**: 8.0 1,740 students/librarian **Guidance Counselors**: 37.8 368 students/counselor	**% Amer Indian**: 1.2 **% Asian**: 1.5 **% Black**: 4.4 **% Hispanic**: 12.0 **% White**: 80.9	National ***Socio-Economic Status*** indicator percentile (100=high): 56th

Lincoln County

[AFTON] **LINCOLN COUNTY S.D. 2**

N ● AFTON WY 83110 ● (307) 886-3811 ● http://www.cyberhighway.net/~lincosd2

Grade Span: KG-12 **Schools**: *Regular* 9 ● *Spec Ed* 0 ● *Alt* 0 **Students**: 2,731 **Total Teachers**: 174 **Student/Classroom Teacher Ratio**: 14.8	**Expenditures/Student**: $5,318 **Librarians**: 2.9 942 students/librarian **Guidance Counselors**: 1.9 1,437 students/counselor	**% Amer Indian**: 0.7 **% Asian**: 0.2 **% Black**: 0.4 **% Hispanic**: 1.2 **% White**: 97.5	National ***Socio-Economic Status*** indicator percentile (100=high): 76th

Natrona County

[CASPER] **NATRONA COUNTY S.D. 1**

970 NORTH GLENN ROAD ● CASPER WY 82601 ● (307) 577-0200 ● http://www.trib.com/WYOMING/NCSD/index.html

Grade Span: KG-12 **Schools**: *Regular* 39 ● *Spec Ed* 1 ● *Alt* 0 **Students**: 12,936 **Total Teachers**: 808 **Student/Classroom Teacher Ratio**: 15.3	**Expenditures/Student**: $5,206 **Librarians**: 9.0 1,437 students/librarian **Guidance Counselors**: 30.4 426 students/counselor	**% Amer Indian**: 0.8 **% Asian**: 0.6 **% Black**: 1.3 **% Hispanic**: 3.8 **% White**: 93.5	National ***Socio-Economic Status*** indicator percentile (100=high): 55th

Park County

[CODY] **PARK COUNTY S.D. 6**

919 CODY AVENUE ● CODY WY 82414 ● (307) 587-4253 ● http://www.wavecom.net/~phs

Grade Span: KG-12 **Schools**: *Regular* 7 ● *Spec Ed* 0 ● *Alt* 0 **Students**: 2,713 **Total Teachers**: 148 **Student/Classroom Teacher Ratio**: 15.5	**Expenditures/Student**: $4,670 **Librarians**: 5.0 543 students/librarian **Guidance Counselors**: 7.0 388 students/counselor	**% Amer Indian**: 0.4 **% Asian**: 0.7 **% Black**: 0.0 **% Hispanic**: 1.7 **% White**: 97.1	National ***Socio-Economic Status*** indicator percentile (100=high): 79th

Sheridan County

[SHERIDAN] **SHERIDAN COUNTY S.D. 2**

PO BOX 919 ● SHERIDAN WY 82801 ● (307) 674-7405

Grade Span: KG-12 **Schools**: *Regular* 10 ● *Spec Ed* 0 ● *Alt* 0 **Students**: 3,564 **Total Teachers**: 215 **Student/Classroom Teacher Ratio**: 15.1	**Expenditures/Student**: $5,258 **Librarians**: 3.0 1,188 students/librarian **Guidance Counselors**: 8.0 446 students/counselor	**% Amer Indian**: 1.1 **% Asian**: 1.0 **% Black**: 0.2 **% Hispanic**: 2.3 **% White**: 95.5	National ***Socio-Economic Status*** indicator percentile (100=high): 60th

Sweetwater County

[GREEN RIVER] **SWEETWATER COUNTY S.D. 2**

400 NORTH 1ST EAST ● GREEN RIVER WY 82935 ● (307) 872-5500 ● http://www.sw2.k12.wy.us

Grade Span: KG-12 **Schools**: *Regular* 14 ● *Spec Ed* 0 ● *Alt* 0 **Students**: 3,769 **Total Teachers**: 239 **Student/Classroom Teacher Ratio**: 12.9	**Expenditures/Student**: $5,841 **Librarians**: 7.0 538 students/librarian **Guidance Counselors**: 10.0 377 students/counselor	**% Amer Indian**: 0.4 **% Asian**: 0.4 **% Black**: 0.1 **% Hispanic**: 8.0 **% White**: 91.1	National ***Socio-Economic Status*** indicator percentile (100=high): 82nd

Sweetwater County

[ROCK SPRINGS] **SWEETWATER COUNTY S.D. 1**

PO BOX 1089 ● ROCK SPRINGS WY 82901 ● (307) 382-2474 ● http://www.sw1.k12.wy.us

Grade Span: KG-12 **Schools**: *Regular* 20 ● *Spec Ed* 0 ● *Alt* 1 **Students**: 5,830 **Total Teachers**: 372 **Student/Classroom Teacher Ratio**: 16.6	**Expenditures/Student**: $5,689 **Librarians**: 7.0 833 students/librarian **Guidance Counselors**: 23.1 252 students/counselor	**% Amer Indian**: 0.5 **% Asian**: 0.5 **% Black**: 1.1 **% Hispanic**: 8.5 **% White**: 89.3	National ***Socio-Economic Status*** indicator percentile (100=high): 70th

Uinta County

[EVANSTON] **UINTA COUNTY S.D. 1**

PO BOX 6002 ● EVANSTON WY 82931-6002 ● (307) 789-7571 ● http://www.webcom.com/~ucedc/schools.htm

Grade Span: KG-12 **Schools**: *Regular* 7 ● *Spec Ed* 0 ● *Alt* 0 **Students**: 3,762 **Total Teachers**: 234 **Student/Classroom Teacher Ratio**: 15.9	**Expenditures/Student**: $5,167 **Librarians**: 1.2 3,135 students/librarian **Guidance Counselors**: 7.9 476 students/counselor	**% Amer Indian**: 1.0 **% Asian**: 0.4 **% Black**: 0.1 **% Hispanic**: 4.8 **% White**: 93.6	National ***Socio-Economic Status*** indicator percentile (100=high): 54th

CITY INDEX (with number of schools)

CITY INDEX (with number of schools)

CITY INDEX (with number of schools)

CITY INDEX (with number of schools)

CITY INDEX (with number of schools)

CITY INDEX (with number of schools)

CITY INDEX (with number of schools)

CITY INDEX (with number of schools)

CITY INDEX (with number of schools)

CITY INDEX (with number of schools)

CITY INDEX (with number of schools)

CITY INDEX (with number of schools)

CITY INDEX (with number of schools)

CITY INDEX (with number of schools)

CITY INDEX (with number of schools)

CITY INDEX (with number of schools)

CITY INDEX (with number of schools)

CITY INDEX (with number of schools)

CITY INDEX (with number of schools)

CITY INDEX (with number of schools)

CITY INDEX (with number of schools)

CITY INDEX (with number of schools)

CITY INDEX (with number of schools)

CITY INDEX (with number of schools)

CITY INDEX (with number of schools)

CITY INDEX (with number of schools)

CITY INDEX (with number of schools)

CITY INDEX (with number of schools)

CITY INDEX (with number of schools)

CITY INDEX (with number of schools)

CITY INDEX (with number of schools)

CITY INDEX (with number of schools)

CITY INDEX (with number of schools)

CITY INDEX (with number of schools)

CITY INDEX (with number of schools)

CITY INDEX (with number of schools)

CITY INDEX (with number of schools)

CITY INDEX (with number of schools)

CITY INDEX (with number of schools)

CITY INDEX (with number of schools)

CITY INDEX (with number of schools)

CITY INDEX (with number of schools)

CITY INDEX (with number of schools)

CITY INDEX (with number of schools)

CITY INDEX (with number of schools)

CITY INDEX (with number of schools)

CITY INDEX (with number of schools)

CITY INDEX (with number of schools)

CITY INDEX (with number of schools)

CITY INDEX (with number of schools)

CITY INDEX (with number of schools)

CITY INDEX (with number of schools)

CITY INDEX (with number of schools)

CITY INDEX (with number of schools)

CITY INDEX (with number of schools)

CITY INDEX (with number of schools)

CITY INDEX (with number of schools)

CITY INDEX (with number of schools)

CITY INDEX (with number of schools)

CITY INDEX (with number of schools)

CITY INDEX (with number of schools)

CITY INDEX (with number of schools)

CITY INDEX (with number of schools)

CITY INDEX (with number of schools)

CITY INDEX (with number of schools)

CITY INDEX (with number of schools)

CITY INDEX (with number of schools)

CITY INDEX (with number of schools)

CITY INDEX (with number of schools)

CITY INDEX (with number of schools)

CITY INDEX (with number of schools)

CITY INDEX (with number of schools)

CITY INDEX (with number of schools)

CITY INDEX (with number of schools)

CITY INDEX (with number of schools)

CITY INDEX (with number of schools)

CITY INDEX (with number of schools)

CITY INDEX (with number of schools)

CITY INDEX (with number of schools)

CITY INDEX (with number of schools)

CITY INDEX (with number of schools)

CITY INDEX (with number of schools)